EMPLOYEE DISMISSAL LAW AND PRACTICE
SECOND EDITION

HENRY H. PERRITT, JR.
Professor of Law
Villanova University School of Law

Wiley Law Publications
JOHN WILEY & SONS
New York · Chichester · Brisbane · Toronto · Singapore

Copyright © 1984, 1987 by John Wiley & Sons, Inc.

All rights reserved. Published simultaneously in Canada.

Reproduction or translation of any part of this work
beyond that permitted by Section 107 or 108 of the
1976 United States Copyright Act without the permission
of the copyright owner is unlawful. Requests for
permission or further information should be addressed to
the Permissions Department, John Wiley & Sons, Inc.

Library of Congress Cataloging in Publication Data:

Perritt, Henry H.
  Employee dismissal law and practice.

  (Trial practice library)
  Includes index.
  Updated ed. of: Employee dismissal. c1984.
  1. Employees, Dismissal of—Law and legislation—
United States. I. Perritt, Henry H. Employee
dismissal. II. Title. III. Series.
KF3471.P47 1987   344.73'012596   86-34019
ISBN 0-471-85099-3   347.30412596

Printed in the United States of America

10 9 8 7 6 5 4 3 2 1

EMPLOYEE DISMISSAL
LAW AND PRACTICE
SECOND EDITION

PREFACE

This book is about employees who get fired and want to sue their former employers. It explains how employees can win their suits and how employers can prevent suits and defend against them if they are brought. During the past fifteen years, a marked trend has developed toward permitting non-union employees to recover for wrongful dismissal in certain circumstances. The trend differs from the largely statutory developments of the 1960s and early 1970s in that many recent wrongful dismissal cases have been decided on state common law contract and tort grounds.

This treatise is designed to fill three needs not currently being met by available literature. First, it offers an analytical treatment of wrongful dismissal doctrines, rather than merely reporting the results of the cases. Law review literature abounds with material on common law wrongful dismissal cases. Few articles, however, sufficiently relate cases to fundamental contract and tort doctrines.

Second, it addresses, at least in general terms, statutory as well as common law doctrines. Real wrongful dismissal cases almost always involve a mixture of common law and statutory claims, and frequently involve collective bargaining agreements as well. A practitioner with specialized knowledge only in employment discrimination, or only in the law of labor agreements, or only in wrongful discharge law, needs a guide to all the legal concepts potentially involved in the cases he or she will be handling. A general practitioner also needs a comprehensive guide to wrongful discharge law to give competent legal services to clients who seek legal remedies for employment termination.

Third, this treatise is intended to be practical as well as theoretical. As an academic lawyer, I am interested intellectually in the emerging common law theories of wrongful dismissal and believe it is useful to articulate the connections between these theories and older doctrines. As a labor law practitioner, I understand the need for practical guidance at least to the relevant questions, if not to the answers, regarding legal theories, evidence, and discovery, spanning the full range of employment termination disputes in both public and private sectors.

I intend the material in the treatise to favor neither plaintiffs nor defendants as classes. Some sections, of course, intentionally marshal the arguments for one side or the other. **Chapter 8**, for example, offers suggestions to employers on how to limit liability. Passages in other chapters stress how a plaintiff employee can present the best possible case.

Since the first edition was written, all but a handful of states have accepted one or more exceptions to the Employment-at-Will Rule, and the analytical principles suggested in the first edition have crystallized in hundreds of state and federal decisions. Accordingly, this edition offers even more specific analytical structure than the first edition did for evaluating cases and evaluates major cases for their conformity to majority and minority rules. The second edition also has been reorganized to make overviews of major theories readily available to readers.

A word about the organization of the book may be useful. **Chapter 1** is an overview of the Employment-at-Will Rule and the three major common law theories for wrongful dismissal. The reader entirely unfamiliar with the subject may wish to begin with §§ **1.2** and **1.17**. **Section 1.12** provides a state-by-state summary.

Chapter 2 identifies the major federal statutes under which employees can recover for discriminatory discharges. It serves as a checklist and starting point for research in employment discrimination law and the relations between federal statutes and state common law claims. **Chapter 3** explains the arbitration process, under which most employees covered by collective bargaining agreements must litigate the fairness of their terminations. The concepts treated in this chapter are important for any discharged employee covered by a collective bargaining agreement. The chapter is written to be useful to labor relations professionals and union grievance committee members as well as counsel.

The new common law theories representing exceptions to the Employment-at-Will Rule are discussed in **Chapters 4, 5,** and **7**. **Chapter 4** discusses common law contract theories for wrongful dismissal, and **Chapter 5** discusses common law tort theories. **Chapter 7** draws upon proof concepts developed in the statutory discrimination, constitutional, and unfair labor practice areas to suggest the directions in which proof rules are developing for common law wrongful dismissal claims. Counsel presenting or defending against a common law claim should consider all three chapters. **Chapters 4** and **5** identify the principal theories of recovery, while **Chapter 7** addresses the manner in which a case can be proven. The discovery checklists in **Appendix B** cover the types of facts to be investigated and possibly used as evidence in a particular case.

Chapter 6 addresses some special problems arising in connection with public employees. It briefly surveys civil service concepts and focuses on the manner in which employees can establish a constitutional infringement. **Chapter 8** is aimed at employers, and offers advice on how personnel policies and procedures might be developed or revised in light of the recent developments in wrongful discharge law.

Chapter 9 is aimed less at practical problems than at shaping the future. It offers a comprehensive legal doctrine for weighing the competing employer and employee interests involved in wrongful dismissal cases and evaluates the alternatives available with respect to wrongful dismissal legislation.

Three appendixes present material of a less analytical nature. **Appendix A** is a table of state statutes limiting employee terminations. **Appendix B** provides a discovery checklist for plaintiff and defendant. **Appendix C** offers draft state and federal statutes reflecting the doctrines developed in **Chapter 9**. **Appendix D** is a checklist for in-house defense counsel written by a prominent practitioner. **Appendix E** is a proposal by a leader of the plaintiff bar for more generous measures of damages. **Appendix F**, written by two distinguished defense counsel, explores application of implied contract theories to enforce employer promises of promotions and compensation arrangements.

A brief comment is appropriate regarding personal pronouns: *he, she, his,* and *her.* I find it cumbersome always to use he-or-she or variants, yet I respect the sensitivity of those who view the conventional use of the masculine pronoun to be sexist. Accordingly, I alternate between the masculine and feminine pronouns in referring to plaintiff, defendant, judge, and arbitrator. The gender of the pronoun is consistent within particular discussions to eliminate confusion.

This is, of course, not the final word on wrongful dismissal. But I hope it is a useful first step in pulling together a great many fragments.

Villanova, Pennsylvania   HENRY H. PERRITT, JR.
January 1987

ACKNOWLEDGMENTS

I received helpful suggestions and criticisms on material for the first edition from several of my colleagues at Villanova Law School: Joseph W. Dellapenna, Peter Goldberger, Charisse R. Lillie, Richard C. Turkington, William D. Valente and Ellen Wertheimer. Deans John E. Murray and Acting Dean Gerald Abraham approved generous student research assistance. Former or present colleagues in the practice of labor law and collective bargaining also provided useful comments on material for the first edition: Dennis J. Morikawa, William P. Hobgood, Richard R. Kasher and James A. Wilkinson. John W. Rowe reviewed several chapters and provided his usual incisive and thought-provoking comments. A number of plaintiff and defense counsel around the country were kind enough to volunteer comments on the first edition and to submit cases they thought, correctly, could improve the presentation in the first edition. The second edition benefits from their suggestions.

Several Villanova law students helped with research for the first edition and its supplements: David G. Arnold, Andrew Bramnick, Joseph E. Chovanes, John J. Del Casale, Frederick J. Gerngross, Kathryn Gover, Paul F. Kulinski, Richard J. Marcolus, Brian E. Meyers, Thomas B. O'Brien, Charles D. Onofry, Bruce L. Silverstein, Jeffrey Stone, Joseph A Piscina, Richard S. Ranieri, Gerard J. Rehel and Laura M. Shemick. I enjoyed working and learning with them.

I particularly want to thank Villanova law students Scott Fegley, Samuel J. McLaughlin, Lisa E. O'Leary, Donald M. Ransom, David C. Shelton, and Jeff Zimskind, who made major contributions to the second edition.

The book would not exist, nor would its quality be nearly as high, without the help of my friend Harry A. Rissetto, who sets a standard of excellence in the practice of law and a standard of decency in dealing with people that any lawyer would benefit from emulating.

More generally, I honor my friend John T. Dunlop, who serves as an important role model for those of us who seek to harness academic learning in service of, rather than in derogation of, the practical needs of people who must make decisions.

Finally, I also want to express my great appreciation to my friend David S. Fortney for his support and to Mitchell T. Bergmann for his encouragement.

H.H.P.

SUMMARY COMMENTS

Chapter 1	Employment at Will	1
Chapter 2	Statutory Protection	41
Chapter 3	Arbitration	119
Chapter 4	Contract Theories	171
Chapter 5	Tort Theories	243
Chapter 6	Special Problems of Public Employment	323
Chapter 7	Problems of Proof	367
Chapter 8	Employer Personnel Policies	457
Chapter 9	Comprehensive Wrongful Discharge Legislation	485
Appendixes		543
Tables		641
Index		709

DETAILED CONTENTS

Chapter 1	**Employment at Will**	
§ 1.1	Introduction	
§ 1.2	Overview of Common Law Wrongful Dismissal Theories	
§ 1.3	Pre-Industrial Revolution Employment Tenure Rule	
§ 1.4	Development of the Employment-at-Will Rule	
§ 1.5	Stages in the Erosion of the Employment-at-Will Rule	
§ 1.6	—Civil Service Protection	
§ 1.7	—Protection of Employees Represented by Trade Unions	
§ 1.8	—Protection against Class-Based Discrimination	
§ 1.9	—Common Law Protection for Private Sector Workers	
§ 1.10	Reasons for Erosion of the Employment-at-Will Rule	
§ 1.11	Influence of Commentators	
§ 1.12	Modern Status of the Employment-at-Will Rule in 50 States	
§ 1.13	Contemporary Role of the Employment-at-Will Rule	
§ 1.14	Choice of Law Principles	
§ 1.15	Major Unresolved Issues	
§ 1.16	Guesses about the Future	
§ 1.17	Checklist for Case Evaluation	
Chapter 2	**Statutory Protection**	
§ 2.1	Introduction	
§ 2.2	Protecting against Class-based Discrimination	
§ 2.3	—Title VII: Basic Concepts	
§ 2.4	—Title VII: Disparate Treatment Examples	
§ 2.5	—Title VII: Sexual Harassment	
§ 2.6	—Age Discrimination in Employment Act: Basic Concepts	
§ 2.7	—Age Discrimination in Employment Act: Examples	
§ 2.8	—Reconstruction Civil Rights Acts: Section 1981	
§ 2.9	—Reconstruction Civil Rights Acts: Section 1985	
§ 2.10	—Handicap Discrimination: Rehabilitation Act	
§ 2.11	—Title VI of the Civil Rights Act of 1964	
§ 2.12	—Handicap Discrimination: State Law	
§ 2.13	—Federal Contractors: Executive Order 11,246	
§ 2.14	—Education Act Amendments	

§ 2.15		Statutes Protecting Employee Conduct
§ 2.16		—National Labor Relations Act
§ 2.17		—Retaliation for Opposing Discrimination
§ 2.18		—Occupational Safety and Health Act
§ 2.19		—Railroad Safety and Liability Acts
§ 2.20		—Environmental Statutes
§ 2.21		—Fair Labor Standards Act
§ 2.22		—Consumer Credit Protection Act
§ 2.23		—Employee Retirement Income Security Act
§ 2.24		—Other Federal Statutes
§ 2.25		Attorneys' Fees
§ 2.26		Implied Private Right of Action from a Statute
§ 2.27		Preemption
§ 2.28		—National Labor Relations Act Preemption
§ 2.29		—Preemption of Tort Claims under § 301 of the Labor Management Relations Act
§ 2.30		—Preemption of Contract Claims under § 301 of the Labor Management Relations Act
§ 2.31		—Preemption of Common Law Claims under the Railway Labor Act
§ 2.32		—Preemption under Discrimination Statutes
§ 2.33		—Preemption under Federal Whistleblower Statutes
§ 2.34		—Preemption under Other Federal Statutes
§ 2.35		Pendent State Claims
§ 2.36		Unemployment Compensation Generally
§ 2.37		—Procedures for Determining Eligibility for Unemployment Benefits
§ 2.38		Considerations in Pursuing Both Statutory and Common Law Relief
Chapter 3		**Arbitration**
§ 3.1		Introduction
§ 3.2		Development of Arbitration in England
§ 3.3		Development of Labor Arbitration in the United States
§ 3.4		Purpose of Labor Arbitration
§ 3.5		Just Cause Standard: General Principles
§ 3.6		—Poor Performance
§ 3.7		—Misconduct on the Job
§ 3.8		—Misconduct Off the Job
§ 3.9		Typical Grievance and Arbitration Procedure
§ 3.10		The Arbitration Hearing
§ 3.11		—Ex Parte Hearings
§ 3.12		Evidence
§ 3.13		—Availability of Exclusionary and Self-Incrimination Rules

DETAILED CONTENTS

§ 3.14	—Medical Evidence
§ 3.15	—Standard of Proof
§ 3.16	—Compulsory Process
§ 3.17	Form and Content of Arbitration Award
§ 3.18	Remedies in Arbitration Awards
§ 3.19	Arbitration under the Railway Labor Act
§ 3.20	Arbitration and the Courts
§ 3.21	—Federal Common Law of Labor Arbitration
§ 3.22	—Arbitration Statutes
§ 3.23	—Compelling Arbitration
§ 3.24	—Judicial Review and Enforcement of Arbitration Awards
§ 3.25	—The Duty of Fair Representation
§ 3.26	—Damages for Breach of the Duty of Fair Representation
§ 3.27	Effect of Arbitration Awards Deciding Statutory Claims
§ 3.28	Handling a Grievance in Practice
§ 3.29	Defending against a Grievance

Chapter 4	**Contract Theories**
§ 4.1	Introduction and Overview of Contract Theories
§ 4.2	Historical Development of Contract Theories
§ 4.3	—Common Law Forms of Action
§ 4.4	—The Consideration Requirement
§ 4.5	—Treatment of Consideration in Collective Bargaining Agreements
§ 4.6	The Promise of Employment Security
§ 4.7	—Express Commitments Made to Specific Employees
§ 4.8	—Promises Derived from Employer Representations Made to Workforce in General
§ 4.9	—Promises Implied from Length of Service and Conduct
§ 4.10	—Disclaimers
§ 4.11	—Covenant of Good Faith and Fair Dealing
§ 4.12	Consideration and Its Substitutes as Validation Devices
§ 4.13	—Unilateral Contracts: Mutuality of Obligation Not Necessary
§ 4.14	—Bargained-for Detrimental Reliance: General Concept
§ 4.15	—Bargained-for Detrimental Reliance: Special Consideration Such as Quitting Another Job or Turning Down Job Offers
§ 4.16	—Bargained-for Detrimental Reliance: Continuing Employment
§ 4.17	—Promissory Estoppel
§ 4.18	—Is Proof of Actual Reliance Necessary, or May It Be Presumed?
§ 4.19	Employer Modification of Promise after Consideration Given
§ 4.20	Statute of Frauds
§ 4.21	What Constitutes a Breach: Generally

§ 4.22	—Breach of Employer Promise
§ 4.23	—Breach of Covenant of Good Faith
§ 4.24	—Who Decides Whether Good Cause Existed
§ 4.25	Suits by Employees Covered by Collective Bargaining Agreements
§ 4.26	Pleading the Plaintiff's Case
§ 4.27	Pleading the Defendant's Case
§ 4.28	Damages

Chapter 5	**Tort Theories**
§ 5.1	Introduction and Overview
§ 5.2	Public Policy Tort Cases Do Not Require Employers to Show Good Cause for Dismissing Employees
§ 5.3	Basic Tort Concepts
§ 5.4	—Development of the Tort Forms of Action
§ 5.5	—The Framework for a Public Policy Tort in Section 870
§ 5.6	—Injury Requirement of Section 870
§ 5.7	—Justification Concept of Section 870
§ 5.8	Categories of Public Policy Torts
§ 5.9	—Labor Statutes as a Basis for Public Policy Torts
§ 5.10	—*External* Public Policy: Jury Duty
§ 5.11	—External Public Policy: Workers' Compensation Claims
§ 5.12	—*External* Public Policy: Termination Jeopardizing Constitutionally Recognized Rights
§ 5.13	—*External* Public Policy: Termination for Private, or Off Duty, Conduct
§ 5.14	*External* versus *Internal* Public Policy Torts for Wrongful Dismissal
§ 5.15	—*Internal* Public Policy: Marshaling the Conflicting Interests
§ 5.16	—*Internal* Public Policy Tort: Protests or Reports to Outside Agencies (Whistleblowing)
§ 5.17	—*Internal* Public Policy Tort: Protests or Reports to Employer
§ 5.18	—*Internal* Public Policy Tort: Refusals to Follow Orders
§ 5.19	Public Policy Torts Are More Than Civil Remedies for Statutory Violations
§ 5.20	Public Policy Tort Protection for Employees Covered by Collective Bargaining Agreements
§ 5.21	Prima Facie Tort: Liability Based on Intent to Harm, Regardless of Public Policy
§ 5.22	Intentional Interference with Contractual Relations
§ 5.23	Intentional Infliction of Emotional Distress
§ 5.24	Fraudulent Misrepresentation (Deceit)
§ 5.25	Defamation
§ 5.26	Invasion of Privacy: Improper Acquisition or Dissemination of Information

DETAILED CONTENTS

§ 5.27	—Invasion of Privacy: Interference with Private Conduct
§ 5.28	Tort Claims for Dismissals Related to AIDS or to Sexual Orientation
§ 5.29	Negligence
§ 5.30	Preemption of State Tort Claims by § 301 of the Labor Management Relations Act
§ 5.31	Pleading the Plaintiff's Case
§ 5.32	Pleading the Defendant's Case
§ 5.33	Damages

Chapter 6   **Special Problems of Public Employment**

§ 6.1	Introduction
§ 6.2	What Is a Public Employer?
§ 6.3	Civil Service Protections: In General
§ 6.4	—Federal Civil Service
§ 6.5	—State and Municipal Civil Service
§ 6.6	—Exhaustion of Administrative Remedies
§ 6.7	Federal Discrimination Statutes
§ 6.8	Reconstruction Era Civil Rights Acts
§ 6.9	Due Process: In General
§ 6.10	—Deprivation of Property Interests
§ 6.11	—Deprivation of Liberty Interests
§ 6.12	—Procedural Due Process Entitlements
§ 6.13	—Substantive Due Process Entitlements
§ 6.14	Interaction of Public Sector Grievance Arbitration and Civil Service Laws
§ 6.15	—Public Sector Grievance and Arbitration Procedures: Exclusivity, Exhaustion and Preclusion
§ 6.16	—Enforceability of Grievance Arbitration Awards
§ 6.17	Sovereign Immunity: In General
§ 6.18	—Suits against the United States and Its Officials
§ 6.19	—Suits against State and Local Governments under § 1983 and Other Federal Statutes
§ 6.20	—Common Law Suits against State and Local Governments and Officials

Chapter 7   **Problems of Proof**

§ 7.1	Introduction
§ 7.2	Basic Proof Concepts
§ 7.3	Pervasiveness of Employer Motive Question
§ 7.4	Statutory and Constitutional Claims: Proof of Motive
§ 7.5	—Public Employee Constitutional Rights

DETAILED CONTENTS

§ 7.6	—Violations of Title VII
§ 7.7	—Violations of the National Labor Relations Act
§ 7.8	—Violations of the Age Discrimination in Employment Act
§ 7.9	—Violations of Other Statutes
§ 7.10	Public Policy Tort: Basic Concepts of Proof
§ 7.11	—Proving Public Policy
§ 7.12	—Proving Jeopardy to Public Policy
§ 7.13	—Proving Lack of Justification: Proving Reason for Dismissal
§ 7.14	—Proving Lack of Justification: Burden of Proof on Reasons for Dismissal and Mixed Motive Problem
§ 7.15	—Proving Justification: Business Necessity
§ 7.16	—Public Policy Tort Jury Instructions
§ 7.17	Common Law Contracts: Basic Concepts of Proof
§ 7.18	—Proving an Express or Implied-in-Fact Promise of Employment Security from Writings or Oral Statements
§ 7.19	—Proving Promise from Conduct
§ 7.20	—Proving Consideration
§ 7.21	—Jury Instructions on Contract Formation
§ 7.22	Proving a Breach: Introduction
§ 7.23	—Proving a Breach: Bad Faith or Unfairness
§ 7.24	—Proving a Breach: Cause for Termination in General
§ 7.25	—Proving a Breach: Proving What the Employee Did
§ 7.26	—Proving a Breach: Who Decides What Is Good Cause
§ 7.27	—Proving a Breach: Burdens of Proof on Cause
§ 7.28	—Jury Instructions on Breach
§ 7.29	Preclusive Effect of Earlier Judicial, Arbitral, and Administrative Decisions
§ 7.30	—Preclusive Effect of Judicial Decisions
§ 7.31	—Preclusive Effect of Arbitral Decisions
§ 7.32	—Preclusive Effect of Administrative Decisions: In General
§ 7.33	—Preclusive Effect of Administrative Decisions: Discrimination Findings
§ 7.34	—Preclusive Effect of Administrative Decisions: Employer Regulatory Compliance
§ 7.35	—Preclusive Effect of Administrative Decisions: Unemployment Compensation
Chapter 8	**Employer Personnel Policies**
§ 8.1	Introduction
§ 8.2	History of Rules Regulating Employees
§ 8.3	Function of Internal Rules
§ 8.4	Rules and Organization Theory
§ 8.5	Contemporary Practices

§ 8.6	Employer Policy on Terminations: In General
§ 8.7	—Disclaimers: Reserving the Right to Dismiss at Will
§ 8.8	—Disclaimers: Limiting Authority to Make Promises
§ 8.9	—Limiting Relief to Internal Remedies
§ 8.10	—Releases
§ 8.11	Contents of Termination and Complaint Policies
§ 8.12	—Substantive Fairness Policies
§ 8.13	—Procedural Fairness Policies: General Principles
§ 8.14	—Procedural Fairness Policies: Suggested Approaches
§ 8.15	Employee Appraisal Programs
Chapter 9	**Comprehensive Wrongful Discharge Legislation**
§ 9.1	Introduction
§ 9.2	Overview of Wrongful Dismissal Doctrine: Substantive and Procedural Fairness
§ 9.3	Is Legislation Needed?
§ 9.4	The Politics of Statutory Reform
§ 9.5	Statutory Models
§ 9.6	—Federal Wrongful Dismissal Statutes
§ 9.7	—State Whistleblower Statutes
§ 9.8	—State Employment Term Statutes
§ 9.9	—State Service Letter Statutes
§ 9.10	—State Just Cause Proposals
§ 9.11	—The British Model
§ 9.12	—The Canadian Model
§ 9.13	Commentators' Models
§ 9.14	—The Summers Concept
§ 9.15	—The Selznick Concept
§ 9.16	—The Bellace Concept
§ 9.17	Judicial Control of Other Types of Associations
§ 9.18	A Proposed Wrongful Dismissal Statute: Introduction
§ 9.19	Legislative Drafting Pitfalls
§ 9.20	Possible Substantive Fairness Standards
§ 9.21	—Just Cause Standard
§ 9.22	—Good Faith Standard
§ 9.23	—Weakness of Simple Standards
§ 9.24	—Enumerated Prohibitions
§ 9.25	Procedural Fairness
§ 9.26	—Preemption, Election, Exhaustion, and Preclusion
§ 9.27	—Deference to Employer Procedures
§ 9.28	—Treatment of Collectively Bargained Arbitration
§ 9.29	—Selection of Forum

DETAILED CONTENTS

§ 9.30 —Integration of Wrongful Dismissal and Unemployment Compensation Systems
§ 9.31 —Burdens of Proof
§ 9.32 —Remedies
§ 9.33 —Costs of Litigation
§ 9.34 Estimation of Case Volume

Appendixes

A. State Statutes
B. Discovery
C. Draft Statutes
D. In-House Counsel Checklist for Wrongful Dismissal Litigation
E. Criticism of the Laws of Damage in Dismissal Cases
F. Implied-in-Fact Contract Theory and the Employment Relation

Tables

Conversion Table First Edition to Second Edition Section Numbers
Cases
Statutes

Index

SHORT REFERENCE LIST

Short Reference	Full Reference
AAA	American Arbitration Association
ADEA	Age Discrimination in Employment Act
AIDS	Acquired Immune Deficiency Syndrome
APA	Administrative Procedure Act
BFOQ	bona fide occupational qualification
BLS	Bureau of Labor Statistics
BMCS	Bureau of Motor Carrier Safety
CCPA	Consumer Credit Protection Act
DOL	Department of Labor
EAT	Employment Appeal Tribunal
EEOC	Equal Employment Opportunity Commission
ERISA	Employee Retirement Income Security Act
FAA	Federal Aviation Act
FELA	Federal Employers' Liability Act
FEPC	Fair Employment Practices Commission
FLSA	Fair Labor Standards Act
FMCS	Federal Mediation and Conciliation Service
FMSHA	Federal Mine Safety and Health Act
FRSA	Federal Railroad and Safety Act
LHWCA	Longshoremen's and Harbor Workers' Compensation Act
LMRA	Labor Management Relations Act
MSPB	Merit Systems Protection Board
NLRA	National Labor Relations Act
NLRB	National Labor Relations Board
NMB	National Mediation Board
NRC	Nuclear Regulatory Commission
OSHA	Occupational Safety and Health Act

SHORT REFERENCE LIST

Title VII	Title VII of the Civil Rights Act of 1964
USAA	United States Arbitration Act
USDA	United States Department of Agriculture

CHAPTER 1

EMPLOYMENT AT WILL

§ 1.1   Introduction
§ 1.2   Overview of Common Law Wrongful Dismissal Theories
§ 1.3   Pre-Industrial Revolution Employment Tenure Rule
§ 1.4   Development of the Employment-at-Will Rule
§ 1.5   Stages in the Erosion of the Employment-at-Will Rule
§ 1.6   – Civil Service Protection
§ 1.7   – Protection of Employees Represented by Trade Unions
§ 1.8   – Protection against Class-Based Discrimination
§ 1.9   – Common Law Protection for Private Sector Workers
§ 1.10 Reasons for Erosion of the Employment-at-Will Rule
§ 1.11 Influence of Commentators
§ 1.12 Modern Status of the Employment-at-Will Rule in 50 States
§ 1.13 Contemporary Role of the Employment-at-Will Rule
§ 1.14 Choice of Law Principles
§ 1.15 Major Unresolved Issues
§ 1.16 Guesses about the Future
§ 1.17 Checklist for Case Evaluation

§ 1.1   Introduction

The most significant employment law development in the last quarter of the twentieth century has been the erosion of the Employment-at-Will Rule[1] and the recognition of a family of common law rights protecting individual employees against wrongful dismissal. Under these wrongful dismissal doctrines, terminated employees may be able to recover damages when they can show that their terminations violated employer promises, jeopardized clear public policies, or, sometimes, when the terminations did not comport with good faith and fair dealing.

---

[1] The Employment-at-Will Rule can be summarized like this: An employer may dismiss an at-will employee for a good reason, a bad reason, or for no reason at all.

These doctrines, or exceptions to the Employment-at-Will Rule, were virtually unknown before about 1970. Until then, an employer could dismiss an at-will employee for any reason or no reason, confident that the law provided the employee no remedy unless one of a handful of statutes prohibiting discrimination was violated. Now, the three wrongful dismissal doctrines, more than a dozen federal statutes, and scores of state statutes provide legal redress when employees can show that their dismissals fit within the factual circumstances covered by the doctrines or the statutes.[2] Nevertheless, the Employment-at-Will Rule is not altogether dead. The law in no American jurisdiction requires private employers to demonstrate just cause for terminating an employee. The obligation to terminate only for just cause is imposed regularly on public sector employers, but it is imposed on private sector employers only by voluntary contract. In other words, the Employment-at-Will Rule continues to provide a presumption, however circumscribed, that a dismissal is legal; it is up to the dismissed employee to rebut that presumption by showing either violation of a common law wrongful dismissal doctrine or violation of a statute.

This chapter addresses the Employment-at-Will Rule and its exceptions. After a section presenting an overview of the common law wrongful dismissal doctrines, the chapter explores the historical development of the Employment-at-Will Rule, explains the pressures leading to its modification, summarizes the current state of the law in fifty states, identifies the major unresolved issues, and concludes with a checklist for evaluation of wrongful dismissal cases.

References link this material to the major sections of the treatise in which the ideas are developed more fully.

§ 1.2 Overview of Common Law Wrongful Dismissal Theories

Three basic common law doctrines permit recovery of damages for wrongful dismissal despite the Employment-at-Will Rule. The first permits a plaintiff to recover for breach of contract when the employer dismisses the employee in violation of promises of employment tenure made orally or implied from a course of conduct or from employee policies or handbooks.[3] This implied-in-fact contract theory requires a plaintiff to plead and prove the following elements:

1. The employer made a promise of employment security
2. The employee gave consideration for the promise in the form of detrimental reliance or otherwise
3. The employer breached the promise by dismissing the employee

---

[2] *See* Wandry v. Bull's Eye Credit Union, 129 Wis. 2d 37, 384 N.W.2d 325, 326 (1986) (noting erosion of employment-at-will rule, citing this treatise).

[3] See **ch. 4**, especially **§§ 4.6–4.24**.

The second common law doctrine allows an employee to recover in tort when the dismissal offends some identifiable public policy.[4] This public policy tort theory requires the plaintiff to plead and prove the following elements:

1. The existence of a clear public policy manifested in a state or federal constitution, statute or administrative regulation, or in the common law
2. That dismissing employees for conduct like that of the plaintiff would jeopardize the public policy
3. That the plaintiff's dismissal was motivated by conduct related to the public policy
4. That the employer lacked overriding legitimate business justification for the dismissal.

The third common law doctrine enables an employee to recover for breach of contract[5] when the employer has violated a *covenant of good faith and fair dealing,* implied in all contracts as a matter of law.[6] Conceptually, the covenant requires that contract rights be exercised in a manner that does not violate the covenant. Thus, even though an employer has the right to terminate an at-will contract for any reason, for no reason, for a good reason, or for a bad reason, the employer also has a duty not to exercise this right unfairly or in bad faith.

Under the broadest view of the doctrine, a dismissed employee need only show: (1) Existence of an employment relationship; (2) Termination of the employment; and (3) Some aspect of the termination that was unfair or in bad faith. Upon such a showing, a jury would be entitled to decide, with only the most general instructions, whether the termination was fair and in good faith.

The trend of wrongful dismissal cases demonstrates a convergence of judicial opinion on the elements of the implied-in-fact contract and public policy tort doctrines. In contrast, substantial differences of opinion exist regarding the implied covenant of good faith and fair dealing.

Despite general agreement on the theoretical elements, the tort cases span a broad range of opinion. Most favorable to the employee is *Cloutier v. Great Atlantic & Pacific Tea Co.*[7] In that case, the court declined to restrict tort recovery to instances in which the dismissal contravened clear public policy pronouncements in statutes. Rather, it decided it "best to allow the citizenry, through the institution of the American jury, to strike the appropriate balance in these difficult cases."[8] In *Novosel v. Nationwide Insurance Co.*,[9] the Third Circuit, applying Pennsylvania

---

[4] See **ch. 5**.

[5] Some courts treat breach of the implied covenant as a tort.

[6] See **ch. 4**, especially **§§ 4.11, 4.23**.

[7] 121 N.H. 915, 436 A.2d 1140 (1981).

[8] *Id.* at 924, 436 A.2d at 1145.

[9] 721 F.2d 894 (3d Cir. 1983). See **§ 5.12** for analysis of public policy tort claims based on constitutional policies.

law, held that a public policy tort claim can be premised on private employer conduct that infringes on rights recognized in the United States Constitution.[10]

At the opposite pole are *Murphy v. American Home Products*,[11] and *Phung v. Waste Management, Inc.*[12] In *Murphy*, the New York Court of Appeals refused to recognize a tort of *abusive discharge*.[13] The court reviewed the trend in other states toward tempering "what is perceived as the unfairness of the traditional rule by allowing a cause of action in tort to redress abusive discharges."[14] It concluded that "whether these conclusions are supportable or whether for other compelling reasons employers should, as a matter of policy, be held liable to at-will employees discharged in circumstances for which no liability has existed at common law, are issues better left to resolution at the hands of the Legislature."[15] In the court's view, the legislature is better equipped than the courts to consider the competing policy positions of various groups in the society and to determine the exact circumstances in which liability is appropriate.[16] *Phung* also appears to reject the public policy tort doctrine, suggesting that courts should defer to legislatures for modifications of the Employment-at-Will Rule. But *Phung* is not as broad as *Murphy*. The Ohio Supreme Court did not say, in the abstract, that it would not recognize a public policy tort. It said that "the allegations herein failed to state a violation of a sufficiently clear public policy to warrant creation of a cause of action in favor of Phung. . . . No jurisdiction has allowed a cause of action to proceed based only on vaguely alleged violations of 'societal obligations.' "[17]

Most of the tort cases fall in between the two poles, permitting the court, rather than the jury, to decide as a matter of law what is the public policy of the state, based on federal or state statutes or constitutions and sometimes on common law principles.[18] The tort cases reviewed in **Chapter 5** all involve difficult questions

---

[10] The *Novosel* case was settled after the district court, on remand, denied the employer's motion for summary judgment. *See* Novosel v. Nationwide Mut. Ins. Co., 118 L.R.R.M. 2779 (W.D. Pa. 1985). Interestingly, the employer argued that it dismissed Novosel for prounion remarks made to nonmanagement personnel, which might have raised additional public policy and preemption issues.

[11] 58 N.Y.2d 293, 448 N.E.2d 86, 461 N.Y.S.2d 232 (1983).

[12] 23 Ohio St. 3d 100, 491 N.E.2d 1114 (1986).

[13] Murphy v. American Home Prods., 58 N.Y.2d at 297, 448 N.E.2d at 87, 461 N.Y.S.2d at 233.

[14] *Id.* at 301, 448 N.E.2d at 89, 461 N.Y.S.2d at 235.

[15] *Id.*

[16] *Id.* at 302, 448 N.E.2d at 89–90, 461 N.Y.S.2d at 235–36.

[17] 23 Ohio St. 3d at ___, 491 N.E.2d at 1117. The membership of the *Phung* court also was unusual. The author of the majority opinion was Justice Dahling, not a regular member of the Supreme Court, sitting on the case in the stead of Justice Douglas, who had written the court of appeals opinion finding a cause of action. So when Justice Dahling is subtracted from the majority, and Justice Douglas added to the dissenters, one obtains a four-three majority in *Phung*, suggesting that the court might reach a different result in another public policy tort case, either because of different facts, or because of minor changes in membership of the court.

[18] See **ch. 5**. *Compare* Lucas v. Brown & Root, Inc., 736 F.2d 1202, 1205 (8th Cir. 1984) (court competent to decide public policy; legislature not only source of public policy) *and* Wagenseller v. Scottsdale Memorial Hosp., 147 Ariz. 370, 710 P.2d 1025 (1985) (court decisions, as well

of the interplay between public policy and employer actions regarding employees. There is a strong trend toward rejecting public policy tort claims based on policies in statutes that provide administrative remedies.

Although legislatures may be more appropriate institutions than courts for making basic policy judgments, there is a long tradition of judges relying on public policy to control the evolution of the common law.[19]

The implied covenant doctrine enjoyed brief popularity and was used by those earliest courts to relax the Employment-at-Will Rule. But as the more traditional and circumscribed implied-in-fact contract and public policy tort doctrines were developed, the implied covenant doctrine has declined in importance. The early implied covenant cases, *Petermann v. Teamsters*[20] and *Monge v. Beebe Rubber Co.*,[21] suggested no real limits to the scope of the implied covenant of good faith and fair dealing. Juries apparently were to be allowed to decide for themselves what constitutes good faith and to decide if the employer's actions meet the standard thus derived by them.[22] Under this approach, the implied covenant doctrine would give employees very broad protection.

Courts willing to relax the Employment-at-Will Rule began to raise doubts about the implied covenant theory in the early 1980s. In *Murphy v. American Home Products*,[23] the New York Court of Appeals disfavored the inconsistency of implying a promise in a breach of contract action that is inconsistent with the manifest intent of the parties.

The Wisconsin Supreme Court recognized the implied covenant doctrine but limited it greatly in *Brockmeyer v. Dun & Bradstreet*.[24] The *Brockmeyer* court concluded that implied covenant recovery should be limited to dismissals "contrary to a fundamental and well-defined public policy as evidenced by existing law."[25] In effect, it used the implied covenant theory to limit damages available under the public policy tort theory.

Now, California, Massachusetts, and Montana are the only states that rely heavily on the implied covenant as the primary wrongful dismissal doctrine, and all impose important limitations on its use.[26]

---

as statutes and constitutions, are sources of public policy) *with* Buethe v. Britt Airlines, Inc., 787 F.2d 1194 (7th Cir. 1986) (Posner, J.) (Indiana public policy tort doctrine provides cause of action for whistleblowers only when a statute creates a right to "blow a particular whistle"—presumably to report a particular type of violation to a particular agency).

[19] Professor Ronald Dworkin is particularly articulate in explaining how judges must consider policy in deciding difficult cases. *See generally* R. Dworkin, Taking Rights Seriously ch.4 (1977).

[20] 174 Cal. App. 2d 184, 344 P.2d 25 (1959).

[21] 114 N.H. 130, 316 A.2d 549 (1974).

[22] Petermann v. Teamsters, 174 Cal. App. 2d at 189, 344 P.2d at 28; Monge v. Beebe Rubber Co., 114 N.H. at 133, 316 A.2d at 552.

[23] 58 N.Y.2d 293, 305, 448 N.E.2d 86, 91, 461 N.Y.S.2d 232, 237 (1983) (accepting implied-in-fact contract theory but rejecting implied covenant).

[24] 113 Wis. 2d 561, 335 N.W.2d 834 (1983).

[25] *Id.* at 573, 335 N.W.2d at 840.

[26] See §§ **4.11, 4.23**.

§ 1.3 Pre-Industrial Revolution Employment Tenure Rule

Before the Industrial Revolution took place in England, circa 1750 to 1850, employment relations were of small importance in the law. Most economic activity was carried on by individual agricultural or commercial units composed of an entrepreneur and, at most, one or two servants.[27] When a master-servant relationship existed, it was treated as a status relationship not entirely unlike that within a family.[28] The master had obligations to his servant that were not purely economic. They included providing adequate shelter for the servant and supervising moral and skills development.[29] Reciprocally, the servant had duties to obey the master as well as to work industriously.[30] The obligations on both sides were not matters of contract between the two parties; they were obligations imposed on each by the common law as a matter of public policy,[31] and therefore the law gave little emphasis to the subjective intent of the parties as to what their relationship should be.

Blackstone summarized the master-servant relationship in 1765:

> The three great relations in private life are, (1) that of master and servant; which is founded in convenience, whereby a man is directed to call in the assistance of others, where his own skill and labor will not be sufficient to answer the cares incumbent upon him; (2) that of husband and wife . . . ; (3) that of guardian and wards. . . .
>
> The first sort of servants therefore, acknowledged by the laws of England, are menial servants; so called from being intra moenia, or domestics. The contract between them and their masters arises upon the hiring. If the hiring be general without any particular time limited, the law construes it to be a hiring for a year; upon a principle of natural equity, that the servant shall serve, and the master maintain him, throughout all the revolutions of the respective seasons; as well when there is work to be done, as when there is not; but the contract may be made for any larger or smaller term.[32]

Consistent with this general practice of defining the terms of the relationship externally, the law limited terminations. Depending on labor market conditions, it

---

[27] *See* P. Mantoux, The Industrial Revolution in the Eighteenth Century 47–56 (rev. ed. 1961) for an account of the pre-Industrial Revolution system of production and commerce.

[28] Note, *Protecting At Will Employees Against Wrongful Dismissal: The Duty to Terminate Only in Good Faith*, 93 Harv. L. Rev. 1816, 1824 (1980); Note, *Tortious Interference with Contractual Relations: The Transformation of Property, Contract and Tort,* 93 Harv. L. Rev. 1510, 1513 (1980) (employment agreements not thought of as contracts, but as status relations), P. Selznick, Law, Society, and Industrial Justice 123–24 (1969).

[29] Note, *Tortious Interference with Contractual Relations: The Transformation of Property, Contract and Tort,* 93 Harv. L. Rev. 1510, 1514 (1980).

[30] *Id.*

[31] Under the prevailing view of master-servant relationships, "it was not contemplated that the parties would design their own relationship. As in the case of marriage, the relation might be entered voluntarily but its character was fixed by law." P. Selznick, Law, Society, and Industrial Justice 123–24 (1969).

[32] W. Blackstone, Commentaries 422, 425 (Christian, 12th ed., vol. 1, 1793) (1st ed. London 1765).

was not uncommon for Parliament to enact statutes prohibiting servants from terminating their relationships with their masters.[33] As late as 1823,[34] it was a crime for an employee to terminate a relationship with a master prematurely.[35] Also, before the Industrial Revolution, civil liability could attach to improper interference with the master-servant relationship. Most of the reported cases deal with third party interference, predominately action by one person to lure away the servant of another.[36] Clearly civil liability could attach to such interference. It is less clear whether a servant could recover damages from a master for premature or improper termination of the relationship.[37] Some of the third party interference cases suggest, however, that civil liability could be imposed in an action by a plaintiff servant against a defendant master.[38]

§ 1.4 Development of the Employment-at-Will Rule

The Industrial Revolution brought large-scale industrial organization and accumulation of capital, changing the basic relationship between employee and employer.[39] It became advantageous for entrepreneurs to employ large numbers of workers.[40] Workers were no longer quasi-family members, but strangers bound to their employers by a more distant and purely economic relationship.[41] The duration of employment became dependent upon the demand for the product.[42] With demand fluctuations determined by market forces rather than by growing seasons, it made little economic sense for public policy to impose an obligation on the employer to continue employment through all four seasons. Employers opposed

---

[33] The 1563 Statute of Artificers required masters to give three months' notice before dismissing domestic servants. P. Selznick, Law, Society, and Industrial Justice, 126, n.10 (1969). The fourteenth century Statute of Laborers forbade servants to quit before the end of their term. This measure was motivated in part by labor shortages resulting from the Black Death. *See* P. Selznick at 126, *citing* 23 Edw. III ch. 2 (18 Jun. 1349).

[34] 4 Geo. IV ch. 34 (1823).

[35] *Id.*

[36] Note, *Tortious Interference with Contractual Relations: The Transformation of Property Contract and Tort,* 93 Harv. L. Rev. 1510, 1514–21 (1980). This action, called enticement, initially was allowed only between persons of equal status, but later developed to permit a servant to maintain an action to protect his own interest in the employment. Lumley v. Gye, 118 Eng. Rep. 749 (Q.B. 1853).

[37] Note, *Tortious Interference with Contractual Relations: The Transformation of Property, Contract and Tort,* 93 Harv. L. Rev. 1510, 1514–21 (1980).

[38] *Id.*

[39] *See* L. Marshall, The Emergence of the First Industrial City: Manchester 1780–1850 (1940) for an account of the transformation of a provincial market town (pop. 25,000) to a major industrial center (pop. 367,232) 70 years later, along with a description of large-scale industrial organization.

[40] *See* H. Wellington, Labor and the Legal Process 7 (1968).

[41] Note, *Protecting At Will Employees Against Wrongful Dismissal: The Duty to Terminate Only in Good Faith,* 93 Harv. L. Rev. 1816, 1824 (1980).

[42] P. Selznick, Law, Society, and Industrial Justice 135–36 (1980).

any general legal obligation to continue employment beyond the length of time needed to meet market demand for the employees' product.

Increased scale of production led to concerted employee action to bargain effectively with larger employers. As it became desirable for employees to organize collectively and to utilize the strike weapon, it became undesirable from their point of view to be bound to a presumed one-year employment.[43] Accordingly, employee interests sought shorter and shorter employment contracts. At one point in the mid-nineteenth century, so-called *minute contracts* in the mining industry were common.[44] Through shorter contracts, striking employees could avoid the civil and potential criminal penalties for breaching or inducing breaches of longer employment contracts.[45]

The Industrial Revolution thus led both parties to the employment relationship to desire greater freedom to negotiate employment terms. These desires coincided with changes in economic theory. Political economists in the seventeenth and eighteenth centuries exhalted the role of market forces in regulating economic activity, rather than public policy and law.[46] The reliance on market forces affected the regulation of labor markets as well as product and capital markets. Maximization of wealth required that producers be free to contract for labor based on the value their product could command in the marketplace.[47] These economic views led to an evolution of legal principles encompassed in the term *freedom of contract*.[48] These principles were enshrined in the United States Constitution for a period of time in a way that prevented federal or state legislatures from regulating employment relations.[49]

---

[43] Feinman, *The Development of the Employment at Will Rule*, 20 Am. J. Legis. Hist. 118, 121–22 (1976).

[44] *Id.*

[45] At common law, employers could enjoin a strike or obtain damages on the grounds that the strike violated employment contracts. *See* H. Perritt, Labor Injunctions ch. 1 (1986).

[46] Every individual, it is evident, can, in his local situation, judge much better [how to direct his energies] than any statesman or lawgiver can do for him." A. Smith, The Wealth of Nations 423 (Mod. Lib. ed. 1937).

> But neither one person, nor any number of persons, is warranted in saying to another human creature of ripe years that he shall not do with his life for his own benefit what he chooses to do with it. . . . The interference of society to overrule his judgment and purposes in what only regards himself must be grounded on general presumptions which may be altogether wrong and, even if right, are as likely as not to be misapplied to individual cases, by persons no better acquainted with the circumstances of such cases than those who look at them merely from without.

J.S. Mill, On Liberty 93 (Bobbs Merrill ed. 1980).

[47] J. Hurst, Law and Markets in United States History 23 (1982).

[48] *Id.* at 35.

[49] *See* Adair v. United States, 208 U.S. 161 (1908) (holding unconstitutional federal legislation prohibiting yellow dog contracts in the railroad industry); Coppage v. Kansas, 236 U.S. 1 (1915) (holding unconstitutional state legislation with same purpose). "In all such particulars the employer and employee have equality of right, and any legislation that disturbs that equality is an arbitrary interference with the liberty of contract which no government can legally justify in a free land." Justice Pitney, in *Coppage,* 236 U.S. at 10–11, quoting with approval Justice Harlan in *Adair,* 208 U.S. 174–75.

§ 1.4 DEVELOPMENT

Complete freedom of contract implies that the terms of an employment relationship, like those of any other economic relationship, should be determined entirely by the parties. Therefore, no presumptions of employment duration, wage levels, or any other factors affecting the substance of the employment relationship should be imposed by public policy or law.[50]

Freedom of contract became a slogan for opposing labor protective legislation. The same forces that were producing a preference for regulation by the marketplace also were diminishing the bargaining power of individual employees.[51] Conceptually, however, it is oversimple to suppose that the legal evolution in favor of freedom of contract was driven by any public policy preference for capital over labor. Rather, it is more accurate to conclude that the move toward freedom of contract and the diminution in employee bargaining power were contemporaneous but largely independent phenomena.

In any event, any legal presumption of employment contract terms not actually contemplated by the parties was at odds with economic freedom. The law responded apace. In 1877, Horace G. Wood wrote an authoritative treatise on the law of master and servant and repudiated the one-year rule articulated by Blackstone.[52] Wood expressed the American rule as follows: "With us the rule is inflexible, that a general or indefinite hiring is *prima facie* a hiring at will . . . "[53] With surprising speed, Wood's rule was adopted by most American jurisdictions.[54] By 1913, Labatt's Commentaries on the Law of Master and Servant concluded that the majority of American courts had rejected the English rule and substituted another presumption: that a general hiring is to be construed as a hiring at will under which

---

[50] Note, *Protecting At Will Employees Against Wrongful Dismissal: The Duty to Terminate Only in Good Faith*, 93 Harv. L. Rev. 1816, 1818–19 (1980).

[51] The increased reliance upon regulation by market forces left more and more details of the employment relationship to be negotiated between the employer and employee, as contrasted with the status relationship between master and servant where the terms of the relationship were supplied by tradition and law. During periods of relative oversupply of labor, individual employees were required to negotiate for terms with employers having substantial bargaining power because of the availability of other potential employees who could work for less. Moreover, the trend toward large-scale enterprise necessitated a switch from individual negotiation of employment conditions to standardization of terms since transaction costs of individual negotiations would be prohibitive for the enterprise. *See generally* Note, *Tortious Interference with Contractual Relations: The Transformation of Property, Contract and Tort*, 93 Harv. L. Rev. 1510, 1514 (1980), Note, *Protecting At Will Employees Against Wrongful Dismissal: The Duty to Terminate Only in Good Faith*, 93 Harv. L. Rev. 1816, 1824 (1980).

[52] H.G. Wood, A Treatise on the Law of Master and Servant (1877).

[53] *Id.* § 134 at 272.

[54] *See, e.g.,* Martin v. New York Life Ins. Co., 148 N.Y. 117, 121, 42 N.E. 416, 417 (1895); P. Selznick, Law, Society, and Industrial Justice 133 (1980), Feinman, *The Development of the Employment At Will Rule*, 20 Am. J. Leg. Hist. 118, 126 (1976) (puzzling origin of Wood's rule; speed of adoption by state courts). The origins of the rule have been characterized as "bizarre" by one judge. *See* Murphy v. American Home Prod. Corp., 58 N.Y.2d 293, 308, 448 N.E.2d 86, 93, 461 N.Y.S.2d 232, 239 (1983) (Meyer, J., dissenting). Critical historical analysis of Wood's rule is provided in Toussaint v. Blue Cross & Blue Shield, 408 Mich. 579, 601–03, 292 N.W.2d 880, 886 (1980).

either party may at any time determine the employment.[55] Application of Wood's version of the new American rule never was free from criticism, however.[56] Modern historians have observed that Professor Wood offered little analysis to justify his rejection of the English tradition.[57] He cited only four American cases as authority for his approach to general hiring, none of which really furnished support.[58]

In time, the force of Wood's rule was increased by transforming it from a rebuttable presumption into a substantive limitation on employment contracts. Wood's articulation of the American rule put it in terms of a presumption.[59] Accordingly, employees could recover for breach of contract by rebutting the presumption through evidence ordinarily sufficient to establish an implied-in-fact contract term. Nevertheless, many American jurisdictions came, in time, to treat the presumption of an employment at will as precluding enforcement of an informal employment contract in most cases.[60] Courts began to construe promises of permanent employment to be promises of indefinite employment. Promises of indefinite employment were construed as too vague to be enforceable, either because there was no

---

[55] "The preponderance of American authority in favor of the doctrine that an indefinite hiring is presumptively a hiring at will is so great that it is now scarcely open to criticism." 1 C. Labatt, Master and Servant § 160 at 519 (1913). Promises of permanent employment similarly were construed as giving rise only to employment terminable at the will of either party. *Id.* § 175 at 551. However, Professor Labatt questioned the soundness of a doctrine that would ignore expectation as an element indicative of intent. *See id.* § 160 at 519.

[56] *See* 1 S. Williston, Contracts § 39 (1921); Wagenseller v. Scottsdale Memorial Hosp., 147 Ariz. 370, 375, 710 P.2d 1025, 1030 (1985) (characterizing foundation of Wood's rule as "unsound").

[57] *See Implied Contract Rights to Job Security,* 26 Stan. L. Rev. 335, 341 n.54 (1974); Toussaint v. Blue Cross & Blue Shield, 408 Mich. 579, 603, 292 N.W.2d 880, 886 (1980) (both criticizing Wood's analysis).

[58] Wood cited Franklin Mining Co. v. Harris, 24 Mich. 115 (1871); Tatterson v. Suffolk Mfg. Co., 106 Mass. 56 (1870); Wilder v. United States, 5 Ct. Cl. 462 (1869); DeBriar v. Minturn, 1 Cal. 450 (1851). *See* H.G. Wood, A Treatise on the Law of Master and Servant § 134 at 272 (1877). "To the extent the issue of the term of employment was even present in these cases, the juries were permitted to determine the duration of the contract from written or oral communications between the parties, usages of trade, the type of employment, and other circumstances." Toussaint v. Blue Cross & Blue Shield, 408 Mich. at 602, 292 N.W.2d at 886. Three of the four cases which Wood cited do not, in fact, support him. In *Franklin Mining Co.* a verdict for plaintiff-employee was affirmed. The court held that employment of at least one year's duration could be inferred from an oral agreement as to yearly salary. The court in *Tatterson* held that the original negotiations between employer and employee were competent evidence to show terms, express or implied, under which the parties continued their relation. *Wilder* is not an employment case. *De Briar* arguably did support Wood's conclusion. There, the former employee was denied recovery because no evidence was offered from which a definite term or promise of termination only for cause could be inferred.

[59] "[I]f the servant seeks to make it out a yearly hiring, the burden is upon him to establish it by proof." H.G. Wood, A Treatise on the Law of Master and Servant § 134 at 272 (1877). *See* Weiner v. McGraw-Hill, Inc., 57 N.Y.2d 458, 466, 443 N.E.2d 441, 446, 457 N.Y.S.2d 193, 198 (1982) (at-will rule, adopted in New York in 1895, as rebuttable presumption); Toussaint v. Blue Cross & Blue Shield, 408 Mich. at 603, 292 N.W.2d at 886 (Wood's rule originally a rebuttable presumption).

[60] In Martin v. New York Life Ins. Co., 148 N.Y. 117, 42 N.E. 416, 417 (1895), Wood was quoted in support of a holding that a general hiring was not to be presumed to be a hiring for a one-year

reliable way to determine whether a breach had occurred, or because such a promise insufficiently showed the parties' intent to be bound, absent special consideration given by the employee in exchange for the promise.[61] Under the special consideration requirement, an indefinite contract could not be enforced unless the employee-plaintiff could show some form of independent consideration beyond performance of his services.[62] In either event, courts refused to permit juries to hear evidence of the parties' informal understanding regarding tenure.[63]

Thus, there were two interrelated theories for preventing recovery for wrongful dismissal on a contract theory: the presumption of an employment at will, and the stringent application of an independent consideration requirement to prevent enforcement of a contract unless independent consideration could be shown.

Of course, social and economic pressures led to legal developments protecting the economic welfare of workers. But these legal developments occurred primarily with respect to collective organization of employees.[64] Collective bargaining facilitated negotiation of collective agreements overriding the employment-at-will status. Development of labor law around collective bargaining relieved social and political pressure to change the law of individual employment relationships. Accordingly, there was little effective pressure to change the legal rules that made it difficult for employees to recover for breach of individual employment contracts.[65]

---

term, merely because the salary was described in terms of an annual rate. Developments in the law of this era are discussed in Weiner v. McGraw-Hill, Inc., 57 N.Y.2d at 462–63, 443 N.E.2d at 443–44, 457 N.Y.S.2d at 195–96, and Toussaint v. Blue Cross & Blue Shield, 408 Mich. at 604, 292 N.W.2d at 887. See Morris v. Lutheran Medical Center, 215 Neb. 677, 680, 340 N.W.2d 388, 391 (1983) (criticizing version of at-will rule that imposes substantive limits on contract formation); Martin v. Federal Life Ins. Co., 109 Ill. App. 3d 596, 440 N.E.2d 998 (1982) (additional consideration requirement should be rebuttable). See §§ **4.12, 4.15** for the rationale behind the additional consideration requirement.

[61] By 1925, the majority rule was described as calling for a contract purporting to be for permanent employment to be "an indefinite hiring terminable at the will of either party," in the absence of "good consideration additional to the services contracted to be rendered," or "additional express or implied stipulation as to the duration of the employment . . ." Annotation, 35 A.L.R. 1432 (1925). The relationship between the form of consideration and the enforceability of the promise is considered in more detail in §§ **4.12–4.18**.

[62] In Adolph v. Cookware Co. of Am., 283 Mich. 561, 568, 278 N.W. 687, 689 (1938), the court stated flatly that additional consideration beyond services rendered was necessary to make a contract for permanent employment enforceable. See Murphree v. Alabama Farm Bureau Ins. Co., 449 So. 2d 1218 (Ala. 1984) (reviewing development of special consideration rule and applying it in a modern case). See §§ **4.12, 4.15**.

[63] See Annotation, 35 A.L.R. 1432 (1925).

[64] The Great Depression constituted the major social pressure resulting in legislation of the New Deal, which, among many other things, promoted the unionization of industry, thereby providing protection to workers covered by collective bargaining agreements. See P. Selznick, Law, Society and Industrial Justice 138 (1980); H. Perritt, Labor Injunctions ch. 2 (1986) (legal and political developments leading up to enactment of the National Labor Relations Act (NLRA).

[65] Since the unions presented a vocal and unified source of pressure compared to individual workers, once legislation was enacted for the benefit of unions, the remaining individual workers lacked an effective political voice. P. Selznick, Law, Society and Industrial Justice 239–40 (1980). See § **9.4** for an analysis of the political calculus of wrongful dismissal policy.

§ 1.5 Stages in the Erosion of the Employment-at-Will Rule

Erosion of the Employment-at-Will Rule began with two defined groups of employees—civil servants and employees represented by trade unions—and then spread to terminations motivated by class membership and defined conduct. Only later were legal protections against wrongful dismissal extended by the common law to employees generally.

§ 1.6 —Civil Service Protection

Civil service protections for federal employees began in 1883 with the Pendleton Act.[66] The Act, however, did not address the question of removals; indeed, Congress rejected a proposal that removals be permitted only for cause.[67] It was not until enactment of the Lloyd-LaFollette Act in 1912[68] that federal employees enjoyed protection against removal except for cause.

Gradually, this basic protection has been extended to virtually all federal and state, and most local government employees.[69] Beginning in the late 1960s, constitutional protections against wrongful dismissal were added to civil service protection, at least for employees below the federal level.[70]

§ 1.7 —Protection of Employees Represented by Trade Unions

Early in the twentieth century, labor interests gained sufficient political power to prompt state legislatures to enact legislation forbidding employer discrimination against employees based on union membership.[71] At the federal level, similar

---

[66] 22 Stat. 403 (1883). *See* Bush v. Lucas, 462 U.S. 367, 381–86 (1983) (describing history of federal civil service system).

[67] *Id.* at 381 n.17.

[68] *Id.* at 383, citing Lloyd-LaFollette Act, 37 Stat. 539, 555, § 6 (1912).

[69] See § **6.5**. *See generally* Note, *Developments in the Law—Public Employment,* 97 Harv. L. Rev. 1611, 1619–68 (1984) (historical and political evolution of civil service).

[70] The requirement under the civil service laws for cause for termination, discussed in §§ **6.3–6.5**, is approximately the same as the substantive due process requirement for a rational relation between the reason for a termination and the legitimate needs of the employing agency, discussed in § **6.13**.

[71] *See* H. Perritt, Labor Injunctions ch. 2 (1986) (development of state and federal legislation protecting concerted employee action); C. Killingsworth, State Labor Relations Acts 10 n.13 (1948). An example was a 1903 Kansas law prohibiting yellow dog contracts. Such laws were held to be an unconstitutional interference with the freedom of contract in Coppage v. Kansas, 236 U.S. 1 (1915).

protective legislation was limited to protection of railroad workers[72] and to divesting federal courts of jurisdiction to enjoin strikes.[73]

By the middle of the 1930s, state and federal legislation ensured that employees could organize collectively to pressure their employers to negotiate improved conditions of employment, including protections against wrongful dismissal.[74] Enactment of the National Labor Relations Act in 1935 took federal labor policy a step further. That Act established as federal policy the promotion of collective bargaining and defined employee rights in detail. Administrative machinery was erected to protect employee rights associated with collective action. Union representation spread in rapidly growing basic industries. The practice of negotiating grievance and arbitration provisions through collective bargaining provided employees with protection against wrongful dismissal.[75] Development of federal labor law ensured that such provisions would be favored in the courts.[76]

§ 1.8 —Protection against Class-Based Discrimination

The civil rights movement led to statutory protection for private sector employees against discriminatory dismissals.[77] Changes in discrimination laws began with federal prohibitions against discrimination in the Unemployment Relief Act of 1933.[78] In 1940, the federal government moved more broadly with the promulgation of Executive Order No. 8587,[79] prohibiting race and religious discrimination in the federal civil service, and in 1941, with Executive Order No. 8802,[80] prohibiting discrimination on the basis of race, creed, color or national origin in employment by war contractors. Nondiscrimination in the civil service was mandated by the Congress in the Ramspeck Act.[81]

Meanwhile, at the state level, New York enacted the first state fair employment practices act in 1945, although it had moved earlier to prohibit employment discrimination in certain industries; for example, public utilities. By the time Title

---

[72] *See* Act of 1898, 30 Stat. 424, held unconstitutional in part in Adair v. United States, 208 U.S. 161 (1908).

[73] Norris LaGuardia Act, 47 Stat. 70 (1932), 29 U.S.C. §§ 101–115 (1982). *See generally* H. Perritt, Labor Injunctions (1986).

[74] *See, e.g.,* National Labor Relations Act, §§ 7, 8(3), 49 Stat. 452 (1935), codified as amended, 29 U.S.C. §§ 157, 158(a)(3) (1982).

[75] The spread of labor arbitration in the United States is discussed more fully in **§ 3.3**.

[76] See **§ 3.20**.

[77] *See* Title VII of the Civil Rights Acts of 1964, 42 U.S.C. § 2000e (1982).

[78] Act of March 31, 1933, 48 Stat. 22, 23.

[79] 5 Fed. Reg. 4445 (1940).

[80] 6 Fed. Reg. 3109 (1941).

[81] 54 Stat. 1211 (1940).

VII of the Civil Rights Act of 1964 had been enacted, more than half the states had fair employment practices legislation.[82]

Overlapping these statutory and executive branch developments were judicial decisions prohibiting race discrimination in collective bargaining, beginning with *Steele v. Louisville & Nashville Railroad Co.*[83] Eventually, by the mid-1970s, statutory protection against discrimination had expanded to a dozen or more specific employee characteristics and types of conduct.[84]

§ 1.9 — Common Law Protection for Private Sector Workers

Further expansion of employment security protections for private sector employees developed at common law, beginning in the mid-1970s. The developments began first under contract theories and later under tort theories. Relatively subtle changes in contract principles applicable to informal agreements of employment were sufficient to permit recovery for wrongful dismissal. All that was necessary was to treat the Employment-at-Will Rule as a rebuttable presumption rather than a substantive bar to breach of contract suits by employees covered by informal contracts. American cases occasionally appeared in the 1920s and 1930s that permitted employees to recover for wrongful dismissal by proving facts that today would be classified as recognizing implied-in-fact contracts for employment tenure.[85]

The public policy tort doctrine developed more recently. Early cases, explored in more detail in **Chapter 5**,[86] permitted tort recovery for instances of employer actions that clearly interfered with societal interests.[87] Gradually, the tort principles developed in the more outrageous cases were applied to less outrageous instances, thereby potentially permitting employee recovery in instances evidencing little more than employee protest of management decisions.

---

[82] *See generally,* Jones, *The Development of Modern Equal Employment Opportunity and Affirmative Action Law: A Brief Chronological Overview,* 20 How. L.J. 74 (1977); M. Sovern, Legal Restraints on Racial Discrimination in Employment 9 (1966).

[83] 323 U.S. 192 (1944) (Railway Labor Act).

[84] *See, e.g.,* Age Discrimination in Employment Act, 29 U.S.C. §§ 621–634 (1982); Rehabilitation Act of 1973, Pub. L. No. 93-112, 87 Stat. 355 (codified as amended in scattered sections of 29 U.S.C.). See generally §§ **2.2–2.14**.

[85] *Compare* Hoffman Speciality Co. v. Pelouze, 158 Va. 586, 594, 164 S.E. 397, 399 (1932) (employment-at-will rule is a rebuttable presumption) *with* Pine River State Bank v. Mettille, 333 N.W.2d 622, 629 (Minn. 1983) (same). *Compare* Norfolk S. Ry. Co. v. Harris, 190 Va. 966, 976, 59 S.E.2d 110, 115 (1950) (consideration present, mutuality irrelevant, where employer promised no arbitrary discharge, in exchange for services) *with* Weiner v. McGraw-Hill, Inc., 57 N.Y.2d 458, 463-64, 443 N.E.2d 441, 444, 457 N.Y.S.2d 193, 196 (1982) (same).

[86] See § **5.10**.

[87] See § **5.5**.

§ 1.9 PROTECTION OF PRIVATE SECTOR WORKERS

The development of modern wrongful dismissal case law begins with *Petermann v. Teamsters*,[88] decided in California in 1959. The *Petermann* court recognized a cause of action under contract principles when the plaintiff alleged a violation of public policy: a discharge for plaintiff's refusal to commit perjury on behalf of the defendant.[89] The court concluded that the employer's conduct breached a covenant of good faith and fair dealing implied in the at-will employment contract by operation of law.

In 1974, the Supreme Court of New Hampshire extended the implied covenant principle derived from *Petermann* to encompass bad faith dismissals more generally, thus balancing the employer's interest in running its enterprise against the employee's interest in continued employment.[90] Three years later, the Massachusetts Supreme Judicial Court, in *Fortune v. National Cash Register Co.*,[91] held that an employer was liable under the implied covenant doctrine on firing an employee for the purpose of reneging on sales commissions.[92]

In 1980, the Supreme Court of Michigan articulated a more traditional wrongful dismissal contract doctrine in *Toussaint v. Blue Cross & Blue Shield*.[93] In that case, the court held that legitimate employee expectations of employment tenure based on the employer's policy statements and handbooks were enforceable in breach of contract actions.

Development of the public policy tort theory for wrongful dismissal occurred after development of the contract theory.[94] The seminal tort case was decided in Oregon in 1975.[95] There the plaintiff was awarded compensatory and punitive damages after being dismissed for requesting jury duty over his employer's objections. The court held that tort liability could arise from employer conduct undermining the public policy in favor of jury service.[96] In *Sheets v. Teddy's Frosted Foods, Inc.*,[97] a 1980 Connecticut case, the court held that a quality control supervisor could recover tort damages if he could prove that his dismissal was caused by his protests of deviations from food labeling requirements. In 1981, the Supreme Court of New Hampshire extended the public policy tort still further by holding that the dismissal of an employee responsible for a store that was burglarized could violate public policy interests in employee safety.[98] There was a background of

---

[88] 174 Cal. App. 2d 184,, 344 P.2d 25 (1959).

[89] *Id.* at 190, 344 P.2d at 28.

[90] Monge v. Beebe Rubber Co., 114 N.H. 130, 316 A.2d 549 (1974).

[91] 373 Mass. 96, 104, 364 N.E.2d 1251, 1257 (1977).

[92] *Id.*

[93] 408 Mich. 579, 292 N.W.2d 880 (1980).

[94] Cases using the tort label, at least, arose later. Arguably, the implied covenant cases, though characterized as breach of contract cases, are really tort cases. The duty imposed on the employer in those cases is derived from public policy rather than from the parties' agreement.

[95] Nees v. Hocks, 272 Or. 210, 536 P.2d 512 (1975).

[96] *Id.* at 219, 536 P.2d at 516.

[97] 179 Conn. 471, 480, 427 A.2d 385, 389 (1980).

[98] Cloutier v. Great Atl. & Pac. Tea Co., 121 N.H. 915, 924, 436 A.2d 1140, 1145 (1981).

disagreements between the plaintiff and his employer over provision of additional security for the store. In 1983, the Third Circuit, applying Pennsylvania law, held that a public policy tort claim could be premised on the free speech policies contained in the United States Constitution.[99]

All the tort developments have not been in the direction of expanded liability, however. The New York Court of Appeals refused, in 1983, to recognize a tort cause of action for wrongful dismissal, believing it to be within the province of the legislature to make the public policy judgments involved.[1] Also, most courts have been reluctant to permit public policy tort cases to be based on policies articulated in statutes providing administrative remedies.[2]

§ 1.10 Reasons for Erosion of the Employment-At-Will Rule

Although identifying the underlying causes for changes in common law rules is speculative at best, it is reasonable to assume that statutory and constitutional developments influenced judges when they decided common law cases. Beginning in the late 1940s American labor law shifted its focus from the protection of collective employee rights to the protection of individual employee rights in certain areas.[3] This shift was evidenced by development of the duty of fair representation which permitted individual employees to recover against their trade union representatives in certain circumstances.[4] Similarly, enactment of the Labor Management Reporting and Disclosure Act in 1959[5] manifested some of the same public policy concerns. The shift towards protection of individual employee rights, as opposed merely to protection of collective rights, obviously was reflected by enactment of Title VII of the Civil Rights Act of 1964,[6] the Age Discrimination in Employment Act of 1967,[7] and subsequent statutes protecting employees against certain other kinds of invidious discrimination.[8]

Beginning in the mid-1950s, the federal courts began to expand constitutional remedies to recognize interests previously unprotected by either statutory or state common law.[9] Some of these expansions afforded government employees protection

---

[99] Novosel v. Nationwide Ins. Co., 721 F.2d 894 (3d Cir. 1983).

[1] Murphy v. American Home Prods., Inc., 58 N.Y.2d 293, 448 N.E.2d 86, 461 N.Y.S.2d 232 (1983).

[2] See § **5.9**.

[3] *See* H. Wellington Labor and the Legal Process (1968).

[4] See § **3.25**.

[5] Pub. L. No. 86-257, 73 Stat. 519, 19 U.S.C. § 401 (1982).

[6] Civil Rights Act of 1964, 42 U.S.C. § 2000e (1982).

[7] Age Discrimination in Employment Act of 1967, 29 U.S.C. §§ 621–634 (1982).

[8] See §§ **2.2–2.14**.

[9] *See, e.g.*, Brown v. Board of Educ., 347 U.S. 483 (1954) (school segregation violates equal protection); Griswold v. Connecticut, 381 U.S. 479 (1965) (prohibiting dissemination of birth control information violates due process); Goldberg v. Kelly, 397 U.S. 254 (1970) (termination of welfare benefits requires procedural due process); Boddie v. Connecticut, 401 U.S. 371 (1971) (fees for

§ 1.10 REASONS FOR EROSION

against wrongful dismissal.[10] This part of the legal evolution resembled common law development in its accommodation of changing social consciousness and the maxim, "every right, when withheld, must have a remedy, and every injury its proper redress."[11] Particularly influential was *Perry v. Sindermann*,[12] which permitted a public employee to establish a constitutionally protected property right based on expectations of employment tenure derived from employer conduct.[13]

These statutory and constitutional legal developments had their impact on judges confronted with the Employment-at-Will Rule. Dealing with new constitutional principles probably made state judges more sensitive to their power to change the common law. In addition, as they became more familiar with applying statutory principles protecting individual employees, it is likely that they became increasingly uneasy with common law rules that barred recovery by individual employees against their employers in circumstances that seemed to the judges unfair or outrageous.[14]

The changes in common law rules necessary to permit such employees to recover were not extreme. As has been noted, the Employment-at-Will Rule depended for its efficacy on special interpretations of presumptions of contract terms and the requirement for consideration.[15] To permit an employee to recover in breach of contract, it really only was necessary to apply to the employment relationship the same basic contract rules respecting implied-in-fact promises and consideration that are applied to other forms of legal relationships.[16] Similarly, as is explored

---

divorce proceedings violate due process); Roe v. Wade, 410 U.S. 113 (1973) (statutes limiting abortion to life-threatening conditions violate due process); Frontiero v. Richardson, 411 U.S. 677 (1973) (denial of dependent quarters allowances to female uniformed service members violates due process).

[10] *See, e.g.,* Wieman v. Updegraff, 344 U.S. 183 (1952) (implying that right to hold public job is property interest protected by Fourteenth Amendment); Slochower v. Board of Higher Educ., 350 U.S. 551 (1956) (discharge of public employee for assertion of Fifth Amendment rights violates due process); Greene v. McElroy, 360 U.S. 474 (1959) (right to private job is liberty or property interest protected from government interference); Keyishian v. Board of Regents, 385 U.S. 589 (1967) (state statute requiring loyalty certification by teachers unconstitutional); Pickering v. Board of Educ., 391 U.S. 563 (1968) (invalidating dismissal of teacher for making public statements).

[11] Bush v. Lucas, 462 U.S. 367, 373 n.10 (1983) (quoting Blackstone). *See also* Parnar v. Americana Hotels, Inc., 65 Haw. 370, 375, 652 P.2d 625, 628 (1982) (plight of unprotected employees led to change in common law rule); Adler v. American Standard Corp., 291 Md. 31, 41–42, 432 A.2d 464, 470 (1981) (need for protection of a majority of employees not otherwise protected).

[12] 408 U.S. 593 (1972). The influence of *Perry* was noted in Toussaint v. Blue Cross & Blue Shield, 408 Mich. 579, 617, 292 N.W.2d 880, 894 (1980).

[13] Constitutional developments are explored in more detail in §§ **6.9–6.13**.

[14] Pine River State Bank v. Mettille, 333 N.W.2d 622, 628–29 (Minn. 1983) (rejection of doctrine requiring additional consideration to support promise of employment tenure).

[15] See § **1.4** (development of Employment-At-Will Rule) and § **4.13** (application of mutuality of obligation to prevent recovery).

[16] In Weiner v. McGraw-Hill, Inc., 57 N.Y.2d 458, 443 N.E.2d 441, 457 N.Y.S.2d 193 (1982), the court permitted a discharged employee to recover in breach of contract for violation of provisions of an employer's handbook. It found it unnecessary to make new law because it understood traditional contract law principles as sufficient to support the cause of action. *Id.* at 462, 443 N.E.2d at 443, 457 N.Y.S.2d at 195.

in more detail in **Chapter 5**,[17] development of the public policy tort required little more than application of generally recognized prima facie tort principles to the specific facts of an individual employment termination.[18]

At the same time, maturation of legal principles in the statutory employment discrimination and labor relations areas helped to reduce concern that imposing liability on employers in certain circumstances would fundamentally undermine the economic system.[19] The body of case law under the antidiscrimination statutes and the National Labor Relations Act provided models for common law principles that adequately protected both the employees' right to recover for wrongful dismissal and the employers' right to dismiss for cause.[20]

Common law recovery for wrongful dismissal was well respected and commonly used in the railroad industry[21] until the 1972 United States Supreme Court decision in *Andrews v. Louisville & Nashville Railroad*.[22] Nevertheless, it does not seem that these railroad wrongful dismissal cases were particularly significant in influencing courts to adopt more general wrongful dismissal principles. Rather, public employee constitutional developments, collective bargaining practices, and employment discrimination law set the stage for the private sector common law developments of the late 1970s and early 1980s.

§ 1.11 Influence of Commentators

The influence of scholarly commentators on the development of the common law is well recognized.[23] For example, Professor Wood apparently played a significant role in promoting the Employment-at-Will Rule.[24] Similarly, a number of law review articles and treatise commentaries written since the mid-1960s were influential in persuading the courts to modify the at-will rule and to permit recovery in both contract and tort.

---

[17] See § **5.5**.

[18] See generally **ch. 5**.

[19] For an expression of this concern, see the dissent in Weiner v. McGraw-Hill, Inc., 57 N.Y.2d 458, 467, 443 N.E.2d 441, 446, 457 N.Y.S.2d 193, 198 (1982), the majority's response, *Id.* at 466 n.7, 443 N.E.2d at 446 n.7, 457 N.Y.S.2d at 198 n.7, and the position of the *amici curiae* in Toussaint v. Blue Cross & Blue Shield, 408 Mich. at 609–10, 292 N.W.2d at 890.

[20] See **ch. 7** for a discussion of the evidentiary limitations of statutory and common law remedies for employment termination.

[21] *See* Moore v. Illinois Cent. R.R., 312 U.S. 630 (1941) (wrongful dismissal action may be maintained by railroad employees); Norfolk S. Ry. Co. v. Harris, 190 Va. 966, 59 S.E.2d 110 (1950) (employment-at-will doctrine is a rebuttable presumption).

[22] 406 U.S. 320 (1972) (statutory arbitration is exclusive forum for railroad employee claims of wrongful dismissal).

[23] *See* C. Jacobs, Law Writers and the Courts (1954) (influence of commentators in establishing liberty of contract as a constitutional limitation on state police power).

[24] *See* Toussaint v. Blue Cross & Blue Shield, 408 Mich. 579, 601–03, 292 N.W.2d 880, 886–87 (1980) (influence of Wood); see also § **1.4** (same).

The seeds of change were sown at about the same time that the employment-at-will doctrine was gaining favor. Oliver Wendell Holmes's formulation of a broad cause of action for intentional torts was the genesis of the prima facie tort concept.[25] As **Chapter 5** suggests, the prima facie tort is the framework within which the public policy tort has been developed.[26] Similarly, contract doctrine always admitted conceptually of a wrongful dismissal cause of action, as Professor Williston recognized as early as 1921.[27] A major push by commentators for easier access to the common law courts by wrongfully dismissed employees developed in the 1960s. Intellectual capital was contributed by Philip Selznick, who opined that the law of employer-employee relations best could be treated in terms of status rather than in terms of contract, analogous to the Blackstone view.[28] Professor Selznick contributed a major treatise in 1969 and had been promoting work in the area since the early 1960s. Professor Selznick's arguments were sketched first in a 1957 paper presented to the American Sociological Association and in a paper presented at the Symposium on Business Policy sponsored by the Harvard Graduate School of Business Administration in 1963.[29] Papers prepared by graduate students working in collaboration with Professor Selznick were published during the same time period.[30] Other articles were written in the early 1960s encouraging the development of legal concepts that would protect employees' interests in private employment.[31]

A 1967 article by Lawrence E. Blades[32] marshalled the arguments for change in application of the Employment-at-Will Rule, and influenced the courts that relaxed the prohibitions on recovery by individual employees in breach of contract or tort actions.[33] Professor Blades argued that large corporate organizations exercise great

---

[25] See Holmes, *Privilege, Malice and Intent,* 8 Harv. L. Rev. 1 (1894).

[26] See § **5.5**.

[27] See 11 S. Williston, Contracts § 1361 (1921); *see also* Note, *Employment Contracts of Unspecified Duration,* 42 Colum. L. Rev. 107, 120–21 (1942).

[28] P. Selznick, Law, Society, and Industrial Justice 271 (1969).

[29] *Id.* at v.

[30] *Id.* at v, citing H. Vollmer, Employee Rights and the Employment Relationship (1960); P. Nonet, The Decline of Contract (unpublished masters thesis, 1964); J. McGillivray, Social Organization and Employee Rights (unpublished Ph.D. dissertation, Dep't of Sociology, Univ. of Calif., Berkeley, 1966).

[31] *See* Reich, *The New Property,* 73 Yale L.J. 733 (1964); Note, *Due Process and the "Right" to a Job,* 46 Va. L. Rev. 323 (1960).

[32] Blades, *Employment at Will vs. Individual Freedom: On Limiting the Abusive Exercise of Employer Power,* 67 Colum. L. Rev. 1404 (1967).

[33] No law review articles were cited in Petermann v. Teamsters, 174 Cal. App.2d 184, 344 P.2d 25 (1959); or in Nees v. Hocks, 272 Or. 210, 536 P.2d 512 (1975). The Blades article and a student work, Comment, *Towards a Property Right in Employment,* 22 Buffalo L. Rev. 1081 (1973), were cited in Geary v. United States Steel Corp., 456 Pa. 171, 176 n.6, 319 A.2d 174, 176 n.6 (1974). The Blades article was cited in Monge v. Beebe Rubber Co., 114 N.H. 130, 133, 316 A.2d 549, 551 (1974) (also citing a 1970 student work, Note, *California's Controls on Employer Abuse of Employee Political Rights,* 22 Stan. L. Rev. 1015 (1970)), and Fortune v. National Cash Register Co., 373 Mass. 96, 101, 364 N.E.2d 1251, 1255 (1977) (also citing

power over individual citizens by virtue of their unlimited right to discharge employees.[34] He criticized as a paradox the lack of legal protections against the abuse of such private power in view of the substantial development of constitutional law during the late 1950s and early 1960s to protect citizens against the abuse of governmental power.[35]

In Professor Blades's view, a private damages remedy for wrongfully dismissed employees was well suited to deter abuse of employer power and to compensate employees injured by such abuses.[36] He was not, however, optimistic that contract law would evolve to permit a remedy because of interpretations of the consideration requirement that require mutuality of obligation before an employee might enforce employer promises of employment tenure in a breach of contract suit.[37] Neither was he optimistic that state or federal legislatures would act to provide an administrative mechanism to adjudicate wrongful dismissal claims, although he thought such a mechanism was desirable.[38]

Accordingly, Professor Blades suggested tort remedies for wrongful dismissal.[39] He argued that the prima facie tort doctrine provided the rubric within which such tort remedies could be developed.[40] He also cited the torts of abuse of process and intentional interference with contractual relations as useful precedents for a wrongful dismissal tort. Both of these torts require courts and juries to identify cases in which wrongful motive produces liability for acts that otherwise are lawful.[41] Having made the case for a wrongful dismissal tort, Professor Blades

---

Blumrosen, *Worker's Rights Against Employers and Unions: Justice Francis—A Judge for Our Season*, 24 Rutgers L. Rev. 480 (1970)). The Blades article was cited by the courts in Harless v. First Nat'l Bank in Fairmont, 246 S.E.2d 270, 275 (W. Va. 1978); Tameny v. Atlantic Richfield Co., 27 Cal. 3d 167, 173 n.7, 610 P.2d 1330, 1333, 164 Cal. Rptr. 839, 842 n.7 (1980) (noting influence of academic commentators); Pierce v. Ortho Pharmaceutical Corp., 84 N.J. 58, 66, 417 A.2d 505, 509 (1980); Sheets v. Teddy's Frosted Foods, 179 Conn. 471, 476, 427 A.2d 385, 387 (1980); Adler v. American Standard Corp., 291 Md. 31, 42, 432 A.2d 464, 470 (1981); Weiner v. McGraw-Hill, Inc., 57 N.Y.2d 458, 463, 443 N.E.2d 441, 444, 457 N.Y.S.2d 193, 196 (1982); Parnar v. Americana Hotels, Inc., 65 Haw. 370, 375, 652 P.2d 625, 628 n.7 (1982) (Blades is seminal); Pine River State Bank v. Mettille, 333 N.W.2d 622, 630 (Minn. 1983); and Wagenseller v. Scottsdale Memorial Hosp., 147 Ariz. 370, 710 P.2d 1025, 1031 (1985) (citing Blades).

[34] Blades, *Employment at Will vs. Individual Freedom: On Limiting the Abusive Exercise of Employer Power*, 67 Colum. L. Rev. 1404–05 (1967).

[35] *Id.* at 1435.

[36] *Id.* at 1413.

[37] *Id.* at 1421.

[38] *Id.* at 1434.

[39] *Id.* at 1422.

[40] *Id.* at 1423. The analytical framework suggested in this treatise for understanding wrongful dismissal tort cases conforms to this view. See § 5.5 (basic approach under § 870 of the Restatement (Second) of Torts), § 5.21 (use of the label prima facie tort).

[41] Blades, *Employment at Will vs. Individual Freedom: On Limiting the Abusive Exercise of Employer Power*, 67 Colum. L. Rev. 1424 (1967).

§ 1.11 COMMENTATORS

proceeded to offer suggestions about the allocations of burdens of proof so as to preserve employers' legitimate need to maintain control over their workforces.[42]

Also influential in pointing out the need for change was a 1976 article by University of Pennsylvania Professor Clyde W. Summers,[43] urging that arbitration remedies be provided by statute for nonunionized employees to adjudicate the fairness of their dismissals.[44] Professor Summers anticipated that the courts would be slow to provide common law remedies.[45] In his view, arbitration of wrongful dismissal claims under collective bargaining agreements had worked well and the process could be extended to the workforce generally.[46]

By late 1986, scores of law review articles explored the subject of employment at will.[47]

---

[42] *Id.* at 1427.

[43] Summers, *Individual Protection Against Unjust Dismissal: Time for a Statute*, 62 Va. L. Rev. 481 (1976). The Summers article was cited on both sides of the question of whether new common law remedies should be made available. The court in Simpson v. Western Graphics Corp., 293 Or. 96, 99, 643 P.2d 1276, 1278 n.1 (1982) (contract providing employment tenure admitted) cited Summers in support of the proposition that new common law remedies might be needed. *Accord,* Ivy v. Army Times, 428 A.2d 831, 833 n.3 (D.C. 1981) (dissent, in denial of petition for rehearing en banc). The court in Jones v. Keogh, 137 Vt. 562, 564, 409 A.2d 581, 582 (1979) cited Summers in support of the proposition that change should be undertaken by the legislature rather than by the courts.

[44] Summers, *Individual Protection Against Unjust Dismissal: Time for a Statute*, 62 Va. L. Rev. 491–99 (1976).

[45] By the end of 1982, Professor Summers, in a conversation with the author of this treatise, observed that the pace of change in the employment-at-will doctrine since his 1976 article rivaled anything that heretofore has occurred in American labor law.

[46] Summers, *Individual Protection Against Unjust Dismissal: Time for a Statute*, 62 Va. L. Rev. 483–84 (1976).

[47] Baldwin, *Fear of Firing—Is There a Cause of Action for Wrongful Discharge in Texas?*, 47 Tex. B.J. 11 (1984); Baxter & Wohl, *A Special Update: Wrongful Termination Tort Claims*, 11 Empl. Rel. L.J. 124 (1985); Bierman & Youngblood, *Employment-at-Will and the South Carolina Experiment*, 7 Indus. Rel. L.J. 28 (1985); Blades, *Employment at Will vs. Individual Freedom: On Limiting the Abusive Exercise of Employer Power*, 67 Colum. L. Rev. 1404 (1967); Blank, *Wrongful Discharge Litigation and Employment-at-Will Rule in Missouri*, 40 J. Mo. B. (1984); Blumrosen, *Workers' Rights Against Employers and Unions: Justice Francis—A Judge for Our Season*, 24 Rutgers L. Rev. 480 (1970); Boyette, *Terminating Employees in Virginia: A Roadmap for the Employer, the Employee, and their Counsel*, 17 U. Rich. L. Rev. 747 (1983); Note, *A Remedy for the Discharge of Professional Employees Who Refuse to Perform Unethical or Illegal Acts: A Proposal in Aid of Professional Ethics*, 28 Vand. L. Rev. 805 (1975); Comment, *Protecting the Private Sector At Will Employee Who "Blows the Whistle": A Cause of Action Based on Determinants of Public Policy*, 1977 Wis. L. Rev. 777 (1977); Catler, *The Case Against Proposals to Eliminate the Employment at Will Rule*, 5 Indus. Rel. L.J. 471 (1983); Copus & Lindsay, *Successfully Defending the Discriminatory/Wrongful Discharge Case*, 10 Employee Rel. L.J. 456 (1985); Crook, *Employment at Will: The "American Rule" and its Application in Alaska*, 2 Alaska L. Rev. 23 (1985); Decker, *At-Will Employment in Pennsylvania—A Proposal for its Abolition and Statutory Regulation*, 87 Dick. L. Rev. 477 (1983); DeGiuseppe, *Recognition of Public Policy Exceptions to the Employment-at-Will Rule*, 11 Fordham Urb. L. J. 721 (1982); DeGiuseppe,

The Effect of the Employment-At-Will Rule on Employee Rights to Job Security and Fringe Benefits, 10 Fordham Urb. L.J. 1 (1981); Estreicher, *Unjust Dismissal Laws: Some Cautionary Notes*, 33 Am. J. Comp. L. 310 (1985); Galvin, *Termination of the Employee at Will*, 26 Law Off. Econ. & Mgt. 80 (1985); Feinman, *The Development of the Employee-at-Will Rule*, 20 Am. J. Legis. Hist. 118 (1976); Glendon & Lev, *Changes in the Bonding of the Employment Relationship: An Essay on the New Property*, 20 B.C.L. Rev. 457 (1979); Greenbaum, *Toward a Common Law of Employment Discrimination*, 58 Temp. L.Q. 65 (1985); Harrison, *The "New" Terminable-at-Will Employment Contract: An Interest and Cost Incidence Analysis*, 69 Iowa L. Rev. 327 (1984); Heinsz, *The Assault on the Employment at Will Doctrine: Management Considerations*, 48 Mo. L. Rev. 855 (1983); Heshizer, *The New Common Law of Employment: Changes in the Concept of Employment*, 36 Lab. L.J. 95 (1985); Heshizer, *The Implied Contract Exception to At-Will Employment*, 35 Lab. L.J. 131 (1984); Hopkins & Robinson, *Employment at Will, Wrongful Discharge, and the Covenant of Good Faith and Fair Dealing in Montana, Past, Present and Future*, 46 Mont. L. Rev. 1 (1985); Jacobs, *Abusive Discharge in New York: Some Confusing Signals From the Courts*, 56 N.Y. St. B.J. 29 (1984); Jenkins, *Federal Legislative Exceptions to the At-Will Doctrine: Proposed Statutory Protection*, 47 Alb. L. Rev. 466 (1983); Madison, *The Employee's Emerging Right to Sue for Arbitrary or Unfair Discharge*, 6 Empl. Rel. L.J. 422 (1981); Mallor, *Punitive Damages For Wrongful Discharge of At Will Employees*, 26 Wm. & Mary L. Rev. 449 (1985); Marrinan, *Employment at Will: Pandora's Box May Have an Attractive Cover*, 7 Hamline L. Rev. 155 (1984); Mennemeier, *Protection from Unjust Discharges: An Arbitration Scheme*, 19 Harv. J. Legis. 49 (1982); Mordsley & Wall, *The Dismissal of Employees Under the Unfair Dismissal Law in the United Kingdom and Labor Arbitration Proceedings in the United States: The Parameters of Reasonableness and Just Cause*, 16 Cornell Int'l L.J. 1 (1983); Naylor, *Employment at Will: The Decay of an Anachronistic Shield for Employers?*, 33 Drake L. Rev. 113 (1983–84); Olsen, *The Public Policies Against Public Policy Wrongful Discharge Claims Premised on State and Federal Employment Statutes*, 62 Den. L.J. 447 (1985); Peck, *Unjust Discharges from Employment: A Necessary Change in the Law*, 40 Ohio St. L.J. 1 (1979); Peck, *Some Kind of Hearing for Persons Discharged from Private Employment*, 16 San Diego L. Rev. 313 (1979); Perritt, *Wrongful Dismissal in Virginia*, 34 Va. Bar News 21 (1985); Perritt, *Employee Dismissal Law in Pennsylvania*, 55 Pa. B.J. 212 (1984); Perritt, *Employee Dismissals: An Opportunity for Legal Simplification*, 35 Lab. L.J. 407 (1984); Pierce, Mann & Roberts, *Employee Termination at Will: A Principled Approach*, 28 Vill. L. Rev. 1 (1982); Power, *A Defense of the Employment at Will Rule*, 27 St. Louis U.L.J. 881 (1983); Robins, *Unfair Dismissal: Emerging Issues in the Use of Arbitration as a Dispute Resolution Alternative for the Nonunion Workforce*, 12 Fordham Urb. L.J. 437 (1983–84); Shemaria-Weber, *A Remedy for Malicious Discharge of the At-Will Employee*, 7 Conn. L. Rev. 758 (1975); Summers, *Individual Protection Against Unjust Dismissal: Time for a Statute*, 62 Va. L. Rev. 481 (1976); Vernon & Gray, *Termination at Will—The Employer's Right to Fire*, 6 Empl. Rel. L.J. 25 (1981); Williams, *Wrongful Termination of Employees at Will: The California Trend*, 78 Nw. U.L. Rev. 259 (1983); *Implied Contract Rights to Job Security*, 26 Stan. L. Rev. 335 (1974); *Discharged Employees: Should They Ever Have Antitrust Standing under Section 4 of the Clayton Act?*, 34 Hastings L.J. 839 (1983); Note, *Employee Handbooks and Employment-at-Will Contracts*, 1985 Duke L.J. 196; *Employee Standing Under Section 4 of the Clayton Act*, 81 Mich. L. Rev. 1846 (1983); Case Note, *Master and Servant—Employment-at-Will Employee's Allegation of Wrongful Termination for Failing to Comply with Illegal Order by Employer States Cause of Action—Hauck v. Sabine Pilots, Inc.*, 16 St. Mary's L.J. 457 (1985); *Missouri's Employment at Will: Vulnerable to Prima Facie Tort?*, 27 St. Louis U.L.J. 1001 (1983); *Standing of the Terminated Employee Employee Under Section 4 of the Clayton Act*, 25 Wm. & Mary L. Rev. 341 (1983); *Unfair Dismissal: Myths and Statistics*, 12 Indus. L.J. 157 (1983); *Employment at Will: An Analysis and Critique of the Judicial Rule*, 68 Iowa L. Rev. 787 (1983); *Contracts—Employee's Discharge Motivated by Bad Faith, Malice or Retaliation Constitutes a Breach of An Employment Contract Terminable at Will*, 43 Fordham L. Rev. 300 (1975); Note, *Protecting At Will Employees Against Wrongful*

§ 1.12 Current Status of the Employment-at-Will Rule in 50 States

More than three-fourths of American jurisdictions now have abandoned the Employment-at-Will Rule as a strict substantive formulation.[48]

Some means of recovery in tort or contract[49] for wrongful dismissal have been recognized in Alabama,[50] Alaska,[51] Arizona,[52] Arkansas,[53] California,[54] Col-

---

Dismissal: The Duty to Terminate Only in Good Faith, 93 Harv. L. Rev. 1816 (1980); Annotation, 51 A.L.R.2d 742 (1957); Annotation, 93 A.L.R.3d 659 (1979); Annotation, 9 A.L.R.4th 329 (1981); Annotation, *Modern Status of Rule that Employer May Discharge At-Will Employee for any Reason*, 12 A.L.R.4th 544 (1982); Note, *Non-Statutory Causes of Action for Employer's Termination of an "At Will" Employment Relationship: A Possible Solution to the Economic Imbalance in the Employer-Employee Relationship*, 24 N.Y.L. Sch. L. Rev. 743 (1979); Note, *A Common Law Action for the Abusively Discharged Employee*, 26 Hastings L.J. 1435 (1975).

[48] *See* Wandry v. Bull's Eye Credit Union, 129 Wis. 2d 37, 384 N.W.2d 325, 326 n.2 (1986); J.R. Simplot Co. v. State, 110 Idaho 762, 718 P.2d 1200 (1986) (citing first edition of this treatise).

[49] Older tort remedies for injury in connection with an employment termination, such as defamation, intentional infliction of emotional distress, intentional interference with contract relations, invasion of privacy, and misrepresentation, are not included in this analysis. They are considered in §§ 5.22–5.29.

[50] In Murphree v. Alabama Farm Bureau Ins. Co., 449 So. 2d 1218 (Ala. 1984), the Alabama Supreme Court reversed summary judgment for the employer and held that relocation of residence in connection with accepting employment might meet the "special consideration" requirement sufficient to make an informal promise of employment tenure enforceable. *Murphree*, 449 So. 2d at 1221. This represents a step toward relaxing the employment-at-will rule. *See* Meeks v. Opps Cotton Mills, Inc., 459 So. 2d 814 (Ala. 1984) (concurring and dissenting opinions discussing merits of reconsidering at-will rule); Scott v. Lane, 409 So. 2d 791 (Ala. 1982) (giving up other employment is sufficient consideration to support a promise of permanent employment). *But see* McCluskey v. Unicare Health Facility, Inc., 484 So. 2d 398 (Ala. 1986) (handbook with express disclaimer did not constitute enforceable promise to dismiss only for cause). While declining to embrace the public policy tort, Alabama courts have been willing to permit dismissed employees to recover on other tort theories. *See* Hall v. Integon Life Ins. Co., 454 So. 2d 1338 (Ala. 1984) (no wrongful dismissal cause of action, but entitled to trial on fraudulent misrepresentation claim based on statements that plaintiff would not be terminated except for gross misconduct—even though written provisons reserved right to terminate at will; also entitled to trial on intentional interference claim, although employment was at will; declining to create tort exception to employment at will); Reich v. Holiday Inn, 454 So. 2d 982 (Ala. 1984) (affirming dismissal of wrongful discharge action despite allegation that employee was dismissed for refusal to pay questionable invoices to avoid taking part in crime; no reason to modify Employment-at-Will Rule); Meredith v. C.E. Walther, Inc., 422 So. 2d 761 (Ala. 1982) (refusal to recognize tort, but hinting willingness to do so).

[51] Knight v. American Guard & Alert, Inc., 714 P.2d 788 (Alaska 1986) (reversing dismissal of complaint on public policy tort theory for security guard allegedly dismissed for reporting drinking, drug use by co-workers; little legal analysis); Eales v. Tanana Valley Medical-Surgical Group, Inc., 663 P.2d 958 (Alaska 1983) (recovery on implied contract theory permitted).

[52] Wagenseller v. Scottsdale Memorial Hosp., 147 Ariz. 370, 710 P.2d 1025 (1985) (reversing dismissal of plaintiff's claim and holding that nurse dismissed for refusing to "moon" could recover on public policy tort, implied-in-fact, and implied covenant theories); Leikvold v. Valley View

orado,[55] Connecticut,[56] the District of Columbia,[57] Hawaii,[58] Idaho,[59] Illinois,[60] Indiana,[61] Iowa,[62] Kansas,[63] Kentucky,[64] Maine,[65] Maryland,[66] Massachusetts,[67]

Hosp., 141 Ariz. 544, 688 P.2d 170 (1984) (recognizing implied-in-fact contract theory based on a personnel manual).

[53] See Lucas v. Brown & Root, Inc., 736 F.2d 1202, 1205 (8th Cir. 1984) (reversing dismissal of wrongful dismissal claims based on public policy theory; tort recovery available for discharge in retaliation for refusal to sleep with foreman); Newton v. Brown & Root, 280 Ark. 337, 658 S.W.2d 370 (1983) (hinting willingness to recognize tort in a case alleging dismissal for protesting safety hazards); Scholtes v. Signal Delivery Serv. Inc., 548 F. Supp. 487, 493–94 (W.D. Ark. 1982) (state law is hospitable to public policy tort concept); Jackson v. Kinark Corp., 282 Ark. 548, 669 S.W.2d 898, 899 (1984) (reversing summary judgment for employer; allegation of handbook promise of employment tenure warrants trial); French v. Dillard Dep't Stores, Inc., 285 Ark. 332, 333, 686 S.W.2d 435, 436 (1985) (suggesting willingness to enforce implied contract, but finding insufficient evidence to withstand summary judgment for employer).

[54] Tameny v. Atlantic Richfield Co., 27 Cal. 3d 167, 610 P.2d 1330, 164 Cal. Rptr. 839 (1980) (discharge for refusal to participate in price fixing plan actionable in tort). Pugh v. See's Candies, Inc., 116 Cal. App. 3d 311, 171 Cal. Rptr. 917 (1981) (implied promise to terminate for good cause only).

[55] Continental Air Lines, Inc. v. Keenan, ___ Colo. ___, ___ P.2d ___, No. 84SC460 (filed Jan. 20, 1987) recognizing implied-in-fact contract theory in handbook case; reversing summary judgment for employer); Brezinski v. F.W. Woolworth Co., 626 F. Supp. 240 (D. Colo. 1986) (Colorado recognizes public policy tort only for exercising statutory right or performing duty; not for age discrimination); Wing v. JMB Management Corp., 714 P.2d 916 (Colo. Ct. App. 1985) (recognizing implied-in-fact contract theory; dictum that dismissal for violation of public policy would sound in contract, not tort); Corporon v. Safeway Stores, Inc., 708 P.2d 1385, 1390 (Colo. Ct. App. 1985) (no claim for unfair dealing under Colorado law, based on failure to follow personnel procedures); Garcia v. Aetna Fin. Co., 752 F.2d 488 (10th Cir. 1984) (Colorado recognizes neither public policy tort, nor implied contract based on failure to follow unilaterally published personnel handbook); Brooks v. Trans World Airlines, 574 F. Supp. 805 (D. Colo. 1983) (handbook can be enforceable under Colorado law on a unilateral contact theory); Lampe v. Presbyterian Medical Center, 41 Colo. App. 465, 590 P.2d 513 (1978) (at will doctrine outweighs general statutory pronouncement that nurses who act improperly will not be relicensed).

[56] Finley v. Aetna Life & Casualty Co., 5 Conn. App. 394, 499 A.2d 64, 73 (employment manual may prohibit dismissal except for just cause), *cert. granted,* 198 Conn. 802, 501 A.2d 1213 (1985); Sheets v. Teddy's Frosted Foods Inc., 179 Conn. 471, 427 A.2d 385 (1980) (tort cause of action stated by quality control supervisor discharged for insistence on compliance with food and drug act).

[57] Newman v. Legal Servs. Corp., 628 F. Supp. 535 (D.D.C. 1986) (the District of Columbia would recognize public policy tort, but dismissal for disagreement with private employer's ideology does not violate public policy); Minihan v. American Pharmaceutical Ass'n, 624 F. Supp. 345 (D.D.C. 1985) (personnel manual and letter offering "permanent" employment not enforceable contract to dismiss only for cause, apparently because of lack of consideration); Washington Welfare Ass'n, Inc. v. Wheeler, 496 A.2d 613, 615 (D.C. 1985) (personnel procedures manual providing for termination for just cause overcomes employment-at-will presumption); Hodge v. Evans Fin. Corp., 707 F.2d 1566 (D.C. Cir. 1983) (plaintiff entitled to trial on allegations of an oral promise of permanent employment), *later appeal,* 778 F.2d 794 (D.C. Cir. 1985); Weaver v. Gross, 605 F. Supp. 210, 216 (D.D.C. 1985) (no public policy tort in District of Columbia).

[58] Parnar v. Americana Hotels, Inc., 65 Haw. 370, 652 P.2d 625 (1982) (reversing summary judgment for employer in public policy tort case); *compare* Kinoshita v. Canadian Pacific Airlines, Ltd., ___ Haw. ___, 724 P.2d 110 (1986) (adopting implied contract theory) *with* Stancil v. Mergenthaler Linotype Co., 589 F. Supp. 78 (D. Haw. 1984) (declining to accept "detrimental reliance exception" to Employment-at-Will Rule; no facts to support exception anyway).

§ 1.12 MODERN STATUS

Michigan,[68] Minnesota,[69] Missouri,[70] Montana,[71] Nebraska,[72] Nevada,[73] New Hampshire,[74] New Jersey,[75] New Mexico,[76] New York,[77] North Carolina,[78] North

---

[59] Watson v. Idaho Falls Consol. Hosp., Inc., 111 Idaho 44, 720 P.2d 632 (1986) (implied contract based on handbook and unilateral contract principles; public policy tort accepted); Whitlock v. Haney Seed Co., 110 Idaho 347, 715 P.2d 1017 (Ct. App. 1986) (explicit oral promise of continued employment rebuts employee-at-will presumption; no discussion of consideration); MacNeil v. Minidoka Memorial Hosp., 108 Idaho 588, 701 P.2d 208 (1985) (no need to decide whether handbook promises were enforceable; dismissal did not violate handbook rules); Verway v. Blincoe Packing Co., 108 Idaho 315, 698 P.2d 377 (1985) (affirming judgment for employees dismissed in violation of employer promise they would not be fired when strike was settled).

[60] Ladesic v. Servomation Corp., 140 Ill. App. 3d 489, 488 N.E.2d 1355 (1986) (refusing another job offer insufficient consideration to support informal promise of employment security under Illinois law); Enis v. Continental Ill. Nat'l Bank, 582 F. Supp. 876 (N.D. Ill. 1984) (suggesting that handbook cannot give rise to contract); Scott v. Sears, Roebuck & Co., 605 F. Supp. 1047, 1053 (N.D. Ill. 1985) (no implied covenant cause of action in Illinois); Kelsay v. Motorola, Inc., 74 Ill. 2d 172, 384 N.E.2d 353 (1978) (tort recovery permitted for firing in retaliation for workers' compensation claim); Palmateer v. International Harvester Co., 85 Ill. 2d 124, 421 N.E.2d 876 (1981) (public policy of reporting thefts).

[61] Morgan Drive Away, Inc. v. Brant, 489 N.E.2d 933 (Ind. 1986) (suggesting Indiana public policy tort may extend no further than dismissals for filing workers compensation claims); Buethe v. Britt Airlines, Inc., 787 F.2d 1194 (7th Cir. 1986) (Indiana public policy tort law does not protect airline copilot for refusing to fly aircraft he believed to violate F.A.A. requirements); Ewing v. Board of Trustees of Pulaski Memorial Hosp., 486 N.E.2d 1094, 1098 (Ind. Ct. App. 1985) (correspondence "guaranteeing" annual salary too vague to be promise of job security when coupled with questionable authority of sender); Hostettler v. Pioneer Hi-bred Inter'l, Inc., 624 F. Supp. 169, 172 (S.D. Ind. 1985) (Indiana does not recognize implied covenant); Frampton v. Central Ind. Gas Co., 260 Ind. 249, 297 N.E.2d 425 (1973) (accepting tort theory for dismissal for filing workers compensation claim).

[62] Albert v. Davenport Osteopathic Hosp., 385 N.W.2d 237, 238–39 (Iowa 1986) (at-will presumption can be overcome by additional consideration such as quitting another job); Haldeman v. Total Petroleum, Inc., 376 N.W.2d 98 (Iowa 1985) (reversing judgment for employee on defamation, emotional distress counts, and affirming dismissal of wrongful dismissal counts); Janda v. Iowa Indus. Hydraulics, Inc., 326 N.W.2d 339 (Iowa 1982) (restatement of general rule in action for travel expense); Abrisz v. Pulley Freight Lines, Inc., 270 N.W.2d 454 (Iowa 1978) (no wrongful dismissal action based on firing for submitting false information).

[63] Baker v. Penn Mut. Life, 788 F.2d 650 (10th Cir. 1986) (Kansas courts unlikely to recognize exceptions to employment at will rule); Anco Constr. Co. v. Freeman, 236 Kan. 626, 693 P.2d 1183, 1186 (1985) (recognizing public policy tort for state-defined interests, but finding claim based on NLRA rights not covered by state tort); Rouse v. Peoples Natural Gas Co., 605 F. Supp. 230, 232 (D. Kan. 1985) (no implied contract cause of action in Kansas based on handbook); Fletcher v. Wesley Medical Center, 585 F. Supp. 1260, 1263–64 (D. Kan. 1984) (refusal to accept implied covenant theory, but declining to dismiss contract claim based on handbook).

[64] Shah v. American Synthetic Rubber Corp., 655 S.W.2d 489 (Ky. 1983) (recognizing implied-in-fact contract theory of recovery, reversing summary judgment for employer); *compare* Firestone Textile Co. v. Meadows, 666 S.W.2d 730 (Ky. 1983) (public policy tort recognized for dismissal for filing workers compensation claim) *and* Brown v. Physicians Mut. Ins. Co., 679 S.W.2d 836, 838 (Ky. Ct. App. 1984) (employee dismissed for reporting violations of Insurance Code to state agency has public policy tort claim) *with* Grzyb v. Evans, 700 S.W.2d 399 (Ky. 1985) (no public policy tort claim for discrimination covered by administrative remedies or based on

Dakota,[79] Ohio,[80] Oklahoma,[81] Oregon,[82] Pennsylvania,[83] South Carolina,[84] South Dakota,[85] Tennessee,[86] Texas,[87] Utah,[88] Vermont,[89] Virginia,[90] Washington,[91] West Virginia,[92] Wisconsin,[93] and Wyoming.[94]

---

constitutional policies protecting free association) *and* Scroghan v. Kraftco Corp., 551 S.W.2d 811 (Ky. App. Ct. 1977) (no tort action for dismissal caused by plans to attend law school).

[65] Larrabee v. Penobscot Frozen Foods, Inc., 486 A.2d 97, 99–100 (Me. 1984) (reversing dismissal of claim for breach of promise to dismiss only for cause; employee entitled to prove such a promise; no tort cause of action for ill will, but public policy tort not ruled out).

[66] Kern v. South Baltimore Gen. Hosp., 66 Md. App. 441, 504 A.2d 1154 (1986) (dismissal for absenteeism due to work-related injury does not contravene public policy represented by statutory provision prohibiting dismissal *solely* for filing workers compensation claim); Adler v. American Standard Corp., 291 Md. 31, 432 A.2d 464 (1981) (tort cause of action exists).

[67] DeRose v. Putnam Management Co., 398 Mass. 205, 496 N.E.2d 428 (1986) (affirming judgment for employee fired for refusing to give false testimony); Maddaloni v. Western Mass. Bus Lines, 386 Mass. 877, 438 N.E.2d 351 (1982) (covenant of good faith; jury verdict for plaintiff affirmed).

[68] *Compare* Covell v. Spengler, 141 Mich. App. 76, 366 N.W.2d 76, 79 (1985) (suggesting that public policy tort is available only when statute expressly prohibits dismissal) *with* Watassek v. Michigan Dep't of Mental Health, 143 Mich. App. 556, 564, 372 N.W.2d 617, 620 (1985) (public policy tort for dismissal of mental health employee for reporting patient abuse; reversing summary judgment for employer); Toussaint v. Blue Cross & Blue Shield, 408 Mich. 579, 292 N.W.2d 880 (1980) (employment tenure implied from handbook).

[69] Pine River State Bank v. Mettille, 333 N.W.2d 622 (Minn. 1983) (implied contract recovery permitted). *Compare* Brookshaw v. South St. Paul Feed, Inc., 381 N.W.2d 33, 36 (Minn. Ct. App. 1986) (jury entitled to decide whether manual containing both disciplinary language and a disclaimer gave rise to unilateral contract) *with* Dumas v. Kessler & Maguire Funeral Home, Inc., 380 N.W.2d 544 (Minn. Ct. App. 1986) (oral statement "we will retire together" too vague to be a promise of employment security).

[70] Haith v. Model Cities Health Corp., 704 S.W.2d 684 (Mo. Ct. App. 1986) (enumeration of reasons for termination of written employment contract did not limit right to terminate at will based on employment-at-will rule); Enyeart v. Shelter Mut. Ins. Co., 693 S.W.2d 120, 123 (Mo. Ct. App. 1985) (reversing dismissal of complaint based on allegations that policy manual promised certain procedures would be followed before termination); Arie v. Intertherm, 648 S.W.2d 142, 153 (Mo. Ct. App. 1983) (contract can be implied from handbook). *Compare* Beasley v. Affiliated Hosp. Prods., 713 S.W.2d 557 (Mo. Ct. App. 1986) (public policy tort pleaded by employee dismissed for refusing to fix raffle) *and* Boyle v. Vista Eyewear, Inc., 700 S.W.2d 859, 876 (Mo. Ct. App. 1985) (permitting public policy tort claim by production worker allegedly dismissed for protesting employer's failure to perform FDA mandated tests on eyeglasses) *with* Dake v. Tuell, 687 S.W.2d 191, 193 (Mo. 1985) (flatly rejecting prima facie tort as vehicle for recovery by at-will employee).

[71] Flanigan v. Prudential Fed. Sav. & Loan Ass'n, ___ Mont. ___, 720 P.2d 257 (1986) (affirming judgment for employee on implied covenant based on proof of arbitrary decision, and on negligence); Nye v. Department of Livestock, 196 Mont. 222, 639 P.2d 498 (1982) (tort recognized); Gates v. Life of Mont. Ins. Co., 196 Mont. 178, 638 P.2d 1063 (1982) (covenant of good faith recognized), *later appeal,* 668 P.2d 213 (1983); Dare v. Montana Petroleum Mktg. Co., ___ Mont. ___, 687 P.2d 1015 (1984) (reversing summary judgment for employer; plaintiff entitled to trial on allegations of (1) promise of job security, and (2) improper reasons for dismissal; covenant of good faith protects reasonable expectations of job security).

[72] Morris v. Lutheran Medical Center, 215 Neb. 677, 680, 340 N.W.2d 388, 391 (1983) (unilateral employer grievance procedures could be enforceable; failure to allege breach in sufficient detail).

§ 1.12 MODERN STATUS 27

But see Mueller v. Union Pac. R.R., 220 Neb. 742, 750-51, 371 N.W.2d 738, (1985) (expressing reluctance to adopt public policy tort theory, but not reaching issue).

[73] Hansen v. Harrah's, 100 Nev. 60, 675 P.2d 394 (1984) (permitting public policy tort for retaliation for filing workers compensation claim); Savage v. Holiday Inn Corp., 603 F. Supp. 311, 314 (D. Nev. 1985) (approving implied covenant claim under Nevada law); Southwest Gas Corp. v. Ahmad, 99 Nev. 594, 668 P.2d 261 (1983) (accepting implied contract theory).

[74] Cilley v. New Hampshire Ball Bearings, Inc., ___ N.H. ___, 514 A.2d 818 (1986) (jury could find public policy tort from evidence that employee was fired for refusing to lie; reversing summary judgment for employee); Cloutier v. Great Atl. & Pac. Tea Co., 121 N.H. 915, 436 A.2d 1140 (1981) (judgment for plaintiff in tort affirmed).

[75] Woolley v. Hoffman-LaRoche, Inc., 99 N.J. 284, 491 A.2d 1257 (1985) (personnel handbook promise to dismiss only for cause can be found by jury to be enforceable contract); Pierce v. Ortho Pharmaceutical Corp., 84 N.J. 58, 417 A.2d 505 (1980) (tort theory recognized).

[76] Vigil v. Arzola, 101 N.M. 687, 687 P.2d 1038 (1984) (reversing dismissal of complaint; breach of contract action based on procedures in personnel manual).

[77] Weiner v. McGraw-Hill, Inc., 57 N.Y.2d 458, 443 N.E.2d 441, 457 N.Y.S.2d 193 (1982) (implied contract theory recognized); Leahy v. Federal Express Corp., 609 F. Supp. 668, 670-71 (S.D.N.Y. 1985) (analyzing cases applying *Weiner*); Murphy v. American Home Prods., 58 N.Y.2d 293, 448 N.E.2d 86, 461 N.Y.S.2d 232 (1983) (no "abusive discharge" tort).

[78] Sides v. Duke Hosp., 74 N.C. App. 331, 328 S.E.2d 818 (1985) (complaint alleging that the university hospital discharged nurse in retaliation for refusal to testify falsely or incompetently at medical malpractice trial states a claim for public policy tort; allegation that nurse changed jobs in reliance on assurances that she could be discharged only for incompetence sufficient to remove breach of contract claim from at-will rule). *Compare* Trought v. Richardson, 78 N.C. App. 758, 338 S.E.2d 617, 619-20 (1986) (hospital policy manual limiting dismissal to cause sufficient allegation of implied contract to survive motion to dismiss), *review denied,* 316 N.C. 557, 344 S.E.2d 18 (1986) *with* Walker v. Westinghouse Elec. Corp., 79 N.C. App. 253, 335 S.E.2d 79, 84 (1985) (failure to prove reliance on gratuitous handbook precludes recovery).

[79] Wadeson v. American Family Mut. Ins. Co., 343 N.W.2d 367 (N.D. 1984) (recognizing covenant of good faith and fair dealing but affirming jury verdict for the defendant).

[80] Mers v. Dispatch Printing Co., 19 Ohio St. 3d 100, 105, 483 N.E.2d 150, 155 (1985) (promissory estoppel may overcome employment-at-will presumption); Phung v. Waste Management, Inc., 23 Ohio St. 3d 100, 491 N.E.2d 1114 (1986) (declining to recognize public policy tort for employee dismissed for reporting water pollution violations).

[81] Vinyard v. King, 728 F.2d 428, 432 (10th Cir. 1984) (constitutionally protected property interest under Oklahoma law created by employee handbook); Langdon v. Saga Corp., 569 P.2d 524 (Okla. Ct. App. 1977) (plaintiff recovery of severance pay under personnel manual implies wrongful dismissal action might succeed). *Cf.* Hall v. Farmers Ins. Exch. 713 P.2d 1027 (Okla. 1986) (finding breach of covenant of good faith in written insurance agency contract; citing Fortune v. National Cash Register Co., 373 Mass. 96, 364 N.E.2d 1251 (1977), and Monge v. Beebe Rubber Co., 114 N.H. 130, 316 A.2d 549 (1974)).

[82] Nees v. Hocks, 272 Or. 210, 536 P.2d 512 (1975) (tort action permitted for discharge caused by jury service).

[83] Novosel v. Nationwide Ins. Co., 721 F.2d 894 (3d Cir. 1983) (Pennsylvania recognizes both public policy tort and implied-in-fact contract theories); Martin v. Capital Cities Media, Inc., 354 Pa. Super. 199, 511 A.2d 830 (1986) (employee handbook does not alter at-will status of employment); Darlington v. General Elec., 350 Pa. Super. 183, 504 A.2d 306, 312, 316 (1986) (citing this treatise); Geary v. United States Steel Corp., 456 Pa. 171, 319 A.2d 174 (1974) (suggesting tort action on other facts); Forman v. BRI Corp., 532 F. Supp. 49 (E.D. Pa. 1982) (implied contract).

In addition, all employees are protected by federal statute from dismissal for certain reasons related to defined characteristics or particular conduct.[95] Most states have statutes affording additional protection of the same sort.[96]

---

[84] Ludwick v. This Minute of Carolina, Inc., 287 S.C. 219, 337 S.E.2d 213 (1985) (recognizing public policy tort for employee dismissed for responding to subpoena from state administrative agency).

[85] Cutter v. Lincoln Nat'l Life Ins. Co., 794 F.2d 352 (8th Cir. 1986) (handbook too general to support inference of promise of employment security); Hopes v. Black Hills Power & Light Co., 386 N.W.2d 490 (S.D. 1986) (performance appraisal procedure gave no rights to employment security; dismissal for disability permissible); Osterkamp v. Alkota Mfg., Inc., 332 N.W.2d 275 (S.D. 1983) (failure to follow policy manual supports breach of contract action).

[86] Clanton v. Cain Sloan Co., 677 S.W.2d 441 (Tenn. 1984) (reversing dismissal of complaint for discharge in retaliation for filing workers compensation claim); Bringle v. Methodist Hosp., 701 S.W.2d 622 (Tenn. Ct. App. 1985) (no implied contract based on handbook reserving discretion over personnel decisions to employer).

[87] Sabine Pilot Serv. Inc. v. Hauck, 687 S.W.2d 733, 735 (Tex. 1985) (reversing summary judgment for employer; employee allegedly dismissed for refusal to violate federal law covering discharge of bilges from water vessel; exception to employment-at-will doctrine exists for employee dismissed for refusal to perform illegal act); Joachim v. AT&T Information Sys., 793 F.2d 113 (5th Cir. 1986) (employee handbook did not alter employment-at-will status); Johnson v. Ford Motor Co., 690 S.W.2d 90, 93 (Tex. Ct. App. 1985) (reversing dismissal of complaint on allegations of oral promises after employment began that termination could occur only for just cause).

[88] Rose v. Allied Dev. Co., 719 P.2d 83 (Utah 1986) (suggesting implied contract or promissory estoppel theories might permit recovery on different facts); Bihlmaier v. Carson, 603 P.2d 790 (Utah 1979) (failure to prove any promise of tenure).

[89] *Compare* Larose v. Agway, Inc., ___ Vt. ___, 508 A.2d 1364 (1986) (unilaterally adopted personnel rules do not support implied-in-fact contract claim; no promissory estoppel because no detrimental reliance) *with* Benoir v. Ethan Allen, Inc., ___ Vt. ___, 514 A.2d 716 (1986) (affirming jury verdict for employee, based on handbook promises) *and* Sherman v. Rutland Hosp., Inc., 146 Vt. 204, 500 A.2d 230 (1985) (affirming jury verdict for employee based on personnel policy manual).

[90] Bowman v. State Bank of Keysville, 229 Va. 534, 331 S.E.2d 797 (1985) (reversing grant of demurrer against plaintiff and accepting public policy tort theory for bank employees dismissed for claiming proxy statements violated state securities laws); Thompson v. American Motor Inns, 623 F. Supp. 409 (W.D. Va. 1985) (handbook enumerating reasons for dismissal and pre-dismissal procedures enforceable under Virginia law); Frazier v. Colonial Williamsburg, 574 F. Supp. 318 (E.D. Va. 1983) (implied contract claim for unfair dismissal goes to jury under Virginia law); Sea-Land Serv. v. O'Neal, 224 Va. 343, 297 S.E.2d 647 (1982) (resignation from one position provided consideration to make promise of another position enforceable).

[91] Thompson v. St. Regis Paper Co., 102 Wash. 2d 219, 685 P.2d 1081 (1984) (adopting implied-in-fact contract and public policy tort theories; rejecting implied covenant theory).

[92] Harless v. First Nat'l Bank, 246 S.E.2d 270 (W. Va. 1978) (retaliatory discharge action is tort); Cook v. Heck's Inc., 342 S.E.2d 453, 458–59 (W. Va. 1986) (handbook statements regarding employment security can be offers of unilateral contract, accepted by employee continuing to work, citing Woolley v. Hoffman-LaRoche, Inc., 99 N.J. 284, 491 A.2d 257 (1985); handbook enumeration of reasons for dismissal could permit jury to infer promise to dismiss only for those reasons; reversing directed verdict for employer); Yoho v. Triangle PWC, Inc., 336 S.E.2d 204 (W. Va. 1985) (no violation of public policy to terminate seniority after absence related to workplace injury).

[93] Bushko v. Miller Brewing Co., ___ Wis. 2d ___, 396 N.W.2d 167 (1986) (complaints against employer practices not enough for claim based on public policy; must show that employee refused

§ 1.12 MODERN STATUS

The following states apparently still honor the Employment-at-Will Rule: Delaware,[97] Florida,[98] Georgia,[99] Louisiana,[1] Mississippi,[2] and Rhode Island.[3]

---

a command to violate public policy); Brockmeyer v. Dun & Bradstreet, Inc., 113 Wis. 2d 343, 335 N.W.2d 834 (1983) (well defined public policy overrides at will rule; contract but not tort action is appropriate); Ferraro v. Koelsch, 119 Wis. 2d 407, 350 N.W.2d 735 (Wis. Ct. App. 1984), *aff'd by different rationale,* 124 Wis. 2d 154, 368 N.W.2d 666 (1985) (jury correctly found that employer and employee agreed to be bound by handbook).

[94] Mobile Coal Producing, Inc. v. Parks, 704 P.2d 702, 707 (Wyo. 1985) (handbook provisions relating to dismissal enforceable as exception to employment-at-will rule); Alexander v. Phillips Oil Co., 707 P.2d 1385 (Wyo. 1985) (reversing summary judgment for employer).

[95] See **ch. 2**.

[96] See **app. A**.

[97] Heideck v. Kent Gen. Hosp., Inc., 446 A.2d 1095 (Del. 1982) (evidence insufficient to overcome employment-at-will presumption); Hanley v. Lamb, 312 A.2d 330 (Del. Super. Ct. 1973) (stock option agreement held to limit employer's rights to dismiss at will). *But see* Heller v. Dover Warehouse Mkt., Inc., 515 A.2d 178, 181 (Del. Super. Ct. 1986) (recognizing implied private right of action under polygraph statute).

[98] Caster v. Hennessey, 727 F.2d 1075, 1077 (11th Cir. 1984) (Florida has rejected the implied doctrine of Toussaint v. Blue Cross & Blue Shield, 408 Mich. 579, 292 N.W.2d 880 (1980); Maguire v. American Family Life Assurance Co., 442 So. 2d 321 (Fla. Dist. Ct. App. 1983) (employer promise not enforceable even though detrimental reliance), *review denied,* 451 So. 2d 849 (Fla. 1984) Smith v. Piezo Technology & Professional Administration, 427 So. 2d 182 (Fla. 1983) (limited recovery for discharge under workers' compensation statute); Muller v. Stromberg Carlson Corp., 427 So. 2d 266 (Fla. Dist. Ct. App. 1983) (employee policy manual not enforceable).

[99] White v. ITT, 718 F.2d 994 (11th Cir. 1983) (no contract action under Georgia law based on handbook), *cert. denied,* 466 U.S. 938 (1984); Anderberg v. Georgia Elec. Membership Corp., 175 Ga. App. 14, ___, 332 S.E.2d 326, 327 (1985) (policy manual cannot alter at-will nature of "permanent" employment); Troy v. Interfinancial, Inc., 171 Ga. App. 763, 320 S.E.2d 872 (1984) (claim that plaintiff fired for refusing to perjure himself in a deposition in another lawsuit; judgment n.o.v. for individual defendant reversed on claim for intentional interference with contract; but affirmed as to corporate defendant because no cause of action for wrongful dismissal); Buice v. Gulf Oil Corp., 172 Ga. App. 93, 322 S.E.2d 103 (1984) (alcoholism policy not binding on employer); Andress v. Augusta Nursing Facilities, 156 Ga. App. 775, 275 S.E.2d 368 (1980) (allegations of improper motive are legally irrelevant); Georgia Power Co. v. Busbin, 242 Ga. 612, 250 S.E.2d 442 (1978) (allegations of improper motive legally irrelevant).

[1] Thebner v. Xerox Corp., 480 So. 2d 454, 457 (La. Ct. App.), (policy manual with disclaimer insufficient to overcome employment-at-will-Rule; promissory estoppel claim rejected for failure to plead detrimental reliance), *cert. denied,* 484 So. 2d 139 (1986); Harris v. Parmley, 480 So. 2d 500 (La. Ct. App. 1985) (anesthesiologist was employee at will, not partner, and thus could be dismissed without reason); Hoover v. Livingston Bank, 451 So. 2d 3, 5 (La. Ct. App. 1984) (applying at-will rule); Arvie v. Century Tel. Enter., Inc., 452 So. 2d 392, 393 (La. Ct. App. 1984) (no implied contract cause of action; issue was what statute of limitations applied); Gil v. Metal Serv. Corp., 412 So. 2d 706 (La. Ct. App. 1982) (no tort cause of action).

[2] Shaw v. Burchfield, 481 So. 2d 247, 254 (Miss. 1985) (informal practice of terminating only for good cause did not modify express written contract providing that "no cause shall be required" for dismissal; suggesting possibility of modifying employment-at-will rule in another case); Kelly v. Mississippi Valley Gas Co., 397 So. 2d 874 (Miss. 1981) (no change in at-will rule until legislature acts).

[3] Rotondo v. Seaboard Foundry, Inc., 440 A.2d 751 (R.I. 1981) (traditional at-will rule reaffirmed).

The highest courts in many of the states still apparently honoring the Employment-at-Will Rule either have not considered the matter recently, or have expressed some willingness to recognize exceptions to the rule in an appropriate case.

§ 1.13 Contemporary Role of the Employment-at-Will Rule

Wide acceptance of common law wrongful dismissal doctrines, such as the public policy tort and the implied-in-fact contract theories, makes it natural to wonder whether the Employment-at-Will Rule has any contemporary vitality in those states that have accepted these theories. It does. This section explains why.

When a terminated employee asserts a public policy tort claim, the balancing analysis explained in § 5.7 weighs the economic interest of the employee in job security against the economic interest of the employer in having the unilateral right to make employment decisions. In addition, as § 5.7 explains, societal interests must be considered. The Employment-at-Will Rule represents a societal interest on the employer's side of the controversy. Unless the employee can marshal a societal interest on the employee's side, the employer wins. Therefore, the Employment-at-Will Rule serves as a policy presumption in a public policy tort case. Unless the employee can show countervailing public policy interests, the Employment-at-Will Rule says that the employer escapes liability.

In an implied in fact contract case,[4] the Employment-at-Will Rule serves to establish a presumption also, though it is a factual presumption rather than a policy presumption. When the evidence shows an indefinite employment relationship, the Employment-at-Will Rule means that the employment is presumed to be terminable unilaterally by the employer without legal liability. Only if the employee can offer evidence of a promise of employment security,[5] reenforced by some form of consideration,[6] is the employee entitled to recover for breach of contract. Absent the Employment-at-Will Rule, the presumption might be in the employee's favor. For example, indefinite employment relationships might be presumed to be terminable only for good cause.

Finally, in implied covenant cases, the Employment-at-Will Rule means that a breach of the covenant can be shown only by evidence of some form of employer misbehavior other than a simple dismissal without just cause.[7] Absent the Employment-at-Will Rule, the covenant theory might permit recovery when the employer fails to show good cause for dismissal.

Although the Employment-at-Will Rule no longer dictates the result in most states, it circumscribes the analysis available to courts and plaintiffs in wrongful dismissal cases.

---

[4] See generally **ch. 4**.

[5] See §§ **4.6–4.10, 7.18, 7.19**.

[6] See §§ **4.12–4.18, 7.20**.

[7] See §§ **4.11, 4.13**.

§ 1.14 Choice of Law Principles

Many employment termination disputes involve more than one state. For example, the employee may be hired in one state and work in another; or the termination may occur in one state, but employment decisions and policies may be set in another. Since jurisdictions differ over adoption of the Employment-at-Will Rule, a court's choice of a particular state's substantive law well may determine whether an employee can recover. This can require a court to make a choice-of-law determination. Choice of law is important only if the outcome would be different under the laws of the different states.[8] But if a wrongful dismissal suit has a considerable likelihood of success in one state but poor likelihood of success in another, a choice of law must be made.

Generally, a court in which the suit is filed will use the choice-of-law principles of its own state in deciding which substantive law to apply to the claim. A federal court, either sitting in diversity or hearing the dismissal suit as a pendent state claim, must apply the substantive law of the state where it sits,[9] including the state's choice-of-law rules.[10]

The appropriate choice-of-law principle depends on whether recovery is sought in tort or contract. The *Restatement (Second) of Conflicts* § 196 contains the general choice-of-law rule for personal service contracts:

> The validity of a contract for the rendition of services and the rights created thereby are determined, in the absence of an effective choice of law by the parties, by the local law of the state where the contract requires that the services, or a major portion of the services, be rendered, unless, with respect to the particular issue, some other state has a more significant relationship under the principles stated in § 6 to the transaction and the parties, in which event the local law of the other state will be applied.

Section 188, which governs contracts generally, adds the place of making and the place of negotiating as additional choice-of-law possibilities.[11]

If a suit is brought in tort, § 145 of the *Restatement (Second) of Conflicts* states that the controlling law is the law of the state which has the most significant

---

[8] *See* Gianaculas v. TWA, Inc., 761 F.2d 1391, 1394 (9th Cir. 1985) (no need to decide which law applies because no recovery under either New York implied-in-fact or California implied covenant doctrines).

[9] Erie R.R. v. Thompkins, 304 U.S. 64 (1938); *but see* Wolk v. Saks Fifth Ave., Inc., 728 F.2d 221, 223 (3d Cir. 1984) (beyond the authority of a federal court adjudicating a state wrongful dismissal case to create new causes of action).

[10] Klaxon Co. v. Stenton Elec. Mfg. Co., 313 U.S. 487 (1941); Rubin v. Rudolf Wolff Commodity Brokers, Inc., 636 F. Supp. 258 (N.D. Ill. 1986) (applying local choice-of-law rules in wrongful dismissal case).

[11] *See* Crossman v. Trans World Airlines, 777 F.2d 1271, 1275 (7th Cir. 1985) (law of forum state requires application of law of place where contract was executed).

relationship to the occurrence and to the parties. Very often this is the state in which the harm or injury occurs.

Courts hearing wrongful dismissal suits gradually are abandoning traditional choice-of-law formalisms such as place of making, place of performance, and occurrence of harm, and are shifting to a more flexible interests analysis.[12] If a governmental interests analysis is appropriate, the choice of law may differ depending on which legal theory is involved. It is important to marshal the governmental interests that might be involved under the different legal theories upon which a wrongful dismissal claim may be brought: implied-in-fact contract, implied covenant of good faith and fair dealing or public policy tort.

Breach of contract under an implied-in-fact contract theory implicates governmental interests in (1) seeing persons injured by the breach receive the benefit of their bargain, and (2) not imposing involuntary obligations on promisors. In addition, states have an interest in applying their own wrongful dismissal law to businesses and workers in their own territory because that law reflects policy determinations resolving conflicts between the interests of the two groups.[13] The first interest is likely to be greatest where the injured person expected to perform and to be paid. The second interest is likely to be greatest where the promisor has the greatest presence. So in a wrongful dismissal action based on an implied-in-fact contract theory, the law of the state where the employee worked is a legitimate candidate under choice-of-law principles.[14] If the employer has its headquarters and principal place of business in another state, that state's law may also be appropriate.

States have two interests in wrongful dismissal tort cases. The first is the interest in punishing and deterring tortious acts. The second is the state's interest in applying its wrongful dismissal law to its businesses and workers.[15] The first interest is likely to be greatest where the allegedly tortious act takes place.[16] This is likely to be the state where the employee was terminated. The second interest is likely to be greatest where the business is located, or where a substantial part of the employees' duties are performed.[17] Because the purpose of the public policy tort is to encourage employee conduct that promotes public policy, however,[18] linkage with the public policy of a particular state probably would give that state the strongest interest in having its substantive law applied. In the vast majority of public policy tort cases, the employee asserts the public policy of the state in

---

[12] *See* Rubin v. Rudolf Wolff Commodity Brokers, Inc., 636 F. Supp. 258 (N.D. Ill. 1986); Rupinsky v. Miller Brewing Co., 627 F. Supp. 1181 (W.D. Pa. 1986); Gillespie v. Equitable Life Assurance Soc'y, 590 F. Supp. 1111 (D. Del. 1984).

[13] *See* Rupinsky v. Miller Brewing Co., 627 F. Supp. 1181, 1184 (W.D. Pa. 1986).

[14] Rubin v. Rudolf Wolff Commodity Brokers, Inc. 636 F. Supp. at 259. (significant interests approach used to select law of place of performance rather than place of making).

[15] *See* Rupinsky v. Miller Brewing Co., 627 F. Supp. at 1184.

[16] *See* Burns v. Preston Trucking Co., Inc., 621 F. Supp. 366, 367 (D. Conn. 1986).

[17] *See* Sivell v. Conwed Corp., 605 F. Supp. 1265 (D. Conn. 1985) (although employee's office moved to New Jersey, substantial part of duties were conducted in Connecticut; Connecticut law applied).

[18] See §§ **5.8–5.19**.

which that employee was terminated. Accordingly, the law of the state of termination would be the most appropriate law to apply in most public policy tort cases.[19]

The implied covenant theory has tort as well as contract characteristics, and therefore the interests involved in recognizing the theory may include punishment and deterrence as well as the interests involved in contract actions. Punishing and deterring persons who act unfairly or in bad faith relates to the place at which the unfair or bad faith act takes place, or where the wrongdoer is located.

§ 1.15 Major Unresolved Issues

Assuming that most courts accept the public policy tort and implied-in-fact contract doctrines in the abstract, five major uncertainties nevertheless must be addressed by courts dealing with wrongful dismissal cases:

1. To what extent will employees suing on an implied-in-fact contract be required to prove, on an individual basis, detrimental reliance?
2. To what extent will the courts permit counsel to be creative with public policy tort theories?
3. Will employees seeking to base public policy torts on statutes that provide administrative remedies be required to resort to the administrative remedies first or exclusively?
4. Will employees covered by collectively bargained just cause and grievance arbitration provisions be permitted to bring public policy torts?
5. Is the implied covenant dead as an independent basis for recovery?

The first question can have substantial impact on the ease with which a dismissed employee can satisfy the requirements of the implied-in-fact contract theory. Frequently, it is not hard to satisfy the promise element; most employers or supervisors make some kind of representations about job security in writing or orally. Most implied-in-fact contract claims fail because the employee is unable to satisfy the consideration requirement by showing detrimental reliance on the promise. The doctrine set out in *Woolley v. Hoffman-LaRoche, Inc.*[20] represents a way of relieving plaintiffs from this important burden. It is not yet clear how enthusiastically courts in other states will follow the example of *Woolley*, or whether they will continue to require detrimental reliance on informal employer promises.

The second question is exemplified by the position taken by the Kentucky Supreme Court[21] and by Circuit Judge Posner.[22] Both narrowly circumscribed the class of

---

[19] *See* Carver v. Sheller-Globe Corp., 636 F. Supp. 368 (W.D. Mich. 1986) (applying law of state in which dismissed; finding no interests of forum state).

[20] 99 N.J. 284, 491 A.2d 1257 (1985); see **§ 4.16**.

[21] Grzyb v. Evans, 700 S.W.2d 399 (Ky. 1985) (no public policy tort claim for discrimination covered by administrative remedies or based on constitutional policies protecting free association).

[22] Buethe v. Britt Airlines, Inc., 787 F.2d 1194 (7th Cir. 1986) (no public policy tort except when statute creates employee right) (Posner, J.).

public policies entitled to serve as a foundation for the public policy tort, requiring that the plaintiff show an explicit statutory grant of rights to employees. **Section 5.19** questions the soundness of this position, considering the large number of cases permitting public policy tort recovery based on statutes protecting consumers or other nonemployee groups. Nevertheless, there is a real possibility that some courts will limit the utility of the public policy tort theory to plaintiffs by defining the allowable sources of public policy narrowly. Alternatively, courts may take an expansive view of sources of public policy, permitting employees to use any policy evidenced by statute, constitution, common law, or industry practice when they can make a convincing argument that the public policy would be jeopardized by permitting employers to dismiss employees for certain types of conduct. Public policy tort cases in Connecticut and New Hampshire suggest that virtually any imaginative employee can articulate a sufficient public policy to force his employer to trial over what, realistically, is a quarrel over practices legitimately within the employer's sole control.

A related question is whether the trend of requiring employees to resort primarily or exclusively to statutory enforcement mechanisms when they allege violation of public policies contained in statutes that also provide enforcement mechanisms will continue.[23]

Another question relating to the public policy tort theory is whether employees covered by collectively bargained just cause and grievance in arbitration procedures will be permitted to bring public policy tort claims for their dismissals. The case law seems about evenly split, with a slight majority of courts permitting dual remedies for such employees.[24]

The last question relates to the viability of the implied covenant theory. In recent years, courts outside a handful of states have been reluctant to use this theory—probably because it is difficult to narrow the role of the jury under it.[25] Courts in those states accepting the theory have seemed inclined to limit it to particular factual circumstances.[26] Probably courts in other states will not reject it, but will not accept it either, leaving it available to cover dismissals in particularly outrageous circumstances that do not fit within the evolving public policy tort or implied-in-fact contract theories. Conversely, it is conceivable that courts might use the implied covenant doctrine to impose a requirement for employers to show just cause to avoid liability for terminating employees. As § **4.9** explains, the doctrine is flexible enough to bear such an interpretation, although no decisional support has emerged so far.

Expansive interpretation of implied-in-fact contract principles present fewer policy risks than expansive interpretation of implied-in-law covenant and public policy tort principles. It is difficult to be upset when an employer is held to promises made explicitly to employees regarding grounds for termination or procedures to

---

[23] See § **5.9**.
[24] See § **5.20**.
[25] See §§ **4.9, 4.23**.
[26] See §§ **4.9, 4.23**.

be followed before termination. In such cases, the employer planted the seeds of liability, and has the power to reduce the liability by changing employment policies and controlling statements made by subordinate employees.

The practical effects of expansive public policy tort and implied covenant development may be perceived as less fair. To be sure, it is difficult to sympathize much with employers who try to force their employees to commit perjury or who dismiss employees in retaliation for exercising statutory or basic citizenship rights. On the other hand, if tort law permits employees to recover damages for dismissals resulting from disagreements with their employers over product design or accounting practices, the courts will be drawn substantially into second guessing basic business decisions made by employers. Courts are not well suited to make these decisions in a market economy.[27]

The spread of the wrongful dismissal doctrine in the common law of the states eventually will lead to pressure for federal or state statutes in order to ensure uniformity or to increase predictability.[28] Common law doctrinal alternatives and possible statutory approaches are considered in **Chapter 9**.

§ 1.16 Guesses about the Future

How the law of wrongful dismissal develops in the future will depend as much on perceptions of fairness and the appropriate balance among competing interests as on legal analysis. Both the public policy tort and implied-in-fact contract doctrines, though rooted in traditional common law principles, afford substantial policy discretion to judges to strike the balance between employer and employee interests at different points along the spectrum of theoretically acceptable possibilities.

Before speculating about the future, it is appropriate to know what is happening now. A study by a committee of the State Bar of California summarized results in wrongful dismissal cases going to juries in that state. The survey covered 41 cases decided in 1980 through 1982. In 32 of the cases, or 78 percent, plaintiffs recovered something. The lowest damage award was $17,000. Punitive damages were awarded in 17 cases. In 13, or 32 percent, of the cases, damage awards exceeded $100,000, and in 6, or nearly 15 percent of the cases, awards exceeded $600,000.[29]

The California figures are representative *of cases that get to the jury*. But the California study did not cover a much larger universe of cases: those that never go to suit and those that do result in litigation but never get to the jury. The future

---

[27] *See* Veno v. Meredith, ___ Pa. Super. ___, 515 A.2d 571, 579 (1986) (quoting this treatise).

[28] *Compare* Cox v. Resilient Flooring Div., 638 F. Supp. 726 (C.D. Cal. 1986) (lamenting flood of wrongful dismissal cases, and opining that ultimate solution is for legislatures to articulate standards) *with* St. Antoine, *The Revision of Employment-at-Will Enters a New Phase*, 36 Lab. L.J. 563 (1985) (common law unlikely to evolve to provide just cause protection, and ideology prevents employers from supporting just cause legislation).

[29] Ad Hoc Committee on Termination at Will and Wrongful Discharge Appointed by the Labor and Employment Law Section of The State Bar of California, To Strike a New Balance 7 (1984).

of wrongful dismissal litigation relates more to that larger universe than to how juries decide.

A later study by the Committee on Individual Rights and Responsibilities in the Workplace of the ABA Section on Labor and Employment Law apparently confined itself to reported appellate cases.[30] It found plaintiff success rates[31] in 1985 to be 38.3 percent in cases based on express contracts, 37.7 percent in cases involving handbooks or policy statements, 30 percent in cases based on oral representations, 30.8 percent in implied covenant cases, and 28.7 percent in public policy tort cases.[32] Success rates declined 12 percent and 15 percent from 1984 to 1985 for implied contract and tort cases respectively.[33] Significantly, implied covenant claims were raised significantly less often in the 1984 cases compared with the 1985 cases.[34]

It is the author's experience that three legal obstacles deter most wrongful dismissal cases[35] from being litigated:

1. The requirement that informal promises of employment security be supported by consideration
2. The requirement for a clear statement of public policy to support tort litigation
3. The statutory preemption of claims based on statutory statements of public policy

Given the judicial momentum, even the most conservative states will probably permit a dismissed employee the opportunity to rebut the presumption of an employment at will if that employee can prove facts permitting an inference of a promise of employment tenure. Very little, if any, expansion of well-accepted principles of contract law is required to allow such proof. Little interference with employer autonomy is threatened. The implied-in-fact contract theory presents less threat to employer prerogatives than implied-in-law covenant and tort theories because employers can forbear to make promises regarding employment tenure, thereby retaining control over exposure to liability.[36] Also, it is reasonably certain that the public policy tort theory will be accepted, at least in a limited way, in most states.

---

[30] *See* 2 The Labor Lawyer 352–54 (1986) (committee report).

[31] The report apparently counted all favorable decisions for plaintiffs in the percentages, including decisions on motions to dismiss and summary judgment.

[32] *Id.*

[33] *Id.*

[34] *Id.* at 354 (implied covenant decisions declined 35 percent from 1984 to 1985).

[35] *Wrongful dismissal case* is used in the sense of an employment termination in which the terminated employee seriously considers legal action.

[36] See **ch. 8**.

§ 1.17 CASE EVALUATION CHECKLIST

Nevertheless, some judges are expressing anxiety about the flood of wrongful dismissal litigation.[37] Such anxiety may stimulate curtailment of wrongful dismissal doctrines.

§ 1.17 Checklist for Case Evaluation

This section suggests threshold questions for use in evaluating employee dismissals.[38] The basic questions are keyed to sections of the treatise that explore legal theories for recovering damages for the dismissal in greater detail, and also are linked to discovery questions in **Appendix B**.

1. Were representations made to the employee about the duration of employment or the circumstances under which employment could be terminated?[39] Such representations might have been made orally at the time of hire or after initial hire, or they might be contained in employee handbooks or employer personnel policy manuals. If such representations were made, the employee may have a claim for breach of an implied-in-fact contract.[40] If the promise requirement can be satisfied, the following questions also must be answered in the affirmative in order for an implied-in-fact contract theory to succeed:

    a. Did the employee know of the employer promise?[41]

    b. Did the employee rely to his detriment on the promise, for example by giving up another job, by turning down job offers, or at least by refraining from looking for other jobs? Such reliance probably is required to show *consideration* for the promise. There is a trend to eliminate this requirement in some states.[42]

    c. Did the employer break the promise by dismissing without just cause, or by failing to afford the procedures that the employer promised would be followed before dismissal?[43]

---

[37] *See* Cox v. Resilient Flooring Div., 638 F. Supp. 726 (C.D. Cal. 1986) (lamenting flood or wrongful dismissal cases, and opining that ultimate solution is for legislatures to articulate standards).

[38] The author of this treatise is developing *expert system* computer software, using artificial intelligence concepts, that permits employment termination cases to be evaluated by using microcomputers.

[39] See Plaintiff's Discovery Questions 1–21, **App. B**.

[40] See §§ **4.6–4.24, 7.17–7.28**.

[41] See §§ **4.12–4.18, 7.20**. Note that some authority, most notably in Woolley v. Hoffman-LaRoche, Inc., 99 N.J. 284, 491 A.2d 1257 (1985), says that knowledge is not required.

[42] See §§ **4.14–4.17**.

[43] §§ **4.21–4.24, 7.22–7.28**.

2. Did the employee make any protests within the employer's organization or to government agencies about products, employer policies, or working conditions, or refuse to follow employer orders that involved detriment to the public welfare?[44] If such protests or refusals were made, it is possible that the dismissal was in retaliation for those protests or refusals. Such circumstances may permit recovery under a public policy tort theory.[45] If a protest or refusal to engage in illegal or detrimental conduct occurred, the following questions must be answered in the affirmative before a public policy tort claim can succeed:

   a. Was the protest or refusal supportive of a public policy articulated in a state or federal statute or constitution?[46]

   b. Are administrative remedies provided for under the statute used as the source of the public policy? If there are, the courts may be reluctant to afford tort relief for the claim.[47]

   c. How did the employee's conduct serve to vindicate the public policy? In other words, how much would the public policy be jeopardized if conduct like the employee's were discouraged by the threat of dismissal?[48]

   d. What proof is there that the public policy-linked conduct was the reason for the dismissal, as opposed to other motivations that might serve legitimate employer interests?[49]

3. Was the employee treated worse than persons of the opposite sex or different races, religions, or ages?[50] If class-based discrimination can be shown, the employee may have a claim under antidiscrimination statutes.[51] If the employee was treated worse than similarly situated persons of other races, sexes, ages, or religions, the following questions must be answered in the affirmative before the employee has a good statutory discrimination claim:

   a. How old was the employee? Only if the employee is age 40 or over does the federal statute protect against age discrimination.[52]

   b. How can the employee show that race, sex, age, or religion was the motivation for the dismissal? Such motivation can be shown by employer statements or by evidence that employees in other race, sex,

---

[44] See Plaintiff's Discovery Questions 22–34, **app. B**.

[45] See §§ **5.8–5.19, 7.10–7.16**. The employee's conduct also might be protected by a federal or state "whistleblower" statute. See §§ **2.15–2.24**.

[46] See § **7.11**.

[47] See §§ **5.9, 7.12**.

[48] See § **7.12**.

[49] See §§ **7.13–7.14**.

[50] See Plaintiff's Discovery Questions 61–65, **app. B**.

[51] See §§ **2.2–2.14**.

[52] See §§ **2.6–2.7**.

age, or religious groups were treated more favorably though they were situated identically with the employee.[53]

    c. Has the employee exhausted administrative procedures that are prerequisite for bringing suit?[54]

4. Was the employee covered by a collective bargaining agreement? Note that what matters is *coverage* by a collective bargaining agreement, not whether the employee was a member of the union that negotiated the collective bargaining agreement. Most collective bargaining agreements contain prohibitions against dismissal without just cause and also require that grievances under the agreement be submitted to arbitration.[55]

5. If these theories cannot be established, it may be possible for the employee to maintain a claim for breach of the implied covenant of good faith and fair dealing. This theory has been disfavored in recent cases, but it still may be available if the manner of the dismissal or the reason for the dismissal was particularly offensive.[56]

6. Has the employee received an award of unemployment compensation? If the employee received unemployment compensation over the employer's protest, it is possible that an administrative agency has decided that the dismissal was not for misconduct. The administrative decision may be entitled to some preclusive effect or evidentiary weight in a trial of the propriety of the dismissal itself.[57]

7. Did the employer communicate detrimental information about the employee to others? If it did, a claim for defamation may be possible.[58]

8. Was the dismissal effected in a particularly outrageous manner? If it was, and if the employee has suffered severe emotional distress, a claim for intentional infliction of emotional distress may be possible.[59]

9. If it can be shown that the employer represented that the job would be secure, knowing that it would not be, a claim for fraudulent misrepresentation may be possible.[60]

10. If the employee was dismissed for private, off-duty conduct, a claim for invasion of privacy or a claim under a variant of the public policy tort may be possible.[61]

---

[53] See §§ 7.4–7.9.
[54] See §§ 2.3, 2.6.
[55] See **ch. 3**; §§ 4.25, 5.20.
[56] See §§ 4.9, 4.23, 7.23.
[57] See §§ 2.37, 7.35.
[58] See § 5.25.
[59] See § 5.23.
[60] See § 5.24.
[61] See §§ 5.26–5.28.

CHAPTER 2

STATUTORY PROTECTION

§ 2.1   Introduction
§ 2.2   Protecting against Class-based Discrimination
§ 2.3   —Title VII: Basic Concepts
§ 2.4   —Title VII: Disparate Treatment Examples
§ 2.5   —Title VII: Sexual Harassment
§ 2.6   —Age Discrimination in Employment Act: Basic Concepts
§ 2.7   —Age Discrimination in Employment Act: Examples
§ 2.8   —Reconstruction Civil Rights Acts: Section 1981
§ 2.9   —Reconstruction Civil Rights Acts: Section 1985
§ 2.10   —Handicap Discrimination: Rehabilitation Act
§ 2.11   —Title VI of the Civil Rights Act of 1964
§ 2.12   —Handicap Discrimination: State Law
§ 2.13   —Federal Contractors: Executive Order 11,246
§ 2.14   —Education Act Amendments
§ 2.15   Statutes Protecting Employee Conduct
§ 2.16   —National Labor Relations Act
§ 2.17   —Retaliation for Opposing Discrimination
§ 2.18   —Occupational Safety and Health Act
§ 2.19   —Railroad Safety and Liability Acts
§ 2.20   —Environmental Statutes
§ 2.21   —Fair Labor Standards Act
§ 2.22   —Consumer Credit Protection Act
§ 2.23   —Employee Retirement Income Security Act
§ 2.24   —Other Federal Statutes
§ 2.25   Attorneys' Fees
§ 2.26   Implied Private Right of Action from a Statute
§ 2.27   Preemption
§ 2.28   —National Labor Relations Act Preemption
§ 2.29   —Preemption of Tort Claims under § 301 of the Labor Management Relations Act

§ 2.30	—Preemption of Contract Claims under § 301 of the Labor Management Relations Act
§ 2.31	—Preemption of Common Law Claims under the Railway Labor Act
§ 2.32	—Preemption under Discrimination Statutes
§ 2.33	—Preemption under Federal Whistleblower Statutes
§ 2.34	—Preemption under Other Federal Statutes
§ 2.35	Pendent State Claims
§ 2.36	Unemployment Compensation Generally
§ 2.37	—Procedures for Determining Eligibility for Unemployment Benefits
§ 2.38	Considerations in Pursuing Both Statutory and Common Law Relief

§ 2.1 Introduction

In contrast with the situation in other industrial countries, general statutory protection in the United States against wrongful discharge does not exist.[1] Several statutes, however, protect employees against adverse employment action based on the employees' membership in a class defined by racial type, gender, religion, national origin, age, or disability,[2] or based on particular conduct, such as participation in union activity or reporting violations of law to administrative agencies.[3] Statutes in most states provide protection similar to that of the federal statutes[4] and, in some instances, afford additional protection against adverse employment action.[5]

This chapter surveys statutory protection against terminations for particular reasons, beginning with statutes prohibiting class-based discrimination[6] and then moving to statutes protecting against retaliation for certain conduct.[7] For each statute, the scope of the protection is identified and the remedial procedures described. Typical cases are discussed to illustrate the factual controversies likely to be presented and to identify certain common problems in proving the causal nexus between the statutorily protected status or conduct and the discharge. This chapter also discusses whether private rights of action can be implied from statutes,[8]

---

[1] See **ch. 9**.

[2] See §§ 2.2–2.14.

[3] See §§ 2.15–2.24.

[4] See **App. A** for a table of state statutes. The text of this chapter identifies the major differences between federal and state approaches.

[5] *E.g.*, Cal. Lab. Code § 1102 (West 1971 & Supp. 1986) (protects against employer action intended to coerce employees into taking a political position).

[6] See §§ 2.2–2.14.

[7] See §§ 2.15–2.24.

[8] See § 2.26.

analyzes federal preemption,[9] and treats pendent state claims.[10] A brief section on unemployment compensation is presented because this is a pervasive statutory remedy for terminated employees, regardless of the reason for the termination. Also, determinations made by unemployment compensation agencies may be entitled to preclusive effect in wrongful dismissal cases.[11] The final section of the chapter identifies practical litigation strategy issues when a single employment termination gives rise to statutory as well as common law claims.

Most of the statutes considered protect against all types of adverse employment action, including failures to hire or promote, discrimination during employment, and discriminatory dismissals. In keeping with the general plan of this treatise, however, only termination of employment is discussed. Moreover, due to the complexities of employment discrimination law, this chapter can do little more than introduce major concepts and identify leading cases.[12]

§ 2.2 Protection against Class-based Discrimination

Federal statutes protecting employees against adverse employment action based on their membership in defined classes include Title VII of the Civil Rights Act of 1964,[13] the Age Discrimination in Employment Act,[14] the Reconstruction Civil Rights Acts,[15] and the Rehabilitation Act of 1973.[16] The coverage, conduct prohibited, remedies available, and procedural requirements of each of these are discussed.

Counsel presented with a wrongful dismissal case should examine the facts carefully to ascertain whether a connection exists between the dismissal and class membership under these statutes. The problems involved in litigating a claim under the statutes, executive orders, and regulations obviously are too complex to be treated exhaustively in one chapter. Counsel handling a case involving the matters presented here is advised to consult specialized research materials.[17]

---

[9] See §§ 2.27–2.34.

[10] See § 2.35.

[11] The preclusive effect of unemployment compensation determinations is addressed in § 7.35. The unemployment compensation system is introduced in this chapter, in §§ 2.36–2.38.

[12] *See* B. Schlei & P. Grossman, Employment Discrimination (1983); H. Eglit, Age Discrimination (1981); W. Diedrich & W. Gaus, Defense of Equal Employment Claims (1982).

[13] 42 U.S.C. §§ 2000e–2000e-17 (1982).

[14] 29 U.S.C. §§ 621–634 (1982).

[15] 42 U.S.C. §§ 1981, 1985(3)(1982); 42 U.S.C. § 1983 (1982) protects against employment discrimination by the states. It is considered in **ch. 6**.

[16] 29 U.S.C. §§ 701–709, 720–724, 730–732, 740, 741, 750, 760–764, 770–776, 780–787, 790–794 (1982).

[17] *See* B. Schlei & P. Grossman, Employment Discrimination Law (1983).

§ 2.3 — Title VII: Basic Concepts

Title VII of the Civil Rights Act of 1964 protects persons against employment discrimination because of their sex, race, religion, or national origin.[18] In every wrongful dismissal case, counsel should consider whether the facts warrant a Title VII claim. Everyone is a member of a *protected class* under Title VII. Whites are protected as well as blacks,[19] males as well as females,[20] Protestants as well as Catholics. All persons are protected by Title VII against a certain type of discrimination: discrimination because of their membership in race, sex, religious, or nationality classes. Adverse action indirectly based on sex also is prohibited, such as pregnancy discrimination and sexual harassment.[21] But the majority view is that discrimination based on sexual preference does not violate Title VII.[22]

The following are covered by Title VII protections: (1) employers in industries affecting commerce, if the employer has 15 or more employees;[23] (2) state and local governments;[24] (3) labor organizations with 15 or more members; (4) labor organizations in industries affecting commerce;[25] and (5) employment agencies.[26] The class of potential plaintiffs is broader than that of employees in the traditional sense.[27] Because the focus of this treatise is on termination of employment, rather than on hiring or promotions, this section considers only Title VII concepts applied to dismissals.

---

[18] Title VII also covers adverse action based on opposition to employment discrimination. 42 U.S.C. § 2000e-2(a) (1982). This aspect of Title VII is discussed in § **2.17** as a statute protecting conduct.

[19] McDonald v. Santa Fe Trail Transp. Co., 427 U.S. 273 (1976). *But see* Livingston v. Roadway Express, Inc., 802 F.2d 1251, 1252 (10th Cir. 1986) (suggesting more stringent proof standards in reverse disparate impact case).

[20] Diaz v. Pan Am. World Airways, Inc., 442 F.2d 385 (5th Cir.) (males as well as females protected), *cert. denied,* 404 U.S. 950 (1971).

[21] See § **2.5**; Bundy v. Jackson, 641 F.2d 934 (D.C. Cir. 1981); Annotation, *Sexual Advances by Employee's Superior as Sex Discrimination within Title VII,* 46 A.L.R. Fed. 224 (1980) (solicitation of sexual favors and other sexual harrassment also violate Title VII). *But see* DeCinto v. Westchester County Medical Center, 807 F.2d 304 (2d Cir. 1986) (Title VII does not prohibit discrimination in favor of boss's lover).

[22] DeSantis v. Pacific Tel. & Tel. Co., 608 F.2d 327 (9th Cir. 1979) (Title VII does not extend to sexual preference discrimination); Blum v. Gulf Oil Co., 597 F.2d 936 (5th Cir. 1979) (discharge for homosexuality not prohibited by Title VII); *but see* Wright v. Methodist Youth Servs., Inc., 511 F. Supp. 307 (N.D. Ill. 1981) (Title VII claim exists for employee terminated for refusing supervisor's homosexual advances); Valdes v. Lumberman's Mut. Cas. Co., 507 F. Supp. 10 (S.D. Fla. 1980) (Title VII may bar treating male and female homosexuals differently). *See generally* Annotation, *Refusal to Hire or Dismissal from Employment on Account of Plaintiff's Sexual Lifestyle or Sexual Preference as Violation of Federal Constitution or Federal Civil Rights Statutes,* 42 A.L.R. Fed. 189 (1979 & Supp. 1985).

[23] *See* Sedlacek v. Hach, 752 F.2d 333, 334 (8th Cir. 1984) (use of *single entity* theory to aggregate employment of apparently distinct employers to get above 15-employee jurisdiction threshold).

[24] 42 U.S.C. §§ 2000e(b), 2000e-2(a) (1982).

[25] *Id.* §§ 2000e(e), 2000e-2(c).

[26] *Id.* §§ 2000e(c), 2000e-2(b).

[27] *See* Doe v. St. Joseph's Hosp., 788 F.2d 411, 422-23 (7th Cir. 1986) (Title VII affords remedy to nonemployee physician for discrimination by hospital, citing Sibley Memorial Hosp. v. Wilson,

§ 2.3   TITLE VII: BASICS

The Civil Rights Act makes it an unlawful employment practice for an employer to dismiss any individual because of race, color, religion, sex, or national origin.[28] The *because of* language establishes as a necessary element a causal link between the individual's membership in a defined class and his or her dismissal.[29] Exemptions are provided for restrictions based on *bona fide occupational qualifications* linked to religion, sex, or national origin,[30] for religious qualifications imposed by religious organizations or religious schools,[31] and for *bona fide seniority or merit systems*.[32] An employer must accommodate religious beliefs or practices only to the extent the accommodation does not interfere unreasonably with the employer's business.[33]

A violation of Title VII can be proved in one of two basic ways: by proving intent to discriminate, or by proving that an employer policy has a disparate impact on a racial, sexual, or other defined group. Proof of intent may be direct,[34] or, as is usually the case, indirect, by proof of disparate treatment. *Disparate treatment* is the name given to the type of proof approved by the Supreme Court in

---

488 F.2d 1338, 1341 (D.C. Cir. 1973)). *See also* Mares v. Marsh, 777 F.2d 1066, 1067 n.1 (5th Cir. 1985) (citing cases applying less stringent test than traditional contractor-employee test in discrimination cases).

[28] 42 U.S.C. § 2000e-2(a)(1). Constructive dismissals can be found even when the employee resigns. *See* Goss v. Exxon Office Sys. Co., 747 F.2d 885, 888 (3d Cir. 1984) (knowingly permitting intolerable conditions amounts to constructive discharge; no specific intent required. Summarizing differences among circuits).

[29] *See* Texas Dep't of Community Affairs v. Burdine, 450 U.S. 248 (1981).

[30] *See* Pullman Standard v. Swint, 624 F.2d 525 (5th Cir. 1980), *rev'd*, 456 U.S. 273 (1982), *on remand*, 692 F.2d 1031 (5th Cir. 1982). A bona fide occupational qualification (BFOQ) is a narrow exception to the general requirement contained in Title VII that employment decisions be gender-, religion-, and national origin-neutral. If applicable, it permits overt discrimination based on sex, religion, or national origin. *See* Dothard v. Rawlinson, 433 U.S. 321 (1977) (BFOQ applies to male-only requirement for maximum security male prison guards; Pirne v. Loyola Univ., 803 F.2d 351 (7th Cir. 1986) (being a Jesuit is BFOQ in Catholic university philosophy department)). Most BFOQ cases under Title VII have involved gender qualifications, because of the rarity with which an employer would perceive a practical need for a religious or national origin qualification. The BFOQ defense is applicable when the essence of the business operation would be undermined by not hiring members of one sex exclusively. Diaz v. Pan Am. World Airways, 442 U.S. 385, 388 (5th Cir.) (no BFOQ for females-only requirement in hiring airline flight attendants), *cert. denied*, 404 U.S. 950 (1971). An employer can rely on the BFOQ exception only by proving that "he had reasonable cause to believe, that is a factual basis for believing, that all or substantially all women would be unable to perform safely and efficiently the duties of the job involved." Weeks v. Southern Bell Tel. & Tel. Co., 408 F.2d 228, 235 (5th Cir. 1969) (no BFOQ for men-only hiring requirement for telephone switchmen). Most BFOQ cases involve hiring decisions rather than terminations.

[31] 42 U.S.C. § 2000e-2(e)(2) (1982).

[32] *Id.* § 2000e-2(h). *See* Zipes v. T.W.A., 455 U.S. 385 (1982); Teamsters v. United States, 431 U.S. 324 (1977).

[33] *See* Protos v. Volkswagen of Am., Inc., 797 F.2d 129, 133–35 (3d Cir. 1986) (reviewing cases from other circuits and finding accomodation to be required).

[34] *See* Cline v. Roadway Express, Inc., 689 F.2d 481, 485 (4th Cir. 1982) (no need for *McDonnell Douglas* disparte treatment proof scheme if direct evidence of intent available; interpreting Title VII concepts in Age Discrimination in Employment Act case).

McDonnell Douglas v. Green.[35] Under the disparate treatment theory,[36] intent may be inferred from circumstantial evidence showing that the plaintiff was treated worse than similarly situated persons in other racial, religious, or gender classes.[37] The circumstantial evidence must be probative of the plaintiff's individual employment situation, however; statistical evidence regarding the workforce in general may not be enough.[38] The employees used for comparison purposes must be similarly situated in all material respects.[39] The plaintiff may be able to prove a Title VII violation even though the person treated more favorably was a member of the same minority group.[40] In every case, however, the plaintiff retains the burden of persuading the factfinder that the adverse employment action was motivated by a prohibited consideration.[41]

Disparate impact is the name given to the theory of discrimination recognized by the Supreme Court in *Griggs v. Duke Power*.[42] Proving a violation of Title VII under a disparate impact theory does not require proof of intent.[43] Instead, it involves showing that persons with the same characteristic as the plaintiff were disadvantaged disproportionately by application of a facially neutral employment policy or practice which cannot be justified by "business necessity."[44] The disparate impact theory is most frequently used in class actions rather than individual actions,[45] but it has been accepted in individual suits.[46]

The Act contemplates two procedural stages: a conciliation stage, conducted under the auspices of state and federal administrative agencies, and a judicial stage,

---

[35] 411 U.S. 792 (1973).

[36] *Id.* at 806.

[37] *Id.* at 804.

[38] *See* Sengupta v. Morrison-Knudson Co., 804 F.2d 1072, 1076 (9th Cir. 1986) (sample size too small); Carmichael v. Birmingham Saw Works, 738 F.2d 1126, 1131 (11th Cir. 1984) ("statistics alone cannot make a case of individual disparate treatment"; hiring, promotion, wage increase case).

[39] *See* Smith v. Monsanto Chem. Co., 770 F.2d 719, 724 (8th Cir. 1985) (overturning jury verdict for employee; employees treated more leniently for violating theft rule either had more seniority or differed in other respects), *cert. denied,* ___ U.S. ___, 106 S. Ct. 1273 (1986).

[40] *See* Nix v. WLCY Radio, 738 F.2d 1181, 1186 (11th Cir. 1984) ("Title VII does not give an employer license to discriminate against some employees on the basis of race or sex merely because he favorably treats other members of the employees' group").

[41] *See* Grubb v. W.A. Foote Memorial Hosp., Inc., 741 F.2d 1486, 1496 (6th Cir. 1984) (district court finding of race discrimination reversed despite evidence of racist remarks by supervisor); Lewis v. Smith, 731 F.2d 1535, 1537-38 (11th Cir. 1984) (direct testimony of discriminatory intent makes *McDonnell-Douglas* inference formula unnecessary).

[42] 401 U.S. 424 (1971).

[43] *Id.* at 432.

[44] *Id.* at 431.

[45] *See* Rissetto, Employment Discrimination Class Actions (BNA) (1979 Yearbook 80). Rissetto explains why the concept of disparate treatment is inherently better suited for individual suits and the concept of disparate impact inherently better suited for class action litigation. *See generally* W. Diedrich & W. Gaus, Defense of Equal Employment Claims (1982).

[46] *See, e.g.,* Craig v. Alabama State Univ., 804 F.2d 682, 686 (11th Cir. 1986); Blizard v. Frechette, 601 F.2d 1217 (1st Cir. 1979).

conducted de novo by the federal courts. An employee who believes she has been discharged because of race, sex, color, religion, or national origin must file a charge with a state agency having jurisdiction over the type of discrimination alleged and may thereafter file with the federal Equal Employment Opportunity Commission (EEOC).[47] Charges filed initially with a state agency must be filed with the EEOC within 300 days after the discharge, but if no state agency has jurisdiction, the charge must be filed with the EEOC within 180 days after the discharge.[48] The Supreme Court has held that the time limits are not jurisdictional.[49] The EEOC has 180 days to seek a conciliation agreement from the employer or to file suit.[50] After 180 days, the charging party is entitled to a right-to-sue letter from the commission, which permits her to file suit on her own behalf in the United States District Court within 90 days after receiving the letter.[51] The EEOC also can file suit on behalf of a charging party.[52] Individual suits are heard de novo, regardless of whether the commission has found merit in the charge.[53] Many state agencies, in contrast, have the power to adjudicate, subject to judicial review.[54] A decision by a state court on a claim that could have been prosecuted before the EEOC is res judicata in a federal court action.[55]

If the commission obtains a conciliation agreement, such an agreement typically waives the employee's right to sue,[56] but it may be enforced judicially in a breach of contract action brought in federal court.[57] In *W.R. Grace & Co. v. Rubber*

---

[47] 42 U.S.C. § 2000e-5(c) (1982). *See* Love v. Pullman Co., 404 U.S. 522 (1972) (EEOC can satisfy requirements by referring charge to state agency); Mohasco v. Silver, 447 U.S. 807 (1979).

[48] 42 U.S.C. § 2000e-5(e) (1982).

[49] Zipes v. T.W.A., 455 U.S. 385 (1982).

[50] 42 U.S.C. § 2000e-5(b) (1982).

[51] *Id.* § 2000e-5(f)(1). The Ninth Circuit has held that federal courts have exclusive jurisdiction over Title VII cases. Valenzuela v. Kraft, Inc., 739 F.2d 434, 435 (9th Cir. 1984) (lack of jurisdiction by state court means federal court lacks removal jurisdiction).

[52] 42 U.S.C. § 2000e-5(f)(1) (1982). 42 U.S.C. § 2000e-6 also authorizes the commission to bring pattern-and-practice suits. *See* B. Schlei & P. Grossman, Employment Discrimination Law 1138 (1983) (explaining requirements for litigation with EEOC as plaintiff).

[53] 42 U.S.C. § 2000e-6(b). *See* Alexander v. Gardner Denver, 415 U.S. 36 (1974). The EEOC's findings are not entitled to any particular deference by the court. McDonnell Douglas v. Green, 411 U.S. 792 (1973).

[54] *See* Rap, Inc. v. District of Columbia Comm'n on Human Rights, 485 A.2d 173, 179 (D.C. 1984) (reversing state agency finding of sex discrimination). See generally **§ 7.33**, considering res judicata effect of adjudicatory state decisions.

[55] Kremer v. Chemical Constr. Co., 456 U.S. 461 (1982). The Ninth Circuit has held that state courts lack jurisdiction over Title VII cases. Valenzuela v. Kraft, Inc., 739 F.2d 434, 435 (9th Cir. 1984) (lack of jurisdiction by state court means federal court lacks removal jurisdiction).

[56] *See* Taylor v. Gordon Flesch Co., 793 F.2d 858, 863 (7th Cir. 1986) (oral settlement agreement reached in state agency proceeding bars Title VII claim).

[57] *See* EEOC v. Henry Beck Co., 729 F.2d 301, 305 (4th Cir. 1984) (predetermination settlement agreement enforceable in federal court by EEOC under Title VII just like conciliation agreement); EEOC v. Safeway Stores, Inc., 714 F.2d 567 (5th Cir. 1983) (district court has jurisdiction over action brought by EEOC under Title VII to enforce conciliation agreement); EEOC v. Liberty Trucking Co., 695 F.2d 1038 (4th Cir. 1982) (same); EEOC v. Pierce Packing Co., 669 F.2d

Workers Local 759,[58] the Supreme Court considered a conflict between a conciliation agreement to which the union was not a party and a collective bargaining agreement. It upheld an arbitration award holding the employer liable for actions taken pursuant to the conciliation agreement that violated the collective agreement. The court reasoned that the employer could have protected itself from conflicting obligations by causing the union to be party to the conciliation agreement before it signed.

Remedies under Title VII include back pay for a period of up to two years[59] and broad injunctive relief.[60] A growing number of circuits also permit front pay in appropriate cases.[61] Jury trials are not available.[62]

§ 2.4 — Title VII: Disparate Treatment Examples

The following discharge cases highlight the Title VII disparate treatment proof concepts articulated by the Supreme Court in *McDonnell Douglas v. Green*[63] and refined in *Texas Department of Community Affairs v. Burdine*.[64] Disparate treatment cases require the plaintiff to prove a prima facie case, after which the employer must articulate a legitimate nondiscriminatory reason for the adverse employment action in order to avoid liability.[65] *Legitimate* may mean no more than non-

---

605, 608 (10th Cir. 1982) (conciliation agreement enforceable, but not preinvestigation "settlement agreement"); EEOC v. Contour Chair Lounge Co., 596 F.2d 809, 816 (8th Cir. 1979) (same). *But see* Parsons v. Yellow Freight Sys., Inc., 741 F.2d 871 (6th Cir. 1984) (plaintiff allegedly discharged in violation of EEOC settlement agreement may not sue for breach of contract without exhausting (unspecified) administrative remedies before EEOC).

[58] 461 U.S. 757 (1983).

[59] 42 U.S.C. § 2000e-5(g) (1981). Back pay should be allowed for the entire two-year period when continuing discrimination is involved. *Cf.* Patterson v. American Tobacco Co., 586 F.2d 300, 304 (4th Cir. 1978) (injunctive relief for continuing violation). However, discrete acts of discrimination before the 300-day filing period do not give rise to back-pay obligations. Inda v. United Air Lines, Inc., 565 F.2d 554, 562 (9th Cir. 1977) (calculation of back pay from first discriminatory act outside filing period was error), *cert. denied,* 435 U.S. 1007 (1978).

[60] 42 U.S.C. § 2000e-5(g) (1982); H. Perritt, Labor Injunctions §§ 14.2–14.4 (1986).

[61] *See* Shore v. Federal Express Corp., 777 F.2d 1155, 1158 (6th Cir. 1985) (front pay is consistent with purposes of Title VII; remanding for further findings to justify front-pay award); Goss v. Exxon Office Sys. Co., 747 F.2d 885, 890 (3d Cir. 1984) (no abuse of discretion to award front pay for a limited time rather than reinstatement).

[62] 42 U.S.C. § 2000e-5(f)(4) assigns the duty to hear and determine the case to the district judge. *See* Blum v. Gulf Oil Co., 597 F.2d 936 (5th Cir. 1979) (motion for jury trial properly denied in civil rights suit brought by discharged former employee who claimed that he was terminated because of his religion and sexual preferences).

[63] 411 U.S. 792 (1973).

[64] 450 U.S. 248 (1981).

[65] See § **7.6** for a fuller discussion.

discriminatory.[66] If the employer articulates such a reason, the employee still can win the case by showing that the proffered reason was a pretext.

Sullivan v. Boorstin[67] involved the Library of Congress and a black employee who was suspended from his job for being absent without filing the requisite form and for engaging in a physical altercation with his supervisor over the incident.[68] Sullivan sued under Title VII for redress of alleged discrimination.[69] He claimed that, subsequent to his firing, similar occurrences between female employees and their female supervisors resulted only in written reprimands.[70] He contended that this disparate treatment was equivalent to sex discrimination.[71] The district court, however, ruled that the library had met its burden of articulating legitimate, non-discriminatory reasons for Sullivan's discharge[72] by distinguishing the plaintiff's actions from those of the female employees.[73]

In *Saucedo v. Brothers Well Service, Inc.*,[74] the district court found that the plaintiff, a Mexican-American, had been discharged in violation of Title VII. His employers had discharged him for violating a de facto "rule" that Spanish could not be spoken on the job.[75] The plaintiff's immediate superior overheard him ask a question in Spanish and informed Saucedo that he (Saucedo) had just resigned.[76] When a fellow employee protested, the supervisor assaulted him.[77] Saucedo's "resignation" subsequently was affirmed by Brothers, and no action was taken against the supervisor.[78] The court's holding was based on the disparate treatment

---

[66] *See* Nix v. WLCY Radio, 738 F.2d 1181, 1187 (11th Cir. 1984) ("The employer may fire an employee for a good reason, a bad reason, a reason based on erroneous facts, or for no reason at all, as long as its action is not for a discriminatory reason.").

[67] 484 F. Supp. 836 (D.D.C. 1980).

[68] *Id.* at 837–39.

[69] *Id.* at 839. Sullivan alleged discrimination in government employment, based on race, color, and sex.

[70] *Id.* at 840. In one incident, two black female employees were given an informal warning for fighting. Another involved a black female employee who was given an informal written warning for fighting with her supervisor, a black female. A third incident involved a white male employee and a black male supervisor, in which only an informal warning was given.

[71] *Id.* at 841.

[72] *Id.* at 843. The library based its decision on Sullivan's own admissions, his threat to his supervisor in the presence of another worker, and the actual injuries suffered by his supervisor; *see id.* at 839.

[73] *Id.* at 840. The court found that the plaintiff had failed to make out a prima facie case; *see id.* at 843. In most cases, the comparison of treatment of the plaintiff with the treatment of other similarly situated employees takes place in the *pretext* part of the proof analysis.

[74] 464 F. Supp. 919 (S.D. Tex. 1979).

[75] *Id.* at 920. The rule was justified by safety considerations in the operation of oil rigs. The rig Saucedo worked on was being repaired, and Saucedo was in the repair shop when the incident occurred. The court considered the location of the incident important. The safety rationale behind the rule would be inapplicable in the repair shop. *Id.* at 921.

[76] *Id.*

[77] *Id.* at 922.

[78] *Id.*

accorded Brothers' employees: Saucedo was discharged for a minor offense, while no action was taken against the supervisor for a major one.[79] The court concluded that Saucedo had been discharged on the basis of racial animus.[80]

In *Reed v. Famous Barr Division*,[81] the plaintiff, a white male,[82] brought an employment discrimination suit alleging that he had been discharged because of his sex.[83] Reed contended that his female supervisor, Knisley, resented males and therefore failed to train him in the same manner as she trained females.[84] He said that, based on her sexual bias, she then recommended that he be fired, and that the defendant, in reliance on Knisley's recommendation, unlawfully discharged him because of his sex.[85] The defendant claimed that Reed, from the first, had indicated resentment at taking orders from a female supervisor.[86] The supervisor concluded after approximately two months, based on direct observation, that Reed's performance justified an unsatisfactory job rating,[87] resulting in termination of his probationary employment.[88] The plaintiff reacted with expletives, stating he was going to "get" his supervisor's job.[89]

The court, assuming the plaintiff's prima facie case, found that the defendant had acted with legitimate business reasons in terminating plaintiff's employment.[90] The court concluded that the public display by the plaintiff, and his threat to the supervisor, made his assertions of sexual discrimination implausible.[91] The court found no disparate treatment in the training Reed had received, although other, female, employees had received more training.[92] Reed's greater formal education and experience reduced the need for such training.[93]

In *Reynolds v. Humko Products*,[94] a white truck driver was fired for drinking on duty. The court of appeals affirmed a judgment for the employer, finding that the plaintiff failed to show disparate treatment because the black employees he

---

[79] *Id.* The court also noted, "[a] rule that Spanish cannot be spoken on the job obviously has a disparate impact on Mexican-Americans."

[80] *Id.*

[81] 518 F. Supp. 538 (E.D. Mo. 1981).

[82] *Id.* at 540.

[83] *Id.*

[84] *Id.* at 542.

[85] *Id.* at 541.

[86] *Id.* at 540. The court concluded the supervisor undoubtedly knew of the plaintiff's attitude.

[87] *Id.* The supervisor's conclusion was based on the plaintiff's lack of interest, inattention to duty, and argumentative nature.

[88] *Id.* at 541.

[89] *Id.* The defendant terminated Reed immediately.

[90] *Id.* The numerous misunderstandings with his supervisor, not fully carrying out his assignments, general lack of cooperation, boredom, and disinterest supported the inference that Reed was unhappy with the limited discretion and repetitive nature of his assignments. *Id.* at 542.

[91] *Id.*

[92] *Id.* The evidence showed Reed received approximately the same number of hours of training as other senior employees in the company.

[93] *Id.*

[94] 756 F.2d 469 (6th Cir. 1985).

offered for comparison were not similarly situated, since their infractions did not involve drinking and the associated safety concerns.

§ 2.5 —Title VII: Sexual Harassment

Although Title VII does not specifically mention sexual harassment it is well settled that such conduct amounts to discrimination on the basis of sex under Title VII.[95] Two types of sexual harassment violate Title VII: sexual harassment creating an offensive working environment; and demand for sexual favors in exchange for favorable treatment.

Sexual harassment creating an offensive working environment is treated as an implicit adverse employment action based on sex.[96] Frequently, *constructive dismissal* results from this type of sexual harassment.[97] In *Bundy v. Jackson*,[98] the court adopted the EEOC's guideline which defines offensive-environment sexual harassment as "such conduct [which] has the purpose or effect of unreasonably interfering with an individual's work performance or creates an intimidating, hostile, or offensive work environment."[99] In this type of sexual harassment action, in order to make out a Title VII violation, the plaintiff must prove the following:

1. The employee belongs to a protected group. This simply means stating that the employee is a man or woman
2. The employee was the subject of unwelcome sexual harassment
3. The sexual harassment was based on sex
4. The sexual harassment affected a term, condition or privilege of employment
5. The employer knew or should have known of the harassment and failed to take remedial action.[1]

---

[95] *See* Meritor Sav. Bank v. Vinson, ___ U.S. ___, 106 S. Ct. 2399 (1986) ("Without question, when a supervisor sexually harasses a subordinate because of the subordinate's sex, that supervisor 'discriminate(s)' on the basis of sex.").

[96] *See* Katz v. Dole, 709 F.2d 251 (4th Cir. 1983). In *Katz,* the court held that an employer's policy or acquiescence in a practice of sexual harassment can constitute a violation of Title VII when such sexual harassment pervades the workplace or is condoned or carried out by supervisory personnel. *Id.* at 254.

[97] Derr v. Gulf Oil Corp., 796 F.2d 340, 344 (10th Cir. 1986) (remanding for application of objective constructive dismissal standard); Schneider v. Jax Shack, Inc., 794 F.2d 383, 385 (8th Cir. 1986) (reversing dismissal of constructive discharge claim); Bishopp v. District of Columbia, 788 F.2d 781, 789 (D.C. Cir. 1986) (articulating standard for constructive discharge).

[98] 641 F.2d 934 (D.C. Cir. 1981), *cited with approval in* Meritor Sav. Bank v. Vinson, ___ U.S. ___, 106 S. Ct. at 2406 (approving EEOC guidelines).

[99] Bundy v. Jackson, 641 F.2d at 947.

[1] *Accord* Meritor Sav. Bank v. Vinson, ___ U.S. ___, 106 S. Ct. 2399 (1986); Jones v. Flagship Int'l, 793 F.2d 714, 719–20 (5th Cir. 1986) (approving elements set forth in text; affirming district court finding of no sexual harassment).

Similar concepts are applied by state courts applying state sex discrimination statutes.[2]

Unwelcome sexual harassment was distinguished from welcome sexual overtures by the Supreme Court in *Meritor Savings Bank v. Vinson*.[3] Vinson testified that her boss made repeated demands on her for sexual favors, fondled her in front of other employees, and raped her. The district court found that the sexual relationship was voluntary. The Supreme Court, approving a reversal of the district court, held that the correct inquiry is whether the complainant indicates that the sexual advances are unwelcome, not whether the actual participation in sexual acts is voluntary.[4] The point is that Title VII prohibits adverse employment action. Only unwelcome sexual overtures can be deemed to be adverse.

The employee must prove that the sexual harassment was based on sex.[5] The essence of a disparate treatment claim under Title VII is that an employee or applicant is intentionally singled out for adverse treatment on the basis of a prohibited criterion; here, sex.[6] In proving a claim for a hostile work environment due to sexual harassment, therefore, the plaintiff must show that but for the fact of her sex, she would not have been the object of sexual harassment.[7] If a supervisor makes sexually harassing gestures to workers of both sexes or if the acts complained of are equally offensive to both sexes, the sexual harassment would not be based upon sex because men and women would be accorded like treatment and therefore the plaintiff would have no Title VII claim.[8]

Sexual harassment claims involving gays or lesbians as perpetrators or victims have not produced many cases. It seems clear that a Title VII violation can be established by showing termination in retaliation for refusal of homosexual favors.[9] It is less clear whether a gay subjected to harassment for sexual preference could make out a Title VII claim. The analysis permitting heterosexuals adversely treated for refusal of homosexual advances to bring Title VII claims does not quite encompass those harassed for sexual preference in bringing Title VII claims. In the former class of cases, sex is the reason for the action; a person of the opposite sex would not have received the same overtures. In the latter class of cases, however, the harassment presumably stems from the preference, not from the sex, and therefore may be more difficult to bring within Title VII's ambit.

The fourth element the plaintiff must prove is that the sexual harassment affected a term, condition, or privilege of employment. This element is satisfied when the

---

[2] *See* Glasgow v. Georgia-Pacific Corp., 103 Wash. 2d 401, 406–07, 693 P.2d 708, 712 (1985).

[3] ___ U.S. ___, 106 S. Ct. 2399 (1986).

[4] *Id.* at ___, 106 S. Ct. at 2406.

[5] Holien v. Sears, Roebuck & Co., 298 Or. 76, 689 P.2d 1292 (1984).

[6] *Id.*

[7] *Id.*

[8] *Id.*

[9] *See* Joyner v. AAA Cooper Transp., 597 F. Supp. 537, 541 (M.D. Ala.), *aff'd without opinion*, 749 F.2d 732 (5th Cir. 1983); Wright v. Methodist Youth Serv., Inc., 511 F. Supp. 307 (N.D. Ill. 1981) (Title VII claim exists for employee terminated for refusing supervisor's homosexual advances); *cf.* Bundy v. Jackson, 641 F.2d at 942 n.7; Barnes v. Costle, 561 F.2d 983, 990 n.55 (D.C. Cir. 1977).

acts complained of create an abusive working environment. Some courts require more proof of pervasiveness and abusiveness when the plaintiff is unable to prove detriment to a tangible economic interest.[10] The fourth element is difficult to distinguish from the second element: proof of unwelcome sexual harassment. Conceptually, the unwelcomeness aspect of the second element is closely related to the fourth element. Conduct amounts to sex discrimination with respect to terms, conditions, or privileges of employment when such conduct has the purpose or effect of unreasonably interfering with an individual's work performance or creates an intimidating, hostile, or offensive work environment.[11]

The second type of sexual harassment violative of Title VII involves demands for sexual consideration in exchange for job benefits.[12] In *Barnes v. Costle*,[13] the D.C. Circuit held that an employer who abolished a female employee's job to retaliate against her resistance of his sexual advances violated Title VII. The *Barnes* court found that plaintiff's retention of her job was conditioned upon submission to sexual relations which the supervisor would not demand from a male employee. In *Horn v. Duke Homes*,[14] the Seventh Circuit concluded that sexual consideration constitutes precisely the kind of artificial, arbitrary, and unnecessary barrier to employment that Title VII was intended to prevent.[15] The court affirmed the district court's holding that the employee's consent to her supervisor's sexual advances was a condition of employment and therefore a violation of Title VII.

In cases in which the plaintiff alleges dismissal in retaliation for a refusal of sexual advances by her supervisor, the plaintiff must show the following to establish a Title VII violation:[16]

1. That she was a victim of sexual harassment attributable to her employer. In *Bundy,* the plaintiff showed this by alleging that the sexual harassment came from the employer's supervisory personnel who had control over promotion and employment decisions
2. That she was dismissed. If this prima facie case is made out, then the employer must articulate legitimate nondiscriminatory reasons for the dismissal

---

[10] *See* Rabidue v. Osceola Refining Co., ____ F.2d ____, 42 Fair Empl. Prac. Cas. (BNA) 631 (6th Cir. 1986) (hostile work environment plaintiff must prove she was actually offended); Jones v. Flagship Int'l, 793 F.2d 714, 720 (5th cir. 1986) (affirming dismissal of sexual harassment claim).

[11] Bundy v. Jackson, 641 F.2d 934, 945-46 (D.C. Cir. 1981). In Meritor Sav. Bank v. Vinson, ____ U.S. ____, 106 S. Ct. 2399 (1986), the Supreme Court held that hostile environment sexual harassment violates Title VII. The Court generally approved the elements described in the preceding paragraphs. *But see* Scott v. Sears, Roebuck & Co., 798 F.2d 210, 213 (7th Cir. 1986) (finding sexual jokes, winks insufficiently abusive to support hostile environment claim).

[12] *See* Meritor Sav. Bank v. Vinson, ____ U.S. at ____, ____, 106 S. Ct. at 2406 (implicitly approving distinction between offensive-environment and quid-pro-quo sexual harassment).

[13] 561 F.2d 983 (D.C. Cir. 1977).

[14] 755 F.2d 599 (7th Cir. 1985).

[15] *Id.* at 603.

[16] These requirements summarize principles developed in this section and in **§ 2.3**.

3. If the employer proffers legitimate nondiscriminatory reasons for the dismissal, the plaintiff has the opportunity to prove that the employer's reasons are a mere pretext for the discrimination.

Most courts have held that an employer is not liable for either of the two types of sexual harassment committed by its employees unless it knows about the conduct and does not take appropriate measures to correct the situation. The knowledge requirement, however, is becoming less prevalent under a trend to hold employers strictly liable for Title VII sexual harassment violations.[17] Strict liability may turn on whether the perpetrator is a supervisor with promotional and hiring power, as opposed to being a rank-and-file employee with no such power. Strict liability is more appropriate for violations by supervisory personnel, while employer knowledge of nonsupervisory sexual harassment should be a prerequisite for liability.

Another factor in determining whether an employer is strictly liable under Title VII is the kind of sexual harassment alleged. Courts properly distinguish between offensive work environment cases and cases involving retaliation for refusal to consent to sexual advances. Employers are more likely to be liable strictly when the plaintiff is discharged for refusing sexual advances. On the other hand, most courts require employer knowledge when the employee is complaining about an offensive work environment.[18] In *Horn v. Duke Homes*,[19] a case holding an employer liable without knowledge of the sexual harassment in which the employee was discharged for refusing to consent to sexual advances, the court said:

> "applying general Title VII principles, an employer is responsible for its acts and those of its agents and supervising employees with respect to sexual harassment regardless of whether the specific acts complained of were authorized or even forbidden by the employer and regardless of whether the employer knew or should have known of their occurrence.[20]

In *Vinson v. Taylor*,[21] the D.C. Circuit expanded strict liability by stating that:

> an employer may be held liable for discrimination accomplished through sexual harassment not only by supervisory employees with authority to hire, promote or

---

[17] *See* Meritor Sav. Bank v. Vinson, ____ U.S. ____, ____, 106 S. Ct. 2399, 2408 (1986) (employers not always automatically liable for supervisor sexual harassment, but absence of notice to employer does not necessarily insulate employer from liability; declining to formulate definitive rule).

[18] *See id.* at ____, 106 S. Ct. at ____ (noting without approving EEOC argument that sexual harassment ought to be treated differently from sexual favor retaliation in determining vicarious liability).

[19] 755 F.2d 599 (7th Cir. 1985).

[20] *Id.* at 604 (quoting EEOC, 29 C.F.R. § 1604.11(c)).

[21] 753 F.2d 141 (D.C. Cir. 1985), *aff'd & remanded sub nom.* Meritor Sav. Bank v. Vinson, ____ U.S. ____, 106 S. Ct. 2399 (1986).

fire but also by supervisors who have or appear to have a significant degree of influence in vital job decisions since ability to direct employees in their work, to evaluate their performances and to recommend personnel actions carries with it attendant power to coerce, intimidate and harass.[22]

An employee may reach this supervisory threshold if he acts or has apparent authority to hire and promote.[23] In *Meritor Savings Bank v. Vinson*,[24] the Supreme Court rejected a rule that employers are strictly liable for sexual harassment by supervisors and held that the district court must apply agency principles to determine employer liability. Other courts have held that knowledge of the sexual harassment is a prerequisite for holding an employer liable for acts of its employees creating an offensive work environment,[25] but the Supreme Court said in *Meritor* that absence of notice to the employer does not necessarily insulate the employer from liability.[26]

§ 2.6 —Age Discrimination in Employment Act: Basic Concepts

The Age Discrimination in Employment Act of 1967 (ADEA)[27] prohibits employers from discriminating because of age against nonexecutive[28] employees[29] over age 40. Members of this age group are protected against any discrimination based on age; thus, it violates the act to favor a 60-year-old over a 45-year-old because of her age just as much as it would to favor a 45-year-old over a 60-year-old.[30]

---

[22] Vinson v. Taylor, 753 F.2d at 150. *See also* Bundy v. Jackson, 641 F.2d 934 (D.C. Cir. 1981) (employer held liable for sexual harassment by supervisory personnel even though employer had no knowledge of such conduct).

[23] *See* Vinson v. Taylor, 753 F.2d at 150.

[24] ____ U.S. ____, 106 S. Ct. 2399 (1986).

[25] *See* Davis v. Western-Southern Ins. Co., 34 F.E.P. Cases (BNA) 97 (N.D. Ohio 1984) (employer liable for offensive working environment only if employer had some knowledge of the activity and failed to act); Katz v. Dole, 709 F.2d 251, 255 (4th Cir. 1983) (in a condition of work case the plaintiff must demonstrate that the employer had actual or constructive knowledge of the existence of a sexually hostile working environment and took no prompt action to remedy the situation).

[26] Meritor Sav. Bank v. Vinson, ____ U.S. at ____, 106 S. Ct. at 2408.

[27] 29 U.S.C. §§ 621–634 (1982).

[28] "Bona fide executives or high policy making employees" are not protected by the ADEA. *See* Whittlesey v. Union Carbide Co., 742 F.2d 724, 726 (2d Cir. 1984) (chief labor counsel found covered by Act under functional analysis of bona-fide-executive exemption).

[29] *Compare* Hyland v. New Haven Radiology Assocs., Inc., 794 F.2d 793 (2d Cir. 1986) (plaintiff found to be employee rather than partner, using "economic realities" test) *with* EEOC v. Zippo Mfg. Corp., 713 F.2d 32 (3d Cir. 1983) (affirming summary judgment for a company which engaged "district managers" for sales work; discharged men were independent contractors not covered by ADEA).

[30] 29 U.S.C. § 631 (1982).

The ADEA applies to all employers with 20 or more employees in an industry affecting commerce,[31] and to state and local governments.[32]

Section 623 expressly precludes liability for discharge based "on a factor other than age" or for "good cause."[33] Employers also are permitted to discriminate based on age when age is a bona fide occupational qualification and to observe the terms of a bona fide seniority system.[34]

ADEA plaintiffs who resign may be able to maintain an ADEA action by showing that they were "constructively discharged."[35]

The EEOC administers the ADEA.[36] Remedies for an ADEA violation are similar to those provided for violation of the Fair Labor Standards Act[37] and include back pay and an additional amount as liquidated damages in the case of willful violations.[38] Most courts of appeals allow front pay for ADEA violations.[39] Some courts also have permitted damages for pain, suffering, and mental distress,[40] although the weight of authority is to the contrary.[41] Similarly, punitive damages

---

[31] *Id.* § 630(b).

[32] *Id.* § 630(b). *See* EEOC v. Wyoming, 460 U.S. 226 (1983); Kelly v. Wauconda Park Dist., 801 F.2d 269, 273 (7th Cir. 1986) (ADEA applies only to governmental employers with 20 or more employees).

[33] 29 U.S.C. § 623(f) (1982).

[34] *Id.* § 623(f)(1) & (2). A defense related to bona fide occupational qualification is business necessity. *See* Nolting v. Yellow Freight Sys., 799 F.2d 1192, 1198 (8th Cir. 1986) (approving jury instruction on business necessity).

[35] *See* Buckley v. Hospital Corp. of Am., 758 F.2d 1525, 1531 (11th Cir. 1985) (jury entitled to decide whether harassment of nurse for age and long years of service so intolerable that constructive discharge resulted).

[36] The statute designates the Secretary of Labor as the public officer responsible for administration of the Act. 29 U.S.C. § 625. However, Reorganization Plan No. 1 of 1978 transferred that authority to the EEOC. Reorganization Plan No. 1 of 1978, § 2, 43 Fed. Reg. 19807, *reprinted in* U.S.C. tit. 5 app., Government Organization and Employees. Questions were raised over the exercise of the authority thus transferred to the EEOC because the transfer was subject to a one-house veto. *Compare* EEOC v. CBS, Inc., 743 F.2d 969 (2d Cir. 1984) (EEOC lacks authority to enforce ADEA because transfer of authority invalid) *with* Muller Optical Co. v. EEOC, 743 F.2d 380 (6th Cir. 1984) (transfer of authority to EEOC was not invalid). The Congress enacted legislation expressly affirming EEOC authority to enforce the ADEA, however. *See* Pub. L. No. 98-532, 98 Stat. 2705 (1984).

[37] 29 U.S.C. §§ 201-217 (1982).

[38] *Id.* § 626(b) (1982).

[39] *See* Whittlesey v. Union Carbide Corp., 742 F.2d 724, 726 (2d Cir. 1984) (citing cases in other circuits; total damages of $242,649 affirmed); Smith v. Consolidated Mut. Water Co., 787 F.2d 1441 (10th Cir. 1986) ($67,000 front-pay award affirmed because reasons articulated, and refusal to award liquidated damages affirmed because violation was not "willful"); Davis v. Combustion Eng'g, Inc., 742 F.2d 916, 922 (6th Cir. 1984) (damages of $88,000 affirmed); EEOC v. Prudential Fed. Sav. & Loan Ass'n, 741 F.2d 1225 (10th Cir. 1984) ($17,000 front-pay award remanded so district court can articulate why front pay more appropriate than reinstatement), *on remand*, 763 F.2d 1166, 1173 (10th cir. 1985).

[40] *See* Buchholz v. Symons Mfg. Co., 445 F. Supp. 706, 713 (E.D. Wis. 1978).

[41] *See* Johnson v. Al-Tech Specialties Steel Corp., 731 F.2d 143, 147 (2d Cir. 1984) (compensatory damages for emotional distress not recoverable); Slatin v. Stanford Research Inst., 590

§ 2.6 AGE DISCRIMINATION: BASICS

have been allowed only by a minority of courts.[42] Broad equitable relief also is available.[43]

Class actions under Federal Rule of Civil Procedure 23 are not available.[44] Instead, a more limited form of class action is permitted under the provisions of the Fair Labor Standards Act.[45] Persons can become members of the litigation class only by taking affirmative steps to opt in.[46]

The theories for proving discrimination are similar to those under Title VII,[47] although it is not completely settled whether disparate impact is available under the ADEA.[48] All the courts of appeal agree that, in disparate treatment cases, the plaintiff must prove that age was a *determining factor* in the adverse employment decision giving rise to the litigation.[49] The plaintiff establishes a prima facie case, in order to survive a motion for a directed verdict, by presenting sufficient evidence from which a jury can draw the inference that age was a determining factor in the employer's action.[50] If the plaintiff makes out such a prima facie case, the employer has the burden of producing evidence tending to show that the adverse employment action was taken for a legitimate, nondiscriminatory reason.[51] If the employer produces such evidence, the plaintiff must show by a preponderance

---

F.2d 1292, 1296 (4th Cir. 1979) (pain and suffering damages not allowed); Vasquez v. Eastern Airlines, Inc., 579 F.2d 107 (1st Cir. 1978); Dean v. American Sec. Ins. Co., 559 F.2d 1036 (5th Cir. 1977), *cert. denied*, 434 U.S. 1066 (1978); Rogers v. Exxon Research & Eng'g Co., 550 F.2d 834 (3d Cir. 1977), *cert. denied*, 434 U.S. 1022 (1978).

[42] *See* Kelly v. American Standard, Inc., 640 F.2d 974 (9th Cir. 1981) (only willful violations); *contra* Walker v. Pettit Constr. Co., 605 F.2d 128 (4th Cir. 1979) (liquidated damages are a substitute for punitive damages), *modified sub nom.* Frith v. Eastern Airlines, 611 F.2d 950 (4th Cir. 1979) (modification involved attorney's fees); Placos v. Cosmair Inc., 517 F. Supp. 1287 (S.D.N.Y. 1981) (no punitive damages allowed).

[43] *See* Criswell v. Western Airlines, Inc., 514 F. Supp. 384 (C.D. Cal. 1981) (permanent injunction); H. Perritt, Labor Injunctions §§ 14.5–14.7 (1986).

[44] *See, e.g.,* McGinley v. Burroughs Corp., 407 F. Supp. 903 (E.D. Pa. 1975).

[45] 29 U.S.C. § 216(b) (1982).

[46] *Id. See* LaChapelle v. Owens-Illinois, Inc., 513 F.2d 286, 289 (5th Cir. 1975).

[47] *See* Cline v. Roadway Express, Inc., 689 F.2d 481, 485 (4th Cir. 1982) (no need for *McDonnell Douglas* disparate treatment proof scheme where direct evidence of intent available; interpreting Title VII concepts in ADEA case). *Compare* Duffy v. Wheeling Pittsburgh Steel Corp., 738 F.2d 1393, 1396 (3d Cir. 1984) (majority opinion; ADEA and Title VII standards the same), *cert. denied*, 469 U.S. 1087 (1984), *with id.* at 1399 (Adams, J., dissenting; ADEA and Title VII proceed from different premises).

[48] *See* Holt v. Gamewell Corp., 797 F.2d 36, 37 (1st Cir. 1986) (disparate impact an allowable mode of proving ADEA violation); Leftwich v. Harris-Stowe State College, 702 F.2d 686, 690 (8th Cir. 1983) (availability of disparate impact theory under ADEA); Geller v. Markham, 635 F.2d 1027 (2d Cir. 1980), *cert. denied*, 451 U.S. 945 (1981) (same).

[49] Cuddy v. Carmen, 694 F.2d 853, 857 n.19 (D.C. Cir. 1982) (citing cases in all the circuits).

[50] *Id.*

[51] *Id.* The employer has the burden of production only in the sense that if the employer remains silent at this stage *and* the trier of fact believes the plaintiff's evidence, the plaintiff is entitled to a verdict. *Id.* at 857 n.21.

of the evidence that the employer's asserted legitimate reason is merely pretext.[52] Throughout the proceedings, the plaintiff-employee retains the burden of persuasion.[53]

The nature and universality of the aging process present some problems for age discrimination litigation not present in race, sex, or religious discrimination. The most basic problem is that there is some negative correlation between age and performance. Deciding whether an employer must make employment decisions based on individual assessments of performance capability as opposed to using age as a proxy for performance capability can be difficult. The case of *Criswell v. Western Airlines, Inc.*,[54] provides a useful example of the legal analysis involved in making such decisions. A related problem is presented by use of proof and causation formulas developed in race discrimination cases in the age context. This problem is explored here and in the discussion of the case of *Laugesen v. Anaconda Co.*[55] in § 2.7.

Procedurally, actions for violation of the ADEA can be brought by private claimants or by the government.[56] The statute has been interpreted to require the government to attempt conciliation before filing suit.[57] Unlike Title VII, no specific time limits are set during which conciliation must be attempted.[58] Private individuals may not file suit unless they have filed charges with the EEOC or with a state agency having jurisdiction.[59] Such administrative charges must be filed within time

---

[52] *Id.* at 857. It is at this stage when the legitimacy of the employer's proffered reason is determined. *See* Coburn v. Pan Am. World Airways, 711 F.2d 339, 343 (D.C. Cir. 1983) (prima facie case, but judgment n.o.v. properly entered for employer because no pretext shown).

[53] 694 F.2d 853, 857; Grubb v. W.A. Foote Memorial Hosp. Inc., 741 F.2d 1486, 1496 (6th Cir. 1984) (district court finding of age discrimination reversed despite evidence of age-based threats by supervisor).

[54] 514 F. Supp 384 (C.D. Cal. 1981).

[55] 510 F.2d 307 (6th Cir. 1975).

[56] 29 U.S.C. § 626(c) (1982).

[57] *Id.* § 626(d). *See* EEOC v. Prudential Fed. Sav. & Loan Ass'n, 741 F.2d 1225, 1228 (10th Cir. 1984) (limited conciliation efforts satisfy requirement); Sedlacek v. Hach, 752 F.2d 333, 335 (8th Cir. 1984) (actual investigation or conciliation attempt by EEOC or state agency not a jurisdictional prerequisite or condition precedent to district court jurisdiction); Marshall v. Sun Oil Co. (Del.), 605 F.2d 1331, 1336 (5th Cir. 1979) (nonjurisdictional conciliation requirements satisfied), *cert. denied,* 444 U.S. 826 (1979); Usery v. Sun Oil Co. (Del.), 423 F. Supp. 125 (N.D. Tex. 1976) (conciliation attempt is a jurisdictional prerequisite), *aff'd in part, rev'd in part,* 605 F.2d 1331 (5th Cir. 1979).

[58] *Compare* 29 U.S.C. § 626(d) (1982) *with* 42 U.S.C. § 2000e-5(b) (1982). *See* Stearns v. Consolidated Management, Inc., 747 F.2d 1105, 1111 (7th Cir. 1984) (ADEA filing requirements not jurisdictional; only a condition precedent; citing cases).

[59] 29 U.S.C. § 626(d) (1982). If the plaintiff files suit before initiating state proceedings, the district court should stay the suit pending completion of state agency action. Oscar Mayer & Co. v. Evans, 441 U.S. 750, 764 (1979). *See* Miller v. International Tel. & Tel. Corp., 755 F.2d 20, 24 (2d Cir. 1985) (untimely claim with EEOC bars ADEA suit—not within 300 days of notice of termination); Whitfield v. City of Knoxville, 756 F.2d 455, 460 (6th Cir. 1985) (ADEA involuntary requirement claim by policeman not barred by res judicata because ADEA/EEOC exhaustion requirement did not permit ADEA claim to be asserted in state court suit in which state discrimination and constitutional claims were rejected); Stearns v. Consolidated Management, Inc., 747

§ 2.7 AGE DISCRIMINATION: EXAMPLES

limits similar to those under Title VII.[60] Sixty days after a charge is filed with the EEOC, suit may be brought in a United States district court.[61] No right-to-sue letter is required before bringing suit on the employee's own behalf, as under Title VII.[62] Unlike Title VII, the ADEA expressly provides for jury trials.[63]

Important questions exist as to the efficacy of a waiver or settlement of an ADEA claim without judicial supervision.[64] The problem arises because of the linkage of ADEA remedies with FLSA remedies. The FLSA disfavors settlement or waiver of rights. The EEOC has published proposed regulations to give effect to knowing and voluntary releases of ADEA claims, supported by consideration.[65]

§ 2.7 —Age Discrimination in Employment Act: Examples

The following two cases illustrate the application of the ADEA in a discharge context. First, in *Laugesen v. Anaconda Co.*,[66] the plaintiff brought an ADEA action after being discharged from employment at age 56.[67] Laugesen was a purchasing manager for Anaconda's Kentucky and New Jersey plants.[68] Because of industry-wide economic difficulties, Anaconda decided to reduce its workforce[69] and discharged Laugesen after combining his job with another.[70] His separation notice contained evaluations which were generally good and listed the primary cause of discharge as "reduction in force" but also noted "too many years on the job. Became too close with vendors. Lacks personal strength."[71] Laugesen's notice formed the basis for his age discrimination case.[72] The plaintiff's case was largely

---

F.2d 1105, 1112 (7th Cir. 1984) (copy of state charge sent to EEOC during 60-day period for state agency action satisfies requirements).

[60] 29 U.S.C. § 626(d)(1), (2) (1982). However, the waiting period for filing suit is 60 days under the ADEA, compared with 180 days under Title VII.

[61] *Id.* § 626(d). An ADEA suit generally must be filed within two years of an ordinary violation, or within three years of a "willful" violation. *See id.* § 626(e), incorporating *id.* § 255(a) (Portal-to-Portal Act of 1947). ADEA actions also can be brought in state court. *See* Burroughs v. Great Atl. & Pac. Tea Co., 462 So. 2d 353 (Ala. 1984).

[62] Compare 29 U.S.C. § 626(c) (1982) with 42 U.S.C. § 2000e-5(f) (1982).

[63] 29 U.S.C. § 626(c)(2) (1982).

[64] *See* Runyan v. National Cash Register Corp., 787 F.2d 1039, 1045 (6th Cir. 1986) (en banc) (private release of ADEA claim can bar ADEA action though unsupervised by court, approving EEOC views expressed in proposed rulemaking); Lancaster v. Buerkle Burch Honda Co., 39 F.E.P. Cas. (BNA) 721 (D. Minn. 1985) (ADEA claim barred by release).

[65] 50 Fed. Reg. 40,870 (1985) (to be codified at 29 C.F.R. § 1627.16).

[66] 510 F.2d 307 (6th Cir. 1975). Another useful example of the structure of an ADEA discharge case is Coburn v. Pan Am. World Airways, 711 F.2d 339, 343 (D.C. Cir. 1983) (prima facie case, but judgment n.o.v. properly entered for employer because no pretext shown).

[67] Laugesen v. Anaconda Co., 510 F.2d at 310.

[68] *Id.*

[69] *Id.*

[70] *Id.* The functions of purchasing agent were combined with those of traffic manager.

[71] *Id.* at 311.

[72] *Id.*

circumstantial, including evidence that he had been replaced by a 39-year-old.[73] He was unable to offer any evidence that directly indicated a policy or intention to use age as a reason for the termination.[74]

The court found that Laugesen had presented a prima facie case,[75] noting the similarity between ADEA and Title VII actions.[76] Laugesen's prima facie case did not shift the burden to the defendant to prove a nondiscriminatory reason for the discharge[77] and thus did not support a directed verdict for Laugesen. Presentation of a prima facie case, however, presented a sufficient factual question for jury consideration.[78] Since Anaconda raised a legitimate defense,[79] claiming economic necessity in reducing its workforce and introducing evidence that Laugesen had received less favorable ratings than the employee who was retained,[80] the court of appeals approved the jury verdict in Anaconda's favor.[81]

Douglas v. Anderson[82] is another example of an age discrimination case in which the employer successfully argued poor performance as a legitimate reason for discharge.[83] The appeals court required more than merely raising a genuine issue of fact to sustain a directed verdict below. The defendant must establish that a jury could not reasonably find that age discrimination was a determining factor in the discharge.[84] *Tribble v. Westinghouse Electric Corp.*[85] is a good example of a discharge case in which a jury award for the plaintiff was affirmed.[86] In *Duffy v. Wheeling Pittsburgh Steel Corp.*,[87] the court held that the plaintiff made out a prima facie case under the ADEA by showing that older employees were laid off while younger employees were retained and affirmed the district court's determination that the employer's proffered reason of poor performance was pretextual. The court merged the pretext inquiry with the intent-to-discriminate inquiry.[88]

---

[73] *Id.* Laugesen testified that his replacement was a younger worker, and that the reduction had the effect of lowering the average age of salaried employees from 43 to 37.

[74] *Id.*

[75] *Id.*

[76] *Id.* The court noted the similarity, but later in its opinion stated it was not deciding whether Congress intended that actions under ADEA must invariably be guided by law applicable to Title VII cases. *Id.* at 312.

[77] *Id.* at 313. According to the court, there are circumstances when the burden of proof may shift; e.g., an admission by the defendant of discrimination, accompanied by assertion of a bona fide occupational qualification as an affirmative defense.

[78] *Id.*

[79] *Id.* at 315.

[80] *Id.* at 310.

[81] *Id.* at 315.

[82] 656 F.2d 528 (9th Cir. 1981).

[83] *Id.* at 534.

[84] *Id.* at 533.

[85] 669 F.2d 1193 (8th Cir. 1982), *cert. denied*, 460 U.S. 1080 (1983).

[86] *See also* Buckley v. Hospital Corp. of Am., 758 F.2d 1525, 1530 (11th Cir. 1985) (jury entitled to decide whether nurse dismissed for misconduct or for age).

[87] 738 F.2d 1393 (3d Cir.), *cert. denied*, 469 U.S. 1087 (1984).

[88] 738 F.2d at 1396.

§ 2.8 CIVIL RIGHTS ACTS: SECTION 1981

Western Air Lines v. Criswell[89] illustrates the operation of the *bona fide occupational qualification* (BFOQ) concept in an ADEA case. The plaintiffs, airline flight engineers, were retired involuntarily upon attaining age 60, although they still possessed the pilot licenses and medical certifications required by the Federal Aviation Administration (FAA).[90] The airline defended the age-60 rule on the ground that it was a BFOQ "reasonably necessary" to the safe operation of the airline.[91] Expert witnesses presented conflicting evidence on whether flight engineers could be screened reliably for health risks on an individual basis.[92] The jury reached a verdict for the plaintiffs, and the court of appeals affirmed. The airline petitioned for certiorari, claiming that the jury instruction was insufficiently deferential to the airline's legitimate concerns for passenger safety.[93]

The Supreme Court rejected the airline's argument, holding that three predicates must be established to support a BFOQ defense in an ADEA case:

1. Reasonable necessity for the restrictions (e.g. risk of incapacitating illness), given the nature of the employer's business
2. The employer is compelled to rely on age as a proxy for the safety-related job qualifications validated in (1) above, because:
    (a) The employer had a factual basis for believing that all or substantially all persons over the age qualification would be unable to perform safely and efficiently, or
    (b) It is impossible or highly impractical to deal with the older employees on an individualized basis.[94]

The Court held that management decisions to use age as a proxy for other job-related factors must be supported by objective justification in court.[95]

§ 2.8 —Reconstruction Civil Rights Acts: Section 1981

Employees who believe they have been discharged because of their race can assert that claim under 42 U.S.C. § 1981. Section 1981 suits can be maintained without satisfying the administrative requirements of Title VII, and the remedies available under § 1981 are broader that those under Title VII. Individual employer agents as well as the employer itself can be defendants.[96]

---

[89] 472 U.S. 400 (1985).

[90] 14 C.F.R. § 61.3(a), (c).

[91] Western Air Lines v. Criswell, 105 S. Ct. at 2747.

[92] *Id.* at 2748.

[93] *Id.* at 2749.

[94] *Id.* at 2753.

[95] *Id.* at 2754.

[96] *See* Al-Khazraji v. St. Francis College, 784 F.2d 505, 518 (3d Cir. 1986) (individual members of tenure committee could be personally liable under § 1981 for religious and national origin discrimination).

Section 1981,[97] originally enacted as part of the Civil Rights Act of 1866,[98] provides protection against racial discrimination largely congruent with that provided by Title VII. It provides, in material part, that "all persons within the jurisdiction of the United States shall have the same right . . . to make and enforce contracts . . . as is enjoyed by white citizens . . . ."[99] In *Jones v. Alfred H. Mayer Co.*,[1] reasoning that the Civil Rights Act of 1866 was enacted pursuant to Congress's power under the Thirteenth Amendment as well as the Fourteenth Amendment,[2] the Supreme Court held that the Civil Rights Act of 1866 covers purely private acts of discrimination. Though *Jones v. Alfred H. Mayer Co.* involved only the application of what now is codified as § 1982, its rationale is applicable to § 1981 as well.[3] The Supreme Court, in *Johnson v. Railway Express Agency*,[4] endorsed the view of several courts of appeals that § 1981 provides a basis for an independent federal cause of action for racial discrimination in employment.[5]

Because § 1981 represents an exercise of congressional power under the Thirteenth Amendment rather than under the commerce clause,[6] a connection with interstate commerce is not a legal prerequisite for coverage. The section affords a remedy against labor unions as well as employers.[7] The characteristics with respect to which discrimination is prohibited by § 1981 are fewer in number than those protected by Title VII. Racial discrimination is prohibited against either blacks or whites.[8] Discrimination against aliens is covered, however, only if it is racial in character.[9] Neither sex discrimination [10] nor age discrimination is covered.[11]

---

[97] 42 U.S.C. § 1981 (1982).

[98] Civil Rights Act of Apr. 9, 1866, ch. 31, 14 Stat. 27.

[99] 42 U.S.C. § 1981 (1982).

[1] 392 U.S. 409 (1973).

[2] *Id.* at 437-39.

[3] General Bldg. Contractors Ass'n v. Pennsylvania, 458 U.S. 375, 387 (1982).

[4] 421 U.S. 454 (1975).

[5] *Id.* at 461. The practical significance of this conclusion is that a plaintiff may bring a suit under § 1981 without satisfying the administrative prerequisites to a Title VII lawsuit, and that the statutes of limitations applicable to § 1981 and to Title VII operate independently without tolling.

[6] *See* Waters v. Steelworkers, 427 F.2d 476 (7th Cir.), *cert. denied,* 400 U.S. 911 (1970).

[7] *See* Henry v. Radio Station KSAN, 374 F. Supp. 260 (N.D. Cal. 1974).

[8] Runyon v. McCrary, 427 U.S. 160 (1976); MacDonald v. Santa Fe Trail Transp. Co., 427 U.S. 273 (1976); Johnson v. Railway Express Agency, 421 U.S. 454 (1975). *But see* Patterson v. McLean Credit Union, 805 F. 2d ___ (4th Cir. 1986) (racial harassment not covered by § 1981).

[9] *See* Alizadeh v. Safeway Stores, Inc., 802 F.2d 111, 114 (5th Cir. 1986) (§ 1981 prohibits discrimination because of marriage to Iranian if based on perception that Iranian is of another race); Al-Khazraji v. St. Francis College, 784 F.2d 505, 514 (3d Cir. 1986) (ethnic Arabs protected by § 1981); Doe v. St. Joseph's Hosp., 788 F.2d 411, 418 (7th Cir. 1986) (discrimination against Korean prohibited by § 1981 if based on race, but not if based on national origin, explaining difference); Bullard v. OMI Georgia, 640 F.2d 632 (5th Cir. 1981); Gonzalez v. Stanford Applied Eng'g, 597 F.2d 1298 (9th Cir. 1979); Manzaneres v. Safeway Stores, Inc., 593 F.2d 968 (10th Cir. 1979) (§ 1981 protects Mexican-Americans).

[10] Bobo v. ITT, Continental Baking Co., 662 F.2d 340 (5th Cir. 1981).

[11] Runyon v. McCrary, 427 U.S. 160 (1976).

§ 2.8 CIVIL RIGHTS ACTS: SECTION 1981

Remedies for violations of § 1981 include injunctive relief[12] and monetary recovery akin to damages.[13] There is no two-year cutoff on potential back-pay recovery as there is under Title VII.[14] Punitive damages may be recoverable.[15]

Until 1982, there was controversy over whether a § 1981 plaintiff could prove a violation under both basic theories available under Title VII: disparate treatment and disparate impact.[16] In *General Building Contractors Association v. Pennsylvania*,[17] the Supreme Court held that liability under § 1981 requires proof of intent to discriminate, thus ruling out the possibility of disparate impact cases.[18]

Actions under § 1981 may be brought directly in state[19] or federal court without exhausting any administrative requirements.[20] Since there is no federal limitations period, the appropriate state limitations period is utilized.[21] Exhaustion of state administrative remedies generally is not required,[22] although a state court judgment on the same operative facts may be res judicata in a § 1981 action.[23] Under

---

[12] Vietnam Fisherman's Ass'n v. Knights of Ku Klux Klan, 518 F. Supp. 993 (S.D. Tex. 1981).

[13] *See* Johnson v. Railway Express Agency, 421 U.S. 454 (1975).

[14] *Id. See* Wilmington v. J.I. Case Co., 793 F.2d 909 (8th Cir. 1986) (affirming jury award of $400,000 compensatory and $40,000 punitive damages in § 1981 case). The applicable state statute of limitations does furnish a cutoff date for monetary recovery with respect to a continuing violation.

[15] *See* Block v. R.H. Macy & Co., 712 F.2d 1241 (8th Cir. 1983); Allen v. Amalgamated Transit Union, Local 788, 554 F.2d 876 (8th Cir.), *cert. denied,* 434 U.S. 891 (1977); Harris v. Richards Mfg. Co., 511 F. Supp. 1193 (W.D. Tenn. 1981), *modified,* 675 F.2d 811 (6th Cir. 1982).

[16] *See* Croker v. Boeing Co., 662 F.2d 975 (3d Cir. 1981).

[17] 458 U.S. 375 (1982).

[18] *Id.* at 389. The Supreme Court reversed a judgment finding liability under § 1981 on a disparate impact theory. The Court's holding that § 1981 requires proof of *purposeful* discrimination presumably permits such proof to be offered indirectly by proving disparate treatment, as well as by direct evidence of intent, though the Court did not say so explicitly. Vicarious liability can be imposed, however. *See* Mitchell v. Keith, 752 F.2d 385, 390 (9th Cir. 1985) (corporation vicariously liable for punitive damages to § 1981 plaintiff based on motive of managerial employee).

[19] DeHorney v. Bank of Am., 777 F.2d 440, 445 (9th Cir. 1985), *withdrawn and reh'g stayed,* 784 F.2d 339 (9th Cir. 1986) (pending decision of California Supreme Court in Foley v. Interactive Data Corp., *petition for review granted,* ___ Cal. 3d ___, 712 P.2d 891, 222 Cal. Rptr. 740 (1986)) (state courts have concurrent jurisdiction with federal courts over § 1981 claims).

[20] Johnson v. Railway Express Agency, 421 U.S. 454 (1975). One case, Young v. ITT Nesbitt Div., 438 F.2d 757 (3d Cir. 1971) suggests that a district court may have discretion to require exhaustion of Title VII administrative procedures before adjudicating a § 1981 claim. But this decision has not been followed and probably is not a good law after *Johnson. See* B. Schlei & P. Grossman, Employment Discrimination 693 (1983).

[21] Johnson v. Railway Express Agency, 421 U.S. at 462.

[22] *See* Goss v. Revlon, Inc., 548 F.2d 405 (2d Cir. 1976), *cert. denied,* 434 U.S. 968 (1977).

[23] *See* Takahashi v. Board of Trustees, 783 F.2d 848 (9th Cir.) (state court judgment finding just cause for dismissal of teacher properly given res judicata effect in subsequent § 1983 action), *cert. denied,* 106 S. Ct. 2916 (1986); Mitchell v. National Broadcasting Co., 553 F.2d 265 (2d Cir. 1977). The Supreme Court expressed agreement with the *Mitchell* holding in Kremer v. Chemical Constr. Co., 456 U.S. 461 (1982), a Title VII case presenting the same legal issue. Similarly, an action under Title VII should bar a subsequent action under § 1981 for the same allegedly discriminatory acts. *Cf.* Nelson v. City of Moss Point, 701 F.2d 556 (5th Cir. 1983) (en banc) (§ 1983 action barred by Title VII; analysis suggests similar result for § 1981 action);

the rationale of *Johnson*,[24] combined with the rationale of *Alexander v. Gardner Denver*,[25] and *McDonald v. City of West Branch*,[26] exhaustion of grievance provisions of collective bargaining agreements is not required.[27] The result is different, however, if the arbitration award is reviewed and affirmed by a state court.[28] A jury trial may be available for certain issues in a § 1981 case.[29]

The factual disputes and order of proof in § 1981 cases are similar to those in Title VII cases.[30]

§ 2.9 — Reconstruction Civil Rights Acts: Section 1985

In a limited set of factual circumstances a discharged employee may be able to maintain an action under 42 U.S.C. § 1985.[31] Judicially created restrictions on the type of employer conduct covered by § 1985 and the rights protected by the section reduce its utility in the typical wrongful discharge case. Nevertheless, two subsections are of possible interest: § 1985(2) and (3). Subsection (3), the broader of the two in concept, provides for a federal right to damages for conspiracies to interfere with governmental or judicial processes, to inhibit the exercise of

---

Clark v. Times Square Stores Corp., 469 F. Supp. 654 (S.D.N.Y. 1979). *See generally* § **7.33** regarding res judicata issues in employment dismissal cases.

[24] Johnson v. Railway Express Agency, 421 U.S. 454 (1975) (Congress intended for § 1981 to remain an independent basis of action, not limited by subsequently enacted Title VII).

[25] 415 U.S. 36 (1974) (adverse arbitration award does not bar Title VII suit).

[26] 466 U.S. 284 (1984) (action under § 1983 not barred by an adverse arbitration award under a collective bargaining agreement).

[27] *See* Wilmington v. J.I. Case Co., 793 F.2d 909, 916 (8th Cir. 1986) (affirming district court refusal to give preclusive effect to arbitration decision in § 1981 case, and rejecting employer's argument that arbitration award gave it a nondiscriminatory reason for dismissal).

[28] *See* University of Tenn. v. Elliott, ___ U.S. ___, 106 S. Ct. 3220 (1986) (unreviewed administrative decision entitled to preclusive effect in § 1983 action but not in Title VII action; Migra v. Warren City School Dist. Bd. of Educ., 465 U.S. 75 (1984) (judgment for employee in state court action for breach of contract barred a susequent action in federal court under § 1983, even though § 1983 basis for recovery not asserted in the state court action.

[29] Plaintiffs seeking compensatory and punitive damages are entitled to a jury trial. *See* Setser v. Novack Inv. Co., 638 F.2d 1137, 1140, *another part modified* (en banc), 657 F.2d 962 (8th Cir.), *cert. denied,* 454 U.S. 1064 (1981). Plaintiffs seeking only equitable remedies such as back pay and reinstatement are not entitled to a jury trial. *See* Moore v. Sun Oil Co., 636 F.2d 154, 156 (6th Cir. 1980).

[30] *See* Pacheco v. Advertisers Lithographing, Inc., 657 F.2d 191, 193-94 (8th Cir. 1981) (employer successfully rebutted plaintiff's prima facie case by showing legitimate, nondiscriminatory reason for plaintiff's suspension); Jackson v. City of Killeen, 654 F.2d 1181 (5th Cir. 1981) (no prima facie case established).

[31] Section 1985 originally was enacted as part of the Ku Klux Klan Act of 1871. Act of Feb. 28, 1871, ch. 99, 16 Stat. 433.

§ 2.9 CIVIL RIGHTS ACTS: SECTION 1985

constitutional or federal statutory rights, or to deprive any person of "the equal protection of the laws or of equal privileges and immunities under the laws."[32] In *Great American Federal Savings & Loan Association v. Novotny*,[33] the Supreme Court held that § 1985(3) extends to purely private conspiracies arising in the employer-employee context.[34]

Three elements of § 1985(3), however, restrict its application in a wrongful discharge situation. First, the injury to the plaintiff must be the result of a conspiracy.[35] Second, the conspiracy must be intended to deprive the plaintiff of substantive federal rights afforded by the Constitution or a federal statute other than § 1985 itself.[36] Third, a discharge cognizable under § 1985 must involve class-based animus.[37]

A conspiracy involves concerted action between or among two or more persons.[38] It is unclear whether the agents of a single corporation can form a conspiracy to terminate a person's employment within the meaning of § 1985(3). The court of appeals in *Novotny* suggested that intracorporate conspiracies are possible,[39] but the majority of the circuits have reasoned that corporate agents, acting within the scope of their employment, cannot conspire.[40]

A discharged employee must allege violation of specific statutory or constitutional rights in order to maintain a § 1985(3) action. The Supreme Court, in *Maine v. Thiboutot*,[41] held that § 1985(3) encompasses deprivation of statutory as well as constitutional rights.[42] It does not, however, cover violations of antidiscrimination

---

[32] 42 U.S.C. § 1985(3) (1982).

[33] 442 U.S. 366 (1979).

[34] 42 U.S.C. § 1985 (1982) originally was divided into three parts (R.S. § 1980, Acts of July 31, 1861, ch. 33, 12 Stat. 284; April 20, 1871, ch. 22, § 2, 17 Stat. 13) and was recodified with alphabetical designations in 1976 (42 U.S.C. § 1985 (1982)). Congress returned to the numbered subsections in 1979 (42 U.S.C. § 1985 (1982)). Because of the change, some articles and cases refer to lettered subsections. This treatise will use the current numbered subsections. *See generally* Comment, *A Construction of Section 1985(c) in Light of its Original Purpose,* 46 U. Chi. L. Rev. 402 (1979).

[35] Griffin v. Breckenridge, 403 U.S. 88 (1971).

[36] Great Am. Fed. Sav. & Loan Ass'n v. Novotny, 442 U.S. 366 (1979).

[37] Griffin v. Breckenridge, 403 U.S. 88 (1971).

[38] *See, e.g.*, 42 U.S.C. § 1985(1) (1982): "If two or more persons in any state or territory *conspire* to prevent . . ." (emphasis added).

[39] Novotny v. Great Am. Fed. Sav. & Loan Ass'n, 584 F.2d 1235 (3d Cir. 1978).

[40] *See* Herrmann v. Moore, 576 F.2d 453 (2d Cir. 1977), *cert. denied,* 439 U.S. 1003 (1978); Dombrowski v. Dowling, 459 F.2d 190 (7th Cir. 1972); Chai v. Michigan Technical Univ., 493 F. Supp. 1137 (W.D. Mich. 1980); *see generally* Comment, *Intracorporate Conspiracies Under 42 U.S.C. § 1985(c): The Impact of Novotny v. Great American Federal Savings and Loan Ass'n,* 13 Ga. L. Rev. 591 (1979); Comment, *Intracorporate Conspiracies Under 42 U.S.C. § 1985(c),* 92 Harv. L. Rev. 470 (1978).

[41] 448 U.S. 1 (1980).

[42] *Id.* at 4.

statutes that contain comprehensive administrative remedies.[43] Violations of state statutory rights are not covered by § 1985(3).[44]

In order to succeed, a § 1985(3) plaintiff also must allege and prove a class-based, invidiously discriminatory animus behind the alleged conspiracy to discharge.[45] The discriminatory animus falls under the § 1985(3) prohibition only when it is against a class which Congress, in 1871, intended to protect. In *Carpenters v. Scott*,[46] the Supreme Court reversed a Fifth Circuit decision finding liability under § 1985(3) for a conspiracy by labor union members to threaten violence against nonunion construction workers.[47] The Supreme Court held that a § 1985(3) claim is not made out by a showing of group-based animus of an economic or commercial nature. The Court declined to embrace the view that § 1985(3) is limited to conspiracies involving racial bias, but it did not define the types of animus that are covered. The opinion hinted that conspiracies aimed at a group because of its political views might be covered.[48] The Court held, however, that when the substantive rights infringed upon are those protected by the Constitution only against governmental interference, there also must be proof that the state is involved in the conspiracy or that the aim of the conspiracy is to influence the activity of the state.[49] Thus, purely private conspiracies interfering with First Amendment rights would not be covered, even if the animus of the conspiracy were political in nature.[50]

Because the *Carpenters* Court left open the question whether the statute covers animus other than racial animus,[51] discharges because of sex,[52] religion, national origin,[53] and age[54] may be cognizable under § 1985 as well as discharges based on race. Some courts have held that discharges based on homosexuality,[55] public

---

[43] Great Am. Fed. Sav. & Loan Ass'n v. Novotny, 442 U.S. 366 (1979). *See* Golden v. Shapell Indus., Inc., 24 F.E.P. Cas. (BNA) 1283 (N.D. Cal. 1980).

[44] *See* Life Ins. Co. of N. Am. v. Reichardt, 591 F.2d 499 (9th Cir. 1979).

[45] *See* Great Am. Fed. Sav. & Loan Ass'n v. Novotny, 442 U.S. 366, 378 (1979) (Powell, J., concurring).

[46] 463 U.S. 825 (1983).

[47] *Id.* at 830–31.

[48] *Id.* at 836.

[49] *Id.* at 833.

[50] *See* Munson v. Friske, 754 F.2d 683, 696 (7th Cir. 1985) (conspiracy against class that submits overtime claims not sufficient); Murphy v. Villanova Univ., 520 F. Supp. 560, 562–63 (E.D. Pa. 1981) (wrongful discharge claim cannot be maintained under § 1985(3) absent allegations of discrimination against a legislatively identified class).

[51] Carpenters v. Scott, 463 U.S. 825, 836 (1983).

[52] *See* Padway v. Palches, 665 F.2d 965 (9th Cir. 1982).

[53] *See* Marlowe v. Fisher Body, 489 F.2d 1057 (6th Cir. 1973).

[54] *See* Pavlo v. Stiefel Laboratories, Inc., 22 F.E.P. Cas. (BNA) 489 (S.D.N.Y. 1979).

[55] *See* DeSantis v. Pacific Tel. & Tel. Co., Inc., 608 F.2d 327 (9th Cir. 1979).

§ 2.9 CIVIL RIGHTS ACTS: SECTION 1985

drunkenness,[56] whistleblowing,[57] and union picketline activity[58] are not within the purview of § 1985.

Actions for violation of § 1985(3) can be brought directly in federal court without exhausting any administrative procedures.[59] However, a § 1985(3) claim may not be used to skirt the administrative procedures contained in Title VII or the Age Discrimination in Employment Act.[60] Remedies available under § 1985(3) include compensatory damages,[61] punitive damages,[62] and injunctive relief.[63] Jury trials may be permitted in certain types of § 1985 claims.[64]

Section 1985(2) prohibits conspiracies aimed at deterring participation in judicial processes.[65] Class-based animus is not a requirement for an action under § 1985(2) involving federal judicial proceedings, but it is for actions involving state judicial proceedings.[66] Thus, employees discharged for resorting to, or testifying in, judicial proceedings may have a § 1985(2) remedy, assuming that they can plead and prove a conspiracy. The courts tend to construe the judicial proceeding requirement narrowly, however.[67]

---

[56] *See* Wager v. Hasenkrug, 486 F. Supp. 47 (D.C. Mont. 1980).

[57] Buschi v. Kirven, 775 F.2d 1240, 1258 (4th Cir. 1985) (state employee "whistleblowers" not a class protected by § 1985(3)).

[58] *See* Daigle v. Gulf State Utils. Co., 794 F.2d 974, 979 (5th Cir. 1986) (discrimination for being a "scab" not covered); Browder v. Tipton, 630 F.2d 1149 (6th Cir. 1980).

[59] *See* Prochaska v. Fediaczko, 458 F. Supp. 778 (W.D. Pa. 1978).

[60] *See* Great Am. Fed. Sav. & Loan Ass'n v. Novotny, 442 U.S. 366, 366-67 (1979). However, there is room for argument that a § 1985(3) action can be maintained for Title VII or ADEA claims extinguished by the running of time limitations or some other technical problem.

[61] *See* Pierce v. Stinson, 493 F. Supp. 609 (E.D. Tenn. 1980).

[62] *See* Great Am. Fed. Sav. & Loan Ass'n v. Novotny, 442 U.S. 366, 376 (1979) (recognizes majority rule that punitive damages not allowed under 42 U.S.C. § 2000e-5, but 42 U.S.C. § 1985(3) authorizes compensatory damages and "punitive damages might well follow" given proper facts).

[63] *See* Scott v. Moore, 680 F.2d 979 (5th Cir. 1982), *rev'd on other grounds,* 463 U.S. 825 (1983); Mizell v. North Broward Hosp. Dist., 427 F.2d 468 (5th Cir. 1970).

[64] A jury trial is allowed under 42 U.S.C. § 1985 (1982) if legal claims are asserted. "Merely because the legal claim is 'incidental' or 'secondary' to the equitable relief sought is not sufficient to abridge the right to trial by jury." Devore v. Edgefield County School Dist., 68 F.R.D. 423, 427 (D.S.C. 1975) (suit by employees against school district after their contract had not been renewed).

[65] 42 U.S.C. § 1985(2) (1982).

[66] Kush v. Rutledge, 460 U.S. 719, 726 (1983). The Supreme Court held that any person prevented by threat from testifying can sue the conspirators making the threat, without the need to prove class-based animus. Class-based animus is a requirement under that part of § 1985(2) prohibiting interference with *state* judicial proceedings, however. *See* Daigle v. Gulf State Utils. Co., 794 F.2d 974, 979 (5th Cir. 1986) (rejecting dismissed employee's claim based on false affidavits in state proceeding).

[67] *See* Daigle v. Gulf State Utils. Co., 794 F.2d at 980 (allegation of interference with NLRB proceedings insufficient); Shoultz v. Monfort of Colo., Inc., 754 F.2d 318, 321 (10th Cir. 1985) (meat inspector discharged by the United States Department of Agriculture (USDA) failed to state § 1985(2) claim against private company's efforts to deter filing of state claim for job-related

§ 2.10 — Handicap Discrimination: Rehabilitation Act

The Rehabilitation Act of 1973[68] prohibits discrimination against individuals perceived to have handicaps by federal contractors, by recipients of federal grants, and by participants in federal programs. *Handicap* is broadly defined to include mental as well as physical impairment.[69] Moreover, § 504 of the Rehabilitation Act[70] prohibits discrimination against any "otherwise qualified handicapped individual . . . under any program or activity receiving Federal financial assistance."[71] Section 505 of the Act makes available the "remedies, procedures, and rights" of Title VI of the Civil Rights Act of 1964.[72]

In *Consolidated Rail Corp. v. Darrone*,[73] the Supreme Court held that a private damage action for employment discrimination against the handicapped can be maintained against an employer receiving federal financial assistance. The Court limited such suits to discrimination in the particular program receiving financial assistance, but rejected the employer's argument that a discrimination suit can be maintained only when the purpose of the federal assistance is to promote employment opportunities.

The Supreme Court applied the particular-program requirement in *United States Department of Transportation v. Paralyzed Veterans*.[74] In that case, which did not involve adverse employment action, the Supreme Court rejected the proposition

---

injuries; § 1985(2) only protects federal court proceedings); Kimble v. D.J. McDuffy, Inc., 648 F.2d 340, 348 (5th Cir. 1981) (en banc) (overturning panel decision and reading § 1985(2) not to apply to discharge for filing workers' compensation claims; no judicial proceeding involved).

[68] 29 U.S.C. §§ 701–709, 720–724, 730–732, 740, 741, 750, 760–764, 770–776, 780–787, 790–794 (1982).

[69] 29 U.S.C. § 707(a) (1982). 45 C.F.R. § 84.3(j) (1982) defines *handicapped person* to include "any person who (i) has a physical or mental impairment which substantially limits one or more major life activities, (ii) has a record of such an impairment, or (iii) is regarded as having such an impairment." 45 C.F.R. § 84.3(j)(2) (1982) defines *physical or mental impairment* to include "(A) any physiological disorder or condition, cosmetic disfigurement, or anatomical loss affecting one or more of the following body systems: neurological; musculoskeletal; special sense organs; respiratory including speech organs; cardiovascular; reproductive, digestive, genito-urinary; hemic and lymphatic; skin; and endocrine; or (B) any mental or psychological disorder, such as mental retardation, organic brain syndrome, emotional or mental illness, and specific learning disabilities." *But see* Forrisi v. Bowen, 794 F.2d 931, 934 (4th Cir. 1986) (acrophobia not a handicap because claimant's own testimony showed he was disqualified for one job and not for others).

[70] 29 U.S.C. § 794 (1982).

[71] *Id.* Only reasonable accommodations need be made, however. *See* Daubert v. United States Postal Serv., 733 F.2d 1367, 1370 (10th Cir. 1984) (§ 504 of Rehabilitation Act permits discharge of employee for preexisting back injury where collective bargaining agreement forecloses accommodation).

[72] 29 U.S.C. § 794a, referring to 42 U.S.C. § 2000d (1982). That section also makes available the remedial provisions of § 717 of the Civil Rights Act of 1964 to persons aggrieved by the failure of a federal agency to act favorably on a complaint of discrimination. 29 U.S.C. § 794 (1982), referring to 42 U.S.C. § 2000e-16 (1982).

[73] 465 U.S. 624 (1984).

[74] ___ U.S. ___, 106 S. Ct. 2705 (1986).

that airlines were covered by the Rehabilitation Act because of their use of airports which receive federal aid directly. The airports were in the programs receiving aid; the airlines were not.[75]

In contrast to § 504, private suits under § 503, which applies to government contractors, are not permitted.[76]

Significant controversy exists as to whether Acquired Immune Deficiency Syndrome (AIDS) is a handicap under the Rehabilitation Act. At least one district court, in permitting a case to go to trial, has assumed that it is.[77] The Justice Department has written a memorandum[78] concluding that § 504 of the Rehabilitation Act prohibits discrimination based on the disabling effects that AIDS and related conditions may have on their victims, but concluding that an individual's real or perceived ability to transmit the disease is not a handicap within the meaning of the statute.

§ 2.11 —Title VI of the Civil Rights Act of 1964

Title VI of the Civil Rights Act prohibits race, sex, religious, and national origin discrimination by employers receiving federal financial assistance.[79] The provisions of Title VI are applied similarly to the Rehabilitation Act.[80]

§ 2.12 —Handicap Discrimination: State Law

Most states have statutes that prohibit employment discrimination against the handicapped.[81] Illinois has an explicit constitutional prohibition against handicap discrimination in employment.[82] A few states limit handicap protection to state

---

[75] *See also* Grove City College v. Bell, 465 U.S. 555, 574 (1984) (applying program-specific limitation in Title IX of the Civil Rights Act to find that only college financial aid program subject to nondiscrimination requirements).

[76] *See* Hodges v. Atchison, T. & S.F. Ry, 728 F.2d 414, 415 (10th Cir.), *cert. denied,* 469 U.S. 822, (1984) (no private right of action under § 503 of Rehabilitation Act) (citing cases from other circuits); D'Amato v. Wisconsin Gas Co., 760 F.2d 1474, 1482 (7th Cir. 1985) (no private right of action under § 503 as third-party beneficiary of affirmative action contract clause).

[77] Shuttleworth v. Broward County, 639 F. Supp. 654 (S.D. Fla. 1986) (denying motions to dismiss claim of Rehabilitation Act violation by employee terminated because he had AIDS).

[78] Jun. 20, 1986 memorandum from Charles J. Cooper, Assistant Attorney General, Office of Legal Counsel, to Ronald E. Robertson, General Counsel, Department of Health and Human Services.

[79] 42 U.S.C. §§ 2000d-1 to 2000d-6 (1982).

[80] See § **2.10**. *See* Doe v. St. Joseph's Hosp., 788 F.2d 411, 420–21 (7th Cir. 1986) (hospital discrimination against physician not covered by Title VI because hospital not the intended beneficiary of federal funds given to hospital; declining to apply 45 C.F.R. §§ 80.4(d)(2), 80.5 purporting to give physicians private right of action against hospitals receiving federal funds).

[81] See **App. A**.

[82] Ill. Const. art. I, § 19.

employees and employees of state contractors or recipients of state assistance.[83] Alabama is the only state to articulate policies in favor of nondiscriminatory employment of the handicapped without creating explicit legal rights or enforcement mechanisms.[84] Delaware is the only state that appears to be without any provisions concerning employment of the handicapped.

State handicap discrimination statutes are of particular interest because federal law prohibits handicap discrimination in employment only by federal grantees and contractors, not by private sector employers in general. Therefore, an employee subject to handicap discrimination is more likely to rely on state law than an employee subject to race, sex, religious, or age discrimination.

Some state handicap statutes include handicap as one of many characteristics for which employment discrimination is prohibited.[85] Others specifically delineate the rights of the handicapped.[86] The remainder of this section highlights typical provisions and identifies variations with important legal consequences.

A typical state handicap statute begins with a policy statement against discrimination of the handicapped in employment.[87] Generally, the courts construe state handicap statutes broadly to further this public policy.[88]

A definitions section typically follows. It is important to be familiar with the definitions of *handicap* and *employer,* which determine the scope of the particular statute. While California limits protection to physical handicaps,[89] Wisconsin's statute, like the federal statute,[90] protects both physical and mental handicaps:

---

[83] See **App. A**.

[84] Ala. Code § 21-5-1 (1984).

[85] Alaska, Arizona, California, Colorado, Connecticut, District of Columbia, Florida, Hawaii, Illinois, Indiana, Iowa, Kansas, Maine, Maryland, Massachusetts, Minnesota, Missouri, Montana, Nebraska, Nevada, New Hampshire, New Mexico, New York, North Dakota, Ohio, Oklahoma, Pennsylvania, Rhode Island, Utah, Vermont, Washington, West Virginia, Wisconsin, and Wyoming. Citations listed in **App. A**.

[86] Arkansas, Georgia, Idaho, Kentucky, Louisiana, Michigan, Mississippi, New Jersey, North Carolina, Oregon, South Carolina, South Dakota, Tennessee, and Virginia. Citations listed in **App. A**.

[87] Cal. Gov't Code § 12920 (West 1980); Pa. Stat. Ann. tit. 43, § 952 (Purdon Supp. 1985); Wis. Stat. Ann. § 111.31 (West Supp. 1985); e.g., Wisconsin provides:

> The legislature finds that the practice of unfair discrimination in employment against properly qualified individuals by reason of their . . . handicap . . . substantially and adversely affects the general welfare of the state . . . .
>
> In the interpretation and application of this subchapter, and otherwise, it is declared to be the public policy of the state to encourage and foster to the fullest extent practicable the employment of all properly qualified individuals regardless of . . . handicap . . . .

Wis. Stat. Ann. §§ 111.31(1) & (3) (West Supp. 1985).

[88] *See* Ray-O-Vac, Div. of E.S.B., Inc. v. Wisconsin Dep't of Indus., Labor & Human Relations, 70 Wis. 2d 919, 931, 236 N.W.2d 209, 215 (1975).

[89] Cal. Gov't Code § 12926(h) (West Supp. 1986). *See* Smithberg v. Merico, Inc., 575 F. Supp. 80, 83 (C.D. Cal. 1983) (heart condition of former employee, who alleged that she was discharged due to her two heart conditions and other physical problems, was "physical handicap" under California statute).

[90] See § **2.10**.

§ 2.12 HANDICAP DISCRIMINATION: STATE LAW

"Handicapped individual" means an individual who:
- Has a physical or mental impairment which makes achievement unusually difficult or limits the capacity to work;
- Has a record of such an impairment; or
- Is perceived as having such an impairment.[91]

A typical definition of *employer* includes the state, state contractors, and grantees as well as private employers.[92] Distinctions are drawn in the private sector as to the number of persons employed, and whether such persons are employed within the state.[93] Most statutes cover employment agencies and labor organizations as well as employers.[94] The statutes commonly provide an exemption for religious, charitable, and/or fraternal organizations.[95] Pennsylvania, however, does not exempt such organizations if they receive any government assistance.[96] The activities proscribed by state handicap statutes generally include: discrimination in the hiring, promoting, or discharging of handicapped employees; requesting any information concerning handicap on a job application; and retaliation for complaining of discriminatory employer policies.[97]

---

[91] Wis. Stat. Ann. §§ 111.32(8)(a), (b), & (c) (West Supp. 1985). *See* American Motors Corp. v. Labor & Indus. Review Comm'n, 119 Wis. 2d 706, 713–14, 350 N.W.2d 120, 123–24 (1984) (*handicap* within meaning of Fair Employment Act is physical or mental condition that imposes limitations on person's ability to achieve); Cronan v. New England Tel. & Tel. Co., 41 F.E.P. Cas. (BNA) 1273 (Mass. Super. Ct. 1986) (AIDS is handicap under Massachusetts law).

[92] Cal. Gov't code § 12926(c) (West Supp. 1986); Ill. Ann. Stat. ch. 68, para. 2-101(B)(c) (Smith-Hurd Supp. 1985); Pa. Stat. Ann. tit. 43, § 954(b) (Purdon Supp. 1985); Wis. Stat. Ann. § 111.32(6)(a) (West Supp. 1985).

[93] Cal. Gov't Code § 12926(c) (West Supp. 1986) ("any person regularly employing five or more persons . . . "); Ill. Ann. Stat. ch. 68, para. 2-101(B)(b) (Smith-Hurd Supp. 1985) ("Any person employing one or more employees when a complainant alleges a civil rights violation due to unlawful discrimination based upon his or her physical or mental handicap unrelated to ability . . . "); Pa. Stat. Ann. tit. 43, § 954(b) (Purdon Supp. 1985) ("any person employing four or more persons within the Commonwealth . . . "); Wis. Stat. Ann. § 111.32(6)(a) (West Supp. 1985) ("any other person . . . employing at least one individual . . . ").

[94] Cal. Gov't Code §§ 12940(d) & (e) (West Supp. 1986); Ill. Ann. Stat. ch. 68, para. 2-101(C) & (D) (Smith-Hurd Supp. 1985); Pa. Stat. tit. 43, §§ 954(d) & (e) (Purdon 1964); Wis. Stat. Ann. §§ 111.32(7) & (9) (West Supp. 1985).

[95] Cal. Gov't Code § 12940(c) (West Supp. 1986) (fraternal organizations not included); Ill. Ann. Stat. ch. 68, para. 2-101(B)(2) (Smith-Hurd Supp. 1985) (exempting religious organizations); Pa. Stat. Ann. tit. 43, § 954(b) (Purdon Supp. 1985) (adds sectarian corporations); Wis. Stat. Ann. § 111.32(6)(b) (West Supp. 1985) (exempting fraternal organizations).

[96] Pa. Stat. Ann. tit. 43, § 954(b) (Purdon Supp. 1985) (Pennsylvania also provides: "The term 'employer' with respect to discriminatory practices based on . . . non-job related handicap or disability, includes religious, fraternal, charitable and sectarian corporations and associations employing four or more persons within the Commonwealth.").

[97] Cal. Gov't Code §§ 12940(a), (b), (d) & (f) (West Supp. 1986) (also proscribing harassment of any physically handicapped employee or applicant; also imposing liability for harassment by coemployees, if agents or supervisors know or should have known of such harassment and fail

Most state statutes give administrative agencies jurisdiction to enforce the statute.[98] The character and procedures of these agencies vary greatly among the states,[99] but most actually adjudicate the discrimination complaint,[1] rather than merely mediating and conciliating like the federal EEOC.[2] A few statutes do not provide for administrative agency oversight; a handicapped person must seek direct relief from the courts.[3]

An employee alleging discrimination under a typical state statute files a complaint with the agency.[4] Most states defer a private cause of action under the statute until the complainant has exhausted the available administrative remedies; failure

---

to take immediate corrective steps; also imposing liability for failure to take all reasonable steps necessary to prevent discrimination and harassment from occurring. *Id.* at §§ (i) & (j)); Ill. Ann. Stat. ch. 68, para. 2-102(A), (B), (C) & para. 6-101(A) (Smith-Hurd Supp. 1985); Pa. Stat. Ann. tit. 43, §§ 955(a), (b), (d) & (j) (Purdon Supp. 1985) (Pennsylvania also proscribes: " . . .any person subject to the act to fail to post and exhibit prominently in his place of business any fair practices notice prepared and distributed by the Pennsylvania Human Relations Commission."); Wis. Stat. Ann. § 111.322 (West Supp. 1985).

[98] Cal. Gov't Code § 12903 (West Supp. 1986) (Fair Employment and Housing Commission); Ill. Ann. Stat. ch. 68, para. 8-101(A) (Smith-Hurd Supp. 1985) (Human Rights Commission); Pa. Stat. Ann. tit. 43, § 956 (Purdon 1964) (Pennsylvania Human Rights Commission; this commission is under the control of a joint committee of the legislature which has extended the original termination date under the Sunset Act of December 31, 1985 by another year); Wis. Stat. Ann. § 111.375(1) (Department of Industry, Labor and Human Relations).

[99] Cal. Gov't code §§ 12903, 12904 & 12905 (West Supp. 1986) (seven members appointed for four-year term; four members constitute a quorum); Ill. Ann. Stat. ch. 68, para. 8-101(A), (C)(3) & (D) (Smith-Hurd Supp. 1985) (nine members appointed for four-year term; majority of members then in office constitute a quorum); Pa. Stat. Ann. tit. 43, § 956 (Purdon 1964) (eleven members appointed for five-year term; six members constitute a quorum).

[1] Cal. Gov't Code § 12967 (West 1980); Ill. Ann. Stat. ch. 68, para. 8-106 (Smith-Hurd Supp. 1985); Pa. Stat. Ann. tit. 43, § 959(f) (Purdon Supp. 1985); Wis. Stat. Ann. § 111.39(c) (West Supp. 1985). Other states include: Alaska, Arizona, Colorado, Connecticut, District of Columbia, Indiana, Iowa, Kansas, Maryland, Massachusetts, Michigan, Minnesota, Missouri, Montana, Nebraska, Nevada, New Hampshire, New Jersey, New Mexico, New York, Ohio, Oklahoma, Oregon, Rhode Island, Tennessee, Utah, Washington, West Virginia, and Wyoming.

[2] The minority of states which follow the federal EEOC model include: Florida, Hawaii, Kentucky, Maine, and Texas.

[3] States which fall into this category include: Georgia, Louisiana, North Carolina, North Dakota, and Virginia.

[4] Cal. Gov't Code § 12960 (West 1980); Ill. Ann. Stat. ch. 68, para. 7-102(A)(1) (Smith-Hurd Supp. 1985) (Illinois uses the term *charge in writing under oath or affirmation* instead of complaint); Pa. Stat. Ann. tit. 43, § 959(a) (Purdon Supp. 1985); Wis. Stat. Ann. § 111.39(1) (West Supp. 1985).

§ 2.12 HANDICAP DISCRIMINATION: STATE LAW

to bring a timely action before the agency bars any future action on such a claim under the statute.[5] Timing requirements vary.[6]

The agencies usually are empowered to promulgate rules and regulations.[7] Judicial review of agency decisions is provided for under the statutes,[8] but is limited to whether the decision is supported by substantial evidence.[9]

---

[5] Upshur v. Love, 474 F. Supp. 332, 343 (N.D. Cal. 1979) (voluntary termination of California Fair Employment Practices Commission investigation of complaint by blind teacher before filing suit against school was failure to exhaust available administrative remedies precluding claim under California Fair Employment Practices Act); Stoecklein v. Illinois Tool Works, Inc., 589 F. Supp. 139, 145 (E.D. Ill. 1984) (failure of plaintiff to exhaust administrative remedies barred cause of action); Yount v. Hesston Corp., 124 Ill. App. 3d 943, 946–47, 464 N.E.2d 1214, 1218 (1984) (no private cause of action under Ill. Const. art. I, § 19, for employment discrimination based on mental handicap, where no record evidence that employee exhausted his adminstrative remedies under the Illinois Human Rights Act); Bruffet v. Warner Communications, Inc., 692 F.2d 910, 919–20 (3d Cir. 1982) (no common law action by an employee for a discharge on basis of handicap or disability and, hence, any remedy was under the Pennsylvania Human Relations Act); Alleman v. T.R.W., Inc., 419 F. Supp. 625, 630 (M.D. Pa. 1976) (Human Relations Act did not provide any remedy by civil action against employer but only remedy through commission action); Lukus v. Westinghouse Elec. Corp., 276 Pa. Super. 232, 278, 419 A.2d 431, 455 (1980) (plaintiff excused from requirement of exhausting administrative remedies under the Human Relations Act because of previous conduct of defendant); Bachand v. Connecticut Gen. Life Ins. Co., 101 Wis. 2d 617, 623–26, 305 N.W.2d 149, 152–54 (Ct. App. 1981) (remedies before Department of Labor, Industry and Human Relations are exclusive); *but cf.* Shanahan v. WITI-TV, Inc., 565 F. Supp. 219, 222–23 (E.D. Wis. 1982) (declining to follow *Bachand;* interpreting Yanta v. Montgomery Ward & Co., 66 Wis. 2d 53, 224 N.W.2d 389 (1974) as allowing implied private cause of action; administrative remedies not exclusive); Elbe v. Wausau Hosp. Center, 606 F. Supp. 1491, 1500 (W.D. Wis. 1985) (agrees with *Shanahan;* Wisconsin Supreme Court has recognized a private right of action under the Wisconsin Fair Employment Act); Kurtz v. City of Waukesha, 91 Wis. 2d 103, 112–16, 280 N.W.2d 757, 762–64 (1979) (statute prohibiting employment discrimination of public school teachers was not exclusive; plaintiff's cause of action under the Fair Employment Act for denial of sick pay during pregnancy-related disability and subsequent discharge not barred).

[6] Cal. Gov't Code § 12960 (West 1980) ("No complaint may be filed after the expiration of one year from the date upon which the alleged unlawful practice . . . occurred; except that this period may be extended for not to exceed 90 days following the expiration of that year, if a person allegedly aggrieved by an unlawful practice first obtained knowledge of the facts of the alleged unlawful practice after the expiration of one year from the date of their occurrence."); Ill. Ann. Stat. ch. 68, para. 7-102(A)(1) (Smith-Hurd Supp. 1985) ("Within 180 days after the date that a civil rights violation allegedly has been committed . . . "); Pa. Stat. Ann. tit. 43, § 959(g) (Purdon Supp. 1985) ("Any complaint filed pursuant to this section must be so filed within ninety days after the alleged act of discrimination."); Wis. Stat. Ann. § 111.39(1) (West Supp. 1985) (" . . . no more than 300 days after the alleged discrimination . . . occurred.").

[7] Cal. Gov't Code § 12930(c) (West Supp. 1986); Ill. Ann. Stat. ch. 68, para. 7-101(A) (Smith-Hurd Supp. 1985); Pa. Stat. Ann. tit. 43, § 957(d) (Purdon 1964); Wis. Stat. Ann. § 111.375 (West Supp. 1985).

[8] Cal. Gov't Code § 12970(e) (West Supp. 1986); Ill. Ann. Stat. ch. 68, para. 8-111(A)(1) & (2) (Smith-Hurd Supp. 1985); Pa. Stat. Ann. tit. 43, § 960 (Purdon Supp. 1985); Wis. Stat. Ann. § 111.395 (West Supp. 1985).

[9] *See* Mahdavi v. Fair Employment Practice Comm'n, 67 Cal. App. 3d 326, 340, 136 Cal. Rptr. 421, 428 (1977) (determinations of fact by an administrative agency must be sustained if supported

An agency conducts an investigation upon receipt of a complaint from an individual, or upon filing its own complaint, depending on the statute governing the respective agency.[10] Most agencies have broad investigatory powers.[11]

The burden of proof issues in a state handicap discrimination case are like those under the ADEA.[12] The Wisconsin Supreme Court, in *Boynton Cab Co. v. Department of Industry*,[13] articulated these elements for a plaintiff employee to establish a prima facie case of employer discrimination:[14]

1. Complainant must be handicapped within the meaning of the Fair Employment Act
2. Complainant must establish that employer's discrimination was on basis of handicap[15]
3. It must appear that the employer cannot justify its alleged discrimination under the statutory exception.[16]

---

by substantial evidence); Burnham City Hosp. v. Human Relations Comm'n, 126 Ill. App. 3d 999, 1103, 467 N.E.2d 635, 637 (1984) (decision of Human Rights Commission cannot be overturned by a reviewing court on basis of sufficiency of proof, unless decision was contrary to the manifest weight of the evidence); Department of Transp. v. Pennsylvania Human Rights Comm'n, 84 Pa. Commw. 98, 100 n.1, 480 A.2d 342, 344 n.1 (1984) (scope of review in discrimination case is to determine whether the Human Rights Commission's adjudication is in accordance with law and whether the fact findings are based on substantial evidence); *but cf.* Anderson v. Labor & Indus. Review Comm'n, 111 Wis. 2d 245, 253, 330 N.W.2d 594, 598 (1983) (reviewing court not bound by the commission's interpretation of the Act (a conclusion of law), but such interpretation will be affirmed if a rational basis for it exists).

[10] Cal. Gov't Code §§ 12960 & 12963 (West Supp. 1986) (individual or agency); Ill. Ann. Stat. ch. 68, para. 7-102(A)(1) (Smith-Hurd Supp. 1985) (individual or agency); Pa. Stat. Ann. tit. 43, §§ 959(a) & (b) (Purdon Supp. 1985) (individual or agency; also providing for commission investigation without a complaint); Wis. Stat. Ann. § 111.39(1) (West Supp. 1985) (individual only).

[11] Cal. Gov't Code §§ 12963.1, 12963.2, 12963.3 & 12963.4 (West 1980 & West Supp. 1986); Ill. Ann. Stat. ch. 68, para. 7-102(C)(2) (Smith-Hurd Supp. 1985); Pa. Stat. Ann. tit. 43, §§ 957(g) & (h) (Purdon 1964 & Purdon Supp. 1985); Wis. Stat. Ann. § 111.39(2) (West Supp. 1985).

[12] See §§ **2.6, 2.7**.

[13] 96 Wis. 2d 396, 291 N.W.2d 850 (1980).

[14] *Id.* at 406, 291 N.W.2d at 855. Pennsylvania has articulated three elements for a plaintiff-employee to establish a prima facie case of employer discrimination in the hiring process. *See* Pennsylvania State Police v. Pennsylvania Human Relations Comm'n, 72 Pa. Commw. 520, 527, 457 A.2d 584, 589 (1983).

[15] For articulation of what plaintiff needs to prove for the second element, *see* Bucyrus-Erie Co. v. State, Dep't of Indus., Labor & Human Relations, Equal Rights Div., 90 Wis. 2d 408, 424–25, 280 N.W.2d 142, 150 (1979) (decision of Department of Industry, Labor and Human Relations that job applicant was physically able safely and efficiently to perform duties of welder at standard set by employer was supported by substantial evidence, and thus Department properly found that employer had unlawfully discriminated).

[16] Exceptions typically include: a bona fide occupational qualification, security regulations of United States or state, handicaps which substantially interfere with the person's ability to perform the job, and handicaps which jeopardize the health and safety of the handicapped employee as well as other employees. Cal. Gov't Code §§ 12940 & (a)(1) (West Supp. 1986) (California also

Once the employee establishes a prima facie case, a rebuttable presumption of employment discrimination arises, and the burden of production shifts to the employer to show a legitimate, nondiscriminatory reason for dismissing the employee.[17] The employee then has the opportunity to prove by a preponderance of the evidence that such legitimate reasons offered by the employer were pretext for discrimination.[18] Ultimately, though, the burden of persuasion remains with the employee.[19]

If the agency, after investigation, does not find probable cause to believe discrimination exists, the case will be dropped.[20] The employee may appeal the decision before the agency[21] and ultimately seek limited judicial review. If the agency finds

---

provides that: "Nothing in this part relating to discrimination in employment shall be construed to require an employer to make any accomodation for an employee who has a physical handicap that would produce undue hardship to the employer." *Id.* § 12994); Ill. Ann. Stat. ch. 68, para. 1-103(I)(1) & 2-104(A) (Smith-Hurd Supp. 1985) (security regulations of United States or Illinois and handicaps which jeopardize the health and safety of the handicapped employee as well as other employees not included); Pa. Stat. Ann. tit. 43, §§ 954(p) & 955 (Purdon Supp. 1985) (handicaps which jeopardize the health and safety of the handicapped employee as well as other employees are not included); Wis. Stat. Ann. §§ 111.34(1)(b), (2)(a), (b) & (c) (West Supp. 1985) (a bona fide occupational qualification and security regulations of United States or Wisconsin are not included, but handicaps which jeopardize the safety of the general public are. Wisconsin also provides that: "Refusing to reasonably accomodate an employee's or prospective employee's handicap unless the employer can demonstrate that the accomodation would pose a hardship on the employer's program, enterprise or business.").

[17] Department of Transp. v. Pennsylvania Human Relations Comm'n, 84 Pa. Commw. 98, 103, 480 A.2d 342, 346 (1984); Winn v. Trans World Airlines, Inc., 75 Pa. Commw. 366, 371, 462 A.2d 301, 304 (1983), *aff'd,* 506 Pa. 138, 484 A.2d 392 (1984) (quoting from the United States Supreme Court in Texas Dep't of Community Affairs v. Burdine, 450 U.S. 248, 254 (1981): "If the trier of fact believes the plaintiff's evidence, and if the employer is silent in the face of the presumption, the court must enter judgment for the plaintiff because no issue of fact remains in the case.").

[18] 84 Pa. Commw. at 103, 480 A.2d at 346.

[19] *Id.*

[20] California's statute only addresses what results from a finding of probable cause, without mentioning what results from a finding of no probable cause. Ill. Ann. Stat. ch. 68, para. 7-102(C)(3) & (D)(2)(a) (Smith-Hurd Supp. 1985) (complaint can also be dismissed for failure of the complainant to attend a factfinding conference held within 120 days after a charge has been brought). Pennsylvania does not address the issue of what happens if the complainant, upon receiving notice of a commission finding that no probable cause exists, fails to respond within 10 days requesting a preliminary hearing before the commission to determine probable cause for crediting the allegations of the complaint. Wisconsin's statute only addresses what results from a finding of probable cause, without mentioning what results from a finding of no probable cause. The statute does provide, however, that: "The department shall dismiss a complaint if the person filing the complaint fails to respond within 20 days to any correspondence from the department concerning the complaint . . . ." Wis. Stat. Ann. § 111.39(3) (West Supp. 1985).

[21] Cal. Gov't Code § 12970(e) (West Supp. 1986) ("Any order issued by the commission shall have printed in its face references to the rights of appeal of any party to the proceedings to whose position the order is adverse."); Ill. Ann. Stat. ch. 68, para. 7-102(D)(2)(a) & para. 8-103 (Smith-Hurd Supp. 1985) ("If the Director determines that there is no substantial evidence, the complaint shall be dismissed and the complainant notified that he or she may seek review of the dismissal order before the Commission. The complainant shall have 30 days from receipt of notice to file

probable cause, it first will attempt conference or conciliation before proceeding to a formal hearing.[22]

If such remedial measures fail, the agency holds a hearing,[23] subject to statutory and constitutional procedural requirements,[24] to decide the case. Upon a finding for the employee, the agency may award: back pay, reinstatement, and, depending on the state, compensatory damages.[25]

If the decision is for the employee, the employer may appeal the decision before the agency[26] and ultimately seek judicial review. If the decision is for the employer, the employee also may appeal the decision before the agency[27] and ultimately seek judicial review.

The relationship between administrative and judicial remedies under state handicap discrimination statutes is diverse and complicated. Once the employee has exhausted his administrative remedies,[28] many statutes give the employee a private

---

a request for review by the Commission."); Pa. Stat. Ann. tit. 43, § 959(c) (Purdon Supp. 1985) (complainant may within 10 days after service of notice of no probable cause file a written request for a preliminary hearing); Wis. Stat. Ann. § 111.39(5)(a) ("Any respondent or complainant who is dissatisfied with the findings and order of the examiner may file a written petition with the department (within 21 days) for review by the commission of the findings and order.").

[22] Cal. Gov't Code § 12963.7(a) (West 1980); Ill. Ann. Stat. ch. 68, para. 7-102(D)(2)(b) (Smith-Hurd Supp. 1985); Pa. Stat. Ann. tit. 43, § 959(c) (Purdon Supp. 1985); Wis. Stat. Ann. § 111.39(4)(b) (West Supp. 1985).

[23] Cal. Gov't Code § 12965 (West Supp. 1986); Ill. Ann. Stat. ch. 68, para. 7-102(F) & para. 8-106(A) (Smith-Hurd Supp. 1985); Pa. Stat. Ann. tit. 43, § 959(d) (Purdon Supp. 1985); Wis. Stat. Ann. § 111.39(4)(b) (West Supp. 1985).

[24] Kropiwka v. Department of Indus., Labor & Human Relations, 87 Wis. 2d 709, 714, 275 N.W.2d 881, 884, cert. denied, 444 U.S. 852 (1979) (proceedings under the Fair Employment Act are subject to due process requirements, which provide that prior to the final disposition of any contested case, all parties shall be afforded an opportunity for a full, fair, public hearing upon reasonable notice).

[25] Cal. Gov't Code § 12970(a) (West Supp. 1986) (compensatory damages not included in statute); Ill. Ann. Stat. ch. 68, para. 8-108(B), (C), (D) & (G) (Smith-Hurd Supp. 1985) (includes compensatory damages and adds payment for all or a portion of costs of maintaining action, including reasonable attorney fees and expert witness fees); Pa. Stat. Ann. tit. 43, § 959(f) (Purdon Supp. 1985) (see Midland Heights Homes, Inc. v. Pennsylvania Human Relations Comm'n, 478 Pa. 625, 387 A.2d 664 (1978) (Human Relations Commission has no statutory authority to award compensatory damages to persons injured by unlawful discrimination)); Wis. Stat. Ann. § 111.39(c) (West Supp. 1985) (compensatory damages not included in statute).

[26] Cal. Gov't Code § 12970(e) (West Supp. 1986); Ill. Ann. Stat. ch. 68, para. 8-107 (Smith-Hurd 1985) (within 30 days); Pa. Stat. Ann. tit. 43, § 959 (Purdon Supp. 1985) (appeals to the agency from a decision after a hearing is not addressed); Wis. Stat. Ann. § 111.39(5)(a) & (b) (West Supp. 1985) (within 21 days).

[27] Cal. Gov't Code § 12970 (West Supp. 1986); Ill Ann. Stat. ch. 68, para. 8-107 (Smith-Hurd 1985); Wis. Stat. Ann. § 111.39(5)(a) (West Supp. 1985).

[28] *Exhaustion* in this context frequently means that the employee has filed a complaint with the administrative agency and that the agency has determined not to proceed to a formal hearing. See Cal. Gov't Code § 12965(b) (West Supp. 1986). See also Yount v. Hesston Corp., 124 Ill. App. 3d 943, 948-49, 464 N.E.2d 1214, 1218 (1984) (employee may not bring private suit for violation of state constitutional prohibition against handicap discrimination without having exhausted administrative procedures); Armstrong v. Freeman United Coal Mining Co., 112 Ill. App. 3d

cause of action.[29] Typically, the private action would be heard by the court de novo, as under Title VII.[30] Other state statutes not only do not require administrative exhaustion, but provide that an employee loses the right to a judicial de novo trial by commencing a proceeding before the state agency and loses the right to an administrative proceeding by bringing an action in court.[31] The courts in some states have difficulty in deciding whether the statutory procedure is meant to be exclusive.[32]

§ 2.13 —Federal Contractors: Executive Order 11,246

Executive Order No. 11,246[33] requires federal contractors to refrain from employment discrimination and to develop affirmative action plans.[34] Most courts have

---

1020, 1022–23, 446 N.E.2d 296, 298 (1983) (plaintiff's complaint under the Illinois Human Rights Act was properly dismissed for failure to exhaust administrative remedies).

[29] Cal. Gov't Code § 12965(b) (West Supp. 1985) ("If an accusation is not issued within 150 days after the filing of a complaint, or if the department earlier determines that no accusation will issue, the department shall . . . indicate that the person claiming to be aggrieved may bring a civil action . . . within one year from the date of such notice."); Pa. Stat. Ann. tit. 43, § 962(c) (Purdon Supp. 1985) ("if a complainant invokes the procedures set forth in this act, that individual's right of action in the courts of the Commonwealth shall not be foreclosed. If within one (1) year after the filing of a complaint with the Commission, the Commission dismisses the complaint or has not entered into a conciliation agreement . . . the Commission must so notify the complainant. On receipt of such a notice the complainant shall be able to bring an action in the courts of common pleas of the Commonwealth based on the right to freedom from discrimination granted by this act.").

[30] See § 2.3 regarding Title VII proceedings. *See* Baker v. Pennsylvania Human Relations Comm'n, 75 Pa. Commw. 366, 462 A.2d 301 (1983), *aff'd as modified,* 507 Pa. 325, 489 A.2d 1354 (1984) (complainant may sue directly for de novo trial, but may not seek judicial review of no probable cause determination).

[31] *See* Fye v. Central Transp., Inc., 487 Pa. Super. 137, 409 A.2d 2 (1979) (affirming dismissal of common law action because employee had filed complaint with Pennsylvania Human Relations Commission); Bruffet v. Warner Communications, Inc., 692 F.2d 910, 916 (3d Cir. 1982) (interpreting *Fye* not to bar recourse to courts for entirely independent statutory or common law claims; but declining to permit public policy tort claim based on handicap discrimination statute).

[32] *Compare* Bachand v. Connecticut Gen. Life Ins. Co., 101 Wis. 2d 617. 623–26, 305 N.W.2d 149, 152–54 (Ct. App. 1981) (no implied private right of action) *with* Shanahan v. WITI-TV, Inc., 565 F. Supp. 219, 222–23 (E.D. Wis. 1982) (implied private right of action separate from proceeding before agency; disagreeing with *Bachand*) *and* Elbe v. Wausau Hosp. Center, 606 F. Supp. 1491, 1500 (W.D. Wis. 1985) (agrees with *Shanahan;* Wisconsin Supreme Court has recognized a private right of action under the Wisconsin Fair Employment Act separate from proceeding before agency) *and* Kurtz v. City of Waukesha, 91 Wis. 2d 103, 112–16, 280 N.W.2d 757, 762–64 (1979) (statute prohibiting employment discrimination of public school teachers was not exclusive, so that plaintiff's cause of action under the Fair Employment Act for denial of sick pay during her pregnancy-related disability and subsequent discharge was not barred).

[33] 30 Fed. Reg. 12,319 (1965), *as amended by* Exec. Order No. 11,375, 32 Fed. Reg. 14,303 (1967); Exec. Order No. 11,478, 34 Fed. Reg. 12,985 (1969); Exec. Order No. 12,086, 43 Fed. Reg. 46,501 (1978); *reprinted in* 42 U.S.C. § 2000c app. at 19-30 (1981).

[34] Written affirmative action plans are required of employers with 50 or more employees and a contract or subcontract amounting to $50,000 or more. 41 C.F.R. § 60-2.1 (1985). On Aug. 25,

refused to recognize a private right of action for violation of the executive order.[35] However, a private individual may be able to bring an action in the nature of mandamus to compel administrative action to enforce the order.[36] A beneficiary of a conciliation agreement under the executive order may be able to enforce it in federal court.[37] In addition, individual back pay relief may be available in suits brought by the government.[38]

§ 2.14 —Education Act Amendments

In 1982, the Supreme Court decided that Title IX of the Education Amendments of 1972[39] prohibits gender discrimination in employment by federally funded education programs.[40] The case in which these statutory provisions were construed, *North Haven Board of Education v. Bell,*[41] involved a tenured teacher in a public school system who was not rehired after a one-year maternity leave. After an investigation, the Department of Health, Education and Welfare (HEW) notified the school system that it was considering administrative enforcement proceedings that could culminate in a cutoff of funding for the school system. The school system sued to prevent the cutoff. The Supreme Court interpreted HEW's regulations[42] as permitting cutoffs only of specific federally funded programs of institutions which had been found in violation of Title IX restrictions.[43]

1981, proposed regulations were published that would limit the written affirmative action plan requirement to employers with 250 employees or more and contracts or subcontracts of $1 million or more. 46 Fed. Reg. 42,968 (1981). A supplemental proposal was published in 1982. 47 Fed. Reg. 17,770 (Apr. 23, 1982). Final action was scheduled for the end of 1986. 51 Fed. Reg. 14,777 (Apr. 21, 1986) (regulatory agenda).

[35] *See* Eatmon v. Bristol Steel & Iron Works, Inc., 769 F.2d 1503, 1515 (11th Cir. 1985) (citing cases); Weiss v. Syracuse Univ., 522 F.2d 397, 410-11 (2d Cir. 1975); Farkus v. Texas Instruments, Inc., 375 F.2d 629 (5th Cir. 1967).

[36] *See* Legal Aid Soc'y v. Brennan, 608 F.2d 1319 (9th Cir. 1979), *cert. denied sub nom.* Chamber of Commerce v. Legal Aid Soc'y, 447 U.S. 921 (1980).

[37] Eatmon v. Bristol Steel & Iron Works, Inc., 769 F.2d 1503, 1514 (11th Cir. 1985) (§ 1331 jurisdiction to enforce conciliation agreement).

[38] *See* United States v. Duquesne Light Co., 423 F. Supp. 507 (W.D. Pa. 1976).

[39] Pub. L. No. 92-318, 86 Stat. 373, 20 U.S.C. § 1681.

[40] North Haven Bd. of Educ. v. Bell, 456 U.S. 512 (1982).

[41] *Id.*

[42] 34 C.F.R. § 86.51-86.61 (recodified in 34 C.F.R. § 106.51-106.61, 45 Fed. Reg. 30,955 (1980)). The Department of Education regulations generally follow the EEOC regulations, 29 C.F.R. § 1604.1-1604.11, and provide that individual complaints are to be referred to the EEOC. 48 Fed. Reg. 3570 (1983) (to be codified at 29 C.F.R. § 1691 and 28 C.F.R. § 42.601-.613).

[43] *See* Grove City College v. Bell, 465 U.S. 555, 574 (1984) (only college financial aid program rather than entire institution subject to Title IX nondiscrimination requirements when federal aid involved came directly to students).

A private right of action is available to enforce the prohibition on sex discrimination by virtue of *Cannon v. University of Chicago*.[44] In *Cannon,* the Court held that female medical school applicants discriminatorily denied admission could sue in federal court for violation of rights protected by Title IX. Suits under Title IX may have advantages over suits under Title VII because Title IX has no time limits for action and no conciliation provisions.[45]

§ 2.15 Statutes Protecting Employee Conduct

A number of federal statutes protect employees engaging in certain types of conduct against retaliatory discharge. The distinction between this type of protection and the protection discussed in §§ 2.2 through 2.14 is that the plaintiff must prove a causal connection between the discharge and protected conduct in the one, and between discharge and membership in a specific class in the other. Counsel presented with a wrongful dismissal claim, in addition to considering whether class-based discrimination occurred, should inquire whether the employee engaged in conduct protected by the statutes discussed in the following sections.

§ 2.16 —National Labor Relations Act

The National Labor Relations Act (NLRA)[46] is the prototype for federal statutes prohibiting adverse employer action against employees based on their conduct. This section addresses those provisions of the NLRA that prohibit a specific type of adverse employer action: termination of employment. Obviously the length of this treatise does not permit exhaustive treatment of this important statute. Counsel interested in complete treatment of the Act should refer to a standard treatise on the subject.[47]

The NLRA was enacted in 1935,[48] amended substantially in 1947,[49] and again in 1959.[50] The original Act defined certain employer actions as unfair labor practices, and these have been retained by the amendments:

---

[44] 441 U.S. 677, 709 (1979). *See* Strong v. Demopolis City Bd. of Educ., 515 F. Supp. 730, 736 (S.D. Ala. 1981) (private right of action for school teacher, based on *Cannon* and court of appeals decision in *North Haven).*

[45] North Haven Bd. of Educ. v. Bell, 456 U.S. 512, 552 (1982) (Powell, J., dissenting).

[46] 29 U.S.C. §§ 151-168 (1982).

[47] *See, e.g.,* Developing Labor Law (C. Morris ed. 1983); H. Perritt, Labor Injunctions (1986); R. Gorman, Basic Text on Labor Law: Unionization and Collective Bargaining (1976).

[48] Wagner Act ch. 372, 49 Stat. 449 (1935) (codified as amended at 29 U.S.C. §§ 151-168 (1982)).

[49] Taft-Hartley Amendments, ch. 120, 61 Stat. 136 (1947).

[50] Landrum-Griffin Amendments, Pub. L. No. 85-257, 73 Stat. 525, 541 (1959).

1. Interfering, restraining or coercing employees in the exercise of rights guaranteed by the Act[51]
2. Discriminating against employees based on their membership in labor organizations[52]
3. Retaliating against employees because they file charges under the Act.[53]

An administrative agency, the National Labor Relations Board (NLRB), has authority to interpret and enforce the Act.[54] The NLRA applies to employers and employees involved in interstate commerce,[55] but enterprises covered by the Railway Labor Act are excluded[56] along with agricultural enterprises[57] and units of state and local governments.[58]

Section 8(a)(1), as labor lawyers generally refer to 29 U.S.C. § 158(a)(1), makes it an unfair labor practice for an employer "to interfere with, restrain, or coerce employees in the exercise of the rights guaranteed in § 7" of the Act.[59] Section 7 protects the right of employees to organize, to bargain collectively, and to engage in other concerted activities.[60]

Violations of § 8(a)(1) can result from violations of other subdivisions of § 8(a)[61] or from other employer conduct interfering with § 7 rights more generally.[62] The NLRB has held that a violation of § 8(a)(1) can occur regardless of the employer's motive.[63] The test is whether the employer engaged in conduct which, it may reasonably be said, tends to interfere with the free exercise of employee rights under the Act.[64] The Supreme Court, however, has been less precise regarding relevance of motive.[65]

---

[51] 29 U.S.C. § 158(a)(1) (1982).

[52] *Id.* § 158(a)(3).

[53] *Id.* § 158(a)(4).

[54] *Id.* § 153 (1982).

[55] *Id.* § 152(6), (7). Board jurisdiction is exercised pursuant to guidelines promulgated by the Board. For a description of what these guidelines are in various industries, *see* Developing Labor Law 1495–1502 (C. Morris ed. 1983).

[56] 29 U.S.C. § 152(2) (1982).

[57] *Id.* § 152(3).

[58] *Id.* § 152(2).

[59] *Id.* § 158(a)(1).

[60] The protections of § 7 are by no means limited to bargaining activities. *See, e.g.*, Misericordia Hosp. Medical Center v. NLRB, 623 F.2d 808 (2d Cir. 1980) (report critical of employer protected under § 7).

[61] *See* NLRB v. Burnup & Sims, 379 U.S. 21 (1964) (application of § 8(a)(1) analysis to a § 8(a)(3) action lacking employer antiunion motivation, derivative § 8(a)(1) violation).

[62] General violations of § 7 can result in an unfair labor practice in violation of § 8(a)(1). *See, e.g.*, NLRB v. Babcock & Wilcox Co., 351 U.S. 105 (1956) (balancing test in union solicitation case).

[63] Cooper Thermometer, 154 NLRB 502, 503 n.2 (1965).

[64] *Id.*

[65] NLRB v. Burnup & Sims, Inc., 379 U.S. 21 (1964) (upholding board's position that good faith is no defense); Textile Workers v. Darlington Mfg. Co., 380 U.S. 263 (1965) (act unlawful even

Section 8(a)(3) treats any action by an employer as an unfair labor practice if the action results in "discrimination in regard to hire or tenure of employment or any term or condition of employment to encourage or discourage membership in any labor organization."[66] A violation occurs when an employer purposefully discourages union membership, but also when discouragement is the "natural consequence of his action."[67] Most § 8(a)(3) cases involve little or no dispute over the employer's action in changing employment tenure; rather the dispute is over the employer's purpose or motive.[68] Though § 8(a)(3) speaks in terms of union membership, discrimination against employees for engaging in concerted activity has long been held to violate the subsection, even if no union is involved.[69]

Section 8(a)(4) creates an unfair labor practice for employer retaliation against an employee for filing charges under the NLRA or for giving testimony in a Board proceeding.[70]

The NLRB has exclusive jurisdiction over charges alleging violation of these provisions of the NLRA. Private judicial relief is limited to review of an NLRB decision.[71] Thus, violation of NLRA rights is asserted in the first instance by filing a charge with the NLRB.[72]

It is important to understand that the range of employee conduct protected by § 7 and therefore against employer retaliation by §§ 8(a)(1) and (3) is broader than union activities. The scope of § 7 is defined by two concepts: *concerted* and *protected*. Sometimes individual employee conduct can be *concerted* within the meaning of § 7, and many subjects related to the workplace are *protected*, even though not directly related to collective bargaining.[73]

In a typical discharge case under the NLRA, the employee alleges that the discharge was motivated by union activity. For example, in *NLRB v. Associated Milk Producers, Inc.*,[74] the employee claimed his dismissal was caused by his support of a union organizing campaign.[75] The employer claimed the dismissal was caused

---

absent discriminatory motive); Republic Aviation Corp. v. NLRB, 324 U.S. 793 (1945) (motive not essential); American Ship Bldg. Co. v. NLRB, 380 U.S. 300 (1965) (emphasis on motive in lockout case); NLRB v. Fleetwood Trailer Co., 389 U.S. 375 (1967) (absence of anti-union motive irrelevant in §§ 8(a)(1), 8(a)(3) case involving striker replacements).

[66] 29 U.S.C. § 158(a)(3) (1982).

[67] Radio Officers Union v. NLRB, 347 U.S. 17, 44–45 (1954).

[68] American Ship Bldg. Co. v. NLRB, 380 U.S. 300, 311 (1965).

[69] *See* NLRB v. Erie Resistor Corp., 373 U.S. 221 (1963); B&R Motor Express v. NLRB, 413 F.2d 1021 (1969) (§ 7 protected four employees who left work together to protest employer refusal to meet).

[70] 29 U.S.C. § 158(a)(4) (1982).

[71] San Diego Bldg. Trades Council v. Garmon, 359 U.S. 236 (1959); Myers v. Bethlehem Shipbuilding Corp., 303 U.S. 41 (1938).

[72] *See* 29 C.F.R. § 102.9, implementing § 10 of the NLRA, 29 U.S.C. § 160 (1982).

[73] *See* Squier Distrib. Co. v. Teamsters Local 7, 801 F.2d 238, 241 (6th Cir. 1986) (reporting embezzlement to sheriff protected when motivated by concerns about job security).

[74] 711 F.2d 627 (5th Cir. 1983).

[75] *Id.* at 628.

by the employee's failure to report an accident.[76] The Board found that the employer failed to show that it would have discharged the employee regardless of his union advocacy and therefore had committed an unfair labor practice under §§ 8(a)(1) and 8(a)(3).[77] In *NLRB v. Bliss & Laughlin Steel Co., Inc.*,[78] one employee active in supporting union representation was dismissed for refusing to perform functions assigned to him in an attempt to make him a supervisor and thus ineligible for inclusion in the bargaining unit. Another union activist was dismissed for being one or two minutes late on a single occasion. The court of appeals had little difficulty in concluding that the NLRB's finding of an unfair labor practice should be sustained, rejecting the employer's claim of legitimate reasons for the adverse employment actions.[79]

Section 7 protects concerted conduct other than union-related employee conduct. The NLRB historically has found certain types of individual employee conduct to be protected by § 7 and therefore within the prohibitions of §§ 8(a)(1) and 8(a)(3).[80] In a case called *Alleluia Cushion Co.*,[81] the Board established a presumption that individual conduct related to workplace issues meets the concerted element of § 7. Even when the conduct clearly is concerted, as when a group of employees act together, however, the subject matter of their efforts must be legitimately related to improvements in working conditions to be protected by § 7.[82]

Beginning in 1984, the Supreme Court and the Board attempted to resolve some confusion over the scope of the *concerted* and *protected* concepts in § 7. In *NLRB v. City Disposal Systems, Inc.*,[83] the Supreme Court held that an individual refusal to drive a truck, motivated by safety concerns and based on a provision in a collective bargaining agreement, was protected by § 7 of the NLRA, and that a discharge for that refusal was an unfair labor practice. In reaching this result, the

---

[76] *Id.* at 630.

[77] *Id.* at 628. The court of appeals enforced the Board's order.

[78] 754 F.2d 229 (7th Cir. 1985).

[79] *See also* NLRB v. Esco Elevators, Inc., 736 F.2d 295, 299 (5th Cir. 1984) (safety complaints rather than fight with coworker was reason for dismissal).

[80] *Compare* NLRB v. Pace Motor Lines, 703 F.2d 28 (2d Cir. 1983) (employee engaged in protected concerted activity when he refused a work assignment after he and other drivers met with the employer in an effort to change safety conditions at work) *and* Ajax Paving Indus., Inc. v. NLRB, 713 F.2d 1214 (6th Cir. 1983) (employee who discussed pay shortage with other employees and then approached management individually was protected), *with* Ontario Knife Co. v. NLRB, 637 F.2d 840, 842 (2d Cir. 1980) (single employee's spur-of-the-moment decision to walk off the job over a work assignment not concerted activity); *Protection of Individual Action as Concerted Activity Under NLRA*, 68 Cornell L. Rev. 369 (1983).

[81] 221 NLRB 999 (1975).

[82] *Compare* Eastex, Inc. v. NLRB, 437 U.S. 556, 565–66 (1978) (distribution of political leaflets protected) *with* Emporium Capwell Co. v. Western Addition Community Org., 420 U.S. 50 (1975) (minority union members who disregarded union grievance procedures to picket the employer for allegedly racist policies were not protected from discharge under § 8(a)(1)).

[83] 465 U.S. 822 (1984).

Court deferred to the NLRB's policy judgment, expressed in *Interboro Contractors, Inc.*[84]

Subsequently, in *Meyers Industries*,[85] the Board overruled *Alleluia Cushion Co.*,[86] and held that individual employee protest action, not engaged in with or on the authority of other employees, is not concerted unless the employee is asserting rights established in a collective bargaining agreement. Thus, under *Meyers Industries*, an individual employee complaining or refusing to work because of perceived violations of state or federal safety statutes or regulations is not protected against dismissal by the NLRA. In *Meyers*, the Board expressly left intact *Interboro's* protection based on collectively bargained rights.[87] The Board's change in treatment of the concerted requirement has not been well received in the courts of appeals.[88]

In order to find a violation of the Act because of a retaliatory dismissal for making complaints on behalf of other employees, the Board need not find that the employee was correct on the merits of the complaint; only that the complaint was made in good faith.[89] Also, in its *NLRB v. City Disposal Systems, Inc.*, the Court acknowledged that conduct otherwise protected by the NLRA may be so disruptive that it loses its protection.[90]

§ 2.17 —Retaliation for Opposing Discrimination

Section 704(a) of the Civil Rights Act of 1964 prohibits discrimination against employees because they either oppose unlawful employment practices of their employers (*opposition clause*) or participate in enforcement procedures under Title VII (*participation clause*).[91] The Age Discrimination in Employment Act contains

---

[84] 157 NLRB 1295 (1966), *enforced,* 388 F.2d 495 (2d Cir. 1967).

[85] 268 NLRB 493 (1984).

[86] 221 NLRB 999 (1975).

[87] *See also* NLRB v. Esco Elevators, Inc., 736 F.2d 295, 300 (5th Cir. 1984) (denying enforcement of NLRB order because no showing that safety complaint related to safety of other employees); Beardon & Co., 272 NLRB 135 (1984) (filing for unemployment compensation is unprotected).

[88] *See* Ewing v. NLRB, 768 F.2d 51, 55–56 (2d Cir. 1985) (Board finding of no unfair labor practice for dismissal for filing an Occupational Safety and Health Act (OSHA) charge remanded to Board for better explanation); Prill v. NLRB, 755 F.2d 941, 956 (D.C. Cir. 1985) (Edwards, J.) (remanding to NLRB for reconsideration of its decision that truck driver dismissed for refusal to drive unsafe truck and for reporting safety violations to state officials was not protected by NLRA) (Bork, J. dissented); Garcia v. NLRB, 785 F.2d 807, 812 (9th Cir. 1986) (refusal by United Parcel Service driver to honk horn in violation of local ordinance was protected activity; suggesting that any refusal to violate the law would be protected).

[89] *See* Interior Alterations, Inc. v. NLRB, 738 F.2d 373, 376 (10th Cir. 1984) (enforcing NLRB order arising from discharge of employees for protesting work assignments).

[90] 465 U.S. at 837.

[91] 42 U.S.C. § 2000e-3(a) (1982); Womack v. Munson, 619 F.2d 1292 (8th Cir. 1980), *cert. denied,* 450 U.S. 979 (1981) (participation clause).

an almost identical antiretaliation provision to § 704(a).[92] Title 42 of U.S.C. § 1981 also has been read to bar retaliation.[93]

To establish a prima facie case under § 704(a), the plaintiff must establish statutorily protected expression,[94] an adverse employment action, and a causal link between the protected expression and the adverse action.[95] The plaintiff has the ultimate burden of persuasion to show that retaliatory motivation was the "but for" cause of the dismissal.[96]

In opposition clause cases, controversy exists over the employee's having to establish an actual violation of law by the employer to satisfy the first element of a prima facie case. The weight of precedent is that the employee merely needs to establish a good faith belief that the employer was violating the law.[97] In addition, the employee must show that the protest engaged in was in fact a protest of the employer's policies, as opposed to a protest of something else,[98] and that the manner of the protest was protected by the Civil Rights Act.[99] Employees responsible for

---

[92] 29 U.S.C. § 623(d) (1982). *See* Setser v. Novack Inv. Co., 638 F.2d 1137 (8th Cir. 1981); Sisco v. J.S. Alberici Constr. Co., Inc., 655 F.2d 146 (8th Cir. 1981), *cert. denied,* 455 U.S. 976 (1982).

[93] *Compare* Benson v. Little Rock Hilton Inn, 742 F.2d 414, 416 (8th Cir. 1984) (employee fired for remarks made in connection with § 1981 claim had a claim for retaliation cognizable under § 1981) (judgment for defendant based on evidence of legitimate motive affirmed by split panel) *and* Choudhury v. Polytechnic Inst., 735 F.2d 38, 43 (2d Cir. 1984) (retaliation proscribed by § 1981) *and* Winston v. Lear Siegler, Inc., 558 F.2d 1266 (6th Cir. 1977) (retaliation against white employee for protesting black employee's discharge cognizable under § 1981), *with* Tramble v. Coverters Ink Co., 343 F. Supp. 1350, 1354 (N.D. Ill. 1972) (retaliation for filing with EEOC not cognizable under § 1981).

[94] *See* Holden v. Owens-Illinois, Inc., 793 F.2d 745 (6th Cir. 1986) (efforts by company equal employment opportunity officer to implement affirmative action plans complying with Executive Order No. 11,246 did not qualify as protected activity under opposition clause).

[95] Jones v. Flagship Int'l., 793 F.2d 714, 724 (5th Cir. 1986); Smalley v. City of Eatonville, 640 F.2d 765, 769 (5th Cir. 1981).

[96] *See* Donnellon v. Fruehauf Corp., 794 F.2d 598 (11th Cir. 1986) (affirming judgment on retaliation claim; employer's stated reasons were pretextual); Jack v. Texaco Research Center, 743 F.2d 1129, 1131 (5th Cir. 1984) (remanding for determination whether reason for dismissal was complaint to EEOC).

[97] Payne v. McLemore's Wholesale & Retail Stores, 654 F.2d 1130 (5th Cir. 1981), *cert. denied,* 455 U.S. 1000 (1982); Berg v. LaCrosse Coller Co., 612 F.2d 1041 (7th Cir. 1980); Sias v. City Demonstration Agency, 588 F.2d 692 (9th Cir. 1978) (actual violation need not be shown); *cf.* Monteiro v. Poole Silver Co., 615 F.2d 4, 8 (1st Cir. 1980) (subjective belief); Hochstadt v. Worcester Found., 545 F.2d 222 (1st Cir. 1976) (balancing test).

[98] *See* Payne v. McLemore's Wholesale & Retail Stores, 654 F.2d 1130 (5th Cir. 1981), *cert. denied,* 455 U.S. 1000 (1982); Monteiro v. Poole Silver Co., 615 F.2d 4 (1st Cir. 1980) (cannot use as a smokescreen to keep from being fired); Silver v. K.C.A., Inc., 586 F.2d 138 (9th Cir. 1978) (cannot be in protest of a coemployee's acts).

[99] A protest may interfere with the employee's performance of a job to such an extent that a discharge on account of the protest is lawful. *See* Wrighten v. Metropolitan Hosps., Inc., 726 F.2d 1346, 1355 (9th Cir. 1984) (district court erred in finding manner of protest so disruptive as to exceed statutory protection); Rosser v. Laboreres, 616 F.2d 221, 223 (5th Cir.), *cert. denied,* 449 U.S. 886 (1980). For a review of cases involving different types of protest, *see* B. Schlei & P. Grossman, Employment Discrimination 549–52 (1983). The burden of proof to show that

promoting employer equal employment opportunity policies may not be protected when they place themselves in positions adversary to their employers.[1]

Procedurally, claims for violation of § 704(a) are handled just like other claims under Title VII, *i.e.*, by a combination of administrative conciliation and judicial remedies.[2]

§ 2.18 —Occupational Safety and Health Act

Section 11(c) of the Occupational Safety and Health Act of 1970 (OSHA)[3] prohibits employers from discharging employees because they file complaints or otherwise exercise rights afforded by the Act. The Federal Mine Safety and Health Act contains a similar prohibition.[4] The OSHA Act gives individual employees the right:

1. To inform the Occupational Safety and Health Administration of unsafe conditions and to request a federal inspection
2. To assist, on a limited basis, OSHA inspectors
3. To aid a court in determining whether certain imminently dangerous conditions exist
4. To bring an action to compel the Secretary of Labor to seek injunctive relief.[5]

In addition, under a regulation promulgated by the Secretary of Labor, employees may have the right to refuse to perform hazardous job activities in certain circumstances.[6] In *Whirlpool Corp. v. Marshall*,[7] the Supreme Court reviewed an action brought by the Secretary of Labor for an injunction against the discipline and suspension of two employees for refusing to work, under § 11(c). The question before the Court was whether the secretary's regulation authorizing employee refusals to work was permissible under the Act.[8] The Court held the regulation to be valid, noting that, while not requiring the employer to pay employees who

---

the form of the protest was inappropriate usually is placed on the defendant employer. Payne v. McLemore's Wholesale & Retail Stores, 654 F.2d 1130 (5th Cir. 1981), *cert. denied*, 455 U.S. 1000 (1982).

[1] *See* Jones v. Flagship Int'l, 793 F.2d 714, 724 (5th Cir. 1986) (no violation of § 704 by employer against equal employment opportunity officer who filed complaint and promoted class action suit).

[2] See § **2.3**; 29 U.S.C. § 623(d).

[3] 29 U.S.C. § 660(c)(1) (1982).

[4] 30 U.S.C. § 815(c) (1982).

[5] *See* 29 U.S.C. §§ 657(f) (unsafe conditions and inspections), 657(b) (right to assist inspectors), 662(d) (action to compel Secretary of Labor to seek injunctive relief).

[6] 29 C.F.R. § 1977.12 (1985).

[7] 445 U.S. 1 (1980).

[8] *Id.* at 4.

refuse to work, it does require an employer not to discriminate against such employees.[9]

The regulation protects only those employees who reasonably believe there was a real danger of death or injury and there was no time to resort to administrative action to remedy the danger.[10] The Court noted that any employee who acts in reliance on the regulation risks discharge if it is subsequently determined that he acted "unreasonably or in bad faith."[11]

In several cases, discharged employees have filed private actions based on § 11(c). The prevailing authority is that no private right of action exists.[12] Rather, an employee must file a complaint with the Secretary of Labor.[13] The language of the statute is unclear as to whether only the secretary has standing to sue to enforce an order finding a violation of § 11(c), or whether an employee also may sue to enforce such an order. In *George v. Aztec Rental Center, Inc.*,[14] the Fifth Circuit reviewed cases from the Second, Fifth, and Sixth Circuits finding no private right of action under § 11(c) and held that only the secretary has standing to sue to enforce an order under § 11(c).

The Federal Mine Health and Safety Act[15] protects against adverse employment action on account of safety complaints.[16] The Secretary of Labor decides if these provisions of the Act have been violated, subject to review by the Federal Mine Safety and Health Review Commission and the courts.[17]

---

[9] *Id.* at 19 n.31.

[10] *Id.* at 4 n.3.

[11] *Id.* at 21.

[12] McCarthy v. Bark Peking, 676 F.2d 42, 47 (2d Cir. 1982) (no recovery because administrative remedies not exhausted); Pavolini v. Bard-Air Corp., 645 F.2d 144, 146 n.3 (2d Cir. 1981) (no private right of action under either OSHA or Federal Aviation Act); Taylor v. Brighton Corp., 616 F.2d 256, 259 (6th Cir. 1980) (no private right of action); Walsh v. Consolidated Freightways, 278 Or. 347, 563 P.2d 1205 (1977) (no common law action based on OSHA statute). No case has been found in which § 11(c) was held to afford a private remedy. However, in Cloutier v. Great Atl. & Pac. Tea Co., 121 N.H. 915, 436 A.2d 1140 (1981), discussed in **§ 5.9**, the duties imposed by OSHA were used to support a tort action by a discharged employee.

[13] 29 U.S.C. § 660(c)(2), Pub. L. No. 91-596, § 11, Dec. 29, 1970, 84 Stat. 1602; 29 C.F.R. § 1977.15. *See* Donovan v. Hahner, Foreman & Harness, Inc., 736 F.2d 1421, 1429 (10th Cir. 1984) (affirming district court judgment for employee; evidence showed reasonable belief in imminent risk and insufficient time to seek OSHA action); Donovan v. George Lai Contracting, Ltd., 629 F. Supp. 121 (W.D. Mo. 1985) (judgment for $6200 for dismissal in retaliation for filing complaint with OSHA); Donovan v. Peter Zimmer Am., Inc., 557 F. Supp. 642 (D.S.C. 1982) (finding employer liable for retaliatory dismissal in suit brought by Secretary of Labor). *See generally* Annotation, *Prohibition of Discrimination Against, or Discharge of, Employee Because of Exercise of Right Afforded by Occupational Safety and Health Act*, 66 A.L.R. Fed. 650 (1984).

[14] 763 F.2d 184, 186 (5th Cir. 1985).

[15] 30 U.S.C. § 820(b)(1) (1982).

[16] *See* Donovan v. Stafford Constr. Co., 732 F.2d 954, 960 (D.C. Cir. 1984) (internal safety complaints protected).

[17] *See* Consolidation Coal Co. v. Federal Mine Safety & Health Review Comm'n, 795 F.2d 364, 368 (4th Cir. 1986) (affirming Commission decision that miner was protected in refusing to work because of good faith belief in hazard to another employee).

§ 2.19 —Railroad Safety and Liability Acts

Section 5 of the Federal Employers' Liability Act[18] voids any contract, rule, regulation, or device intended to exempt the employer from liability under the Act. Section 10 of the Act[19] contains similar language prohibiting contracts intended to prevent employees from furnishing information regarding an injury or death of any employee to a person in interest.[20] The section further makes it a crime, punishable by a fine of up to $1,000 and imprisonment of up to one year, to threaten, to intimidate, or to discharge an employee for furnishing such information. It is not entirely clear whether either § 5 or § 10 supports a private right of action. An early California district court case said no.[21] A more recent Fifth Circuit case, *Hendley v. Central of Georgia Railroad*,[22] stated that a private plaintiff is entitled to an injunction preventing his discharge.[23] *Hendley* has been distinguished and its holding questioned by the Sixth,[24] Seventh,[25] and Eighth[26] Circuits. In *Gonzalez v. Southern Pacific Transportation Co.*,[27] moreover, the Fifth Circuit held that a Railway Labor Act (RLA) arbitrator's factual decision could be given preclusive effect in a suit under the FELA for an injunction against dismissal.

Section 212 of the Federal Railroad Safety Act[28] prohibits a covered carrier from discharging an employee because such employee has filed a complaint under the Act or testified in proceedings under the Act.[29] The section also prohibits discharge for refusal by an employee to work when confronted by a hazardous condition.[30] Disputes over the application of § 212 are settled by grievance arbitration under the Railway Labor Act.[31] An employee must elect the protections provided by § 212 or "any other provision of law."[32]

---

[18] 45 U.S.C. § 55 (1982).

[19] *Id.* § 60.

[20] *Id.*

[21] Greenwood v. Atchison, T. & S.F. Ry., 129 F. Supp. 105, 107 (S.D. Cal. 1955).

[22] 609 F.2d 1146 (5th Cir. 1980), *cert. denied,* 449 U.S. 1093 (1981).

[23] *Id.* at 1152. In *Hendley,* the plaintiff was held to be entitled to an injunction blocking implementation by the employer of an arbitration award rendered under the Railway Labor Act. Stark v. Burlington, 538 F. Supp. 1061 (D. Colo. 1982), applied the same principle.

[24] *See* Minehart v. Louisville & N. R.R., 731 F.2d 342, 345 (6th Cir. 1984) (FELA retaliatory discharge claim is a minor dispute, which must be heard by an adjustment board, not by a federal court).

[25] *See* Lancaster v. Norfolk & W. Ry., 773 F.2d 807, 815 (7th Cir. 1985) (Posner, J.) (FELA grants no private right of action for wrongful dismissal); Jackson v. Consolidated Rail Corp., 717 F.2d 1045, 1050 (7th Cir. 1983) (no retaliatory discharge claim under FELA).

[26] *See* Landfried v. Terminal R.R. Ass'n, 721 F.2d 254 (8th Cir. 1983) (retaliatory discharge claim not cognizable under FELA), *cert. denied,* 466 U.S. 928 (1984).

[27] 773 F.2d 637, 645 (5th Cir. 1985) (on rehearing).

[28] 45 U.S.C. § 441(a) (1982).

[29] *Id.*

[30] *Id.* § 441(b).

[31] *Id.* § 441(c); *see* Railway Labor Act, 45 U.S.C. § 153 (1982).

[32] 45 U.S.C. § 441(d) (1982).

§ 2.20 —Environmental Statutes

Most of the major federal environmental statutes have provisions protecting employees from discharge or other retaliation for reporting environmental violations by their employers.[33] Complaints alleging violation of these employee protection provisions are made to the Secretary of Labor, who is authorized to afford relief which may include reinstatement[34] and, in some cases, monetary relief beyond back pay.[35] The judicial enforcement procedures vary, but only one statute expressly provides for a private right of action.[36] The Clean Air Act permits an employee who has obtained an administrative order from the Secretary of Labor to sue in United States district court for its enforcement.[37]

Little case law exists interpreting these provisions. One Third Circuit case suggests only that the time limit for filing complaints with the Secretary of Labor alleging retaliatory discharge should be strictly construed.[38]

§ 2.21 —Fair Labor Standards Act

Section 215(a)(3) of Title 29[39] declares it to be unlawful to discharge an employee for filing a complaint, instituting a proceeding, or for testifying in connection with

---

[33] Clean Air Act, 42 U.S.C. § 7622(a) (1982); Clean Water Act, 33 U.S.C. § 1367 (1982); Resource Conservation and Recovery Act, 42 U.S.C. § 6971 (1982); Toxic Substance Control Act, 15 U.S.C. § 2622 (1982). Administrative regulations have been promulgated to cover procedures for filing complaints, in 29 C.F.R. § 24.1–.9, which also cover employees in the nuclear industry. The regulations define those who may complain, set times for institution of complaints, and outline the format for hearings.

[34] 42 U.S.C. § 7622(b)(1) (1982).

[35] The Toxic Substance Control Act provision, 15 U.S.C. § 2622 (1982), is unique in that it expressly provides for exemplary damages. The Clean Air Act provision expressly provides for recovery of expenses and attorneys' fees associated with bringing the complaint before the Secretary of Labor. 42 U.S.C. § 7622 (1982). 29 C.F.R. § 24.6(b)(2) purports to permit the Secretary of Labor to order compensatory damages as well as expenses and attorneys' fees.

[36] The regulations, 29 C.F.R. § 24.8(b)(1) purport to confer a civil right upon persons on whose behalf the Secretary of Labor issues a final order, and to confer jurisdiction over the enforcement of such orders on the district courts. There is apparently no case law on the validity of these regulations, which would ordinarily be accorded some deference by a court. *But cf.* Doe v. St. Joseph's Hosp., 788 F.2d 411, 420–21 & n.17 (7th Cir. 1986) (declining to apply 45 C.F.R. §§ 80.4(d)(2), 80.5 purporting to give physicians private right of action against hospitals receiving federal funds).

[37] 42 U.S.C. § 7622(e) (1982). 29 C.F.R. § 24.8(b)(1) would permit any such employee bringing a complaint under various protection statutes to sue to enforce an order. The more general citizen suit provisions of the Clean Air Act, 42 U.S.C. § 7604 (1982), do not create a private right of action to challenge a retaliatory discharge because that section requires an allegation of a violation of an emission standard or limitation, or of an order issued with respect to such a standard or limitation. Moreover, the relief contemplated by that section is a judicial order compelling compliance with an emission standard or limitation.

[38] School Dist. v. Marshall, 657 F.2d 16 (3d Cir. 1981).

[39] 29 U.S.C. § 215(a)(3).

a Fair Labor Standards Act violation.[40] The courts agree that an employee may maintain a private civil action for violation of this section and recover back pay and obtain reinstatement.[41] In *Love v. RE/MAX of America, Inc.*,[42] the Fifth Circuit held that a violation of § 215(a)(3) occurs for discharge of an employee who makes a good faith, though mistaken, internal protest of disparate treatment of women. The FLSA disfavors settlement or waiver of rights.[43] Attorneys' fees are recoverable.[44]

§ 2.22 —Consumer Credit Protection Act

Section 304 of the Consumer Credit Protection Act[45] provides that no employer may discharge any employee because his or her earnings have been subjected to garnishment for any one indebtedness.[46] The Secretary of Labor enforces the prohibition through the Wage and Hour Division. The weight of authority says that no private right of action exists for violation of § 304,[47] although there is some authority to the contrary.[48]

§ 2.23 —Employee Retirement Income Security Act

Section 510 of the Employee Retirement Income Security Act (ERISA)[49] prohibits any person from discharging a benefit plan participant or beneficiary for exercising

---

[40] *Id.*

[41] *See* Mitchell v. Robert DeMario Jewelry, Inc., 361 U.S. 288, 293 (1960) (employee dismissed in retaliation for asserting FLSA rights can recover lost wages as well as being reinstated); Wirtz v. Ross Packaging Co., 367 F.2d 549 (5th Cir. 1966); Hayes v. McIntosh, 604 F. Supp. 10, 19 (N.D. Ind. 1984) (judgment for employee dismissed in violation of FLSA for refusal to compromise back pay claim); Marshall v. Georgia Southwestern College, 489 F. Supp. 1322 (M.D. Ga. 1980); Brennan v. Braswell Motor Freight Lines, Inc., 396 F. Supp. 704 (N.D. Tex. 1975); Wirtz v. C.H. Valentine Lumber Co., 236 F. Supp. 616 (E.D.S.C. 1964) (court may enter injunction, order reinstatement and award back pay).

[42] 738 F.2d 383, 387 (10th Cir. 1984).

[43] *See* Runyan v. National Cash Register Corp., 787 F.2d 1039 (6th Cir. 1986) (en banc) (analyzing FLSA settlement and waiver precedent in context of ADEA case).

[44] 29 U.S.C. § 216(b).

[45] 15 U.S.C. § 1674.

[46] *Id.*

[47] *See* LeVick v. Skaggs Co., 701 F.2d 777, 780 (9th Cir. 1983) (no private right of action; declining to follow earlier Ninth Circuit case); McCabe v. City of Eureka, 664 F.2d 680 (8th Cir. 1981) (applying Cort v. Ash, 422 U.S. 66 (1975), factors to find no private right of action); Smith v. Cotton Bros. Backing Co., Inc., 609 F.2d 738 (5th Cir.) (applying *Cort* factors to find no private right of action), *cert. denied,* 449 U.S. 821 (1980). The *Cort v. Ash* formula is discussed in **§ 2.26**.

[48] Ellis v. Glover & Gardner Constr. Co., 562 F. Supp. 1054, 1065 (M.D. Tenn. 1983) (awarding back pay and reinstatement for violation of § 304).

[49] 29 U.S.C. § 1140 (1982).

rights under the Act or under a plan subject to the Act.[50] This covers two types of situations: (1) retaliatory dismissals for asserting ERISA rights; and (2) dismissals to prevent benefit payments under pension plans or "welfare plans" like severance or health insurance plans. Private civil actions may be maintained for violation of the section.[51] In *Bittner v. Sadoff & Rudoy Industries*,[52] the court affirmed a dismissal of an ERISA § 510 claim, finding that the employee had been fired, not for suing under ERISA, but for filing a state common law suit seeking punitive damages.[53]

In *Amaro v. Continental Can Co.*,[54] the court held that employees claiming they were laid off to cut short accrual of pension benefits in violation of ERISA were not barred from litigating their claim in federal court by an adverse arbitration award.[55]

Attorneys' fees are available under ERISA.[56]

§ 2.24 —Other Federal Statutes

The Veterans Reemployment Act[57] protects reemployed veterans against discharge without cause for a period of one year after reemployment. Covered employees

---

[50] *Id.*

[51] *See* West v. Butler, 621 F.2d 240 (6th Cir. 1980); Garry v. TRW, Inc., 603 F. Supp. 157, 162 (N.D. Ohio 1985) (alleged termination to prevent receipt of pension states ERISA claim for wrongful dismissal); McKay v. Capital Cities Communications, Inc., 605 F. Supp. 1489, 1490 (S.D.N.Y. 1985) (same); Grywczynski v. Shasta Beverages, Inc., 606 F. Supp. 61, 63 (N.D. Cal. 1984) (dismissal allegedly as part of company wide "purge" to deprive of pension rights states a claim under § 510 of ERISA; no need to exhaust remedies under plan); Kross v. Western Elec. Co., Inc., 534 F. Supp. 251 (N.D. Ill. 1982), *aff'd in part, rev'd in part,* 701 F.2d 1238 (7th Cir. 1983); McGinnis v. Joyce, 507 F. Supp. 654 (N.D. Ill. 1981); Calhoun v. Falstaff Brewing Corp., 478 F. Supp. 357 (E.D. Mo. 1979) (suit maintainable for discharge to prevent vesting).

[52] 728 F.2d 820 (7th Cir. 1984).

[53] *Id.* at 825.

[54] 724 F.2d 747 (9th Cir. 1984).

[55] *Id.* at 749.

[56] 29 U.S.C. § 1132(g) (1982). *See* Smith v. CMTA-IAM Pension Trust, 746 F.2d 587 (9th Cir. 1984) (reversing district court for failure to consider remedial purposes of ERISA in denying attorneys' fees; not a dismissal case).

[57] 38 U.S.C. § 2021(b)(1) (draftees). 38 U.S.C. § 2024 (1982) provides similar rights for persons enlisting in the armed forces.

§ 2.24 OTHER STATUTES

are authorized to file suit in United States district court to enforce the protection.[58] Federal employees have additional remedies.[59]

A provision of the Energy Reorganization Act of 1974[60] prohibits licensees of the Nuclear Regulatory Commission and their contractors from discharging employees for commencing or participating in proceedings to enforce nuclear safety requirements.[61] The protection includes internal protests[62] made in a reasonable manner.[63] This employee protection is enforced by the Secretary of Labor in the first instance.[64] If the Secretary of Labor issues an enforcement order on an employee's behalf, either the Secretary of Labor or the employee may maintain a civil action to enforce it.[65]

A provision of the Asbestos School Hazard Detection and Control Act of 1980[66] prohibits state or local educational agencies receiving assistance under the Act from discharging employees because the employees bring asbestos problems to the attention of the public.[67] How the prohibition is to be enforced is not clear.

Federal jurors are protected against dismissal by reason of their jury service.[68]

---

[58] 38 U.S.C. § 2022 (1982). *See generally* Carter v. United States, 407 F.2d 1238 (D.C. Cir. 1968) (employer has burden of proof to show cause for discharge; predecessor section); Weber v. Logan County Home for the Aged, 623 F. Supp. 711 (D.N.D. 1985) (finding that nurse was dismissed because of National Guard membership, despite evidence of legitimate reasons for employer dissatisfaction); Henry v. Anderson County, 522 F. Supp. 1112 (E.D. Tenn. 1981) (employer has burden). Recovery of attorneys' fees is not authorized by the statute. *See* Wimberly v. Mission Broadcasting Co., 523 F.2d 1260, 1262 (10th Cir. 1975); Witter v. Pennsylvania Nat'l Guard, 462 F. Supp. 299, 306 (E.D. Pa. 1978).

[59] 38 U.S.C. § 2023 (1982) authorizes the Federal Office of Personnel Management to issue orders providing for employment and back pay to federal employees denied employment in violation of the Act.

[60] 42 U.S.C. § 5851 (1983).

[61] *Id.*

[62] *See* Kansas Gas & Elec. Co. v. Brock, 780 F.2d 1505, 1513 (10th Cir. 1985) (Energy Reorganization Act of 1974 protects employees for filing complaints with employers as well as with federal agencies), *cert. denied*, ___ U.S. ___, 106 S. Ct. 3311 (1986); *id.* at 1508, 1514 (district courts must enforce Secretary's order in actions brought by complaining employee). *But see* Brown & Root, Inc. v. Donovan, 747 F.2d 1029, 1031 (5th Cir. 1984) (employee not protected against dismissal for internal corporate reports; recognizing disagreement with Ninth Circuit).

[63] *See* Dunham v. Brock, 794 F.2d 1037 (5th Cir. 1986) (affirming administrative finding that dismissal was for insubordination and therefore not in violation of the Act).

[64] 42 U.S.C. § 5851(b) (1982). *See, e.g.,* Kansas Gas & Elec. Co. v. Brock, 780 F.2d 1505, 1509 (10th Cir. 1985) (citing memorandum of understanding between DOL and NRC to coordinate handling of employee complaints, 47 Fed. Reg. 54,585), *cert. denied*, ___ U.S. ___ 106 S. Ct. 3311 (1986); Consolidated Edison Co. v. Donovan, 673 F.2d 61 (2d Cir. 1982) (Secretary's reinstatement order upheld); Mackowiak v. University Nuclear Sys., Inc., 735 F.2d 1159, 1163 (9th Cir. 1984) (remanding Secretary of Labor's dismissal of complaint alleging retaliation for internal safety complaint).

[65] 42 U.S.C. §§ 5851(d), (e) (1982).

[66] 20 U.S.C. § 3608 (1982).

[67] *Id.*

[68] 28 U.S.C. § 1875 (1982), *as amended by* Pub. L. No. 97-463, 96 Stat. 2531 (1983), providing for attorneys' fees.

STATUTORY PROTECTION

The Longshoremen and Harbor Workers Compensation Act[69] prohibits retaliatory dismissals on account of a claim for compensation under the Act.[70]

The Surface Transportation Assistance Act[71] protects against retaliation for safety complaints and refusals to operate unsafe equipment. Complaints of retaliatory employment action must be filed with the Secretary of Labor.[72] The Bankruptcy Act prohibits discrimination against employees for filing bankruptcy.[73]

§ 2.25 Attorneys' Fees

Pursuing wrongful discharge claims under the statutes discussed in this chapter can have an important advantage over asserting the same claims under common law contract[74] or tort[75] theories. Attorneys' fees are not generally recoverable in common law suits in the United States.[76] Most of the statutes treated in this chapter, however, expressly permit recovery of attorneys' fees in certain circumstances.[77] Title VII expressly authorizes recovery of attorneys' fees.[78] In addition, the Civil Rights Attorney's Fees Awards Act of 1976[79] permits recovery of attorneys' fees in actions brought under the Reconstruction Era Civil Rights Acts.[80] The Civil

---

[69] 33 U.S.C. §§ 902(3), (4) (1982).

[70] 33 U.S.C. § 948a (1982). *See* Buchanan v. Boh Bros. Constr. Co., 741 F.2d 750 (5th Cir. 1984) (denying wrongful dismissal recovery because retaliation was for filing claim under Jones Act rather than under the LHWCA).

[71] 49 U.S.C. § 2305 (1982).

[72] *See* Roadway Express, Inc. v. Donovan, 603 F. Supp. 249, 253 (N.D. Ga. 1985) (granting injunction against enforcement of Secretary's order temporarily reinstating truck driver as violative of procedural due process).

[73] 11 U.S.C. § 525 (1982). *See* Iticho v. First Nat'l Bank, No. AP 85-533 (W.D. Cal., filed Oct. 9, 1986) (finding violation and ordering reinstatement).

[74] Common law contract theories are discussed in **ch. 4**.

[75] Common law tort theories are discussed in **ch. 5**.

[76] *See* Alyeska Pipeline Serv. Co. v. Wilderness Soc'y, 421 U.S. 240 (1975) for a discussion of the American rule on attorneys' fees as court costs. *See generally* S. Speiser, Attorneys' Fees, ch. 12 (Allowance of Fees as Costs; Recovery from Opponent), ch. 13 (Allowance of Fees as Damages) (1973).

[77] The sections discussing individual statutes state whether attorneys' fees are recoverable.

[78] *See* § 706(k) of the Civil Rights Act of 1964, 42 U.S.C. § 2000-e5(k) (1982); Eichman v. Linden & Sons, Inc., 752 F.2d 1246, 1248 (7th Cir. 1985) (district court properly denied attorneys' fees to defendant after plaintiff voluntarily dismissed sex and age discrimination suit following discovery).

[79] 42 U.S.C. § 1988 (1982). *See generally* B. Schlei & P. Grossman, Employment Discrimination, ch. 39 (Attorney's Fees) at 1446–1522 (1983) (discussion of rules for attorneys' fees under discrimination statutes in various circumstances).

[80] *See generally* City of Riverside v. Rivera, ___ U.S. ___, 106 S. Ct. 2686 (1986); Hensley v. Eckerhart, 461 U.S. 424 (1983) (general concepts for award of attorneys' fees under 42 U.S.C. § 1988); Webb v. Board of Educ., 471 U.S. 234 (1985) (42 U.S.C. § 1983 plaintiff not entitled to attorneys' fees expended in optional administrative litigation before local school board; unlike Title VII, which may require pursuit of state administrative remedies).

Rights Attorney's Fees Awards Act also permits attorneys' fees to be taxed against plaintiffs.[81] Attorneys' fees are recoverable under the ADEA.[82]

Under the National Labor Relations Act, litigation costs and attorneys' fees ordinarily are not recoverable.[83] In cases involving frivolous employer defenses or outrageous employer conduct, however, the NLRB may order reimbursement of costs and attorneys' fees as part of its remedy.[84]

Trial court discretion to award attorneys' fees under these statutes may include discretion to prevent an attorney from receiving a windfall in the form of a contingent fee plus a statutory fee award. The prevailing view is that a private contingent fee arrangement may provide for more than the statutory award, but that any statutory fee award should be applied against the amount due under the contingent fee contract.[85]

§ 2.26 Implied Private Right of Action from a Statute

Statutes protecting employees from certain employer conduct sometimes contain no explicit provisions affording the employee a remedy for violation of the statute. Or the statute may vest enforcement authority in administrative or criminal prosecutorial officials. In such cases, the problem can be presented as to whether the individual employee has an implied private right of action to sue for damages for violation of the statute.

This is a different—and narrower—question from the question whether a public policy tort may be based on the policy articulated in a statute.[86] The distinction between the implied right of action question and the public policy tort question can be illustrated by the contrast between *Moniodis v. Cook*,[87] a case recognizing an employee's right to recover for a dismissal in violation of a statute prohibiting compulsory polygraph examinations, and *Sheets v. Teddy's Frosted Foods*,[88] a case permitting an employee to recover for a dismissal in retaliation for his complaining about employer violations of truth-in-labeling statutes.

---

[81] *See* Munson v. Friske, 754 F.2d 683, 698 (7th Cir. 1985) (affirming award of $45,095 attorneys' fees against § 1983/§ 1985 plaintiff); Steinberg v. St. Regis/Sheraton Hotel, 583 F. Supp. 421, 426 (S.D.N.Y. 1984) (awarding $30,000 attorneys' fees to defendant in frivolous ADEA case, $10,000 of which was assessed against plaintiffs' attorney).

[82] *See* B. Schlei & P. Grossman, Employment Discrimination 528 (1983). *See* Richardson v. Alaska Airlines, Inc., 750 F.2d 763, 765 (9th Cir. 1984) (ADEA authorizes attorneys' fees only against employers, not against union that opposed settlement agreement).

[83] *See* Developing Labor Law at 1680 (citing cases).

[84] *See id.* (citing cases).

[85] *See* Wilmington v. J.I. Case Co., 793 F.2d 909, 923 (8th Cir. 1986) (modifying district court order to provide that statutory fee award to be applied against amounts due under contingent fee agreement).

[86] See §§ **5.19; 7.11**.

[87] 64 Md. App. 1, 494 A.2d 212, 216 (1985).

[88] 179 Conn. 471, 427 A.2d 385 (1980).

Moniodis is an implied-right-of-action case. *Sheets* is a public policy tort case. Moniodis was within the class expressly protected by the statute: employees potentially subject to polygraph tests. The duty established by the statute was an employer duty not to dismiss employees for refusing to take polygraph exams. The only thing missing from the statute was an express right to sue for damages, the penalties being criminal. In *Sheets,* on the other hand, the duty imposed by the statute had nothing to do with employment policy; it related to product quantity. The class protected by the statute was consumers of cereal, not employees like Sheets. While an implied-right-of-action question might arise under the statute involved in the *Sheets* case it would involve suits by consumers, not by dismissed employees. As a result, the public policy tort question presented to the *Sheets* court was broader, and different in character, from the implied-private-right-of-action question presented in *Moniodis* and the other cases discussed in this section.

The implied-right-of-action concept is particularly important in federal courts, which lack general jurisdiction over common law actions, and therefore may lack power to develop public policy torts. In state court, it may not make much difference to a particular plaintiff or defendant whether the court is implying a private right of action from a statute or recognizing a public policy tort based on the statute, though the analysis is different.

Section 874A of the *Restatement (Second) of Torts* gives an analytical framework for addressing the implied private right of action question. It states:

> When a legislative provision protects a class of persons by proscribing or requiring certain conduct but does not provide a civil remedy for the violation, the court may, if it determines that the remedy is appropriate in furtherance of the purpose of the legislation and needed to assure the effectiveness of the provision, accord to an injured member of the class a right of action, using a suitable existing tort action or a new cause of action analogous to an existing tort action.[89]

A court must consider several factors before borrowing the policy of a legislative provision to accord an injured party a right of action. First, the court must find that the plaintiff is a member of the class protected by the statute.[90] Second, the court must determine whether the tort remedy provided is "consistent with the legislative provision, appropriate for promoting its policy and needed to assure its effectiveness."[91] In making this determination, the court considers whether the legislature intended to satisfy the statutory objectives exclusively through the designated procedure and the administrative process.[92] Finally, in a federal question

---

[89] Restatement (Second) of Torts § 874 (1979).

[90] This requirement distinguishes the implied-right-of-action question from the public policy tort question, as explained earlier in this section.

[91] Restatement (Second) of Torts § 874A comment h (1979).

[92] "If application of the legislation has been placed in the hands of an administrative agency, for example, this may have been done with the intent that the agency exercise a discretionary enforcement or treat the matter from an administrative standpoint." Restatement (Second) of Torts § 874A comment g (1979). In Carrillo v. Illinois Bell Tel. Co., 538 F. Supp. 793 (N.D. Ill. 1982), the court dismissed pendent state claims premised on the public policy contained in state antidiscrimination statutes because of uncertainty as to how state courts would treat such claims

§ 2.26 PRIVATE RIGHT OF ACTION

action initiated in the federal courts, the court must give attention to whether state remedies provide adequate relief.[93]

Courts usually are reluctant to recognize an implied private right of action when the statute establishes comprehensive administrative remedies available to dismissed employees. Sometimes, however, it is not altogether clear whether the court is rejecting a private right of action *under* a statute, or declining to recognize a public policy tort cause of action derived from the policies of the statute.[94]

In *Cort v. Ash*,[95] the Supreme Court approved the Restatement § 874A concept:

---

and because the "very completeness of the statutory remedies for employment discrimination that are codified in [the state statute] argue against the application of the tort to employment discrimination cases." *Id.* at 799.

[93] "[T]here would seem to be no reason why a state court could not modify a state common law tort on the basis of a policy promoted by a federal statute or utilize a federal statute in application of the principle of negligence per se." Restatement (Second) of Torts § 874A comment g (1979). Thus a federal court considering the federal question of whether a private right of action should be implied under a federal statute should consider the degree to which state tort law affords relief based on a public policy tort furthering the statutory intent. Note, however, that although a distinction must be made between state and federal court consideration of § 874A, "the principle set forth in this Section applies in the federal courts as well as the state courts." *Id.* at comment g. Of course in a diversity action, the federal court would be obligated to apply state law, as it thought state courts would apply it. Bruffett v. Warner Communications, Inc., 692 F.2d 910 (3d Cir. 1982).

[94] *See* Wolk v. Saks Fifth Ave., 728 F.2d 221, 223 (3d Cir. 1984) (no common law tort claim based on the Pennsylvania Human Relations Act because statute provides own administrative remedies); Delaney v. Taco Time Int'l, Inc., 297 Or. 10, 16, 681 P.2d 114, 117–18 (1984) (suggesting public policy tort appropriate only where no statutory remedies exist); Walsh v. Consolidated Freightways, 278 Or. 347, 563 P.2d 1205 (1977) (no tort recovery for discharge of an employee for complaining about unsafe working conditions because the employee had adequate administrative remedy); Covell v. Spengler, 141 Mich. App. 76, 366 N.W.2d 76, 80 (1985) (whistleblower protection act provides exclusive remedy; no independent tort or implied covenant cause of action for conduct protected by Act); Melley v. Gillette Corp., 19 Mass. App. 511, 475 N.E.2d 1227, 1229–30 (1985) (no public policy tort for age discrimination prohibited by state statute; must seek administrative remedies); Gutierrez v. City of Chicago, 605 F. Supp. 973, 980 (N.D. Ill. 1985) (no public policy tort claim to protect rights already protected by state and federal civil rights statutes); Crews v. Memorex Corp., 588 F. Supp. 27, 28 (D. Mass. 1984) (Massachusetts implied covenant cause of action not available where statutory remedy exists for age discrimination); Medina v. Spotnail, Inc., 591 F. Supp. 190, 198 (N.D. Ill. 1984) (no tort claim for conduct within Illinois Human Rights Act); Kamens v. Summit Stainless, Inc., 586 F. Supp. 324, 329–30 (E.D. Pa. 1984) (no implied covenant cause of action for dismissal allegedly violative of FLSA and ADEA). *But see* Savage v. Holiday Inn Corp., 603 F. Supp. 311, 313 (D. Nev. 1985) (age and sex discrimination in violation of statute states public policy tort claim under Nevada law); Wynn v. Boeing Military Airplane Co., 595 F. Supp. 727, 729 (D. Kan. 1984) (Kansas public policy tort cause of action available for race discrimination covered by Title VII and 42 U.S.C. § 1981). Additional cases, and more analysis of the public policy tort cases appear in §§ **5.8–5.19**.

[95] 422 U.S. 66 (1975) (rejecting private cause of action for damages against corporate directors under a criminal statute prohibiting corporations from making certain expenditures during political campaigns). *See also* Brezinski v. F.W. Woolworth Co., 626 F. Supp. 240 (D. Colo. 1986) (*Cort v. Ash* analysis used to find implied private right of action under Colorado age discrimination statute); Heller v. Dover Warehouse Mkt., Inc., 515 A.2d 178, 180 (Del. Super. Ct. 1986) (*Cort* analysis to find implied right of action under state polygraph statute).

In determining whether a private remedy is implicit in a statute not expressly providing one, several factors are relevant. First, is the plaintiff one of the class for whose *especial* benefit that statute was enacted, [citations omitted] that is, does the statute create a Federal right in favor of the plaintiff? Second, is there any indication of legislative intent, explicit or implicit, either to create such a remedy or to deny one? Third, is it consistent with the underlying purposes of the legislative scheme to imply such a remedy for the plaintiff? And finally, is the cause of action one traditionally relegated to state law, in an area basically the concern of the states, so that it would be inappropriate to infer a cause of action based solely on Federal law?[96]

Private rights of action have been recognized or denied under a variety of federal statutes. Typical is the analytical process used to find implied rights under the Railway Labor Act.[97]

In *Burke v. Compania Mexicana de Aviacion, S.A.*,[98] an individual employee sued his employer for wrongful discharge, alleging that the employer had violated the Railway Labor Act by firing him for trying to organize a union.[99] The district court dismissed his complaint for failure to state a claim upon which relief could be granted.[1] For purposes of the appeal, it was conceded that the employer's action violated § 2 of the Act,[2] which gives employees the right to organize and prohibits employers from interfering with that right.[3] The Ninth Circuit held that a private right of action could be implied under the Act because no congressional intent could be found that limits the remedies for violation of § 2 to the criminal sanctions expressly provided therein.[4] The court reasoned that imposition of criminal penalties would be inadequate to protect the organizational rights of the discharged employee. "The only remedies adequate fully to effectuate the congressional purpose in this case are those requested by Burke—damages and reinstatement."[5] *Burke* is an example of a plaintiff who is clearly a member of the protected class not having real remedies in the absence of an implied right of action.

---

[96] Cort v. Ash, 422 U.S. at 78 (emphasis in original). In Transamerica Mortgage Advisors, Inc. v. Lewis, 444 U.S. 11, 15 (1979), the Court, although not rejecting the *Cort* factors, stressed that the question of "whether a statute creates a cause of action, either expressly or by implication, is basically a matter of statutory construction."

[97] *See generally* Arouca, *Damages for Unlawful Strikes Under the Railway Labor Act,* 32 Hastings L.J. 779, 791 nn. 42 & 43, 794-95 (1981). *But see* Nelson v. Piedmont Aviation, 750 F.2d 1234, 1236 (4th Cir. 1984) (RLA does not protect applicant for employment from discrimination due to strike breaking activities). The typical means of enforcing the Railway Labor Act is an injunction. *See* H. Perritt, Labor Injunctions ch. 6 (1986).

[98] 433 F.2d 1031 (9th Cir. 1970).

[99] *Id.* at 1032.

[1] *Id.* at 1031.

[2] *Id.* at 1032.

[3] 45 U.S.C. § 152 (1982).

[4] Burke v. Compania Mexicana de Aviacion, S.A., 433 F.2d at 1033.

[5] *Id.* at 1034. *See also* Stepanischen v. Merchants Despatch Transp. Corp., 722 F.2d 922, 924 (1st Cir. 1983) (implied right of action under Railway Labor Act recognized to remedy discharge in retaliation for union organizing activities) (citing cases in other circuits); Rachford v. Evergreen Int'l Airlines, 596 F. Supp. 384, 386 (N.D. Ill. 1984) (RLA does not protect concerted safety protest by airline employee).

§ 2.26 PRIVATE RIGHT OF ACTION

The following cases are typical of same analysis excluding an implied private right of action. In *Schrachta v. Curtis*,[6] the Seventh Circuit joined a host of other federal courts in holding that the Civil Service Reform Act does not create private right of action. Also, in *Le Vick v. Skaggs Co.*[7] the Ninth Circuit refused to imply a private right of action under the Consumer Credit Protection Act[8] for an employee who had his wages subjected to garnishment.[9] In denying a private right of action, the court applied the principles of *Transamerica Mortgage Advisors, Inc. v. Lewis*[10] to find that Congress intended only that the Secretary of Labor, not private parties, enforce the antidischarge provisions of the statute.[11] In both of these cases, the plaintiff was a member of the statutorily protected class, but statutory remedies were found to be adequately protective of the rights granted. In *Shoultz v. Monfort of Colorado, Inc.*,[12] the Tenth Circuit found no implied private right of action under the Federal Meat Inspection Act[13] for a meat inspector discharged by the United States Department of Agriculture (USDA) for a private company's efforts to induce his dismissal. Among other things, the court noted that the plaintiff was not a member of the class—consumers—that the statute was designed to protect.[14]

Absent a finding that Congress intended the remedies provided by a statute to be exclusive, satisfaction of the four factors expressed in § 874A and *Cort* should allow a private right of action to further the policy contained in a legislative provision. When statutes contain an express restriction against discharge and do not establish an administrative procedure to vindicate that right, the courts probably always will find a private cause of action. When an antiretaliation prohibition in the statute is not express, the question of a private right of action is a closer one, although a public policy tort might be based on the policy inherent in the statute.[15]

Disagreement among the circuits exists as to whether a discharged employee has standing to bring an action for treble damages under the antitrust laws.[16] In *Ostrofe v. Crocker Co.*,[17] the Ninth Circuit held that the congressional purpose was served by permitting an employee who was blacklisted for refusal to participate in a price-fixing conspiracy to maintain such an action.[18] In *In re Industrial Gas*

---

[6] 752 F.2d 1257, 1258 (7th Cir. 1985).

[7] 701 F.2d 777 (9th Cir. 1983).

[8] 15 U.S.C. § 1674(a) (1982). See **§ 2.22**.

[9] Le Vick v. Skaggs Co., 701 F.2d at 777.

[10] 444 U.S. 11 (1979).

[11] Le Vick v. Skaggs Co., 701 F.2d at 780.

[12] 754 F.2d 318, 323 (10th Cir. 1985).

[13] 21 U.S.C. § 601 (1982).

[14] Shoultz v. Monfort of Colo., Inc., 754 F.2d at 324.

[15] *But see* Larrabee v. Penobscot Frozen Foods, Inc., 486 A.2d 97, 100 (Me. 1984) (no private right of action under unemployment fraud statute.).

[16] The issue in these cases was not whether a private right of action existed at all, but whether the plaintiff was the proper person to maintain an action. Nevertheless, the mode of analysis is analogous, turning on congressional intent.

[17] 670 F.2d 1378 (9th Cir. 1982), *vacated & remanded*, 460 U.S. 1007 (1983), *on remand*, 740 F.2d 739 (9th Cir. 1984) (adhering to original decision), *cert. dismissed*, 469 U.S. 1200 (1985).

[18] 670 F.2d at 1384.

Antitrust Litigation,[19] the Seventh Circuit disagreed, in part because the plaintiff was not within the *target zone* of the conspiracy[20] and in part because of the attenuated causal nexus between the antitrust violation and the employee's dismissal.[21]

§ 2.27 Preemption

Preemption is the converse of implied private rights of action, addressed in the preceding section. Implied private rights of action under a statute reinforce the plaintiff's claim; preemption under a statute divests the plaintiff of a claim otherwise existing at common law. The existence of statutory remedies for employment termination may preclude resort to common law judicial remedies. *Preemption,* the name generally given to this statutory preclusion, arises when a statutory remedy and a common law remedy exist for the same conduct. Preemption of state law by federal law results from applying the supremacy clause of the United States Constitution.[22] Moreover, the preemption doctrine may involve application of the *primary jurisdiction* doctrine,[23] which occurs when an administrative agency has been authorized by statute to address the same factual circumstances as a common law court.

To give concreteness to the general principles of preemption applicable to the statutes addressed in this chapter, it is useful to consider the practical context within which preemption becomes an issue. The plaintiff files a common law action for wrongful discharge in tort[24] or contract[25] in state court.[26] The defendant moves to dismiss on the grounds that the state court lacks jurisdiction[27] or that no cause of action exists from the facts pleaded.[28] A somewhat different situation occurs when an employee seeks to litigate part of a claim in a state court and part in an administrative forum or to litigate the same claim twice. That situation presents problems of res judicata and mootness.[29]

Usually, preemption occurs in labor law when a scheme of federal regulation is determined to be so pervasive as to make reasonable the inference that Congress

---

[19] 681 F.2d 514 (7th Cir. 1982).

[20] *Id.* at 519.

[21] *Id.* at 520.

[22] U.S. Const. art. VI.

[23] *See* United States v. Western Pac. R.R., 352 U.S. 59 (1956) (explaining difference between *exhaustion* and exclusive *primary jurisdiction*).

[24] Tort theories are discussed in **ch. 5**.

[25] Contract theories are discussed in **ch. 4**.

[26] The preemption analysis is the same if the state court action is removed to federal court.

[27] This would be an assertion that state court jurisdiction is preempted.

[28] This would be an assertion that, while the state court may retain jurisdiction, the cause of action is preempted.

[29] See §§ **7.29–7.35**, regarding res judicata and related preclusion issues. These problems are more likely to occur in the employment discrimination area, where federal preemption is not a problem. See § **2.32**.

left no room for the state to supplement it[30] or when the state policy is likely to produce a result inconsistent with the objective of the federal statute.[31] If either is true, the supremacy clause of the United States Constitution precludes application of state law.[32]

The doctrine of primary jurisdiction, which involves concepts additional to federal supremacy, arises when the legislature has empowered an administrative agency, rather than the courts, to decide certain questions.[33] The doctrine can be applied to state as well as federal administrative agencies.[34] Usually, primary jurisdiction in an administrative agency will be found to exist when the agency has specialized policy responsibilities or expertise which should be applied to the dispute.[35] On the other hand, the inability of an administrative agency to afford the particular type of relief sought in a judicial action militates against a finding of primary jurisdiction.[36]

Preemption is most likely to be found when an employee seeks to assert a state claim that is also the subject of an unfair labor practice under federal law.[37] Preemption is also at issue when an employee covered by a collective bargaining agreement brings a common law action for wrongful discharge.[38] Primary jurisdiction may be at issue when an employee brings a common law action for a discharge involving discrimination within the jurisdiction of a state or federal antidiscrimination agency.[39]

When a particular case is considered, it is important to clarify whether the state cause of action or only certain state remedies are preempted, as opposed to the jurisdiction of the state court being preempted. In many cases, the state court will retain jurisdiction, even if it must apply federal law. In *Clafin v. Houseman,* the

---

[30] *See* Napier v. Atlantic Coast Line, 272 U.S. 605 (1926).

[31] *See* Rice v. Santa Fe, 331 U.S. 218, 230 (1947); Allis Chalmers v. Lueck, 471 U.S. 202, ___ n.9, 105 S. Ct. 1904, 1912 n.9 (1985); Cloverleaf Butter v. Patterson, 315 U.S 148 (1942).

[32] Florida Lime & Avocado Growers v. Paul, 373 U.S. 132 (1963).

[33] *See* Nader v. Allegheny Airlines, 426 U.S. 290 (1976); Texas & Pac. Ry. v. Abilene Cotton, 204 U.S. 426 (1907).

[34] *See* Bell Tel. & Tel. Co. v. Mobile Am. Corp., 291 So. 2d 199 (Fla. 1974).

[35] *See* Nader v. Allegheny Airlines, 426 U.S. 290 (1976).

[36] *Compare* Texas State Fed'n of Labor v. Brown & Root, 246 S.W.2d 938 (Tex. Civ. App. 1952), *with* J.&J. Enters. v. Martignetti, 369 Mass. 535, 341 N.E.2d 645 (1976).

[37] See § **2.16**.

[38] *See* Allis Chalmers v. Lueck, 471 U.S. 202 (1985).

[39] *See* Wolk v. Saks Fifth Ave., 728 F.2d 221, 223 (3d Cir. 1984) (no common law tort claim based on the Pennsylvania Human Relations Act because statute provides administrative remedies); Gutierrez v. City of Chicago, 605 F. Supp. 973, 980 (N.D. Ill. 1985) (no public policy tort claim to protect rights already protected by state and federal civil rights statutes); Crews v. Memorex Corp., 588 F. Supp. 27, 28 (D. Mass. 1984) (Massachusetts implied covenant cause of action not available where statutory remedy exists for age discrimination); Medina v. Spotnail, Inc., 591 F. Supp. 190, 198 (N.D. Ill. 1984) (no tort claim for conduct within Illinois Human Rights Act); Fye v. Central Transp., Inc., 487 Pa. 137, 409 A.2d 2 (1979) (resort to state antidiscrimination agency precludes subsequent resort to equity court). *See also* Kofoid v. Woodard Hotels, Inc., 78 Or. App. 283, 716 P.2d 771, 774 (1986) (distinguishing preemption from nonexistence of tort claim because societal interests adequately protected by statutory procedure).

Supreme Court held that state courts have concurrent jurisdiction with federal courts over federal questions, unless state court jurisdiction is "excluded by express provision"[40] or because it is incompatible with federal policy. Application of federal preemption doctrines by state courts under the *Clafin* rule is best described as involving preemption of the state cause of action. In other cases, the jurisdiction of the state court to adjudicate the matter is foreclosed.[41] This is best described as preemption of jurisdiction.[42] In still other cases, the state court retains jurisdiction, and the state cause of action is not preempted, but certain remedies are preempted.[43]

§ 2.28 — National Labor Relations Act Preemption

The National Labor Relations Act (NLRA), discussed in § 2.16, establishes a comprehensive federal regulatory mechanism to govern the rights of employees and employers to engage in collective bargaining.[44] A state common law action for wrongful discharge is preempted by federal law if the plaintiff employee is covered by the federal statutes[45] and if the employer conduct at issue in the state action bears a close relation to collective bargaining.

One type of preemption question is presented when an employee brings a state common law tort action alleging conduct that arguably is protected or prohibited by the NLRA.[46] For example, a worker in a nonunion plant fired for seeking support for a union on his own time would almost surely have a potential remedy under §§ 8(a)(1) and 8(a)(3) of the NLRA. Another example would be a discharge prompted by an employee's complaint to the National Labor Relations Board (NLRB) against his or her employer, which would give rise to a § 8(a)(4) charge

---

[40] 93 U.S. 130, 136 (1876).

[41] *See* Gulf Offshore Co. v. Mobil Oil Co., 453 U.S. 473, 477–78 (1981) (no exclusive federal court jurisdiction).

[42] *See* Belknap, Inc. v. Hale, 463 U.S. 491, 497 n.5 (1983) and cases cited therein (policy requiring the subject matter to be heard by the Board, not by the state courts).

[43] *See id.* at 511 n.13 (state court can decide breach of contract claim but may not order specific performance if that would conflict with NLRB order).

[44] See §§ **2.29, 2.30, 4.25, 5.20,** and **3.21** for additional discussion of preemption in the context of arbitral and judicial relief for breach of labor agreements.

[45] *See generally* Cox, *Federalism in the Law of Labor Relations,* 67 Harv. L. Rev. 1297 (1954). If the state lawsuit involves conduct regulated by the unfair labor practice provisions of the NLRA, the state court jurisdiction is preempted. If the state lawsuit alleges breach of a collective bargaining agreement, state court jurisdiction is not preempted, but the state court must apply federal common law. If the collective agreement contains no arbitration procedure, the state court hearing the breach of contract suit should apply general contract law principles. *See* Smith v. Kerrville Bus Co., 709 F.2d 914, 917 (5th Cir. 1983) (implication of *for cause* limitation on discharges under collective agreement lacking arbitration procedure). See §§ **2.29–2.30,** for a discussion of § 301 preemption.

[46] *See* San Diego Bldg. Trades Council v. Garmon, 359 U.S. 236 (1959). Belknap, Inc. v. Hale, 463 U.S. 491 (1983) involved this type of preemption question in the context of a state lawsuit

under the NLRA. Even if the state court has accepted the wrongful discharge cause of action, the federal statute preempts its jurisdiction.[47]

An individual action for wrongful discharge does not involve conduct arguably protected or prohibited by the NLRA unless the plaintiff participated in an NLRB proceeding or engaged in some form of concerted conduct with other employees.[48] Additionally, the state court action can proceed, even if it involves conduct potentially regulated under the NLRA, if the state court action involves matters of special interest to the state. This might be the case with an action for intentional infliction of emotional distress or an action for defamation,[49] or if the treatment of the conduct under the NLRA is reasonably clear.[50] State statutory claims are treated similarly.[51]

Supervisors are not covered by the NLRA, but in a limited class of cases, employer conduct that forces supervisors to discourage concerted action protected by the NLRA may be an unfair labor practice, leading to preemption.[52]

---

for breach of contract, as well as in tort. In *Belknap,* striker replacements brought a lawsuit in state court for breach of contract and misrepresentation after they were discharged to make way for returning strikers. The Supreme Court held that the state suit was not preempted, even though unfair labor practices might be involved, potentially resulting in an NLRB order to reinstate the strikers. Reaching a different result, the Court found preemption in Operating Eng'rs Local 926 v. Jones, 460 U.S. 669 (1983). The discharged employee brought a state tort action against his former union, alleging that the union wrongfully had procured his discharge. The Court found that the union's conduct arguably was within the reach of the NLRB. *Id.* at 678–79. *See* Satterfield v. Western Elec. Co., 758 F.2d 1252, 1254 (8th Cir. 1985) (tort claim for intentional interference with contractual relations by employee fired for distribution of right-to-work literature preempted; conduct was protected by § 7 of the NLRA)

[47] Wisconsin Dep't. of Indus. v. Gould, Inc., ___ U.S. ___, 106 S. Ct. 1057 (1986) (states preempted from using spending power to penalize firms found by NLRB to have violated NLRA).

[48] *See* § **2.16**; *See also* Anco Constr. Co. v. Freeman, 236 Kan. 626, 693 P.2d 1183, 1185 (1985) (tort claim for dismissal for individual protest over wage rates under Davis-Bacon Act preempted by NLRA).

[49] *See* Farmer v. Carpenters Local 25, 430 U.S. 290 (1977). *But see* Vane v. Nocella, 303 Md. 362, 494 A.2d 181 (1985) (supervisor's common law tort claim against union officer for intentional interference with contractual relations preempted by NLRA); Collins v. MBPXL Corp., 9 Kan. App. 2d 363, 679 P.2d 746, 752 (1984) (emotional distress claim arising from fact of discharge rather than manner of discharge preempted by NLRA).

[50] *See generally* Sears, Roebuck & Co. v. San Diego County Dist. Council of Carpenters, 436 U.S. 180 (1978), *on remand,* 25 Cal. 3d 317, 599 P.2d 676, 158 Cal. Rptr. 370 (1979), *cert. denied,* 447 U.S. 935 (1980). The *Sears* case involved unusual facts, in that the employer potentially was without a remedy. It is likely that preemption would be found to exist if an employer fires an employee for union activity, notwithstanding that the treatment of the firing is reasonably clear under the NLRA. *But see* Martin v. Capital Cities Media, Inc., 354 Pa. Super. 199, 511 A.2d 830, 834 (1986) (no preemption; dismissal of charge by NLRB, common law claims for breach of contract and tort, growing out of dismissal of newspaper employee for placing ad in rival "strike" paper).

[51] *See* Ruiz v. Miller Curtain Co., 686 S.W.2d 671, 675 (Tex. Ct. App. 1985) (state statutory claim for dismissal in retaliation for filing workers compensation claim preempted by NLRA).

[52] *See* Sitek v. Forest City Enters., Inc., 587 F. Supp. 1381, 1385 (E.D. Mich. 1984) (supervisor's public policy tort claim for discharge on account of refusal to engage in union busting was preempted by NLRA).

§ 2.29 — Preemption of Tort Claims under § 301 of the Labor Management Relations Act

Another type of preemption case is presented when an employee covered by a collectively bargained grievance and arbitration clause brings a state common law action for wrongful discharge.[53] A series of United States Supreme Court cases makes it reasonably clear that, while a state court may adjudicate a state breach of contract suit in such circumstances,[54] it must apply federal law.[55] This requires the state court to defer to any grievance and arbitration procedures contained in the collective bargaining agreement.[56] Thus, an employee entitled to resort to grievance and arbitration remedies under a collective agreement must follow those procedures before proceeding in a state breach of contract lawsuit.[57] An arbitration award in the employer's favor cannot be attacked collaterally in a state action absent unusual circumstances such as fraud.[58]

State tort actions for employer conduct covered by the arbitration clause are treated somewhat differently, particularly when the tort claim grows out of the manner in which the collective agreement was administered.[59] In *Garibaldi v. Lucky*

---

[53] Additional analysis of preemption of wrongful dismissal tort claims by § 301 of the Labor Management Relations Act (LMRA) appears in § **5.20**.

[54] Charles Dowd Box Co. v. Courtney, 368 U.S. 502 (1962).

[55] § 301 of the Labor Management Relations Act, 29 U.S.C. § 185 (1982), has been interpreted as requiring the application of federal common law to the enforcement of collective bargaining agreements. *See* Textile Workers Union v. Lincoln Mills, 353 U.S. 448 (1957); Teamsters Local 174 v. Lucas Flour, 369 U.S. 95, 103 (1962). The substantive state cause of action is preempted by federal common law.

[56] Avco Corp. v. Aerolodge No. 735, 390 U.S. 557 (1968); Steelworkers v. American Mfg. Co., 363 U.S. 564 (1960); Steelworkers v. Warrior & Gulf Navigation Co., 363 U.S. 574 (1960); Steelworkers v. Enterprise Wheel & Car Corp., 363 U.S. 593 (1960).

[57] Teamsters Local 174 v. Lucas Flour Co., 369 U.S. 95 (1962).

[58] Frazier v. Ford Motor Co., 364 Mich. 648, 651, 112 N.W.2d 80, 82 (1961). A breach of the duty of fair representation by the union would permit the arbitration award to be attacked. See § **3.25** for a discussion of the fair representation concept.

[59] *See* Varnum v. Nu-Car Carriers, ___ F.2d ___, 123 L.R.R.M. (BNA) 3068 (11th Cir. 1986) (no § 301 preemption of fraud claim because based on pre-employment conduct); Johnson v. Hussman Corp., ___ F.2d ___, 123 L.R.R.M. (BNA) 3074 (8th Cir. 1986) (workers compensation retaliation claim preempted becaused depends on analysis of collective agreement); Truex v. Garrett Freightlines, Inc., 784 F.2d 1347 (9th Cir. 1985) (state tort claims for harassment and intentional infliction of emotional distress preempted because alleged employer conduct related to interpretation and administration of collective bargaining agreement); Bale v. General Tel. Co., 795 F.2d 775, 780 (9th Cir. 1986) (tort claims for fraud and negligent misrepresentation preempted because dependent on analysis of terms of collective bargaining agreement); Morris v. Owens-Illinois, 544 F. Supp. 752, 757–58 (S.D. W. Va. 1982) (state tort claim for intentional infliction of emotional distress preempted because dispute essentially related to discharge covered by grievance and arbitration provisions of the collective bargaining agreement); Spielmann v. Anchor Motor Freight, Inc., 551 F. Supp. 817, 826 (S.D.N.Y. 1982) (state claim for emotional distress preempted); Dinger v. Anchor Motor Freight, Inc., 501 F. Supp. 64, 72 (S.D.N.Y. 1980)

Food Stores, Inc.,[60] the Ninth Circuit held that a public policy tort claim for wrongful dismissal was not preempted by the availability of a collectively bargained arbitration provision, even though the plaintiff-employee arbitrated his claim and received an adverse award. The employee, a truck driver, claimed that he was discharged for reporting a shipment of adulterated milk to local health officials after his supervisors ordered him to deliver it. The court found that the state's interests in the health and safety policy involved were the type of state interests recognized as not preempted in *Farmer v. Carpenters Local 25*.[61] It observed that the result might be different if the state claim were premised on an implied covenant or other contractual theory.[62] It concluded that:

> a claim grounded in state law for wrongful termination for public policy reasons poses no significant threat to the collective bargaining process . . . . The remedy is in tort, distinct from any contractual remedy an employee might have under the collective bargaining contract. It furthers the state's interest in protecting the general public—an interest which transcends the employment relationship.[63]

Garibaldi is not as broad as it might seem on first reading. First of all, *Garibaldi* has no application at all to a state claim based on breach of an implied contract rather than public policy tort.[64] Second, in *Buscemi v. McDonnell Douglas Corp.*,[65] a different panel of the same court reached an apparently contrary result without any serious discussion of *Garibaldi*. It affirmed the district court's conclusions (1) that the state claim really was one for violation of the collective agreement and therefore that arbitration was the exclusive remedy; and (2) that the state claim, based on retaliation for passing out petitions and voicing coemployee complaints, was within the exclusive jurisdiction of the NLRB. The apparent conflict between *Garibaldi* and *Buscemi* can be reconciled because Buscemi's claim seemed to invoke no state policy other than the policy incorporated in § 7 of the NLRA.

Similarly, in *Olguin v. Inspiration Consolidated Copper Co.*,[66] Judge Wisdom, writing for the panel, held that a state public policy tort claim was preempted by

---

(tort claim for intentional infliction of emotional distress barred because it represented an attempt to sidestep the collectively bargained grievance and arbitration machinery); Fisher v. Illinois Office Supply Co., 130 Ill. App. 3d 996, 474 N.E. 2d 1263, 1266 (1984) (letter prepared for use in grievance procedure not absolutely privileged under preemption doctrine; common law conditional privilege applied in employee's defamation action); Embry v. Pacific Stationery & Printing Co., 62 Or. App. 113, 659 P.2d 436 (1983) (no exception to grievance procedure exhaustion requirement for public policy torts).

[60] 726 F.2d 1367 (9th Cir. 1984), *cert. denied,* 471 U.S. 1099 (1985).

[61] 430 U.S. 290 (1977).

[62] 726 F.2d at 1374.

[63] *Id.* at 1375.

[64] *See* Williams v. Caterpillar Tractor Co., 786 F.2d 928, 933 n.3 (9th Cir. 1986) (distinguishing *Garibaldi* in breach of implied contract case), *cert. granted,* ____ U.S. ____, No. 86-526 (Nov. 17, 1986).

[65] 736 F.2d 1348 (9th Cir. 1984).

[66] 740 F.2d 1468 (9th Cir. 1984).

federal labor law favoring arbitration. The employee claimed he was fired for complaining about mine safety conditions and engaging in concerted labor activity. Judge Wisdom distinguished *Garibaldi* because the tort claim in *Garibaldi* was premised on the state's interest in enforcing local health regulations, while the plaintiff in *Olguin* premised his tort claim only on two federal statutes that contained their own remedial mechanisms.[67] Similarly, in *Moore v. General Motors Corp.*,[68] the court of appeals held that an employee's state common law claim for fraudulent misrepresentation was preempted by federal law because the underlying rights supporting the claim were based on the collective bargaining agreement.

§ 2.30 — Preemption of Contract Claims under § 301 of the Labor Management Relations Act

Employees covered by collective bargaining agreements generally may not make individual contracts of employment because of the potential for conflict with collective bargaining.[69] This means that an implied-in-fact contract promising employment security is precluded by an applicable collective bargaining agreement, and hence that a common law claim for breach of an implied contract is preempted by § 301 of the LMRA,[70] which provides for enforcement of collective bargaining agreements. The preemption of state law is so complete under § 301 that preempted state law actions brought in state court may be removed to federal court, despite the general rule against preemption removal.[71]

Employees covered by collective bargaining agreements may be promoted to supervisory positions outside the unit of employees covered by the collective agreement. When that happens, the employee may bring a common law action on his individual contract of employment if adjudicating the common law claim does not require the court to interpret the collective agreement.[72]

---

[67] *Id.* at 1475.

[68] 739 F.2d 311 (8th Cir. 1984).

[69] J.I. Case Co. v. NLRB, 321 U.S. 332, 337 (1944); Malia v. RCA Corp., 794 F.2d 909, 912 (3d Cir. 1986) (stating general principle but finding no preemption).

[70] 29 U.S.C. § 185 (1982).

[71] *See* Williams v. Caterpillar Tractor Co., 786 F.2d 928, 932 (9th Cir. 1986) (finding no preemption because alleged implied contract arose when employee was not covered by collective agreement). *See also* Bartley v. University Asphalt Co., Inc., 111 Ill. 2d 318, 330, 489 N.E.2d 1367, 1372 (1986) (civil conspiracy suit against union growing out of termination for cooperating with FBI investigation of union and employer preempted by § 301 of LMRA).

[72] *See* Malia v. RCA Corp., 794 F.2d 909, 912 (3d Cir. 1986) (employee claiming breach of promise that he could return from supervisory position into bargaining unit could maintain common law claim) (split panel).

§ 2.31 —Preemption of Common Law Claims under the Railway Labor Act

Railroad and airline employees are covered by the Railway Labor Act (RLA)[73] rather than by the National Labor Relations Act (NLRA).[74] The RLA contains no unfair labor practice provisions, but it does contain statutory grievance resolution procedures.[75] After a period during which dismissed employees covered by the RLA could elect between statutory arbitration remedies and common law actions for wrongful dismissal,[76] the Supreme Court decided, in *Andrews v. Louisville & Nashville Railroad*,[77] that common law actions for wrongful dismissals, based on the collective bargaining agreement, are preempted by the RLA.[78]

Preemption is less certain, however, with respect to common law tort actions or statutory claims growing out of a dismissal.[79] A common law breach of contract claim involves a controversy squarely within the jurisdiction of the statutory grievance forum; a common law tort claim, though arising out of a discharge, might involve operative facts and legal theories different from the claim cognizable in the grievance forum. If the employee could make such a showing with respect to his tort claim, it should not be preempted.[80] A tort claim for mental distress, unrelated to interpretation of the collective bargaining agreement, is not within the exclusive jurisdiction of an RLA adjustment board.[81] Nor, as Judge Posner

---

[73] 45 U.S.C. §§ 151–164, 181–188 (1982).

[74] 29 U.S.C. §§ 151–168 (1982).

[75] 45 U.S.C. § 153 (1982).

[76] Moore v. Illinois Cent. R.R., 312 U.S. 630 (1941).

[77] 406 U.S. 320 (1972) (overruling *Moore*).

[78] *Id.* at 323–24. *See* Woolridge v. National R.R. Passenger Corp., 800 F.2d 647 (7th Cir. 1986) (breach of contract and implied covenant claims preempted); Hodges v. Atchison, T. & S.F. Ry., 728 F.2d 414, 417 (10th Cir.), *cert. denied*, 469 U.S. 822 (1984) (Railway Labor Act precludes suit as third party beneficiary of nondiscrimination contract between employer and government).

[79] *See, e.g.*, Beers v. Southern Pac. Transp. Co., 703 F.2d 425 (9th Cir. 1983) (emotional distress claim preempted).

[80] *Id.* at 428. *But see* Jackson v. Consolidated Rail Corp., 717 F.2d 1045 (7th Cir. 1983) (state tort remedy for discharge in retaliation for filing FELA claim preempted by Railway Labor Act); Majors v. United States Air, 544 F. Supp. 752 (D. Md. 1982) (employee tort action for false imprisonment and defamation preempted by RLA's broad grievance arbitration scheme); Cummings v. National R.R. Passenger Corp., 343 Pa. Super. 137, 148, 494 A.2d 393, 396 (1985) (state claims for breach of allegedly separate employment contracts not justiciable by state court; RLA adjustment board has exclusive jurisdiction).

[81] *See* Buell v. Atchison, T. & S.F. Ry., 771 F.2d 1320, 1323 (9th Cir. 1985) (reversing district court and permitting claim for mental distress resulting from supervisory harassment to proceed under Federal Employers' Liability Act); Peterson v. Air Line Pilots' Ass'n, 759 F.2d 1161, 1170 (4th Cir. 1985) (state claim for intentional interference with contract preempted by Railway Labor Act; essentially identical to fair representation claim against union for forcing discharge

put it, would a battery claim be preempted even though it grew out of an altercation between an RLA employee and his or her supervisor.[82]

Similarly, statutory claims may not be preempted by the RLA if they do not involve interpretation or application of a collective agreement.[83]

§ 2.32 —Preemption under Discrimination Statutes

State common law actions seeking damages or other relief for conduct that violates federal antidiscrimination statutes are not preempted. Title VII of the Civil Rights Act of 1964[84] supplements whatever other relief may exist under federal or state law.[85] Nevertheless, questions of primary jurisdiction are likely to arise when a plaintiff seeks to premise a public policy tort action for wrongful discharge on the policy contained in a state or federal antidiscrimination statute.[86] It is important to note, however, that Title VII preempts state laws that are inconsistent with it because they *require* discrimination.[87]

A second civil rights statute, 42 U.S.C. § 1985, has similarly been interpreted not to preempt state law remedies.[88]

---

by carrier). *See generally* Lewy v. Southern Pac. Transp. Co., 799 F.2d 1281, 1290-91 (9th Cir. 1986) (surveying RLA discharge preemption cases).

[82] Jackson v. Consolidated Rail Corp., 717 F.2d 1045, 1059 (7th Cir. 1983) (Posner, J., dissenting). *But cf.* Graf v. Elgin, J. & E. Ry., 790 F.2d 1341, 1345-46 (7th Cir. 1986) (Posner, J.) (federal court decides whether state tort claim is preempted) (finding tort claim premised on federal liability statute preempted).

[83] *But see* Stephens v. Norfolk & W. Ry., 792 F.2d 576, 581 (6th Cir. 1986) (finding claim based on state handicap discrimination statute preempted by RLA; collective agreement established physical qualifications); Flight Attendants v. Pan Am. World Airways, Inc., 789 F.2d 139 (2d Cir. 1986) (claim of suspension in violation of RLA duty to negotiate with union within exclusive jurisdiction of adjustment board).

[84] 42 U.S.C. § 2000e-7 (1982).

[85] *See* Frazier v. Colonial Williamsburg Found., 574 F. Supp. 318 (E.D. Va. 1983) (state implied contract claim for wrongful dismissal not preempted by Title VII). *Cf.* Johnson v. Railway Express, 421 U.S. 454, 459 (1975); Alexander v. Gardner Denver, 415 U.S. 36, 48 (1974).

[86] See §§ **5.8-5.19** for a discussion of the public policy tort concept. Implying a federal private right of action from a federal statute is discussed in § **2.26**. Rice v. United Ins. Co., 465 So. 2d 1100, 1102 (Ala. 1984) (Title VII does not displace tort claim for intentional infliction of emotional distress).

[87] *See* Hays v. Potlatch Forests, Inc., 465 F.2d 1081, 1082 (8th Cir. 1972) (tortured construction of state overtime pay statute to avoid conflict with federal sex discrimination law); California Fed. Sav. & Loan Ass'n v. Guerra, 758 F.2d 390, 396 (9th Cir. 1985) (California statute requiring employers to grant four months' pregnancy leave not sexually discriminatory; not preempted by Title VII), *aff'd*, ___ U.S. ___, 55 U.S.L.W. 4077 (Jan. 13, 1987).

[88] Jackson v. Cox, 540 F.2d 209, 210 (5th Cir. 1976); Holland v. Beto, 309 F. Supp. 785 (S.D. Tex. 1970) (prisoner rights).

§ 2.32 PREEMPTION—DISCRIMINATION STATUTES

A third civil rights statute, 42 U.S.C. § 1981, also does not preempt state remedies. The coexistence of § 1981 with state laws is illustrated by *Neulist v. County of Nassau*,[89] in which the court noted:

> One of the purposes underlying [§ 1981] was "to provide a remedy in the federal courts supplementary to any remedy any state might have." [citing McNeese v. Board of Education, 373 U.S. 668, 672 (1963)] We believe that a common law action for malicious prosecution brought in this state may co-exist with a pending Federal Civil Rights Action based upon the same facts.[90]

Finally, a fourth statute, the Age Discrimination in Employment Act (ADEA),[91] does not preempt state common law causes of action.[92] Section 623(a) of the ADEA states, "Nothing in this chapter shall affect the jurisdiction of any agency of any state performing like functions with regard to discriminatory employment practices on account of age except that upon commencement of action under this chapter such action shall supersede any state action."[93]

In addition, "the ADEA permits concurrent rather than sequential state and federal administrative jurisdiction in order to expedite the processing of age discrimination claims . . . . The purpose of expeditious disposition would not be frustrated were ADEA claimants required to pursue state and federal administrative remedies simultaneously."[94]

It is apparent that a plaintiff may elect to pursue remedies under state statutes or common law for conduct that also might entitle the plaintiff to remedies available under federal antidiscrimination statutes. Thus, although preemption is not likely to be a serious problem for a wrongful dismissal plaintiff who claims discrimination for which there is a statutory remedy, election of remedies and associated res judicata problems should be considered.[95] Moreover, a plaintiff who gets complete relief in a common law action or under a federal statute would be precluded, on the grounds of mootness,[96] from asserting the same claim again in another forum. A plaintiff who gets partial relief may be prevented from seeking

---

[89] 50 A.D.2d 803, 375 N.Y.S.2d 402 (1975).

[90] *Id.* at 804, 375 N.Y.S.2d at 403.

[91] 29 U.S.C. § 623 (1982).

[92] Cancellier v. Federated Dep't Stores, 672 F.2d 1312, 1318 (9th Cir. 1982). The structure of the ADEA indicates congressional intent not to preempt state statutory claims because of the deferral procedure. See § 2.6. Wolber v. Service Corp., 612 F. Supp. 235, 237 (D. Nev. 1985) (refusing to dismiss pendent state public policy tort claim in action under ADEA).

[93] 29 U.S.C. § 623(a) (1982).

[94] Oscar Mayer v. Evans, 441 U.S. 750, 757 (1979).

[95] See § 2.38 on issues involving common law and statutory claims growing out of the same dismissal, and §§ 7.29–7.35 on res judicata. *See* B. Schlei & P. Grossman, Employment Discrimination, ch. 29 at 1073–1091 (Election and Exhaustion of Remedies) (1983).

[96] Mootness is a judicially developed doctrine. *See* B. Schlei & P. Grossman, Employment Discrimination at 1074 n.11, and accompanying text (citing cases).

additional relief on the same claim in a different forum by the doctrine of merger.[97] A plaintiff who loses may encounter the doctrine of bar[98] and be precluded from litigating the same claim again in a different forum. In addition, courts are reluctant to permit public policy tort causes of action to be derived from statutes providing their own remedies.[99]

The Ninth Circuit has held that state courts lack jurisdiction over Title VII cases.[1]

§ 2.33 — Preemption under Federal Whistleblower Statutes

Several federal statutes explicitly prohibit adverse action against employees because they assert rights under, or report violations of, the statutes.[2] Most of these statutes authorize an administrative agency to prosecute violations, and therefore the rationale exists for finding that state public policy tort claims based on the statutes are preempted. In *Wheeler v. Caterpillar Tractor Co.*,[3] however, the Illinois Supreme Court concluded that the whistleblower provisions of the Energy Reorganization Act[4] did not preempt a state public policy tort based on a dismissal for refusal to work with allegedly unsafe nuclear equipment. The court reasoned that Congress meant to leave open the possibility of punitive damages under state law, applying *Silkwood v. Kerr-McGee Corp.*[5]

Similarly, in *Kilpatrick v. Delaware County Society for Prevention of Cruelty*,[6] the district court held that the retaliatory dismissal provisions of the Occupational Safety and Health Act do not preempt a state public policy tort claim based on the federal Act.

---

[97] The case law is not entirely clear whether the doctrine of merger precludes subsequent resort to federal forums by a discrimination victim who has obtained partial relief in a state forum. *See id.* at 1083 n.20 (citing cases), 1089.

[98] *See* Kremer v. Chemical Constr. Co., 456 U.S. 461 (1982) (Title VII claim barred by state court judgment rejecting state statutory discrimination claim arising from same conduct). In Allen v. Greenville County, 712 F.2d 934 (4th Cir. 1983), the Fourth Circuit held that a claim of discriminatory contract termination under 42 U.S.C. §§ 1981 and 1983 was barred by a judgment in a state common law breach of contract suit. The discrimination claim was not raised in the state litigation though it could have been.

[99] *See* § **5.9**, citing cases.

[1] Valenzuela v. Kraft, Inc., 739 F.2d 434, 435 (9th Cir. 1984) (lack of jurisdiction by state court means federal court lacks removal jurisdiction).

[2] *See* §§ **2.15–2.24**.

[3] 108 Ill. 2d 502, 485 N.E.2d 372 (1985), *cert. denied*, 106 S. Ct. 1641 (1986).

[4] *See* § **2.24**.

[5] 464 U.S. 238 (1984).

[6] 632 F. Supp. 542 (E.D. Pa. 1986).

A majority rule is emerging that the availability of administrative relief under federal statutes militates against implying a cause of action under the statute[7] or permitting public policy tort claims based on the statute, but that congressional intent does not require preemption of state causes of action.

§ 2.34 —Preemption under Other Federal Statutes

Other statutes preempt state wrongful dismissal claims under analytical principles similar to those used for NLRA, RLA, and discrimination preemption cases. Public policy tort claims based on ERISA's prohibition against dismissing employees to deprive them of pension or welfare plan benefits[8] apparently are preempted.[9] Cases involving other statutes reach the same result.[10]

§ 2.35 Pendent State Claims

Under the doctrine of *Hurn v. Oursler*,[11] state common law claims arising out of the same transaction as a federal claim may be litigated by the federal court having jurisdiction over the federal claim.[12] In *Gibbs v. United Mine Workers*,[13] this pendent jurisdiction doctrine was expanded to enable the federal court to exercise jurisdiction over state law claims whenever the state and federal claims "derive from a common nucleus of operative fact" and are such that a plaintiff "would ordinarily be expected to try them all in one judicial proceeding."[14] Although the federal courts have the power to hear the state claims[15] under these circumstances, pendent jurisdiction is a doctrine of discretion, not of right.[16] The discretion is to be exercised by the federal courts, not by the states, however.[17]

---

[7] See § **2.26**.

[8] 29 U.S.C. § 1140 (1982).

[9] *See* Baker v. Kaiser Aluminum & Chem. Corp., 608 F. Supp. 1315, 1318 (N.D. Cal. 1984); Authier v. Ginsberg, 757 F.2d 796, 800 (6th Cir. 1985) (ERISA preempts state public tort claim by plan fiduciary dismissed for inquiries to attorney).

[10] *See* LeSassier v. Chevron USA, Inc., 776 F.2d 506, 510 (5th Cir. 1985) (retaliatory discharge provision of Longshoremen's and Harbor Workers' Compensation Act preempts state remedy).

[11] 289 U.S. 238 (1933). *See generally* C. Wright, Handbook of Law of the Federal Courts § 19 at 73–76 (1976); Shepard's Manual of Federal Practice §§ 1.109–1.110 (1979 and Supp. 1982).

[12] Hurn v. Oursler, 289 U.S. at 246.

[13] 383 U.S. 715 (1966).

[14] *Id.* at 725.

[15] *Id.*

[16] *Id.* at 726.

[17] *See* Thompkins v. Stuttgart School Dist. No. 22, 787 F.2d 439, 441 (8th Cir. 1986) (federal court has pendent jurisdiction despite state statute purporting to vest state courts with exclusive jurisdiction).

The test for pendent jurisdiction requires a two-step determination: first, whether the court has the power to hear the state law claims;[18] and second, whether the court in its discretion should hear them. The court's discretion is influenced by a number of factors. The principal justification of the doctrine "lies in considerations of judicial economy, convenience and fairness to litigants; if these are not present a federal court should hesitate to exercise jurisdiction over state claims . . . ."[19] If state issues clearly predominate, the state issues should be dismissed without prejudice.[20] The same result obtains from application of the *abstention* doctrine.[21] Federal courts are reluctant to hear unsettled questions of state law in exercising their pendent jurisdiction.[22] This is probably the most important barrier to wrongful dismissal plaintiffs' desiring their state claims to be heard in federal court.

The doctrine of pendent jurisdiction allows a wrongful dismissal plaintiff with a claim that gives rise to federal question jurisdiction to have the federal court try related state common law claims.[23] Federal courts may be especially reluctant to try pendent claims when federal question jurisdiction is based on Title VII of the Civil Rights Act of 1964.[24] In *Jong-Yul Lim v. International Institute of Metropolitan Detroit*,[25] the plaintiff alleged a Title VII claim and a state common law claim premised on breach of contract.[26] The plaintiff sought both legal and equitable relief,[27] with legal relief available only under the state claims.[28] The

---

[18] The federal court has the power to hear the pendent claim if the federal issues are substantial and if the state and federal claims derive from a common nucleus of operative fact, such that the plaintiff ordinarily would be expected to try all the claims in one judicial proceeding. Phillips v. Smalley Maintenance Serv., Inc., 711 F.2d 1524, 1531 n.4 (11th Cir. 1983) (quoting *Gibbs*).

[19] *Id.*

[20] *Id.* Dismissal *without prejudice* means that the plaintiff is free to pursue the claims independently in state court.

[21] *See* DeHorney v. Bank of Am., 777 F.2d 440, 445 (9th Cir. 1985), *withdrawn & stayed by* 784 F.2d 339 (9th Cir. 1986) (pending decision of California Supreme Court in Foley v. Interactive Data Corp., *petition for review granted*, ___ Cal. 3d ___, 712 P.2d 891, 222 Cal. Rptr. 740 (1986)) (federal court properly refused to abstain deciding state common law questions in employee dismissal case).

[22] *See* Thibodeau v. Foremost Ins. Co., 605 F. Supp. 653, 661 (N.D. Ind. 1985) (pendent state claims presenting unresolved questions of state law on implied-in-fact-contract and public policy tort dismissed from ADEA suit); Borumka v. Rocky Mountain Hosp. & Medical Serv., 599 F. Supp. 857, 859 (D. Colo. 1984) (pendent jurisdiction not exercised over state public policy tort claims based on state discrimination statute in ADEA case).

[23] Frequently, when plaintiffs have a federal statutory claim, they also have a factual basis for a common law contract or tort claim, as discussed in **chs. 4** and **5**. In such cases, the plaintiff should plead the state claims in the federal suit as pendent claims.

[24] 42 U.S.C. § 2000e-5(f)(3) (1982).

[25] 510 F. Supp. 722 (E.D. Mich. 1981).

[26] *Id.* at 723.

[27] *Id.*

[28] *Id.*

§ 2.35 PENDENT CLAIMS 111

court, recognizing that Title VII permits only equitable relief and specifically excludes jury trials,[29] stated, "The limited grant of relief under Title VII is an indication of congressional intent to negate the exercise of pendent jurisdiction over the plaintiff's state law claims."[30] The court held that exercising pendent jurisdiction in the circumstances before it would thwart the congressional mandate of adjudicating Title VII claims in an expedited manner:[31] the rationale for exclusion of jury trials.

An indication of judicial uncertainty in the area of pendent jurisdiction is shown by *Hall v. Board of Commissioners.*[32] In *Hall,* the plaintiff alleged a Title VII claim and a state common law claim for breach of an employment contract.[33] The plaintiff alleged she was fired for circulating a proposed affirmative action plan for the county.[34] She also alleged the discharge was a result of sex discrimination and discrimination based on a physical disability.[35] The court held that the federal and state claims met the *Gibbs* test,[36] stating, "All of plaintiff's claims concern the same historical conduct and time period."[37]

In the hope of receiving a jury trial on all of the claims together, civil rights plaintiffs have always had an incentive to assert pendent jurisdiction over related state claims. The Supreme Court's decision in *Kremer v. Chemical Construction Co.*[38] gives a Title VII claimant an additional incentive to assert pendent jurisdiction over state claims. In *Kremer,* the Court held that an adverse decision by state courts on a state fair employment practices claim must be given preclusive effect in a subsequent Title VII suit. Therefore, a plaintiff may wish to proceed to federal

---

[29] *Id.* at 725, referring to 42 U.S.C. § 2000e-5(f)(4) (1982).

[30] *Id.* at 725.

[31] *Id.* at 726. *See also* Bouchet v. National Urban League, Inc., 730 F.2d 799, 806 (D.C. Cir. 1984) (affirming refusal to exercise jurisdiction over state claims for defamation and sexual harassment in Title VII sex discrimination suit).

[32] 509 F. Supp. 841 (E.D. Md. 1981).

[33] *Id.* at 849.

[34] *Id.* at 843.

[35] *Id.*

[36] Gibbs v. United Mine Workers, 383 U.S. 715 (1966).

[37] Hall v. Board of Comm'rs, 509 F. Supp. at 850; *see also* Thompkins v. Stuttgart School Dist. No. 22, 787 F.2d 439, 442 (8th Cir. 1986) (presumption against exercise of pendent jurisdiction in Title VII cases because no jury; but same principle inapplicable in § 1981 case); Phillips v. Smalley Maintenance Serv., 711 F.2d 1524 (11th Cir. 1983). In *Phillips,* the appellant claimed the trial court erred in exercising pendent jurisdiction over a plaintiff's state claims of battery and intentional infliction of emotional distress in a Title VII case. The court stated it was unusual for a court to decline to exercise pendent jurisdiction and affirmed the lower court verdict for a discharged plaintiff who claimed sex discrimination was the motivating factor of the discharge. *See also* Medina v. Spotnail, Inc., 591 F. Supp. 190, 195 (N.D. Ill. 1984) (pendent jurisdiction over state claims for defamation, intentional interference with contract, breach of implied contract, and public policy tort exercised in Title VII case).

[38] 456 U.S. 461 (1982).

court after exhausting state administrative remedies rather than proceeding in state court and possibly losing the right to a federal forum.[39]

Plaintiffs with both age discrimination and common law claims have less of an incentive than Title VII plaintiffs to seek pendent jurisdiction in order to get a federal jury trial; they are entitled to a jury trial on their age discrimination claim.[40]

Pendent jurisdiction should be distinguished from an aspect of basic federal question jurisdiction, under which a federal court has jurisdiction where a federal question is an essential part of the plaintiff's state common law claim.[41] This might be the case, for example, if a state tort claim were based on the public policy contained in the federal Constitution or in a federal statute.[42] It is reasonably clear that a state tort claim can be premised on public policy articulated in a federal statute.[43] Using this relationship between the state cause of action and federal substantive law to support federal question jurisdiction would essentially translate a public policy tort question into a question of whether a private right of action should be implied under the federal statute.[44] Broader scope is more likely to be afforded to a state public policy theory than to a federal implied-private-right-of-action theory. Thus, where the state public policy tort claim is premised on federal statutory policy, the plaintiff may wish to file in state court, and the defendant may wish to remove to federal court.

§ 2.36 Unemployment Compensation Generally

A dismissed employee, under the appropriate state unemployment compensation law, usually can obtain unemployment compensation benefits if the dismissal was

---

[39] *See* Thomas v. Kroger Co., 583 F. Supp. 1031, 1036 (S.D. W. Va. 1984) (28 U.S.C. § 1445(c) bars removal of workers' compensation retaliation action); Roberts v. Citicorp Diners Club, Inc., 597 F. Supp. 311, 315 (D. Md. 1984) (remanding workers' compensation retaliation claim; removal jurisdiction barred by 28 U.S.C. § 1445(c)).

[40] See § 2.6.

[41] *Compare* Smith v. Kansas City Title & Trust Co., 255 U.S. 180 (1921) (federal question jurisdiction exists) *with* Gully v. First Nat'l Bank, 299 U.S. 109 (1936) (no federal jurisdiction). See § 2.26; *see generally* C. Wright, Handbook of Federal Courts § 17 (1976).

[42] *But see* Buethe v. Britt Airlines, Inc., 749 F.2d 1235, 1239–40 (7th Cir. 1984) (possibility that dismissal of copilot for insisting on compliance with FAA regulations would involve questions of federal law not enough to create federal question jurisdiction, or to justify pendent jurisdiction where state law question was one of first impression), *later appeal,* 787 F.2d 1194 (7th Cir. 1986) (Indiana public policy tort law does not protect airline copilot for refusing to fly aircraft he believed to violate FAA requirements).

[43] *See, e.g.,* Sheets v. Teddy's Frosted Foods, Inc., 179 Conn. 471, 427 A.2d 385 (1980) (claim based partially on OSHA); Adler v. American Standard Corp., 538 F. Supp. 572 (D. Md. 1982) (plaintiff may rely on federal law for source of public policy to support state tort claim); see generally §§ 5.8–5.19.

[44] See § 2.26.

for any reason *other* than misconduct connected with work.[45] Misconduct in the unemployment compensation context has been defined as "an act of wanton or willful disregard of the employer's interests or of the employee's duties and obligations to the employer."[46] This and the next section examine state determinations of a discharged employee's eligibility for unemployment compensation. The preclusive effect[47] of these determinations in a subsequent suit for wrongful discharge by the employee is considered in § 7.35.

Unemployment compensation is the ultimate system of no-fault employment dismissal legislation. Terminated employees are entitled to receive modest economic relief to ease the burden of losing their jobs. Only those dismissed because of egregious fault are denied relief. The adjudications required to administer the system are relatively simple. Accordingly, unemployment compensation is interesting not only because of its potential preclusive effect on subsequent wrongful dismissal litigation, but also because it can serve as a model of wrongful dismissal legislation.[48]

Eligibility for unemployment compensation benefits is defined by state and federal law under the cooperative state-federal system.[49] Generally, the claimant's unemployment must be involuntary in order for him to collect benefits, but it cannot have been caused by the claimant's misconduct.[50]

§ 2.37 —Procedures for Determining Eligibility for Unemployment Benefits

Federal law,[51] like most state statutes,[52] requires that claimants have an opportunity for a fair hearing to dispute the denial of benefits, but does not prescribe

---

[45] Staff of Sen. Comm. on Finance, 94th Cong., 2d Sess., Staff Data and Materials on Unemployment Compensation Amendments of 1976 (H.R. 10,210) 12. *See generally* 76 Am. Jur. 2d *Unemployment Compensation* §§ 52–58 (1975) (misconduct as ground for denial of benefits).

[46] Gunderman v. Pennsylvania Unemployment Compensation Bd. of Review, ___ Pa. Commw. ___, 505 A.2d 1112, 1114 (1986).

[47] The term *preclusive effect* encompasses the concepts of merger, bar, direct and collateral estoppel. *See* Restatement (Second) of Judgments, introductory note to ch. 3 (1982).

[48] See generally § **9.30**.

[49] Social Security Act §§ 301–303, 42 U.S.C. §§ 501–504; Act, §§ 901–908, 42 U.S.C. §§ 1101–1108 (1982). For a detailed history of the federal and state statutes, *see* Witte, *Development of Unemployment Compensation,* 55 Yale L.J. 21 (1945). Every state has an unemployment compensation statute, enabling state employers to receive a 90 percent tax credit on the federal unemployment tax. 1B Unempl. Ins. Rep. (CCH) ¶ 1020 (Sept. 22, 1980).

[50] Federal Unemployment Tax Act, 26 U.S.C. § 3304(a)(10) (1982).

[51] 42 U.S.C. § 503(a)(3) (1982).

[52] *E.g.* Miss. Code Ann. § 71-5-19 (1972) (affording parties reasonable opportunity for fair hearing where the rules of evidence will be strictly followed); Cal. Unemp. Ins. Code § 1334 (West 1982); N.J. Stat. Ann. § 43:21-6(f) (West 1982) (rules for deciding claims and appeals to be prescribed by board of review).

the procedures for the fair hearings. Typical state procedural provisions[53] require the employee to file a claim with the appropriate agency[54] and require the agency to evaluate the claim promptly[55] and to notify both the employer and the claimant of the claimant's eligibility.[56] If either party appeals the determination, the agency sets a hearing date and takes evidence on the circumstances of the unemployment.[57] Since it is to the employer's detriment[58] for the claim to be granted, there is ample incentive for the employer to attempt to disqualify the claimant.

If either side is dissatisfied with the second determination, about half the states provide for a further appeal to a review board.[59] These boards can administer oaths, subpoena witnesses and documents, and take depositions.[60] Where there is no further administrative appeal, the case can be appealed to state court in every state.[61] In most states, the reviewing court must affirm the administrative decision if it is supported by evidence and is not erroneous as a matter of law.[62]

---

[53] *See, e.g.,* Miss. Code Ann. §§ 71-5-517 to -533 (1972); Cal. Unemp. Ins. Code §§ 1326–1332 (1972 and West Supp. 1983); Ill. Ann. Stat. ch. 48, paras. 450–520 (Smith-Hurd Supp. 1983); N.J. Stat. Ann. § 43:21-6 (West Supp. 1983).

[54] *See, e.g.,* Miss. Code Ann. § 71-5-515 (1972); Cal. Unemp. Ins. Code § 1326 (West 1972); Ill. Ann. Stat. ch. 48, para. 450 (Smith-Hurd 1966); N.J. Stat. Ann. § 43:21-6(a) (West Supp. 1983).

[55] *See, e.g.,* Miss. Code Ann. § 71-5-517 (Supp. 1983); Cal. Unemp. Ins. Code § 1328 (West 1972); Ill. Ann. Stat. ch. 48, paras. 451–452 (Smith-Hurd Supp. 1983); N.J. Stat. Ann. § 43:21-6(b)(1) (West Supp. 1983).

[56] *See, e.g.,* Miss. Code Ann. § 71-5-517 (1972); Cal. Unemp. Ins. Code § 1328 (West 1972); Ill. Ann. Stat. ch. 48, paras. 451–452 (Smith-Hurd 1966); N.J. Stat. Ann. § 43:21-6(b)(1) (West Supp. 1983).

[57] *See, e.g.,* Miss. Code Ann. §§ 71-5-517, -519, -521 (1972); Cal. Unemp. Ins. Code § 1334 (West 1972) (providing for a fair hearing); Ill. Ann. Stat. ch. 48, para. 471 (Smith-Hurd Supp. 1983); N.J. Stat. Ann. § 43:21-6(c) (West Supp. 1983) (no specific provision for taking of evidence); *see also* N.J. Admin. Code tit. 12, § 16-10.4 (1976) (detailed hearing procedure to be followed by hearing examiner).

[58] The amount the employer pays into the state's unemployment compensation system is determined in part by how many of the employer's ex-employees are awarded compensation. 1B Unempl. Ins. Rep. (CCH) ¶ 1120 (Sept. 16, 1982).

[59] *Id.* ¶ 2020 (Feb. 24, 1976).

[60] *Id. See* Miss. Code Ann. § 71-5-527 (1972) (does not specifically confer powers, but code provides for payments of witness fees to those subpoenaed); Cal. Unemp. Ins. Code § 1953 (West 1972); Ill. Ann. Stat. ch. 48, para. 500, 503 (Smith-Hurd 1966) (permits claims adjudicator, as well as appeals referee, to administer oaths, subpoena witnesses and documents, and take depositions); N.J. Stat. Ann. § 43:21-6 (West Supp. 1983) (no mention of powers); *but see* N.J. Admin. Code tit. 12, § 16-10.5 (1976) (hearing officer has power to issue subpoenas, compel attendance of witnesses and production of documents, may administer oaths, examine, and cross-examine witnesses).

[61] 1B Unempl. Ins. Rep. (CCH) ¶ 2020 at 4544 (Feb. 24, 1976).

[62] *Id.*

§ 2.38 Considerations in Pursuing Both Statutory and Common Law Relief

Frequently, a dismissal will give rise to possible statutory claims discussed in this chapter as well as common law claims discussed in **Chapters 4** and **5**. When this happens, counsel for the dismissed employee must decide whether to pursue all claims in the same legal proceeding, if possible, or whether to pursue two or more claims in parallel proceedings. The problem is complicated if the employee also is covered by a collective bargaining agreement and has a possible claim under it.[63]

The range of choices is narrowed by time limits and exhaustion requirements accompanying statutory and collectively bargained rights. Race, sex, religious, and national origin claims under Title VII of the Civil Rights Act must be filed with the EEOC within 180 days after the allegedly discriminatory action.[64] Claims of age discrimination under the ADEA must be filed with the EEOC within 180 days.[65] One hundred eighty days after a Title VII claim is filed with the EEOC, the claimant is entitled to a right-to-sue letter from the commission. After receiving such a letter, the claimant must file suit in federal court within 90 days.[66] The ADEA permits a claimant to file suit within 60 days after filing a charge with the EEOC.[67] No right-to-sue letter is required. Limitation periods for the Reconstruction era Civil Rights Acts are determined under state law. Time limits for filing claims under other federal statutes are similarly short. For example, unfair labor practice claims must be filed with the NLRB within six months of the alleged unfair labor practice.[68]

The longest of the time limits for major federal statutes (under Title VII) is one year and three months before suit must be filed in court. Typical limitation periods for common law tort and contract actions are one to six years.[69] This means that an employee with a possible statutory claim must move more quickly to assert the statutory claim than to assert common law claims.

Collective bargaining agreements provide their own time limits—typically short ones—within which grievances must be filed and within which arbitration must be requested if the grievance is denied. Under *Del Costello v. Teamsters*,[70] if an

---

[63] See **ch.3**.

[64] 42 U.S.C. § 2000e-5(e) (1982). The section extends the time limit for EEOC filing to 300 days in deferral states. See **§ 2.3**.

[65] 29 U.S.C. § 626(d) (1982).

[66] 42 U.S.C. § 2000e-5(f) (1982).

[67] 29 U.S.C. § 626(d) (1982).

[68] *Id.* § 160(b) (NLRB lacks jurisdiction over unfair labor practice committed more than six months prior to filing). *See also* Rose v. Secretary of Labor, 800 F.2d 563 (6th Cir. 1986) (applying 30-day deadline under Energy Reorganization Act).

[69] Limitations periods for state common law actions are discussed later in this section.

[70] 462 U.S. 151 (1983).

employee wishes to challenge the handling of a grievance on an unfair representation theory, a claim must be filed within six months. Therefore, claims under collective agreements also typically must be pursued more quickly than common law claims.

Statutes of limitation for common law tort actions typically range from one to three years. Determining the limitation period for public policy tort actions requires deciding whether the limitation for injury to intangible personal interests is most appropriate, or whether the limitation for physical injury is more appropriate. Typically, the former limitation period is shorter.[71] Statutes of limitations for common law breach of contract actions are longer than for tort actions. They range from two to six years,[72] with shorter limitation periods sometimes specified for oral, as compared with written, contracts.[73]

These time limits militate in favor of pursuing statutory and collectively bargained claims first, before common law claims are pursued. There are risks, however, in pursuing statutory and collective agreement claims entirely separately from possible common law claims. The predominant risk is that facts would be adjudicated or admitted which would have preclusive or estoppel effect in subsequent common law litigation.[74]

In addition, Title VII claimants are not entitled to a jury trial on their Title VII claims. Those federal statutes prohibiting retaliatory dismissal may not permit de novo judicial trial on the merits at all. Rather, access to the courts may be limited to judicial review of administrative decisions. Therefore, a claimant may wish to pursue associated common law claims as pendent claims to a Title VII or ADEA action, in order to get a jury trial on the basic facts leading to the dismissal.[75]

---

[71] *Compare* Cal. Civ. Proc. Code § 340 (West 1982) (one year for libel, slander, assault); Cal. Civ. Proc. Code § 338 (West 1982) (three years for trespass to chattel, slander of title, false advertising); N.Y. Civ. Prac. L. & R. § 215 (McKinney Supp. 1986) (one year for assault, battery, false imprisonment, slander, libel, violation of right of privacy); 42 Pa. Cons. Stat. Ann. § 5522 (Purdon Supp. 1986) (six months for suit against government); 42 Pa. Cons. Stat. Ann. § 5523 (Purdon Supp. 1986) (one year for libel, slander, invasion of privacy) *with* N.Y. Civ. Prac. L. & R. § 214 (McKinney Supp. 1986) (three years for all other forms of personal injury); 42 Pa. Cons. Stat. Ann. § 5524 (Purdon Supp. 1986) (two years for assault, battery, false imprisonment, malicious prosecution).

[72] *See* N.Y. Civ. Prac. L. & R. § 213 (McKinney Supp. 1986) (six years except as provided by the U.C.C.); 42 Pa. Cons. Stat. Ann. § 5525 (Purdon Supp. 1986) (four years for oral contract); 42 Pa. Cons. Stat. Ann. § 5526 (Purdon Supp. 1986) (five years for contract for sale of property); 42 Pa. Cons. Stat. Ann. § 5527 (Purdon Supp. 1986) (six years for written contract).

[73] *Compare* Cal. Civ. Proc. Code § 339 (West 1982) (two years for oral contract) *with* Cal. Civ. Proc. Code § 337 (West 1982) (four years for written contract).

[74] See §§ **7.29–7.35** regarding preclusion issues such as res judicata and collateral estoppel.

[75] See § **2.35** regarding pendent claims. Federal courts may have limited authority to remand pendent state claims if the federal claim is meritless. *See* Boyle v. Carnegie Mellon Univ., 648 F. Supp. 1318 (W.D. Pa.), *mandamus denied,* No. 85-3619 (3d Cir. 1986).

It probably would be difficult to litigate common law claims in connection with review of administrative determinations on retaliatory dismissal statutes.

The principal economic advantage of statutory claims is that attorneys' fees may be available. This may facilitate obtaining adequate counsel for a claimant who has a relatively modest damages claim.

Obviously, if the dismissed employee prefers a federal to a state forum, it would be desirable to pursue federal statutory claims and accompany them with pendent claims for common law wrongful dismissal. There is some doubt whether state courts have jurisdiction to hear Title VII discrimination claims.[76]

It is important for counsel evaluating a dismissal case to understand statutory, collectively bargained, and common law theories so that intelligent choices can be made with respect to forum selection and timing of multiple claims.

---

[76] See § 2.3.

CHAPTER 3

ARBITRATION

§ 3.1   Introduction
§ 3.2   Development of Arbitration in England
§ 3.3   Development of Labor Arbitration in the United States
§ 3.4   Purpose of Labor Arbitration
§ 3.5   Just Cause Standard: General Principles
§ 3.6   —Poor Performance
§ 3.7   —Misconduct on the Job
§ 3.8   —Misconduct Off the Job
§ 3.9   Typical Grievance and Arbitration Procedure
§ 3.10 The Arbitration Hearing
§ 3.11 —Ex Parte Hearings
§ 3.12 Evidence
§ 3.13 —Availability of Exclusionary and Self-Incrimination Rules
§ 3.14 —Medical Evidence
§ 3.15 —Standard of Proof
§ 3.16 —Compulsory Process
§ 3.17 Form and Content of Arbitration Award
§ 3.18 Remedies in Arbitration Awards
§ 3.19 Arbitration under the Railway Labor Act
§ 3.20 Arbitration and the Courts
§ 3.21 —Federal Common Law of Labor Arbitration
§ 3.22 —Arbitration Statutes
§ 3.23 —Compelling Arbitration
§ 3.24 —Judicial Review and Enforcement of Arbitration Awards
§ 3.25 —The Duty of Fair Representation
§ 3.26 —Damages for Breach of the Duty of Fair Representation
§ 3.27 Effect of Arbitration Awards Deciding Statutory Claims
§ 3.28 Handling a Grievance in Practice
§ 3.29 Defending against a Grievance

§ 3.1 Introduction

Arbitration is the predominant method of resolving wrongful dismissal disputes involving employees covered by collective bargaining agreements. Whether the arbitration forum is available for such disputes depends on the collective bargaining agreement;[1] but more than 90 percent of such agreements provide for arbitration. Typically, such agreements include a prohibition against dismissals without *just cause.* The arbitration tribunal decides whether just cause existed. A considerable body of decisional law has grown up defining the just cause concept.

Federal law developed under § 301 of the Labor Management Relations Act preempts state law, but state courts have concurrent jurisdiction with federal courts to apply this body of common law. Two overriding principles characterize § 301 labor arbitration law. The first is that disputes are presumed to be arbitrable. The second is that arbitration awards will not be invalidated except in extraordinary circumstances. Accordingly, the following principles govern the interaction between federal and state common law when a terminated employee is covered by a collective bargaining agreement:

1. The employee may not maintain a common law action based on breach of contract theories without resorting to arbitration where it is provided[2]
2. The employee may be able to maintain a public policy tort action even though he also has an arbitration remedy[3]
3. An arbitration award is subject to an extremely deferential standard of judicial review[4]
4. An employee may be able (a) to avoid the obligation to arbitrate or (b) to litigate the merits of a wrongful dismissal claim despite an adverse arbitration award if the employee can show a breach of the duty of fair representation owed by the union to all employees in the bargaining unit.[5] Duty of fair representation claims must be brought within six months of the conduct allegedly violating the union's duty.

This chapter considers resolution of employee discharge disputes under collectively bargained grievance and arbitration procedures. After reviewing the development of arbitration, it explains how grievance and arbitration procedures work and the interaction between such contractual procedures and judicial relief. Specific

---

[1] Whether the collective agreement provides for arbitration of a particular dispute is a question to be decided by a court, not by the arbitrator. *See* AT&T Technologies, Inc. v. Communications Workers, ___ U.S. ___, 106 S. Ct. 1415 (1986).

[2] See §§ **2.30, 4.25**.

[3] See §§ **2.29, 5.20**.

[4] See § **3.24**.

[5] See § **3.25**.

attention is given to the development by arbitrators of the concept of just cause for dismissal. This concept serves as a useful basis from which to evaluate alternative standards for deciding common law or statutory actions for wrongful dismissal.

Arbitration, which refers to the settlement of disputes by private decisionmakers, is of two types: *interest* arbitration and *rights* or *grievance* arbitration. Interest arbitration is a process for deciding disputes over new contracts. The interest arbitrator imposes contract terms on the parties.[6] Interest arbitration is rarely used in the private sector.[7] Frequently it is employed as an alternative to strikes in public sector collective bargaining for groups of employees who are not permitted to strike. Rights arbitration, more frequently called grievance arbitration in the United States, is a process for deciding disputes over existing contracts. As such, it is an alternative to breach of contract suits and is commonly used. Nearly all American collective bargaining agreements contain grievance procedures, and most of these terminate with arbitration.[8] Increasingly, this form of arbitration also is becoming popular in the United States as an alternative to judicial trials for a wide variety of disputes.[9]

A further distinction should be made between arbitration, on the one hand, and mediation or conciliation on the other. *Arbitration* refers to a process that results in a decision by a third party. *Mediation* or *conciliation* refers to a process in which a third party confines himself to assisting the parties in resolving their own dispute through negotiation. The distinction was not made early in the development of the processes. The term arbitration was used to refer to what we today would call mediation or conciliation as well as to what we would call arbitration.

§ 3.2 Development of Arbitration in England

Arbitration was recognized as a method of dispute resolution long before trade unions emerged.[10] Reference to arbitration under judicial supervision became

---

[6] *See* International Labour Office, Conciliation and Arbitration Procedures in Labor Disputes 5 (1980). Ordinarily interest arbitration is concerned with impasses arising during the negotiation of new collective bargaining agreements. It can be involved, however, in formulating new terms and conditions of employment during the term of a contract. *See* Bakery Salesmen v. ITT Continental Baking Co., 692 F.2d 29 (6th Cir. 1982) (approving arbitration award compelling change in management policy).

[7] Exceptions are found in newspaper publishing and in the "Experimental Negotiating Agreement" in the basic steel industry, which included interest arbitration beginning in 1974.

[8] P. Prasow & E. Peters, Arbitration and Collective Bargaining at xi (1983).

[9] *See Abstracts for Background Papers,* National Conference on the Lawyer's Changing Role in Resolving Disputes (unpublished manuscript from Harvard Law School conference, Oct. 14-16, 1982); Waxman, *Moving the Apart Together, Alternatives to Litigation,* 7 District Law. 28 (1983).

[10] Kyd on Awards at 4 (1808) (asserting that English rules of arbitration and award originated in the Code of Justinian).

common in England beginning with the reign of Charles II (1660–1685).[11] Finality of awards was strengthened in 1698 when a statute was enacted providing for punishment by contempt of a party refusing to comply with an award entered in arbitration under a voluntary submission.[12]

Arbitration in England evolved as a part of equity procedure in connection with the mode of taking evidence out of the court's presence before trial. It gradually developed an independent existence. There were several reasons why arbitration emerged from equity and became common in seventeenth century England.[13] Equity, unlike the common law courts, was centralized in London. Accordingly, it was desirable to find means of gathering factual proof without forcing nonparty witnesses to come to London. Moreover, only two judges sat in Chancery: the Chancellor himself and the Master of the Rolls.[14] Using written interrogatories framed by the parties, lay citizens were commissioned to conduct secret depositions of witnesses. The evidence thus obtained formed proof upon which the case could be decided.[15]

As the caseload increased, chancellors found it natural to extend the responsibilities of lay commissioners by allowing them to actually resolve the cases in which they were to hear evidence.[16] Such decisions by nonjudges amounted to arbitration. By the middle of the sixteenth century, it was fairly common to commission laypersons to hear and end cases in this manner, by arbitration.[17]

The use of arbitration was favored especially in two types of cases which were thought to be unsuitable for judicial resolution: family conflicts and commercial disputes. Commercial disputes frequently involved complex accounting issues for which special skills were needed. Equity pleading was slow and too complex for speedy resolution of these disputes.[18] At the same time, the attractiveness of arbitration as an alternative to common law resolution of disputes was increased by the simultaneous development of more detailed and restrictive rules of procedure and evidence for the judicial system.[19] Both the Chancery and Privy

---

[11] *Id.* at 21.

[12] *Id.* at 21, 9 & 10 William III c.15 S.1.

[13] *See* J. Dawson, A History of Lay Judges 145–72 (1960).

[14] *Id.* at 171.

[15] *Id.* at 153–54.

[16] *Id.* at 153–64.

[17] *Id.* at 164. Typically, if the referees could not resolve a case, they were to report their proceedings and opinions to the Chancellor. However, it was also common for the Chancellor to compel compliance by the parties with the arbitration proceedings and to induce them to accept the arbitration awards by imposing substantial bonds which would be forfeited in the event of noncompliance. *Id.* at 165.

[18] *Id.* at 166–68. Equity procedure frequently involved multiple hearings and consideration of evidence separately with respect to each pleading. *See* C. Langdell, Equity Pleading at 27–50 (1883) (contrasting equity and common law pleading).

[19] *Compare* Kyd on Awards at 22–23 *with* Kyd at 21.

Council[20] organized arbitration commissions of merchants to deal with merchants' cases.[21]

Arbitration was used to resolve labor disputes at an early time in England.[22] Prosecuted for attempting to organize employees in 1699, the Hatters removed the case from the Lord Mayor's court to the Assizes by writ of certiorari where Lord Chief Justice Holt referred the dispute to arbitration. The arbitration award provided for an increase in rates of pay and termination of legal proceedings.[23]

A 1799 act[24] provided for arbitration of wage disputes. Apparently, the provision never was put into effect because of opposition by management, which claimed the measure tended toward recognition of trade unions and toward fixing of wages.[25]

By the middle of the nineteenth century, according to House of Commons committees in 1856 and 1860, workers in all trades were disposed to support the principle of voluntary submission to arbitration.[26] By 1875, employers regularly participated in boards of conciliation and arbitration.[27]

The English trade union movement strove for arbitration of wage disputes from 1850 to 1876 because an arbitrator's award, although not legally binding, "puts an end to individual bargaining (over wages) and thus excludes, from influence on the terms of employment, the exigencies of particular workmen."[28] Arbitration was employed on 20 separate occasions to settle the conditions of future wage contracts. On every occasion the arbitrator's award was accepted by both employers and employees.[29]

Commentators were not optimistic, however, that either interest or rights arbitration would become prevalent. They thought frequent reference to interest arbitration unlikely because capitalists and workers would not be able to adopt identical assumptions as to the proper basis of wages.[30] The commentators thought rights

---

[20] The Privy Council was the descendant of the medieval King's Council. By the time of the Restoration, it exercised appellate jurisdiction over courts in the Channel Islands, the American colonies, and in India. In addition, it had powers to enforce treaty privileges. Thus it had special concern with merchants involved in foreign trade. T. Plucknett, A Concise History of the Common Law 205–06 (1956). Authority over appeals from the equity courts had passed to the House of Lords shortly after the Restoration. *Id.* at 202.

[21] J. Dawson, A History of Lay Judges 167–68 (1960).

[22] *Arbitration* had a less definite meaning in the labor context than in the judicial context. The word frequently was used to refer to any system of resolving employment disputes on a collective basis.

[23] S. Webb & B. Webb, The History of Trade Unionism 29 (1894).

[24] 40 Geo. III 90.

[25] S. Webb & B. Webb, The History of Trade Unionism 71 (1894).

[26] *Id.* at 227.

[27] *Id.* at 337.

[28] S. Webb & B. Webb, Industrial Democracy 224 (1897).

[29] *Id.* at 232.

[30] *Id.* at 237. *See generally* Fuller, *The Forms and Limits of Adjudication,* 92 Harv. L. Rev. 353 (1978) (explaining that any form of adjudication is ill suited to resolve interest disputes because of the lack of rules of decision).

arbitration would not take root because the "promptitude, technical efficiency, and the expensiveness of an impartial outsider is inferior to the joint meeting of the salaried secretaries [staff officials] of either side."[31] In modern terminology, commentators believed arbitration inferior to collective bargaining.

Despite this pessimistic view about the future of arbitration, recourse to an impartial umpire as conciliator was viewed as a way for collective bargaining to begin in circumstances where both employer and employee representatives mistrusted one another too much to meet bilaterally. Neither side's dignity would be offended by appearing before an eminent person sitting virtually in a judicial capacity. Moreover, it would be regarded as only natural that the arbitrator should ask for each side to present its case in fairly precise terms with statistical support. In such a fashion, collective bargaining would proceed. The result would be a form of conciliation rather than an arbitration award.[32]

Ironically, labor arbitration is not common in England today, because of the availability of statutory remedies for unfair dismissal.[33]

§ 3.3 Development of Labor Arbitration in the United States

In the United States, the distinctions among grievance (rights) arbitration, interest arbitration, conciliation, and collective bargaining emerged relatively recently. At first, *arbitration* was a term used generally for any formal, collective dealing between employers and employees.[34] Thus understood, arbitration was utilized to resolve wage disputes involving Pittsburgh iron puddlers, Massachusetts boot and shoe workers, and coal miners in the anthracite coal fields as early as the 1860s and 1870s.[35] Some, though not all, of these instances involved use of a third party, such as a judge.[36]

Arbitration did not always succeed, but it was favored in many crucial industries as an alternative preferred to strikes.[37] The Congress embraced it for railroad disputes in the 1888 Arbitration Act.[38] By 1900, a group of leaders from industry,

---

[31] S. Webb & B. Webb, Industrial Democracy 238 (1897).

[32] *Id.* at 238–40. *Conciliation* refers to a practice of a third party assisting the disputing parties to reach their own agreement. *Arbitration* refers to a process in which the third party actually decides the case.

[33] See § **9.11**.

[34] Braden, *Arbitration and Arbitration Provisions,* N.Y.U. Second Annual Conference on Labor 355, 356–57 (1949); R. Fleming, The Labor Arbitration Process 1 (1965).

[35] R. Fleming, The Labor Arbitration Process 2 (1965).

[36] *Id.*

[37] *Id.* at 3.

[38] Arbitration Act, 25 Stat. 501 (1888).

labor, and the government were organizing conferences to promote arbitration as a method of ensuring industrial harmony.[39] By 1901, 17 states had enacted statutes establishing *boards of arbitration,* which were really mediation agencies, and the trend continued in the years following.[40]

Arbitration as a separate function emerged with the report of the United States Strike Commission, appointed by President Roosevelt in 1902 to deal with a five-month long anthracite coal strike.[41] The commission recommended the establishment of a permanent bipartite board to resolve disputes.[42] When necessary, an impartial umpire would render a binding decision.[43] This basic concept for an industry-wide arbitration system in anthracite coal production has continued to the present.[44]

However, the distinction between interest arbitration and rights arbitration remained blurred. In the newspaper industry at about the same time, permanent arbitration machinery was established in the early 1900s. The adoption of typesetting machinery in the years before and after 1900 led to industrial unrest.[45] In an effort to reduce strikes, the industry agreed to a two-tier bipartite system of local boards and a national board.[46] If the national board could not agree, a neutral was selected to preside. A majority decision was binding on both sides to the dispute.[47] The newspaper industry is one of the few in which labor and management regularly have used interest arbitration.[48]

---

[39] R. Fleming, The Labor Arbitration Process 3 (1965).

[40] *Id. See* Nolan & Abrams, *American Labor Arbitration: The Early Years,* 35 U. Fla. L. Rev. 373, 389 (1983). Interest arbitration of private sector interest disputes was adopted by the legislatures of Pennsylvania in 1893, of Colorado in 1915, and of Kansas in 1920. J Loewenberg, W. Gershenfeld, H. Glasbeck, B. Heppel & K. Walker, Compulsory Arbitration 145 (1976), citing Pa. Stat. Ann. tit. 43, pp. 721–26 (Purdon 19____); 1915 Colo. Sess. Laws ch. 180; 1920 Kan. Sess. Laws ch. 29. The Pennsylvania compulsory arbitration feature was declared unconstitutional by the state courts in 1909, Wise v. Pressed Steel Car Co., 19 Dist. 112 (1909), and the Kansas statute was declared unconstitutional by the United States Supreme Court in 1923. Chas. Wolff Packing Co. v. Court of Industrial Relations, 262 U.S. 522 (1923); 267 U.S. 552 (1925).

[41] R. Fleming, The Labor Arbitration Process 3 (1965).

[42] *Id.* at 3–4. The recommendation did not distinguish between arbitration of rights disputes and arbitration of interest disputes.

[43] *Id.* at 4.

[44] *Id.*

[45] *Id.* at 5. For an excellent history of union policy during this change, *see* Barrett, *The Introduction of the Linotype, reprinted in* J. Commons, Trade Unionism and Labor Problems 250 (1905).

[46] R. Fleming, The Arbitration Process 6 (1965). *Bipartite* means composed of equal numbers of labor and management representatives.

[47] *Id.*

[48] *See* Milwaukee Newspaper & Graphic Communications Union Local 23 v. Newspapers, Inc., 586 F.2d 19, 21 (7th Cir. 1978) (interest arbitration not a mandatory subject of bargaining); NLRB v. Columbus Printing Pressmen, 543 F.2d 1161, 1166 (5th Cir. 1976) (same); Winston-Salem Printing Press v. Piedmont Publishing Co., 393 F.2d 221 (4th Cir. 1968) (interest arbitration agreement enforceable).

In the New York apparel industry, permanent machinery for conciliation and arbitration was established in 1910 under the guidance of Louis D. Brandeis.[49] The machinery, which collapsed in a strike during 1916, was revived after World War I and eventually spread to the entire industry.[50]

In the 1920s, interest in commercial arbitration stimulated further interest in labor arbitration and focused the meaning of the term more specifically on rights, as opposed to interest, disputes. In addition, a distinction began to emerge more clearly between voluntary, or *contractual* arbitration, and compulsory arbitration, imposed by statute.[51] The emphasis was on contractual arbitration, especially after the United States Supreme Court held a Kansas compulsory arbitration statute to be unconstitutional.[52] The American Arbitration Association was formed in 1926 and was called upon almost immediately by the Actors Equity Association and by other entertainment unions to handle contract disputes.[53]

Legislation covering railroad labor relations set the pattern for federal government action[54] and, by 1926, crystallized the distinction between grievance and interest arbitration. As noted above, arbitration in the broad sense had been a feature of such legislation since 1888.[55] The 1920 Transportation Act,[56] followed by the Railway Labor Act of 1926,[57] distinguished for the first time between grievances and interest disputes.[58] Arbitration was required for grievance disputes.[59] This contributed to a clearer understanding of the appropriate role of labor arbitration.

The National Labor Relations Act,[60] enacted in 1935, was silent on the legal status of arbitration.[61] However, the trend toward wider use of grievance arbitration was accelerated in 1937 when the United Auto Workers and General Motors

---

[49] R. Fleming, The Labor Arbitration Process 7 (1965).

[50] *Id.* at 8.

[51] *Id. at 12.*

[52] Chas. Wolff Packing Co. v. Court of Industrial Relations, 262 U.S. 522, 540-42 (1923), 267 U.S. 552 (1925).

[53] R. Fleming, The Labor Arbitration Process 12 (1965). It is not clear whether the type of arbitration pursued in the entertainment industry was rights or interest arbitration.

[54] *See generally* H. Perritt, Labor Injunctions ch. 2 (1986) (pre-1930 history of government intervention in labor disputes).

[55] The Arbitration Act, 25 Stat. 501 (1888), provided for federally funded voluntary arbitration, and temporary factfinding commissions appointed by the President. It was followed by the Erdman Act of 1898, 30 Stat. 424, and the Newlands Act of 1913, 38 Stat. 103, both of which provided for voluntary arbitration. *See generally* Perritt, *Ask and Ye Shall Receive: The Legislative Response to the Northeast Rail Crisis,* 28 Vill. L. Rev. 271 (1983); Perritt, *Ploughshares into Swords from Buffalo Forge?,* 12 Transp. L.J. 219 (1982).

[56] Ch. 91, 41 Stat. 456 (1920).

[57] Ch. 347, 44 Stat. 577 (1926).

[58] Ch. 347, 44 Stat. 578 (1926).

[59] *Id.*

[60] Ch. 372, 49 Stat. 449.

[61] The NLRA was amended in 1947, among other things, to recognize the usefulness of arbitration. *See* § 203(d), ch. 120, 61 Stat. 154.

reached an agreement that included a grievance procedure, the final step of which was referral of disputes to an impartial umpire.[62]

By 1941, it was estimated that 62 percent of collective agreements contained grievance procedures with arbitration as the final step.[63]

During World War II the National War Labor Board, as a matter of policy, sought to induce labor and management to include grievance arbitration clauses in their contracts.[64] Subsequently, enactment of § 301 of the Labor Management Relations Act in 1947[65] and the Supreme Court's *Textile Workers v. Lincoln Mills*[66] decision in 1957 facilitated the adoption of grievance arbitration as the standard means of resolving disputes in organized industries. Section 301, on its face, merely gave federal courts jurisdiction to hear suits for breach of collective bargaining agreements. The *Textile Workers v. Lincoln Mills* decision permitted the development of a federal common law for application of § 301, which eventually included a strong preference for enforcing collectively bargained arbitration agreements.

Recently, a series of experiments has been conducted with mediation as an alternative to arbitration. In these experiments, the increasingly formal arbitration process is reserved for those rights disputes that cannot be settled through more informal means.[67]

§ 3.4 Purpose of Labor Arbitration

Employees favor union representation to obtain a measure of security in their employment. A union contract which contains both a wage scale and a seniority clause assures the worker that his pay and employment tenure will be decided not by the whim of the employer but by the terms agreed to by both the employer and the employees.

A *grievance,* which may be resolved by arbitration, is an assertion that the collective bargaining agreement has been violated.[68] Grievances may involve disputes over the application of contract language relating to pay rates or seniority or they may involve contractual limitations on disciplinary action taken against an employee. This chapter focuses on disciplinary grievances.

---

[62] R. Fleming, The Labor Arbitration Process 13-14 (1965).

[63] *Id.* at 13.

[64] *Id.* at 15; D. Mills, Government Labor and Inflation 237-41 (1975); Freidin & Ulman, *Arbitration and the War Labor Board,* 58 Harv. L. Rev. 309 (1945).

[65] Ch. 120, 61 Stat. 156, § 203(d) of the Act, 29 U.S.C. § 173(d), states that arbitration is the "desirable method for settlement of disputes arising over the application or interpretation of an existing collective bargaining agreement." This obviously refers only to rights arbitration.

[66] 353 U.S. 448 (1957). See § **3.21** for a discussion of the significance of this case.

[67] *See* Goldberg, *Mediation of Grievances Under a Collective Bargaining Contract: An Alternative to Arbitration,* 77 Nw. U. L. Rev. 270 (1982).

[68] F. Elkouri & E.A. Elkouri, How Arbitration Works 109 (1973).

Grievance and arbitration procedures in collective agreements guarantee that the contractual provisions the parties agreed upon will be enforced, without requiring resort to breach of contract actions in the ordinary courts. Employers generally favor arbitration provisions because they permit peaceful resolution of disputes without strikes.[69] Both parties benefit from the likelihood that arbitrators will develop specialized expertise in the practices of the industry in which the grievances arise.

The usual contractual grievance procedure provides an injured employee the opportunity to have his dispute heard in a swift and relatively inexpensive form by a neutral arbitrator or panel of arbitrators. The union is obligated to represent all employees fairly, with no cost to the employee for an individual grievance.[70]

§ 3.5 Just Cause Standard: General Principles

Most collective bargaining agreements permit an employee to be discharged only for cause or just cause,[71] and if the agreement fails so to state, most arbitrators imply it so as to avoid the danger of sustaining disciplinary action at the employer's whim.[72] Many contracts also contain progressive discipline clauses, which impose a kind of procedural due process requirement of an escalating series of disciplinary steps before discharge may be imposed.[73] Even if progressive discipline is not required explicitly, contracts frequently enumerate cardinal sins for which

---

[69] Strikes over arbitrable grievances may be enjoined. *See* H. Perritt, Labor Injunctions chs. 4, 5 (1986).

[70] See **3.25** for a discussion of the fair representation concept.

[71] For example, the Western States Area Over-the-Road Motor Frieght Supplemental Agreement, art. 46, § 1, between the Teamsters Union and trucking companies provides, "The employer shall not discharge nor suspend any employee without just cause . . . ." Substantive types of just cause are discussed in §§ **3.6–3.8**. Two excellent and current treatises point to arbitration cases dealing with specific types of just cause: F. Elkouri & E. A. Elkouri, How Arbitration Works (1973); J. Redeker, Discipline: Policies and Procedures (1983).

[72] Cameron Iron Works Inc., 25 Lab. Arb. (BNA) 295, 301 (1955) (Boles, Arb.). In Smith v. Kerrville Bus Co., 709 F.2d 914, 919 (5th Cir. 1983), *later appeal,* 748 F.2d 1049 (5th Cir. 1984), the court held that a trial court similarly could imply a just cause requirement from aspects of an employment relationship that suggest job security.

[73] F. Elkouri & E.A. Elkouri, How Arbitration Works 630 (1973). For example, the Western States Area Over-the-Road Motor Freight Supplemental Agreement between the Teamsters Union and trucking companies provides:

> [The employer] . . . in respect to discharge or suspension shall give at least one warning notice of the complaint against such employee to the employee in writing . . . except that no warning notice need be given to an employee before he is suspended or discharged if the cause of such suspension or discharge is (a) dishonesty; (b) drunkenness; (c) recklessness resulting in a serious accident while on duty; (d) the carrying of unauthorized passengers; (e) unprovoked physical assault on a supervisory employee; (f) selling, transporting or use of illegal narcotics while in the employment of the employer; (g) willful, wanton, or malicious damage to the employer's property. Art. 46, § 1.

§ 3.5 JUST CAUSE STANDARD

no prior warning is necessary before an employer can dismiss an employee.[74] From such a prescription, it is easy to draw the inference that employees committing lesser offenses are to be subjected to progressive discipline. Among the most common *cardinal sins* are dishonesty, insubordination, using drugs or drinking alcohol while on duty, fighting, using company vehicles without permission, and possessing firearms on company property. Misconduct of equal magnitude also can result in discharge for cause.[75]

In determining that an employer's discipline of an employee was for cause, the arbitrator usually considers two elements. The arbitrator first must make a factual determination as to whether the employee committed the act alleged and then make the determination as to whether the act committed was of a character to warrant the discipline imposed.[76]

The ultimate penalty that can be assessed for wrongdoing is dismissal.[77] Dismissal is recognized to be the extreme industrial penalty since the employee's job, contractual benefits, and future employability are at stake.[78] In cases of dismissal, the burden almost always is on the employer to prove wrongdoing, and always so when the agreement requires just cause for dismissal. The quantum of required proof, however, is an unsettled issue.[79]

After determining whether the specific offense constitutes just cause for discipline, the arbitrator must then decide whether dismissal was appropriate, as opposed to a lesser penalty. Some arbitrators will not substitute their judgment for that of management unless the penalty is excessive or unreasonable, an abuse of discretion, or a departure from disciplinary procedure.

A set of guidelines was articulated in one case to suggest when the arbitrator should substitute her own judgment for that of the employer. A negative answer to any one or more of the following questions signifies that just cause does not exist.

1. Did the company give to the employee the forewarning or foreknowledge of the possible or probable disciplinary consequences of the employee's conduct?

The pattern of progressive discipline usually is established at each work place. For example, one employer may use a written warning, followed by a one-day suspension, followed by discharge; another may use an oral warning, followed by a three-day suspension, followed by discharge. Some contracts require a preliminary suspension before discharge with a hearing during the suspension period.

[74] *See* the list of causes enumerated in preceding note.

[75] Genuine Parts Co., 79 Lab. Arb. (BNA) 220, 224 (1982) (Reed, Arb.).

[76] Some contracts, such as in basic steel, do not give the arbitrator the authority to modify discipline imposed. If the arbitrator determines that the employee was guilty of the offense alleged, the employer's discipline stands.

[77] Lesser penalties include warnings and suspensions.

[78] Stylemaster, Inc., 79 Lab. Arb. (BNA) 76, 77–78 (1982) (Winton, Arb.).

[79] See §§ **3.12, 3.15**.

2. Was the company's rule reasonably related to (a) the orderly, efficient, and safe operation of the company's business, and (b) the performance that the company might properly expect of the employee?
3. Did the company, before administering discipline to an employee, make an effort to discover whether the employee did in fact violate or disobey a rule or order of management?
4. Was the company's investigation conducted fairly and objectively?
5. At the investigation did the company decisionmaker obtain substantial and compelling evidence or proof that the employee was guilty as charged?
6. Has the company applied its rules, orders, and penalties evenhandedly and without discrimination to all employees?
7. Was the degree of discipline administered by the company in a particular case reasonably related to (a) the seriousness of the employee's proven offense, and (b) the service record of the employee in his service with the company?[80]

Although these guidelines are not followed uniformly, arbitrators usually agree that the inconsistent enforcement of company rules is improper and often set aside discipline upon proof of discriminatory enforcement.[81] Some arbitrators set aside management decisions when the employee was denied due process rights in the investigatory procedure.[82]

Even when management acts only after careful deliberation and in the full light of all the facts and without any evidence of bias, haste, or lack of emotional balance, arbitrators may intervene if the management decision offends the sense of justice of ordinary reasonable persons.[83]

Increasingly, alcoholism and drug abuse are recognized by arbitrators as defenses for offenses that otherwise would warrant dismissal. In such cases, however, reinstatement and back pay usually are contingent on the employee completing a recognized rehabilitation program.[84]

§ 3.6 — Poor Performance

Arbitrators generally permit an employee to be terminated for poor performance, but only if certain prerequisites are met. First, in advance of any termination, the

---

[80] Genuine Parts Co., 79 Lab. Arb. (BNA) 220, 224–25 (1982) (Reed, Arb.); Enterprise Wire Co., 46 Lab. Arb. (BNA) 359, 362–65 (1966) (Daugherty, Arb.).

[81] Akron Beacon Journal Publishing Co., 85 Lab. Arb. (BNA) 314, 317, 318 (1985) (Oberdank, Arb.) (discharge of driver for involvement in fatal accident improper because employer did not discharge other employees involved in serious accidents).

[82] *See* O. Fairweather, Practice & Procedure in Labor Arbitration 312 (1983) (Chapter 13 "Due Process Considerations").

[83] Freuhauf Trailer Co., 16 Lab. Arb. (BNA) 666, 670 (1951) (Donely, Arb.).

[84] J. Redeker, Discipline: Policies and Procedures 81 (1983).

§ 3.6 POOR PERFORMANCE

employer should establish a reasonable standard pursuant to which employee performance can be measured.[85] Second, in order to give the employee a chance to improve performance, the employer should undertake progressive discipline before resorting to termination.[86] This general approach to poor performance as a ground for dismissal applies to dismissals for absenteeism or tardiness,[87] carelessness,[88] poor attitude,[89] or poor relations with customers.[90]

---

[85] J. Redeker, Discipline: Policies and Procedures 220 (1983). While a company may have advanced a reasonable standard by which to measure employee performance, however, it is arbitrary to base a discharge on inaccurate information relating to employee performance. Dresser Indus., Inc., 83 Lab. Arb. (BNA) 577, 580 (1984) (Harrison, Arb.).

[86] J. Redeker, Discipline: Policies and Procedures 223 (1983). *See also* F. Elkouri & E.A. Elkouri, How Arbitration Works 661 (1973) (incompetence) (table of arbitration cases); Southwest Elec. Co., 54 Lab. Arb. (BNA) 195, 196 (1969) (Bothwell, Arb.) ("[t]he objective in progressive discipline is to encourage the employee to meet minimum standards of conduct and work performance established by the employer. Most offenses do not warrant discharge for the first offense. In the case of most offenses, the employee should not be terminated unless disciplinary penalties less severe than discharge have failed over a period of time to cause the employee to meet these minimum standards."). Progressive discipline includes lesser penalties such as warnings or suspensions leading up to discharge. *But see* Weyerhaeuser Co., 83 Lab. Arb. (BNA) 365 (1984) (Shearer, Arb.) (discharge for being absent three days without notifying his employer; no progressive discipline used).

[87] *See* J. Redeker, Discipline: Policies and Procedures 55 (1983); F. Elkouri & E.A. Elkouri, How Arbitration Works 652 (1973) (table of arbitration cases); Naval Air Rework, 72 Lab. Arb. (BNA) 1266 (1979) (Mire, Arb.) (upholding two-day suspension against grievant who provided no evidence to support claim that his car had broken down, causing tardiness, and who had record of being late). With respect to tardiness and absenteeism from work, the progressive discipline may be a company policy of tolerating a maximum limit of absenteeism beyond which the employee will be discharged. General Elec. Co., 74 Lab. Arb. (BNA) 290 (1979) (MacDonald, Arb.) (employer properly discharged employee after fourth written warning notice for absenteeism and tardiness, who offered no excuse for his absence and did not try to improve his attendance).

[88] *See* J. Redeker, Discipline: Policies and Procedures 109 (1983); F. Elkouri & E.A. Elkouri, How Arbitration Works 660 (1973) (negligence) (table of arbitration cases); Wheeling-Pittsburgh Steel Corp., 83 Lab. Arb. (BNA) 318, 322 (1984) (Leahy, Arb.) (discharge reduced to a 90-day suspension for helper who was not available to assist a trainee, resulting in molten steel being poured over work area causing over $2 million damage; 90-day suspension would teach helper not to be casual about his job); Furr's, Inc., 83 Lab. Arb. (BNA) 279 (1984) (Daughton, Arb.) (employer improperly discharged a food clerk who admitted mistake in forgetting to ring up immediately a customer's purchase in violation of the company policy but had attempted to correct her error after realizing her mistake).

[89] *See* J. Redeker, Discipline: Policies and Procedures 99 (1983); Town House Apartments, 83 Lab. Arb. (BNA) 538 (1984) (Roumell, Arb.) (employer properly discharged assistant maintenance supervisor for attitude problem as evidenced when he bought cigarettes in the lobby before responding to an emergency bell on a boiler and when he arrived late to help push a van away from an egress).

[90] *See* F. Elkouri & E.A. Elkouri, How Arbitration Works 666 (1978) (abusing customers) (table of arbitration cases); Charles Todd Uniform Rental Serv. Co., 77 Lab. Arb. (BNA) 144 (1981) (Hutcheson, Arb.) (employer properly discharged employee who persisted in preaching his religious faith to customers after grievant had been previously warned and suspended for the same problem); Capital Area Transp. Auth., 79 Lab. Arb. (BNA) 665 (1982) (Fieger, Arb.) (grievant's discharge reduced to loss of 30 days' pay where bus driver took passenger to the bus parking

§ 3.7 —Misconduct on the Job

Arbitrators permit employees to be dismissed for misconduct on the job[91] if the employer can demonstrate the relationship between the misconduct and the accomplishment of the employer's business purposes,[92] and if progressive discipline is followed for less serious types of misconduct. Fighting and threatening assaults may impact the employer's business interests sufficiently to justify discharge.[93] However, when the grievant is provoked into the fight, discharge may not be appropriate.[94]

Certain types of misconduct, such as insubordination[95] and theft,[96] are presumed to have the requisite impact on the employer's business interests. Others, such as poor dress or grooming,[97] gambling,[98] falsification of records,[99] or possession

---

garage, insisted that she let him drive her to her destination and then dropped her off in an area away from that destination.) When the conduct is egregious, discharge with no progressive discipline may be warranted. Greyhound Lines, Inc., 79 Lab. Arb. (BNA) 422 (1982) (Larkin, Arb.) (employer properly discharged a bus operator who evicted a passenger and continued to threaten bodily harm to the passenger while he was filing a complaint at the dispatcher's office).

[91] *Misconduct* is used in the text in a generic sense. It sometimes is used in arbitration cases in a narrower sense, to refer to conduct that has the potential for physical injury and property damage. *See* J. Redeker, Discipline: Policies and Procedures 194 (1983).

[92] For example, dismissals for abusive, profane, or obscene language are permitted only where the employer can show that the language tends to disrupt production. *See* Fairchild Indus., 75 Lab. Arb. (BNA) 288 (1980) (Groshong, Arb.) (plant rule subjected employees to discharge for improper conduct, and employer properly discharged employee who repeatedly shouted indecent and vulgar language in the employee lunch room causing female employees to complain and avoid the lunchroom).

[93] Alvey, Inc., 74 Lab. Arb. (BNA) 835, 838 (1980) (Roberts, Arb.) ("[i]n the absence of mitigating circumstances, fighting is generally regarded as an industrial felony. This is true because the company has an obligation to maintain a safe working place for its employees."); General Elec. Co., 71 Lab. Arb. (BNA) 884 (1978) (Abrams, Arb.) (employer properly discharged grievant who struck coemployee with the flat side of a machete during an argument).

[94] Union Camp Corp., 71 Lab. Arb. (BNA) 883 (1978) (Hardy, Arb.) (discharge reduced to suspension without pay where grievant was provoked into a fight by a racial slur); Hilo Coast Processing Co., 74 Lab. Arb. (BNA) 236 (1980) (Tanake, Arb.) (grievant was properly discharged for threatening to assault coemployee who was late in picking up the grievant from his job site at the end of his shift); St. Regis Paper Co., Consumer Prods. Div., 74 Lab. Arb. (BNA) 1281 (1980) (Kaufman, Arb.) (grievant was properly discharged for threatening to rape fellow worker).

[95] J. Redeker, Discipline: Policies and Procedures 170 (1983). *See* Concrete Pipe Prods., Daily Lab. Rep. 2 (Sept. 18, 1986) (Caraway, Arb.) (approving dismissal of employee for refusing to take drug test).

[96] *Id.* at 119 (dishonesty); F. Elkouri & E.A. Elkouri, How Arbitration Works 659 (1973) (table of arbitration cases).

[97] *See* J. Redeker, Discipline: Policies and Procedures 132 (1983).

[98] *Id.* at 158; F. Elkouri & E.A. Elkouri, How Arbitration Works 666 (1973) (table of arbitration cases).

[99] *See* J. Redeker, Discipline: Policies and Procedures 120 (1983) (suggesting that one factor is the detrimental effect of the dishonest act).

of drugs or alcohol[1] may justify discharge only if the employer can demonstrate a nexus between a prohibition of the conduct and the employer's legitimate business interests. This analysis also applies to immoral or indecent acts performed while on duty.[2] In addition, for these offenses, progressive discipline is likely to be required before termination is effected.

§ 3.8 —Misconduct Off the Job

Arbitrators uphold discharges for off-the-job conduct only when the employer can show a clear relationship between the conduct and legitimate employer interests.[3] For example, moonlighting is not grounds for dismissal, unless the employer can show a conflict of interest or adverse effect on job performance.[4] Disloyalty, publicly expressed, may subject the employee to dismissal if the effect on the employer's public image is sufficiently serious.[5] Immoral conduct off the job cannot be the basis for dismissal unless the employer can show an adverse effect on business operations.[6]

---

[1] *Id.* at 81 (alcohol) and 147 (drugs) (both suggesting factors such as effect on orderly operation of employer's business and reputation of employer); F. Elkouri & E.A. Elkouri, How Arbitration Works at 664 (drugs) and 665 (alcohol) (1973) (table of arbitration cases).

[2] Anaconda Copper Co., N. M. Div., 78 Lab. Arb. (BNA) 690 (1982) (Cohen, Arb.) (grievant properly discharged where he persistently harassed a female coworker with obscene gestures and demeaning slurs); Fisher Foods, Inc., 80 Lab. Arb. (BNA) 133 (1983) (Abrams, Arb.) (employee who touched the breast of a sales representative from a product distributor was properly discharged). *But see* Dayton Power & Light Co., 80 Lab. Arb. (BNA) 19 (1982) (Heinsz, Arb.) (discharge penalty too severe for employee who pinched female coworker's breast when employee had 28 years of service and no prior problems with this type of misconduct) *and* Powermatic Houdaille, Inc., 71 Lab. Arb. (BNA) 54 (1978) (Cocalis, Arb.) (when plant rule subjected employees to immediate discharge for immoral conduct, discharge was too severe for employee who made lewd gesture to female coworker).

[3] *See* F. Elkouri & E.A. Elkouri, How Arbitration Works 616 (1973); Indian Head, Inc., 71 Lab. Arb. (BNA) 82, 85 (1978) (Rimer, Arb.) ("[a]rbitrators have long held that what an employee does on his own time and off company premises is not a proper basis for disciplinary action unless it can be shown that the employee's conduct has an adverse effect on the company's business or reputation, the morale and well being of other employees, or the employee's ability to perform his regular duties.").

[4] *See* J. Redeker, Discipline: Policies and Procedures 215 (1983) ("[g]enerally speaking, an employee's off-duty activities are not open to question by an employer.").

[5] *Id.* at 106; F. Elkouri & E.A. Elkouri, How Arbitration Works 660 (1973) (table of arbitration cases).

[6] *Compare* Bazor Express, Inc., 46 Lab. Arb. (BNA) 307, 309 (1966) (Duff, Arb.) ("romantic exploits" had no bearing on job as truck driver) *and* Hughes Air Corp., 73 Lab. Arb. (BNA) 148 (1979) (Barsamian, Arb.) (single offduty homosexual act insufficient cause for discharge of airline flight attendant) *with* Gas Serv. Co., 39 Lab. Arb. (BNA) 1025, 1028–29 (1962) (Granoff, Arb.) ("sordid private life," required to enter customers' homes). *See generally* F. Elkouri & E.A. Elkouri, How Arbitration Works 616 (1973).

This nexus between off duty misconduct and adverse effect upon business operations may be a standard which is explicitly provided for in the collective bargaining agreement or one which fairly may be implied by the arbitrator. For example, in *Social Security Administration*,[7] the arbitrator concluded that *good cause* incorporated the standard that employees may be removed only for those causes which would affect the efficiency of the service. Under this standard, a grievant's immoral or even illegal sexual activity while off duty generally is not grounds for discharge.[8]

Likewise, when the off duty misconduct involves criminal action which does not affect the employer's business, discharge is not appropriate.[9] Instances of off duty misconduct which sufficiently involve employer interests to justify discharge involve threats and assaults on supervisors, crimes which reflect the employee's inability to perform his duty, and crimes which affect the company's reputation.[10]

---

[7] 80 Lab. Arb. (BNA) 725 (1983) (Lubic, Arb.).

[8] *See* Community College, 85 Lab. Arb. (BNA) 687 (1985) (Goldberg, Arb.) (college not warranted in dismissing tenured professor for arrest for homosexual solicitation away from employer's premises; even if students and faculty knew of arrest, college failed to show unfitness to teach); Ralph's Grocery Co., 77 Lab. Arb. (BNA) 867, 870 (1981) (Kaufman, Arb.) (employer had no cause to discharge assistant bookkeeper who allegedly spent the night with the manager of the store after they had attended an employee's party in which a "lesbian show" had allegedly occurred. "A bargaining unit employee's off duty and off the property conduct, of course, is not subject to discipline or discharge unless it adversely affects the operation of the employer's business."); Hughes Air Corp, 73 Lab. Arb. (BNA) 148 (1979) (Barsamian, Arb.) (employer improperly discharged male flight attendant who made a homosexual advance to a 15-year-old hotel employee where no passenger or prospective passenger complained and incident had no affect on grievant's ability to perform his duties); Social Sec. Admin., 80 Lab. Arb. (BNA) 725 (1983) (Lubic, Arb.) (employee improperly discharged where his conviction for illegal sexual activity with a seven-year-old child had no effect on the agency's efficiency).

[9] *See* Nugent Sand Co., 71 Lab. Arb. (BNA) 585 (1978) (Kanner, Arb.) (employee improperly discharged for felony conviction for possession of drugs with the intent to deliver, occurring while on sick leave); Indian Head, Inc., 71 Lab. Arb. (BNA) 82 (1978) (Rimer, Arb.) (employer improperly discharged grievant who was arrested for possession of marijauna while off duty; company failed to show detrimental impact on the company despite the fact that the grievant violated a company rule prohibiting use of illegal drugs by its employees). *But see* Joy Mfg. Co., 68 Lab. Arb. (BNA) 697 (1977) (Freeman, Arb.) (employer properly discharged employee who was convicted of selling marijuana where employer showed that the employee's return to the workforce would seriously damage the employer's drug and alcohol rehabilitation program); Livingston Export Packing, Inc., 83 Lab. Arb. (BNA) 270 (1984) (Ives, Arb.) (employee's discharge upheld where the employee had marijauna in his car on company premises immediately before he was arrested off company premises).

[10] *See* Heaven Hill Distilleries, Inc., 74 Lab. Arb. (BNA) 42 (1980) (Beckman, Arb.) (employee who struck a supervisor in the face and threatened to cut the plant manager's throat while at a local restaurant was properly discharged); Central Soya Co., 74 Lab. Arb. (BNA) 1084 (1980) (Cantor, Arb.) (employer properly discharged employee who swerved in front of his foreman's car on the way to work and also threatened to kill him); Safeway Stores, Inc., 74 Lab. Arb. (BNA) 1293 (1980) (Doyle, Arb.) (employer properly discharged food clerk who demonstrated dishonesty by being convicted for breaking and entering another store); Southern Bell Tel. &

§ 3.9 Typical Grievance and Arbitration Procedure

The grievance machinery usually consists of a series of steps to be taken within specified time limits, with the last step being arbitration.[11] The exact nature of the procedure depends on the structure of the company, the agreement, and the needs and desires of the parties, but most follow a fairly definite pattern. As a first step, the grievant usually takes the grievance to the foreman or immediate supervisor for settlement; if no settlement is reached, the grievant goes through successive steps within the management and union hierarchy, and if necessary, to arbitration.[12] The union representative may file a written grievance on behalf of the grievant, either at the first step or in later steps, depending on the contract.

It is basic to the concept of collective bargaining under the National Labor Relations Act (NLRA) that the union, rather than the employee, controls the grievance process. The union's status as the exclusive representative of the employees contemplates such control. The union has the right, and arguably the responsibility, to determine whether an employee's grievance has merit. In an appropriate case, the union can elect not to prosecute a grievance—even one involving discharge. That decision is binding on the employee absent a breach of the duty of fair representation.[13] Many grievances start out with an individual employee complaint at step one, but involve a discretionary determination by the union whether or not to proceed with the grievance at steps two or three.

Some agreements contain no time limits for presentation of grievances; others specify the time within which each step of the grievance process must be completed. It is not uncommon for agreements to provide different time limits for different types of grievances.[14]

Tel. Co., 75 Lab. Arb. (BNA) 409 (1980) (Seibel, Arb.) (repairman who made obscene phone calls to customers was properly discharged since employer's business would be affected adversely if it dispatched grievant to provide telephone service). *But see* Wisconsin Tissue Mills, 63 Lab. Arb. (BNA) 917 (1974) (Hilpert, Arb.) (employer improperly discharged employee who assaulted the personnel manager during a company picnic).

[11] For example, § 7.2 of the 1980–1983 Eastern Area Cement Haul Agreement of the Teamsters provides for a four-step process which is illustrative of the grievance procedure. Step one requires the presentation of a written grievance by the employee or the employee's shop steward to the foreman within seven days of the incident giving rise to the grievance. The foreman must make a written disposition of the grievance within three calendar days. Step two involves presenting the grievance to the union business agent and the employer's terminal manager within five days of the completion of step one. Step three permits an appeal to a panel of a "Joint Area Committee," composed of three employer and three union representatives. If the matter is not resolved at this step, Article 8 of the National Master Freight Agreement permits final resort to the permanent National Grievance Committee, composed of equal numbers of employer and Teamster representatives. The procedure is unusual in that it does not provide for binding arbitration by a neutral as the final step, but otherwise it is typical of grievance procedures.

[12] F. Elkouri & E.A. Elkouri, How Arbitration Works 120 (1973).

[13] See § 3.25 for a discussion of the fair representation concept.

[14] F. Elkouri & E.A. Elkouri, How Arbitration Works 146–47 (1973).

Unless restricted by the agreement, the grievant, the union, and the company are free to select the individuals who are to serve as their respective grievance representatives.[15] There is no clear answer as to when the right to union representation first accrues to the grievant. The cases fall roughly into three categories:

1. Cases in which the agreement is found to provide for the presence of a union representative at a pregrievance stage (*pregrievance stage* is that time before which management's discipline has been assessed)
2. Cases in which the employee has no right to union representation, unless the agreement provides otherwise, until after discipline has been assessed
3. Cases in which the employee has a right, even if not traced directly to the agreement, to union representation as early as the investigation stage.[16]

Employees have a statutory right to union representation at the earliest stage which may result in discipline against the employee. This is the *Weingarten* rule.[17] Discipline against an employee for refusing to participate in a meeting with a supervisor or other employer representative without such representation is an unfair labor practice.[18] Employees also may have contractual rights to certain types of representation or representation at certain procedural stages. Violation of these rights could invalidate discipline resulting from the proceeding at which representation was denied wrongfully or invalidate other decisions made at such a proceeding.

Whether an employer has the duty to meet with individual employees for the purpose of settling a grievance over the objections of the union has been the subject of some confusion. A proviso to § 9(a) of the NLRA[19] states:

> . . . any individual employee . . . shall have the right at any time to present grievances to his or her employer and to have such grievances adjusted, without the intervention of the bargaining representative, as long as the adjustment is not inconsistent with the terms of the collective bargaining agreement then in effect.

This proviso can be interpreted in two ways. The first interpretation would permit an employee to compel arbitration as a statutorily vested right notwithstanding the union's refusal to process the grievance.[20] Under this interpretation, no agreement between the union and the employer can deprive the employee of the right to have a grievance handled. If the union and the employer have created a right to arbitration in the collective agreement, this interpretation gives the employee

---

[15] *Id.* at 200.

[16] *Id.* at 128.

[17] *See* NLRB v. Weingarten, Inc., 420 U.S. 251 (1975); Garment Workers v. Quality Mfg. Co., 420 U.S. 276 (1975).

[18] NLRB v. Weingarten, Inc., 420 U.S. at 262.

[19] § 9(a), National Labor Relations Act, 29 U.S.C. § 159(a).

[20] *See* Summers, *Individual Rights in Collective Agreements and Arbitration,* 37 N.Y.U. L. Rev. 362 (1962); Donnely v. United Fruit Co., 40 N.J. 61, 190 A.2d 825 (1963).

the individual right to compel arbitration.[21] This interpretation has not been well received by courts.[22]

Under a second interpretation, an individual may not process his own grievance to arbitration absent acquiescence of both the employer and the union.[23] Rather than conferring a right upon an employee to compel compliance with the grievance machinery up to and including arbitration, § 9(a) of the NLRA permits an employee to take his grievances to the employer and authorizes the employer to hear them.[24]

Under § 9(a), the union is the exclusive bargaining representative of all employees in the bargaining unit for the purposes of collective bargaining.[25] Because the grievance procedure is recognized as an integral part of the collective bargaining process,[26] the union should control the grievance procedure. This rationale is also applied to prohibit an employee from using independent counsel in the grievance or arbitration process.[27] Proponents of this view say that channeling grievances through the union leads to sound labor relations by screening out frivolous grievances,[28] enhancing the employer's confidence in the union's authority,[29] and enhancing the union's prestige with the employees.[30]

The conflicting interpretations illustrate a tension in NLRA law between the rights of the employees as individuals and the rights of the employees collectively, as embodied by the union. *Smith v. Evening News Association*[31] allows an individual employee to bring a suit under § 301 for breach of the collective bargaining agreement. In such a suit, federal law, including the deference to arbitration, would be applied by the court.[32] This does not mean, however, that an individual employee should have the right under § 9(a) to utilize the collectively bargained grievance

---

[21] F. Elkouri & E.A. Elkouri, How Arbitration Works 130-31 (1973).

[22] *See* Vaca v. Sipes, 386 U.S. 171, 190 n.13 (1967) (specifically noting *Donnely v. United Fruit Co.* decision and declining to follow it).

[23] *See* Cox, *Rights Under a Labor Agreement,* 69 Harv. L. Rev. 601, 621-24 (1956). *Compare* Eichelberger v. NLRB, 765 F.2d 851, 856 (9th Cir. 1985) (union's negligence did not prevent plaintiff from pursuing her own grievance) *with* Seymor v. Olin Corp., 666 F.2d 202, 207 n.2 (5th Cir. 1985) (employer need not entertain individual grievances outside contractual procedure, providing union will represent grievant); Black-Clawson Co. v. Machinists, Lodge 355, 313 F.2d 179 (2d Cir. 1962).

[24] Black-Clawson Co. v. Machinists, Lodge 355, 313 F.2d at 185.

[25] § 9(a), National Labor Relations Act, 29 U.S.C. § 159(a).

[26] Steelworkers v. Warrior & Gulf Navigation Co., 363 U.S. 574, 581 (1960).

[27] *See* Castelli v. Douglas Aircraft Co., 752 F.2d 1480, 1483 (9th Cir. 1985) (union may retain or exclude counsel as long as it does not violate the duty of fair representation). *But see* Taylor v. Missouri Pac. R.R., 794 F.2d 1082 (5th Cir. 1986) (agreement may not limit representation by another union). *See generally* § **3.25**.

[28] *See* Vaca v. Sipes, 386 U.S. 171, 191 (1967).

[29] *Id.*

[30] *See* Republic Steel v. Maddox, 379 U.S. 650, 653 (1965).

[31] 371 U.S. 195 (1962).

[32] *Id.*

procedure.[33] To permit the employer to handle grievances with individual employees and to secure interpretations of the collective agreement at odds with the one preferred by the union would amount to an individual contract of employment that conflicts with the collective agreement. This is prohibited under the holding of *J.I. Case Co. v. NLRB*.[34]

§ 3.10 The Arbitration Hearing

Arbitration is a private proceeding and the hearing is not as a rule open to the public. However, all persons having a direct interest in the case ordinarily are entitled to attend the hearing. Other persons, such as observers, may be permitted to attend the hearing with permission of the arbitrator and the parties.[35] When the union or union attorney presents the grievant's case, the union usually does not permit the grievant's private attorney to attend.

No fixed rules exist for setting the date and locale for an arbitration hearing.[36] The arbitrator ordinarily tries to accommodate the time and place most convenient for the parties. In some cases the collective agreement states the time and place at which an arbitration hearing must be held, but for the most part, the selection of time and place is not so formally circumscribed.

The arbitration hearing usually takes place in a conference room large enough to accommodate eight to ten people. The arbitrator or panel of arbitrators, the employer's representatives in charge of processing grievances, and the grievant and/or the union representatives usually are present. There is some authority for the proposition that each party (the union and the management) has the right to be represented in arbitration proceedings by persons of its own choosing.[37] Under this conception, if either party chooses, it may retain the services of an attorney. Under the practice in most industries, however, the grievant is represented by the union rather than by a private attorney. If either party plans to be represented by an attorney, the other party as a courtesy should be informed.

The hearing room itself is frequently some neutral site chosen by the parties in order to minimize interruptions that can occur when a hearing is held at the employer's place of business or at a union hall. Some parties, however, choose

---

[33] *See* Broniman v. Great Atl. & Pac. Tea Co., 353 F.2d 559, 562 (6th Cir. 1965) (employee may not compel employer to adjust grievance directly with individual employee under the authority of § 9(a)).

[34] 321 U.S. 332, 337 (1944). *See* Bowen v. United States Postal Serv., 459 U.S. 212, 225 n.14 (1983) (whether employee can present grievance directly depends on agreement, but resolution cannot be inconsistent with agreement).

[35] F. Elkouri & E.A. Elkouri, How Arbitration Works 202 (1973).

[36] *Id.* at 202.

[37] Bronx County Pharmaceutical Ass'n, 16 Lab. Arb. (BNA) 835, 838 (1951) (Singer, Arb.) (arbitrator proceeded with the hearing without one of the parties, who refused to appear in the same room with counsel for the opposition).

§ 3.10 THE HEARING

to arbitrate at the company site or union hall to reduce costs, to make witnesses and records more easily accessible, and to minimize the time necessary for any visit by the arbitrator to the site of the dispute.

The arbitrator ordinarily sits at the head of the conference table. The arbitrator wears a business suit, not robes, and can be addressed by name, or by the title sir or ma'am. The arbitrator is not addressed as *your honor.* The arbitrator rules on all questions of procedure, from the order of witnesses to the admissibility of evidence, and ultimately decides the victor and the amount of the award.[38]

In dismissal cases, management presents its case first. Written opening statements occasionally are used by grievants. If they are used, copies of the statement are distributed to the arbitrator and the adversary. The grievant's representative[39] then reads the statement aloud. The statement usually contains a request for specific relief and the reason the grievant is entitled to such relief. After each opening statement, the adversary is given an opportunity to respond; the skillful respondent avoids simply reacting to the opponent's claims and instead presents a specifically designed case.

After the opening statements have been given and management has presented its case, the grievant's representative is given the chance to present all relevant evidence and testimony.[40] In the case of testimony, the form of questioning can be as formal or casual as the grievant desires.[41] Whether testimony is taken under oath is at the option of the arbitrator and the parties.[42] Leading questions on direct examination are permitted, although they naturally diminish the probative value of the testimony. After direct testimony, the adversary has the right to cross examine the witness. Since the arbitration itself is considerably less formal than a trial, cross examination is not subject to the judicial rules of evidence. The arbitrator thus decides when the types of questions posed in a cross examination should be limited. Since normally there is little or no discovery before the hearing, the questioning can easily become protracted and unfocused; it is necessary for the arbitrator to retain control.[43]

---

[38] *See* Hoteles Conado Beach v. Union de Tronquistas Local 901, 763 F.2d 34, 39 (1st Cir. 1985) (general rule is that arbitrator has authority to limit cumulative testimony, affirming vacation of award); O. Fairweather, Practice and Procedure in Labor Arbitration 161 (1983).

[39] The role of the grievant vis-a-vis the union at the arbitration hearing is unsettled. For example, under some collective bargaining agreements, the grievant may have an attorney present but the attorney is not permitted to participate in the hearing. In most cases where discipline is at issue, the arbitrator will ask the grievant whether anything needs to be added to the case presented by the union.

[40] *See* § **3.12**.

[41] A.L.I.-A.B.A., A Lawyer's Guide To Commercial Arbitration 58 (1977).

[42] *See* F. Elkouri & E.A. Elkouri, How Arbitration Works 221–22 (1973); O. Fairweather, Practice and Procedure in Labor Arbitration 180 (1983). If the collective agreement requires, or precludes, sworn testimony, it governs the procedure to be used.

[43] *See* Mailhandlers v. United States Postal Serv., 751 F.2d 834, 841 (6th Cir. 1985) (arbitrator can limit cumulative evidence, duration of hearing).

After the evidentiary part of the hearing, the parties usually are given the opportunity to present closing statements. Sometimes posthearing briefs also are submitted, depending on the arbitrator's wishes and the custom in the industry.

§ 3.11 — Ex Parte Hearings

In exceptional cases, the arbitrator may hold a hearing in the absence of a party who refuses to participate. The rationale for permitting ex parte proceedings is that a party should not be able to frustrate the arbitration process by refusing to attend.[44] Of course adequate notice of the hearing must be given.[45]

§ 3.12 Evidence

Arbitrators need not observe legal rules of evidence strictly unless the parties expressly require it in the contract.[46] Parties arbitrating under the rules of the American Arbitration Association (AAA) are subject to AAA Rule 28 which provides in part, "[t]he arbitrator shall be the judge of the relevancy and materiality of the evidence offered and conformity to legal rules of evidence shall not be necessary."[47] The result is that in most cases any evidence or testimony which is pertinent to the case and helpful to the arbitrator may be admitted into the proceedings.[48]

Arbitrators generally are flexible with respect to evidence. The parties usually are given great latitude in presenting any type of evidence they consider will strengthen their case.[49] The AAA's code of ethics[50] also reflects this view by providing that "[a]n arbitrator must provide a fair and adequate hearing, which assures that both parties have sufficient opportunity to present their respective evidence and argument."[51] The arbitrator may, however, exclude evidence which is clearly immaterial.[52]

Arbitrators usually accept all evidence submitted by the parties while reserving a response to the opposing party's objections of relevance or by agreeing to admit

---

[44] *See* Heat & Frost Insulators v. General Pipe Covering, 613 F. Supp. 858 (D. Minn. 1985).

[45] *Id.* at 860.

[46] Harvey Aluminum, Inc. v. Steelworkers, 263 F. Supp. 488 (C.D. Cal. 1967); *see also* Instrument Workers v. Minneapolis-Honeywell Co., 54 L.R.R.M. (BNA) 2660, 2661 (E.D. Pa. 1963).

[47] F. Elkouri & E.A. Elkouri, How Arbitration Works 253 (1973).

[48] *Id.* at 253.

[49] *See* Shulman, *Reason, Contract and Law in Labor Relations*, 68 Harv. L. Rev. 999, 1017 (1955).

[50] Code of Professional Responsibility for Arbitrators of Labor Management Disputes of the National Academy of Arbitrators, American Arbitration & Federal Mediation and Conciliation Service (1974).

[51] *Id.* at 19.

[52] F. Elkouri & E.A. Elkouri, How Arbitration Works 255 (1973).

the evidence "for what it is worth,"[53] thus allowing the arbitrator to evaluate the challenged evidence in light of the whole record and avoiding the possibility of excluding evidence initially deemed not to be germane to the case, which later becomes relevant in light of subsequent evidence.[54] In addition, by accepting all reasonable material evidence, the arbitrator decreases the possibility that his award will be vacated or overturned. Many state statutes and the Uniform Arbitration Act provide for vacating an award on grounds that the arbitrator refused to hear all relevant evidence.[55] However, the arbitrator can force the parties to stick to the issues and to explain why proffered evidence is relevant and material.

An arbitrator may, of course, refuse to admit evidence deemed not relevant or lacking in probative value. Moreover, if the parties fail to submit what turns out to be relevant and probative evidence within the time limits set for submitting evidence, the issuance of the award prior to receipt of the requested data may not be grounds for vacating the award if the court finds that the arbitrator has in fact been informed fully as to the facts and issues in the case.[56]

It is within the province of the arbitrator to determine the weight, relevancy, and authenticity of evidence.[57] These determinations require the arbitrator to consider the demeanor of witnesses, to discern whether any witnesses speak from firsthand knowledge or from the basis of hearsay, and to determine the weight and credibility to be given to any data or evidence submitted.

Hearsay evidence is almost always admitted, but the arbitrator usually qualifies its reception by informing the parties that it is admitted only "for what it is worth." Although it is impossible to predict how the arbitrator in an individual case will weigh hearsay evidence, in many cases very little weight is given to such evidence, and it is unlikely that an arbitrator will render a decision supported by hearsay evidence alone.[58]

Arbitrators do decide some cases on the basis of circumstantial evidence.[59] The need for circumstantial evidence to support the dismissal of employees for instigating an unauthorized strike is explained as follows:

> Because of the secret nature of the offense of these men, proof is extremely difficult. It does not follow from this that mere suspicious circumstances may take the place of proof . . . I think it follows that something less than the most direct and the most positive proof is sufficient; in other words, that, just as in cases of fraud

---

[53] *Id.* at 279; O. Fairweather, Practice and Procedure in Labor Arbitration 180 (1983).

[54] F. Elkouri & E.A. Elkouri, How Arbitration Works 255 (1973).

[55] *Id.* at 256; Uniform Arbitration Act § 12(a)(4), 7 U.L.A. 140 (West 1985). See **§ 3.22** regarding states adopting Uniform Arbitration Act.

[56] *In re* Aranson, 6 Lab. Arb. (BNA) 1033 (1946) (Botein, Arb.).

[57] Andrew Williams Meat Co., 8 Lab. Arb. (BNA) 518, 519 (1947) (Chency, Arb.).

[58] F. Elkouri & E.A. Elkouri, How Arbitration Works 279-80 (1973).

[59] Circumstantial evidence is evidence less than direct proof of the asserted facts, from which the existence of the asserted facts can be inferred. McCormick on Evidence § 185, at 435 (E. Cleary ed. 1984).

and conspiracy, legitimate inferences may be drawn from such circumstances as a prior knowledge of the time set for the strike. Unusual actions in circulating among the employees just prior to 9:30, communications of the time set to employees, and signals, however surreptitious, given at that hour. Mere prior guilty knowledge of the time set would not alone be sufficient since presumably many of the employees must have been told of the time a half hour, an hour or several hours in advance. Nor would merely being the first in a department to quit at the stroke of 9:30, standing alone, be sufficient. A wave of the hand, which might be reasonably interpreted . . . as a signal to the others to go out . . . would of itself be insufficient. But these or other suspicious circumstances, in combination, and especially in case of known leaders in the union's affairs, may be sufficient to convince the reasonable mind of guilt.[60]

If the arbitrator wishes to base a decision on circumstantial evidence, however, he "must exercise extreme care so that by due deliberation and careful judgment he may avoid making hasty or false deductions. If the evidence producing the chain of circumstances pointing [to guilt] is weak and inconclusive, no probability of fact may be inferred from the combined circumstances."[61]

§ 3.13 — Availability of Exclusionary and Self-Incrimination Rules

There is a substantial amount of disagreement concerning whether evidence obtained by allegedly improper methods may be used as a basis for an arbitration award. In one case, a female employee was discharged for violating a rule against possession of dangerous knives on company premises. The company obtained knowledge of the employee's possession of the knife by unilaterally seizing and searching her locker and her purse. The arbitrator held that such evidence was inadmissable because "knowledge, even though incriminating, if acquired through such illegitimate procedures, is of questionable validity in bringing action against the individual."[62]

In another case,[63] however, a similar search and seizure was upheld. An employee was escorted to the guard office and told to empty his pockets. The incriminating evidence thus obtained was a factor in his dismissal, which was upheld. Some arbitrators have held that constitutional rights regarding search and seizure can only be asserted against the government in criminal cases and are not available to employees in dismissal cases.[64] The theory underlying this reasoning was

---

[60] Stockholm Pipe Fittings Co., 4 Lab. Arb. (BNA) 744, 746–47 (1946) (McCoy, Arb.).

[61] South Penn Oil Co., 29 Lab. Arb. (BNA) 718, 721 (1957) (Duff, Arb.).

[62] Campbell Soup Co., 2 Lab. Arb. (BNA) 27, 31 (1946) (Lohman, Arb. Panel Chairman); *see also* Ross-Meehan Foundries, 55 Lab. Arb. (BNA) 1078, 1080 (1970) (King, Arb.).

[63] Jones & Laughlin Corp., 29 Lab. Arb. (BNA) 778 (1957) (Cahn, Arb. Panel Chairman).

[64] Lockheed Aircraft Corp., 27 Lab. Arb. (BNA) 709 (1956) (Maggs, Arb.).

articulated in *Hennis Freight Liners*,[65] in which the arbitrator stated that "the company is manifestly entitled to inquire into facts which suggest their employees are involved in the theft of company property."[66] Application of constitutional protections in arbitration cases is conceptually a matter of interpreting the contract. When the contract itself provides for compliance with "applicable laws," the arbitrator may construe this as requiring the employer to honor constitutional limitations.[67]

The supremacy of company rights has been extended to situations where the employer devises a plan to bait or entrap an employee violating company policy.[68] Arbitrators generally take the view that evidence obtained by various forms of secret surveillance will be admitted and, where reliable, will be given weight.[69]

The prevailing view is that employees enjoy no privilege against self-incrimination in arbitration hearings, though there is sharp disagreement among arbitrators.[70] The absence of such a privilege can create a dilemma for both employee and employer when there are contemporaneous arbitration and criminal proceedings involving the same operative facts. Generally, if the employee does not testify in his own behalf, for whatever reason, the arbitrator is entitled to draw an adverse inference from the failure.[71]

§ 3.14 —Medical Evidence

In many cases, the opposing parties provide the arbitrator with differing medical opinions on the same subject matter. The consensus among arbitrators is not to resolve the conflicts but to uphold the employer's position if it acted in good faith pursuant to good faith medical advice from its medical expert:[72]

> The judgment of the plant physician is entitled to great weight. He is conversant with the requirements of the occupation involved and the risks inherent in such work. It is generally held that where there is a conflict in the views of qualified physicians, whose veracity there is no reason to question, the company is entitled to rely on the views of its own medical advisers.[73]

---

[65] 44 Lab. Arb. (BNA) 711 (1964) (McGury, Arb.).

[66] *Id.* at 714.

[67] *See* Postal Workers v. United States Postal Serv., 789 F.2d 1, 3 (D.C. Cir. 1986) (reversing district court and approving arbitrator's imposition of *Miranda* warning requirement) (Edwards, J.).

[68] Borg-Warner Corp., 3 Lab. Arb. (BNA) 423, 484–85 (1944) (Gilden, Arb.).

[69] F. Elkouri & E.A. Elkouri, How Arbitration Works 285 (1973).

[70] *Id.* at 267–68; O. Fairweather, Practice and Procedure in Labor Arbitration 318–24 (1983) (discussing due process considerations).

[71] F. Elkouri & E.A. Elkouri, How Arbitration Works 266 (1973).

[72] F. Elkouri & E.A. Elkouri, How Arbitration Works 292 (1973), quoting Hughes Aircraft Corp., 49 Lab. Arb. (BNA) 535 (1967) (Doyle, Arb.).

[73] 49 Lab. Arb. at 539.

Thus, from the arbitrator's standpoint, an employer acts in good faith if it has given the employee fair notice and an opportunity to overcome the employer's findings. Under this view, the employee is only entitled to present additional medical evidence to the employer in an attempt to change the employer's mind.

The arbitrator must take into account special factors bearing on the reliability of medical evidence. Such things as the contemporaneity or the extensiveness of the examination can alter the weight to be given the evidence. The opinion of a specialist usually carries added weight. The testimony of a neutral third party physician carries greater weight than the testimony of a doctor whose services were procured just for the purposes of the particular grievance. And finally, certificates of examination are given significant weight in determining whether an employee's absence from work is to be excused due to illness.[74]

§ 3.15 — Standard of Proof

Arbitrators require, almost universally, that the employer bear the burden of proving cause for dismissal. There is less agreement as to the standard of proof.

In some cases proof beyond a reasonable doubt has been required.[75] In other cases a lesser degree of proof has been required, such as a preponderance of the evidence, or clear and convincing evidence, or evidence sufficient to convince a reasonable mind of guilt.[76] In most cases, the violation charged and the arbitrator's attitude will establish the requisite standard of proof.

One arbitrator believes it seems reasonable and proper to hold that alleged misconduct of a kind which carries the stigma of general social disapproval as well as disapproval under accepted canons of plant discipline should be clearly and convincingly established by the evidence. Reasonable doubts raised by the proofs should be resolved in favor of the accused. This may mean that the employer will at times be required, for want of sufficient proof, to withhold or rescind disciplinary action which in fact is fully deserved, but this kind of result is inherent in any civilized system of justice.[77]

In another case, in which the employee was discharged for possession of marijuana while on the employer's premises, the arbitrator held that "the great weight of arbitral authority requires that the proof offered must be beyond a reasonable doubt in cases involving criminal conduct."[78] If however, the alleged offense is not recognized by the criminal law or does not otherwise involve moral turpitude, proof beyond a reasonable doubt should not be required by arbitrators.[79]

---

[74] F. Elkouri & E.A. Elkouri, How Arbitration Works 293–94 (1973).

[75] F. Elkouri & E.A. Elkouri, How Arbitration Works 621 (1973).

[76] Id.

[77] Kroger Co., 25 Lab. Arb. (BNA) 906, 908 (1955) (Smith, Arb.).

[78] Air Force Logistics Command, 75 Lab. Arb. (BNA) 597, 602 (1980) (Johannes, Arb.).

[79] F. Elkouri & E.A. Elkouri, How Arbitration Works 622–23 (1973).

§ 3.16 COMPULSORY PROCESS

The Arbitration Agreement provides that the Arbitrator shall determine whether there was reasonable cause for the discharge. It does not seem to us that in the making of such determination, we should be bound by a doctrine of the criminal law as to proof beyond a reasonable doubt. We think the issue we have to decide in any particular case is: Is the employee guilty, and if so, is the act that he committed serious enough to justify discharge?[80]

Attempts have been made to establish general guidelines for proof requirements. After reviewing an array of opinions regarding burden of proof, one arbitrator concluded that the standard to be applied to cases where the alleged activity was not criminal in nature is clear and convincing evidence: less than beyond a reasonable doubt but more than the ordinary prima facie case and preponderance test. The level of minimum proof is based on the notion that "imposition of a lesser burden than clear and convincing proof fails to give consideration to the harsh effects of summary discharge upon the employee in terms of future employment."[81]

There is considerable disagreement among arbitrators concerning the role of the doctrine of collateral estoppel.[82] This can be important in a discharge arbitration when the employee has been acquitted in a criminal prosecution.

§ 3.16 —Compulsory Process

Production of evidence germane to an arbitration case generally presents no problems. The parties, eager to have the arbitrator decide the issue in their favor, present all the evidence they consider relevant and probative to their side. Occasionally, however, relevant and material testimony or other evidence may be withheld. In some cases when special circumstances are found to exist (e.g., information withheld in order to prevent criminal incrimination or disclosure of trade secrets or classified defense matters), the arbitrators refuse to order the production of evidence.[83] When special circumstances do not exist, however, the arbitrator's ability to order production is limited. Usually, arbitrators lack subpoena power.[84] The arbitrator may request the production of evidence, but the parties are under no obligation to meet that request. If a party does refuse evidence, however, the significance of that refusal to provide the requested data or evidence may be reflected in the arbitrator's decision as indicated by Arbitrator Saul Wallen:

> An arbitrator has no right to compel the production of documents [it might be otherwise if the arbitration is carried out under an arbitration statute] by either side. He

---

[80] Southern Bell Tel. & Tel. Co., 25 Lab. Arb. (BNA) 85, 87 (1955) (Alexander, Arb.).

[81] General Tel. Co. of Cal., 73 Lab. Arb. (BNA) 531, 533 (1979) (Richman, Arb.).

[82] *See* O. Fairweather, Practice and Procedure in Labor Arbitration 269–72 (1983).

[83] F. Elkouri & E.A. Elkouri, How Arbitration Works 264 (1973).

[84] § 7 of the Uniform Arbitration Act provides for arbitral subpoenas. See notes to § 3.22 for a list of states adopting the Act.

may, however, give such weight as he deems appropriate to the failure of a party to produce documents on demand. The degree of weight to be attached to such failure will depend upon the relevancy of the documents requested to the issues at hand. If the information withheld appears to be strongly pertinent, the withholding of it may be vital in the making of a decision. If it is of doubtful relevancy and merely represents an attempt by one party to probe through the files of another on the mere chance that its position may be generally strengthened thereby, then the failure to produce such records should be disregarded.[85]

§ 3.17 Form and Content of Arbitration Award

After the hearing is closed, the arbitrator renders a decision by weighing the evidence heard at the hearing. Normally the arbitrator's decision is written, but need not elaborate on the arbitrator's reasoning.[86] The arbitrator may not receive further evidence without first reopening the case or run the risk of having his award vacated on appeal.[87] An arbitrator is not bound by precedent.[88]

§ 3.18 Remedies in Arbitration Awards

If an arbitrator finds that an employee has been dismissed without cause, in violation of the collective bargaining agreement, he may order whatever relief is provided in the agreement for such wrongful dismissal.[89] In this context, the arbitrator's remedial powers are limited by the agreement that grants jurisdiction in the first instance.[90] Even where the agreement is silent on remedies, it generally is accepted that an arbitrator in a dismissal case may award back pay and reinstatement if he finds the discharge to have been improper.[91]

In addition, the arbitrator has considerable flexibility to tailor relief to fit the situation, provided the relief is not wholly inconsistent with the agreement.[92] Punitive

---

[85] American Tel. & Tel. Co., 6 Lab. Arb. (BNA) 31, 43 (1947) (Wallen, Arb.).

[86] Wallace v. Civil Aeronautics Bd., 755 F.2d 861, 864 (11th Cir. 1985).

[87] F. Elkouri & E.A. Elkouri, How Arbitration Works 273 (1973).

[88] *See* Wyman Gordon Co. v. Steelworkers, 613 F. Supp. 626 (N.D. Ill. 1985).

[89] *See* Electrical Workers Local 369 v. Olin Corp., 471 F.2d 468, 471–72 (6th Cir. 1972) (remand to arbitrator to determine method of calculating back pay, per agreement); *see generally* F. Elkouri & E.A. Elkouri, How Arbitration Works 648 (1973).

[90] *See* Operating Eng'rs v. Shank-Artukovich, 751 F.2d 364, 366 (10th Cir. 1985); St. Louis Theatrical Co. v. St. Louis Theatrical Bhd. Local 6, 715 F.2d 405, 408 (8th Cir. 1983) (arbitrator, in setting aside discharge penalty, exceeded its authority under agreement).

[91] Kane Gas Light & Heating Co. v. International Bhd. of Fireman & Oilers, 687 F.2d 673, 679–80 (3d Cir. 1982); Kroger Co. v. Teamsters Local 661, 380 F.2d 728, 731–32 (6th Cir. 1967); Sugar Creek Packing, Inc. v. Food & Allied Workers, 526 F. Supp. 809, 814 (S.D. Ohio 1981); Durabond Prods., Inc. v. Steelworkers, 421 F. Supp. 76, 79 (N.D. Ill. 1976) (agreement silent).

[92] *See* Miller Brewing Co. v. Brewery Workers Local 9, 739 F.2d 1159, 1163 (7th Cir. 1984) (arbitrator must have at least implicit authority to give relief awarded if it is to stand) (Posner, J.);

damages,[93] or attorneys' fees,[94] however, rarely are appropriate, unless the agreement expressly provides for them.

§ 3.19 Arbitration under the Railway Labor Act

Airlines and railroads are not covered by the National Labor Relations Act (NLRA) or Labor Management Relations Act (LMRA).[95] Rather, they are covered by the Railway Labor Act (RLA),[96] which requires arbitration of minor disputes,[97] which include most disputes over dismissals.

The legal theory underlying LMRA arbitration, moreover, is different from arbitration under the RLA. Arbitration under the LMRA is consensual; unless the parties agree to arbitration of certain types of disputes, they have the right to litigate those disputes in common law breach-of-contract actions.[98] Under the RLA, arbitration of such disputes is required by statute and leaves no room for judicial resolution.[99]

Section 3 of the RLA covers railroads[1] and establishes an administrative agency, the National Railroad Adjustment Board (NRAB),[2] to arbitrate disputes not referred to boards of adjustment (arbitration panels) established by agreement.[3] Legally, the different types of arbitration panels are treated identically.[4] Section 204 covers airlines[5] and imposes a duty on airlines and labor organizations to establish boards

---

Compo Machining Co. v. Machinists Local 1926, 536 F.2d 330, 333–34 (10th Cir. 1976) (combination of suspension and back pay); Gulf States Tel. Co. v. Electrical Workers Local 1692, 416 F.2d 198, 201–02 (5th Cir. 1969) (reduction of back pay rather than discharge).

[93] *See* Norfolk & W. Ry. Co. v. B.R.A.C., 657 F.2d 596, 602 (4th Cir. 1981).

[94] *See* Samini Line Ltd. v. Altamar Navegacion S.A., 605 F. Supp. 72 (S.D.N.Y. 1985) (nonlabor case).

[95] Railroad Trainmen v. Jacksonville Terminal Co., 394 U.S. 369, 376–77 (1969) (railroads); Marriott In-Flite Servs. v. Air Transp. Div. Local 504, 557 F.2d 295 (2d Cir. 1977) (airlines).

[96] 45 U.S.C. § 151 *et seq.* (1982).

[97] Minor disputes are disputes over the interpretation or application of existing collective agreements. They are contrasted with *major disputes,* those over the establishment of new terms and conditions of employment. *See* Elgin, J. & E. Ry. v. Burley, 325 U.S. 711, 723 (1945). The distinction corresponds to the distinction between *grievance* or *rights* disputes, and *interest* disputes. *See* F. Elkouri & E.A. Elkouri, How Arbitration Works 251 (1973).

[98] AT&T Technologies, Inc. v. Communications Workers, ___ U.S. ___, 106 S. Ct. 1415 (1986); Nolde Bros., Inc. v. Bakery Workers, 430 U.S. 243, 250–51 (1977).

[99] A.L.P.A. v. Northwest Airlines, 627 F.2d 272, 275 (D.C. Cir. 1980).

[1] 45 U.S.C. § 153 (1982).

[2] *Id.*

[3] Detroit & Toledo Shore Line R.R. v. U.T.U., 413 F. Supp. 681 (E.D. Mich. 1976).

[4] Murray v. Consolidated Rail Corp., 736 F.2d 372 (6th Cir. 1984) (NRAB has no power to review decision of Special Board of Adjustment); Baltimore & A. R.R. v. National Mediation Bd., 321 F. Supp. 51 (D. Md. 1970).

[5] 45 U.S.C. § 184 (1982).

of adjustment.[6] Airline boards of adjustment are legally identical to railroad boards of adjustment.[7]

Railroad arbitration panels function largely in an appellate capacity by reviewing decisions made by the employers, based on evidence taken before a company hearing officer.[8] Airline arbitration panels function more like those agreed to under the LMRA, with the arbitrators taking evidence.[9]

The interaction between the duty of fair representation and the finality of arbitration awards under the RLA is not entirely clear,[10] though the RLA is interpreted to impose a duty of fair representation identical to the duty imposed under the LMRA.[11] However, the conceptual basis under the LMRA for allowing judicial determination of the underlying dispute between employee and employer, once a breach of the duty of fair representation has been proven, is not applicable to the RLA because arbitration of grievances is statutory rather than contractual.[12] Some courts of appeals, nevertheless, permit judicial resolution of otherwise arbitrable discharge controversies in the context of RLA fair representation suits.[13] Others require that such disputes be determined separately in arbitration, if at all.[14]

§ 3.20 Arbitration and the Courts

Arbitration is (except for grievance arbitration under the Railway Labor Act) a creature of contract. A contract to arbitrate may be enforced against a reluctant party in the courts. Also, sheriffs and marshals will not execute arbitration awards, so enforcement of arbitration awards against a reluctant party requires a judicial

---

[6] I.A.M. v. Central Airlines, 372 U.S. 682 (1963).

[7] Hunt v. Northwest Airlines, 600 F.2d 176 (8th Cir.), *cert. denied,* 444 U.S. 946 (1979).

[8] *See* F. Elkouri & E.A. Elkouri, How Arbitration Works 100 n.104 (1973).

[9] Of course, the parties and the arbitrator can agree to utilize the transcript generated at an earlier step in the grievance procedure.

[10] Raus v. B.R.C., 663 F.2d 791, 796 (8th Cir. 1981) (characterizing law as confusing when claim against Railway Labor Act carrier for breach of contract is joined with fair representation claim against union).

[11] See § **3.25**.

[12] *See* Kaschak v. Consolidated Rail Corp., 707 F.2d 902, (6th Cir. 1983).

[13] *See, e.g., id.* at 902; Richins v. Southern Pac. Co., 620 F.2d 761 (10th Cir. 1980), *cert. denied,* 449 U.S. 1110 (1981). *Accord,* Hennebury v. T.W.U., 485 F. Supp. 1319 (D. Mass. 1980).

[14] *See* Goclowski v. Penn Cent. Transp. Co., 571 F.2d 747 (3d Cir. 1978); Harrison v. U.T.U., 530 F.2d 558 (4th Cir. 1975); Dorsey v. Chesapeake & O. R.R., 476 F.2d 243 (4th Cir. 1973). *Accord,* Connor v. B.R.A.C., 496 F. Supp. 154 (M.D. Pa. 1980). Also interesting in this regard is Martino v. Transport Workers, 505 Pa. 391, 480 A.2d 242 (1984), in which the Pennsylvania Supreme Court held that the only remedy for a public employee claiming both wrongful discharge and a breach of his union's duty of fair representation is an order compelling arbitration. It based its departure from federal law under the LMRA as interpreted by *Vaca v. Sipes,* 386 U.S. 171 (1967), as justified by the mandatory nature of public employee grievance arbitration under the Pennsylvania statute—precisely the distinction between the Railway Labor Act and the LMRA. *See id.* at 405, 480 A.2d at 249.

proceeding to get a judgment or decree which sheriffs and marshals will enforce. Special rules for such legal proceedings in support of labor arbitration have been developed by statute and federal common law. **Sections 3.21** through **3.27** describe the development of the law of arbitration, explain the role of statutory law, introduce the concept of the duty of fair representation, suggest how arbitration can be compelled to proceed, and explain the basic guidelines for judicial review of arbitration awards.

§ 3.21 —Federal Common Law of Labor Arbitration

This section addresses the legal status of arbitration. It begins by explaining the status of collective bargaining agreements as legally enforceable contracts at common law. The section then reviews the early development of a federal common law of labor contracts under § 301 of the Labor Management Relations Act (LMRA). Finally, it identifies the leading decisions by the United States Supreme Court establishing the propositions that collectively bargained arbitration ordinarily provides the exclusive process in which breach of contract claims can be adjudicated and that state common law contract actions cannot frustrate the primacy of arbitration.

At common law, collective bargaining agreements were enforceable under four major theories. The first was that the agreements created *usages* which bound both employer and union.[15] The second viewed the union as the agent of the individual employee and as capable of bargaining and suing for the employee on the contract.[16] The third theory treated the members of a union as third-party beneficiaries of the collective bargaining agreement,[17] and the fourth simply treated the contract as any other contract between two suitable parties.[18]

Some state courts, however, refused to enforce collective bargaining agreements on a variety of grounds, among them lack of consideration,[19] the policy against

---

[15] Hudson v. Cincinnati Ry., 152 Ky. 711, 154 S.W. 47 (1913). A dismissed engineman was held to have had an individual contract with the employer railroad, and the collective bargaining agreement was "merely a memorandum of rates of pay and regulations," and one of the ingredients of the contract.

[16] Mueller v. Chicago & N.W. Ry., 194 Minn. 83, 259 N.W. 798 (1935). "The contract having been made by the representative of the brotherhood on behalf of the [employees], plaintiff is entitled to sue on the contract as one made in his behalf by a duly authorized agent. . . ." *Id.* at 85, 259 N.W. at 799.

[17] Gulla v. Barton, 164 A.D. 293, 149 N.Y.S. 952 (1924) (holding that a workman, ignorant of the existence of a collective bargaining agreement between the union of which he was a member and the employer, had a claim for back wages, since he was a party intended to be benefited by the agreement).

[18] Schlesinger v. Quinto, 201 A.D. 487, 194 N.Y.S. 401 (1922) (injunction against employer association). *See also* Goldman v. Cohen, 222 A.D. 631, 227 N.Y.S. 311 (1928) (holding that because the union had no adequate remedy at law, and if no injunction were to issue, union would suffer irreparable damages, injunction should issue).

[19] Wilson v. Airline Coal Co., 215 Iowa 855, 246 N.W. 753 (1933).

enforcement of personal service contracts,[20] restraint of trade,[21] illusory promises,[22] and inability of a voluntary association to sue or be sued.[23] In 1947, prompted by the difficulties of enforcement in some state courts, Congress passed the Taft-Hartley Act.[24] Section 301 of the Act[25] conferred jurisdiction on federal courts to hear suits for breach of collective bargaining agreements. But Congress did not make plain whether it intended federal courts to use state contract law in considering these cases, or whether it intended to create substantive federal law for the court to use.[26]

The Supreme Court, in *Textile Workers v. Lincoln Mills*,[27] decided the question by holding that Congress intended for federal courts to use federal common law, "which the courts must fashion from the policy of our national labor laws."[28] Courts could use state law as guidance, but any state law would be absorbed as federal law.[29]

After *Textile Workers v. Lincoln Mills,* both employer and union were subject to the federal common law of labor in suits to enforce collective bargaining agreements. The question then arose to what extent courts would resolve contract disputes when the contract in question included dispute resolution provisions or arbitration clauses.

In three cases decided in 1960, the Supreme Court placed limits on the courts' ability to decide disputes when the parties had agreed to use arbitration. In *Steelworkers v. American Manufacturing Co.*,[30] the first of the *Steelworkers Trilogy,* the Court barred federal courts from deciding the merits of a grievance filed under contracts with arbitration provisions and restricted them to inquiring whether the claim, on its face, was covered by the contract provisions.[31] If the claim was covered by the contract, the correct action for the court was to order arbitration. In

---

[20] Schwartz v. Driscoll, 217 Mich. 384, 186 N.W. 522 (1922) (injunction stayed pending trial on merits); Schwartz v. Cigar Makers, 219 Mich. 589, 189 N.W. 55 (1922) (injunction rejected on merits).

[21] Connors v. Connolly, 86 Conn. 641, 86 A. 600 (1913).

[22] Moran v. Lasete, 221 A.D. 118, 223 N.Y.S. 283 (1927).

[23] Worthington Pump & Mach. Corp. v. Local 259, 63 F. Supp. 411, 413 (D. Mass. 1945); Pullman Standard Car Mfg. Co. v. Local 2928, 152 F.2d 493 (7th Cir. 1945).

[24] Labor Management Relations Act of 1947, Pub. L. No. 101, 61 Stat. 136 (1947) (amending the National Labor Relations Act, 29 U.S.C. §§ 141–197 (1982).

[25] 29 U.S.C. § 185 (1982).

[26] For an excellent discussion of the desired impact of § 301, *see* Cox, *Some Aspects of the Labor Management Relations Act, 1947,* 61 Harv. L. Rev. 274, 303 (1947).

[27] 353 U.S. 448 (1957).

[28] *Id.* at 456.

[29] *Id.* at 457.

[30] 363 U.S. 564 (1960). The district court had denied an arbitration request because it deemed the grievance, under the terms of the contract, to be without merit. *Id.* at 567.

[31] *Id.* at 568. "[The court] is confined to ascertaining whether the party seeking arbitration is making a claim which on its face is governed by the contract. . . . The agreement is to submit all grievances to arbitration, not merely those which the court will deem meritorious."

§ 3.21 FEDERAL COMMON LAW OF LABOR

Steelworkers v. Warrior & Gulf Navigation Co.,[32] the Court narrowed the grounds for denial of an arbitration request by holding that expressed congressional preference for arbitral rather than judicial resolution of disputes required courts to deny requests only in the presence of an express provision or the "most forceful evidence of a purpose to exclude the claim from arbitration."[33] Finally, in *Steelworkers v. Enterprise Wheel & Car Corp.*,[34] the Court held that courts could not refuse to enforce arbitration awards merely because the accompanying opinion was vague as to the exact contract provision from whence the award had sprung.[35]

Immediately after the Court decided the *Steelworkers Trilogy*, the question arose as to whether the *Lincoln Mills* doctrine of a federal common law of labor relations should apply when the action was brought in state court. In *Teamsters v. Lucas Flour Co.*,[36] the Court held that state courts must also apply the federal common law of labor by stating that in its view Congress "intended doctrines of federal labor law uniformly to prevail over inconsistent local rules."[37] The Court cited as authority the general policy of promotion of industrial peace. Thus, the Court bound state courts as well as federal courts to the *Steelworkers Trilogy* principles, requiring that parties to collective bargaining agreements utilize privately negotiated dispute resolution procedures before resorting to judicial remedies.[38]

When a court is asked to determine the arbitrability of a case covered by federal law, the reviewing court is limited to deciding only whether the reluctant party agreed to arbitrate the grievance or agreed to give the arbitrator the power to make the award rendered.[39] Any doubts the court may have over whether the arbitration clause covers the asserted dispute should be resolved in favor of coverage.[40] It is clear that reviewing courts should not weigh the merits of the grievance.[41]

---

[32] 363 U.S. 574 (1960).

[33] *Id.* at 585.

[34] 363 U.S. 593 (1960).

[35] *Id.* at 598: "A mere ambiguity in the opinion accompanying an award, which permits the inference that the arbitrator may have exceeded his authority, is not a reason for refusing to enforce the award." The Court later in its opinion indicated its preference for the arbitrator's construction of the contract: "It was the arbitrator's construction which was bargained for; and so far as the arbitrator's decision concerns construction of the contract, the courts have no business in overruling him because their interpretation of the contract is different from his." *Id.* at 599. In W.R. Grace & Co. v. Rubber Workers Local 759, 461 U.S. 757 (1983), the Supreme Court reaffirmed this basic approach, even though the arbitration award at issue conflicted with a Title VII conciliation agreement.

[36] 369 U.S. 95 (1962).

[37] *Id.* at 104.

[38] For an example of a state court application of this principle, *see* Burkhart v. Mobil Oil Corp., 143 Vt. 123, 463 A.2d 226 (1983) (employee not attempting to utilize arbitration procedure may not bring suit for wrongful dismissal).

[39] *See* AT&T Technologies, Inc. v. Communications Workers, ___ U.S. ___, 106 S. Ct. 1415 (1986) (courts, not arbitrators, decide whether dispute is substantively arbitrable).

[40] Steelworkers v. Warrior & Gulf Navigation Co., 363 U.S. 574 (1960).

[41] Steelworkers v. American Mfg. Co., 363 U.S. 564 (1960).

Under federal law, the question of substantive arbitrability[42] is for the court to decide unless it is reserved expressly, by the collective agreement, to the arbitrator.[43] In addition, even in cases where the court does have the power of review and where arbitrability cannot be determined without delving into the merits of the grievance, the arbitrator is allowed to make the initial determination.[44]

Questions of procedural arbitrability, however, are questions for the arbitrator and not the courts, as resolution of these also involves consideration of the merits of the dispute.[45]

§ 3.22 — Arbitration Statutes

Aside from § 301 of the Taft-Hartley Act, there are two additional sources of statutory law from which federal or state courts may derive authority in connection with arbitration disputes: the United States Arbitration Act (USAA)[46] and state arbitration acts.

The USAA is intended to facilitate voluntary arbitration of disputes[47] and, by its terms, does not apply to labor arbitration.[48] It has, however, been used to fill out the interstices of federal labor law and to expand the authority of federal courts to grant relief sufficient to permit labor arbitration of disputes.[49]

---

[42] *Substantive arbitrability* refers to the question of whether the subject matter of the grievance is covered by the collectively bargained arbitration clause. In contrast, *procedural arbitrability* refers to whether arbitration of the claim is precluded because of failure to meet procedural requirements such as time limits.

[43] *See* AT&T Technologies, Inc. v. Communications Workers, ___ U.S. ___, 106 S. Ct. 1415 (1986) (courts, not arbitrators, must decide substantive arbitrability).

[44] For a discussion of the respective roles of arbitrator and court, *see* O. Fairweather, Practice and procedure in Labor Arbitration 97 (1983).

[45] John Wiley & Sons v. Livingston, 376 U.S. 543, 555–59 (1964).

[46] 43 Stat. 883, 9 U.S.C. §§ 1-14 (1982).

[47] *See* Scherk v. Alberto-Culver Co., 417 U.S. 506, 510–11 (1974); Textile Workers v. Lincoln Mills, 353 U.S. 448, 466 (1957) (Frankfurter, J., dissenting). *See generally* H.R. Rep. No. 96, 68th Cong., 1st Sess. 1 (1924); Sturges & Murphy, *Some Confusing Matters Relating to Arbitration under the United States Arbitration Act,* 17 Law & Contemp. Probs. 580 (1952).

[48] USAA § 1 says, "nothing herein contained shall apply to contracts of employment of seamen, railroad employees, or any other class of workers engaged in foreign or interstate commerce." 9 U.S.C. § 1. *See* Justice Frankfurter's dissent in Textile Workers v. Lincoln Mills, 353 U.S. 448, 466 (1957). *See* Sturges & Murphy, *Some Confusing Matters Relating to Arbitration under the United States Arbitration Act,* 17 Law & Contemp. Probs. 605 (1952).

[49] General Elec. Co. v. Electrical Workers Local 205, 353 U.S. 547, 548 (1957) (discussion of use of USAA to supply substantive law); Grahams Serv. Co. v. Teamsters Local 975, 700 F.2d 420 (8th Cir. 1982) (USAA utilized to decide action to vacate arbitration award); Bethlehem Mines Corp. v. United Mine Workers, 344 F. Supp. 1161, 1166 (W.D. Pa. 1972), *aff'd,* 494 F.2d 726 (3d Cir. 1974) (selection of arbitrator); Textile Workers v. American Thread Co., 113 F. Supp. 137, 142 (D. Mass. 1953) (appointment of arbitrator). *But see* Miller Brewing Co. v. Brewery

§ 3.22 ARBITRATION STATUTES

In addition, 25 states have statutes furthering voluntary arbitration.[50] Many of these are derived from the Uniform Arbitration Act.[51] The Uniform Arbitration Act either contains or provides for a limitation period,[52] for the appointment of

---

Workers Local 9, 739 F.2d 1159, 1162 (7th Cir. 1984) (though USAA excludes expressly only transportation industry workers, it is superseded by § 301 of LMRA) (Posner, J.); San Diego County Dist. Council v. Cory, 685 F.2d 1137, 1141–42 (9th Cir. 1982) (questioning use of USAA); Service Employees v. Office Center Servs., Inc., 670 F.2d 404, 406–07 n.6 (3d Cir. 1982) (same).

[50] In addition to the states adopting the Uniform Arbitration Act, California has a statute providing for the judicial enforcement of arbitration agreements, including those contained in labor contracts. See Cal. Civ. Proc. Code §§ 1281–1288 (West 1982). So does New York. See N.Y. Civ. Prac. L. & R. §§ 7501–7514 (McKinney 1980).

[51] 7 U.L.A. 1 (West 1978 & 1982 Supp.). The following table shows the states that have adopted the Uniform Arbitration Act, and the statutory citation for the Act in each state:

Jurisdiction	Statutory Citation
Alaska	Alaska Stat. §§ 09.43.010 to 09.43.180 (1985)
Arizona	Ariz. Rev. Stat. Ann. §§ 12-1501 to 12-1518 (1982)
Arkansas	Ark. Stat. Ann. §§ 34-511 to 34-532 (Supp. 1985)
Colorado	Colo. Rev. Stat. §§ 13-22-201 to 13-22-223 (Supp. 1985)
Delaware	Del. Code Ann. tit. 10, §§ 5701–5725 (1975)
District of Columbia	D.C. Code Ann. §§ 16-4301 to 16-4319 (1981)
Idaho	Idaho Code §§ 7-901 to 7-922 (1979)
Illinois	Ill. Ann. Stat. ch. 10, §§ 101–123 (Smith-Hurd 1975)
Indiana	Ind. Code Ann. §§ 34-4-2-1 to 34-4-2-22 (West 1983)
Kansas	Kan. Stat. Ann. §§ 5-401 to 5-422 (1982)
Maine	Me. Rev. Stat. Ann. tit. 14, §§ 5927–5949 (1980)
Maryland	Md. Cts. & Jud. Proc. Code Ann. §§ 3-201 to 3-234 (1984)
Massachusetts	Mass. Gen. Laws Ann. ch. 251, §§ 1–22 (West 1959)
Michigan	Mich. Comp. Laws Ann. §§ 600.5001 to 600.5035 (West 1968)
Minnesota	Minn. Stat. Ann. §§ 572.08–572.30 (West Supp. 1985)
Missouri	Mo. Ann. Stat. §§ 435.350–435.470 (Vernon Supp. 1986)
Nevada	Nev. Rev. Stat. §§ 38.015–38.205 (1986)
New Mexico	N.M. Stat. Ann. §§ 44-7-1 to 44-7-22 (1978)
North Carolina	N.C. Gen. Stat. §§ 1-567.1 to 1-567.20 (1983)
Oklahoma	Okla. Stat. Ann. tit. 15, §§ 801–818 (West Supp. 1985)
Pennsylvania	42 Pa. Cons. Stat. Ann. §§ 7301–7320 (Purdon 1982)
South Carolina	S.C. Code Ann. §§ 15-48-10 to 15-48-240 (Law. Co-op. Supp. 1985)
South Dakota	S.D. Codified Laws Ann. §§ 21-25A-1 to 21-25A-38 (1978)
Tennessee	Tenn. Code Ann. §§ 29-5-301 to 29-5-320 (Supp. 1985)
Texas	Tex. Rev. Civ. Stat. arts. 224 to 238-6 (Vernon 1973)
Wyoming	Wyo. Stat. §§ 1-36-101 to 1-36-119 (1977)

[52] The Uniform Arbitration Act provides in § 12 that an action to vacate an award must be brought within 90 days after delivery of a copy of the award. 7 U.L.A. 140 (1985).

arbitrators,[53] for the enforcement of subpoenas issued by an arbitrator,[54] for the payment of arbitration expenses,[55] and for the confirmation[56] and review[57] of arbitration awards. These provisions can be applied by state or federal courts consistent with concepts of the supremacy of federal labor law so long as such application is "not inconsistent with federal labor policies."[58] Usually it is determined that "application of the state rule is pragmatic and consistent with . . . principles of federalism."[59]

There is less case law in support of utilizing state statutes or the USAA in Railway Labor Act controversies. Nevertheless, the same preemption principles should permit use of such statutory law to prevent frustration of the arbitral process.[60]

§ 3.23 — Compelling Arbitration

It is settled under both the LMRA and the Railway Labor Act[61] that an injunction is available under federal common law to compel specific performance of an agreement to arbitrate.[62] In the usual case, an injunction will suffice when a dispute is arbitrable and one party refuses to arbitrate. There are cases, however, in which specific performance of the collective agreement is inadequate. For example, one party may frustrate the arbitration process by refusing to cooperate in the selection of an arbitrator.[63]

---

[53] Uniform Arbitration Act § 3 provides for appointment of arbitrators by a court if the arbitration agreement fails to provide for appointment, or if the method of appointment provided for in the agreement fails. 7 U.L.A. 96 (1985).

[54] Uniform Arbitration Act § 7 authorizes arbitrators to issue subpoenas and permits enforcement of such subpoenas. 7 U.L.A. 114 (1985).

[55] Uniform Arbitration Act § 10 provides for the payment of fees and expenses as determined by the arbitrator. 7 U.L.A. 131 (1985).

[56] Uniform Arbitration Act § 11 provides for the confirmation of an arbitration award unless an action to vacate or modify/correct the award is brought within the time limits set by §§ 12 and 13. 7 U.L.A. 133 (1985).

[57] Uniform Arbitration Act § 12 provides five limited bases for judicial vacation of an arbitration award. 7 U.L.A. 140–41 (1985). *See generally* Annotation, 22 A.L.R.4th 366 (1983).

[58] *See* Service Employees v. Office Center Servs., Inc., 670 F.2d at 409.

[59] *Id.*

[60] *Cf.* Railroad Trainmen v. Jacksonville Terminal, 394 U.S. 369, 380–81 (1969) (general principles of relation between federal and state law in a strike situation).

[61] *See* Locomotive Eng'rs v. Missouri-Kansas-Texas R.R., 363 U.S. 528 (1960); Railroad Trainmen v. Central of Ga. Ry., 305 F.2d 605 (5th Cir. 1962).

[62] Steelworkers v. Warrior & Gulf Navigation Co., 363 U.S. 574, 577 (1960); Textile Workers v. Lincoln Mills, 353 U.S. 448, 458 (1957). In the case of railroads, the injunction would be to compel performance of a statutory duty rather than to enforce an agreement. See § **3.19**; *see also* H. Perritt, Labor Injunctions ch.6 (1986) (discussing injunctions under the Railway Labor Act).

[63] *See, e.g.,* Bethlehem Mines Corp. v. United Mine Workers, 344 F. Supp. 1161, 1166 (W.D. Pa. 1972), *aff'd*, 494 F.2d 726 (3d Cir. 1974) (dispute over selection of arbitrator); Deaton Truck

§ 3.23 COMPELLING ARBITRATION

Occasionally, one party may invoke the arbitration clause of the collective agreement by demand or notice of intent to arbitrate, and the other party may resist that demand on the ground that the dispute is not arbitrable. The resisting party may contend that the case does not involve any of the types of disputes covered by the arbitration clause, that some condition precedent must first be met before the dispute can go to arbitration, or that timely notice of intent to arbitrate has not been given.[64]

Resolution of the issue of arbitrability may be made by either an arbitrator or the courts. If an appointing agency is named in the arbitration clause, the challenge may be filed with it. The agency may then appoint an arbitrator to resolve the dispute over arbitrability. There is no requirement, however, that the agency appoint an arbitrator. The agency will look to the collective agreement, the dispositions of the two parties, and all other surrounding circumstances and choose what it believes to be the efficient method. Most commonly, the appointing agency will direct that the parties raise the arbitrability issue with the arbitrator and will then exercise its ministerial responsibilities by appointing the arbitrator and noticing the time and place of the hearing.

The courts may become concerned with arbitrability questions in three ways: (1) the party challenging arbitrability may seek an injunction against arbitration; (2) the party demanding arbitration may seek an injunction compelling the other party to arbitrate;[65] and (3) the issue may be considered when an award is taken to court for review or enforcement.[66] When the question of arbitrability is presented in a suit for an injunction to prevent or to compel arbitration, the standards for judicial consideration of the question are well established by the *Steelworkers Trilogy*.[67] A court may decide that the dispute is not arbitrable only if the collective agreement provides the "most forceful evidence of a purpose to exclude the claim from arbitration."[68] But in *AT&T Technologies, Inc. v. Communications Workers*,[69] the Supreme Court stressed that courts rather than arbitrators must decide

---

Line v. Teamsters Local 612, 314 F.2d 418, 422–23 (5th Cir. 1962) (appointment of arbitrator); Textile Workers v. American Thread Co., 113 F. Supp. 137, 142 (D. Mass. 1953) (Wyzanski, J.) (appointment of arbitrator). A remedy for this problem is available if the collective bargaining agreement provides that arbitration is to be conducted under the rules of the American Arbitration Association. The AAA will appoint an arbitrator unilaterally and permit ex parte arbitration when one party refuses to proceed. *See* Rules 12 and 27, American Arbitration Association, Voluntary Labor Arbitration Rules 4, 7 (1979). See § **3.11**, regarding ex parte arbitration. If that happens, the opposing party must either sue to enjoin the arbitration proceeding or sue to vacate the ensuing award.

[64] F. Elkouri & E.A. Elkouri, How Arbitration Works 169 (1973).

[65] These procedural contexts are discussed in this section.

[66] F. Elkouri & E.A. Elkouri, How Arbitration Works 170–71 (1973). Judicial review of arbitration awards is treated in § **3.24**.

[67] See § **3.21**.

[68] Steelworkers v. Warrior & Gulf Navigation Co., 363 U.S. 574, 585 (1960).

[69] ___ U.S. ___, 106 S. Ct. 1415 (1986).

whether a dispute is substantively arbitrable since a party is not obligated by the LMRA to arbitrate disputes it has not agreed to arbitrate.

Thus, if a dismissed employee is covered by a collective bargaining agreement with an arbitration clause, the union usually can compel the employer to deal with a claim of wrongful dismissal through the grievance and arbitration process. Procedurally, the union would commence a suit for injunction under § 301 in state or federal court[70] and base claims for additional relief on the appropriate provisions of the United States Arbitration Act (USAA)[71] or on a state arbitration statute.[72] An individual employee probably does not have standing to compel arbitration, because the union is entitled to control the collectively bargained arbitration process.[73] Accordingly, if the union refuses to prosecute a grievance through arbitration on behalf of a dismissed employee, the employee may be without a remedy[74] unless the employee can show a breach of the duty of fair representation.[75]

Frequently, unions ask the courts to enjoin adverse employer action pending arbitration. The general rule prohibits such relief unless the arbitration process will be frustrated without preservation of the status quo by injunction.[76] If the employee has obtained an arbitration award and if the employer refuses to comply with it, an injunction compelling compliance with the award can be sought.[77]

§ 3.24 — Judicial Review and Enforcement of Arbitration Awards

When an arbitration award has issued, it may be enforced in an action for specific performance of the underlying collective bargaining agreement under § 301 of the Labor Management Relations Act (LMRA),[78] or under § 3 of the Railway

---

[70] See § 3.21.

[71] As explained in § 3.22, the USAA can be used as a guide for developing federal common law under § 301 of the LMRA.

[72] Uniform Arbitration Act §§ 11–19 specify the procedure to be used under the Act. 7 U.L.A. 133–217 (1985).

[73] Smith v. Evening News Ass'n, 371 U.S. 195 (1962) did not decide the type of claims individual employees could assert under § 301. *Id.* at 204 (Black, J., dissenting). Hines v. Anchor Motor Freight, Inc., 424 U.S. 554, 562–63 (1976) strongly suggests individual employees can compel or sidestep arbitration only if they can prove breach of the duty of fair representation.

[74] *See* Feller, *A General Theory of the Collective Bargaining Agreement,* 61 Calif. L. Rev. 663, 774 (1973) (argument that individual employee is not entitled to enforce collective agreement).

[75] See § 3.25 regarding the duty of fair representation.

[76] Industrial Workers v. Exxon, 712 F.2d 161, 165 (5th Cir. 1983) (vacating injunction against employer action in benefits dispute). *See* H. Perritt, Labor Injunctions § 5.10 at 183 (1986).

[77] See § 3.24 regarding review and enforcement of arbitration awards.

[78] 29 U.S.C. § 185 (1982). Individual employees, as opposed to the union representing them, may have difficulty in maintaining a suit for enforcement of an arbitration award. In Diaz v. Schwerman Trucking Co., 709 F.2d 1371 (11th Cir. 1983), the court held that district court could not

§ 3.24 JUDICIAL REVIEW AND ENFORCEMENT

Labor Act.[79] A party resisting the arbitration award may bring a statutory action to impeach the award.[80] In either type of judicial proceeding, the court may be required to review the award to determine whether it should be enforced.

Suits brought by employees seeking to avoid, on fair representation grounds,[81] the effects of adverse arbitration awards must be brought within six months after the cause of action accrues.[82] Presumably, suits brought to vacate awards for other reasons, or to enforce them, would be governed by the appropriate state statute of limitations.[83]

In either an enforcement or a review proceeding, it is not permissible for the court to review the arbitrator's decision on the merits.[84] There are, however, certain limited grounds that will permit the arbitration award to be vacated.[85]

Enforcement of an award can be denied if the dispute is not arbitrable,[86] if the arbitration decision did not draw its essence from the collective bargaining agreement,[87] if the award violates public policy,[88] or if there was fraud or corruption involved.[89] Some courts also vacate awards for gross defects in procedure or rationality.[90] These grounds are construed very strictly, which makes it difficult to defeat

---

enforce an arbitration award in a suit brought by the individual employees benefited thereby absent a factual finding that the union breached its duty of fair representation.

[79] 45 U.S.C. § 153 (1982).

[80] *See* § 7 Uniform Arbitration Act; Railway Labor Act § 3, first (q), 45 U.S.C. § 153, first (q) (1982).

[81] See §§ **3.25–3.26**.

[82] *See* DelCostello v. Teamsters, 462 U.S. 151 (1983).

[83] *DelCostello* leaves this question unclear.

[84] Steelworkers v. Enterprise Wheel & Car Corp., 363 U.S. 593, 596 (1960).

[85] *See generally* O. Fairweather, Practice and Procedure in Labor Arbitration 585 (1983) (Ch. 21, dealing with vacation, enforcement, or correction of arbitration awards).

[86] Steelworkers v. Enterprise Wheel & Car Corp., 363 U.S. at 597; Amalgated Meat Cutters v. Great W. Food Co., 712 F.2d 122, 124 (5th Cir. 1983).

[87] Young Radiator Co. v. U.A.W., 734 F.2d 321, 325 (7th Cir. 1984) (reversing order enforcing award and remanding to arbitrator to address proper question); Miller Brewing Co. v. Brewery Workers Local 9, 739 F.2d 1159, 1162 (7th Cir. 1984) (Posner, J.) (explaining what the test means); Amalgated Meat Cutters v. Great W. Food Co., 712 F.2d at 124.

[88] Amalgamated Meat Cutters v. Great W. Food Co., 712 F.2d at 124 (reversing order enforcing arbitration award on public policy grounds). *Compare* Misco, Inc. v. Paperworkers, 768 F.2d 739, 742 (5th Cir. 1985) (affirming refusal to enforce award requiring reinstatement of dangerous equipment operator who had marijuana on company premises) *and* Longshoremen v. Pacific Maritime Ass'n, 773 F.2d 1012, 1021 (9th Cir. 1985) (arbitration award invalidated because conflicted with NLRB decision) *with* Vosch v. Werner Continental, Inc., 734 F.2d 149, 155 n.10 (3d Cir. 1984) (reversing district court for vacating arbitration award and reinstating employee on public policy grounds).

[89] *See* O. Fairweather, Practice and Procedure in Labor Arbitration 619 (1983); Annotation, 22 A.L.R.4th 366 (1983).

[90] *See* Mailhandlers v. United States Postal Serv., 751 F.2d 834, 843 (6th Cir. 1985) (clear misstatement of undisputed historical fact, serving as basis of award, necessitates vacating award).

the implementation of an award.[91] Generally, attorneys' fees are not recoverable in an action to enforce an arbitration award unless the employer unjustifiably refused to comply with the award.[92]

Judicial review of Railway Labor Act grievance arbitration awards is provided for expressly by § 3, First (q), of the Railway Labor Act,[93] and is even narrower than review of contractual arbitration awards under § 301 of the LMRA.[94]

§ 3.25 —The Duty of Fair Representation

An exception to the exclusivity of the arbitral process has been created when the union frustrates the efficacy of the collectively bargained procedure. A dismissed employee, who loses a grievance after an arbitration hearing or whose union has declined to arbitrate the grievance, may sue her employer for wrongful dismissal and the union for violating its duty of fair representation. Thus, the grievant may ask the court to relitigate the merits of the grievance and may recover only if the court is convinced that the union improperly represented her in processing the grievance and that the employer had no just cause in dismissing the grievant.[95]

The duty of fair representation was first established by the Supreme Court under the Railway Labor Act in *Steele v. Louisville & Nashville Railroad*.[96] The duty derives from the statutory principle of exclusive representation under which the majority union is the exclusive bargaining representative, even for those employees

---

[91] Postal Workers v. United States Postal Serv., 789 F.2d 1 (D.C. Cir. 1986) (Edwards, J.) (reversing district court, and upholding arbitrator's imposition of *Miranda* warning requirement); Amalgamated Meat Cutters v. Great W. Food Co., 712 F.2d at 124; Mailhandlers v. United States Postal Serv., 751 F.2d at 841 (even if arbitrator dozed briefly during hearing, no prejudice shown).

[92] *See* Amalgamated Meat Cutters v. Great W. Food Co., 712 F.2d at 125 (reversing award of attorneys' fees).

[93] 45 U.S.C. § 153(q) (1982).

[94] *See* Jones v. Seaboard Sys. R.R., 783 F.2d 639, 642 (6th Cir. 1986) (neither due process nor abuse-of-discretion nor arbitrary-and-capricious claims permit review of NRAB decision); Sheffens v. Railway Clerks, 797 F.2d 442, 447 (7th Cir. 1986) (evidentiary challenge insufficient to permit review); Locomotive Eng'rs v. St. Louis S.W. Ry., 757 F.2d 656, 661 (5th Cir. 1985) (review of RLA adjustment board decisions among "the narrowest known to the law") (suggesting gross violation of due process might be a basis for vacating award); Anderson v. National R.R. Passenger Corp., 754 F.2d 202, 203 (7th Cir. 1985) (showing that public law board decision is "without foundation in reason or fact" would permit invalidation on grounds that board acted outside jurisdiction, but employee failed to make such a showing); Myron v. Consolidated Rail Corp., 752 F.2d 50, 53 (2d Cir. 1985) (adjustment board did not act outside its jurisdiction or in violation of Railway Labor Act by upholding dismissal of union officer who solicited personal injury suits against employer in separate capacity as attorney); Henry v. Delta Air Lines, 759 F.2d 870, 873 (11th Cir. 1985) (failure to support impeachment of adjustment board award based on bias or refusal to consider personnel file).

[95] Hines v. Anchor Motor Freight, Inc., 424 U.S. 554, 570–71 (1976).

[96] 323 U.S. 192 (1947). See **§ 3.19** for a fuller discussion of Railway Labor Act arbitration.

§ 3.25 DUTY OF FAIR REPRESENTATION 159

in the unit that oppose that union.[97] The duty of fair representation was later extended to the National Labor Relations Act (NLRA) in *Ford Motor Co. v. Huffman*.[98] The duty imposed on the union is to "make an honest effort to serve the interests of all its members without hostility to any."[99] The union's powers always are subject to complete good faith and honesty of purpose in the exercise of its discretion.[1] The Supreme Court later elaborated on the nature of the statutory duty in *Humphrey v. Moore*[2] and *Vaca v. Sipes*.[3]

To prove a breach of a union's duty of fair representation, the record must show by substantial evidence that the union was motivated in its actions by hostility, malice or bad faith. Proof that the union may have acted negligently or exercised poor judgment is not enough to support a claim of unfair representation.[4] The Supreme Court said that an arbitrator's decision, even if erroneous, must stand, unless "the employee's representation by the union had been dishonest, in bad faith or discriminatory."[5]

A union that refuses to arbitrate a grievance must have a rational explanation for its conduct, especially if there is arguable hostility between the grievant and union officials. Moreover, although a union need not arbitrate all its grievances, it should investigate all evidentiary leads submitted by the grievant.[6]

When the union proceeds to arbitration, it has a reasonable ambit of action: the union need not have an attorney at the arbitration hearing nor permit the grievant to bring an attorney to participate in the hearing.[7] The grievant may not second guess the representative's or the attorney's selection of evidence or choice of relevant

---

[97] *Id.* at 198–99; Ford Motor Co. v. Huffman, 345 U.S. 330, 337–38 (1953).

[98] 345 U.S. 330 (1953).

[99] *Id.* at 337.

[1] *Id.* at 337–38.

[2] 375 U.S. 335 (1964) (interpretation of duty in negotiation of contract changes).

[3] 386 U.S. 171, 191 (1967) (no breach of duty by good faith refusal to take a grievance to arbitration).

[4] *See* Camacho v. Ritz-Carlton Water Tower, 786 F.2d 242 (7th Cir.), *cert. denied*, ___ U.S. ___, 106 S. Ct. 3282 (1986) (must prove intentional misconduct to show breach of duty of fair representation); Graf v. Elgin, J. & E. Ry. Co., 697 F.2d 771, 778–79 (7th Cir. 1983) (breach of duty requires more than negligence); Early v. Eastern Transfer, 669 F.2d 552, 555 (1st Cir. 1983). This is a correct statement of the prevailing standard. Increasingly, however, courts are willing to find a breach of the duty of fair representation when the union has been negligent. *See, e.g.*, Drutrisac v. Caterpillar Tractor Co., 749 F.2d 1270 (9th Cir. 1983) (negligence enough to show a breach of duty of fair representation); Ruzicka v. General Motors Corp., 523 F.2d 306, 310 (6th Cir. 1975); *see generally* O. Fairweather, Practice and Procedure in Labor Arbitration 700–04 (1983) (discussing shift in standard from bad faith to negligence).

[5] Hines v. Anchor Motor Freight, Inc., 424 U.S. 554 (1976).

[6] *Id.*

[7] Castelli v. Douglas Aircraft Co., 752 F.2d 1480, 1483 (9th Cir. 1985) (no breach of duty of fair representation where union investigated charges for only 1.5 hours before arbitration hearing, committed tactical errors in cross examining employer's witness, and refused grievant's request for either union-retained counsel or to have his own counsel present); DelCasal v. Eastern

testimony.[8] The union need not sue to overturn an arguably erroneous arbitration award.[9] The grievance process need not be error-free; some degree of negligence on the part of the union is permissible.[10] The union is required only to represent the grievants adequately in the arbitration hearing.[11]

§ 3.26 — Damages for Breach of the Duty of Fair Representation

In a fair representation/wrongful dismissal case, both the employer and the union will be liable for damages if the court finds that the union has violated its duty of fair representation in processing the grievance and the employer wrongfully dismissed the grievant. The employer pays back pay that accrues prior to the hypothetical date upon which an arbitrator would have issued an award had the employee's union properly handled the grievance. The union is liable for the remainder of the back pay liability, expenses, and attorneys' fees caused by its breach.[12]

The Supreme Court established the guidelines for awarding and apportioning damages in fair representation suits in a series of cases.[13] In the premiere case, *Vaca v. Sipes,* a union refused to arbitrate the grievance of a dismissed employee. The Court held the union was not liable because it had not breached its duty of fair representation. The Court also held that the union was not liable for damages solely attributable to the employer's breach of contract because "[t]hough the union [may have] violated a statutory duty in failing to press the grievance, it is the employer's unrelated breach of contract which triggered the controversy and which caused this portion of the employee's damages."[14] In apportioning damages the court held that:

Airlines, Inc., 634 F.2d 295, 301 (5th Cir.), *cert. denied,* 454 U.S. 892 (1981) (union need not provide attorneys to grievants, but if it provides them for members it must also provide them for nonmembers); Walden v. Teamsters Local 71, 468 F.2d 196 (4th Cir. 1972).

[8] Teamsters Local 542, 223 N.L.R.B. 533 (1976).

[9] Fountain v. Safeway Stores, 555 F.2d 753 (9th Cir. 1977).

[10] Griffin v. U.A.W., 469 F.2d 181, 183 (4th Cir. 1972).

[11] *See* Hines v. Anchor Motor Freight, Inc., 424 U.S. 554, 571 (1976); Smith v. Hussman Refrigerator Co., 619 F.2d 1229, 1241 (8th Cir. 1980).

[12] Bowen v. United States Postal Serv., 459 U.S. 212, 230 (1983) (concurring and dissenting opinion, characterizing holding of majority).

[13] *Id.* Vaca v. Sipes, 386 U.S. 171 (1967); Czosek v. O'Mara, 397 U.S. 25, 28–29 (1970); Hines v. Anchor Motor Freight, Inc., 424 U.S. 554 (1976).

[14] Vaca v. Sipes, 386 U.S. at 197.

§ 3.26 DAMAGES FOR BREACH OF DUTY

[t]he governing principle, then, is to apportion liability between the employer and the union according to the damages caused by the fault of each. Thus, damages attributable solely to the employer's breach of contract should not be charged to the union, but increases if any in those damages caused by the union's refusal to process the grievance should not be charged to the employer.[15]

Two rules emerge from *Vaca*: (1) if there is a breach of contract caused by the employer's wrongful dismissal of an employee, back pay is primarily the employer's liability;[16] and (2) if the employee is lawfully dismissed by the employer, the employee cannot recover back pay from the employer or the union, regardless of either's breach of duty. Thus, *Vaca* places a dual burden on the employee to prove both wrongful dismissal and the union's breach of its duty.

Three cases subsequent to *Vaca* illustrate the application of the two-pronged requirement. In *Czosek v. O'Mara*,[17] the court found both a wrongful dismissal and a breach of the duty of fair representation by the union, and held that the grievant could recover back pay from the employer and, from the union, any extra expenses incurred that were caused by the union's breach.

In *Hines v. Anchor Motor Freight, Inc.*,[18] the Supreme Court reaffirmed its position that the grievant has a dual burden of proof. "To prevail against either the company or the Union, petitioners must not only show that their discharge was contrary to the contract but must also carry the burden of demonstrating breach of duty by the union."[19] Damages against the union are, therefore, inextricably tied to the breach of contract claim. Thus, absent an allegation that employees were unfairly represented in the grievance, the courts must accept the arbitrator's decision upholding the dismissal. Having done so, the courts can then only conclude that since the employer lawfully dismissed the employee, the employee suffered no compensable damage from any breach of the union's duty.

In 1983, the Supreme Court decided *Bowen v. United States Postal Service*,[20] holding a union primarily liable for that part of a wrongfully dismissed employee's damages caused by the failure of the union fairly to represent him. The Court found that, under *Vaca*, the union could be found liable since its actions increased the grievant's losses, and, allocating damages against both the employer and the union, remanded the case for judgment.

---

[15] *Id.* at 197–98.
[16] *Bowen* casts doubt on this proposition. *See* Bowen v. United States Postal Serv., 459 U.S. at 212.
[17] 397 U.S. 25, 29 (1970).
[18] 424 U.S. 554 (1976).
[19] *Id.* at 570–71.
[20] 459 U.S. 212 (1983).

§ 3.27 Effect of Arbitration Awards Deciding Statutory Claims

From time to time, an employee covered by a collective bargaining agreement with a grievance and arbitration clause is dismissed in circumstances that suggest both a violation of the collective agreement and possible violation of federal or state statutes (discussed in **Chapter 2**). The contract claim must be arbitrated rather than litigated judicially, as explained in §§ 3.21 and 3.19. Usually, however, the associated statutory claim may be decided de novo by an appropriate court, even if the statutory claim has been decided by the arbitrator.[21]

This split jurisdiction is the result of the basic holding of the United States Supreme Court in *Alexander v. Gardner Denver*,[22] in which an employee was held to be entitled to litigate anew his claim of racial discrimination in violation of Title VII of the Civil Rights Act of 1964, despite having been unsuccessful in arbitration of the same claim.[23] An identical result has been reached by the Sixth Circuit in a case in which the arbitrator did not decide the statutory question of discrimination but decided the facts on which a discrimination claim would be based under 42 U.S.C. § 1981.[24]

In *Barrentine v. Arkansas-Best Freight System*,[25] the Supreme Court decided that an employee retains the right to a judicial trial of his wage claims under the Fair Labor Standards Act, despite an adverse arbitration award on the same issue.[26] *Barrentine,* combined with *Alexander v. Gardner Denver,* are strong authority for the proposition that court litigation of any statutory claim of improper employment termination is not barred by arbitration of the same claim.[27] The result may be different when the statutory claim arises under the National Labor Relations

---

[21] *See generally* O. Fairweather, Practice and Procedure in Labor Arbitration 643 (1983) (Ch. 22 "DeNovo Reviews in a Court").

[22] 415 U.S. 36 (1974).

[23] *Id.* at 59–60. *See generally* Oppenheimer & LaVan, *Arbitration Awards in Discrimination Disputes*, 34 Arb. J. 12 (1979). One should distinguish the situation involved in W.R. Grace & Co. v. Rubber Workers Local 759, 461 U.S. 757 (1983), in which the Supreme Court upheld an arbitration award enforcing a collective bargaining agreement that conflicted with a Title VII conciliation agreement.

[24] Becton v. Detroit Terminal of Consol. Freightways, 687 F.2d 140, 141–42 (6th Cir. 1982).

[25] 450 U.S. 728 (1981).

[26] *Id.* at 736–37.

[27] *See also* United States Bulk Carriers, Inc. v. Arguelles, 400 U.S. 351 (1971) (seaman may assert wage claim in federal court under the Seaman's Wage Act even though he had not previously pursued collectively bargained arbitral remedies); McKinney v. Missouri-Kansas-Texas R.R., 357 U.S. 265, 268–70 (1958) (employee returning from military service need not pursue grievance and arbitration procedures prior to asserting seniority rights in federal court under Universal Military Training and Service Act). *But see* Devine v. White, 697 F.2d 421, 437–39 (D.C. Cir. 1983) (deference paid to public sector employee arbitration award interpreting civil service statute);

§ 3.27 AWARDS DECIDING STATUTORY CLAIMS   163

Act. In such a case, the National Labor Relations Board may defer to the arbitration award.[28] The NLRB and the courts have struggled to develop a deferral formula that adequately protects the role of arbitration while preserving a public forum to decide public law issues.[29]

In *McDonald v. City of West Branch*,[30] the Supreme Court held that an action under 42 U.S.C. § 1983 is not barred by an adverse arbitration award under a collective bargaining agreement. It implied, however, that the result might be different if the arbitration award were reviewed and affirmed by a state court.[31]

Thus, in general, an arbitration decision will not preclude a suit based on federal or state statutes. Nevertheless, an arbitration award may be given substantial evidentiary weight.[32]

Most of the courts to consider public policy tort claims by employees who had arbitrated the legitimacy of their terminations under collective bargaining agreements reached conclusions similar to those reached by the Court in *Alexander v. Gardner Denver,* for similar reasons.[33] Many courts, however, deny access to

---

Mahan v. Reynolds Metals, 569 F. Supp. 488, 488–90 (E.D. Ark. 1983) (arbitration of benefits claim bars subsequent litigation of same claim under ERISA).

[28] *See* NLRB v. Plasterers Local 79, 404 U.S. 116, 136 (1971); Hammermill Paper Co. v. NLRB, 658 F.2d 155 (3d Cir. 1981), *cert. denied,* 460 U.S. 1080 (1983); NLRB v. Container Corp. of Am., 649 F.2d 1213, 1215 (6th Cir. 1981); Roadway Express, Inc. v. NLRB, 647 F.2d 415, 418–23 (4th Cir. 1981); Ad-Art, Inc. v. NLRB, 645 F.2d 669, 674–77 (9th Cir. 1980); Hospital Employees v. NLRB, 613 F.2d 1102, 1107 (D.C. Cir. 1979); United Technologies Corp., 268 N.L.R.B. 557 (1984) (prearbitration deferral); Olin Corp., 268 N.L.R.B. 268 (1984) (postarbitration deferral). *See generally* Note, *The NLRB and Deference to Arbitration,* 77 Yale L.J. 1191 (1968).

[29] *See* Taylor v. NLRB, 786 F.2d 1516 (11th Cir. 1986) (vacating NLRB order deferring to arbitration award denying grievance of truck driver dismissed for refusal to drive unsafe truck); *id.* at 1518–20 (reviewing history of deferral doctrine and rejecting *Olin Corp.* standard); Dair v. NLRB, 801 F.2d 1404, 1408 (D.C. Cir. 1986) (board must articulate rationale for deferring to arbitration award applying different remedial doctrine from board's).

[30] 466 U.S. 284 (1984).

[31] Reinforcing this possibility is Migra v. Warren City School Dist. Bd. of Educ., 465 U.S. 75, (1984), in which the court held that a judgment for the employee in a state court action for breach of contract barred a subsequent action in federal court under § 1983, even though the § 1983 basis for recovery was not asserted in the state court action.

[32] *See* Barrentine v. Arkansas-Best Freight Sys., 450 U.S. at 743 n.22; Alexander v. Gardner-Denver, 415 U.S. at 60 n.21; Gonzalez v. Southern Pac. Transp. Co., 773 F.2d 637, 645 (5th Cir. 1985) (on rehearing) (RLA arbitrator's award deciding outcome determinative facts entitled to preclusive effect in suit for retaliation under federal railroad liability act). A recent study concluded that few arbitration awards involving statutory issues are overturned, but that in about half the cases the award is given little evidentiary weight. Hoyman & Stallworth, *Arbitrating Discrimination Grievances,* 106 Monthly Lab. Rev. 3 (Oct. 1983).

[33] *See* Garibaldi v. Lucky Food Stores, 726 F.2d 1367 (9th Cir. 1984) (denying preclusive effect to arbitration award in public policy tort suit by truck driver dismissed for refusing to deliver

the courts on a public policy tort claim for employees already protected against wrongful dismissal by collective bargaining agreements.[34]

Moreover, an arbitration award may be invalidated to the extent it was based on the arbitrator's view of *external law* rather than on the collective bargaining agreement.[35] There is a disagreement among commentators and arbitrators on the appropriate role of external law in the arbitration process. Elkouri and Elkouri conclude that arbitrators are entitled to refer to *external* substantive law in deciding cases.[36] Two overlapping theories support such external reference. The first, and broadest, theory considers that arbitrators are like other authorities deciding claims of right: they are bound by the constitution, statutes, and the common law as well as by the terms of the instrument creating their jurisdiction.[37] The second, and narrower, theory considers that arbitrators must apply the terms of the instrument giving them jurisdiction, but that they are permitted (and may be obligated) to refer to external law to construe the contract.[38] Professor St. Antoine has explained that this theory obligates parties to honor the arbitrator's interpretation of external law when the arbitrator must apply external law to interpret the contract.[39]

Both theories draw support from the principle that an arbitrator cannot order performance of an illegal act and that contracts contravening public policy are unenforceable. In other words, if an arbitrator construes a contract so that it creates obligations or rights that contravene external law, any order resulting from such an interpretation would be impeachable on that ground.

World Airways v. Teamsters[40] is an example of the interaction between a collective agreement and external law. In that case, the airline suspended and demoted a 747 captain for a series of incidents indicating deterioration of judgment that posed a threat to life if he were to remain a pilot in command. The captain grieved

---

load of spoiled milk; tort and grievance present different issues), *cert. denied,* 471 U.S. 1099 (1985). See §§ **2.29, 5.20**.

[34] See § **5.20, 7.12**, explaining how jeopardy element of public policy tort is hard to satisfy when other protections against wrongful dismissal exist.

[35] *See* Bottini v. Sadore Management Corp., 764 F.2d 116, 121 (2d Cir. 1985) (Title VII claim outside scope of arbitration); United States Steel & Carnegie Pension Fund v. McSkining, 759 F.2d 269, 271 (3d Cir. 1985) (arbitrator exceeded authority by deciding claim based on ERISA rather than collective bargaining agreement).

[36] F. Elkouri & E.A. Elkouri, How Arbitration Works 321-23 (1973).

[37] *Id.* at 326 (quoting Arbitrator Howlett); O. Fairweather, Practice and Procedure in Labor Arbitration 437 (1983) (quoting Archibald Cox).

[38] *Id.* at 325-27 (describing views of Arbitrators Meltzer and Mittenthal).

[39] *See* Postal Workers v. United States Postal Serv., 789 F.2d 1, 6 (D.C. Cir. 1986 (Edwards, J.) (reversing district court and approving arbitral application of *Miranda* warning requirement), *citing* St. Antoine, *Judicial Review of Labor Arbitration Awards: A Second Look at Enterprise Wheel and its Progeny,* 75 Mich. L. Rev. 1137 (1977).

[40] 578 F.2d 800 (9th Cir. 1978).

§ 3.27 AWARDS DECIDING STATUTORY CLAIMS 165

the demotion and suspension and the adjustment board invalidated the suspension, ordering the airline to retrain the captain and to give him an opportunity to requalify. The district court vacated that portion of the board award that compelled the airline to retrain and provide an opportunity to requalify. The Ninth Circuit affirmed, based on its determination that the Federal Aviation Act and FAA regulations "clearly places the responsibility upon the airline to determine whether or not a pilot possesses the judgment to serve as a Pilot-in-Command."[41] "The arbitrator usurped this responsibility."[42]

In *Flight Attendants v. American Airlines, Inc.*,[43] the court affirmed an order compelling an airline to arbitrate application of a "no beard" rule. American Airlines had threatened to dismiss flight attendant Hagerty unless he shaved his beard. Hagerty filed a grievance, claiming that the "no beard" rule was unreasonable. Before the matter was arbitrated, the FAA issued an advisory circular finding that "the presence of beards . . . that affect the mask-to-face seal in crewmembers required to perform at optimum levels during flight at altitudes where supplemental oxygen is required, is not compatible with aviation safety."[44] American refused to submit the Hagerty claim to arbitration, claiming that the "no beard" rule concerned an air passenger safety issue which is not subject to arbitration.[45] American cited *World Airways v. Teamsters* in support of its position that it had the unilateral duty to determine employee fitness related to public safety, but the Ninth Circuit was unwilling to accept American's construction of *World Airways v. Teamsters*. The applicable labor agreement permitted covered employees to grieve "*any* action of the company" (emphasis in original). Moreover, the Ninth Circuit noted, the FAA circular did not expressly prohibit the wearing of beards by flight attendants; rather it indicated that "wearing of beards has some safety implications." It reasoned that a record on the nature and scope of the safety implications of the challenged rule should be developed in arbitration. Then, if the arbitrator's decision should "exceed the scope of his authority or be inconsistent with federal aviation law," judicial review would be available under *World Airways v. Teamsters*.[46]

---

[41] 578 F.2d at 803.

[42] *Id.*

[43] 767 F.2d 1331 (9th Cir. 1985).

[44] *Id.* at 1333.

[45] *Id.*

[46] *Id.* at 1334. *See also* Johns-Manville Sales Corp. v. Machinists Local 1609, 621 F.2d 756 (5th Cir. 1980) (affirming refusal to vacate arbitration award invalidating employer's no-smoking rule; managerial prerogative did not allow rule because not mandated by specific OSHA requirement; distinguishing *World Airways*); Trailways Southeastern Lines, Inc. & Amalgamated Transit Union, 83-2 Arb. (CCH) ¶ 8519 (1983) (Gibson, Arb.) (violation of state motor carrier regulations pertaining to alcoholism amounted to just cause for dismissal).

§ 3.28 Handling a Grievance in Practice

In light of the matters discussed in this chapter, this section offers practical suggestions for the handling of a grievance on behalf of an employee.

The grievance itself should be presented in writing with enough specificity to notify management of contract violations alleged.[47] A written grievance establishes a record and avoids possible distortion of the grievance in the course of possible appeals. The relief sought should be stated in broad general terms but not so broad as to leave the employer unsure of what the grievant is seeking. A full remedy in a dismissal case would include reinstatement with full seniority rights, back pay, payment to health and pension funds, and removal of discharge notice from the employee's file. Time limitations in filing the grievance should be strictly followed as failure to observe them may result in dismissal of the grievance if the failure is protested. If both parties have been careless in observing time limits in the past, however, an arbitrator may hesitate to enforce them strictly until notice has been given by a party of intent to demand strict adherence to the contractual requirements.

Both parties should be knowledgeable concerning the facts of the grievance.[48] Good preparation also assists the parties in achieving the primary goals of the grievance procedure: (1) learning the other party's position on the grievance and its view of the facts, and (2) resolving the dispute without the necessity of resorting to arbitration. Preparation should include identifying any witnesses, reviewing the past conduct of the grievant, and obtaining information about the treatment of other employees engaging in the same conduct. It may be desirable to obtain written statements from potential witnesses in order to reduce the harm to the grievant's case if the witnesses subsequently become reluctant to testify in the grievant's behalf.

The individual grievant and his representative can achieve their goals best by using the grievance machinery fully. Smart grievance tactics include:

1. Taking detailed notes during meetings with the employer and/or preparing a written summary of the meetings as soon as they are over
2. Requesting from the employer all information that is necessary and relevant to processing the grievance (these can include payroll records, job records, discharge or disciplinary writeups, correspondence to and from the employer)

---

[47] F. Elkouri & E.A. Elkouri, How Arbitration Works 145 (1973). This is less important in dismissal cases than in disputes over contract language. In a dismissal case, the employee claim frequently says little more than, "I was unjustly dismissed."

[48] *Id.* at 197; *see also* J. Axelrod, Wrongful Discharge in the Union Environment, Let the Firer Beware: Seminar on Wrongful Discharge at 13–14 (Dec. 6, 1982) (unpublished manuscript available in Villanova Law School Pulling Law Library).

3. Preparing a summary of both the grievant's and the employer's view of the facts surrounding the grievance
4. Considering whether additional facts are relevant and/or how to resolve factual inconsistencies
5. Making written requests of the employer for information that the employer proffered at the meeting between the two parties (the employer is required by the NLRA to release such information).[49]

Even if these efforts do not produce a victory for the dismissed employee, they help protect the union in a possible suit for breach of its duty of fair representation.[50]

The right to obtain information is an invaluable tool but it remains useless unless invoked. Therefore, once the grievant or union determines that certain information is relevant and/or necessary to contract administration, it should be requested. The union should combine with its request for information an offer to reimburse the employer for reproduction costs in order to avoid an employer refusal to submit to the request on financial grounds. The union may, if it wishes to avoid reproduction costs itself, request, in the alternative, the right to inspect the records of the employer at the employer's place of business, reserving the right to copy or have copied, at the union's expense, those records it needs.

Requests for information often are met with claims of confidentiality or privilege. Such claims usually are no defense to production of information. Once a union can show that the information requested is relevant, necessary, or both, to its function as a collective bargaining representative, § 8(a)(5) of the NLRA requires the employer to disclose that information.[51] The duty of disclosure also applies to information needed by the union to determine whether to take a grievance to arbitration. The employer's duty to provide information may continue after the arbitration process has begun: "The duty of an employer to furnish information relevant to the processing of the grievance does not terminate when the grievance is taken to arbitration."[52]

If the parties are unable to settle their dispute through the grievance procedure, the dispute normally is taken to arbitration by a joint submission of the parties.[53]

---

[49] *See* NLRB v. Acme Indus. Co., 385 U.S. 432, 435–36 (1967); C. & P. Tel. Co. v. NLRB, 687 F.2d 633 (2d Cir. 1982).

[50] See § **3.25** for a discussion of the duty of fair representation.

[51] C. & P. Tel. Co. v. NLRB, 687 F.2d 633 (2d Cir. 1982) (requiring company to give union information concerning employee disciplined for improper conduct in connection with grievance over same).

[52] *Id.* at 635, quoting Cook Paint & Varnish Co. v. NLRB, 648 F.2d 712, 716 (D.C. Cir. 1981). *See also* R. Fleming, The Labor Arbitration Process 170 (1965).

[53] The submission is an agreed-to statement of the question. This sets the substantive ground rules for the arbitrator. If the parties cannot agree on a submission, the arbitrator will formulate the question to be decided.

The parties may agree on an arbitrator. If they do not, the services of either the Federal Mediation and Conciliation Service (FMCS) or, for railroads and airlines, the National Mediation Board (NMB), may be requested by either or both parties to the dispute by contacting the offices of either agency.[54] However, the FMCS prefers to act upon a request from both parties.[55] The FMCS provides a form (FMCSR-43) on which to submit a request. The arbitration request form requires general identifying information about the parties and information describing the dispute.[56] If the parties are unable to agree on a panel of arbitrators, both agencies nominate a list from their pool of arbitrators' registers. Next, the parties choose the arbitrators from the list. If the parties are unable to agree, either agency appoints the arbitrators directly.[57] A similar procedure is followed by the American Arbitration Association when the collective agreement provides for arbitration under the auspices of that body.[58]

The grievant's representative should prepare for an arbitration hearing by developing the facts and arguments to be presented in connection with two questions: did the employee engage in the conduct alleged by the employer, and was the discipline imposed on the employee fair? Witnesses should be prepared carefully. The employee's record should be summarized in a manner that will persuade to the arbitrator that a less severe form of discipline was appropriate. The employer's past handling of similar offenses should be explained to the arbitrator if this reinforces the impression that the grievant was treated especially harshly.

§ 3.29 Defending against a Grievance

An employer should structure a strategy for dealing with dismissal grievances around the criteria for judging just cause discussed in §§ 3.5 through 3.8. It is wise to post all workplace rules so that employees clearly have notice. In addition, it may be desirable to require a supervisor to consult with the personnel department before dismissing any employee. It may be preferable to adopt a policy prohibiting all peremptory dismissals; if a discharge is contemplated, the employee can be suspended with a hearing held during the suspension to decide the question of dismissal. Such a procedure gives both sides a chance for reflection.

On first contact with a supervisor desiring to dismiss an employee, the personnel specialist should get complete information about the employee and the grounds asserted for the dismissal. This information should include the names of witnesses

---

[54] 29 C.F.R. § 1202.1; 29 C.F.R. § 1404.10 (1982).

[55] *Id.* § 1404.10.

[56] *Id.* §§ 1202.10, 1404.11(D).

[57] *Id.* §§ 1209.9, 1404.13.

[58] American Arbitration Association, Voluntary Labor Arbitration Rules (1979), Rule 12, p.4.

§ 3.29 DEFENDING AGAINST A GRIEVANCE

to alleged misconduct, information about the employee's past record, and copies of the applicable collective agreements, if necessary.

If a decision is made to dismiss the employee, the employer should decide whether written witness statements are desirable to preserve potentially useful testimony. A letter informing the employee of the dismissal is almost always important in subsequent arbitration. The employer should weigh the pros and cons of providing detail as to the grounds for the dismissal. The advantage of detail is that it builds a record that the employee had notice sufficient to enable him to assert available defenses in subsequent grievance steps. In addition, the discharge letter frequently is the first comprehensive narrative of the facts that an arbitrator will see. The disadvantage of too much specificity is that evidence presented at a subsequent arbitration hearing may not conform to the charges in the letter.

During prearbitration handling of the grievance, personnel specialists may wish to maintain their distance from the process, both to avoid becoming witnesses in a subsequent arbitration hearing and to preserve their neutrality in the event that they must decide the matter on its merits in subsequent grievance stages. Supervisory personnel who actually handle grievances, however, should be trained carefully about the factors that arbitrators look at in determining whether to sustain or overrule a dismissal.

If the grievance is not resolved and arbitration is requested, the employer should address a number of basic issues. Historical information on potential arbitrators should be obtained from the Bureau of National Affairs (BNA) or Commerce Clearing House (CCH) labor services or from other employers that have experience with the arbitrators. Such groundwork enables the employer to exercise intelligently its role in the arbitration selection process. Witnesses should be prepared carefully for the arbitration hearing. A trial brief should be prepared for guidance of the employer's advocate, if not for submission to the arbitrator.

Preparation for the hearing should focus on two separate questions to be decided by the arbitrator: is there proof of the event alleged by the employer, and was the discipline imposed reasonable? Evidence on the first question should be marshalled in the same way that evidence is marshalled to prove any contested facts. Evidence concerning the second question should address the seriousness of the infraction for the employer's operation and the fairness of the discipline in light of the way other employees have been treated in the past.

Sometimes the question is presented whether an arbitrator may consider evidence and arguments not presented at earlier stages in the grievance procedure. As a practical matter, the sophistication of representation increases as the grievance proceeds, and this often results in the refinement of arguments and the unearthing of additional evidence. The general rule is that such evidence may be considered by the arbitrator, provided that the opposing party is given ample time to prepare a response and that there is no indication that the evidence was withheld deliberately.[59]

---

[59] F. Elkouri & E.A. Elkouri, How Arbitration Works 258 (1973).

In the hearing itself, advocates who are lawyers should avoid the temptation to be aggressive with regard to matters of procedure and evidence; rarely are arbitrators influenced favorably toward the company by such tactics, and rarely is evidence excluded.

If an unfavorable award is entered, and the employer can articulate reasons why reconsideration is appropriate, the employer should consider requesting the arbitrator to reconvene the proceeding. If the arbitration hearing is reconvened, the employer can register its dissatisfaction with the arbitrator and possibly request a reduction in the penalty.[60]

---

[60] *But see* Sacks, *Book Review,* 59 Conn. B.J. 327 (1985) (reviewing this treatise, and disagreeing with suggestion).

CHAPTER 4
CONTRACT THEORIES

§ 4.1   Introduction and Overview of Contract Theories
§ 4.2   Historical Development of Contract Theories
§ 4.3   —Common Law Forms of Action
§ 4.4   —The Consideration Requirement
§ 4.5   —Treatment of Consideration in Collective Bargaining Agreements
§ 4.6   The Promise of Employment Security
§ 4.7   —Express Commitments Made to Specific Employees
§ 4.8   —Promises Derived from Employer Representations Made to Workforce in General
§ 4.9   —Promises Implied from Length of Service and Conduct
§ 4.10 —Disclaimers
§ 4.11 —Covenant of Good Faith and Fair Dealing
§ 4.12 Consideration and Its Substitutes as Validation Devices
§ 4.13 —Unilateral Contracts: Mutuality of Obligation Not Necessary
§ 4.14 —Bargained-for Detrimental Reliance: General Concept
§ 4.15 —Bargained-for Detrimental Reliance: Special Consideration Such as Quitting Another Job or Turning Down Job Offers
§ 4.16 —Bargained-for Detrimental Reliance: Continuing Employment
§ 4.17 —Promissory Estoppel
§ 4.18 —Is Proof of Actual Reliance Necessary, or May It Be Presumed?
§ 4.19 Employer Modification of Promise after Consideration Given
§ 4.20 Statute of Frauds
§ 4.21 What Constitutes a Breach: Generally
§ 4.22 —Breach of Employer Promise
§ 4.23 —Breach of Covenant of Good Faith
§ 4.24 —Who Decides Whether Good Cause Existed
§ 4.25 Suits by Employees Covered by Collective Bargaining Agreements
§ 4.26 Pleading the Plaintiff's Case
§ 4.27 Pleading the Defendant's Case
§ 4.28 Damages

§ 4.1 Introduction and Overview of Contract Theories

Under the emerging wrongful dismissal case law, common law contract doctrines permit dismissed employees to recover damages when their employers violate commitments to discharge only for cause or only through certain procedures. Claims under this family of theories are described best as *implied-in-fact contract* claims.[1] Dismissed employees sometimes also can recover for violation of an *implied-in-law covenant of good faith and fair dealing* when they persuade juries that their employers acted unfairly. Employers can limit liability for implied-in-fact contracts through their control of personnel policies and other types of commitments. Employer control over the reach of the implied covenant is limited.

When a formal written contract of employment has been entered into, courts historically have accepted the proposition that discharge of the employee before the end of the contract can give rise to liability under ordinary breach of contract principles.[2] Most employees, however,[3] are not covered by formal contracts of employment, and the employment-at-will doctrine frequently prevents recovery for wrongful dismissal. The Employment-at-Will Rule says that informal promises of permanent or indefinite or lifetime employment are presumed to establish only an employment at will, which can be terminated at any time for any reason or for no reason. To recover on a breach of contract theory, the employee must establish the following elements in order to overcome the presumption of an employment at will:[4]

1. A promise to employ for a particular period of time or to terminate only for certain reasons or through certain procedures[5]
2. Enforceability of the promise because consideration was given or through a doctrine that avoids the requirement of consideration[6] and
3. Breach of the promise.[7]

---

[1] The nomenclature is somewhat misleading. Some breach of contract cases for wrongful dismissal are based on express promises of employment security.

[2] A. Corbin, Corbin on Contracts § 958 (1952). If an employee is dismissed wrongfully by an employer, a total breach occurs for which only a single action lies; judgment being obtainable for all wages past due and for all future promised wages less what can be earned by reasonable effort in similar employment. *See* Toussaint v. Blue Cross & Blue Shield, 408 Mich. 579, 610, 292 N.W.2d 880, 890 (1980) (court would enforce written contract).

[3] For suits alleging breaches of collective bargaining agreements, see § 4.25.

[4] See **ch. 1** for a discussion of the employment-at-will doctrine.

[5] See §§ **4.6–4.9**; Rompf v. John Q. Hammons Hotels, Inc., 685 P.2d 25, 28–29 (Wyo. 1984) (detrimental reliance shown by quitting other job unavailing where no promise of employment security).

[6] See §§ **4.12–4.18**; Restatement (Second) of Contracts § 71 (1979) (requirement of exchange; types of exchanges) and *id.* § 90 (promise reasonably inducing action or forbearance).

[7] See §§ **4.21–4.24**; A. Corbin, Corbin on Contracts § 958 at 937 (1952).

§ 4.1 INTRODUCTION

The Statute of Frauds[8] or federal preemption[9] may bar recovery even when these elements are established.

The first two elements are the most difficult for the plaintiff in a wrongful dismissal contract action. The promise element can be satisfied in several ways. The first and simplest way is to present evidence of an explicit promise made to the individual employee-plaintiff, orally or in writing.[10]

Absent evidence of an express promise made to a specific employee, there are two conceptual approaches to finding a promise implied in fact.[11] The first concept implies a promise from employer statements made to a workforce in general, such as are frequently contained in personnel manuals or handbooks.[12] Cases adopting this approach are discussed in § **4.8**. The second concept, less frequently accepted by the courts, implies a promise to continue the employment from a course of dealing over a considerable period of time.[13] Under this approach, substantial weight is given to the length of the employee's service as exemplified by the cases discussed in § **4.9**.

Even if a promise cannot be proven or implied in fact, a limited promise to act in good faith and consistent with public policy may be implied in law.[14] Cases involving the covenant of good faith and fair dealing may be found in § **4.11**.

Unless the employee can show a promise of continued employment, termination cannot be a breach of the employment contract. As one commentator has said:

> In the case of employment contracts without fixed duration it seems to be universally held that only an employment at will is created. In other words there is no contract at all since "refusal on either side to perform is not a breach, being merely exercise of the reserved power to terminate."[15]

Thus, the first question in a wrongful dismissal case is simply whether the employer promised any kind of employment security. Of course the employee would have a right to recover wages for work already performed under a contract, either in a suit for breach or under quasi-contract principles.[16] But, in order to establish

---

[8] See § **4.20**. *See also* A. Corbin, Corbin on Contracts §§ 446–447 (1952).

[9] See §§ **4.25** and **2.27–2.34**.

[10] See § **4.7**.

[11] Questions can arise as to exactly what part of the contract is being implied. This subject is discussed at the end of this section.

[12] See § **4.8**.

[13] See § **4.9**.

[14] See § **4.11**.

[15] L. Simpson, Contracts § 48 at 74 (1965).

[16] The label *quasi-contract* is applied to the common law action requiring payment for a benefit received. Its logic depends on a contract implied in law to prevent unjust enrichment. *See* J. Murray, Murray on Contracts § 9 at 15–16 (1974).

a right to recover for termination by the employer, the employee must prove an express or implied duration term for the oral or written contract.

The second element, consideration, is problematic for plaintiffs because of great variation in the requirements imposed by courts. The law of most jurisdictions requires the employee to prove something more than mere performance of services for the employer. Moreover, some courts equate the consideration requirement with mutuality of obligation. Under this approach, rejected by all commentators and thoughtful judicial opinion writers, courts ask only if the employment relationship qualifies as a bilateral contract—an exchange of a promise for a promise.[17] Because most employees do not promise to remain in their employer's employ, no bilateral contract exists. An employer promise of employment tenure is not supported by any reciprocal promise by the employee.[18]

Recovery for wrongful dismissal on a breach of contract theory depends on showing that the consideration requirement has been met or avoided in a way not encompassed by the bilateral contract concept.[19] Modern wrongful dismissal cases permit the consideration requirement to be met (1) under the unilateral contract theory of bargained-for reliance,[20] or (2) under the closely related promissory estoppel theory.[21]

Nearly all states allow consideration to be shown by proof of conduct above and beyond performing the ordinary job duties, such as quitting another job or turning down alternative job offers. If such special consideration is established, the promise of employment security is enforced even in the most conservative states.[22] In a growing number of states, continuation of employment after knowing of a promise of employment security is consideration for the employer's promise. The rationale is that the continued performance of service is a detriment suffered by the employee which was bargained for by the employer. Even when the bargained-for aspect cannot be met, the employer's promise can be enforced under the promissory estoppel doctrine, contained in § 90 of the *Restatement (Second) of Contracts,* if the employee's conduct in reliance on the promise was reasonable, and reasonably should have been expected by the employer.[23]

Most factual situations can be addressed satisfactorily by applying traditional contract law consideration doctrines without the need for more exotic theories. The real dispute between employer and employee will be factual: whether the employer promised employment tenure in order to induce the employee to accept

---

[17] A. Corbin, Corbin on Contracts § 142 at 205–06 (1952).

[18] See **§ 4.13** explaining why this analysis is not appropriate for most employment contracts.

[19] For a concise explanation of the difference between a bilateral contract and a unilateral contract, see J. Murray, Murray on Contracts § 6 (1974).

[20] See §§ **4.12–4.16**.

[21] See § **4.17**.

[22] See §§ **1.12, 4.15**.

[23] See § **4.17**.

§ 4.1 INTRODUCTION

or continue employment[24] or whether the employer reasonably could expect the employee to rely detrimentally on its promise.[25]

In other factual circumstances, either the promise or consideration element cannot be met, and the plaintiff will assert a covenant of good faith and fair dealing, which supplies both promise and consideration as a matter of law, if the covenant is applicable.[26] If the plaintiff can prove a promise and the existence of consideration, he still must prove a breach. Establishing a breach depends on the theory used to establish a promise. If relying on a contract implied in law, the so-called covenant of good faith and fair dealing,[27] the plaintiff must show that the reasons for dismissal offended public policy or otherwise were not in good faith.[28] If the plaintiff relies on an explicit promise or a promise implied in fact from a course of dealing or from policy statements, establishing a breach requires the employee to show that the dismissal violated the promise, the custom, or the policy statements, respectively.[29]

The term *implied-in-fact contract* needs to be probed a little. It is not always clear what element of a common law contract is being implied in wrongful dismissal cases carrying that name.[30]

In some cases the *promise* element is implied. This is so when no express promise is made, but only more general promises of long term employment or a course of dealing in which employment security is provided. In other cases, however, the promise of employment security is express and it makes no sense to say that a promise is being implied.

In many cases, the *consideration* element is implied. Most frequently, the bargained-for aspect of consideration is not express, and must be implied. For example in *Toussaint v. Blue Cross & Blue Shield*[31] and in *Woolley v. Hoffman-LaRoche, Inc.*[32] the courts were willing to infer that an employer makes an offer of employment security to the workforce in general in order to induce that workforce to remain in its employ. In some cases, it may be appropriate to imply reliance. This is the only way to explain the cases holding that a plaintiff in an implied-in-fact

---

[24] This employer purpose must be shown to establish bargained-for detriment, under traditional consideration requirements.

[25] This expectation must be shown to meet the promissory estoppel requirements of Restatement (Second) of Contracts § 90.

[26] See § **4.11**.

[27] See § **4.23**.

[28] See §§ **4.11, 4.23, 7.23**.

[29] See §§ **4.22, 4.24, 7.24–7.28**.

[30] J. Calamari & J. Perillo, The Law of Contracts 19–20 (1977) (when the parties manifest their agreement by their conduct the contract is said to be implied in fact); J. Murray, Murray on Contracts § 9 at 14–15 (1974). *See also* Erickson v. Goodell Oil. Co., 384 Mich. 207, 180 N.W.2d 798 (1970).

[31] 408 Mich. 579, 292 N.W.2d 880 (1980); see § **4.16**.

[32] 99 N.J. 284, 491 A.2d 1257 (1985). See § **4.16**.

contract case need not prove knowledge of the employer's promise in order to show the reliance link between the detrimental conduct and the promise.

Rarely would the breach element be implied. To do so would permit damages to be recovered without proof of wrongful conduct.

§ 4.2 Historical Development of Contract Theories

Before considering the three requirements identified in § **4.1**, it is useful to review the historical development of actions in contract. As in any area of the law that is changing rapidly, such as wrongful dismissal, both plaintiff and defendant counsel can advise clients and convince courts more effectively if they can place recent developments in their own and other jurisdictions in historical context. The purpose of §§ **4.3** through **4.5** is to identify major conceptual underpinnings of modern contract theory and to refer the reader to other sources for a more detailed treatment.

A limitation on the employer's right to dismiss an employee, such as a just cause standard for dismissal, can come explicitly from a promise, or it can be implied in a contract that seems to promise unconditional employment for a period of time. Implying important terms of employment contracts has a long history. For example, formal contracts of employment, enforced in the heyday of the employment-at-will rule, could be terminated for just cause without the employer being liable. This employer right was implied by law. Implying a right to terminate for just cause was necessary to protect employers from being obligated to continue employment for life or otherwise for indefinite terms without having the power to dismiss unless the employee breached the contract.[33] The implied-in-fact contract doctrine similarly implies a term: a limitation on the employer's right to dismiss.

In considering the history of the employment-at-will rule, it is helpful to recall that contract law does not take all promises seriously: if you sue me for reneging on an invitation to come to dinner, it is unlikely you will recover. The employment-at-will rule reflected a policy judgment that informal promises of informal employment security should not be taken seriously by the law, unless the employee offers an indication that both parties meant for their deal to be enforced.[34]

§ 4.3 — Common Law Forms of Action

Under the system of common law pleading, three causes of action evolved into what is now called contract: covenant, special assumpsit, and indebitatus assumpsit.[35]

---

[33] *See* Ohanian v. Avis Rent a Car System, Inc., 779 F.2d 101, 108 (2d Cir. 1985) (explaining distinction between employee breach and existence of just cause).

[34] Validation devices, such as consideration, for promises of employment security are discussed in §§ **4.4** and **4.12–4.17**.

[35] *See* G. Gilmore, The Death of Contract (1974); S. Milsom, Historical Foundations of the Common Law 243–360 (1981). The two forms of assumpsit emerged from the tort writ of trespass

§ 4.3 COMMON LAW

Covenant lay for the recovery of damages for breach of a promise under seal.[36] Special assumpsit lay for the recovery of damages for breach of a simple contract, either express or implied in fact.[37] Contracts *implied in fact* were those implied from the conduct of the parties because their course of conduct showed agreement.[38] Indebitatus assumpsit lay for the recovery of damages for a breach of a promise implied in law.[39] Involving circumstances other than explicit agreement between the parties and sometimes involving circumstances that actually negated the existence of any agreement,[40] promises *implied in law* were quasi-contractual rather than contractual.

Consideration as a means of contract validation was not universally required; it was linked only with assumpsit. Theoretically, indebitatus assumpsit required consideration in the sense that the plaintiff must have performed some act obligating the defendant to pay for the value of the plaintiff's act.[41] Special assumpsit, as finally developed, enforced promises only when they were based on consideration, and consideration was an essential allegation for the cause of action.[42] Consideration was not, however, an essential element in covenant; promises made in writing under seal were enforced simply as promises.[43]

As a result of historical development, the legal elements of a modern contract are those of the special assumpsit action. Covenant fell into disuse because most states abolished, by statute, the effectiveness of the private seal and because of procedural limitations such as lack of a jury trial.[44] Indebitatus assumpsit evolved

---

on the case beginning in the 15th century. T. Plucknett, A Concise History of the Common Law 636-48 (5th ed. 1956). Covenant was much older. S. Milsom, Historical Foundations of the Common Law at 365.

[36] J. Koffler & A. Reppy, Common Law Pleading § 144 at 303–04 (1969); S. Milsom, Historical Foundations of the Common Law 247 (1981).

[37] J. Koffler & A. Reppy, Common Law Pleading § 162 at 319 (1969); S. Milsom, Historical Foundations of the Common Law 249 (1981).

[38] J. Koffler & A. Reppy, Common Law Pleading § 172 at 338 (1969).

[39] *Id.* § 173 at 339.

[40] *Id.* § 172 at 338. For a discussion of the implied-in-fact/implied-in-law distinction, *See* Restatement (Second) of Contracts § 4 (1979).

[41] J. Koffler & A. Reppy, Common Law Pleading § 173 at 339 (1969).

[42] *Id.* § 163 at 320.

[43] T. Plucknett, A Concise History of the Common Law 634 (5th ed. 1956); J. Koffler & A. Reppy, Common Law Pleading § 162 of 320 (1981).

[44] J. Koffler & A. Reppy, Common Law Pleading § 153 at 308 (1981); S. Milsom, Historical Foundations of the Common Law 314–15 (1981). Plaintiffs preferred assumpsit because all they had to do was convince a jury that there was a contract. T. Plucknett, A Concise History of the Common Law 647 (5th ed. 1956).

into the general remedy for quasi-contractual obligations,[45] while special assumpsit developed into the basic remedy for breach of contract, express or implied in fact.[46]

These early characteristics of contract theories pertain to a modern wrongful dismissal action because they show the willingness of the law: to imply obligations as a matter of law, in indebitatus assumpsit; to imply undertakings from conduct as well as from verbal expressions, in special assumpit; and to permit recovery without proof of consideration, in covenant.[47]

§ 4.4 — The Consideration Requirement

Consideration as a contract validation device is associated with the *bargain* theory of contract. In 1870, after American jurisdictions began to abolish common law pleading,[48] Dean Christopher Langdell undertook to articulate a general theory of contract, synthesizing the diverse requirements of the several separate causes of action.[49] His ideas were developed further by Oliver Wendell Holmes, Jr. and Professor Samuel Williston.[50] Under this general theory, consideration, a concept recognized earlier by Kent, Story, and others,[51] became a tool for narrowing the range of contractual liability.[52] Absent consideration, the person to whom the promise was made (the promisee) had no legal right or claim. Thus, in order to enforce the original promise, the promisee must make a return promise, or suffer a detriment, and the parties also must understand the second promise or the detriment as the motive or inducement for the original promise.[53] This bargain theory of consideration was reflected in § 75 of the original *Restatement of Contracts*.[54]

---

[45] Stone v. White, 301 U.S. 532 (1937). Justice Stone noted that *indebitatus assumpsit* "has been gradually expanded as a medium for recovery upon every form of quasi-contractual obligation in which the duty to pay money is imposed by law, independently of contract, express or implied in fact." *Id.* at 354.

[46] J. Koffler & A. Reppy, Common Law Pleading § 171 at 334 (1969).

[47] For further exposition of the proposition that consideration was only one of several validation devices, *see* J. Murray, Murray on Contracts § 72 at 139–42 (1974).

[48] J. Koffler & A. Reppy, Common Law Pleading § 6 at 24 (1969) (though antiquated, common law pleading remains the foundation of modern code pleading at both the state and federal level).

[49] G. Gilmore, The Death of Contract 12 (1974). A similar effort already was underway in England. T. Plucknett, A Concise History of the Common Law 652 (5th ed. 1956).

[50] G. Gilmore, The Death of Contract 14 (1974).

[51] *Id.* at 111 n.34.

[52] *Id.* at 21. This historical view is that of Professor Gilmore. Other commentators view the development of the consideration requirement as something of a historical accident, intended to identify those promises that should be enforced. *See, e.g.,* J. Murray, Murray on Contracts § 72 at 141–42 (1974); T. Plucknett, A Concise History of the Common Law 651 (5th ed. 1956).

[53] G. Gilmore, The Death of Contract 20 (1974); *See* J. Murray, Murray on Contracts § 79 at 158–60 (1974) for a discussion of when a detriment is bargained for.

[54] G. Gilmore, The Death of Contract 21 (1974).

As the *Restatement of Contracts* was being formulated, however, scholars and judges recognized that liability for breach of contract frequently was imposed in cases not fitting the bargain theory of consideration. Judge Benjamin Cardozo and Professor Arthur Corbin led the effort to expand the theory of contract to accommodate the circumstances under which promises could be implied and enforced without consideration in the bargain sense. An early result was the inclusion of § 90 of the original *Restatement of Contracts*,[55] articulating the *promissory estoppel* theory of contract enforcement. During the 1960s, the *Restatement of Contracts (Second)* was drafted in a fashion that diminished the importance of consideration and enhanced the flexibility of § 90.[56] The doctrine of promissory estoppel began to supply a theoretical basis for enforcing promises unsupported by consideration in the traditional sense.[57] Promissory estoppel allows a person to whom a promise is made to enforce the promise if it can be shown that the promisee reasonably relied on the promise, regardless of whether the reliance was bargained for.

Recently, Charles Fried has undertaken to reformulate a theory of contract based purely on the enforcement of promises. He explains why the law may not wish to enforce casual promises yet should enforce serious promises without regard to consideration. Consideration, in his view, offers no coherent basis for deciding which promises to enforce.[58]

It is fair to say that the law of implied-in-fact contracts associated with employment terminations is moving subtly away from the bargain theory of contract to promissory estoppel, and even beyond, toward a Fried-type principle that would omit altogether inquiry into consideration. Nevertheless, most courts purport to honor the bargain theory by permitting various types of inferences to be drawn from the promise itself.[59]

§ 4.5 —Treatment of Consideration in Collective Bargaining Agreements

During the same period that general contract principles were being developed, suits were being brought for breach of collective bargaining agreements.[60] Before

---

[55] *Id.* at 60–65.

[56] *Id.* at 69–76. For a review of the doctrinal implications of the evolution of § 90, *see* Feinman, *Promissory Estoppel and Judicial Method,* 97 Harv. L. Rev. 678 (1984).

[57] G. Gilmore, The Death of Contract 60–66 (1974).

[58] C. Fried, Contract as Promise 38 (1981). *But see* 1 A. Corbin, Corbin on Contracts § 111 at 496 (1950) (opining that the consideration doctrine, for all its flaws, will continue to be the means used by the law to decide which promises to enforce). *See generally* Feinman, *Promissory Estoppel and Judicial Method,* 97 Harv. L. Rev. 678 (1984) (review of doctrinal implications of the evolution of promissory estoppel).

[59] See § **4.18**, citing cases requiring no direct evidence of reliance.

[60] *See* H. Perritt, Labor Injunctions § 1.12 (1986).

the National Labor Relations Act[61] and the Labor Management Relations Act[62] provided a statutory regulatory mechanism and expressly made collective agreements enforceable,[63] the courts regularly held that collective agreements were enforceable against both the employer and the union.[64] The most common means of dealing with the consideration requirement was to imply a promise by the union not to call a strike or demand changes in employment conditions during the term of the agreement.[65] In reality, however, the consideration requirement was deemed satisfied, as a matter of policy preference in favor of enforceability.[66]

§ 4.6 The Promise of Employment Security

The analytical starting point in a wrongful dismissal breach of contract action is to decide what the employer has promised: specifically, whether the employer has offered or promised employment tenure or promised to terminate the employment relationship only for certain reasons or after exhaustion of certain procedures.[67] It is easy to conclude that the employer, at least by implication, has promised to pay for services actually performed; the harder question is whether the employer has promised something more—employment tenure. The case law indicates that the promise of employment tenure can be found in specific oral commitments to an individual employee,[68] in employer representations made to the workforce in

---

[61] 29 U.S.C. §§ 151-169 (1982).

[62] Labor Management Relations Act of 1947, Pub. L. No. 80-101, 61 Stat. 136 (codified as amended in scattered sections of 29 U.S.C. §§ 141-187 (1982)).

[63] Section 301 of the 1947 LMRA, 29 U.S.C. § 185 (1982), explicitly made collective bargaining agreements enforceable. In Textile Workers v. Lincoln Mills, 353 U.S. 448 (1957), the Supreme Court held that federal common law should govern enforcement of collective bargaining agreements. §§ **2.30, 3.21**, and **4.25** review the contemporary relationship between federal and state law in this area.

[64] Plumbers v. Kahme, 6 N.Y.S.2d 589 (N.Y. Sup. Ct. 1937) (injunction against a strike); Harper v. I.B.E.W. Local 520, 48 S.W.2d 1033 (Tex. Civ. App. 1932) (enforcement against employer); Goldman v. Cohen, 222 A.D. 631, 227 N.Y.S. 311 (1928) (injunction granted against employer lockout); Schlesinger v. Quinto, 201 A.D. 487, 194 N.Y.S. 401 (1922) (injunction granted against employer association); Nederlandsch ASM v. Stevedores, 265 F. 397 (E.D. La. 1920) (damages awarded employer after strike); Gilchrist v. Metal Polishers, 113 A. 320 (N.J. Ch. 1919) (injunction against strike); Rice, *Collective Labor Agreements in American Law,* 44 Harv. L. Rev. 572 (1931); Cox, *Rights Under a Labor Agreement,* 69 Harv. L. Rev. 601, 603 (1956).

[65] Harper v. I.B.E.W. Local 520, 48 S.W.2d at 1040; Nederlandsch ASM v. Stevedores, 265 F. at 400; Note, 11 N.Y.L.Q. 262, 263 (1933); Note, 41 Yale L.J. 1221, 1225 (1932).

[66] The opinions cited in the two preceding notes show the heavy reliance placed by the courts on policy considerations. The Yale note concludes that collective agreements ought to be enforced and then suggests ways of dealing with the consideration problem. Note, 41 Yale L.J. 1221, 1225 (1932).

[67] Absent such a promise, the employment is presumed to be terminable at will. See **ch. 1**.

[68] See **§ 4.7**.

§ 4.6 THE PROMISE

general,[69] less often from a course of dealing over a long period of service,[70] or in a legally implied covenant of good faith.[71]

Analytically, it is useful to distinguish between express promises of employment security and more general statements from which a promise of employment security can be inferred.[72] A promise implied in fact may be entitled to less serious treatment legally than an express one. Accordingly, the search for consideration as a validation device may be more stringent for implied-in-fact promises than for express promises.[73]

The implied covenant of good faith and fair dealing, discussed in § **4.11**, is a special implied-in-law promise. It is a substitute for an express or implied-in-fact promise by the employer.[74] The implied promise imposes a legally enforceable obligation not to exercise the otherwise unlimited power of termination in bad faith or for reasons offending public policy. This implied covenant concept resembles a tort theory more than a contract theory because it tests the defendant's compliance with a duty imposed through public policy rather than with a promise voluntarily made. This may explain some of the confusion in early wrongful dismissal cases between contract and tort.[75]

The following four sections deal with express promises (§ **4.7**), promises implied in fact from employer representations (§ **4.8**), promises implied in fact from length of service and conduct (§ **4.9**), and promises implied in law by the covenant of good faith and fair dealing (§ **4.11**). Disclaimers as a way of negating promises are analyzed in § **4.10**. The question of how an employer can change a promise, once made and relied upon by employees, is dealt with in § **4.19**.

A growing number of cases involve efforts to use the implied-in-fact contract theory to support recovery for promises other than a promise of employment security; e.g., promises of promotions or pay raises. Some courts are reluctant to accept such efforts.[76]

---

[69] See § **4.8**.

[70] See § **4.9**.

[71] See § **4.11**.

[72] *See* Broussard v. C.A.C.I., Inc., 780 F.2d 162 (1st Cir. 1986) (express promise of employment security distinguished from implied promise derived from negotiations and handbook; latter insufficient to support wrongful dismissal claim); *but see* Myrtle Springs Reverted Indep. School Dist. v. Hogan, 705 S.W.2d 707 (Tex. Ct. App. 1985) (written school board policies limiting reasons for dismissal become part of individual teacher's contract).

[73] This validation question is addressed in §§ **4.12–4.14**.

[74] *See* Wagenseller v. Scottsdale Memorial Hosp., 147 Ariz. 370, 381, 710 P.2d 1025, 1036 (1985) (implied-in-law term does not depend on party intent).

[75] *See* Tameny v. Atlantic Richfield Co., 27 Cal. 3d 167, 176–77, 610 P.2d 1330, 1334–35, 164 Cal. Rptr. 839, 843–44 (1980) (relationship between tort and contract bases for recovery); Brockmeyer v. Dun & Bradstreet, Inc., 113 Wis. 2d 561, 574, 335 N.W.2d 834, 841 (1983) (same).

[76] *Compare* Banas v. Matthews Int'l Corp., 348 Pa. Super. 464, 502 A.2d 637 (1985) (reversing judgment for employee; dismissal for appropriation of employer property pursuant to implied promise that such appropriation was permissible distinguished from violation of implied promise of job security) *with* Sepanske v. Bendix Corp., 147 Mich. App. 819, 826, 384 N.W.2d 54, 58

§ 4.7 — Express Commitments Made to Specific Employees

Sometimes a direct oral promise of employment security can be shown. For example, in *Terrio v. Millinocket Community Hospital*,[77] the Supreme Judicial Court of Maine affirmed a jury verdict for a plaintiff in a wrongful dismissal suit. It held that an oral statement by the employer's agent that the plaintiff was secure in her job "for the rest of her life," in "the context of her long service in a position of substantial responsibility . . . provided the critical evidentiary support for her contract claim."[78]

In *Toussaint v. Blue Cross & Blue Shield*[79] and in its companion case, *Ebling v. Masco Corp.*,[80] the Supreme Court of Michigan found sufficient factual evidence to permit a jury to imply a contract based on assurances that termination would occur for "just cause only."[81] In *Toussaint*, there were two independent promises, either of them apparently sufficient: an oral promise and a personnel policy handbook.[82] Regarding the oral promise, the court held:

> When a prospective employee inquires about job security and the employer agrees that the employee shall be employed as long as he does the job, a fair construction is that the employer has agreed to give up his right to discharge at will without assigning a cause and may discharge only for cause.[83]

In *Weiner v. McGraw-Hill, Inc.*,[84] the New York Court of Appeals reversed a decision by the Appellate Division of the state supreme court and held that an employee who relied on oral representations and an employee handbook promising

---

(1985) (unilateral employer policies established enforceable contract right to return to certain position on return from leave; relying on Toussaint). **App. F** discusses this.

[77] 379 A.2d 135 (Me. 1977).

[78] *Id.* at 138. *But cf.* Pinsof v. Pinsof, 107 Ill. App. 3d 1031, 438 N.E.2d 525 (1982) (stock purchase agreement and death benefits not sufficient to show existence of lifetime contract). Griffith v. Sollay Found. Drilling, Inc., 373 So. 2d 979, 982 (La. Ct. App. 1979) (alleged understanding of permanent employment unenforceable under traditional rule that a promise of permanent employment created an indefinite hiring, terminable at will). *See also* Annotation, 60 A.L.R.3d 226, § 3 (1974).

[79] 408 Mich. 579, 292 N.W.2d 880 (1980).

[80] 408 Mich. 579, 292 N.W.2d 880 (1980); the opinion of the Michigan Supreme Court addresses both the *Toussaint* and *Ebling* cases.

[81] 408 Mich. at 599, 292 N.W.2d at 885.

[82] "A provision of an employment contract providing that an employee shall not be discharged except for cause is legally enforceable . . . such a provision may become part of the contract either by express agreement, oral or written, or as a result of an employee's legitimate expectations grounded in an employer's policy statements." *Id.* at 598, 292 N.W.2d at 885. The written assurances contained in the handbook are considered in § **4.8**.

[83] *Id.* at 610, 292 N.W.2d at 890.

[84] 57 N.Y.2d 458, 443 N.E.2d 441, 457 N.Y.S.2d 193 (1982).

discharge only for just cause had a claim in contract.[85] Weiner had been assured in the initial employment interview that McGraw-Hill terminated employees only for just cause.[86]

In *Ohanian v. Avis Rent a Car System, Inc.*,[87] the Second Circuit, applying New York law, suggested that promises of employment security made to individual employees are entitled to greater weight than promises made to the workforce in general.[88]

§ 4.8 —Promises Derived from Employer Representations Made to Workforce in General

An employer's promise of continued employment made to the workforce in general can support a wrongful dismissal claim premised on breach of contract. In most of the cases permitting plaintiff recovery, the defendant-employer communicated a promise through an employee handbook that employment would be terminated only for cause or only after exhaustion of certain procedures. In other cases, the alleged promise was communicated to a group of employees, frequently in connection with changes in corporate organization.[89]

In a number of cases, the plaintiffs recovered based on general statements of employer policies that promised continued employment. *Toussaint v. Blue Cross & Blue Shield*,[90] *Weiner v. McGraw-Hill, Inc.*,[91] *Pine River State Bank v. Mettille*[92] and *Wagenseller v. Scottsdale Memorial Hospital*[93] are the leading cases.[94] In *Toussaint* and in *Weiner v. McGraw-Hill, Inc.* there were oral promises made directly to the employee in addition to general promises contained in the handbooks.[95]

---

[85] *Id.* at 462, 443 N.E.2d at 443, 457 N.Y.S.2d at 195. The handbook aspect of Weiner v. McGraw-Hill, Inc. is addressed in **§ 4.8**.

[86] *Id.* at 460, 443 N.E.2d at 442, 457 N.Y.S.2d at 194.

[87] 779 F.2d 101, 108 (2d Cir. 1985).

[88] *Id.* at 109. Promises made to the workforce in general, however, are more likely to be in writing and thus less likely to raise Statute of Frauds problems. *Id.* at 119 (Wyatt, J., dissenting). See **§ 4.20** regarding the Statute of Frauds.

[89] *See* Chastain v. Kelly-Springfield Tire Co., 733 F.2d 1479 (11th Cir. 1984) (assurances by new corporate parent too indefinite to enforce as a promise of permanent employment under Alabama law).

[90] 408 Mich. 579, 292 N.W.2d 880 (1980).

[91] 57 N.Y.S.2d 458, 443 N.E.2d 441, 457 N.Y.S.2d 193 (1982).

[92] 333 N.W.2d 622 (Minn. 1983).

[93] 147 Ariz. 370, 710 P.2d 1025 (1985).

[94] *Compare* Richardson v. Charles Cole Memorial Hosp., 320 Pa. Super. 106, 466 A.2d 1084 (1983) (policies in handbook are not of a contract of employment) *with* Staggs v. Blue Cross, 61 Md. App. 381, 392, 486 A.2d 798, 803-04 (1985) (reversing summary judgment for employer; personnel policy memorandum setting forth procedures to be followed before termination may give rise to contractual obligation).

[95] The effect of these explicit promises is considered in **§ 4.7**.

In *Toussaint*,[96] the Supreme Court of Michigan found sufficient factual evidence to permit a jury to imply a contract based on assurances that termination would occur for "just cause only."[97] In *Toussaint*, there were two independent promises, either of them apparently sufficient: an oral promise and a personnel policy handbook.[98] The *Toussaint* court emphasized that the written obligation was voluntarily undertaken by the employer when it decided to promulgate formal policies limiting its right of termination at will, even if the oral promise had not been made.[99]

In *Weiner v. McGraw-Hill, Inc.*,[1] the decision by the Appellate Division of the state supreme court was reversed by the New York Court of Appeals, which held that an employee who relied on oral representations and an employee handbook promising discharge only for just cause had a claim in contract.[2] Weiner's employment application specified that employment would be subject to the provisions of McGraw-Hill's "Handbook on Personnel Policies and Procedures," which stated, "the company will resort to dismissal for just and sufficient cause only . . . "[3]

The importance to employees and the hidden danger to employers of statements made in a company handbook standing alone, i.e., without any oral representations to an employee, was underscored by the Minnesota Supreme Court in *Pine River State Bank v. Mettille*.[4] The court ruled that disciplinary procedures contained in an employee handbook distributed to employees were a legally enforceable promise not to dismiss employees without following the procedures.[5] In *Wagenseller v. Scottsdale Memorial Hospital*,[6] the court reversed dismissal of plaintiff's claim and held that a nurse dismissed for refusing to "moon" could recover on implied-in-fact contract theory based on employee manual. *Wagenseller* and *Pine River* illustrate handbook promises relating to pretermination procedures, as contrasted with the promises related to grounds for termination in *Toussaint* and *Weiner*.

Other jurisdictions also have recognized the significance of employer handbooks. The Supreme Judicial Court of Maine accepted the proposition, in *Knowles v. Unity College*,[7] that unilateral issuance by a university employer of policies could give rise to legally enforceable contractual obligations. However, in the case before

---

[96] The opinion of the Michigan Supreme Court addresses both the *Toussaint* and Ebling v. Masco Corp. cases.

[97] Toussaint v. Blue Cross & Blue Shield, 408 Mich. at 599, 292 N.W.2d at 885.

[98] "A provision of an employment contract providing that an employee shall not be discharged except for cause is legally enforceable . . . such a provision may become part of the contract either by express agreement, oral or written, or as a result of an employee's legitimate expectations grounded in an employer's policy statements." *Id.* at 598, 292 N.W.2d at 885.

[99] *Id.* at 614, 292 N.W.2d at 892. *See also* Simpson v. Western Graphics Corp., 293 Or. 96, 643 P.2d 1276 (1982) (employee, by handbook's terms, could only be fired for just cause, but employer could define just cause; parties stipulated handbook was binding).

[1] 57 N.Y.2d 458, 443 N.E.2d 441, 457 N.Y.S.2d 193 (1982).

[2] *Id.* at 462, 443 N.E.2d at 443, 457 N.Y.S.2d at 195.

[3] *Id.* at 460, 443 N.E.2d at 442, 457 N.Y.S.2d at 194.

[4] 333 N.W.2d 622 (Minn. 1983).

[5] *Id.* at 631.

[6] 147 Ariz. 370, 383, 710 P.2d 1025, 1036 (1985).

[7] 429 A.2d 220 (Me. 1981).

§ 4.9 IMPLIED PROMISES

it, the court affirmed a finding that the university expressly had forborne to adopt policies guaranteeing tenure.[8] In *Thompson v. St. Regis Paper Co.*,[9] the Supreme Court of Washington held that an employer handbook can establish enforceable obligations to the extent that it leads employees to expect specific treatment in specific situations, as opposed merely to articulating general policies.[10] The Supreme Court of Idaho, in *Watson v. Idaho Falls Consolidated Hospitals*,[11] affirmed a judgment for an employee based on handbook provisions that enumerated the reasons for which employment could be terminated. The Supreme Court of Vermont did likewise in *Benoir v. Ethan Allen, Inc.*[12] The appellate courts of Oklahoma, in *Langdon v. Saga Corp.*[13] and *Dangott v. ASG Industries, Inc.*,[14] stated that employer manuals or policy statements affording severance pay were enforceable.

In a number of other cases, oral promises and handbooks have been combined with other factors in support of the promise element.[15]

Affirmative action commitments distributed to employees are potentially fertile sources of implied promises.[16] The promise in the handbook must be reasonably specific, however, to support an implied contract claim.[17] In most of the cases discussed in this section, the promise element was easy to satisfy; the employer had communicated reasonably explicit assurances that employment would be terminated only for cause or only after exhaustion of certain procedures.

§ 4.9 —Promises Implied from Length of Service and Conduct

There are a few cases that suggest that length of service can be a strong factor leading a court to imply a promise of continued employment.[18] In none of these

---

[8] *Id.* at 223.

[9] 102 Wash. 2d 219, 685 P.2d 1081, 1087–88 (1984).

[10] *See also* Woolley v. Hoffman-LaRoche, Inc., 99 N.J. 284, 491 A.2d 1257 (1985) (personnel handbook promise to dismiss only for cause can be found by jury to be enforceable contract).

[11] 11 Idaho 44, 720 P.2d 632 (1986).

[12] ___ Vt. ___, 514 A.2d 716 (1986) (handbook setting forth procedures required cause for dismissal).

[13] 569 P.2d 524 (Okla. Ct. App. 1977).

[14] 558 P.2d 379 (Okla. 1976).

[15] Cleary v. American Airlines, 111 Cal. App. 3d 443, 447, 168 Cal. Rptr. 722, 724 (1980) (employer regulation); Pugh v. See's Candies, 116 Cal. App. 3d 311, 171 Cal. Rptr. 917 (1981) (oral promise).

[16] *See* Fitzgerald v. Norwest Corp., ___ Minn. App. ___, 382 N.W.2d 290, 293 (1986) (affirmative action statement in handbook sufficiently definite to permit jury to decide whether constituted enforceable promise), *review denied* (Apr. 24, 1986).

[17] *See* Ellis v. El Paso Natural Gas Co., 754 F.2d 884, 886 (10th Cir. 1985) (personnel manual promising "balanced compensation program . . . to attract, motivate and retain" competent employees was too indefinite to support implied contract claim for wrongful dismissal; applying New Mexico law).

[18] Older cases relying on longevity are collected in a student work: Note, *Implied Contract Rights to Job Security*, 26 Stan. L. Rev. 335, 361–65 (1974). The authors of that note conclude that

cases is length of service used by itself to imply such a promise; rather it is used with other conduct by the employer to establish a course of dealing from which such a promise can be inferred.[19]

It is a well accepted principle of contract law that a promise may be inferred from conduct. Professor Williston put it this way: "Any conduct from which a reasonable person in the offeree's position would be justified in inferring a promise in return for a requested act . . . amounts to an offer."[20] There need be no request for the performance of services; if it is known that the services are being rendered with the expectation of pay, the person benefited is liable.[21]

It is a question of fact whether a reasonable person would understand that the services were being performed in exchange for fair compensation.[22] Professor Corbin agreed, pointing out that the only difference between express and implied-in-fact contracts is in the mode of proof of the promise.[23] The authors of the *Restatement* agreed with these general propositions:

> Conduct as Manifestation of Assent
> (1) The manifestation of assent may be made wholly or partly by written or spoken words or by other acts or by failure to act.
> (2) The conduct of a party is not effective as a manifestation of his assent unless he intends to engage in the conduct and knows or has reason to know that the other party may infer from his conduct that he assents.
> (3) The conduct of a party may manifest assent even though he does not in fact assent. In such cases a resulting contract may be voidable because of fraud, duress, mistake, or other invalidating cause.[24]

There are a number of cases adopting these principles in the employment context to imply a promise to continue employment under the same terms as those provided

---

longevity in these cases generally was used as a basis to infer either an implied contract or special consideration. *See also* Roberts v. Wake Forest Univ., 55 N.C. App. 430, 435, 286 S.E.2d 120, 123, *review denied*, 305 N.C. 586, 292 S.E.2d 571 (1982) (business usage may support promise of employment tenure; evidence insufficient to show such usage).

[19] *See* Hunt v. I.B.M. Mid America Employees Fed. Credit Union, 384 N.W.2d 853 (Minn. 1986) (no evidence of past practices to flesh out meaning of vague handbook promises; reinstating summary judgment for employer).

[20] S. Williston, Williston on Contracts § 36 (3d ed., Jaeger ed. 1956), citing Horacek v. Smith, 33 Cal. 2d 186, 199 P.2d 929 (1948) (recovery of back salary).

[21] S. Williston, Williston on Contracts § 36 at n.13 (3d ed., Jaeger ed. 1956). It should be noted that Williston views this situation as one of implied-in-fact promise rather than treating it as quasi-contract.

[22] S. Williston, Williston on Contracts § 36 at 14 (3d ed., Jaeger, ed. 1956).

[23] A. Corbin, Corbin on Contracts § 18 at 40–41 (1963).

[24] Restatement (Second) of Contracts § 19 (1979). Comment (a) makes it clear that the principle contained in § 19 applies to implication of a promise by conduct, as well as implication of the acceptance of a promise.

§ 4.9 IMPLIED PROMISES

for in a completed express contract,[25] to pay for services rendered,[26] or to continue certain monetary benefits according to past practice.[27]

It is also a recognized principle of contract law that a course of dealing between the parties gives context to their conduct, "which is fairly to be regarded as establishing a common basis of understanding for interpreting their expressions and other conduct."[28] This principle was used by the Supreme Court of the United States to imply a promise of employment tenure in *Perry v. Sindermann*.[29] In his tenth year of employment after a succession of one-year contracts,[30] Sindermann was notified that his contract for a state college teaching position would not be renewed.

> The college had no formal tenure system, but Mr. Sindermann alleged that a "de facto tenure system" had been established by custom and practice and by a statement in the college's faculty guide encouraging faculty members "to feel that [they have] permanent tenure as long as [their] teaching services are satisfactory."[31]

The Supreme Court held that Sindermann was entitled to prove his claim that the college had fostered the understanding that the employment of persons in his position would be continued unless "cause" existed for their termination.[32] It reasoned that a contract can be implied from the promissor's words and conduct, even though no formal agreement exists.[33]

In *Board of Regents v. Roth*,[34] decided the same day as *Perry*, the Court applied the same analytical principles, but reached the opposite result. The Court held that, based on the course of dealing between Roth and his employer, he had no legitimate expectation of continued employment beyond the one-year term of his contract.

Several private sector wrongful discharge cases also looked to the totality of the course of dealing between employer and employee to determine if a promise of employment tenure could be inferred.[35] Length of service has been viewed as

---

[25] *See* Cinefot, Int'l Corp. v. Hudson Photographic Indus., 13 N.Y.2d 249, 196 N.E.2d 54, 246 N.Y.S.2d 345, 6 A.L.R.3d 1347 (1963) (citing Corbin § 18), Harper v. Cedar Rapids Tel. Co., 244 N.W.2d 782, 789 (Iowa 1976) (conduct extending employment contract; discussion of burdens of proof and presumptions).

[26] *See* Annotation, *Services Rendered by Attorneys*, 78 A.L.R.2d 318 (1961).

[27] *See* Annotation, *Regular Payment of Bonuses*, 66 A.L.R.3d 1075 (1975).

[28] Restatement (Second) of Contracts § 233 (1979). Section 223 appears in Chapter 9, *The Scope of Contractual Obligations*, Topic 4, *Scope as Affected by Usage*. The introductory note to Chapter 9 states that the parties' intention arises from context, and usages are an important part of the context.

[29] 408 U.S. 593 (1972). This case is discussed in greater detail in **§ 6.10**.

[30] *Id.* at 594.

[31] *Id.* at 600.

[32] *Id.* at 602–03.

[33] *Id.* at 601–02.

[34] 408 U.S. 564 (1972).

[35] Restatement (Second) of Contracts § 18 (manifestation of mutual assent), § 19 (conduct as manifestation of assent) and § 24 (offer defined) (1979); *see also* A. Corbin, Corbin on Contracts

establishing a course of dealing[36] from which a promise can be implied in fact or as a factor influencing application of an implied covenant of good faith. The cases discussed in this section seem to blur these two separate legal concepts, but they all emphasize length of service to some degree as a way of deriving or reinforcing a promise of employment tenure.

In *Delzell v. Pope*,[37] the plaintiff was fired from his job as secretary of the executive board of the Tennessee Baptist Convention after 13 years of service. Relying in part on the payment of an annual salary and the presumption that the pay period indicates the duration of an employment contract,[38] the court found an implied contract for a one-year term. The court also said, noting the length of the plaintiff's service, "it would be most unreasonable to infer that he was employed upon a month-to-month basis and was subject to dismissal on a moment's notice."[39] It concluded that the plaintiff's suit was premised upon an implied understanding "based on a course of conduct between the complainant and the Board, and *was of sufficient duration to bind the parties.*" (Emphasis added.)[40]

The California Court of Appeal, in *Cleary v. American Airlines, Inc.*,[41] reversed a trial court order sustaining a demurrer to a breach of contract claim. The employee alleged that he entered into an oral contract with American Airlines by which he became a permanent employee.[42] The *Cleary* court concluded that employment contracts, like all contracts, include an implied covenant of good faith and fair dealing.[43] The court attached importance to the plaintiff's 18 years of service by stating, "[t]ermination of employment without legal cause after such a period of time offends the Implied-in-law Covenant of Good Faith and Fair Dealing."[44]

In *Pugh v. See's Candies, Inc.*,[45] The California Court of Appeal reversed a nonsuit entered against a plaintiff-employee who alleged that he was fired in breach of contract and for reasons which offended public policy. Mr. Pugh was terminated with no reason given after 32 years of employment. There had been a continuing

---

§ 13 (1952). Restatement (Second) of Contracts § 19 (1979) (conduct as manifestation of assent); *see also* Corbin § 13, § 34 at 53–54, Restatement (Second) of Contracts § 19 (1979) (conduct as manifestation of assent). Proof issues relating to contract causes of action are considered in §§ **7.17–7.28**.

[36] "A course of dealing is a sequence of previous conduct between the parties to an agreement which is fairly to be regarded as establishing a common basis of understanding" between the parties, and as such may give meaning to or supplement or qualify their agreement. Restatement (Second) of Contracts § 223 (1979).

[37] 200 Tenn. 641, 294 S.W.2d 690 (1956).

[38] *Id.* at 651, 294 S.W.2d at 694. See **ch. 1** for an explanation of the presumption of contract duration from pay arrangements.

[39] *Id.* at 649, 294 S.W.2d at 693.

[40] *Id.*

[41] 111 Cal. App. 3d 443, 168 Cal. Rptr. 722 (1980).

[42] *Id.* at 447, 168 Cal. Rptr. at 724. In addition to length of service, the court also inferred a promise from an employer "regulation."

[43] *Id.* at 453, 168 Cal. Rptr. at 728. See § **4.11** for a discussion of the covenant.

[44] *Id.* at 455, 168 Cal. Rptr. at 729.

[45] 116 Cal. App. 3d 311, 171 Cal. Rptr. 917 (1981).

practice of not terminating administrative personnel except for good cause. The court began its contract analysis with the proposition that the employer's right to terminate a contract at will is subject to a limitation that the dismissal not be "contrary to the terms of the agreement, expressed or implied."[46] The court was willing to find a contract because "the presumption that an employment contract is intended to be terminable at will is subject, like any presumption, to contrary evidence."[47] In determining whether there exists an implied-in-fact promise for continued employment, the court concluded that the personnel policies or practices of the employer, the employee's longevity of service, actions or communications by the employer reflecting assurances of continued employment, and the practices of the industry in which the employee is engaged can be considered.[48] The court found the result in this case, as in *Cleary*, to be "explainable in traditional contract terms: the employer's conduct gave rise to an implied promise that it would not act arbitrarily in dealing with its employees."[49]

These cases suggest that length of service, combined with other factors, can be a strong force leading courts to infer an employer promise of employment tenure.[50] It is difficult to conclude, however, that length of service by itself suffices to meet the promise element because of the presence in virtually all of the cases of explicit assurances of employment tenure, either orally or in written employer policies.

§ 4.10 —Disclaimers

Of course, employers are free to avoid promises of employment tenure. Disclaimers are one way employers attempt to preclude such promises from being enforceable. Disclaimers are express statements, usually in employment applications or in employee handbooks, that put employees on notice that general statements or

---

[46] *Id.* at 322, 171 Cal. Rptr. at 922.

[47] *Id.* at 324, 171 Cal. Rptr. at 924.

[48] *Id.* at 327, 171 Cal. Rptr. 925–26.

[49] *Id.* at 329, 171 Cal. Rptr. 927. Comerio v. Beatrice Foods Co., 600 F. Supp. 765, 769 (E.D. Mo. 1985) (*Cleary* and *Pugh* require more longevity than three years and some proof of assurances of continued employment; applying California law).

[50] *Compare* Kent Jenkins Sales, Inc. v. Angelo Bros. Co., 804 F.2d 482, 485 (8th Cir. 1986) (proof of concern about job security, plus ambigious employer letter enough to establish jury question under Arkansas law). Allegri v. Providence-St. Margaret Health Center, 9 Kan. App. 2d 659, 684 P.2d 1031, 1036 (1984) (nonverbal course of conduct can support inference of promise of employment security; summary judgment for employer reversed) *with* Adams v. Budd Co., 583 F. Supp. 711, 714 (E.D. Pa. 1984) (practice of promoting from within and retaining employees until retirement insufficient to establish implied contract, applying Pennsylvania law); Sprott v. Avon Prods., Inc., 596 F. Supp. 178, 183 (S.D.N.Y. 1984) (encouragement, rewards for long service do not overcome employment-at-will presumption under New York law).

conduct suggesting a commitment of employment security should not be relied upon by the employees. In *Novosel v. Sears, Roebuck & Co.*,[51] the federal court applied *Toussaint v. Blue Cross & Blue Shield*[52] and found that an employment application which expressly reserved the employer's right to terminate with or without cause and, precluding informal agreements to the contrary, negated any possibility of an implied agreement to dismiss only on certain grounds.[53] Written or oral assurances of continued employment, however, may vitiate the effect of a disclaimer. The Michigan intermediate appellate court, in *Schipani v. Ford Motor Co.*,[54] affirmed a trial court denial of a motion for summary judgment by holding that it was a question for the jury whether informal assurances of employment until retirement constituted an implied contract, despite a letter from the employer expressly reserving the right to terminate at any time.[55]

Obviously, the content and timing of both the promise and the disclaimer are important.[56] In *Ohanian v. Avis Rent a Car System, Inc.*,[57] the court affirmed a jury finding that a written disclaimer executed after an oral promise of employment security was made did not constitute a contract.

---

[51] 495 F. Supp. 344 (E.D. Mich. 1980).

[52] 408 Mich. 579, 292 N.W.2d 880 (1980).

[53] Novosel v. Sears, Roebuck & Co., 495 F. Supp. at 346. *See also* Castiglione v. Johns Hopkins Hosp., ___ Md. App. ___, ___, 517 A.2d 786, 793 (1986) (disclaimer in handbook precluded implied-in-fact claim); Thompson v. St. Regis Paper Co., 102 Wash. 2d 219, 231, 685 P.2d 1081, 1088 (1984) (employers can avoid enforceability of handbooks by stating conspicuously that they are not intended to be enforceable; Scott v. Sears, Roebuck & Co., 798 F.2d 210, 215 (7th Cir. 1986) (disclaimer in employment application precludes implied covenant claim under Illinois law); Cutter v. Lincoln Nat'l Life Ins. Co., 794 F.2d 352, 355 (8th Cir. 1986) (affirming judgment n.o.v. for employer under South Dakota law; written employment agreement provided for termination with or without cause).

[54] 102 Mich. App. 606, 302 N.W.2d 307 (1981).

[55] The letter said, "I understand that my employment is not for any definite time, and may be terminated any time, without advance notice by either myself or Ford Motor Company," *Id.* at 610, 302 N.W.2d at 309. *But see* Longley v. Blue Cross & Blue Shield, 136 Mich. App. 336, 356 N.W.2d 20, 22 (1985) (plaintiff's deposition testimony that she read and believed statement that employer could dismiss with or without cause precluded trial on implied contract theory); Reid v. Sears, Roebuck & Co., 790 F.2d 453, 461 (6th Cir. 1986) (giving effect, under Michigan law, to disclaimer in employment application despite later communication of assurances of employment security); Ringwelkski v. Sears, Roebuck & Co., 636 F. Supp. 519, 520 (E.D. Mich. 1985) (same); Ledl v. Quik Pik Food Stores, Inc., 133 Mich. App. 529, 349 N.W.2d 529, 531 (Mich. App. 1984) (agreement acknowledging unenforceability of employer's promises of employment security made seven years earlier precluded recovery for termination based on breach of implied promise).

[56] *See* Murray v. Kaiser Aluminum & Chem. Corp., 591 F. Supp. 1550, 1554 (S.D. W. Va. 1984) (written contract providing for continued employment as long as "mutually agreeable" permitted unilateral termination by employer for any reason).

[57] 779 F.2d 101, 108 (2d Cir. 1985).

§ 4.11 —Covenant of Good Faith and Fair Dealing

Section 205 of the *Restatement (Second) of Contracts* states, "Every contract imposes upon each party a duty of good faith and fair dealing in its performance and its enforcement."[58] The commentary to § 205 states:

> Subterfuges and evasions violate the obligation of good faith in performance even though the actor believes his conduct to be justified. But the obligation goes further: bad faith may be overt or may consist of inaction, and fair dealing may require more than honesty. A complete catalogue of types of bad faith is impossible, but the following types are among those which have been recognized in judicial decisions: evasions of the spirit of the bargain, lack of diligence and slacking off, willful rendering of imperfect performance, abuse of a power to specify terms, and interference with or failure to cooperate in the other party's performance.[59]

Although § 205 and its commentary do not address employment contracts, or exercise of the power to terminate a contract, the section's concept has been used by several courts to imply an employer obligation not to discharge employees wrongfully. It represents a way of implying a promise of employment tenure as a matter of law. The implied covenant theory is of major significance in wrongful dismissal law because it represents a way to place employment tenure beyond the employer's control[60] and because it widens the spectrum of employer conduct that may be considered to constitute a breach.[61]

---

[58] Restatement (Second) of Contracts (1979). The Reporter's Note to § 205 cites Fortune v. National Cash Register Co., 373 Mass. 96, 364 N.E.2d 1251 (1977) discussed in this section, as an example of the application of the section.

[59] *Id.*, comment d.

[60] *See* Wagenseller v. Scottsdale Memorial Hosp., 147 Ariz. 370, 381, 710 P.2d 1025, 1036 (1985) (covenant does not depend on party intent); Murphy v. American Home Prods. Corp., 58 N.Y.2d 293, 304–05, 448 N.E.2d 86, 91–92, 461 N.Y.S.2d 232, 237–38 (1983) (rejecting implied covenant as inconsistent with parties' intent); J. Calamari & J. Perillo, The Law of Contracts 19–20 (1977) (a contract implied in law is not a contract at all but an obligation imposed by law to do justice even though it is clear that no promise was ever made or intended. The principal function of an implied-in-law contract is generally said to be that of prevention of unjust enrichment). *See* J. Murray, Murray on Contracts § 9 at 14–15 (1974). *See also* Bradkin v. Leverton, 26 N.Y.2d 192, 257 N.E.2d 643, 309 N.Y.S.2d 192 (1970). Restatement (Second) of Contracts § 205 (1979). *See generally* C. Fried, Contract as Promise ch. 6 (1981).

[61] *Compare* Brockmeyer v. Dun & Bradstreet, Inc., 113 Wis. 2d 561, 573, 335 N.W.2d 834, 840–41 (1983) (no breach of implied covenant unless clear public policy violated by discharge) *with* Wagenseller v. Scottsdale Memorial Hosp., 147 Ariz. 370, 385, 710 P.2d 1025, 1039 (1985) (holding that covenant does not require good cause for termination as some California cases do, but not articulating definitive limits); Gates v. Life of Montana Ins. Co., 196 Mont. 178, 638 P.2d 1063, 1067 (1982) (breach of implied covenant by discharge without following handbook procedures that were not contractually binding), *later appeal,* 668 P.2d 213 (1983).

The implied covenant idea is broad enough in theory to impose on employers an obligation to dismiss only for good cause as a matter of law.[62] It is a small step to translate good faith and fair dealing into terminating employment only for legitimate employer related reasons; i.e., good cause.

Despite this theoretical potential for the covenant doctrine, in no jurisdictions have the courts taken it that far. Indeed, the supreme courts of Arizona,[63] Connecticut,[64] and North Dakota[65] have expressly disavowed any idea that a breach of the covenant can be shown merely by showing dismissal without good cause.

The 1959 California case, *Petermann v. Teamsters*,[66] frequently is cited as the seminal case in the modern wrongful dismissal revolution.[67] In *Petermann*, the plaintiff was employed by a union as a business agent. He claimed that he was dismissed for refusing to commit perjury before a committee of the state legislature.[68] The trial court granted the defendant's motion for a judgment on the pleadings.[69]

The court of appeals noted that the plaintiff's breach of contract cause of action was predicated on an employment contract that did not contain any fixed period of duration. It quoted the usual rule: "Generally, such a relationship is terminable at will of either party for any reason whatsoever," and went on to say: "However, the right to discharge an employee under such contract may be limited by statute or by considerations of public policy."[70] The court acknowledged that the public policy concept is vague, but characterized it as "that principle of law which holds that no citizen can lawfully do that which has a tendency to be injurious to the public or against the public good."[71] The court easily concluded that allowing an employer to dismiss an employee for refusing to commit perjury offends public

---

[62] *See* Wagenseller v. Scottsdale Memorial Hosp., 147 Ariz. 370, 384, 710 P.2d 1025, 1039 (1985) (California cases come close to good cause interpretation of covenant).

[63] *Id.* at 385, 710 P.2d at 1040 (accepting covenant but declining to interpret so as to require good cause to escape liability).

[64] *See* Magnan v. Anaconda Indus., Inc., 193 Conn. 558, 479 A.2d 781, 782 (1984) (no action for breach of implied covenant wholly upon discharge without just cause).

[65] *See* Wadeson v. American Family Mut. Ins. Co., 343 N.W.2d 367, 370 (N.D. 1984) (approving jury instruction on good faith, rejecting the unsuccessful plaintiff's argument that the covenant requires the employer to discharge only for good cause).

[66] 174 Cal. App. 2d 184, 344 P.2d 25 (1959).

[67] A Westlaw search in June 1986 showed 147 citations to *Petermann*. When *Petermann* was decided, it already was well established that the presumption of an indefinite employment contract, terminable at will, can be overcome by evidence of the parties' intent to restrict the power of termination. **Chapter 1** discusses the presumption of an employment-at-will. Sections **4,8, 4.9** and **7.18** discuss ways of rebutting the presumption, through factual evidence.

[68] Petermann v. Teamsters, 174 Cal. App. 2d at 187, 344 P.2d at 26.

[69] *Id.*

[70] *Id.* at 188, 344 P.2d at 27.

[71] *Id.*

policy.[72] Thus, in the absence of any factual evidence of an actual employer promise of employment security, the court implied a promise not to dismiss for policy-offensive reasons.

Monge v. Beebe Rubber Co.[73] was another early case applying the covenant. The Supreme Court of New Hampshire considered a jury verdict in favor of the plaintiff in a suit for breach of an employment contract for an indefinite period of time. The court found sufficient evidence for the jury to conclude that the plaintiff's dismissal was motivated by her refusal to "go out with" her foreman.[74] After a brief discussion of the need to modify the employment-at-will rule, the court held "that a termination by the employer of a contract of employment at will which is motivated by bad faith or malice or based on retaliation, is not in the best interests of the economic system or the public good and constitutes a breach of the employment contract."[75] Again, the promise of employment tenure was implied in law.

In *Fortune v. National Cash Register Co.*,[76] the Massachusetts Supreme Judicial Court held that a trial court committed no error in submitting the issue of bad faith termination of an employment-at-will contract to the jury. The plaintiff was employed under a written salesman's contract which was terminable at will, without cause, by either party on written notice. The defendant apparently admitted the existence of a legally enforceable contract. The court held that the plaintiff, in spite of the literal wording of the contract, was entitled to a jury determination on his employer's motives in terminating him.[77] The premise for the employer's obligation not to discharge in bad faith was a legally implied covenant. In support of its conclusion, the court cited statutory provisions requiring good faith respecting contracts under the Uniform Commercial Code and motor vehicle franchise contracts and a number of cases assuming or implying a requirement of good faith

---

[72] *Id.* at 189, 344 P.2d at 27–28. The employer argued that the reason for the dismissal had nothing to do with the policy-offensive ground of refusal to commit perjury. Whether it relied in good faith on a legitimate reason for the dismissal was a question of fact.

[73] 114 N.H. 130, 316 A.2d 549 (1974).

[74] *Id.* at 133–34, 316 A.2d at 552.

[75] *Id.* at 133, 316 A.2d at 551. In Howard v. Dorr Woolen Co., 120 N.H. 295, 414 A.2d 1273 (1980), the court limited the *Monge* approach to reasons for discharge that clearly offend public policy, thus virtually merging the doctrine with the public policy tort doctrine discussed in **ch. 5**. Howard v. Dorr Woolen Co., 120 N.H. at 297, 414 A.2d at 1274.

[76] 373 Mass. 96, 364 N.E.2d 1251 (1977). Fortune v. National Cash Register Co. is cited in the Reporter's notes to § 205 of the Restatement (Second) of Contracts (1979).

[77] *Id.* at 101, 364 N.E.2d at 1255–56; ". . . Fortune argues that, in spite of the literal wording of the contract, he is entitled to a jury determination of NCR's motives in terminating his services under the contract and in finally discharging him. We agree. We hold that NCR's written contract contains an implied covenant of good faith and fair dealing, and a termination not made in good faith constitutes a breach of the contract."

in contract performance.[78] The Massachusetts Supreme Judicial Court also cited *Monge*[79] and § 231 of the *Restatement (Second) of Contracts*.[80]

The California Court of Appeal concluded, in *Cleary v. American Airlines, Inc.*,[81] that employment contracts, like all contracts, include an implied covenant of good faith and fair dealing. Having concluded generally that the plaintiff's contract included a covenant of good faith, the court decided that an important factor in construing the covenant was the plaintiff's 18 years of service: "Termination of employment without legal cause after such a period of time offends the implied-in-law covenant of good faith and fair dealing."[82]

In *Gates v. Life of Montana Insurance Co.*,[83] the Supreme Court of Montana used an implied covenant of good faith and fair dealing to obligate the employer to follow policies in its personnel handbook.[84]

In *Dare v. Montana Petroleum Marketing Co.*,[85] the court reversed summary judgment for the employer and held that the plaintiff was entitled to a trial on allegations of (1) a promise of job security, and (2) improper reasons for dismissal. It held that the covenant of good faith protects reasonable expectations of job security, and can be based on objective manifestations by the employer relied on by employee. The covenant, it said, is not limited to employment handbook promises. The plaintiff alleged no specific promise of employment security, only raises and other conduct indicating satisfaction with performance.

This line of cases suggests that the covenant of good faith and fair dealing can be used to supply a promise of employment tenure which cannot be proven from

---

[78] *Id.* at 102, 364 N.E.2d at 1256, citing U.C.C. § 1-203 (every conduct or duty within this Act imposes an obligation of good faith in its performance or enforcement); Mass. Gen. L. ch. 93B, § 4(3)(c) (1984) (good faith in motor vehicle franchise termination).

[79] Monge v. Beebe Rubber Co., 114 N.H. 130, 316 A.2d 549 (1974).

[80] *See* Restatement (Second) of Contracts § 205 (1979). This section was identified as § 231 in the tentative draft cited by the *Fortune* court. The court declined to speculate whether the good faith requirement is implicit in every contract for employment at will. Fortune v. National Cash Register Co., 373 Mass. at 104–05, 364 N.E.2d at 1257. *See* Cook v. Alexander & Alexander of Conn., Inc., 40 Conn. Supp. 246, 488 A.2d 1295, 1297 (1985) (denying motion to dismiss *Fortune*-like implied covenant pleading).

[81] 111 Cal. App. 3d 443, 453, 168 Cal. Rptr. 722, 728 (1980).

[82] *Id.* at 455, 168 Cal. Rptr. at 729. *Cleary* subsequently has been construed to imply a covenant of good faith and fair dealing only when (1) longevity of employment is present, or (2) the employer has promulgated a policy for adjudicating employee disputes. *See* Shapiro v. Wells Fargo Realty Advisors, 152 Cal. App. 3d 467, 479, 199 Cal. Rptr. 613, 619 (1984) (affirming demurrer).

[83] 196 Mont. 178, 638 P.2d 1063 (1982).

[84] *Id.* at 183, 638 P.2d at 1067. The court found that the handbook policies were not enforceable on a traditional contract theory since the handbook was distributed after plaintiff was hired. Similar analysis was used in Rulon-Miller v. I.B.M., 162 Cal. App. 3d 241, 208 Cal. Rptr. 524 (1984) to affirm a $300,000 verdict for an employee dismissed for dating an employee of a competing firm. The court held that the dismissal violated the implied covenant of good faith and fair dealing because it contravened the employer's policy of not interfering in employees' private, off-the-job conduct.

[85] ___ Mont. ___, 687 P.2d 1015 (1984).

§ 4.11 GOOD FAITH AND FAIR DEALING

the facts. Most of the cases predate wide acceptance of the implied-in-fact contract and public policy tort theories, though some jurisdictions continue to embrace the implied covenant doctrine broadly.[86] Such use of the implied covenant theory is potentially more far-reaching than either the implied-in-fact contract[87] or the public policy[88] tort doctrines.

Significant resistance to the implied covenant doctrine is manifest, however.[89] In *Murphy v. American Home Products, Inc.*,[90] the New York Court of Appeals refused to imply a covenant of good faith and fair dealing when it would be inconsistent with other terms of the contractual relationship. The court reasoned, "It would be incongruous to say that an inference may be drawn that the employer impliedly agreed to a provision which would be destructive of his right of termination."[91] The court of appeals declined to imply such a covenant as a matter of law for the same reasons it declined to recognize a public policy tort theory for wrongful dismissal—its belief that the legislature was the appropriate branch of government to weigh the policy factors involved.[92]

Other courts have questioned the need for the covenant theory, now that more traditional theories such as implied-in-fact contract and public policy tort are recognized widely. For example, in *Thompson v. St. Regis Paper Co.*,[93] the Supreme Court of Washington, while adopting the implied-in-fact contract theory and the public policy tort theory, refused to adopt the implied covenant theory because its bad faith concept is "amorphous," and because it might be internally inconsistent with actual conduct or promises. In *Bertrand v. Quincy Market Cold Storage & Warehouse Co.*,[94] the federal court concluded that, under Massachusetts law, an implied covenant of good faith and fair dealing is not appropriate when collectively bargained arbitration exists as a remedy for wrongful dismissal. The court reasoned that the collective agreement gave greater protections against wrongful

---

[86] *See* Crenshaw v. Bozeman Deaconess Hosp., ___ Mont. ___, 693 P.2d 487 (1984) (affirming jury verdict of $125,000 compensatory and $25,000 punitive damages for respiratory therapist discharged during probationary period) (covenant of good faith and fair dealing applies to probationary employees) (plaintiff need not show violation of public policy to prove breach of covenant of good faith and fair dealing).

[87] The similarity between the treatment of the covenant of good faith in contract cases and tort analysis is obvious. In both types of analysis, a duty is imposed as a matter of public policy, rather than by agreement between the parties.

[88] *See* Crenshaw v. Bozeman Deaconess Hosp., ___ Mont. ___, 693 P.2d 487 (1984) (plaintiff need not show violation of public policy to prove breach of covenant of good faith and fair dealing).

[89] *See* Hunt v. I.B.M. Mid America Employees Fed. Credit Union, 384 N.W.2d 853 (Minn. 1986) (majority of jurisdictions have rejected covenant for sound policy reasons; suggesting it might be available if facts imply contract for permanent employment).

[90] 58 N.Y.2d 293, 448 N.E.2d 86, 461 N.Y.S.2d at 232 (1983).

[91] *Id.* at 304–05, 448 N.E.2d at 91, 461 N.Y.S.2d at 237.

[92] *Id.* at 302, 448 N.E.2d at 89, 461 N.Y.S.2d at 235.

[93] 102 Wash. 2d 219, 227, 685 P.2d 1081, 1086 (1984).

[94] 728 F.2d 568, 571 (1st Cir. 1984).

dismissal than the covenant, and therefore that there was no reason to utilize the covenant.[95]

Three major ways of limiting the covenant have evolved. The first is still awaiting clarification by the California Supreme Court. A number of intermediate appellate cases in California suggest that the covenant is available only for employees with long service[96] and/or for employees working in places where some kind of expectation has reasonably arisen that dismissal will be only for certain reasons or will occur only after following certain procedures.[97] It is not altogether clear from the case law whether these are conjunctive requirements or whether either will suffice by itself. It also is not clear what qualifies as long service. Five years seems to be a safe figure. But California may join a few other jurisdictions in which the covenant exists only when there is some type of employer conduct or communication suggesting employment security.[98]

The second mode of limiting the covenant is to make it available only in cases in which an employee is deprived of compensation for past service. This approach, appearing mainly in Massachusetts decisions,[99] would transform the covenant into a quasi-contract doctrine rather than a wrongful dismissal doctrine.

---

[95] Kamens v. Summit Stainless, Inc., 586 F. Supp. 324, 329-30 (E.D. Pa. 1984) (no implied covenant cause of action for dismissal allegedly violative of FLSA and ADEA); High v. Sperry Corp., 581 F. Supp. 1246, 1248 (S.D. Iowa 1984) (claim for breach of implied covenant distinct from statutory age discrimination claim, though based on same facts; can be maintained independently of statutory procedures under Iowa law); Price v. United Parcel Serv., Inc., 601 F. Supp. 20, 23 (D. Mass. 1984) (no implied covenant claim under Massachusetts law for employee covered by collective agreement); Azzi v. Western Elec. Co., 19 Mass. App. Ct. 406, 474 N.E.2d 1166, 1169 (1985) (implied covenant cause of action does not exist for employee covered by collective bargaining agreement).

[96] *Compare* DeHorney v. Bank of America, 777 F.2d 440, 448 (9th Cir. 1985) (employment for nine months insufficient to trigger implied covenant under California law), *withdrawn and rehearing stayed,* 784 F.2d 339 (9th Cir. 1986), *with* Gray v. Superior Court (Cipher Data), 181 Cal. App. 3d 813, 226 Cal. Rptr. 570, 573-74 (1986) (lengthy service not essential to cause of action based on implied covenant); *and* Foley v. Interactive Data Corp., *review granted,* ___ Cal. 3d ___, 712 P.2d 891, 222 Cal. Rptr. 740 (1986).

[97] *See* Shapiro v. Wells Fargo Realty Advisors, 152 Cal. App. 3d 467, 479, 199 Cal. Rptr. 613, 619 (1984) (affirming demurrer; construing *Cleary* to imply a covenant of good faith and fair dealing only when (1) longevity of employment is present, or (2) the employer has promulgated a policy for adjudicating employee disputes).

[98] *See* Gates v. Life of Mont. Ins. Co., 196 Mont. 178, 638 P.2d 1063, 1067 (1982) (breach of implied covenant by dismissal without following handbook procedures that were not contractually binding). *Accord,* Murphy v. American Home Prods. Corp., 58 N.Y.2d 293, 304-05, 448 N.E.2d 86, 91-92, 461 N.Y.S.2d 232, 237-38 (1983) (rejecting implied covenant as inconsistent with parties' intent).

[99] *Compare* McCone v. New England Tel. & Tel. Co., 393 Mass. 231, ___, 471 N.E.2d 47, 50 (1984) (suggesting that implied covenant claim lies only to deny employer financial windfall resulting from denial to employee of compensation for past services) *and* Wakefield v. Northern Telecom, Inc., 769 F.2d 109 (2d Cir. 1985) (New York law permits implied covenant claim for a dismissal motivated by desire to deprive employee of commissions) *with* De Rose v. Putnam Mgmt. Co., 398 Mass. 205, 496 N.E.2d 428 (1986) (Massachusetts implied covenant covers dismissals violating public policy as well as dismissals financially benefiting employer).

The third approach, reflected in decisions in a number of states, is that breach of the covenant can be shown only by violation of a public policy. In *Magnan v. Anaconda Industries, Inc.*,[1] the Supreme Court of Connecticut held that an employee, hired under a contract of indefinite duration, cannot maintain a cause of action in contract for breach of an implied covenant of good faith and fair dealing based wholly upon a discharge without just cause.[2] The court suggested that a cause of action for breach of the implied covenant is identical to a public policy tort cause of action.[3] Under this approach, the covenant doctrine adds little if anything to the public policy tort.[4] In Wisconsin, the covenant is used instead of the public policy tort in order to limit damages.[5]

Yet another strategem for limiting the implied covenant is to conclude that it is applicable only to contracts for a fixed term, and not to at-will contracts or contracts for an indefinite term.[6] This approach is not consistent with the *Restatement,* which clearly contemplates application of the covenant to powers reserved to one party under the contract. Such reserved powers conceptually include the power to terminate.

It is likely that the courts in most jurisdictions will not afford definitive guidance as to the limits of the implied covenant doctrine, while being cautious in accepting it in particular cases. This would make the doctrine potentially available for egregious cases not meeting the requirements of implied-in-fact contract or public policy tort, and may preserve its potential for imposing a duty to dismiss only for good cause.

§ 4.12 Consideration and Its Substitutes As Validation Devices

Part of the idea of offer and acceptance or *meeting of the minds* in contract theory is to require that a promise be supported by some sort of validation device before the law enforces it. A competing approach to promise enforcement has received little support in the cases: essentially to forget about validation devices and enforce employer promises of employment security merely upon proof the employer made

---

[1] 193 Conn. 558, 479 A.2d 781 (1984).

[2] *Id.* at ___, 479 A.2d at 782.

[3] *Id.* at ___ n.25, 479 A.2d at 791 n.25.

[4] *See* Wagenseller v. Scottsdale Memorial Hosp., 147 Ariz. 370, 710 P.2d 1025 (1985) (reversing dismissal of plaintiff's claim and holding that nurse dismissed for refusing to "moon" could recover on implied covenant theory because public policy violated, but declining to accept broader California implied covenant doctrine); Howard v. Dorr Woolen Co., 120 N.H. 295, 297, 414 A.2d 1273, 1274 (1980) (limiting Monge v. Beebe Rubber Co. approach to reasons for discharge that clearly offend public policy).

[5] *See* Brockmeyer v. Dun & Bradstreet, Inc., 113 Wis. 2d 561, 573, 335 N.W.2d 834, 840–41 (1983) (no breach of implied covenant unless clear public policy violated by discharge).

[6] *See* Vallone v. Agip Petroleum Co., 705 S.W.2d 757, 759 (Tex. Ct. App. 1986) (good faith obligation may be implied in contracts for a fixed term, but not in contracts for an indefinite term).

them.[7] This approach is supported by few cases.[8] The most common validation device is *consideration*: something given in return for a promise. This may be a return promise or it may be conduct.[9] It may be any benefit or detriment that is given in exchange for a promise.[10] The benefit may be a promise to pay a sum of money or may be the performance of an act; for example, repairing an automobile. The detriment can be forebearance to do anything that one has a legal right to do; for example, refraining from using tobacco. The motive for the consideration requirement, as for alternative validation devices, is essentially evidentiary. If a party has given something in return for a promise it is more likely that both parties meant for the promise to be enforced.[11] When something has been given in return for a promise, it also seems fairer to enforce the promise.[12]

The concept of the *bargained-for exchange* is important to grasp before analysis of the consideration requirement in wrongful dismissal suits makes sense. Intuitively, the bargained-for idea is easily understood when two parties sit down at a table and say to each other, "If I give you this what will you give to me in return?" and eventually reach a deal. It is more difficult to grasp when one party makes a promise without saying anything explicit to the other about what is expected in return, and then the other engages in some sort of conduct in reliance on the promise. Yet that is precisely the circumstance found in most implied-in-fact contract cases involving wrongful dismissal allegations.

When one party makes a promise and the other party responds with conduct, a unilateral contract may have arisen. In the unilateral contract context, the bargained-for question is the following: Did the party making the promise make it *for the purpose of inducing* a certain kind of conduct?[13] If such a purpose was present, then the reliance was "bargained for."

If, for example, I am concerned that my employees may defect to another employer who pays higher salaries and offers more secure employment, I may make a general commitment to the workforce that no one will be laid off. In such circumstances, it is reasonable to infer that my promise was made for the purpose of inducing employees to turn down offers to go to the competitor and to remain in my employ. In contrast, I might make the same commitment to the workforce

---

[7] C. Fried, Contract as Promise 39 (1981) (enforcement of promises on the basis of fairness).

[8] One case apparently adopting the Fried approach is Whitlock v. Haney Seed Co., 110 Idaho 347, 715 P.2d 1017 (Ct. App. 1986) (explicit oral promise of continued employment rebuts employee-at-will presumption; no discussion of consideration).

[9] See § **4.13** for analysis of the difference between bilateral (promise given in return) and unilateral (conduct given in return) contracts.

[10] There must be a promise, or finding consideration is of no avail to the plaintiff. *See* Walker v. Modern Realty of Mo. 675 F.2d 1002, 1004 (8th Cir. 1982) (recognizing promissory estoppel theory, but denying recovery because no promise of continued employment).

[11] *See* Darlington v. General Elec. Co., 350 Pa. Super. 183, 504 A.2d 306, 312, 316 (1986) (analysis of role of consideration in evidencing party intent to be bound) (quoting this treatise on order of proof in implied contract case).

[12] See § **4.4**, discussing the history of the consideration requirement.

[13] *See* Ross v. Montana R.R., ____ Pa. Super. ____, ____, 516 A.2d 29, 31 (1986) (failure to present evidence that employer made promise for purpose of inducing employee to turn down job offer defeats consideration).

§ 4.12 CONSIDERATION SUBSTITUTES

and one employee might rely on it by passing up a scholarship for postgraduate education. In this circumstance, it would not be reasonable to infer that I made the general commitment for the purpose of inducing the giving up of the scholarship. In the first hypothetical, the reliance (turning down other job offers) would be bargained for. In the second hypothetical, the reliance (passing up the scholarship) would not be bargained for.

Even when reliance is not bargained for in this sense, it nevertheless may have legal effect as a validation device,[14] under the promissory estoppel idea reviewed in § **4.17**. Promissory estoppel does not contemplate that the reliance is bargained for, only that it should have been anticipated by a reasonable promissor and that the reliance itself be reasonable.

These validation ideas, bargained-for reliance and reasonable detrimental reliance, arise in two slightly different contexts with employment at will. In one context, the reliance is something over and above mere continuation of employment. Courts have had an easier time finding that unusual types of reliance serve as a validation device for a promise of employment security. In the second context, the reliance is merely continuing employment. It may be reasonable to infer that the employer meant to induce continuation of employment although there is nothing unusual about it. It has been more difficult for courts to accept mere continuation of employment, as opposed to some unique form of reliance, as an adequate validation device because, not being unusual, it has less evidentiary value.

The special consideration requirement was a means of insisting upon especially obvious validation for unusual types of employment promises.[15] The idea was that most employers would not make promises of employment security, or not intend to be bound by such promises. Therefore, for an allegation of such a promise to be taken seriously there should be an especially credible validation device. The most obvious such device was special consideration: paying money or doing something out of the ordinary beyond merely undertaking or continuing the employment relationship. This special consideration requirement was misunderstood by some courts and transformed into a substantive rule: the employment-at-will rule.

Virtually all courts accept the general proposition that employee action or forbearance in reliance on employer promises of employment tenure (i.e., *detriment* or *detrimental reliance*) meets the consideration requirement. This result falls within the mainstream of contract doctrine; a detriment always has been deemed to be consideration if it is bargained for.[16] *Bargained for* can mean that the parties actually negotiated over the exchange of the promise for the detriment or merely

---

[14] Restatement (Second) of Contracts § 18 (manifestation of mutual assent), § 19 (conduct as manifestation of assent) and § 24 (offer defined) (1979); *see also* C. Corbin, Corbin on Contracts § 13 (1952). Restatement (Second) of Contracts § 19 (1979) (conduct as manifestation of assent); *see also* Corbin § 13; Corbin § 34 at 53–54, Restatement (Second) of Contracts § 19 (1979) (conduct as manifestation of assent). Proof issues relating to contract causes of action are considered in §§ **7.17–7.28**.

[15] *See* Albert v. Davenport Osteopathic Hosp., 385 N.W.2d 237, 238–39 (Iowa 1986) (at-will presumption can be overcome by additional consideration such as quitting another job).

[16] Weiner v. McGraw-Hill, Inc., 57 N.Y.2d 458, 464, 443 N.E.2d 441, 444, 457 N.Y.S.2d 193, 196 (1982); Pine River State Bank v. Mettille, 333 N.W.2d 622 (Minn. 1983).

that the promise was made for the purpose of inducing the detriment. But even as courts have accepted the general proposition that detrimental reliance meets the consideration requirement, the special consideration requirement has lingered.[17]

Requiring special consideration creates a potential *Catch 22* situation, and therefore can be a creative device for courts or defendants to defeat implied-in-fact contract claims. It is highly likely that an employer makes a general promise of employment security for the purpose of inducing greater stability in the workforce. Therefore, it is intuitively logical to conclude that continuation of employment was bargained for. On the other hand, all employees generally continue their employment, and therefore continuation of employment has the least value as an evidentiary validation device. But if a court insists upon special consideration, it insists upon a type of conduct less likely to have been the real motive for the employer's promise. Accordingly, a court that wants to frustrate satisfaction of the requirements for an implied-in-fact contract claim can be rigorous both with respect to special consideration and to inferences regarding the employer's motivation for making the promise.

Another type of detrimental reliance is distinguished from the type just discussed because it concededly is not bargained for. Sometimes promises inducing this type of detrimental reliance are enforced even though the bargain element of the traditional consideration requirement is not present. The doctrine permitting such promises to be enforced is sometimes loosely called *promissory estoppel*.

In none of the circumstances discussed is mutuality of obligation present. All of them involve unilateral contracts, in which there is a promise by one party and no promise by the other party. Mutuality of obligation is irrelevant in determining whether such contracts should be enforced.[18]

§ 4.13 —Unilateral Contracts: Mutuality of Obligation Not Necessary

A *bilateral contract* is one in which the consideration for a promise is another promise.[19] A *unilateral contract* is one in which the consideration for a promise

---

[17] *See* Ross v. Montana R.R., ____ Pa. Super. ____, ____, 516 A.2d 29, 32 (1986) (failure to identify consideration over and above performance of duties defeats effort to rebut employment-at-will presumption).

[18] *See* Pine River State Bank v. Mettille, 333 N.W.2d 622 (Minn. 1983); Weiner v. McGraw-Hill, Inc., 57 N.Y.2d 458, 464, 443 N.E.2d 441, 444, 457 N.Y.S.2d 193, 196 (1982); J. Murray, Murray on Contracts § 90 at 190–95 (1974). Section 79(c) of the Restatement (Second) of Contracts (1979) repudiates the mutuality concept. *See also* Pugh v. See's Candies, Inc., 116 Cal. App. 3d 311, 325, 171 Cal. Rptr. 917, 924 (1981); Cleary v. American Airlines, Inc., 111 Cal. App. 3d 443, 448–49, 168 Cal. Rptr. 722, 725 (1980); Hepp v. Lockheed-California Co., 86 Cal. App. 3d 714, 150 Cal. Rptr. 408 (1978).

[19] *See* Ferraro v. Koelsch, 119 Wis. 2d 407, 350 N.W.2d 735 (Ct. App. 1984), *aff'd by different rationale*, 124 Wis. 2d 154, 368 N.W.2d 666 (1985) (promise to comply with company rules adequate consideration for employer's promise not to dismiss).

is an act or forbearance to act.[20] The important difference between the two types of contract is that only in the bilateral contract is there *mutuality of obligation*,[21] which means that both parties are under an obligation to perform their promises.[22]

In employment law, it is essential to recognize that usually there is an exchange of a promise (by the employer) for performance (by the employee)—a unilateral rather than a bilateral contract;[23] the modern view is that mutuality of obligation has little to do with the enforceability of a contract in a wrongful dismissal case.[24]

A necessary prerequisite to sound unilateral contract analysis is to put aside the mutuality of obligation concept.[25] The court in *Toussaint v. Blue Cross & Blue Shield*[26] rejected an argument that mutuality of obligation is a prerequisite to a valid contract, concluding instead that enforceability depends on whether the employee has given consideration for the employer's promise of employment. It pointed out that a traditional mutuality requirement would mean that an employer

---

[20] Unilateral contract means that the employer makes a promise in exchange for performance, rather than in exchange for another promise. C. Corbin, Corbin on Contracts § 21 at 31 (1952) (offeror of reward for return of article is bound by a contract just as soon as the offeree has returned the article with intent to accept the offer). For an explanation of the distinction between bilateral and unilateral contracts, see J. Murray, Murray on Contracts § 6 at 9–11 (1974). In Weiner v. McGraw-Hill, Inc., 57 N.Y.2d 458, 443 N.E.2d 441, 457 N.Y.S.2d 193 (1982), the New York Court of Appeals reasoned that the employer's promise of employment tenure becomes enforceable as soon as the employee enters upon employment. See also § **4.15**; Restatement (Second) of Contracts § 72 (1979); J. Calamari & J. Perillo, the Law of Contracts 17–18 (1977). Every contract involves at least two contracting parties. In some contracts, however, only one party has made a promise and therefore only that party is subject to a legal obligation. Such a contract is said to be unilateral. If both parties have made promises the contract is bilateral.

[21] Mutuality of obligation requires that unless both parties to a contract are bound, neither is bound. Black's Law Dictionary 920 (5th ed. 1979). C. Corbin, Corbin on Contracts § 152 at 221 (1952). Under the view of the Second Restatement, mutuality of obligation is irrelevant. Restatement (Second) of Contracts § 81(c) (1979). *Accord,* Pine River State Bank v. Mettille, 333 N.W.2d 622, 629 (Minn. 1983); Weiner v. McGraw-Hill, Inc., 57 N.Y.2d 458, 464, 443 N.E.2d 441, 444, 457 N.Y.S.2d 193 196 (1982); Toussaint v. Blue Cross & Blue Shield, 408 Mich. 579, 599–600, 292 N.W.2d 880, 885 (1980).

[22] Because of antipeonage principles, courts are reluctant to find enforceable promises by employees to continue their employment. If such an employee promise is found to exist, of course the employee would be liable in damages for breaking the promise.

[23] See §§ **4.15, 4.16**; *see also* Restatement (Second) of Contracts § 72 (1979). To be rigorous about terminology, unilateral contract is relevant only with respect to bargained-for consideration because it implies a conscious exchange. The more general detrimental reliance or promissory estoppel theory can make a promise enforceable without a bargained-for exchange; hence promissory estoppel does not necessarily involve a unilateral contract.

[24] See §§ **4.14, 4.15**. T. Plucknett, A Concise History of the Common Law 634 (5th ed. 1956); J. Koffler & A. Reppy, Common Law Pleading § 162 at 320 (1969).

[25] For a discussion of the confusion surrounding the mutuality of obligation concept, *see* Pine River State Bank v. Mettille, 333 N.W.2d at 629–30 (Minn. 1983); Weiner v. McGraw-Hill, Inc., 57 N.Y.2d at 464, 443 N.E.2d at 444, 457 N.Y.S.2d at 196 (1982); J. Murray, Murray On Contracts § 90 at 190–95 (1974). The concept has been repudiated by § 79(c), Restatement (Second) of Contracts (1979). *See* Toussaint v. Blue Cross & Blue Shield, 408 Mich. 579, 600, 292 N.W.2d 880, 885 (1980).

[26] 408 Mich. 579, 292 N.W.2d 880 (1980).

never could enter into a legally enforceable agreement to terminate the employment only for cause, a position contrary to precedent.[27]

Virtually all the cases discussed in this chapter used unilateral contract principles to enforce the employer's obligations. The case law[28] treats the employer's representations as an offer of a unilateral contract which becomes enforceable upon performance of regular employment duties by the employee,[29] or the giving of some form of special consideration, such as quitting another job or turning down another job offer.[30]

The concurring opinion in *Toussaint*[31] expressly addressed the unilateral contract concept. In holding that the employer's policy manual was enforceable, it reasoned that "there is no contractual requirement that the promisee do more than perform the act upon which the promise is predicated in order to legally obligate the promisor."[32] In this case, the only act required of the employee was to perform the normal duties of an employee. The *Pine River State Bank v. Mettille*[33] opinion also contains a good analysis of unilateral contract principles,[34] as do the West Virginia Supreme Court's opinion in *Cook v. Heck's Inc.*,[35] and the Idaho Supreme Court's opinion in *Watson v. Idaho Falls Consolidated Hospitals, Inc.*[36]

§ 4.14 — Bargained-for Detrimental Reliance: General Concept

Suffering a detriment, when it is bargained for, always has sufficed as consideration.[37] Under this approach, the employer is viewed as offering employment security in order to induce the employee to accept or continue employment.[38] In

---

[27] *Id.* at 609, 292 N.W.2d at 890.

[28] *See, e.g.,* Pine River State Bank v. Mettille, 333 N.W.2d 622 (Minn. 1983) (interpretation of authority).

[29] See § **4.16**.

[30] See § **4.15**.

[31] Toussaint v. Blue Cross & Blue Shield, 408 Mich. at 630, 292 N.W.2d at 900.

[32] *Id.* at 631, 292 N.W.2d at 900.

[33] 333 N.W.2d 622 (Minn. 1983).

[34] *Id.* at 627. Scholtes v. Signal Delivery Serv., Inc., 548 F. Supp. 487, 491–92 (W.D. Ark. 1982), also contains a useful discussion of the unilateral contract concept.

[35] 342 S.E.2d 453, 458–59 (W. Va. 1986) (handbook statements regarding employment security can be offers of unilateral contract, accepted by employee continuing to work, citing *Woolley*).

[36] 111 Idaho 44, 720 P.2d 632, 636 (1986) (mutuality of obligation irrelevant; appropriate framework is unilateral contract).

[37] *See* Weiner v. McGraw-Hill, Inc., 57 N.Y.2d 458, 464, 443 N.E.2d 441, 444, 457 N.Y.S.2d 193, 196 (1982); Hamer v. Sidway, 124 N.Y. 538, 27 N.E. 256 (1891).

[38] *See* Langdon v. Saga Corp., 569 P.2d 524, 527 (Okla. Ct. App. 1977) (affirming jury award for termination allowances and accrued vacation pay; employer's personnel manual was "offer for a unilateral contract accepted by the Plaintiff's continuing to work . . . and foregoing his option of termination." Benefits offered were calculated to induce employees to increase production and remain with the company).

effect, the employer has made an offer or series of offers of a unilateral contract.[39] Consequently, the employer is saying to the employee, "If you come to work tomorrow I will pay you for tomorrow's work *and* continue your employment." The employee accepts the offer when she comes to work.[40] But the essence of the bargained-for idea is that the employer made the offer, or promise, for the purpose of inducing the reliance.[41]

This bargained-for reliance is to be distinguished from a situation in which the employer had no such purpose, but the employee nevertheless reasonably relied to her detriment on the same promise. Under the concept of *promissory estoppel*, a promise may be enforced *without* a showing that the purpose of the employer's promise was to induce reliance.[42]

Both detrimental reliance approaches are supported by the wrongful dismissal case law. The theoretical distinction between these two approaches is subtle. The section in the *Restatement (Second) of Contracts* requiring consideration is flexible enough to accommodate detrimental reliance even when it is not bargained for: "The word 'consideration' often has been used with meanings different from that given here. It is often used merely to express the legal conclusion that a promise is enforceable."[43] The traditional consideration concept, however, generally implies a bargained-for exchange.[44] In the wrongful dismissal context, this implies that the employer offer employment security in order to induce the employee to accept or continue employment.[45]

Section 90 of the *Restatement*[46] eliminates the requirement that detriment must be bargained for, when the promisor reasonably should expect the reliance to occur and when the detrimental reliance is reasonable.[47]

Modern contract theory easily enforces employer promises of employment tenure that result in employee detriment in the form of reliance on those promises. Whether the label used is promissory estoppel or bargained-for consideration, the legal and factual inquiries are similar:[48] Has the employer promised continued employment

---

[39] See § **4.13**.

[40] Restatement (Second) of Contracts § 72 (1979) states, "any performance which is bargained for is consideration." See § **4.16**.

[41] This is sometimes referred to as the *detriment inducing the promise*. An example would be an employer who says to prospective employees, "If you quit your present job and come to work for me, I promise not to dismiss you without cause."

[42] See § **4.17**; Restatement (Second) of Contracts § 90 (1979). As explained in the notes to § 90, promissory estoppel is a misnomer for the concept that detrimental reliance on a promise, even if it is not bargained for, can make the promise enforceable. Nevertheless, the term is in wide use and will be employed in this chapter for simplicity of exposition.

[43] Restatement (Second) of Contracts § 71 comment a (1979).

[44] *Id.* § 71, comment b.

[45] In a bargained-for exchange, not only does the promise by A induce the performance by B, the performance by B also must induce the promise by A. *See* J. Murray, Murray on Contracts § 80 (1974).

[46] This is frequently referred to as the promissory estoppel section.

[47] Promissory estoppel and wrongful dismissal cases applying it are considered in § **4.17**.

[48] See §§ **4.15–4.17**. The factual inquiry in a traditional consideration analysis includes an inquiry whether the employee reliance was bargained for. Restatement (Second) of Contracts § 71,

and has the employee reasonably relied on that promise by becoming and remaining an employee? If the answer to both questions is "yes," the employer's promise will be enforceable as a matter of contract theory.

Sea-Land Service, Inc. v. O'Neal[49] illustrates the bargained-for detrimental reliance concept, although its facts are atypical of dismissal actions. The plaintiff brought a breach of contract action[50] against her employer after she resigned one position in order to accept another with the same employer.[51] The court found that the employer "promised her that, if she resigned from the one position, she would be employed in the other."[52] It found that the plaintiff's act of resigning furnished adequate consideration for the employer's promise to employ her in the other job and cited the rule of law as follows:

> Where one makes a promise conditioned upon the doing of an act by another, and the latter does the act, the contract is not void for want of mutuality, and the promisor is liable . . . . Upon the performance of the condition by the promisee, the contract becomes clothed with a valid consideration which renders the promise obligatory.[53]

The reliance in *Sea-Land* was bargained for because the context of the employer's promise indicated that it was made for the purpose, possibly among others, of inducing the employee to incur the detriment of resigning.

Sea-Land involved breach of a promise to hire rather than a dismissal. The court's analysis, however, deals directly with the concept of a bargained-for detriment as consideration for an employer's promise. In the usual wrongful dismissal case, the employee argues that the same analytical approach requires that an employer's promise of employment tenure be enforced under traditional consideration principles if it is coupled with a bargained-for reliance by the employee. Moreover, the reliance asserted by the plaintiff-employee may be the quitting of another job, as in *Sea-Land*, refusing other job offers, or any other forbearance to exercise any legal right.

Toussaint v. Blue Cross & Blue Shield[54] involved a more complex analysis but reached essentially the same conclusion as *Sea-Land*. In *Toussaint*, the court held that the employee's agreement to come to work for the employer and remain in its employ is sufficient to meet the consideration requirement.[55] The facts involved the employee's quitting another job, and the court's opinion do not make it entirely

---

comment b (1979); *i.e.,* whether the employer promised employment tenure in order to induce the employee to accept or continue employment.

[49] 224 Va. 343, 297 S.E.2d 647 (1982).

[50] She also included a count for fraud.

[51] Sea-Land Serv., Inc. v. O'Neal, 224 Va. at 349, 297 S.E.2d at 650.

[52] *Id.*

[53] *Id.* at 350, 297 S.E.2d at 651.

[54] 408 Mich. 579, 292 N.W.2d 880 (1980).

[55] *Id.* at 610, 292 N.W.2d at 890.

clear whether this was a necessary type of reliance or whether mere continuation of employment would have sufficed.[56] The court said:

> We hold that employer statements of policy, such as the Blue Cross supervisory manual and guidelines, can give rise to contractual rights in employees without evidence that the parties mutually agreed that the policy statements would create contractual rights in the employee, and, hence, although the statement of policy is signed by neither party, can be unilaterally amended by the employer without notice to the employee, and contains no reference to a specific employee, his job description or compensation, and although no reference was made to the policy statement in pre-employment interviews and the employee does not learn of its existence until after his hiring.[57]

Language in the opinion suggests a conclusion that the employee's reliance was bargained for, in the sense that the promise (of employment tenure) was made for the purpose of inducing the detriment (continuing in the employer's employ).

The handful of courts refusing to permit implied-in-fact contract recovery to be based on employee handbooks in any circumstances have used the bargained-for exchange requirement as their rationale, apparently insisting on some form of verbal communication between employer and employee to evidence a bargain.[58] The Pennsylvania intermediate appellate court has been particularly dogmatic in this position.[59]

§ 4.15 —Bargained-for Detrimental Reliance: Special Consideration Such as Quitting Another Job or Turning Down Job Offers

Some courts accept the unilateral contract/detrimental reliance framework but apply a rule that additional consideration[60] is required to make a promise of employment tenure enforceable.[61] Even before the modern wrongful dismissal revolution began, it generally was accepted that a promise of continued employment was

---

[56] See § **4.16**.

[57] Toussaint v. Blue Cross & Blue Shield, 408 Mich. at 614–15, 292 N.W.2d at 892 (the inference that the policies and procedures in the manual were relied on by Toussaint is supported by his testimony that he was handed the manual in the course of a conversation in which he inquired about job security).

[58] See Larose v. Agway, Inc., ____ Vt. ____, 508 A.2d 1364, 1366 (1986) (stipulation that handbook was unilaterally issued precludes any factual issue as to whether assurances contained in the handbook were bargained for).

[59] See Martin v. Capital Cities Media, Inc., 354 Pa. Super. 199, 511 A.2d 830, 836 (1986) (inquiry into consideration unnecessary; employee could not reasonably conclude that unilaterally promulgated handbook was intended to be binding).

[60] Sometimes called *special consideration* or *individual consideration*.

[61] Pugh v. See's Candies, Inc., 116 Cal. App. 3d 311, 325–26, 171 Cal. Rptr. 917, 925 (1981). See Roberts v. Atlantic Richfield Co., 88 Wash. 2d 887, 895, 568 P.2d 764, 769 (1977); Pine

enforceable when an employee gave consideration in addition to services.[62] For example, the surrender of a personal injury or a contract claim against the employer or the abandonment of an earlier business conducted by the employee satisfied the concept of additional consideration.

Applying this theory of unilateral contract to the employment situation, the employee would argue that the employer, through oral promises of continued employment or through a personnel manual, made an offer of a unilateral contract that became enforceable according to its terms when the employee engaged in some conduct above and beyond performance of regular employment obligations. In *Murphree v. Alabama Farm Bureau Insurance Co.*,[63] the court reviewed the special consideration requirement, noting that in some early cases giving up other employment with knowledge of the new employer amounted to special consideration. It reversed summary judgment for the employer, concluding that relocation in connection with acceptance of employment might satisfy the "special consideration" requirement.[64]

In *Weiner v. McGraw-Hill, Inc.*,[65] the court found traditional consideration requirements to be satisfied by detrimental reliance.[66] The court held that four factors necessitated the conclusion that a cause of action in contract was stated. Two of these related to consideration: the allegation that the plaintiff was induced to leave his former job by McGraw-Hill's representations and the allegation that the plaintiff rejected other offers of employment in reliance on the job security assurance.[67]

In other cases reliance, in addition to performance of services, was found sufficient to make a promise of employment security enforceable. In *O'Neill v. ARA Services, Inc.*,[68] the plaintiff alleged that he left his former employment and worked for the defendant for two years in reliance on a promise that he would be transferred to a management position after two years.[69] The federal district court, applying

---

River State Bank v. Mettille, 333 N.W.2d 622, 628-29 (Minn. 1983) (independent consideration not an absolute requirement).

[62] *See* Roberts v. Atlantic Richfield Co., 88 Wash. 2d at 894, 568 P.2d at 769. In Pine River State Bank v. Mettille, 333 N.W.2d at 628-29, the court concluded that the rule of independent consideration is a rule of construction, not an absolute requirement.

[63] 449 So. 2d 1218, 1220-21 (Ala. 1984).

[64] *Id.* at 1221. *But cf.* Walker v. Modern Realty, 675 F.2d 1002 (8th Cir. 1982) (relocation did not create enforceable promise).

[65] 57 N.Y.2d 458, 457 N.Y.S.2d 193, 443 N.E.2d 441 (1982).

[66] The court noted that the absence of mutuality, because the employee was free to quit his job at any time, did not matter; the relevant inquiry was whether there was consideration. *Id.* at 463-64, 443 N.E.2d at 444, 457 N.Y.S.2d at 196.

[67] Two others related to the promise element: the incorporation of the job security assurance into his employment application and the allegation that the plaintiff, in his role as a supervisor, always had been instructed to comply strictly with the personnel procedures when recommending that a subordinate be dismissed. *Id.* at 465-66, 443 N.E.2d at 445, 457 N.Y.S.2d at 197.

[68] 457 F. Supp. 182 (E.D. Pa. 1978).

[69] *Id.* at 184.

§ 4.16 DETRIMENTAL RELIANCE: BARGAINED FOR 207

Pennsylvania law,[70] held that if these allegations were established at trial, the trier of fact could conclude that the "parties intended plaintiff's employment in management to extend for a reasonable period of time."[71] This language suggests a conclusion that the reliance was bargained for.

The intermediate Michigan appellate court, in *Rowe v. Noren Pattern & Foundry Co.*,[72] reversed a trial court dismissal of a wrongful discharge claim premised on detrimental reliance on the employer's job offer.[73] The court held that the plaintiff's having given up a "virtually assured position and pension for the rest of his life" in order to take a job with the defendant was sufficient to take the case out of the employment-at-will doctrine.[74] Promissory estoppel was not mentioned, and the facts would permit an inference that the employee's reliance was bargained for.

Courts in many states continue to insist upon special consideration, despite the trend toward allowing the consideration to be met from mere continuation of employment. The typical ways of meeting the special consideration requirement are: quitting another job, especially if benefits are lost; relocating;[75] or turning down other job offers. The best position for a plaintiff required to show special consideration is to have evidence that something tangible was given up, especially if the plaintiff thought specifically about the promise of employment security when that something was given up.

§ 4.16 — Bargained-for Detrimental Reliance: Continuing Employment

The doctrine of additional consideration sometimes has led to the erroneous notion that a promise of employment tenure must be supported by its own consideration,

---

[70] *Id.* at 185–86:

Under Pennsylvania law, the determination of the terms of a disputed oral contract is the exclusive function of the jury as a question of fact; the legal effect of the agreement is the province of the courts as a matter of law. McCormack v. Jermyn, 351 Pa. 161, 40 A.2d 477 (1945). Plaintiff here has alleged an oral agreement, various assurances and commitments, a letter of confirmation, various modifications, a rate of pay, and an official title. Plaintiff's complaint will not be dismissed without giving him an opportunity to prove the existence of facts and circumstances which together may show a definite employment contract.

[71] *Id.* at 185. *But cf.* Walker v. Modern Realty, 675 F.2d 1002 (8th Cir. 1982) (promissory estoppel of no avail unless a promise of employment tenure can be found).

[72] 91 Mich. App. 254, 283 N.W.2d 713 (1979).

[73] *Id.* at 256, 283 N.W.2d at 714–15.

[74] *Id.* at 263, 283 N.W.2d at 718. *See also* Martin v. Federal Life Ins. Co., 109 Ill. App. 3d 596, 440 N.E.2d 998 (1982) (enforceable contract existed if employee gave up other offer in reliance on employer's promise of permanent employment).

[75] *But cf.* Walker v. Modern Realty, 675 F.2d 1002 (8th Cir. 1982) (relocation did not create enforceable promise).

separate from consideration for other promises in the employment agreement. A majority view of contract doctrine is to the contrary:

> "A single and undivided consideration may be bargained for and given as the agreed equivalent of one promise or of two promises or of many promises." Thus there is no analytical reason why an employee's promise to render services, or his actual rendition of services over time, may not support an employer's promise both to pay a particular wage (for example) and to refrain from arbitrary dismissal.[76]

Thus, it is important to recognize that the issue regarding consideration in an employment contract is whether the entire package of promises made by one party is supported by consideration. Each discrete promise need not be supported by separate consideration.

As explained in the preceding section, many states require a showing of special consideration in the form of quitting another job or turning down job offers to validate an employer promise of job security. Several cases, however, clearly indicate that the employer's promise can be validated merely by continuing employment.

In *Woolley v. Hoffman-LaRoche, Inc.*,[77] the New Jersey Supreme Court concluded that consideration to support a handbook promise to dismiss only for cause was inherent in the nature of the handbook, which apparently was intended to discourage unionization. The court held that reliance by employees in general should be presumed, and need not be shown in individual cases. The *Woolley* analysis is unexceptional in one respect and strange in another. The unexceptional part of *Woolley* relates to acceptance of the premise that a bargained-for exchange in the unilateral contract context can be shown by a general promise of employment security on one side and mere continuation of employment on the other. As explained earlier, the most likely motive for an employer to make a promise of employment security to the workforce in general is that the promise will encourage employees to continue their employment. Thus the bargained-for exchange characterization for this kind of reliance on the promise is logical.

Other courts before *Woolley* found continuation of employment sufficient to satisfy the bargained-for detriment requirement. *Pine River State Bank v. Mettille*[78] involved an employee handbook distributed to the plaintiff employee after he was on the job.[79] The Supreme Court of Minnesota held that the employee, by continuing his employment thereafter, furnished consideration sufficient to support the handbook promises of employment tenure.[80] The language of the court's opinion

---

[76] Pugh v. See's Candies, Inc., 116 Cal. App. 3d 311, 325–26, 171 Cal. Rptr. 917, 925 (1981) (quoting Corbin). "The fact that there are many promises given in exchange for the one consideration does not make it insufficient as to any of them." A. Corbin, Corbin on Contracts § 125 at 535 (1963).

[77] 99 N.J. 284, 491 A.2d 1257 (1985).

[78] 333 N.W.2d 622 (Minn. 1983).

[79] *Id.* at 624.

[80] *Id.* at 627.

§ 4.16 DETRIMENTAL RELIANCE: BARGAINED FOR 209

does not invoke the promissory estoppel doctrine, and its reasoning suggests the inference that the employee's reliance on the employment tenure promise was bargained for in the sense that the employer's promise was intended to cause employees to continue their employment.

In *Hepp v. Lockheed-California Co.*,[81] the court held that continued employment in reliance on an employer rehire policy would make the policy enforceable if the jury found that reliance in fact occurred.[82] Central to the court's reasoning was the proposition that such policies are intended to induce employees to accept or to continue their employment and that intent makes the reliance bargained for.

Similarly, in *Southwest Gas Corporation v. Ahmad*,[83] the court reasoned that, while the plaintiff-employee was free to leave her employment yet remained after receiving a handbook containing a promise of employment tenure, there was consideration.[84] Also, in *Gorrill v. Icelandair/Flugleidir*,[85] the Second Circuit, applying New York law, stated that an employee relying on an implied contract theory need not show reliance through leaving another job or rejection of job offers. Rather, "appellees continued to render their services to appellants, thereby satisfying the requirement of valid consideration . . . ."[86] *Toussaint v. Blue Cross & Blue Shield*[87] also may be authority for the *Woolley* approach, although the opinion is somewhat murky, and the facts involved quitting another job.[88] The supreme court of Hawaii, in *Kinoshita v. Canadian Pacific Airlines, Ltd.*,[89] embraced the idea that employer policies can be legally enforceable without evidence of reliance beyond continued performance of work, and without evidence of employee awareness. The employer had distributed specific policies to its workforce in order to discourage them from

---

[81] 86 Cal. App. 3d 714, 150 Cal. Rptr. 408 (1978).

[82] *Id.* at 719–20, 150 Cal. Rptr. at 411:

[T]he rehiring policy was not merely a guideline for the benefit of management but a positive inducement for employees to take and continue employment with defendant . . . "It is well settled in this state that, where the employer has a pension plan and the employee knows of it, continued employment constitutes consideration for the promise to pay the pension" (citations omitted). Under such reasoning there was a triable issue of fact whether plaintiff gave consideration by continuing employment in reliance on defendant's policy.

[83] 99 Nev. 594, 668 P.2d 261 (1983).

[84] *Id.* at 595, 668 P.2d at 262. In a dissenting opinion, Steffen, J., argued that Ahmad's "non-exercise of a pre-existing legal right was neither bargained for nor given in exchange for any promise." *Id.* at 597, 668 P.2d at 263. Thus, there was an essentially factual dispute within the court as to whether the lower court had correctly found the detriment suffered by Ahmad to have been bargained for. *See also* Thompson v. St. Regis Paper Co., 102 Wash. 2d 219, 685 P.2d 1081, 1088 (1984) (suggesting that inducement to an employee to remain on the job and not *actively* seek other employment is enough).

[85] 761 F.2d 847, 852 (2d Cir. 1985).

[86] *Id.*

[87] 408 Mich. 579, 292 N.W.2d 880 (1980).

[88] *Id.* at 610, 292 N.W.2d at 890 (employer's statements not to dismiss as long as employee "did his job" and employee's meeting that requirement was construed to create an agreement whereby employer could only dismiss employee for cause).

[89] 724 P.2d 110 (Hawaii 1986), *after certification,* 803 F.2d 471 (9th Cir. 1986).

voting for union representation and had told the employees that the policies gave rise to enforceable contractual obligations.[90]

Woolley has crystallized the distinction between special consideration and merely continuing employment. The courts in other states are beginning to take a position on whether mere continuation of employment is sufficient to support a promise.[91]

Because of the function of consideration as a validation device for promises, there is theoretical justification for linking the special consideration requirement to the clarity of the promise. If the promise of employment security is relatively specific, there is less reason to insist on special consideration, and continuation of employment should serve to validate the promise. Conversely, if the promise is ambiguous, it may be appropriate to insist on special consideration such as quitting another job or giving up a specific job offer.

§ 4.17 —Promissory Estoppel

Section 90 of the *Restatement (Second) of Contracts* sets forth the promissory estoppel concept:

> A promise which the promisor should reasonably expect to induce action or forebearance on the part of the promisee . . . and which does induce such action or forebearance is binding if injustice can be avoided only by enforcement of the promise.[92]

---

[90] 724 P.2d at 113–14.

[91] *See* Watson v. Idaho Falls Consol. Hosp., Inc., 111 Idaho 44, 720 P.2d 632, 636 (1986) (continuation of employment sufficient, citing *Woolley*); Brookshaw v. South St. Paul Feed, Inc., 381 N.W.2d 33, 36 (Minn. Ct. App. 1986) (employee accepts an offer contained in a handbook by remaining on the job); Hunt v. I.B.M. Mid America Employees Fed. Credit Union, 384 N.W.2d 853 (Minn. 1986) (distinguishing special consideration case from implied contract case like Pine River State Bank v. Mettille; implying nothing more than performance of services necessary when promise sufficiently specific; reinstating summary judgment for employer because handbook promise too vague); Cook v. Heck's Inc., 342 S.E.2d 453, 458–59 (W. Va. 1986) (handbook statements regarding employment security can be offers of unilateral contract, accepted by employee continuing to work, citing *Woolley*); Thompson v. American Motor Inns, 623 F. Supp. 409 (W.D. Va. 1985) (consideration for handbook promises supplied by continued work after reading handbook; citing *Woolley* approvingly). *But see* Sabetay v. Sterling Drug, Inc., 114 A.D.2d 6, 497 N.Y.S.2d 655, 657 (1986) (lack of knowledge of handbook precludes implied contract claim because both inducement and reliance must be shown); Banas v. Matthews Int'l Corp., 348 Pa. Super. 464, 487, 503, 502 A.2d 637, 649, 658 (1985) (Beck, J., dissenting) (arguing that Pennsylvania should follow *Woolley* and find consideration from continuation of employment after publication of handbook promise).

[92] Restatement (Second) of Contracts § 90 (1979). A's promise can be enforced as long as the promise by A induces reliance by B, regardless of whether the prospect of B's action induces A's promise; *i.e.*, without the reliance being bargained for. See § **4.14** for an explanation of the bargained-for idea.

§ 4.17 PROMISSORY ESTOPPEL

The comments to § 90 of the *Restatement (Second)* explain that the section permits detrimental reliance to supply legal validation for promises,[93] even when the reliance is not bargained for.[94]

As some courts have recognized, the promissory estoppel doctrine rarely is necessary to deal with the consideration issue because it is easy to infer that an employer promises employment tenure for the purpose of inducing employees to accept or continue their employment.[95] Nevertheless, promissory estoppel analysis has been used in many cases[96] and can be necessary for a dismissed employee to win an implied-in-fact contract case.[97] An example would be an employer who issues a policy requiring cause for dismissal to supervisors with the purpose of regulating supervisor behavior. It may be reasonable to expect that nonsupervisory employees will rely on the policy if they know of it, but the policy is not issued for the purpose of affecting nonsupervisory employee actions or decisions.

---

[93] *Id.*, comment a; 1 A. Corbin, Corbin on Contracts § 195 (1950) (the concept that action in reliance makes a promise enforceable is consistent with the most common of all the definitions of consideration).

[94] Henderson, *Promissory Estoppel and Traditional Contract Doctrine,* 78 Yale L.J. 343, 359 (1969) (§ 90 should serve as a distinct basis of liability without regard to theories of bargain, contract or consideration). *See* Jones v. East Center for Community Mental Health, Inc., 19 Ohio App. 3d 19, 482 N.E.2d 969 (1984) (finding no consideration, but finding promissory estoppel).

[95] Commentators have observed that Restatement (Second) § 90 is used in many cases when there is no occasion to invoke it because the promise is supported by bargained-for consideration. *See* L. Fuller & M. Eisenberg, Basic Contract Law 23 (1981). *But see* Jones v. East Center for Community Mental Health, Inc., 19 Ohio App. 3d 19, 482 N.E.2d 969 (1984) (finding no consideration because handbook not distributed for purpose of inducing reliance, but finding promissory estoppel). The New York Court of Appeals observed that detriment long has satisfied the consideration requirement, and that most promissory estoppel cases can be explained with mainstream consideration analysis. Weiner v. McGraw-Hill, Inc., 57 N.Y.2d 458, 465 n.6, 443 N.E.2d 441, 445 n.6, 457 N.Y.S.2d 193, 197 n.6 (1982).

[96] *See* Thebner v. Xerox Corp., 480 So. 2d 454, 457 (La. Ct. App. 1986) (promissory estoppel claim based on policy manual rejected for failure to plead detrimental reliance), *cert. denied,* 484 So. 2d 139 (1986); Minihan v. American Pharmaceutical Ass'n, 624 F. Supp. 345, 350 (D.D.C. 1985) (promissory estoppel permits judgment for annual leave, after rejecting implied contract to be dismissed only for cause); D'Ulisse-Cupo v. Board of Directors of Notre Dame High School, 6 Conn. App. 153, 503 A.2d 1192, 1196 (1986) (approving promissory estoppel theory; reversing trial court), *cert. granted,* 199 Conn. 806, 508 A.2d 32 (1986); Eklund v. Vincent Brass and Aluminum Co., 351 N.W.2d 371 (Minn. Ct. App. 1984) (reversing summary judgment for employer, based in part on § 90 promissory estoppel theory); Litman v. Massachusetts Mut. Life Ins. Co., 739 F.2d 1549 (11th Cir. 1984) (using § 90 as authority to find enforceable promise of employment security, based on promissory estoppel theory, applying Massachusetts law); Ackman v. Ohio Knife Co., 589 F. Supp. 768, 771 (S.D. Ohio 1984) (Ohio promissory estoppel "is not based upon a contract," and therefore is a way of avoiding Employment-at-Will Rule); Scholtes v. Signal Delivery Serv., Inc., 548 F. Supp. 487, 492 (W.D. Ark. 1982) (promissory estoppel obviates need for consideration).

[97] *See* Continental Air Lines, Inc. v. Keenan, ___ Colo. ___, ___ P.2d ___, No. 84SC460 (filed Jan. 20, 1987) (handbook can be enforced on promissory estoppel theory when requisites of bargain are not met); J. Murray, Murray on Contracts § 93 at 203 (1974).

In *Grouse v. Group Health Plan, Inc.*,[98] the Supreme Court of Minnesota reversed a trial court dismissal of a promissory estoppel claim brought by a pharmacist who quit his job to accept an offer by the defendant.[99] The defendant filled the job with someone else before the plaintiff could report to work.[1] The Minnesota Supreme Court held that Grouse was entitled to recover damages for his lost income from the job he quit and from declining an offer of employment elsewhere.[2] The court expressly used the term promissory estoppel and cited § 90 of the *Restatement*[3] as authority for its approach.[4] The court's factual analysis focuses only on the plaintiff's reliance on the employer's promise and ignores the employer's purpose in making the promise. This is the crucial factual distinction between promissory estoppel and bargained-for detriment; in the former, the plaintiff need not show that the promise was made for the purpose of inducing his reliance, only that he in fact relied and that the reliance was reasonable.[5]

In *Mers v. Dispatch Printing Co.*,[6] the Ohio Supreme Court expressly held that promissory estoppel is a viable theory for overcoming the employment-at-will presumption. It characterized the theory this way: "The test . . . is whether the employer should have reasonably expected its representation to be relied upon by its employee and, if so, whether the expected action or forbearance actually resulted and was detrimental to the employee."[7]

---

[98] 306 N.W.2d 114 (Minn. 1981). *See also* Kulins v. Malco, 121 Ill. App. 3d 520, 527, 459 N.E.2d 1038, 1045 (1984) (promissory estoppel used to freeze severance pay formula); McCauley v. Thygerson, 732 F.2d 978, 981 (D.C. Cir. 1984) (affirming dismissal of promissory estoppel claim by discharged employee because doctrine applies to governmental entities only in a restricted form).

[99] In the court's view the principle of contract law applicable was promissory estoppel: We . . . hold . . . that . . . the appellant had a right to assume he would be given a good faith opportunity to perform his duties to the satisfaction of respondent once he was on the job. He was not only denied that opportunity but resigned the position he already held in reliance on the firm offer which respondent tendered him." Grouse v. Group Health Plan, Inc., 306 N.W.2d at 114.

[1] *Id.* at 115–16. On December 4, 1975, Grouse accepted respondent's offer to work as a pharmacist at Group Health's St. Louis Park Clinic. Grouse informed respondent that two weeks' notice to his present employer would be necessary. On December 15, Grouse called respondent and reported that he was free to begin work. Respondent informed Grouse that someone else had been hired.

[2] *Id.* at 116. These are *reliance,* rather than *expectation,* damages. This may be the reason the court used promissory estoppel: it permits more flexibility respecting damages than traditional contract theories. *See* Restatement (Second) of Contracts § 90 comment d and Reporter's Notes (1979); J. Murray, Murray on Contracts § 92 at 200 (1974).

[3] See **§ 4.4** for a history of § 90 of the Restatement.

[4] Grouse v. Group Health Plan, Inc., 306 N.W.2d at 116.

[5] Section 90 of the Second Restatement also requires that the promise be one that the "promisor should reasonably expect to induce action or forbearance."

[6] 19 Ohio St. 3d 100, 105, 483 N.E.2d 150, 155 (1985).

[7] *Id.* at 105, 483 N.E.2d at 155. *See also* Finley v. Aetna Life & Casualty Co., 5 Conn. App. 394, 499 A.2d 64, 73 (1985) (promissory estoppel claim should have been submitted to jury on evidence of 24 years of employment, and refusal of other job offers), *cert. granted,* 198 Conn. 802, 501 A.2d 1213 (1985).

§ 4.18 PROOF OF RELIANCE

The promissory estoppel doctrine, however, is a way of meeting only the consideration requirement, not a way of supplying a promise.[8] Moreover, promissory estoppel requires proof of reliance[9] and reasonableness of the reliance.[10]

§ 4.18 —Is Proof of Actual Reliance Necessary, or May It Be Presumed?

There are two ideas encompassed by the bargained for exchange phrase: *bargaining* and *exchange*. The bargaining idea is taken care of by the employer's motive in making the promise. The exchange idea means that the conduct undertaken by the employee must be undertaken in reliance on the promise. If the employee does not know about the promise, it hardly can be said that the conduct is undertaken in reliance on the promise. If this formula for validating promises is followed, the question of employee knowledge of the promise must be material—and indeed outcome determinative.[11] *Woolley v. Hoffman-LaRoche, Inc.*,[12] says that the employee need not prove knowledge of the employer's promise of employment security.[13] The *Woolley* court's disinterest in whether or not the plaintiff knew of the promise is difficult to harmonize with either the bargained-for reliance or promissory estoppel theories.

---

[8] *See* Chastain v. Kelley-Springfield Tire Co., 733 F.2d 1479, 1485 (11th Cir. 1984) (finding promissory estoppel doctrine of no aid to plaintiff where promise too indefinite to be enforced); Walker v. Modern Realty, 675 F.2d 1002, 1004 (8th Cir. 1982) (promissory estoppel at issue only where a promise has been made).

[9] *See* Larose v. Agway, Inc., ___ Vt. ___, 508 A.2d 1364, 1366 (1986) (failure to plead or testify as to awareness of personnel manual or detrimental change in position in reliance on manual defeats promissory estoppel claim).

[10] *See* Rose v. Allied Dev. Co., 719 P.2d 83, 87 (Utah 1986) (subjective understanding by employee that he could work and attend night school not sufficiently justified to permit promissory estoppel claim).

[11] *See* Falcone v. Columbia Pictures Indus., Inc., 805 F.2d 115, 119 (2d Cir. 1986) (relocation from Florida to New York fails as consideration because failed to show would not have moved absent employer's promise of employment security) (New York law); Lakeside v. Freightliner Corp., 612 F. Supp. 10, 12–13 (D. Or. 1984) (handbook distributed to managers but not to employees not intended to be part of employment contract and therefore could not support breach of contract claim for wrongful dismissal); Gianaculas v. T.W.A., Inc., 761 F.2d 1391, 1394 (9th Cir. 1985) (affirming dismissal of implied-in-fact claim under New York law because reliance not alleged); Price v. Mercury Supply Co., 682 S.W.2d 924, 933–34 (Tenn. Ct. App. 1984) (bargain theory of consideration requires that the promise must induce reliance; past services cannot be induced by a new promise therefore insufficient consideration to support promise of employment tenure).

[12] 99 N.J. 284, 491 A.2d 1257 (1985).

[13] *Id.* at 304–05 n.10, 491 A.2d at 1268 n.10. *See also* Kinoshita v. Canadian Pac. Airlines, Ltd., 724 P.2d 110, 117 (9th Cir. 1986) (employees not required to show knowledge of standard employer policy).

In *Wagenseller v. Scottsdale Memorial Hospital*,[14] the court held that reliance is only one way of establishing enforceability of policy manual promise. It rejected the necessity for proof of reliance in fact as an element of a breach of contract action.[15]

In *Dangott v. ASG Industries, Inc.*,[16] the court reasoned that an employer policy affording severance pay for a reduction in force was enforceable on a unilateral contract theory.[17] This was so even though the plaintiff had no actual knowledge of the policy because "publication . . . is the equivalent of constructive knowledge on the part of all employees not specifically excluded."[18] The court found consideration in the benefit to the employer of a "stable, contented labor force,"[19] a condition presumably induced by the severance pay policy.

Disinterest by these courts in employee knowledge of the employer's promise is either a mistake, or it represents an unarticulated move toward a new substantive rule of employment contracts.[20] Under such a rule, the employer, like an administrative agency,[21] would be bound by its rules until they validly are changed. The publication of the rules to those to be bound by them would make no difference.[22]

§ 4.19 Employer Modification of Promise after Consideration Given

The problem with the unilateral contract[23] approach taken in virtually all implied-in-fact contract cases is that the employer's promise of employment tenure may become unchangeable as soon as the employee performs service after the promise

---

[14] 147 Ariz. 370, 710 P.2d 1025 (1985).

[15] *See also* Enyeart v. Shelter Mut. Ins. Co., 693 S.W.2d 120, 123 (Mo. Ct. App. 1985) (employer must observe published policies with regard to all employees regardless of whether they knew of policies when hired).

[16] 558 P.2d 379 (Okla. 1976) (reinstating trial court judgment in favor of dismissed plaintiff for severance pay).

[17] *Id.* at 384.

> It is fundamental that one who accepts the benefits of a contract must assume the detriments. Consideration is present: the benefit to ASG is a stable contented labor force, its price, pension rights or severance pay. Oklahoma by statute indicates such a factual situation will support a contract.

[18] *Id.* at 383.

[19] *Id.* at 384.

[20] *See* Watson v. Idaho Falls Consol. Hosp., Inc., 111 Idaho 44, 720 P.2d 632, 636 (1986) (suggesting special rule for enforcing unilateral promises of employment security may be appropriate; citing *Woolley*).

[21] The administrative law analogy is explained more fully in § **4.19**.

[22] Woolley v. Hoffman-LaRoche, Inc., 99 N.J. at 304–05 n.10, 491 A.2d at 1268 n.10 (employee's knowledge of employer promise of job security irrelevant).

[23] See § **4.13** for an explanation of the unilateral contract idea.

§ 4.19 EMPLOYER MODIFICATION

is made.[24] The courts in *Toussaint v. Blue Cross & Blue Shield*[25] and *Pine River State Bank v. Mettille*[26] sought to avoid this result by stating that the employer could change its employment tenure policy at any time. It is challenging to characterize the nature of the bargain in a way that such a change by the employer would not be a breach of the contract that became enforceable as soon as the employee accepted or continued employment in reliance thereon. In *Helle v. Landmark, Inc.*,[27] the court said that an employer remained free to modify a promise of severance pay prospectively by giving adequate notice, but it did not explain how such a change would not defeat unilateral contract rights which the court found to be vested based on past service.

One possible theoretical basis for permitting the employer to change promises of employment security is to conclude that there is a *substitute contract*[28] when the employer makes the change: the employer makes a new offer of a unilateral contract when the change is made, and the employee accepts the change by continuing to work.[29] There are, however, conceptual difficulties with the substitute contract idea. First, a substitute contract is not effective to discharge obligations under a preexisting contract unless the party giving up something receives consideration.[30] What benefit or detriment does the employer suffer when it modifies the employment security promise in its own favor? Second, the efficacy of the employee's acceptance of the change depends on merely continuing employment being sufficient consideration to support an employer promise, and not all courts are willing to accept this mode of employee acceptance.[31] The substitute contract approach is of limited utility.

A better conceptual solution is to characterize the employer's promise something like this: "I promise I will not dismiss you without cause (or without exhausting specified procedures) unless I change this policy before you are discharged."[32]

---

[24] *See* St. Antoine, *The Revision of Employment-at-Will Enters a New Phase*, 36 Lab. L.J. 563 (1985) (discussing possibility that employer assurances might be frozen when employees give consideration).

[25] 408 Mich. 579, 619, 292 N.W.2d 880, 895 (1980).

[26] 333 N.W.2d 622, 627 (Minn. 1983).

[27] 15 Ohio App. 3d 1, 13, 472 N.E.2d 765, 777 (1984).

[28] *See* Restatement (Second) of Contracts §§ 278, 279 (1979); J. Murray, Murray on Contracts § 253 at 515 (1974) (new informal contract discharges obligations under old contract if new contract has essential requisites of contract).

[29] *See* General Mills, Inc. v. Hathaway, 694 S.W.2d 96, 99 (Tex. Ct. App. 1985) (when employee continued to work after change in commission formula, he accepted new formula as a matter of law; applying Employment-at-Will Rule).

[30] *See* Restatement (Second) of Contracts ch. 12 intro. note, § 273 (1979).

[31] See §§ **4.14–4.16**.

[32] Such a formulation receives support from language in the *Toussaint* and *Pine River State Bank* opinions. "Employers can make known to their employees that personnel policies are subject to unilateral changes by the employer." Toussaint v. Blue Cross & Blue Shield, 408 Mich. at 619, 292 N.W.2d at 894–95. "Language in the handbook itself may reserve . . . the right to amend or modify the handbook provisions." Pine River State Bank v. Mettille, 333 N.W.2d at 627. *See* Farrell v. Automobile Club, ___ Mich. App. ___, ___ N.W.2d ___ (No. 82916,

Such a characterization is consistent with *Toussaint* and *Pine River State Bank*, and with *Bullock v. Automobile Club of Michigan*,[33] in which the employer was held to reserve the right to change unilaterally promulgated policies either by express reservation or by practice of periodic changes that gives employees notice they are subject to change.

One is tempted to draw an analogy to administrative law, where an agency is bound by its rules, but always remains free to change the rules prospectively through proper procedures. Valid administrative regulations are binding upon the agency that issues them.[34] This basic administrative law principle explains why Judge Gesell, in *Nader v. Bork*,[35] held the discharge of Watergate Special Prosecutor Archibald Cox to be illegal.[36] Once the Attorney General promulgated the regulation that the Watergate Special Prosecutor could be fired only for extraordinary improprieties, the Attorney General was bound by his own regulation even though the Attorney General did not have to promulgate such a regulation and absent such a regulation, the Attorney General would have had the authority to fire Cox at any time and for any reason.[37] Agencies have wide discretion in amending or revoking their regulations,[38] as long as they meet the requirements set by administrative law for issuing them in the first place.[39] But until modified or revoked, the regulations must be followed by the issuing agency.[40]

Closer to employment law is the concept that an employer making benefit promises can reserve the right to withdraw or change the promises. The question of an implied employer reservation of a right to change a promise made to employees arises frequently under the Employee Retirement Income Security Act (ERISA).[41] ERISA commonly is associated with pension plans, but it also applies to another category of plans called "welfare benefit plans." Such plans are subject to the reporting and disclosure, fiduciary, enforcement, and administration requirements of ERISA,[42] but are not covered by the vesting, participation, or funding requirements of the Act.[43]

---

filed Oct. 6, 1986) (evidence warranted jury determination that employer had not reserved right to modify).

[33] 146 Mich. App. 711, 720–21, 381 N.W.2d 793, 797 (1985).

[34] Nader v. Bork, 366 F. Supp. 104, 108 (D.D.C. 1973) (agency regulation has the force and effect of law and is binding upon the body that issues it).

[35] *Id.*

[36] *Id.* at 108.

[37] *Id.*

[38] Such discretion, however, is not absolute. *See id.* at 108–09 (order revoking the Office of Watergate Special Prosecutor replaced by a virtually identical regulation as arbitrary and unreasonable).

[39] *See* Motor Vehicle Mfrs. Ass'n v. State Farm Mut., 463 U.S. 29, 42, 48–49 (1982) (agencies must be given ample latitude to "adapt their rules and policies to the demands of changing circumstances,"); United States v. O'Brien, 391 U.S. 367, 380 (1968) (regulations may be modified or revoked from time to time by administrative discretion).

[40] Note, *Violations By Agencies of Their Own Regulations*, 87 Harv. L. Rev. 629, 629–30 (1974).

[41] 29 U.S.C. §§ 1001–1461 (1982).

[42] *Id.* §§ 1003, 1021, 1101, 1131.

[43] *Id.* §§ 1051, 1081.

§ 4.19 EMPLOYER MODIFICATION

Because ERISA does not impose a vesting requirement for welfare benefit plans, the employer has the right to change the terms of the benefit plan unilaterally after the collective agreement expires,[44] without violating ERISA.[45]

The employer can, however, restrict its right to make modifications when it establishes the benefit plan and defines how rights to receive benefits would vest. In *Sutton v. Weirton Steel Division*,[46] a group of employees unsuccessfully sued under ERISA for severance benefits aggregating $300 million, in connection with a corporate reorganization.[47] The employer had modified the welfare benefit plans to avoid triggering liability on the transfer.[48] "Congress . . . has not prohibited an employer who is also a fiduciary from exercising the right accorded other employers to renegotiate or amend, as the case may be, unfunded contingent benefits payable before normal retirement age. . . . [Such] changes . . . are not to be reviewed by fiduciary standards."[49]

In *Amato v. Western Union International, Inc.*,[50] the court reversed dismissal of a statutory enforcement claim under § 502 of ERISA, concluding that trial was appropriate on claims that preconditions for amendment had not been met.

What these cases say about employee benefit promises is this: The right of an employer to change such benefits before the activity giving rise to them is limited

---

[44] Obligations to contribute to welfare benefit plans, once undertaken, are independent of any collective bargaining agreement, though they may be modified by subsequent collective agreements. *See* Viggiano v. Shenango Chica Div., 750 F.2d 276, 280 (3d Cir. 1984) (requiring arbitration of whether employer's duty to continue hospital premium payments survived expiration of collective bargaining agreement). Of course, welfare benefit plans may be established for employees not covered by collective bargaining agreements, but most of the cases involve collectively bargained plans.

[45] The ERISA cases addressing this issue addressed it in the context of disputes over two other questions: first, whether the welfare benefits plan was subject to ERISA at all, and second, whether the plan was part of a collective bargaining agreement. These issues are not directly pertinent to the question whether the employer reserved the right to change the plan, but the reader should be aware that they were the dominant issues in the cases.

[46] 724 F.2d 406 (4th Cir. 1983).

[47] *Id.* at 410.

[48] *Id.*

[49] *Id.* at 411. In support of its conclusion that National retained the right under ERISA to modify the contingent benefits, the Fourth Circuit cited Fentron Indus., Inc. v. National Shopmen Pension Fund, 674 F.2d 1300, 1306 (9th Cir. 1982) (disapproving cancellation of pension past service credits); Fine v. Semet, 699 F.2d 1091, 1093 (11th Cir. 1983) (affirming district court determination that past practice did not give rise to enforceable right to lump sum distribution of pension benefits upon breakup of law firm); and distinguished (without analysis) Dependahl v. Falstaff Brewing Corp., 491 F. Supp. 1188, 1196–97 (E.D. Mo 1980), *modified,* 653 F.2d 1208 (8th Cir. 1981).

[50] 773 F.2d 1402 (2d Cir. 1985). The court approved dismissal of state law claims for early pension benefits because they were preempted. The court noted that ERISA gives a federal cause of action, under federal common law, for breach of contracts establishing an ERISA covered plan, but found that, because the plan agreement clearly contemplated the possibility of amendment, no such common law claim was established on the facts.

only if the contract establishing the benefits clearly restricts such right, or if the employer exercises any right to amend in contemplation of the activity.[51]

Similar analytical principles are applied to enforce certain benefits under a collective agreement after the agreement giving rise to them expires. Postexpiration enforcement results from the concept that the right to such benefits *vests* upon the event triggering benefits payments and therefore is enforceable by beneficiaries or their representatives regardless of whether the collective bargaining agreement giving rise to such benefits still is in existence. Employees covered by § 301 of the Labor Management Relations Act (LMRA) can sue in federal court to enforce their rights to vested benefits. In *Allied Chemical Workers Local 1 v. Pittsburgh Plate Glass Co.*,[52] the Supreme Court held that retiree benefits are not mandatory subjects of bargaining covered by § 8(a)(5) of the NLRA. Accordingly, an employer may change such benefits unilaterally without bargaining with the union representing its employees. On the other hand, such benefits may be vested, subjecting the employer to an obligation to bargain with the retirees individually before changing the benefits, or to liability for breach of contract if it changes the benefits unilaterally.[53]

These cases say that employers may modify promises concerning employee benefit plans, unless the original promise restricted the employer's rights to modify, or, under *Dependahl v. Falstaff Brewing Corp.*,[54] the employer's motivation for exercising its right to amend a plan is to avoid obligations anticipated by the approach of the triggering event.

The administrative law, ERISA, and collectively bargained-individual right analogies suggest the following principles to guide employer modification of employment security promises in the implied-in-fact contract wrongful dismissal context: (1) The employer should be presumed to have reserved the right impliedly to modify the employment security promise any time before a termination is effected; and (2) A course of conduct involving successive employer modification is evidence that the right to modify was reserved and that employees could not reasonably expect otherwise.

A prudent employer will make sure that any written statements regarding employment security or the circumstances under which terminations will be effected include express warnings that the procedures and policies are subject to modification. An

---

[51] *See* Dependahl v. Falstaff Brewing Corp., 491 F. Supp. at 1196–97 (finding a violation because employer modified in contemplation of event that would vest right to receive benefits), *modified,* 653 F.2d 1208 (8th Cir. 1981).

[52] 404 U.S. 157 (1971).

[53] *Id.* at 181 n.20. *See* Anderson v. Alpha Portland Indus., Inc., 727 F.2d 177 (8th Cir. 1984), *reh'g en banc,* 752 F.2d 1293 (1985) (retirees may sue directly to enforce collectively bargained benefit rights without exhausting grievance and arbitration procedures under collective agreement); Bower v. Bunker Hill Co., 725 F.2d 1221 (9th Cir. 1984) (reversing summary judgment for employer; payment of medical benefits during strike and other evidence could support finding that benefits were vested, despite expiration of collective agreement when company ceased operations); U.A.W. v. Yard-Man, Inc., 716 F.2d 1476 (6th Cir. 1983) (construing expired collective agreement as promising continuing benefits to retirees, extending beyond expiration of agreement), *cert. denied,* 465 U.S. 1007 (1984).

[54] 491 F. Supp. 1188 (E.D. Mo. 1980).

aggressive plaintiff in a wrongful dismissal case will argue that the employer was bound by employment security statements unless the employer expressly reserved the right to modify.

§ 4.20 Statute of Frauds

Even if the contract formation[55] problem is resolved in the employee's favor, the Statute of Frauds presents a potential obstacle to enforceability. All the American states except Louisiana, Maryland, and New Mexico have copied § 4 of the English Statute of Frauds.[56] In Maryland and New Mexico, the statute is enforced by judicial decision.[57] Section 4 of the original English Statute of Frauds, enacted in 1677,[58] provided that

> no action shall be brought . . . (5) upon any agreement that is not to be performed within the space of one year from the making thereof; (6) unless the agreement upon which such action shall be brought, or some memorandum or note thereof, shall be in writing and signed by the party to be charged therewith. . . .[59]

Generally, an oral contract for a specific term longer than one year violates the statute.[60] However, an oral contract for an indefinite term usually is held not to violate the statute because it *might* be performed fully within a one-year period.[61]

Because the Statute of Frauds can prevent the enforcement of an otherwise valid contract,[62] it is worth brief consideration. Although some commentators have suggested that the purpose of the statute was to prevent the enforcement of casual promises,[63] generally the purpose of the statute is viewed as requiring reliable

---

[55] *Contract formation* refers to the establishment of the promise and consideration elements in a breach of contract case.

[56] Restatement (Second) of Contracts ch. 5, statutory note at 282 (1979).

[57] *Id.*

[58] *Id.* ch. 5, statutory note at 281.

[59] *Id.*

[60] *Id.* § 130; 2 A. Corbin, Corbin on Contracts §§ 444–459 (1950 & Supp. 1971); 3 S. Williston, Williston on Contracts § 495 (1960). The test is the duration from the time of making to the time of completion of the promised performance. If by the terms of the agreement performance on either side is to continue beyond a year, the entire contract is unenforceable if oral. *See also* Annotation, *Oral Contract for Personal Services,* 28 A.L.R.2d 878 (1953).

[61] Restatement (Second) of Contracts § 130 comment a, illustration 2 (1979). A orally promises to work for B, and B promises to employ A during A's life at a stated salary. The promises are not within the one-year provisions of the statute, since A's life may terminate within one year. *See also* 2 A. Corbin, Corbin on Contracts §§ 444–446 (1950 & Supp. 1971).

[62] *See* Savodnik v. Korvettes, Inc., 488 F. Supp. 822, 824 (E.D.N.Y. 1980) (oral employment contracts for more than one year are unenforceable because of Statute of Frauds); Molder v. Southwestern Bell Tel. Co., 665 S.W.2d 175, 177 (Tex. Ct. App. 1983) (oral contract of employment security barred by Statute of Frauds); Anselmo v. Manufacturers Life Ins. Co., 595 F. Supp. 541, 548 (W.D. Mo. 1984) (oral contract for three years unenforceable under Statute of Frauds).

[63] *See* Rabel, *The Statute of Frauds and Comparative Legal History,* 63 L.Q. Rev. 174, 185 (1947).

evidence of a contract.[64] Most courts interpreting § 4 have concluded that the test depends not on what actually happens but on what *could* have happened.[65] In other words, when the contract was entered into, was there any possibility that it could have been performed within a year? If there is, it is not within the statute.[66]

Thus, under the majority view, the Statute of Frauds should not be a barrier to the plaintiff in a wrongful dismissal contract action. This is so because most employment contracts involved in such actions are indefinite in duration. The events permitting their termination—existence of cause for dismissal or exhaustion of the predischarge procedures—may occur within a year.[67] A recent decision by the D.C. Circuit, *Hodge v. Evans Financial Corp.*,[68] held that enforcement of an oral contract for employment until retirement was barred by the Statute of Frauds. The panel opinion distinguished a contract for life. This distinction seems analytically unpersuasive, for the reasons articulated by Judge Wald in dissent.[69]

On the other hand, the Statute of Frauds could be a problem if the existence of conditions for dismissal is viewed not as terminating the contract[70] but as excusing the employer's obligation to perform. Also, a promise of employment security

---

[64] Restatement (Second) of Contracts ch. 5, statutory note at 286 (1979). *See also* Hening, *The Original Drafts of the Statute of Frauds*, 61 U. Pa. L. Rev. 283 (1913).

[65] Owenboro Shovel & Tool Co. v. Moore, 154 Ky. 431, 157 S.W. 1121 (1913) (plaintiff orally promised to saw 50,000 ties in 250 days. The court said, "In determining whether a contract falls within the Statute of Frauds, the inquiry is not directed toward ascertaining whether or not the contract would actually be performed within a year but whether or not it could be performed within a year." *Id.* at 434, 157 S.W. at 1123. In Martin v. Federal Life Ins. Co., 109 Ill. App. 3d 596, 440 N.E.2d 998 (1982), the defendant argued that if the employee's oral contract was for more than one year's service, the Statute of Frauds barred its enforcement. The court found that since the employee could have retired or quit within the year, the statute was no bar. *See also* 2 A. Corbin, Corbin on Contracts, § 444 n.4 (1950 & Supp. 1971); J. Murray, Murray on Contracts § 319 at 658 (1974).

[66] *See* Murphy v. American Home Prods., Inc., 58 N.Y.2d 293, 305 n.2, 448 N.E.2d 86, 92 n.2, 461 N.Y.S.2d 232, 238 n.2 (1983) (reversing and holding Statute of Frauds no bar, but denying recovery on other grounds); Weiner v. McGraw-Hill, Inc., 57 N.Y.2d 458, 463, 443 N.E.2d 441, 444, 457 N.Y.S.2d 193, 196 (1982); Restatement (Second) of Contracts § 130 (1979); 2 A. Corbin, Corbin on Contracts § 444 (1950 & Supp. 1971); 3 S. Williston, Williston on Contracts § 495 (1960); J. Murray, Murray on Contracts § 319 at 658 (1974). Price v. Mercury Supply Co., 682 S.W.2d 924, 932 (Tenn. Ct. App. 1984) (Statute of Frauds no bar).

[67] *See* Ohanian v. Avis Rent a Car Sys., Inc., 779 F.2d 101, 108 (2d Cir. 1985) (implied contract not within Statute of Frauds because cause for termination might exist within one year). *But see* Evans v. Fluor Distrib. Co., 799 F.2d 364 (7th Cir. 1986) (implied contract to employ until age 65 barred by Statute of Frauds because not capable of performance within one year).

[68] 778 F.2d 794 (D.C. Cir. 1985).

[69] *Id.* at 804. *See also* Harris v. Arkansas Book Co., 287 Ark. 353, 700 S.W.2d 41, 44 (1985) (oral contract made 20-30 years before dismissal for employment until age 70 barred by Statute of Frauds, affirming judgment n.o.v. for employer. No analysis).

[70] Completion of performance within a year is to be distinguished from an event excusing performance. The possibility of such an event occurring within a year does not take a contract outside the Statute of Frauds. J. Murray, Murray on Contracts § 319 at 660-61 (1974). Similarly, an option to terminate the contract, exercisable by only one party, may not take a contract outside the statute. *Id.* at 661-62.

arising from a handbook can be treated as a written contract, entirely outside the Statute of Frauds.[71]

§ 4.21 What Constitutes a Breach: Generally

Once a terminated employee proves a promise to continue employment, satisfies the consideration requirement, and deals with the Statute of Frauds problem, a successful breach of contract action then requires proof of a breach of the promise.[72] What constitutes a breach depends on the theory used to establish the promise: breach of an explicit or implied-in-fact employer promise is conceptually different from a breach of an implied covenant of good faith and fair dealing.

Express or implied-in-fact promises usually obligate the employer to continue the contract of employment until the occurrence of a condition subsequent:[73] the employer no longer has the economic need for anyone in the employee's job,[74] the employee engages in misconduct, or the employee's job performance is unsatisfactory. All three items are classified as just cause for dismissal. Alternatively, of course, the employer could promise merely that it would follow certain procedures in terminating employees.[75] Under either of the promises, dismissal of the employee for any other reason (in the case of a just cause promise) or without following the procedures (in the case of a promise to follow procedures) constitutes a breach.[76]

The implied covenant approach is more general than the implied-in-fact promise approach. It defines, from public policy, a set of reasons for which termination is *not* permitted, leaving all other conditions not addressed explicitly by the parties

---

[71] *See* Ohanian v. Avis Rent a Car Sys., Inc., 779 F.2d at 119 (Wyatt, J. dissenting). *But see* Rubin v. Rudolf Wolff Commodity Brokers, Inc., 636 F. Supp. 258, 260 (N.D. Ill. 1986) (written memorandum alleged to satisfy Statute of Frauds did not permit action for breach of promise of employment security because it did not mention employment security).

[72] *See* Darlington v. General Elec., 350 Pa. Super. 183, 504 A.2d 306, 316 (1986) (quoting this treatise on order of proof in implied contract case). Proof of a breach is considered in **§§ 7.22–7.28**. This section considers basic concepts of breach of the employer's promise.

[73] J. Calamari & J. Perillo, The Law of Contracts 385 (1977). A condition subsequent is any fact the existence or occurrence of which by agreement of the parties operates to discharge a duty of performance after it has become absolute. *See also* Restatement of Contracts § 250(b) (1932); J. Murray, Murray on Contracts § 139 at 283–84 (1974).

[74] In Grubb v. W.A. Foote Memorial Hosp., Inc., 741 F.2d 1486, 1500 (6th Cir. 1984), the Sixth Circuit suggested that the rationale of *Toussaint* would not extend naturally to a layoff. Rather, the court observed, *Toussaint* involves removal of an employee from a position that continues to exist, while a layoff involves elimination of the position itself. *See also* Rompf v. John Q. Hammons Hotels, Inc., 685 P.2d 25, 29 (Wyo. 1984) (no breach of handbook procedures by discharge for economic reasons).

[75] *See* Pine River State Bank v. Mettille, 333 N.W.2d 622, 631 (Minn. 1983).

[76] Taylor v. General Motors Corp., 588 F. Supp. 562, 566 (E.D. Mich. 1984) (dismissal for refusal to obey order to return to work is good cause).

as permissible reasons.[77] Of course, the relative breadth or narrowness of the class of prohibited reasons, as compared with the class of permissible reasons, depends on the way the implied covenant is applied. A breach of the implied covenant is shown by proving a dismissal for one of the prohibited reasons.

§ 4.22 —Breach of Employer Promise

Litigation of the breach question when an implied-in-fact contract claim is asserted requires testing the employer's conduct against its promise to see if the two are congruent. If the employer promised to terminate employees only after one month's notice and one month's notice was not given, there is a breach. If the employer promised to terminate only after a review by the CEO and terminates without such a review, there is a breach. If the employer promised to terminate only for cause and terminates without cause there is a breach.

It is important not to confuse promises of pretermination procedures with promises of dismissal only for cause. If the employer has promised that an employee will not be dismissed until certain procedures have been followed, the fact question in determining whether there was a breach of this promise is whether the procedures were followed and not whether there was cause for the discharge.[78] This was the situation in *Pine River State Bank v. Mettille*,[79] in which the court pointed out the fallacy of allowing termination for cause in violation of promised procedures or requiring cause for dismissal even when the promised procedures had been followed.[80]

§ 4.23 —Breach of Covenant of Good Faith

As explained in § **4.11**, substantial differences exist in applying the covenant of good faith and fair dealing to employment termination cases. Conceptually, the implied-in-law covenant of good faith and fair dealing is breached when an employer terminates an employee without a reason rationally related to the employer's legitimate business interests. In simpler terms, the covenant is breached when an employee is dismissed without good cause. Virtually no case authority exists for

---

[77] See § **4.11**.

[78] *See* Gates v. Life of Montana Ins. Co., 196 Mont. 178, 638 P.2d 1063 (1982), *later appeal*, 668 P.2d 213 (1983) (citing Fortune v. National Cash Register Co., 373 Mass. 96, 364 N.E.2d 1251 (1977) and holding that when an employer created policies on discharge, a jury question existed as to whether the employer afforded the plaintiff the process required by the policies); Damrow v. Thumb Coop. Terminal Inc., 126 Mich. App. 354, 337 N.W.2d 338, *appeal denied*, 418 Mich. App. 899 (1983) (breach of procedural promise in handbook shown; judgment for employer reversed). *See also* Osterkamp v. Alkota Mfg. Co., 332 N.W.2d 275, 277 (S.D. 1983) (approving jury instruction limiting the question to whether procedures were followed).

[79] 333 N.W.2d 622 (Minn. 1983).

[80] *Id.* at 631 n.7 (distinguishing *Toussaint*).

§ 4.23 BREACH: GOOD FAITH

this broad interpretation of the covenant doctrine, however. In fact, the argument that a breach of the covenant can be shown merely by proving a dismissal without just cause has been rejected by three state supreme courts.[81] While rejecting this proposition, favorable to employees and with enormous implications for employers, the courts have not decided covenant cases on principles that permit an alternative breach prescription for the covenant doctrine. Some courts say that the covenant is breached only when jeopardy to public policy is shown. But this approach reduces the covenant to another name for the public policy tort theory, perhaps with limitations on damages.

Other courts say that a breach of the covenant can be established only by showing that an employer has failed to follow employer promulgated procedures that have led to reasonable expectations by employees.[82] But it is not clear what this interpretation adds to the implied-in-fact contract doctrine, especially when it is supplemented by promissory estoppel concepts.

Massachusetts courts have suggested that a breach of the covenant can be shown only when the employer has acted to deprive the employee of compensation that has been earned by past performance. But this interpretation makes the covenant redundant of quasi contract doctrines.

In sum, it is not possible to offer a definition of the covenant of good faith and fair dealing that makes it an intelligible alternative theory for wrongful dismissal, and also is supported by the case law.[83]

The early cases suggested that a breach of the covenant could be shown by a nearly infinite variety of employer decisions, which in the opinion of the factfinder, contravened good faith or fair dealing. The *Cleary v. American Airlines*[84] court said, "Termination of employment without legal cause after such a period of time[85] offends the Implied-in-law Covenant of Good Faith and Fair Dealing."[86] In *Fortune v. National Cash Register Co.*,[87] the Massachusetts Supreme Judicial Court held that a trial court committed no error in submitting the issue of bad

---

[81] *See* Wagenseller v. Scottsdale Memorial Hosp., 147 Ariz. 370, 385, 710 P.2d 1025, 1040 (1985) (accepting covenant but declining to interpret so as to require good cause to escape liability); Magnan v. Anaconda Indus., Inc., 193 Conn. 558, 479 A.2d 781, 782 (1984) (no action for breach of implied covenant wholly upon discharge without just cause); Wadeson v. American Family Mut. Ins. Co., 343 N.W.2d 367, 370 (N.D. 1984) (approving jury instruction on good faith, rejecting the unsuccessful plaintiff's argument that the covenant requires the employer to discharge only for good cause).

[82] *See* Grayson v. American Airlines, Inc., 803 F.2d 1097 (10th Cir. 1986) (claim that employer implemented procedures maliciously permits trial of implied covenant theory under Oklahoma law, even if economic cause for termination).

[83] *But see* Flanigan v. Prudential Fed. Sav. & Loan Ass'n, ___ Mont. ___, 720 P.2d 257, 261 (1986) (suggesting standard for implied covenant is whether employer had fair and honest reason for dismissal, contrasting apparently objective good cause standard for implied-in-fact contract claim).

[84] 111 Cal. App. 3d 443, 168 Cal. Rptr. 722 (1980).

[85] The plaintiff had 18 years of service.

[86] Cleary v. American Airlines, 111 Cal. App. 3d at 455, 168 Cal. Rptr. at 729.

[87] 373 Mass. 96, 364 N.E.2d 1251 (1977).

faith termination of an employment-at-will contract to the jury.[88] It found sufficient evidence, although the evidence was conflicting, to permit the jury rationally to infer that the plaintiff's termination was motivated by the employer's desire to pay as little as it could of the commissions that the plaintiff had earned.[89] The Montana courts are inclined to this broad view. In *Crenshaw v. Bozeman Deaconess Hospital*,[90] the Montana Supreme Court affirmed a jury verdict of $125,000 compensatory and $25,000 punitive damages for a respiratory therapist discharged during a probationary period, finding that the covenant of good faith and fair dealing applies to probationary employees, and that the plaintiff need not show violation of public policy to prove breach of the covenant of good faith and fair dealing. Some California cases still take the broad view.[91] The California Supreme Court apparently will decide the degree to which such limitations on the covenant doctrine exist in that state.[92]

More recent cases take a more restrictive view, generally rejecting claims that the covenant is violated unless the employer can show good cause.[93]

Some states require proof of a violation of public policy to show a breach of the covenant. This was, of course, the factual context of *Petermann v. Teamsters*,[94] which gave the implied covenant its start as a wrongful dismissal doctrine. Other more recent decisions limit the implied covenant to situations jeopardizing public policy. Borrowing a statutory age discrimination standard to determine the boundaries of the contractual good faith obligation, in *McKinney v. National Dairy Council*,[95] the district court approved a jury finding that the covenant of good faith

---

[88] *Id.* at 101, 364 N.E.2d at 1255–56: "We hold that NCR's written contract contains an Implied Covenant of Good Faith and Fair Dealing, and a termination not made in good faith constitutes a breach of the contract."

[89] *Id.* at 105, 364 N.E.2d at 1258.

[90] ___ Mont. ___, 693 P.2d 487 (1984).

[91] *See* Khanna v. Microdata Corp., 170 Cal. App. 3d 250, 264,, 215 Cal. Rptr. 860, 869 (1985) (finding breach of covenant when employee was dismissed for suing employer, without showing of public policy violation). *Contra* Foley v. Interactive Data Corp., 174 Cal. App. 3d 282, 219 Cal. Rptr. 866 (1985) (disagreement with analysis used in *Khanna*), *review granted,* ___ Cal. 3d ___, 712 P.2d 891, 222 Cal. Rptr. 740 (1986).

[92] That court will resolve the conflict between Khanna v. Microdata Corp., 170 Cal. App. 3d 250, 215 Cal. Rptr. 860 (1985) (finding breach of covenant when employee was dismissed for suing employer, without addressing public policy) and Foley v. Interactive Data Corp., 174 Cal. App. 3d 282, 219 Cal. Rptr. 866 (1985) (disagreement with analysis used in *Khanna*), *review granted,* ___ Cal. 3d ___, 712 P.2d 891, 222 Cal. Rptr. 740 (1986).

[93] *See* Rompf v. John Q. Hammons Hotels, Inc., 685 P.2d 25, 28 (Wyo. 1984) (no breach of implied covenant by discharge for economic reasons); Wadeson v. American Family Mut. Ins. Co., 343 N.W.2d 367 (N.D. 1984) (rejecting argument that the covenant of good faith and fair dealing imposes an obligation on the employer to discharge only for just cause); Zick v. Verson Allsteel Press Co., 623 F. Supp. 927, 929 (N.D. Ill. 1985) (covenant of good faith does not impose an obligation to "be nice or to behave decently in a general way.") *Id.* at 929.

[94] 174 Cal. App. 2d 184, 344 P.2d 25 (1959). See § **4.11**.

[95] 491 F. Supp. 1108 (D. Mass. 1980). The employee claimed that the employer indicated to him in his job interview that NDC could provide him with stable employment. The court construed those representations into an implied covenant of good faith and proceeded to apply Mass. Gen. L. ch. 149, § 24A (1982) as a means to define stable employment.

§ 4.23 BREACH: GOOD FAITH

was breached by a dismissal because of age.[96] In *Maddaloni v. Western Massachusetts Bus Lines*,[97] an intermediate court approved a jury finding of a breach of the good faith covenant for a termination to avoid payment of bonuses.[98] In *Brockmeyer v. Dun & Bradstreet, Inc.*,[99] the court held that a covenant of good faith and fair dealing is violated when the discharge "is contrary to a fundamental and well-defined public policy as evidenced by existing law."[1] The New Hampshire Supreme Court limited the scope of the implied covenant in that state in *Howard v. Dorr Woolen Co.*,[2] In *Magnan v. Anaconda Industries, Inc.*,[3] the Supreme Court of Connecticut suggested that a cause of action for breach of the implied covenant is identical to a public policy tort cause of action.[4]

Other states require a showing that the employer has violated some understanding about how employees would be handled, though not perhaps a sufficiently clear procedure to support a claim for breach of an implied-in-fact contract.[5] For example, in *Pugh v. See's Candies*[6] and *Cancellier v. Federated Department Stores, Inc.*,[7] the courts found a breach of the implied covenant because a longterm employee was discharged without notice or compliance with customary procedures. The Supreme Court of Montana found, in *Gates v. Life of Montana Insurance Co.*,[8] that an implied covenant of good faith and fair dealing would be breached by the employer's failure to follow policies in its personnel handbook.[9]

There is case law in Massachusetts suggesting that no breach of the covenant occurs except when the employer acts to deprive an employee of earned compensation.[10] In theory, a breach of the implied covenant could be shown if the employer acts with specific intent to harm the employee, as discussed in § **5.21**.

---

[96] McKinney v. National Dairy Council, 491 F. Supp. at 1121.

[97] 12 Mass. App. Ct. 236, 422 N.E.2d 1379 (1981), *modified,* 386 Mass. 877, 438 N.E.2d 351 (1982).

[98] *Id.* at 241, 422 N.E.2d at 1382. The employee brought an action against the employer for breach of a written contract under which plaintiff was employed by defendant bus company as general manager and which was terminable at will. The contract provided for enhanced compensation to plaintiff upon the acquisition of Interstate Commerce Commission rights deemed advantageous by the employer who, in turn, after reaping the benefits, dismissed plaintiff to end the extra pay.

[99] 113 Wis. 2d 561, 335 N.W.2d 834 (1983).

[1] *Id.* at 573, 335 N.W.2d at 840.

[2] 120 N.H. 295, 297, 414 A.2d 1273, 1274 (1980) (limiting Monge v. Beebe Rubber Co. approach to reasons for discharge that clearly offend public policy).

[3] 193 Conn. 558, 479 A.2d 781 (1984).

[4] 193 Conn. at ___ n.25, 479 A.2d at 791 n.25.

[5] *See* Gray v. Superior Court (Cipher Data), 181 Cal. App. 3d 813, 821, 226 Cal. Rptr. 570, 573 (1986) (jury, not court, decides whether failure to follow procedures in personnel manual is breach of covenant).

[6] 116 Cal. App. 3d 311, 171 Cal. Rptr. 917 (1981).

[7] 672 F.2d 1312 (9th Cir. 1982), *cert. denied,* 459 U.S. 859 (1982).

[8] 196 Mont. 178, 638 P.2d 1063 (1982), *later appeal,* 668 P.2d, 213 (1983).

[9] *Id.* at 183, 638 P.2d at 1067. The court found that the handbook policies were not enforceable on a traditional contract theory.

[10] *See* McCone v. New England Tel. & Tel. Co., 393 Mass. 231, 471 N.E.2d 47, 50 (1984) (suggesting that implied covenant claim lies only to deny employer financial windfall resulting from denial to employee of compensation for past services); De Rose v. Putnam Mgmt. Co., 398 Mass.

§ 4.24 — Who Decides Whether Good Cause Existed

The breach question raises important questions of institutional responsibility when the promise was to dismiss only for cause. The court and jury potentially are in the position of making decisions as to what efficient management of the employer's enterprise reasonably requires, balancing legitimate employer needs against legitimate employee interests.[11]

When the obligation not to dismiss for certain reasons arises from the implied covenant, the court and jury decide whether the external standard was met, though probably giving substantial latitude to the term *good faith*.

When the employer promised to dismiss only for cause, courts and juries can decide whether cause for dismissal existed by considering the body of labor arbitration precedent, much of which involves interpretation of express or implied commitments to dismiss only for just cause.[12] In determining that an employer's discipline of an employee was for cause, an arbitrator usually considers two elements. The arbitrator first must make a factual determination as to whether the employee committed the act alleged and then make the policy determination as to whether the act committed was of a character that would warrant the discipline imposed.[13]

The same two elements of cause regularly receive consideration in three other types of cases: those involving civil service, public employee constitutional rights, and statutory discrimination.[14] There also, courts distinguish between review of the factual questions relating to employee conduct or performance, and policy questions relating to what conduct or performance should amount to cause for termination. Substantially more discretion is given to the employer on the policy question.[15]

In all types of cases in which good cause for dismissal is disputed, there are these two separate questions: (1) whether the employee engaged in the conduct the employer alleges; and (2) whether that conduct constitutes just cause for termination of employment. The first question is a straightforward fact dispute. The second question requires employer interests to be balanced against employee interests, with appropriate consideration of the public interest on both sides.[16]

205, 496 N.E.2d 428 (1986) (Massachusetts implied covenant doctrine covers dismissals violating public policy and dismissals financially benefiting employer); Siles v. Travenol Laboratories, 13 Mass. App. 354, 433 N.E.2d 103, *writ denied*, 386 Mass. 1103, 440 N.E.2d 1176 (1982) (evidence did not support jury finding of wrongful dismissal).

[11] See generally §§ **7.22–7.28** for a more complete treatment of a breach and the respective roles of judge and jury.

[12] See §§ **3.5–3.8**. Staton v. Amax Coal Co., 122 Ill. App. 3d 631, 634, 461 N.E.2d 612, 615 (1984) (reversing summary judgment for employer and remanding for trial of whether *cause* for dismissal existed, suggesting that standards be borrowed from labor arbitration decisions).

[13] See § **3.5**.

[14] See generally **ch. 2** (statutory claims); **ch. 6** (public employee dismissal cases).

[15] See § **6.4**.

[16] See generally discussion of the *justification* idea in § **7.13**.

§ 4.24 BREACH: WHO DECIDES

The issues are illustrated by the approach utilized by the court in *Toussaint v. Blue Cross & Blue Shield*.[17] The court discussed the first component, what were the facts of the breach issue, as follows:

> Where the employer claims that the employee was discharged for specific misconduct—intoxication, dishonesty, insubordination—and the employee claims that he did not commit the misconduct alleged, the question is one of fact: did the employee do what the employer said he did?[18] Where the employer alleges that the employee was discharged for one reason—excessive tardiness—and the employee presents evidence that he was really discharged for another reason— because he was making too much money in commissions—the question also is one of fact . . . . The [fact finder] is always permitted to determine the employer's true reason for discharging the employee.[19]

The court had more difficulty with the second question—what constitutes just cause. When the employer, as in *Toussaint*, has promised to dismiss only for cause, the court cannot decide the breach issue without second guessing to some degree the policy question of what amounts to good cause for termination. If the judicial factfinder is permitted to decide de novo whether there was good cause for discharge, there is the danger that it will substitute its judgment for the employer's. "While the promise to terminate employment only for cause includes the right to have the employer's decisions reviewed, it does not include a right to be discharged only with the concurrence of the communal judgment of the jury."[20] On the other hand, if the factfinder is prohibited from finding a breach when the employer's decision to dismiss was not unreasonable under the circumstances, the promise to dismiss only for good cause effectively is transformed into a satisfaction contract.[21] The *Toussaint* court opted to let the factfinder decide whether the reason proffered by the employer amounts to good cause.[22]

In *Simpson v. Western Graphics Corp.*,[23] the Oregon Supreme Court agreed that the question of breach of a just cause promise involves the two questions posed earlier in this section.[24] But the Oregon court concluded that it was for the employer, and not for the court, to decide the factual question of what conduct occurred. It affirmed a trial court conclusion that "to constitute just cause, the employer . . . must make a good faith determination of a sufficient cause for discharge based on facts reasonably believed to be true and not for any arbitrary, capricious or

---

[17] 408 Mich. 579, 292 N.W.2d 880 (1980). The *Toussaint* court discussed the question in terms of what a jury should decide, but its analytical framework is equally applicable to a bench trial.

[18] *Id.* at 621, 292 N.W.2d at 896.

[19] *Id.* at 622, 292 N.W.2d at 896. This is the *mixed motive* problem, considered in **ch. 7**.

[20] *Id.*

[21] *Id.* at 622–23, 292 N.W.2d at 896.

[22] *Id.* at 623, 292 N.W.2d at 896.

[23] 293 Or. 96, 643 P.2d 1276 (1982).

[24] *Id.* at 100, 643 P.2d at 1278.

illegal reason."[25] The court did not expressly address the issue of who is to decide what amounts to just cause,[26] but merged the two parts of the just cause inquiry.

In the labor arbitration arena, the question is what the parties agreed to: the arbitrator's decision regarding what constitutes just cause or the employer's? This also should be the question in an implied-in-fact contract case. If the factfinder concludes that the employer promised that it would determine in good faith the grounds for termination, then the factfinder should do no more than decide whether that determination was made in good faith. If, on the other hand, the factfinder decides that the employer promised to terminate only according to some external standard, then the factfinder is acting appropriately in deciding whether the external standard was met.

§ 4.25 Suits by Employees Covered by Collective Bargaining Agreements

Union employees usually can assert wrongful dismissal breach of contract claims because their collective bargaining agreements almost always provide protection against dismissal without just cause.[27] Principles of federal labor law,[28] however, dictate that these claims be addressed in virtually all cases by arbitrators rather than by courts.[29]

Collective bargaining agreements are negotiated between employers and unions, but individual employees covered by the agreements may sue to enforce them in some circumstances.[30] A suit for breach of a collective bargaining agreement can be maintained in state as well as federal court.[31] A state court, however, is required to apply federal law,[32] and federal law requires that collectively bargained

---

[25] *Id.* at 99, 643 P.2d at 1278.

[26] *Id.* at 100, 643 P.2d at 1278.

[27] See § **3.5**.

[28] As this section suggests, suits for breach of collective bargaining agreements raise federal preemption questions. The preemption issue is discussed fully in §§ **2.27–2.31**.

[29] Most American collective bargaining agreements contain grievance and arbitration provisions. See §§ **3.2–3.4** for a discussion of the development and the purpose of arbitration.

[30] *See* Smith v. Evening News Ass'n, 371 U.S. 195 (1962). The theory under which individual employees can litigate issues arising under collective agreements is far from clear. *See* Feller, *A General Theory of the Collective Bargaining Agreement*, 61 Calif. L. Rev. 663, 774 (1973).

[31] Dowd Box Co. v. Courtney, 368 U.S. 502, 508–09 (1962). The Court, in construing § 301 of the Labor Management Relations Act of 1947, which gives federal district courts jurisdiction over suits for violation of contracts between an employer and a labor union in an industry affecting commerce, stated that the legislative history makes clear that the basic purpose of § 301(a) was not to limit but to expand the availability of forums. "Moreover, there is explicit evidence that Congress expressly intended not to encroach upon the existing jurisdiction of the state courts." *Id.* at 509.

[32] This is true only if the employment relationship affects interstate commerce, since the reach of the Labor Management Relations Act is so limited. Humphrey v. Moore, 375 U.S. 335, 342–44 n.6 (1964). The Court determined that since the action was one arising under § 301 of the LMRA, the case is controlled by federal law even though brought in the state court. *See also* Textile Workers

grievance and arbitration procedures be exhausted before a breach of contract claim is addressed judicially.[33] Moreover, after exhaustion of arbitral remedies, federal law requires a court hearing a breach of contract claim to give virtually preclusive effect to the arbitration award.[34]

Therefore, an individual employee is unlikely to be able to get a judicial adjudication of a breach of contract claim based on a collective agreement that contains a grievance arbitration clause.[35] The only significant exception is where the employee can plead a breach of the duty of fair representation by the union.[36]

Union v. Lincoln Mills, 353 U.S. 448 (1957) (substantive law to apply under § 301(a) is federal law, which the courts must fashion from the policy of the national labor laws; any state law compatible with the purpose of § 301 may be the source of a rule that will best effectuate the federal policy; any state law applied, however, will be absorbed as federal law and will not be an independent source of private rights).

[33] *See* Clayton v. Automobile Workers, 451 U.S. 679, 681 (1981); Republic Steel v. Maddox, 379 U.S. 650 (1965); *cf.* Steelworkers v. Warrior & Gulf Navigation Co., 363 U.S. 574 (1960) (federal policy under § 301 justifies construing the arbitration clause as hospitably as possible toward sending the case to arbitration). *See also* Vaca v. Sipes, 386 U.S. 171, 184 (1967) ("If the wrongfully discharged employee himself resorts to the courts before the grievance procedures have been fully exhausted, the employer may well defend on the ground that the exclusive remedies provided by such a contract have not been exhausted."); Dinger v. Anchor Motor Freight, Inc., 501 F. Supp. 64 (S.D.N.Y. 1980) (breach of contract suit precluded by contractual arbitration procedure available to employee); Burkhart v. Mobil Oil Corp., 143 Vt. 123, 463 A.2d 226 (1983) (employee who has not attempted to arbitrate claim under collective agreement may not sue under agreement for wrongful dismissal); Bertrand v. Quincy Mkt. Cold Storage & Warehouse Co., 728 F.2d 568, 571 (1st Cir. 1984) (under Massachusetts law, employee must present his claim for breach of employment contract to an arbitrator and could not elect to sue independently on an implied covenant of good faith and fair dealing). *See also* Azzi v. Western Elec. Co., 19 Mass. App. Ct. 406, 474 N.E.2d 1166, 1169 (1985) (implied covenant cause of action does not exist for employee covered by collective bargaining agreement). The Railway Labor Act yields similar results. *See* Union Pac. R.R. v. Sheehan, 439 U.S. 89 (1978); Andrews v. Louisville & N.R.R., 406 U.S. 302 (1972).

[34] Steelworkers v. Enterprise Wheel & Car Corp., 363 U.S. 593, 596 (1960): "The refusal of courts to review the merits of an arbitration award is the proper approach to arbitration under collective bargaining agreements. The federal policy of settling labor disputes by arbitration would be undermined if courts had the final say on the merits of awards." *See also* Steelworkers v. Warrior & Gulf Navigation Co., 363 U.S. 574, 582 (1960). *See generally* Annotation, 22 A.L.R.4th 366 (1983). Similar results are obtained under the Railway Labor Act. *See* Union Pac. R.R. v. Sheehan, 439 U.S. 89 (1978).

[35] A suit can be brought, however, if the collective agreement does not provide for arbitration. *See* Smith v. Kerrville Bus Co., Inc., 709 F.2d 914 (5th Cir. 1983), *later appeals,* 748 F.2d 1049, 1055 (5th Cir. 1984), 799 F.2d 1079 (5th Cir. 1986); Lumber Prod. Workers Local 2812 v. Missoula White Pine Sash Co., 734 F.2d 1384 (9th Cir. 1984) (finding no collectively bargained restriction on employer's common law right to dismiss); McQuitty v. General Dynamics Corp., 204 N.J. Super. 514, 499 A.2d 526 (1985) (after collective bargaining agreement expired, employer's telegram establishing conditions of employees' return to work contained no promise of job security).

[36] See § **3.25**; Vaca v. Sipes, 386 U.S. 171, 185–86 (1967) (courts have no jurisdiction to try alleged employer violations of the contract before the grievance and arbitration machinery has been exhausted, unless the failure to exhaust has been precipitated by the union's failure to represent the aggrieved employee fairly and without arbitrary discrimination); Clayton v. Automobile Workers, 451 U.S. 679, (1981); Hines v. Anchor Motor Freight, 424 U.S. 554 (1976). *Cf.* Huffman

It is permissible for the court to hear and to decide the breach of contract claim if it determines that the union has breached its duty of fair representation.[37] Assuming there has been a breach of the duty of fair representation, the court has jurisdiction to hear the breach of contract claim, either before or after arbitration.[38]

The rationale for this exception is that it would be futile to require the employee to exhaust arbitral remedies when the union, which superintends the arbitration process, is not willing to be a fair advocate for the employee.[39] Similarly, it would be unfair to require the employee to be bound by an arbitration award tainted by the union's misconduct.

It is not clear that the fair representation exception exists for collective bargaining agreements under the Railway Labor Act (RLA), which covers railroads and airlines.[40] Under the RLA, it may be necessary for the breach of contract claim to be presented to an arbitration panel while the court determines the fair representation claim.[41]

The foregoing principles assume that the employee's breach of contract suit is premised on violation of the collective bargaining agreement. Some terminated employees have attempted to avoid these federal preemption and deference to arbitration principles by claiming breach of an individual contract of employment independent of the collective agreement. Such arguments rarely succeed because of the holding of *J.I. Case Co. v. NLRB*[42] that individual contracts of employment

---

v. Westinghouse Elec. Corp., 752 F.2d 1221, 1224 (7th Cir. 1985) (no suit for breach of collective agreement merely because union failed to call strike after conclusion of "open ended" grievance process without arbitration as terminal step; must show fair representation breach. Not a discharge case).

[37] Vaca v. Sipes, 386 U.S. at 186: "The wrongfully discharged employee may bring an action against his employer in the face of a defense based upon the failure to exhaust contractual remedies, provided the employee can prove that the union as bargaining agent breached its duty of fair representation in its handling of the employee's grievance." *See also* Hines v. Anchor Motor Freight, Inc., 424 U.S. 554, 569, 570 (1976). In DelCostello v. Teamsters, 462 U.S. 151 (1983), the Supreme Court explained that the employee asserts two causes of action, even if he sues only the employer: the breach of the duty of fair representation and breach of the collective bargaining agreement. The employee must prove breach of the fair representation duty in order to succeed on the breach of collective agreement claim. *Id.* at 165.

[38] The duty of fair representation and its relation to judicial decision of wrongful dismissal claims is considered more fully in §§ **3.25, 3.26**.

[39] Vaca v. Sipes, 386 U.S. at 186:

> We cannot believe that Congress . . . intended to confer upon unions such unlimited discretion to deprive injured employees of all remedies for breach of contract. Nor do we think that Congress intended to shield employers from the natural consequences of their breaches of bargaining agreements by wrongful union conduct in the enforcement of such agreements.

See also Hines v. Anchor Motor Freight, 424 U.S. at 567: "The union's breach of duty relieves the employee of an express or implied requirement that disputes be settled through contractual grievance procedures . . . ."

[40] See § **3.19**.

[41] *Id.*, § **3.25**.

[42] 321 U.S. 332 (1944).

significantly different from a collective agreement covering the same employee may not be enforced.[43]

§ 4.26 Pleading the Plaintiff's Case

Details of the pleadings submitted by the plaintiff obviously depend on the procedures of the jurisdiction within which the action is brought. *Notice pleading* is more permissive than *fact pleading*. Under notice pleading, there is no requirement to plead facts sufficient to constitute a cause of action, but only that there "be a short and plain statement of the claim showing that the pleader is entitled to relief."[44] A pleading that satisfies fact pleading requirements, however, also will satisfy notice pleading requirements,[45] and it is prudent intellectual discipline for counsel to plead available facts to support each element of all the causes of action asserted.

This section suggests some general points to be considered by counsel for the plaintiff.[46] In addition to the contract theories considered here, the plaintiff should consider pleading, in the same action, the statutory and tort theories discussed in **Chapters 2** and **5**.[47]

The complaint should allege the basic factual requisites for any breach of contract action. The facts pleaded in an actual case must be objective facts, not merely plaintiff's belief.[48] In addition to facts supporting jurisdiction and venue, the complaint should allege:

1. The making of a promise and the date on which it was made
2. The terms of the promise, specifically focusing on obligations relating to employment security[49]
3. Consideration or a substitute for consideration[50]
4. The performance by the plaintiff of any conditions precedent
5. The facts showing the defendant's breach[51]
6. The injury to the plaintiff resulting from the defendant's breach

---

[43] *Id.* at 339.

[44] Dioguardi v. Durning, 139 F.2d 774 (2d Cir. 1944); Conley v. Gibson, 355 U.S. 41, 47–48 (1957) (detailed facts not required).

[45] *See* Brezinski v. F.W. Woolworth Co., 626 F. Supp. 240, 243 (D. Colo. 1986) (implied contract claims adequately pleaded under federal rules; notice pleading concept).

[46] Proof issues are discussed in **ch. 7**. This section is confined to pleading issues.

[47] See **§ 2.38** regarding the issues raised by terminations presenting both statutory and common law claims.

[48] *See* Vallone v. Agrip Petroleum Co., 705 S.W.2d 757 (Tex. Ct. App. 1986) (allegation of plaintiff's belief that employment would be secure insufficient; affirming judgment on pleadings for employer).

[49] See §§ **4.6–4.10**.

[50] See §§ **4.12–4.19**.

[51] See §§ **4.21–4.23**.

7. Damages
8. Relief requested.[52]

The plaintiff has the burden of pleading and proving the facts to support an inference of a contract for continued employment. Employment-at-will is a legal presumption, not an affirmative defense.[53]

In considering how to apply these principles to an actual case, it is useful to separate allegations relating to the promise element, the consideration element, and the breach element. In addition, it is useful to discuss pleading issues in the context of a concrete hypothetical set of facts.

Suppose the plaintiff's employer promulgated a handbook of employment policies containing two relevant items: (1) that no employee would be terminated without cause and (2) that no employee would be terminated except after review of the grounds for termination by the chief personnel officer. Suppose further that the plaintiff was dismissed by a supervisor, that the chief personnel officer did not review the dismissal, and that the grounds asserted for the termination were the plaintiff's active advocacy, on her own time, of nuclear disarmament.

The plaintiff should plead two separate counts for breach of contract. The first should allege a promise of dismissal only under certain conditions.[54] Separate factual allegations under this heading would cover the publication of the handbook and its communication to the plaintiff. The plaintiff also should plead the specific terms of the promise.[55] This heading requires that the plaintiff characterize the nature of the commitment to dismiss only for cause. The plaintiff also should consider alleging any facts that support a course of dealing by the employer with the employee, or with other employees, which the employer reasonably should have expected would give rise to employee expectations of dismissal only for cause.[56] For example, if no employee ever was terminated without cause, this should be alleged.

Count 2 should differ from count 1 only in the nature of the promise alleged. In count 2, the plaintiff should allege the making of a promise to dismiss only after review of the grounds for termination by the chief personnel officer. As in count 1, the plaintiff should identify the rules relating to pretermination review by the chief personnel officer. The plaintiff also should consider alleging any facts that support a course of dealing by the employer with the employee, or with other employees, which the employer reasonably should have expected would give rise to employee expectations of no dismissal before certain procedures are followed. For example, if no employee ever was terminated without a pretermination review by the chief personnel officer, this should be alleged.

---

[52] *See* J. Koffler & A. Reppy, Common Law Pleading 274 (1969). *See* Am. Jur. Practice and Pleading Forms, *Contracts* § 68.

[53] *See* Rice v. Grant County Bd. of Comm'rs, 472 N.E.2d 213, 215 (Ind. Ct. App. 1984) (pleading and proof of duration of employment part of plaintiff's prima facie case; employment at will not affirmative defense).

[54] This allegation would correspond to the first item on the list shown at the beginning of this section.

[55] This would correspond to the second item on the list.

[56] Such facts would support the theory for implying a promise discussed in § **4.9**.

In relation to the consideration issue (allegation #3), the plaintiff should assert facts in both counts supporting as many of the theories discussed in §§ **4.12** through **4.18** as possible. In the hypothetical situation, the plaintiff should allege that the reason for the employer's handbook rules was to induce employees to continue their employment and to forego their right to accept other jobs. This would establish the bargained-for aspect of consideration. In addition, plaintiff should assert that it was reasonable for the employer to expect that the handbook rules would induce employee reliance. This assertion supports an aspect of the promissory estoppel theory.[57] The plaintiff also should assert that she continued in employment and any other facts showing actual reliance on the handbook, such as quitting a previous job or refusing other job offers. This would establish either the detrimental reliance aspect of unilateral contract consideration or detrimental reliance for promissory estoppel.[58]

Facts should be pleaded that establish a breach of the employer's promises.[59] Failure to plead facts establishing a breach is, of course, fatal to a contract claim.[60] In count 1, the plaintiff should allege that off-duty advocacy of nuclear disarmament[61] does not constitute cause for dismissal, and thus that dismissal for this reason breached the *for cause* promise in the handbook. In count 2, breach of the pretermination review promise contained in the handbook should be alleged.

In addition, the plaintiff may add a third count for breach of an implied covenant of good faith and fair dealing.[62] This allegation states that the motive for the dismissal contravenes the covenant to act in good faith and consistent with public policy, specifically the public policy associated with the right to free speech.

The plaintiff should anticipate an argument that an implied condition precedent to continued employment was satisfactory job performance (allegation #4). Accordingly, plaintiff should allege that her work was satisfactory.

Pleading facts that establish injury[63] and damages[64] (allegation #7) is straightforward. The prayer for relief is similarly simple and should contain a request that the court award damages, including front pay, and, if desired, reinstatement.[65]

---

[57] *See* Ross v. Montana R.R., ____ Pa. Super. ____, 516 A.2d 29, 31 n.1 (1986) (failure to plead or argue promissory estoppel precludes appellate court from considering it).

[58] See §§ **4.12–4.17**. *See* Thebner v. Xerox Corp., 480 So. 2d 454, 457 (La. Ct. App.), *cert. denied*, 484 So. 2d 139 (1986) (promissory estoppel claim based on policy manual rejected for failure to plead detrimental reliance); Edwards v. Citibank, 74 A.D.2d 553, 554, 425 N.Y.S.2d 327, 328 (Kupferman, J., dissenting), *appeal dismissed*, 51 N.Y.2d 875, 414 N.E.2d 400, 433 N.Y.S.2d 1020 (1980).

[59] This corresponds to item number 5 on the list at the beginning of this section.

[60] *See* Gaulden v. Emerson Elec. Co., 284 Ark. 149, 151, 680 S.W. 2d 92, 94 (1984) (failure to allege timely notice to employer of inability of truck driver to make assigned run due to illness fails to put in question employer's just cause for dismissal for failure to make run).

[61] If warranted, the employee also could deny that he did advocate nuclear disarmament. This goes to the first part of the cause question, discussed in § **4.24**.

[62] See §§ **4.11, 4.23**.

[63] This corresponds to item number 6 on the list at the beginning of this section.

[64] This corresponds to item number 7 on the list at the beginning of this section.

[65] See § **4.28** for a discussion of damages and equitable relief available under a contract theory.

§ 4.27 Pleading the Defendant's Case

If the case is brought in a jurisdiction that continues to adhere firmly to the traditional Employment-at-Will Rule,[66] the defendant's first line of defense is to file a demurrer or an equivalent motion appropriate to the jurisdiction asserting that the plaintiff has failed to state a claim upon which relief can be granted. A motion in the nature of a demurrer asserts that the facts pleaded by the plaintiff, taken as true, do not entitle him to recover under any recognized legal theory. Success on such a motion keeps the case away from a jury which is likely to be sympathetic to the dismissed plaintiff. The timing of such a motion should be determined by the forum's procedural rules and the defendant's litigation strategy.[67]

The defendant's strongest arguments are likely to relate to the promise and consideration elements; whether there was a breach is more likely to involve factual disputes. The factual allegations in the complaint should be scrutinized carefully to determine if they fall short of the requirements of the implied-promise case law[68] and the doctrines of bargained-for detriment and promissory estoppel.[69] If the case is brought in a jurisdiction that insists upon mutuality of obligation,[70] the defendant also should argue that the facts pleaded by the plaintiff do not show mutuality of obligation and that this is fatal to a contract cause of action.

If the plaintiff asserts facts supporting an allegation that an implied covenant of good faith and fair dealing was breached, the employer should consider arguing in a threshold motion that the facts pleaded do not make out a breach of the covenant as a matter of law, for example, that the plaintiff has failed to plead long service, violation of public policy, or deprivation of earned commissions.[71] In a notice pleading jurisdiction, these arguments are more likely to be presented at the summary judgment, rather than the pleading, stage.

If a responsive pleading is filed, either because the demurrer is denied or because the defendant elects to file such a pleading in conjunction with a demurrer, the defendant also should concentrate on contesting the existence of facts necessary to a finding of a promise, the consideration or a substitute therefor, and the breach.[72]

---

[66] See § 1.12.

[67] Motions for summary judgment may be considered more seriously than demurrers in notice-pleading jurisdictions.

[68] See §§ 4.6–4.10 for discussion of implied promise theories.

[69] See §§ 4.12–4.18 for discussion of consideration theories. For the consequences of a failure to plead effectively, see Washington Welfare Ass'n v. Poindexter, 116 L.R.R.M. 3438 (D.C. App. 1984) (employer who failed to argue in trial court that personnel manual was not enforceable promise to dismiss only for just cause, arguing instead only that just cause existed, could not challenge jury verdict for plaintiff on that basis).

[70] See § 4.13 for a discussion of mutuality of obligation in the context of a unilateral contract.

[71] Cases imposing such prerequisites on the covenant of good faith and fair dealing are discussed in § 4.11.

[72] Obviously, whether the defendant admits or denies depends on an honest understanding of the facts. Ordinarily, the defendant will be without knowledge sufficient to form a belief regarding the factual basis of promissory estoppel and bargained-for detriment claims. The defendant also should be alert to separating allegations of fact from conclusions of law. The latter can be denied as such.

In responding to each allegation in the complaint, the defendant must understand why the allegation is made and what theories it will tend to support.

In denying consideration, the defendant should pay careful attention to the elements of promissory estoppel or bargained-for detriment and to the unilateral contract doctrine as recognized in the jurisdiction and as found in the leading cases discussed in §§ 4.12 through 4.19. For pleading purposes, the bargained-for detriment and promissory estoppel theories should be treated the same. If the plaintiff has argued that she detrimentally relied on defendant's representations, the defendant should, if possible, deny the facts supporting the conclusion that such detrimental reliance occurred. If the conduct asserted as detrimental reliance by the plaintiff occurred, the defendant should deny that the motivation for the promise of employment security was to induce such conduct, thereby defeating the bargained-for aspect of detrimental reliance.[73]

If promissory estoppel might be relied upon, the reasonableness of the plaintiff's expectations of continued employment are likely to present a factual question. Crucial facts should be denied, if they can be, or the plaintiff otherwise put to proof under the forum's procedure.[74] If it is appropriate to assert the unreasonableness of the plaintiff's reliance on the defendant's representations in an affirmative defense, this should be done. As a part of the reasonableness question, the defendant should plead, as an affirmative defense, the advisory, nonbinding character of any representations relied on by the plaintiff and allege a general course of dealing, custom, and practice that should have put the plaintiff on notice that employment was terminable at will.

The pleader may have difficulty in determining whether a particular matter is an affirmative defense. Precedent, rules, or statutes in any particular jurisdiction should provide the answer. The Federal Rules of Civil Procedure provide that the failure of consideration and the Statute of Frauds are affirmative defenses[75] and must be stated specifically by the defendant. If it is uncertain whether something must be pleaded affirmatively, it may be that the best course is to plead affirmatively as a precaution, since affirmative defenses are waived if not pleaded. The danger of this route lies in the fact that a few jurisdictions impose the burden of proof on one who pleads affirmatively.[76]

Even if the plaintiff establishes the existence of an enforceable contract,[77] the defendant's obligation to perform may be excused by an event such as the plaintiff's misconduct, poor performance, or other justification.[78] The defendant should allege the occurrence of such events as affirmative defenses. For example, under

---

[73] See § 4.14.

[74] J. Koffler and A. Reppy, Common Law Pleading 543 (1969).

[75] Fed. R. Civ. P. 8(c) (affirmative defenses).

[76] F. James v. G. Hazard, Civil Procedures § 7.8 (2d ed. 1974); J. McCoid II, Civil Procedure 242 (1974).

[77] See §§ 4.6–4.19.

[78] A. Corbin, Corbin on Contracts § 628 at 587 (1952) (conditions subsequent are those facts and events that terminate the right to immediate performance and also the right to judicial remedy). Defense counsel for bank employers should not forget that a federal statute, 12 U.S.C. § 24 Fifth (1976), may permit dismissal regardless of whether there is a contract guaranteeing job security.

the hypothetical facts given in § **4.26**, the defendant should allege that the plaintiff's off-duty activities adversely affected the employer's business and, therefore, constitute just cause for dismissal.

§ 4.28 Damages

Compensation in the form of money damages for disappointed expectations is the usual remedy for breach of contract.[79] *Expectation damages* are measured by the financial position the plaintiff would have occupied had the contract been performed fully.[80] In general, the injured promisee is entitled to recover the economic equivalent of the performance promised plus any losses incurred or gains prevented through the failure of performance.[81] Punitive damages usually are not permitted for breach of contract[82] or for emotional distress or mental suffering unless it is evident to the breaching party that such injury is likely to flow from the breach.[83]

Section 347 of the *Restatement (Second) of Contracts* states the general rule for measuring damages in a breach of contract action:

See McGeehan v. Bank of N.H., 123 N.H. 83, 86–87, 455 A.2d 1054, 1055 (1983) (dismissal permissible despite explicit one-year contract).

[79] J. Murray, Murray on Contracts § 221 at 442 (1974).

[80] *Id. Reliance* damages are available as an alternative in some cases. *See id.* § 233 at 446; Restatement (Second) of Contracts § 90, comments (1979).

[81] J. Murray, Murray on Contracts § 221 at 442 (1974). This formula has produced relatively modest damage awards in leading cases. *See, e.g.,* Toussaint v. Blue Cross & Blue Shield, 408 Mich. 579, 292 N.W.2d 880 (1980) ($72,835); Pine River State Bank v. Mettille, 333 N.W.2d 622 (Minn. 1983) ($27,675). Gulf Consol. Int'l, Inc. v. Murphy, 658 S.W.2d 565 (Tex. 1983) (general rule: present cash value of contract if it had not been breached, less amounts employee could earn elsewhere through reasonable diligence). In Grouse v. Group Health Plan, Inc., 306 N.W.2d 114 (Minn. 1981), the Supreme Court of Minnesota held that the plaintiff was entitled to recover damages for his lost income from the job he quit and from declining an offer of employment elsewhere. *Id.* at 116. These are *reliance,* rather than *expectation,* damages. This may be the reason the court used promissory estoppel: it permits more flexibility respecting damages than traditional contract theories. *See* Restatement (Second) of Contracts § 90 comment d and Reporter's Notes (1979); J. Murray, Murray on Contracts § 92 at 200 (1974). See § **4.17** for a discussion of § 90 of the Restatement.

[82] The rule is stated in 5 A. Corbin, Corbin on Contracts § 1077 at 438 (19___). *But see* 11 S. Williston, Williston on Contracts § 1340 at 209–13 (1960); J. Murray, Murray on Contracts § 231 at 470–71 (1974); Dvorak v. Pluswood Wis., Inc., 121 Wis. 2d 218, 358 N.W.2d 544, 546 (1984) (punitive damages not available); Cappiello v. Ragen Precision Indus., Inc., 192 N.J. Super. 523, 471 A.2d 432, 436–37 (1984) (punitive damages recoverable for termination in breach of commission contract because of egregious conduct); Crenshaw v. Bozeman Deaconess Hosp., ___ Mont. ___, 693 P.2d 487 (1984) (affirming jury verdict of $125,000 compensatory and $25,000 punitive damages for respiratory therapist discharged during probationary period. Tort damages permitted for breach of implied covenant).

[83] Restatement (Second) of Contracts § 353 (1979); J. Murray, Murray on Contracts § 232 at 471 (1974). In Monge v. Beebe Rubber Co., 114 N.H. 130, 316 A.2d 549 (1974), the jury's awarding of $1,083.80 attributable to mental suffering was deemed improper because such damages are not generally recoverable in a contract action. *Id.* at 134, 316 A.2d at 552. *See also* Valentine

Subject to the limitations stated in §§ 350-53,[84] the injured party has a right to damages based on his expectation interest as measured by

(a) the loss in the value to him of the other party's performance caused by its failure or deficiency, plus

(b) any other loss, including incidental or consequential loss, caused by the breach, less

(c) any cost or other loss that he has avoided by not having to perform.[85]

An important limitation on application of the general rule is contained in § 352:

Damages are not recoverable for loss beyond an amount that the evidence permits to be established with reasonable certainty.[86]

Expectation damages in a wrongful dismissal case require the factfinder to project how long the employee would have been employed but for the employer's breach. This is an inherently speculative undertaking.[87]

The uncertainty problem when a plaintiff avoids the Employment-at-Will Rule by establishing an implied-in-fact contract of employment security is not uncertainty with respect to earnings, but uncertainty with respect to the duration of the contract. This source of uncertainty is unique to informal contracts for indefinite employment; when breach of an express contract for a definite term is involved, the duration of the contract is clear.

The tension between the expectation damages principle and the uncertainty proviso is illustrated by two recent implied contract cases: *Ohanian v. Avis Rent a Car*

---

v. General Am. Credit, Inc., 420 Mich. 256, 362 N.W.2d 628, 629 (1984) (mental distress damages not recoverable for termination of implied contract, though foreseeable).

[84] Section 350 deals with avoidability; § 351 deals with unenforceability; § 352 deals with uncertainty, and is discussed more fully later in this section. Section 353 deals with damages for emotional injury or loss.

[85] Several illustrations to § 347 make it clear that the drafters intended the principle articulated by the section to be applied to personal service contracts. Illustrations 3, 9, 13, and 14 deal with a contract to employ someone for $10,000 to supervise the production of a crop. The employer in the illustrations fires the employee at the beginning of the season. All of the illustrations say that the dismissed employee is entitled to $10,000 in damages, less earnings for other jobs made possible by the breach, and less unemployment compensation if state legislative policy so permits.

[86] The illustrations to § 352 do not deal with employment contracts. Illustration 7, however, involves a contract between A and B, under which B is to be A's exclusive agent for the sale of machine tools in a specified territory and A is to supply B with machine tools at specified prices. If A repudiates the agreement, replacing B with C, the illustration states, "B can use evidence as to sales and profits made by him before the repudiation and made by C after the repudiation in attempting to prove his lost profits with reasonable certainty. It would be more difficult, although not necessarily impossible, for B to succeed in this attempt if his agency were not exclusive."

[87] *Compare* Renny v. Port Huron Hosp., ___ Mich. ___, ___, N.W. 2d ___, No. 74884 (Dec. 1986) (affirming $100,000 jury award of front pay for breach of implied just cause contract); Washington Welfare Ass'n, Inc. v. Wheeler, 496 A.2d 613, 617 (D.C. 1985) ($26,000 jury award for future earnings under contract terminable only for just cause allowed to stand) *with* Gram v. Liberty Mut. Ins. Co., 391 Mass. 333, 335, 461 N.E.2d 796, 798 (1984) (reversing $325,000 judgment for dismissed employee on grounds that proper measure is not same as earnings for lifetime employment).

System, Inc.,[88] and *Sepanske v. Bendix Corp.*[89] In *Ohanian*, the Second Circuit, applying New York law, affirmed a jury award of $304,393 to an Avis regional vice president, based on breach of a contract for lifetime employment. The contract arose from negotiations over a transfer in which an employer representative said, "[U]nless he screwed up badly, there is no way he was going to get fired . . . he would never get hurt here in this company."[90] When the plaintiff was fired, his annual salary was $68,400. The jury found that the present value of the plaintiff's lost wages was $245,409. The Second Circuit approved instructing the jury that it was to compute the amount plaintiff would have received until the natural end of the plaintiff's contract, subtracting from this amount anything Ohanian would receive from other employment. *Ohanian*, therefore, is a paradigmatic illustration of the expectation damages principle in an implied-in-fact contract case.

The uncertainty issue was involved directly in *Sepanske*. The plaintiff had been promised employment in an equivalent job after he returned from a leave of absence. The jury found that the job offered on his return was not equivalent. The appellate court reversed an award of $75,206 in damages. It held that the plaintiff was entitled to an award of nominal damages only for breach of the employment contract:

> Plaintiff's expectation under the contract was to be restored to his old job or to an at-will position which was equivalent to or better than his [old] position . . . but he had no actionable expectation that any such restoration would be permanent. The position was still at will—one which the employer was free to alter or terminate without consequence. . . . The jury's damage assessment in such a situation amounts to pure speculation. There is no tangible basis upon which damages may be assessed where plaintiff's expectation was for an at-will position which could have been changed or from which he could have been terminated without consequence.[91]

The difference between *Ohanian* and *Sepanske* is the (admittedly subtle) difference between assessing damages for termination of an at-will employment contract and assessing damages for breach of a promise of employment security. In *Sepanske*, the jury was in the position of estimating when Sepanske's employer might wish to exercise its unilateral right to terminate Sepanske. That was too speculative an undertaking to pass muster. In *Ohanian*, the jury was in the position of estimating the likelihood—or the timing—that Ohanian might "screw up," permitting the employer to terminate the employment. That was not too speculative an undertaking.

The point is not that there is a special rule for computing damages for breach of an implied-in-fact contract of employment, as compared with breach of a contract for a definite term; on the contrary, the rule is the same. But most implied-in-fact contracts are based on rather general assurances of employment until a contingency

---

[88] 779 F.2d 101, 108 (2d Cir. 1985).
[89] 147 Mich. App. 819, 829, 384 N.W.2d 54, 58 (1985).
[90] 779 F.2d 101, 104 (2d Cir. 1985).
[91] 147 Mich. App. 819, 829, 384 N.W.2d at 59.

§ 4.28 DAMAGES

occurs—frequently the existence of just cause for termination, or the completion of certain procedures. Evaluating the probability of the contingency occurring and its timing is inherently more uncertain than determining when a certain number of years or months will elapse.

Some courts avoid speculation by denying front pay altogether. In *Brockmeyer v. Dun & Bradstreet, Inc.*,[92] the court concluded that reinstatement and back pay were the most appropriate remedies for wrongful dismissal in violation of a public policy.[93] *Brockmeyer* precludes damages for the executory portion of the employment contract and substitutes specific performance in the form of reinstatement.

Notably, however, there is a trend in statutory employment discrimination cases to award front pay.[94]

Compensatory damages for breach of contract usually are calculated as the plaintiff's lost earnings minus earnings from any work after the dismissal[95] plus any expenses reasonably incurred in seeking work.[96] For instance, in *Osterkamp v. Alkota Manufacturing, Inc.*,[97] the court upheld a jury verdict of $30,000 for a dismissed employee, stating that the undisputed testimony was that the plaintiff had been earning $13,000 per year, was unemployed for 11 months, and had obtained a new job for $10,500 per year.[98] He was expected to be able to work for 14 more years. The court stated that the damages for breach of contract were "clearly supported by sufficient evidence."[99] Damages awarded under this theory can be substantial.[1] In *Brewster v. Martin Marietta Aluminum Sales, Inc.*,[2] the court affirmed a $740,000 damages award for breach of implied contract, reasoning that the plaintiff's injured reputation and psyche could interfere with her obtaining

---

[92] 113 Wis. 2d 561, 335 N.W.2d 834 (1983).

[93] *Id.* at 575, 335 N.W.2d at 841.

[94] See §§ **2.3, 2.6**.

[95] A. Corbin, Corbin on Contracts § 958 at 847, § 1095 at 516 (multivolume ed. 1951). The dismissed employee must make a reasonable effort to find new employment in order to recover the full amount of lost wages from the employer. The burden of proof is on the employer to show that similar employment could have been obtained. *Id.* § 1095 at 518. Unemployment benefits, in contrast, may not be an offset. *See* Hall v. Hotel l'Europe, Inc., 69 N.C. App. 664, 667, 318 S.E.2d 99, 102 (1984) (affirming refusal of trial judge to admit evidence of unemployment benefits in jury trial resulting in verdict for employee). *See* Adams v. Frontier Airlines Fed. Credit Union, 691 P.2d 352, 353 (Colo. Ct. App. 1984) (affirming judgment of $109,000 for balance of three-year contract).

[96] 11 S. Williston, Contracts § 1359 at 311 (1960); J. Murray, Murray on Contracts § 228 at 465 (1974).

[97] 332 N.W.2d 275 (S.D. 1983).

[98] *Id.* at 279.

[99] *Id.* at 278. The court evaluated the verdict in light of a jury instruction stating that the "measure of damages is the unpaid wages due under the contract. But if the Plaintiff has been able to secure other employment, then the measure of damages is the difference between the wages agreed to be paid and the wages received under the new employment." *Id.*

[1] *See, e.g.*, Chastain v. Kelly-Springfield Tire Co., 733 F.2d 1479, 1481 (11th Cir. 1984) (reversing, on other grounds, a judgment for the plaintiff on a jury verdict of $170,000).

[2] 145 Mich. App. 641, 378 N.W.2d 558, 567 (1985).

other employment before retirement. The award represented about half her expected earnings from the terminated position until retirement.[3]

In some cases, the dismissed employee seeks only termination pay.[4]

The concept of mitigation of damages in a breach of a contract suit permits the dismissing employer to pay less in damages than it might otherwise.[5] Theoretically, the employee has no duty to search for a new job, but if the employee does not, damages will be less.[6] The burden of proof is on the employer to show that the employee could have earned an income after the dismissal.[7] In *Juvenile Diabetes Research Foundation v. Rievman*,[8] the Florida District Court of Appeals upheld a judgment for two dismissed workers in the face of allegations on appeal that the workers had formed a new corporation immediately after dismissal, had continued in the same work, and had subsisted on donations.[9] The court found the burden to be on the defendant to plead and prove mitigation of the employees' damages at trial, and, since it had not, the judgment was not erroneous.[10] The dismissed employee may not be charged with compensation obtainable from a significantly inferior position under the mitigation rule, however.[11]

Under the American rule,[12] attorneys' fees ordinarily are not recoverable in a breach of contract action.[13] Federal Rule of Civil Procedure 11 permits sanctions to be imposed on counsel for advancing frivolous claims. The rule permits counsel to advance good faith arguments for the extension, modification, or reversal of

---

[3] *See also* Ohanian v. Avis Rent a Car Sys., Inc., 779 F.2d 101, 110 (2d Cir. 1985) (affirming judgment of $304,693 in implied contract case, based on jury estimate of what plaintiff would have received until "natural end" of contract); *but see* Myrtle Springs Reverted Indep. School Dist. v. Hogan, 705 S.W.2d 707 (Tex. Ct. App. 1985) (damages for diminished earning capacity and mental distress not recoverable in contract action); Sepanske v. Bendix Corp., 147 Mich. App. 819, 829, 384 N.W.2d 54, 59 (1985) (jury award of front pay for breach of obligation to return to former position purely speculative and therefore invalid, because employer free to terminate at any time. Split panel).

[4] *See, e.g.*, Staton v. Amax Coal Co., 122 Ill. App. 3d 631, 461 N.E.2d 612 (1984) (reversing summary judgment for employer and remanding for trial of whether cause for dismissal existed).

[5] *See* J. Murray, Murray on Contracts § 227 at 460 (1974). The concept is similar to that of avoidable consequences. 11 S. Williston, Williston on Contracts § 1359 at 306 n.2 (1960).

[6] 11 S. Williston, Williston on Contracts § 1360 at 312 (1960); 5 A. Corbin, Corbin on Contracts § 1095 at 518 (multivolume ed. 1951).

[7] 5 A. Corbin, Corbin on Contracts § 1095 at 518 (multivolume ed. 1951).

[8] 370 So. 2d 33 (Fla. Dist. Ct. App. 1979).

[9] *Id.* at 35.

[10] *Id.* at 37.

[11] *See* Flanigan v. Prudential Fed. Sav. & Loan Ass'n, ___ Mont. ___, 720 P.2d 257, 265 (1986) (no duty to accept inferior employment).

[12] *See* Alyeska Pipeline Serv. Co. v. Wilderness Soc'y, 421 U.S. 240 (1975) for a discussion of the American Rule regarding attorneys' fees as court costs. *See generally* S. Speiser, Attorneys' Fees chs. 12 (allowance of fees as costs; recovery from opponent) & 13 (allowance of fees as damages) (1973).

[13] See generally § **2.25** regarding attorneys' fees under remedial statutes.

§ 4.28 DAMAGES

existing law, but some courts have nevertheless imposed sanctions based on nothing more than a conclusion that the legal argument advanced lacked merit.[14]

In any case, calculation of damages is fact-dependent. Analogies can be found in arbitration awards and in National Labor Relations Board and court decisions adjudicating claims under remedial statutes discussed in **Chapter 2**.

Reinstatement also may be available in contract actions. Although the usual rule in contract law prohibits specific performance when the parties are master and servant,[15] this has been criticized as based on inadequate reasoning.[16] Few common law wrongful dismissal cases, aside from *Brockmeyer v. Dun & Bradstreet, Inc.*, deal with the availability of reinstatement as a remedy.[17]

---

[14] Albright v. Upjohn Co., 788 F.2d 1217 (6th Cir. 1986) (reversing denial of Rule 11 sanctions for failure to investigate facts; nonemployment case); Jones v. Continental Corp., 789 F.2d 1225 (6th Cir. 1986) (assessment of fees against plaintiff counsel for sloppy pleading, refusal to narrow issues for trial); Golden Eagle Distrib. Co. v. Burroughs Corp., 801 F.2d 1531 (9th Cir. 1986) (no Rule 11 sanctions for failure to cite contrary precedent or for failure to acknowledge that argument requires extension of existing law); *See* Zick v. Verson Allsteel Press Co., 623 F. Supp. 927, 932-33 (N.D. Ill. 1985) (sanctions imposed for arguing that federal court should find covenant of good faith appropriate under Illinois law). The *Zick* case is an obvious misapplication of Rule 11, in that the court's opinion demonstrates the colorability of the counsel's argument.

[15] Restatement (Second) of Contracts § 367 comment b (1979) (rule barring specific performance of employee's promise sometimes used to bar specific performance of employer's promise where personal supervision involved).

[16] *See* D. Dobbs, Remedies 929 (1973). Professor Dobbs notes that damages are sometimes inadequate, cooperation between employer and employee is not always required, supervision of the employee by the employer is not always required, and mutuality of obligation is a discredited theory. He advocates a case-by-case analysis of requests for specific performance in master-servant cases. *Id.* at 931.

[17] In Duhon v. Slickline, Inc., 449 So. 2d 1147, 1153 (La. Ct. App. 1984), the court held that breach of a written employment contract could be remedied by either specific performance or damages. *See also* Decker, *Reinstatement as a Remedy for a Pennsylvania Employer's Breach of a Handbook or an Employment Policy,* 90 Dick. L. Rev. 41 (1985).

CHAPTER 5

TORT THEORIES

§ 5.1   Introduction and Overview
§ 5.2   Public Policy Tort Cases Do Not Require Employers to Show Good Cause for Dismissing Employees
§ 5.3   Basic Tort Concepts
§ 5.4   —Development of the Tort Forms of Action
§ 5.5   —The Framework for a Public Policy Tort in Section 870
§ 5.6   —Injury Requirement of Section 870
§ 5.7   —Justification Concept of Section 870
§ 5.8   Categories of Public Policy Torts
§ 5.9   —Labor Statutes as a Basis for Public Policy Torts
§ 5.10 —*External* Public Policy: Jury Duty
§ 5.11 —*External* Public Policy: Workers' Compensation Claims
§ 5.12 —*External* Public Policy: Termination Jeopardizing Constitutionally Recognized Rights
§ 5.13 —*External* Public Policy: Termination for Private, or Off Duty, Conduct
§ 5.14 *External* versus *Internal* Public Policy Torts for Wrongful Dismissal
§ 5.15 —*Internal* Public Policy: Marshaling the Conflicting Interests
§ 5.16 —*Internal* Public Policy Tort: Protests or Reports to Outside Agencies (Whistleblowing)
§ 5.17 —*Internal* Public Policy Tort: Protests or Reports to Employer
§ 5.18 —*Internal* Public Policy Tort: Refusals to Follow Orders
§ 5.19 Public Policy Torts Are More Than Civil Remedies for Statutory Violations
§ 5.20 Public Policy Tort Protection for Employees Covered by Collective Bargaining Agreements
§ 5.21 Prima Facie Tort: Liability Based on Intent to Harm, Regardless of Public Policy
§ 5.22 Intentional Interference with Contractual Relations
§ 5.23 Intentional Infliction of Emotional Distress
§ 5.24 Fraudulent Misrepresentation (Deceit)
§ 5.25 Defamation

§ 5.26	Invasion of Privacy: Improper Acquisition or Dissemination of Information
§ 5.27	—Invasion of Privacy: Interference with Private Conduct
§ 5.28	Tort Claims for Dismissals Related to AIDS or to Sexual Orientation
§ 5.29	Negligence
§ 5.30	Preemption of State Tort Claims by § 301 of the Labor Management Relations Act
§ 5.31	Pleading the Plaintiff's Case
§ 5.32	Pleading the Defendant's Case
§ 5.33	Damages

§ 5.1 Introduction and Overview

Courts in all but six states[1] recognize a private right of action for dismissals that jeopardize a specific public policy interest of the state. This category of tort liability is called the *public policy tort*. Intentional tort principles permit a plaintiff to recover only by showing that a legally protected right of the plaintiff was harmed by an act of the defendant and that the defendant lacked justification for his act.[2] Until the public policy tort theory was accepted by the courts, dismissed employees could recover in tort only if they could show that their dismissals were accompanied by conduct or a state of mind sufficient to satisfy traditional tort categories such as intentional interference with contractual relations,[3] intentional infliction of emotional distress,[4] fraudulent misrepresentation,[5] defamation,[6] or invasion of privacy.[7] None of these traditional theories permitted the employee to recover for the dismissal itself. The newer public policy tort theory permits a dismissed employee to recover for the dismissal itself.

The *public policy tort*[8] is a specific application of the *prima facie tort*.[9] The public policy tort permits recovery by a dismissed employee only when the dismissal violates a clear public policy of the state.[10] The prima facie tort allows

---

[1] See § **1.12** for a state-by-state summary.

[2] The analytical framework is given by § 870 of the Restatement (Second) of Torts (1979), discussed more extensively in §§ **5.5–5.7**.

[3] See § **5.22**.

[4] See § **5.23**.

[5] See § **5.24**.

[6] See § **5.25**.

[7] See § **5.26**.

[8] See §§ **5.8–5.20**.

[9] See § **5.21**. As § **5.21** explains, the prima facie label is not new, but its application to wrongful dismissal suits is new.

[10] See §§ **5.8–5.20**.

recovery if the employer dismissed the employee with malice and without justification.[11]

Public policy tort cases require courts to balance employee, employer and societal interests under a formula presented in § 870 of the *Restatement (Second) of Torts*.[12] To win a public policy tort case for wrongful dismissal, the employee must show:

1. The existence of a clear and substantial public policy
2. Which would be jeopardized if employers were allowed to escape liability for terminating employees in circumstances like that involving the plaintiff,[13] and
3. Lack of legitimate employer interest (other than the Employment-at-Will Rule) justifying the dismissal.

The balancing process can be symbolized by the scales of justice. On the employee's side of these scales is an obvious economic interest in employment. On the employer's side is an obvious economic interest in running the business as the employer sees fit. If the employee asserts no other interest, society places an additional interest on the employer's side of the scales: the Employment-at-Will Rule, representing society's interest in market forces as the best way to promote efficient enterprise. This is sufficient to tip the scales in favor of the employer and against the employee. If, however, the employee can add a societal interest to her side of the scales, she may win, depending on the weightiness of the interest. Of course, the employer may assert additional justification for the dismissal on the employer's side, which may tilt the scales back in the employer's favor. Liability is imposed on the employer whenever the interests of the terminated employee and the public outweigh the interests of the employer.

The public policy tort formula is illustrated well by comparing two cases: *Geary v. United States Steel Corp.*,[14] a 1974 Pennsylvania Supreme Court case, and *Sheets v. Teddy's Frosted Foods, Inc.*,[15] a 1980 Connecticut Supreme Court case.

Geary claimed that he was fired because he protested the marketing of tubular casings without further testing, a protest based on his belief that the casings would be dangerous. His protests were directed to his superiors and ultimately to a company vice president. The Supreme Court of Pennsylvania agreed with the trial court that United States Steel was not liable. There was no clear public policy relating to safe design of tubular steel products, and even if there were, the policy would

---

[11] *Malice* is a legal term of art meaning little more than the mental state motivating harmful conduct in the absence of justification. See § **5.21**.

[12] See § **5.5** for an analysis of § 870.

[13] Separating the policy existence and jeopardy inquiries first was suggested to the author by a student law review note, which proposed a two-dimensional analysis for evaluating public policy tort claims. *Guidelines for a Public Policy Exception to the Employment at Will Rule: The Wrongful Discharge Tort,* 13 Conn. L. Rev. 617, 635 (1980–1981) (suggesting assessment of the clarity and substantiality of the public policy involved and the degree to which the public policy would be contravened by the dismissal).

[14] 456 Pa. 171, 319 A.2d 174 (1974).

[15] 179 Conn. 471, 427 A.2d 385 (1980).

not be jeopardized by dismissing employees in circumstances such as those involving Geary. Mr. Geary had no special responsibilities or expertise related to product design. He was a salesman. Moreover, it looked like the employer was promoting legitimate interests by dismissing Geary. The court concluded that the "most natural inference from the chain of events recited in the complaint is that Geary had made a nuisance of himself, and the company discharged him to preserve administrative order in its own house."[16] So Geary was unable to satisfy any of the three elements for a public policy tort.

The *Sheets*[17] case was quite different. Sheets was a quality control director and operations manager of a producer of frozen food products, who was fired after complaining to his employer about substandard raw materials and underweight components in finished products.[18] These deviations caused a violation of state labeling statutes.[19] In reversing the trial court's striking of the plaintiff's complaint, the supreme court distinguished *Geary*.[20] State statutes unambiguously mandated truth in labeling of food products. This satisfied the first element: clarity of public policy. Sheets' job responsibilities directly covered product quality.[21] Dismissing him, therefore, could chill conduct necessary to realization of the policy represented by the statutes. This satisfied the second element: jeopardy to the public policy.[22]

In some states, the highest courts have decided that judges and juries are not the appropriate institutions to make the public policy judgments required in deciding whether dismissals should give rise to tort liability.[23] Courts in most states, however, *have* been willing to make those policy judgments—or have said they might be willing to do so in appropriate cases. This chapter does not reject the proposition that legislatures rather than courts should make the policy judgments;[24] instead, it offers an analytical framework explaining how those policy judgments can be made by courts in a principled fashion.

The chapter begins with the interest-balancing concepts of tort law generally[25] and explains how the interest-balancing formula of § 870 of the *Restatement* can

---

[16] Geary v. United States Steel Corp., 456 Pa. at 180, 319 A.2d at 178.

[17] Sheets v. Teddy's Frosted Foods, Inc., 179 Conn. 471, 427 A.2d 385 (1980).

[18] *Id.* at 472–73, 427 A.2d at 386.

[19] Conn. Uniform Food Drug and Cosmetic Act, Conn. Gen. Stat. § 19-222 (1977) (current version at § 21a-102 (1985) (a food shall be deemed to be misbranded: (a) if its labeling is false or misleading in any particular)).

[20] Geary v. United States Steel Corp., 456 Pa. 171, 319 A.2d 174 (1974).

[21] Sheets v. Teddy's Frosted Foods, Inc., 179 Conn. at 479, 427 A.2d at 388.

[22] The employer claimed Sheets was dismissed for unsatisfactory performance, thus arguably raising a specific justification defense, but the supreme court did not address this defense in detail.

[23] Most notably New York, and perhaps Ohio. See § **1.12** for a state-by-state summary. *See* Veno v. Meredith, ___ Pa. Super. ___, 515 A.2d 571, 579 (1986) (quoting this treatise on risks of courts involving themselves in internal disputes).

[24] Indeed **ch. 9** argues that legislatures should enact wrongful dismissal statutes, rationalizing the law in this area, and consolidating litigation relating to a single employment termination.

[25] See § **5.5**.

§ 5.2 NO GOOD CAUSE REQUIREMENT

be applied in the employment context.[26] It probes specific categories of public policy tort cases and explains how the cases in each category can be understood under the three-element formula introduced in this section.[27] It also reviews federal preemption,[28] pleading,[29] and damage[30] issues relating to the public policy tort.

In addition to public policy tort, dismissed employees frequently assert that employer conduct associated with the termination should give rise to liability under traditional tort theories. Use of these theories in employee dismissal cases is also considered in this chapter.[31]

§ 5.2 Public Policy Tort Cases Do Not Require Employers to Show Good Cause for Dismissing Employees

The public policy tort concept does not require an employer to prove cause for dismissal to escape liability in a public policy tort action. Employers terminate employees in three basic types of situations:

1. When the employer has no reason for terminating the employee; i.e., when the termination is entirely arbitrary
2. When the employer has cause for the termination in the sense that term has been defined by labor arbitrators[32]
3. When the employer's reason for the discharge is employee conduct protected by public policy.

The public policy tort only prohibits dismissals in the third category, and the employee bears the burden of proof.[33] The typical collective bargaining agreement[34] or civil service system[35] prohibits any dismissal except one falling into the second category, and burdens the employer to show that the dismissal falls into the second category. Arbitrary dismissal, a dismissal for no reason, would not be permissible under either collective bargaining or public employment arrangements. In contrast, the public policy tort permits terminations falling within the first category. The public policy tort concept does not impose an obligation on employers to dismiss only for just cause.[36]

---

[26] See §§ 5.5–5.7.
[27] See §§ 5.8–5.20.
[28] See § 5.30.
[29] See §§ 5.31–5.32.
[30] See § 5.33.
[31] See §§ 5.21–5.29.
[32] See §§ 3.5–3.8, collecting labor arbitration cases defining *just cause*.
[33] Questions of the order and burdens of proof are discussed in **ch. 7**.
[34] See §§ 3.5–3.8 for a discussion of cause under collective bargaining agreements.
[35] See §§ 6.3–6.6 regarding civil service dismissals.
[36] *See* Ellis v. El Paso Natural Gas Co., 754 F.2d 884, 886 (10th Cir. 1985) (New Mexico law does not permit tort claim for retaliatory dismissal by employee allegedly dismissed in retaliation

§ 5.3 Basic Tort Concepts

Understanding development of the public policy tort requires an appreciation of the evolution of the theory of tort law in the United States. In an area of the law that changes as rapidly as that relating to wrongful dismissal, it is important to be able to engage the client or the court in a dialogue about the intellectual context of common law developments in other jurisdictions and to express the reasons why a particular court should or should not recognize a type of claim for which recovery has been denied in the past. Sections **5.4** and **5.5** provide the background inherent in such a dialogue.

§ 5.4 —Development of the Tort Forms of Action

Tort is a residual category of legal claim basically comprising those legal wrongs that are not criminal and not based on contract.[37] Before the middle of the nineteenth century, it was possible to define the categories of recognized torts by means of the writ system which was at the foundations of common law pleading.[38] Thus, recovery was permitted for battery, assault, false imprisonment, and other intentional torts by satisfying the particular elements required by the common law courts in England.[39] Under common law pleading, some flexibility for new or unnamed torts was provided by the form of action, *trespass on the case,* which was defined in terms of general concepts such as conduct, state of mind, causation, and damage, rather than being limited only to specific types of legal injury or intent. *Case* was a residual category of tort, theoretically covering any injury indirectly caused by culpable conduct.[40] The case concept expanded only modestly, however, to encompass new torts because of the tendency of most American courts to restrict themselves to traditionally recognized forms of action.[41]

With the abolition of both common law pleading and forms of action beginning in New York in 1848,[42] the scope of tort theory became broad enough to encompass almost any injury inflicted on one party by another. One manifestation of this flexibility was the development of negligence in the United States.[43] But the law

---

for protesting employer's violation of its own compensation policies; plaintiff acknowledged no public policy implicated).

[37] W. Prosser, Handbook of the Law of Torts 2 (5th ed. 1984).

[38] *Id.* § 4 at 19.

[39] These are causes of action recognized under the form of action called *trespass.*

[40] W. Prosser, Handbook of the Law of Torts § 7 at 28-30 (5th ed. 1984).

[41] W. Prosser, Handbook of the Law of Torts § 4 at 19 (5th ed. 1984). "The old attitude still persisted, however, that the substance of the plaintiff's right is determined and limited by the possibility of a remedy under the common law forms."

[42] *See* L. Friedman, A History of American Law 342-44 (1973). In 1848, the New York Legislature adopted a Code of Procedure. By 1894, 22 states had adopted the basic principles of the New York Code. *See* J. Pomeroy, Remedies and Remedial Rights by the Civil Action 28 (1894). *See generally* C. Wright, Handbook of the Law of the Federal Courts § 62 at 291-92 (1976).

[43] L. Friedman, A History of American Law 409-27 (1973).

§ 5.4 DEVELOPMENT OF TORT FORMS

continued to impose limitations based on fault and causation, and restricted the universe of legally protected rights as a matter of public policy.

Because of these limitations, new intentional torts were recognized slowly. After the abolition of common law pleading, a spirited debate ensued over whether common law courts should permit recovery for injury-producing conduct that could not be pigeonholed easily into the traditional categories. Some commentators, exemplified by Professor Salmond in England, characterized the class of torts as *closed* and basically limited to the torts for which a cause of action existed under common law pleading.[44] Others, led by Professor Pollock in England and Justice Holmes in the United States, argued that recovery should be permitted for any injury-producing conduct meeting requisite, but abstract, tests of intent, causation, and damage.[45] Justice Holmes summed up his view in the 1904 case, *Aikens v. Wisconsin*: "the intentional infliction of temporal damages . . . requires a justification if the defendant is to escape. . . . "[46] This expansive view is expressed today by § 870 of the *Restatement (Second) of Torts*, which sets forth the following general principle for intentional torts:

> One who intentionally causes injury to another is subject to liability to the other for the injury: if his conduct is generally culpable and not justifiable under the circumstances. This liability may be imposed although the actor's conduct does not come within a traditional category of tort liability.[47]

The courts have neither frozen tort law in its state as of 1870 nor adopted § 870 wholeheartedly. Some new intentional common law torts, such as invasion of privacy[48] and intentional infliction of emotional distress,[49] have been developed and generally accepted in this century. Many statutorily implied private rights of action have been recognized by federal and state courts.[50] These rights of action are new torts, limited by the policies and rights articulated in the statutes.[51] Despite these innovations, the courts have been reluctant to relax entirely the traditional constraints on liability, such as requiring a label for the tort theory or finding liability only in egregious factual situations.

The public policy tort is a new tort struggling for definition and recognition. Courts are applying analytical concepts that guided the development of other intentional torts, after common law pleading was abandoned, to refine the public

---

[44] J. Salmond, Law of Torts § 2 at 8–10 (7th ed. 1928).

[45] F. Pollock, Law of Torts 16–18 (14th ed. 1939).

[46] Aikens v. Wisconsin, 195 U.S. 194, 204 (1904).

[47] Restatement (Second) of Torts § 870 (1979). Comment a to § 870 explains that the section is intended to set forth a unifying principle for the development of recently created intentional torts.

[48] *See id.* § 870 comment a (1979).

[49] *See id.*

[50] See generally **§ 2.26 & 5.19** respecting these statutory torts.

[51] Implied private rights of action under statutes are considered more fully in **§§ 2.26–2.19**. When courts imply such rights of action they impose on the defendant a legal duty to act, or to refrain from acting, borrowed from the statute. Or, viewed from the other side, the statute creates a legal right in the plaintiff which would not exist without the statute.

policy tort cause of action, though sometimes imperfectly and inarticulately. Those general, guiding concepts are the place to begin considering the public policy tort for wrongful dismissal.

§ 5.5 — The Framework for a Public Policy Tort in Section 870

Two general concerns inhibiting courts from recognizing new tort causes of action constrain the public policy tort. First, the interest the plaintiff claims was invaded should be one that legal institutions should protect. This proposition is dealt with in § 870 of the *Restatement (Second) of Torts* by use of the word *injury*, which means harm to a legally protected interest.[52] Second, the conduct of the defendant should be such that imposition of liability is appropriate. Section 870 deals with this proposition by using two terms: *culpable* and *not justifiable*.[53]

These two concerns are addressed by § 870's three components that collectively describe a public policy inquiry by the court: (1) injury to another, (2) the culpable character of the employer's conduct, and (3) the unjustifiable character of the employer's conduct under the circumstances.[54] The injury requirement is evaluated separately in § 5.6. The culpability and unjustifiability requirements are considered in § 5.7.

§ 5.6 — Injury Requirement of Section 870

The first element under § 870 is the existence of *injury*. Injury exists only if two predicates are satisfied: (1) injury in fact, (2) involving legally protected interests.[55]

Injury in fact usually is present, because the plaintiff has been deprived of employment involuntarily. Of course, the plaintiff must be dismissed rather than having resigned in order to satisfy the injury in fact requirement.[56]

---

[52] Restatement (Second) of Torts § 870 comment e (1979(. The blackletter statement for this section speaks of an injury to another, noting that the use of the term *injury* in this section means that the harm must be to a legally protected interest of the plaintiff. *See also* Proceedings, 53rd Annual Meeting, The American Law Institute 66 (1977) (preadoption discussion of § 870). Injury is defined in Restatement (Second) of Torts § 7 (1979).

[53] § 870 comment e speaks of the culpable character of the actor's conduct and the unjustifiable character of his conduct under the circumstances.

[54] Restatement (Second) of Torts § 870 comment e (1979).

[55] *Injury* is defined in Restatement (Second) of Torts § 7 (1979) as the invasion of a legally protected interest. *See id.* § 870 comment e (1979).

[56] *See* Beye v. Bureau of Nat'l Affairs, 59 Md. App. 642, 653, 477 A.2d 1197, 1201 (1984) (discharge required to state a claim for "abusive discharge", recognizing possibility of meeting requirement by showing constructive discharge), *cert. denied,* 301 Md. 369, 484 A.2d 274 (1984); Staggs v. Blue Cross of Md., Inc., 61 Md. App. 381, 387, 486 A.2d 798, 800–01 (1985) (resignation may in fact be a discharge if coerced; dangerous working conditions not essential); Scheller

But injury in fact is insufficient under § 870; the injury also must involve legally protected interests. Employers have argued that the termination of an employment at will cannot be injury because the employee has no legally recognizable interest in continuation of employment. Without injury, the remaining elements of § 870 need not be evaluated. Deciding whether dismissal of an at-will employee infringes legally protected interests determines whether tort recovery will be permitted under any circumstances.[57] Public policy tort cases permitting recovery for wrongful dismissal frequently are labeled as expansive because the courts historically were reluctant to recognize a general, legally protectable interest in continued employment.[58] This reluctance is embodied in the Employment-at-Will Rule.[59] The interest in employment, however, has long been given protection in certain circumstances, and the courts have not questioned seriously that invasion of this interest sometimes amounts to injury, as the term is used in § 870.[60] For example, the plaintiff's interest in employment receives legal protection in the tort of intentional interference with contractual relations.[61] Moreover, interference with the plaintiff's interest in employment is compensable in a defamation action[62] and in connection with other traditionally recognized torts.[63] It is only a modest logical step to move from these types of legal protection to the conclusion that deprivation of employment satisfies the legal injury requirement of § 870 in some circumstances.[64]

---

v. Health Care Serv. Corp., 138 Ill. App. 3d 219, 222, 485 N.E.2d 26, 30 (1985) (refusing to permit public policy tort recovery on constructive discharge concept).

[57] The leading recent wrongful dismissal case denying, in effect, the existence of injury is Murphy v. American Home Prods. Corp., 58 N.Y.2d 293, 461 N.Y.S.2d 232, 448 N.E.2d 86 (1983).

[58] *See generally* Geary v. United States Steel Corp., 456 Pa. 171, 319 A.2d 174 (1974); *Protecting At Will Employees Against Wrongful Discharge: The Duty to Terminate Only in Good Faith*, 93 Harv. L. Rev. 1816 (1980); Blades, *Employment at Will vs. Individual Freedom: On Limiting the Abusive Exercise of Employer Power*, 67 Colum. L. Rev. 1404 (1967).

[59] See § **1.4**.

[60] *Injury* is defined in Restatement (Second) of Torts § 7 (1979) as the invasion of a legally protected interest. *See id.* § 870 comment e (1979). The leading recent wrongful dismissal case denying, in effect, the existence of injury is Murphy v. American Home Prods. Corp., 58 N.Y.2d 293, 461 N.Y.S.2d 232, 448 N.E.2d 86 (1983).

[61] *See* Restatement (Second) of Torts § 766 comment d (1979). In the early cases, the plaintiff usually was the employer, but recovery on this tort theory also is permitted by the employee. *See Tortious Interference with Contractual Relations in the Nineteenth Century: The Transformation of Property, Contract, and Tort*, 93 Harv. L. Rev. 1510, 1522, (1980). See § **5.22**.

[62] *See* Restatement (Second) of Torts § 575 comment b, illustration 2 (1979). In fact, harm to one's profession or employment was recognized as sufficiently serious to support an action for slander per se, without proof of special damages. *See* Restatement (Second) of Torts § 573 (1979).

[63] *See* McKinney v. Kimberly-Clark Corp., 449 So. 2d 790 (Ala. Civ. App. 1982) (recovery for wrongful dismissal of at-will employee permitted in conjunction with action for malicious prosecution against employer), *aff'd*, 449 So. 2d 794 (1983).

[64] A roughly analogous problem is presented when a plaintiff claims deprivation of public employment in violation of the Constitution. Public employees have no constitutional right to a government job, but once they have been given such a job, they may not be deprived of it in violation of due process guarantees. See generally §§ **6.9–6.10**. As in tort analysis, the existence of the legal interest depends to some degree on the type of interference threatened. As suggested in § **1.8**, constitutional developments respecting public employees probably influenced courts hearing tort claims by private sector employees.

It is important to realize that interaction exists between the injury and culpability inquiries.[65] It is not enough that the plaintiff has a right not to be dismissed for the conduct alleged. If it were, the public policy tort would be little more than an inquiry into the existence of a specific employee right not to be dismissed. The common law courts accepting the public policy tort have framed a broader inquiry.[66]

§ 5.7 —Justification Concept of Section 870

Most of the analytical emphasis in public policy tort cases is placed not on the injury requirement but on defining employer-defendant conduct for which liability should be imposed. Although § 870 provides a basic structure for assessing the defendant's conduct,[67] its neatness is somewhat misleading. Section 870 legitimates a policy inquiry by the courts, but its terms merely suggest the kind of employer conduct the court may take into account in its policy analysis.

The culpability and unjustifiability requirements together describe an evaluative process involving three factors: the nature and significance of the interests promoted by the employer's conduct, the character of the means used by the employer, and the employer's motive. The first factor is concerned primarily with applying the black letter term *not justifiable*. The second and third factors, along with the injury to the plaintiff, are equally significant in applying the black letter term *culpable*.[68]

Ultimately, two public policy issues must be determined by the court: what type of social harm can be reduced by imposing liability for dismissing the employee,[69] and what type of employer justification should exculpate the employer despite the social harm?[70]

The structure of § 870 offers little guidance to separate the concept of culpability from the concept of justification in the wrongful dismissal context. There was considerable debate among members of the American Law Institute over inclusion of both *culpable* and *not justifiable* because of a concern that the terms mean the same thing.[71] The American Law Institute, however, decided to use both,[72] possibly to negate the requirement for the defendant to produce evidence of an excuse or justification when the plaintiff alleges and proves intentional injury[73] and to permit dismissal of a claim when the plaintiff fails to prove culpability.

---

[65] § 870 comment e (all three black letter terms involved in evaluative balancing).

[66] See § **5.19** distinguishing the public policy tort from the implied right of action inquiry.

[67] Restatement (Second) of Torts § 870 (1979).

[68] *Id.* Comment e actually presents four factors to be considered in the evaluative process. The first relates to injury. The second, third, and fourth are set forth here.

[69] This relates to the first two elements, clarity and jeopardy, identified in § **5.1**.

[70] This relates to the third element, absence of justification, identified in § **5.1**.

[71] *See* Proceedings, 53rd Annual Meeting, The American Law Institute 67–78 (1977) (criticism of *culpable* as being circular, and Reporter's response that it is circular).

[72] *Id.* at 87 (motion to delete word *culpable* defeated).

[73] *Id.* at 81 (Freund argument that culpable would permit claim to be dismissed without requiring defendant to show justification).

§ 5.7 JUSTIFICATION CONCEPT

It is hornbook law that a defendant is not subject to liability for an intentional tort unless he intends both the act and the consequences;[74] this intent supplies legal culpability. When a defendant intentionally does an act with substantial certainty that certain consequences will result, he is held legally to intend the consequences.[75] Usually, when an employer decides to terminate an employee, the decision is not reached for the purpose of causing the employee to be without a job; rather, the employer makes the decision for personal or business reasons. The employer's act certainly is intentional, but the most that usually can be inferred about the employer's state of mind regarding the consequences is that the employer does the act substantially certain that the consequences of unemployment will result.[76] The employer does not really care, in the typical case, whether the employee gets another job; the employer just wants to terminate the particular employment relationship.[77] This is sufficient to supply intent to cause the consequence of unemployment. But intent to cause employment termination is not enough. The metaphorical scales of justice[78] require more than a tension between economic interests if the employee is to recover from the employer. In a balancing process, the culpability analysis—the assessment of the employer's intent—tends to merge with an analysis of the employer's justification for its act. In some cases, of course, culpability or absence of justification is easier to discern. Sometimes the employer has a subjective intent to chill socially desirable employee conduct. In some cases, the employer has a subjective intent to hurt the employee in a personal way. When this type of intent can be proven, a higher level of culpability exists, directly implicating societal interests.

The comments to § 870 endorse a balancing of interests. If the interests served by the employer's conduct outweigh the interests endangered by its conduct, then *justification* exists, and the employer's actions also are likely to be characterized as not improper or wrongful and, therefore, not *culpable*. Usually in a wrongful dismissal case, the defendant can point to strong interests served by maximum freedom for employers to remove unsatisfactory employees at the employer's sole discretion.[79] When the motive for the dismissal can be shown, however, to be unrelated to job performance, then the interests on the defendant's side of the case

---

[74] " 'Intent,' as it is used throughout the Restatement of Torts, has reference to the consequences of an act rather than the act itself." Restatement (Second) of Torts § 8A comment a.

[75] *Id.* comment b.

[76] "Intent is not, however, limited to consequences which are desired. If the actor knows that the consequences are certain, or substantially certain, to result from his act, and still goes ahead, he is treated by the law as if he had in fact desired to produce the result." *Id.* The quoted language seems an apt description of the employer's state of mind in the usual employment termination situation.

[77] In exceptional cases, however, the employer may affirmatively desire to inflict injury on the employee. This is considered further in **§ 5.21**.

[78] See **§ 5.1**, describing the scales of justice metaphor.

[79] *See* Martin v. Capital Cities Media, Inc., 354 Pa. Super. 199, 511 A.2d 830, 843 (1986) (even though Constitution allows one to speak freely, it also allows employer to discharge employee whose speech offends employer, generally presenting need for employer flexibility); Cox v. Resilient Flooring Div., 638 F. Supp. 726 (C.D. Cal. 1986) (lamenting flood of wrongful dismissal cases); Adler v. American Standard Corp., 291 Md. 31, 42, 432 A.2d 464, 470 (1981);

diminish.[80] Moreover, when the plaintiff can show that the dismissal jeopardizes important public policy interests as well as the plaintiff's economic interests, the balance of interests tilts substantially in the plaintiff's favor.[81] When the interests are tilted in the plaintiff's favor, the defendant's conduct may be said to be *culpable* and to lack *justification*.

It is easy to see why such an interest-balancing approach permits recovery for dismissals that infringe on clear public policy. Upon concluding that the employer was motivated by the employee's jury service, or refusal to commit perjury, the court finds that the employer's legitimate interests in sustaining the dismissal have diminished, and the employee's—and society's—interests opposing the dismissal have increased.

The public policy tort cases weigh the relationship between the defendant-employer's conduct and interests of legitimate concern against the interests endangered by the dismissal. The cases that use the prima facie tort theory also can be seen as focusing both on the defendant-employer's motive and the legitimate interest justifying the dismissal.[82] The prima facie tort concept allows liability to be premised on specific intent to inflict injury, plus absence of legitimate motivation; the plaintiff need not show societal interests reflected in public policy to tip the balance in the employee's favor.[83] Despite separate labels, the public policy tort and prima facie tort inquiries really represent two different factual paradigms triggering liability under the culpability and justification formula of § 870.[84]

Although few courts recognizing a public policy tort cause of action for wrongful dismissal have relied explicitly on § 870 of the *Second Restatement*,[85] the analysis of virtually all the cases is consistent with § 870's doctrine of balancing interests to see if injurious conduct should give rise to liability.

§ 5.8 Categories of Public Policy Torts

Public policy tort cases fall into three general groups. In the first group of cases, the employee was dismissed in violation of a statutory grant of rights directly pertinent to the employment relationship.[86] In the second group, the employee was

---

Pierce v. Ortho Pharmaceutical Corp., 84 N.J. 58, 71–72, 417 A.2d 505, 511–12 (1980); Geary v. United States Steel Corp., 456 Pa. 171, 183, 319 A.2d 174, 180 (1974).

[80] See generally cases discussed in §§ **5.8–5.20**.

[81] See generally cases discussed in §§ **5.8–5.20**.

[82] See § **5.21**.

[83] This application of the prima facie tort concept has been recognized only by a few courts. See § **5.21**.

[84] Restatement (Second) of Torts § 870 comment e (1979). The conduct must first be improper or wrongful; it must be blameworthy, not in accord with community standards of right conduct. The conduct must also not be excusable or justifiable; a privilege should not be applicable. The two terms, culpable and justifiable, are together descriptive of the evaluative process that the court must follow.

[85] See §§ **5.8–5.20**.

[86] See § **5.9**.

dismissed for engaging in activities outside the workplace, affirmatively protected by public policy.[87] In the third group of cases, the employee was dismissed for opposing employer conduct that contravened public policy.[88]

Other classifications of public policy tort cases are used by courts and commentators.[89] The useful distinctions in these typologies are preserved in this chapter's subcategories of the internal public policy tort.[90]

§ 5.9 —Labor Statutes as a Basis for Public Policy Torts

Some public policy tort cases involve public policy interests directly related to the employer employee relationship and employee termination rights clearly articulated in statutes. These cases can be decided in the plaintiff's favor with the least expansion of existing law because the courts are doing little more than grafting tort remedies onto existing statutory rights of the plaintiff-employee or defendant-employer. When a statute creates a right in an employee not to be subject to certain types of employer conduct, implied private right of action principles may permit the employee to recover damages for violation of the right.[91] Some federal statutory rights, however, preempt state law.[92]

Early cases in California and elsewhere permitted employees to recover damages for violation of certain statutory rights. *Glenn v. Clearman's Golden Cock Inn, Inc.*[93] and *Krystad v. Lau*[94] implied a private civil remedy for violation of a state criminal statute protecting the right of employees to organize.[95] *Montalvo v.*

---

[87] See §§ 5.10–5.13.

[88] Cases falling into this category involve employee protests to the employer, reporting of employer violations to governmental agencies, or refusal to obey orders. See §§ **5.14–5.18**.

[89] One useful classification divides the cases into four groups: (1) terminations for employee refusal to perform criminal acts or acts contrary to public policy; (2) terminations for reporting employer violations of law or public policy, either to the employer or to governmental agencies; (3) terminations for acts that public policy encourages; e.g., the jury duty cases; and (4) retaliatory terminations for seeking governmental benefits; e.g., the worker's compensation cases. *See* Boyle v. Vista Eyewear, Inc., 700 S.W.2d 859, 874–75 (Mo. Ct. App. 1985) (permitting public policy tort claim by production worker allegedly dismissed for protesting employer's failure to perform FDA mandated tests on eyeglasses). *See also* Delaney v. Taco Time Int'l, 297 Or. 10, 18, 681 P.2d 114, 117 (1984) (dividing public policy torts into three classes).

[90] See §§ **5.14–5.18**.

[91] See § **2.26** (explaining private right of action analysis); § **5.19** (distinguishing implied private right of action analysis from public policy tort analysis).

[92] The unfair labor practice provisions of the National Labor Relations Act, 29 U.S.C. § 158 (1982), and the retaliation provisions of ERISA, 29 U.S.C. §§ 1140, 144(a) (1982), are notable examples. See §§ **2.28** (NLRA preemption) & **2.34** (ERISA preemption).

[93] 192 Cal. App. 2d 793, 798, 13 Cal. Rptr. 769, 772 (1961).

[94] 65 Wash. 2d 827, 846, 400 P.2d 72, 83 (1965).

[95] *See also* Watson v. Idaho Falls Consol. Hosps. Inc., 111 Idaho 44, 720 P.2d 632, 637 (1986) (affirming judgment for nurse, suggesting public policy tort would exist for dismissal because of union organizing activity).

Zamora[96] implied a civil action for retaliation against an employee for exercising his rights under a minimum wage statute. *Cleary v. American Airlines, Inc.*[97] held that the public policy necessary to support a tort claim for wrongful dismissal could be found in statutory protection of union activities. *Perks v. Firestone Tire & Rubber Co.*[98] and *Polsky v. Radio Shack*[99] applied Pennsylvania law to find a tort cause of action for dismissing, or threatening to dismiss, an employee for refusing to take a polygraph test in contravention of a Pennsylvania criminal statute prohibiting such dismissals. *Savodnik v. Korvettes, Inc.*,[1] applied New York law to find a tort cause of action for a plaintiff who was terminated in order to prevent vesting of his pension in contravention of the spirit of New York and federal pension statutes.

In *Cloutier v. Great Atlantic & Pacific Tea Co.*,[2] the Supreme Court of New Hampshire derived a public policy tort from two different labor statutes, even though the connection with the statutes was tenuous. Cloutier was fired from his job as store manager after the store safe had been burglarized. The court premised the public policy opposing his dismissal on the federal Occupational Safety and Health Act.[3] It reasoned that Cloutier's conduct furthered employee safety because he did not force those in charge of the store in his absence "to imperil themselves by making bank deposits."[4] In addition, the court found that A & P, by holding the plaintiff responsible for the store seven days per week, violated the spirit of a state statute requiring employers to give their employees a day off.[5] *Cloutier* did not involve an express statutory provision saying "no employee shall be terminated. . . ." It did involve employee rights granted by the statutes, however: the right to a safe workplace, and the right to a day of rest.

Public policy tort cases involving labor statutes present a paradox:[6] statutes specifically creating employee rights to be free from dismissal for certain reasons generally

---

[96] 7 Cal. App. 3d 69, 75–76, 86 Cal. Rptr. 401, 404–05 (1970).

[97] 111 Cal. App. 3d 443, 454–56, 168 Cal. Rptr. 722, 729 (1980).

[98] 611 F.2d 1363 (3d Cir. 1979).

[99] 666 F.2d 824 (3d Cir. 1981). *But see* Ising v. Barnes Hosp., 674 S.W.2d 623, 625 (Mo. Ct. App. 1984) (no liability for dismissal over refusal to sign consent form for polygraph test; no state statute like Pennsylvania's).

[1] 488 F. Supp. 822, 826 (E.D.N.Y. 1980). It is not clear that the holding of *Savodnik* survives the refusal of the New York Court of Appeals to recognize a cause of action for the tort of wrongful dismissal. *See* Murphy v. American Home Prods. Corp., 58 N.Y.2d 293, 461 N.Y.S.2d 232, 448 N.E.2d 86 (1983). *But see* Titsch v. Reliance Group, Inc., 548 F. Supp. 983, 985 (S.D.N.Y. 1982) (holding that it was necessary, for purposes of claim of interference with pension rights, for plaintiff to allege that interference was a motive for the discharge).

[2] 121 N.H. 915, 436 A.2d 1140 (1981).

[3] *Id.* at 923, 436 A.2d at 1145.

[4] *Id.*

[5] *Id.* at 923–24, 436 A.2d at 1145.

[6] *See* Grzyb v. Evans, 700 S.W.2d 399 (Ky. 1985) (suggesting public policy tort limited to violation of specific statutory rights, but finding that statute granting rights preempted common law claim because it provided administrative remedies).

establish their own remedial schemes. Courts are reluctant to permit public policy tort recovery for violation of labor statutes containing their own administrative remedies, though a major exception exists in Illinois.

Generally, employees have been unsuccessful in attempts to base public policy tort recovery on rights against retaliatory employer action established by occupational safety and health statutes.[7] Public policy tort suits based on policies contained in antidiscrimination statutes have led to mixed results, probably because of the general principle that such statutes were meant to supplement rather than to supplant other remedies for employment discrimination.[8] Most of the cases do not permit independent public policy tort recovery.[9] But cases can be found reaching the opposite result.[10] Other types of labor statutes may or may not serve as a source of public policy for the public policy tort, depending on the clarity of the right

---

[7] *See* Walsh v. Consolidated Freightways, Inc., 278 Or. 347, 563 P.2d 1205 (1977) (no tort recovery for discharge of employee for complaining about unsafe working conditions because adequate administrative remedy); Corbin v. Sinclair Mkt., Inc., 684 P.2d 265 (Colo. Ct. App. 1984) (no public policy tort pleaded under state employee safety statutes providing administrative remedies).

[8] *See* § 2.32 (no preemption by federal discrimination statutes).

[9] *See* Kofoid v. Woodard Hotels, Inc., 78 Or. App. 283, 716 P.2d 771, 774 (1986) (distinguishing preemption from nonexistence of tort claim because societal interests adequately protected by statutory procedure; no public policy tort claim for sex discrimination); Murray v. Commercial Union Ins. Co., 782 F.2d 432 (3d Cir. 1986) (no public policy tort claim for age discrimination; Pennsylvania administrative remedies are exclusive); Guevara v. K-Mart Corp., 629 F. Supp. 1189 (S.D. W. Va. 1986) (no public policy tort in West Virginia for discrimination covered by state human rights statute); Salazar v. Furr's, Inc., 629 F. Supp. 1403, 1408 (D.N.M. 1986) (no public policy tort under New Mexico law for pregnancy discrimination covered by Title VII); Atkins v. Bridgeport Hydraulic Co., 5 Conn. App. 643, 501 A.2d 1223, 1226 (1985) (public policy against age discrimination adequately enforceable through statutory remedies; no independent public policy tort exists); Gutierrez v. City of Chicago, 605 F. Supp. 973, 980 (N.D. Ill. 1985) (no public policy tort claim to protect rights already protected by state and federal civil rights statutes); Tombollo v. Dunn, 342 N.W.2d 23, 25 (S.D. 1984) (no tort cause of action for sexual harassment within jurisdiction of state human rights commission); Fischer v. Sears, Roebuck & Co., 107 Idaho 197, 687 P.2d 587 (Ct. App. 1984) (no common law claim for dismissal in violation of state age discrimination statute); Mein v. Masonite Corp., 124 Ill. App. 3d 617, 464 N.E.2d 1137 (1984) (no public policy tort for violation of state age discrimination statute), *aff'd*, 109 Ill. 2d 1, 485 N.E.2d 312 (1985); Melley v. Gillette Corp., 19 Mass. App. Ct. 511, 475 N.E.2d 1227, 1229-30 (1985) (no public policy tort for age discrimination prohibited by state statute; must seek administrative remedies); Wolk v. Saks Fifth Ave., Inc., 728 F.2d 221, 223 (3d Cir. 1984) (common law tort claim cannot be based on the Pennsylvania Human Relations Act because that statute provides its own administrative remedies); Crews v. Memorex Corp., 588 F. Supp. 27, 28 (D. Mass. 1984) (Massachusetts implied covenant cause of action not available where statutory remedy exists for age discrimination); Medina v. Spotnail, Inc., 591 F. Supp. 190, 198 (N.D. Ill. 1984) (no tort claim for conduct within Illinois Human Rights Act); Schroeder v. Dayton-Hudson Corp., 448 F. Supp 910 (E.D. Mich. 1977) (no state action permitted).

[10] *See* Savage v. Holiday Inn Corp., 603 F. Supp. 311, 313 (D. Nev. 1985) (age and sex discrimination in violation of statute states public policy tort claim under Nevada law); Wolber v. Service Corp., 612 F. Supp. 235, 237 (D. Nev. 1985) (Nevada law permits public policy tort claim based on state age discrimination statute); Wynn v. Boeing Military Airplane Co., 595 F. Supp. 727, 729 (D. Kan. 1984) (Kansas public policy tort cause of action available for race discrimination covered by Title VII and § 1981); Placos v. Cosmair, Inc., 517 F. Supp. 1287 (S.D.N.Y. 1981) (age claim permitted).

established[11] and the availability of administrative or other statutory remedies, which would weaken the jeopardy element of the public policy tort.[12]

Public policy tort cases involving labor statutes do not present difficulties regarding the clarity of public policy; the statutes directly grant employee rights. The dominant issue in public policy tort cases based on labor statutes involves the second element (jeopardy), requiring a finding that the dismissal would interfere substantially with realization of the public policy.[13] If the statute establishing the public policy contains its own remedies, it is less likely that tort liability is necessary to prevent dismissals from interfering with realization of the statutory policy. The Oregon Supreme Court emphasized the jeopardy factor in *Walsh v. Consolidated Freightways*.[14]

A major exception to the tendency to find administrative remedies adequately protective of public policies articulated in labor statutes is *Wheeler v. Caterpillar Tractor Co.*[15] In that case the Illinois Supreme Court permitted a public policy tort claim to be based on the federal nuclear safety statute, even though that statute contains an explicit whistleblower protection provision enforced by the Secretary of Labor. The Illinois Supreme Court held that a public policy tort claim as well as statutory remedies exists for a dismissal in response to an employee refusal to work near allegedly unsafe nuclear equipment, though the employee made no complaint to the Nuclear Regulatory Commission. The court offered little analysis in support of its holding. The result in *Wheeler v. Caterpillar Tractor Co.*[16] is hard to reconcile with the analytical structure of the public policy tort. While the public policy in favor of protecting employees from exposure to nuclear radiation is clear under federal statutory law, the statute provides an administrative mechanism

---

[11] This implicates the first element, clarity, identified in § **5.1**.

[12] *See* Covell v. Spengler, 141 Mich. App. 76, 366 N.W.2d 76, 80 (1985) (whistleblower protection act provides exclusive remedy; no independent tort or implied covenant cause of action for conduct protected by act); Kamens v. Summit Stainless, Inc., 586 F. Supp. 324, 329–330 (E.D. Pa. 1984) (no implied covenant cause of action for dismissal allegedly violative of FLSA and ADEA).

[13] See § **5.1** identifying three elements for public policy tort.

[14] 278 Or. 347, 563 P.2d 1205 (1977) (no recovery permitted for discharge over safety complaint because adequate administrative remedies), *distinguished in* Delaney v. Taco Time Int'l, 297 Or. 10, 681 P.2d 114 (1984) (recovery permitted for discharge over refusal to sign defamatory statement against coemployee because no administrative remedy). *Compare* Mein v. Masonite Corp., 124 Ill. App. 3d 617, 464 N.E.2d 1137 (1984) (no public policy tort for violation of state age discrimination statute), *aff'd,* 109 Ill. 2d 1, 485 N.E.2d 312 (1985); *with* Wolber v. Service Corp., 612 F. Supp. 235, 237 (D. Nev. 1985) (Nevada law permits public policy tort claim based on state age discrimination statute). *See also* Corbin v. Sinclair Mktg., Inc., 684 P.2d 265 (Colo. Ct. App. 1984) (no public policy tort pleaded under state employee safety statutes providing administrative remedies); Price v. Carmack Datsun, Inc., 124 Ill. App. 3d 979, 464 N.E.2d 1245 (1984) (no cause of action for discharge in retaliation for filing group health insurance claim, despite effort to bring within policy of state insurance regulatory statutes and ERISA; expressing doubt whether federal statute can be basis for state public policy), *aff'd,* 109 Ill. 2d 65, 485 N.E.2d 359 (1985).

[15] 108 Ill. 2d 502, 485 N.E.2d 372 (1985), *cert. denied,* ___ U.S. ___, 106 S. Ct. 1641 (1986).

[16] *Id.*

to protect employees from retaliatory dismissal, mitigating any jeopardy to public policy if employers avoid tort liability.

The result in *Cloutier v. Great Atlantic & Pacific Tea Co.*,[17] is also difficult to reconcile with general public policy tort principles. The public policies against work on Sunday and against employee safety risks from holdups are vague. The degree of interference with those policies resulting from Cloutier's dismissal is highly speculative. And the countervailing employer interests in disciplining supervisory employees for economic losses for which they are responsible seem colorable. These conclusions would point in the direction of no liability for A & P, but the New Hampshire court reached the opposite result.

When a tort suit for wrongful dismissal is premised on the public policy reflected in statutes promoting collective bargaining, the possibility of federal preemption arises. Preemption is virtually certain if the public policy tort is based on rights granted in the National Labor Relations Act and enforceable by the National Labor Relations Board, unless the claim is based on an important state interest, and represents little potential for interfering with uniform federal regulation of labor relations.[18] This is a different problem from a public policy tort claim which potentially sidesteps collectively bargained grievance and arbitration procedures,[19] and from the question whether the public policy tort should protect employees already protected by collective bargaining agreements, as a matter of common law.[20]

§ 5.10 —*External* Public Policy: Jury Duty

The first public policy tort cases to attract wide attention involved public policy interests of the society generally, as opposed to statutorily defined interests of employees in their employment relationships. Unlike the public policy tort cases discussed in § 5.9, these cases did not involve labor statutes reflecting a public policy balance already struck by the legislature, but required the courts to balance broad social interests against private employer interests. Not surprisingly, the social interests won when they were sufficiently clear and when the dismissal of the plaintiff-employee seemed likely to interfere with those interests. These cases were easier to decide in the employee's favor under § 870 of the *Restatement (Second)*

---

[17] *Cloutier* is discussed earlier in this section.

[18] Compare Farmer v. Carpenters Local 25, 430 U.S. 290, 305 (1977) (defamation suit not preempted) with Dinger v. Anchor Motor Freight, Inc., 501 F. Supp. 64, 66 (S.D.N.Y. 1980) (state tort claim probably would be preempted if also an unfair labor practice). *But see* Sherman v. St. Barnabas Hosp., 535 F. Supp. 564, 576–77 (S.D.N.Y. 1982) (holding that because a pending NLRB complaint was not identical to the wrongful dismissal claim, court could entertain the wrongful dismissal action). See § **2.28** for a deeper analysis of NLRA preemption.

[19] *Compare* Republic Steel Corp. v. Maddox, 379 U.S. 650, 653 (1965) (state suit for breach of collective bargaining agreement governed by federal law, which requires exhaustion of grievance procedures) *with* Vaughn v. Pacific Northwest Bell Tel. Co., 289 Or. 73, 83, 611 P.2d 281, 287 (1980) (tort claim for discharge in retaliation for filing workers' compensation claim not preempted). See generally §§ **2.29, 2.30, 4.25**, and **5.20** regarding § 301 preemption.

[20] See § **5.20**.

of Torts concepts than cases involving disputes entirely within the workplace,[21] because the employer was trying to use workplace-based power to influence conduct outside the workplace having an attenuated bearing on legitimate employer interests.

One early jury duty claim was unsuccessful. In *Mallard v. Boring*,[22] the plaintiff was discharged for volunteering for jury service. Deferring to the legislature,[23] the court refused to accept the public policy tort argument. But a decade later, public policy tort plaintiffs were successful in cases involving jury duty and workers' compensation in Indiana,[24] Oregon,[25] Illinois,[26] Michigan,[27] Idaho,[28] Pennsylvania,[29] Kansas,[30] and New Jersey.[31]

The elements of a public policy tort[32] are met in the jury duty cases because permitting employers to dismiss their employees for serving jury duty has the potential for significant disruption of the jury system. In jury duty cases, however, the jeopardy element is mitigated since nonemployed persons still would be available to serve on juries.[33]

One of the best reasoned jury duty cases is *Nees v. Hocks*.[34] In *Nees,* the Supreme Court of Oregon affirmed a jury verdict for compensatory damages on evidence

---

[21] See §§ 5.14–5.18 for analysis of these internal public policy tort cases.

[22] 182 Cal. App. 2d 390, 6 Cal. Rptr. 171 (1960). Petermann v. Teamsters, 174 Cal. App. 2d 184, 344 P.2d 25 (1959) frequently is credited as being the first modern case to recognize a civil claim for wrongful dismissal premised on public policy. *Petermann* was a breach of contract rather than a tort case. In Tameny v. Atlantic Richfield Co., 27 Cal. 3d 167, 181, 610 P.2d 1330, 1338, 164 Cal. Rptr. 839, 847 (1980) (Clark, J., dissenting), the California Supreme Court extended the basic concept of *Petermann* to permit recovery in tort.

[23] 182 Cal. App. 2d at 396, 6 Cal. Rptr. at 175.

[24] Frampton v. Central Ind. Gas Co., 260 Ind. 249, 297 N.E.2d 425 (1973).

[25] Nees v. Hocks, 272 Or. 210, 536 P.2d 512 (1975).

[26] Kelsay v. Motorola, Inc., 74 Ill. 2d 172, 384 N.E.2d 353 (1978).

[27] Hrab v. Hayes-Albion Corp., 103 Mich. App. 90, 302 N.W.2d 606 (1981); Sventko v. Kroger Co., 69 Mich. App. 644, 245 N.W.2d 151 (1976).

[28] Jackson v. Minidoka Irrigation, 98 Idaho 330, 563 P.2d 54 (1977) (while denying recovery in the case before it, the court said the discharges for filing workers' compensation claims or for serving on a jury would violate public policy and therefore support civil actions).

[29] Reuther v. Fowler & Williams, Inc., 255 Pa. Super. 28, 386 A.2d 119 (1978).

[30] Murphy v. City of Topeka-Shawnee County Dept. of Labor Servs., 6 Kan. App. 2d 488, 630 P.2d 186 (1981) (court recognized a cause of action for an employee alleging termination for filing a workers' compensation claim).

[31] Lally v. Copygraphics, 85 N.J. 668, 428 A.2d 1317 (1981) (common law action for wrongful discharge exists for an employee fired for filing a workers' compensation claim).

[32] See § 5.1 for a description of the three elements: clarity of public policy, jeopardy to the policy, and lack of justification.

[33] *Guidelines for a Public Policy Exception to the Employment at Will Rule: The Wrongful Discharge Tort,* 13 Conn. L. Rev. 617, 637 (1980–1981). Also, Harry A. Rissetto, of Morgan, Lewis & Bockius, has pointed out to the author of this treatise that most jury service statutes compel service by those called and not excused. This also mitigates the jeopardy factor of the public policy tort.

[34] 272 Or. 210, 536 P.2d 512 (1975).

from which the jury could have found that the "defendants discharged plaintiff because, after being subpoenaed, and contrary to the defendant's wishes, plaintiff told the clerk she would like to serve and did serve on jury duty."[35] The only legal question was whether the community's interest in having its citizens serve on jury duty was so important that an employer who interferes with that interest should be required to compensate the dismissed employee for damages suffered.[36] Through a two-step logical process, the court answered the question in the affirmative by focusing, first, on the existence of the public policy interest, and second, on the interference with that interest flowing from the dismissal.[37] As to the existence of the public policy, the court found that the jury system and jury duty "are regarded as high on the scale of American institutions and citizen obligations."[38] It relied on state constitutional guarantees of jury trial, on statutes limiting the grounds for which a potential juror could be excused from service,[39] and on an Illinois case and a Massachusetts statute subjecting employers to contempt penalties for dismissing employees absent because of jury duty.[40] Notably, the court found the public policy to be derived from a number of different sources taken together rather than a single, clear legislative statement regarding employer interference with jury service.

As to interference with the public interest in jury duty, the court reasoned that the jury system would be affected adversely if an employer were permitted with impunity to dismiss an employee for fulfilling a jury service obligation.[41] Without a specific citation, the court utilized the interest-balancing philosophy embodied in § 870 of the *Restatement*[42] though declining to base its analysis on the justification concept.[43]

Most courts permit public policy tort recovery for dismissals in retaliation for jury service.[44] When a statute exists prohibiting employer retaliation against employees for serving on juries, as it does at the federal level,[45] the analysis of

---

[35] *Id.* at 212, 536 P.2d at 513.

[36] *Id.* at 215, 536 P.2d at 514.

[37] These are the first two elements of the public policy tort identified in § 5.1.

[38] 272 Or. at 219, 536 P.2d at 516.

[39] *Accord,* Reuther v. Fowler & Williams, Inc., 255 Pa. Super. 28, 33, 386 A.2d 119, 121 (1978) (discharged employee entitled to present to the jury evidence that he had been discharged in retaliation for having taken a week off from work to serve on jury duty; citing *Nees v. Hocks* approvingly, and deriving public policy from Pennsylvania and United States constitutional guarantees of jury trial and a statute providing penalties for failure to appear for jury service).

[40] 272 Or. at 219, 536 P.2d at 516.

[41] *Id.*

[42] Restatement (Second) of Torts § 870 (1979).

[43] 272 Or. at 214, 536 P.2d at 514.

[44] *See, e.g.,* Reuther v. Fowler & Williams, Inc., 255 Pa. Super. 28, 386 A.2d 119 (1978); Jackson v. Minidoka Irrigation, 98 Idaho 330, 563 P.2d 54 (1977). *See also* Wiskotoni v. Michigan Nat'l Bank–West, 716 F.2d 378 (6th Cir. 1983) (discharge for being subpoenaed to testify before grand jury violates public policy).

[45] See § 2.26.

the public policy tort becomes the same as is appropriate for other instances in which employees are dismissed in derogation of specific rights granted by statute.[46]

Essentially the same reasoning used in the jury duty cases permits public policy tort recovery in other circumstances in which dismissal can jeopardize interests related to effective functioning of the judicial system. In *Ludwick v. This Minute of Carolina, Inc.*,[47] the Supreme Court of South Carolina used reasoning similar to that used in the jury duty cases to recognize a public policy tort for employees dismissed for responding to subpoenas from state administrative agencies. In *Sides v. Duke Hospital*,[48] the court held that discharging a nurse in retaliation for a refusal to testify falsely or incompletely at a medical malpractice trial gives rise to a claim for public policy tort. Dismissal for refusing to commit perjury is a public policy tort, as well as a possible breach of an implied covenant of good faith and fair dealing.[49] But other cases involving access to the courts have reached different outcomes. In *Kavanagh v. KLM Royal Dutch Airlines*,[50] the court declined to permit a public policy tort based on the general public policy favoring right to counsel and access to the courts. The plaintiff claimed he was fired for retaining an attorney and threatening to sue his employer over a wage payment dispute.

§ 5.11 —*External* Public Policy: Workers' Compensation Claims

Public policy tort recovery is usually permitted for dismissals for filing workers' compensation claims or similar claims for workplace-related injuries. These cases involve conflicting interests more directly related to the workplace than do jury duty cases, which pitted employer interests against societal interests in the jury system. The workers' compensation cases do not, however, involve matters at the core of managerial control, as in the internal public policy tort cases, discussed in §§ **5.14** through **5.18**. One also could classify the workers' compensation cases with the cases involving direct grant of employee rights[51] on the grounds that the workers' compensation system represents a balance struck by the legislature respecting conflicting rights between employer and employee. Filing a workers' compensation claim, however, involves participation in dispute resolution machinery established by the state. Accordingly, the cases resemble somewhat the jury duty cases. Also, the workers' compensation system is essentially an external set of legal institutions intended to compensate employees. The no-fault aspects dilute

---

[46] See § **5.9**.

[47] 287 S.C. 219, 337 S.E.2d 213 (1985).

[48] 74 N.C. App. 331, 328 S.E.2d 818, *review denied*, 314 N.C. 331, 333 S.E.2d 490 (1985).

[49] See §§ **4.11, 4.23** for analysis of the implied covenant theory.

[50] 566 F. Supp. 242 (N.D. Ill. 1983).

[51] See § **5.9**.

any direct regulatory character,⁵² thus distinguishing these cases from those involving express employee rights not to be dismissed.⁵³

The workers' compensation cases meet the first factor of the public policy test (clarity and substantiality) because the policy in favor of permitting employees to file workers' compensation claims is expressed by statute. The first element thus is satisfied more easily with a workers' compensation case than with a jury duty case. Workers' compensation cases meet the second factor (interference with public policy) because the policy would be completely frustrated if employers were free to dismiss employees for filing claims.⁵⁴

The first workers' compensation public policy tort case was *Frampton v. Central Indiana Gas Co.*,⁵⁵ decided in 1973. The Indiana Supreme Court held that a cause of action existed even though the statutes in question provided neither civil nor criminal penalties for retaliatory sdischarges.⁵⁶ The court's emphasis on the jeopardy element was apparent:

> The Act creates a duty in the employer to compensate employees for work-related injuries (through insurance) and a right in the employee to receive such compensation . . . . If employers are permitted to penalize employees for filing workmen's compensation claims . . . employees will not file claims for justly deserved compensation—opting, instead, to continue their employment without incident. The end result, of course, is that the employer is effectively relieved of his obligation.⁵⁷

Thus, it found, employee rights and employer duties contained in the state workers' compensation acts would be jeopardized if employers could retaliate against employees for filing claims.

Similarly, in 1976, the Court of Appeals of Michigan reversed a trial court grant of summary judgment against the plaintiff in *Sventko v. Kroger Co.*,⁵⁸ holding that the public policy embodied in the workers' compensation statute would be undermined if employers, by dismissing employees,⁵⁹ were permitted to discourage them from realizing the rights created by the statute. And in 1978, in *Kelsay v. Motorola, Inc.*,⁶⁰ the Illinois Supreme Court reversed a panel of the intermediate

---

⁵² *See* Clanton v. Cain Sloan Co., 677 S.W.2d 441 (Tenn. 1984) (reversing dismissal of complaint for dismissal in retaliation for filing workers' compensation claim).

⁵³ See § **5.9**.

⁵⁴ *See also* Morgan Drive Away, Inc. v. Brant, 479 N.E.2d 1336 (Ind. Ct. App. 1985) (public policy tort for dismissal in retaliation for suing for back wages), *reversed,* 489 N.E.2d 933 (Ind. 1986) (declining to extend public policy tort beyond workers' compensation retaliation).

⁵⁵ 260 Ind. 249, 297 N.E.2d 425 (1973). In Scott v. Union Tank Car, 402 N.E.2d 992 (Ind. Ct. App. 1980), the court held that the action in Indiana is a tort, rather than a contract, action.

⁵⁶ Frampton v. Central Ind. Gas Co., 260 Ind. 249, 252, 297 N.E.2d 425, 427, 428 (1973).

⁵⁷ *Id.* at 251, 297 N.E.2d at 427.

⁵⁸ 69 Mich. App. 644, 245 N.W.2d 151 (1976).

⁵⁹ *Id.* at 647, 245 N.W.2d at 153.

⁶⁰ 74 Ill. 2d 172, 384 N.E.2d 353 (1978).

appellate court and held that implementing the public policy of the state workers' compensation statute required a cause of action for retaliatory dismissals.[61] It concluded that the legislature, even in the absence of an explicit statutory proscription against such dismissals, could not have intended that employers should be able to discourage employees from filing claims.[62]

In *Darnell v. Impact Industries*,[63] the Illinois Supreme Court held that dismissal for filing workers' compensation claims against a former employer is a tort. Depriving an employee of future job opportunities chills exercise of the right to file claims just as much as termination of present employment.

The public policy tort doctrine also has been adopted as part of federal admiralty law in *Smith v. Atlas Off-Shore Boat Service, Inc.*,[64] a 1981 Fifth Circuit case. There, the court reasoned that an employer "should not be allowed to use his absolute discharge right to retaliate" against a seaman for filing a suit against his employer under the Jones Act.[65] The court reviewed and found persuasive the state decisions discussed in this section.

The balance of interests is different, however, when an employee is dismissed for being unable to perform a job rather than being dismissed for filing a claim, even when the inability stems from a workplace injury. In *Clifford v. Cactus Drilling Corp.*,[66] the Michigan Supreme Court held that no public policy tort was committed when the employee was dismissed for a work-related injury. The plaintiff received compensation for the injury, and the court concluded that the dismissal could not have chilled exercise of the right to file for workers' compensation.[67] The *Clifford* court concluded that a dismissal for absence resulting from a workplace injury interferes less with the public policy in favor of employee freedom for workers' compensation than a dismissal for filing a claim. Because of the lower degree of "chill," it excluded this type of dismissal from the public policy tort.[68] Thus the plaintiff was unable to satisfy the second element of the public policy tort: showing jeopardy to the public policy.[69] Dismissal for inability to perform job duties also involves greater employer justification, based on legitimate employer

---

[61] *Id.* at 181, 384 N.E.2d at 357.

[62] *Id.* at 182, 384 N.E.2d at 357.

[63] 105 Ill. 2d 158, 473 N.E.2d 935 (1984).

[64] 653 F.2d 1057 (5th Cir. Aug. 1981).

[65] *Id.* at 1062. *Smith* has been limited, however, to cases in which the discharged employee's employment was covered by the Jones Act at the time of his dismissal. In Buchanan v. Boh Bros. Constr. Co., 741 F.2d 750 (5th Cir. 1984), the court held that an employee dismissed from maritime employment for filing a Jones Act claim against a previous employer had no legal claim under the *Smith* holding because Buchanan was not discharged from a job as a seaman, and thus was outside the admiralty jurisdiction of the federal court. It affirmed the district court's dismissal of his claim without prejudice to his rights to sue in state court. *Id.* at 752.

[66] 419 Mich. 356, 353 N.W.2d 469 (1984).

[67] *Id.* at 360–61, 353 N.W.2d at 471.

[68] !d. at 360–61, 353 N.W.2d at 471.

[69] The three elements for a public policy tort are described in **§ 5.1**.

interests. Thus the plaintiff-employee's position on the third element of the public tort also is weaker.

The logic of the workers' compensation dismissal cases should permit recovery for employees dismissed for suing their employers for back wages under state statutes.[70] The right to collect wages is chilled by threat of dismissal, just as the right to file claims. Courts may be reluctant to extend the analysis justifying recovery by employees filing workers' compensation claims to other, apparently similar, situations, however. In *Kavanagh v. KLM Royal Dutch Airlines*,[71] the court declined to permit a public policy tort based on the general public policy favoring right to counsel and access to the courts. The plaintiff claimed he was fired for retaining an attorney and threatening to sue his employer over a wage payment dispute.

Some state statutes expressly create a cause of action for employees dismissed in retaliation for filing workers' compensation claims.[72] Actions under such statutes do not necessitate use of public policy tort analysis.[73] Other state statutes prohibit retaliatory dismissals but do not expressly create a cause of action. Claims under such statutes should be evaluated like other dismissal claims involving express statutory grant of rights.[74]

When administrative remedies are available for discharges resulting from the filing of workers' compensation claims, some courts have required plaintiffs to resort to those administrative remedies.[75] This type of preclusion involves different analysis from the conclusion that the compensatory provisions of a workers' compensation statute preclude claims for certain types of injury.[76]

---

[70] *See* Morgan Drive Away, Inc. v. Brant, 479 N.E.2d 1336 (Ind. Ct. App. 1985) (approving public policy tort for dismissal in retaliation for suing for back wages); *reversed,* 489 N.E.2d 933 (Ind. 1986) (declining to expand Indiana public policy tort beyond workers compensation retaliation).

[71] 566 F. Supp. 242 (N.D. Ill. 1983).

[72] The federal Fair Labor Standards Act has an express provision prohibiting retaliatory dismissal. See **§ 2.21**.

[73] *See* Wilson v. Riverside Hosp., 18 Ohio St. 3d 8, 479 N.E.2d 275 (1985) (recognizing cause of action for retaliation under state workers' compensation statute expressly creating right to sue); VanTran Elec. Corp. v. Thomas, 708 S.W.2d 527 (Tex. Ct. App. 1986) (violation of workers' compensation statutory prohibition of retaliatory dismissal); Webb v. Dayton Tire & Rubber Co., 697 P.2d 519 (Okla. 1985) (accepting claim for dismissal in violation of statute); Hansome v. Northwestern Coop. Co., 679 S.W.2d 273 (Mo. 1984) (affirming judgment for employee under statute); Ducote v. J.A. Jones Constr. Co., 471 So. 2d 704 (La. 1985) (reinstating judgment for employee under statute prohibiting retaliation for filing workers' compensation claim).

[74] See **§ 2.26** (implying private right of action for violation of statutory rights); **§ 5.19** (difference between these two approaches).

[75] *See* MacDonald v. Eastern Fine Paper, Inc., 485 A.2d 228, 230 (Me. 1984) (Maine statute provides exclusive remedy for dismissal in retaliation for workers' compensation claim; no independent tort cause of action); Portillo v. G.T. Price Prods., Inc., 131 Cal. App. 3d 285, 182 Cal. Rptr. 291 (1982) (exclusive remedy for dismissal in retaliation for filing a workers' compensation claim lies before the Workers' Compensation Appeal Board).

[76] *See also* Crews v. Memorex Corp., 588 F. Supp. 27, 30 (D. Mass. 1984) (emotional distress tort claim by dismissed employee barred by state workers' compensation statute).

§ 5.12 —*External* Public Policy: Termination Jeopardizing Constitutionally Recognized Rights

The external public policy tort concept logically extends to wrongful dismissal lawsuits in which the employment termination offends policies embodied in the United States or state constitutions. The precedent for such an application is mixed, largely because it generally is agreed that the Constitution does not protect persons against purely private conduct.[77] There is no logical reason, however, why the Bill of Rights[78] cannot be used as a foundation for public policy to permit tort recovery. Indeed, its guarantee of jury trial was used for this purpose in *Nees v. Hocks*.[79]

A public policy tort based on the First Amendment to the United States Constitution was recognized under Pennsylvania law in *Novosel v. Nationwide Insurance Co.*[80] The Third Circuit held that an employee who was dismissed for refusing to participate in an employer-directed lobbying campaign had a legitimate claim upon which relief could be granted.[81] The court reasoned that the public policy tort concept as recognized in *Nees v. Hocks* includes dismissals that chill rights contained in the United States and state constitutions.[82]

The first element of the analytical structure for a public policy tort,[83] clarity of the policy, was met in *Novosel* because "the protection of an employee's freedom of political expression would appear to involve no less compelling a societal interest than the fulfillment of jury service or the filing of a workers' compensation claim."[84] The second element, jeopardy, was met because of the chilling effect

---

[77] For example, the First Amendment does not protect persons against purely private conduct. *See* Barr v. Kelso-Burnett Co., 106 Ill. 2d 520, 526, 478 N.E.2d 1354, 1357 (1985) (free speech provisions of state and federal constitutions cannot support public policy tort because they reflect public policy only against governmental interference); Carpenters v. Scott, 463 U.S. 825 (1983) (violation of First Amendment rights cannot be shown under 42 U.S.C. § 1985(3) unless the state was involved in the deprivation). *See* Annotation, 51 A.L.R.2d 742 (1957).

[78] U.S. Const. amends. I–X.

[79] 272 Or. 210, 536 P.2d 512 (1975) (tort recovery permitted for discharge in retaliation for jury service). *See* § **5.10**. However, in Chin v. American Tel. & Tel. Co., 96 Misc. 2d 1070, 1075, 410 N.Y.S.2d 737, 741 (1978), the court declined to find public policy support for a tort action from the First Amendment. For early dicta that a tort remedy does exist for dismissals based on constitutionally protected acts, *see* Boniuk v. New York Medical College, 535 F. Supp. 1353 (S.D.N.Y. 1982), and Brink's Inc. v. City of N.Y., 533 F. Supp. 1123 (S.D.N.Y. 1982). It is not clear what vitality these New York cases have since the New York Court of Appeals has rejected the concept of a public policy tort in Murphy v. American Home Prods., 58 N.Y.2d 293, 448 N.E.2d 86, 461 N.Y.S.2d 232 (1983). *Cf.* Gil v. Metal Serv. Corp., 412 So. 2d 706, 708, (La. Ct. App. 1982) (dicta that a whistleblower might be constitutionally protected from dismissal under the free speech clause).

[80] 721 F.2d 894 (3d Cir. 1983).

[81] *Id.* at 897.

[82] *Id.*

[83] See § **5.1** for an analysis of the three elements.

[84] Novosel v. Nationwide Ins. Co., 721 F.2d at 899.

§ 5.12 CONSTITUTIONAL RIGHTS 267

that threat of employment termination can have on expression.[85] On the record before the court of appeals, the employer had suggested no particular justification for the dismissal, permitting an inference that it was solely motivated by Novosel's political expression.[86]

Another approach to using constitutional rights as a basis for recovery against private employers is reflected by the 1979 California case, *Gay Law Students Association v. Pacific Telephone & Telegraph Co.*,[87] In that case, the California Supreme Court used constitutionally recognized interests to support civil relief in an employment case.[88]

Gay Law Students utilized tort principles to protect employee interests premised in the constitution. The court implied the cause of action from state and federal constitutional guarantees of equal protection and of association.[89] It found the public utility sufficiently protected by the state to impose constitutional constraints on its employment policies.[90] Next, the court found that discrimination against homosexuals as a class was sufficiently unrelated to legitimate employer interests as to violate equal protection guarantees under a minimal scrutiny analysis.[91]

Alternatively, it found that discrimination against homosexuals based on their open profession of their sexual orientation or on their membership in gay advocacy groups violated statutory guarantees of political freedom.[92]

---

[85] *Id.* at 900.

[86] The *Novosel* case was settled after the district court, on remand, denied the employer's motion for summary judgment. *See* Novosel v. Nationwide Mutual Insurance Co., 118 L.R.R.M. 2779 (W.D. Pa. 1985). Interestingly, the employer argued that it dismissed Novosel for prounion remarks made to nonmanagement personnel, which might have raised additional public policy and preemption issues.

[87] 24 Cal. 3d 458, 595 P.2d 592, 156 Cal. Rptr. 14 (1979).

[88] *Id.* at 474–75, 595 P.2d at 602, 156 Cal. Rptr. at 24:

> [T]he California Constitution precluded a public utility's management from automatically excluding all homosexuals from consideration for employment positions. . . . [A]ny person who has been injured by an illegal public utility practice may institute a court action to recover monetary damages. . . . Moreover . . . we believe that plaintiff's request for injunctive relief can properly be maintained. . . .

[89] *Id.* at 467, 595 P.2d at 597–99, 156 Cal. Rptr. at 19–21.

[90] *Id.* at 469, 595 P.2d at 599, 156 Cal. Rptr. at 21. This represents application of the symbiotic relationship governmental involvement approach to finding state action. See § **6.2** regarding the symbiotic relationship concept. The Supreme Court of the United States has decided that regulation of a public utility by the state does not bring the utility's acts within the ambit of federal constitutional protections. Accordingly, the *Gay Law Students* case must be viewed as a direct application of only the California Constitution, or else a tort case importing public policy from the federal Constitution.

[91] *Id.* at 470, 595 P.2d at 599, 156 Cal. Rptr. at 21:

> Protection against the arbitrary foreclosing of employment opportunities lies close to the heart of the protection against "second class citizenship" which the equal protection clause was intended to guarantee. An individual's freedom to work and earn a living has long been recognized as one of the fundamental and most cherished liberties enjoyed by the members of our society.

[92] *Id.* at 486–89, 595 P.2d at 609–11, 156 Cal. Rptr. at 32–33.

The case has not been followed generally in other jurisdictions when the question of discrimination against gay employees has been presented.[93] *Gay Law Students* presents an analytical approach which could result in requiring employers to justify the connection between their legitimate business needs and class-based dismissal in circumstances in which the dismissal occurs because of the exercise of First Amendment rights. In addition, it suggests a conceptual path, later adopted by the *Novosel* court, for imposing on private employers the obligation not to dismiss employees for exercising their free speech and associational rights outside the workplace through an interest-balancing analysis consistent with that suggested by § 870 of the *Restatement (Second) of Torts*.[94] This conceptual path involves using federal or state constitutions as a source of public policy from which a public policy tort can be constructed.[95]

Some other courts have considered the possibility of public policy tort recovery based on constitutional rights, but authority supporting this approach is sparse.[96] Some courts have either flatly rejected the *Novosel* approach, or have been reluctant to use it.[97]

---

[93] The basis for the *Gay Law Students* decision was the governmental character of the public utility employer. This allowed an equal protection analysis. For a discussion of when an apparently private employer is deemed to be the government for purposes of constitutional rights adjudication, see **§ 6.2**.

[94] Restatement (Second) of Torts § 870 (1979).

[95] This is precisely the analytical technique utilized by courts that use a statute as a source of public policy, as discussed in **§§ 5.9 & 5.11**.

[96] Ring v. River Walk Manor, Inc., 596 F. Supp. 393, 396 (D. Md. 1984) (remanding to state court for decision whether Maryland public policy tort claim exists for dismissal in retaliation for exercise of free speech rights; settled before trail); Jones v. Memorial Hosp. Sys., 677 S.W.2d 221 (Tex. Ct. App. 1984) (reversing summary judgment for employer; state and federal constitutional protection of free speech affords cause of action for nurse dismissed for newspaper article expressing personal views, perhaps without proof that employer was "public entity"); Hunter v. Port Auth. of Allegheny County, 277 Pa. Super. 4, 11, 419 A.2d 631, 635 (1980) (public policy tort might lie against a private employer based on a provision of Article I, § 1 of the Pennsylvania Constitution, guaranteeing "an individual's right to engage in any of the common occupations of life." *Id.* at 14 n.5, 419 A.2d at 636 n.5 (analogy to public policy tort analysis in earlier private employer cases); Shaitelman v. Phoenix Mut. Life Ins. Co., 517 F. Supp. 21, 24 (S.D.N.Y. 1980) (implying that a dismissal to restrict an employee's political beliefs, activities, or associations would be cognizable under New York law as a tort; cited approvingly for that proposition in Kovalesky v. A.M.C. Associated Merchandising Corp., 551 F. Supp. 544, 547 (S.D.N.Y. 1982)). Subsequently, in Murphy v. American Home Prods., 58 N.Y.2d 293, 448 N.E.2d 86, 461 N.Y.S.2d 232 (1983), the New York Court of Appeals refused to recognize the public policy tort concept. The *Shaitelman/Kovalesky* analysis, however, continues to support the proposition that, in a jurisdiction that does recognize the public policy tort concept, a constitutional right can be the source of public policy for the tort.

[97] *See* Patton v. J.C. Penny Co., 301 Or. 117, 719 P.2d 854 (1986) (no public policy tort for employee dismissed for dating coworker; rejecting argument that constitutional rights to privacy and association and state action infringement cases represent sufficiently clear public policy); Martin v. Capital Cities Media, Inc., 354 Pa. Super. 199, 511 A.2d 830, 843 (1986) (even though Constitution allows one to speak freely, it also allows employer to discharge employee whose speech offends employer); Ferguson v. Freedom Forge Corp., 604 F. Supp. 1157, 1160 (W.D. Pa. 1985) (dismissal for associating with former company president does not state public policy claim based on First Amendment freedom of association); Barr v. Kelso-Burnett Co., 106 Ill. 2d 520,

Novosel, and the other cases cited, are consistent with the analytical approach embodied in the public policy tort. The law of evidence contemplates that judges may interpret public policy from a wide variety of sources.[98] As the *Novosel* opinion points out, societal interests in free political expression are at least as strong as societal interests in jury service and workers' compensation claims.[99] Thus, it is relatively easy to conclude that the first element, clarity of public policy, is met. As to the second element, jeopardy, both *Novosel* and *Gay Law Students Association v. Pacific Telephone & Telegraph Co.*[1] are correct that dismissal (or refusal to hire) has a direct deterrent impact on exercise of speech and associational rights for which public policy is made clear by the federal Constitution.[2] On the other hand, employer justification, the third element, may override the societal interests embodied in the first two elements.[3] *Harman v. LaCrosse Tribune*[4] is a clear case in which the employer's interests in proper service to clients overrode public policy in the employee's favor. The court held that public policy based on the constitutional right of free speech was overridden by the lawyers' code of professional responsibility when a lawyer-employee of the law firm attacked a client in a press release.[5]

§ 5.13 —*External* Public Policy: Termination for Private, or Off Duty, Conduct

It is reasonable to classify any case involving not a conflict over employer business policies, but use of employer power to interfere with employee private choice, as involving *external* public policy torts, though the conduct leading up to the discharge might have occurred wholly within the workplace. Only a few courts have premised public policy tort recovery on the public policy in favor of employee

---

526, 478 N.E.2d 1354, 1357 (1985) (free speech provisions of state and federal constitutions cannot support public policy tort because reflect public policy only against governmental interference); Harman v. LaCrosse Tribune, 117 Wis. 2d 448, 344 N.W.2d 536 (1984) (public policy based on Constitution overridden by lawyers' code of professional responsibility when employee of law firm attacked client in press release).

[98] See § 7.11 for a fuller discussion of the manner in which public policy can be proven.

[99] Novosel v. Nationwide Ins. Co., 721 F.2d at 899.

[1] 24 Cal. 3d 458, 595 P.2d 592, 156 Cal. Rptr. 14 (1979).

[2] U.S. Const. amend. I.

[3] In Novosel v. Nationwide Ins. Co., 721 F.2d 894 (3d Cir. 1983), the employer did have a legitimate interest in seeing the employee present its position to the legislature, but the court decided the employee's First Amendment interests were stronger.

[4] 117 Wis. 2d 448, 344 N.W.2d 536 (1984).

[5] For an interesting analysis of employer interests in tension with public policy interests, albeit in the context of an alleged statutory violation, see Brown & Root, Inc. v. Donovan, 747 F.2d 1029, 1035 (5th Cir. 1984) (pointing out that whistleblowing to government agencies has less impact on employment policies than internal quarrel over employer policies).

privacy.[6] This would be consistent with the public policy tort approach,[7] though perhaps a court might be more willing to reach a result favorable to the plaintiff within the framework of the invasion of privacy tort.[8]

In *Slohoda v. United Parcel Service, Inc.*,[9] the court reversed summary judgment for the employer, and held that inquiry by an employer into extramarital sexual activities could give rise to tort liability if the employee were discharged for that reason. Thus the invasion of privacy associated with a dismissal for private sexual conduct was used as the foundation for a public policy tort.

Another example, assisted by a particular statutory policy, is *Lucas v. Brown & Root, Inc.*,[10] in which the court of appeals, reversing the district court, found a public policy tort pleaded under Arkansas law when the plaintiff claimed she was fired for refusing to sleep with her foreman. The court premised the public policy on state statutes prohibiting prostitution, reasoning that compelling sexual favors as the price of keeping one's job effectively compels exchange of sex for money—the target of the prostitution statutes.

In *Wagenseller v. Scottsdale Memorial Hospital*,[11] a nurse dismissed for refusing to "moon" on an off duty rafting trip could recover on public policy tort theory, based on criminal statute prohibiting indecent exposure. Because of the statute, the first element, clarity of policy, was met. The second element also was met, because permitting the dismissal would have discouraged compliance with the criminal statute. And the third element was little problem because the employer was able to marshal no argument independently justifying the dismissal.

The external public policy tort cases involving off duty conduct or private choice present weaker claims under the three elements of the analytical framework than

---

[6] The sources of public policy favoring employee privacy are federal and state constitutions, the invasion of privacy tort (discussed in §§ 5.26 & 5.27), and statutes against maintenance or disclosure of certain information in personnel records (as noted later in this section).

[7] The opinion in Geary v. United States Steel Corp., 456 Pa. 171, 319 A.2d 174 (1974) suggests that "there are areas of an employee's life in which his employer has no legitimate interest. An intrusion into one of these areas by virtue of the employer's power of discharge might plausibly give rise to a cause of action." *Id.* at 184, 319 A.2d at 180. This hints at a privacy approach. Stronger support is provided by Slohoda v. United Parcel Serv., Inc., 193 N.J. Super. 586, 590, 475 A.2d 618, 622 (App. Div. 1984), *appeal after remand,* 207 N.J. Super 145, 504 A.2d 53 (1986), in which the court reversed summary judgment for the employer, and held that inquiry by an employer into extramarital sexual activities could give rise to tort liability if the employee were discharged for that reason. Thus the invasion of privacy associated with a dismissal for private sexual conduct was used as the foundation for a public policy tort. *But see* Patton v. J.C. Penney Co., 301 Or. 117, 719 P.2d 854 (1986) (no public policy tort for employee dismissed for dating coworker; rejecting argument that constitutional rights to privacy and association and state action infringement cases represent sufficiently clear public policy); Karren v. Far West Fed. Sav., 79 Or. App. 131, 717 P.2d 1271 (1986) (dismissal for becoming engaged to marry does not involve rights as employee; therefore does not support public policy tort).

[8] For fuller development of this idea, see § 5.27.

[9] 193 N.J. Super. 586, 590, 475 A.2d 618, 622 (App. Div. 1984), *appeal after remand,* 207 N.J. Super. 145, 504 A.2d 53 (1986).

[10] 736 F.2d 1202, 1205 (8th Cir. 1984).

[11] 147 Ariz. 370, 710 P.2d 1025 (1985).

cases involving political expression.[12] Privacy interests are less clearly manifested in constitutions and statutes than freedom of political expression. Thus the first element is more difficult to meet, unless a specific statute can be brought to bear, as in *Wagenseller* and *Lucas v. Brown & Root, Inc.* The jeopardy element is equally strong, however, because threats of dismissal have as much chilling effect on private choice as on political expression. Also, the likelihood of independent employer justification in the type of case addressed in this section is even weaker than in *Novosel* itself, where the employer wished to present a political position related to its economic interests.

The approach suggested in this section would be buttressed in a state having a personnel records statute such as Illinois.[13] The Illinois statute prohibits employers from keeping records on the nonemployment activities of employees. This manifests public policy that private off duty conduct is none of the employer's business, unless there is some specific connection with the employer's legitimate interests.

Dismissals affecting employee privacy, such as dismissals for sexual orientation,[14] can be addressed not only in the framework of an external public policy tort, but also within the framework of the tort of invasion of privacy,[15] where the clarity-of-policy inquiry is resolved in the cause of action itself.

§ 5.14 *External* versus *Internal* Public Policy Torts for Wrongful Dismissal

Many wrongful dismissal cases involve disputes wholly internal to the workplace, as contrasted with dismissals arising from conduct outside, and unrelated to, the workplace. These cases may be classified as *internal* public policy tort cases. The public policy torts cases discussed in §§ **5.9** through **5.13** involved employer conduct that tended to chill employee activity outside the workplace in a way found to be detrimental to public policy. The common bond of public policies favoring jury duty and workers' compensation is that they are not essentially regulatory programs aimed at employer conduct. Accordingly, when an employer dismisses an employee for conduct in connection with these outside-the-workplace activities, the employer can be said to be overreaching with the power of dismissal into some area of private concern to the employee or public concern to the state, or both, with which the employer has no direct legitimate business interest.[16] Thus, a balancing of interests, discussed in § **5.7**, weighs the employer's somewhat diminished interest against interests external to the workplace recognized by the legislature as valid. Cases falling in this branch of the public policy area were classified as

---

[12] See § **5.12**.

[13] 48 Ill. Ann. Stat. para. 2009 (Smith-Hurd Supp. 1986) (prohibiting employers from keeping records of nonemployment activities).

[14] See § **5.28**.

[15] See § **5.27**.

[16] The employer has some incidental interest in the worktime lost due to jury service or in the cost of paying workers' compensation insurance premiums.

external public policy tort cases because they involve a public policy extrinsic to the employer's operation.[17]

In the external public policy tort cases, the interests of the employer in escaping liability (the third factor) are relatively weak. This is what distinguishes the external public policy tort category from the internal public policy tort category. In the external category, the conduct for which the employee is dismissed is largely or entirely external to the employment relationship, and the interests of the employer in controlling that conduct are correspondingly weak. This is not to say that the employer has no interests worthy of consideration; the employer retains at all times the interest in complete freedom to decide whom to employ. But this interest is little more than the interest in retention of the Employment-at-Will Rule. The relatively strong public policy interests, combined with the ever-present economic interests of the employee, outweigh the relatively weak interests of the employer in the decided cases in the external public policy tort category.

The internal public policy tort category involves public policy interests entirely internal to the employer's business. Courts considering claims in this category must focus exclusively on interactions within the workplace, where the employer interests in managing the business conflict more directly with policies favoring particular business practices, than in external public policy tort cases. Most of the internal public policy tort cases involve employee objections to employer policies. Under the interest-balancing approach discussed in § **5.7**, the courts must evaluate the employer's claim that it, rather than the employee, should be entitled to formulate policy for its business.[18] While there is some temporal overlap, most of the internal public policy tort cases were decided after, and drew upon, the external public policy tort cases.

The distinction between the judicial tasks involved in the two types of public policy tort cases was drawn in *Geary v. United States Steel Corp.*,[19] a 1974 Pennsylvania Supreme Court case. Geary protested the sale of unsafe steel products by his employer, and was fired. His protests were directed to his superiors and ultimately to a vice president. The trial court dismissed his complaint for wrongful discharge.[20] The Supreme Court of Pennsylvania affirmed. Its analysis was based on the proposition that the employer has a privilege, "hitherto regarded as virtually absolute," to terminate its employees.[21] In order for Geary to win, the court must impose "limitations on this privilege for reasons of policy."[22] The court concluded that the "most natural inference from the chain of events recited in

---

[17] *External* public policy torts are discussed in §§ **5.10** & **5.11** (jury duty and workers' compensation claims), **5.12** (constitutional rights), and **5.13** (private, off duty conduct).

[18] *See* Brown & Root, Inc. v. Donovan, 747 F.2d 1029, 1035 (5th Cir. 1984) (pointing out that protecting whistleblowing has less impact on employment policy than protecting employee in internal quarrel over employer policies; statutory violation).

[19] 456 Pa. 171. 319 A.2d 174 (1974).

[20] *Id.* at 173, 319 A.2d at 175.

[21] *Id.* at 175, 319 A.2d at 176.

[22] *Id.* at 177, 319 A.2d at 177.

the complaint is that Geary had made a nuisance of himself, and the company discharged him to preserve administrative order in its own house."[23]

Under these circumstances, the court decided that public policy considerations militated against permitting Geary to recover, primarily because of the deleterious effect tort liability would have on an employer's legitimate interest in preserving and protecting its own internal procedures.[24]

The court hinted, however, that it might have reached a different conclusion if an external public policy tort had been alleged. It pointed to areas of an employee's life in which the employer has no legitimate interest, particularly if some recognized facet of public policy is threatened.[25]

Thus, the *Geary* court denied recovery in circumstances involving employer-employee arguments about employer policy, but suggested liability might exist if elements of an external public policy tort were satisfied.[26] The *Geary* court was reluctant to strike the interest balance in a way that would deprive the employer of autonomy to make product decisions.[27] Its reluctance was reinforced by Geary's manner of protest—his making a nuisance of himself. This nuisance factor weakened Geary's position on the third element, justification.[28] Overall, *Geary* suggests a less sympathetic judicial stance toward internal public policy torts than toward external public policy torts.

§ 5.15 —*Internal* Public Policy: Marshaling the Conflicting Interests

Internal public policy tort cases involve the three elements of the public policy tort in different ways, depending on how the employee seeks to protest or change employer practices. In all of the internal public policy tort cases, the public policy asserted relates directly to the employer's business decisions rather than to conduct outside the workplace. Therefore, in all the internal cases, the employer begins

---

[23] *Id.* at 180, 319 A.2d at 178.

[24] *Id.* at 181, 319 A.2d at 179.

> Given the rapidity of change in corporate personnel in the areas of employment not covered by labor agreements, suits like the one at bar could well be expected to place a heavy burden . . . on the legitimate interest of employers in hiring and retaining the best personnel available. The everpresent threat of suit might well inhibit the making of critical judgments by employers concerning employee qualifications.

[25] *Id.* at 184, 319 A.2d 180:

> It may be granted that there are areas of an employee's life in which his employer has no legitimate interest. An intrusion into one of these areas by virtue of the employer's power of discharge might plausibly give rise to a cause of action, particularly where some recognized facet of public policy is threatened.

[26] The *Geary* opinion does not utilize the external public policy label. Discussion in the opinion, however, fits within the external public policy category developed in §§ **5.10–5.14**.

[27] Geary v. United States Steel Corp., 456 Pa. at 181, 319 A.2d at 179.

[28] See § **5.1** for an explanation of the three elements of the public policy tort.

with a relatively strong interest in making business decisions unilaterally. To overcome this employer interest in the balancing process, the plaintiff must show strong public policy interests as revealed by the first two elements.

In some cases, the courts are unable to identify a sufficiently clear public policy to necessitate evaluation of the second element (jeopardy) of the public policy tort.[29] In other cases, the public policy is clear, but the degree of interference with the policy potentially resulting from the dismissal is questionable. Sometimes jeopardy to public policy resulting from dismissing an employee is modest because of the availability of nonemployee channels to enforce the policy involved. In situations in which chilling employee action by threat of dismissal would have little or no impact on the public policy, recovery is not permitted.[30] Cases in which the employee is fired for taking a position on securities issues, or corporate record keeping,[31] or on a matter as to which the employee has no special responsibility or expertise, illustrate instances when the public policy jeopardy resulting from employer conduct allegedly violating public policy is too slight to justify recovery.

In contrast, tort liability is appropriate in those cases in which the dismissed employee has special responsibilities in connection with the policy asserted and/or there is a low probability of effective enforcement of the public policy by outside agencies acting on their own. These factual characteristics strengthen the employee's position on the second element, jeopardy.

Internal public policy tort cases can be classified into three subordinate categories: those involving employee protests or reports on employer policies to outside agencies,[32] those involving employee protests or reports to the employer,[33] and those involving employee refusal to obey employer orders.[34] The category involving reports to outside agencies presents stronger arguments on the jeopardy element than the other two categories because of the likelihood that enforcement agencies depend on employee tips. Cases involving reports or protest to employer representatives present weaker jeopardy elements because the link between internal appeals and realization of public policy is weaker. Cases involving refusal to obey orders present much weaker plaintiff arguments on the justification element because of the obvious legitimacy of the employer's interest in having employees follow orders. Sufficiency of the plaintiff's position on the first element, clarity of public policy, generally does not vary according to subcategory.

---

[29] *See* Barr v. Kelso-Burnett Co., 106 Ill. 2d 520, 478 N.E.2d 1354 (1985) (no public policy tort for dismissal in retaliation for protesting layoff policies).

[30] Recovery should not be permitted in such cases because no harm to public policy exists to balance against the employer's interest in running its business. See § **5.7**. Adams v. Budd Co., 583 F. Supp 711, 716 (E.D. Pa. 1984) (no public policy tort for pointing out product defects when no violation of law and no indication employer attempted to hide them).

[31] Campbell v. Ford Indus., 274 Or. 243, 546 P.2d 141 (1976); Murphy v. American Home Prods. Corp., 58 N.Y.2d 293, 448 N.E.2d 86, 461 N.Y.S.2d 232 (1983).

[32] See § **5.16**.

[33] See § **5.17**.

[34] See § **5.18**.

There are a few cases, of course, that do not fit easily into any of the categories. In *Nye v. Department of Livestock*,[35] for example, a public employee was permitted to maintain a public policy tort action. The court found that administrative personnel rules could be the source of a public policy, and that violation of those rules contravened the policy.[36]

§ 5.16 —*Internal* Public Policy Tort: Protests or Reports to Outside Agencies (Whistleblowing)

Internal public policy tort cases involving employee reports of employer misconduct to outside agencies present relatively strong arguments on the jeopardy element because of the likelihood that agencies charged with public policy enforcement depend on such reports. Such cases also usually are strong on the clarity element because the employee's ability to identify a specific agency to receive his complaints suggests that the employee was able to identify a specific public policy. The justification element in such cases is likely to be mixed, because of the employer's legitimate interests in avoiding adverse publicity, receiving loyalty from employees, and having a chance to correct improper practices before public agencies become involved.

In 1981, the Supreme Court of Illinois decided *Palmateer v. International Harvester Co.*[37] Palmateer was terminated after supplying information to local law enforcement authorities about possible criminal activities, not specified, by a fellow employee. He alleged that his termination was in retaliation for his cooperation with the criminal justice authorities.[38]

The trial court dismissed his complaint, and the intermediate appellate court affirmed. The supreme court reversed.[39] Reasoning that the public policy supporting a wrongful discharge cause of action "must strike at the heart of a citizen's social rights, duties, and responsibilities" before the tort will be allowed,[40] the court concluded that "there is no public policy more basic, nothing more implicit in the concept of ordered liberty . . . than the enforcement of a state's criminal

---

[35] 196 Mont. 222, 639 P.2d 498 (1982).

[36] *Id.* at 228, 639 P.2d at 502.

[37] 85 Ill. 2d 124, 421 N.E.2d 876 (1981).

[38] *Id.* at 127, 421 N.E.2d at 877:

> According to the complaint, Palmateer was fired both for supplying information to local law enforcement authorities that an IH employee might be involved in a violation of the Criminal Code of 1961 (Ill. Rev. Stat. 1979, ch. 38, par. 1-1 et. seq.) and for agreeing to assist in the investigation and trial of the employee if requested.

[39] The *Palmateer* court was broadening the circumstances in which the earlier Illinois decision of Kelsay v. Motorola, Inc., 74 Ill. 2d 172, 384 N.W.2d 353 (1978), would apply.

[40] Palmateer v. International Harvester Co., 85 Ill. 2d at 130, 384 N.E.2d at 878-79.

code."[41] While no specific constitutional or statutory provisions in Illinois required a citizen to take an active part in the ferreting out and prosecution of crime, "public policy nevertheless favors citizen crime fighters."[42] Therefore, the court held that Palmateer had stated a cause of action for wrongful dismissal.[43]

McQuary v. Bel Air Convalescent Home, Inc.[44] was a case involving a threat to engage in whistleblowing. A nursing home in-service training director claimed she was fired for threatening to report patient abuse to a state enforcement agency. The clarity element of the public policy tort was met by a state statute prohibiting mental and physical abuse and requiring that nursing home patients be treated with respect and dignity.[45] The jeopardy element was met because the statute was interpreted to obligate persons with knowledge of violations to report them to the enforcement agency. Threats of dismissal would chill exercise of that reporting obligation.[46]

§ 5.17 — *Internal* Public Policy Tort: Protests or Reports to Employer

The second subcategory of public policy tort cases involves employee complaints or reports within the workplace regarding conduct allegedly contravening public policy.

Harless v. First National Bank[47] involved an employee allegedly fired solely for protesting his employer's practice of making illegal loan charges in contravention of state and federal regulations.[48] He complained to higher bank officers and

---

[41] *Id.* at 132, 384 N.E.2d at 879. It is difficult to conclude from the facts reported whether the criminal conduct was remote from the employer's main business decisions or intertwined with them. If the criminal conduct was remote, the interest balancing would have involved weighing purely public concerns in favor of criminal prosecution against diminished employer interests: an external public policy analysis. If the criminal conduct involved conduct by other employees adverse to the employer, the interest balancing would have required deciding whether an employer should be free to decide whether to prosecute or to utilize internal disciplinary procedures: an internal public policy analysis.

[42] *Id.* at 132, 384 N.E.2d at 880.

[43] *Id.* at 133, 384 N.E.2d at 880.

[44] 69 Or. App. 107, 684 P.2d 21, 23 (1985). The appeals court reversed a jury verdict for the nursing home, finding erroneous an instruction that the jury could not find for the plaintiff unless it found that there was, in fact, patient abuse.

[45] *Id.* at 111, 684 P.2d at 23.

[46] *Id.* at 111, 684 P.2d at 23.

[47] 246 S.E.2d 270 (W. Va. 1978).

[48] *Id.* at 272. The plaintiff's complaint contained two counts. The first count alleged that his discharge was in retaliation for his efforts to bring to the attention of and require his employer to operate in compliance with the state and federal consumer credit and protection laws. The second count claimed that the employer's conduct leading up to the discharge amounted to intentional, malicious and outrageous conduct which caused the plaintiff severe emotional distress. *Harless*

§ 5.17   REPORTS TO EMPLOYER   277

ultimately to a member of the board of directors.[49] The trial court dismissed his complaint.[50] The Supreme Court of West Virginia concluded that:

> the rule giving the employer the absolute right to discharge an at will employee must be tempered by the further principle that where the employer's motivation for the discharge contravenes some substantial public policy principle, then the employer may be liable to the employee for damages occasioned by the discharge.[51]

It found a "clear and unequivocal" public policy expressed by the West Virginia consumer protection statute[52] and reasoned that employees of lending institutions covered by the act who seek to ensure compliance with the act, cannot be discharged without being furnished a cause of action for such discharge.[53] The court did not address the jeopardy element, but it is reasonable to conclude that policies governing bank credit charges depend to a substantial degree on bank employee compliance. So dismissal of an employee for insisting on such compliance reasonably can be said to jeopardize the policy. Subsequently, a jury verdict in Harless's favor was affirmed.[54]

In *Thompson v. St. Regis Paper Co.*,[55] the Supreme Court of Washington, reversing summary judgment for the employer, held that an employee could recover in tort if he could show that his dismissal was premised on his instituting an accurate accounting system in compliance with the federal Foreign Corrupt Practices Act of 1977.[56] The *Thompson* court emphasized the jeopardy factor.[57] The possible jeopardy to public policy arose because the plaintiff's dismissal might discourage other controllers from complying with the statute.[58]

In *Bowman v. State Bank of Keysville*,[59] the Supreme Court of Virginia reversed grant of demurrer against the plaintiff and accepted a public policy tort theory for bank employees dismissed for claiming proxy statements violated state securities laws. The clarity element of the public policy tort was satisfied by a state statute

---

is treated as an internal public policy case because the bank discharged Harless for conduct in the workplace; his protests of the bank's policies were internal.

[49] *Id.* at 272.

[50] *Id.*

[51] *Id.* at 275.

[52] *Id.* at 275–76 (citing West Virginia Consumer Credit and Protection Act, W. Va. Code § 46A-1-101 (1986)). "We have no hesitation in stating that the legislature intended to establish a clear and unequivocal policy that consumers of credit covered by the Act were to be given protection." *Id.* at 276.

[53] *Id.* at 276.

[54] Harless v. First Nat'l Bank, 289 S.E.2d 692 (W. Va. 1982) (affirming verdict respecting liability, but reversing and remanding on damage issues).

[55] 102 Wash. 2d 219, 685 P.2d 1081, 1090 (1984).

[56] Pub. L. No. 95-213, 91 Stat. 1494 (1977).

[57] This is the second element of the public policy tort. See § **5.1**.

[58] Thompson v. St. Regis Paper Co., 102 Wash. 2d at ___, 685 P.2d at 1090.

[59] 229 Va. 534, 331 S.E.2d 797 (1985).

giving corporate shareholders the right to vote.[60] The jeopardy element was met because, "for the goal of the statute to be realized and the public policy fulfilled, the shareholder must be able to exercise this right without fear of reprisal from corporate management which happens also to be the employer."[61]

In *Sheets v. Teddy's Frosted Foods, Inc.*,[62] a quality control director and operations manager of a food processor was dismissed for complaining to his employer about substandard raw materials and underweight components in food products.[63] The employer practices he complained about caused a violation of state labeling statutes.[64] In reversing the trial court's striking of the plaintiff's complaint, the Supreme Court of Connecticut emphasized that plaintiff Sheets's job responsibilities directly covered product quality and that, because of the mislabeled food products, [65] he might have been exposed to criminal liability under the state statute governing food labeling. "[A]n employee should not be put to an election whether to risk criminal sanction or to jeopardize his continued employment."[66] The clarity element was met in *Sheets* by the state statute; the jeopardy element was met because of the plaintiff's special responsibilities for ensuring compliance.

In several cases, however, courts concluded that employee-employer disputes over policy involved only management disputes and not matters clothed with public policy.[67] In *Adler v. American Standard Corp.*,[68] the Court of Appeals of Maryland, on certification of the question from a federal district court, held that Maryland recognizes a cause of action for wrongful dismissal when the motivation for the dismissal contravenes a clear mandate of public policy.[69] A plaintiff, however, does not state a cause of action by alleging that he was dismissed for protesting falsification of corporate records.[70] The court reasoned that a general allegation that corporate records were falsified is not specific enough to establish the violation of a state statute intended to protect purchasers of corporate securities;[71] nor

---

[60] *Id.* at 540, 331 S.E.2d at 801, citing Va. Code Ann. § 13.1-32 (repealed as of Jan. 1, 1986, Va. Code Ann. § 13.1-32 (1985)).

[61] *Id.* at 540, 331 S.E.2d at 801.

[62] 179 Conn. 471, 427 A.2d 385 (1980).

[63] *Id.* at 472-73, 427 A.2d at 386.

[64] Conn. Uniform Food Drug and Cosmetic Act, Conn. Gen. Stat. § 19-222, now codified at § 21a-93 (1985) (a food shall be deemed to be misbranded: (a) If its labeling is false or misleading in any particular).

[65] Sheets v. Teddy's Frosted Foods, Inc., 179 Conn. at 479, 427 A.2d at 388.

[66] *Id.* at 480, 427 A.2d at 389.

[67] In addition to the cases discussed in the text, *see* Giudice v. Drew Chem. Corp., 210 N.J. Super. 32, 509 A.2d 200 (1986) (failure to identify specific public policy jeopardized by dismissal for internal protest of corporate president's misconduct precludes recovery on public policy tort theory); Petrick v. Monarch Printing Corp., 143 Ill. App. 3d 1, 10, 493 N.E.2d 616, 621 (1986) (affirming summary judgment for employer; no public policy implicated by internal disagreement over financial accounting, stockholder disclosure).

[68] 291 Md. 31, 432 A.2d 464 (1981).

[69] *Id.* at 47, 432 A.2d at 473.

[70] *Id.* at 46, 432 A.2d 472-73.

[71] *Id.*

§ 5.17   REPORTS TO EMPLOYER   279

was the court willing to infer judicially a general public policy against the doctoring of corporate records.[72] Accordingly, Adler's complaint failed because his discharge did not contravene a sufficiently clear mandate of public policy.[73]

Geary v. United States Steel Corp.[74] has already been discussed.[75] Geary claimed that he was fired because he protested against the marketing of tubular casings without further testing, a protest based on his belief that the casings would be dangerous. His protests were directed to his superiors and ultimately to a vice president. The Supreme Court of Pennsylvania was unable to find a clear public policy jeopardized by Geary's termination, and further concluded that the "most natural inference from the chain of events recited in the complaint is that Geary had made a nuisance of himself, and the company discharged him to preserve administrative order in its own house."[76] Under these circumstances, the court decided that public policy considerations did not support recovery by Geary, primarily because of the deleterious effect tort liability would have on an employer's legitimate interest in preserving and protecting its own internal procedures.[77] Thus Geary failed on all three elements of the public policy tort. The clarity of the public policy involved was insubstantial. The jeopardy to public policy was small because Geary had no special responsibility or expertise. The employer's justification was substantial because of the disruptive manner of Geary's protest.

In *Suchodolski v. Michigan Consolidated Gas Co.*,[78] the plaintiff was denied relief for a dismissal resulting from his reporting of questionable accounting practices.[79] The Supreme Court of Michigan held that recovery would be limited to circumstances in which a person was dismissed because of his exercise of a statutory right. It found the case before it to involve only a "corporate management dispute," and declined to elevate the code of ethics of internal auditors into a statement of public policy.[80]

---

[72] *Id.*

[73] *Id.* In Teays v. Supreme Concrete Block, Inc., 51 Md. App. 166, 441 A.2d 1109 (1982), *Adler* was interpreted to require particularity in the pleadings to make out a cause of action for wrongful dismissal. *See also* Murphy v. American Home Prods. Corp., 58 N.Y.2d 293, 448 N.E.2d 86, 461 N.Y.S.2d 232 (1982) *and* Titsch v. Reliance Group, Inc., 548 F. Supp. 983 (S.D.N.Y. 1982) for disputes over internal corporate account procedures.

[74] 456 Pa. 171, 319 A.2d 174 (1974).

[75] See § **5.14**.

[76] Geary v. United States Steel Corp., 456 Pa. at 180, 319 A.2d at 178.

[77] *Id.* at 181, 319 A.2d at 179.

[78] 412 Mich. 692, 316 N.W.2d 710 (1982).

[79] The reported opinion does not specify to whom the reports were made. Other facts of the case suggest, however, that the plaintiff's protests were primarily, if not entirely, internal.

[80] Suchodolski v. Michigan Consol. Gas Co., 412 Mich. at 696, 316 N.W.2d at 712. *Accord,* Martin v. Platt, 179 Ind. App. 688, 386 N.E.2d 1026 (1979) (allegation of kickbacks; report to supervisor's boss); Campbell v. Eli Lilly & Co., 413 N.E.2d 1054 (Ind. Ct. App. 1980), *aff'd,* 421 N.E.2d 1099 (1981) (controversy over safety of drugs sold by employer; report by employee's counsel to employer's counsel); Gil v. Metal Serv. Corp., 412 So. 2d 706 (La. Ct. App. 1982), *cert. denied,* 414 So. 2d 379 (La. 1982) (refusal to remove foreign markings from steel represented to be domestic; communicated to supervisor); Maus v. National Living Centers, Inc., 633 S.W.2d 674 (Tex. Ct. App. 1982) (care of patients in nursing home; complaint made to supervisor).

In the 1980 case of *Kenneally v. Orgain*,[81] the Supreme Court of Montana affirmed a trial court dismissal of a suit brought by an employee fired for complaining about inadequate customer service. The supreme court could find no public policy violated by the discharge of Kenneally "unless it may be considered that the public is hurt when a corporation allows sales of its machines to be made upon promises of adequate service and maintenance and then fails (to perform)."[82]

In *Rachford v. Evergreen International Airlines*,[83] the federal court held that no tort was pleaded under Illinois law for a discharge in retaliation for aircraft safety complaints. The court reached the dubious conclusion that a state has no interest in enforcing federal law.

The results in the cases involving employee protests or reports to the employer can be rationalized according to the clarity and substantiality of the public policy interest involved,[84] according to the jeopardy to that policy potentially resulting from the dismissal of the plaintiff,[85] and for the countervailing employer interests in escaping liability for the dismissal.[86]

Geary, Suchodolski, Adler, Kenneally, and *Rachford* were decided in the defendants' favor. In all but *Rachford,* the public policy invoked by the plaintiff was vague: the policy in favor of safe steel tubing in *Geary,* the policy in favor of correct corporate record keeping in *Suchodolski* and *Adler,* and the policy in favor of good customer service in *Kenneally.* Even if the public policy had been clearer (and it was clear, at least at the federal level, in *Rachford*), the degree of jeopardy resulting from the dismissals was low because of the availability of other enforcement mechanisms relating to product safety, corporate accounting, securities regulation, and aircraft safety.[87] Moreover, in each of these three cases, the employer had a strong interest in making the tradeoffs involved in product design or delivery, accounting policy decisions, and aircraft operations. So the plaintiffs had weak arguments on all three elements of the public policy tort.

Harless, Bowman, Sheets, Cloutier, and *Thompson* were decided in favor of the plaintiff. In all except *Cloutier,* the public policy was clear: statutory and regulatory proscriptions against excessive loan charges in *Harless,* statutory promotion of shareholder freedom in *Bowman,* the statutory policy against adulterated or mislabeled food in *Sheets.* The degree of interference with the policy resulting from the dismissals was arguable in these cases because of the availability of

---

[81] 186 Mont. 1, 606 P.2d 127 (1980).

[82] *Id.* at 6, 606 P.2d at 129.

[83] 596 F. Supp. 384, (N.D. Ill. 1984). The employee made three internal complaints, two to a vice president of the employer and another to coemployees. The employer claimed the employee made a report to the FAA. The court found it unnecessary to resolve the factual conflict.

[84] This is the first element of the public policy tort. See § 5.1.

[85] This is the second element of the public policy tort. See § 5.1.

[86] This is the third element of the public policy tort. See § 5.1. *See* Bushko v. Miller Brewing Co., 396 N.W.2d 167, 170 (Wis. 1986) (public policy claim only for refusing to commit illegal act, not for internal safety protest, broadly rejecting internal protest subcategory in implied covenant case).

[87] Similarly, it can be argued that the degree of interference with the policy was low in *Keneally* because the market adequately deals with customer service.

administrative enforcement agencies. Nevertheless, it is likely that effective enforcement of regulations such as those involved depends to some degree on the conduct of persons with intimate knowledge of the regulated activities. If pro-compliance conduct is chilled by threat of dismissal, a lower degree of compliance is likely.

In *Suchodolski* and *Adler,* rejection of the employees' claims is explainable more logically by the difference in the clarity of the public policy involved. If a clear enough public policy had been found, the degree of interference would have been as high as in the cases resolved in the employees' favor.

In internal protest cases, it is important to be clear about the type of employee conduct that allegedly furthers public policy. It is not disclosure of wrongdoing, to permit enforcement agencies to punish employers, it is communication within the employer's own organization, which promotes compliance. Even if enforcement agencies have adequate means to detect noncompliance, employee awareness of regulatory requirements and advocacy of compliance to supervisors and coemployees is an important guarantee that the underlying public policy will be realized. The facts of *Sheets* illustrate this point well. Truth-in-labeling policies can be realized most efficiently through vigilance by quality control personnel in the regulated companies, rather than by after-the-fact imposition of sanctions on violators.

Bowman v. State Bank of Keysville[88] is a special case on the jeopardy element. The plaintiffs were shareholders as well as employees. Thus, using the employment connection to interfere with their freedom as shareholders more directly jeopardized the public policy in favor of shareholder freedom than if they had not been shareholders.

The employee's position on the justification element in internal protest cases is relatively strong, compared with the employee's position on justification in external report or refusal of orders cases. Employers have a legitimate interest in having employees follow orders, and in inhibiting adverse publicity. Neither of these interests is jeopardized when an employee makes internal protests, though one or both are when an employee refuses to obey orders or reports employer violations to outside agencies.

§ 5.18 —*Internal* Public Policy Tort: Refusals to Follow Orders

The third subcategory of internal public policy tort cases involves employees who refuse to follow employer orders in circumstances in which following the orders would contravene public policy.

---

[88] 229 Va. 534, 331 S.E.2d 797 (1985) (reversing grant of demurrer against plaintiff and accepting public policy tort theory for bank employees dismissed for claiming proxy statements violated state securities laws).

In the 1980 California Supreme Court case, *Tameny v. Atlantic Richfield Co.*,[89] the plaintiff alleged that his employer fired him for refusing to participate in an illegal scheme to fix retail gasoline prices.[90] The trial court dismissed the plaintiff's tort claim, an intermediate court of appeals affirmed, but the California Supreme Court reversed.[91] The court stressed the harm to public policy that could result from permitting employers to use their power of discharge to compel employees to commit criminal acts.[92] The clarity element was met by the antitrust laws. The jeopardy element was met because the conduct refused was itself criminal.

Pierce v. Ortho Pharmaceutical Corp.[93] involved refusal by a medical doctor to conduct research on a product containing saccharin because of her belief that saccharin presents health risks. She admitted the varied medical opinions on the effects of saccharin and alleged neither a violation of any specific regulatory or statutory standard nor a violation of her professional code of conduct.[94] The Supreme Court of New Jersey accepted the premise that an employee has a cause of action for wrongful dismissal when the dismissal is contrary to a "clear mandate" of public policy.[95] An employee, in order to avoid dismissal under the theory, must identify "a specific expression of public policy."[96] The court found that public policy could be expressed in legislation, judicial decisions, and administrative decisions, rules, or regulations.[97] Moreover, "[i]n certain instances, a professional code of ethics may contain an expression of public policy."[98]

But in the opinion of the court, the "controversy at Ortho involved a difference in medical opinions."[99] This, it concluded, was not entitled to public policy protection because of the disorder that would result in drug research if employees could

---

[89] 27 Cal. 3d 167, 610 P.2d 1330, 164 Cal. Rptr. 839 (1980).

[90] *Id.* at 170–71, 610 P.2d at 1331–32, 164 Cal. Rptr. 840–41.

[91] *Id.* at 171–72, 610 P.2d at 1332, 164 Cal. Rptr. at 841. It cited California cases, beginning with Petermann v. Teamsters, 174 Cal. App. 2d 184, 344 P.2d 25 (1959) and cases from other states recognizing a public policy grounded on a breach of contract action or an external public policy tort, in support of its conclusion that recovery should be permitted for a wrongful dismissal on internal public policy tort grounds. *Id.* at 172–76, 610 P.2d at 1333–35, 164 Cal. Rptr. at 842–44. It did not, however, engage in further analysis of whether the precedent should be applied to the facts before it.

[92] *Id.* at 178, 610 P.2d at 1336–37, 164 Cal. Rptr. at 845–46.

[93] 84 N.J. 58, 417 A.2d 505 (1980).

[94] *Id.* at 73–74, 417 A.2d at 513.

[95] *Id.* at 72, 417 A.2d at 512.

[96] *Id.*

[97] *Id.*: "We hold that an employee has a cause of action for wrongful discharge when the discharge is contrary to a clear mandate of public policy. The sources of public policy include legislation; administrative rules, regulations or decisions; and judicial decisions."

[98] *Id.* In Kalman v. Grand Union Co., 183 N.J. Super. 153, 443 A.2d 728 (1982), the court held that a pharmacist might be able to maintain a cause of action in tort if he could show that he was fired for refusing to violate the state code of professional ethics for pharmacists.

[99] Pierce v. Ortho Pharmaceutical Corp., 84 N.J. at 75, 417 A.2d at 513.

§ 5.18   REFUSALS TO FOLLOW ORDERS   283

refuse to perform work that contravened only their personal morals.[1] As in *Geary v. United States Steel Corp.*,[2] the court was unwilling to strike the balance of interests against the employer on matters related to product design.[3]

The difference between the court's permitting recovery in *Tameny*[4] and denying recovery in *Pierce*[5] can be explained by consideration of the tension between the first and third elements of the public policy tort—the difference in the interests that were balanced.[6] Not only is the public policy opposing price fixing clearer, and older, than the public policy against the use of saccharin, but it is reasonable to conclude that the employer's legitimate interest in price fixing is weaker than its interests in determining product characteristics.

In *Delaney v. Taco Time International, Inc.*,[7] a jury verdict for the plaintiff was reinstated, and the court held that the plaintiff proved a public policy tort on evidence that he was fired for refusing to sign a false and arguably defamatory statement regarding a sexual proposition made to him by a subordinate employee. The absence of other remedies influenced the court to permit common law tort recovery. It distinguished an earlier Oregon case[8] in which the court refused to permit tort recovery for discharge of an employee for complaining about unsafe working conditions because the employee had an adequate administrative remedy.[9] The clarity element was met by the special place given common law defamation in the state constitution.[10] The jeopardy element was satisfied because threat of job loss could cause the employee to commit a tort that directly contravened public policy.[11]

The refusal of orders cases present sharp conflict between the clarity-of-policy and jeopardy elements of the public policy tort on the one hand, and the justification element on the other hand. Employers have a legitimate interest in having employees obey orders. Whether the public policy depends on employee refusal

---

[1] *Id.* at 75–76, 417 A.2d at 514: "The thrust of Dr. Pierce's complaint is not that saccharin is dangerous, but that it is controversial. . . ."

[2] 456 Pa. 171, 319 A.2d 174 (1974).

[3] Pierce v. Ortho Pharmaceutical Corp., 84 N.J. at 76, 417 A.2d at 514.

[4] Tameny v. Atlantic Richfield Co., 27 Cal. 3d. 167, 610 P.2d 1330, 164 Cal. Rptr. 839 (1980).

[5] Pierce v. Ortho Pharmaceutical Corp., 84 N.J. 58, 417 A.2d 505 (1980).

[6] While not citing § 870 of the Restatement, the *Pierce* court expressly recognized the need to balance different interests in acknowledging the public policy basis for a tort of wrongful dismissal. Restatement (Second) of Torts § 870 (1979); Pierce v. Ortho Pharmaceutical Corp., 84 N.J. at 71, 417 A.2d at 511: "In recognizing a cause of action to provide a remedy for employees who are wrongfully discharged, we must balance the interests of the employee, the employer and the public." In *Geary*, the interests being balanced were the interests of the employer in controlling his workforce, against the interests of the employee in job security. The same was true in *Tameny*, but the result was different because of weaker employer interests.

[7] 297 Or. 10, 681 P.2d 114 (1984).

[8] Walsh v. Consolidated Freightways, Inc., 278 Or. 347, 563 P.2d 1205 (1977).

[9] Delaney v. Taco Time Int'l, Inc., 297 Or. at 15, 681 P.2d at 117–18.

[10] *Id.* at 17, 681 P.2d at 118.

[11] *Id.*

to carry out certain orders is a question that deserves special scrutiny. If the evidence shows that the employee was explicitly ordered to commit a clearly illegal act, public policy requires that the employer interest in employee obedience give way.[12] But when the conduct involved has a more tenuous link with public policy, courts should be wary of permitting damages for employees who refuse to obey orders.

Some cases involve refusal of orders as well as other issues. In *Vosch v. Werner Continental, Inc.*,[13] the Third Circuit reversed the district court and found no cause of action under federal motor carrier safety regulations sufficient to justify reinstatement of a dismissed truck driver. The driver violated employer orders to be available for work, claiming that federal regulations entitled him to a rest period free from work calls.

Cloutier v. Great Atlantic & Pacific Tea Co.[14] can be considered a case involving specific statutory grant of employee rights,[15] or it can be considered a case involving employee noncompliance with employer orders. Cloutier was a grocery store manager fired after the store safe had been burglarized. The employer claimed that Cloutier neglected store security, violating employer policies. The court derived the public policy opposing his dismissal from the federal Occupational Safety and Health Act.[16] It reasoned that Cloutier's conduct furthered employee safety because he did not force those in charge of the store in his absence "to imperil themselves by making bank deposits".[17] In addition, the court found that A & P, by holding the plaintiff responsible for the store seven days per week, violated the spirit of a state statute requiring employers to give their employees a day off.[18] Cloutier arguably refused to obey orders when he did not ensure the bank deposits were made.

In these cases, the other issues make it easier for courts to sidestep the direct conflict between employer interests and public policy by manufacturing a direct employee right to engage in the conduct opposed by the employer, rather than characterizing the cases as involving a refusal to obey orders.

§ 5.19 Public Policy Torts Are More Than Civil Remedies for Statutory Violations

It is important to understand that the courts in the external and internal public policy cases discussed in §§ 5.10 through 5.18 are creating new torts rather than merely implying additional remedies for violations of particular statutes, as in the labor

---

[12] *See* Beasley v. Affiliated Hosp. Prods., 713 S.W.2d 557 (Mo. Ct. App. 1986) (recognizing cause of action for employee dismissed for opposing employer rigging of contest; genesis of public policy was statute aimed at protecting contest participants).

[13] 734 F.2d 149 (3d Cir. 1984).

[14] 121 N.H. 915, 436 A.2d 1140 (1981).

[15] *Cloutier* is analyzed as a case involving statutory employee rights in § 5.9.

[16] Cloutier v. Great Atl. & Pac. Tea Co., 121 N.H. at 923, 436 A.2d at 1145.

[17] *Id.*

[18] *Id.* at 923-24, 436 A.2d at 1145.

statute cases discussed in § 5.9. They are looking to statutes and to other materials to determine the direction of public policy, but they then are deciding for themselves what conduct should result in liability. The public policy tort approach was described well by the Oregon Supreme Court in *Burnette v. Walsh*:

> The establishment by courts of a civil cause of action based on a criminal or regulatory statute is not premised upon legislative intent to create such an action. . . . [T]he court should recognize that it is being asked to bring into existence a new type of tort liability on the basis of its own appraisal of the policy considerations involved.[19]

Subsequently, the Oregon Supreme Court expressly embraced a public policy tort category involving jeopardy to rights of society generally, contrasting it with another category involving express employee rights.[20] The public policy tort is to be distinguished from imposition of tort liability for violation of a statutory provision, envisioned in § 874A of the *Restatement (Second) of Torts*,[21] and a similar approach adopted by the United States Supreme Court.[22] The more limited approach summarized in these *Restatement* sections is discussed in § 2.26.

Traditionally, courts deciding whether to imply a private right of action concentrated on whether the plaintiff was a member of the class protected by a particular statute. If the plaintiff was, then the commission of the prohibited act or the omission to perform the duty established by the statute gave rise to tort liability, absent special factors militating against liability.[23] More recently, under § 874A of the *Second Restatement*[24] the analysis has expanded beyond the protected class inquiry to focus on legislative intent, and the Supreme Court's formula in *Cort v. Ash*.[25] When a private right of action is implied under a statute, it is limited to the class protected thereby and linked directly to the duties and rights created by a single statute.[26] For example, in the Railway Labor Act cases discussed in § 2.26, the courts determined that a private damages remedy should be implied to further the express statutory prohibition on employer interference with employee organization.[27]

---

[19] 284 Or. 705, 588 P.2d 1105 (1978).

[20] Delaney v. Taco Time Int'l, Inc., 297 Or. 10, 17, 681 P.2d 114, 118 (1984).

[21] Restatement (Second) of Torts § 874A (1979).

[22] *See* Cort v. Ash, 422 U.S. 66 (1975).

[23] Restatement of Torts § 286 comment e (1934).

[24] Restatement (Second) of Torts § 874A (1979).

[25] 422 U.S. 66 (1975).

[26] Restatement (Second) of Torts § 874A comment b (1979). Emphasis on legislative intent frequently results in finding tort remedy not to be appropriate, especially when the legislature creates other remedies. *See* Bruffett v. Warner Communications, Inc., 692 F.2d 910 (3d Cir. 1982), in which the Third Circuit refused to find a tort remedy under Pennsylvania law for a dismissal arguably violating the state statute prohibiting discrimination on the basis of handicap.

[27] For a holding that an employee who alleged his dismissal was in violation of the Sherman Antitrust Act could maintain an action for treble damages under the Act itself, not as a tort remedy, *see* Ostrofe v. H.S. Crocker Co. Inc., 670 F.2d 1378 (9th Cir. 1982), *vacated and remanded*, 460 U.S. 1007 (1983), *and* Shaw v. Russell Trucking Line Inc., 542 F. Supp. 776 (W.D. Pa.

The public policy tort analysis is different. The starting point for a public policy tort may be a legislative declaration of policy, but its reach is determined not by the legislature[28] but by judicial reasoning and perceptions of public policy.[29] Also, implied remedies under statutes generally are limited to the class protected by the statute; public policy torts protect employees for conduct which furthers policies that ultimately aim to protect other classes.[30]

The public policy tort approach is inherently more flexible than the statutory implication approach. Depending as it does on the court's assessment of public policy rather than legislative intent, the public policy tort permits the courts to expand the remedy to new classes of plaintiffs and to conduct beyond those addressed by a single statute.

In *Buethe v. Britt Airlines, Inc.*,[31] Circuit Judge Posner took too narrow a view. He interpreted Indiana public policy tort doctrine as providing a cause of action for whistleblowers only when a statute creates a right to "blow a particular whistle"—presumably to report a particular type of violation to a particular agency. The panel for which he wrote thus affirmed a district court dismissal of a diversity action brought by an airline copilot dismissed for refusing to fly an aircraft the copilot believed to violate FAA safety standards. The problem with the Posner formulation, permitting public policy tort recovery only when the statute manifesting the public policy grants a right implicitly or explicitly to employees, is that it narrows formulation of the public policy tort too much to accommodate the major cases.[32] For example, the courts are prepared to allow employees to recover in whistleblowing situations when the public policy protects the public against tainted food. In these circumstances, the statute grants a right in the employee only insofar as the employee is a member of the consuming public. Yet, employees dismissed for refusing to deliver tainted food or for reporting employers who produce tainted food can establish public policy tort liability. This is so not because the statute protects employees as a class, but because the protections of the statute would be jeopardized if employee conduct of the sort involved is chilled by the threat of dismissal.[33]

1982) (citing *Ostrofe*). *Contra* Callahan v. Scott Paper Co., 541 F. Supp. 550 (E.D. Pa. 1982); Perry v. Hartz Mountain Corp. 537 F. Supp. 1387 (S.D. Ind. 1982); Bichan v. Chemetron Corp., 681 F.2d 514 (7th Cir. 1982).

[28] This is because the public policy analysis requires a balancing of interests to determine if the employer's action was jusitified. See § 5.7. There is no logical reason why this analytical approach need be limited by statutory expressions.

[29] *See* Wandry v. Bull's Eye Credit Union, 129 Wis. 2d 37, 42 n.6, 384 N.W.2d 325 , 328 n.6 (1986) (public policy tort can be broader than statutory prohibition).

[30] *See* Beasley v. Affiliated Hosp. Prods., 713 S.W.2d 557 (Mo. Ct. App. 1986) (recognizing cause of action for employee dismissed for opposing employer rigging of contest, even though genesis of public policy was statute aimed at protecting contest participants).

[31] 787 F.2d 1194 (7th Cir. 1986).

[32] *See* Wandry v. Bull's Eye Credit Union, 129 Wis. 2d at 42 n.6, 384 N.W.2d at 328 n.6 (can have public policy tort even if statute does not expressly prohibit discharge).

[33] *See* Beasley v. Affiliated Hosp. Prods., 713 S.W.2d 557 (Mo. Ct. App. 1986) (employee fired for opposing employer rigging of contest has claim, although genesis of public policy was statute protecting contest participants).

Most courts are reluctant to permit public policy tort recovery, however, when the statute allegedly supplying the public policy provides administrative remedies.[34] This reluctance should be understood as relating to the jeopardy element of the public policy tort, rather than to the nature of the public policy involved, legislative intent, or to the class granted rights by the statute.

§ 5.20 Public Policy Tort Protection for Employees Covered by Collective Bargaining Agreements

When an employee covered by a collective bargaining agreement seeks recovery on a public policy tort theory, two problems are presented. The first relates to federal preemption.[35] The second relates to the scope of the public policy tort as a matter of common law. This section addresses the second problem. Some courts, while recognizing the public policy tort doctrine for at-will employees, have refused to extend it to employees covered by collective bargaining agreements.[36]

In *Midgett v. Sackett-Chicago, Inc.*,[37] the Supreme Court of Illinois held that an employee covered by a collectively bargained grievance and arbitration procedure may bring a public policy tort action for wrongful dismissal. The case involved a dismissal allegedly in retaliation for filing a workers' compensation claim, but the court's analysis extends broadly to public policy torts in general. The court rejected arguments that arbitration is an adequate avenue of relief for employees dismissed in violation of public policy, that exhaustion of contractual remedies should be required as a prerequisite to adjudication of a tort claim, and that

---

[34] See § **5.9**, citing numerous cases; Vosch v. Werner Continental, Inc., 734 F.2d 149 (3d Cir. 1984) (reversing district court and finding no cause of action under federal motor carrier safety regulations sufficient to justify reinstatement of dismissed truck driver). *Vosch* was treated by the Third Circuit as an implied-right-of-action case.

[35] Preemption is addressed in §§ **2.29** & **5.30**.

[36] *Compare* Lamb v. Briggs Mfg., 700 F.2d 1092, 1094–95 (7th Cir. 1983) (public policy tort not available under Illinois law for employee covered by collectively bargained good cause and arbitration provisions because rationale lacking) *and* Herring v. Prince Foods-Canning Div., 611 F. Supp. 177, 180 (D.N.J. 1985) (no public policy tort protection available under New Jersey law for employee covered by collectively bargained *just cause* protection), *and* Phillips v. Babcock & Wilcox, 349 Pa. Super. 351, 503 A.2d 36 (1986) (no public policy tort under Pennsylvania law for employee covered by collective agreement) *and* Smith v. Greyhound Lines, Inc., 614 F. Supp. 558, 560–61 (W.D. Pa. 1984) (no public policy tort under Pennsylvania law for employee covered by collective agreement) *and* Mouser v. Granite City Steel Div., 121 Ill. App. 3d 834, 838, 460 N.E.2d 115, 117 (1984) (rationale for public policy tort not present where arbitral remedy exists for unjust discharge) *with* Garibaldi v. Lucky Food Stores, Inc., 726 F.2d 1367 (9th Cir. 1984), *cert. denied,* 471 U.S. 1099 (1985) (state public policy action available despite adverse arbitration award) *and* Midgett v. Sackett-Chicago, Inc., 105 Ill. 2d 143, 473 N.E.2d 1280 (1984) (employee covered by collectively bargained grievance and arbitration procedure may bring public policy tort action for wrongful dismissal) *and* Phillips v. Babcock & Wilcox, 349 Pa. Super. 351, 355, 503 A.2d 36, 38 (1986) (Spaeth, J., dissenting). *See also* Elia v. Industrial Personnel Corp., 125 Ill. App. 3d 1026, 1029–30, 466 N.E.2d 1054, 1057–58 (1984) (suggesting that if public policy tort claim were raised and resolved in grievance process, separate public policy tort claim might be barred).

[37] 105 Ill. 2d 143, 473 N.E.2d 1280 (1984).

permitting common law relief would undermine the federal policy promoting arbitration. The issue of federal preemption was not considered by the supreme court because it had not been raised below.

§ 5.21 Prima Facie Tort: Liability Based on Intent to Harm, Regardless of Public Policy

The prima facie tort concept may permit an employee to recover for a dismissal even when the employee cannot satisfy the elements of the public policy tort. It is suggested earlier[38] in this chapter that § 870 of the *Restatement (Second) of Torts*[39] provides the concept for the public policy tort basis of recovery for wrongful dismissal. The underlying theory of intentional tort liability is labeled the prima facie tort in New York and a few other jurisdictions.[40] Prima facie tort originally referred to the broad concept embodied in § 870, but the prima facie label has come to be associated with the requirements that the actor be motivated by specific intent to cause harm (malice) and that the plaintiff prove special damages.[41] These restrictions have been criticized by commentators and by some courts.[42] Prima facie tort may be a species of tort different from the public policy concept in New York, Pennsylvania, and a few other jurisdictions.[43]

Pennsylvania law has developed the specific intent to harm as a facet of prima facie tort doctrine separate from the public policy tort, though recovery rarely

---

[38] See § **5.5**.

[39] Restatement (Second) of Torts § 870 (1979).

[40] *Id.* § 870 comment a (characterizing New York prima facie tort requirements as more rigid than § 870). South Carolina apparently recognizes a variant that its courts call "economic duress." *See* Troutman v. Facetglas, Inc., 281 S.C. 598, 603, 316 S.E.2d 424, 426–27 (1984) (affirming nonsuit because employee failed to show that breach-of-contract suit would provide inadequate remedy).

[41] *See* Forkosch, *An Analysis of the "Prima Facie Tort" Cause of Action*, 42 Cornell L.Q. 465, 475 (1957) (comparison of general doctrine with more restricted New York version). *Special damages,* as distinguished from *general damages,* are actual damages that must be pleaded and proved by the plaintiff. General damages can be presumed to result from the tort complained of. *See* Black's Law Dictionary 353–54 (5th ed. 1979).

[42] *See* Nees v. Hocks, 272 Or. 210, 213, 536 P.2d 512, 514 (1975) (permitting tort recovery for dismissal in retaliation for jury service; criticizing the New York approach of transforming the prima facie tort into a new category of tort with special restrictions); Brown, *The Rise and Threatened Demise of the Prima Facie Tort Principle*, 54 Nw. U.L. Rev. 563 (1959–60).

[43] In Chin v. American Tel. & Tel. Co., 96 Misc. 2d 1070, 410 N.Y.S.2d 737 (1978), the court distinguished between *prima facie tort* and *abusive discharge. Id.* at 1073–74, 410 N.Y.S. at 739–40. In Geary v. United States Steel Corp., 456 Pa. 171, 319 A.2d 174 (1974), the court seems to distinguish between the prima facie and public policy bases of recovery in its analysis, but makes use of neither label. Anselmo v. Manufacturers Life Ins. Co., 595 F. Supp. 541, 548–49 (W.D. Mo. 1984) (prima facie tort unavailable under Missouri law for termination of at-will employment).

has been allowed on proof of specific intent alone.[44] In *McNulty v. Borden, Inc.*,[45] the plaintiff alleged that he was dismissed for refusal to participate in an illegal price rebating scheme.[46] The United States District Court for the Eastern District of Pennsylvania, applying Pennsylvania law, denied a motion to dismiss.[47] Under *Geary v. United States Steel Corp.*,[48] the court held that the plaintiff's allegation of discharge because of his refusal to cooperate in the illegal pricing arrangement,

> *together with the allegation that the defendant made false statements to others which were designed maliciously to injure plaintiff's ability to obtain new employment,* if proved at trial, could support a conclusion by the trier of fact that defendant's discharge of plaintiff was motivated by a specific intent to cause harm to the plaintiff. (Emphasis added.)[49]

In *Geary,* the court credited Geary's argument that tort liability can be imposed based on the defendant's motive but concluded that the averments in his complaint did not amount to specific intent on the part of the company "to harm Geary or to achieve some other proscribed goal."[50] Specific intent, the court suggested, could vitiate any privilege the employer otherwise might have under the abuse of privilege concept.[51]

Tourville v. Inter-Ocean Insurance Co.[52] reads *Geary* as recognizing both a public policy tort and a separate tort cause of action based on a specific intent to harm.[53] The court discussed, rather inconclusively, how inference of intent to harm can be supported, given its conclusion that mere intent to terminate employment is not enough. In *Rossi v. Pennsylvania State University*[54] and *Yandl v. Ingersoll*

---

[44] A careful review of Pennsylvania cases supports this conclusion. *See* Perritt, *Employee Dismissal Law in Pennsylvania,* 55 Pa. Bar Q. 212 (1984); *see also* Brown, *The Rise and Threatened Demise of the Prima Facie Tort Principle,* 54 Nw. U.L. Rev. 563, 566 (1959–1960); Note, *The Prima Facie Tort Doctrine,* 52 Colum. L. Rev. 503, 509 (1952); Forkosch, *An Analysis of the "Prima Facie Tort" Cause of Action,* 42 Cornell L.Q. 465, 471 (1957).

[45] 474 F. Supp. 1111 (E.D. Pa. 1979). The *McNulty* court did not use the prima facie tort label, but seems to have focused on the need for a specific intent to cause harm—an element of the prima facie tort as it is applied in New York.

[46] *Id.* at 1113–14.

[47] *Id.* at 1120.

[48] 456 Pa. 171, 319 A.2d 174 (1974).

[49] McNulty v. Borden, Inc., 474 F. Supp. at 1118–19.

[50] Geary v. United States Steel Corp., 456 Pa. 171, 319 A.2d 174 (1974).

[51] *Id.* at 178, 319 A.2d at 177:
> Appellant . . . argues that a court should recognize the abuse of the privilege in a particular instance, and grant damages accordingly. To this extent, appellant's proffered analogy to cases involving the malicious abuse of recognized rights seem apt enough. The difficulty is that the averments of Geary's complaint do not add up to specific intent.

[52] ___Pa. Super. ___, 508 A.2d 1263 (1986).

[53] *Id.* at ___, 508 A.2d at 1265.

[54] 340 Pa. Super. 39, 55–56, 489 A.2d 828, 837 (1985).

Rand Co.,[55] the courts explicitly accepted the major premise that specific intent to harm might support the cause of action, while finding the pleadings or the facts inadequate to support recovery under the premise.

The reference to specific intent in these cases suggests that the scope of the prima facie tort might be broader than the public policy tort. The prima facie tort might permit recovery, without the plaintiff being required to prove that a public policy was offended by the dismissal, whenever the plaintiff could prove actual intent to harm the employee as the motive for the dismissal.[56]

The public policy tort theory is merely a specific application of the prima facie tort theory,[57] and there is no reason that it is the exclusive way of satisfying the requirements of § 870 of the *Restatement* in a dismissal case. The potentially broader scope of the prima facie tort approach may be difficult to realize, however. Should a dismissed employee not be able to show a strong public policy that would be undermined by permitting the employer to escape liability,[58] then the plaintiff must have evidence of a specific intent to harm the employee to avoid the balance being struck in the employer's favor. Such evidence is hard to come by.

In *Murphy v. American Home Products Corp.*,[59] the Court of Appeals affirmed dismissal of a prima facie tort count for failing to allege that the "discharge was without economic or social justification."[60] This language suggests that a plaintiff may be able to show *malice* merely by showing an absence of legitimate business justification for the employer's decision to terminate. Such an interpretation would, however, make the prima facie tort a theory permitting recovery for any dismissal not supported by just cause, a result obviously not favored by the *Murphy* court.[61] In *Dake v. Tuell*,[62] the Supreme Court of Missouri flatly rejected the prima facie tort as a vehicle for recovery by an at-will employee.

---

[55] 281 Pa. Super. 560, 579–80, 422 A.2d 611, 620–21 (1981).

[56] *See* Costello v. Shelter Mut. Ins. Co., 697 S.W.2d 236, 239 (Mo. Ct. App. 1985) (heated argument and dissatisfaction with activities in association not enough to show malice or actual intent to injure); Kumpf v. Steinhaus, 779 F.2d 1323 (7th Cir. 1985) (termination to satisfy greed of supervisor for larger share of commissions does not violate public policy).

[57] The public policy tort theory and the prima facie tort theory are merely different ways of expressing the interest-balancing approach suggested by the Restatement (Second) of Torts § 870 (1979), and discussed in §§ **5.5–5.7**.

[58] The approach to the public policy tort theory discussed at §§ **5.8–5.19** requires establishment of a clear public policy, rooted in a statute or another official statement of policy. Conceptually, there is no reason for this requirement under the prima facie tort theory, but the lack of an external public policy interest makes it more likely that the balance of interests will be struck in the employer's favor.

[59] 58 N.Y.2d 293, 448 N.E.2d 86, 461 N.Y.S.2d 232 (1983).

[60] *Id.* at 303–04, 448 N.E.2d at 90–91, 461 N.Y.S.2d at 236–37. The court also said that the prima facie tort theory should not be allowed to circumvent its holding that New York does not recognize the tort of wrongful discharge. *Id.*

[61] See §§ **1.13 & 5.2** regarding the relationship between the public policy tort and good cause.

[62] 687 S.W.2d 191, 193 (Mo. 1985).

§ 5.22 Intentional Interference with Contractual Relations

In appropriate circumstances, a dismissed employee may seek tort damages for intentional interference with contractual relations, typically when individual supervisors or other individuals are named as defendants. The principal problem with this tort in the wrongful dismissal context is that agents of the employer have a conditional privilege to cause termination of an employee's contract of employment.

This tort has been recognized for more than 100 years[63] and presently is treated in §§ 766 through 767 of the *Restatement (Second) of Torts*.[64]

In order to be liable, the defendant must have acted with knowledge of the contract[65] and for the primary purpose of interfering with it.[66] The comments in the *Restatement* make it clear that the essence of this basis for tort recovery is that the interference be *improper,* a term meant to embody the same interest-balancing process as is required under § 870.[67]

It seems reasonably clear that the action can be maintained for interference with an employment contract terminable at will, though the matter is not free from doubt.[68]

---

[63] *See* Restatement (Second) of Torts § 766 comment c (1979); *Tortious Interference with Contractual Relations in the Nineteenth Century: The Transformation of Property, Contract, and Tort,* 93 Harv. L. Rev. 1510 (1980).

[64] Section 766 deals with the general rule. Section 766A treats interference with another's performance of his own contract. Section 766B treats interference with prospective contractual relations. Section 767 addresses the factors to be considered in determining whether the interference was "improper."

[65] Restatement (Second) of Torts § 766 comment i (1979).

[66] *Id.* comment j.

[67] Introductory Note to Restatement (Second) of Torts, ch. 37 (1979). *See* Harman v. LaCrosse Tribune, 117 Wis. 2d 448, 344 N.W.2d 536 (1984) (newspaper's inducement of law firm representing it to dismiss lawyer who attacked paper in press release was not wrongful; lawyer-plaintiff violated duty of loyalty to client); Gordon v. Lancaster Osteopathic Hosp. Assoc., 340 Pa. Super. 253, 265, 489 A.2d 1364, 1370 (1985) (allegation of lack of justification enough for trial on intentional interference claim; letters from medical staff asking board to terminate privileges of pathologist). The plaintiff is required to plead impropriety. *See* Sharon Steel Corp. v. V.J.R. Co., 604 F. Supp. 420, 421 (W.D. Pa. 1985) (dismissal of counterclaim by dismissed employee for intentional interference for failure to plead "absence of privilege").

[68] *See* W. Prosser, *Handbook of the Law of Torts* § 129 at 932 (4th ed. 1971); 86 C.J.S. *Torts* § 44 at 966 nn. 18–21 (1954 & Supp. 1986); Restatement (Second) of Torts § 766 comment g (1979). *Compare* Wagenseller v. Scottsdale Memorial Hosp., 147 Ariz. 370, 386, 710 P.2d 1025, 1041 (1985) (permitting intentional interference claim though employment was at will) *and* Todd v. South Carolina Farm Bureau Mut. Ins. Co., 283 S.C. 155, 164, 321 S.E.2d 602, 607 (1984) (contract terminable at will is a contract upon which action for intentional interference may be brought), *later appeal,* 287 S.C. 190, 336 S.E.2d 472 (1985) *and* West Virginia Glass Specialty Co. v. Guice & Walshe, Inc., 170 Ga. App. 556, 317 S.E.2d 592 (1984) (even though employment relationship is at-will, action for third party interference may lie, though not proven)

A potentially insuperable difficulty for a plaintiff seeking damages for wrongful dismissal under this theory is in persuading a court that the theory can be utilized against a party to the contract which is being interfered with. The *Restatement* and the cases limit the theory to third party interference rather than including interference by the other party.[69] If the tort were not so limited it would be transformed into a breach of contract action with a motive element.

The historical context of this tort, and its widespread use in labor disputes, gives support to the idea that it will support recovery when a fellow employee has caused an employment relationship to be broken.[70] It is doubtful, however, whether the action can be maintained against an employer's agent (e.g., a supervisor) who acted within the scope of his employment.[71] This is because of doubt as to whether

---

and Troy v. Interfinancial, Inc., 171 Ga. App. 763, 320 S.E.2d 872 (1984) (jury award of $50,000 compensatory and $70,000 punitive damages, and $20,000 attorney's fees, for wrongful discharge on proof that superior had fired plaintiff for refusing to perjure himself in a deposition in another lawsuit; judgment n.o.v. for individual defendant reversed on claim for intentional interference with contract) *and* Hall v. Integon Life Ins. Co., 454 So. 2d 1338 (Ala. 1984) (no wrongful dismissal cause of action, but entitled to trial on intentional interference claim; matters not that employment was at will) *and* Kemper v. Worcester, 106 Ill. App. 3d 121, 435 N.E.2d 827 (1982) *and* La Rocco v. Bakwin, 108 Ill. App. 3d 723, 439 N.E.2d 537 (1982) *with* Kaminski v. United Parcel Serv., 120 A.D.2d 409, 501 N.Y.S.2d 871, 873 (1986) (no claim for intentional interference under New York law when employment contract was terminable at will) *and* Murray v. Bridgeport Hosp., 40 Conn. Supp. 56, 480 A.2d 610 (1984) (intentional interference count stricken because supervisors cannot interfere with employer's contract) *and* Pinsof v. Pinsof, 107 Ill. App. 3d 1031, 438 N.E.2d 525 (1982) (holding that in the absence of any written agreement as to lifetime employment, plaintiff could not maintain an action for tortious interference with contractual relations; employee/employer relationship was familial).

[69] Ross v. Life Ins. Co., 273 S.C. 764, 766, 259 S.E.2d 814, 815 (1979) (action will not lie against employer for dismissal); Geary v. United States Steel Corp., 456 Pa. 171, 177, 319 A.2d 174, 177 (1974) (limited to strangers to the relationship); Dryden v. Tri-Valley Growers, 65 Cal. App. 3d 990, 998, 135 Cal. Rptr. 720, 725–26 (1977) (can be maintained only against third party, not party to contract); *accord* Janmort Leasing Inc. v. Econo-Car Int'l., 475 F. Supp. 1282, 1292 (E.D.N.Y. 1979). *But see* Elbe v. Wausau Hosp. Center, 606 F. Supp. 1491, 1503 (W.D. Wis. 1985) (Wisconsin law permits intentional interference claim by employee against officers and directors of corporation). *Cf.* Welch v. Kennedy Piggly Wiggly Stores, Inc., 63 Bankr. 888 (W.D. Va. 1986) (dismissing claim of tortious interference with employment contract, but refusing to dismiss tortious interference claim for employer conspiracy to obtain adverse polygraph results in order to frustrate pursuit of unemployment compensation benefits).

[70] *See* Introductory note to Restatement (Second) of Torts, ch. 37 (1979); *Tortious Interference with Contractual Relations in the Nineteenth Century: The Transformation of Property, Contract, and Tort,* 93 Harv. L. Rev. 1510 (1980). A secondary employer who promotes the dismissal of a union member by a primary employer may also be liable. *See* Shaw v. Russell Trucking Line, Inc., 542 F. Supp. 776 (W.D. Pa. 1982).

[71] Raab v. Keystone Ins. Co, 271 Pa. Super. 185, 412 A.2d 638 (1979); *but see* dissenting opinion in *id.* at 191, 412 A.2d at 641 (Spaeth, J., dissenting). Weaver v. Gross, 605 F. Supp. 210, 216 (D.D.C. 1985) (no intentional interference action against agent of employer); Fletcher v. Wesley Medical Center, 585 F. Supp. 1260, 1262 (D. Kan. 1984) (no intentional interference action against employer's agent); Todd v. South Carolina Farm Bureau Mut. Ins. Co., 283 S.C. 155, 164, 321 S.E.2d 602, 607 (1984) *cert. granted,* 285 S.C. 84, 328 S.E.2d 479 (1985) ("settled

an agent (e.g., a supervisor) acting within the scope of his duties is considered a third party or is the employer, and thus immune from suit.[72]

Even if an employer agent is considered to be a third party, the agent may be privileged to induce termination.[73] Unlike defamation and other intentional torts, the tort of intentional interference with contractual relations has not developed definite rules as to the existence of a privilege.[74] The existence of a privilege depends on whether the interference is improper under the circumstances;[75] that is, whether the conduct should be permitted despite its harmful effect. In other words, the privilege abuse analysis is the same as the analysis of the impropriety element in testing whether the plaintiff has made out a prima facie case. If the evidence shows that the defendant's conduct is determined to be *improper* within the meaning of § 767, it cannot show that a privilege existed. Conversely, if the interference was privileged, the plaintiff cannot establish an element of the tort.

The *Restatement* has developed a number of factors a court may consider in determining impropriety:

1. The nature of the actor's conduct
2. The actor's motive
3. The interests of the other with which the actor's conduct interferes
4. Social and contractual interests

---

beyond dispute'' that action for intentional interference will not lie against party to contract), *verdict for plaintiff reinstated,* 287 S.C. 190, 336 S.E.2d 472 (1985).

[72] Raab v. Keystone Ins. Co., 271 Pa. Super. 185, 412 A.2d 638 (1979); *but see* dissenting opinion in *id.* at 191, 412 A.2d at 641 (Spaeth, J., dissenting); *see also* Wells v. Thomas, 569 F. Supp. 426 (E.D. Pa. 1983) (managerial employees acting in their official capacities were not third parties); DeHorney v. Bank of Am., 777 F.2d 440, 446 (9th Cir. 1985) (privilege shielding corporate agent from liability for inducing corporation to terminate employment contract not abused by honest though erroneous report of employee theft), *withdrawn & rehearing stayed,* 784 F.2d 339 (9th Cir. 1986); Kumpf v. Steinhaus, 779 F.2d 1323 (7th Cir. 1985) (privilege of corporate agents to interfere with corporate employment contract may be lost by personal motivation, hypothetically to punish employee for refusal to marry daughter, but not for "greed" mixed with corporate motivations, discussing Wisconsin law in terms of whether extraneous motive must be exclusive or merely present); Hogan v. Forsyth Country Club Co., 79 N.C. App. 483, 340 S.E.2d 116 (1986) (suggesting plaintiff should have pleaded intentional interference with employment contract against coemployee who made sexual advances, culminating in plaintiff's dismissal), *review denied,* 317 N.C. 334, 346 S.E.2d 140 (1986).

[73] While justification is usually treated as a matter of defense, some courts may treat the tort of malicious interference as requiring the plaintiff to show interference without justification. In this event, a plaintiff is well advised to include a lack of justification on the defendant's part in his pleading. Otherwise, the plaintiff's complaint may not withstand a motion to dismiss for failure to state a claim. *See* Restatement (Second) of Torts § 767, comment a (1979). *See also* Sharon Steel Corp. v. V.J.R. Co., 604 F. Supp. 420 (W.D. Pa. 1985) (defendant's responsibility to plead and prove absence of privilege in intentional interference with contract counterclaim).

[74] *See* Restatement (Second) of Torts § 767 comment b (1979).

[75] *Accord* Wagenseller v. Scottsdale Memorial Hosp., 147 Ariz. 370, 387, 710 P.2d 1025, 1043 (1985) (analysis should be in terms of impropriety rather than of privilege and abuse; reversing grant of summary judgment for supervisor on intentional interference claim).

5. The interests sought to be advanced by the actor
6. The relations between the parties.[76]

In the case of an agent, it is argued that the privilege should be conditioned upon the agent's having acted to protect his principal's welfare, thus imposing liability where such purpose was absent.[77] It is in this situation that the interests sought to be advanced by the actor become relevant.

The factor most relevant to the employment situation is the relations between the parties. For example, a coemployee or agent may be privileged if he was in a position which required and permitted him to make evaluations and judgments about fellow employees.[78] Thus, there is a privilege to give advice to withdraw or alter a contractual relationship when that advice is requested or the defendant is in a position to justify his advice.[79] The boundary of this privilege is arguably exceeded when advice is volunteered, improper means are used,[80] or an improper motive is operative.[81]

What this all means is the following: If an agent is legally indistinguishable from the employer, then no liability can exist for intentional interference with a contract. One cannot interfere with one's own contract. In contrast, if the agent is a legally separate person, whether the agent can be liable for interfering with the employer's contract with another employee depends on the agent's motive in interfering. If the motive was to promote the employer's legitimate interests, the interference was not improper and therefore not a tort. In other words, the interference was privileged.

---

[76] Restatement (Second) of Torts § 767 (1979).

[77] Note, *Torts—Agent's Liability to Third Party for Inducing Breach of Contract by Principal,* 89 U. Pa. L. Rev. 250 (1940); Prosser argues that "an impersonal or disinterested motive of a laudable character may protect the defendant in his interference." W. Prosser & P. Keeton, Prosser and Keeton on Torts § 129 at 985 (5th ed. 1984); *see* Wampler v. Palmerton, 250 Or. 65, 439 P.2d 601 (1968) ("it is obvious that if the action or advice is to serve other interests than those of the corporation there can be no immunity because it is not rendered for the purpose which gives birth to the immunity.")

[78] *See* Sharon Steel Corp. v. V.J.R. Co., 604 F. Supp. 420 (W.D. Pa. 1985) (privilege when officer of employer in a position to make evaluations); Wells v. Thomas, 569 F. Supp. 426 (E.D. Pa. 1983) (defendants, as supervisors of plaintiff, were privileged to evaluate performance, discuss plaintiff's position among themselves, and pass their evaluation on to their supervisors).

[79] *See* W. Prosser & P. Keeton, Prosser and Keeton on Torts § 129 at 985 (5th ed. 1984).

[80] *See* Straube v. Larson, 287 Or. 357, 600 P.2d 371 (1979) (privilege does not extend when employee makes alleged misstatements of fact); *but see* DeHorney v. Bank of America, 777 F.2d 440, 446 (9th Cir. 1985), *withdrawn pending decision in* Foley v. Interactive Data Corp., 174 Cal. App. 3d 282, 219 Cal. Rptr. 866 (1985), *review granted,* ___ Cal. 3d ___, 712 P.2d 891, 222 Cal. Rptr. 740 (1986) (privilege shielding corporate agent from liability for inducing corporation to terminate employment contract not abused by honest though erroneous report of employee theft).

[81] *See* Kumpf v. Steinhaus, 779 F.2d 1323 (7th Cir. 1985) (privilege of corporate agents to interfere with corporate employment contract may be lost by personal motivation, hypothetically to punish employee for refusal to marry daughter, but not for "greed" mixed with corporate motivations, discussing Wisconsin law in terms of whether extraneous motive must be exclusive or merely present); Hogan v. Forsyth Country Club Co., 79 N.C. App. 483, 340 S.E.2d 116 (1986)

§ 5.23 Intentional Infliction of Emotional Distress

The tort of intentional infliction of emotional distress[82] may permit employee recovery. The requirements of the tort are not satisfied in most dismissal cases, but could be met in the extraordinary case in which the employer's conduct was outrageous and the employee suffered unusual emotional distress as a result.[83]

Liability under this theory is discussed in §§ 46 and 47 of the *Restatement (Second) of Torts*. In addition to causation, § 46 requires the existence of three elements in order for the plaintiff to make out a prima facie case. First, the defendant's conduct must be extreme and outrageous.[84] Second, the defendant must act with the intent to cause emotional distress or with substantial certainty that distress will result from the conduct.[85] Third, severe emotional distress must result from the defendant's conduct.[86]

When employees seek to recover for their dismissals on this theory,[87] the plaintiff usually has difficulty in establishing that the employer's conduct was sufficiently "extreme and outrageous" to satisfy that element.[88] For example, in

---

(suggesting plaintiff should have pleaded intentional interference with employment contract against coemployee who made sexual advances, culminating in plaintiff's dismissal), *review denied,* 317 N.C. 334, 346 S.E.2d 141 (1986).

[82] *See* W. Prosser, *Handbook of the Law of Torts* § 12 (1971); 74 Am. Jur. 2d *Torts* § 32 (1974). As to application of the concept to employer/employee disputes, *see* Annotation, 86 A.L.R.3d 454 (1978). The differences between this tort and wrongful discharge are summarized in Harless v. First Nat'l Bank, 289 S.E.2d 692, 705 (W. Va. 1982).

[83] *But see* Carrillo v. Illinois Bell Tel. Co., 538 F. Supp. 793 (N.D. Ill. 1982) (dismissing intentional infliction of emotional distress claim, noting that the state did not recognize such a tort in an employment-at-will situation); Murphy v. American Home Prods. Corp., 58 N.Y.2d 293, 303, 448 N.E.2d 86, 90, 461 N.Y.S.2d 232, 236 (1983) (denying recovery on emotional distress claim, not only because the employer's action was not sufficiently outrageous, but also because a plaintiff should "not be allowed to . . . subvert the traditional at-will contract rule").

[84] Restatement (Second) of Torts § 46 comment d (1965). Todd v. South Carolina Farm Bureau Mut. Ins. Co., 283 S.C. 155, 167, 321 S.E.2d 602, 610-12 (1984), *cert. granted,* 328 S.E.2d 479 (1985) (judge, not jury, decides in first instance whether outrageousness element is satisfied; fabricating adverse information about employee and forcing to take stress evaluation test not outrageous), *verdict for plaintiff reinstated,* 287 S.C. 190, 336 S.E.2d 472 (1985).

[85] Restatement (Second) of Torts § 46 comment i (1965). Recklessness also satisfies the fault requirement. *Id.*

[86] *Id.* § 46 comment j. For a case in which a discharged employee failed to state a claim for this tort because his distress was no more than typical of other discharged employees, *see* Eklund v. Vincent Brass & Aluminum Co., 351 N.W.2d 371, 379 (Minn. Ct. App. 1984).

[87] *See generally,* Annotation, 86 A.L.R.3d 454 (1978). *See* Brinks Inc. v. City of New York, 533 F. Supp. 1123, 1125 (S.D.N.Y. 1982) (allegations of demotion, harassment and verbal abuse insufficient to withstand a motion for summary judgment). *See also* Gates v. Life of Montana Ins. Co., 196 Mont. 178, 638 P.2d 1063 (1982), *later app.,* 668 P.2d 213 (1983); Murray v. Bridgeport Hosp., 40 Conn. Supp. 56, 480 A.2d 610 (1984) (wrongful dismissal counts stricken but emotional distress count, based on failure to evaluate, retained); Perry v. Hartz Mountain Corp., 537 F. Supp. 1387 (S.D. Ind. 1982).

[88] *See* Patton v. J.C. Penney Co., 301 Or. 117, 719 P.2d 854 (1986) (dismissal of employee for dating coworker did not exceed bounds of socially acceptable conduct); Hogan v. Forsyth Country

American Road Service Co. v. Inmon,[89] the Alabama Supreme Court held that it was error for the trial court to deny the defendant's motion for a directed verdict in an action by a former employee for intentional infliction of emotional distress.[90] Although an employer has "no license to treat an employee in an extreme and outrageous manner,"[91] the court held that showing that the employer's investigation of the employee was disorganized and humiliating was not enough to show outrageousness within the requirement of § 46.[92] In addition, the court found that the plaintiff failed to show that the employer had intended to inflict emotional distress.[93]

In contrast, the Arkansas Supreme Court, in *M.B.M. Co. v. Counce,*[94] while denying recovery on a public policy wrongful dismissal theory,[95] held that summary judgment for the defendant was improper on an intentional infliction of emotional distress theory.[96] Applying § 46 of the *Restatement,*[97] the court reasoned that a claim that the employee submitted to a polygraph examination after her dismissal and that the employer refused to pay her accrued wages created a question of fact for the jury on the question of outrageousness.[98] Similarly, in *Contreras v. Crown Corp.,*[99] the Washington Supreme Court held that racial slurs and accusations of theft were within the parameters of the outrageousness element of § 46.[1]

Club Co., 79 N.C. App. 483, 340 S.E.2d 116, 121–23 (1986) (sexual advances, physical touching, and threat with knife on refusal of advances sufficiently outrageous to present jury question; shouting, throwing menus are not), *review denied,* 317 N.C. 334, 346 S.E.2d 141 (1986); Haldeman v. Total Petroleum, Inc., 376 N.W.2d 98 (Iowa 1985) (reversing jury verdict for dismissed employee on emotional distress count; conduct insufficiently outrageous); Gibson v. Hummel, 688 S.W.2d 4, 8 (Mo. Ct. App. 1985) (requiring employee to submit to polygraph test after serious inventory shortages not sufficiently outrageous).

[89] 394 So. 2d 361 (Ala. 1980).

[90] *Id.* at 365.

[91] *Id.* at 364.

[92] *Id.* at 368. *See also* Corder v. Champion Road Mach. Int'l, 283 S.C. 520, 523, 324 S.E.2d 79, 80 (1984) (threat to fire for filing workers' compensation claims not sufficiently outrageous); Fletcher v. Wesley Medical Center, 585 F. Supp. 1260, 1262 (D. Kan. 1984) (age discrimination does not satisfy outrage element under Kansas law); Hurst v. Farmer, 40 Wash. App. 116, 118, 697 P.2d 280, 282 (1985) (telling employee he was being dismissed for sexual harassment not sufficiently outrageous).

[93] American Road Serv. Co. v. Inmon, 394 So. 2d at 367.

[94] 268 Ark. 269, 596 S.W.2d 681 (1980).

[95] *Id.* at 279, 596 S.W.2d 683–84. The court suggested that it would recognize the public policy theory, but denied recovery because the plaintiff could not establish what public policy had been violated by her dismissal.

[96] *Id.* at 280, 596 S.W.2d at 687–88.

[97] *Id.,* 596 S.W.2d at 687.

[98] *Id.* at 281, 596 S.W.2d at 688; *but see* Harris v. Arkansas Book Co., 287 Ark., 353, 356, 700 S.W.2d 41, 43 (1985) (claim of intentional infliction of emotional distress cannot be predicted on dismissal itself).

[99] 88 Wash. 2d 735, 565 P.2d 1173 (1977).

[1] *Id.* at 741–42, 565 P.2d at 1177. *See also* Howard Univ. v. Best, 117 L.R.R.M. 3241 (D.C. 1984) (sexual harassment can give rise to jury question of whether intentional infliction of emotional

A paradigm of a successful emotional distress cause of action in the employment context is *Agis v. Howard Johnson Co.*[2] The Massachusetts Supreme Judicial Court reversed the trial court and permitted the plaintiff to proceed to trial on an action for the intentional infliction of emotional distress. She was the first employee to be discharged as part of a plan to fire all waitresses in alphabetical order until the person responsible for certain thefts was discovered.[3]

The severity-of-distress element also is difficult for a plaintiff to satisfy.[4] In some states a claim for intentional infliction of emotional distress for employer conduct is precluded by the workers' compensation laws.[5]

§ 5.24 Fraudulent Misrepresentation (Deceit)

A dismissed employee may be able to claim fraudulent misrepresentation, sometimes referred to as *deceit* or *fraud*.[6] In jurisdictions still honoring a strong form of the Employment-at-Will Rule, an employee may be able to recover on a fraudulent misrepresentation theory even though recovery is unlikely on a public policy tort or implied-in-fact contract theory.[7]

This also is an attractive theory for dismissed employees even in jurisdictions recognizing the public policy tort and the implied-in-fact contract theories because it presents a dilemma for the employer. The more the employer seeks to avoid

---

distress occurred, but supervisor's interference with performance of duties insufficiently outrageous to create jury question); Caproom v. G.D. Searle Co., ___ F. Supp. ___, No. 84-0640-Civ-Marcus (S.D. Fla, filed Nov. 21, 1986) (ridiculing complaints about employer practices endangering children; and threatening to "disappear" employee permitted jury to find outrageous conduct); Moffett v. Gene B. Glick Co., 604 F. Supp. 229, 237 (N.D. Ind. 1984) (threats of physical violence on account of interracial relationship states claim for intentional infliction of emotional distress).

[2] 371 Mass. 140, 355 N.E.2d 315 (1976).

[3] *Id.* at 146–47, 355 N.E.2d at 320.

[4] *See* Polk v. Yellow Freight Sys., 801 F.2d 190, 196 (6th Cir. 1986) (crying and intensified religious conviction insufficient to satisfy Restatement severity of distress standard); Moniodis v. Cook, 64 Md. App. 1, 15–16, 494 A.2d 212, 219–220 (1985) (explaining why one plaintiff but not others met severity-of-distress requirement); Morris v. Hartford Courant Co., 200 Conn. 676, 513 A.2d 66 (1986) (failure to allege risk of illness or bodily harm defeats claim for intentional infliction of emotional distress).

[5] *See, e.g.,* Bertrand v. Quincy Mkt. Cold Storage & Warehouse Co., 728 F.2d 568, 572 (1st Cir. 1984) (applying Massachusetts law).

[6] *But see* Shipper v. Avon Prods., Inc., 605 F. Supp. 701, 706 (S.D.N.Y. 1985) (*Murphy*, by rejecting public policy tort, bars state claims for fraudulent misrepresentation, breach of contract).

[7] *See* Hall v. Integon Life Ins. Co., 454 So. 2d 1338 (Ala. 1984) (no wrongful dismissal cause of action, but entitled to trial on fraudulent misrepresentation claim based on statements that plaintiff would not be terminated except for gross misconduct—even though written provisions reserved right to terminate at will); Moore v. General Motors Corp., 739 F.2d 311 (8th Cir. 1984) (federal law preempts state law claim for fraud based on employer's promise of a job).

liability on an implied-in-fact contract theory,[8] the greater the likelihood that it admits facts sufficient to establish fraudulent misrepresentation.

The elements of this tort are set forth in § 525 of the *Restatement (Second) of Torts*:

> One who (1) fraudulently makes (2) a misrepresentation of fact, opinion, intention or law (3) for the purpose of inducing another to act or to refrain from action in reliance upon it, is subject to liability to the other in deceit for pecuniary loss caused to him by his (4) justifiable reliance upon the misrepresentation.[9]

Application of these principles is illustrated by a 1968 California case[10] in which the plaintiff, owner of a jewelry store, was induced by promises of a weekly paycheck and a yearly bonus to close his shop and go to work for another jewelry store owner. The plaintiff was discharged after two weeks. Reasoning that because the employment was terminable at will the plaintiff could not have been injured, the trial court dismissed the plaintiff's suit. Holding that the pleadings stated a cause of action sounding in fraud,[11] the appellate court reversed.

This theory of recovery could be asserted by plaintiffs in cases involving employee handbooks containing promises of employment tenure.[12] In the face of an employer's contention that a handbook is not part of an employment contract,[13] the plaintiff-employee could claim fraudulent misrepresentation since the employer represented that the policies set forth in the handbook would be followed. The plaintiff would have to show that the defendant knew that terminations would not be carried out pursuant to the handbook.[14] The employee also must show that the employer intended to induce the employee to enter employment when the representation was made[15] and that the employee relied on the representation in accepting employment.[16]

---

[8] See **ch. 4**.

[9] Restatement (Second) of Torts § 525 (1977). *See* Stancil v. Mergenthaler Linotype Co., 589 F. Supp. 78, 85 (D. Haw. 1984) (testimony of plaintiff that he was not misled by assurances of employment security defeats fraudulent misrepresentation claim).

[10] Bondi v. Jewels by Edwar, Ltd., 267 Cal. App. 2d 672, 73 Cal. Rptr. 494 (1968).

[11] The court stated that the cause of action was predicated upon a promise made without any intention of performance. It gauged the complaint as adequately pleading the requisite elements of (1) a promise, (2) lack of intent to perform, (3) intent to induce, (4) justifiable reliance by plaintiff, (5) nonperformance, and (6) injury to plaintiff. *Id.* at 677, 73 Cal. Rptr. at 498.

[12] See **§ 4.8**.

[13] *See, e.g.,* Toussaint v. Blue Cross & Blue Shield, 408 Mich. 579, 292 N.W.2d 880 (1980) (handbook part of employment contract); Gates v. Life of Montana Ins. Co., 196 Mont. 178, 638 P.2d 1063 (1982), *later app.,* 668 P.2d 213 (1983) (handbook distributed after employment began not part of contract). *But see* White v. I.T.T., 718 F.2d 994 (11th Cir. 1983) (no fraud claim under law if underlying promise in handbook is unenforceable).

[14] *See* Restatement (Second) of Torts § 526 (1976) for a detailed discussion of the state of mind required.

[15] *See* Broussard v. C.A.C.I., Inc., 780 F.2d 162 (1st Cir. 1986) (no claim of fraudulent concealment under Maine law for general promises of employment security accompanied by policy to permit supervisors to dismiss for any reason).

§ 5.24 FRAUDULENT MISREPRESENTATION

Plaintiff must show that reliance was reasonable,[17] and that a pecuniary loss was suffered when the employer failed to perform as represented.[18]

In *Mueller v. Union Pacific Railroad*,[19] the plaintiff claimed that the employer expressly promised him that there would be no retaliation if he disclosed misconduct by other employees. The court held that he adequately pleaded a fraud claim when he subsequently was dismissed in violation of the representation. In *Brooks v. TWA*,[20] the court denied the employer's motion for summary judgment on a fraud count, reasoning that the employee might be able to prove intent to deceive and reasonable reliance.

In *Shelby v. Zayre Corp.*,[21] a terminated employee sought to escape the effect of an exculpatory clause in an employment application by pursuing a claim for fraudulent misrepresentation. The employment application stipulated that, "I agree . . . my employment and compensation can be terminated, with or without cause, and with or without notice, at any time. . . . I understand that no . . . representative of your company has any authority to enter into any other agreement with me . . . ."[22] The employee claimed that the assistant manager who hired her had promised that she would have permanent employment, knowing that the representation of permanent employment was false, and that she had quit her previous job in reliance on that representation. The Supreme Court of Alabama affirmed judgment for the employer, finding that any reliance on the supervisor's statement was unreasonable, since the plaintiff admitted reading and understanding the quoted provision of the employment application.[23] By negative implication, the court's analysis supports recovery for fraudulent misrepresentation in a case in which reliance on such representations was reasonable.

In *Maley v. John Hancock Mutual Life Insurance Co.*,[24] the district court, applying Pennsylvania law, found that the plaintiff failed to sustain a fraudulent misrepresentation claim as a matter of law. The plaintiff claimed that he was induced to relinquish his employment by employer representations that he would qualify for disability benefits. The court found that the employer did not promise that

---

[16] *See id.* The reliance element of misrepresentation should be satisfied by reliance sufficient to satisfy the consideration requirement in a breach of contract suit. See § **4.12–4.18**. *See* Brooks v. Trans World Airlines, 574 F. Supp. 805, 114 L.R.R.M. 3136 (D. Colo. 1983) (factual question regarding reliance); Moffett v. Gene B. Glick Co., 604 F. supp. 229, 238 (N.D. Ind. 1984) (no fraudulent misrepresentation claim for giving employee incorrect reasons for her dismissal—no detrimental reliance); Collins v. M.B.P.X.L. Corp., 9 Kan. App. 2d 363, 679 P.2d 746, 752 (1984) (fraud claim fails for lack of detrimental reliance).

[17] *See* Restatement (Second) of Torts § 537 (1976).

[18] *See id.* §§ 546, 548A.

[19] 220 Neb. 742, 753–54, 371 N.W.2d 732, 740 (1985).

[20] 574 F. Supp. 805 (D. Colo. 1983).

[21] 474 So. 2d 1069 (Ala. 1985).

[22] *Id.* at 1070.

[23] *Id.* at 1071.

[24] 609 F. Supp. 621, 625 (E.D. Pa. 1985).

disability benefits would be paid, and that, in any event, there was no intent to defraud the plaintiff.[25]

It is important to note that, in some jurisdictions, no actionable wrong occurs when the representation is a promise to act in the future.[26] Generally, this tort requires misrepresentations as to current or past facts, but an exception to this rule applies when the promise is made with a present intent not to perform.[27]

In *Briggs v. Mid-State Oil Co.*,[28] employees terminated after a merger brought an action premised on misrepresentation to recover severance pay. The employees claimed that the employer falsely promised that severance pay would be paid to employees dismissed after the merger and that they had relied to their detriment on the promise. The trial court entered summary judgment for the defendant. The appellate court affirmed, based on the plaintiffs' failure to allege, or to adduce evidence during discovery, that they had forborne to look for, or to accept, other employment in reliance on the employer's representations. This failure, the court found, defeated the reasonable reliance element of misrepresentation.[29]

§ 5.25 Defamation

A dismissed employee may be able to recover damages for defamation. Such an action would not be based on the dismissal itself but on acts leading to the dismissal or following it. Section 558 of the *Restatement (Second) of Torts* sets forth the following elements:

To create liability for defamation there must be:
(a) a false and defamatory statement concerning another;
(b) an unprivileged publication to a third party;
(c) fault amounting at least to negligence on the part of the publisher; and

---

[25] *Id.*

[26] *See generally* Annotation, 24 A.L.R.3d 1412 (1969 & Supp. 1983); 37 Am. Jur. 2d, *Fraud and Deceit* §§ 45, 72 (1968 & Supp. 1983).

[27] The jurisdictions refusing to recognize the exception hold that the unfulfilled promise is a mere unexecuted intention. 37 Am. Jur. 2d, *Fraud and Deceit* § 72 (1968). *See* Restatement (Second) of Torts § 544 (1976) (statement of intention). *See also* 5 Am. Jur. Proof of Facts 2d 727, *Promissory Fraud* (1975 & Supp. 1983). *See also* Cannon v. Geneva Wheel & Stamping Corp., 172 Ga. App. 20, 322 S.E.2d 69, 70 (1984) (fraud cannot be based on unenforceable promise of employment security); Jacobs v. Georgia-Pacific Corp., 172 Ga. App. 319, 323 S.E.2d 238 (1984) (same); Price v. Mercury Supply Co., 682 S.W.2d 924, 934 (Tenn. Ct. App. 1984) (same).

[28] ___ N.C. App. ___, 280 S.E.2d 501 (1981).

[29] *Id.* at 504–05. *See also* Crossman v. Trans World Airlines, 777 F.2d 1271, 1276 (7th Cir. 1985) (reversing denial of judgment n.o.v. for employer on fraudulent misrepresentation claim; no evidence of detrimental reliance on employer representation).

§ 5.25   DEFAMATION   301

(d) either actionability of the statement irrespective of special harm or the existence of special harm caused by the publication.[30]

Obviously the dismissed employee must show that a false and *defamatory* statement was made for a defamation action to succeed. For the purposes of this element "[a] communication is defamatory if it tends so to harm the reputation of another as to lower him in the estimation of the community or to deter third persons from associating or dealing with him."[31]

In addition to a defamatory statement, the plaintiff also must show *fault* by the defendant. Liability may be imposed only if the publisher either knew the statement was false and defamed the plaintiff, acted in reckless disregard of whether the statement was false and whether it defamed the plaintiff, or acted negligently in failing to ascertain truth or falsity and defamatory tendency.[32] This limitation on liability results from the First Amendment of the United States Constitution.[33] The common law generally ignored intent or other fault and concentrated on whether the communication was in fact false and tended to injure the plaintiff's reputation.[34]

Assuming the existence of a false statement and the requisite fault with respect to falsity, the crucial issue in wrongful dismissal/defamation cases involve whether an "unprivileged publication to a third party,"[35] and fault with respect to publication, occurred. The common law historically required proof of fault, amounting at least to negligence, with respect to publication.[36] Though some differences remain

---

[30] Restatement (Second) of Torts § 558 (1977).

[31] *Id.* § 559; Keddie v. Pennsylvania State Univ., 412 F. Supp. 1264 (M.D. Pa. 1976) (letters relating to denial of tenure sent within university administration and to advisors did not tend to lower estimation of plaintiff; also found privileged). Gordon v. Lancaster Osteopathic Hosp. Ass'n, 340 Pa. Super. 253, 262, 489 A.2d 1364, 1368–69 (1985) (letter of no confidence not defamatory).

[32] Restatement (Second) of Torts § 580B (1977). This section applies both to private parties and to public persons, when the statement about the public person deals with a purely private part of life.

[33] *Id.* § 580B comment c. The Constitution has been held to restrict even more severely liability for statements about public officials, candidates for office, and public figures. *See id.* § 580A comment a, discussing New York Times Co. v. Sullivan, 376 U.S. 254 (1964), in which the Court held that liability could be imposed only when the plaintiff could show that the publisher knew the statement was false and it defamed the plaintiff, or that the publisher acted in reckless disregard of these matters. *See* Philadelphia Newspapers, Inc. v. Hepps, ___ U.S. ___, 106 S. Ct. 1558 (1986) (common law rule that defendant bears burden of proving truth unconstitutional in an action by a private figure against a media defendant on a matter of public concern). (5–4 decision; Burger, C.J., Stevens, White, Rehnquist, J.J. dissenting); Anderson v. Liberty Lobby, Inc., ___ U.S. ___, 106 S. Ct. 2505 (1986) (plaintiff must offer affirmative evidence, under *clear and convincing* standard, to withstand motion for summary judgment).

[34] Restatement (Second) of Torts § 580B comment b (1977).

[35] *Id.* § 558(b). *See* Perry v. Hartz Mountain Corp., 537 F. Supp. 1387 (S.D. Ind. 1982) (plaintiff failed to allege time and place of defamatory statement and therefore failed to state a claim for defamation) *and* Williams v. Delta Haven, Inc., 416 So. 2d 637 (La. Ct. App. 1982) (failure to allege publication of defamatory remarks with malice failed to state a claim).

[36] *See* Restatement (Second) of Torts § 580B comment b (1977).

in the legal standards to be applied to written, as opposed to oral, communication, these differences are not likely to be important within the context of wrongful dismissal.

Conceptually, communication of a defamatory statement to one person suffices for the publication requirement.[37] Some case law, however, indicates that communication from one person to another within the same business enterprise will not suffice for publication.[38] A significant trend is emerging that permits the publication requirement to be satisfied by showing that an employer issued a communication to the plaintiff, knowing that the plaintiff would have to publish it in order to get another job.[39]

The most difficult question in employment termination defamation involves the applicability of a *privilege*. There is a well-recognized conditional privilege for an employer to communicate information about its employees.[40] The privilege can be lost by communicating information if the actor knows it to be false or if the actor acts in reckless disregard as to its truth or falsity.[41] Of course this collapses the abuse-of-privilege inquiry into the fault constitutionally required for a prima facie case of defamation.[42] In addition, the privilege can be lost if the person communicating defamatory material does not act for the purpose of furthering the interest

---

[37] *Id.* § 577 (1977); W. Prosser, *Handbook of the Law of Torts* § 113 at 766 (4th ed. 1971).

[38] Denver Public Warehouse Co. v. Holloway, 34 Colo. 432, 83 P. 131 (1905); Munsell v. Ideal Food Stores, 208 Kan. 909, 494 P.2d 1063 (1972); *see also* Restatement (Second) of Torts § 596 (1977) (conditional privilege when several persons having a common interest in a particular subject matter correctly or reasonably believe there is information another sharing that interest should know). *Compare* Howard Univ. v. Best, 484 A.2d 958 (D.C. 1984) (insufficient evidence of publication to persons outside employer to sustain dismissed plaintiff's burden of proof) *with* Ramos v. Henry C. Beck Co., 711 S.W.2d 331, 335 (Tex. Ct. App. 1986) (status as employee may have relevance to question of privilege, but has no bearing on issue of publication).

[39] *See* Lewis v. Equitable Life Assurance Soc'y, 389 N.W.2d 876, 888 (Minn. 1986) (accepting "compelled self-publication doctrine"); *see also* Neighbors v. Kirksville College of Osteopathic Medicine, 694 S.W.2d 822, 825 (Mo. Ct. App. 1985) (publication of "service letter" only to dismissed employee sufficient to satisfy publication element where it is intended that contents of letter will be disclosed to prospective employers); McKinney v. County of Santa Clara, 110 Cal. App. 3d 787, 798, 168 Cal. Rptr. 89, 94 (1980) (compulsion for self-publication foreseeable by defendant can satisfy publication requirement); Belcher v. Little, 315 N.W.2d 734, 738 (Iowa 1982) (jury decides whether "compulsion" for self-publication existed).

[40] Montgomery v. Big B, Inc., 460 So. 2d 1286, 1288 (Ala. 1984) (conditional privilege applicable to reports from polygraph operator to employer).

[41] Restatement (Second) of Torts § 600 (1977). Russell v. Geis, 251 Cal. App. 2d 560, 59 Cal. Rptr. 569 (1967) (privilege lost by publication of a deliberate lie). *See also* Adler v. American Standard Corp., 538 F. Supp. 572 (D. Md. 1982) (proof of falsity and malice would overcome privilege attached to in house publication or statements made to facilitate personnel administration).

[42] Banas v. Matthews Int'l Corp., 348 Pa. Super. 464, 469, 502 A.2d 637, 639 (1985) (negligence sufficient to show abuse of conditional privilege; recognizing that, because burdens to establish defamation and abuse of a conditional privlege are the same, privilege loses any meaning).

§ 5.25   DEFAMATION

which the privilege is intended to protect.[43] Thus, if an employer disseminates adverse information more broadly than is necessary for legitimate personnel purposes, the employer has acted beyond the scope of its privilege and may be liable.[44]

In addition, there is an absolute privilege for employer statements made in the course of judicial proceedings, which has been extended by some courts to cover statements made in connection with administrative proceedings such as those involving unemployment compensation.[45]

The jury determines whether the matter in question was true or false.[46] The court determines whether the occasion upon which the defendant published the defamatory matter gives rise to a privilege, and the jury decides whether the employer abused its conditional privilege.[47] For example, in *Biggins v. Hanson*,[48] the dissemination of a foreman's interoffice memorandum dismissing an employee for threatening to sabotage equipment—to the employer's personnel manager, the foreman's superior and the business manager of the employee's union—was held to be privileged. A jury verdict in favor of the plaintiff-employee was reversed because of lack of evidence that the privilege was abused.[49]

---

[43] Restatement (Second) of Torts § 603 (1977). Vail v. Pennsylvania R.R., 103 N.J.L. 213, 136 A. 425 (1927). Stepanischen v. Merchants Despatch Transp. Corp., 722 F.2d 922, 933 (1st Cir. 1983) (abuse of employer's qualified privilege would be established by proof of anti-union animus).

[44] *See* Stearns v. Ohio Sav. Ass'n, 15 Ohio App. 3d 18, 20, 472 N.E.2d 372, 375 (1984) (affidavit evidence of publication to persons outside qualified privilege and of malice sufficient to withstand motion for summary judgment); McCone v. New England Tel. & Tel. Co., 393 Mass. 231, 471 N.E.2d 47, 51 (1984) (publication of adverse performance appraisals to department head within qualified privilege).

[45] *See* Peytan v. Ellis, 200 Conn. 243, 248, 510 A.2d 1337, 1339 (1986) (employer's statement responding to request of state unemployment compensation agency absolutely privileged; extending absolute privilege applicable to judicial proceedings).

[46] Restatement (Second) of Torts § 617 (1977).

[47] *Id.* § 619. *Compare* Lewis v. Equitable Life Assurance Soc'y, 389 N.W.2d 876, 890 (Minn. 1986) (approving jury verdict finding abuse of qualified privilege in discharge case but disapproving instruction allowing jury to decide whether employer entitled to privilege) *and* Fisher v. Illinois Office Supply Co., 130 Ill. App. 3d 996, 1002, 474 N.E.2d 1263, 1266-67 (1984) (dismissed employee entitled to trial on claim that conditional privilege was abused by letter from employer to union because employer knew letter to be false or recklessly disregarded whether it was true or false) *and* Litman v. Massachusetts Mut. Life Ins. Co., 739 F.2d 1549, 1561 (11th Cir. 1984) (jury entitled to decide whether motive in making statement was likely to trigger privilege); Florida law, applied in connection with a wrongful dismissal suit) *with* Haldeman v. Total Petroleum, Inc., 376 N.W.2d 98 (Iowa 1985) (reversing jury verdict for dismissed employee on defamation count; insufficient evidence to overcome privilege); Frankson v. Design Space Int'l, 394 N.W.2d 140 (Minn. 1986) (insufficient evidence of malice to overcome conditional privilege).

[48] 252 Cal. App. 2d 16, 59 Cal. Rptr. 897 (1967).

[49] *Id.*

In contrast, in *Poledna v. Bendix Corp.*,[50] the court upheld a trial judge's charge to the jury that, although a statement of the reasons for discharging an employee might be conditionally privileged if made to other employees who had responsibility for the hiring or firing of employees, the making of such communications to fellow employees in general about an employee who had been discharged for sleeping on the job and for theft was not privileged.

§ 5.26 Invasion of Privacy: Improper Acquisition or Dissemination of Information

A dismissed employee may be able to maintain a tort action for invasion of privacy. Established precedent should permit recovery on a privacy theory if information related to the dismissal was obtained or disseminated in an improper manner. Like defamation, a traditional invasion of privacy action probably would not be brought for the dismissal itself but for other acts connected with the dismissal. Section **5.27** considers extension of privacy concepts to permit an employee to recover for the dismissal itself when the effect of the dismissal is to intrude into matters for which the employee has a reasonable expectation of privacy.

There are four accepted variants of the tort of invasion of privacy:

1. Intrusion upon seclusion
2. Appropriation of name or likeness
3. Publicity given to private life
4. Publicity placing a person in false light.

These are discussed in §§ 652B, 652C, 652D, and 652E respectively of the *Restatement (Second) of Torts*.

Appropriation of name or likeness is unlikely to be involved in a dismissal situation,[51] and the false light variant is difficult to distinguish from defamation.[52] Accordingly, a dismissed employee is most likely to benefit from the intrusion and publicity given to private life variants.

---

[50] 360 Mich. 129, 103 N.W.2d 789 (1960).

[51] *But see* Haith v. Model Cities Health Corp., 704 S.W.2d 684 (Mo. Ct. App. 1986) (approving denial of summary judgment on claim by dismissed physicians that employer appropriated their names for use in grant application).

[52] There may be a few differences between false light and defamation. *See* Restatement (Second) of Torts § 652E comment b (1979) (not necessary that plaintiff be defamed in order to recover on false light theory). For example, a statement that might not be defamatory might nevertheless permit recovery on a false light theory, e.g., saying that one is a Democrat when he is a Republican. Also, pleading requirements dealing with colloquium and innuendo may not be applicable in a strict sense to false light. Finally, special damages almost certainly are not required to make out false light claim.

§ 5.26 PRIVACY: ACQUISITION OF INFORMATION

The intrusion variant of invasion of privacy consists of an intentional interference with the plaintiff's private affairs in a manner "that would be highly offensive to a reasonable man;"[53] it does not depend on any publicity given to the information collected about the plaintiff. Most of the cases accepting the intrusion variant of the privacy tort have involved intrusion (not necessarily physical) into a physical area with respect to which the plaintiff had a reasonable expectation of privacy. Most of the cases also involved acquisition of information.[54] Thus, if an employee were dismissed for reasons related to her private life, and the employee could prove that her employer had in some way unreasonably investigated her private life, a claim could be made under established precedent.[55] Wiretapping has been held to constitute an invasion of privacy, but the factual circumstances are very important.[56] Polygraph examinations similarly may constitute an invasion of privacy depending on the subjects inquired about.[57] Photographs taken on the job, however, have been held in a few cases not to constitute an invasion of privacy.[58]

The publicity variant of invasion of privacy involves making public information about the plaintiff that would be highly offensive to a reasonable person and is not of legitimate concern to the public.[59] It is distinguished from defamation in that the information publicized need not be false, and the publication must be to the public at large.[60] It is different from the intrusion variant of invasion of

---

[53] Restatement (Second) of Torts § 652B (1977). In Phillips v. Smalley Maintenance Servs., Inc., 711 F.2d 1524, 1532 (11th Cir. 1983), the Alabama Supreme Court, on certification, adopted the Second Restatement respecting privacy torts, and held that "acquisition of information from a plaintiff is not a requisite element of a § 652B cause of action." *Id.* at 1534.

[54] *See* Froelich v. Werbin, 219 Kan. 461, 464-65, 548 P.2d 482, 485 (1976) (must have intrusion into physical seclusion for intrusion tort to lie).

[55] In Court v. Bristol-Myers Co., 385 Mass. 300, 431 N.E.2d 908 (1982), recovery on this theory was denied. The employer had dismissed the plaintiff after he refused to answer personal questions on a questionnaire. The court held that, since there had been no disclosure by the employee to the employer, there had been no invasion. *See generally* Annotation, 13 A.L.R.3d 1025 (1967).

[56] *See generally* Annotation, 11 A.L.R.3d 1296 (1967); Awbrey v. Great Atl. & Pac. Tea Co., 505 F. Supp. 604 (N.D. Ga. 1980) (tort action for wiretapping implied under Georgia law, even though there was no disclosure). *But see* Simmons v. Southwestern Bell Tel. Co., 452 F. Supp. 392 (W.D. Okla. 1978) (private employer cannot violate constitutional privacy guarantees against monitoring telephone calls). Title III of the 1968 Omnibus Cirme Control Act, Pub. L. No. 90-351, 82 Stat. 197 makes it a crime for any person to intercept conversations, 18 U.S.C. § 2511 (1982), and authorizes civil actions for interceptions violating the statute. 18 U.S.C. § 2520 (1982). Conceivably, therefore, a public policy tort could be based on the statutory policies. See §§ **5.12–5.13**.

[57] *See* O'Brien v. Papa Gino's, 780 F.2d 1067 (1st Cir. 1986) (approving judgment for invasion of privacy based on jury finding that polygraph examination regarding off-the-job drug use was highly offensive).

[58] DeLury v. Kretchover, 66 Misc. 2d 897, 899, 322 N.Y.S.2d 517, 519 (Sup. Ct. 1971); Truxes v. Kenco Enter., 80 S.D. 104, 119 N.W.2d 914, 919 (1963); Thomas v. General Elec. Co., 207 F. Supp. 792 (W.D. Ky. 1962).

[59] Restatement (Second) of Torts § 652D (1977).

[60] *Id.*

privacy in that publicity must exist.[61] Accordingly, if an employer communicated to large numbers of people private information about the plaintiff-employee in connection with the employee's dismissal, a claim might be established under this theory.[62]

Section 652C of the *Second Restatement* affords the defendant in an action for invasion of privacy the same conditional privileges available in a defamation action. Thus, an employer can defend an action for invasion of privacy by showing that its conduct was reasonably necessary to the effective management of its business.[63]

In *Bratt v. International Business Machines Corp.*,[64] the court, applying Massachusetts law, held that disclosure of information obtained when an employee used IBM's *open door* internal grievance machinery was not an invasion of privacy because the information disclosed was not "intimate" or "highly personal." It affirmed summary judgment for the employer on this allegation. It also held that disclosure of mental problems to supervisors was no invasion of privacy because they had a legitimate need to know, affirming summary judgment for the employer on that count also.[65] It reversed summary judgment respecting disclosure of psychiatric problems by the company doctor to supervisors, however. It held that the expectation of privacy was much greater with respect to information disclosed in the doctor-patient setting, particularly when company policy reinforced the employee's expectation that such communications would not be divulged. The court also noted that privacy interests of the employee also might be outweighed by legitimate interests of the employer. The required balancing should be undertaken by the factfinder.

§ 5.27 — Invasion of Privacy: Interference with Private Conduct

The concepts embodied in the privacy tort can be extended logically beyond the facts of the decided cases to provide much broader protection for unfairly dismissed

---

[61] Restatement (Second) of Torts § 652D comment a (1977).

[62] *Cf.* Anderson v. Low Rent Hous. Comm'n, 304 N.W.2d 239 (Iowa 1981) (false light theory, recovery permitted, public employer).

[63] It is not quite as simple as § 652C suggests. In the context of an intrusion tort involving wiretapping, the business purpose of the employer's action probably would not be a defense. Defenses to the false light privacy tort should track the privileges for defamation, but the constitutional privileges for defamation are difficult to apply logically to the publicity privacy tort, in which the information need not be false to make out a prima facie case. *See* Restatement (Second) of Torts § 652D Special Note on Relation of § 652D to the First Amendment of the Constitution (1979). Conversely, the legitimate public concern defense, generally recognized in connection with the privacy tort, may permit somewhat broader defenses in a privacy action than in a defamation action. *See id.* § 652D comment d.

[64] 785 F.2d 352 (1st Cir. 1986).

[65] *Id.* at 360. The need to know made the disclosure to superiors privileged.

employees. *Restatement* § 652B does not refer to information acquisition; it refers more broadly to "interference with private affairs."[66]

To give concreteness to a discussion of this possibility, it is useful to begin with a hypothetical situation. Suppose an employee were dismissed for private sexual conduct that had no plausible connection with her ability to perform the job.[67] The off duty conduct might involve a gay lifestyle or it might involve marital infidelity. If the employer gained knowledge of the conduct without intrusive investigative action, the cases involving electronic surveillance would not be directly on point.[68] If the employer made no disclosure of the reasons for the dismissal, the privacy cases involving publicity similarly would be of little aid to the plaintiff. The employee could, however, build upon the intrusion variant of the privacy tort to argue that she should be able to recover.[69]

The plaintiff's argument would be: By recognizing the intrusion variant of the invasion of privacy tort, the courts have recognized that I have a legal interest in pursuing my private activities without unjustified interference. By depriving me of my employment on account of these private activities, my employer is interfering with my private conduct just as surely as if she spied on me; indeed the harm from the spying would be less direct: the spying would harm me only because I would fear that she would take adverse action against me based on the fruits of her spying. That adverse action, in concrete form, is what I have suffered in this case.[70] Unless my employer can justify this intrusion into my private life by the needs of her business, she should be subjected to liability for invasion of privacy.[71]

---

[66] *But see* Corder v. Champion Road Mach. Int'l, 283 S.C. 520, 523, 324 S.E.2d 79, 80 (1984) (threat to fire for filing workers' compensation claims does not make out intrusion sufficient to support invasion of privacy action).

[67] The hypothetical presents a factual situation that would not amount to *cause* under civil service laws or collective bargaining agreements, and would not satisfy substantive due process in public employment. Employers subject to those duties are required to demonstrate some nexus between the private conduct and the employee's job performance. See §§ **3.8, 6.4–6.5 & 6.13**. This also is the same factual situation covered by the *off duty conduct* provisions of the proposed wrongful dismissal statutes. See **app. C**.

[68] In the cases discussed in Annotation, 13 A.L.R.3d 1025 (1967), the surveillance was an essential factual element.

[69] *See, e.g.,* O'Brien v. Papa Gino's, 780 F.2d 1067 (1st Cir. 1986) (approving judgment for invasion of privacy based on jury finding that polygraph examination regarding off-the-job drug use was highly offensive).

[70] Imposing an economic cost for the exercise of rights has been found to be an interference in other contexts. In Thomas v. Review Bd. of Ind. Employment Sec. Div., 450 U.S. 707 (1981), the Supreme Court held that denial of unemployment benefits to a Jehovah's Witness who quit his job rather than work on military projects violates the First Amendment. The Court reasoned that substantial, though indirect, pressure on a person for exercise of religious beliefs amounted to interference in violation of the free exercise clause.

[71] This justification concept is virtually identical to the basic justification concepts discussed in § **5.7**. In the privacy context, the interests to be balanced against the employer's asserted interests are

Courts confronted with public employee dismissals have accepted an analysis much like this, based on the constitutionally protected liberty interest of privacy.[72]

The Massachusetts Supreme Judicial Court considered the boundary between an information acquisition privacy tort and a broader privacy tort in *Cort v. Bristol-Myers Co.*,[73] but did not resolve the question whether information acquisition is a prerequisite to recovery. In that case, the court denied recovery to plaintiffs who had been asked to provide private information on an employer questionnaire, largely because the employees had refused to give the requested information.[74] The analysis used by the court, however, in reaching this conclusion started with this premise: "In short, if Bristol-Myers had no right to ask the questions that the plaintiffs declined to answer, Bristol-Myers could be liable for discharging the plaintiffs for their failure to answer those questions."[75] The court proceeded to suggest a balancing of the degree of intrusion into the privacy rights of the employee against the relevancy of the information sought as it pertains to the business purposes of the employer.[76] Because *Bristol-Myers* involves pursuit of information, it is not direct authority for the proposition that the privacy tort more broadly involves the "right to be left alone."[77]

Nevertheless, a case involving acquisition of information is barely distinguishable from a case involving use of information. In *Whalen v. Roe*,[78] Justice Stevens said that constitutional privacy cases involve two different kinds of interests: avoiding disclosure of personal matters, and independence in making certain kinds of important decisions.[79] The second type of interest is involved in the hypothetical situation discussed in this section. The privacy tort should recognize this second

---

the employee's interests in privacy. Thus the analysis proceeds just like the public policy tort discussed in §§ **5.8–5.19**, except that privacy is substituted for the statutory public policy.

[72] *Compare* Briggs v. North Muskegon Police Dept., 563 F. Supp. 585 (W.D. Mich. 1983) (Gibson, J.) (dismissal for cohabitation violates constitutional right of privacy) *and* Golden v. Board of Educ., 285 S.E.2d 665, 669 (W. Va. 1981) (discharge by public employer for private conduct violated privacy concepts) *and* Shuman v. City of Philadelphia, 470 F. Supp. 449 (E.D. Pa. 1979) (same), *with* Graves v. Duganne, 581 F.2d 222, 224 *on rehearing* 620 F.2d 749 (10th Cir. 1978) (nonrenewal of teacher contract because of off duty conduct no invasion of privacy because no direct attempt to regulate conduct; Griswold v. Connecticut, 381 U.S. 479 (1965) (distinguished) *and* Shawgo v. Spradlen, 701 F.2d 470, 482–83 (5th Cir. 1983) (rational connection between legitimate police department needs and prohibiting cohabitation between officers). *See* Hafen, *The Constitutional Status of Marriage, Kinship and Sexual Privacy—Balancing the Individual and Social Interests*, 81 Mich. L. Rev. 463, 517–44 (1983); Karst, *The Freedom of Intimate Association*, 89 Yale L.J. 624, 673, 682 (1980) (discussion of values involved in nonmarital and homosexual relationships); Annotation, 9 A.L.R.4th 614 (1981).

[73] 385 Mass. 300, 431 N.E.2d 908 (1982).

[74] *Id.* at 302–03, 431 N.E.2d at 910.

[75] *Id.* at 307, 431 N.E.2d at 912.

[76] *Id.* at 308, 431 N.E.2d at 912.

[77] *See* Restatement (Second) of Torts § 652B comment d (1979). *See generally* Gavison, *Privacy and the Limits of Law*, 89 Yale L.J. 421, 448 (1980) (part of privacy concept is promoting liberty of action).

[78] 429 U.S. 589 (1977).

[79] *Id.* at 599–600.

interest in connection with unfair dismissals. Discharge of an employee for private conduct not affecting his employer's interests interferes with the employee's right to make certain kinds of important decisions, and the employee should be permitted to recover in tort.[80]

An intermediate appellate court in New Jersey has endorsed the plausibility of this theory under both invasion of privacy and public policy tort theories. In *Slohoda v. United Parcel Service,*[81] the court reversed summary judgment for the employer, and held that inquiry by an employer into extramarital sexual activities could give rise to tort liability if the employee were discharged for that reason.

In *Wilson v. Taylor,*[82] the court held that a police officer's relationship with a woman whom he was dating was an interest protected by the First Amendment to the United States Constitution. "We conclude that dating is a type of association which must be protected by the first amendment's freedom of association."[83]

A similar result was reached under a contract theory in *Rulon-Miller v. IBM,*[84] in which the court affirmed a $300,000 verdict for an employee dismissed for dating an employee of a competing firm. The court held that the dismissal violated the implied covenant of good faith and fair dealing because it contravened the employer's policy of not interfering in employees' private, off-the-job conduct.

The same rationale ought to be applied to permit recovery for dismissal of employees for marital status, sexual orientation, or lifestyle, unless the employer can show how such matters impair legitimate employer interests. Such an approach would be consistent with the reasoning and results of labor arbitration cases.[85]

§ 5.28 Tort Claims for Dismissals Related to AIDS or to Sexual Orientation

The AIDS crisis[86] has caused concern among employers and employee groups as to the legal implications of dismissing persons with AIDS, and the closely related

---

[80] *See* Moffett v. Gene B. Glick Co., 604 F. Supp. 229, 236 (N.D. Ind. 1984) (harassment for interracial relationship states invasion of privacy intrusion claim).

[81] 193 N.J. Super. 586, 590, 475 A.2d 618, 622 (App. Div. 1984), *later appeal,* 207 N.J. Super. 145, 504 A.2d 53 (1986).

[82] 733 F.2d 1539 (11th Cir. 1984).

[83] *Id.* at 1544. *See also* Cybyske v. Independent School Dist. No. 196, 347 N.W.2d 256, 262 (Minn. 1984), *cert. denied,* 469 U.S. 933 (1984) (dismissal because of spouse's political views infringes freedom of assocation). *But see* Patton v. J.C. Penney Co., 301 Or. 117, 719 P.2d 854 (1986) (no public policy tort for employee dismissed for dating coworker; rejecting argument that constitutional rights to privacy and association and state action infringement cases represent sufficiently clear public policy); Karren v. Far West Fed. Sav., 79 Or. App. 131, 717 P.2d 1271 (1986) (dismissal for becoming engaged to marry does not invovle rights as employee; therefore does not support public policy tort).

[84] 162 Cal. App. 3d 241, 208 Cal. Rptr. 524 (1984).

[85] See § **3.8**.

[86] AIDS is an acronym for Acquired Immune Deficiency Syndrome. As of the end of 1986 the disease is incurable and almost inevitably fatal. By some estimates, as many as two million Americans

question of the legal permissibility of dismissing persons on the basis of homosexual lifestyles.[87] A variety of legal theories analyzed in this treatise potentially limit employer freedom to terminate employment based on AIDS or sexual orientation. This section summarizes them, and directs counsel to the substantive portions of the treatise for further research.

One can crystallize the legal issues best by considering two hypothetical situations: (1) an employee who does not have AIDS dismissed because he is gay, and (2) a nongay employee dismissed because she has AIDS.

The legal arguments available to an employee dismissed because of sexual orientation are as follows:[88]

1. Dismissal for such a reason violates Title VII of the Civil Rights Act.[89] Title VII has been interpreted by most courts as not prohibiting sexual orientation discrimination.[90] Legislation has been introduced to amend Title VII expressly to prohibit such discrimination.[91] Nevertheless, Title VII can be used as a basis for litigating sexual orientation dismissals when gay employees suffer employment discrimination because of involvement in gay organizations of a religious nature,[92] or, perhaps, when gay employees have been subjected to harassment because of their sexual orientation.[93] In addition, commentators have suggested a Title VII theory based on the disparate impact upon males which accompanies sexual orientation discrimination[94]

---

have been exposed to the AIDS virus, and the number of persons infected could increase to 5–10 million by 1995. Not all persons exposed to the virus develop the disease. Available medical evidence suggests that from 4 to 19 percent of those exposed develop the disease. An additional 25 percent develop AIDS Related Complex, a set of related symptoms that is not necessarily fatal. Memorandum from Charles J. Cooper, Assistant Attorney General, Office of Legal Counsel, to General Counsel of Department of Health and Human Services (Jun. 20, 1986) at 3–5 [the DOJ Memo].

[87] Homosexual males are a high-risk group for AIDS exposure, though the disease is by no means limited to the homosexual part of the population.

[88] Obviously, some of the arguments are available only in particular factual situations.

[89] 42 U.S.C. §§ 2000e to 2000e(17) (1982).

[90] See § 2.3.

[91] See H.R. 230, 99th Cong., 1st Sess. (1986); S. 1432, 99th Cong., 1st Sess. (1986).

[92] See Dorr v. First Kentucky Nat'l Corp., 796 F.2d 179 (6th Cir. 1986) (Title VII prohibits dismissal because of religious beliefs although religious organization geared towards the particular needs of homosexuals).

[93] Cf. Joyner v. A.A.A. Cooper Transp., 597 F. Supp. 537 (M.D. Ala.) (unwelcome homosexual harassment violates Title VII), aff'd, 749 F.2d 732 (11th Cir. 1983); Wright v. Methodist Youth Serv. Inc., 511 F. Supp. 307 (N.D. Ill. 1981) (discharge of male employee for rejecting sexual advances from male supervisor violated Title VII prohibition of sex discrimination). It is more difficult to make the logical connection between harassment based on sexual orientation and sex discrimination, than to make the logical connection in the cited cases, which involved harassment of males because they were male.

[94] The theory rests on the higher incidence of homosexuality reported in the male population combined with an easier employer access to such information through arrest and military records.

§ 5.28 SEXUAL ORIENTATION

2. Dismissal for such a reason violates state or local discrimination statutes[95]
3. Dismissal for such a reason permits damages to be recovered for the tort of invasion of privacy[96]
4. Dismissal for such a reason permits damages to be recovered under the public policy tort theory[97]
5. Dismissal for such a reason violates an employer promise under the implied-in-fact contract theory.[98] Some large employers have made promises specifically relating to sexual orientation[99]
6. Dismissal for such a reason violates the implied covenant of good faith and fair dealing[1]
7. Dismissal for such a reason violates a collectively bargained prohibition against dismissal without just cause[2]
8. Dismissal of a public employee for such a reason violates civil service protections and constitutional due process and equal protection guarantees.

For a more complete discussion of the disparate impact theory, see § 2.3; Note, *Challenging Sexual Preference Discrimination in Private Employment,* 41 Ohio St. L.J. 501, 505–07 (1980).

[95] Although 44 cities and 12 counties have some type of gay rights protection, most of the ordinances do not protect gay employees in the private sector. Rivera, *Queer Law: Sexual Orientation Law in the Mid-Eighties* Part I, 10:3 U. Dayton L. Rev. 459, 480–83 (1985). Philadelphia and Detroit are the notable exceptions. California, New York, Ohio and Pennsylvania have executive orders protecting state employees from discrimination based on sexual orientation. *Id.* Wisconsin and the District of Columbia have enacted nondiscrimination clauses in employment, covering private as well as public employment, based on sexual orientation. Wis. Stat. Ann. §§ 111.321, 111.322 & 111.36 (West Supp. 1985); D.C. Code Ann. § 1-2512 (1981).

[96] § 5.27 explains why employment terminations on account of private, off duty sexual practices or decisions violates the elements of the intrusion variant of the invasion of privacy tort recognized in the Restatement (Second) of Torts.

[97] Gay employees in this context would present a number of public policies that could be jeopardized by their dismissals. They would not assert a policy in favor of being gay. Rather, they could argue: The common law recognizes an individual's right to be free from unnecessary invasions into her privacy (See § 5.26). State and federal constitutions recognize a similar right to privacy and also protect freedom of association (see § 5.12), and freedom of expression (see § 5.12). In addition, the general policy of nondiscrimination embodied in state and federal statutes could be used as the basis for a public policy tort. See § 5.9.

[98] See § 4.22. Promises to dismiss only for just cause would be breached by dismissals for sexual orientation unless the employer can show how the sexual orientation interferes with legitimate employer interests.

[99] The National Gay Task Force has compiled a list of employers who have voluntary nondiscrimination policies based on sexual orientation. Gay employees who are dismissed on the basis of their sexual orientation by these employers could satisfy requirements of an action for breach of an implied-in-fact contract by arguing that they remained in their positions in reliance upon their employer's nondiscrimination policies.

[1] See §§ 4.11, 4.23.

[2] See **ch. 3**. Most union contracts have a provision whereby employers can dismiss employees only for just cause; gay union employees, covered by such a provision, who are subsequently dismissed on the basis of their sexual orientation, would have a cause of action against their employers by arguing that such dismissal was not for just cause. Unions have an obligation to represent gay employees in presenting grievances because of a duty of fair representation. See § 3.8.

Employees dismissed for AIDS would have an additional argument based on local, state, or federal handicap discrimination prohibitions.[3]

Decisional law and legal doctrine do not give gay employees or AIDS victims any special protections not enjoyed by employees in general. But neither are gay employees or AIDS victims entitled to any less protection or subject to any greater employer intrusion into their private lives than other employees, based on their sexual orientation or disease.

The Supreme Court's decision in *Hardwick v. Bowers*[4] does not foreclose this analysis. In *Hardwick,* a 5-4 decision, the Supreme Court held that the United States Constitution does not confer a fundamental right upon homosexuals to engage in sodomy.[5] Journalists have characterized the case as having broad implications for the rights of gay employees to be free of adverse action based on sexual orientation. The right to be free from adverse employment action, however, and the right to engage in sodomy are separate rights. Legislatures have handled the two rights differently. For example, the District of Columbia has both a sodomy prohibition statute[6] and a statute prohibiting employment discrimination based on sexual orientation.[7]

Hardwick does not preclude the possibility of a successful argument, based on the federal Constitution, that the right to privacy precludes employment discrimination based on sexual orientation. More importantly, *Hardwick* says nothing about rights based on state constitutions or the common law. Rights granted by the federal Constitution, state constitutions[8] and the common law, although similar in many significant ways, are not exactly the same. Therefore, gay employees may find that state constitutions or the common law afford privacy rights sufficient to permit relief for employment discrimination based on sexual orientation, even if the federal Constitution does not protect against such employment discrimination. *Hardwick* does not foreclose state law developments in the direction suggested in this section based on state constitutional privacy interests or privacy interests recognized by the common law. Section **5.27** suggests a particular application of the intrusion variant of the common law invasion of privacy tort, and thus does not depend on the United States Constitution as the starting point.

§ 5.29 Negligence

In a handful of cases, plaintiffs have succeeded in wrongful dismissal suits based on a negligence theory. The leading case is *Flanigan v. Prudential Federal Savings*

---

[3] See §§ **2.10, 2.12**. Thomas v. Atascadero Unified School Dist., ____ F. Supp. ____, Civ. 86-6609 (C.D. Cal. 1986) (preliminary granted) (Stotter, J.).

[4] 106 S. Ct. 2841 (1986).

[5] *Id.* at 2843.

[6] D.C. Code Ann. § 22-3502 (1981).

[7] *Id.* § 1-2512 (1981).

[8] *See* Novosel v. Nationwide Ins. Co., 721 F.2d 894, 899 (3d Cir. 1983) (public policy can be based on either U.S. Constitution or Pennsylvania Constitution, suggesting the two sources are independent).

and Loan Association,[9] in which the Montana Supreme Court held that the plaintiff was entitled to present a negligence theory to the jury based on evidence that the employer's supervisors committed 13 different violations of the employer's personnel policies in terminating the plaintiff.[10]

In other cases, a court found that the failure of the plaintiff's supervisor to inform him of the potential for dismissal because of his negative performance appraisals constituted negligence.[11] The duty to the plaintiff arose from the contractual relations between the plaintiff and his employer.[12] Liability in negligence could exist even without breach of contract. In another case, negligence was established by the manner in which an employer investigated the facts supporting a discharge for insubordination, disruptive conduct and poor performance.[13]

The negligence theory has not proved fruitful for many terminated employees, because of a judicial reluctance to permit its use.[14]

§ 5.30 Preemption of State Tort Claims by § 301 of the Labor Management Relations Act

When an employee covered by a collective bargaining agreement asserts a tort claim for wrongful dismissal, the question may arise whether the tort claim is preempted by § 301 of the Labor Management Relations Act.[15] This is a different question from that of whether a tort claim is preempted by the National Labor Relations Act because the conduct giving rise to the tort also is an unfair labor practice under that NLRA. The question of NLRA preemption is addressed in **§ 2.28**. Section 301 preemption of tort claims also is a different question from § 301 preemption of state breach of contract claims, addressed in **§ 4.25,** and

---

[9] ___ Mont. ___, 720 P.2d 257 (1986).

[10] *Id.* at ___, 720 P.2d at 263.

[11] Chamberlain v. Bissell, Inc., 547 F. Supp. 1067, 1081 (W.D. Mich. 1982).

[12] *Id. See also* Brooks v. Trans World Airlines, 574 F. Supp. 805, 810 (D. Colo. 1983) (summary judgment for employer denied on negligence count based on duty arising from handbook). *But cf.* Lieber v. Union Carbide Corp., 577 F. Supp. 562 (E.D. Tenn. 1983) (notice to employees that performance appraisals would be given did not establish legal obligation to make appraisals; suit by retiree for increased pension benefits on grounds that performance appraisals would have induced better performance and salary increases).

[13] Crenshaw v. Bozeman Deaconess Hosp., ___ Mont. ___, 693 P.2d 487 (1984) (affirming jury verdict of $125,000 compensatory and $25,000 punitive damages for respiratory therapist discharged during probationary period).

[14] Brewster v. Martin Marietta Aluminum Sales, Inc., 145 Mich. App. 641, 668, 378 N.W.2d 558, 569 (1985) (no cause of action for "negligent breach of contract" when no breach of duty other than breach of contract).

[15] 29 U.S.C. § 185 (1982). **§ 2.28** discusses the related question of preemption of tort claims for conduct covered by the NLRA. **§§ 2.31–2.34** discuss preemption of common law claims by other federal statutes. **§§ 2.30, 3.21** and **4.25** discuss preemption of common law contract claims by § 301 of the L.M.R.A.

from the question of whether a public policy tort should be available to employees already protected by collective bargaining agreements.[16]

The Supreme Court considered § 301 preemption of state tort claims in *Allis-Chalmers v. Lueck*.[17] *Allis-Chalmers v. Lueck* involved a tort action for bad faith handling of disability claims under a collectively bargained disability plan. The collective agreement establishing the plan contained a typical grievance procedure terminating in binding arbitration, but the employee did not file a grievance. The Wisconsin Supreme Court held that the tort was not preempted because, under Wisconsin law, "the tort of bad faith is distinguishable from a bad faith breach of contract claim. . . . violation of the labor agreement was irrelevant to the issue of whether the defendants exercised bad faith in the manner in which they handled [the] claim."[18]

The Supreme Court of the United States reversed. It concluded that the policies behind § 301 could be implemented only if the preemptive effect of § 301 extends beyond suits alleging breach of contract:

> Questions relating to what the parties to a labor agreement agreed, and what legal consequences were intended to flow from breaches of that agreement, must be resolved by reference to uniform federal law, whether such questions arise in the context of a suit for breach of contract or in a suit alleging liability in tort.[19]

Because the duty to process disability claims was entirely a creature of the collective bargaining agreement, the court concluded that acceptance of an independent state tort for violation of the duty would violate the preemption concept articulated in the quoted part of the opinion. The court cautioned, however:

> In extending the pre-emptive effect of § 301 beyond suits for breach of contract, it would be inconsistent with congressional intent under that section to pre-empt state rules that proscribed conduct, or establish rights and obligations independent of a labor contract.[20]

Allis-Chalmers v. Lueck was applied by the Seventh Circuit in *Mitchell v. Pepsi-Cola Bottlers, Inc.*,[21] holding that a state tort claim for terminating employment under a collective bargaining agreement was preempted by § 301, and in *Vantine v. Elkhart Brass Manufacturing Co.*,[22] finding a tort claim for dismissal in retaliation for filing a workers' compensation claim preempted by § 301.

In *Garibaldi v. Lucky Food Stores, Inc.*,[23] the Ninth Circuit held that a truck driver's public policy tort claim was not preempted by § 301 even though his

---

[16] See § **5.20**.
[17] 471 U.S. 202, 105 S. Ct. 1904 (1985).
[18] *Id.* at 1909.
[19] *Id.* at 1911.
[20] *Id.* at 1912.
[21] 772 F.2d 342, 347 (7th Cir. 1985), *cert. denied*, ___ U.S. ___, 106 S. Ct. 1266 (1986).
[22] 762 F.2d 511, 518 (7th Cir. 1985).
[23] 726 F.2d 1367 (9th Cir. 1984), *cert. denied*, 471 U.S. 1099 (1985).

dismissal had been upheld by an arbitrator. The court reasoned that the tort claim, arising from a dismissal for reporting a load of spoiled milk to health authorities, was distinct from his right to be dismissed only for just cause under the collective bargaining agreement.

The following rules of thumb synthesize § 301 preemption of wrongful dismissal tort litigation:

1. If the tort claim depends for its legal efficacy on a just cause or other employment security provision in a collective agreement, the tort claim is preempted
2. If the tort claims grows out of the administration of a collective agreement, it is also preempted[24]
3. If, on the other hand, the tort claim is entirely independent of collectively bargained rights and obligations, in the sense that the same facts involving an employee not covered by a collective agreement would permit recovery, then the tort claim is not preempted by § 301.[25]

Of course, the tort claim nevertheless may be preempted by the NLRA.[26] Moreover, the common law tort may be construed as not protecting employees already protected by collective bargaining agreements.[27]

§ 5.31 Pleading the Plaintiff's Case

Plaintiffs seeking recovery on one of the traditional tort theories should separately allege facts supporting each of the elements.[28] The specificity with which facts

---

[24] *See* Truex v. Garrett Freightlines, Inc., 784 F.2d 1347 (9th Cir. 1986) (state tort claims for harassment and intentional infliction of emotional distress preempted because alleged employer conduct related to interpretation and administration of collective bargaining agreement); Bartley v. University Asphalt Co., Inc., 111 Ill. 2d 318, 333, 489 N.E.2d 1367, 1372 (1986) (civil conspiracy suit against union growing out of termination for cooperating with FBI investigation of union and employer preempted by § 301 of L.M.R.A.).

[25] This is essentially the point urged by Alan J. Haus in his article *NLRA Preemption of State Wrongful Discharge Claims,* 34 Hastings L.J. 635 (1983). *See also* Anderson v. Ford Motor Co., 803 F.2d 953, 957 (8th Cir. 1986) (state law fraud claims by laid-off employees not preempted by § 301 of L.M.R.A.).

[26] See § **2.28**.

[27] This possibility is explored in § **5.20**. *Compare* Phillips v. Babcock & Wilcox, 349 Pa. Super. 351, 503 A.2d 36 (1986) (no public policy tort under Pennsylvania law for employee covered by collective agreement) *and* Smith v. Greyhound Lines, Inc., 614 F. Supp. 558, 560–61 (W.D. Pa. 1984) (same) *and* Herring v. Prince Foods-Canning Div., 611 F. Supp. 177, 180 (D.N.J. 1985) (no public policy tort protection available under New Jersey law for employee covered by collectively bargained "just cause" protection) *with* Midgett v. Sackett-Chicago, 105 Ill. 2d 143, 473 N.E.2d 1280 (1984) *and* Phillips v. Babcock & Wilcox, 349 Pa. Super. 351, 503 A.2d at 38 (Spaeth, J., dissenting).

[2b] *See* M. Dichter, A. Gross, D. Morikawa & S. Sauntry, Employee Dismissal Forms and Procedures (1986) for more extensive discussion of pleading and other pretrial issues.

should be pleaded depends on the theory of pleading utilized in the forum state.[29] *Notice pleading* is more permissive than fact pleading. Under notice pleading, there is no requirement to plead facts sufficient to constitute a cause of action, but only that there "be a short and plain statement of the claim showing that the pleader is entitled to relief."[30] A pleading that satisfies fact pleading requirements, however, also will satisfy notice pleading requirements,[31] and it is prudent intellectual discipline for counsel to plead available facts to support each element of all the causes of action asserted. Even if the forum state uses notice pleading, the plaintiff can reduce the likelihood of dismissal by being specific as to facts supporting each element of a public policy tort, anticipating the particular theory to be urged on the court.[32] The plaintiff also should be careful to plead all the traditional theories that may be justified by the facts.[33]

Plaintiffs seeking recovery on a public policy tort theory discussed in §§ **5.8** through **5.19** should plead facts supporting the three basic requirements for recovery: existence of a public policy, jeopardy to the public policy that would result if liability is not imposed for the discharge, and absence of legitimate employer interests justifying the discharge.[34]

First, the plaintiff should allege the existence of the specific public policy asserted as the basis for the action, linking it, if possible, to a statute of the state whose law is to be applied. In most cases, courts are willing to recognize public policy embodied in a statute as a basis for tort recovery. If no such statute is available,

---

[29] Not only pleading rules, but other pretrial procedural steps should be considered. *See, e.g.*, Snuffer v. Motorists Mut. Ins. Co., 636 F. Supp. 430, 431 (S.D.W. Va. 1986) (published order clarifying legal theories for trial, resulting from pretrial conference).

[30] Dioguardi v. Durning, 139 F.2d 774 (2d Cir. 1944); Conley v. Gibson, 355 U.S. 41, 47–48 (1957) (detailed facts not required).

[31] *See* Brezinski v. F.W. Woolworth Co., 626 F. Supp. 240, 243 (D. Colo. 1986) (implied contract claims adequately pleaded under federal rules; notice pleading concept).

[32] *Compare* Milton v. Illinois Bell Tel. Co., 101 Ill. App. 3d 75, 77, 427 N.E.2d 829, 831-33 (1981) (plaintiff alleged eight separate ways in which his employer punished him for refusing to falsify work reports; appellate court found these factual allegations established the elements of outrageous conduct necessary for recovery) *with* Rossi v. Pennsylvania State Univ., 340 Pa. Super. 39, 489 A.2d 828, 837 (1985) (failure to allege specific intent to harm negates possible claim for prima facie tort).

[33] *See* Hogan v. Forsyth Country Club Co., 79 N.C. App. 483, 340 S.E.2d 116 (1986) (suggesting plaintiff should have pleaded intentional interference with employment contract, based on coemployee sexual advances), *review denied*, 317 N.C. 334, 346 S.E.2d 141 (1986); Holden v. Owens-Illinois, Inc., 793 F.2d 745, 754 (6th Cir. 1986) (dismissal of state public policy tort claim because of failure to plead theory, despite pleading fraud, misrepresentation, and breach of contract).

[34] Staggs v. Blue Cross of Maryland, Inc., 61 Md. App. 381, 486 A.2d 798, 800 (1985) (public policy tort not pleaded in trial court, and therefore may not be raised on appeal); Cloutier v. Great Atl. & Pac. Tea Co., 121 N.H. 915, 436 A.2d 1140 (1981) suggests that a plaintiff also must allege bad faith or malice. *Id.* at 921, 436 A.2d at 1143. Such an allegation, though it may not be required under the three-part formula explained in § **5.1**, helps tilt the balance of interests in the plaintiff's favor. See §§ **5.7, 5.21**.

the plaintiff should make specific reference to an administrative regulation, a formal professional code of ethics, or a provision of the state or federal constitution.[35]

Second, the plaintiff should allege factually how his dismissal interferes with the public policy asserted. In most cases, this will require the plaintiff to articulate how the conduct which resulted in the dismissal is necessary for the realization of the public policy or how chilling of such conduct will jeopardize public policy.[36]

When pleading clarity of the policy and jeopardy, the plaintiff should bear in mind the fatal flaw in the complaint in *Adler v. American Standard Corp.*[37]

> His complaint does not recite, with the requisite degree of specificity, the manner in which . . . statutory enactments were offended so as to constitute a violation of the public policy of this State. The bald allegations of Adler's complaint do not provide a sufficient factual predicate for determining whether any declared mandate of public policy was violated.[38]

Similarly, in *Pierce v. Ortho Pharmaceutical Corp.*,[39] the plaintiff failed to allege violation of specific standards or to allege that continuing her research would "constitute an act of medical malpractice or violate any statute."[40]

Third, the plaintiff's exercise of rights protected by the public policy should be alleged as the exclusive reason for his dismissal. The plaintiff must plead that the public policy-linked conduct motivated the dismissal.[41]

This will satisfy the third element of the analytical approach under which the plaintiff must show that a public policy exists, that the dismissal jeopardizes the public policy, and that the employer lacks justification. Proof and evidentiary problems on causation are discussed in detail in **Chapter 7**.

Facts showing good work performance by the employee support the third factor (absence of justification). Facts showing hostility or unreasonableness in the manner of the dismissal also support factor number three and buttress a possible independent claim under the the prima facie tort doctrine.[42] Such facts should be

---

[35] *See* Rice v. Grant County Bd. of Comm'rs, 472 N.E.2d 213, 215 (Ind. Ct. App. 1984) (plaintiff must plead and prove statutory right with which dismissal interferred); Gordon v. Lancaster Osteopathic Hosp. Assoc., 340 Pa. Super. 253, 256, 489 A.2d 1364, 1371 (1985) (public policy must be pleaded to state a claim); Sharon Steel Corp. v. V.J.R. Co., 604 F. Supp. 420, 421 (W.D. Pa. 1985) (dismissal of counter claim by dismissed employee for public policy tort for failure to plead public policy).

[36] See §§ **5.1, 7.12** explaining the jeopardy element.

[37] 291 Md. 31, 432 A.2d 464 (1981).

[38] *Id.* at 44, 432 A.2d at 471.

[39] 84 N.J. 58, 417 A.2d 505 (1980).

[40] *Id.* at 74, 417 A.2d at 513.

[41] *See* Thomas v. Zamberletti, 134 Ill. App. 3d 387, 390, 480 N.E.2d 869, 871 (1985) (affirming dismissal of complaint for failure to allege wrongful motivation).

[42] The requirements for pleading a prima facie tort are discussed in § **5.21**. Under this approach, the plaintiff would be required to plead and prove malice to overcome the defendant's allegation

pleaded, if possible. If no public policy was implicated by the dismissal, the plaintiff should consider pleading facts from which an inference of specific intent to harm can be drawn, supporting recovery under the more general variant of the prima facie tort.[43]

§ 5.32 Pleading the Defendant's Case

Appendix D contains a checklist for employer in-house counsel to use in evaluating a wrongful dismissal claim.[44]

Depending on the law of the jurisdiction in which the case arises, the defendant's first line of defense probably will be a legal argument that the plaintiff's pleading does not state a claim upon which relief can be granted. Accordingly, the defendant should file a demurrer or a similar motion appropriate in the jurisdiction to test the legal sufficiency of the plaintiff's claim. In support of such a demurrer or motion, the defendant should present the arguments suggested by the cases discussed in §§ **5.8** through **5.20**. Fundamentally, the defendant can argue that no form of public policy tort for wrongful dismissal should be recognized. Defendant would argue that termination of an employment-at-will cannot amount to legal injury within the meaning of § 870 of the *Restatement (Second) of Torts*.

If the jurisdiction recognizes the public policy tort or the prima facie tort, however, the defendant still can argue that the plaintiff's allegations are insufficient to make a claim. If confronted with a claim based on the public policy theories,[45] the defendant should assert that the claimed public policy does not exist or that the plaintiff's dismissal will not jeopardize realization of the policy. If the plaintiff has failed to plead lack of justification for the dismissal, the defendant should argue that demonstrating lack of justification is part of the plaintiff's burden of production in a prima facie case.[46] In preparing a responsive pleading, the defendant should deny any factual allegations she can and thereby seek to defeat the plaintiff's prima facie case. In addition, if confronted with a claim based on either a public policy theory or the prima facie tort theory, the defendant should assert, as an affirmative

---

of justification. Anselmo v. Manufacturers Life Ins. Co., 595 F. Supp. 541, 548 (W.D. Mo 1984) (must plead lack of justification to state claim for prima facie tort).

[43] See § **5.21**.

[44] *See also* M. Dichter, A. Gross, D. Morikawa & S. Sauntry, Employee Dismissal Forms and Procedures (1986) for treatment of other pretrial issues.

[45] See §§ **5.8–5.19**.

[46] See §§ **5.5** & **5.7**, discussing the approach suggested in Restatement (Second) of Torts § 870. A somewhat different order of proof, with implications for pleading a prima facie tort, is discussed in § **5.21**. Under this approach, the plaintiff would be required to plead and prove malice to overcome the defendant's allegation of justification.

§ 5.33 DAMAGES

defense,[47] her justification for the dismissal. The affirmative defense of justification should be presented in the form of specific factual allegations related to the plaintiff's poor performance, misconduct, or other unsuitability for the position, or it should be presented to underscore the reasons why the plaintiff's public policy-linked conduct could not be tolerated within the defendant's legitimate business interests. Problems of proof and evidence in connection with justification are considered more fully in **Chapter 7**.

Claims premised on traditional common law tort theories[48] should be dealt with in the customary manner by challenging the facts on which the plaintiff's prima facie case is based and by asserting recognized affirmative defenses.

§ 5.33 Damages

It is fundamental that those who suffer legally recognized injuries are entitled to damages.[49] Early public policy tort cases neglected the question of compensatory damages.[50] Generally, however, courts have awarded compensatory damages for the tort of wrongful dismissal which include lost earnings, lost future earnings, expenses of finding a new job, and mental anguish. An example of compensatory damages being awarded is *Harless v. First National Bank*,[51] in which the court upheld an award of $25,000. The court, although striking an award of punitive damages,[52] found that the bank's act gave rise to damages for emotional distress[53] in addition to damages for loss of wages.[54] In *Smith v. Atlas Off-Shore Boat Service*,

---

[47] At common law, this would be a plea in confession and avoidance, presenting justification and excuse. *See* J. Koffler & A. Reppy, Common Law Pleading § 245 (1969).

[48] See §§ **5.22–5.29**.

[49] D. Dobbs, Law of Remedies § 3.1 (1973).

[50] *See* Harless v. First Nat'l Bank, 289 S.E.2d 692 (W. Va. 1982): "The law regarding the measure of damages that may be recovered for the tort of retaliatory discharge is rather sparse. Most courts have merely addressed the issue of whether a cause of action exists. . . . " *See* Alaniz v. San Isidro Indep. School Dist., 589 F. Supp. 17, 19–20 (S.D. Tex. 1983) (approving $51,017 back pay, $50,000 compensatory damages for mental anguish, and reinstatement as appropriate remedies in a public employee dismissal case litigated under § 1983), *aff'd*, 742 F.2d 207 (5th Cir. 1984).

[51] 289 S.E.2d 692 (W. Va. 1982).

[52] *Id.* at 703. The court found punitive damages should not be awarded automatically in retaliatory dismissal cases, holding that the employee must prove "further egregious conduct on the part of the employer" to collect punitive damages. It also struck the award for "outrageous conduct," believing it duplicated the award for retaliatory dismissal.

[53] *Id.* at 702: "We believe that the tort of retaliatory discharge carries with it a sufficient indicia of intent, thus, damages for emotional distress may be recovered as a part of the compensatory damages." *See also* Cagle v. Burns & Roe, Inc., 106 Wash. 2d, 911, 726 P.2d 434, (1986) (emotional distress damages recoverable for public policy tort).

[54] 289 S.E.2d at 699, 700 n.13.

Inc.,[55] the Fifth Circuit found that a retaliatory dismissal entitled a fired employee to damages for job search expenses, lost earnings, and future lost earnings.[56] Punitive damages usually are not permitted for breach of contract[57] but often are allowed in tort suits.[58] Several courts have indicated that punitive damages are appropriate in wrongful dismissal tort actions.[59] For example, in *Kelsay v. Motorola, Inc.*,[60] the court held that punitive damages in wrongful dismissal actions could be assessed, but not retroactively, since it would be unfair to punish employers for actions that they did not know were wrong. The Supreme Court of Appeals of West Virginia has concluded[61] that punitive damages can be awarded only when the plaintiff can demonstrate "wanton, willful or malicious conduct"[62] by the employer. The trend thus appears to be toward allowing punitive damages for the public policy tort. Unresolved, however, is whether the *malice* required for liability will satisfy the *malice* required for punitive damages.[63]

If the employer is a partnership, the concept of joint and several liability permits a successful public policy tort plaintiff to recover from each member of the partnership as well as from the partnership.[64]

A February 1984 study by a special committee of the State Bar of California reported on a survey of California wrongful dismissal cases proceeding to a jury

---

[55] 653 F.2d 1057 (5th Cir. 1981).

[56] *Id.* at 1064. The court cautioned in a footnote that damages for lost future earnings must be based on the likely duration of the old employment. *See* O'Brien v. Papa Gino's, 780 F.2d 1067 (1st Cir. 1986) (approving judgment for plaintiff of $385,000 in lost wages on public policy/privacy claim and $50,000 compensatory damages on defamation claim); Schubbe v. Diesel Serv. Unit Co., 71 Or. App. 232, 692 P.2d 132, 135 (1984) (affirming back pay damages of $20,417 for dismissal on account of filing workers' compensation claim).

[57] The rule is stated in A. Corbin, Corbin on Contracts § 1077 at 438 (1964). *But see* S. Williston, Contracts § 1340 at 209–13 (1968); *and* Taylor v. Atchison, T.&.S. F. Ry., 92 F. Supp. 968 (W.D. Mo. 1950) (holding that punitive damages were permissible in a contract suit for wrongful dismissal under theory that liability in tort could coexist with liability in contract).

[58] Punitive or exemplary damages are limited to cases in which the tortfeasor's conduct is outrageous or evil in nature, and are designed to punish the wrongdoer and deter him from repeating the action. *See* Restatement (Second) Tort § 908, comment b (1979).

[59] Clanton v. Cain Sloan Co., 677 S.W.2d 441 (Tenn. 1984) (punitive damages for retaliatory discharge available in the future but not in this case); Pierce v. Ortho Pharmaceutical Corp., 84 N.J. 58, 417 A.2d 505 (1980); Nees v. Hocks, 272 Or. 210, 536 P.2d 512 (1975); Kelsay v. Motorola, Inc., 774 Ill. 2d 172, 384 N.E.2d 353 (1978).

[60] 74 Ill. 2d 172, 384 N.E.2d 353 (1978).

[61] Harless v. First Nat'l Bank, 289 S.E.2d 692 (W. Va. 1982).

[62] *Id.* at 703.

[63] *See* Malik v. Apex Int'l Alloys, Inc., 762 F.2d 77, 80 (10th Cir. 1985) (affirming judgment of $50,000 compensatory, and $75,000 punitive damages in workers' compensation retaliation case, finding that *malice* means wrongful action done intentionally without just cause or excuse); Moniodis v. Cook, 64 Md. App. 1, 494 A.2d 212, 221 (1985) (affirming punitive damages judgment on evidence that employer, knowing of statutory prohibition, nevertheless dismissed employees for refusing polygraph exam).

[64] *See* Reed v. Sale Memorial Hosp. & Clinic, 698 S.W.2d 931, 939 (Mo. Ct. App. 1985) (tort claim under statutory no-retaliation provision of workers' compensation statute).

verdict. In 53 percent of the plaintiff verdicts, punitive damages were awarded. In 76 percent of that 53 percent, awards were greater than $100,000, and in 35 percent, awards exceeded $600,000.[65]

The computation of damages is likely to be a particular problem under a misrepresentation theory, because of confusion between contract and tort theories.[66]

Under the American Rule,[67] attorneys' fees ordinarily are not recoverable in a tort action.[68]

Reinstatement is available in common law actions as a form of injunctive relief.[69] The availability of injunctive relief in tort cases depends on a variety of factors,[70] but it is foreseeable that courts, when faced with requests for orders to reinstate employees in the public policy tort context, will refer to the contract rule[71] and decline to order reinstatement.

---

[65] State Bar of California Labor and Employment Law Section, To Strike a New Balance: A Report of the Adhoc Committee on Termination at Will and Wrongful Discharge 7 (Feb. 8, 1984).

[66] The majority rule is to permit *benefit of the bargain* damages, a measure equivalent to that used in an action for breach of an employment contract, Restatement (Second) of Torts § 549 (Appendix) (1977); see § **4.28**; *see also* Andolsun v. Berlitz School of Languages, Inc., 196 A.2d 926 (D.C. 1964). A competing rule permits recovery only of out-of-pocket expenses, based on the premise that the plaintiff should be restored to her position as it existed before the misrepresentation occurred. Restatement (Second) of Torts § 549(1)(a) (1977); Hanlon v. MacFadden Publications, Inc., 302 N.Y. 502, 99 N.E.2d 546 (1951). The Restatement (Second) of Torts adopted a compromise position, which gives "the plaintiff the option of either the out-of-pocket or the benefit-of-the bargain rule in any case in which the latter measure can be established by proof in accordance with the usual rules of certainty in damages." Restatement (Second) of Torts § 549 comment h (1977). Some courts refuse to adopt either of these rules and prefer a more flexible measure adapted to the circumstances of each case. *See* Espaillat v. Berlitz Schools of Languages, Inc., 383 F.2d 220 (D.C. Cir. 1967); Annotation, 24 A.L.R.3d 1388, 1392 (1969).

[67] *See* Alyeska Pipeline Serv. Co. v. Wilderness Soc'y, 421 U.S. 240 (1975) for a discussion of the American Rule regarding attorney's fees as court costs. *See generally* S. Speiser, Attorney's Fees, ch. 12 (allowance of fees as costs; recovery from opponent), ch. 13 (allowance of fees as damages) (1973).

[68] See generally § **2.25** regarding attorney's fees under remedial statutes.

[69] " 'Injunctive relief,' as used in this section, includes both mandatory and prohibitory injunctions." Restatement (Second) of Torts ch. 48, Note on Terminology (1977).

[70] *Id.* § 936:
    (a) the nature of the interest to be protected,
    (b) the relative adequacy to the plaintiff of injunction and other remedies,
    (c) any unreasonable delay by the plaintiff in bringing suit,
    (d) any related misconduct on the part of the plaintiff,
    (e) the relative hardship likely to result to defendant if an injunction is granted and to plaintiff if it is denied,
    (f) the interests of third persons and of the public, and
    (g) the practicability of framing and enforcing the order or judgment.

[71] *See* Restatement (Second) of Contracts § 367 comment b (1979) (rule barring specific performance of employee's promise sometimes used to bar specific performance of employer's promise when personal supervision involved). *But see* D. Dobbs, Remedies 929 (1973). Professor Dobbs notes that damages are sometimes inadequate, cooperation between employer and employee is not always required, supervision of the employee by the employer is not always required, and

Federal Rule of Civil Procedure 11 permits sanctions to be imposed on counsel for advancing frivolous claims. The rule permits counsel to advance good faith arguments for the extension, modification, or reversal of existing law, but some courts have nevertheless imposed sanctions based on nothing more than a conclusion that the legal argument advanced lacked merit. *Zick v. Verson Allsteel Press Co.* [72] used the rule to impose sanctions for arguing that federal court should find covenant of good faith appropriate under Illinois law. The *Zick* case is an obvious misapplication of Rule 11, in that the court's opinion demonstrates the colorability of the counsel's argument.

---

that mutuality of obligation is a discredited theory. He advocates a case-by-case analysis of requests for specific performance in master-servant cases. *Id.* at 931.

[72] 623 F. Supp. 927, 932–33 (N.D. Ill. 1985).

CHAPTER 6
SPECIAL PROBLEMS OF PUBLIC EMPLOYMENT

§ 6.1   Introduction
§ 6.2   What Is a Public Employer?
§ 6.3   Civil Service Protections: In General
§ 6.4   —Federal Civil Service
§ 6.5   —State and Municipal Civil Service
§ 6.6   —Exhaustion of Administrative Remedies
§ 6.7   Federal Discrimination Statutes
§ 6.8   Reconstruction Era Civil Rights Acts
§ 6.9   Due Process: In General
§ 6.10 —Deprivation of Property Interests
§ 6.11 —Deprivation of Liberty Interests
§ 6.12 —Procedural Due Process Entitlements
§ 6.13 —Substantive Due Process Entitlements
§ 6.14 Interaction of Public Sector Grievance Arbitration and Civil Service Laws
§ 6.15 —Public Sector Grievance and Arbitration Procedures: Exclusivity, Exhaustion and Preclusion
§ 6.16 —Enforceability of Grievance Arbitration Awards
§ 6.17 Sovereign Immunity: In General
§ 6.18 —Suits against the United States and Its Officials
§ 6.19 —Suits against State and Local Governments under § 1983 and Other Federal Statutes
§ 6.20 —Common Law Suits against State and Local Governments and Officials

§ 6.1   Introduction

This chapter considers wrongful dismissal claims by public employees. Public employees enjoy greater protection against wrongful dismissal than private sector employees, though the doctrine of sovereign immunity[1] mitigates the greater protections to some degree. Public employees, like private sector employees, can sue to recover damages for breach of contract[2] and for tortious conduct.[3] In addition, many public employees are protected by civil service systems against dismissal without cause, and all are protected by the United States Constitution against infringement of property or liberty interests without due process.

This chapter does not repeat substantive tort and contract material discussed in **Chapters 4, 5** and **7**. Instead, it deals with legal issues unique to public employers. As a threshold matter, it considers who is and who is not a public employee. It reviews, in general terms, the types of protections typically provided under state or federal civil service systems and federal discrimination statutes. Next, the chapter considers constitutional protections against wrongful dismissal available to public employees, which are not generally available to private sector employees because their employers' actions are not state action. Then, it considers some special problems of grievance arbitration. The chapter concludes by considering problems of sovereign immunity.

§ 6.2 What Is a Public Employer?

Because employees of public employers enjoy protections against wrongful dismissal that generally are greater than those enjoyed by private sector employees,[4] it may be important for a plaintiff-employee or a defendant-employer in a particular case to establish that the employer is or is not *public* for purposes of making those protections available. The courts have occasion to decide the meaning of public employer in four different contexts:

1. In deciding whether an employer's personnel decisions are covered by state or federal civil service statutes[5]
2. In deciding whether an employer's labor relations are covered by a state labor relations statute[6]

---

[1] Immunity is discussed in §§ **6.17–6.20**.

[2] Contract theories are discussed in **ch. 4**. Gutierrez v. City of Chicago, 605 F. Supp. 973, 977 (N.D. Ill. 1985) (statutory status as at-will public employee can be altered by informal understanding of job security).

[3] Tort theories are discussed in **ch. 5**.

[4] See §§ **6.3–6.6** (civil service protection) and §§ **6.9–6.13** (constitutional protections). Conversely, government employers may enjoy immunities not enjoyed by private employers. See §§ **6.17–6.20**.

[5] See §§ **6.3–6.6**.

[6] The usual question is whether collective bargaining is covered by federal law because the employer is private, and affects commerce, or is covered by a state public employee labor relations statute. *See, e.g.,* U.T.U. v. Long Island R.R., 455 U.S. 678 (1982) (rejecting applicability of strike prohibition under state public employee bargaining law); Baker Bus Serv., Inc. v. Keith, 416 A.2d 727, 731 (Me. 1980) (private school bus company found to be *alter ego* of city and thus subject to state collective bargaining statute); *In re* New York Pub. Library v. New York P.E.R.B.,

3. In deciding whether the employer may be a defendant in a lawsuit brought under 42 U.S.C. § 1983
4. In deciding whether the doctrine of sovereign immunity applies.[7]

The most difficult of these is likely to be the third: is an employer's action a state action sufficient to trigger constitutional due process and equal protection rights?

The availability of federal constitutional protections for state and local government under federal civil rights law depends on whether the state was the employer.[8] This subject is worthy of detailed discussion.

An element of a prima facie case under § 1983 is that *state action* be involved in the context of a dismissal from employment.[9] State action can be found not only when the state or other governmental entity is the employer, but also when an apparently private entity, having a *symbiotic relationship*[10] with the state or performing a *state function*,[11] is the employer.

The *symbiotic relationship* and *nexus* approaches to finding state action in the activities of an otherwise private entity focus on the degree of involvement by the state in the activities of the defendant entity. Thus, in *Burton v. Wilmington Parking Authority*,[12] the Court found so much state entanglement in the operations of the defendant as to amount to "that degree of state participation and involvement" which it was the design of the Fourteenth Amendment to condemn.[13] Emphasizing that the state regulatory body overseeing the utility had not ordered the challenged practice, in *Jackson v. Metropolitan Edison Co.*[14] the Court held that termination of service by a public utility was not state action. The Court offered what has come to be called the *nexus* test: "[T]he inquiry must be whether there is a sufficiently close nexus between the State and the challenged action of the

---

37 N.Y.2d 752, 755–57, 337 N.E.2d 136, 138, 374 N.Y.S.2d 625, 628 (1975). (Fuchsberg, J., dissenting, in collective bargaining case). The rights of a terminated employee might be affected by the resolution of the question because of the treatment of arbitration provisions in a collective bargaining agreement. Both federal and state law provide for the enforcement of arbitration awards finding discharges to be wrongful, but a collective bargaining agreement negotiated under the belief it was covered by the NLRA might not comply with state law, or questions might arise as to the lawfulness of the union's representation status. See §§ **6.14–6.16**.

[7] See §§ **6.17–6.20** for a discussion of sovereign immunity.

[8] The Constitution only creates rights vis-a-vis the government, and the principal civil rights law permitting damages for infringement of constitutional rights only covers governmental "persons." 42 U.S.C. § 1983 (1982).

[9] *See* Rendell-Baker v. Kohn, 457 U.S. 830, 837 (1982) (discharge of teachers and counselor by private school receiving 90 percent of funds from state not state action); *see generally* S. Nahmod, Civil Rights and Civil Liberties Litigation § 2.01 at 34 (1979).

[10] S. Nahmod, Civil Rights and Civil Liberties Litigation § 2.05 (1979).

[11] *Id.* § 2.06.

[12] 365 U.S. 715 (1961).

[13] *Id.* at 724.

[14] 419 U.S. 345 (1974).

regulated entity so that the action of the latter may be fairly treated as that of the State itself."[15]

An alternative approach to finding state action is the *public function* test. According to this test, the act of a private entity constitutes state action when the entity performs a function traditionally associated with the sovereign. This test originated in the case of *Marsh v. Alabama*[16] but has been circumscribed in recent cases.[17]

Three cases involving adverse employment action illustrate the boundaries of these methods of finding state action. In *Janusaitis v. Middlebury Volunteer Fire Department*,[18] the Second Circuit found state action in the dismissal of a firefighter by a volunteer fire department. The court found that "fire protection is a function so traditionally associated with sovereignty that its performance, even by an otherwise 'private' entity, constitutes state action."[19] Having found state action under the public function test, it found it unnecessary to apply the nexus or symbiotic relationship tests.[20]

Conversely, in *Musso v. Suriano,* the Seventh Circuit found no state action in the dismissal of an employee by a private nursing home.[21] The court held that receipt of extensive state and federal funding combined with regulation and licensing were not enough to constitute state action under *Jackson v. Metropolitan Edison Co.*[22] and *Flagg Brothers Inc. v. Brooks.*[23]

In *Lubin v. Crittenden Hospital Association*,[24] the Eighth Circuit held that a § 1983 action could not be maintained against a private, nonprofit hospital for adverse action affecting the plaintiff's staff privileges in the hospital. The court concluded that the hospital's action was not state action under the nexus, symbiotic relationship, or public function tests.[25]

The Supreme Court has emphasized that the determination of whether an entity is public for § 1983 purposes must be made on a case-by-case basis. Counsel in close cases must therefore be prepared to address the two basic questions: is a

---

[15] *Id.* at 351.

[16] 326 U.S. 501 (1946).

[17] Flagg Bros., Inc. v. Brooks, 436 U.S. 149 (1978) (self-help disposal of goods under the Uniform Commercial Code not a public function); Hudgens v. NLRB, 424 U.S. 507 (1976) (operation of shopping centers and malls not a public function); Jackson v. Metropolitan Edison Co., 419 U.S. 345 (1974) (heavily regulated public utility with a monopoly not performing a public function).

[18] 607 F.2d 17 (2d Cir. 1979).

[19] *Id.* at 22.

[20] *Id.*

[21] 586 F.2d 59, 60 (7th Cir. 1978) (three cases consolidated on appeal). *See also* Rendell-Baker v. Kohn, 457 U.S. 830 (1982) (similar result on similar facts); Harris v. Hubbert, 588 F.2d 167 (5th Cir. 1979) (no state action when Alabama Education Association transferred supervisory employee over employee's objections).

[22] 419 U.S. 345 (1974).

[23] 436 U.S. 149 (1978).

[24] 713 F.2d 416 (8th Cir. 1983).

[25] *Id.* at 418.

§ 6.3 Civil Service Protections: In General

Most public employees below the policymaking level enjoy protection against wrongful dismissal by virtue of civil service statutes. The structure of federal civil service is somewhat different from state, municipal and teacher systems. The concepts underlying the protection afforded against wrongful dismissal are similar, however, in all civil service systems.

Civil service protection usually exists for certain positions. The federal Civil Service Reform Act applies to "all appointive positions in the executive, judicial and legislative branches of the Government of the United States."[27] Occasionally controversies arise over coverage.[28] Coverage under state statutes is more varied than federal coverage but can be determined by reference to the specific civil service statutes involved.[29]

Two distinct questions are presented with respect to terminations made under civil service statutes: Did the requisite cause for termination exist, and were the required procedures followed in effecting the termination?[30] Counsel in a particular case should ascertain the grounds for dismissal permitted in the applicable statute and the procedures specified for deciding whether a termination should be effected.

---

[26] *See* Myron v. Consolidated Rail Corp., 752 F.2d 50, 54 (2d Cir. 1985) (government control of stock of private railroad, and monitoring of financial performance not enough to make employment decisions of railroad "state action"); Anderson v. National R.R. Passenger Corp., 754 F.2d 202, 204 (7th Cir. 1985) (action by Amtrak is not action by federal government, even though government controls Amtrak's board of directors); Edwards v. Lutheran Senior Serv. of Dover, Inc., 603 F. Supp. 315 (D. Del. 1985) (neither *nexus* nor *symbiotic relationship* tests met by funding, regulation of public housing enterprise by state agency).

[27] 5 U.S.C. § 2101(1) (1982).

[28] *See* Doe v. United States Dep't of Justice, 753 F.2d 1092, 1100 (D.C. Cir. 1985) (government attorney, excepted from civil service protections, failed to show violation of departmental regulations in manner in which her discharge was effected); Windsor v. Tennessean, 726 F.2d 277 (6th Cir. 1984) (United States Attorney not entitled to civil service protection but can maintain action against supervisor in personal capacity, on appropriate facts); McCauley v. Thygerson, 732 F.2d 978, 981 n. (D.C. Cir. 1984) (Federal Home Loan Mortgage Corporation not covered by civil service but nevertheless a federal government employer); Anselmo v. Ailes, 344 F.2d 607 (2d Cir. 1965) (application of federal civil service law to technicians controlled by state).

[29] *See, e.g.,* Ala. Code § 36-26-10 (1977) (positions in the service of the state); Wyatt v. Bronner, 500 F. Supp. 817 (M.D. Ala. 1980) (coverage of building commission employees under state civil service law); *see generally* 15A Am. Jur. 2d §§ 13–14 (1976 & Supp 1986); Annotation, 134 A.L.R. 1149 (1982 Supp.).

[30] Analytically, the two questions are similar to the questions of substantive and procedural due process. The first concerns the rational relationship between the grounds asserted for dismissal and the legitimate interests of the employer. The second concerns whether the procedures were adequate for a reliable determination of whether the asserted cause for dismissal in fact existed. See §§ **6.12–6.13** for a discussion of substantive and procedural due process.

The federal system will be considered first; then some general observations will be offered about state, municipal and teacher systems.[31]

§ 6.4 — Federal Civil Service

The federal Civil Service Reform Act of 1978[32] allows the dismissal of a federal employee only "for such cause as will promote the efficiency of the service."[33] The same act provides federal employees with statutory protection against reprisals for "whistleblowing."[34]

In addition to guaranteeing employees that they will not be dismissed without cause, the federal Act specifies in some detail the procedural steps that must be taken before an employee[35] can be terminated. The federal statute provides for the following procedural guarantees:

1. Advance notice of the proposed personnel action
2. An opportunity for the employee to respond orally and in writing and to present evidence
3. Representation by counsel
4. A written decision and reasons supporting it from the employing agency
5. A right to appeal to the Merit Systems Protection Board (MSPB), and ultimately
6. A right to judicial review of the administrative decision by the MSPB.[36]

MSPB and judicial review serve the purpose of ensuring that the administrative agencies had substantial evidence to support two separate determinations: that the employee actually committed the conduct complained of and that removal based

---

[31] It plainly is not feasible in the space available to give even general treatment to the civil service laws of all 50 states. The modest objective of this section is to explain major concepts and to identify likely issues to facilitate counsel's entry into the research resources covering the law of a particular jurisdiction. *See generally Defending Civil Service Employee From Discharge,* 24 Am. Jur. *Trials* § 421 (1977). *See also,* Note, *Developments in the Law—Public Employment,* 97 Harv. L. Rev. 1611 (1984) (reviewing evolution of civil service, collective bargaining and constitutional protections with respect to public employees).

[32] 5 U.S.C. §§ 7501 (1982).

[33] *Id.* §§ 7503, 7513(a).

[34] *Id.* § 2301(b)(9).

[35] Probationary employees enjoy substantially less procedural protection than permanent employees. *See* Mastriano v. F.A.A., 714 F.2d 1152, 1155 (Fed. Cir. 1983) (probationary employees may not appeal to MSPB); Connolly v. United States, 554 F. Supp. 1250, 1257 (Ct. Cl. 1982) (probationary employees are pointedly excluded from panoply of procedural rights to appeal adverse personnel actions).

[36] 5 U.S.C. § 7513 (1982). *See* Bush v. Lucas, 462 U.S. 367, 386–87 (1983) (explaining procedural steps).

§ 6.4   FEDERAL CIVIL SERVICE   329

on the misconduct will promote the efficiency of the service.[37] The standards of review permit the employing agency substantial discretion in determining what constitutes cause for dismissal, particularly in the second determination, as long as the agency articulates a rational basis for its conclusion.

The operation of statutory protections respecting cause for discharge is illustrated by four federal cases. As these cases show, the federal civil service system requires an employer (1) to ascertain the facts in a reliable way, and (2) to terminate employment only for conduct bearing a logical nexus with ability to perform governmental duties. In *Risner v. Federal Aviation Administration*,[38] the court affirmed an MSPB determination that a Federal Aviation Administration employee had been properly dismissed for disruptive workplace conduct, holding that the statute was satisfied when the agency had "a rational basis for discharging an employee."[39]

In *Hoska v. United States Department of the Army*,[40] the court overturned an MSPB determination in part because the employer had failed to establish any nexus between the employee's allegedly "improper or indiscreet" behavior and his ability to protect classified information.[41] Therefore, the employee's security clearance was revoked improperly and his discharge based on the security clearance revocation could not stand.[42]

Similarly, in *Bonet v. United States Postal Service*,[43] the court refused to sustain an MSPB determination because there was no nexus shown between the employee's off-duty conduct and his job performance.[44] It reasoned that a dismissal in the petitioner's circumstances required some showing in the record of a nexus between sexually indecent conduct with minors and an adverse reflection on the image of the United States Postal Service[45] which the Postal Service had made no attempt to do.[46]

In *Abrams v. Department of the Navy*,[47] the court vacated a decision of the MSPB involving the dismissal of an employee for conviction of criminal offenses resulting

---

[37] Sherman v. Alexander, 684 F.2d 464, 468 (7th Cir. 1982). James v. F.E.R.C., 747 F.2d 1581, 1583 (Fed. Cir. 1984) (decision of MSPB upholding dismissal of profane and abusive employee adequately articulated nexus between conduct and efficiency of service); Hunt v. Department of Health & Human Servs., 758 F.2d 608, 611 (Fed. Cir. 1985) (violation of anti-gambling regulation, even for first offense, punishable by dismissal); Beard v. General Servs. Admin., 801 F.2d 1318, 1322 (Fed. Cir. 1986) (MSPB does not determine de novo whether discharge was appropriate; rather, it reviews agency decision for reasonableness).

[38] 677 F.2d 36 (8th Cir. 1982) (per curiam).

[39] *Id.* at 38.

[40] 677 F.2d 131 (D.C. Cir. 1982).

[41] *Id.* at 134.

[42] *Id.*

[43] 661 F.2d 1071 (5th Cir. 1981).

[44] *Id.* at 1074.

[45] *Id.* at 1075.

[46] *Id.* (presumption utilized).

[47] 714 F.2d 1219 (3d Cir. 1983).

from an off-duty shooting in a card game. The court held that the employing agency could rely on a presumption of a nexus between such off-duty conduct and an impairment of the employee's ability to do his job. It reversed the MSPB's conclusion that the employee had adequately rebutted the nexus by testimony that his own job performance was unaffected. The court reasoned that "[a]n employee may remain at his post only if he can show that his off-duty misconduct will not impede the agency's achievement of its goals directly or indirectly . . . ."[48]

Procedural deficiencies are not grounds for overturning the employer's decision unless they affect the employee's ability fairly to contest the factual basis for discharge.[49] Therefore, noncompliance with notice requirements is measured by the effect it has on an employee's ability to defend against the charges.[50] Likewise, while judicial evidentiary rules are not strictly enforced, the nature of the evidence used against the employee must provide a fair opportunity for rebuttal.[51] Similarly, requirements for a specific statement of reasons for adverse action are deemed met when the procedure followed permits meaningful appellate review.[52]

Federal employees who prevail in protesting adverse employment action may be entitled to attorneys' fees at the discretion of the MSPB.[53]

§ 6.5 — State and Municipal Civil Service

State civil service statutes are generally similar in concept to the federal system[54] but usually provide for multiple civil service systems: a unitary system for state employees, multiple systems for employees of individual municipalities, and a separate system or systems for school teachers.[55] Virtually all of these systems

---

[48] *Id.* at 1223. *But see* McLeod v. Department of Army, 714 F.2d 918, 921 (9th Cir. 1983) (illegality of marijuana possession not sufficient to establish nexus).

[49] *See* Doyle v. Veterans Admin., 667 F.2d 70, 72 (Ct. Cl. 1981) (harmless procedural errors).

[50] *Compare* Sherman v. Alexander, 684 F.2d 464, 471 (7th Cir. 1982) (notice adequate to permit defense) *with* Burkett v. United States, 402 F.2d 1002, 1006–07 (Ct. Cl. 1968) (notice inadequate; different statute). *See* Conner v. United States Civil Serv. Comm'n, 721 F.2d 1054, 1056 (6th Cir. 1983) (procedural lapses did not prejudice employee).

[51] *See* Cooper v. United States, 639 F.2d 727, 730 (Ct. Cl. 1980) (hearsay too remote to amount to substantial evidence).

[52] *See* Cecil v. Department of Transp., 767 F.2d 892, 894 (Fed. Cir. 1985) (rejecting several procedural challenges to MSPB decision on a group of air traffic controller dismissal appeals); Kump v. Department of Transp., 767 F.2d 889, 891 (Fed. Cir. 1985) (failure to show prejudice from five-day notice of opportunity to make oral response); Mendelson v. Macy, 356 F.2d 796, 798 (D.C. Cir. 1966) (punishment for falsifying time records not arbitrary or unreasonable because of documentation supporting conclusion).

[53] 5 U.S.C. § 7701(g)(1) (1982). *See* Sterner v. Department of Army, 711 F.2d 1563 (Fed. Cir. 1983) (employee "prevailed" but MSPB did not abuse discretion in denying fees).

[54] *See generally* 15A Am. Jur. 2d, *Civil Service* § 61–67 (grounds for dismissal), §§ 68–71 (procedure for dismissal) (1976).

[55] *See* 15A Am. Jur. 2d, *Civil Service* § 9 (1976); 68 Am. Jur. 2d, *Schools* §§ 149–160 (1973 & 1982 Supp.). Civil service protection for state and local emloyees is growing. In 1955 only

provide for some form of tenure, permitting dismissal only for cause.[56] For example, the California civil service statute provides state employees with tenure "during good behavior"[57] and contains a list of 22 enumerated reasons for dismissal.[58] The California statute covering primary and secondary school teachers also provides for tenure,[59] though the list of enumerated reasons is somewhat more restrictive on what constitutes cause for removal.[60] In contrast, the California statute governing municipal and county civil service merely authorizes the local authority to establish civil service systems without specifying whether such systems must guarantee dismissal only for cause.[61] All three statutes establish or require an administrative mechanism within which employees can adjudicate the legality of adverse action.[62]

The arrangement in Pennsylvania is similar, except that it fills in the details of the municipal civil service systems and leaves it to local authorities to administer the systems.[63] Virginia's structure for municipal systems requires counties and municipalities to establish personnel systems conforming to the state system and to submit those systems to the state personnel director for approval.[64]

Some state statutes, including Alabama's, on their face do not require that there be cause for dismissal, only that a supervisor may dismiss a classified employee whenever the supervisor considers the "good of the service will be served by" the dismissal.[65] The provision, however, has been interpreted judicially to require

---

23 states had civil service laws covering approximately 65 percent of full time state employees. In 1970, 84 percent of the cities, 83 percent of the counties, and 96 percent of the states had adopted some type of merit system. H. Edwards, R. Clark & C. Craver, Labor Relations Law in the Public Sector, 347 n.2 (1979).

[56] Under most systems, the tenure protections do not extend to probationary employees. *See, e.g.,* Cal. Gov't Code § 19500 (West 1980), which gives tenure to every *permanent employee,* defined in § 18528 as an employee who is retained after the completion of a probationary period.

[57] Cal. Gov't Code § 19500 (West 1980).

[58] *Id.* § 19572.

[59] Cal. Educ. Code § 44882 (West 1980) (tenure after three years).

[60] *Id.* § 44932 (West 1980) (enumerating grounds for separation of tenured teacher).

[61] Cal. Gov't Code §§ 45001–45010 (West 1980) (authorizing establishment of municipal civil service systems); Cal. Gov't Code §§ 31103–31116 (authorizing establishment of county civil service systems).

[62] Cal. Gov't Code §§ 19574, 19575, 19578 (West 1980) (state employees); Cal. Gov't Code § 31108 (West 1980) (county employees); Cal. Educ. Code § 44932 (West 1980) (teachers).

[63] Pa. Stat. Ann. tit. 53 §§ 12621–12638 (first class cities); §§ 23431–23453 (second class cities); §§ 39401–39408 (third class cities); §§ 55644–55645 (first class townships) (Purdon 1957 & 1983–1984 Supp.).

[64] Va. Code Ann. § 15.1–17.1 (1981).

[65] Ala. Code § 36-26-27 (1975) (covering state employees):

> An appointing authority may dismiss a classified employee whenever he considers the good of the service will be served thereby, for reasons which shall be stated in writing, served on the affected employee and a copy furnished to the director, which action shall become a public record.

In Alabama, municipal law enforcement officers are subject to systems adopted by local authorities. Ala. Code § 11-43-182 (Supp 1986). *See* Chandler v. City of Lanett, 424 So. 2d 1307 (Ala.

that employees be given advance notice with reasonable specificity as to what will constitute grounds for dismissal.[66] Thus construed, such a statute is not materially different in effect from a statute expressly prohibiting dismissal except for cause. The employing agency may define *cause* by articulating a rational relationship between the grounds it asserts as cause and the needs of the civil service.

Obviously, what constitutes cause for dismissal will depend on the details of the applicable statute or ordinance and judicial decisions interpreting it. The requirement, developed under the federal system, that some relationship exist between the cause asserted for dismissal and the performance of an employee's duties also is applied by state courts.[67] The employer, in order to sustain a dismissal, is required to find that the employee actually engaged in the alleged conduct, and that the conduct constitutes cause for dismissal because of a nexus with the needs of the employing agency.

As with the federal civil service, procedural irregularities are evaluated according to the effect they have on the employee's rights. Thus, in *Department of Corrections v. Gandy*,[68] the Florida District Court of Appeals held that, although the governing statute required certified mail delivery,[69] the hand delivery of a notice of dismissal was not enough of a procedural defect to invalidate the dismissal. And in *Sanders v. Broadwater*,[70] the Alabama appeals court affirmed the dismissal of a state worker who claimed his dismissal notice was too vague for him to challenge. The court found the notice adequate for the employee's defense preparation.[71] In *Gee v. Alabama State Tenure Commission*,[72] a board of education was

---

1982) (personnel manual qualifies as civil service system). Teachers are subject to a separate system under state law, which is administered by local boards of education. Ala. Code §§ 16-24-2 to 16-24-10 (1977).

[66] *See* Simpson v. Van Ryzin, 289 Ala. 22, 265 So. 2d 569 (1972).

[67] *See* Stanton v. State Personnel Bd., 105 Cal. App. 3d 729, 164 Cal. Rptr. 557 (1980) (nexus must be established between misconduct and harm to the service); Blake v. State Personnel Bd., 25 Cal. App. 3d 541, 102 Cal. Rptr. 50 (1972) (upholding dismissal of state employee for inappropriate off-duty behavior in front of other agency employees); State Tenure Comm'n v. Madison County Bd. of Educ., 282 Ala. 658, 673, 213 So. 2d 823, 835 (1968) (cause includes any cause which bears reasonable relation to teacher's fitness); West Virginia Dept. of Corrections v. Lemasters, 313 S.E.2d 436, 440 (W. Va. 1984) (reversing order of civil service commission reinstating prison guard who provided firearms to prisoner); *Compare* Foley v. Philadelphia Civil Serv. Comm'n, 55 Pa. Commw. 594, 423 A.2d 1351 (1980) (facts proven do not constitute just cause) *with* In re Priest, 47 Pa. Commw. 320, 408 A.2d 547 (1979), *aff'd*, 497 Pa. 202, 439 A.2d 671 (1982) (off-duty drug offense amounts to cause) *and* Holliday v. Civil Serv. Comm'n, 121 Ill. App. 3d 763, 776, 460 N.E.2d 358, 366 (1984) (deferring to civil service commission determination that failure of tax collector to disqualify himself from assignment involving wife's business was cause for dismissal).

[68] 374 So. 2d 1081 (Fla. Dist. Ct. App. 1979).

[69] The statute, Fla. Stat. Ann. § 110.061(2)(b) (West 1977), requires notice to be sent to the dismissed employee "by certified mail with return receipt requested," (now renumbered Fla. Stat. Ann. § 110.227(4) (West 1982)).

[70] 402 So. 2d 1035 (Ala. Civ. App. 1981).

[71] *Id.* at 1036. The court also noted that the defense made to the charges was excellent, "addressing squarely the deficiencies." Id.

[72] 419 So. 2d 227 (Ala. Civ. App.), *cert. denied*, 419 So. 2d 227 (Ala. 1982).

not required to make specific findings of fact because its notice to a teacher was sufficiently specific to permit the State Tenure Commission to determine whether the evidence supported the charges.[73]

But in *Chavers v. State Personnel Board*,[74] the Alabama Court of Civil Appeals reversed the state's dismissal of a clerk because the letter of dismissal had come not from the clerk's appointing authority but from her immediate supervisor.[75] The court reasoned that the employee was entitled to the exercise of discretion by the higher authority. It is not sufficient merely to identify the procedural flaw; the person complaining should be able to articulate how the procedural error prejudiced her ability to show that cause for dismissal did not exist.

When a civil service statute requires the employer to follow certain procedures in termination, the purpose is to specify the means for determining whether grounds for the discharge exist. Such requirements properly are construed in light of that connection.[76]

Even if an employee cannot bring an action based on civil service regulations, she may be able to premise a public policy tort claim[77] or an implied-in-fact contract claim[78] on the personnel regulations of the agency.

§ 6.6 —Exhaustion of Administrative Remedies

Employees alleging violation of statutory rights under the federal civil service laws must pursue administrative remedies, seeking judicial review only after exhaustion of those remedies.[79] In *Bush v. Lucas*,[80] the Supreme Court held that federal employees have no direct nonstatutory remedy for violations of constitutional rights;

---

[73] *Id.* at 228. *Compare* Brown v. Alabama State Tenure Comm'n, 349 So. 2d 56, 58 (Ala. Civ. App. 1977) (inadequate notice of proposed action) *with* Elliott v. Kupferman, 58 Md. App. 510, 524, 473 A.2d 960, 967-68 (1984) (procedural irregularities not materially harmful to employee's rights).

[74] 357 So. 2d 662 (Ala. Civ. App.), *cert. denied,* 357 So. 2d 664 (Ala. 1978).

[75] Ala. Code § 36-26-27(a) (1977).

[76] Such a conception is consistent with the treatment of procedural due process in Mathews v. Eldridge, 424 U.S. 319, 335 (1976). See § **6.12**.

[77] *See* Nye v. Department of Livestock, 196 Mont. 222, 639 P.2d 498 (1982) (agency's personnel regulations were a source of public policy, and agency's failure to follow them constituted a public policy tort). See §§ **5.8–5.20** for discussion of public policy tort concepts.

[78] *See* Petrovich v. New Canaan Bd. of Educ., 189 Conn. 585, 589, 457 A.2d 315, 317-18 (1983) (contract theory permitted back pay award for nontenured teacher).

[79] *See* Borrell v. United States Int'l Communications Agency, 682 F.2d 981 (D.C. Cir. 1982) (nontenured employees do not have implied private right of action under Civil Service Reform Act); Shoultz v. Monfort of Colo., Inc., 754 F.2d 318, 325 (10th Cir. 1985) (no implied right of action under constitution for meat inspector discharged by the United States Department of Agriculture due to private company's efforts to induce his dismissal; employee must resort to civil service remedies).

[80] 462 U.S. 367 (1983). *But see* Kotarski v. Cooper, ___ F.2d ___ (9th Cir. Sept. 16, 1986) (*Bush v. Lucas* does not preclude *Bivens* action by probationary employee). *Compare* Spagnola v. Mathis, ___ F.2d ___ (D.C. Cir. 1986) (*Bivens* action available for First Amendment

they must litigate those rights in the administrative processes provided under the civil service statutes. Review of administrative determinations usually is narrow. In the federal system, courts affirm "rational decisions to dismiss federal employees if applicable procedures were followed and substantial evidence supports the [agency's] determination."[81]

Employees alleging a violation of statutory rights under state civil service laws need not exhaust state administrative remedies before bringing a suit under 42 U.S.C. § 1983 for violation of constitutional rights;[82] however, the merits of the constitutional claim may depend on the content of the state civil service statute involved.[83]

Employees must exhaust administrative remedies with respect to other types of statutory claims, however.[84] Also, if the employee appeals an administrative decision to the state courts, the employee may not bring a § 1983 action subsequently based on the same theories adjudicated by the state court.[85]

§ 6.7 Federal Discrimination Statutes

Both Title VII of the Civil Rights Act of 1964[86] and the Age Discrimination in Employment Act (ADEA)[87] cover federal, state, and local government employees.

---

violation) *with* Hubbard v. United States E.P.A., ___ F.2d ___ (D.C. Cir. 1986) (*Bivens* action not available).

[81] Jones v. Farm Credit Admin., 702 F.2d 160, 162 (8th Cir. 1983) (dismissal for insubordination affirmed).

[82] *See* Patsy v. Florida Bd. of Regents, 457 U.S. 496, 516 (1982). The availability of such procedures may, however, defeat the claim that procedural due process has not been satisfied. *See* Cohen v. City of Philadelphia, 736 F.2d 81, 86 (3d Cir. 1984), *cert. denied,* 469 U.S. 1019 (1984) (due process satisfied by availability of appeal in state court system); Lewis v. Hillsborough Transit Auth., 726 F.2d 668, 669 (11th Cir. 1984), *cert. denied,* 469 U.S. 822 (1984) (finding no due process violation because of availability of collectively bargained and administrative procedures; distinguishing exhaustion). *But see* Averyt v. Doyle, 456 So. 2d 1096, 1098 (Ala. Civ. App. 1984) (state employee constitutional claims must be presented in civil service administrative hearing, not in court).

[83] This is so because the property claim asserted in a § 1983 suit usually depends on expectations created by the civil service laws. See § **6.10**.

[84] *See* Boyd v. United States Postal Serv., 752 F.2d 410, 413 (9th Cir. 1985) (federal employee must exhaust administrative remedies with respect to handicap discrimination claim; reinstatement case).

[85] *See* Carbonell v. Louisiana Dep't of Health & Human Servs., 772 F.2d 185, 188 (5th Cir. 1985) (§ 1985 claim in essence a request to review decision of state court, which is beyond jurisdiction of lower federal courts).

[86] 42 U.S.C. §§ 2000e- 1 to 2000e-17 (1982). Title VII was amended by the Equal Employment Opportunity Act of 1972, Pub. L. No. 92-261, 86 Stat. 111 (1972), to expand its coverage to most federal, state, and local government employees. State and local governments were included by changing the definition of *person* in § 701(a). Federal employees were included by adding a new § 717.

[87] 29 U.S.C. §§ 621–633a (1982). The ADEA was amended by the Age Discrimination in Employment Act Amendments of 1978, Pub. L. No. 95-256, 92 Stat. 189 (1978) to bring most federal

The differences between application of these statutes to private sector employees and to public sector employees are minor.

Proof standards for Title VII claims are the same for public and private employers.[88] The enforcement machinery for federal employees is different from that for private, state, and municipal employees. It involves the employing agency, in conjunction with the Equal Employment Opportunity Commission (EEOC), in making a determination whether a violation of the Civil Rights Act occurred.[89]

The ADEA applies to state and local government employers in exactly the same manner that it applies to private employers.[90] It applies to the federal government with two material differences: there is an independent enforcement mechanism created under the Merit Systems Protection Board,[91] and there is no upper age limit on the ADEA protections.[92]

§ 6.8 Reconstruction Era Civil Rights Acts

Sections 1981, 1983 and 1985 of Title 42[93] are potent protections for public employees. These sections, however, have only limited application to discrimination expressly prohibited by other, more recent statutes, and to private sector interference with public employment. Federal employees may not bring actions for race discrimination under the Reconstruction Era Civil Rights Acts. The Supreme Court has held that Title VII is the exclusive remedy for such discrimination.[94] There also is some authority for the proposition that Title VII is the exclusive remedy for discrimination by state and local governments, although the majority rule is to the contrary.[95]

---

and state and local government employees within the ADEA's coverage. State and local government employees were added by changing the definition of *employee* under § 11(f) of the ADEA. Federal employees were added by a new § 15, 29 U.S.C. § 633a (1982). Extension of the Act to state and local employees was held to be constitutional in EEOC v. Wyoming, 460 U.S. 226 (1983).

[88] New York City Transit Auth. v. Beazer, 440 U.S. 568, 578 (1979) (government employer must use criteria connected with position to evaluate fitness); Dothard v. Rawlinson, 433 U.S. 321, 331 n.14 (1977) (arbitrary height and weight requirements for prison guards violate Title VII).

[89] *See* 29 C.F.R. § 1613 (1982).

[90] The definitional section was changed to include employees of state and local governments as employees. 43 Fed. Reg. 60,901 (1978).

[91] 29 U.S.C. § 633a (functions of Civil Service Commission transferred to EEOC, Reorg. Plan No. 1 of 1978, § 2, 43 Fed. Reg. 19,807 (1978)). When a civil service appeal includes allegations of discrimination, 5 U.S.C. § 7702 provides for a decision by the Merit Systems Protection Board subject to review by the EEOC.

[92] 29 U.S.C. § 633a(a) (1982 Supp.).

[93] Popularly known as the *Reconstruction Era Civil Rights Acts*.

[94] Brown v. G.S.A., 425 U.S. 820 (1976).

[95] *See* Day v. Wayne County Bd. of Auditors, 749 F.2d 1199, 1204 (6th Cir. 1984) (Title VII provides the exclusive remedy when the only § 1983 violation is based on a violation of Title VII); Torres v. Wisconsin Dep't of Health & Social Serv., 592 F. Supp. 922, 928 (E.D. Wis. 1984) (no § 1983 suit for discrimination covered by Title VII). *But see* Ratliff v. City of Milwaukee,

Also, it can be difficult to base a § 1983 claim on alleged interference with employment by private sector parties. *Shoultz v. Monfort of Colorado, Inc.*[96] involved a meat inspector employed by the United States Department of Agriculture (USDA), dismissed after the USDA received complaints about the way he was doing his job at the facilities of a private company to which he was assigned. The inspector claimed that a private company whose meat he was inspecting conspired with USDA to interfere with the performance of his duties, in violation of 42 U.S.C. § 1985(1).[97] The court of appeals affirmed the district court's dismissal of the inspector's § 1985(1) claim, finding that the statute was not intended to cover complaints made through proper government channels about federal employees' performance of their duties.

§ 6.9 Due Process: In General

Public employees enjoy protections against wrongful dismissal derived from the Constitution of the United States. The Fourteenth Amendment prohibits any state from depriving a person of life, liberty, or property without *due process of law*.[98] The Fifth Amendment contains a similar restriction on actions by the federal government.[99] Persons suffering legal injury because of a violation of these constitutional provisions can maintain an action against states and their subdivisions under § 1983 of Title 42[1] and against the federal government under the general federal question jurisdictional statute.[2]

Applying these general principles to public employees who believe they have been discharged wrongfully requires examination of four questions:

---

795 F.2d 612, 624 (7th Cir. 1986) (plaintiff may sue public employer for violations of Fourteenth Amendment under § 1983 even though same facts suggest a violation of Title VII); Trigg v. Fort Wayne Community Schools, 766 F.2d 299, 302 (7th Cir. 1985) (great weight of authority says one can sue under both Title VII and § 1983); Green v. Illinois Dep't of Transp., 609 F. Supp. 1021, 1027 (N. D. Ill. 1985) (when same conduct violates both Title VII and rights granted elsewhere, can bring both Title VII and § 1983 actions) (explaining *Day* and disagreeing with *Torres*).

[96] 754 F.2d 318, 321 (10th Cir. 1985).

[97] Claims under 42 U.S.C. § 1985 are addressed in **§ 2.9**.

[98] U.S. Const. amend. XIV, § 1.

[99] U.S. Const. amend. V.

[1] It is necessary for the plaintiff to allege that rights "secured by the Constitution and laws" of the United States were violated under color of state law with some specificity for jurisdiction to exist. Maine v. Thiboutout, 448 U.S. 1 (1980) (rights protected under § 1983 include rights deriving from federal statutory law); Williams v. Treen, 671 F.2d 892 (5th Cir. 1982) (state prisoner action, based on allegations that refusal of medical treatment was "cruel and unusual punishment"); White v. Thomas, 660 F.2d 680 (5th Cir.) (§ 1983 provides a remedy for deprivation of constitutional rights), *cert. denied,* 455 U.S. 1027 (1982); Dorak v. Shapp, 403 F. Supp. 863 (M.D. Pa. 1975) (§ 1983 provides a remedy for deprivation of rights granted by state statute).

[2] The general federal question statute is 28 U.S.C. § 1331 (1982). The district courts have jurisdiction over specific federal questions by virtue of various statutes. *See* Wright & Miller, Federal

§ 6.10 PROPERTY INTERESTS

1. Was there deprivation of a property interest?[3]
2. Was there deprivation of a liberty interest?[4]
3. Was due process observed in a procedural sense?[5]
4. Was due process observed in a substantive sense?[6]

A due process violation can be established only if question one *or* two can be answered in the affirmative.[7] Once a property or liberty infringement has been shown, however, a violation can be shown *either* by procedural *or* substantive shortcomings. Each of these questions is addressed separately in the sections that follow.

§ 6.10 — Deprivation of Property Interests

The Fifth and Fourteenth Amendments guarantee against the deprivation of property without due process of law.[8] Public employment can be a property interest entitled to constitutional protection when the employee has a reasonable expectation, created by the employer, of continued employment, subject to termination only for cause, or to termination only by way of statutorily defined procedures.

In a public employee dismissal case, proving infringement of a property interest is conceptually similar to proving breach of an implied-in-fact contract at common law.[9] The plaintiff claiming a constitutional violation must show (1) that a property interest in the job existed—usually resulting from a state promise of employment security, and (2) deprivation of the property interest by breach of the promise.[10]

Practice and Procedure, Civil § 1210 (1969). The Supreme Court, in Bivens v. Six Unknown Agents, 403 U.S. 388 (1971), held that a plaintiff alleging violation of his constitutional right to be free from unreasonable searches under the Fourth Amendment had an implied right of action in the district courts, even though no federal statute specifically conferred jurisdiction over such a claim. *See also* Carlson v. Green, 446 U.S. 14 (1980), for the Court's recent discussion of relief for constitutional violations. In Bush v. Lucas, 462 U.S. 367 (1983), the Court held that a federal employee must litigate constitutional claims administratively within the civil service system, rather than by bringing actions directly in court.

[3] See § **6.10**.

[4] See § **6.11**.

[5] See § **6.12**.

[6] See § **6.13**.

[7] *See* Hewitt v. Grabicki, 794 F.2d 1373, 1380 (9th Cir. 1986) (two step analysis: first determine whether liberty or property interest, then apply balancing test to decide what process is due).

[8] U.S. Const. amends. V, XIV, § 1.

[9] See §§ **4.6–4.24**.

[10] These two requirements are analogous to (1) proving a promise (§§ **4.6–4.11**) and (2) proving a breach (§§ **4.21–4.24**).

The property interest created by an expectation of continued employment subject to termination only for cause is illustrated by two Supreme Court cases, *Board of Regents v. Roth*[11] and *Perry v. Sindermann*.[12]

In *Perry v. Sindermann,* Sindermann was notified in his tenth year of employment after a succession of one-year contracts that his contract for a state college teaching position would not be renewed.[13] The college had no formal tenure system, but Sindermann alleged that a de facto tenure system had been established by custom and practice, and by a statement in the college's faculty guide encouraging faculty members "to feel that [they have] permanent tenure as long as [their] teaching services are satisfactory."[14] The Supreme Court held that Sindermann was entitled to prove his claim that the college had fostered the understanding that the employment of persons in his position would be continued unless cause existed for their termination.[15] It reasoned that a property interest can arise from a contract and that a contract can be implied from the promisor's words and conduct even though no formal agreement exists.[16]

In *Board of Regents v. Roth*,[17] decided the same day as *Sindermann,* the Court applied the same analytical principles but reached the opposite result. Roth was hired to teach at a state university for a term of one year. He was informed without explanation that his contract would not be renewed. He sued to require the university to give reasons for not renewing his contract and to afford him a hearing.[18] The Court held that Roth had no property interest in continued employment beyond the one-year term of his contract. The terms of his contract "specifically provided that [Roth's] employment was to terminate on June 30. They did not provide for contract renewal absent 'sufficient cause.' Indeed they made no provision for renewal whatsoever."[19] Moreover, there was no state statute or university rule or policy that created any legitimate expectation of reappointment.[20] "Thus the terms of [Roth's] appointment secured absolutely no interest in re-employment for the next year."[21]

The Supreme Court missed an opportunity to refine its *Roth* and *Sindermann* holdings further in *Vail v. Board of Education*.[22] In *Vail,* the school board offered a prospective coach a one-year contract, with an assurance of a one-year extension.[23]

---

[11] 408 U.S. 564 (1972).

[12] 408 U.S. 593 (1972).

[13] *Id.* at 594.

[14] *Id.* at 600.

[15] *Id.* at 602–03.

[16] *Id.* at 601–02.

[17] 408 U.S. 564, 569 (1972).

[18] *Id.* at 578.

[19] *Id.*

[20] *Id.*

[21] *Id.*

[22] 706 F.2d 1435 (7th Cir. 1983), *aff'd by an equally divided Court,* 466 U.S. 377 (1984).

[23] Mr. Vail gave up his old job, which he had held for 10 years, and took a salary cut to move himself and his family to the school district. The court found that Vail had relied on the board's

§ 6.10 PROPERTY INTERESTS

The Seventh Circuit found the board's act of not renewing his contract deprived Vail of a property interest without due process[24] and affirmed the lower court's award of damages. Judge Posner argued in a forceful dissent, however, that contract rights are not property within the intendment of the Fourteenth Amendment.[25] To hold otherwise, he concluded, would turn every claim for breach of an employment contract by a public employer into a federal claim under § 1983. The Supreme Court granted certiorari and affirmed by an equally divided court.[26]

The contrast between *Roth* and *Sindermann* demonstrates that a due process claim based on deprivation of an expectation of continued employment absent cause must be supported by facts showing a legitimate expectation of continued employment. The analysis is similar to that involved in satisfying the promise and breach elements of a common law claim for breach of an implied-in-fact contract.[27] The first step is to show that the state made a reasonably explicit promise of employment security.[28] As with common law implied-in-fact contract analysis, the unilateral expectations of the employee are not sufficient to establish the promise/property element.[29] The second step is to show a deprivation of the property interest by

---

promise, and the board's actions worked to deny his legitimate expectations of continued employment. *Id.* at 1440.

[24] Vail was afforded no hearing and given no explanation for the action. *Id.* at 1436.

[25] *Id.* at 1450–52 (Posner, J., dissenting).

[26] 466 U.S. 377 (1984).

[27] See §§ **4.21–4.24, 7.22**, and **7.28**. *Compare* McCauley v. Thygerson, 732 F.2d 978, 980–81 (D. C. Cir. 1984) (strong policies against applying contract theories, including promissory estoppel, to federal government employer; suggesting property interest must be based on statute rather than private contract) *with* Vinyard v. King, 728 F.2d 428, 432 (10th Cir. 1984) (constitutionally protected property interest under Oklahoma law created by employee handbook), *and* Whitfield v. Finn, 731 F.2d 1506, 1509 (11th Cir. 1984) (dismissed police officer entitled to trial on whether employee created property interest under Alabama law).

[28] *Compare* Bueno v. City of Donna, 714 F.2d 484, 492 (5th Cir. 1983) (personnel policies authorizing termination for just cause create property right) *with* Ogletree v. Chester, 682 F.2d 1366, 1369–71 (11th Cir. 1982) (no property interest in job created under state law by oral promises and by regulations that were "not explicit enough concerning conduct and disciplinary procedures") *and* Ratliff v. City of Milwaukee, 795 F.2d 612, 624 (7th Cir. 1986) (probationary employee does not have entitlement to continued employment under Wisconsin law, hence no property interest) *and* Blanton v. Griel Memorial Psychiatric Hosp., 758 F.2d 1540, 1544 (11th Cir. 1985) (probationary employee under Alabama civil service system does not have property interest, despite some limitations on reasons for removal), *and* Munson v. Friske, 754 F.2d 683, 693 (7th Cir. 1985) (no property interest shown by temporary employee) *and* Beckham v. Harris, 756 F.2d 1032, 1038 (4th Cir. 1985) (service "at pleasure of commission" does not involve a property interest) *and* Brockert v. Skornicka, 711 F.2d 1376, 1384 (7th Cir. 1983) (rule providing dismissal for certain reasons may not preclude dismissal for other reasons) *and* Osman v. Hialeah Hous. Auth., 785 F.2d 1550 (11th Cir. 1986) (since attorney can be dismissed by client at any time, attorney employed by public agency has no property interest in job under Florida law).

[29] *See* Martin v. Unified School Dist. No. 434, 728 F.2d 453, 455 (10th Cir. 1984) (series of eleven one-year contracts combined with unilateral expectation of further renewals not sufficient to create property interest).

showing that the state broke its promise. If the state promised to dismiss only for cause, the employee can show a deprivation of the resulting property interest by showing dismissal without cause. When an ordinance or statute specifies the reasons for which an employee may be discharged, most courts will construe it to limit discharges for other, nonspecified reasons.[30] If the state promised to dismiss only after following certain procedures, the employee can show a deprivation by showing failure to follow the procedures.

Establishing deprivation of a property interest is closely interrelated with showing lack of procedural or substantive due process.[31] It can be difficult to decide what questions are essentially factual, leading to the question of whether deprivation occurred, and which questions are legal, leading to the question of whether the procedures afforded comported with the minimum constitutional requirements. In *Cleveland Board of Education v. Loudermill*,[32] the Court made it clear that the adequacy of procedure leading to deprivation of a property interest is to be tested by federal constitutional standards. This means that an employee promised that employment will not be terminated unless certain factual predicates, such as good cause, exist is entitled by the federal Constitution to procedures adequate to determine the existence of the factual predicates with reasonable accuracy.[33]

Codd v. Velger[34] is a good example of how a particular termination can be evaluated differently based on property interests, on liberty interests, or procedurally. In *Codd*, the Court denied a claim for a hearing by a dismissed policeman because he had never disputed the alleged misinformation in his file, which he claimed had prevented him from gaining or keeping subsequent positions. The Court's discussion focused on deprivation of liberty, but the dissenters would have found a property interest in the employment under New York law, which barred arbitrary and capricious dismissals. Prohibiting arbitrary and capricious dismissals could be viewed as establishing a right to be dismissed only if certain factual predicates exist, requiring constitutionally acceptable minimum procedures under *Cleveland Board of Education v. Loudermill*.[35] Or it could be viewed as promising only to exhaust certain procedures before dismissal.[36]

---

[30] *See* Lentsch v. Marshall, 741 F.2d 301, 304 (10th Cir. 1984) (property infringement shown).

[31] Substantive due process is considered in § **6.13**. Procedural due process is considered in § **6.12**.

[32] 470 U.S. 532 (1985). This case is discussed more fully in § **6.12**.

[33] See § **6.12** for development of this idea. In Riggs v. Commonwealth of Ky., 734 F.2d 262, 265 (6th Cir. 1984), *cert. denied*, 469 U.S. 857 (1984), the court held that no property interest was infringed by a layoff because the statute permitting layoffs did not require *cause* for layoff (though it did set up other factual prerequisites, such as lack of funds or work).

[34] 429 U.S. 624 (1977).

[35] *But cf.* Dorr v. County of Butte, 795 F.2d 875, 878 (9th Cir. 1986) (neither procedures for termination nor purely subjective conclusion that cause exists for termination creates property interest in job; applying Cleveland Bd. of Educ. v. Loudermill). *Loudermill* is discussed later in this section and in § **6.12**.

[36] *See* Codd v. Velger, 429 U.S. at 639 (Stevens, J., dissenting).

A certain amount of confusion over whether a property interest could be circumscribed procedurally at the time it was created[37] resulted from the Supreme Court decisions in *Arnett v. Kennedy*[38] and *Bishop v. Wood*,[39] but was eliminated by *Cleveland Board of Education v. Loudermill*.[40] In *Arnett*, a federal civil service employee alleged his constitutional due process rights were violated by the discharging agency's dismissal procedures. In an opinion joined by Chief Justice Burger and Justice Stewart, Justice Rehnquist reasoned that the employee's statutory right to be discharged only for cause was "inextricably intertwined" with the limited termination procedures mandated by Congress for removal.[41] Thus, the employee's property interest was an interest in his job only until a condition subsequent—exhaustion of the statutory procedures—occurred. Since the statute's procedures were honored, the discharge was made correctly without any constitutional invasion.[42] Arnett got all that he was legitimately entitled to expect.[43]

Cleveland Board of Education v. Loudermill states that constitutional scrutiny of procedures cannot be defeated by arguing that the property interest was circumscribed by procedural limitations. But this case still leaves room for an *Arnett*-type argument when the extent of the promise was to follow procedures rather than dismissing only for certain reasons.[44]

§ 6.11 —Deprivation of Liberty Interests

Even if dismissed public employees cannot support claims that they have been deprived of their *property* interests, they nevertheless may be able to show a deprivation of *liberty* interests.[45] This branch of the due process analysis differs from the property branch in that the claimant is relieved of the burden of proving as

---

[37] For a general discussion of the Arnett v. Kennedy and Bishop v. Wood definitions of defeasible property job interests, see Van Alstyne, *Cracks in "The New Property": Adjudicative Due Process in the Administrative State,* 62 Cornell L. Rev. 445, 460 (1977).

[38] 416 U.S. 134 (1974).

[39] 426 U.S. 341 (1976).

[40] 470 U.S. 532 (1985). This case is discussed more fully in **§ 6.12**.

[41] Arnett v. Kennedy, 416 U.S. at 153.

[42] *Id.* at 154.

[43] *Id.* at 158.

[44] *See* Hogue v. Clinton, 791 F.2d 1318, 1324 (8th Cir. 1986) (grievance procedures create no expection of continued employment, hence no property interest).

[45] "A public employee, even one who is not tenured and could be discharged for no reason, may nevertheless demand reinstatement if he proves that protected conduct under the First Amendment was [the reason for his discharge]." Bryant v. St. Helena Parish School Bd., 561 F. Supp. 239, 244 (M.D. La. 1983). *See* Ratliff v. City of Milwaukee, 795 F.2d 612, 625 (7th Cir. 1986) (employee failing to establish property interest nevertheless may assert deprivation of liberty interest); Loehr v. Ventura County Community College Dist., 743 F.2d 1310, 1317 (9th Cir. 1984) (failure to demonstrate property interest does not defeat properly asserted liberty interest claim).

a factual matter that the interest in liberty existed. Existence of constitutional liberty interests is a question of law, not fact. Therefore, the only showing required of a public employee basing a due process claim on a liberty deprivation is to show that a recognized liberty interest was impaired by the state.[46] *Liberty* in the public employment context includes First Amendment rights of political expression,[47] of association,[48] and religious freedom, and *penumbral* rights of privacy[49] and reputation.[50]

Two common liberty-based due process challenges to public employment termination involve freedom of expression and reputation. It is a deprivation of the liberty interest in political expression to dismiss a public employee, without due process, for expressing political opinions.[51]

When public employees claim that their dismissals infringe on First Amendment liberty interests without due process, the court hearing the claims must engage in a multiple step analysis. First, the employees must demonstrate that their conduct was protected. Second, the employees must demonstrate that such protected

---

[46] The claimant may be required to show infringement of the liberty interest through factual proof. *See* Hogue v. Clinton, 791 F.2d 1318, 1322 (8th Cir. 1986) (remanding to district court to determine if stigmatizing charges were made public, a prerequisite to infringement of liberty interest in reputation).

[47] *See* Connick v. Myers, 461 U.S. 138 (1983); Pickering v. Board of Educ., 391 U.S. 563 (1968).

[48] *See* Keyishian v. Board of Regents, 385 U.S. 589 (1967); Wilson v. Taylor, 733 F.2d 1539, 1544 (11th Cir. 1984) (police officer's relationship with a woman whom he was dating was an interest protected by First Amendment's freedom of association); Saye v. St. Vrain Valley School Dist., 785 F.2d 862, 867 (10th Cir. 1986) (dismissal for union activity infringes liberty interest in free association unless substantial state interest involved).

[49] *Privacy,* in the constitutional setting, was defined in *Whalen v. Roe,* 429 U.S. 589 (1977). *See* Hollenback v. Carnegie Free Library, 439 U.S. 1052 (1978) (denial of certiorari, Brennan & Marshall, JJ., dissenting); *see generally* Wilkinson & White, *Consititutional Protection for Personal Lifestyles,* 62 Cornell L. Rev. 563, 618 (1977). In Hardwick v. Bowers, ___ U.S. ___, 106 S. Ct. 2841 (1986), a sharply divided Court held that a state criminal statute prohibiting sodomy did not infringe the privacy interests of homosexual plaintiffs. Even when a liberty or property interest cannot be established, however, a public employee can recover for denial of equal protection. Swift v. United States, ___ F. Supp. ___, 42 Fair Empl. Prac. Cas. (BNA) 787 (D.D.C. 1986) (employee of White House contractor fired for homosexuality entitled to recover on equal protection theory unless government can show rational basis for termination).

[50] *See* Bishop v. Wood, 426 U.S. 341, 345 (1976); Norton v. Macy, 417 F.2d 1161 (D.C. Cir. 1969) (reputation is a liberty interest).

[51] Connick v. Myers, 461 U.S. 138 (1983). *See also* Bueno v. City of Donna, 714 F.2d 484 (5th Cir. 1983) (discharge of workers for refusal to support official's candidacy violative of workers' liberty interests); Grossart v. Dinaso, 758 F.2d 1221, 1235 (7th Cir. 1985) (town bookkeeper dismissed for insufficient loyalty, energy, in support of political ambitions of supervisor did not suffer infringement of liberty interests); Soderbeck v. Burnett County, 752 F.2d 285, 288 (7th Cir. 1985) (Posner, J.) (affirming jury verdict for plaintiff fired by sheriff who defeated her husband in election; jury entitled to find she was not a policymaker and therefore not within Elrod v. Burns, 427 U.S. 347 (1980)).

§ 6.11 LIBERTY INTERESTS 343

conduct was a substantial or motivating factor in the decision to dismiss them. Third, the employer has the opportunity to show that the dismissals would have occurred even in the absence of the protected conduct.[52] As explained in § 7.5, the order of proof is similar to the order of proof for a common law public policy tort claim.

Under *Connick v. Myers*,[53] the first step in deciding whether the conduct was protected involves two subordinate inquiries: (1) whether the speech addressed a "matter of public concern,"[54] and (2) whether the interest of the employees in speaking outweighed the interest of the public employer in promoting the efficiency of the public service.[55] The inquiry into whether the speech is protected is a question of law to be decided by the judge, not a question of fact to be decided by the jury.[56] Appropriate questions of fact should be submitted to the jury in separate interrogatories.[57] The truth or falsity of the statements is not directly at issue however, except as it bears on the tendency of the speech to undermine effective governmental functioning.[58]

The critical threshold inquiry in this branch of the liberty analysis is to determine whether the communication by the employee involved matters of public concern.[59] The nature of the inquiry is illustrated by *Connick v. Myers*[60] in which an assistant district attorney was fired for circulating a questionnaire among her fellow workers that impliedly criticized the district attorney's policy on personnel transfers.[61] The Court held that Myers' communication, with one exception, did

---

[52] *See* Roberts v. Van Buren Pub. Schools, 773 F.2d 949, 953–54 (8th Cir. 1985).

[53] 461 U.S. 138 (1983).

[54] *See* Munson v. Friske, 754 F.2d 683, 689 n.3 (7th Cir. 1985) (suggesting that submission of overtime claim not protected by First Amendment).

[55] Roberts v. Van Buren Pub. Schools, 773 F.2d at 954; McPherson v. Rankin, 786 F.2d 1233, 1239 (5th Cir. 1986) (interest of constable's office in maintaining efficiency and morale outweighed by low-level clerk's First Amendment right to make remark approving assassination attempt against President Reagan in private conversation). This balancing can be part of deciding whether the conduct is protected by the Constitution, or part of the substantive due process analysis assuming the conduct is protected. See § 6.13 regarding substantive due process.

[56] Roberts v. Van Buren Pub. Schools, 773 F.2d at 954 (reversing district court for permitting jury to decide protected nature of speech).

[57] *Id. See also* Day v. South Park Indep. School Dist., 768 F.2d 696, 697 (5th Cir. 1985) (teacher's grievance protesting performance evaluation did not involve matter of public concern and therefore was not protected speech).

[58] *See* Buschi v. Kirven, 775 F.2d 1240, 1248 (4th Cir. 1985) (district judge properly excluded evidence of truth or falsity of statements determined to involve matters of public concern).

[59] The term more frequently used in the literature on constitutional law is *political speech*. The *Connick* court, however, discussed the issue in terms of "matters of public concern," and the Court's usage will be employed.

[60] 461 U.S. 138 (1983).

[61] *Id.* at 141.

not "fall under the rubric of matters of 'public concern'."[62] Instead, it involved her anger over a grievance of primary interest only to her.[63]

Once speech on a matter of public concern is established, the governmental employer nevertheless can escape liability by showing sufficient state interests in taking the adverse employment action despite its effect on free expression.[64]

It also is a deprivation of liberty to accomplish a discharge in a manner that injures the public employee's reputation.[65] The interaction of this type of injury and the predeprivation hearing requirement is complex. In *Codd v. Velger*,[66] the Court suggested that the plaintiff alleging an injury to the liberty interest in reputation must plead and prove falsity. Justice Stevens, in dissent, suggested a multifaceted analysis of the interests being protected.[67]

---

[62] *Id.* at 148. *Compare* Gomez v. Texas Dep't of Mental Health, 794 F.2d 1018, 1022 (5th Cir. 1986) (communication of internal memorandum regarding length of patient stay to employee of another agency did not involve matter of public concern) *and* Terrell v. University of Tex. Sys. Police, 792 F.2d 1360, 1362 (5th Cir. 1986) (entries in personal diary involving personnel policy disagreements did not satisfy public concern requirement) *and* Saye v. St. Vrain Valley School Dist., 785 F.2d 862, 866 (10th Cir. 1986) (discussion of teacher's aide time allocation with parents not protected speech because not a matter of public concern and not raised in public forum) *and* Wilson v. City of Littleton, 732 F.2d 765, 769 (10th Cir. 1984) (police officer's wearing of black shroud on badge to mourn death of another officer did not involve matter of public concern, thus no balancing necessary under *Connick*) *with* Eiland v. City of Montgomery, 797 F.2d 953 (11th Cir. 1986) (poem by police officer criticizing mayor in election year was protected; and potential disruptive effect insufficient to outweigh interests in speaking) *and* Cox v. Dardanelle Pub. School Dist., 790 F.2d 668, 673 (8th Cir. 1986) (teacher criticism of principal involved educational policy as well as parochial disciplinary matters and therefore was of public concern) *and* Sykes v. McDowell, 786 F.2d 1098, 1105 (11th Cir. 1986) (deputy sheriff's refusal to speak in support of sheriff's election was protected speech; affirming damages judgment) *and* Brockell v. Norton, 732 F.2d 664, 668 (8th Cir. 1984) (public nature of police radio dispatcher's report of stolen test to another police department outweighed his employer's interest in chain of command; whistleblowers entitled to special First Amendment protection) *and* Berdin v. Duggan, 701 F.2d 909 (11th Cir. 1983) (worker who spoke to mayor in relative privacy and subsequently was discharged won damages for the violation of his free speech rights), *cert. denied,* 464 U.S. 893 (1983).

[63] Connick v. Myers, 461 U.S. at 148.

[64] *See* Cox v. Dardanelle Pub. School Dist., 790 F.2d at 673–74 ("employee's interest in freely commenting on matters of public concern must generally give way to the state's interest in efficiently fulfilling its responsibilities where the employee's speech significantly impairs her ability to perform her duties, disrupts working relationships and harmony among co-workers, or otherwise impedes the normal operations of the institution"; finding insufficient state interest).

[65] *See* Bishop v. Wood, 426 U.S. 341, 345 (1976); Doe v. United States Dep't of Justice, 753 F.2d 1092, 1102 (D.C. Cir. 1985) (dismissal of government attorney for unprofessional conduct adversely affects liberty interest); Beckham v. Harris, 756 F.2d 1032, 1038 (4th Cir. 1985) (admission/self-accusation negates harm to reputation/liberty interest). Martin v. Unified School Dist. No. 434, 728 F.2d 453, 456 (10th Cir. 1984) (reputational injury resulting from inferences drawn from dismissal alone not sufficient injury to liberty interest to trigger constitutional protections).

[66] 429 U.S. 624 (1977).

[67] *Id.* at 631, 634 nn.4–5, 638 n.11. The Supreme Court refused to consider the issue in Guard v. Kilburn, 5 Ohio St. 3d 21, 448 N.E.2d 1153, *cert. denied,* 464 U.S. 893 (1983).

§ 6.11 LIBERTY INTERESTS

Wells v. Doland[68] provides an example of the liberty interest in reputation. Professor Wells sued the president of the university where he had been employed after he was refused tenure and terminated. He alleged that the reasons given for his termination "attacked 'his good name, reputation, and integrity so as to possibly deprive him of future state employment [and] caus[ed] damage to his professional reputation . . .' "[69] Holding that Professor Wells had no property interest in his continued employment, the court of appeals affirmed the district court. It reversed, however, the district court's summary judgment for the employer on Wells's liberty interest argument. It held that Wells was entitled to an opportunity to prove certain elements of liberty impairment:

1. That he was stigmatized
2. That the stigma was a result of the discharge process[70]
3. That the charges were made public
4. That he was denied a meaningful hearing to clear his name.[71]

On remand, the district court was required to order the university to provide Wells with a hearing to clear his name, if these four elements of liberty impairment were established.[72]

As noted, an employee usually must prove publication of the stigmatizing information,[73] although in some cases, silence may create a sufficient risk of reputation injury to entitle the employee to a hearing.[74]

---

[68] 711 F.2d 670 (5th Cir. 1983).

[69] *Id.* at 673; Lawson v. Sheriff of Tippecanoe County, 725 F.2d 1136, 1139 (7th Cir. 1984) ("when a state fires an employee for stated reasons likely to make him all but unemployable in the future . . . the consequences are so nearly those of formally excluding him from his occupation that the law treats the state's action (as a deprivation of liberty)).

[70] *See* Laureano-Agosto v. Garcia-Caraballo, 731 F.2d 101, 104 (1st Cir. 1984) (public comments harmful to reputation made after discharge, as opposed to comments made in the course of discharging an employee, do not invoke due process guarantees).

[71] Wells v. Doland, 711 F.2d at 676. As a part of establishing the stigma element, the plaintiff must show that the charges were false. *Id.* at 676 n.7. As a part of the fourth element, the plaintiff must show that the injury to reputation resulted from denial of procedural protection. *Id.* at 677.

[72] *Id.* at 676-77. The court made it clear that reinstatement and/or back pay were not appropriate remedies for the claimed infringement of the liberty interest in reputation.

[73] *See* Ratliff v. City of Milwaukee, 795 F.2d 612, 626 (7th Cir. 1986) (failure to prove publication sufficient to reach future potential employers or community at large).

[74] *See* Guard v. Kilburn, 5 Ohio St. 3d 21, 448 N.E.2d 1153, *cert. denied,* 464 U.S. 893 (1983). In *Guard,* a police chief who was dismissed requested a name-clearing hearing after media speculation as to the reasons for his dismissal. The city gave no explanation for its action. The Ohio Supreme Court held that he was entitled to a hearing. *But see* Hogue v. Clinton, 791 F.2d 1318, 1322 (8th Cir. 1986) (remanding to district court to determine if stigmatizing charges were made public, a prerequisite to infringement of liberty interest in reputation).

An employee may not premise a harm-to-reputation claim on damaging testimony at the hearing on his dismissal.[75] The Sixth Circuit has held that the jury should decide whether an employee is entitled to a name-clearing hearing, based on its findings about whether the employee was stigmatized by the public employer.[76]

In addition to dismissals for political expression or dismissals injuring reputation, it is a deprivation of liberty to discharge an employee for membership in an organization.[77] It also appears to be a deprivation of liberty to terminate a public employee for purely private conduct when the employee's interest in privacy is involved.[78]

§ 6.12 — Procedural Due Process Entitlements

Assuming that dismissed public employees can demonstrate deprivation of liberty or property interests as explained in §§ **6.10** and **6.11**, they further must demonstrate that the deprivation occurred without *due process*. There are two aspects of due process: procedural and substantive.[79] Procedural rights to which the employee might be entitled have been identified by Circuit Judge Friendly:

1. An unbiased tribunal
2. Notice of the proposed action and grounds asserted for it
3. An opportunity to present reasons why the proposed action should not be taken

---

[75] *See* Lentsch v. Marshall, 741 F.2d 301, 304 (10th Cir. 1984) (defendant in § 1983 discharge case immune from suit based on derogatory statements before civil service commission hearing).

[76] *See* Burkhart v. Randles, 764 F.2d 1196, 1200 (6th Cir. 1985) (reversing district court for failure to give jury instructions quoted in margin).

[77] *See* Abood v. Board of Educ., 431 U.S. 209 (1979); Elrod v. Burns, 427 U.S. 347 (1976); Healy v. James, 408 U.S. 169, 181 (1972) (freedom of association protected by First Amendment).

[78] It is difficult to separate the liberty interest in off-duty personal autonomy from the substantive due process problem involved in terminating a property interest for reasons unrelated to public need. The substantive due process concept is discussed in § **6.13**. Several cases arguably establish a liberty interest. *See* Littlejohn v. Rose, 768 F.2d 765, 769 (6th Cir. 1985) (reversing directed verdict for employer; dismissal of teacher for impending divorce infringed on liberty interest in privacy), *cert. denied*, ___ U.S. ___, 106 S. Ct. 1260 (1986); Brantley v. Surles, 765 F.2d 478, 482 (5th Cir. 1985) (dismissal of public school cafeteria manager for sending son to private school violated liberty interest); Andrews v. Drew Mun. Separate School Dist., 507 F.2d 611 (5th Cir. 1975) (unwed schoolteacher); Fisher v. Snyder, 476 F.2d 375 (8th Cir. 1973) (schoolteacher having "male guests"); Saal v. Middendorf, 427 F. Supp. 192 (N.D. Cal. 1977) (discharge from Navy for homosexuality); *see generally* Annotation, 42 A.L.R. Fed. 189 (1979). Hardwick v. Bowers, ___ U.S. ___, 106 S. Ct. 2841 (1986) raises doubts about the breadth of a privacy-based liberty challenge, but leaves intact a substantive due process claim based on property deprivation. In *Hardwick*, a sharply divided Court held that a state criminal statute prohibiting sodomy did not infringe on the privacy interests of homosexual plaintiffs.

[79] Substantive due process is addressed in § **6.13**.

§ 6.12 PROCEDURAL DUE PROCESS

4. The right to present evidence, including the right to call witnesses
5. The right to know opposing evidence
6. The right to cross-examine adverse witnesses
7. A decision based exclusively on the evidence presented
8. The right to counsel
9. A requirement that the tribunal prepare a record of the evidence presented
10. A requirement that the tribunal prepare written findings of fact and reasons for its decision[80]

Which of these rights will be applicable depends on the gravity of the deprivation threatened, the accuracy of the determination resulting from procedures actually used, and the improvement in accuracy resulting from additional procedures, and the harm to the administrative effectiveness resulting from imposition of additional procedural requirements.[81]

In *Cleveland Board of Education v. Loudermill*,[82] the Supreme Court rejected the proposition that state-created property interests could be limited by the procedures defined in conjunction with those interests. It thus laid to rest the "bitter-with-the-sweet" concept of Justice Rehnquist's opinion in *Arnett*. The Court held that the categories of substance and procedure under the Fifth and Fourteenth Amendments are distinct:

> "Property" cannot be defined by the procedures provided for its deprivation any more than can life or liberty. The right to due process "is conferred, not by legislative grace but by constitutional guarantee. While the legislature may elect not to confer a property interest in public employment, it may not constitutionally authorize the deprivation of such an interest, once conferred, without appropriate procedural safeguards."[83]

---

[80] Friendly, *Some Kind of Hearing*, 123 U. Pa. L. Rev. 1267 (1975).

[81] Mathews v. Eldridge, 424 U.S. 319 (1976). See Rodgers v. Norfolk School Bd., 755 F.2d 59, 63 (4th Cir. 1985) (procedural due process satisfied despite deprivation of chance to confront and cross-examine because notice of charges, explanation of evidence, two opportunities to contest case were received); Lew v. Kona Hosp., 754 F.2d 1420, 1424 (9th Cir. 1985) (hearing before termination of staff privileges satisfied procedural due process, in part because plaintiff consented to procedures actually followed); Lee v. Western Reserve Psychiatric Habilitation Center, 747 F.2d 1062, 1069 (6th Cir. 1984) (notice of patient sexual abuse charges, opportunity to respond, satisfied procedural due process despite lack of cross-examination, right to call witnesses, absence of impartial decisionmaker); Cha-Tsu Siu v. Johnson, 748 F.2d 238, 244 (4th Cir. 1984) (denial of tenure leading to dismissal inherently requires exercise of professional judgment, not trial-type adversarial fact finding). *But see* Gattis v. Gravett, 806 F.2d 778, 781 (8th Cir. 1986) (legislative deprivation of property interest inherently satisfies procedural due process).

[82] 470 U.S. 532 (1985), 105 S. Ct. 1487.

[83] *Id.* at 1493 (quoting Powell concurrence in *Arnett v. Kennedy*.)

The Supreme Court held that procedural entitlements may not be limited by the definition of the property interest. In addition, it offered specific guidance on what procedures the constitution guarantees in connection with dismissal of a public employee with a property interest in her job.

First, the employee is entitled to some kind of pretermination hearing.[84] This hearing need not definitively resolve the propriety of the dismissal, but should permit a "determination of whether there are reasonable grounds to believe that the charges against the employee are true and support the proposed action."[85] It must include oral or written notice of the charges against the employee, an explanation of the employer's evidence, and an opportunity for the employee to present her side of the story. The majority declined to require that the pretermination procedures also include an opportunity to confront and cross-examine witnesses and to present witnesses in behalf of the employee, as urged by Justice Marshall in his concurring opinion.[86] Justice Brennan suggested, however, that when an employee contests the facts allegedly justifying dismissal, as opposed merely to contesting the validity of the discharge penalty for admitted facts, due process might require some opportunity before dismissal to produce contrary records or testimony, or even to confront an accuser in front of the decisionmaker.[87] The Brennan opinion illustrates application of the marginal-improvement-to-accuracy element of the *Mathews v. Eldridge* formula.

Oral notice and an opportunity to respond orally can satisfy the *Cleveland Board of Education v. Loudermill* pretermination hearing requirements.[88] But the posttermination hearing must be more formal.[89]

Once the federal due process requirements of notice and hearing have been satisfied, violation of additional procedural requirements imposed by state law do not give a federal constitutional claim.[90]

---

[84] *Id;* Buschi v. Kirven, 775 F.2d 1240, 1256 (4th Cir. 1985) (*Loudermill* requirement for pretermination procedure satisfied by offer of individual interview which was rejected by counsel insisting on group interview).

[85] Cleveland Bd. of Educ. v. Loudermill, 470 U.S. at 545-46.

[86] *Id.* at 548.

[87] *Id.* at 552-53.

[88] Deretich v. Office of Admin. Hearings, 798 F.2d 1147, 1152 (8th Cir. 1986) (pretermination procedures adequate; employee ignored invitation to respond); Riggins v. Board of Regents of Univ. of Neb., 790 F.2d 707, 711 (8th Cir. 1986) (informal opportunity to hear charges by supervisor and to offer her side of story satisfied *Loudermill* requirement for pretermination procedures); Kelly v. Smith, 764 F.2d 1412, 1414 (11th Cir. 1985).

[89] Kelly v. Smith, 764 F.2d at 1415 (reversing district court for failure to permit dismissed employee to confront accuser in presence of decisionmaker); Agarwal v. Regents of Univ. of Minn., 788 F.2d 504, 508 (8th Cir. 1986) (university met procedural due process requirements: notice of reasons for termination sufficient to permit evidence to be presented in opposition; names of those making allegations against employee and factual basis for the charges; reasonable opportunity to present testimony; hearing before impartial board).

[90] *See* Franceski v. Plaquemines Parish School Bd. 772 F.2d 197, 200 (5th Cir. 1985).

When constitutional scrutiny of statutory or regulatory procedural protection is appropriate, *Mathews v. Eldridge* suggests that the plaintiff be able to articulate the deficiency of the procedures actually used. For example, the plaintiff may argue that the procedures were inadequate in determining whether the predicate for termination of employment (usually cause) existed. Alternatively, the plaintiff may argue that the procedures were inadequate to protect a liberty interest; for example, to permit the plaintiff to clear her name and thus to protect her reputation.[91]

Occasionally, the question arises whether collectively bargained remedies satisfy procedural entitlements. Frequently, the courts find that they do.[92]

Pre-deprivation procedures are not required when the deprivation occurs because of a random, unpredictable act, rather than pursuant to state policy, but they may be required when the deprivation occurs through application of state policy.[93]

§ 6.13 — Substantive Due Process Entitlements

The substantive due process entitlement requires that the government should not take action that is wholly unrelated to legitimate public interests.[94] Substantive due process scrutiny of a government action involves a case-by-case balancing of the nature of the individual interest allegedly infringed, the importance of the government interests furthered, the degree of infringement, and the sensitivity of the government entity responsible for the regulation to more carefully tailored alternative means of achieving its goal.[95] While substantive due process has declined

---

[91] *Compare* Wells v. Doland, 711 F.2d 670 (5th Cir. 1983) *and* Greene v. Finley, 749 F.2d 467, 470 (7th Cir. 1984) (dismissal based on outcome of criminal trial affords employee all the process that was due) *with* Doe v. United States Dep't of Justice, 753 F.2d 1092, 1112 (D.C. Cir. 1985) (government attorney dismissed for unprofessional conduct did not receive adequate opportunity to refute charges and to clear her name when given no advance notice of evidence against her or opportunity to produce her own evidence).

[92] *See* Papapetropoulous v. Milwaukee Transp. Serv. Inc., 795 F.2d 591, 600 (7th Cir. 1986) (interruption of cross-examination of witness in arbitration proceeding did not render arbitration procedurally inadequate; arbitrator relied on other evidence; existence of state action dubious); Lewis v. Hillsborough Transit Auth., 726 F.2d 668 (11th Cir. 1984), *cert. denied*, 469 U.S. 822 (1984) (finding collectively bargained procedures adequate, in conjunction with administrative procedures; denial of rehearing).

[93] *See* Lee v. Western Reserve Psychiatric Habilitation Center, 747 F.2d 1062, 1068 (6th Cir. 1984).

[94] Major v. Hampton, 413 F. Supp. 66, 69 (E.D. La. 1976); *see* J. Nowak, R. Rotunda & J. Young, Constitutional Law 404 (1978). The term *substantive due process* frequently is used to refer to the rights asserted by the plaintiff, as well as to the requirement of a rational balancing between these rights and state interests. The term is used in this section only with respect to the rationality requirement. Plaintiff interests are considered as property or liberty interests in §§ **6.10 & 6.11**.

[95] Beller v. Middendorf, 632 F.2d 788, 807 (9th Cir. 1980); McMurphy v. City of Flushing, 802 F.2d 191 (6th Cir. 1986) (interests of city outweighed interests of policeman in carrying out vendetta against superior officers and mayor); Deretich v. Office of Admin. Hearings, 798 F.2d 1147, 1152 (8th Cir. 1986) (state interest in avoiding appearance of impropriety outweighed hearing examiner's freedom of association to be part of law firm).

as a constitutional basis for scrutinizing economic regulation, it still is available to protect individual rights against irrational government action.[96] This rationality requirement can be applied to deprivations of property or of liberty. The liberty interests usually involve fundamental rights, such as those prescribed in the Bill of Rights, privacy and association.[97]

Major v. Hampton[98] is an example of this substantive due process analysis. Major was discharged from his job with the Internal Revenue Service (IRS) for behavior that tended "to discredit himself or the Service," after it was discovered that he engaged in sexual relationships with females during off-duty hours.[99] The court began its review of the discharge with the proposition, "The type of off-duty conduct on which a governmental employer may base a discharge of its employees is limited to actions that at least could rationally be considered likely to discredit them or the government."[1] It found no evidence that Major's actions were calculated to arouse, or did in fact arouse, odium for the employee or the IRS. Accordingly, it found that the record demonstrated no rational basis for the conclusion reached by the government resulting in Major's discharge.[2]

Application of these concepts is illustrated further by *Beller v. Middendorf*[3] and *Norton v. Macy*.[4] Both involved dismissals from government service for homosexuality. In *Norton,* the court was unable to find a sufficient rational connection between the plaintiff's off-duty homosexual conduct and the "efficiency of the service" to justify a dismissal.[5] It suggested, however, that another case, in which a federal employee openly flaunts or carelessly displays unorthodox sexual conduct in public, might cause sufficient embarrassment to the agency to justify discharge under a substantive due process analysis.[6] In *Beller,*[7] the court found sufficient connection to justify the dismissal, based on the special needs of the naval service, in which the plaintiff was employed.[8]

Connick v. Myers[9] illustrates the type of analysis the Supreme Court endorses to determine whether a public employer has a rational reason for effecting a

---

[96] *See* Agarwal v. Regents of Univ. of Minn., 788 F.2d 504, 507 (8th Cir. 1986) (rejecting substantive due process challenge by tenured state university professor terminated for incompetence); Norton v. Macy, 417 F.2d 1161 (D.C. Cir. 1969); J. Nowak, R. Rotunda & J. Young, Constitutional Law 409 (1978).

[97] J. Nowak, R. Rotunda & J. Young, Constitutional Law 409 (1978).

[98] 413 F. Supp. 66 (E.D. La. 1976).

[99] *Id.* at 67.

[1] *Id.*

[2] *Id.* at 71.

[3] 632 F.2d 788 (9th Cir. 1980).

[4] 417 F.2d 1161 (D.C. Cir. 1969).

[5] *Id.* at 1167.

[6] *Id.* at 1168; *see, e.g.,* McConnell v. Anderson, 451 F.2d 193 (8th Cir. 1971), *cert. denied,* 405 U.S. 1046 (1972) (discharge of university instructor justified by open advocacy of gay rights).

[7] Beller v. Middendorf, 632 F.2d 788 (9th Cir. 1980).

[8] *Id.* at 812.

[9] 461 U.S. 138, 146 (1983).

discharge when liberty interests are involved. Myers was discharged from her job as an assistant district attorney after she circulated a questionnaire among her fellow workers that implied criticism of her supervisors for effecting transfers. She claimed that she was discharged for exercising her free speech rights. The district attorney claimed she was discharged for insubordination.[10]

The Court found that one aspect of the questionnaire sufficiently involved a matter of public concern to be protected by the First Amendment.[11] The Court derived, however, from *Pickering v. Board of Education*,[12] a balancing test in which the infringement on the employee's right of expression is balanced against the state's justification for effecting the dismissal.[13] The Court found sufficient justification for Myers' dismissal in the potential disruption to the office resulting from her questionnaire.[14]

§ 6.14 Interaction of Public Sector Grievance Arbitration and Civil Service Laws

In the private sector, an employee entitled to collectively bargained grievance arbitration must resort to the arbitration procedure to assert a wrongful dismissal claim instead of suing for common law breach of contract.[15] In contrast, remedies under federal discrimination laws are cumulative with collectively bargained arbitration remedies.[16]

In the public sector, exclusivity of arbitration remedies[17] is somewhat weaker because of the prevalence of statutory civil service protections against wrongful

---

[10] The communication contained in the questionnaire was the reason for the discharge under both views. Accordingly, Connick v. Myers did not involve a "mixed motive" discharge as in Mt. Healthy City School Dist. v. Doyle, 429 U.S. 274 (1977). See § **7.5**. Instead, it involved a balancing of First Amendment interests against state interests respecting a single reason for dismissal.

[11] Conick v. Myers, 461 U.S. at 149.

[12] 391 U.S. 563 (1968).

[13] Connick v. Myers, 461 U.S. at 142. The Colorado Supreme Court used the *Pickering* test in Johnson v. Jefferson County Bd. of Health, 662 P.2d 463 (Colo. 1983), *later appeal,* 674 P.2d 952 (1984). Finding the lower court had failed to weigh a dismissed public health officer's free speech rights against the county's interests in discipline and efficiency when it denied reinstatement pending the outcome of a trial, the court vacated the lower court dismissal and remanded.

[14] Connick v. Myers, 461 U.S. at 154. *See also* McMullen v. Carson, 754 F.2d 936, 939 (11th Cir. 1985) (clerical employee of sheriff's office dismissed for public statement supporting Ku Klux Klan had no meritorious § 1983 claim; need for public confidence in sheriff's office outweighed plaintiff's First Amendment rights).

[15] See §§ **2.30, 3.1, 3.21, 4.25**.

[16] See § **3.27**.

[17] Approximately 80 percent of public sector collective agreements contain grievance arbitration clauses. *See* Craver, *The Judical Enforcement of Public Sector Grievance Arbitration,* 58 Tex. L. Rev. 329, 330 (1980).

discharge.[18] Two issues arise: first, whether a dismissed public employee is barred from utilizing statutory procedures because of the existence of collectively bargained grievance and arbitration procedures, or vice versa;[19] and second, whether such an employee, having utilized the collectively bargained procedures and won, can enforce an award in his favor, even though it conflicts in some respects with the statutory provisions.[20]

How these issues will be resolved in a given case is difficult to predict. Whether a statutory right or grant of power can be interpreted by an arbitrator depends largely on the public policy of the state, as reflected in the statute at issue.

§ 6.15 — Public Sector Grievance and Arbitration Procedures: Exclusivity, Exhaustion and Preclusion

If public sector employees were allowed to utilize both contractual arbitration and statutory civil service procedures to test the wrongfulness of terminations, an inefficient duplication of remedies and potentially conflicting decisions in the same cases could result.[21] This problem can be avoided by applying election-of-remedies or waiver concepts.[22] A public employee is, however, permitted to pursue both types of procedure when the two forums decide different questions.[23]

---

[18] See §§ 6.3–6.5. Of course an employee may not be limited to an arbitral forum with respect to constitutional claims discussed in §§ 6.9–6.13.

[19] See § 6.15.

[20] See § 6.16. The question of arbitral decisions on public law issues is considered more generally in § 3.27.

[21] See Craver, *The Judicial Enforcement of Public Sector Grievance Arbitration*, 58 Tex. L. Rev. 329, 341 n.58 (1980).

[22] See Rodriguez v. MSPB, 804 F.2d 673, 675 (Fed. Cir. 1986) (federal employee must elect either arbitration or MSPB review; cannot have both); Commonwealth v. Social Servs. Union, 82 Pa. Commw. 200, 209, 475 A.2d 1333, 1337 (1984) (arbitrator had jurisdiction over dismissal even though civil service commission had found statutory violation and ordered separation from service); Waterbury Teachers Ass'n v. City of Waterbury, 164 Conn. 426, 435, 324 A.2d 267, 271 (1973); Gorham v. City of Kansas City, 225 Kan. 369, 375–77, 590 P.2d 1051, 1057–58 (1979); City of Yonkers v. Cassidy, 44 N.Y.2d 784, 377 N.E.2d 475, 406 N.Y.S.2d 32 (1978); Board of Educ. v. Associated Teachers of Huntington, Inc., 30 N.Y.2d 122, 132, 282 N.E.2d 109, 115, 331 N.Y.S.2d 17, 25 (1972). *But see* City of Poughkeepsie School Dist. v. Poughkeepsie Pub. Teachers Ass'n, 35 N.Y.2d 599, 605–07, 324 N.E.2d 144, 146–47, 364 N.Y.S.2d 492, 495–97 (1974); Ridley School Dist. v. Ridley Educ. Ass'n, 84 Pa. Commw. 117, 123, 479 A.2d 641, 644 (1984) (parties can provide for arbitral resolution of statutory claims regarding suspensions). *See generally* Pegnetter & Hayford, *State Employee Grievances and Due Process: An Analysis of Contract Arbitration and Civil Service Review Systems*, 29 S.C.L. Rev. 305 (1978).

[23] See A.F.S.C.M.E. Council 96 v. Arrowhead Regional Corrections Bd., 356 N.W.2d 295 (Minn. 1984) (discharged public employee has right to both collectively bargained arbitration and veterans preference administrative hearing); Jerviss v. School Dist. No. 294, 273 N.W.2d 638, 647 (Minn. 1978); Pennsylvania Labor Relations Bd. v. West Middlesex Area School Dist., 55 Pa. Commw. 404, 423 A.2d 781 (1980).

§ 6.15 PROCEDURES

A final decision under a statutory procedure may bar subsequent resort to grievance procedures,[24] but an employer or employee should not be permitted to avoid a collectively bargained grievance procedure merely because the dispute is covered by civil service laws.[25] An example of the exclusivity of bargained-for arbitration procedures is *Antinore v. New York*,[26] in which a public employee asserted as unconstitutional an arbitration clause in his union's collective bargaining agreement. The employee alleged that the clause and the state law permitting the clause to supersede state civil service procedures deprived him of due process, since the arbitration procedures did not provide him with certain protections.[27] The intermediate appellate court held that an employee may waive due process rights, provided the waiver is not against public policy.[28] The court noted that orderly labor relations could be disrupted by requiring civil service procedures in addition to bargained-for procedures. The court also mentioned a public policy in favor of arbitration because of its simplicity and rapidity.[29] The court held that the employee had waived his statutory rights to civil service review by reason of the arbitration clause.[30]

A related issue is the preclusive effect of arbitration awards in subsequent actions based on the Constitution. In *McDonald v. City of West Branch*,[31] the Supreme Court held that an action under § 1983 is not barred by an adverse arbitration award under a collective bargaining agreement. It implied, however, that the result might be different if the arbitration award were reviewed and affirmed by a state court. Reinforcing this possibility is *Migra v. Warren City School District Board of Education*,[32] in which the court held that a judgment for the employee in a state

---

[24] Pennsylvania Labor Relations Bd. v. Neshaminy School Dist., 43 Pa. Commw. 377, 403 A.2d 1003 (1979).

[25] Pittsburgh Joint Collective Bargaining Comm. v. City of Pittsburgh, 481 Pa. 66, 391 A.2d 1318 (1978), *rev'g* 351 A.2d 304 (1976) (discharge held to be arbitrable, reversing Commonwealth Court).

[26] 49 A.D.2d 6, 371 N.Y.S.2d 213, *aff'd* 358 N.E.2d 268 (1975).

[27] The plaintiff and the lower court attacked the absence of a requirement that the arbitrator state the reasons for the decision, the requirement that either party desiring a transcript of the arbitration proceedings provide for it at his own expense, the absence of a requirement that the arbitrator be bound by rules of law, and the lack of explicit assurances of the right to present witnesses or to confront witnesses in the arbitration procedures as violative of due process.

[28] Antinore v. New York, 49 A.D.2d at 10, 371 N.Y.S.2d at 216.

[29] *Id.* at 11, 371 N.Y.S.2d at 217:

> Indeed, far from violating public policy, the binding arbitration procedures provided by the agreement between the state and CSEA must be viewed as advancing the public good by the expedition of the resolution of disciplinary disputes in a simpler, more prompt manner than would attend their disposition by [the Civil Service Law].

[30] *Id.* at 12, 371 N.Y.S.2d at 218. *See also* Pedersen v. South Williamsport Area School Dist., 677 F.2d 312 (3rd Cir. 1982), *cert. denied*, 459 U.S. 972 (1982) (when employee knew of right to appeal to school board, he waived his hearing rights by selecting arbitration by union).

[31] 466 U.S. 284 (1984).

[32] 465 U.S. 75 (1984).

court action for breach of contract barred a subsequent action in federal court under § 1983, even though the § 1983 basis for recovery was not asserted in the state court action. In reaching this result, the Court applied state judgment-preclusion rules.[33]

The duty of fair representation may interact with grievance and arbitration procedures in the public sector differently from the interaction under federal law applicable to the private sector.[34] For example, if a state statute requires the arbitration of grievance disputes, the remedy in a successful fair representation suit may be an order compelling arbitration rather than a judicial decision of the underlying wrongful dismissal claim.[35]

Conversely, a state may decline to adopt the federal requirement that breach of the union's duty of fair representation is a prerequisite to a judicial action for wrongful dismissal.[36]

But at least one court of appeals has opined that basic principles applicable to private sector labor arbitration should be applied in the public sector.[37]

§ 6.16 —Enforceability of Grievance Arbitration Awards

Courts afford substantial deference to public sector grievance arbitration awards,[38] though less in some instances than is accorded private sector awards.[39] When the

---

[33] *See also* Holmes v. Jones, 738 F.2d 711, 714 (5th Cir. 1984) (state court decision on outcome-determinative facts precludes relitigation of same facts in federal suit under § 1983).

[34] See §§ **3.25** & **3.26** regarding the duty of fair representation generally; Treasury Employees v. Federal Labor Relations Auth., 800 F.2d 1165 (D.C. Cir. 1986) (duty of fair representation for federal employee union same as for private sector union).

[35] *See* Martino v. Transport Workers, 505 Pa. 391, 480 A.2d 242 (1984) (refusing to follow Vaca v. Sipes, 386 U.S. 171 (1967), and holding that appropriate remedy in a wrongful discharge case is to require arbitration of the claim). *Cf.* Warren v. A.F.G.E. Local 1759, 764 F.2d 1395, 1399 (11th Cir. 1985) (federal courts lack jurisdiction over fair representation claim by federal employee against union).

[36] *See* Casey v. City of Fairbanks, 670 P.2d 1133, 1138 (Alaska 1983) (due process requires that employee be permitted to sue employer directly when pursuit of grievance procedure would be futile; no need to show breach of duty of fair representation).

[37] *See* Salary Policy Employee Panel v. T.V.A., 731 F.2d 325, 330 (6th Cir. 1984).

[38] Joint School Dist. v. Jefferson Educ. Ass'n, 78 Wis. 2d 94, 117–18, 253 N.W.2d 536, 547 (1977); *See* Craver, *The Judicial Enforcement of Public Sector Grievance Arbitration,* 58 Tex. L. Rev. 329, 345–47 (1980).

[39] *See* Philadelphia Hous. Auth. v. Security Officers, 500 Pa. 213, 216, 455 A.2d 625, 627 (1983) ("manifestly unreasonable" award vacated); County of Allegheny v. Allegheny City Prison Employees Indep. Unions, 476 Pa. 27, 381 A.2d 849 (1978). The difference can be explained most satisfactorily by recalling that private sector arbitration awards are reviewed under federal common law. State public employee arbitration awards are reviewed under state law, where the public policy issues may be different.

§ 6.16 ARBITRATION AWARDS 355

arbitration award is based on statutory provisions rather than contract language, less deference is appropriate.[40] Obviously, awards that contravene public policy will not be enforced.[41]

Some courts have concluded that arbitration awards significantly limiting a public employer's statutory right to terminate employees should not be enforced, reasoning either that the award contravenes public policy[42] or that a public employer may not bargain away certain authority and thus disputes are not arbitrable.[43] On the other hand, an arbitration award that applies the same limitations contained in civil service laws is entitled to judicial deference.[44]

In *Taylor v. Crane*,[45] the California Supreme Court struck a compromise between a city's assertion that its charter gave the city manager the sole power to discipline employees and a police officers' union's assertion that any dispute could be submitted to an arbitrator under the collective bargaining agreement.[46] The court,

---

[40] Hunt v. Department of Health & Human Servs., 758 F.2d 608, 611 (Fed. Cir. 1985) (standards for review of arbitrator's decision same as standards for review of Merit Systems Protection Board decision); Devine v. White, 697 F.2d 421, 433 (D.C. Cir. 1983) (Edwards, J.) (judicial review of federal sector arbitration awards for errors in interpreting law or regulation, if error has substantial impact); County College of Morris Staff Ass'n v. County College of Morris, 100 N.J. 383, 392, 495 A.2d 865, 870 (1985) (vacating arbitration award reducing discipline for failure to follow "progressive discipline" concepts not explicitly provided for in collective bargaining agreement). *See* Craver, The Judicial Enforcement of Public Sector Grievance Arbitration, 58 Tex. L. Rev. 329, 349 (1980). *But see* Maine School Dist. No. 33 v. Teacher Ass'n, 395 A.2d 461, 463 (Me. 1978) (award to be sustained even if based on erroneous legal principles, if parties bargained for arbitrator's interpretation of law).

[41] *See* United States Postal Serv. v. Postal Workers, 736 F.2d 822, 825 (1st Cir. 1984) (refusing enforcement of arbitration award which reinstated employee who stole Postal Service funds); Board of Educ. v. Yonkers Fed'n. of Teachers, 46 N.Y.2d 727, 729, 385 N.E.2d 1297, 1298, 413 N.Y.S.2d 370, 371 (1978); Wisconsin Employee Relations Comm'n v. Teamsters Local 567, 75 Wis. 2d 602, 612–13, 250 N.W.2d 696, 701–02 (1977).

[42] *Compare* Antinore v. New York, 49 A.D.2d 6, 371 N.Y.S.2d 213 (1975) (arbitration procedure furthers public policy) *with* Philadelphia Hous. Auth. v. Security Officers, 500 Pa. 213, 216, 455 A.2d 625, 627 (1983) ("manifestly unreasonable" award vacated).

[43] School Comm. of Danvers v. Tyman, 372 Mass. 106, 111, 360 N.E.2d 877, 880 (1977) (decision not to renew teacher contract not arbitrable because cannot be delegated by school committee). *But see* Board of Educ. v. Philadelphia Fed'n of Teachers, 464 Pa. 92, 346 A.2d 35 (1975) (no violation of delegation doctrine to arbitrate validity of teacher dismissal). In the federal sector the legality of grievance arbitration clauses depends on whether they prevent or unreasonably delay management action. *See* Veterans Admin. Medical Center v. Federal Labor Relations Auth., 675 F.2d 260, 262–63 (11th Cir. 1982); Department of Defense v. Federal Labor Relations Auth., 659 F.2d 1140, 1158 (D.C. Cir. 1981).

[44] *See* Taylor v. Crane, 24 Cal. 3d 442, 595 P.2d 129, 155 Cal. Rptr. 695 (1979); Westbrook School Comm'n v. Westbrook Teachers Ass'n, 404 A.2d 204 (Me. 1979).

[45] 24 Cal. 3d 442, 595 P.2d 129, 155 Cal. Rptr. 695 (1979).

[46] The agreement provided for preliminary negotiation, submission to an adjustment board, and finally, submission to an arbitrator whose decision would be final and binding to the extent permitted by the charter of the city.

hearing a suit to enforce an arbitrator's award reinstating a discharged officer,[47] held that although the city charter's provision on its face gave the city manager sole discretion to discipline, the arbitration clause in the contract could be reconciled with the charter by giving the manager the absolute power to initiate disciplinary proceedings, and the arbitrator the power of review.[48] While the city argued that permitting the arbitrator to decide whether the action taken was proper would delegate the city's powers illegally, the court construed the charter as permitting the city to do anything not specifically prohibited. The court was probably influenced by the fact that the city's agreement to arbitrate required the arbitrator to use the city's personnel regulations as his rules for decision.[49]

§ 6.17 Sovereign Immunity: In General

Litigation asserting wrongful dismissal claims against public employers necessarily involves the doctrine of sovereign immunity, which says that the sovereign cannot be sued unless it has consented.[50] Sovereign immunity is potentially at issue regardless of whether a wrongful discharge suit is based on statutory claims discussed in **Chapter 2**, on tort or contract claims discussed in **Chapters 4** and **5**, or on constitutional or civil service claims discussed in this chapter. Sovereign immunity is, however, treated somewhat differently in each context depending on whether the defendant is the federal government, a state, a subordinate entity of a state, or an individual federal or state official.

Despite the sovereign immunity doctrine, suits against federal, state, and local government entities and their officials are allowed in many instances. Four independent doctrines permit such suits:

1. The defendant government itself may have consented to suit by legislative enactment[51]
2. States can be sued if Congress so authorizes pursuant to powers granted in the Thirteenth or Fourteenth Amendments[52]

---

[47] The police officers' association sued for confirmation of the award, while the city sought a declaratory judgment that it was void. The lower court found that the city manager had the sole power to discipline or remove city employees. Taylor v. Crane, 24 Cal. 3d at 446, 595 P.2d at 131, 155 Cal. Rptr. at 700.

[48] *Id.* at 451, 595 P.2d at 134–135, 155 Cal. Rptr. at 702.

[49] *Id.* at 446, 595 P.2d at 131, 155 Cal. Rptr. at 700.

[50] United States v. Testan, 424 U.S. 392, 399 (1976). *See* Owen v. City of Independence, 445 U.S. 622, 645 n.28 (1980) (history of sovereign immunity concept). *See generally* 72 Am. Jur. 2d States §§ 90–125 (1974 & 1985 Supp.).

[51] Restatement (Second) of Torts §§ 895A(2) & 895B(2) (1979).

[52] *See* Owen v. City of Independence, 445 U.S. 622, 647 (1980).

3. Certain units of government may not enjoy immunity at all[53]
4. Most public officials, as individual defendants, enjoy only a qualified immunity.[54]

Sections **6.18** through **6.20** deal first with the federal government as a defendant, then with state and local governments when suit is brought under a federal statute, and finally, when suit is brought against state or local governments under state common law.

§ 6.18 —Suits against the United States and Its Officials

Suits against the United States may be permitted because Congress has waived sovereign immunity. The Tucker Act[55] permits suits for breach of contract, and the Federal Tort Claims Act[56] allows suits for negligence. Section 702 of the Administrative Procedure Act[57] eliminates sovereign immunity in suits for injunctive or declaratory relief brought to review administrative agency action.[58] This last statutory provision removes federal government immunity in suits brought

---

[53] *Id.* at 648 (municipalities). Monell v. Department of Social Servs., 436 U.S. 658, 690 (1978) (local government units not part of state).

[54] Gomez v. Toledo, 446 U.S. 635 (1980).

[55] 24 Stat. 505 (1877), 96 Stat. 669 (1982) (codified as amended at 28 U.S.C. § 1346 (district courts) and 28 U.S.C. § 1491 (United States Claims Court) (1982). Sections 1346 and 1491 give jurisdiction to the district courts and to the United States Claims Court, respectively, over "any claim against the United States founded either upon the Constitution, or any Act of Congress or any regulation of an executive department, or upon any express or implied contract with the United States, or for liquidated or unliquidated damages in cases not sounding in tort." *Id.* § 1491. The section extends to employment contracts. United States v. Hopkins, 427 U.S. 123 (1967) Relief can include reinstatement and back pay. Smith v. United States, 654 F.2d 50 (Ct. Cl. 1981). But the Civil Service Reform Act of 1978, 5 U.S.C. § 7703 (1982) divested the Claims Court of § 1491 jurisdiction over federal employee personnel cases, when the employee status is either probationary or tenured. There are, however, certain employees whose employment status, or the subject matter of their dispute, still allows actions for back pay and other damages to be brought to the Claims Court under the Tucker Act. *See* McClary v. United States, 775 F.2d 280, 283 (Fed. Cir. 1985) (upholding dismissal of appeal concerning demotion because CSRA requires employee to follow procedures for appeal outlined in 5 U.S.C. § 7703 (1982), but reversing dismissal of § 1491 claim for reimbursement of moving expenses, based on the existence of a money-mandating pay statute addressing moving expenses).

[56] 28 U.S.C. § 1346(b) (1982).

[57] 5 U.S.C. § 702 (1982).

[58] *Id.*

to review administrative determinations respecting dismissals in contravention of civil service rights. It does not, however, permit suits for damages.[59] None of these statutes waives immunity for tort damages actions not involving negligence; therefore, intentional tort claims seeking damages are barred by sovereign immunity.

A plaintiff may be able to avoid the sovereign immunity doctrine when it has not been waived by suing an officer or employee of the United States instead of the United States itself.[60] Suits against individuals employed by the government sometimes are dismissed, however, because they are found really to be suits against the United States,[61] or because the United States is an indispensable party.[62]

Despite the general immunity of the federal government to suit (absent statutory waiver), its officials enjoy only a more limited immunity when sued as individuals. In *Butz v. Economou*,[63] the Supreme Court held that federal officials in the executive branch enjoy only a qualified immunity for actions growing out of their violation of constitutional rights.[64] The Court extended absolute immunity, however, to persons performing the functions of judging, deciding to prosecute, and presenting evidence in administrative proceedings.[65]

In practice, this means that an employee alleging wrongful dismissal by a federal agency or instrumentality has several ways around the sovereign immunity problem. The employee can litigate the dismissal administratively and seek judicial review of the administrative decision.[66] The employee may sue under the back

---

[59] *See* McCartin v. Norton, 674 F.2d 1317, 1322 (9th Cir. 1982).

[60] *See, e.g.*, United States v. Lee, 106 U.S. 196 (1882).

[61] *See, e.g.*, Larson v. Domestic & Foreign Commerce Corp., 337 U.S. 682 (1949). It is more likely that suits against federal officers in their official capacities as opposed to suits against them in their individual capacities will be found to be, in reality, suits against the United States. Likewise, it is more likely that a suit for injunctive relief against an individual will be found to be a suit against the United States, than a suit for damages. *See generally* S. Nahmod, Civil Rights and Civil Liberties Litigation § 6.04 at 171–72 (1979 and 1985 Supp.) (discussing suits against individual officials of municipal governments).

[62] *See, e.g.*, Mine Safety Appliances Co. v. Forrestal, 326 U.S. 371 (1945).

[63] 438 U.S. 478 (1978).

[64] *Id.* at 507. The same officials may be absolutely immune from state common law liability, however. *Id.* at 495.

[65] *Id.* at 508.

[66] *See e.g.*, Abrams v. Department of Navy, 714 F.2d 1219 (3d Cir. 1983), in which a discharged employee protested his discharge through the administrative process with the Merit Systems Protection Board (MSPB), and ultimately petitioned the court of appeals for review of the MSPB decision. In *Bush v. Lucas*, 462 U.S. 367 (1983), the Supreme Court suggested that this is the preferred method for obtaining judicial consideration of the legitimacy of a discharge of a civil service employee.

§ 6.19 — Suits against State and Local Governments under § 1983 and Other Federal Statutes

pay statutes, in which case the Tucker Act waives immunity.[67] Or, the employee may be able to sue an individual official in tort.[68]

Suits against state and local governments in federal court for violation of rights granted by federal law raise complex issues: regarding sovereignty reserved to the states by the Eleventh Amendment and regarding powers to regulate state conduct expressly granted Congress by the post Civil War Amendments to the Constitution. In general, employees may sue municipalities in federal court under 42 U.S.C.

---

[67] 28 U.S.C. § 1491 (1982 & Supp. 1984) gives the United States Claims Court jurisdiction over claims for money damages against the United States. This section, often referred to as the Tucker Act, allows jurisdiction in the Claims Court for actions founded on an act of Congress, the Constitution, any regulation of an executive department, a liquidated or unliquidated damages claim in cases not sounding in tort, or any express or implied contract with the United States. The Civil Service Reform Act of 1978, 5 U.S.C. § 7703, divested the Claims Court of § 1491 jurisdiction over federal employee personnel cases, when the employee status is either probationary or tenured. There are, however, certain employees whose employment status, or the subject matter of their dispute, still allows actions for back pay and other damages to be brought to the Claims Court under the Tucker Act. *See* Fausto v. United States, 783 F.2d 1020, 1023 (Fed. Cir. 1986) (non-preference eligible employee of the Department of the Interior properly asserted Claims Court jurisdiction of his claim under the Tucker Act because the plaintiff sued under an enabling executive department regulation, and the plaintiff sought the back pay award under an existing money-mandating pay statute) *on rehearing,* 791 F.2d 1554 (Fed. Cir. 1986); McClary v. United States, 775 F.2d 280, 283 (Fed. Cir. 1985) (upholding dismissal of appeal concerning demotion because CSRA requires employee to follow procedures for appeal outlined in 5 U.S.C. § 7703, but reversing dismissal of § 1491 claim for reimbursement of moving expenses, based on the existence of a money-mandating pay statute addressing moving expenses). *See also* Schuhl v. United States, 3 Cl. Ct. 207 (1983) (plaintiff-employee did not state a valid claim under § 1491 based on theories of promissory estoppel and breach of employment contract); Connelly v. United States, 554 F. Supp. 1250 (Cl. Ct. 1982), *cert. denied,* 465 U.S. 1065 (1984) (Claims Court has no jurisdiction to review dismissals of probationary or tenured federal employees since enactment of the CSRA, but may have jurisdiction to review dismissal that violates the First Amendment).

[68] An employee covered by federal civil service procedures may have difficulty maintaining such an action directly in court however. In Bush v. Lucas, 462 U.S. 367 (1983), the Supreme Court held that the Congress intended the remedies under the civil service laws to be exclusive. This conclusion implies that the Congress has not consented to direct suit by employees on tort or contract theories. *See also* Hewitt v. Grabicki, 794 F.2d 1373, 1382 (9th Cir. 1986) (federal officials, operating within outer perimeter of authority, are absolutely immune from state or common law tort liability). As *Grabicki* suggests, federal officials may enjoy absolute immunity from state common law liability while enjoying only qualified immunity from liability arising from federal constitutional torts.

§ 1983, but sovereign immunity sharply limits other types of suit in federal court against municipal or state instrumentalities.

The Eleventh Amendment to the United States Constitution provides that the federal judicial power does not extend to suits brought by individuals against states. In *Edelman v. Jordan*,[69] the Supreme Court held that the Eleventh Amendment precludes federal courts from entering orders that require the direct disbursement of state funds.[70] The Court also has suggested that injunctive relief directly against a state is barred.[71] Prospective injunctive relief against state officials, however, is not barred.[72] The Eleventh Amendment thus prevents employees from maintaining common law suits against states in the federal courts.[73] Suits against such employers based on federal statutes enacted under powers granted to the Congress by the Fourteenth Amendment are permitted, however, if the Congress has manifested an intention that state immunity be overridden. Important examples are 42 U.S.C. § 1983, and Title VII of the Civil Rights Act of 1964.[74]

In *Fitzpatrick v. Bitzer*,[75] the Supreme Court considered whether Title VII of the Civil Rights Act of 1964 could be applied to the states consistent with the Eleventh Amendment. The Court had little difficulty with the proposition that the Fourteenth Amendment, having been adopted later in time than the Eleventh Amendment, gives Congress the power to authorize damages against states as a means of enforcing the substantive guarantees of the Fourteenth Amendment. The question then becomes whether the Congress *has* authorized such damages—a question of statutory construction. Because the 1972 amendments to Title VII on their face authorized suit against state and local governments, the *Fitzpatrick* Court concluded that the Eleventh Amendment does not bar suits for back pay under Title VII. However, it distinguished § 1983 and earlier cases construing that statute with the Eleventh Amendment.

The Supreme Court has reached somewhat different conclusions regarding the treatment of sovereign immunity under § 1983, depending on whether the defendant is the state, a municipality, or an individual state official.

---

[69] 415 U.S. 651 (1974). *See generally* McGuire, *Public Employee Actions and the Eleventh Amendment*, 14 Urb. Law. 89 (1982).

[70] Edelman v. Jordan, 415 U.S. at 671. Quern v. Jordan, 440 U.S. 332 (1979) reaffirmed the holding of *Edelman* in light of *Monell v. Department of Social Servs.*, 436 U.S. 658 (1978).

[71] *See* Cory v. White, 457 U.S. 85 (1982) (interpleader against a state barred by Eleventh Amendment).

[72] Edelman v. Jordan, 415 U.S. at 677; *Ex parte* Young, 209 U.S. 123 (1908). *See* Lee v. Western Reserve Psychiatric Habilation Center, 747 F.2d 1062, 1066 (6th Cir. 1984) (Eleventh Amendment does not bar prospective injunction against use of flawed dismissal procedures; nor does it bar awarding attorneys' fees).

[73] Of course, the Eleventh Amendment is no bar to suit in state court.

[74] *See* Fitzpatrick v. Bitzer, 427 U.S. 445, 451–56 (1976).

[75] *Id.*

§ 6.19 SUITS AGAINST STATE AND LOCAL

In *Monell v. Department of Social Services*,[76] the Court held that municipalities and other local governments are not immune from suit under § 1983.[77] The Court also held, however, that a local government may not be sued under § 1983 for an injury inflicted solely by its employees or agents, unless their actions fairly may be said to represent official policy.[78] In *Owen v. City of Independence*,[79] the Supreme Court held that municipalities enjoy no qualified immunity for actions taken, even in good faith, that violate constitutional rights.[80] One rationale for the Court's decision was the unfairness of imposing financial liability on individual municipal officers and employees.[81]

In *Owen,* the city manager fired the police chief with the knowledge and consent of city council.[82] Chief Owen sued under 42 U.S.C. § 1983 for dismissal in violation of his civil rights, naming the city as a defendant. The district court and court of appeals denied relief against the city,[83] but the Supreme Court reversed. Holding that, "by including municipalities within the class of persons subject to liability for violations of the Federal Constitution and laws,"[84] Congress abolished municipal sovereign immunity in civil rights cases. Thus the Court found the city could be liable to Chief Owen.[85] Subsequently, in *City of Oklahoma City v. Tuttle,*[86] the Supreme Court, in concurring opinions, held that municipalities are liable under

---

[76] 436 U.S. 658 (1978).

[77] It specifically held also that local government officials sued in their official capacities enjoy no greater immunity than the governmental entities which they serve. *Id.* at 690 n.55. *Monell* has been harmonized with Monroe v. Pape, 365 U.S. 167 (1961) (municipalities not covered at all by § 1983), *overruled,* Monell v. Department of Social Servs., 436 U.S. 658 (1978), in Quern v. Jordan, 440 U.S. 332, 338 (1979). *But see* Riggs v. Commonwealth of Ky., 734 F.2d 262, 265 (6th Cir. 1984), *cert. denied,* 469 U.S. 857 (1984) (state is immune from suit under § 1983).

[78] Monell v. Department of Social Servs., 436 U.S. at 694. *See also* Berdin v. Duggan, 701 F.2d 909 (11th Cir.) (because city ordinances permitted the mayor unbridled discretion over hiring and firing, the city was liable), *cert. denied,* 464 U.S. 893 (1983). *Cf.* City of Oklahoma City v. Tuttle, 471 U.S. 808 (1985) (no recovery under § 1983 for police officer shooting; no showing that city condoned police behavior).

[79] 445 U.S. 622 (1980).

[80] *Id.* at 650.

[81] *Id.* at 657.

[82] *Id.* at 628–29. The city manager, after initiating an investigation of the police department, presented the results to council and was given express authority to take action against the persons involved in the improprieties.

[83] *Id.* at 634. The courts found the city could not have known that its actions were unconstitutional at the time the action was taken, since Perry v. Sinderman, 408 U.S. 593 (1972), and Board of Regents v. Roth, 408 U.S. 564 (1972), had not yet been decided. They declined to hold the city liable for its good faith denial of a hearing for the aggrieved police chief.

[84] Owens v. City of Independence, 445 U.S. at 647–48.

[85] *Id.* at 657. The court's decision was partly based on the theory that the public is better held liable for a municipality's constitutional violations than the municipality's individual officers. *Id.*

[86] 471 U.S. 808 (1985), 105 S. Ct. 2427.

§ 1983 only when the plaintiff can show that the municipality as an entity, and not just an individual agent of the municipality, violated constitutional rights.[87]

It would seem that a municipality could not be held liable for punitive damages in a wrongful dismissal suit instituted under 42 U.S.C. § 1983 in light of the Supreme Court's holding in *City of Newport v. Fact Concerts.*[88]

These decisions involving municipal liability under § 1983 impliedly leave the sovereign immunity of states intact.[89]

Section 1983 has been construed as permitting suits against individual state officials, however.[90] Municipal officials, enjoying no more immunity than their employers, already are without immunity under *Monell v. Department of Social Services.* The Eleventh Amendment was held to permit suit against state officials in *Ex parte Young.*[91] Subsequently, in *Scheuer v. Rhodes*[92] and a number of subsequent cases,[93] the Supreme Court held that most state officials are entitled only to a qualified immunity in suits brought under § 1983. In *Scheuer* and *Wood v. Strickland,*[94] the Court held that the immunity does not exist if the official "knew or reasonably should have known that the action he took within his sphere of official responsibility would violate the rights of [the plaintiff], or if he took the action with the malicious intention to cause a deprivation of constitutional rights

---

[87] *Id.* at 2441 (Brennan, J., concurring).

[88] 453 U.S. 247 (1981). Among the considerations was the nondeterrent effect of such damages on a municipality, the incapacity of a city to bear malice, the more effective deterrence of punishing individual city officers, the cost to the taxpayer of official folly, and the windfall potentiality of assessing damages against an entity possessed of unlimited taxing power.

[89] *See* Quern v. Jordan, 440 U.S. 332, 338 (1979); Fitzpatrick v. Bitzer, 427 U.S. 445, 452 (1975); Riggs v. Commonwealth of Ky., 734 F.2d 262, 265 (6th Cir. 1984) (state is immune from suit under § 1983), *cert. denied,* 469 U.S. 857 (1984). McGuire, *Public Employee Actions and the Eleventh Amendment,* 14 Urb. Law. 125 (1982). As the McGuire article explains, the status of school districts and other such entities depends on state law. *Id.* at 93-101. *See* Patsy v. Florida Bd. of Regents, 457 U.S. 496, 520-32 (1982) (Powell, J., dissenting).

[90] *See* Jorden v. National Guard Bureau, 799 F.2d 99 (3d Cir. 1986) (reviewing immunity standards for state military officers in both damages actions and injunction suits). It can make a difference whether individuals are sued in their individual capacities or their official capacities. Suit against a named person in his official capacity is more likely to be found to be a suit against the government entity employing him. Suit against a person in his individual capacity is less likely to be found to be a suit against the government entity. Similarly, suits against individuals for damages are more likely to be permitted than suits for equitable relief. *See* S. Nahmod, Civil Rights and Civil Liberties Litigation § 6.04 at 172 (1979). *See* Riggs v. Commonwealth of Ky., 734 F.2d 262, 265 (6th Cir. 1984), *cert. denied,* 469 U.S. 857 (1984) (state is immune from suit under § 1983).

[91] 209 U.S. 123 (1908).

[92] 416 U.S. 232 (1974).

[93] Procunier v. Navarette, 434 U.S. 555 (1978) (prison officials); Imbler v. Pachtman, 424 U.S. 409 (1976) (police officers); O'Connor v. Donaldson, 422 U.S. 563 (1975) (state hospital superintendent); Wood v. Strickland, 420 U.S. 308 (1975) (local school board members).

[94] 420 U.S. 308 (1975).

or other injury to the [plaintiff].'"[95] In *Gomez v. Toledo*,[96] the Supreme Court held that the qualified immunity of a public official must be pleaded and proved by the defendant.[97] Certain classes of state officials, however, such as legislators, judges, prosecutors, and witnesses in judicial proceedings, are absolutely immune from suit under § 1983.[98]

§ 6.20 —Common Law Suits against State and Local Governments and Officials

Whether a state or its instrumentality is immune from a tort or contract action brought in its own courts is a matter of state constitutional, statutory and common law.[99] The doctrine of sovereign immunity has been eroded substantially by the legislatures and courts, especially as it applies to municipalities.[1] The doctrine retains greater vitality with respect to state governments, but there also it has been relaxed considerably.[2]

There is a strong trend toward abolition of the doctrine of sovereign immunity with respect to contracts entered into by state or local entities.[3] There is some

---

[95] *Id.* at 322. Davis v. Scherer, 468 U.S. 183 (1984) (showing of violation of clear state regulation not sufficient to overcome qualified immunity); Buschi v. Kirven, 775 F.2d 1240, 1256 (4th Cir. 1985) (*Loudermill* requirement for pretermination procedure sufficiently uncertain that violation by individual would be within qualified privilege). *See also* Malley v. Briggs, ___ U.S. ___, 106 S. Ct. 1092 (1986) (reviewing *objective reasonableness* standard for qualified immunity applicable to both state and federal officials under § 1983); Berdin v. Duggan, 701 F.2d 909, 913 (11th Cir.) (mayor liable for dismissing a city worker who spoke to him about the need for additional workers; mayor "should have known . . . that his action was . . . impermissible."), *cert. denied*, 464 U.S. 893 (1983).

[96] 446 U.S. 635 (1980).

[97] The plaintiff in a § 1983 action against a person possibly possessing a qualified immunity need only plead that the defendant deprived the plaintiff of a federal right while acting under the color of state law. The burden to prove good faith as an affirmative defense is placed on the defendant since establishing a qualified immunity defense usually depends on proving facts within the defendant's knowledge and control. Gomez v. Toledo, 446 U.S. at 640-41.

[98] Briscoe v. LaHue, 460 U.S. 325 (1983) (police officer witness is immune).

[99] *See* Restatement (Second) of Torts § 895B, comment c (1979). *See, e.g.*, Hutchinson v. Board of Trustees of Univ. of Ala., 288 Ala. 20, 256 So. 2d 281 (1971) (constitutional immunity, legislature cannot consent); Ill. Const. art. 13, § 4 (constitutional waiver); Campbell v. State, 259 Ind. 55, 284 N.E.2d 733 (1972) (judicially abolished).

[1] *See* Restatement (Second) of Torts § 895B, comment b (1979).

[2] *See* Restatement (Second) of Torts ch. 45A, Introductory Note (1979).

[3] *See* Restatement (Second) of Contracts § 8 comment c (1981); Shepard's Civil Actions Against State Governments § 2.29 at 57 (1982).

authority for the proposition that the doctrine never was applied as strongly to contract liability as to tort liability.[4]

The modern trend toward elimination of sovereign immunity for most tort actions began in 1945 in New York[5] and gained acceptance with a 1961 California decision.[6] The general rule affording immunity to state governments in tort actions is set forth in § 895B of the *Restatement (Second) of Torts*. The Appendix to § 895B contains a state-by-state summary of the status of the doctrine. Generally, state instrumentalities other than municipalities, such as universities, boards and commissions, enjoy the same degree of immunity as the state itself, except as provided in legislation specific to the agency.[7]

The relaxation of the immunity doctrine for municipalities relates to the historical distinction between proprietary and governmental functions of municipalities.[8] The former were not covered by the immunity doctrine, and the latter were. Beginning in Florida in 1957,[9] a growing number of states have abolished sovereign immunity for governmental as well as proprietary activities of municipalities.[10] There is growing acceptance of the view that local government entities do not enjoy sovereign immunity, except for legislative, judicial, or policy matters. This view is reflected in § 895C of the *Restatement (Second) of Torts*.[11] Some states clothe certain geographic subdivisions, however, such as counties and school

---

[4] *See* E. McQuillan, The Law of Municipal Corporations § 29.123 at 558 (1981). Some courts hold that the state waives its sovereign immunity by entering into a contract. Shepard's Civil Actions Against State Governments § 3.27 (1982). *See* Myrtle Springs Reverted Indep. School Dist. v. Hogan, 705 S.W.2d 707 (Tex. Ct. App. 1985) (contract damages, but not tort damages recoverable from school board because of sovereign immunity); Watassek v. Michigan Dept. of Mental Health, 143 Mich. App. 556, 372 N.W.2d 617, 621 (1985) (sovereign immunity in Michigan does not bar wrongful discharge sounding in contract or in intentional tort). *Compare* Carter v. Board of Trustees of Univ. of Ala., 431 So. 2d. 529, 531 (Ala. 1983) (breach of contract suit against state instrumentality for wrongful dismissal barred by sovereign immunity) *and* Yellow Cab Co. v. City of Chicago, 186 F.2d 946, 948–49 (7th Cir. 1951) (tort immunity may extend to contract liability) *with* Jones v. State Bd. of Regents, 385 N.W.2d 240, 242 (Iowa 1986) (state waives sovereign immunity by entering into contract) *and* Spaur v. City of Greeley, 150 Colo. 346, 372 P.2d 730 (1962) (sovereign immunity no longer exists as to state contracts) *and* Cahill v. Board of Educ., 187 Conn. 94, 102, 444 A.2d 907, 912 (1982) (doctrine of sovereign immunity does not bar teacher's suit against board of education for breach of contract).

[5] Bernardine v. City of New York, 294 N.Y. 361, 62 N.E.2d 604 (1945).

[6] Muskopf v. Corning Hosp. Dist., 55 Cal. 2d 211, 359 P.2d 457 11 Cal. Rptr. 89, (1961). *See* Restatement (Second) of Torts § 895B, comment b (1979).

[7] *See* Restatement (Second) of Torts § 895B, comment g (1979).

[8] Restatement (Second) of Torts § 895C, comments a–e (1979).

[9] Hargrove v. Town of Cocoa Beach, 96 So. 2d 130 (Fla. 1957) (superseded by statute as stated in Cauley v. Jacksonville, 403 So. 2d 329 (Fla. 1981)).

[10] *See* Restatement (Second) of Torts § 895C, comment f (1979).

[11] Restatement (Second) of Torts § 895C (1979). The Reporter's Note in the Appendix to § 895B contains a state-by-state survey of the doctrine as it pertains to local governments.

districts, with the same immunity as the state, which usually is greater than that afforded municipalities.[12]

Generally, public officials sued individually enjoy the same immunity as the governmental entity by which they are employed.[13] The applicability of the immunity in a particular case, however, depends on whether the official was performing a discretionary act, whether he was operating within the scope of his authority, and whether he was acting in good faith.[14]

Accordingly, the justiciability of a suit against a state, subordinate entity, or official employed thereby, for wrongful dismissal premised on tort or breach of contract, will be determined by the status of the sovereign immunity doctrine in that state. Even if sovereign immunity bars such a suit, the same operative facts usually will make out a claim of violation of due process cognizable under 42 U.S.C. § 1983, where sovereign immunity is a matter of federal law.[15]

---

[12] Restatement (Second) of Torts § 895C, comment a (1979).

[13] Restatement (Second) of Torts § 895D, comment j (1979). *See* Cahill v. Board of Educ., 187 Conn. 94, 101, 444 A.2d 907, 912 (1982) (doctrine of sovereign immunity applied to agents of state and municipalities to same extent as to state or municipality itself for breach of contract).

[14] *See* Restatement (Second) of Torts § 895D, comments a–j (1979), for a discussion of these factors and their application. *See, e.g.,* Elliott v. Kupferman, 58 Md. App. 510, 526, 473 A.2d 960, 967 (1984) (individual municipal officials found immune to suit for dismissing police chief; discretionary acts, no malice).

[15] *See* Vinyard v. King, 728 F.2d 428, 432 (10th Cir. 1984) (remanding for consideration of whether individual supervisor's conduct permits award of compensatory and punitive damages resulting from dismissal of public employee). In *Vail,* Judge Posner argued in a forceful dissent, however, that contract rights are not property within the intendment of the Fourteenth Amendment. Vail v. Board of Educ., 706 F.2d 1435, 1450–52 (7th Cir. 1983) (Posner, J., dissenting). To hold otherwise, he concluded, would turn every claim for breach of an employment contract by a public employee into a federal claim under § 1983.

CHAPTER 7

PROBLEMS OF PROOF

§ 7.1   Introduction
§ 7.2   Basic Proof Concepts
§ 7.3   Pervasiveness of Employer Motive Question
§ 7.4   Statutory and Constitutional Claims: Proof of Motive
§ 7.5   —Public Employee Constitutional Rights
§ 7.6   —Violations of Title VII
§ 7.7   —Violations of the National Labor Relations Act
§ 7.8   —Violations of the Age Discrimination in Employment Act
§ 7.9   —Violations of Other Statutes
§ 7.10 Public Policy Tort: Basic Concepts of Proof
§ 7.11 —Proving Public Policy
§ 7.12 —Proving Jeopardy to Public Policy
§ 7.13 —Proving Lack of Justification: Proving Reason for Dismissal
§ 7.14 —Proving Lack of Justification: Burden of Proof on Reasons for Dismissal and Mixed Motive Problem
§ 7.15 —Proving Justification: Business Necessity
§ 7.16 —Public Policy Tort Jury Instructions
§ 7.17 Common Law Contracts: Basic Concepts of Proof
§ 7.18 —Proving an Express or Implied-in-Fact Promise of Employment Security from Writings or Oral Statements
§ 7.19 —Proving Promise from Conduct
§ 7.20 —Proving Consideration
§ 7.21 —Jury Instructions on Contract Formation
§ 7.22 Proving a Breach: Introduction
§ 7.23 —Proving a Breach: Bad Faith or Unfairness
§ 7.24 —Proving a Breach: Cause for Termination in General
§ 7.25 —Proving a Breach: Proving What the Employee Did
§ 7.26 —Proving a Breach: Who Decides What Is Good Cause
§ 7.27 —Proving a Breach: Burdens of Proof on Cause
§ 7.28 —Jury Instructions on Breach

§ 7.29 Preclusive Effect of Earlier Judicial, Arbitral, and Administrative Decisions
§ 7.30 —Preclusive Effect of Judicial Decisions
§ 7.31 —Preclusive Effect of Arbitral Decisions
§ 7.32 —Preclusive Effect of Administrative Decisions: In General
§ 7.33 —Preclusive Effect of Administrative Decisions: Discrimination Findings
§ 7.34 —Preclusive Effect of Administrative Decisions: Employer Regulatory Compliance
§ 7.35 —Preclusive Effect of Administrative Decisions: Unemployment Compensation

§ 7.1 Introduction

This chapter explores the types and levels of proof that will suffice to make out a case for wrongful dismissal under the legal theories discussed in preceding chapters, and the possibility that earlier proceedings may foreclose de novo consideration of proof. The emphasis is on emerging common law theories, but more established constitutional and statutory proof concepts are reviewed first, both because of their independent importance as bases for recovery and to establish a baseline from which the common law alternatives can be evaluated. This chapter concentrates on presumptions, burdens of proof, and permissible inferences that can be drawn from direct evidence. Counsel should tailor trial strategy in a particular case to the facts of the case and the availability of witnesses, documents, and other forms of proof.[1]

Two proof problems occur under several legal theories of wrongful dismissal: how to prove motive for a dismissal and how to prove a promise of employment security. Proving motive is common to tort theories and most statutory theories, and can be important in certain contract cases. The motive issue is treated in several sections of this chapter.[2]

Proof of a promise of employment security is discussed only in two sections (see §§ **7.18** and **7.19**), though such proof may be necessary not only for a common law contract claim, but also to establish a property interest as a prerequisite

---

[1] **App. B** contains discovery checklists for both plaintiff and defendant that should assist in developing factual evidence. M. Dichter, A. Gross, D. Morikawa & S. Sauntry, Employee Dismissal Forms and Procedures (1986) provides practical litigation tools supplementing the concepts presented in this chapter.

[2] See §§ **7.4–7.9, 7.13–7.15, 7.23**.

to recovery against a public employer under a due process theory.[3] In both instances, the chapter gives appropriate cross references.

One type of proof problem occurs only in tort cases: proof of public policy. This problem does not arise in statutory or constitutional cases because the legislature or the people, respectively, already have declared public policy. In contract cases, public policy is a less prominent issue because the parties have defined their obligations by contract. In tort cases, the courts must define public policy for individual cases. Accordingly, the public policy tort sections of this chapter contain more extensive treatment of public policy proof than other sections.

Many of the common law cases discussed do not involve posttrial review; instead, they involve review of decisions on motions to dismiss, for judgment on the pleadings or for summary judgment. Cases terminated without trial nevertheless are helpful in defining proof requirements because of the principle that factual allegations of the pleadings are to be taken as true to test the legal sufficiency of the pleading.[4] Thus, such cases help to define the boundaries of a successful factual case.

§ 7.2 Basic Proof Concepts

In order to discuss the problems of proof in wrongful dismissal most effectively, a common vocabulary is desirable. This section defines some concepts necessary to the discussion of proof, and contrasts different interpretations of the concepts.

One should remember that the *burden of proof* is divided into two parts—the burden of producing evidence (burden of *production*) and the burden of persuading the finder of fact (burden of *persuasion*).[5] One also should remember that *prima facie* in the wrongful dismissal context may have more than one meaning. The term *prima facie tort*[6] is used by some courts to refer to a form of tort liability in which the plaintiff can recover by showing intentional injury and lack of justification, regardless of whether the defendant's conduct falls within a recognized tort category.

Apart from a label for a residual tort category, *prima facie* means two different things regarding the strength of the case presented by the plaintiff.[7] The first meaning

---

[3] See § **7.5**. See also § **6.10**.

[4] *See* Haines v. Kerner, 404 U.S. 519, 521 (1972) (civil rights prisoner action); Paolino v. Channel Home Centers, 668 F.2d 721, 722 (3d Cir. 1981).

[5] C. McCormick, Handbook on the Law of Evidence § 336 at 948–49 (E. Cleary ed. 1984).

[6] See §§ **5.5, 5.21**.

[7] C. McCormick, Handbook on the Law of Evidence § 342 at 803 n. 26 (E. Cleary ed. 1984); 9 J. Wigmore, Wigmore on Evidence § 2494 at 378 (Chadbourne rev. 1981).

is that the plaintiff, who has pleaded well, has produced evidence at trial sufficient to permit reasonable persons to *infer* the ultimate fact to be proved.[8] Thus, a motion for a directed verdict by defendant must be denied if the plaintiff has a prima facie case,[9] but the jury still may find for the defendant even if the defendant puts on no evidence.

The second meaning assigned to prima facie is that a presentation of a prima facie case by the plaintiff shifts the burden of production.[10] Some authorities, if the plaintiff pleads correctly and produces evidence supporting the allegations, would create a *presumption* in the plaintiff's favor, and unless the defendant brings forth evidence to rebut the presumption, would permit a directed verdict for the plaintiff.[11] Application of this concept obviously is advantageous to the plaintiff. Many authorities also would shift the burden of persuasion to the defendant when a presumption for the plaintiff exists,[12] requiring the defendant to carry an even heavier load.

Legal reasoning and factfinding rely heavily on the drawing of *inferences.* In most cases, factfinders must infer ultimate fact conclusions from direct evidence of conduct or mental state. Juries are permitted to draw inferences when evidence is presented that would lead a reasonable person to conclude that the ultimate fact is more likely than not to have existed. For example, if the employer praises the employee's work record the day before the employee files a claim for workers' compensation, and dismisses the employee the day after, one can infer that the filing of the workers' compensation claim, rather than poor work performance, was the motive for the dismissal.

Justification presents another definitional problem. In the public policy tort context, liability rests in part on the lack of justification for the defendant's act in the circumstances.[13] Under usual tort theory, however, the concept of justification as a privilege ordinarily would require the defendant to present evidence on the justifiable nature of his act as an affirmative defense.[14]

---

[8] C. McCormick, Handbook on the Law of Evidence § 338 at 789–90 (E. Cleary ed. 1984).

[9] 9 J. Wigmore, Wigmore on Evidence § 2494 at 379 (Chadbourne rev. 1981).

[10] *Id.;* C. McCormick, Handbook on the Law of Evidence § 342 at 803 (E. Cleary ed. 1984).

[11] *See* C. McCormick, Handbook on the Law of Evidence § 342 at 803 n.26 (E. Cleary ed. 1984); 9 J. Wigmore, Wigmore on Evidence § 2494 at 379 (Chadbourne rev. 1984).

[12] C. McCormick, Handbook on the Law of Evidence § 342 at 803 (E. Cleary ed. 1984).

[13] Restatement (Second) of Torts § 870 (1979) requires the court to balance the injury, the culpable nature of the behavior, and the actor's justification in the circumstances to find whether the action complained of is tortious.

[14] *Id*. Section 890 states that "one who otherwise would be liable for a tort is not liable if he acts in pursuance of and within the limits of his own or of a privilege of another that was properly delegated to him."

§ 7.3 Pervasiveness of Employer Motive Question

In most dismissal situations, an employee has a legal remedy only on a showing that the dismissal was for a particular reason.[15] The employer's motive[16] thus is at issue if the employee claims that she was dismissed in retaliation for her exercise of rights to engage in concerted action protected by the National Labor Relations Act or conduct such as whistleblowing shielded by statute.[17] Motive also is at issue if the employee claims a violation of discrimination statutes; these statutes prohibit discrimination on the basis of the employee's membership in a race, sex, religion, national origin, age, or handicap class.[18] Motive also is at issue if the employee seeks common law relief on a public policy tort theory,[19] alleging that the employer dismissed the employee for a reason that jeopardizes public policy. Discharge for any of these reasons will be referred to in the discussion that follows as dismissal for a *prohibited reason.*

In prohibited reason cases, an employer is most likely to defend on the factual basis that the employee was dismissed for other than the prohibited reason. If the employer claims that the prohibited reason played no role in the dismissal decision, legal questions are presented on standards of proof and the allocation of responsibility between judge and jury. The same questions are presented in more complex form if the evidence shows that the prohibited reason played some role, along with other, legitimate, reasons, in the termination decision. This is the *mixed motive* problem.

The National Labor Relations Board has explained the difference between *pretext* and *mixed motive* cases.[20] In a pretext case the employer's asserted justification

---

[15] This is true of all the statutes discussed in **ch.2**; when a breach of an implied covenant of good faith and fair dealing is alleged, as discussed in **§ 4.9**; and when a public policy tort is alleged, as discussed in **ch. 5**. The need for the employee to prove a prohibited reason for the dismissal is the essential difference between the current state of the law regarding employee dismissals and what the law would be if dismissals were prohibited except for good cause. See **§§ 1.13, 5.2, ch. 9**. The burden of pleading and proof is on the plaintiff to show prohibited reason. The burden of pleading and proof would be on the employer to show good cause.

[16] Use of the term *motive* is not meant to imply a specific intent by an employer to interfere with protected rights; rather, it implies that the employer's reason for the dismissal was conduct or a characteristic that is protected.

[17] National Labor Relations Act, as amended by the Labor-Management Relations Act of 1947 (Taft-Hartley Act) 29 U.S.C. §§ 151–169 (1982). See **§§ 2.15–2.24**, relating to statutes protecting against discharge in retaliation for specified conduct.

[18] See **§§ 2.2–2.14**, relating to statutes protecting against class-based discharge.

[19] See **§§ 5.8–5.20**, relating to public policy tort theories.

[20] Wright Line & Bernard R. Lamoureux, 251 N.L.R.B. 1083, 1083 n.4 (1980). The Supreme Court has suggested that pretext and mixed motive cases are different. In mixed motive cases, it is appropriate to shift the burden to the employer to prove that the illegal motive did not actuate the adverse employment action; in pretext cases, it is not appropriate to shift the burden to the employer.

of a legitimate business reason is found to be wholly without merit—pretextual, in other words.[21] If the employer assertion has at least some merit, the case becomes a mixed motive case, and the issue is one of the standard of proof necessary for the employer's defense to be sustained.[22]

Common law cases require more from the decisionmaker than statutory cases. Statutes prohibiting certain types of dismissal define the prohibited reasons for dismissal more or less clearly,[23] and judicial analysis is necessary only to allocate burdens of proof and to define the role of the jury, if jury trials are involved.[24] In public policy tort actions for wrongful dismissal, there is no explicit statutory definition of prohibited reasons for dismissal.[25] The judiciary must decide what reasons for dismissal are impermissible, and must also decide the proof and jury role questions.

§ 7.4 Statutory and Constitutional Claims: Proof of Motive

In order to explore the alternative legal standards for proving motive[26] in wrongful dismissal cases, it is appropriate to begin with the case law relating to dismissals violating statutes or the Constitution. This body of law is more completely developed than the body of law involving public policy torts or implied-in-fact contract claims, in which many of the leading cases involve only the question of whether a cause of action exists, not how the plaintiff proves a case. Sections **7.5** through **7.9** address the standards of proof for dismissals of public employees for exercising constitutional rights, for discriminatory dismissals under Title VII, for unfair labor practices, and for violations of the federal age discrimination act. The chapter then reviews, against this relatively settled backdrop, the proof requirements for common law claims.

NLRB v. Transportation Management Corp., 462 U.S. 393, 400 n.5 (1983) (distinguishing Texas Dep't of Community Affairs v. Burdine, 450 U.S. 248 (1981)).

[21] 462 U.S. at 400 n.5.

[22] *Id.*

[23] See **ch. 2**.

[24] *See, e.g.,* Wright Line & Bernard R. Lamoureux, 251 N.L.R.B. 1083 (1980) (NLRA burdens of proof); Tuohy v. Ford Motor Co., 675 F.2d 842 (6th Cir. 1982) (jury role in age case).

[25] See §§ **2.26, 5.19**, distinguishing implied private rights of action for statutory violations from public policy tort actions.

[26] Use of the term *motive* usually does not mean a specific intent by an employer to interfere with constitutionally protected rights; instead, it implies that the employer's reason for the dismissal was conduct or a characteristic that is protected.

§ 7.5 —Public Employee Constitutional Rights

Public employee cases involving constitutional rights are discussed in **Chapter 6**. In many of those cases, in order to recover, the plaintiff must establish a property right in his job resulting from employer promises. Proving such a property interest involves many of the proof problems involved in establishing a contract.[27] These problems are considered in **§§ 7.18** and **7.19**. Only the motive question is considered in this section. Motive is important in a lawsuit for violation of constitutional rights when a plaintiff alleges that his dismissal interferes with liberty interests protected by the Constitution, such as free speech, religion, or privacy.[28]

When public employees claim that their dismissals infringed First Amendment liberty interests without due process, the court hearing the claims must engage in a multiple step analysis. First, the employees must demonstrate that their conduct was protected. Second, the employees must demonstrate that such protected conduct was a substantial or motivating factor in the decision to dismiss them. Third, the employer may show that the dismissals would have occurred even in the absence of the protected conduct.[29] Under *Connick v. Meyers*,[30] the first step of deciding whether the conduct was protected involves two subordinate inquiries: does the speech address a "matter of public concern," and does the interest of the employees in speaking outweigh the interest of the public employer in promoting the efficiency of the public service.[31] The inquiry regarding whether the speech is protected is a question of law to be decided by the judge, not a question of fact to be decided by the jury.[32] Appropriate questions of fact should be submitted to the jury in separate interrogatories.[33]

The main fact question is therefore why the employer dismissed the employee: because of protected conduct or for another reason. Usually some evidence exists permitting an inference that protected conduct played some role in the employer's decision, but the employer asserts that a legitimate reason was the real reason.

The mixed motive problem was addressed in *Mt. Healthy City School District v. Doyle*,[34] which also presented the order of proof related to other elements. The United States Supreme Court announced a *but for* causation standard for cases

---

[27] *See* Vinyard v. King, 728 F.2d 428, 432 (10th Cir. 1984) (constitutionally protected property interest under Oklahoma law created by employee handbook).

[28] Motive also is important in deciding if there has been no taking of a property interest without due process because *cause* existed for dismissal. See **§ 6.13**.

[29] Roberts v. Van Buren Pub. Schools, 773 F.2d 949, 953–54 (8th Cir. 1985) (explaining Connick v. Myers order of proof).

[30] 461 U.S. 138 (1983). The case of Connick v. Myers is discussed in **§§ 6.11** and **6.13**.

[31] Roberts v. Van Buren Pub. Schools, 773 F.2d at 954.

[32] *Id.* (reversing district court for permitting jury to decide protected nature of speech).

[33] *Id.*

[34] 429 U.S. 274 (1977). Public employee dismissals are discussed generally in **ch. 6**.

involving dismissal of a public employee for exercising First Amendment rights to free speech. The district court ordered Doyle reinstated because his exercise of First Amendment rights had played "a substantial part in the decision" not to renew his contract as a school teacher, even though other legitimate reasons existed for terminating his employment.[35] Although the court of appeals affirmed, the Supreme Court reversed. The Court expressed concern that a "rule of causation which focuses solely on whether protected conduct played a part . . . in a decision not to rehire, could place an employee in a better position as a result of the exercise of constitutionally protected conduct than he would have occupied had he done nothing."[36] In the Court's view, the constitutional interests at stake are sufficiently vindicated if an employee like Doyle is placed in "no worse" position because of his exercise of constitutional rights.[37]

Accordingly, the Court formulated the following order of proof for cases in which an employee claims the dismissal was because of constitutionally protected conduct. The plaintiff has the burden of showing that the conduct was constitutionally protected and that this conduct was a motivating factor in the employer's decision to terminate.[38] If the plaintiff meets that burden, the employer can escape liability if it shows, by a preponderance of the evidence, that it would have reached the same decision even in the absence of the protected conduct.[39] This approach to proof can be applied in any case alleging any type of constitutional infringement, as well as in the statutory contexts discussed in the following sections. The approach also is quite similar to the approach to proving a public policy tort.[40]

An employee seeking recovery for liberty infringement must present evidence to support the following propositions:

1. The employee engaged in certain conduct
2. The conduct was protected

---

[35] Mt. Healthy City School Dist. v. Doyle, 429 U.S. at 281–85. One reason for Doyle's dismissal was his telephone call to a radio station, in which he communicated the substance of a memorandum relating to teacher dress and appearance that the school principal had circulated to various teachers. Doyle understood that the subject was to be settled by joint teacher-administration action. The other reason asserted for his dismissal was Doyle's penchant for arguing with fellow teachers, school cafeteria employees, and students.

[36] *Id.* at 285.

[37] *Id.*

[38] *Id.* at 287.

[39] *Id. See* Sykes v. McDowell, 786 F.2d 1098, 1100 n.1 (11th Cir. 1986) (quoting jury instructions on reasons for dismissal in First Amendment case); Balicao v. University of Minn., 737 F.2d 747, 749 (8th Cir. 1984) (sudden and unprecedented criticism of work adequately supports inference of motive to discriminate for protected speech, but proof of deficient work rebutted inference).

[40] See § 7.13.

3. The conduct was at least part of the motivation for the employer's decision to terminate the employee.

Testimony by the employee plaintiff should be enough to establish the first proposition.[41] The second proposition requires legal analysis by the court, and turns more on precedent and characterization of conduct than proof. The third proposition frequently is the most difficult one for the employee to establish. An inference of prohibited motive can be drawn from circumstantial evidence[42] or from admissions by the employer decisionmakers.[43] An obvious precondition for establishing prohibited motive is to prove that the employer was aware of the protected conduct.[44]

§ 7.6 —Violations of Title VII

Section 703 of the Civil Rights Act of 1964[45] prohibits adverse employment actions—including terminations—"because of" race, color, religion, national origin, or sex.[46] Section 706(g) of the same act precludes relief if the adverse employment action was taken for "any reason other than" discrimination.[47] The employee claiming a violation has the burden of proving class membership was the reason for the adverse employer action. Similarly, in a suit for retaliation in violation of § 704,[48] the plaintiff has the ultimate burden of persuasion to show that retaliatory motivation was the "but for" cause of the dismissal.[49]

---

[41] Ordinarily the employer does not contest the employee's version of what the employee did. If a factual dispute exists on this point, testimony of additional witnesses may be necessary to reinforce the credibility of the employee's testimony.

[42] *See* Cox v. Dardanelle Pub. School Dist., 790 F.2d 668, 675–76 (8th Cir. 1986) (memoranda in personnel file referred to protected conduct; also, only those employees engaging in protected conduct were subjected to adverse employer action).

[43] *Id.* (supervisor admitted protected conduct was part of motivation).

[44] *See id.* at 676 (ultimate decisionmaker was not aware of protected conduct, but would not have been presented with recommendation to take adverse action but for initiative of subordinate decisionmaker, who was aware).

[45] 42 U.S.C. §§ 2000e-1 to 2000e-17 (1982).

[46] *Id.* § 2000e-2(a) (1) & (2). See §§ **2.3** and **2.5** for a discussion of Title VII.

[47] 42 U.S.C. § 2000e-5(g) (1982).

[48] *Id.* § 2000e-3.

[49] *See* Jack. v. Texaco Research Center, 743 F.2d 1129, 1131 (5th Cir. 1984) (remanding for determination whether reason for dismissal was complaint to EEOC); Mitchell v. Baldridge, 759 F.2d 80, 86 (D.C. Cir. 1985) (causation part of prima facie retaliation case may be established by showing that the employer had knowledge of employee's protected activity and that adverse personnel action took place shortly after that activity); Ross v. Communications Satellite Corp., 759

The Supreme Court has offered relatively detailed guidance as to standards of proof under the statute, and these standards have been applied by lower courts in factual circumstances involving several reasons for an adverse employer action, some legitimate and some discriminatory.

In *McDonnell Douglas v. Green*,[50] the Court recognized that a Title VII plaintiff rarely will be able to offer direct evidence of a discriminatory employer motive. Accordingly, it held that a plaintiff can make out a prima facie case in a refusal to hire situation by showing that:

1. The prospective employee is a member of a protected class
2. The job applicant applied for and was qualified for a vacant position
3. The applicant was rejected despite her qualifications
4. The defendant employer continued to seek applicants with the defendant's qualifications.[51]

The *McDonnell Douglas* prima facie concept is applied, with necessary modifications, to cases involving dismissal.[52]

In 1981, the Supreme Court explained the *McDonnell Douglas* concepts in *Texas Department of Community Affairs v. Burdine*.[53] *Burdine* reached the Supreme Court after the United States Court of Appeals for the Fifth Circuit reversed a judgment for the defendant in a dismissal case, applying its rule that the defendant in a Title VII case bears the burden of proving by a preponderance of the evidence the existence of legitimate, nondiscriminatory reasons for the challenged employment action.[54] The Supreme Court disagreed.

The ultimate burden of persuading the trier of fact that the defendant intentionally discriminated against the plaintiff, it held, remains at all times with the plaintiff.[55] Therefore, the *McDonnell Douglas*[56] three-element order of proof means that first, the plaintiff must produce evidence according to the *McDonnell Douglas* formula.[57] This, if sufficient to permit a factfinder to infer discrimination, raises a rebuttable presumption of discrimination.[58] The formula is flexible, and permits

---

F.2d 355, 366 (4th Cir. 1985) (adopting *but for* test in retaliation case; expressly rejecting *any part at all* test).

[50] 411 U.S. 792 (1973).

[51] *Id.* at 802.

[52] Texas Dep't of Community Affairs v. Burdine, 450 U.S. 248, 254 n.7 (1981).

[53] 450 U.S. 248 (1981).

[54] *Id.* at 252.

[55] *Id.* at 253.

[56] McDonnell Douglas v. Green, 411 U.S. 792 (1973).

[57] Texas Dep't of Community Affairs v. Burdine, 450 U.S. at 252–53. *See also* Walters v. City of Atlanta, 803 F.2d 1135, 1142 (11th Cir. 1986) (can prove discrimination by direct evidence).

[58] *Id.* at 254.

§ 7.6 TITLE VII VIOLATIONS

an inference of discriminatory motive from any reasonably probative circumstantial evidence.[59]

The burden then shifts to the defendant to produce evidence that the plaintiff was rejected, or someone else was preferred, for a legitimate nondiscriminatory reason.[60] "It is sufficient to rebut the stage one presumption if the defendant raises a genuine issue of fact legally sufficient to permit judgment for the defendant as to whether it discriminated against the plaintiff."[61]

Third, the plaintiff must have the opportunity to demonstrate that the legitimate reasons proffered by the employer in stage two were "not the true reason for the employment decision."[62] The plaintiff may do this directly by persuading the fact-finder that a discriminatory reason more likely motivated the employer, or indirectly, by showing that the employer's proffered explanation is unworthy of credence.[63] The employee need not introduce new evidence to show pretext, but may do it through cross examination or argument.[64]

Though the Court's language is broad enough to encompass a case in which there were two or more real reasons for a dismissal, the *Burdine* analysis focuses

---

[59] *See* Wilmington v. J.I. Case Co., 793 F.2d 909, 920 (8th Cir. 1986) (statistical expert testimony showing disparity between black representation in workforce and incidence of terminations of black employees); Donnellon v. Fruehauf Corp., 794 F.2d 598, 601 (11th Cir. 1986) (short period of time between protected conduct and dismissal permitted inference that retaliation was motive).

[60] 450 U.S. at 252–53. *Legitimate* may mean no more than nondiscriminatory. *Compare* Nix v. WLCY Radio, 738 F.2d 1181, 1187 (11th Cir. 1984) ("The employer may fire an employee for a good reason, a bad reason, a reason based on erroneous facts or for no reason at all, as long as its action is not for a discriminatory reason.") *with* Jennings v. Tinley Park Community Consol. School Dist. 146, 796 F.2d 962, 967 (7th Cir. 1986) (defendant must offer legitimate reason, not merely any nondiscriminatory reason; remanding for consideration whether disloyalty was legitimate reason when employee prepared report critical of employer policies).

[61] 450 U.S. at 252–53. Though the burden of persuasion never shifts to the employer, the employer must proffer reasonably clear and specific reasons for the adverse employment action to overcome the prima facie case. Conner v. Fort Gordon Bus Co., 761 F.2d 1495, 1499 (11th Cir. 1985) (finding employer's reasons sufficiently clear and specific to support district court's judgment for employer; split panel).

[62] Texas Dep't of Community Affairs v. Burdine, 450 U.S. at 256. This usually is called *pretext*.

[63] *Id. See also* Rap, Inc. v. District of Columbia Comm'n on Human Rights, 485 A.2d 173, 178 (D.C. 1984) (use of weapon by wife in fight with husband justifies employer in firing her and only reprimanding him); Miles v. M.N.C. Corp., 750 F.2d 867, 876 (11th Cir. 1985) (reversing judgment for employer; employer must show by preponderance of evidence a lack of racial motivation for failure to recall from layoff, when plaintiff showed illegal motivation from racial slur by supervisor, workforce statistics, and subjective personnel decisions).

[64] *See* Donnellon v. Fruehauf Corp., 794 F.2d 598, 601 (11th Cir. 1986) (totality of evidence, including plaintiff's cross-examination of defendant's witnesses sufficient to permit finding of pretext; rejecting employer's argument that new evidence by plaintiff was required); Jadison v. Missouri Pac. R.R., 803 F.2d 401, 406 (8th Cir. 1986) (insufficient evidence to show pretext); Waddell v. Small Tube Prods., Inc., 799 F.2d 69, 74 (3d Cir. 1986) (proof of pretext shown in religious discrimination retaliation case); Davis v. State Univ., 802 F.2d 638, 642–43 (2d Cir. 1986) (pretext not shown in retaliation case).

on single-reason dismissals.[65] Earlier, in *McDonald v. Santa Fe Trails Transportation Co.*,[66] the court articulated a "but for" test when multiple reasons were present.[67] Nevertheless, there remains some confusion among the circuits about the standard to be utilized in mixed motive Title VII cases. Present standards range from the Fifth Circuit's "significant factor" test[68] to the First Circuit's adoption of the "but for" standard of *Mt. Healthy City School District v. Doyle*.[69] The once fashionable "any part at all" test is now a minority test.[70]

The matter is free from neither doubt nor criticism, but it seems likely that Title VII requires proof that the prohibited motive was the "but for" cause of the adverse employer action, like public employee liberty infringement[71] and National Labor Relations Act § 8(a) causation standards:[72] the discharged employee must show

---

[65] "The [*Burdine*] Court discussed only the situation in which the issue is whether either illegal or legal motives, but not both, were the true motives behind the decision. It thus addressed the pretext case." NLRB v. Transportation Management Corp., 462 U.S. 393, 400 n.5 (1983). *See* Brodin, *The Standard of Causation in the Mixed-Motive Title VII Action: A Social Policy Perspective*, 82 Colum. L. Rev. 292, 300–01 n.40 (1982).

[66] 427 U.S. 273 (1976). Two white employees claimed they were subjected to unequal treatment when they were discharged for stealing from a company shipment while a black employee also involved in the theft was retained.

[67] *Id.* at 282 n.10. *See also* Brodin, *The Standard of Causation in the Mixed-Motive Title VII Action: A Social Policy Perspective*, 82 Colum. L. Rev. 292, 302 (1982).

[68] Whiting v. Jackson State Univ., 616 F.2d 116, 121 (5th Cir. 1980). A white instructor brought a reverse discrimination action challenging his dismissal at a predominantly black university: "Title VII is not violated simply because an impermissible factor plays some part in the employer's decision. The forbidden taint need not be the sole basis for the action to warrant relief, but it must be a significant factor."

[69] Mack v. Cape Elizabeth School Bd., 553 F.2d 720 (1st Cir. 1977). A teacher alleged that the Board's refusal to renew her teaching contract after maternity leave constituted sex discrimination in violation of Title VII. The court held that the ultimate burden is on the plaintiff to show "not merely that impermissible factors entered into the decision not to renew her contract, but that they were determinative; viz., that but for them she would have been re-employed." *Id.* at 722. *See* Grubb v. W.A. Foote Memorial Hosp., 741 F.2d 1486, 1494 (6th Cir. 1984) (reversing district court finding of Title VII violation because court effectively required proof by defendant that decision to eliminate plaintiff's job would have been reached regardless of any racism by supervisor); Brodin, *The Standard of Causation in the Mixed-Motive Title VII Action: A Social Policy Perspective*, 82 Colum. L. Rev. 292, nn.75-79 (1982).

[70] United States v. Hayes Int'l Corp., 6 Fair Empl. Prac. Cas. (BNA) 1328, 1330 (N.D. Ala. 1973), *aff'd*, 507 F.2d 1279 (5th Cir. 1975) ("any part at all" test). *See* Brodin, *The Standard of Causation in the Mixed-Motive Title VII Action: A Social Policy Perspective*, 82 Colum. L. Rev. 292, nn.75-79 (1982); Ross v. Communications Satellite Corp., 759 F.2d 355, 366 (4th Cir. 1985), (adopting *but for* test in retaliation case; expressly rejecting *any part at all* test). *But see* Bibbs v. Block, 778 F.2d 1318, 1319, 1323–25 (8th Cir. 1985) (en banc) (reversing district court for requiring proof that race was a determining factor; *any part at all* sufficient to prove violation; *but for* necessary for remedy of retroactive promotion and back pay).

[71] *See* Mack v. Cape Elizabeth School Bd., 553 F.2d 702 (1st Cir. 1977). See also § **7.5**.

[72] Legislative history suggests similar causation analysis. Section 706(g) of Title VII was patterned after the remedial provisions of the National Labor Relations Act, as amended by the

§ 7.7 NLRA VIOLATIONS

that a prohibited motive was present, and the employer can escape liability if it can show the discharge would have occurred anyway, for legitimate reasons. The burdens of proof are, however, somewhat different.[73]

§ 7.7 —Violations of the National Labor Relations Act

Proof of prohibited motive is an element of unfair labor practices under the National Labor Relations Act (NLRA) and under state public employee collective bargaining statutes. Sections 8(a)(1), 8(a)(3) and 8(a)(4) of the NLRA are typical of the statutory protections at issue in dismissal cases.[74] Section 8(a)(1) prohibits adverse employer action against an employee because the employee exercises rights to engage in concerted action.[75] Section 8(a)(3) prohibits employer discrimination against an employee to encourage or discourage membership in a labor organization. Section 8(a)(4) prohibits discrimination against an employee because he or she has filed charges or given testimony under the NLRA. Section 10(e) of the NLRA, however, expressly says that no remedies under the Act shall exist for dismissals effected for cause.[76] The three paragraphs of § 8(a) define three different unfair labor practices. An element of each is a slightly different prohibited motive. The prohibited motive element in all three can be inferred from evidence of conduct making it more likely than not the prohibited motive existed.[77]

The mixed motive problem has received much attention in unfair labor practice cases. One line of state public employee cases holds that a discharge is illegal if union activity played *any* part in the employer's decision to fire, even if the employer also had legitimate reasons to terminate the employee.[78] Several early NLRA cases

---

Labor-Management Relations Act of 1947, 29 U.S.C. §§ 151-169 (1982). *See* Albemarle Paper Co. v. Moody, 422 U.S. 405, 419 n.11 (1975) (citing cases). In addition, the legislative history of § 8(a)(3) of the NLRA evidences a general concern similar to that of the Congress that enacted Title VII, that the employer's prerogatives be preserved and that interferences with personnel decisions be limited to that necessary to correct discriminatory practices. See § **7.7**.

[73] As § **7.7** explains in more detail, the Title VII approach places a lighter burden on the plaintiff to make out a prima facie case, but never shifts the burden to the defendant.

[74] 29 U.S.C. §§ 158(a)(1), 158(a)(3), 158(a)(4) (1982).

[75] Employee rights are defined in § 7 of the NLRA, 29 U.S.C. § 157 (1982).

[76] *Id.* § 160(e).

[77] Some Board law and commentary suggests that § 8(a)(1) violations, not involving violations of other paragraphs of § 8(a), may be found regardless of the employer's motive, whenever the "employer engaged in conduct which, it may reasonably be said, tends to interfere with the free exercise of employee rights under the Act." American Freightways Co., 124 N.L.R.B. 146 (1959). Oberer, *The Scienter Factor in Sections 8(a)(1) and (3) of the Labor Act: Of Balancing Hostile Motive, Dogs and Tails,* 52 Cornell L.Q. 491 (1967), 1 Developing Lab. L. 75-78 (2d ed. 1983).

[78] *See, e.g.,* Muskego-Norway Consol. Schools v. Wisconsin Employee Relations Bd., 35 Wis. 2d 540, 562, 151 N.W.2d 617, 628 (1967). The Supreme Court determined that the school board's

were in accord,[79] and generally the NLRB used what is called an "in part" test for a a number of years.[80] In 1980, however, in *Wright Line & Bernard R. Lamoureux*,[81] the NLRB adopted the standard of *Mt. Healthy City School District v. Doyle*[82] for cases arising under §§ 8(a)(1) and (3) of the NLRA.

The *Wright Line* Board observed that the *Mt. Healthy* causation standard eliminates the need to distinguish between *pretext* and *dual motive* cases.[83] In both types of cases the NLRB held that the employer's asserted justification for the dismissal should be viewed as an affirmative defense.[84] In a pretext case the employer's asserted justification of a legitimate business reason is found to be wholly without merit—pretextual, in other words.[85] If the affirmative defense has at least some merit, the case becomes a dual motive case, and the issue becomes one of the standard of proof necessary for the employer's affirmative defense to be sustained.[86] The Board viewed dual motive cases as more difficult because it is those cases in which the legitimate interests of the parties most directly conflict.[87] Nevertheless, the Board saw no need to use different standards of proof for the two different types of cases.[88]

---

failure to renew a teacher's teaching contract was motivated by the teacher's activities as chairman of the welfare committee of an employee organization and not by any shortcomings the teacher may have had as a teacher nor by his difference with certain policies of the school board and supervisory personnel. Thus the *any reason* standard expressed by the court may be dictum.

[79] *See* NLRB v. Great E. Color Lithographic Corp., 309 F.2d 352, 355 (2d Cir. 1962). Substantial evidence supported the finding that the employees were discharged for attending a union organizing meeting. Despite the fact that the employer had other legitimate reasons for discharging the employees, the court was satisfied that the employer violated §§ 2(11), 8(a)(1), 8(a)(3) of the NLRA.

[80] Wright Line & Bernard R. Lamoureux, 251 N.L.R.B. 1083, 1084 (1980).

[81] *Id.*

[82] 429 U.S. 274 (1977).

[83] Wright Line & Bernard R. Lamoureux, 251 N.L.R.B. at 1083 n.4.

[84] *Id.* at 1084 n.5.

[85] *Id.*

[86] *Id.*

[87] *Id.*

[88] *Id.* at 1083. Subsequently the Supreme Court approved the NLRB's use of *Mt. Healthy*, while suggesting that pretext and dual motive cases are different. In mixed motive cases, it is appropriate to shift the burden to the employer to prove that the illegal motive did not actuate the adverse employment action; in pretext cases, it is not appropriate to shift the burden to the employer. NLRB v. Transportation Management Corp., 462 U.S. 393, 400 n.5 (1983) (distinguishing Texas Dep't of Community Affairs v. Burdine, 450 U.S. 248 (1981)).

§ 7.7 NLRA VIOLATIONS

The Board reviewed the conflict that had developed in some judicial circuits between the "in part" test[89] and a "dominant motive" test.[90] The Board reasoned that the confusion flowing from this conflict could be alleviated by adopting the *Mt. Healthy* test for dismissals allegedly violating §§ 8(a)(1) and (3).[91] Under its view of the *Mt. Healthy* standard, the general counsel of the Board, acting on behalf of the discharged employee, has the initial burden to make out a prima facie case.[92] The general counsel can do this by showing that the employer relied to some extent on the employee's protected activity in deciding to dismiss the employee.[93] The burden then shifts to the employer to "demonstrate that the decision would have been the same in the absence of protected activity."[94] As the Board noted, the decision as to who bears the burden of proof frequently is outcome determinative.[95] The Board considered the *Mt. Healthy* test consistent with the approach, not yet formally embraced by the Supreme Court, followed by the courts of appeals in discrimination cases.[96] In *National Labor Relations Board v. Transportation Management Corp.*,[97] the Supreme Court approved the *Wright Line* order of proof.

There is a difference between the burdens of proof in *Wright Line* and in *McDonnell Douglas v. Green*.[98] Under *Wright Line,* the general counsel (plaintiff) must prove unlawful motive. Then the burden of proof shifts to the employer to establish its affirmative defense. This puts a greater initial burden on the general counsel than under the *McDonnell Douglas v. Green* standard, in which the plaintiff has a light burden to establish a prima facie case. But *Wright Line* places a heavier burden on the respondent (defendant) once the general counsel has made

---

[89] Wright Line & Bernard R. Lamoureux, 251 N.L.R.B. at 1084: "The in part test provides that if a discharge is motivated, 'in part' by the protected activities of the employee the discharge violates the act even if a legitimate business reason was also relied on." *See also* Youngstown Osteopathic Hosp., 224 N.L.R.B. 574, 575 (1976), *enforcement denied,* 574 F.2d 891 (6th Cir. 1978).

[90] Wright Line & Bernard R. Lamoureux, 251 N.L.R.B. at 1085. The dominant motive test provides that "when both a 'good' and 'bad' reason for discharge exist the burden is upon the General Counsel to establish that, in the absence of protected activities, the discharge would not have taken place."

[91] *Id.*

[92] *Id.*

[93] *Id.*

[94] *Id.* n.14. *See, e.g.,* Vokas Provision Co. v. NLRB, 796 F.2d 864 (6th Cir. 1986) (declining to enforce NLRB order; employer did not terminate employees in retaliation for attending representation hearing, but rather for causing an unjustified disruption of work when employees left work without subpeona).

[95] Wright Line & Bernard R. Lamoureux, 251 N.L.R.B. at 1086.

[96] *Id.*.

[97] 462 U.S. 393 (1983).

[98] 411 U.S. 792 (1973). McDonnell Douglas v. Green is the leading Supreme Court statement on the burden of proof under Title VII of the Civil Rights Act of 1964. This is discussed in **§ 7.6**.

his case than does *McDonnell Douglas*. Under the second stage of the *McDonnell Douglas* formula, the defendant has a light burden to articulate some nondiscriminatory reason. The ultimate burden of persuasion remains with the plaintiff under *McDonnell Douglas*; the defendant is not required to prove, as an affirmative defense, that a legitimate motive was the reason for the dismissal.[99]

The effect of *Wright Line* is to put a heavier burden on the plaintiff at the outset and shift the burden to the defendant to prove absence of pretext. If *Wright Line* were used in the Title VII arena, there probably would be a greater number of dismissals at the close of the plaintiff's case.

§ 7.8 — Violations of the Age Discrimination in Employment Act

Section 4 of the Age Discrimination in Employment Act (ADEA)[1] prohibits adverse employment actions, including dismissals, because of age. Section 4 of the ADEA states that it is not unlawful to dismiss an individual "for good cause."[2]

The courts have developed a determining factor standard of proof, and most circuits borrow Title VII concepts to define the necessary prima facie showing.[3] The Sixth Circuit, in the seminal case of *Laugesen v. Anaconda Co.*,[4] however, refused to use Title VII concepts,[5] suggesting that the plaintiff's initial burden should be heavier because of the inevitable biological necessity for older workers to be replaced with younger workers.[6] The Fifth Circuit, in *McCorstin v. United States Steel Corp.*,[7] also rejected strict adherence to the *McDonnell Douglas v. Green*

---

[99] Cline v. Roadway Express, Inc., 689 F.2d 481, 485-86 (4th Cir. 1982) (employer's proffered motive in age discrimination case is neither an affirmative defense nor an effort to rebut a presumption of discrimination).

[1] *See* 29 U.S.C. § 623(a) (1982). See also § **2.6**.

[2] *See* 29 U.S.C. § 623(f)(3).

[3] *See* 58 A.L.R. Fed. 99 (1982); see also § **2.7**; Duffy v. Wheeling Pittsburgh Steel Corp., 738 F.2d 1393, 1396 (3d Cir. 1984), *cert. denied,* 469 U.S. 1087 (1984) (Title VII and ADEA mixed motive proof concepts the same); Palmer v. United States, 794 F.2d 534 (9th Cir. 1986) ("The criteria applied to a Title VII discrimination claim also apply to claims arising under the ADEA." (citations omitted)).

[4] 510 F.2d 307 (6th Cir. 1975).

[5] *Id.* at 312. *Accord,* Cline v. Roadway Express, Inc., 689 F.2d 481, 486 (4th Cir. 1982) (refusal to follow constricted "three-state minuet" of McDonnell Douglas v. Green in ADEA case).

[6] Laugesen v. Anaconda Co., 510 F.2d at 312-13 n.14. *See also* LaGrant v. Gulf & W. Mfg. Co., 748 F.2d 1087, 1090 (6th Cir. 1984) (Sixth Circuit has repeatedly rejected strict adherence to the *McDonnel Douglas* criteria for ADEA claims; such adherence could bar worthy suits as well as support unworthy ones); Blackwell v. Sun Elec. Corp., 696 F.2d 1176, 1179 (6th Cir. 1983) (Laugesen v. Anaconda Co. states that employment decisions involving age may reflect the result of the universal progression of aging rather than represent discrimination).

[7] 621 F.2d 749, 754 (1980).

§ 7.8 AGE DISCRIMINATION VIOLATIONS

criteria,[8] but suggested a lighter burden on the plaintiff[9] because of the possibility that age discrimination can be more subtle than race, sex, or religious discrimination.[10]

Of course the evidence from which the jury infers that age was a determining factor must be logically probative of that conclusion.[11]

In mixed motive cases, the determining factor standard is close to the *Mt. Healthy* "but for" test. The common sense meaning of the phrase *determining factor* excludes an interpretation that it means any factor at all. Language in some appellate opinions precludes any interpretation that would require a showing that age was the sole reason.[12] The but for interpretation is the most logical interpretation.[13]

---

[8] *Id.* at 754.

[9] "In those (ADEA) cases, however, when it [*McDonnell Douglas* criteria] was not intended to apply and, factually, cannot apply, the plaintiff must enjoy more leeway in a presentation of a prima facie case." *Id.*

[10] The Fifth Circuit cited instances in which an employer replaces the older employee not with a much younger employee but with an employee only five years younger. *Id. See also* Mistretta v. Sandia Corp., 649 F.2d 1383, 1386 (10th Cir. 1981) (termination of older employees based on poor performance ratings was discriminatory because the performance ratings, although objective in nature were inherently discriminatory; reasoning suggests adherence to the lighter burden of proof of McCorstin v. United States Steel Corp.). *See generally* B. Schlei & P. Grossman, Employment Discrimination 498 (1983). *Compare* Stacey v. Allied Stores Corp., 768 F.2d 402, 409 (D.C. Cir. 1985) (reversing judgment n.o.v. for employer; sufficient evidence for jury to find pretext) *with* Graham v. F.B. Leopold Co., 602 F. Supp. 1423, 1425 (W.D. Pa. 1985) (granting summary judgment for employer; employee failed to raise triable issue of fact after employer articulated legitimate reason for dismissal).

[11] *Compare* Guthrie v. J.C. Penny Co., 803 F.2d 202, 208 (5th Cir. 1986) (sufficient evidence of pretext) *and* McNeil v. Economics Laboratory, Inc., 800 F.2d 111, 115 (7th Cir. 1986) (sufficient evidence of pretext) *and* Powell v. Rockwell Int'l Corp., 788 F.2d 279, 283 (5th Cir. 1986) (jury validly could find that removal of company document in violation of company rules was pretext for dismissal for filing age discrimination complaint, based on employer threats, more lenient treatment of supervisor for violating different company rules) *with* Merkel v. Scovill, Inc., 787 F.2d 174 (6th Cir. 1986) (reversing denial of motion for judgment n.o.v. in employer's favor) *and* Ridenour v. Lawson Co., 791 F.2d 52, 57 (6th Cir. 1986) (reversing jury verdict for plaintiff-employee; employee terminated during a corporate reorganization could not show his age was a determining factor in the defendant corporation's decision to terminate) *and* Brieck v. Harbison-Walker Refractories, 624 F. Supp. 363, 365–66 (W.D. Pa. 1985) (evidence that discharged employee with slightly more seniority than younger employee reinstated after layoff was overcome by evidence older employee had slightly worse work record; no prima facie case; summary judgment for employer).

[12] *See* Dale v. Chicago Tribune Co., 797 F.2d 458, 464 (7th Cir. 1986) (ADEA plaintiff need not prove that age was the only factor motivating his discharge, but must prove that age was *determining factor*); Smith v. Consolidated Mut. Water Co., 787 F.2d 1441, 1442 (10th Cir. 1986) (determining factor); Cuddy v. Carmen, 694 F.2d 853, 857 n.22 (D.C. Cir. 1982) (determining factor does not mean sole reason).

[13] *See* Maxfield v. Sinclair Int'l, 766 F.2d 788, 791 (3d Cir. 1985) (explaining determining factor as "but for" cause in jury instruction), *cert. denied,* ___ U.S. ___, 106 S. Ct. 796 (1986); Cline v. Roadway Express, Inc., 689 F.2d 481, 485 (4th Cir. 1982) (*determining factor* means "but for").

Most circuits also permit proof of an ADEA violation under the disparate impact theory, under which motive is irrelevant.[14]

§ 7.9 — Violations of Other Statutes

Proof standards similar to those discussed in §§ 7.4 through 7.8 are used to assess the reasons for dismissal under other statutes considered in **Chapter 2**. For example, in *Love v. RE/MAX of America, Inc.*,[15] the court of appeals affirmed a finding of retaliatory dismissal under the Equal Pay Act,[16] on evidence that the plaintiff was fired within two hours after the employer received her memorandum containing a pay increase request and a copy of the Equal Pay Act. "The causal connection may be demonstrated by evidence of circumstances that justify an inference of retaliatory motive, such as protected conduct closely followed by adverse action."[17]

Title VII proof standards are applied to retaliation claims under § 1981, in which the issue is whether the discrimination occurred because of the employee's assertion of statutory rights, not because of racial characteristics.[18]

§ 7.10 Public Policy Tort: Basic Concepts of Proof

In most public policy tort cases, the plaintiff's major problem will be surviving a motion for dismissal on the pleadings, a motion for summary judgment, or a motion for a directed verdict. Accordingly, major cases involving the question

---

[14] *See* Holt v. Gamewell Corp., 797 F.2d 36, 38 (1st Cir. 1986) (plaintiff in disparate impact age case must prove that a facially neutral practice has a significant discriminatory impact on members of the protected class); Palmer v. United States, 794 F.2d 534, 538-39 (9th Cir. 1986) (discriminatory motive need not be shown under disparate impact theory, but plaintiff must prove disparate impact rather than merely raising inference); Krodel v. Young, 748 F.2d 701, 709 (D.C. Cir. 1984) (statistical evidence is crucial in disparate impact cases, in which plaintiff need not prove discriminatory intent), *cert. denied,* ___ U.S. ___, 106 S. Ct. 62 (1985); Leftwich v. Harris-Stowe State College, 702 F.2d 686, 690 (8th Cir. 1983) ("to establish a prima facie case of age discrimination . . . [a] Plaintiff need only demonstrate that a facially neutral employment practice actually operates to exclude from a job a disproportionate number of persons protected by the ADEA."); Geller v. Markham, 635 F.2d 1027 (2d Cir. 1980), *cert. denied,* 451 U.S. 945 (1981).

[15] 738 F.2d 383, 386 (10th Cir. 1984).

[16] 29 U.S.C. § 215(a)(3) (1982).

[17] *Id.*

[18] *See* Mitchell v. Keith, 752 F.2d 385, 391 (9th Cir. 1985) (determining factor or but for jury instruction appropriate for § 1981 race discrimination case); Choudhury v. Polytechnic Inst. of N.Y., 735 F.2d 38, 44-45 (2d Cir. 1984).

§ 7.10   PUBLIC POLICY TORT   385

of whether a cause of action for public policy tort is presented by the pleadings, supplemented by discovery, are useful, even though they do not involve trial proof.[19]

Chapter 5 grouped public policy tort cases into three categories: those involving labor statutes,[20] those involving *external* public policy torts,[21] and those involving *internal* public policy torts.[22] The principal difference among these categories is that public policy interests in the employee's favor are greatest and the employer's justification for dismissal is least when the dismissal contravenes a policy in a labor statute.[23] The public policy interests in the employee's favor are likely to be weakest and the employer's justification likely to be greatest when an internal public policy tort is alleged.[24] The external public policy tort is likely to involve an intermediate level of public policy interests in the employee's favor and justification for the employer.[25]

Chapter 5 presents a three-element formula that explains the results in virtually all of the decided cases in all three categories.[26] This formula provides the appropriate framework within which to consider proof of a public policy tort.[27] Under the first element, the plaintiff proves the existence of a clear public policy.[28] Under the second element, the plaintiff proves that discouraging the conduct in which she engaged would jeopardize the public policy.[29] Under the third element, the plaintiff proves lack of justification for the dismissal.[30] These three factors resemble

---

[19] *See, e.g.*, Nees v. Hocks, 272 Or. 210, 536 P.2d 512 (1975).

[20] See § **5.9**.

[21] See §§ **5.10–5.13**.

[22] See § **5.14–5.18**. Internal public policy torts can be further subdivided into cases involving employee refusal of orders (§ **5.18**); employee complaints to employers (§ **5.17**); and employee complaints to outside agencies (§ **5.16**).

[23] The legislature, by prohibiting certain employer conduct in these statutes, such as dismissing employees for union activity, or forcing employees to take lie detector tests, already has struck the public policy balance in favor of the employee. But the jeopardy element frequently is weak in labor statute cases because of the availability of statutory administrative remedies. See § **5.9**.

[24] The employer's interest in unfettered control over employees is greater when a dispute between employee and employer involves matters of product design or business recordkeeping.

[25] Most of these cases involve dismissals for off-the-job conduct. In these cases, the employer's legitimate concern is less.

[26] See § **5.1**. Pleading issues associated with these three factors are treated in §§ **5.31** and **5.32**.

[27] This chapter focuses on proof problems associated with the public policy tort. Proof of a prima facie tort and of the traditional torts such as intentional interference with contractual relations, defamation, invasion of privacy, and misrepresentation are addressed in the cases cited in **ch.5** or in Restatement (Second) of Torts, and in a number of treatises on tort law. *See, e.g.*, W. Prosser, Handbook on Torts (1974).

[28] This is the *clarity* element.

[29] This is the *jeopardy* element. *See* Wiskotoni v. Michigan Nat'l Bank W., 716 F.2d 378, 383 (6th Cir. 1983) (articulating second element within analytical framework consistent with that suggested in the text).

[30] This is the *absence of justification* element.

the elements of a constitutional liberty infringement case.[31] The clarity and jeopardy elements primarily involve questions of law and policy; most factual disputes implicate the absence of justification element.

The ultimate burden of persuasion remains with the plaintiff on all three elements.[32] The burden of production also should rest with the plaintiff with respect to the first two elements. The burden of production respecting justification is more controversial and is addressed in § 7.14.

The plaintiff, as a part of her initial burden, must satisfy the judge about public policy and jeopardy elements, and must also offer sufficient evidence from which lack of justification can be inferred by the jury as constrained by instructions from the judge. If the plaintiff meets this burden, she can survive a motion for directed verdict. To summarize the public policy tort proof analysis:

1. The first element, clarity of public policy, presents a question of law
2. The second element, jeopardy to public policy, also presents a question of law
3. The third element, absence of justification, presents factual questions relating to employer motive and business needs.

§ 7.11 —Proving Public Policy

In a public policy tort case, the threshold question is what public policy might be jeopardized[33] if the plaintiff's dismissal were allowed to go uncompensated. This is the *clarity* element. The public policy is necessary to overcome the employer's interest in running its business as it sees fit.[34] Thus, as the following

---

[31] As explained in § 7.5, in a liberty infringement case, the plaintiff has the burden of showing that the conduct was constitutionally protected and that this conduct was a motivating factor in the employer's decision to terminate. If the plaintiff meets that burden, the employer can escape liability if it shows, by a preponderance of the evidence, that it would have reached the same decision even in the absence of the protected conduct.

[32] *See* Thompson v. St. Regis Paper Co., 102 Wash. 2d 219, 232, 685 P.2d 1081, 1089 (1984) (employee must demonstrate that discharge was motivated by policy-offensive reasons, then employer may prove discharge was for other reasons); Moore v. McDermott, Inc., 481 So. 2d 602 (La. 1986) (timing of dismissal and evidence of disparate treatment supported inference that termination was for filing workers' compensation claim); Cleary v. American Airlines, 111 Cal. App. 3d 443, 168 Cal. Rptr. 722 (1980) (plaintiff in wrongful dismissal action sounding in both contract and tort "has the burden of proving that he was terminated unjustly"; employer "will have its opportunity to demonstrate that it did in fact exercise good faith and fair dealing.") *Id.* at 456, 168 Cal. Rptr. at 729; Restatement (Second) of Torts § 870 comment j (1979). *See* C. McCormick, Handbook on the Law of Evidence § 337 (E. Cleary 2d ed. 1972).

[33] The *degree* of jeopardy is the subject of the second element, discussed in § 7.12.

[34] *See* Turner v. Letterkenny Fed. Credit Union, 351 Pa. Super. 51, 505 A.2d 259 (1985) (reversing judgment on jury verdict for employee; dismissal for poor relations with subordinates did not involve public policy).

§ 7.11 PUBLIC POLICY

cases make clear, a threshold requirement for a tort plaintiff is establishing the public policy on which to base the tort. Then the judge, rather than the jury, should decide what public policy is.[35] It is elementary that the judge may take judicial notice of law.[36] "The heavy footed common law system of proof by witnesses and authenticated documents is too slow and cumbrous for the judge's task of finding what the applicable law is."[37]

The plaintiff must identify the public policy with particularity. In *Adler v. American Standard Corp.*,[38] the Maryland Court of Appeals rejected Adler's claim because he did not identify with sufficient specificity the public policy allegedly violated by his discharge.[39] The federal district court[40] subsequently found that Adler, in an amended complaint, had pleaded with the requisite specificity the public policy connection with his discharge.[41] He alleged specific misconduct by his employer, identified eight federal and three state statutes violated by the misconduct, and alleged that his discharge specifically occurred to prevent the plaintiff from exposing the misconduct.[42]

The clarity element can be satisfied in three basic ways, with diminishing effectiveness:

1. By identifying a specific provision of a statute, constitution or administrative regulation[43]
2. By synthesizing from several different statutes or constitutional provisions[44]
3. By identifying a right or mode of conduct covered by a traditional common law cause of action.[45]

---

[35] This existence of public policy question is analogous to the question in negligence cases of whether a duty exists, which also is decided by the court. *See* Cordle v. General Hugh Mercer Corp., 325 S.E.2d 111 (W. Va. 1984) (whether dismissal for refusal to take polygraph test is question for judge rather than jury). *But see* Cloutier v. Great Atl. & Pac. Tea Co., 121 N.H. 915, 924, 436 A.2d 1140, 1145 (1981) (jury decides the public policy question). The *Cloutier* dissent pointed out that no public policy opposing the dismissal was proven, and that, in any event, the legal authority states that the public policy question is for the court, not the jury. *Id.* at 926, 927, 436 A.2d at 1147. The dissent is right about the precedent.

[36] Wandry v. Bull's Eye Credit Union, 129 Wis. 2d 37, 42, 384 N.W.2d 325, 327 (1986) (whether public policy is fundamental and well defined is an issue of law for the court).

[37] C. McCormick, Handbook on the Law of Evidence § 335 at 776 (F. Cleary 2nd ed. 1972).

[38] 291 Md. 31, 432 A.2d 464 (1981).

[39] *Id.* at 44, 432 A.2d at 471. The plaintiff alleged that his employer was motivated to discharge him solely by its desire to conceal improprieties and illegal activities. *Id.* at 34, 432 A.2d at 466.

[40] The case originally was brought in federal court. The question of whether a wrongful discharge action exists under Maryland law was certified to the Maryland Court of Appeals.

[41] 538 F. Supp. 572 (D. Md. 1982).

[42] *Id.* at 577-78. The district court's ruling addressed pleading rather than proof issues. Necessarily, however, the court began with a conclusion of what Adler would have to prove at trial.

[43] The policy in favor of freedom to file workers' compensation claims is an example.

[44] The policy in favor of broad representation on juries is an example.

[45] Defamation or right to privacy are examples.

Whenever a plaintiff can point to a specific statutory or constitutional provision as the source of public policy, the plaintiff's showing on the clarity element is strong.[46] When the source of public policy is statutory, constitutional, or administrative, counsel first pleads the existence of the policy with specificity, and then, in supporting memoranda or at trial, cites the appropriate part of the statute, constitution or regulation that expresses the public policy.[47] Of course, counsel should explain to the judge the reasoning process by which the public policy asserted derives from express statutory language.[48]

---

[46] *See* Kilpatrick v. Delaware County Soc'y for Prevention of Cruelty to Animals, 632 F. Supp. 542, 546 (E.D. Pa. 1986) (finding OSHA policy protecting employee complaints about workplace safety adequate basis for public policy tort claim under Pennsylvania Law); Moniodis v. Cook, 65 Md. App. 1, 10, 494 A.2d 212, 216 (1985) (termination for refusal to take polygraph examination within clear public policy of statutory prohibition); Cordle v. General Hugh Mercer Corp., 325 S.E.2d 111 (W. Va. 1984) (dismissal for refusal to take polygraph test violates public policy, based on statute); Schmidt v. Yardney Elec. Corp., 4 Conn. App. 69, 492 A.2d 512, 515 (1985) (dismissal for revealing insurance fraud to parent corporation within common law and statutory policy against fraudulent conduct).

[47] *See* Authier v. Ginsberg, 757 F.2d 796, 799 (6th Cir. 1985) (federal ERISA is source of Michigan's state public policy in wrongful dismissal case; finding state cause of action preempted); Adler v. American Standard Corp., 538 F. Supp. 572, 578 (D. Md. 1982) (federal antitrust, tax, and corrupt practices statutes could be relied upon as a source of public policy); Cloutier v. Great Atl. & Pac. Tea Co., 121 N.H. 915, 923, 436 A.2d 1140, 1145 (1981) (public policy could be borrowed from the federal OSHA statute); Cancellier v. Federated Dep't Stores, 672 F.2d 1312, 1318 (9th Cir. 1982) (state tort claims premised in part on the policy of the federal age discrimination statute, *cert. denied*, 459 U.S. 859 (1983); Thompson v. St. Regis Paper Co., 102 Wash. 2d 219, 232, 685 P.2d 1081, 1090 (1984) (public policy sufficient to permit tort recovery could be found in the federal Foreign Corrupt Practices Act); Johnson v. World Color Press, Inc., 147 Ill. App. 3d 746, 498 N.W.2d 576 (1986) (disclosing violation of federal securities laws meets clarity requirement). *But see* Rachford v. Evergreen Int'l Airlines, 596 F. Supp. 384 (N.D. Ill. 1984) (no tort pleaded under Illinois law for discharge in retaliation for aircraft safety complaints; state has no interest in enforcing federal law); Bruffett v. Warner Communications, Inc., 692 F.2d 910, 918–19 (3d Cir. 1982) (declining to permit tort recovery under state law for a dismissal that also arguably was violative of a state statute prohibiting discrimination on the basis of handicap). See §§ **2.27–2.34** for a discussion of potential federal preemption problems when a federal statute is used as the source of public policy.

[48] *Compare* Fulford v. Burndy Corp., 623 F. Supp. 78 (D.N.H. 1985) (denying motion to dismiss suit alleging termination of employment in retaliation for personal injury suit against employer; state constitution guaranteeing access to courts adequately states public policy) *and* Wandry v. Bull's Eye Credit Union, 129 Wis. 2d 37, 42, 384 N.W.2d 325, 327 (1986) (statute need not expressly protect employee from dismissal to be basis for public policy tort; dismissing bank teller for refusing to cover loss caused by bad check she cashed with supervisor's approval contravened public policy; cause of action pleaded) *and* Knight v. American Guard & Alert, Inc., 714 P.2d 788 (Alaska 1986) (reversing dismissal of complaint on public policy tort theory for security guard allegedly dismissed for reporting drinking, drug use by coworkers; little legal analysis) *with* Gould v. Campbell's Ambulance Serv., 111 Ill. 2d 54, 488 N.E.2d 993 (1986) (retaliation for complaints that fellow ambulance technician failed to meet qualifications set by city ordinance does not state public policy tort claim; municipal ordinance insufficient indication of policy of state) *and* Patton v. J.C. Penney Co., 301 Or. 117, 719 P.2d 854 (1986) (no public policy tort for employee dismissed for dating coworker; rejecting argument that constitutional rights to privacy and association and state action infringement cases represent sufficiently clear public policy) *and*

§ 7.11 PUBLIC POLICY

Courts sometimes may be reluctant to extend the public policy beyond that expressed in the plain language of a statute,[49] or to permit a public policy tort plaintiff to derive a public policy from a statutory or constitutional provision protecting persons other than employees.[50] In *Buethe v. Britt Airlines, Inc.*,[51] Circuit Judge Posner interpreted Indiana public policy tort doctrine as providing a cause of action for whistleblowers only when a statute creates a right to "blow a particular whistle"—presumably to report a particular type of violation to a particular agency. The panel for which he wrote thus affirmed a district court dismissal of a diversity action brought by an airline copilot dismissed for refusing to fly an aircraft the copilot believed to violate FAA safety standards. As **§ 5.19** explains, this is too narrow a view of the public policy concept to reflect accurately the tenor of the mainstream public policy tort cases. The nexus between the public policy and the employee's conduct properly is addressed in analyzing the jeopardy element[52] rather than the clarity element.

Though most of the public policy tort cases have looked to state law as a source of public policy, some have permitted the tort to be premised on public policies contained in federal statutes. For example, in *Adler v. American Standard Corp.*,[53] the court held that federal antitrust, tax, and corrupt practices statutes could be relied upon as a source of public policy, specifically saying that no federal preemption question was presented.[54] Similarly, in *Cloutier v. Great Atlantic and Pacific Tea Co.*,[55] the court suggested public policy could be borrowed from the federal OSHA statute.[56] In *Cancellier v. Federated Department Stores*,[57] the court

---

Hogan v. Forsyth Country Club Co., 79 N.C. App. 483, 340 S.E.2d 116, 126 (1986) (dismissal to resolve personal conflict growing out of alleged sexual harassment does not sufficiently involve public policy to permit claim; must establish policy prohibiting employee act or requiring employee act), *review denied,* 317 N.C. 334, 346 S.E.2d 140 (1986) *and* Morris v. Hartford Courant Co., 200 Conn. 676, 513 A.2d 66, 68 (1986) (false accusations of criminal conduct not related to clear statutory or judicial policy) *and* Gillespie v. St. Joseph's Univ., ____ Pa. Super. ____, 513 A.2d 471 (1986) (same) *and* Salazar v. Furr's, Inc., 629 F. Supp. 1403, 1409 (D.N.M. 1986) (public policy tort to dismiss to deprive of pension benefits, but not for being married to employee of competitor) *and* Thomas v. Zamberletti, 134 Ill. App. 3d 387, 390, 480 N.E.2d 869, 872 (1985) (public policy against dismissal for seeking emergency medical attention not shown from statutes requiring hospitals to provide emergency care and requiring motorists to provide assistance to accident victims).

[49] *See* Kern v. South Baltimore Gen. Hosp., 66 Md. App. 441, 504 A.2d 1154 (1986) (dismissal for absenteeism due to work-related injury does not contravene public policy represented by statutory provision prohibiting dismissal *solely* for filing workers' compensation claim).

[50] *See* Karren v. Far West Fed. Sav., 79 Or. App. 131, 717 P.2d 1271 (1986) (dismissal for becoming engaged to marry does not involve rights as employee; therefore does not support public policy tort).

[51] 787 F.2d 1194 (7th Cir. 1986).

[52] See § **7.12**.

[53] 538 F. Supp. 572, 578 (D. Md. 1982).

[54] *Id.* at 578.

[55] 121 N.H. 915, 436 A.2d 1140 (1981).

[56] *Id.* at 923, 436 A.2d at 1145.

[57] 672 F.2d 1312, 1318 (9th Cir.), *cert. denied,* 459 U.S. 859 (1982).

apparently permitted state tort claims to be premised in part on the policy of the federal age discrimination statute. In *Thompson v. St. Regis Paper Co.*,[58] the Supreme Court of Washington, reversing summary judgment for the employer, held that an employee could recover in tort if he could show that his dismissal was premised on his instituting an accurate accounting system in compliance with the federal Foreign Corrupt Practices Act of 1977.[59] And, in *Wheeler v. Caterpillar Tractor Co.*,[60] the Illinois Supreme Court permitted a public policy tort claim to be based on the federal nuclear safety statute.

When the statute or constitution does not expressly prohibit the employer conduct or protect the employee conduct,[61] it also is necessary to explain to the judge the reasoning process by which the public policy asserted can be inferred from the language of the statute, using legislative history as appropriate.[62] This blurs to some extent the clarity-of-public-policy element with the jeopardy element. Strictly speaking, the only question in the existence-of-public-policy element is whether the public policy exists, regardless of whether it has anything to do with employer-employee relations. The connection between employee dismissals and the public policy properly should be reserved for the analysis of the jeopardy element. In *Wiskotoni v. Michigan National Bank West*,[63] the court found a public policy in favor of appearance before a grand jury. Its analysis is illustrative. The point is not whether grand jury appearances have anything to do with firing employees; the point is that there *is* a public policy favoring grand jury appearances. And in *Lucas v. Brown & Root, Inc.*,[64] the court of appeals, reversing the district court, found a public policy tort pleaded under Arkansas law when the plaintiff claimed she was fired for refusing to sleep with her foreman. The court premised the public policy on state statutes prohibiting prostitution.[65] Similarly, in *Bowman*

---

[58] 102 Wash. 2d 219, 685 P.2d 1081, 1090 (1984).

[59] 15 U.S.C. §§ 78m, 78dd-1, 78dd-2, 78ff (1982).

[60] 108 Ill. 2d 502, 485 N.E.2d 372 (1985), *cert. denied*, ___ U.S. ___, 106 S. Ct. 1641 (1986).

[61] *See* Cook v. Alexander & Alexander of Conn., Inc., 40 Conn. Supp. 246, 488 A.2d 1295, 1296 (1985) (denying motion to dismiss claim arising out of discharge to deprive of bonuses; violative of public policies reflected in state wage payment statute). Such express prohibition or protection generally is found only in labor statutes. See § **5.9** (public policy torts based on labor statutes). Other categories of public policy tort require the analysis explained in the text to establish the nexus between the policy and the workplace dispute.

[62] *See* J. Hurst, Dealing with Statutes 31–65 (1982); R. Dickerson, The Interpretation and Application of Statutes 135–69 (1975); J. Sutherland, Statutory Construction ch. 48 (C.D. Sands ed., 3d ed. 1975).

[63] 716 F.2d 378, 381–82 (6th Cir. 1983) (Michigan law).

[64] 736 F.2d 1202, 1205 (8th Cir. 1984).

[65] It reasoned that compelling sexual favors as the price of keeping one's job effectively compels exchange of sex for money—the target of the prostitution statutes. This reasoning process is part of the jeopardy analysis discussed in § **7.12**. *But see* Rossi v. Pennsylvania State Univ., 340 Pa. Super. 39, 54, 489 A.2d 828, 836 (1985) (no public policy shields barrage of complaints about management of public university even though waste of tax dollars implicated).

v. *State Bank of Keysville*,[66] it was clear that Virginia public policy promoted honest proxy statements, regardless of whether it prohibited employers from dismissing employees who complained about dishonest ones. *Novosel v. Nationwide Insurance Co.*[67] is a good example of this reasoning process when a constitutional basis for public policy is asserted.[68]

The public policy tort cases involving dismissals for protesting violation of food labeling or bank loan interest rate statutes are examples of this type of public policy proof. In these cases, statutory duties[69] are imposed on an employer primarily to protect a class other than employees. It is necessary in analysis of the jeopardy element of the public policy tort[70] to show why certain employee conduct must not be chilled by the threat of discharge in order to further the public policy.[71]

A plaintiff faces greater difficulty satisfying the clarity element when the public policy asserted is not expressed in positive law; for example, when the policy derives either directly or indirectly from professional guidelines such as the physician's Hippocratic Oath, or the attorney's Code of Professional Responsibility. If the public policy asserted is manifest on the face of a document containing such guidelines, all that is necessary is to ask the court to take judicial notice of the guidelines and of the proposition that the guidelines promote the public welfare rather than merely promoting the economic interests of a particular group.[72] If the asserted public policy is not clear from the face of such official guidelines, the plaintiff must ask the court to infer the public policy, which presumably also is within the ambit of the judge's responsibility rather than the jury's duties.[73]

---

[66] 229 Va. 534, 331 S.E.2d 797 (1985) (reversing grant of demurrer against plaintiff and accepting public policy tort theory for bank employees dismissed for claiming proxy statements violated state securities laws).

[67] 721 F.2d 894 (3d Cir. 1983). The *Novosel* case was settled after the district court, on remand, denied the employer's motion for summary judgment. *See* Novosel v. Nationwide Ins. Co., 118 L.R.R.M. 2779 (W.D. Pa. 1985). Interestingly, the employer argued that it dismissed Mr. Novosel for prounion remarks made to nonmanagement personnel, which might have raised additional public policy and preemption issues.

[68] *See also* Jones v. Memorial Hosp. Sys., 677 S.W.2d 221 (Tex. Ct. App. 1984) (reversing summary judgment for employer; state and federal constitutional protection of free speech affords cause of action for nurse dismissed for newspaper article expressing personal views, perhaps without proof that employer was "public entity"); Ring v. River Walk Manor, Inc., 596 F. Supp. 393, 396 (D. Md. 1984) (remanding to state court for decision whether Maryland public policy tort claim exists for dismissal in retaliation for exercise of free speech rights). *But see* Barr v. Kelso-Burnett Co., 106 Ill. 2d 520, 527–28, 478 N.E.2d 1354, 1357 (1985) (free speech provisions of state and federal constitutions cannot support public policy tort because they reflect public policy only against governmental interference).

[69] A prohibition is a duty to refrain from acting.

[70] See § **7.12**.

[71] *See* Perry v. Hartz Mountain Corp., 537 F. Supp. 1387, 1389 (S.D. Ind. 1982) (public policy tort pleaded by alleged dismissal for refusal to engage in conspiracy violative of antitrust laws).

[72] Judicial notice of such official professional standards should be permissible under Rule 201 of the Federal Rules of Evidence and similar state evidence rules.

[73] In Pierce v. Ortho Pharmaceutical Corp., 84 N.J. 58, 417 A.2d 505 (1980), the court declined to draw the inference from the Hippocratic Oath desired by the plaintiff. *Id.* at 76, 417 A.2d at 514.

The most difficult case is where the plaintiff seeks to have recognized as public policy something which is not contained in a constitution or statute[74] nor in officially promulgated professional guidelines. In these circumstances, the court must decide what public policy is from its own perception of community values and consideration of competing interests. This seems to be what the courts did in the implied covenant contract cases of *Fortune v. National Cash Register Co.*[75] and *Monge v. Beebe Rubber Co.*[76] The plaintiff also might present evidence resembling evidence of custom and practice in an industry, and the factfinder would decide the public policy question, in line with *Cloutier v. Great Atlantic and Pacific Tea Company.*[77] Courts are reluctant to play this role or to have juries play this role in the absence of any statutory, constitutional, administrative agency, or professional standards authority.[78]

Authority exists, however, for the proposition that courts are entitled to decide what the applicable public policy is, even when competing interests must be weighed with little explicit guidance from a constitution or statute.[79] Such an approach is

---

[74] *See* Cipov v. International Harvester Co., 134 Ill. App. 3d 522, 526, 481 N.E.2d 22, 24 (1985) (no public policy tort for dismissal for refusal to take polygraph examination in absence of statute); Wyant v. S.C.M. Corp., 692 S.W.2d 814, 816 (Ky. Ct. App. 1985) (no public policy tort claim for supervisor, dismissed for asserting subordinate's right to overtime compensation absent showing of statutory right to overtime pay).

[75] 373 Mass. 96, 364 N.E.2d 1251 (1977).

[76] 114 N.H. 130, 316 A.2d 549 (1974). These cases are discussed in § **4.9**.

[77] 121 N.H. 915, 436 A.2d 1140 (1981).

[78] *See* Veno v. Meredith, ___ Pa. Super. ___, 515 A.2d 571, 579 n.3 (1986) (citing this treatise); Gillespie v. Equitable Life Assurance Soc'y, 590 F. Supp. 1111, 1115 (D. Del. 1984) (no violation of public policy to dismiss for arrest, before conviction; Pennsylvania law); Barr v. Kelso-Burnett Co., 106 Ill. 2d 520, 478 N.E.2d 1354 (1985) (no public policy tort for dismissal in retaliation for protesting layoff policies); Price v. Carmack Datsun, Inc., 124 Ill. App. 3d 979, 464 N.E.2d 1245 (1984) (no cause of action for discharge in retaliation for filing group health insurance claim, despite effort to bring within policy of state insurance regulatory statutes and ERISA; expressing doubt whether federal statute can be basis for state public policy), *aff'd*, 109 Ill. 2d 65, 485 N.E.2d 359 (1985); Rachford v. Evergreen Int'l Airlines, 596 F. Supp. 384 (N.D. Ill. 1984) (no tort pleaded under Illinois law for discharge in retaliation for aircraft safety complaints; state has no interest in enforcing federal law); Powers v. Delnor Hosp., 135 Ill. App. 3d 317, 321, 481 N.E.2d 968, 972 (1985) (no public policy violated when employer lies to at-will employee about reasons for dismissal); Ising v. Barnes Hosp., 674 S.W.2d 623, 625 (Mo. Ct. App. 1984) (no liability for dismissal for refusal to sign consent form for polygraph test; no state statute); Todd v. South Caroline Farm Bureau Mut. Ins. Co., 283 S.C. 155, 174, 321 S.E.2d 602, 613 (1984) (in absence of statute, no public policy violated by forcing employee to take polygraph test), *rev'd on other grounds*, 287 S.C. 190, ___, 336 S.E.2d 472, 473 (1985) (intentional interference with contract).

[79] *See* Lucas v. Brown & Root, Inc., 736 F.2d 1202, 1205 (8th Cir. 1984) (court competent to decide public policy; legislature not only source of public policy); Wagenseller v. Scottsdale Memorial Hosp., 147 Ariz. 370, 710 P.2d 1025 (1985) (reversing dismissal of plaintiff's claim and holding that nurse dismissed for refusing to "moon" could recover on public policy tort theory, based on criminal statute prohibiting indecent exposure. Court decisions, as well as statutes and constitutions, are sources of public policy).

suggested by the comments to § 870 of the *Restatement (Second) of Torts*.[80] Public policy determined by the courts is also the approach suggested by Professor Corbin: "In determining what public policy requires, there is no limit whatever to the 'sources' to which the court is permitted to go; and there is no limit to the 'evidence' that the court may cause to be produced. . . ."[81] The argument for a judge inferring public policy from the common law is especially strong when the rights involved already are recognized in other mature tort categories such as invasion of privacy.[82]

This essentially has the judge serving the function of a legislature, and many courts may be reluctant to make the value judgments involved.[83] Nevertheless, it is preferable for the judge, rather than the jury, to make the decisions. If judges make the value judgments, appellate review can promote consistency and predictability. If juries make the value judgments in individual cases, their decisions will be largely immune from appellate review.

§ 7.12 —Proving Jeopardy to Public Policy

In addition to establishing the existence of a public policy, the plaintiff also must show how the public policy would be jeopardized if employers were allowed to dismiss employees for the conduct in which the plaintiff engaged.[84] This *jeopardy* element is the second factor in the three-factor formula developed in **Chapter 5**.

Conceptually, proving jeopardy involves proving several subordinate factual propositions:

1. That the plaintiff engaged in particular conduct, such as an act while off duty, protesting employer policy, or refusing an employer order
2. That the conduct proven in step one furthers the public policy asserted, either because the public policy directly promotes the conduct (as in the public policy in favor of jury service), or because the conduct is necessary to effective enforcement of the public policy (as in a public policy

---

[80] See § 5.5–5.7.

[81] A. Corbin, Corbin on Contracts § 1375 at 1165 (1962) (determining public policy for purpose of deciding legality of contract.)

[82] See § **5.26**; Schmidt v. Yardney Elec. Corp., 4 Conn. App. 69, 492 A.2d 512, 515 (1985) (dismissal for revealing insurance fraud to parent corporation within common law and statutory policy against fraudulent conduct); Delaney v. Taco Time International, 297 Or. 10, 681 P.2d 114 (1984) (recovery permitted for discharge over refusal to sign defamatory statement against co-employee because no administrative remedy). *Cf.* Morris v. Hartford Courant Co., 200 Conn. 676, 513 A.2d 66, 68 (1986) (suggesting clarity element can be met by judicially created policy).

[83] *See* Murphy v. American Home Prods., 58 N.Y.2d 293, 448 N.E.2d 86, 461 N.Y.S.2d 232, (1983) (refusing to recognize abusive discharge tort, preferring to leave the question to legislature).

[84] See § **5.1** for an overview of the three elements of a public policy tort.

against excess consumer loan charges depending on vigilance by bank employees)

3. That threat of dismissal will discourage the conduct.

Ordinarily, the plaintiff will have no great difficulty proving that he engaged in the conduct alleged by the plaintiff or refused to engage in conduct requested by the employer.[85] The conduct, of course, must relate to the asserted public policy.[86] If there is a dispute over the plaintiff's conduct or over employer knowledge of the conduct, the jury must resolve the conflict as a matter of fact. Other aspects of jeopardy analysis present legal and policy questions for the judge.[87]

Assuming that the only reason for the dismissal was the plaintiff's conduct or refusal,[88] the plaintiff must establish that the public policy asserted by the plaintiff would be jeopardized.[89]

The jeopardy analysis can be illustrated by workers' compensation and jury duty cases. The public policy involved in public policy torts based on workers' compensation statutes is the statutory policy in favor of workers receiving compensation for work-related injury. If employers are allowed to terminate employees who file workers' compensation claims, filing of claims and therefore receipt of compensation will be discouraged, and the purpose of the statute jeopardized. In jury duty cases, the public policy is to have a cross section of the citizenry serve on juries. If employers are allowed to terminate their employees when they serve on juries, the policy in favor of having all groups on juries will be jeopardized.[90] Then the question becomes whether such dismissal jeopardizes the public policy to such a degree that tort damages are appropriate.

Suppose the plaintiff alleges that he was fired for protesting accounting irregularities. He will have established a public policy in favor of integrity and accuracy in corporate recordkeeping, the clarity element of the formula. The first element is no different from a workers' compensation or jury duty case; statutes, constitutional provisions, or the common law can be the source of the public policy.[91]

---

[85] Of course the plaintiff also must show employer knowledge of conduct to have a plausible motive argument. See §§ **7.3–7.9** regarding proof of motive.

[86] *See* Gray v. Superior Court, 181 Cal. App. 3d 813, 226 Cal. Rptr. 570 (1986) (employee offered insufficient evidence to show employer conduct contravened public policy evidenced in state discrimination statute).

[87] *See* Wiskotoni v. Michigan Nat'l Bank W., 716 F.2d 378, 383 (6th Cir. 1983) (Michigan law; court decided question discussed in text).

[88] Establishing the reason for the dismissal and the mixed motive problem are treated in §§ **7.13–7.15**. Motive is assumed in this section to isolate the jeopardy element analytically.

[89] In *Wiskotoni,* the court articulated the jeopardy factor separately from the existence factor. Wiskotoni v. Michigan Nat'l Bank W., 716 F.2d at 388. The issue was whether public policy was jeopardized by dismissing an employee for being subpoenaed by a grand jury.

[90] Nonemployees would not be discouraged from serving on juries, so whether jeopardy is shown depends on the framing of the public policy as having a cross section of citizens on juries, as opposed to having an adequate number of jurors.

[91] See § **7.11**.

§ 7.12 PROVING JEOPARDY

The jeopardy analysis is a bit different, however. He must also establish that if employees were effectively discouraged from protesting accounting irregularities, this would jeopardize the public policy. To make this showing, he must argue that other means for promoting the policy, such as regulatory requirements for audits, criminal penalties, and rights of shareholders and creditors to maintain private civil actions, are inadequate. In *Bowman v. State Bank of Keysville*,[92] the court concluded that permitting employers to dismiss employees for claiming that proxy statements violated state securities laws would chill the freedom of shareholder decisionmaking protected by the securities laws. A similar jeopardy analysis was at work in *Townsend v. L.W.M. Management, Inc.*,[93] in which the court approved a common law tort claim for a dismissal associated with a polygraph examination, reasoning that criminal prosecution under the polygraph statute giving rise to the public policy is discretionary with the prosecutor, and therefore less than a complete remedy for the employee dismissed in violation of the statutory policy.

The ease or difficulty with which the jeopardy element can be satisfied depends on how much the public policy will be jeopardized if the employer conduct is discouraged. In an external public policy tort case, the fit between the policy and the conduct may be tight. For instance, if the plaintiff asserts the public policy in favor of political expression and alleges that he was discharged for off-duty advocacy of a candidate for public office, it is relatively easy to conclude that chilling this conduct jeopardizes the asserted policy. The policy is limited to promotion of the conduct. In other external public policy cases, the fit between the policy and the conduct may be much looser. Suppose, for example, that the plaintiff was discharged for getting a divorce. He may have little difficulty in establishing a public policy permitting divorces.[94] It will be more difficult to establish that the disincentive to divorce resulting from employee terminations for that reason jeopardizes the public policy.

When the plaintiff fails to match the conduct with the public policy, no jeopardy can be shown. This occurs, for example, in cases involving dismissal for workplace injuries compensable under the workers' compensation system rather than dismissals for filing workers' compensation claims.[95]

The jeopardy analysis involves a mixture of fact and policy. The degree of jeopardy depends on fact questions such as how many employers will dismiss employees even if there is no tort liability, how frightened the employees will be about the possibility of discharge, and how important employee conduct is in furthering the public policy. But these facts are prospective in nature, more like those involved in any policy decision than like retrospective facts usually decided by

---

[92] 229 Va. 534, 331 S.E.2d 797 (1985).

[93] 64 Md. App. 55, 63, 494 A.2d 239, 244 (1985).

[94] Of course, a policy *permitting* divorce is weaker support for the plaintiff's jeopardy analysis than a policy *promoting* divorce. But the plaintiff would have considerable difficulty satisfying the clarity element if the policy is characterized as one *promoting* divorce.

[95] *See* Yoho v. Triangle P.W.C., Inc., 336 S.E.2d 204 (W. Va. 1985) (no violation of public policy to terminate seniority after absence related to workplace injury).

juries.[96] These matters could be questions of fact for the jury, but it seems better to include them in the policy-balancing analysis that is the responsibility of the judge.[97]

When the statute allegedly supplying the public policy provides administrative remedies, the jeopardy element is much weakened.[98] A major exception is *Wheeler v. Caterpillar Tractor Co.*,[99] in which the Illinois Supreme Court permitted a public policy tort claim to be based on the federal nuclear safety statute, even though that statute contains an explicit whistleblower protection provision enforced by the Secretary of Labor. The court was motivated, in major part, by the unavailability of punitive damages under the administrative procedures. Also, jeopardy analysis depends on the availability of actual administrative remedies to redress the claim asserted by the public policy tort plaintiff.[1]

Similarly, the degree of interference can be low because of the availability of collectively bargained remedies for unjust dismissal.[2] In *Mouser v. Granite City Steel Division*,[3] the court concluded that the rationale for the public policy tort is not present when an arbitral remedy exists for unjust discharge. A later decision by the Illinois Supreme Court in *Midgett v. Sackett-Chicago, Inc.*,[4] held that

---

[96] The distinction is exactly that between *legislative* and *adjudicative* facts in administrative law. See K. Davis, 2 Administrative Law Treatise § 12.3 (1978).

[97] *See* Kilpatrick v. Delaware County Soc'y for Prevention of Cruelty to Animals, 632 F. Supp. 542, 546 (E.D. Pa. 1986) (judge's conclusion that few employees would have courage to report suspected occupational hazard to government agency if threatened with dismissal; no actual prospect of chilling effect mentioned).

[98] See cases cited in § **5.9**; Kofoid v. Woodard Hotels, Inc., 78 Or. App. 283, 716 P.2d 771, 774 (1986) (distinguishing preemption from nonexistence of tort claim because societal interests adequately protected by statutory procedure; no public policy tort claim for sex discrimination); Atkins v. Bridgeport Hydraulic Co., 5 Conn. App. 643, 501 A.2d 1223, 1226 (1985) (public policy against age discrimination adequately enforceable through statutory remedies; no independent public policy tort exists); Welch v. Brown's Nursing Home, 20 Ohio App. 3d 15, 17, 484 N.E.2d 178, 180 (1985) (availability of administrative remedies for retaliation based on complaint of nursing home violations precluded common law action); Murray v. Commercial Union Ins. Co., 782 F.2d 432 (3d Cir. 1986) (no public policy tort claim for age discrimination; Pennsylvania administrative remedies are exclusive).

[99] 108 Ill. 2d 502, 485 N.E.2d 372 (1985), *cert denied*, ___ U.S. ___, 106 S. Ct. 1641 (1986).

[1] *See* Moniodis v. Cook, 64 Md. App. 1, 494 A.2d 212, 218 (1985) (administrative remedies available only for applicants; does not preclude tort claim by dismissed employee).

[2] *See* Phillips v. Babcock & Wilcox, 349 Pa. Super. 351, 503 A.2d 36 (1986) (no public policy tort under Pennsylvania law for employee covered by collective agreement); *but see id.* at 38 (Spaeth, J., dissenting); Herring v. Prince Foods-Canning Div., 799 F.2d 120 (3d Cir. 1986) (no public policy tort protection available under New Jersey law for employee covered by collectively bargained *just cause* protection); Smith v. Greyhound Lines, Inc., 614 F. Supp. 558, 560–61 (W.D. Pa. 1984) (no public policy tort under Pennsylvania law for employee covered by collective agreement).

[3] 121 Ill. App. 3d 834, 838, 460 N.E.2d 115, 117 (1984).

[4] 105 Ill. 2d 143, 473 N.E.2d 1280 (1984).

§ 7.13 LACK OF JUSTIFICATION: REASON FOR DISMISSAL

an employee covered by a collectively bargained grievance and arbitration procedure may bring a public policy tort action for wrongful dismissal.[5]

If the employee is dismissed for asserting an incorrect view of public policy, the possibility of jeopardy to public policy from a dismissal is reduced.[6] On the other hand, the dismissed employee may need only a good faith belief that a violation occurred, and not be required to prove there actually was a violation.[7]

The jeopardy analysis focuses exclusively on jeopardy to the public policy. Disruption to the employer's business occasioned by the public policy-linked conduct is considered separately as a part of analysis of the justification element.[8]

§ 7.13 —Proving Lack of Justification: Proving Reason for Dismissal

The third element of the public policy tort requires the plaintiff to show that the employer lacked justification for the dismissal.[9] The justification issue potentially presents two types of fact questions: the actual reason for the dismissal[10] and the business necessity for discharging the plaintiff, even if protected conduct[11] was the reason for the dismissal.[12] The plaintiff should be able to make out a prima facie case by showing (1) protected conduct, and (2) that the defendant offered no explanation for the dismissal.

The comments to § 870[13] of the *Restatement (Second) of Torts* state that it is the plaintiff's burden to plead and prove the elements of the prima facie case,[14] and the defendant's burden to plead and prove the existence of any privilege that may be applicable.[15] These two propositions potentially conflict respecting proof

---

[5] *But see* Elia v. Industrial Personnel Corp., 125 Ill. App. 3d 1026, 1029, 466 N.E.2d 1054, 1057 (1984) (suggesting that if public policy tort claim were raised and resolved in grievance process, separate public policy tort claim might be barred).

[6] *See* Alford v. Harold's Club, 99 Nev. 670, 674, 669 P.2d 721, 724 (1983) (employees dismissed for refusal to comply with employer's tip pooling policy cannot recover for wrongful dismissal because employer's policy legal under state statute).

[7] *See* McQuary v. Bel Air Convalescent Home, Inc., 69 Or. App. 107, 111, 684 P.2d 21, 24 (1985) (employee protected for reporting what employee believes in good faith are violations of nursing home patient statute; not required to prove actual violations).

[8] See §§ **7.15–7.16**.

[9] See §§ **1.2, 5.1**.

[10] See § **7.13**.

[11] *Protected conduct* is involved only if both the clarity and jeopardy elements of the public policy tort have been resolved in the plaintiff's favor.

[12] See § **7.15**.

[13] Restatement (Second) of Torts § 870 (1979). This section provides the doctrine for the public policy tort. See §§ **5.5–5.7**.

[14] Restatement (Second) of Torts § 870 comment j (1977).

[15] *Id.* § 870, comments j, n.

of justification. Because lack of justification is an element of the prima facie case under § 870, the comments suggest that the plaintiff has the burden of producing evidence showing lack of justification. Yet conceptually, justification is a privilege, and the comments also say that the defendant has the burden with respect to privileges.[16]

Consideration of the allocation of responsibility between judge and jury helps explicate the order of proof respecting justification.[17] Comment k requires the judge to engage in the interest balancing process to determine whether tort liability will exist for a dismissal in the circumstances alleged by the plaintiff and to decide what privileges will apply.[18] Justification is a privilege. The jury is limited to applying the rules and standards laid down by the judge to the facts that it finds to exist.[19] The relationship between legal justification and factual cause for the dismissal will be embodied in the jury instructions. Thus, the jury will decide the employer's true reasons for dismissing the plaintiff, as a matter of fact. Or, if the impact of the plaintiff's conduct on the defendant's business is a factual issue,[20] the jury will decide that as a matter of fact. The judge will decide, as a part of her balancing responsibility, whether the employer had legal justification.

It is desirable for the judge to retain control over the balancing process. Only in this way can the appellate courts retain adequate control over the direction in which the public policy balance is struck. If juries are allowed to strike the balance in individual cases, the constraints on employer discretion will be unpredictable and the outcomes largely immune from appellate review.

The best authority drawn from public policy tort cases and analogies with statutory or common law prohibited motive cases says that a public policy tort plaintiff, to recover for wrongful dismissal, must prove that the public policy-linked employee conduct was the determining factor in her termination. Such an approach is consistent with the apparent convergence on the but for test in statutory dismissal

---

[16] *Id.* § 870, comments e, j. Comment e sets forth the requirement that the actor's conduct be unjustifiable, and the burden of proving this apparently is carried by the plaintiff. Comments j and n, however, recognize that it is the defendant's burden to plead and prove privilege as a defense in order to justify her conduct.

[17] The public policy tort cases vary somewhat in the faithfulness with which they honor this allocation of responsibility between judge and jury. *See* Cloutier v. Great Atl. & Pac. Tea Co., 121 N.H. 915, 436 A.2d 1140 (1981) (jury decides not only the factual reason for the dismissal, but also the question of whether it contravened public policy. *Accord,* Cilley v. New Hampshire Ball Bearings, Inc., ____ N.H. ____, 514 A.2d 818 (1986). The approach limiting the jury to factual questions, suggested in this and following sections, is most consistent with the underlying philosophy of § 870 and the nature of wrongful dismissal disputes.

[18] *Id.* § 870, comment k. Comment j notes that recognized privileges for the established torts that are most analogous to the newly created tort will usually be held applicable to the new tort, but a deliberate decision must be made as to this issue. Comment k would charge the judge with this decision.

[19] *Id.*

[20] This involves issues of *business justification,* discussed in **§ 7.15**.

§ 7.13 LACK OF JUSTIFICATION: REASON FOR DISMISSAL

cases,[21] which is available as an easy model for common law courts to follow. A but for requirement permits the plaintiff greater latitude than a sole reason requirement. The but for standard does not require the plaintiff to convince the jury that the employer had no legitimate reason for the dismissal—an unrealistic burden.

Though a plaintiff should prove that public policy-linked conduct was the but for reason for the dismissal, the plaintiff need not prove prohibited motive by direct evidence.[22] The plaintiff can raise an inference that a prohibited motive was at work[23] by proceeding with a modification of the *McDonnell Douglas v. Green*[24] concepts developed under Title VII. The same reason for permitting indirect proof of motive relied upon by the *McDonnell Douglas* court is equally applicable to a public policy tort plaintiff: direct evidence of motive is likely to be within the exclusive possession and control of the defendant-employer.[25]

If the plaintiff can show that she engaged in protected activity,[26] or refused to engage in prohibited activity after her employer requested her to,[27] and was dismissed, it should be permissible for the finder of fact, in the absence of evidence from the employer, to infer that the reason for the dismissal was the public policy-linked activity.[28] It should, however, be necessary for the plaintiff to show by direct evidence that the defendant had knowledge of the activity, because such evidence should be within the plaintiff's reach.

Under the approach suggested here, the plaintiff can make out a prima facie case, permitting the jury to infer lack of justification, by indirect evidence.[29] Under these circumstances, the judge would deny a directed verdict for the defendant

---

[21] See §§ **7.4–7.9**. Melchi v. Burns Int'l Sec. Serv., Inc., 597 F. Supp. 575, 581 (E.D. Mich. 1984) (Title VII order of proof used for retaliatory discharge case under Michigan whistleblower statute).

[22] *See* Moore v. McDermott, Inc., 481 So. 2d 602 (La. 1986) (timing of dismissal and evidence of disparate treatment supported inference that termination was for filing workers' compensation claim); Roseborough v. N.L. Indus., 10 Ohio St. 3d 142, 143, 462 N.E.2d 384, 387 (1984) (involvement of employer in paying benefits enough to support statutory claim for dismissal in retaliation for workers' compensation claim; formal filing of claim not necessary); Hicks v. Tulsa Dynaspan, Inc., 695 P.2d 17, 19 (Okla. Ct. App. 1985) (seeking medical treatment sufficiently indicates intent to file workers' compensation claim to permit action for retaliatory dismissal); 29 Am. Jur. 2d *Evidence* § 365 (1967). Ways in which illegal motive can be inferred from indirect evidence also are considered in many unfair labor practice and Title VII discrimination cases. See §§ **2.2, 2.24**.

[23] I.e., that public policy-linked conduct was a reason for the dismissal.

[24] 411 U.S. 792 (1973). See § **7.6**.

[25] See § **7.6**.

[26] E.g., reporting to the employer (§ **5.17**) or reporting to outside enforcement agencies (§ **5.16**).

[27] See § **5.18**.

[28] *See* Polk v. Yellow Freight System, Inc., 801 F.2d 190, 197 (6th Cir. 1986) (timing alone insufficient evidence of retaliation to present jury question, but timing plus employer knowledge is sufficient).

[29] *See* Parnar v. Americana Hotels, Ind., 65 Haw. 370, 652 P.2d 625 (1982).

if she had determined the validity of the public policy asserted[30] and determined that the public policy would be jeopardized if employers discouraged the conduct engaged in by the plaintiff.[31] If the employer offers proof of other reasons for the dismissal, not linked with public policy, or if the employer offers proof of business necessity for the discharge, even though it involved public policy, the jury gets to decide the factual issues, which will decide the outcome within the balance struck by the judge in the jury instructions.

Other commentators have made suggestions on proof of justification which confuse to some extent the reason for the dismissal with the analysis of the business necessity affirmative defense.[32] Nevertheless, they provide some helpful guidance.[33]

§ 7.14 — Proving Lack of Justification: Burden of Proof on Reasons for the Dismissal and Mixed Motive Problem

The first step in the plaintiff's obligation to prove lack of justification is to convince the factfinder that he would not have been dismissed except for the conduct protected by the public policy.[34] Otherwise, the dismissal would be justified under the third element of the three-factor formula.[35] In most cases, the evidence permits inferences that dismissal was motivated both by protected conduct *and* by one or more legitimate reasons. Leading public policy tort cases disagree to some extent

---

[30] This is the clarity element of the public policy tort. See §§ **5.1, 7.11**.

[31] This is the second element of the public policy tort. See §§ **5.1, 7.12**.

[32] See § **7.15** for treatment of the business necessity defense.

[33] *See Protecting At-Will Employees Against Wrongful Discharge: The Duty to Terminate Only in Good Faith,* 93 Harv. L. Rev. 1816, 1842–43 (1980); Blades, *Employment At-Will vs. Individual Freedom: On Limiting the Abusive Exercise of Employer Power,* 67 Colum. L. Rev. 1404, 1429 (1967) (suggesting that in all cases the plaintiff-employee be required to prove by affirmative and substantial evidence that her dismissal was motivated by improper reasons). Professor Blades also considers the possibility of holding the plaintiff to a higher than usual standard of proof, such as clear and convincing evidence. He suggests establishing a legal presumption that the dismissal was for a proper cause, a presumption that would be reduced in force as the length of the employee's past service increased. *Id.* at 1430. Blades hypothesizes that in a situation where an employee had served a company faithfully for 30 years, a jury would be quite justified in finding little merit in an explanation that the employee was fired for chronic inefficiency and incompetence. Common experience may lead employers to disagree with Professor Blades's hypothesis.

[34] *Protected conduct* means that both the clarity and jeopardy elements have been resolved in the plaintiff's favor.

[35] If there is no causal nexus between the public policy and the termination, the plaintiff has failed to mobilize any interest to offset the Employment-at-Will Rule in the balancing process. See § **5.7**.

§ 7.14 LACK OF JUSTIFICATION: BURDEN OF PROOF 401

on whether the protected conduct must be proven to have been the *sole* reason for the dismissal, or a "but for," "dominant," or a "substantial" reason.

As § **7.13** suggested, the most appropriate test is whether the protected conduct was a *determining factor* in the employer's discharge decision. This standard, borrowed from age discrimination case law, means that the protected conduct must be proven to have been a but for reason for the dismissal. In considering the appropriate standard of proof, it is essential to recall that the judge decides the existence of public policy and jeopardy elements, that the plaintiff retains the ultimate burden of persuasion, and that the plaintiff also bears the burden of producing evidence from which lack of justification can be inferred.

One case clearly supports the proposition that the plaintiff need only offer evidence from which the jury can infer that the public policy-protected conduct was a determining factor in his discharge. In *Parnar v. Americana Hotels, Inc.*,[36] the court held that Hawaii recognizes liability in tort when the dismissal of an employee violates a clear mandate of public policy.[37] It found the relevant public policy in that case in federal antitrust statutes.[38] The court held that summary judgment for the defendant was improper when the plaintiff offered evidence that she was dismissed and sent back to the mainland in the middle of a Justice Department investigation of the trade practices of her employer. The jury could infer wrongful motivation for the plaintiff's dismissal, even though the employer offered plausible legitimate reasons.[39] This suggests a kind of *res ipsa loquitur* approach, consistent with the burdens of production and persuasion summarized at the end of § **7.13**. If the plaintiff offers evidence from which a wrongful motivation can be inferred, the employer has the opportunity to weaken the inference by offering evidence of other reasons for the dismissal. The burden of persuasion remains with the plaintiff.

In *Harless v. First National Bank*,[40] the West Virginia Supreme Court of Appeals reviewed a judgment entered on a jury verdict for the plaintiff, after it earlier had remanded the case for trial.[41] The plaintiff maintained that his discharge was solely because of his attempts to require the bank to comply with federal and state laws.[42] The bank offered five legitimate reasons for dismissing the plaintiff.[43] The

---

[36] 65 Haw. 370, 652 P.2d 625 (1982).

[37] *Id.* at 380, 652 P.2d at 631.

[38] *Id.*

[39] *Id.* at 381, 652 P.2d at 632. *See also* Schubbe v. Diesel Serv. Unit Co., 71 Or. App. 232, 235, 692 P.2d 132, 134 (1984) (judge sitting as factfinder properly found filing of workers' compensation claim was but for reason for dismissal, after disbelieving other reasons proffered by employer).

[40] 289 S.E.2d 692 (W. Va. 1982) (plaintiff-employee alleged discharge prompted by effort to require bank to comply with consumer credit laws).

[41] Harless v. First Nat'l Bank, 246 S.E.2d 270 (W. Va. 1978).

[42] Harless v. First Nat'l Bank, 289 S.E.2d at 696.

[43] *Id.*

court held that there were sufficient facts to go to the jury, although the court did not decide whether the plaintiff, in order to recover, had to prove to the jury's satisfaction that the illegitimate reason for firing him was a determining factor.[44]

But in *Thompson v. St. Regis Paper Co.*,[45] the Supreme Court of Washington, reversing summary judgment for the employer, said, "Once the employee has demonstrated that his discharge may have been motivated by reasons that contravene a clear mandate of public policy, the burden shifts to the employer to prove that the dismissal was for reasons other than those alleged by the employee."

The determining factor standard suggested in this section is not accepted universally. Some courts would require a finding that the protected conduct was the sole reason for the discharge.[46] In *Firestone Textile Co. v. Meadows*,[47] there is a suggestion that jury instructions in public policy tort cases should permit liability to be found only if the public policy-linked reason was the sole reason for dismissal. In *Sabine Pilot Service, Inc. v. Hauck*,[48] the Texas Supreme Court, recognizing a public policy tort for the first time, held that the plaintiff must prove that the discharge was for "no other reason" than the public policy-linked reason. In *Reuther v. Fowler and Williams*,[49] the intermediate appellate court of Pennsylvania reversed a nonsuit against a defendant who claimed he was terminated for going on jury duty. The nonsuit had been granted because the trial court viewed the evidence at the close of the plaintiff's case as showing that his employer had fired him not because he had served jury duty, but because he had been discourteous and inconsiderate in failing to notify his employer that he would be absent for one week.[50] The appellate court reviewed the evidence and concluded that a jury could have drawn two contradictory inferences: first, that the plaintiff was discharged for being absent without giving notice, or second, that the plaintiff was fired for failing to seek excuse from jury service.[51] Significantly, the court suggested that recovery could be permitted only if the public policy-linked reason is the *sole* reason for a discharge.[52] "[E]ven when an important public policy is involved, an employer may discharge an employee if he has a separate, plausible, and legitimate reason for doing so."[53]

---

[44] *Id.*

[45] 102 Wash. 2d 219, 232–33, 685 P.2d 1081, 1089 (1984).

[46] Frequently the language used by the courts is ambiguous. For example, in Wiskotoni v. Michigan Nat'l Bank W., 716 F.2d 378, 383 (6th Cir. 1983) (Michigan law), the court held that the jury was entitled to find the "real reason" among two proffered reasons. This could mean determining factor or it could mean sole reason.

[47] 666 S.W.2d 730, 734 (Ky. 1983) (concurring opinion of Vance, J.).

[48] 687 S.W.2d 733, 735 (Tex. 1985).

[49] 255 Pa. Super. 28, 386 A.2d 119 (1978) (jury duty retaliation case).

[50] *Id.* at 33, 386 A.2d at 121.

[51] *Id.* at 34, 386 A.2d at 121.

[52] *Id.*, 386 A.2d at 121–22.

[53] *Id.*, 386 A.2d at 122 *citing* Geary v. United States Steel Corp., 456 Pa. 171, 319 A.2d 174 (1974).

§ 7.14 LACK OF JUSTIFICATION: BURDEN OF PROOF

A number of other cases contain dicta suggesting that the plaintiff cannot recover unless the jury finds that the public policy-linked reason was the sole reason for dismissal. *Frampton v. Central Indiana Gas Co.*[54] says that tort recovery is permitted when an employee is discharged solely for exercising a statutorily conferred right.[55] In *Sventko v. Kroger Co.*,[56] language in the majority opinion,[57] along with some elaboration in the concurring opinion,[58] suggests that at trial a plaintiff must prove that a reason offending public policy was the sole reason for his termination. In *Tameny v. Atlantic Richfield Co.*,[59] there is opinion language and a footnote[60] suggesting that tort recovery is permitted only when the plaintiff can show that a reason offending public policy was the sole reason for the dismissal.

The case law on the standard of proof respecting motive is far from uniform. There is substantial support for the alternative possibilities that when plaintiff and defendant present evidence of competing motives, the plaintiff cannot recover unless the jury finds either that the public policy-linked motive was the sole reason for dismissal, or that it was a determining factor in the dismissal.

A determining factor standard is better than a sole reason standard because of the practical likelihood that any employer has multiple reasons for dismissing an employee.[61]

Notwithstanding employer concerns to the contrary, none of the public policy tort cases suggests that the employer must prove to the jury's satisfaction that there

---

[54] 260 Ind. 249, 297 N.E.2d 425 (1973) (plaintiff-employee was injured on job and filed a workers' compensation claim. One month after receiving a settlement for her injury, she was fired from her employment without a reason being given).

[55] *Id.* at 253, 297 N.E.2d at 428.

[56] 69 Mich. App. 644, 245 N.W.2d 151 (1976) (workers' compensation retaliation case).

[57] *Id.* at 649, 245 N.W.2d at 154. The procedural posture of this case bound the court to accept as true all of the plaintiff's factual allegations as well as any conclusions which would reasonably be drawn therefrom, i.e., that the plaintiff had been discharged solely in retaliation against her filing a workers' compensation claim. Reversal of summary judgment for the defendant was in this light.

[58] *Id.* at 650 n.2, 245 N.W.2d at 154 n.2. Allen, J. suggested in his concurrence that a legitimate and equally plausible reason for terminating the at-will employment relationship might be inferred from the allegation. He added that a jury should be instructed to find no cause of action if it accepts the alternative explanation for termination.

[59] 27 Cal. 3d 167, 610 P.2d 1330, 164 Cal. Rptr. 839 (1980).

[60] *Id.* at 171 n.3, 610 P.2d at 1332 n.3, 164 Cal. Rptr. at 841 n.3. In review of the trial court's sustaining of the defendant's demurrer, the California Supreme Court was bound to accept the plaintiff's reasonably drawn conclusion that the "sole reason" for the plaintiff's dismissal was his refusal to commit unlawful acts. The footnote intimates that something less than this assertion would prove inadequate and justify the sustaining of the demurrer. It follows, then, that recovery for the plaintiff would only exist upon a showing at trial that retaliation was the sole cause of his termination.

[61] Wright Line v. Bernard R. Lamoureux, 251 N.L.R.B. 1083, 1087 (1980) (rarely can it be said that a decision is motivated solely by a single concern), *enforced,* 662 F.2d 899 (1st Cir. 1981), *cert. denied,* 455 U.S. 989 (1982).

was just cause for the dismissal. In *Sheets v. Teddy's Frosted Foods, Inc.*,[62] the court, in holding that a tort cause of action existed for wrongful dismissal, was careful to distinguish between a rule that would require an employer in all instances to proffer a proper reason for dismissal, amounting to just cause,[63] and a rule permitting a plaintiff to recover only if he can prove a demonstrably *improper* reason for dismissal, a "reason whose impropriety is derived from some important violation of public policy."[64] It rejected the just cause rule in favor of the latter, more limited, public policy rule.[65]

§ 7.15 —Proving Justification: Business Necessity

Circumstances can arise, especially in the internal public policy category,[66] in which the employer does not deny that the reason for the dismissal was the employee's public policy-linked conduct, but asserts that legitimate business reasons nevertheless outweigh the public policy and justify the dismissal.[67] This is the *business necessity* defense. This defense differs from the mixed motive problem addressed in § 7.14. In the mixed motive case, the employer asserts that the real motive for the dismissal had nothing to do with public policy. In the business necessity case, the employer admits that the dismissal related to public policy protected conduct, but asserts that employer interests in the circumstances should override the

---

[62] 179 Conn. 471, 427 A.2d 385 (1980) (plaintiff-employee, quality control director for employer, alleged dismissal in retaliation for his insistence that employer comply with requirements of the Connecticut Uniform Food, Drug and Cosmetic Act).

[63] *Id.* at 475, 427 A.2d at 386; proof of the existence of just cause is considered in *Dismissal of Attorney with Just Cause,* 31 Am. Jur. Proof of Facts 2d 125 (1981) and in §§ **3.5–3.8** (arbitrator-applied cause standard). See also § **5.2** (no just cause requirement in public policy tort cases).

[64] Sheets v. Teddy's Frosted Foods, Inc., 179 Conn. at 475, 427 A.2d at 387. Because of the similarity of the motive issue in wrongful dismissal cases and intentional interference cases, some useful guidance as to proof of improper motive can be found in 21 Am. Jur. Proof of Facts 2d 509 (1980).

[65] Sheets v. Teddy's Frosted Foods, Inc., 179 Conn. at 474, 427 A.2d at 386. The court noted that the just cause rule was not at stake in this litigation as it was not alleged by the plaintiff, and that further, the Connecticut legislature had refused to interpolate such a requirement into contracts of employment.

[66] *Internal* public policy torts are defined in §§ **5.14–5.18**. The distinction among internal public policy, external public policy, and public policy based on labor statutes is reviewed in § **5.8** and **7.10**.

[67] *See* Alexander v. Kay Finlay Jewelers, Inc., 208 N.J. Super. 503, 506 A.2d 379 (1986) (dismissal of employee for filing suit in salary dispute did not offend public policy; employer had legitimate interest in being free of harassment from employee suits). For an interesting analysis of employer interests in tension with public policy interests, albeit in the context of an alleged statutory violation, see Brown & Root, Inc. v. Donovan, 747 F.2d 1029, 1035 (5th Cir. 1984) (pointing out the difference in impact on employment policies between protecting whistleblowing to government agencies as opposed to internal quarrels over employer policies).

§ 7.15 JUSTIFICATION: NECESSITY

public policy jeopardy. If circumstances under which the employee was terminated present questions of business necessity, fact issues should be resolved by the jury, with the judge retaining control over balancing the employee, employer, and public policy interests. The employee should retain the burden of persuasion in convincing the jury that her conduct was not unreasonably disruptive to the employer's legitimate business needs.

A clear example of the business necessity defense is *Harman v. LaCrosse Tribune*,[68] in which the employer's interests in proper service to clients overrode public policy in the employee's favor. The court held that public policy based on a constitutional right of free speech was overridden by the lawyers' code of professional responsibility when a lawyer-employee of the law firm attacked a client in a press release. Another example is *Geary v. United States Steel Corp.*,[69] in which the employer apparently was willing to admit that it fired Geary for his protests of safety defects in the employer's steel tubing products, but asserted that the manner of his protest was sufficiently unreasonable to justify his dismissal. The Supreme Court of Pennsylvania, affirming dismissal of the plaintiff's complaint, concluded that the most natural inference to be drawn from the facts recited by the plaintiff was that he "had made a nuisance of himself, and the company discharged him to preserve administrative order in its own house."[70] It hinted that the outcome might be different if a plaintiff presented evidence from which it could be inferred that "the company fired Geary for the specific purpose of causing him harm, or coercing him to break [a] law."[71]

Such cases present questions like those in statutory sex, religion, or age discrimination cases, in which the employer admits that the defined characteristic (sex, religion, or age) was the reason for the dismissal, but defends on the grounds that the defined characteristic was a "bona fide occupational qualification" for the position from which the plaintiff employee was excluded.[72] Another analogy is found in statutory retaliation cases, in which the employer admits that employee protest of the general type protected by statute was the reason for the dismissal, but defends on the ground that the form or nature of the protest was so disruptive to the employer's legitimate business interests that it should not be liable.[73]

---

[68] 117 Wis. 2d 448, 344 N.W.2d 536 (1984).

[69] 456 Pa. 171, 319 A.2d 174 (1974). Geary was fired after protesting that tubular steel products manufactured by his employer were unsafe. The Pennsylvania Supreme Court affirmed a lower court dismissal of his action.

[70] *Id.* at 180, 319 A.2d at 178. According to the court, the facts allegedly showed only that there was a dispute over the merits of the new product and Geary had expressed his own point of view, bypassing his immediate superiors, and taking his case to a company vice president.

[71] *Id.*

[72] Application of the bona fide occupational qualification defense in an age discrimination action is discussed in § 2.7. To prevail with the defense, the employer must show that the discharge because of age was "reasonably necessary" to its business operations.

[73] § 2.17 discusses statutory prohibitions against retaliation for protesting discrimination. The courts have held that a protest of this type may interfere with the employee's performance of her job

In these statutory cases, the employer must establish an affirmative defense, which means that the employer has the burden of persuasion.[74]

In public policy tort cases, the burden of persuasion remains with the plaintiff-employee on all three elements, including when mixed motive is involved. But if the employer admits protected conduct was the determining factor in the dismissal but defends on business necessity grounds, the employer should have the burden of persuasion on that defense. In effect, the employer is saying that something special about its business gives it an interest strong enough to override public policy, even though the plaintiff met her burden on all three elements of the public policy tort. The evidence of the special circumstances of the employer's business would be within the employer's control. Therefore, it is fair to put the burden of production on the employer. The burden of persuasion also should be placed on the employer because the proposition advanced by the employer is disfavored as contrary to public policy, and counter-intuitive.[75]

The types of factual inquiry in a public policy tort business necessity case are similar to those in statutory bona fide occupational qualification or business necessity cases. In both, the strength of the employer's asserted business necessity[76] defense will turn on facts such as the disruption to the employer's business that would result from permitting the plaintiff-employee's conduct to continue[77] and the availability of measures other than dismissal (such as transferring the employee to another part of the employer's business) to reduce the business impact of the employee's conduct.

In *Geary*-type facts, the employer would argue that protest over product design was effected in such a way as to jeopardize managerial authority to make the final decision over product design. In the words of the Pennsylvania Supreme Court,

---

to such an extent that a dismissal on the basis of the protest is lawful. *See* Rosser v. Laboreres, 616 F.2d 221, 223 (5th Cir. 1980), *cert. denied,* 449 U.S. 886 (1980). A similar limitation is applied under the National Labor Relations Act. *See* Emporium Capwell Co. v. Western Addition Community Org., 420 U.S. 50 (1975). For a review of cases involving different types of protest, see B. Schlei & P. Grossman, Employment Discrimination 549–52 (1983). In Novosel v. Nationwide Mutual Ins. Co., 721 F.2d 894 (3d Cir. 1983), *on remand,* 118 L.R.R.M. 2779 (W.D. Pa. 1985), the employer argued that it dismissed the plaintiff for prounion remarks made to nonmanagement personnel, defending itself against a public policy tort claim based on the First Amendment.

[74] In retaliation cases under Title VII, the burden of proof to show that the form of the protest was inappropriate usually is placed on the defendant employer. Payne v. McLemore's Wholesale & Retail Stores, 654 F.2d 1130 (5th Cir. Sept. 1981), *cert. denied,* 455 U.S. 1000 (1982).

[75] C. McCormick, McCormick on Evidence § 336 at 948–49 (E. Cleary ed. 3d ed. 1984) (discussing factors leading to placing burden of proof on one party or the other).

[76] The term *business necessity* is used as a term of art in *disparate impact* race, sex, and religion cases. See § **2.3**. It is used here in a more general sense because the term is more evocative than "bona fide occupational qualification."

[77] *See* Novosel v. Nationwide Ins. Co., 721 F.2d 894, 901 (3d Cir. 1983) (trial court should consider the effect of the public policy-protected conduct on efficient employer operations).

the employer would argue that the employee "made a nuisance of himself," instead of reasonably advocating public policy.[78] If believed by the jury, the employer would face no liability for the dismissal, even though it was established that the employee's conduct was protected by public policy, and that the conduct was the determining factor in the dismissal.[79]

In *Cisco v. United Parcel Service, Inc.*,[80] for example, the court affirmed dismissal of a public policy tort claim. The employee was terminated after being acquitted of theft and trespass involving a UPS customer. The court reasoned that, even though dismissal for an unsubstantiated criminal charge might violate public policy in Pennsylvania, the employer had an overriding interest in protecting its reputation and business activity which might be jeopardized by a mere arrest of one of its employees.[81]

In another, somewhat facetious, hypothetical situation, an employee might bring poisonous snakes to work and be dismissed for that reason. If the employee claimed a public policy in favor of free exercise of religious beliefs and that the policy would be jeopardized by firing an employee for snake handling required by the employee's religion,[82] and the employer admitted the employee was fired for bringing snakes to work,[83] the employer still could win under the justification factor of the three-factor formula. In deciding the justification question, the jury would be required to decide, as a matter of fact, whether the presence of the snakes in the workplace disrupted the employer's operations because of the effect on customers or other employees, including supervisors. Such disruption might be found not to exist, for example, if the employer's business were a pet shop. The jury also might have to decide, as a matter of fact, whether the employer reasonably could have taken action other than dismissal to minimize the disruptive effect on its business. For example, if the employer had both a pet shop and a boutique, and the employee worked in the boutique, the employee might be able to convince the jury that the employer's proffered business necessity defense should not exculpate it from wrongful dismissal liability because it could have transferred the employee to the pet shop rather than dismissing the employee.

---

[78] Geary v. United States Steel Corp., 456 Pa. 171, 180, 319 A.2d 174, 178 (1974).

[79] *See* Galante v. Sandoz, 196 N.J. Super. 568, 570, 483 A.2d 829, 830 (1984) (dismissal under equitably administered absenteeism policy does not give rise to public policy tort, though absence was occasioned by workers' compensation injury); Slover v. Brown, 140 Ill. App. 3d 618, 621, 488 N.E.2d 1103, 1105 (1986) (same).

[80] 328 Pa. Super. 300, 476 A.2d 1340 (1984).

[81] *Id.* at 307–08, 476 A.2d at 1344. *See also* Kinoshita v. Canadian Pac. Airlines, Ltd., 803 F.2d 471, 475 (9th Cir. 1986) (airline justified in dismissing for suspicion of drug abuse, based on company's need for good reputation); Alexander v. Kay Finlay Jewelers, Inc., 208 N.J. Super. 503, 506 A.2d 379 (1986) (dismissal of employee for filing suit in salary dispute did not offend public policy; employer had legitimate interest in being free of harassment from employer suits).

[82] These are the first two elements of the public policy tort: clarity and jeopardy. See §§ **5.1** and **7.10**.

[83] This assumption is made to simplify the illustration by eliminating the mixed motive fact issue treated in § **7.14**.

For cases in which business necessity is at issue, the jury instructions should be framed so that the jury makes the necessary factual decisions and the judge retains the ultimate responsibility for balancing employer, employee, and public policy interests.[84]

§ 7.16 — Public Policy Tort Jury Instructions

The public policy tort proof concepts discussed in §§ 7.10 through 7.15 can be illustrated most concretely by reviewing jury instructions from public policy tort cases, and from statutory discrimination cases involving factual issues similar to those in public policy tort cases.[85]

This section contains seven jury instructions. The first two permit the jury to decide public policy as well as factual issues. The third limits the jury to factual questions within a public policy framework decided by the judge. The fourth and fifth instructions deal with a determining factor or "but for" requirement on motive for the dismissal. The final two instructions address the business necessity defense discussed in § 7.15.

Sections 7.11 and 7.12 say that the judge should engage in the interest-balancing required to decide whether the public policy asserted by the wrongful dismissal plaintiff should be recognized, and whether allowing the plaintiff's conduct to be a reason for dismissal will jeopardize the public policy. An opposing view would permit the jury to decide these questions as well as the factual question of what was the employer's reason for dismissing the employee. This opposing view was accepted by the Supreme Court of New Hampshire in *Cloutier v. Great Atlantic & Pacific Tea Co.*[86] In that case, the following instruction was approved on appeal:

> In all employment contracts, whether at will such as this one, or for definite term, our Court has said—and that is speaking of the New Hampshire Supreme Court—that the employer's interests in running his business as he sees fit must be balanced against the interests of the employee in maintaining his employment and the public's interest in maintaining a proper balance between the two. . . . First you have to ask yourself, based on the evidence that you have heard, whether or not this is a situation where the employee was terminated or discharged because he performed an act that public policy would encourage, or refused to do that which public policy

---

[84] §§ 7.11, 7.12, and 7.14 explain why the judge should retain this responsibility. The Oregon Supreme Court suggests agreement with this allocation of responsibility between judge and jury. *See* Nees v. Hocks, 272 Or. 210, 218 n.2, 536 P.2d 512, 516 n.2 (1975).

[85] More jury instructions can be found in M. Dichter, A. Gross, D. Morikawa & S. Sauntry, Employee Dismissal Forms and Procedures (1986). *See also* Caproon v. G.D. Searle Co., ___ F. Supp. ___, No. 84-0640-CIV-MARCUS, slip op. at 11 (S.D. Fla. Nov. 11, 1986) (instruction on constructive dismissal).

[86] 121 N.H. 915, 436 A.2d 1140 (1981). *Accord,* Cilley v. New Hampshire Ball Bearings, Inc., ___ N.H. ___, 514 A.2d 818 (1986).

§ 7.16 JURY INSTRUCTIONS

would condemn. I will go over this again because you have to keep that concept in mind. Was there a situation here, and you have heard the evidence, where Mr. Cloutier performed an act that public policy would encourage or refused to perform an act or do that which public policy would condemn.[87]

The breadth of the *Cloutier* instruction may be explained by the trial judge's view that the proper legal framework for the case was breach of contract and covenant of good faith and fair dealing. The complete instruction, including the second part of the test on which the judge instructed the jury,[88] makes it clear that he saw the case in that framework. If one conceives of the public policy question as merely a specific example of a bad faith dismissal, it may seem reasonable to permit the jury to decide the entire question.[89] On the other hand, if one views the legal framework in public policy tort terms, a more limited role for the jury, as suggested in §§ **7.10** through **7.15**, is preferable.

Sometimes it is difficult to distinguish between submitting legal questions to the jury and submitting ultimate questions of fact. In some states, procedural rules militate in favor of submitting ultimate fact questions rather than evidentiary fact questions to the jury. Thus in *Reed v. Sale Memorial Hospital and Clinic*,[90] the court approved this instruction: "[I]f you believe . . . that plaintiff . . . exercised certain of her rights under the Workers Compensation Law by filing a claim for compensation . . . ." as involving an ultimate fact question rather than a legal question.[91]

An instruction that limits the jury to deciding the factual question of the employer's reason for the dismissal of the plaintiff is illustrated by proposed instructions submitted in *Harless v. First National Bank*:[92]

---

[87] Other parts of the instruction gave as examples of reasons that would offend public policy: firing a person for accepting jury duty, firing a person for filing for unemployment compensation, firing a person for attempting to lawfully organize a union, firing an employee because of a refusal of sexual advances, firing a person because of refusal to violate the criminal law of the state. Trial transcript at 294–95, Cloutier v. Great Atl. & Pac. Tea Co., 121 N.H. 915, 436 A.2d 1140 (1981).

[88] The second part of the test on which the judge instructed the jury was that "the discharge must have been motivated out of malice or bad faith or in retaliation." The instruction required that both tests be satisfied if the jury was to find liability. Trial transcript at 296, Cloutier v. Great Atl. & Pac. Tea Co., 121 N.H. 915, 436 A.2d 1140 (1981).

[89] *See* O'Brien v. Papa Gino's, 780 F.2d 1067 (1st Cir. 1986) (quoting with approval broad jury instruction in New Hampshire public policy case). *See also* M. Dichter, A. Gross. D. Morikawa & S. Sauntry, Employee Dismissal Forms and Procedures §§ 8.5–8.8 (1986) (instructions letting jury decide aspects of public policy).

[90] 698 S.W.2d 931 (Mo. Ct. App. 1985).

[91] *Id.* at 937.

[92] 289 S.E.2d 692 (W. Va. 1982) (affirming verdict respecting liability, but reversing and remanding on damage issues).

> The law of this state provides that an oral contract of employment is terminable at will by any party to it. Therefore, you are instructed there is no liability on the part of the defendants . . . for the alleged retaliatory discharge of John Harless unless that discharge was motivated solely by a desire on the part of [the defendants] to retaliate for the alleged efforts of John Harless to obtain compliance with the West Virginia Consumer Protection Act.[93]
>
> If you believe from a preponderance of all the evidence in this case that the motive or basis for the termination of John Harless was other than his alleged effort to secure compliance with the West Virginia Consumer Protection Act, then your verdict should be for the defendants . . . .[94]

The plaintiff objected to the use of the word "solely" in the first quoted paragraph, but otherwise found the instruction unobjectionable. Deletion of the word "solely" would be necessary if the instruction is to embody the determining factor standard suggested in §§ 7.13 and 7.14. It is evident from the first quoted paragraph of the instruction that the court already has found that the asserted public policy exists, and that dismissing the plaintiff would jeopardize the public policy—the first two elements of the public policy tort.[95]

Treatment of the mixed motive problem[96] is illustrated by a portion of a jury instruction given in an age discrimination case:[97]

> The Plaintiff must show by preponderance of the evidence that the University refused to reappoint or promote the Plaintiff because of her age. The Plaintiff is not required to prove that the refusal to reappoint or promote her was based solely on her age. Rarely can it be said that a person making a decision is motivated solely by a single concern or even that a particular purpose was the dominant or primary one. The Plaintiff is required to prove only that her age was a substantial or motivating factor in the decision not to reappoint or promote . . . .[98]

Such an instruction is a useful beginning in presenting the jury with a but for standard in a wrongful dismissal case, if the appropriate words for the public policy-

---

[93] Defendants Wilson and Schulte Instruction No. 4, Civil Action No. 77-C-243, Cir. Ct. of Marion County, W. Va.

[94] Defendants Wilson and Schulte Instruction No. 5, Civil Action No. 77-C-243, Cir. Ct. of Marion County, W. Va. A similar instruction was approved in Wiskotoni v. Michigan Nat'l Bank W., 716 F.2d 378, 381 (6th Cir. 1983) (Michigan law; dismissal for being subpoenaed by grand jury).

[95] See § 5.1; see also M. Dichter, A. Gross. D. Morikawa & S. Sauntry, Employee Dismissal Forms and Procedures § 8.13 (1986) (quoting Wiskotoni v. Michigan Nat'l Bank W., 716 F.2d 378, 381 (6th Cir. 1983) on sole reason requirement after court found that dismissal for obeying subpoena from grand jury satisfied clarity and jeopardy elements).

[96] See § 7.14.

[97] Smith v. University of N.C., 632 F.2d 316, 331 (4th Cir. 1980) (employer won, thus harmless error to instruct that employer had burden of persuasion to establish that age was not the "but for" reason).

[98] The instruction went on to impose the burden of persuasion on the defendant-employer respecting the but for nature of age.

§ 7.16 JURY INSTRUCTIONS

linked conduct were substituted for the word *age*. The but for test could be made clearer by the addition of the following:

> Age has to be what we call a but for element in the decision. It's not the only element, not the only major element, but, in order for the plaintiff to recover, age must be either the basis of the decision or one of the things which played a significant part in arriving at the decision. It has to be a producing cause. It has to be one of the factors which brought about the decision, one of the factors without which he would not have been [dismissed].[99]

Section 7.15 discussed the situation in which the defendant-employer defends on the ground that the plaintiff-employee's conduct exceeded the bounds of reasonableness and therefore that the employer's interests in maintaining workplace harmony and managerial authority outweighed the public policy interests. In such a case, a jury instruction similar to the following should be given, in addition to other appropriate instructions presented in this section:

> Even though the plaintiff's conduct was clothed with a public policy interest, the law does not give an employee unlimited license to complain at any and all times and places.[1] You may not find for the plaintiff unless you find from a preponderance of the evidence that you have heard that the following additional requirements were met. First you must conclude that the employee reasonably believed that he was protesting a violation of the [public policy as found by the judge].[2] Second, you must find that the manner of the protest did not exceed the bounds of that which was reasonably necessary to call to the employer's attention[3] the possibility of a violation of this [public policy as found by the judge].

This instruction might be modified to permit the employee to recover also if the employee reasonably believed it to be necessary to report the apparent violation of public policy to official authorities after a refusal by the employer to act on the employee's complaint. The instruction might be given as a special jury interrogatory to permit the judge to retain control over the balancing of the public policy against the disruption to the employer's business associated therewith.

---

[99] Spagnuolo v. Whirlpool Corp., 641 F.2d 1109, 1112 n.1 (4th Cir. 1981) (judgment on verdict for employee affirmed). For additional ADEA jury instructions, *see* Tribble v. Westinghouse Elec. Corp., 669 F.2d 1193, 1197 (8th Cir. 1982); Haring v. C.P.C. Int'l, Inc., 664 F.2d 1234, 1237 (5th Cir. 1981); Goodman v. Heublein, Inc., 645 F.2d 127, 130 (2d Cir. 1981).

[1] The first sentence is taken from the court's observation in Hochstadt v. Worcester Found. for Experimental Biology, Inc., 545 F.2d 222, 233 (1st Cir. 1976). The remainder of the instruction is a composite of concepts developed in statutory discrimination cases.

[2] This part of the instruction would be tailored to match the employee conduct: external protest, off-duty conduct, refusal of orders, etc. See **§§ 5.8–5.20**, analyzing different factual contexts for public policy tort.

[3] This part of the instruction would be tailored to match the type of employee conduct involved.

In other situations identified in § **7.15**, the issue will not be the reasonableness of the manner of protest, but the impact of protected conduct. In such cases, an instruction like the one presented below could be given:

> You may not find for the plaintiff unless you also find that the disruption to the employer's legitimate business needs arising from the employee's conduct was reasonable in light of all the circumstances. In this connection, you may consider whether the employer could have taken steps to permit the employee's conduct while reducing the adverse impact on customers or other employees and whether the conduct of the employee seemed reasonably necessary to a person in the employee's position.

This instruction also might be given in the form of a special interrogatory to permit the judge to retain control over the balancing instinct in the justification analysis.

§ 7.17 Common Law Contracts: Basic Concepts of Proof

Sections 7.18 through **7.28** consider proof problems associated with the implied-in-fact contract theory.[4] If the plaintiff-employee pleads as suggested in § **4.26**, the employee has alleged that the defendant-employer made a promise to continue the plaintiff's employment,[5] that the employee gave consideration or a substitute for consideration for the entire employment contract,[6] and that there was a breach of the employer's promise.[7] Proving a breach will not necessarily involve showing that the employer dismissed the employee for a particular motive; it may involve nothing more than negating the possibility that the employer had cause to dismiss the employee, or that the employer followed promised procedures.

In one respect, contract cases require the finder of fact to decide more than is required in tort cases. The factfinder must decide if there was a legally enforceable obligation before deciding if the employer breached it by terminating the employee.[8] In tort cases, the existence of a duty is a legal question, and the factfinder only need decide if the employer's conduct breached the duty.[9] In addition, the jury in a breach of contract case usually must decide whether there was cause for the dismissal—assuming the contract entitled the employee to be retained absent cause. What constitutes good cause is not at issue in a tort case.

---

[4] See **ch. 4**.
[5] See §§ **4.6–4.11**.
[6] See §§ **4.12–4.18**.
[7] See §§ **4.21–4.24**. For pleading the plaintiff's case, see § **4.26**.
[8] See §§ **7.18–7.19** (establishing the duration of the employment contract for a reasonable period of time).
[9] Restatement (Second) of Torts § 328B(b) (court determines duty), § 328C(b) (jury determines breach) (1977).

In a wrongful dismissal breach of contract action, the plaintiff must show that a legally enforceable contract existed. **Sections 7.18** through **7.20** build on the legal concepts introduced in **Chapter 4** to deal with two difficult proof problems confronting a plaintiff in the typical wrongful dismissal action: proving a promise of employment security, and proving consideration or an alternative way of satisfying the consideration requirement. **Sections 7.22** through **7.28** deal with proving a breach.

The order and burdens of proof in a wrongful dismissal action based on contract theory follow basic proof principles in any contract action.[10] The plaintiff has the burden of proving the existence of a contract,[11] satisfaction of all conditions precedent to the defendant's performance,[12] and breach.[13] The defendant has the burden of proving any excuse for performance,[14] such as satisfaction of any conditions subsequent.[15] Each of these burdens refers to producing evidence; the plaintiff retains the ultimate burden of persuasion.[16]

§ 7.18 —Proving an Express or Implied-in-Fact Promise of Employment Security from Writings or Oral Statements

All of the leading cases permitting a plaintiff to reach trial on a wrongful dismissal claim premised on breach of contract have treated the employment-at-will concept as a rebuttable presumption.[17] Rebuttal of the presumption occurs when the plaintiff offers proof of a promise of employment security sufficient to persuade the trier of fact that such a promise was made. It is important to realize that the promissory

---

[10] *See* Darlington v. General Elec., 350 Pa. Super. 183, 203–04, 504 A.2d 306, 316 (1986) (quoting author of this treatise on order of proof in implied contract case).

[11] *See Offeree's Acceptance of Contract Offer,* 27 Am. Jur. Proof of Facts 2d 559 (1981).

[12] A. Corbin, Corbin on Contracts § 749 at 703 (1952).

[13] *See Offeree's Acceptance of Contract Offer,* 27 Am. Jur. Proof of Facts 2d 559 (1981).

[14] *See generally Implied Promise Not to Terminate At-Will Employment Without Cause,* 34 Am. Jur. Proof of Facts 2d 259 (1983).

[15] A. Corbin, Corbin on Contracts § 749 at 703 (1952).

[16] C. McCormick, Handbook on the Law of Evidence § 336 at 783–84, § 337 at 786 (E. Cleary ed 2d ed. 1972).

[17] *See* Toussaint v. Blue Cross & Blue Shield, 408 Mich. 579, 600, 614–15, 292 N.W.2d 880, 885, 892 (1980); Weiner v. McGraw-Hill, Inc., 57 N.Y.2d 458, 466, 443 N.E.2d 441, 446, 457 N.Y.S.2d 193, 198 (1982); Hartman v. C.W. Travel, Inc., 792 F.2d 1179, 1181 (D.C. Cir. 1986) (presumption of terminability at will applies only when there is no other evidence of party intent; reversing district court because of provision providing for review of the employment relationship after one year).

estoppel doctrine is a way of satisfying the consideration element, not the promise element.[18]

When the promise of employment is based on an express written contract, the analysis is basically the same as when implied promises are involved.[19] A formal written contract, however, may vitiate the reasonableness of relying on other promises.[20]

Three basic factual situations were considered in **Chapter 4**:

1. The employer made an oral or written statement to the individual employee expressly referring to employment security
2. The employer made oral or written statements to the workforce in general from which a promise of employment security can be inferred
3. No statements were made, but employer and employee conduct supports an inference of a mutual expectation of employment security.

In the first enumerated situation, a plaintiff can prove by direct evidence a promise to employ for a specified time, or to dismiss him only for certain reasons, or only after the exhaustion of certain procedures based on evidence of the writings or oral statements.[21] In most cases, however, the plaintiff must convince the trier of fact that a promise of employment security should be implied from more general statements, perhaps reinforced by conduct.[22] Evidence must be strong enough to

---

[18] *See* Banas v. Matthews Int'l Corp., 348 Pa. Super. 464, 486 n.12, 502 A.2d 637, 648 n.12 (1985) (doctrine cannot supply promise); see also § **4.17**.

[19] *See* Cleasby v. Leo A. Daly Co., 221 Neb. 254, 376 N.W.2d 312 (1985) (two-year express contract construed to contain an implied right to dismiss for just cause); *see* Bader v. Alpine Ski Shop, 505 A.2d 1162 (R.I. 1986) (written employment contract found to be terminable at will).

[20] *See* Armstrong v. Richland Clinic, Inc., 42 Wash. App. 181, 709 P.2d 1237, 1239 (1985), *review denied*, 105 Wash. 2d 1009 (1986) (medical center business manager covered by express written contract not entitled to implied contract claim based on handbook or to implied covenant claim); Shaw v. Burchfield, 481 So. 2d 247, 254 (Miss. 1985) (informal practice of terminating only for good cause did not modify express written contract providing that ''no cause shall be required'' for dismissal; suggesting possibility of modifying Employment-at-Will Rule in another case).

[21] See § **4.7**; Mueller v. Union Pac. R.R., 220 Neb. 742, 752, 371 N.W.2d 732, 739 (1985) (promise not to retaliate if employee disclosed misconduct by other employees); Buchanan v. Martin Marietta Corp., 494 A.2d 677 (Me. 1985) (affirming jury verdict for plaintiff based on finding of promise of employment security, based only on plaintiff's testimony that employer promised continuous service until retirement); Stoetzel v. Continental Textile Corp., 768 F.2d 217, 221 (8th Cir. 1985) (sufficient evidence of oral offer and acceptance of employment security promise to support jury verdict for plaintiff under Missouri law; quoting jury instruction); Hall v. Hotel l'Europe, Inc., 69 N.C. App. 664, 318 S.E.2d 99, 101 (1984) (trial court properly admitted parol evidence of promise of employment security because letter agreement was silent on duration of employment); Terrio v. Millinocket Community Hosp., 379 A.2d 135 (Me. 1977) (statements by employer representative).

[22] See §§ **4.8–4.9**. For instance, in Toussaint v. Blue Cross & Blue Shield, a contract was implied from a general statement of employer policies. In Delzell v. Pope, 200 Tenn. 641, 294 S.W.2d

§ 7.18   PROVING PROMISE   415

permit the factfinder to infer the making of a promise.[23] When the promise is based on written language, as in an employee handbook, it is the judge's function to

---

690 (1956), the court found an implied one-year contract from the pay period and length of service. In Pugh v. See's Candies, Inc., 116 Cal. App. 3d 311, 171 Cal. Rptr. 917 (1981), a contract was implied from the employer's practice of terminating only for cause. In Wiskotoni v. Michigan Nat'l Bank W., 716 F.2d 378 (6th Cir. 1983), the court approved, under Michigan law, a jury verdict inferring a promise to dismiss only for cause from evidence of a practice of dismissing only for cause and from a handbook that stated only that probationary employees could be dismissed for dissatisfaction with their work. *Id.* at 385–86. *See also* Ohanian v. Avis Rent a Car Sys., Inc., 779 F.2d 101, 109 (2d Cir. 1985) (oral statement that future was secure in absence of "screw-up" sufficiently definite when accompanied by intent to convince employee to relocate and subsequent relocation); Cook v. Heck's Inc., 342 S.E.2d 453, 458–59 (W. Va. 1986) (handbook enumeration of reasons for dismissal could permit jury to infer promise to dismiss only for those reasons; reversing directed verdict for employer); Brookshaw v. South St. Paul Feed, Inc., 381 N.W.2d 33, 36 (Minn. Ct. App. 1986) (jury entitled to decide whether manual containing both disciplinary language and a disclaimer gave rise to unilateral contract).

[23] *See* Ellis v. El Paso Natural Gas Co., 754 F.2d 884, 886 (10th Cir. 1985) (personnel manual promising "balanced compensation program . . . to attract, motivate and retain" competent employees was too indefinite to support implied contract claim for wrongful dismissal; applying New Mexico law); Hunt v. I.B.M. Mid America Employees Fed. Credit Union, 384 N.W.2d 853 (Minn. 1986) (handbook vaguely referring to immediate dismissal for serious offenses and referring to probation but not clearly promising probation before dismissal too vague to be enforced; facts of Pine River State Bank v. Mettille distinguished); Oakley v. St. Joseph's Hosp., 116 A.D.2d 911, 498 N.Y.S.2d 218 (1986) (promise "to provide, insofar as possible, continuous employment to all whose work proves satisfactory" insufficiently specific under New York law); Hopes v. Black Hills Power & Light Co., 386 N.W.2d 490 (S.D. 1986) (performance appraisal procedure gave no rights to employment security; dismissal for disability permissible); Darlington v. General Elec., 350 Pa. Super. 183, 203–04, 504 A.2d 306, 316 (1986) (analysis of degree of specificity required in promise, in combination with other factors signifying party intent; quoting author of this treatise on order of proof in implied contract case); Murray v. Commercial Union Ins. Co., 782 F.2d 432 (3d Cir. 1986) (testimony of assurances of "a future and lifetime career" and of employment for "as long as I wanted" too vague to support implied contract, applying Pennsylvania law); Sabetay v. Sterling Drug, Inc., 114 A.D.2d 6, 497 N.Y.S.2d 655, 656 (1986) (restricted circulation policy manual insufficiently specific regarding tenure) *appeal granted,* 68 N.Y.2d 605, 497 N.E.2d 708, ___ N.Y.S.2d ___ (1986); Ewing v. Board of Trustees of Pulaski Memorial Hosp., 486 N.E.2d 1094, 1098 (Ind. Ct. App. 1985) (correspondence *guaranteeing* annual salary too vague, when coupled with questionable authority of sender); Brieck v. Harbison-Walker Refractories, 624 F. Supp. 363 (W.D. Pa. 1985) (allegations that employer said not to worry about layoffs and promised to reward for good performance insufficient to overcome at-will presumption under Pennsylvania law); Dumas v. Kessler & Maguire Funeral Home, Inc., 380 N.W.2d 544 (Minn. Ct. App. 1986) (oral statement "we will retire together" too vague to be a promise of employment security); Kay v. United Technologies Corp., 757 F.2d 100, 102 (6th Cir. 1985) (no just cause promise shown by president's letter exhorting good performance, performance evaluation system, and deposition testimony regarding purpose of performance evaluation system; applying Michigan law); Bakker v. Metropolitan Pediatric, 355 N.W.2d 330, 331 (Minn. Ct. App. 1984) (long service and good performance reviews not enough to imply a contract under Pine River State Bank v. Mettille); Ruch v. Strawbridge & Clother, Inc., 115 L.R.R.M. 2044 (E.D. Pa. 1983) (code of conduct for employees does not establish promise of employment security; applying Pennsylvania law).

construe the language if it is unambiguous and if there is no extrinsic evidence of a course of dealing offered.[24]

In *Pine River State Bank v. Mettille*,[25] the Minnesota Supreme Court decided that an employee handbook establishing predischarge procedures amounted to a unilateral offer of employment security when distributed to an employee after he had begun his employment.[26] The court concluded that general provisions of the handbook relating to disciplinary policy did not constitute an offer, but were general statements of policy. It found, however, that provisions of the handbook section entitled "Disciplinary Policy" did set out in definite language an offer of a unilateral contract for procedures to be followed in job termination.[27] While the supreme court accepted, as the law of the case, the trial court's jury instruction that the employer must have intended the handbook to be binding before the jury could find that it became part of the employment contract, the supreme court's discussion implies that it believed such intention was not material to finding the handbook constituted an offer.[28]

Toussaint v. Blue Cross & Blue Shield[29] illustrates evidence offered to establish an implied promise to continue an employment until cause existed for termination. The Michigan Supreme Court actually heard two appeals: Toussaint's and Ebling's.[30] The majority found the two cases factually indistinguishable.[31] Both Ebling and Toussaint testified that they inquired about job security when they were hired. Toussaint testified that he was told he would be with the company as long as he did his job. Ebling testified that he was told that if he was doing the job he would not be dismissed. The supreme court found that this testimony created an issue of fact for the jury—whether there was an agreement for a contract of employment terminable only for cause.[32] The court went further than holding that the testimony alone created the basis for a favorable jury verdict. It also held that merely promulgating an employment manual and policy that promised job security—even if the plaintiff employee did not know of the particulars of the

---

[24] *See* Hunt v. I.B.M. Mid America Employees Fed. Credit Union, 384 N.W.2d 853, 856 (Minn. 1986) (construction of unambiguous handbook language solely for court; reinstating summary judgment for employer).

[25] 333 N.W.2d 622 (Minn. 1983).

[26] *Id.* at 630.

[27] *Id. See also* Lewis v. Equitable Life Assurance Soc'y, 361 N.W.2d 875, 880 (Minn. Ct. App. 1985) (handbook prohibiting discharge without unheeded warnings and specifying that only serious misconduct could be ground for immediate dismissal specific enough).

[28] Pine River State Bank v. Mettille, 333 N.W.2d at 630 n.6.

[29] 408 Mich. 579, 292 N.W.2d 880 (1980).

[30] *Id.* at 595, 292 N.W.2d at 883. (Toussaint was employed by Blue Cross and Ebling was employed by Masco Corporation).

[31] *Id.* at 597, 292 N.W.2d at 884 (Toussaint's case, if anything, was stronger because he was handed a manual of Blue Cross personnel policies which reinforced the oral assurance of job security. Also, Toussaint was employed for five years while Ebling was employed for only two years).

[32] *Id.*

§ 7.18   PROVING PROMISE   417

policy—permitted the factfinder to conclude that there was an enforceable promise to continue employment until cause existed for dismissal.[33] Accordingly, under the apparent rule in *Toussaint,* the plaintiff could meet the burden to prove a promise simply by introducing the policy manual, even without testimonial evidence of explicit promises made to the employee.[34]

In *Weiner v. McGraw-Hill, Inc.,*[35] the court had little difficulty finding that the promise element was satisfied. The court pointed to an oral assurance of employment security when the plaintiff was hired,[36] to a statement in the plaintiff's employment application form incorporating by reference handbook provisions promising no dismissal without cause,[37] and to a course of dealing in which the plaintiff was instructed not to dismiss his subordinates without cause,[38] any one of which should have sufficed as a promise that could be enforced if the other requisites of a contract could be proven.

While the interpretation of an unambiguous contract is a matter of law for the court, the plaintiff must adduce evidence from which a reasonable jury can find, as a matter of fact, that a contract existed.[39] The promise in the handbook must be reasonably specific to support an implied contract claim.[40] The type of evidence that will suffice to meet the plaintiff's burden on the promise element is illustrated by two cases reaching opposite results. In *Cook v. Heck's, Inc.,*[41] the supreme court of appeals reversed a directed verdict for the defendant entered at the conclusion of the plaintiff's evidence. The testimony showed that the defendant distributed a handbook to employees, and a copy of the handbook was admitted into evidence. The handbook contained a list of 41 different types of conduct for which dismissal could result.[42] There was additional testimony from a former executive of the defendant's that employees could be dismissed only for committing one of the 41 infractions, and that no one had been fired without cause during his long association with the defendant.[43] Testimony conflicted as to whether the handbook

---

[33] *Id.*

[34] *Id.* at 614, 292 N.W.2d at 892 (the court held that employer statements of policy, such as the Blue Cross Supervisory Manual and Guidelines, can give rise to contractual rights in employees without evidence that the parties mutually agreed that the policy statements would create contractual rights in the employee).

[35] 57 N.Y.2d 458, 443 N.E.2d 441, 457 N.Y.S.2d 193 (1982).

[36] *Id.* at 460, 443 N.E.2d at 442, 457 N.Y.S.2d at 194.

[37] *Id.*

[38] *Id. But see* O'Connor v. Eastman Kodak Co., 65 N.Y.2d 724, 481 N.E.2d 549, 492 N.Y.S.2d 9 (1985) (no promise of employment security established by popular perception or by performance appraisal system).

[39] *See* Cook v. Heck's, Inc., 342 S.E.2d 453, 457 (W. Va. 1986) (quoting rule).

[40] *See* cases cited at the beginning of this section.

[41] 342 S.E.2d 453 (W. Va. 1986).

[42] *Id.* at 455–56 (reviewing evidence).

[43] *Id.* at 456.

applied to the plaintiff.[44] The court concluded that the jury should decide whether the handbook applied, and that the jury could infer a promise to dismiss only for cause from the enumeration of reasons for dismissal described in the handbook itself as "complete."[45]

In *Cutter v. Lincoln National Life Insurance Co.*,[46] also a handbook case, the court applied South Dakota law to affirm a judgment n.o.v. for the employer. The handbook provided that there would be an immediate investigation of misconduct and that termination could result. The court distinguished this from a handbook explicitly promising dismissal only for just cause, or a handbook setting forth specific procedures to be followed before termination from which a just cause promise could be inferred.[47] It effectively drew the boundary of permissible factual inferences so as to require direct evidence of an explicit just cause promise, or direct evidence of a comprehensive procedural system involving terminations.

Some courts, notably the intermediate appellate court in Pennsylvania, are unwilling to permit the promise element to be satisfied by a statement in a handbook without some other evidence of employer intent to make a legally enforceable promise.[48]

Forman v. B.R.I. Corp.,[49] is an example of a case permitting the jury wide latitude to infer a promise from relatively general evidence. The plaintiff survived a motion for summary judgment in her wrongful dismissal breach of contract claim. She offered testimony from her own deposition that she had conversations during the interview process in which the defendant's agents told her that the job would be a good one in which to "stay and grow," and expressed concern that she would accept the job and "not stay." The court held that the evidence could permit a jury to find a promise of employment for the duration of the defendant's five year business plan sufficient to overcome the Pennsylvania presumption of an employment at will.[50]

The plaintiff's testimony, if credible, should be enough to establish a promise unless the employer contradicts the plaintiff's testimony by testimony from other witnesses. But if a written agreement exists, the parol evidence rule may bar evidence of prior or contemporaneous oral promises.[51] Also, the plaintiff may negate

---

[44] *Id.*

[45] *Id.* at 459.

[46] 794 F.2d 352 (8th Cir. 1986).

[47] *Id.* at 355–56.

[48] *See* Martin v. Capital Cities Media, Inc., 354 Pa. Super. 199, 511 A.2d 830, 838, 841 (1986) (unreasonable for employee to believe handbook is legally binding unless it says so, or other evidence indicates employer intention to be bound).

[49] 532 F. Supp. 49 (E.D. Pa. 1982).

[50] *Id.* at 51.

[51] *Compare* Ohanian v. Avis Rent a Car Sys., Inc., 779 F.2d 101, 109 (2d Cir. 1985) (letter containing disclaimer did not bar evidence of oral promise of employment security under parol evidence rule) *with* Whitehead v. Telesphere Int'l, Inc., 611 F. Supp. 961, 965 (N.D. Ill. 1985) (applying Texas parol evidence rule to exclude evidence of employment security promises inconsistent with letter of understanding).

the existence of a promise by admissions made in trial testimony or discovery.[52] This possibility shows defendants the need for effective cross-examination.

When a plaintiff wants to satisfy the promise element under the implied covenant of good faith and fair dealing, proof of any prerequisite to the applicability of the covenant in the particular jurisdiction,[53] such as length of service, must be offered.[54]

A growing number of cases involve efforts to use the implied-in-fact contract theory to support recovery for promises other than a promise of employment security. These cases are discusses in **Appendix F**. Some courts are reluctant to accept such efforts.[55]

§ 7.19 — Proving Promise from Conduct

Proving the promise element from conduct alone, without statements addressing employment security, is difficult. There is theoretical support for the proposition that promises can be implied from conduct, but few wrongful dismissal cases permit it.[56] It is a well accepted principle of contract law that a promise may be inferred from conduct. Professor Williston put it this way: "Any conduct from which a reasonable person in the offeree's position would be justified in inferring a promise in return for a requested act . . . amounts to an offer."[57] There need be no request for the performance of services; if it is known that the services are being rendered with the expectation of pay, the person benefited is liable.[58]

Professor Williston further believes that a question of fact arises regarding whether a reasonable person would understand that the services were being performed in exchange for fair compensation.[59] Professor Corbin agreed, pointing out that the

---

[52] *See* Deschler v. Brown & Williamson Tobacco Co., 797 F.2d 695, 696 (8th Cir. 1986) (plaintiff's admission that he understood the contract to be at-will at the time he signed it undermined credibility of plaintiff's claim); Rubin v. Rudolf Wolff Commodity Brokers, Inc., 636 F. Supp. 258, 261 (N.D. Ill. 1986) (plaintiff's deposition testimony showed no promise of employment security).

[53] **§ 4.11** explains the different prerequisites imposed by some courts.

[54] *See* Flanigan v. Prudential Fed. Sav. & Loan Ass'n, ___ Mont. ___, 720 P.2d 257, 262 (1986) (evidence of 28 years of service enough to make covenant applicable).

[55] *See* Banas v. Matthews Int'l Corp., 348 Pa. Super. 464, 502 A.2d 637 (1985) (reversing judgment for employee; dismissal for appropriation of employer property pursuant to implied promise that such appropriation was permissible distinguished from violation of implied promise of job security).

[56] *See* Overman v. Flour Constructors, Inc., 797 F.2d 217 (5th Cir. 1986) (testimony by plaintiff that he "understood" that he would be employed for duration of construction project failed to meet substantial evidence requirement to support jury verdict under Louisiana law).

[57] S. Williston, Williston on Contracts § 36 (3d ed. 1961), *citing* Horacek v. Smith, 33 Cal. 2d 186, 199 P.2d 929 (1948) (recovery of back salary).

[58] S. Williston, Williston on Contracts § 36 at n.13 (3d ed. 1961). Williston views this situation as one of implied-in-fact promise rather than treating it as quasi-contract.

[59] *Id.* § 36 at 14.

only difference between express and implied-in-fact contracts is in the mode of proof of the promise.[60] Professor Corbin would allocate the responsibility of judge and jury in the following fashion:

1. If the actions and conduct are undisputed, the plaintiff will ask the court to draw the inference that the parties acted because they felt they had a deal.
2. The defendant is not entitled to go to the jury unless he or she can offer a competing inference that attributes the actions of the parties to some other motivation.[61]

The authors of the *Restatement (Second) of Contracts* agreed with these general propositions:

> Conduct as Manifestation of Assent (1) The manifestation of assent may be made wholly or partly by written or spoken words or by other acts or by failure to act. (2) The conduct of a party is not effective as a manifestation of his assent unless he intends to engage in the conduct and knows or has reason to know that the other party may infer from his conduct that he assents. (3) The conduct of a party may manifest assent even though he does not in fact assent. In such cases a resulting contract may be voidable because of fraud, duress, mistake, or other invalidating cause.[62]

An additional principle of general contract law reinforces these arguments: the principle that a course of dealing between the parties gives context to their conduct "which is fairly to be regarded as establishing a common basis of understanding for interpreting their expressions and other conduct."[63] This principle was used by the Supreme Court of the United States to imply a promise of employment security in *Perry v. Sindermann*.[64] Some private employer cases have accepted proof consistent with the same principles.

There are a number of cases adopting these principles in the employment context to imply a promise to continue employment under the same terms as those provided for in a completed express contract,[65] to pay for services rendered,[66] to dismiss

---

[60] A. Corbin, Corbin on Contracts § 18 at 40-41 (1952).

[61] *Id.* § 18 at 17 (Kaufman Supp. 1982).

[62] Restatement (Second) of Contracts § 19 (1979). Comment a makes it clear that the principle contained in § 19 applies to implication of a promise by conduct, as well as implication of the acceptance of a promise.

[63] *Id.* § 223. Section 223 appears in Chapter 9, "The Scope of Contractual Obligations," Topic 4, "Scope as Affected by Usage." The introductory note to ch. 9 says that the parties' intention arises from context, and usages are an important part of the context.

[64] 408 U.S. 593 (1972). This case is discussed in greater detail in **§ 6.10**.

[65] *See* Cinefot Int'l Corp. v. Hudson Photographic Indus., 13 N.Y.2d 249, 196 N.E.2d 246 N.Y.S.2d 345, 6 A.L.R.3d 1347 (1963) (citing A. Corbin, Corbin on Contracts § 18 (1952)); Harper v. Cedar Rapids Tel. Co., 244 N.W.2d 782, 789 (Iowa 1976) (conduct extending employment contract; discussion of burdens of proof and presumptions).

[66] *See* Annotation, 78 A.L.R.2d 318 (1961).

during probation only for the reasons justifying the probation,[67] or to continue certain monetary benefits according to past practice.[68]

Nonverbal conduct alone may be sufficient to establish a promise of employment security.[69] But vague expressions of hope that the employment relationship will be satisfactory are not sufficient to establish the promise element.[70] Nor can the plaintiff avoid the need to prove a promise by buttressing his consideration proof.[71] Some authority exists for the proposition that the fixing of salary on an annual basis, supported by other evidence, permits a promise to be inferred that the employment was to last for that term.[72]

The strongest authority for permitting a promise of employment security to be inferred from conduct is *Wayne v. Rollins International, Inc.*,[73] in which the appeals court said:

> Evidence was presented that [the plaintiff] worked for [the employer] for six years during which he had been consistently assured that his work was satisfactory and that no reason was provided to [the plaintiff] for his termination. This evidence was sufficient to raise the inference that [the plaintiff] was terminated in violation of an implied-in-fact promise that he would not be discharged without good cause.[74]

The nature of the case suggests, however, that the court may have been confusing the implied-in-fact and implied covenant theories of recovery.

§ 7.20 —Proving Consideration

As explained in **Chapter 4**, after the plaintiff suing for breach of contract has proved that a promise of employment security was made,[75] the plaintiff must prove

---

[67] *See* Brewster v. Martin Marietta Aluminum Sales, Inc., 145 Mich. App. 641, 378 N.W.2d 558, 565 (1985) (probation for poor work performance was commitment to dismiss only for good cause).

[68] *See* Annotation, 66 A.L.R.3d 1075 (1975).

[69] *See* Farrell v. Automobile Club, ___ Mich. App. ___, ___ N.W.2d ___, No. 82916 (Oct. 6, 1986) (evidence of practices, assurances sufficient to present jury question on obligation not to dismiss for failing to meet new quota); Allegri v. Providence-St. Margaret Health Center, 9 Kan. App. 2d 659, 684 P.2d 1031, 1036 (1984) (nonverbal course of conduct can support inference of promise of employment security; summary judgment for employer reversed).

[70] *See* Hillsman v. Sutter Community Hosps., 153 Cal. App. 3d 743, 750, 200 Cal. Rptr. 605, 609 (1984) ("We look forward to a long, pleasant, and mutually satisfactory relationship . . . " insufficient to show promise of employment security).

[71] *Id.* at 752–53, 200 Cal. Rptr. at 611 (showing "independent consideration" does not eliminate the need to prove an express or implied promise).

[72] *See* Stearns v. Ohio Sav. Ass'n, 15 Ohio App. 3d 18, 19–20, 472 N.E.2d 372, 374 (1984) (annual salary combined with active recruitment of employee from another job sufficient evidence of promise of employment term to withstand motion for summary judgment).

[73] 169 Cal. App. 3d 1, 215 Cal. Rptr. 59 (1985).

[74] 169 Cal. App. 3d at 18, 215 Cal. Rptr. at 69 (1985).

[75] See §§ **4.6–4.11**. *See* Rompf v. John Q. Hammons Hotels, Inc., 685 P.2d 25, 28–29 (Wyo. 1984) (detrimental reliance shown by quitting other job unavailing when no promise of employment

that the entire contract of employment, including the promise of tenure, is supported by consideration.[76] Otherwise, the promise is not legally enforceable. A common way of establishing consideration for promises of employment security is to show under various theories,[77] that the plaintiff-employee detrimentally relied on the defendant-employer's promise.[78] This section considers the various ways in which such reliance can be demonstrated. It does not consider the infrequent and conceptually trivial case in which a plaintiff can prove money consideration or a promise to remain in the defendant's employ.[79]

Proving detrimental reliance can be subdivided into proving three subordinate factual predicates:

1. The plaintiff knew of the employer's promise
2. The plaintiff engaged in conduct that was detrimental to the plaintiff or beneficial to the employer
3. The conduct was motivated by knowledge of the employer's promise.[80]

Usually, the plaintiff's testimony will establish these elements, though credibility concerns can make supporting evidence desirable.

Application of the doctrine contained in *Woolley v. Hoffman-LaRoche, Inc.*[81] materially simplifies the plaintiff's proof problem, because *Woolley* says that the plaintiff need not show detrimental reliance beyond merely continuing employment. A significant number of other cases say that the consideration requirement can be met by merely continuing employment.[82] The majority rule, however, requires proof on all three elements: knowledge, detriment, and nexus.

Knowledge of the employer's promise is a theoretical prerequisite to detrimental reliance, though *Woolley v. Hoffman LaRoche, Inc.*[83] suggests that the knowledge

---

security); *see* Darlington v. General Elec., 350 Pa. Super. 183, 203–04, 504 A.2d 306, 316 (1986) (quoting author of this treatise on order of proof in implied contract case).

[76] See §§ **4.12–4.18**.

[77] See §§ **4.12–4.18**.

[78] See §§ **4.12–4.18**.

[79] See § **4.13** regarding mutuality of obligation. *But see* Ferraro v. Koelsch, 119 Wis. 2d 407, 350 N.W.2d 735 (Ct. App. 1984), *aff'd by different rationale*, 124 Wis. 2d 154, 368 N.W.2d 666 (1985) (promise to comply with company rules adequate consideration for employer's promise not to dismiss).

[80] *But see* Larose v. Agway, Inc., ___ Vt. ___, 508 A.2d 1364 (1986) (affirming summary judgment for employer; no evidence or allegation of employee knowledge or change in position). See generally § **4.18**.

[81] 99 N.J. 284, 491 A.2d 1257 (1985).

[82] *See* Woolley v. Hoffman LaRoche, 99 N.J. 284, 491 A.2d 1257 (1985), *modified*, 101 N.J. 10, 499 A.2d 515 (1985); Brookshaw v. South St. Paul Feed, Inc., 381 N.W.2d 33, 36 (Minn. Ct. App. 1986) (employee accepts an offer contained in a handbook by remaining on the job); Thompson v. American Motor Inns, 623 F. Supp. 409 (W.D. Va. 1985) (consideration for handbook promises supplied by continued work after reading handbook; citing *Woolley* approvingly). Other authority for this approach is found in § **4.16**.

[83] 99 N.J. 284, 491 A.2d 1257 (1985).

§ 7.20   PROVING CONSIDERATION   423

requirement can be dispensed with.[84] Some language in *Woolley* notwithstanding, both the consideration and promissory estoppel theories require proof that the plaintiff knew of the promise when the alleged detrimental reliance occurred. Otherwise, the conduct hardly can be said to be in reliance on the promise.[85]

In *Weiner v. McGraw-Hill, Inc.*[86] the court found that the plaintiff's affidavit testimony would support a factual conclusion that detrimental reliance occurred in two respects. First, the plaintiff quit his previous job and lost accrued benefits in reliance on McGraw-Hill's promise. Second, the plaintiff rejected other offers of employment after he was at McGraw-Hill.[87]

In *Toussaint v. Blue Cross & Blue Shield*,[88] there is less explicit discussion of consideration than of the question whether the employer promised employment security. Based on the facts and the court's general discussion, however, it seems safe to conclude that the court found the consideration element satisfied by Toussaint's coming to work at Blue Cross in reliance on the assurances of employment security made to him before he took the job.[89]

In *Pine River State Bank v. Mettille*,[90] the court had little difficulty in concluding that "by continuing to stay on the job, although free to leave, the employee supplied the necessary consideration . . . ."[91]

Proof of the elements of promissory estoppel[92] is not greatly different from proving traditional detrimental reliance, except that the factfinder need not find that inducing the employee detriment was the purpose of the employer promise, only that it was reasonable for the employer to expect employee reliance.

As **Chapter 4** explains, reliance can satisfy, or substitute for, the consideration requirement in two different ways. First, if the reliance is bargained for, it meets

---

[84] *Compare* Pine River State Bank v. Mettille, 333 N.W.2d 622, 626 n.4 (Minn. 1983) (dissemination of the handbook to the plaintiff crucial factor in permitting an offer to be inferred, distinguishing Minnesota's earlier case of Cederstrand v. Lutheran Bhd., 263 Minn. 520, 117 N.W.2d 213 (1962) in which personnel manual not distributed to employees not an offer to employees) *with* Toussaint v. Blue Cross & Blue Shield, 408 Mich. 579, 292 N.W.2d 880 (1980) (merely publishing handbook may establish enforceable contract, though employee has no knowledge of specific provisions). See § **4.18**.

[85] *See* Sabetay v. Sterling Drug, Inc., 114 A.D.2d 6, 497 N.Y.S.2d 655, 657 (1986) (lack of knowledge of handbook precludes implied contract claim because both *inducement* and reliance must be shown), *appeal granted*, 68 N.Y.2d 605, 497 N.E.2d 708, ___ N.Y.S.2d ___ (1986).

[86] 57 N.Y.2d 458, 443 N.E.2d 441, 457 N.Y.S.2d 193 (1982).

[87] *Id.* at 461, 443 N.E.2d at 442-43, 457 N.Y.S.2d at 194-95. *But see* Salanger v. U.S. Air, 611 F. Supp. 427, 431 (N.D.N.Y. 1985) (judgment for defendant under Weiner v. McGraw-Hill, Inc. because plaintiff not induced to leave other employment by assurances of job security).

[88] 408 Mich. 579, 292 N.W.2d 880 (1980).

[89] This seems a fair reading of the court's analysis even though it says reliance need not be shown. *See id.* at 613 n.25, 292 N.W.2d at 892 n.25.

[90] 333 N.W.2d 622 (Minn. 1983).

[91] *Id.* at 627. *But see* Ferguson v. Freedom Forge Corp., 604 F. Supp. 1157, 1161 (W.D. Pa. 1985) (abstaining from looking for another job not sufficient detrimental reliance to support Pennsylvania implied contract claim).

[92] See § **4.17**.

traditional consideration requirements.[93] Second, if it is not bargained for, but nevertheless is reasonable, it satisfies the consideration requirement under the promissory estoppel concept of § 90 of the *Restatement (Second) of Contracts*.[94] Put differently, detrimental reliance satisfies the traditional bargain requirement only if the prospect of reliance induces the promise, in addition to the promise inducing the reliance.

In *Litman v. Massachusetts Mutual Life Insurance Co.*,[95] the court affirmed a jury verdict for the plaintiff on a promissory estoppel theory, holding that whether reliance on an oral promise was reasonable, and whether "injustice could only be avoided by the imposition of appropriate damages," were questions for the jury on sharply conflicting testimony. It also found that the plaintiff's investment of substantial time, energy, and money, and borrowing money in reliance on the defendant's promise of employment security, permitted the jury to find reliance under the formula contained in § 90 of the *Restatement (Second) of Contracts*.[96]

The plaintiff's safest course is to persuade the factfinder to draw the inference that the employer promised employment security for the purpose of inducing employees to rely on the promise by accepting or continuing employment.[97] This would prove the bargained for aspect of the reliance. As a fallback position, plaintiff should understand that this inference is not necessary to a promissory estoppel theory, which is satisfied merely by proof of reasonable reliance by the plaintiff on the defendant's promise, without regard to a showing of the defendant's purpose in making the promise. Under a promissory estoppel theory, however, the plaintiff must show that his reliance was reasonable.[98] Reliance that is inconsistent with practice in a particular workplace does not satisfy the promissory estoppel requirements because it is unreasonable.[99]

§ 7.21 — Jury Instructions on Contract Formation

As §§ **4.2** and **4.16** explain, the promise and consideration elements in a breach of contract case are related. Both elements have to do with contract formation.

---

[93] Reliance in these cases is detriment sufficient to satisfy the consideration requirement, if bargained for. See § **4.14**.

[94] See § **4.17**.

[95] 739 F.2d 1549, 1559 (11th Cir. 1984).

[96] *Id.*

[97] When a promise of tenure is made after the plaintiff already is employed, a finding of reliance is likely to be artificial, unless there is evidence that the promise was made in response to some threat by the plaintiff to quit. A more natural inference is that the plaintiff remained with the job because of simple inertia, rather than in reliance on the new promise of employment security. Stancil v. Mergenthaler Linotype Co., 589 F. Supp. 78, 84 (D. Haw. 1984) (no showing of justifiable detrimental reliance through sale of car, furniture at loss).

[98] *See* Finley v. Aetna Life & Casualty Co., 5 Conn. App. 394, 499 A.2d 64, 73 (1985) (promissory estoppel claim should have been submitted to jury on evidence of 24 years of employment, and refusal of other job offers).

[99] *See* Brower v. Holmes Transp., Inc., 140 Vt. 114, 118, 435 A.2d 952, 954 (1981) (any reliance would have been unreasonable).

§ 7.21 JURY INSTRUCTIONS

The consideration requirement is imposed as a validation device to permit the court to conclude that a promise should be taken seriously in the sense that the law should enforce it. Accordingly, appropriate jury instructions may combine the promise and consideration elements, asking the jury to decide whether the employer's promise is enforceable.[1] *Sherman v. Rutland Hospital, Inc.*[2] approved the following jury instruction on a policy manual:

> An employment contract at will may be terminated by either party with or without cause at any time unless the parties have contracted that certain procedures must take place before discharge. . . . The first question for you to decide is whether the disciplinary and dismissal procedures in the Personnel Policy Manual form a binding and enforceable part of Mr. Sherman's employment contract.

Despite the interrelatedness of the promise and consideration elements, it is preferable for jury instructions to separate the factual questions relating to the promise element from the factual questions involved in the consideration element. The following instruction embodies that separation:

> The first thing you have to decide is whether the employer promised job security. You may find such a promise only if you believe from the evidence that the employer said that it would dismiss employees only for cause [or only for certain reasons] [or only after following certain procedures] for the purpose of inducing employees to continue their employment. You have to decide two things in the plaintiff's favor in order to decide that a promise of employment security was made. First, you have to decide that the employer actually promised job security. Second, you must find that the employer's motivation in making this promise was to cause employees to continue their employment.[3]

An instruction more favorable to the plaintiff on the promise element would borrow from the suggestion in *Woolley* and *Toussaint* that mere publication of a promise is sufficient, without regard to employee knowledge:

> You may find that a promise of employment security was made only if you find that the employer communicated to the employee directly or if you find that the employer published to the work force in general, a statement indicating that employees would be dismissed only for cause, only for certain reasons, or only after following certain procedures. You need not find the plaintiff knew about this promise.[4]

---

[1] *See* M. Dichter, A. Gross, D. Morikawa, & S. Sauntry, Employee Dismissal Forms and Procedures §§ 8.25–8.33 (1986) (general instructions on contract formation, rebuttal of employment-at-will presumption).

[2] 146 Vt. 204, 500 A.2d 230, 232 (1985).

[3] *See also* M. Dichter, A. Gross, D. Morikawa, & S. Sauntry, Employee Dismissal Forms and Procedures §§ 8.35–8.46 (1986) (instructions relating to various ways in which promise can be proven).

[4] *See generally* Finley v. Aetna Life & Casualty Co., 5 Conn. App. 394, 499 A.2d 64, 72 n.8 (1985) (quoting plaintiff's requested handbook instruction and characterizing it as close to correct, but erroneous to the extent it suggested that the handbook was enforceable as a matter of law); Murphy v. Publicker Indus., Inc., ___ Pa. Super. ___, 516 A.2d 47, 51 (1986) (jury instruction failed to emphasize consideration requirement).

Instructions on the consideration element should separate the knowledge, detrimental reliance, and nexus components of the detrimental reliance idea.

The following instruction would be appropriate for bargained-for consideration or for promissory estoppel. A bargained-for consideration theory would need an additional instruction discussed later in this section:

> In addition to deciding whether the employer promised employment security, you must also decide whether the employee relied on this promise to the employee's detriment. This is called *detrimental reliance.* You may find detrimental reliance only if you decide from all the evidence that three things happened.
>
> First, you may find detrimental reliance only if you find that the employee knew about the employer's promise of employment security.[5]
>
> Second, in addition to deciding whether the employee knew about the promise, you may find detrimental reliance only if you find in addition that the employee acted in a way that benefitted the employer or that the employee gave up something of benefit to the employee. For example, you may find from the evidence that the employee passed up another job offer in order to remain with the employer making the promise. Or, you may find that the employee quit another job to come to work for the employer making the promise. Alternatively, you may find detrimental reliance from the simple fact that the employee continued employment with the employer making the promise.[6]
>
> Third, you may not find for the employee on the detrimental reliance question unless you also find based on all the evidence that the *reason* the employee gave up something or conferred some benefit on the employer was the employer's promise. In other words, you may find detrimental reliance only if you find that the employee gave up something or conferred some benefit on the employer primarily *because of* the employer's promise of employment security.

If promissory estoppel is the theory relied upon, the following instruction should also be given:

> You may not find that detrimental reliance existed unless you also find that the employee's reliance on the employer's promise of employment security was reasonable considering all the circumstances.

If the theory is bargained-for detrimental reliance, the following instruction should be given in conjunction with the other promise instructions:

> You may find that a legally enforceable promise was made only if you find that the employer made the promise (the statements to the employee or the things said in the handbook) for the purpose of causing the type of detrimental reliance you found occurred in the case. If the type of detrimental reliance by the employee was unanticipated or not particularly desired by the employer, you may not find that an enforceable promise was made.

---

[5] This sentence would be deleted from the instruction if the *Woolley/Toussaint* approach is followed. See § **4.18**.

[6] Whether this sentence is included depends on whether the jurisdiction permits mere continuation of employment to satisfy the consideration element. See § **4.16**.

An instruction more favorable to the defendant on the bargained-for aspect of detrimental reliance is suggested by the opinion of the Iowa Supreme Court in *Wolfe v. Graether*:[7]

> Even if you find additional consideration in the form of something of value given up by the plaintiff, you may not find an enforceable promise unless you also find that it was the intention of both the employer and the employee, or, unless this was the employee's intention and the employer should reasonably have known that it was.

§ 7.22 —Proving a Breach: Introduction

Liability for breach of contract is imposed without regard to fault.[8] Thus, motive, in the sense of subjective mental state, is irrelevant. When an employee who has been promised employment security is dismissed, however, the objective reason for the dismissal is likely to be relevant to a determination of whether there was a breach of the employment agreement. The employer's reason or motive is of concern in two slightly different respects: First, the employee may allege that the dismissal was motivated by a reason that violates a covenant, implied in law, of good faith and fair dealing.[9] Second, the employee may allege that the contract of employment, express or implied in fact, permitted dismissal only for certain reasons, and the employer fired him for some other reason.[10]

In either event, deciding the employer's reason for the dismissal is essential to deciding the case. Proof of a reason violating the covenant of good faith and fair dealing is discussed in § 7.23. Proof of the absence of cause is discussed in §§ 7.24–7.28.

§ 7.23 —Proving a Breach: Bad Faith or Unfairness

The plaintiff can recover on an implied covenant theory only by showing that the employer breached the covenant. It is not enough to show an absence of good cause; the plaintiff must prove bad faith or unfairness. The burden of persuasion on bad faith or unfairness rests with the employee.[11]

---

[7] 389 N.W.2d 643, 657 (Iowa 1986) (reversing judgment for plaintiff on jury verdict because of failure to instruct as text suggests); Olin v. Prudential Ins. Co., 781 F.2d 1, 3 (1st Cir. 1986) (quoting jury instructions and interrogatories in implied contract case); Benoir v. Ethan Allen, Inc., ___ Vt. ___, 514 A.2d 716 (1986) (approving instruction on contract formation, but not quoting it).

[8] Restatement (Second) of Contracts § 235 (1981) (nonperformance need not be willful or even negligent to be a breach).

[9] See § 4.23.

[10] See §§ 4.21–4.22, 4.24.

[11] *See* Kravetz v. Merchants Distrib., Inc., 387 Mass. 457, 462, 440 N.E.2d 1278, 1281 (1982) (burden of proving bad faith or unfair dealing in breach of an implied covenant rests with the plaintiff employee).

In *Fortune v. National Cash Register Co.*,[12] an implied covenant of good faith case, the court approved submitting the question of motive to the jury in simple terms: "Did the Defendant act in bad faith when it decided to terminate the plaintiff's contract . . . ?"[13] It was willing to permit the jury to infer bad faith—an intent to deprive the plaintiff of legitimately earned commissions—from the termination of the plaintiff one day after a large order was obtained on which commissions would have been due.[14] Similarly, in *Monge v. Beebe Rubber Co.*,[15] the court was willing to give the jury a fairly free hand in finding bad faith or malice from the circumstances.[16] The dissent disagreed that such an inference rationally could be drawn from the evidence.[17] In *Khanna v. Microdata Corp.*,[18] the court affirmed a jury verdict for the plaintiff, holding that a breach of the covenant was established by proof that the plaintiff was fired for suing his employer.[19]

One case suggests that the question of whether the implied covenant of good faith and fair dealing was breached can merge into the question of whether handbook procedures were followed. In *Gates v. Life of Montana Insurance Co.*,[20] the court held that an employee handbook, which promised that dismissal for certain causes would not occur without a warning, did not create a contractual obligation binding on the employer. It held, however, that discharge of the plaintiff in violation of the handbook presented a "genuine issue of material fact which precludes a summary judgment, i.e., whether the respondent failed to afford appellant the process required [by the handbook] and if so, whether the respondent

---

[12] 373 Mass. 96, 364 N.E.2d 1251 (1977).

[13] *Id.* at 100, 364 N.E.2d at 1255.

[14] *Id.* at 103, 364 N.E.2d at 1256-57 (the fact that the dismissal was after a portion of the bonus vested still creates a question for the jury on the defendant's motive in terminating the employment). *Compare* Tenedios v. Wm. Filene's Sons Co., 20 Mass. App. Ct. 252, 479 N.E.2d 723, 726 (1985) (arbitrary firing for suspicion of theft from employer does not breach covenant under *Fortune* doctrine) *with* DeRose v. Putnam Management Co., 398 Mass. 205, 496 N.E.2d 428, 431 (1986) (breach of implied covenant can be established by showing public policy violation; coercion to testify in a particular way).

[15] 114 N.H. 130, 316 A.2d 549 (1974).

[16] *Id.* at 133-34, 316 A.2d at 552 (the court said that the foreman's overtures and capricious firing, the seeming manipulation of job assignments, and the apparent connivance of the personnel manager in this course of events all supported the jury's conclusion that the dismissal was maliciously motivated). *See also* Gray v. Superior Court, 181 Cal. App. 3d 813, 226 Cal. Rptr. 570 (1986) (employee offered insufficient evidence to show violation of public policy evidenced in state discrimination statute by showing the employee was not insubordinate and handbook procedures were not followed, but stated a claim for breach of implied covenant because these claims are based on questions of fact, not law; reversing grant of demurrer).

[17] *Id.* at 134-35, 316 A.2d at 552 (the dissent believed that a reasonable person could not find for the plaintiff on the evidence of the case, that the substance of the plaintiff's claim is that she was dismissed because she did not accept the invitation of her foreman to go out with him, and that it is not reasonable to find that this single refusal was the reason for the termination of plaintiff's employment).

[18] 170 Cal. App. 3d 250, 262, 215 Cal. Rptr. 860, 869 (1985).

[19] *Compare* Foley v. Interactive Data Corp., 174 Cal. App. 3d 282, 219 Cal. Rptr. 866 (1985) (disagreement with analysis used in Khanna v. Microdata Corp.).

[20] 196 Mont. 178, 638 P.2d 1063 (1982).

§ 7.23 BREACH: BAD FAITH 429

thereby breached the covenant of good faith and fair dealing."[21] Similarly, in *Rulon-Miller v. I.B.M.*,[22] the court affirmed a $300,000 verdict for an employee dismissed for dating an employee of a competing firm. The court held that the dismissal violated the implied covenant of good faith and fair dealing because it contravened the employer's policy of not interfering in employees' private, off-the-job conduct. Other courts, however, decline to equate a violation of employer policies with a breach of the covenant of good faith.[23]

There is some authority for the proposition that the jury can infer bad faith from an unexplained dismissal. This approach has the effect of transforming the implied covenant into a requirement that an employer demonstrate good cause for dismissal, a proposition rejected by most courts. In *Wadeson v. American Family Mutual Insurance Co.*,[24] the court approved a jury instruction on good faith, rejecting the unsuccessful plaintiff's argument that the covenant requires the employer to discharge only for good cause.[25] Similarly, in *Magnan v. Anaconda Industries, Inc.*,[26] the Supreme Court of Connecticut held that an employee, hired under a contract of indefinite duration, cannot maintain a cause of action in contract for breach of an implied covenant of good faith and fair dealing based wholly upon a discharge without just cause.[27] The court suggested that a cause of action for breach of the implied covenant is identical to a public policy tort cause of action.[28]

In *Flanigan v. Prudential Federal Savings & Loan Ass'n*,[29] the Montana Supreme Court distinguished between dismissal without good cause, which it rejected as a standard for breach of the implied covenant, and arbitrary dismissal, which it found proven from conflicting employer testimony that the employee was dismissed for poor performance and that the employee was dismissed as part of a layoff without concern for performance.[30]

Accordingly, to prove a breach, the plaintiff needs to offer more than proof of dismissal and legal argument on the implied covenant doctrine. The plaintiff

---

[21] *Id.* at 184–85, 638 P.2d at 1066–67.

[22] 162 Cal. App. 3d 241, 208 Cal. Rptr. 524 (1984).

[23] *Compare* Hall v. Farmers Ins. Exch., 713 P.2d 1027 (Okla. 1986) (finding breach of covenant of good faith in written insurance agency contract by termination of agent to deprive agent of earned commissions; citing *Fortune* and *Monge*) and DeHorney v. Bank of Am., 777 F.2d 440, 451 (9th Cir. 1985) (withdrawn) (deviations from internal regulations sufficient to support jury question on implied covenant theory, suggesting jury should decide whether just cause for dismissal existed) *with* Gianaculas v. T.W.A., Inc., 761 F.2d 1391, 1394 (9th Cir. 1985) (affirming summary judgment for employer under California law).

[24] 343 N.W.2d 367 (N.D. 1984).

[25] *Id.* at 370.

[26] 193 Conn. 558, 479 A.2d 781 (1984).

[27] *Id.* at ___, 479 A.2d at 782.

[28] *Id.* at ___ n.25, 479 A.2d at 791 n.25. *But see* Crenshaw v. Bozeman Deaconess Hosp., ___ Mont. ___, 693 P.2d 487 (1984) (affirming jury verdict of $125,000 compensatory and $25,000 punitive damages for respiratory therapist discharged during probationary period; plaintiff need not show violation of public policy to prove breach of covenant of good faith and fair dealing).

[29] ___ Mont. ___, 720 P.2d 257 (1986).

[30] *Id.* at ___, 720 P.2d at 260.

must have evidence that the dismissal was effected in an extreme manner, or for the purpose of depriving the employee of earned commissions, or in violation of the usual employer procedures, or for a nonwork-related reason, such as off-duty conduct.

§ 7.24 —Proving a Breach: Cause for Termination in General

In most wrongful dismissal cases litigated on a breach of contract theory, motive in the subjective sense of good or bad faith is not at issue. Rather, the issue is the objective one of whether the employer kept its promise. It is important to know what the promise was: whether the employer has promised to dismiss only for cause as opposed to promising only that certain procedures will be followed. For example, in *Pine River State Bank v. Mettille*,[31] the court was careful to distinguish *Toussaint v. Blue Cross & Blue Shield*.[32] *Toussaint* involved a promise to dismiss only for cause. *Mettille* involved a promise to dismiss only after the exhaustion of certain procedures, without regard to cause.[33] The court had little difficulty in concluding as a matter of law that a breach occurred because the employer made no attempt to follow the procedures before dismissing the plaintiff.[34] In *Grubb v. W.A. Foote Memorial Hospital, Inc.*,[35] the Sixth Circuit suggested that the rationale of *Toussaint* would not extend naturally to a layoff. Rather, the court observed, *Toussaint* involved removal of an employee from a position that continued to exist, while a layoff involves elimination of the position itself.[36]

As § 4.24 explains, proof of a breach usually involves two issues: proof of what the employee actually did and proof of what constitutes good cause for dismissal. The first is almost entirely factual. The second is a mixed fact and law question.

§ 7.25 —Proving a Breach: Proving What the Employee Did

Frequently, the employer and the employee will disagree as to the performance or conduct of the employee. This is a separate question from whether the

---

[31] 333 N.W.2d 622 (Minn. 1983).

[32] 408 Mich. 579, 292 N.W.2d 880 (1980).

[33] Pine River State Bank v. Mettille, 333 N.W.2d at 626. *See also* Salanger v. U.S. Air, 611 F. Supp. 427, 431 (N.D.N.Y. 1985) (no breach of promises in personnel policies because promised grievance procedures made available).

[34] Pine River State Bank v. Mettille, 333 N.W.2d at 631. *See also* Damrow v. Thumb Coop. Terminal, Inc., 126 Mich. App. 354, 337 N.W.2d 338 (1983) (breach of procedural promise in handbook shown; judgment for employer reversed).

[35] 741 F.2d 1486, 1500 (6th Cir. 1984).

[36] *See also* Rompf v. John Q. Hammons Hotels, Inc., 685 P.2d 25, 29 (Wyo. 1984) (no breach of handbook procedures by discharge for economic reasons).

performance or conduct amounted to good cause for dismissal. *Toussaint v. Blue Cross & Blue Shield*[37] says that when the employer claims that the employee was dismissed for specific misconduct,[38] e.g., intoxication, dishonesty, or insubordination, and the employee claims that he did not commit the alleged misconduct, the question is one of fact for the jury: Did the employee do what the employer said he did?[39] Similarly, when the employer alleges that the employee was dismissed for one reason, e.g., excessive tardiness, and the employee presents evidence that the dismissal was for another reason, e.g., making too much money in commissions, the question is one of fact for the jury.[40] Under this approach, the jury is permitted to determine the employer's true reason for dismissal.[41] *Toussaint* has been interpreted as placing the burden of proof on the employer to show cause once the plaintiff has met the other requirements of the implied-in-fact contract.[42]

Toussaint is not the only view of the jury's role. The Oregon Supreme Court, for example, disagrees with the Michigan Supreme Court. Oregon would permit the employer unilaterally to determine the facts at issue in the question of whether cause existed for dismissal. The jury would decide only whether the employer made its decision in good faith.[43]

---

[37] 408 Mich. 579, 292 N.W.2d 880 (1980).

[38] *Id.* at 621, 292 N.W.2d at 896 (citing Martin v. Southern R.R., 240 S.C. 460, 126 S.E.2d 365 (1962), in which the Supreme Court of South Carolina held that although the defendant railroad had complied with the collective bargaining agreement by conducting an investigation to determine whether the discharged employee had violated a rule against use of intoxicants, the employee was entitled to have a jury pass on the issue of whether he in fact violated the rule, and if he had not, he was entitled to recover for wrongful discharge). The *Toussaint* court did not, however, discuss the burden of proof.

[39] Toussaint v. Blue Cross & Blue Shield, 408 Mich. at 621, 292 N.W.2d at 896.

[40] *Id.* at 622, 292 N.W.2d at 896 (citing Ward v. Consolidated Food Corp., 480 S.W.2d 483) (Tex. Ct. App. 1972), in which the court held that when the employer claimed that the employee was discharged for failure to correct sanitation deficiencies and the employee claimed that he was discharged to prevent his exercise of a stock option and so that the new president could bring in his own men, the question of cause was for the jury). *Accord,* Smith v. Kerrville Bus Co., 709 F.2d 914, 916 (5th Cir. 1983) (breach of collective bargaining agreement not providing for arbitration).

[41] *Compare* Danzer v. Professional Insurors, Inc., 101 N.M. 178, 182, 679 P.2d 1276, 1281 (1984) (trial court decides cause for dismissal and whether just cause existed; written contract) *with* Adams v. Frontier Airlines Fed. Credit Union, 691 P.2d 352, 354 (Colo. Ct. App. 1984) (jury, not employer, decides whether employee was incompetent).

[42] *See* Rasch v. City of East Jordan, 141 Mich. App. 336, 367 N.W.2d 856 (1985) (once plaintiff proves implied contract to dismiss only for just cause, defendant has burden of proving just cause; reversing trial court).

[43] *See* Simpson v. Western Graphics Corp., 53 Or. App. 205, 211, 631 P.2d 805, 808 (1981), *aff'd,* 293 Or. 96, 643 P.2d 1276 (1982) (when reviewing a dismissal decision of a private employer in a contract case, the factfinder need only find that there was substantial evidence to support the employer's decision and that the employer believed that evidence and acted in good faith in dismissing the worker and need not also determine that what the employer believed was true).

The Oregon Supreme Court has the better view:[44] The employer's fact decision should be scrutinized to determine whether it was made in good faith, rather than permitting its factual decision to be second-guessed in a fullblown trial.

§ 7.26 —Proving a Breach: Who Decides What Is Good Cause

Once the true facts regarding the employee's conduct or performance have been determined, the question then arises: What is good cause for dismissal, and who should decide? Two leading cases allocate responsibility for deciding these fact questions somewhat differently.

One possibility is to let the jury decide what constitutes good cause.[45] But if the jury is permitted to decide whether there is good cause for the discharge, there is the danger that it will substitute its decision for the employer's.[46] The *Toussaint* court apparently was willing to run this risk, noting that the employer could provide for binding arbitration on the issues of cause and damages in its policy statement.[47] In *Fleming v. Kids and Kin Head Start*,[48] the court held that an employer does not have unilateral right to decide what just cause means in the absence of specific contract language giving that right. Presumptively, the court decides.

Following the *Toussaint* approach in all implied-in-fact contract cases would expand the role of the jury beyond deciding whether the contract was breached. The right to be dismissed only for cause or only after exhaustion of certain procedures is established in contract cases by voluntary employer conduct or statements. Absent evidence that the employer also promised third party determination of the facts (as in collectively bargained arbitration clauses), a jury should not be allowed to decide the facts preceding the dismissal de novo. To permit de novo review adds to the employer's promise and modifies the contract. The only proper question for the jury is whether there was a breach; i.e., whether the employer lived up to its promise.

Deciding the breach question means deciding if the employer faithfully has followed any pretermination procedures it promised to follow, or if the employer has decided in good faith what the facts are and defined cause reasonably. Of course,

---

[44] *Compare* Simpson v. Western Graphics Corp., 53 Or. App. 205, 631 P.2d 805 (1981), *aff'd*, 293 Or. 96, 643 P.2d 1276 (1982) (deference to employer decision) *with* Toussaint v. Blue Cross & Blue Shield, 408 Mich. 597, 292 N.W.2d 880 (1980) (jury decides).

[45] Toussaint v. Blue Cross & Blue Shield, 408 Mich. 597, 622, 292 N.W.2d 880, 896 (1980). *See also* M. Dichter, A. Gross, D. Morikawa & S. Sauntry, Employee Dismissal Forms and Procedures §§ 8.54, 8.58 (1986) (instructions permitting the jury to decide what constitutes good cause, depending on its view of what employer interests are legitimate).

[46] Toussaint v. Blue Cross & Blue Shield, 408 Mich. at 622, 292 N.W.2d at 896.

[47] *Id.* at 624, 292 N.W.2d at 897. The Fifth Circuit, applying federal labor law, agreed that the factfinder should weigh evidence of misconduct against mitigating factors. Smith v. Kerrville Bus. Co., 709 F.2d 914, 920 n.4 (5th Cir. 1983).

[48] 71 Or. App. 718, 723, 693 P.2d 1363, 1366 (1985).

there may also be cases in which employer conduct and employee expectations may be relevant to the question of how the promise to dismiss only for cause should be interpreted, and this may present a jury question over the promise element of the case, as distinguished from the breach element. In other words, the jury may infer that the employer promised to define good cause in some way. There also may be cases in which the employer promised that an objective or external standard would be followed in determining good cause. If such a promise is proven, then it is entirely proper for the jury to decide what constitutes good cause.

A good model of the appropriate role for the jury is *Video Electronics, Inc. v. Tedder*,[49] regarding breach of a written employment contract. The court found that (1) the court, rather than the jury, should construe the contract, and (2) the jury should decide whether the employer's decision to dismiss was reasonable, unless the employer had reserved the right in the contract (under the court's construction) to be the sole judge as to the grounds for dismissal, in which case the jury could decide only whether the employer acted in good faith.

When the promise is found to permit dismissal only for cause, but is silent as to what constitutes cause, the jury should engage in a limited review of the employer's interpretation of the good cause standard. To do otherwise would vitiate the employer's promise, as the *Toussaint* court observed. The jury should not, however, substitute its judgment for the employer's in defining good cause. A jury instruction on this question should require the jury to consider the nexus between the conduct asserted by the employer as justifying dismissal and the legitimate needs of the employer's business.[50] Regardless of the jury's role, there must be evidence to support its verdict.[51]

§ 7.27 —Proving a Breach: Burdens of Proof on Cause

The burden of proof on the existence of cause for the termination can be placed on either the plaintiff-employee or the defendant-employer. The plaintiff is burdened to plead and prove the absence of cause if the question is viewed as an essential

---

[49] 470 So. 2d 4, 6 (Fla. Dist. Ct. App. 1985).

[50] *See* Staton v. Amax Coal Co., 122 Ill. App. 3d 631, 634–35, 461 N.E.2d 612, 615 (1984) (suggesting that cause exists only when (1) notice has been given as to the grounds for dismissal, (2) similar conduct by different employees is treated similarly, and (3) the conduct was detrimental to the discipline and efficiency of employer; reversing summary judgment for employer and remanding for trial of whether *cause* for dismissal existed; suggesting that the burden of proof is on the employer to show cause). This is the same approach followed in public employee dismissal cases in which civil service statutes or regulations require cause as a prerequisite to dismissal. See §§ **6.3–6.5**.

[51] *See* Ferraro v. Koelsch, 119 Wis. 2d 407, 350 N.W.2d 735 (Ct. App. 1984) *aff'd by different rationale,* 124 Wis. 2d, 154, 368 N.W.2d 666 (1985) (no evidence to support jury verdict for the employee; all evidence showed the employee violated rules explicitly set forth in handbook as grounds for dismissal, and that the employer met its obligation to investigate).

part of establishing breach of the employer's promise of employment security.[52] The defendant, on the other hand, is burdened to plead and prove cause for dismissal if the question is viewed as one of establishing a condition subsequent that excuses the defendant's obligation to perform the promise of continued employment.[53] Treating existence of cause as a condition subsequent probably is more appropriate for promises of employment for life or for a definite term than for promises to employ until cause for dismissal exists.

How this burden of proof question is resolved well may be outcome-determinative. It is not beyond the realm of possibility, for example, that neither the plaintiff nor the defendant corporate employer will have evidence on the reason for the plaintiff's discharge, if the employer assumed at the time that no cause legally was necessary to justify termination of what it viewed as an employment at will. Such a case might go to the factfinder with no evidence on the cause question. The party on whom the burden of production is imposed would therefore lose as a matter of law.

The case law on which party bears the burdens is sparse and inconclusive. Precedent from arbitration hearings imposes the burden on the employer to prove cause for discharge.[54] Courts may be reluctant, however, to follow this precedent in order to assuage concerns about the economic effect the new wrongful discharge doctrines may have on employers.[55]

Evidence law commentators suggest that the placement of burdens of proof should turn on several factors, such as the "policy of handicapping disfavored contentions,"[56] imposing the burden on the party with best access to relevant knowledge,[57] and imposing the burden in accordance with "judicial estimate of the probabilities of the situation."[58] Two of these three factors[59] would militate in favor of imposing the burden of proving the absence of cause for dismissal on the plaintiff.

---

[52] *See* C. McCormick, Handbook on the Law of Evidence § 337 at 785 (E. Cleary ed. 2d ed. 1972). *See* Wyman v. Osteopathic Hosp. of Me., Inc., 493 A.2d 330, 335 (Me. 1985) (affirming judgment for employer based on employee's failure to sustain burden of proof that dismissal was without just cause).

[53] Comment e to § 224 of the Restatement (Second) of Contracts explains that the term *condition subsequent* is not used in the Second Restatement. Rather, the concept is treated in § 230 under the heading, "Event that Terminates a Duty."

[54] F. Elkouri & E.A. Elkouri, How Arbitration Works 621 (3d ed. 1973); see also §§ **3.5-3.8**.

[55] *See, e.g.,* Weiner v. McGraw-Hill, Inc., 57 N.Y.2d 458, 467, 443 N.E.2d 441, 447, 457 N.Y.S.2d 193, 199 (1982) (Wachtler, J., dissenting); Toussaint v. Blue Cross & Blue Shield, 408 Mich. 579, 623-24, 292 N.W.2d 880, 896-97 (1980); Pine River State Bank v. Mettille, 333 N.W.2d 622, 630 (Minn. 1983).

[56] *See* C. McCormick, Handbook on the Law of Evidence § 337 at 786-87 (E. Cleary ed. 2d ed. 1972). The policy probably accounts for the requirement that the defendant has the burden with respect to matters such as contributory negligence, the statute of limitations, and truth in defamation.

[57] *Id.* at 787. The defendant commonly must bear the burden of proof of payment, of discharge in bankruptcy, and in license cases. But very often, a party is required to plead and prove matters peculiarly within the opponent's knowledge.

[58] *Id.* The risk of failure of proof may be placed on the party who contends the more unusual event has occurred. For instance, where a gift is alleged in a business relationship, the burden of proving donative intent is placed on the party claiming the gift.

[59] The first and third.

§ 7.27 BREACH: BURDENS ON CAUSE

Several appellate cases offer guidance as to the burdens of proof imposed on plaintiff and defendant concerning cause for termination. In *Pugh v. See's Candies, Inc.*,[60] the court, concluding that there were facts from which a jury could determine the existence of an implied promise of continued employment,[61] gave guidance on burdens of proof the trial court might confront on remand. The court stated that the plaintiff bears the ultimate burden of proving that the termination was wrong.[62] The court then cited Title VII cases[63] in allocating the order of proof. After the plaintiff has demonstrated a prima facie case of wrongful termination in violation of the contract of employment, the burden of production shifts to the defendant to show the reason for the termination.[64] Next, the plaintiff might attack the defendant's proffered explanation, either on the grounds that it is a pretext or on the grounds that it is insufficient to meet the employer's obligation under the contract or applicable legal principles.[65] The court cautioned, however, that the legitimate exercise of managerial discretion not be interfered with and that "good cause in the context of Mr. Pugh's case is 'quite different from the standard applicable in determining the propriety of an employee's termination under a contract for a specified term.' "[66] The court characterized the appropriate standard of cause as "a fair and honest cause or reason, regulated by good faith on the part of the [employer]."[67]

In *Kravetz v. Merchants Distributors, Inc.*,[68] the Massachusetts Supreme Judicial Court reversed a judgment entered on a jury verdict for the plaintiff in a wrongful dismissal suit. The trial judge instructed the jury that the defendant-employer had the burden of proving that the plaintiff-employee did not perform satisfactorily. This was prejudicial error, the appellate court held, because, "the jury may well have concluded, incorrectly, that [the employer] had the burden of proving that it had good cause to discharge [Kravetz]."[69] The Supreme Court reversed, saying that the employer was entitled to a clear instruction that the burden was on the plaintiff to prove that the defendant terminated the employment without cause.[70]

---

[60] 116 Cal. App. 3d 311, 171 Cal. Rptr. 917 (1981).

[61] *Id.* at 329, 171 Cal. Rptr. at 927 (facts from which the jury could find implied promise were: the duration of employment, commendations and promotions employee received, apparent lack of any direct criticism of his work, the assurances given, and the employer's acknowledged policies).

[62] *Id.* at 329–30, 171 Cal. Rptr. at 927.

[63] *Id.* at 330, 171 Cal. Rptr. at 927 (citing McDonnell Douglas Corp. v. Green, 411 U.S. 792 (1973)).

[64] Pugh v. See's Candies, Inc., 116 Cal. App. 3d at 329, 171 Cal. Rptr. at 927.

[65] *Id.*

[66] *Id.* at 330, 171 Cal. Rptr. at 928. The court added that where, as here, the employee occupies a sensitive managerial or confidential position, the employer must of necessity be allowed to exercise subjective judgment.

[67] *Id. See* Capone v. Cheesebrough Pond's, Inc., 112 A.D.2d 779, 781, 492 N.Y.S.2d 277, 279 (1985) (absence for 31 percent of available working time is good cause for dismissal), *appeal dismissed,* 67 N.Y.2d 904, 492 N.E.2d 1230, 501 N.Y.S.2d 814 (1986).

[68] 387 Mass. 457, 440 N.E.2d at 1278 (1982).

[69] *Id.* at 462, 440 N.E.2d at 1281.

[70] *Id.* at 462–63, 440 N.E.2d at 1281.

This burden on the plaintiff to prove the absence of cause may not be as onerous as it seems. In an early Vermont case,[71] the court held that the plaintiff has the burden of proving "his faithful performance of that contract and his wrongful discharge from the engagement by the defendant."[72] The court went on, however, to say: "Had the plaintiff satisfied the jury of his adequate fulfillment of his undertaking, in the absence of anything to the contrary, the jury might infer that there was no sufficient cause for the defendant to discharge him."[73] This observation raises the possibility that a wrongful discharge plaintiff could satisfy his burden by showing good job performance. For example, the plaintiff could introduce evidence of satisfactory performance appraisals. This showing would not only meet the plaintiff's burden, but effectively would shift the burden (of production) to the defendant to articulate the cause for the discharge. The court held, however, that it was error for the trial court to establish a presumption in the plaintiff's favor. Therefore, the court reversed because of the following jury instruction:

> The burden of proving just cause of the discharge of the employee generally rests upon the employer, and where the employee enters upon his duties and continues until he is dismissed, he need not prove that he performed his duties as a presumption arises that such is the fact, and the burden of proving a sufficient cause of his discharge is on the employer, and this burden does not shift to the employee by reason of the allegations in his complaint that he was dismissed without good cause.[74]

§ 7.28 —Jury Instructions on Breach

In a breach of contract case,[75] where the breach assertedly results from violation of the covenant of good faith and fair dealing, one of two types of jury instruction can be given on the breach issue. The first type would permit a verdict for the plaintiff-employee if the jury concludes that the dismissal violated public policy. This type is illustrated by the portion of the *Cloutier v. Great Atlantic & Pacific Tea Co.*[76] instruction quoted in § 7.16. A jury instruction defining good faith in

---

[71] Lambert v. Equinox House, Inc., 126 Vt. 229, 227 A.2d 403 (1967) (reversing a wrongful discharge judgment for the plaintiff).

[72] *Id.* at 231, 227 A.2d at 404.

[73] *Id. See* Washington Welfare Ass'n, Inc. v. Wheeler, 496 A.2d 613, 616 (D.C. 1985) (jury could infer lack of good cause for dismissal on conflicting evidence regarding whether plaintiff was disruptive).

[74] Lambert v. Equinox House, Inc., 126 Vt. at 231, 227 A.2d at 404. *See also* Schmidly v. Perry Motor Freight, Inc., 735 F.2d 1086, 1087 (8th Cir. 1984) (affirming, as consistent with Arkansas law, jury instruction burdening plaintiff to prove absence of willful misconduct or employer's lack of good faith in believing employee conduct detrimental to the employer).

[75] A variety of jury instructions can be found in M. Dichter, A. Gross, D. Morikawa & S. Sauntry, Employee Dismissal Forms and Procedures §§ 8.47–8.69 (1986).

[76] Trial Transcript at 296, Cloutier v. Great Atl. & Pac. Tea Co., 121 N.H. 915, 436 A.2d 1140 (1981).

terms of public policy was reviewed sympathetically in *Magnan v. Anaconda Industries, Inc.*,[77] in which the Supreme Court of Connecticut held that an employee, hired under a contract of indefinite duration, cannot maintain a cause of action in contract for breach of an implied covenant of good faith and fair dealing based wholly upon a discharge without just cause.[78] The court suggested that a cause of action for breach of the implied covenant is identical to a public policy tort cause of action.[79]

The second type of implied covenant instruction would permit a verdict for the plaintiff-employee if the jury finds a more specific mental state. This approach also is illustrated by the *Cloutier* instructions:

> Was the termination of the employment, the contract of employment at will, by the employer, A & P, motivated by bad faith or malice or based on retaliation. Now, I have just used a term of art, and that word "malice" may bother some. So I am going to define that for you as meaning actual malice or ill will, hatred, hostility, or some evil motive on the part of the defendant. . . .[80]

In *Wadeson v. American Family Mutual Insurance Co.*,[81] the court approved a jury instruction on good faith, rejecting the unsuccessful plaintiff's argument that the covenant permits the employer to discharge only for good cause.[82] It impliedly approved the following jury instruction:

> North Dakota law recognizes an implied covenant of good faith and fair dealing in all contracts. In employment contracts, this means that neither party may do anything in bad faith that will injure the rights of the other to receive the benefits of the employment agreement. In order for Wayne Wadeson to prevail on this count, the preponderance of the evidence must show that he was dealt with unfairly and in bad faith in the termination of his employment contract. Factors which you may consider in determining whether Defendants breached their duty of good faith and fair dealing to Wayne Wadeson are duration of employment, commendations and promotions or lack thereof, employee evaluations, job performance, existing personnel policies, and any assurances or representations by the defendants that shows an implied promise by the employer not to act arbitrarily or unfairly in terminating his employment contract. The law, however, does not forbid a termination for legal cause related to the employer's legitimate interest in running the business.[83]

---

[77] 193 Conn. 558, 479 A.2d 781 (1984).

[78] *Id.* at ____, 479 A.2d at 782.

[79] *Id.* at ____ n.25, 479 A.2d at 791 n.25.

[80] Trial Transcript at 293, Cloutier v. Great Atl. & Pac. Tea Co., 121 N.H. 915, 436 A.2d 1140 (1981).

[81] 343 N.W.2d 367 (N.D. 1984).

[82] *Id.* at 370.

[83] *Id.* at 369.

The third type of implied covenant instruction would permit the jury to find a breach if it finds that the employee was dismissed for off-duty conduct bearing no relation to legitimate employer interests.[84]

In an implied-in-fact contract case in which the breach assertedly results from lack of cause for termination, an instruction like the one presented in *Pine River State Bank v. Mettille*[85] should be given:

> It is the law that . . . an employer has the right to establish its own standards of performance, and if the defendant [employee] was not performing his work according to those standards, the bank would have good or just cause to terminate him for non-performance. And this is true even though some other employer might not have had as high standards, and it's true even though you, the jury, might feel that the bank's standards were too high. In order to breach standards of performance, an employee must know what the standards are, and in order to terminate for good cause, an employee must not only have breached the standards of performance, but the employer must have uniformly applied its standards of performance to all employees.
>
> If you find that the defendant has sustained his burden of proof and has proven that the bank terminated him without good or just cause under the circumstances shown by the evidence and the law I have just given you, [then your verdict should be for the employer].[86]

This instruction reserves to the employer virtually unlimited latitude to define just cause. It is appropriate to require in addition that the cause asserted by the employer bear a reasonable relationship to its business needs. Thus, the instruction quoted above can be supplemented by the following language:

> You may not find that the employer had cause to discharge the plaintiff unless you find that the reason given by the employer for the dismissal related to the employer's business. If you find that the reason given related only to the employee's off- the-job activities, and that the employer has no legitimate interest in those activities, then you may not find that cause existed.

In *Roach v. Consolidated Forwarding Co.*,[87] the court affirmed the following jury instruction on the meaning of *just cause*, in a suit for breach of fair representation by the union, and breach of a collective bargaining agreement by the employer:

---

[84] *See* M. Dichter, A. Gross, D. Morikawa & S. Sauntry, Employee Dismissal Forms and Procedures § 8.62 (1986) (citing Rulon Miller v. I.B.M., 162 Cal. App. 3d 241, 208 Cal. Rptr. 524 (1984)).

[85] 333 N.W.2d 622 (Minn. 1983). Giving the just cause instruction was found to be error by the appellate court, because the employer was found not to have promised to terminate only for cause. Nevertheless, the instruction is a good example of an instruction in which the existence of cause appropriately is at issue.

[86] *Id.*, affirming instruction given by trial court (instruction not quoted in appellate opinion).

[87] 665 S.W.2d 675 (Mo. Ct. App. 1984).

As used in these instructions, the term "just cause" means a real cause or basis for dismissal as distinguished from an arbitrary whim or caprice—that is, a cause or ground that a reasonable employer, acting in good faith under the collective bargaining agreement here in question, would regard as good and sufficient reason for terminating the services of an employee.[88]

In *Osterkamp v. Alkota Mfg. Co.*,[89] the court approved the following instruction in a case in which the breach allegation was premised on the employer's failure to follow the procedures in a personnel handbook:

The reason for Plaintiff's discharge is not material to the resolution of the issue in this case. The only issue to be resolved by you is whether or not Plaintiff's discharge from his employment was in violation of Defendant's own rules and regulations, and if so, whether or not Plaintiff sustained any damages thereby.[90]

§ 7.29 Preclusive Effect of Earlier Judicial, Aribitral, and Administrative Decisions

The following sections consider the doctrine of res judicata in the context of wrongful dismissal litigation. The doctrine is important to wrongful dismissal plaintiffs and defendants because of the multiple sources of legal right and multiple forums usually involved in employee dismissals. A good example of what employers sometimes call the *many bites at the apple* problem is found in *Olguin v. Inspiration Consolidated Copper Co.*[91] Olguin was a welder who claimed he was fired for protesting safety violations and for engaging in union activity. He filed a retaliatory discharge complaint with the federal Mine Safety and Health Administration, an unfair labor practice charge alleging retaliatory dismissal with the NLRB, a grievance under his collective bargaining agreement, and a lawsuit in state court for wrongful dismissal including both public policy tort and contract counts. In such cases, it is inevitable that one forum will decide its case before the other forums decide theirs. Then the question is presented: What effect should the first decision have on subsequent litigation? This is the broad question of res judicata.

Res judicata is an affirmative defense to be pleaded and proven by the person asserting it.[92]

The section begins by explaining the doctrine of res judicata and its components: bar, merger, and collateral estoppel. The section then highlights the application of these concepts to three common situations. In the first situation, a claim has been adjudicated by a state court and subsequently one of the parties brings another

---

[88] *Id.* at 679 n.7.

[89] 332 N.W.2d 275, 277 (S.D. 1983).

[90] *Id.*

[91] 740 F.2d 1468 (9th Cir. 1984).

[92] Fed. R. Civ. P. 8 (c); J. Friedenthal, M. Kane & A. Miller, Civil Procedure § 14.3 at 617 (1985).

state or federal court claim.[93] In the second situation a federal or state court action is brought following an arbitration decision.[94] In the third situation a suit is brought in either state or federal court following a determination by an administrative agency,[95] including cases in which the earlier decision was made by an unemployment compensation tribunal.[96] In all three situations, courts must decide whether res judicata should be applied to preclude the subsequent suit or the relitigation of certain issues.

The res judicata doctrines of bar, merger, and collateral estoppel are designed to ensure that there will be a point at which litigation ends. Under the definitions of bar and merger, final merits determination of a cause of action precludes relitigation between the same parties of that cause of action and any allegation or defense which was or might have been presented in the first suit. A merits judgment for the defendant *bars*[97] a subsequent attempt by the plaintiff to relitigate the same cause of action,[98] while a judgment for the plaintiff *merges*[99] with his cause of action and prevents its assertion in a later suit.[1] When the second suit between the same parties involves a different cause of action, the absolute barriers of bar and merger are inapplicable and the first judgment can be given only limited res judicata effect under the *collateral estoppel* doctrine,[2] which precludes relitigation only as to questions which actually were litigated and determined in the first suit. Therefore, the doctrines of bar and merger are used to preclude subsequent *claims* while collateral estoppel precludes the relitigation of *issues* already determined.

Terminology relating to the preclusive effect of earlier litigation can be confusing. Modern usage distinguishes between *claim preclusion,* usually associated with the term *res judicata,* and *issue preclusion,* usually associated with the term *collateral estoppel.*[3]

Collateral estoppel can be asserted either by plaintiffs or defendants. Offensive use of collateral estoppel occurs when a plaintiff seeks to foreclose a defendant from relitigating an issue the defendant has previously litigated unsuccessfully in another action against the same or a different party. Defensive use of collateral

---

[93] See § 7.30.

[94] See § 7.31.

[95] See §§ 7.32–7.35.

[96] See § 7.35.

[97] See Restatement (Second) of Judgments § 19 (1982).

[98] See Kremer v. Chemical Constr. Co., 456 U.S. 461 (1982) (doctrine of bar applied to preclude Title VII claim for discrimination litigated unsuccessfully in state court).

[99] See Restatement (Second) of Judgments § 18 (1982).

[1] See Thibodeau v. Foremost Ins. Co., 605 F. Supp. 653, 659 (N.D. Ind. 1985) (breach of contract and abusive discharge claims precluded by earlier judgment in employee's favor for breach of contract).

[2] See Restatement (Second) of Judgments §§ 27–29 (1982 & Supp. 1984).

[3] See United States v. Mendoza, 464 U.S. 154, 158 n.3 (1984) (distinguishing res judicata from collateral estoppel, citing Restatement (Second) of Judgments § 27 (1982).)

estoppel occurs when a defendant seeks to prevent a plaintiff from relitigating an issue the plaintiff has previously litigated unsuccessfully in another action against the same or a different party.[4] Collateral estoppel can prevent relitigation of either law or facts conclusively determined in prior litigation, though an exception for *unmixed questions of law* may permit relitigation of pure legal questions in subsequent cases involving unrelated claims.[5]

§ 7.30 —Preclusive Effect of Judicial Decisions

The full faith and credit clause of the United States Constitution, Article IV, Section 1, requires states to give full faith and credit to the judicial proceedings of every other state. The law to be applied in determining the effect of a judgment under this clause generally is determined by the choice-of-law rules of the forum state of the first action.

A federal statute, 28 U.S.C. § 1738 (1982), requires that federal courts give full faith and credit to state court judgments.[6] Generally, § 1738 requires that federal courts apply the law of the state in which the original judgment was issued to determine its preclusive effect. "Congress has specifically required all federal courts to give preclusive effect to state-court judgments whenever the courts of the State from which the judgments emerged would do so."[7]

The question of the preclusive effect of state court judgments usually arises when a state common law judgment is followed by a statutory claim in federal court, especially when the federal claim is based on 42 U.S.C. § 1983. This section begins with § 1983 suits, when the plaintiff has litigated common law or statutory claims in state court and seeks subsequently to maintain a § 1983 action premised on property interests based on the same common law or statutory rights.[8]

Smith v. Updegraff[9] was such a case. Smith was fired as a deputy sheriff. He claimed the events leading up to his dismissal resulted from a conspiracy among local civil service commissioners, the sheriff and other deputies, and the county attorney. Smith had contested his firing in a hearing before the civil service

---

[4] United States v. Mendoza, 464 U.S. at 159 n.4.

[5] United States v. Stauffer Chem. Co., 464 U.S. 165, 171 (1984).

[6] The predecessor to § 1738 originally was enacted in 1790. *See* Kremer v. Chemical Constr. Corp., 456 U.S. 461, 466 n.6 (1982); *see also* Annotation, *Supreme Court's Views as to Res Judicata or Collateral Estoppel Effect of State Court Judgments on Federal Courts,* 72 L. Ed. 2d 911 (1983).

[7] Kremer v. Chemical Constr. Corp., 456 U.S. at 482.

[8] See § **6.10** for a discussion of the property interest concept in § 1983 suits. *See* Takahashi v. Board of Trustees, 783 F.2d 848 (9th Cir. 1986) (state court judgment finding just cause for dismissal of teacher properly given res judicata effect in subsequent § 1983 action), *cert. denied,* ___ U.S. ___, 106 S. Ct. 2916 (1986).

[9] 744 F.2d 1354 (8th Cir. 1984).

commission, which upheld the dismissal. He then appealed the commission determination in state court, resulting in a determination that substantial evidence supported the commission finding that there was no employer bad faith, arbitrary or capricious action, abuse of discretion, or violation of due process—typical standards for judicial review of an administrative agency decision.[10]

In the federal suit, the defendants appealed the refusal by the district judge to find Smith's claims barred by the doctrines of res judicata and collateral estoppel. The Eighth Circuit agreed with the basic proposition that federal courts must give state court judgments the same preclusive effect they are given under state law, but rejected the defendants' arguments. It found two requirements for res judicata under state law missing in the case before it. First, it determined that the defendants in the federal suit were not parties to the civil service commission proceeding. Second, it found that Smith did not have, in his state judicial proceeding, a "full legal opportunity for an investigation and determination of the matters" he raised in his federal suit. The second conclusion derived from the fact that the state court was limited to evidence presented before the commission.[11]

The Eighth Circuit also rejected the defendant's collateral estoppel argument. It found that the issue raised in the federal suit was not the same as the issue litigated in the state suit. "No constitutional issues were raised or actually litigated before the Commission or the Jasper County District Court. Moreover, . . . because the Jasper County Court's review was limited by [state statute], it could not consider the issues of conspiracy and deprivation of constitutional rights; the review was limited to evidence before the Commission offered in support of Smith's discharge."[12]

In *Whitfield v. City of Knoxville*,[13] the court found an ADEA involuntary retirement claim by a police officer not barred by res judicata because the ADEA/EEOC exhaustion requirement did not permit an ADEA claim to be asserted in a state court suit in which state discrimination and constitutional claims were rejected.

Conversely, in *Gahr v. Trammel*,[14] the court found a teacher's § 1983 suit precluded by a state court decision in which the teacher had an opportunity to present his constitutional arguments and in which the state court completely litigated the essential factual elements of a constitutional claim by deciding that the dismissal was not arbitrary or capricious.[15]

As these examples indicate, the predominant issue, when a state court judgment is offered to preclude litigation of part or all of a subsequent wrongful dismissal

---

[10] *Id.* at 1361.

[11] *Id.* at 1362. (This conclusion is difficult to reconcile with the conclusion in Kremer v. Chemical Constr. Corp. giving res judicata effect to a similar state court judgment reviewing an administrative agency decision under a similarly limited standard of review.)

[12] *Id.* at 1363.

[13] 756 F.2d 455, 460 (6th Cir. 1985).

[14] 796 F.2d 1063 (8th Cir. 1986).

[15] *Id.* at 1070. *See also* Deretich v. Office of Admin. Hearings, 798 F.2d 1147, 1153 (8th Cir. 1986) (administrative decision precludes § 1983 claim); Burney v. Polk Community College,

suit in federal court, is whether the state court actually litigated the claims or issues to be asserted in federal court.

The most difficult situation conceptually is one in which a state judicial decision involves review of an administrative decision under a deferential standard of review. This was the situation involved in *Kremer v. Chemical Construction Co.*,[16] in which the Court held that a federal court hearing a Title VII suit must give preclusive effect to a state court decision refusing to overturn a state agency decision finding no discrimination. The state court in *Kremer* did not reach the merits of the discrimination claim, but merely reviewed the agency decision under a typically deferential standard of review.

§ 7.31 —Preclusive Effect of Arbitral Decisions

Section 84 of the *Restatement (Second) of Judgments* (1982) states the general rule for the res judicata effect of arbitration awards: "A valid and final award by arbitration has the same effects under the rules of *res judicata,* subject to the same exceptions and qualifications, as a judgment of a court." The section provides four exceptions to the general rule under which arbitration awards do not have preclusive effect, though there is no reason that the award cannot be introduced as evidence. The preclusive effect of arbitration awards is interesting in common law wrongful dismissal cases because employers increasingly may wish to avoid litigation by implementing employee grievance and arbitration procedures.[17] As yet, there is little caselaw on the effect of employer procedures that require employees to exhaust internal grievance and arbitration remedies, as is suggested in § **8.9**.

Despite the *Restatement's* general rule, arbitration awards generally do not have preclusive effect in statutory or public policy tort cases—for essentially the same reasons.

In *Alexander v. Gardner-Denver Co.*,[18] the Supreme Court held that an adverse arbitration award did not bar a subsequent Title VII suit. The Court reasoned that the Title VII statutory rights are distinct from collectively bargained contractual rights even though "both were violated as a result of the same factual occurrence."[19] It also found arbitral forums inferior to federal courts for the litigation of federal

---

728 F.2d 1374, 1380 (11th Cir. 1984) (state court judgment affirming administrative decision precludes subsequent § 1983 suit); Yancy v. McDevitt, 802 F.2d 1025, 1030 (8th Cir. 1986) (adjudicatory administrative decision bars §§ 1981, 1983 claim). *But see* Scroggins v. Kansas Dep't of Human Resources, 802 F.2d 1289, 1293 (10th Cir. 1986) (administrative decision, affirmed by state court under arbitrary and capricious standard of review, not entitled to preclusive effect in Title VII, §§ 1981, 1983, 1985 suit because not narrowly focused on discrimination claim).

[16] 456 U.S. 461 (1982).

[17] § **8.9** discusses the merits and prevalence of such procedures.

[18] 415 U.S. 36 (1974).

[19] *Id.* at 49–50.

statutory rights. The Court reached the same conclusion in a Fair Labor Standards Act case, *Barrentine v. Arkansas-Best Freight System*.[20] State court review of an arbitration award makes no difference; the employee still is entitled to a de novo trial of a Title VII claim in federal court.[21] An adverse arbitration award can be given great weight in determining whether the plaintiff's evidence shows discrimination, however.[22]

The rationale of these cases suggests the same right to de novo trial of any federal statutory claim.[23] In *Amaro v. Continental Can Co.*,[24] the plaintiffs brought suit in federal court alleging that they were laid off to prevent accumulation of pension credits in violation of ERISA. Earlier, they had arbitrated their layoff and the arbitrator had found no violation of the collective bargaining agreement.[25] The district court dismissed the suit, finding the ERISA claim precluded by the arbitrator's decision. The Ninth Circuit reversed, finding the ERISA statutory claim to be independent of the contractual claim decided by the arbitrator.[26]

The same approach has been followed when public employees sue for violation of constitutional rights after unsuccessfully arbitrating.[27]

The *Gardner-Denver* rationale was applied by the Ninth Circuit in *Garibaldi v. Lucky Food Stores, Inc.*[28] in support of its conclusion that an adverse arbitration award did not bar a subsequent state tort action for wrongful dismissal. The court reasoned that California's interest in recognizing the public policy tort cause of action is the "enforcement of the underlying statute or policy, not the regulation of the employment relationship." Therefore, it concluded that the arbitrator had decided different issues from those decided in the wrongful dismissal suit. Subsequent cases agree.

The inclination of courts to permit public policy tort lawsuits to proceed despite adverse arbitration awards is somewhat surprising, given the historical preference for arbitration to resolve labor disputes. One can conclude that the trend is motivated by a desire not to subject the individual employee to union discretion in the handling of a claim. Or, one can conclude that, as one of my students put it on his final examination, "The arbitrator's expertise is the law of the shop, not the law of the land." Under this view, public policy issues ought to be decided by courts, not by arbitrators.

---

[20] 450 U.S. 728 (1981).

[21] *See* Bottini v. Sadore Management Corp., 764 F.2d 116, 121 (2d Cir. 1985).

[22] *See* Darden v. Illinois Bell Tel. Co., 797 F.2d 497, 504 (7th Cir. 1986) (affirming summary judgment for employer Title VII, based in large part on weight given to arbitration award).

[23] *See* Wilmington v. J.I. Case Co., 793 F.2d 909, 918 (8th Cir. 1986) (adverse arbitration award not entitled to preclusive effect in § 1981 case, nor did it give employer prima facie nondiscriminatory reason for adverse employment action; permissible to introduce award into evidence, however).

[24] 724 F.2d 747 (9th Cir. 1984).

[25] *Id.* at 748.

[26] *Id.* at 749.

[27] *See* McDonald v. City of West Branch, 466 U.S. 284 (1984).

[28] 726 F.2d 1367, 1375-76 (9th Cir. 1984), *cert. denied*, 471 U.S. 1099 (1985).

In contrast to statutory and public policy tort claims, individual common law claims for wrongful dismissal based on contract theories should not be entitled to a judicial forum when a collectively bargained forum is available. The preclusion argument is stronger with respect to this category of claims than with respect to tort claims.[29]

§ 7.32 —Preclusive Effect of Administrative Decisions: In General

The third basic context in which the preclusion issue can arise involves an assertion that an administrative agency decision bars relitigation in a judicial forum. These kinds of issues arise:

1. In public employee discharge cases in which the employee has administrative remedies under civil service laws and regulations[30]
2. In connection with statutory discrimination suits in which the claimant has pursued administrative remedies at the state level before bringing suit in federal court[31]
3. In connection with public policy torts based on statutes giving administrative agencies enforcement authority[32] or
4. When unemployment compensation claims have been denied based on the employee's conduct.[33]

Section 83 of the *Restatement (Second) of Judgments* (1982) presents the general rule with respect to the res judicata effect of decisions by administrative agencies:

> A valid and final adjudicative determination by an administrative tribunal has the same effects under the rules of *res judicata,* subject to the same exceptions and qualifications, as a judgment of a court.

Subsection (2) of Section 83 limits the effect of the general rule to administrative determinations involving the "essential elements of adjudication," including the right to present evidence and argument and to rebut opposing evidence and argument. The section also provides for exceptions to the general rule when the

---

[29] *Cf.* Olguin v. Inspiration Consol. Copper Co., 740 F.2d 1468, 1474 (9th Cir. 1984) (to the extent that a policy manual is inconsistent with the collective bargaining agreement, the latter controls).

[30] See § **6.6**. *See* Gorin v. Osborne, 756 F.2d 834, 836 (11th Cir. 1985) (§ 1983 claim barred by res judicata effect of state court decision affirming state personnel board on *any evidence* to support decision; following Kremer v. Chemical Construction Corp., 456 U.S. 461 (1982)).

[31] This issue is explored in § **7.33**.

[32] For example, an employee may complain that she was fired for complaints about the safety of employer products. In the employee's lawsuit, the court may be presented with a determination by the cognizant administrative agency respecting the product safety question. See § **7.34**.

[33] See § **7.35**.

remedial scheme of a subsequent claim permits assertion of that claim notwithstanding a decision on the first claim; and if giving preclusive effect to the administrative determination would be "incompatible with legislative policy." Some of the reasons why legislative policy might militate against preclusive effect are discussed in connection with unemployment compensation tribunal decisions in § 7.35.

Generally, the Supreme Court has allowed administrative agency decisions that are adjudicatory in character to be given res judicata or collateral estoppel effect.[34] The diverse nature of administrative tribunals makes reliable application of general concepts difficult, however.[35]

§ 7.33 — Preclusive Effect of Administrative Decisions: Discrimination Findings

Statutory discrimination cases involving earlier administrative decisions implicate two Supreme Court decisions: *Kremer v. Chemical Construction Co.*[36] and *McDonnell Douglas Corp. v. Green.*[37] In *McDonnell Douglas*, the Supreme Court held that a finding of no probable cause by the EEOC is not preclusive in a subsequent suit for race discrimination under Title VII because the EEOC does not have an adjudicatory function under Title VII. In *Kremer*, the Court held that a federal court hearing a Title VII suit must give preclusive effect to a state court decision refusing to overturn a state agency decision finding no discrimination. The state court in *Kremer* did not reach the merits of the discrimination claim, but merely reviewed the agency decision under a typically deferential standard of review. The administrative decision in *Kremer*, however, was adjudicatory, unlike EEOC determinations.

The pure effect of an administrative decision rejecting a discrimination claim, without an intervening judicial review, was the subject in *University of Tennessee v. Elliott.*[38] The plaintiff was dismissed from his job in a state university extension service, and claimed racial discrimination under Title VII and § 1983. A state administrative proceeding ensued, at which an administrative law judge held that

---

[34] *See* United States v. Utah Constr. & Mining Co., 384 U.S. 394, 422 (1966) (giving collateral estoppel effect to contract review board decision in case subsequently heard by Court of Claims).

[35] *See, e.g.*, Thomas v. Washington Gas Light Co., 448 U.S. 261, 283 (1980) (denying res judicata effect to award of Virginia workers' compensation commission because of limited jurisdiction of commission); McDonnell Douglas Corp. v. Green, 411 U.S. 792 (1973) (EEOC finding of no reasonable cause to believe discrimination occurred not binding on federal court; EEOC does not have adjudicatory function); Nasem v. Brown, 595 F.2d 801, 807 (D.C. Cir. 1979) (denying offensive collateral estoppel effect of administrative determination of discriminatory motive because agency did not permit live testimony or cross-examination); Athan v. P.A.T.C.O., 672 F.2d 706, 711 (8th Cir. 1982) (reversing trial court for permitting offensive collateral estoppel as to element of tort not actually decided by administrative agency which did decide all other elements of tort).

[36] 456 U.S. 461 (1982).

[37] 411 U.S. 792 (1973).

[38] ___ U.S. ___ 106 S. Ct. 3220 (1986).

he lacked jurisdiction to decide the federal civil rights claims but nevertheless heard evidence on the claimed racial motivation in order to decide whether the university had legitimate grounds for termination. The administrative law judge determined that the dismissal was not racially motivated, and that decision was affirmed by the ultimate administrative authority.[39] Elliott did not seek review of the administrative decision in state court, electing to pursue federal remedies in federal court. The district court granted summary judgment for the university, based on the administrative decision. The Supreme Court, agreeing with the Sixth Circuit, held that unreviewed state administrative proceedings do not have preclusive effect on Title VII claims. It reached a different conclusion, however, respecting the § 1983 claim, holding "that when a state agency acting in a judicial capacity resolves disputed issues of fact properly before it which the parties have had an adequate opportunity to litigate, federal courts must give the agency's factfinding the same preclusive effect to which it would be entitled in the State's courts."[40]

Elliott is inconsistent with *Buckhalter v. Pepsi-Cola General Bottlers*,[41] holding that an Illinois Fair Employment Practices Commission (FEPC) decision was entitled to res judicata effect in a Title VII/§ 1981 proceeding.[42] The *Elliott* opinion does not mention *Buckhalter,* but neither does it suggest any reason to treat governmental employers differently from private employers in terms of relitigating Title VII matters already decided by state administrative agencies. The rationale of *Buckhalter,* distinguishing non-adjudicatory EEOC decisions from adjudicatory state administrative agency decisions, has been undermined by the reasoning of *Elliott,* but the identity of the employer in *Elliott* leaves room to argue that *Buckhalter* should be followed when private employers are involved.

§ 7.34 —Preclusive Effect of Administrative Decisions: Employer Regulatory Compliance

As **Chapter 5** explains, public policy tort claims for wrongful dismissal must be founded on employee efforts to promote public policy. Many of these cases involve employee protests of alleged employer violations of federal or state health or safety statutes.[43] Typically, some enforcement responsibility under such statutes is vested in administrative agencies. In many such cases, the administrative agency does not decide directly whether the employee's dismissal was retaliatory.[44] If the statute does contain whistleblower retaliation protection, serious preemption problems[45]

---

[39] The administrative law judge was the assistant to a vice president of the defendant university, and the ultimate decisionmaker was the university's Vice President for Agriculture. The proceedings were held under the state's administrative procedure act.

[40] ___ U.S. at ___, *quoting* United States v. Utah Constr. & Mining Co., 384 U.S. 394, 422 (1966).

[41] 768 F.2d 842 (7th Cir. 1985).

[42] *Id.* at 853.

[43] See §§ **5.16–5.18**.

[44] Unless the statute contains an express prohibition against retaliatory dismissal, see §§ **2.15–2.24**.

[45] See §§ **2.27, 2.34**.

and problems with the jeopardy element of the public policy tort[46] confront the plaintiff.

Even if the administrative agency does not decide the legality of the employment termination, it may decide whether the employer conduct complained of by the employee violates the statute from which public policy is derived. In such cases, decisionmaking responsibility between the wrongful dismissal court and the health or safety enforcement agency must be allocated.

In *Gaibis v. Werner Continental, Inc.*,[47] the plaintiff-truck drivers claimed they were dismissed under circumstances that violated regulations promulgated under the Federal Motor Carrier Safety Act relating to duty time. The collective bargaining agreement covering the plaintiffs' employment made violation of federal safety regulations a breach of the agreement. The district court stayed the action challenging an arbitration award in the defendant's favor pending a decision of the Bureau of Motor Carrier Safety (BMCS), within the Department of Transportation, on whether the employer's practices violated the Federal Motor Carrier Safety Regulations. The BMCS decided that no violations occurred. The district judge concluded that he was not bound by the administrative determination.[48] He considered the question of interpretation of the regulations to be a legal question fully within the competence of the court to decide. The Third Circuit reversed on the grounds that no private right of action existed under the federal statute, and did not reach the question of the weight to be given to the decisions of an administrative agency in such circumstances.

In *Cavoli v. A.R.A. Services, Inc.*,[49] the plaintiff claimed he was dismissed from his job as a corporate pilot because he complained about poor maintenance of corporate aircraft. The district court concluded, under the primary jurisdiction doctrine, that Cavoli's lawsuit should be stayed until the Federal Aviation Administration could apply its expertise to determine whether there had been violations of its

> highly complex regulations governing airworthiness and airplane maintenance. . . . The agency may find that the plaintiff's concerns were frivolous, in which case we would be disposed to find that his discharge was justified. Or the agency may find that there were violations, in which case, taking the remainder of the complaint as true, the court or a jury might be disposed to find that the discharge was wrongful.[50]

The court did not say that the FAA's decisions would be conclusive, only that they would be helpful in putting the court in a more educated position.

Gaibis and *Cavoli* raise the question, but neither gives the answer. Three questions should be asked to apply the *Restatement* principles to the administrative decision:

---

[46] See § **5.9**.

[47] 565 F. Supp. 1538 (W.D. Pa. 1983), *rev'd sub nom.* Vosch v. Werner Continental, 734 F.2d 149 (3d Cir. 1984).

[48] *Id.* at 1548.

[49] Civil No. 83-3764 (D.N.J. letter opinion filed Jan. 24, 1984).

[50] *Id.*

§ 7.34 ADMINISTRATIVE DECISIONS

1. Is the same fact issue presented in both the administrative and in the subsequent judicial proceeding?
2. Was the administrative decision adjudicatory in nature?
3. Were the parties the same in both proceedings?

The fact-identity issue depends on the type of protection public policy affords to employees. If employees are protected against retaliatory dismissal only[51] when they *correctly* believe their employers are violating the law, then agency decisions on the violation resolve a fact question in the public policy tort suit: whether there was a regulatory violation by the employer. In that event, agency decisions on the underlying violation may be given collateral estoppel effect on the employer violation question.

But in public policy tort cases, the issue is not whether the employee was correct on her complaints; rather the issue is whether the employee's right to complain without fear of retaliation promotes public policy.[52] If the employee's protest is frivolous, public policy is not served by protecting her from retaliation by the employer.[53] But if good faith employee belief and conduct motivated the termination, public policy may be served by protecting the employee from retaliation even if the employee turns out to be wrong.[54] Accordingly, even when an administrative agency has been given responsibility for applying public policy, the agency's decision on the legality of the employer's conduct should not be outcome determinative in a related public policy tort case, though it may be helpful in deciding whether the employee's conduct was reasonable.

Most federal statutes expressly protecting against retaliatory dismissal have been construed to protect good faith, though meritless, protest. For example, in cases arising under § 8(b)(4) of the National Labor Relations Act, an employee protesting violations of the NLRA need not be correct on her assertions of a violation; she need only make the protest in good faith.[55] A similar rule is followed under

---

[51] The discussion assumes an internal public policy tort claim involving complaints to employer officials or to outside agencies of the sort discussed in §§ 5.16 and 5.17.

[52] This is the jeopardy element of the public policy tort explained in §§ 5.1 & 7.12.

[53] *See* Alford v. Harold's Club, 99 Nev. 670, 674, 669 P.2d 721, 724 (1983) (employees dismissed for refusal to comply with employer's tip pooling policy cannot recover for wrongful dismissal because employer's policy legal under state statute).

[54] *Compare* McQuary v. Bel Air Convalescent Home, Inc., 69 Or. App. 107, 111, 684 P.2d 21, 24 (1985) (employee protected for reporting what employee believed in good faith were violations of nursing home patient statute; not required to prove actual violations to recover on public policy tort claim) *and* Johnson v. World Color Press, Inc., 147 Ill. App. 3d 746, 498 N.W.2d 575 (1986) (need not show violation of securities laws actually occurred in public policy tort case) *with* Walker v. Westinghouse Elec. Corp., 79 N.C. App. 253, 335 S.E.2d 79, 86 (1985) (lack of evidence of state or federal violations precluded recovery on public policy tort claim based on safety complaints).

[55] *See* Interior Alterations, Inc. v. NLRB, 738 F.2d 373, 376 (10th Cir. 1984) (enforcing NLRB order arising from discharge of employees for protesting work assignments).

the Fair Labor Standards Act,[56] under the Occupational Safety and Health Act,[57] and under Title VII.[58]

If the same concepts are applied in public policy tort cases, an administrative finding of a serious violation would be persuasive evidence that the employee's concern was reasonable. An administrative finding of no violation may support an argument that the employee's complaint was frivolous. A decision on the merits of the employer's conduct by the responsible administrative agency may assist the court in deciding whether the employee's complaint was frivolous or made in good faith.

Under the *Restatement* principles, the administrative decision must be adjudicatory to be entitled to preclusive effect. Nevertheless, an administrative agency finding of no probable cause to proceed further may help the court hearing the public policy tort claim decide whether the employee's belief and conduct were reasonable.

§ 7.35 — Preclusive Effect of Administrative Decisions: Unemployment Compensation

One of the most common administrative decisions preceding a wrongful dismissal suit is a decision by an unemployment compensation agency.[59] Depending on the content of the decision, either the employee or the employer may wish to argue that it precludes litigation of certain issues in a subsequent wrongful dismissal suit.[60] General principles of res judicata applicable to administrative agency decisions are applicable in such cases.[61]

Preclusion is appropriate only if the unemployment compensation decision was final and adjudicatory in character. Most state unemployment compensation procedures provide for an adjudicatory hearing, followed by administrative and judicial

---

[56] *See* Love v. RE/MAX of Am., Inc., 738 F.2d 383, 387 (10th Cir. 1984) (violation of 29 U.S.C. § 215(a)(3) for discharge of employee making good faith, though mistaken, internal protest of disparate treatment of women).

[57] *Compare* Whirlpool Corp. v. Marshall, 445 U.S. 1, 21 (1980) (employee making bad faith refusal to work because of OSHA violation subject to discharge) *with* Donovan v. Hahner, Foreman & Harness, Inc., 736 F.2d 1421, 1429 (10th Cir. 1984) (affirming judgment for employee; evidence showed reasonable belief in imminent risk).

[58] *See* Payne v. McLemore's Wholesale & Retail Stores, 654 F.2d 1130 (5th Cir. Sept. 1981) (plaintiff in § 504 suit need not prove defendant actually committed Title VII violations; reasonable belief is sufficient), *cert. denied,* 455 U.S. 1000 (1982). See generally **§ 2.17.**

[59] Unemployment compensation systems are discussed in §§ **2.36–2.37**.

[60] *See* Roberts v. Wake Forest Univ., 55 N.C. App. 430, 286 S.E.2d 120, 124 (1982), *review denied,* 305 N.C. 586, 292 S.E.2d 571 (1982) (doctrine of res judicata inapplicable to unemployment compensation agencies; plaintiff unsuccessfully urged that agency benefits award was res judicata in wrongful dismissal suit). For a discussion of administrative preclusion in the context of unemployment compensation and collective bargaining agreements, *see* Note, *Issue Preclusion: Unemployment Compensation Determinations and Section 301 Suits,* 31 Case W. Res. L. Rev. 862 (1981).

[61] These principles are described in **§ 7.29**.

review.[62] Most state unemployment compensation procedures also meet the res judicata requirement[63] that adequate notice be given to the parties.[64] Although most states permit the employer to appear at the hearing, state regulations on hearing procedures and evidence should be examined closely in order to determine if the presentation of evidence and argument requirements[65] have been satisfied.

The *Restatement* also requires a fair hearing. This involves a formulation of issues of law and fact,[66] application of rules to the proceedings,[67] finality,[68] and other procedural elements as may be necessary to constitute a fair hearing.[69]

The first requirement for preclusive effect, a final adjudicatory decision, is likely to be met. The other requirements are more difficult to satisfy, however.

The parties to a contested unemployment compensation claim usually are the claimant-employee and the state agency.[70] The employer may be an active participant in contesting entitlement to compensation, but usually is not a formal party. Therefore, the party identity requirement of preclusion is not strictly met.[71] The motivation for the party identity requirement is to ensure that the party against whom the first decision may have preclusive effect had an incentive and an opportunity to litigate the question fully.[72] If the employer asserts an unemployment

---

[62] See § **2.37**. One must be careful about finality, however. Some states permit reconsideration of determinations for a set time period. 1B Unempl. Ins. Rep. (CCH) ¶ 2020 at 4544 (Feb 24, 1976). *See* Miss. Code Ann. § 71-5-523 (1973) (allowing board of review to affirm, modify or set aside any appeals tribunal decision, with no apparent time limitation); Cal. Unemp. Ins. Code § 1336 (West 1972) (language similar to that of Mississippi); Ill. Ann. Stat. ch. 48, para. 453 (Smith-Hurd Supp. 1983) (permitting claims adjudicator to reconsider findings within 13 weeks, and determination of eligibility within one year); N.J. Stat. Ann. § 43:21—6(b)(1) (West Supp. 1983) (decision final seven days after made); *see also* N.J. Admin. Code tit. 12, § 20-4.5 (19___) (board of review may reconsider appeals tribunal decision on own motion, but only within 10 days of the date of decision).

[63] Restatement (Second) of Judgments § 83(2)(a) (1982).

[64] Some require notice to be given to the discharging employer only, while others require notice to be given to all employers for whom the claimant worked during his *base year*. 1B Unempl. Ins. Rep. (CCH) ¶ 2020 at 4541 (Feb. 24, 1976). *See, e.g.*, Miss. Code Ann. § 71-5-517 (1972); Cal. Unemp. Ins. Code §§ 1334, 1336 (West 1972); Ill. Ann. Stat. ch. 48, para. 474 (Smith-Hurd 1966); N.J. Stat. Ann. § 43:21-6 (West Supp. 1983).

[65] Restatement (Second) of Judgments § 83(2)(b) (1982).

[66] *Id.* § 83(2)(c).

[67] *Id.*

[68] *Id.* § 83(2)(d).

[69] *Id.* § 83(2)(e).

[70] See § **2.37**.

[71] In some states, appeals are taken in the names of employer and employee, although Ohio, Connecticut, Louisiana and Michigan name the employer as a party on appeal. The name in which the appeal is taken, however, does not determine the parties to an action under Restatement (Second) of Judgments § 41(1)(d) (1982):

  (1) A person who is not a party to an action but who is represented by a party is bound by and entitled to the benefits of a judgment as though he were a party (if the representative is): . . .

  (d) An official or agency invested by law with authority to represent the person's interests.

[72] J. Friedenthal, M. Kane & A. Miller, Civil Procedure § 14.13 at 682-83 (1985).

compensation decision against the claimant-employee in a subsequent proceeding, this rationale is satisfied; the claimant was a party to the administrative proceeding, and had every incentive to litigate his entitlement to unemployment compensation fully. If the claimant-employee asserts a favorable compensation decision against the employer in a subsequent proceeding, the party identity criterion is not literally satisfied, but it nevertheless may be fair to hold the employer to the decision when the employer in fact challenged the entitlement to compensation and fully participated in the administrative proceeding.

At most, elements of an unemployment compensation decision are entitled to issue preclusion effect. An unemployment compensation decision is not entitled to claim-preclusion effect[73] in a subsequent wrongful dismissal action because the nature of the claims is fundamentally different:[74] a claim for statutory compensation based on the status of unemployment, versus a claim for compensation based on tort or breach of contract principles. But administrative decisions on certain fact questions necessary to decide entitlement to unemployment compensation may be entitled to issue-preclusion effect in the subsequent common law action if they satisfy the requirements for collateral estoppel.[75]

The *Restatement* precludes relitigation of an issue once it has been *actually litigated* and the issue determined was *essential to the judgment*.[76]

Two such issues frequently are outcome determinative in the unemployment compensation proceeding, and also material to the wrongful dismissal action: whether the employee was involuntarily terminated, and whether the employee engaged in misconduct.[77]

The parameters of the factual question whether the employee was terminated involuntarily usually are the same as between the unemployment compensation

---

[73] § **7.29** explains the difference between issue preclusion and claim preclusion. Issue preclusion frequently is referred to as *collateral estoppel*.

[74] Section 26(c) permits a second action on the same claim when the plaintiff was unable to rely on a certain theory of the case or to seek a certain remedy or form of relief within the subject matter jurisdiction of the tribunal.

[75] *See, e.g.,* Hill v. Coca Cola Bottling Co., 786 F.2d 550 (2d Cir. 1986) (judicially confirmed finding by New York unemployment compensation agency that employee was terminated for just cause did not preclude litigation of Title VII and §§ 1981 and 1983 claims, but state finding was binding on fact question of whether employee violated company policy; insufficient opportunity to litigate claims in administrative tribunal).

[76] Restatement (Second) of Judgments § 27 (1982). Of course, there are exceptions to this preclusion rule: If review of the determination was not possible, no preclusion, if the determination was one of law, and the two actions involve claims substantially unrelated, no preclusion; if the procedures of determination are markedly different, no preclusion; if the burden of persuasion changes significantly, or if the public policy demands rehearing, no preclusion; finally, if at the time of the first action, the second was not foreseeable, or if the first adversary had an inadequate opportunity to have a fair hearing, no preclusion. *See* Lewis v. I.B.M., 393 F. Supp. 305 (D. Or. 1974) (holding that lack of incentive to litigate vigorously, unforeseeability of estoppel barred preclusion); DeMarco v. Thatcher Furnace Co., 102 N.J. Super. 258, 245 A.2d 773 (1968) (holding that change in burden of proof, inter alia, barred preclusion).

[77] Misconduct is grounds for denying unemployment compensation in most states. See § **2.36**.

proceeding and the wrongful dismissal suit.[78] Accordingly, if the unemployment compensation tribunal decides that an employee quit voluntarily, this ought to be given preclusive effect in a subsequent wrongful dismissal action,[79] unless some policy reason can be found for not applying issue-preclusion principles. Similarly, if the unemployment compensation tribunal decides that an employee was dismissed, this also ought to be given preclusive effect.[80]

A denial of employment benefits for misconduct requires a determination of the following factors: that the claimant was engaged in certain conduct;[81] that the claimant was discharged;[82] that the claimant's conduct was the reason for the dismissal;[83] that the conduct was *misconduct*;[84] and that the misconduct was connected with the claimant's work.[85]

In a public policy tort case, these discrete fact issues match up well with the fact questions relating to the justification element of the tort.[86] In an implied-in-fact contract case, the fact issues may match with the fact questions relating to the breach element of the contract claim, depending on the nature of the employer's promise of employment security.[87] In a contract case, however, the employer's promise may have allowed it to dismiss for reasons not qualifying as misconduct in the unemployment compensation proceeding, in which case a finding of no misconduct would be immaterial to the question of breach.

Different burdens of proof, however, may militate against preclusive effect, even if certain fact issues are identical. In the unemployment compensation proceeding, the burden of proof usually is on the employer to prove that the dismissal was caused by misconduct[88] and in the wrongful dismissal action, on the employee to prove that the dismissal was for an impermissible reason. This supports an

---

[78] Compare § **2.36** (types of termination qualifying for unemployment compensation) with §§ **4.21** and **5.6** (constructive dismissal concept).

[79] *See also* Rotert v. Jefferson Fed. Sav. & Loan Ass'n, 623 F. Supp. 1114, 1119 (D. Conn. 1985) (state unemployment agency determination that termination was voluntary precludes ADEA constructive discharge suit).

[80] *But cf.* Colorado Springs Coach Co. v. Colorado Civil Rights Comm'n, 35 Colo. App. 378, 536 P.2d 837 (1975) (barring later civil rights action).

[81] Kempfer, *Disqualifications for Voluntary Leaving and Misconduct,* 55 Yale L.J. 147, 160 (1945).

[82] *Id.* at 161.

[83] *Id.*

[84] *Id.*

[85] *Id.* Usually, the burden of proving willful misconduct is on the employer. 76 Am. Jur. 2d *Unemployment Compensation* § 92 at 1010 (1975). *See, e.g.,* Orloski v. Pennsylvania Unemployment Compensation Bd. of Review, 52 Pa. Commw. 254, 257, 415 A.2d 720, 721 (1980).

[86] See §§ **5.8–5.18, 7.13–7.16** (employee engaged in certain conduct was dismissed for that reason, and employer lacked business-necessity justification for the dismissal).

[87] See §§ **4.24, 7.22–7.28** (employee performed or acted in a certain way, was dismissed for that performance or action, and such reason not allowed under employer's promise).

[88] Usually, the burden of proving willful misconduct is on the employer. 76 Am. Jur. 2d *Unemployment Compensation* § 92 at 1010 (1975). *See, e.g.,* Orloski v. Pennsylvania Unemployment Compensation Bd. of Review, 52 Pa. Commw. 254, 257, 415 A.2d 720, 721 (1980).

argument that an administrative finding of no misconduct should not be entitled to preclusive effect in a subsequent wrongful dismissal action.

The main stumbling block to giving preclusive effect to unemployment compensation decisions is based on legislative policy. Issue preclusion is not permitted when a legislative policy exists to the effect that the unemployment compensation adjudication is not be to accorded conclusive effect, or that the second tribunal be free to make an independent determination of the issue.[89] There may be an important legislative policy that militates against preclusion of wrongful dismissal litigation based on unemployment benefit determinations. The possibility of such preclusion would create an incentive for employees and employers to litigate unemployment claims aggressively, thus substantially increasing the burden on the unemployment claims process.

It seems obvious that the preclusive effect of unemployment compensation proceedings on subsequent wrongful dismissal suits is highly fact- and policy-sensitive, and can be resolved only through a careful examination of state procedures, the unemployment compensation proceeding's records,[90] and the issues to be determined in the wrongful dismissal suit.

Among the few reported cases dealing with this preclusion issue are two New York cases: *Ryan v. New York Telephone Co.*[91] and *Bernstein v. Birch Wathen School.*[92] In *Ryan,* the Court of Appeals held that a determination by an unemployment compensation tribunal barred a subsequent suit for wrongful discharge. Unemployment compensation was denied because Ryan was guilty of unauthorized removal and possession of company property, and was discharged for that reason. The court concluded that this determination, entitled to collateral estoppel effect, "is dispositive of the fact that Ryan's termination from employment resulted from and was justified by his misconduct. Consequently, justification being a defense to the tort of wrongful discharge, the determination constitutes a basis for dismissal of these causes of action as well."[93]

In *Bernstein,* a teacher was barred from litigating her wrongful discharge suit involving a written contract of employment because an earlier unemployment compensation decision had found the employment termination to be voluntary. The court distinguished cases in which *award* of unemployment compensation was not

---

[89] Restatement (Second) of Judgments § 83(4) (1982). California has enacted a statute depriving unemployment compensation decisions of preclusive effect. A.B. 3950, to be effective Jan. 1, 1987.

[90] *See, e.g.,* Miss. Code Ann. § 71-5-525 (1972) (prescribing recording of testimony for disputed claim, but delaying transcription until appeal); Cal. Unemp. Ins. Code § 1952 (West 1972); Ill. Ann. Stat. ch. 48, para.520 (Smith-Hurd Supp. 1983) (requiring that a full and complete record be kept of all proceedings for disputed claims, and that a typewritten copy be prepared on appeal); N.J. Stat. Ann. § 43:21-6(f) (West Supp. 1983).

[91] 62 N.Y.2d 494, 467 N.E.2d 487, 478 N.Y.S.2d 823 (1984).

[92] 71 A.D.2d 129, 132 (1979), *aff'd,* 51 N.Y.2d 932, 415 N.E.2d 982, 434 N.Y.S.2d 994 (1980).

[93] Ryan v. New York Tel. Co., 62 N.Y.2d at 503, 467 N.E.2d at 492, 478 N.Y.S.2d at 828. *See also* Rotert v. Jefferson Fed. Sav. & Loan Ass'n, 623 F. Supp. 1114, 1119 (D. Conn. 1985) (state unemployment agency determination that termination was voluntary precludes ADEA constructive discharge suit).

given preclusive effect in subsequent wrongful dismissal actions because the issues were not identical as between the two adjudications.

In *Chatelain v. Mount Sinai Hospital*,[94] the district court refused to give collateral estoppel effect to an unemployment compensation finding of dismissal for misconduct because the administrative decision was not judicially reviewed and because of procedural infirmities in administrative proceeding casting doubt on its fairness.[95]

In *Ross v. Communications Satellite Corp.*,[96] the court construed Maryland law to preclude collateral estoppel effect of an unemployment compensation administrative determination, affirmed by a state court. The unemployment compensation agency had determined that a Title VII plaintiff was dismissed for misconduct, and not because of his race or sex. The court of appeals, reversing the district court, concluded that the statutory issues were different, as between the Title VII claim and the unemployment compensation issue. The former statute was concerned with motive, and the latter statute was concerned with conduct.[97]

The Ninth Circuit provided an extensive analysis of res judicata principles in an unemployment compensation preclusion case in *Mack v. South Bay Beer Distributors*.[98] Mack had been denied unemployment compensation after a hearing before an administrative law judge who found that he was dismissed for misconduct and wanton neglect of his employer's interests.[99] Mack, without seeking state court review of the administrative determination, filed suit in federal court, alleging violation of the federal age discrimination act and breach of contract under state law.[1] The district court dismissed the complaint, taking judicial notice of the unemployment compensation decision. The court of appeals, while approving the

---

[94] 580 F. Supp. 1414 (S.D.N.Y. 1984).

[95] *Id.* at 1416–17. *See also* Roberts v. Wake Forest Univ., 55 N.C. App. 430, 436, 286 S.E.2d 120, 124 (1982), *review denied* (administrative finding of entitlement to unemployment benefits not preclusive in wrongful dismissal suit because issues different); Donovan v. Peter Zimmer Am., Inc., 557 F. Supp. 642, 652–53 (D.S.C. 1982) (no res judicata or collateral effect to state conciliation effort or to state unemployment compensation determination in OSHA retaliation case because former was not adjudicatory, and latter concerned different legal issues).

[96] 759 F.2d 355, 362 (4th Cir. 1985).

[97] *See also* Hill v. Coca Cola Bottling Co., 786 F.2d 550 (2d Cir. 1986) (judicially confirmed finding by New York unemployment compensation agency that employee was terminated for just cause did not preclude litigation of Title VII and §§ 1981 and 1983 claims, but state finding was binding on fact question of whether employee violated company policy; insufficient opportunity to litigate claims in administrative tribunal); Heath v. John Morrell & Co., 768 F.2d 245, 248 (8th Cir. 1985) (reversing district court for giving res judicata effect to unemployment compensation board decision in Title VII and § 1981 case; state board had no jurisdiction over discrimination law issues).

[98] 798 F.2d 1279 (9th Cir. 1986). *See also* Polk v. Yellow Freight Sys., Inc., 801 F.2d 190, 192 (6th Cir. 1986) (unemployment compensation tribunal finding of misconduct given preclusive effect in statutory retaliation case).

[99] *Id.* at 1281.

[1] The district court dismissed the state claim without prejudice under its discretion to decline pendent jurisdiction. Thus the state claim was not before the Ninth Circuit.

procedure of judicial notice of such administrative decisions, reversed. It found, as a matter of federal common law, that decisions of state unemployment compensation tribunals are not entitled to issue- or claim-preclusion effect primarily because of the informal nature of such proceedings. It noted that an employee's incentive to litigate unemployment compensation vigorously is less than the incentive to litigate statutory or common law dismissal claims because of the smaller stakes involved in the former. In addition, it was reluctant to create an incentive for both employers and employees "to litigate every employment benefits claim as if it encompassed a discrimination suit. Should this come to pass, the board may find it difficult to adjudicate unemployment benefit claims expeditiously."[2] *Mack,* therefore, is a clear example of denying preclusive effect for policy reasons, as suggested earlier in this section.

---

[2] Mack v. South Bay Beer Distrib., 798 F.2d at 1284.

CHAPTER 8

EMPLOYER PERSONNEL POLICIES

§ 8.1   Introduction
§ 8.2   History of Rules Regulating Employees
§ 8.3   Function of Internal Rules
§ 8.4   Rules and Organization Theory
§ 8.5   Contemporary Practices
§ 8.6   Employer Policy on Terminations: In General
§ 8.7   —Disclaimers: Reserving the Right to Dismiss at Will
§ 8.8   —Disclaimers: Limiting Authority to Make Promises
§ 8.9   —Limiting Relief to Internal Remedies
§ 8.10 —Releases
§ 8.11 Contents of Termination and Complaint Policies
§ 8.12 —Substantive Fairness Policies
§ 8.13 —Procedural Fairness Policies: General Principles
§ 8.14 —Procedural Fairness Policies: Suggested Approaches
§ 8.15 Employee Appraisal Programs

§ 8.1   Introduction

This chapter considers employer personnel policies and procedures.[1] Such employer procedures have significant legal consequences in employee dismissal suits. More importantly, employer personnel procedures often determine whether dismissed employees are motivated to litigate the legality of their terminations.

Employers who follow three basic rules of thumb are unlikely to be held liable for wrongful dismissal:

1. Don't make promises you don't want to keep
2. Don't ask your employees to break the law
3. Investigate employee complaints fully.

---

[1] The same subject is considered in M. Dichter, A. Gross, D. Morikawa & S. Sauntry, Employee Dismissal Forms and Procedures ch. 1 (1986).

These rules of thumb can be reflected in employer rules. More generally, employers manage organizations through rules. This chapter begins with the history of formal rules in large private enterprises, emphasizing policies regarding employee compliance with employer rules and employee complaints of improper treatment by their supervisors. Then practical reasons for employer rules are summarized with consideration given to some of the knowledge generated by organization theorists. The chapter then addresses several basic questions regarding the design of a modern employer's personnel policies.

The initial focus is on employer rules of all kinds, not just on those rules relating directly to personnel. There are two reasons for this approach: the same organizational needs justify both types of rules and nonconformity with a general rule frequently is asserted as the basis for adverse personnel action. The relationship between general rules and personnel actions can be at the heart of a wrongful dismissal controversy.

This treatise is concerned with only one aspect of enterprise management: employee retention. Therefore, the emphasis in the latter part of this chapter is on rules governing employee discipline and dismissal, and on rules governing employees' rights to obtain higher-level review of lower-level decisions to terminate them. Nevertheless, it should be remembered that cause for dismissing an employee well may arise from the employee's violation of some other type of rule respecting the general conduct of the business.

§ 8.2 History of Rules Regulating Employees

Possible legal liability for employment decisions has led employers to formalize workplace governance by establishing rules. Rules also are desirable as a basic management technique. Employee dismissal policies are likely to be embodied in rules. For example, an employer rule may state that noone will be dismissed without just cause, that noone will be dismissed because of race, or that noone can be dismissed until the personnel department approves the dismissal.

The importance of employer rules makes it appropriate to consider the historical evolution of formal employer personnel policies. Employer personnel policies developed largely in response to the increased size and scope of work organizations. The core of personnel policy was the statement of formal rules regulating employee activities. These rules were supplemented in time by additional rules and procedures intended to facilitate decisions regarding employee rewards and discipline. A clear example of this course of development is found in the railroad industry, considered at the end of this section.

Few large private sector organizations existed until technological advances, expansion of markets,[2] and reform of the laws of incorporation made such organizations

---

[2] Technological advances in production and market expansion made possible by technological advances in transportation together were the sources of the Industrial Revolution.

economically advantageous and practically feasible.[3] When markets were localized the typical business enterprise operated from a single plant or office and performed a single function. Market mechanisms controlled the activities of such enterprises and coordinated them with the activities of other firms.[4] As markets expanded and production technology became more complex, it became advantageous for a single enterprise to operate at multiple locations and to perform multiple functions. Interaction among the different components of such a firm were controlled by internal bureaucratic mechanisms rather than by the market.[5]

Professor Alfred Chandler has studied the transformation of American enterprise into large bureaucratic organizations and offers several propositions germane to the function of formal personnel policies.[6] One proposition is that "the advantages of internalizing the activities of many business units within a single enterprise could not be realized until a managerial hierarchy had been created."[7] Rules were necessary to the functioning of such a hierarchy. Internal procedures for developing and administering workplace rules replaced legislative and judicial mechanisms. Bureaucratic control replaced arms-length market relations.[8] The same phenomenon occurs in all societies as they industrialize. John Dunlop and his co-authors observed:

> At any one time, the rights and duties of workers and of managers, indeed of all those in the hierarchy, must be established and understood by all those involved in the hierarchy. . . . The industrial system creates an elaborate "government" at the work place and work community. It is often said that primitive societies have extensive rules, customs, and taboos, but a study of the industrial society reflects an even greater complex and a different set of detailed rules.[9]

The railroad industry developed such a hierarchy of rules early in its history. Railroads were among the first enterprises in which geographic dispersion of operations made supervision difficult without a web of rules and procedures to coordinate activities and to provide a mechanism for dealing with rule-breakers.[10] Although collective bargaining developed early among railroad operating employees, it was employer initiative, not unions, that led to the establishment of formal procedures for enforcing rules and for adjudicating grievances. "No

---

[3] A. Chandler, The Visible Hand: The Managerial Revolution in American Business 6–8 (1977) (reasons for development of modern enterprise structure); *id.* at 14 (nature of traditional enterprise); J. Hurst, Law and Markets in United States History 106–07 (1982) (replacement of bargaining among atomized units by rules in larger enterprise organizations). See §§ **1.3** & **1.4** for a fuller discussion of the development of modern labor markets.

[4] A. Chandler, The Visible Hand: The Managerial Revolution in American Business 3 (1977).

[5] *Id.;* J. Hurst, Law and Markets in United States History 50 (1982).

[6] A. Chandler, The Visible Hand: The Managerial Revolution in American Business 6 (1977).

[7] *Id.* at 7.

[8] *Id.*

[9] C. Kerr, J. Dunlop, F. Harbison & C. Myers, Industrialism and Industrial Man 41 (1960).

[10] A. Chandler, The Visible Hand: The Managerial Revolution in American Business 79 (1977).

other business enterprise, or for that matter few other nonbusiness institutions, had ever required the coordination and control of so many different types of units carrying out so great a variety of tasks that demanded such close scheduling."[11] By the middle of the nineteenth century, eastern railroads had begun to develop elaborate organizations with precise written rules to govern employees' work.[12] The Pennsylvania Railroad was at the forefront of developing and refining new organizational concepts.[13]

In 1915, the Pennsylvania Railroad presented a report on its personnel practices to the United States Commission on Industrial Relations.[14] The context makes it clear that the railroad was defending itself against criticism that it opposed unionization of its nonoperating employees. The report described a procedure under which employees accused of responsibility for accidents or of "derelictions of duty" initially were subjected to investigation of facts and circumstances by a discipline committee of five or six division officers. This committee, if it found misconduct, would recommend a penalty to the division superintendent, who would choose the discipline. Employees were entitled to advance notice of discipline, and, if dissatisfied, could appeal initially to the superintendent, thence to the general superintendent and ultimately to the general manager.[15]

Employees also could present grievances concerning compensation, discipline, or working conditions to the division superintendent with rights of appeal to the general superintendent, and ultimately to the general manager.[16] In addition, the railroad had in place a system of military-style "efficiency reports" on supervisory employees which resulted in the preparation of approximately 1,300 annual performance appraisals.[17]

As other large industrial, transportation, and commercial enterprises developed, they followed a similar pattern. In 1950, Peter Drucker said with confidence, "[T]he enterprise is also a governmental institution necessarily discharging political functions. . . . The authority in the enterprise . . . is a law making body, laying down rules for the individual's behavior and for the settlement of conflicts."[18] By the early 1950s it was estimated that half to two-thirds of larger firms had written personnel policies,[19] and a substantial portion of the nonunion firms also had formal employee grievance procedures.[20]

---

[11] *Id.* at 94.

[12] *Id.* at 97–107.

[13] *Id.*

[14] The Pennsylvania Railroad, The Pennsylvania Railroad: Its Policies Toward its Employees (1915).

[15] *Id.* at 34–35.

[16] *Id.* at 43.

[17] *Id.* at 38–39.

[18] P. Drucker, The New Society 44–45 (1950).

[19] P. Selznick, Law, Society & Industrial Justice 86 (1969) (citing W. Spriegel and A. Dale, Personnel Practices in Industry (1954)).

[20] P. Selznick, Law, Society & Industrial Justice 91 (1969).

§ 8.3 Function of Internal Rules

Economic activity can be carried on in small units without rules.[21] Entrepreneurs or their agents often apply discretion and make each decision on its merits. When the number of employees is relatively small, their activities can be directed in a similarly individualized fashion. When organizations get larger, however, the feasibility of discretionary decisionmaking diminishes if the organization's activities are to be coordinated. There are two reasons for this. First, increased size of the organization multiplies the number of business decisions that must be made beyond the capacity of any one or a few top management officials to make them. Second, delegation of decisionmaking authority to lower-level employees creates the risk of inconsistency and confusion unless top authority provides guidance and limits discretion.

In large organizations, formal rules explain management policy to all employees and reduce the number of individual cases to be decided by top managers. Large organizations need rules to manage operations, marketing, procurement, capital investment, accounting, and public relations functions. They also need personnel rules to control supervisory discretion with respect to compensation, time off, other benefits, promotions, and discipline. The perceived need for formal personnel rules has been increased by the growing body of state and federal law that may impose liability on the employing organization for unfair treatment of employees.[22] An employer, by internal rule, prohibits supervisory action that may result in legal liability for the employer.

§ 8.4 Rules and Organization Theory

The development of large organizations spurred efforts to develop a theory of organizational structure and function. Several competing schools of thought have emerged, each based on a different model of organizational behavior. The classical *administrative model* emphasized formal organization structure and clear definition of individual responsibilities. It stressed principles such as unity of command, authority, division of labor, unity of direction, and the like.[23] The *bureaucratic*

---

[21] The introduction to § **8.2** explained why rules are important when employers face potential legal liability because of personnel decisions.

[22] See §§ **1.2** & **1.12** for an overview of common law theories and **ch. 2** for statutory sources of liability.

[23] A complete list of Fayol's 14 principles of management can be found in J. Stoner, Management 43 (1982). *See, generally,* L. Gulick & L. Urwick, Papers on the Science of Administration (1937); L. Urwick, The Elements of Administration (1943); H. Fayol, General and Industrial Management 19-42 (1949); F. Taylor, Scientific Management (1911). Professor Simon gives a critical review of the classical theory in chapter 2, ''Problems of Administrative Theory,'' H. Simon, Administrative Behavior (2d ed. 1957).

model, offered initially by Max Weber,[24] emphasized the development of a rational-legal bureaucracy to govern large organizations.[25] Weber's bureaucratic model complemented the administrative model.

A more recent *human relations model* deemphasized formal structures. It rejected the notion of the worker as a machine. This model sought a work environment that would encourage self-motivation and willing conformity to organizational norms, and proposed a management style that was participatory and employee-centered.[26] The *Theory Z* management method is a logical extension of the human relations model, aiming at increased commitment to the employer through employee satisfaction. Sometimes called consensus management or Japanese style management, the Theory Z model seeks to improve overall productivity by allowing blue collar employees to participate in what are typically managerial functions.[27] These employee participation plans take many forms, but are most commonly associated with quality of work life circles, or *quality circles.*[28] The Japanese style of management, which involves every level of employee in the corporate decisionmaking process, inspired the American experimentation with quality circle plans.[29] Many quality circle programs have not lived up to management expectations, but there is evidence that quality circle systems can increase productivity.[30] The mixed success of American quality circle plans may be the result of a fundamental misconception about the true nature of Japanese consensus-style management.[31]

Several organizational systems models treat organizations as task performers with a structure and style to be determined by the nature of the task or by the technology required to accomplish it.[32] Variants of this view treat organizations as information processing organisms in which decisionmakers seek to reduce

---

[24] M. Weber, The Theory of Social and Economic Organization (1947).

[25] P. Selznick, Law, Society & Industrial Justice 76–82 (1969).

[26] *Id.* at 99; D. McGregor, The Human Side of Management (1960); R. Likert, New Patterns of Management (1961).

[27] Ferguson-Gaal, *Codeterminism: A Fad or a Future in America,* 10 Emp. Rel. L.J. 176, 181 (1984).

[28] *Id.* at 182. *See also* Rosenberg-Rosenstein, *Participation and Productivity: An Empirical Study,* 33 Indus. & Lab. Rel. Rev. 255, 362–64 (1980) (percentage increase of productivity is influenced by the number in the group and the frequency of meetings).

[29] 33 Indus. & Lab. Rel. Rev. at 362–64.

[30] Rosenberg-Rosenstein, *Participation and Productivity: An Empirical Study,* 33 Indus. & Lab. Rel. Rev. 255, 361–63 (1980): Ferguson-Gaal, *Codeterminism: A Fad or a Future in America,* 10 Emp. Rel. L.J. 176, 192 (1984) (emphasizing the importance of management cooperation).

[31] Ferguson-Gaal, *Codeterminism: A Fad or a Future in America,* 10 Emp. Rel. L.J. 176, 183–84 (1984). *See generally* Yang, *Demystifying Japanese Management Practices,* 6 Harv. Bus. Rev. 172 (1984). Mr. Yang gives an illuminating account of the sub-systems at work under the surface of the Japanese consensus-style management system. He makes the interesting observation that some Japanese corporations are currently looking to adopt Western management styles in an effort to become more competitive.

[32] *See* J. Thompson, Organizations in Action (1967); J. Woodward, Industrial Organization: Theory and Practice 122 (1965) (optimal organization structure depends on technology).

uncertainty.[33] Still others analyze organizational behavior in political terms in which actors enhance their power through political alliances.[34]

Under all of these more recent models, rules reduce the load of decisionmaking on top managers by permitting routine treatment of recurring problems.[35] Moreover, all models accept the need for rules to reduce uncertainty and to promote rational management of the enterprise as a whole.[36] A study of the effect of unionization on productivity within the cement industry supports this contention.[37] A review of management style and procedure in several cement plants reveals that after unionization, a more businesslike attitude on the part of supervisors and an increased predictability of work rules occurred.[38] The result was an increase in plant productivity.[39]

Under all of the organization theories, management aims at two potentially conflicting goals. The first is to increase order by reducing individual variation in employee performance.[40] This goal is served by standardizing production methods and enforcing individual compliance with these standards. This necessarily occurs at the expense of individual autonomy.[41] Single-minded pursuit of this goal is frequently, though somewhat inaccurately, characterized as *Theory X* management.[42]

The second goal is to improve employee commitment to the organization in order to mobilize workforce energies fully.[43] One corollary of this goal is to reduce

---

[33] *See* J. Galbraith, Designing Complex Organizations (1973).

[34] *See* J. Pfeffer, Power in Organizations (1981) (political view of organization behavior).

[35] *See* C. Perrow, Complex Organizations: A Critical Essay 23-30 (1972) (need for rules). *See also* Clark, *The Impact of Unionization on Productivity: A Case Study*, 33 Indus. & Lab. Rel. Rev. 464 (1980) (significant changes in management and personnel procedures, in the form of standardized rules, led to productivity gains).

[36] *See generally,* P. Selznick, Law, Society & Industrial Justice 75-120 (1969) ("management and governance"); R. Ullrich & G. Wieland, Organization Theory and Design 103-132 (ch. 5, "Control") (1980); J. March & H. Simon, Organizations ch. 6 (1958); A. Gouldner, Patterns of Industrial Bureaucracy 157 (1954) (functions of bureaucratic rules: explanation, screening, remote control, punishment legitimation); C. Perrow, Complex Organizations: A Critical Essay 23-30 (1972) (same).

[37] Clark, *The Impact of Unionization on Productivity: A Case Study*, 33 Indus. & Lab. Rel. Rev. 464, 467 (1980).

[38] *Id.*

[39] *Id.*

[40] *Cf.* P. Selznick, Law, Society & Industrial Justice 79-80 (1969) (limitations on supervisor discretion).

[41] "The organization . . . takes from the individual some of his decisional autonomy and substitutes for it an organization decision-making process." H. Simon, Administrative Behavior 8 (2d ed. 1957). *See* R. Ullrich & G. Wieland Organization Theory and Design 109 (1980).

[42] D. McGregor, The Human Side of Management 33-44 (1960). Theory X is a label used by Professor McGregor for a set of assumptions about worker motivation and behavior that conclude that workers need negative stimuli to function productively. It is frequently used also as a label for management styles that result from adoption of those assumptions.

[43] P. Selznick, Law, Society & Industrial Justice 97 (1969).

employee turnover by promoting employee satisfaction. Single-minded pursuit of this goal is frequently characterized as *Theory Y* management.[44]

Systems of personnel rules serve both the order-increasing and the employee-commitment goals. Rules provide one method of standardizing employee production and punishing deviations from the standards without depending unduly on the idiosyncracies of supervisors. The rules must be applied consistently to achieve the underlying goals of predictability and order.[45] Rules also increase employee morale. By reducing the opportunity for arbitrary supervisory action, rules can enhance the perception of fairness.[46] When coupled with supervisory training and procedures for appealing adverse supervisory actions, rules promote a perception that employees are treated with respect and concern.[47]

§ 8.5 Contemporary Practices

A typical large organization has two general types of formal rules: those circumscribing employee authority or activities and those governing the treatment of employees. Falling in the first category are rules that define how customers are to be treated, how capital expenditures are to be authorized, how purchases are to be made, how assets are to be transferred, how accounting information is to be collected and reported, how information may be disclosed outside the organization, and how subordinate employees are to be hired and managed. Falling in the second category are rules respecting salaries, fringe benefits, vacations and holidays, discipline, performance evaluation, and involuntary termination.

Two types of employee treatment rules are of interest: those limiting the grounds for which an employee may be terminated and those specifying the procedures that must be followed in connection with a termination. The first type of rule is substantive; the second is procedural.[48] To give concreteness to the discussion that follows, an example of each type is useful. The rule involved in *Weiner v. McGraw-Hill, Inc.*[49] contained elements of both substance and procedure:

> The company will resort to dismissal for just and sufficient cause only, and only after all practical steps toward rehabilitation or salvage of the employee have been

---

[44] Theory Y is a label used by Professor McGregor for a set of assumptions about worker motivation and behavior that concludes that workers are self-motivated in a supportive environment. It frequently is also used as a label for a democratic style of management. *See* D. McGregor, The Human Side of Management 45–57 (1960).

[45] P. Selznick, Law, Society & Industrial Justice 79–80, 83 (1969).

[46] *Id.* at 102–03.

[47] *Id.* at 96–99.

[48] The distinction between substantive rules and procedural rules is developed more fully in § **9.2**.

[49] 57 N.Y.2d 458, 443 N.E.2d 441, 457 N.Y.S.2d 193 (1982). This case is discussed in **ch. 4**.

§ 8.5 CONTEMPORARY PRACTICES

taken and failed. However, if the welfare of the company indicates that dismissal is necessary, then that decision is arrived at and is carried out forthrightly.[50]

The employee manual relied upon in a 1981 Utah Supreme Court case[51] concentrated on procedure. It outlined four steps of progressive discipline: oral warning, written warning, suspension, and discharge.[52]

Some form of self-imposed substantive fairness[53] criterion is common. Robert Coulson, president of the American Arbitration Association, commissioned an informal survey of termination practices by major nonunion employers.[54] "Every personnel executive interviewed said that there had to be a reason for discharge, using terms such as 'cause' or 'just cause'."[55]

In addition to substantive fairness criteria, complaint or grievance procedures also are common. An employee complaint or grievance system is procedural rather than substantive; whether exhaustion of the procedure is a condition precedent to termination depends, of course, on the interpretation given to the procedure.

In 1980, Harvard Professor Foulkes published a study of about two dozen large nonunion companies' personnel policies.[56] He found two companies that had formal grievance procedures culminating in arbitration with the company paying the arbitrator's fee. Two other companies had appeal boards to which employees could take their grievances. These boards made recommendations to the presidents of the companies.[57] Almost all the other companies had some form of formal procedure for resolving employees' complaints.[58] In one, the office of the chief executive officer (CEO) receives several hundred complaints in a typical year. Investigators assigned to the CEO's office look into the complaints.[59]

A 1980 study by the Conference Board[60] reported that about half the union companies had a complaint system for nonunion employees and that more than two-thirds

---

[50] *Id.* at 460–61, 443 N.E.2d at 442, 457 N.Y.S.2d at 194.

[51] Piacitelli v. Southern Utah State College, 636 P.2d 1063 (Utah 1981).

[52] *Id.* at 1065–66.

[53] The concepts of substantive and procedural fairness are explained in § **9.2**. *Substantive fairness* means that action will be taken against employees only for certain reasons bearing a legitimate relationship to the employer's business requirements. *Procedural fairness* means that the employer will provide for procedures that develop the facts respecting any adverse action reliably.

[54] *See* R. Coulson, The Termination Handbook 119–20 (1981). The survey involved companies in diverse industries, drawn from the roster of the New York Personnel Management Association.

[55] *Id.* at 121.

[56] F. Foulkes, Personnel Policies in Large Nonunion Companies (1980).

[57] *Id.* at 300.

[58] *Id.*

[59] *Id.* at 302–03.

[60] The Conference Board, Nonunion Complaint Systems: A Corporate Appraisal, Report No. 770 (1980). The survey was conducted in 1979 and covered 652 companies with some union presence and 96 nonunion companies. *Id.* at 4.

of the nonunion companies had such a system.[61] The main reason given for establishing systems was to reduce the involvement of parties or agencies outside the company in resolving employee complaints.[62]

The complaint procedures were used relatively infrequently. Respondents to the Conference Board survey reported that fewer than five percent of the employee populations used complaint systems.[63] Professor Foulkes found, however, that the procedures were well accepted and valuable for three reasons: they gave top management better information on how the organization was functioning; "the mere threat of a formal grievance case created pressures and incentives for informal problem solving;" and the availability of a credible grievance system improved employee attitudes toward the company.[64] Foulkes concluded that a formal complaint procedure is "essential, especially in today's environment."[65]

In addition to procedures for handling employee complaints, most sophisticated personnel policies also provide for a systematic method of evaluating employee performance. The policy presented below, similar to that of a middle-sized New York bank, is illustrative:

> The performance of all nonofficer employees will be reviewed each year during the quarter in which they were employed with an effective raise beginning the first week of the following quarter.
>
> You are entitled to know where you stand as far as your performance is concerned and know exactly what your supervisor thinks of the job you do. Your supervisor will evaluate your performance and meet with you to discuss your strong and weak points.
>
> You will then have the opportunity to write your comments on the rating form. You will be notified at a later date of any salary change considered appropriate by management.

§ 8.6 Employer Policy on Terminations: In General

Sections **8.7** through **8.15** are intended to raise issues that employers should consider in reviewing their personnel policies and rules in light of the emerging law of wrongful dismissal. The first step in designing a rational set of personnel policies is to make a reasoned choice respecting the two employee relations goals discussed

---

[61] *Id.*

[62] *Id.* at 3.

[63] *Id.* at 35. The systems were used rarely in connection with terminations, unless arbitration was provided as the terminal step. *Id.* at 41.

[64] F. Foulkes, Personnel Policies in Large Nonunion Companies 321 (1980).

[65] *Id.* at 322.

briefly in § **8.3** and **8.4**: the goal of preserving order and authority and the goal of increasing employee commitment and morale. These goals must be weighed against the liability that can result from a judicial determination that employer rules constitute an enforceable contract between the employer and individual employees.

Employers can provide two basic types of protection: they can ensure substantive fairness and they can ensure procedural fairness.[66] *Substantive fairness* means that action will be taken against employees only for certain reasons bearing a legitimate relationship to the employer's business requirements. *Procedural fairness* means that the employer will provide for procedures that develop the facts respecting any adverse action reliably, including an opportunity for the employee to present his side of the controversy.

Relatively detailed policies, affording significant substantive fairness protection to employees, can minimize the chances that a dismissal will occur that results in public policy tort[67] or statutory discrimination[68] liability. On the other hand, such detailed policies are more likely to result in liability being imposed for breach of contract[69] if the policies are not followed to the letter.

Similarly, detailed employer policies regarding procedural fairness enhance the likelihood that an external tribunal may defer to the employer's decision on the facts. But such detail increases the likelihood of some misapplication of the procedures that may result in liability for breach of contract for not following the promised procedures.[70]

Three different types of personnel policy bear on dismissal decisions: termination policies, grievance policies, and appraisal policies. Termination policies are discussed in §§ **8.7** through **8.14**. They usually are activated by a preliminary decision of a supervisory employee that a subordinate should be terminated. Grievance policies, also discussed in §§ **8.7** through **8.14**, usually are activated by the employee, frequently in connection with a management decision other than a decision to dismiss the grievant. Appraisal policies, discussed in § **8.15**, almost always are activated by the employer, usually on a periodic basis, and are not limited to termination issues. Though each type of procedure serves a different purpose, the subject matter of each overlaps. The information and the decisions involved with each type of procedure can be relevant to a dismissal and can influence the outcome of postdischarge litigation.

Regardless of which of the three types of procedure is being considered, certain general issues should be addressed. These issues, covered in §§ **8.7** through **8.9**, have clear liability implications.

---

[66] The concepts of substantive and procedural fairness are explained in § 9.2.
[67] See **ch. 5**.
[68] See §§ **2.2–2.14**.
[69] See **ch. 4**.
[70] See §§ **4.21–4.24**.

§ 8.7 —Disclaimers: Reserving the Right to Dismiss at Will

An employer may wish to ensure, to the maximum extent possible, that its personnel policies and rules are not legally enforceable because they create no reasonable expectations that they are binding. Sears, Roebuck and Company's[71] employment application language is illustrative:

> In consideration of my employment, I agree to conform to the rules and regulations of Sears, Roebuck and Co., and my employment and compensation can be terminated, with or without cause, and with or without notice, at any time, at the option of either the Company or myself.[72]

Another example is modeled after a middle-sized New York bank's personnel guide:

> The Bank has the option to terminate your employment at any time, especially during your probation, if your supervisor feels you are not progressing well enough to perform your duties successfully. Other reasons for termination may include, but are not limited to, attitude, adherence to Bank policy, attendance and punctuality.

Similar language has been used by other employers and has protected them against liability.[73]

As § 4.10 explains, the legal effect of disclaimers depends on their negating the reasonableness of employee reliance on subsequent employer statements or conduct that otherwise might support an inference of a promise of employment security.

In many cases, the dispute over the legal effect to be given a disclaimer will be basically factual. In *Longley v. Blue Cross & Blue Shield of Michigan*,[74] for example, the plaintiff's deposition testimony—that she read and believed a statement that the employer could dismiss with or without cause—precluded trial on an implied contract theory.

---

[71] Novosel v. Sears, Roebuck & Co., 495 F. Supp. 344 (E.D. Mich. 1980), discussed in § 4.10.

[72] *Id.* at 346. *See also* Ringwelkski v. Sears, Roebuck & Co., 636 F. Supp. 519 (E.D. Mich. 1985) (disclaimer reserving the employer's right to terminate employment without cause was sufficient to defeat claim under Michigan law).

[73] *See* Holloway v. K-Mart Corp., 113 Wis. 2d 143, 334 N.W.2d 570 (1983). *See also* Leahy v. Federal Express Corp., 609 F. Supp. 668, 671–72 (S.D.N.Y. 1985) (statement in application reserving right to terminate precluded action based on personnel manual representations); Ferraro v. Koelsch, 119 Wis. 2d 407, 350 N.W.2d 735, 736 (Ct. App. 1984) ("I agree that my employment may be terminated by this Company at any time without liability . . . " contained in application precludes enforceable employment tenure based on subsequently distributed handbook), *aff'd by different rationale*, 124 Wis. 2d 154, 368 N.W.2d 666 (1985).

[74] 136 Mich. App. 336, 340, 356 N.W.2d 20, 22 (1985).

§ 8.8 —Disclaimers: Limiting Authority to Make Promises

For employee relations reasons, an employer may be unwilling to state clearly that its employment policies and rules are unenforceable; a statement like that used by Sears (see § 8.7) undermines the morale-boosting effect of any statement that discharge will be only for cause. Equally important, if an employer has promulgated carefully developed written policies respecting employment tenure, that should preclude the possibility that informal communication by a recruiter or supervisor will negate any exculpatory clause.

In many of the cases discussed in **Chapter 4** in which employees sought to enforce employer obligations arising from employer policies and handbooks, oral statements from lower-level employees were offered as evidence of an employer promise to discharge only for cause or only after certain procedures were followed.[75] Management can eliminate the apparent authority of lower level employees to make such promises.

In *Schipani v. Ford Motor Co.*,[76] the court said express disclaimers in a handbook may negate informal oral assurances, but left open the possibility that such oral assurances may supersede written disclaimers, resulting in estoppel.[77]

To be effective, a statement similar to that below should be included in employment applications or other written documents communicated to employees when they first enter service. Language from the Sears, Roebuck and Company employment application is illustrative:

> I understand that no store manager or representative of Sears, Roebuck and Co., other than the president or vice-president of the Company, has any authority to enter into any agreement for employment for any specified period of time, or to make any agreement contrary to the foregoing.[78]

Such a provision can shield the employer from liability for fraudulent misrepresentation[79] as well as for breach of an implied-in-fact contract.[80] In *Shelby v. Zayre*

---

[75] See § 4.7.

[76] 102 Mich. App. 606, 613, 302 N.W.2d 307, 310 (1981).

[77] *Compare* Reid v. Sears, Roebuck & Co., 588 F. Supp. 558, 561 (E.D. Mich. 1984) (acknowledgement of employer's right to terminate without cause signed 17 years before discharge did not preclude employee from showing legitimate expectation of continued employment, but summary judgment for employer because no such showing) *with* Eller v. Houston's Restaurants, 117 L.R.R.M. 2651 (D.D.C. 1984) (plaintiff entitled to trial on question of whether employer assurances of employment security vitiated application form statement that employees could be dismissed at any time for any reason).

[78] Novosel v. Sears, Roebuck & Co., 495 F. Supp. 344, 346 (E.D. Mich. 1980).

[79] See § 5.24.

[80] See §§ 4.21–4.24.

Corp.,[81] a terminated employee sought to escape the effect of an exculpatory clause in an employment application by pursuing a claim for fraudulent misrepresentation. The employment application stipulated that, "I agree . . . my employment and compensation can be terminated, with or without cause, and with or without notice, at any time . . . . I understand that no . . . representative of your company has any authority to enter into any other agreement with me . . . ."[82] The employee claimed that the assistant manager who hired her had promised that she would have permanent employment, knowing that the representation of permanent employment was false, and that she had quit her previous job in reliance on that representation. The Supreme Court of Alabama affirmed judgment for the employer, finding that any reliance on the supervisor's statement was unreasonable, since the plaintiff admitted reading and understanding the quoted provision of the employment application.[83] The language limiting authority thus was outcome determinative.

§ 8.9 —Limiting Relief to Internal Remedies

Employer dismissal policies may contain two components: they may limit the reasons for which an employee may be dismissed, and they may prescribe dismissal procedures.[84] Either component may turn out to be an enforceable promise. It may be in the employer's interest to offer either kind or both kinds of promise but to limit an employee's right to obtain de novo review of the employer's compliance with the limitation in an external forum.

If an employer wishes to assure employees that they will be terminated only for cause, it must face the risk that such a promise will be enforceable legally. The employer should be able, however, to avoid having a judge or jury decide what constitutes cause and whether the facts of a particular case amount to cause.[85] General principles of contract construction are consistent with literal enforcement of the following language:

---

[81] 474 So. 2d 1069 (Ala. 1985).

[82] *Id.* at 1070.

[83] *Id.* at 1071.

[84] These two types of limitation relate, respectively, to substantive fairness and procedural fairness, discussed more fully in § **9.2**.

[85] The reasoning of the court in Toussaint v. Blue Cross & Blue Shield, 408 Mich. 579, 292 N.W.2d 880 (1980), strongly supports the proposition that employers may limit their liability by adequate notice that appropriately conditions employee expectations. The court's language regarding modification of employment policies is cast in terms of making it known to employees that the policies can be modified unilaterally, resulting in the employees having "no legitimate expectation that any particular policy would remain in force." *Id.* at 619, 292 N.W.2d at 895. Similarly, the court concluded that an employer could avoid the perils of jury determination of just cause by "providing for an alternative method of dispute resolution," such as binding arbitration. *Id.* at 624, 292 N.W.2d at 897. §§ **7.25–7.26** discuss more generally the allocation of responsibility for deciding what constitutes cause for dismissal between employer and court.

§ 8.9 LIMITING RELIEF

> In consideration of my employment, I understand and accept that "cause" for my termination will be determined to exist or not to exist within the sole discretion of my employer. I waive any rights I may have to obtain court determination or review of an employer finding that there is cause for my dismissal.[86]

If an employer elects to require pretermination exhaustion of certain procedures, or to afford an internal complaint procedure, it may wish to limit an employee's right to relitigate the dismissal in the courts by the inclusion of language similar to the following:

> In consideration of my employer affording me certain rights to obtain higher level review of supervisory actions adverse to me, including a possible decision to terminate my employment, I waive any rights I may have to obtain court review of the appropriateness of such adverse action, and will utilize the internal company procedures as the exclusive means of protesting adverse supervisory action, including discharge. The internal procedures provide an adequate opportunity for the true facts to be determined and for me to present my side of any controversy. I will accept the determination resulting from such internal procedures as final and binding, and waive any right I may have to protest such a determination or to obtain review of it in any proceeding outside the company.[87]

If the internal procedures terminate in arbitration, an employee agreement to be bound by the arbitration should be enforceable in any jurisdiction that has adopted the Uniform Arbitration Act.[88]

Nevertheless, even if such election of remedies language is included prominently in employer policy statements, employment applications, and otherwise made known to employees, it may not be effective if an employee asserts a violation of federal statutes because the Supreme Court has concluded that certain federal statutory rights cannot be waived before they arise.[89] Such statutory rights may be subject

---

[86] This language should achieve a result substantially the same as that reached by the court in Simpson v. Western Graphics Corp., 293 Or. 96, 643 P.2d 1276 (1982).

[87] *See* Khalifa v. Henry Ford Hosp., ___ Mich.App. ___, ___ N.W.2d ___, No. 84582 (Dec. 2, 1986) (final and binding decision by employee grievance council established by unilateral employer policy barred suit for breach of implied-in-fact contract even though judicial-type procedures not followed) (split panel).

[88] Section 1 of the Uniform Arbitration Act provides that agreements to arbitrate shall be binding. Section 12 of the Act strictly limits judicial review of awards entered under such an agreement. The notes to § **3.22** list the jurisdictions that have adopted the Act. It is also possible to argue that the United States Arbitration Act, 9 U.S.C. §§ 1–4 (1982), discussed in § **3.22**, obligates states to enforce arbitration agreements. *See* Southland Corp. v. Keating, 465 U.S. 1 (1984) (invalidating state statute making arbitration agreements unenforceable).

[89] *See* Alexander v. Gardner-Denver, 415 U.S. 36 (1974). This case involved race discrimination in violation of Title VII of the Civil Rights Act of 1964. Barrentine v. Arkansas-Best Freight Sys., Inc., 450 U.S. 728 (1981), involved claims to compensation for work time under the Fair Labor Standards Act. In both cases, the Supreme Court held that employees retain the right to

to waiver, however, in individual cases after they arise.[90] Even if a purported waiver is found to be legally ineffective in subsequent litigation, any arbitration award in the employer's favor should be entitled to some evidentiary weight in a wrongful dismissal lawsuit.[91] Accordingly, this language also should be included prominently on forms used to commence internal review of an adverse employment action and on any settlement document.

Also, employers should recognize that fair review procedures may not insulate them from vicarious liability based on misconduct by supervisory employees.[92]

§ 8.10 —Releases

Disclaimers, discussed in §§ **8.8** and **8.9**, are preventive in character: they attempt to preclude the possibility of a legal right to employment security arising in the first place. An employee release is a contract in which a discharged employee abandons claims against a former employer after they have arisen,[93] in exchange for benefits such as severance pay or continuation of salary and benefits for a period of time.[94]

---

litigate the statutory claims in federal court, regardless of whether the claims arguably are covered by collectively bargained arbitration procedures. Both cases are discussed in §§ **3.27 & 7.31**.

[90] *See* Alexander v. Gardner-Denver, 415 U.S. at 52 n.15. *But see* Barrentine v. Arkansas-Best Freight Sys., Inc., 450 U.S. 728 (1981). *Barrentine* could be read to preclude voluntary resort to arbitration by an individual *after* a claim arose. The Court's opinion contains strong language, however, about the "non-waivable" nature of statutory claims. It also questions the competence of arbitrators to resolve such claims in a manner adequately protecting employee rights. *See generally* McClendon v. Continental Group, Inc., 602 F. Supp. 1492, 1505 (D.N.J. 1985) (ERISA dismissal claims cannot be waived by submitting to arbitration); O. Fairweather, Practice and Procedure in Labor Arbitration 643 (1983) (de novo judicial review of disputes submitted to arbitration).

[91] *See* Barrentine v. Arkansas-Best Freight Sys., Inc., 450 U.S. 728, 743 n.22 (1981) (quoting footnote 21 from Alexander v. Gardner Denver to same effect); Darden v. Illinois Bell Tel. Co., 797 F.2d 497, 504 (7th Cir. 1986) (approving "great weight" given to arbitration award by district judge in deciding to dismiss Title VII claim; arbitrator fully considered race discrimination under collective agreement prohibiting discrimination); Gonzalez v. Southern Pac. Transp. Co., 773 F.2d 637, 645 (5th Cir. 1985) (on rehearing) (Railway Labor Act arbitrator's award deciding outcome-determinative facts entitled to preclusive effect in suit for retaliation under federal railroad liability act).

[92] *See* Mitchell v. Keith, 752 F.2d 385, 388-89 (9th Cir. 1985) (good faith decision by management committee cannot insulate employer from liability if managerial employee acted with racially discriminatory motivation).

[93] Costa v. Stephens-Adamson, Inc., 142 Ill. App. 3d 798, 801, 491 N.E.2d 490, 492 (1986) (employer release did not prohibit employer reports after release signed).

[94] M. Dichter, A. Gross, D. Morikawa & S. Sauntry, Employee Dismissal Forms and Procedures § 1.34 (1986). Employee releases should be distinguished from disclaimers which are express statements, generally in employment applications or employee handbooks, that put employees on notice that general statements should not be relied upon by employees. See § **4.10**.

§ 8.10 RELEASES

Absent a clear showing of duress, employee releases generally are effective in barring implied-in-fact contract claims against employers,[95] to the extent that such claims are within the scope of the agreement,[96] but may not be as effective in barring public policy tort claims.[97] In *LaBeach v. Beatrice Foods Co.*,[98] a former employee sued for wrongful discharge and sought to avoid the effect of a release by a claim of "economic duress."[99] The court held that as a matter of law there was no duress where the plaintiff asserted only that the company's vast economic power and refusal to pay his claims until a release was signed amounted to economic duress. Under Illinois law, the court found that to establish a claim of duress, there must be a wrongful act or threat which forces a person to act against his own will.[1]

Similarly, in *Anselmo v. Manufacturers Life Insurance Co.*,[2] a former employee brought an action against his former employer for breach of contract and fraudulent misrepresentation.[3] The Eighth Circuit held that as matter of law there was no duress when the former employee, an experienced business person, took the release home, consulted a lawyer, and returned the signed release the next day, although he was told by the employer that he must sign the release or be denied references and severance pay.[4]

---

[95] *See* Anselmo v. Manufacturers Life Ins. Co., 771 F.2d 417, 420 (8th Cir. 1985) (no duress when employee, an experienced businessperson, took agreement home and consulted both wife and attorney before signing); LaBeach v. Beatrice Foods Co., 461 F. Supp. 152, 156 (S.D.N.Y. 1978) (under Illinois law, to prove economic duress a person must show that duress left him "bereft of the quality of mind essential to the making of a contract;" the key question being whether the party had a choice).

[96] Costa v. Stephens-Adamson, Inc., 142 Ill. App. 3d 798, 801, 491 N.E.2d 490, 493 (1986) (employer release of claims existing prior to or arising subsequent to date of discharge did not bar employer from giving negative reference concerning employee's job performance).

[97] *See* Kellums v. Freight Sales Centers, Inc., 467 So. 2d 816 (Fla. Dist. Ct. App. 1985) (exculpatory clause in employment application releasing former employers from all liability for furnishing such information did not bar slander claim by applicant against former employer, as application of release to slander action would violate public policy).

[98] 461 F. Supp. 152 (S.D.N.Y. 1978).

[99] *Id.* at 156. After negotiation with the president of Beatrice, LaBeach had received $122,210 in exchange for a signed release of all claims. Shortly thereafter, LaBeach commenced an action against Beatrice for $100,000. Beatrice sought summary judgment based on the release. The court found that whether particular facts are sufficient to support a claim of duress is a question of law to be decided by the court, while the question of whether the facts alleged actually exist is a question of fact to be decided by the factfinder. *Id.* at 156-57.

[1] *Id.* at 156.

[2] 771 F.2d 417 (8th Cir. 1985).

[3] *Id.* at 419. In *Anselmo,* it was disputed whether a contract which allowed for termination at will or three letters which appeared to guarantee at least three years' employment governed Anselmo's employment. The court declined to reach the question, holding that the release signed by Anselmo in exchange for four weeks' severance pay barred all of his claims arising over the termination). *Id.* at 419.

[4] *Id.* at 420.

Courts, however, consistently have held that the scope of employee releases is limited to the intentions of the parties as set forth on the face of the agreement.[5] In *Beauvoir v. Rush-Presbyterian-St. Luke's Medical Center*,[6] an employee brought a claim for retaliatory discharge after being discharged for bringing numerous workers' compensation claims against his employer. The court refused to allow a release of workers' compensation claims to be used to bar a claim of retaliatory discharge, holding that general language of release in a settlement agreement will not be construed to defeat the clear intentions of the parties at the time the release was executed.[7]

The effectiveness of releases also has been limited by public policy. In *Kellums v. Freight Sales Centers, Inc.*,[8] a former employee brought an action alleging that his former employer made defamatory statements to a prospective employer. The court held that language in an employment application releasing all parties from all liability resulting from furnishing information could not be used to bar a defamation claim. To do so would violate public policy.[9] This line of authority raises serious doubts about the effectiveness of releases against any intentional tort claim, including public policy tort claims. Also, as § **2.6** explains, releases of certain federal statutory claims are disfavored as a matter of policy.

---

[5] Beauvoir v. Rush-Presbyterian-St. Luke's Medical Center, 137 Ill. App. 3d 294, 484 N.E.2d 841 (1985).

[6] *Id.*

[7] *Id.* at 304, 484 N.E.2d at 847. In *Beauvoir*, the plaintiff worked in a laboratory in the defendant's hospital and contracted hepatitis. After filing several worker's compensation claims, the plaintiff entered into a settlement contract with the defendant under which he agreed to release all worker's compensation claims against the hospital in exchange for $25,000. The plaintiff was then discharged from the hospital. The release states:

> . . . to avoid futher litigation the respondent agrees to pay and the petitioner agrees to accept the sum of $25,000.00 in a lump sum for . . . any and all claims for occupational disease during employment by respondent in full settlement of any and all claims of any kind, nature and description, including medical expenses as a result of the alleged exposure and disability and all known or unknown injuries which allegedly [sic] resulted from said alleged exposure and petitioner hereby releases the respondent from any and all claims under Workmen's Occupational Diseases Act of Illinois for said alleged exposure and disability and petitioner assumes to pay for all medical, surgical and hospital services incurred. . . .

Id. at 847. The hospital relied on the language "all claims of any kind" and "to avoid further litigation" to establish that the release was broad enough to cover retaliatory discharge.

[8] 467 So. 2d 816 (Fla. Dist. Ct. App. 1985).

[9] *Id.* at 817. The court found that a party may "by an exculpatory clause, absolve itself of liability for negligence, but an attempt to absolve itself from liability for an intentional tort is against public policy." *Id.* (citations omitted). The court found that slander is a quasi-intentional tort and that in this case it was alleged that the defendant "knowingly and maliciously" made the slanderous statements. The court held that it would therefore be in violation of public policy to apply the release in this situation. *Cf.* Costa v. Stephens-Adamson, Inc., 142 Ill. App. 3d 798, 491 N.E.2d 490, 493 (1986) (release of claims existing prior to or arising subsequent to date of discharge did not bar employer from giving negative reference concerning employees job performance).

§ 8.11 Contents of Termination and Complaint Policies

Assuming that the employer decides for management reasons to have a policy limiting its right to dismiss employees and is prepared to have compliance with the policy legally enforced, consideration should be given to some basic elements for the policy. The policy should be spelled out in reasonable detail, drafted carefully by someone with knowledge of the case law of wrongful dismissal. If termination and complaint policies already exist, they should be reviewed by someone with knowledge of the case law, and modified accordingly. The basic question that should be asked of top management by the reviewer is: Are you willing to have this particular provision legally enforced against you?

As a general matter, the policy should make it clear who has authority to promulgate changes in the policy or to authorize deviations in individual cases. For example, general changes might be authorized only in directives bearing a number and signed by the chief executive officer or another appropriate official. Deviations in individual cases might require the authorization of a specifically identified official in the personnel department.

An analytical framework for design of private employer termination policies has been suggested in § 8.6: such policies must address the questions of substantive fairness and procedural fairness. An elaborate approach to both questions is suggested by the entitlements, summarized by the Supreme Court,[10] of federal civil service employees. These entitlements presumably represent the maximum protection that any private employer might wish to provide. Most private employers would be extremely reluctant to limit their managerial flexibility to such an extent. Nevertheless, the scope and detail of the civil service system provides a conceptual model from which private employers may extract if they wish.

> A federal employee in the competitive service may be removed or demoted "only for such cause as will promote the efficiency of the service." The regulations . . . required that an employee be given 30 days' written notice of a proposed discharge . . . accompanied by the agency's reasons and a copy of the charges. The employee then had the right to examine all disclosable materials that formed the basis of the proposed action, the right to answer the charges with a statement and supporting affidavits, and the right to make an oral non-evidentiary presentation to an agency official. The regulations required that the final agency decision be made by an official higher in rank than the official who proposed the adverse action. The employee was entitled to notification in writing stating which of the initial reasons had been sustained.
>
> The next step was a right to appeal to the [Civil Service Commission, which] was required to hold a trial-type hearing at which the employee could present witnesses,

---

[10] Bush v. Lucas, 462 U.S. 367 (1983).

cross-examine the agency's witnesses, and secure the attendance of agency officials, and then to render a written decision.[11]

The federal civil service system addresses both substantive and procedural fairness. A private employer should consider both subjects, as discussed below, when drafting or reviewing employment termination policies.

§ 8.12 —Substantive Fairness Policies

The concept of substantive fairness contemplates that employees may be dismissed only for reasons that bear a reasonable relationship to the employer's legitimate business needs.[12] To formulate a policy respecting substantive fairness, the employer need only decide in advance the reasons for which employees may be dismissed. One of two basic approaches may be taken. The first approach involves identifying particular reasons for which dismissal will not occur, such as race, sex, age, religion, marital status, sexual orientation, serving on juries, and other characteristics or conduct presently protected by statute, case law, and privacy concepts. Of course, this list can be expanded to include any reason that the employer believes should be prohibited, such as any private not conduct affecting work performance or the reputation of the employer.[13]

The other basic approach is to provide that terminations will occur only for cause. The policy should make it clear how the existence of cause will be determined. The substantive content of cause can be defined specifically in the policy by using concepts and rules developed by arbitrators hearing dismissal cases under collectively bargained cause language[14] and cause and substantive due process concepts developed for civil service employees[15] as reference points.

Alternatively, the term *cause* can be left undefined in the written personnel policy, leaving it to be defined on a case-by-case basis. Such case-by-case definition will impose additional burdens on the procedural aspects of the policy.[16] The language from the personnel handbook involved in *Weiner v. McGraw-Hill, Inc.*[17] illustrates a policy requiring cause, but not specifying what cause is: "The company will

---

[11] *Id.* at 386–87 (citations omitted). The private sector analogue of the civil service commission appeal would be an appeal of a dismissal decision to the chief personnel officer.

[12] The concept of substantive fairness is developed more fully in §§ **9.21** and **9.20–9.24**.

[13] Language embodying a reasonably comprehensive list of such reasons can be borrowed from § 5 of the proposed state and federal statutes in **App. C**. Reasons found by arbitrators to justify discharge are discussed in §§ **3.5–3.8**.

[14] See § **3.5–3.8**.

[15] See §§ **6.3–6.5** (civil service) and **6.13** (due process).

[16] See § **8.13**.

[17] 57 N.Y.2d 458, 443 N.E.2d 441, 457 N.Y.S.2d 193 (1982).

resort to dismissal for just and sufficient cause only, and only after all practical steps toward rehabilitation or salvage of the employee have been taken and failed."[18]

One commentator advises against defining cause in advance. Reasoning that a court may conclude that only those offenses similar to the examples are to be considered as cause for dismissal, James Redeker recommends that employers in nonunion plants not list specific examples as cause for summary dismissal.[19] He has drafted language for use in employment manuals that he believes would adequately protect the employer's interest in defending against wrongful dismissal actions[20] but believes its use would negate any feeling of security the employer seeks to encourage in the workforce.[21]

The disadvantage of not defining cause in advance is that supervisors retain substantial discretion to decide what is good cause. One sets up a kind of common law system without decisional reporting or a way to enforce stare decisis. Unless a central authority reviews decisions being made under an undefined just cause standard, the employer risks arbitrary supervisor action, making successful disparate treatment type challenges more likely.[22]

§ 8.13 — Procedural Fairness Policies: General Principles

Management also should consider procedural fairness in connection with its termination policies and its complaint or grievance policies. The procedures afforded in a well designed employee complaint or grievance policy may provide procedural fairness in connection with terminations without any separate termination appeals procedure.

Procedural fairness respecting terminations does not imply anything mysterious; it merely means that an employer should decide, in advance, the sort of notice

---

[18] *Id.* at 460, 443 N.E.2d at 442, 457 N.Y.S.2d at 194. As the quoted language makes clear, the McGraw-Hill policy also required progressive discipline in addition to cause as a prerequisite to termination.

[19] J. Redeker, Discipline: Policies and Procedures 47 (1983). An example of a court implying a promise to dismiss only for cause from much more limited express language is Wiskotoni v. Michigan Nat'l Bank W., 716 F.2d 378 (6th Cir. 1983). The bank's employee handbook said only that probationary employees could be dismissed for dissatisfaction with their work. *Id.* at 385–86.

[20] J. Redeker, Discipline: Policies and Procedures 46 (1983).

[21] One of Redeker's premises is that an appearance of fair disciplinary procedures is important to discourage unionization, enhance productivity, and avoid lawsuits. *Id.* at 42, 47.

[22] Disparate treatment is a way of proving violation of discrimination statutes. See § 2.3. It also presumably could show breach of an implied-in-fact contract or, more likely, breach of an implied covenant of good faith. See §§ 7.22–7.28.

an employee will receive when termination is contemplated,[23] who will make the dismissal decision,[24] and what kind of opportunity the employee will have to present her side of the story. The two purposes of any dismissal procedure are to provide a reliable means of deciding facts with respect to substantive questions and to give employees a sense of fair treatment. These purposes may be served without imposing an elaborate judicial-like procedure.

It is important to ensure that employee grievance procedures are linked appropriately with employee termination procedures. Frequently, as in the case of the Blue Cross manual in *Toussaint v. Blue Cross & Blue Shield*,[25] the termination and grievance procedures appear in separate sections of the policy statement and are not related clearly to each other. An example of a more integrated policy (though one which led to a judgment against the employer when it did not follow the policy) is the one at issue in *Pine River State Bank v. Mettille*.[26] This is how the Supreme Court of Minnesota described it:

> The key section, central to this case, is entitled "Disciplinary Policy." This section provides for what appears to be a three-stage procedure consisting of reprimands for the first and second "offense" and thereafter suspension or discharge, but discharge only "for an employee whose conduct does not improve as a result of the previous action taken." The section concludes with the sentence, "In no instance will a person be discharged from employment without a review of the facts by the Executive Officer."[27]

§ 8.14 — Procedural Fairness Policies: Suggested Approaches

Procedurally, two basic approaches to grievance and termination policies can be followed. One approach is to require higher approval *before* dismissal as well as exhaustion of certain remedial efforts short of dismissal. This is the approach

---

[23] Notice implies that the employee receive enough information that he has a practical opportunity to know what factual arguments would be relevant to the discharge decision. See § **6.12**.

[24] Procedural fairness suggests that this should be an unbiased decisionmaker. See generally § **6.12** and Judge Friendly's article cited in that section. Usually this means only that an official of the employer other than the employee's immediate supervisor make the decision.

[25] 408 Mich. 579, 292 N.W.2d 880 (1980). Three separate sections of the employer's policy manual dealt with terminations, employee complaint procedures, and disciplinary procedures. Their language was overlapping and inconsistent. *See id.* at 641, 292 N.W.2d at 905.

[26] 333 N.W.2d 622 (Minn. 1983).

[27] *Id.* at 626.

§ 8.14 PROCEDURAL FAIRNESS: APPROACHES

followed by Pine River State Bank in the case of *Pine River State Bank v. Mettille*.[28] Another example of this approach is that used by a large New York bank, which states that gross misconduct, as determined by the regional/functional officer and Director of Human Resources, is grounds for immediate dismissal. The second approach is to provide for postdecision review by higher levels of authority within the organization.

Under the first approach (pretermination procedures), for example, no terminations could be permitted without approval of the personnel department. The personnel department could require documentation of the reason for the discharge and possibly, on a case-by-case basis, a period of probation during which accomplishment of specific improvement goals by the employee would be monitored.[29] If the circumstances make it undesirable for the employee to continue in service until the pretermination review is complete, the employer's policy may provide for suspension while the termination decision is being made.

Under the second approach (posttermination procedures), a number of different possibilities exist for internal review of the termination decision.[30] Such procedures are desirable because they permit top management to monitor lower-level compliance with policies, because they may prevent outside litigation of employment decisions, and because they enhance morale.[31] One possibility is to provide a procedure for employees to file complaints of unfair treatment with the personnel department.[32] If this approach is followed, it may be desirable to provide for shared authority in hearing and deciding the grievance; such authority should be shared between a responsible personnel department official and a line manager superior to the supervisor involved in the grievance. Otherwise, if the personnel department is permitted to decide the matter unilaterally, line management may not retain an acceptable level of authority to manage.[33]

Another possibility is to provide for filing of employee complaints with a line manager superior to the complainant's immediate supervisors. Under this approach,

---

[28] 333 N.W.2d 622 (Minn. 1983).

[29] This would be similar to the concept of progressive discipline increasingly required by arbitrators as a prerequisite to discharge. See §§ **3.5–3.8**.

[30] The Conference Board, Nonunion Complaint Systems: A Corporate Appraisal, Report No. 770 (1980), identified four major types of employee complaint systems: (1) open door; (2) a series of steps with ultimate appeal to line management at the same facility; (3) a series of steps with ultimate appeal to a disinterested employer official; and (4) a series of steps with ultimate appeal to arbitration. *Id.* at 10–34 (reproducing policy manuals from companies utilizing each type).

[31] See §§ **8.3–8.4**.

[32] The Conference Board study found systems with ultimate appeal to a third party within the company to be the most favored. The third party might be the personnel department or it might be senior corporate management. The Conference Board, Nonunion Complaint Systems: A Corporate Appraisal 16, Report No. 770 (1980).

[33] Maintaining supervisory morale in the administration of employee complaint systems was identified in the Conference Board study as a continuing problem. *See id.* at 44.

the personnel department might provide a staff advisory function to the person with whom the grievance is filed.[34]

The level at which the appeal process stops can depend on the needs of the particular organization. It is not uncommon, as noted in § 8.5, for the ultimate decision authority to be the chief executive officer. In very large organizations, it may be preferable to designate a lower-level line officer or chief personnel officer as the ultimate decisionmaker. A few companies utilize a committee, sometimes with employee representation, as the ultimate or penultimate decisionmaker.[35]

Arbitration is another possibility for the final decision process in the termination proceedings. Relatively few companies provide arbitration as an ultimate decision step for nonunion employee complaints. Two notable systems are those employed by Trans World Airlines[36] and by Northrop Aviation.[37] The Conference Board study, which reported on both systems, said that many executives of companies not using arbitration felt that no system "can be entirely credible without arbitration."[38] Arbitration costs more and invades ultimate management authority to a greater extent than other systems.[39] A system can be structured, however, to limit the arbitrator's jurisdiction to deciding whether an existing corporate policy was applied properly and to bar any decision as to whether the policy itself is fair or justifiable.[40]

Robert Coulson, president of the American Arbitration Association, has proposed, for nonunion employees, a grievance procedure terminating in arbitration. He also suggests other alternatives that involve neutral decisionmakers but which do not bind management.[41]

James Redeker proposes yet another termination or grievance system. The first step provides the employee with a written statement of facts, giving the exact nature

---

[34] For example, in the Xerox "Open Door" procedure, the corporate personnel department is responsible for monitoring complaints to make sure they are investigated properly. *Id.* at 13 (reproducing a portion of Xerox policy manual).

[35] *See* F. Foulkes, Personnel Policies in Large Nonunion Companies 300 (1980).

[36] The TWA system (in the case of terminations) provides for a "system board of adjustment," composed of a company industrial relations representative, another noncontract employee selected by the complaining employee, and a neutral arbitrator who functions as a chairman. The Conference Board, Nonunion Complaint Systems: A Corporate Appraisal 22, Report No. 770 (1980) (reproducing TWA personnel manual excerpts).

[37] The Northrop procedure provides for selection of an arbitrator by agreement between the employee and the company, or, failing agreement, through the Federal Mediation and Conciliation Service. *Id.* at 32 (reproducing Northrop personnel manual excepts).

[38] *Id.* at 20.

[39] *Id.* at 18.

[40] The Northrop manual states, "The arbiter's function is to determine whether company policies, practices, rules or regulations have been complied with in the case of the employee filing the grievance. . . . The arbiter . . . will have no power to change [the policies]." *Id.* at 32 (reproducing Northrop personnel manual excerpts).

[41] R. Coulson, The Termination Handbook 195-98 (1981).

of the violation of company rules. The employee would be able to respond to the charge within a set time period with failure to respond meaning the employee accepts the discipline. If the employee chooses to dispute the charge or the discipline, he can choose the help of any uninvolved supervisor.[42] The employee can use outside counsel at his own expense and only for the last step in the process—arbitration. The employee would pay for half the arbitration cost, up to $300, to be deposited at the time demand for arbitration is made.[43]

Redeker also suggests a committee approach which would permit employees who dispute charges or penalties to appeal to a mixed group of supervisors and employees[44] with a tie-breaking vote to the management chair. The committee would conduct a hearing with the involved supervisor and employee present and render a decision.[45]

§ 8.15 Employee Appraisal Programs

A systematic procedure for evaluating employee performance on a periodic basis has a number of advantages in connection with terminations.[46] By forcing supervisors to evaluate subordinates formally, it reduces the likelihood of arbitrary supervisory action. It increases the likelihood that employees will be evaluated according to criteria decided upon by top management and enumerated as part of the appraisal policy. It conditions employee expectations so that a marginal employee

---

[42] The company would have the power to prevent overuse of favorite supervisors by declaring, with supporting documentation, that the supervisor was being overused and could require the employee to pick another, or could assign one from a rotating roster. J. Redeker, Discipline: Policies and Procedures 49 (1983).

[43] The cost would be high enough to discourage frivolous demands, in Redeker's opinion. *Id.* He also recommends a strict rule barring fellow employees from contributing to the aggrieved employee's cause, since such a rule would prevent the formation of groups with sufficient money to advance frivolous grievances. Such a rule almost certainly would violate the National Labor Relations Act, as to employees covered by the Act.

[44] The employee and the personnel director would select two members each, with a high level manager as moderator. *Id.* at 50. *See* Khalifa v. Henry Ford Hosp., ___ Mich.App. ___, ___ N.W.2d ___, No. 84582 (Dec. 2, 1986) (final and binding decision by employee grievance council established by unilateral employer policy barred suit for breach of implied-in-fact contract even though judicial-type procedures not followed) (split panel).

[45] Redeker points out that this system is economical, has a measure of due process, and would help supervisors become consistent in their operation of the disciplinary system. *Id.* Such a system apparently was used by the employer in Green v. American Cast Iron Pipe Co., 446 So. 2d 16 (Ala. 1984) (affirming jury verdict for employer in wrongful discharge action premised on irregularities by joint discipline committee).

[46] *See Study of Court Decisions in Cases Involving Employee Performance Appraisal Systems,* 248 Daily Lab. Rep. (BNA) E-1 (Dec. 26, 1984), summarizing Field & Holley, *The Relationship of Performance Appraisal System Characteristics to Verdicts in Selected Employment Discrimination Cases,* 25 Acad. Mgmt. J. 392 (1982).

will be less surprised if dismissed. It creates a documentary record, or *paper trail,* that can be used in internal disciplinary procedures and in external litigation over adverse personnel decisions.

But employee appraisal systems can create a number of risks unless they are properly designed and managed. Probably the greatest risk is that appraisal forms will show good employee performance and thus will undercut the legitimacy of a subsequent decision to dismiss the employee.[47] Another risk is that a discharge will be found to violate the employer's policies because of a failure to follow the appraisal procedures carefully. A third risk is that a discharged employee may claim that a failure to inform the employee of the risk of discharge constitutes negligence.[48] Appraisal systems can be improved in several ways. These suggestions are intended to improve the accuracy and consistency of employee appraisals and to reduce the possibility of liability for negligence in implementing the system, as discussed in § 5.29.

1. Regular written appraisals should be made for all employees or for all employees not represented by a labor organization
2. Written appraisals should be approved by line management one level above the supervisor doing the appraisal, before the appraisal is communicated to the employee
3. Employees should be appraised according to explicit criteria that are demonstrably job-related
4. Supervisors performing the appraisal should have available to them, and be required to utilize where relevant, quantitative data on attendance and productivity. If quantitative data are neither available nor relevant, materials illustrative of the quality of the employee's performance should be used
5. Employees should sign the appraisal form to evidence the fact that the appraisal has been communicated to them. If an employee refuses to sign, another supervisor can be invited to witness the oral communication of the appraisal to the employee and this supervisor-witness can sign the form
6. An audit mechanism should be used to control the incidence of inflated appraisals. One possibility is to impose a frequency distribution on each supervisor providing that a certain percentage of employees can be rated as "outstanding" and that a certain percentage must be rated as

---

[47] *See* Douglas v. Anderson, 656 F.2d 528 (9th Cir. 1981) (sufficient evidence of unsatisfactory performance to be of legitimate concern to employer). *See also Discrimination Under Age Discrimination in Employment Act,* 10 Am. Jur. Proof of Facts 2d 1, 27 (1976) (sample witness examination to support age discrimination claim by testimony of good performance ratings); Annotation, 32 A.L.R. Fed. 7 (1977 & 1982 Supp.).

[48] See § **5.29** regarding recovery of tort damages for such negligence; Lieber v. Union Carbide Corp., 577 F. Supp. 562 (E.D. Tenn. 1983) (notice to employees that performance appraisals would be given did not establish legal obligation to make appraisals; suit by retiree for increased pension benefits on grounds that performance appraisals would have induced better performance and salary increases).

§ 8.15 EMPLOYEE APPRAISAL

"marginal."[49] Another possibility is to monitor the appraisals statistically, and to counsel a supervisor informally if she seems to be giving inflated appraisals

7. The interrelationship between the salary administration program and possible terminations should be considered explicitly. It is common for supervisors to give inflated performance appraisals in order to justify salary increases they believe to be necessary to retain average employees. Such a result can be incompatible with an accurate assessment of the employee's performance

8. When an employee is rated as marginal or unsatisfactory, a necessary part of the appraisal system should be the development of formal goals for employee improvement, agreed to by the employee. Recording goals and evaluating performance toward them can materially strengthen the employer's position in litigation if the employee's performance does not improve.

Copies of evaluation forms actually used by representative companies are available from commercial publishers.[50]

The relationship between an appraisal system and termination policies and procedures should be considered carefully. In some instances, performance appraisals and a termination will have no connection; the former will concern performance, and the latter will involve misconduct. In other cases, when a decision to terminate is based on poor performance, the employee may buttress a wrongful dismissal claim on the pretermination appraisal results. It may be possible for an employer to uncouple the appraisal system from the termination decision by a clearly articulated personnel rule that makes one independent from the other. Such an approach would make little sense in terms of a rational personnel policy, though it might have some narrow legal attraction.

On the other hand, a sound appraisal system can improve the employer's position in wrongful dismissal litigation because it provides documentary evidence in support of the decision to terminate. A sound system also can prevent litigation because it enhances self-discipline and encourages good supervisor-subordinate communication.

---

[49] An employee's effort to challenge an appraisal system because of a requirement that appraisals conform to a specific statistical distribution failed in McCone v. New England Tel. & Tel. Co., 393 Mass. 231, 471 N.E.2d 47, 50 (1984) (poor appraisals resulting in dismissal failed to state an implied covenant claim).

[50] *See* Warren, Gorham & Lamont, Modern Personnel Forms, ch. 8 (On-the-Job Evaluations) (1976 and 1982 Supp); Bureau of National Affairs, Performance Appraisal Programs (PPF Survey No. 135) (1983).

CHAPTER 9

COMPREHENSIVE WRONGFUL DISCHARGE LEGISLATION

§ 9.1	Introduction
§ 9.2	Overview of Wrongful Dismissal Doctrine: Substantive and Procedural Fairness
§ 9.3	Is Legislation Needed?
§ 9.4	The Politics of Statutory Reform
§ 9.5	Statutory Models
§ 9.6	—Federal Wrongful Dismissal Statutes
§ 9.7	—State Whistleblower Statutes
§ 9.8	—State Employment Term Statutes
§ 9.9	—State Service Letter Statutes
§ 9.10	—State Just Cause Proposals
§ 9.11	—The British Model
§ 9.12	—The Canadian Model
§ 9.13	—Commentators' Models
§ 9.14	—The Summers Concept
§ 9.15	—The Selznick Concept
§ 9.16	—The Bellace Concept
§ 9.17	Judicial Control of Other Types of Associations
§ 9.18	A Proposed Wrongful Dismissal Statute: Introduction
§ 9.19	Legislative Drafting Pitfalls
§ 9.20	Possible Substantive Fairness Standards
§ 9.21	—Just Cause Standard
§ 9.22	—Good Faith Standard
§ 9.23	—Weakness of Simple Standards
§ 9.24	—Enumerated Prohibitions
§ 9.25	Procedural Fairness
§ 9.26	—Preemption, Election, Exhaustion, and Preclusion
§ 9.27	—Deference to Employer Procedures
§ 9.28	—Treatment of Collectively Bargained Arbitration

§ 9.29	—Selection of Forum
§ 9.30	—Integration of Wrongful Dismissal and Unemployment Compensation Systems
§ 9.31	—Burdens of Proof
§ 9.32	—Remedies
§ 9.33	—Costs of Litigation
§ 9.34	Estimation of Case Volume

§ 9.1 Introduction

This chapter addresses statutory reform[1] of the law of wrongful dismissal, offering a basic policy matrix for dealing with both substantive and procedural questions.[2]

The chapter proposes a substantive standard of wrongful dismissal which would incorporate presently recognized protections for employees without disregarding the needs of employers.[3] It contemplates forcing all legal claims growing out of a single employment termination into a single proceeding.[4]

The proposed statutory approach stops short of requiring employers to establish just cause for terminating employees,[5] thus rejecting models represented by English and Canadian wrongful dismissal statutes,[6] civil service,[7] most collective bargaining agreements,[8] and the suggestions of many commentators.[9] Instead, it suggests a carefully circumscribed set of reasons for which dismissal would *not* be permitted,[10] and also a means of enforcing employer promises of employment tenure.[11]

The chapter begins by explaining the difference between substantive and procedural fairness. It then assesses the need for enactment of statutory law,[12] and considers the politics that will determine whether, and in what form, such

---

[1] Many of the concepts in the suggested doctrine and the substantive portions of the draft statutes in **App. C** could be adopted by courts as common law rules for decision in the absence of legislation, consistent with the common law and statutory concepts developed in **chs. 2–7**.

[2] *See* § **9.2**.

[3] *See* §§ **9.20–9.24**.

[4] *See* § **9.26**.

[5] Requiring cause for dismissal is an element of substantive fairness, discussed generally in § **9.20**. A specific proposal respecting substantive fairness is presented in § **9.24**.

[6] The British statute is discussed in § **9.11**. The Canadian statute is discussed in § **9.12**.

[7] See §§ **6.3–6.6**.

[8] See § **3.5–3.8**.

[9] See, e.g., Professor Clyde Summers' proposal, discussed in § **9.14**, and the other proposals described in §§ **9.15–9.16**.

[10] See § **9.24** for an explanation of this requirement. Specific statutory language effecting such a requirement is contained in § 5(2) of the draft state and federal statutes, contained in **App. C**.

[11] See § **9.24** for an explanation of this requirement. Specific statutory language effecting such a requirement is contained in § 5(b) of the draft state and federal statutes, contained in **App. C**.

[12] See § **9.3**.

legislative action may occur.[13] A summary of the contents of statutes enacted, and bills considered, by state legislatures is presented.[14] Statutory wrongful dismissal doctrines in Britain,[15] Canada,[16] and proposed by American commentators[17] are reviewed, as well as the ways the courts have dealt with internal decisions of other private associations.[18] After making the case for an enumerated prohibitions approach to substantive fairness, the chapter evaluates alternative means to force claims related to a single termination to be tried in a single proceeding. Finally, the chapter projects the types of caseloads that might be anticipated if statutes such as those contained in **Appendix C** were enacted by the Congress or in all 50 states.[19]

§ 9.2 Overview of Wrongful Dismissal Doctrine: Substantive and Procedural Fairness

This section identifies the two conceptual components of a wrongful dismissal doctrine. It does not propose that these components be enforced fully against employers. A proposed doctrine is developed in **§§ 9.20** through **9.24**. When an employer's decision to terminate an employee is questioned, two aspects of the decision can be scrutinized. The first is substantive: Did the reason relied upon by the employer for the termination bear a rational relationship to the employer's business needs?[20] The second is procedural: Did the employer ascertain and evaluate the existence of the reason asserted by him in a manner likely to result in a reasonably accurate factual decision?[21] For ease in exposition, the first aspect is called

---

[13] See **§ 9.4**.

[14] See **§§ 9.5–9.10**.

[15] See **§ 9.11**.

[16] See **§ 9.12**.

[17] See **§§ 9.13–9.16**.

[18] See **§ 9.17**.

[19] See **§ 9.34**.

[20] This concept is the same as the substantive due process test applied to public employee discharges (see **§ 6.13**), and to the concept of cause applied under civil service statutes (see **§§ 6.3–6.5**), and under collective bargaining agreements (see **§§ 3.5–3.8**). The concept is used here in a general sense, rather than in its more restricted constitutional sense, in which state action usually is a prerequisite. The Constitution requires due process only by governments, as distinguished from private sector employers. Bifurcation of the dismissal decision into these substantive and procedural questions has been accepted by courts trying wrongful dismissal cases. *See, e.g.,* Simpson v. Western Graphics Corp., 293 Or. 96, 100, 643 P.2d 1276, 1278 (1982).

[21] This concept is the same as the procedural due process test applied to public employee discharges. See **§ 6.12**. Here the concept is used in a general sense, rather than in its more restricted constitutional sense, in which state action usually is a prerequisite. "The rules and principles of procedural fairness . . . all are designed to promote the correct decision of disputes. All of them tend to ensure that facts will be found more accurately or that evaluations will be made more reasonably and impartially than would be the case if they were not in force." Grey, *Procedural Fairness and Substantive Rights,* Nomos XVIII, Due Process 182, 184 (1977).

substantive fairness, and the second aspect is called *procedural fairness.* Unless the law imposes a substantive fairness test, procedural fairness has limited utility.[22]

Choosing a substantive fairness standard involves a balancing process, in which the need for an employer to have broad discretion to make dismissal decisions is weighed against the harm to the employee adversely affected by the decision. The use of a balancing process implies that one should be able to identify the interests being weighed. Commonly, the rights and needs thus drawn into the balance must be recognized as *legitimate* if the law is to take them into account. Defining the scope of legitimate rights and needs accomplishes the hardest part of the substantive fairness analysis.

The analytical process involved is embraced by the prima facie tort concept, recognized in § 870 of the *Restatement of Torts.*[23] The prima facie tort concept provides for the imposition of liability on one who intentionally, without justification, causes legal injury to another.[24] The *Restatement* drafters contemplated that a court would engage in a balancing process, in which the legal injury to the plaintiff would be weighed against the legitimate needs of the defendant attempting to justify her

---

[22] "It makes sense to impose special procedural controls from outside the authoritative decision-making institution . . . only when the substantive right placed at hazard has its source outside the decision making institution itself." Grey, *Procedural Fairness and Substantive Rights,* Nomos XVIII, Due Process 182, 202 (1977). John Rawls identifies two criteria for "perfect procedural justice:" (1) an independent criterion for a just outcome, and (2) a procedure that is certain to give that outcome. J. Rawls, A Theory of Justice 85 (1971). Rawls's first criterion illustrates what the text calls substantive fairness and his second criterion illustrates procedural fairness. Rawls's formulation makes the relationship between the two concepts apparent. Procedural fairness can serve values other than accuracy in determining the existence of substantive fact, however. For example, there may be value in the perception of just treatment when an employee is afforded an opportunity to present her position. Or procedural fairness may ensure that an agent of the employer at a policymaking level makes the ultimate termination decision. *See* Michelman, *Formal and Associational Aims in Procedural Due Process,* Nomos XVIII, Due Process 126, 127–28 (1977) (due process can serve values other than accuracy in determining substantive rights).

[23] Another example is constitutional substantive due process analysis. In substantive due process analysis, the needs of the state are weighed against the rights of the individual claiming denial of due process. See Beller v. Middendorf, 632 F.2d 788, 807 (9th Cir. 1980); Major v. Hampton, 413 F. Supp. 66, 69 (E.D. La. 1976); J. Nowak, R. Rotunda & J. Young, Constitutional Law 404 (1978). See generally **§ 6.13**. The balancing process is not necessary unless the person claiming denial of due process can implicate rights recognized as appropriate for constitutional protection. *See* Connick v. Myers, 461 U.S. 138 (1983); Loehr v. Ventura County Community College Dist., 743 F.2d 1310, 1317 (9th Cir. 1984) (failure to demonstrate property interest does not defeat a properly asserted liberty interest claim). *See* Cleveland Bd. of Educ. v. Loudermill, 470 U.S. 532 (1985); Perry v. Sindermann, 408 U.S. 593 (1972); Board of Regents v. Roth, 408 U.S. 564 (1972). Once either of these rights is shown to be involved, the decision under scrutiny can be sustained only if a legitimate state interest in making the scrutinized decision can be shown. *Compare* Connick v. Myers, 461 U.S. at 154 (decision justified) *with* Norton v. Macy, 417 F.2d 1161 (D.C. Cir. 1969) (decision not justified). The analogy between the property or liberty interest in constitutional analysis and the individual right in substantive fairness analysis is obvious. Similarly, the legitimate state interest is analogous to the institutional employer need in substantive fairness analysis.

[24] Restatement (Second) of Torts § 870 (1979). See generally **§§ 5.5–5.7**.

§ 9.2 OVERVIEW: FAIRNESS

action.[25] In prima facie tort analysis, as in constitutional due process analysis, legitimacy enters into the equation on both the plaintiff's and the defendant's sides. If the plaintiff has been hurt in some way not recognized as legal injury, prima facie tort will afford the plaintiff no damages and no injunction.[26] Once the plaintiff proves legal injury (and causation, of course), if the defendant cannot offer legally recognized justification, her conduct will subject her to liability.[27]

In prima facie tort analysis, the challenger of a decision cannot obtain scrutiny by legal institutions unless he or she can show impairment of an interest formally recognized by the law. The defender can be successful only if she shows that the decision was supported by interests formally recognized by the law.

The history of employment law in the United States has been the history of adding legally recognized employee interests. Once a new category of interests is recognized, these interests are weighed against legitimate employer interests—either in a statutory formula or in individual cases. The courts and legislatures have expanded recognized employee interests in the following ways:

First, when the reason for the termination is based on a racial, religious, gender or age characteristic, or when it is based on certain conduct, the legislature has said that the termination is at least prima facie illegal, and has afforded remedies to employees terminated for these reasons, unless the employer can offer overriding justification.[28]

Second, termination by a public employer is prima facie illegal when the reason for the termination is conduct within constitutional guarantees against governmental interference with free speech, association, privacy and religion.[29] A governmental employer must offer legally adequate justification to escape liability.

Third, when the reason for the termination is conduct that is protected by public policy,[30] the discharge is a tort, unless the employer can offer justification.[31]

Fourth, when the employer has promised that it will terminate only for certain reasons, or only after following certain procedures, the employee's expectations created thereby will be protected by enforcing the employer's promise in a common law breach of contract suit.[32] If the employer is the government, its promises

---

[25] *Id.* comment k.

[26] *Id.* comment e. See § **5.6**.

[27] *Id.* See § **5.7**.

[28] Statutory prohibitions against class-based discharges are considered in §§ **2.2–2.14**. Statutory prohibitions against conduct-based discharges are considered in §§ **2.15–2.24**.

[29] These *liberty* interests are considered in § **6.11**. Use of the term *prima facie* indicates that the employer can assert sufficiently compelling state interests to justify the invasion of liberty interests. Assessing the justification is at the heart of substantive due process analysis. See § **6.13**.

[30] **Chapter 5** classifies the public policy torts into two major categories: internal and external, and subclassifies internal public policy torts into those involving reports of employer misconduct to public agencies, those involving internal complaints, and those involving refusal of employer orders.

[31] The public policy tort concept is considered in **ch. 5**.

[32] Contract theories are considered in **ch. 4**.

may be enforced under the constitutional guarantee against governmental deprivation of property without due process.[33]

Fifth, when a private sector employer acts in bad faith, or for reasons extraneous to workplace management, to deprive an employee of compensation, a common law action for breach of an implied covenant of good faith and fair dealing may lie.[34] In several of the enumerated interests, employee interests are reinforced by societal interests in favor of certain types of conduct by employees. Formulating a standard for substantive fairness in wrongful discharge legislation requires consideration of all of the recognized interests enumerated above.[35]

Opposing these interests are employer and societal interests favoring effective management of organizations. *Free enterprise* (the preference for regulating economic relations by market forces instead of by law) is a societal value on the employer's side. The free enterprise value militates against legal regulation of discharge decisions regardless of whether an employer can justify a particular discharge. These interests require that employees not be shielded from the consequences of their poor performance or misconduct and that supervisors not be deterred from exercising their managerial responsibilities by the inconvenience of litigating employees claims.[36] An employer should be allowed to remove an employee in pursuit of these interests when such interests outweigh the adverse effect on legitimate employee interests.

Substantive fairness requires that an employer satisfy an external criterion which requires at a minimum that the employer use its power over the employment relation in a way that does not jeopardize important social policies, and at most that the employer's decision meet objective criteria of rationality.[37]

If a policy direction is chosen that imposes any type of substantive fairness standard on employers, the problem of procedural fairness must be addressed.[38] This is so because the substantive fairness concept requires that certain facts be present as a prerequisite for termination, or that certain facts be excluded from consideration in the termination decision. If the substantive fairness requirement is to be meaningful, the manner in which termination decisions are made must be controlled.

---

[33] Due process protection of property rights rooted in promises of employment tenure is considered in § **6.10**.

[34] See § **4.11**.

[35] §§ **9.20–9.24** consider the alternatives for a statutory substantive fairness standard.

[36] See Note, *Limiting the Right to Terminate At Will Employees—Have the Courts Forgotten the Employer?*, 35 Vand. L. Rev. 201 (1982).

[37] The minimum approach is exemplified by the public policy tort, addressed in **ch. 5**. The maximum approach encompasses just cause proposals discussed in § **9.21**.

[38] Under the present system, procedural fairness works like this: Substantive rights defined by statute are applied by administrative agencies and courts. Substantive rights defined by the Constitution and by tort law are applied by the courts. Contract rights are applied by arbitrators if they arise under collective bargaining agreements, and by courts otherwise. But there is much uncertainty regarding the respective roles of employers, judges, and juries with respect to decisionmaking. See §§ **7.13–7.16** (torts), **7.22–7.28** (contracts). Moreover, there is a need for simplification in the external machinery available to review employer decisions.

§ 9.2 OVERVIEW: FAIRNESS

The issue of procedural fairness in private employment termination decisions primarily involves a choice between deferring to decisions made by the employer through employer-selected procedures as contrasted with retrying the termination decision in an external forum.

Procedural fairness is a relative rather than an absolute concept.[39] At a minimum, it requires some external check on the decisionmaking procedures utilized by employers as a counterweight to natural employer interests potentially antagonistic to employee interests.[40] Procedural fairness can be ensured by a review of procedures used by the employer, or it can involve a de novo decision by an external tribunal. Determining the appropriate level of procedural fairness requires a balancing of values. Accuracy-promoting mechanisms must not be imposed beyond the point at which the costs or delays involved outweigh the benefits from the additional accuracy they secure.[41]

Two polar alternatives can be identified. The first alternative, least intrusive into employer prerogatives but also the least protective of fairness, would be to permit employers to make discharge decisions, immune from significant external review, as long as they follow *some* formal process embodying the rudiments of procedural fairness; e.g., giving notice, appointing an unbiased decisionmaker, and providing an opportunity for the employee to tell her side of the story to that decisionmaker.[42] The other alternative would be more intrusive, but also would enhance the protection afforded to employees. It would involve a trial de novo of the fairness of the dismissal decision by the jury in a regular court of law, following the usual rules of evidence.[43]

---

[39] *See* Grey, *Procedural Fairness and Substantive Rights,* Nomos XVIII, Due Process 182, 184–85 (1977).

[40] *Id.* at 187.

[41] *Id.* at 184. Acceptance of this proposition is reflected in the balancing approach to procedural due process adopted by the Supreme Court in Mathews v. Eldridge, 424 U.S. 319 (1976), and discussed in **§ 6.12**.

[42] This is similar to the minimum due process required for student suspensions in Goss v. Lopez, 419 U.S. 565, 581 (1975) (notice of charges, explanation of evidence against student, and an opportunity to present student's side of story). *But see* Bethel School Dist. No. 403 v. Fraser, ____ U.S. ____, 106 S. Ct. 3159 (1986) (rejecting student due process challenge; school discipline code can accommodate informal student-teacher relationship; need not be as detailed as criminal statute). The text suggests including only the first three rights identified in Judge Friendly's list of ingredients of procedural due process (see **§ 6.12**): (1) an unbiased tribunal, (2) notice, and (3) an opportunity to present reasons why the proposed actions should not be taken. The Oregon Supreme Court has embraced a related approach in Simpson v. Western Graphics Corp., 293 Or. 96, 100, 643 P.2d 1276, 1278 (1982), though it is not clear that it would impose *any* procedural requirements, as opposed to deferring to the employer regardless of the procedure followed. An alternative, adopted by the Montana Supreme Courts in Gates v. Life of Mont. Ins. Co., 196 Mont. 178, 638 P.2d 1063 (1982), *later appeal,* 668 P.2d 213 (1983), permits the employer to define the procedures for decisionmaking, but lets the jury decide whether the employer followed them.

[43] Essentially this is the approach adopted by the Michigan Supreme Court in Toussaint v. Blue Cross & Blue Shield, 408 Mich. 579, 621–23, 292 N.W.2d 880, 896 (1980) (jury decides facts,

An intermediate approach to procedural fairness can be borrowed from administrative law.[44] Under this approach, the employer could adopt procedures meeting generic requirements of procedural fairness.[45] Employer decisions reached under such procedures[46] would be accepted unless they were arbitrary and capricious[47] or made in bad faith.[48] The approach selected for procedural fairness should minimize interference with employer prerogatives while providing a means of imposing some external procedural constraint of proven workability.[49]

It is conceptually important, though difficult in practice, to separate the substantive from the procedural inquiry. Ensuring a high degree of procedural fairness by de novo review of the termination decision in an external tribunal tends unavoidably to impose an external standard of substantive fairness. A prominent example is the propensity of labor arbitrators to find an implied just cause standard for dismissals under collective bargaining agreements, even when the agreements

---

and whether facts amount to cause). Obviously, even if a jury is to decide the termination question de novo, presumptions and burdens of proof materially affect the relative weight given to employer and employee interests. *See* Grey, *Procedural Fairness and Substantive Rights,* Nomos XVIII, Due Process 182, 183 (1977). Presumptions and burdens of proof are discussed in **ch. 7**.

[44] The administrative law analogy is imperfect. Judicial review of administrative agency decisions proceeds from constitutional due process and legislative delegation doctrines, and is intended to enforce compliance with the agency's statutory mandate. External review of private employer decisions would be premised instead on public policy principles derived through the common law or expressed in statutes.

[45] The Administrative Procedure Act (APA) imposes detailed procedural requirements for adjudication; *see* 5 U.S.C. §§ 554, 556–557 (1982), but the courts allow agencies some discretion respecting compliance with these requirements. *See* Richardson v. Perales, 402 U.S. 389, 409–10 (1971); American Trucking Ass'ns v. United States, 627 F.2d 1313, 1321 (D.C. Cir. 1980) (agencies have broad discretion to fashion own procedures); Verkuil, *The Emerging Concept of Administrative Procedure,* 78 Colum. L. Rev. 258, 313 (1978) (noting flexibility provided by present APA adjudication requirements). Even more flexibility is permitted under procedural due process constitutional requirements. *See* Schweiker v. McClure, 456 U.S. 188 (1982) (agency adjudicatory functions can be delegated to private hearing officer pursuant to statute without violating due process); Mathews v. Eldridge, 424 U.S. 319 (1976); Richardson v. Perales, 402 U.S. 389 (1971) (informal adjudication by the Social Security Administration).

[46] Whether the employer followed procedure adopted voluntarily or imposed on it externally is of course a discrete question. *See* Gates v. Life of Mont. Ins. Co., 196 Mont. 178, 638 P.2d 1063 (1982), *later appeal,* 668 P.2d 213 (1983) (jury should decide whether employer followed its own policies).

[47] One of the difficulties with the administrative model is that it tends toward imposition of greater procedural obligations, over time, on the decisionmaker. For example, a requirement that a factual decision be supported by *substantial evidence* (*see* Universal Camera v. NLRB, 340 U.S. 474 (1951)), implies that a record must be generated which, in turn, implies certain procedural requirements. *See* Camp v. Pitts, 411 U.S. 138 (1973). *See generally* Pittston Stevedoring Corp. v. Dellaventura, 544 F.2d 35 (2d Cir. 1976), for Judge Friendly's discussion of the standards for judicial review of administrative agency action. Pittston Stevedoring Corp. v. Dellaventura was not appealed; the companion cases were affirmed, 432 U.S. 249 (1977).

[48] *See* Gates v. Life of Mont. Ins. Co., 196 Mont. 178, *later appeal,* 668 P.2d 213 (1983) (covenant of good faith violated by failure to follow procedures).

[49] *See* Mathews v. Eldridge, 424 U.S. 319 (1976) (approving long-standing decisional procedures without rejecting the concept of external review).

contain no such standard explicitly.[50] It is easier to keep the two aspects of fairness separate if a policy decision respecting substantive fairness is made first, before a policy decision is made respecting procedural fairness.

These policy decisions can be made by legislatures, as they have been respecting race, sex and age discrimination, or they can be made by the courts in the context of individual lawsuits.

§ 9.3 Is Legislation Needed?

The need for additional legislation to protect employees from wrongful dismissal has diminished as exceptions to the Employment-at-Will Rule have been recognized.[51] Legislative action may be desirable, however, to consolidate existing protections against wrongful discharge and to simplify litigation.

The preceding chapters of this treatise analyzed the growing body of law covering wrongful discharge that largely has supplanted the Employment-at-Will Rule.[52] Several federal statutes protect employees from discharge due to their membership in defined classes or due to specified conduct.[53] Public employees enjoy general protection under civil service statutes and under the Constitution.[54] Private sector employees in about 45 states can recover under contract[55] and tort[56] theories, depending on the reasons for their discharges and on representations made to them by their employers.

The existing legal framework is both incomplete and duplicative, however. The several statutes and common law doctrines define substantive fairness in different ways and ensure procedural fairness largely by providing forums within which the termination decisions can be tried de novo. Some employees can relitigate the fairness of their dismissals several times in several different forums.[57] Other

---

[50] See § 3.5.

[51] The cumulative effect of statutory, collectively bargained, and common law protections for employees is reasonably comprehensive in more than two-thirds of the states. See § 1.12. Thus, the lack of protection motivating the Summers and Blades proposals has changed to a substantial degree. Summers, *Individual Protection Against Unjust Dismissal: Time for a Statute,* 62 Va. L. Rev. 481, 482–83 (1976) (criticizing lack of common law protection for nonunion employees); Blades, *Employment at Will vs. Individual Freedom: On Limiting the Abusive Exercise of Employer Power,* 67 Colum. L. Rev. 1404, 1413 (1967) (noting lack of common law protection for workers).

[52] But see § 1.13 explaining how the Rule still is outcome determinative under the three principal common law theories.

[53] See ch. 2.

[54] See ch. 6.

[55] See ch. 4.

[56] See ch. 5.

[57] *See* University of Tenn. v. Elliot, ___ U.S. ___, 106 S. Ct. 3220 (1986) (unreviewed state administrative decision not entitled to preclusive effect in Title VII case); Alexander v. Gardner-Denver, 415 U.S. 36 (1974) (both collectively bargained arbitration and Title VII available for same claim); NLRB v. Plasterers Local 79, 404 U.S. 116, 136 (1971) (unfair labor practice and arbitration potentially available for same claim); Johnson v. Railway Express Agency, 421 U.S.

employees have no remedy at all, regardless of the unfairness of their dismissals.[58] Employers are subjected to multiple challenges by some employees, and are unable to predict with any confidence the probable liability flowing from different causes of action. Few existing mechanisms for adjudicating wrongful discharge claims give appropriate deference to collectively bargained or unilaterally established procedures designed to protect employees.[59]

It will be difficult to improve the uniformity of common law rules of decision for the substantive and procedural fairness criteria without legislation, although the common law produces reasonably uniform "majority rules" over time.[60] Also, it would be impossible to consolidate the law of wrongful dismissal into a single body of law, applied by efficient adjudicatory mechanisms, without legislation, because much of the existing law is statutory in origin.

The strongest argument for legislation, therefore, is an essentially conservative argument arising from the need for more order and predictability. The existing diversity and fragmentation of forums benefits neither employees nor employers.

Employees face a bewildering set of choices. Employee counsel must make difficult guesses about the best order in which to pursue different kinds of claims and the degree to which particular legal arguments should be presented or omitted from the claim presented to any particular forum.

Employers face the prospect of litigating the appropriateness of a dismissal many times, under different legal theories, in different forums, as noted earlier in this section.

The time has come for institutional reform, if not substantive reform. The merits of various forms of legislation to rationalize the substantive law of wrongful dismissal have been addressed in other writings. These proposals range from a prohibition against dismissing employees without just cause, perhaps a bit too revolutionary, to statutes essentially codifying the common law of wrongful dismissal in order to prohibit dismissals jeopardizing clear public policies and to prohibit dismissals violating employer promises of employment security.

For now, the overriding need is to channel litigation over the legality of a particular employment determination into a single forum, which can decide with finality the related common law, federal statutory, and state statutory legal issues presented.

---

454 (1975) (Title VII and 42 U.S.C. § 1981 available for same discrimination claim); W.R. Grace & Co. v. Rubber Workers Local 759, 461 U.S. 757 (1983) (conflicting arbitration award and Title VII decree allowed to stand); Belknap v. Hale, 463 U.S. 491 (1983) (potentially conflicting unfair labor practice proceeding and state lawsuit by discharged striker replacements permitted). *See generally* B. Schlei & P. Grossman, Employment Discrimination 1073 (1983) (election and exhaustion of remedies).

[58] This would be the case for employees in those states continuing to recognize the Employment-at-Will Rule as a substantive legal doctrine, who cannot bring their cases within the statutory protections. See § **1.12** for a state-by-state summary of common law theories.

[59] In other words, present law adopts too intrusive an approach to the procedural fairness question identified in § **9.2**.

[60] The contract law requirement of consideration is an obvious example. See § **4.4**. A more recent example is the acceptance of four types of tortious invasion of privacy. *See* Restatement (Second) of Torts §§ 652A–652E (1979).

Despite the compelling logic of such a move, it is not easy politically or technically to do this. Various interest groups have a proprietary attitude toward particular tribunals. For example, organized labor, despite its aggressive criticism of the National Labor Relations Board, probably would be reluctant to see unfair labor practice adjudication handled by another tribunal. Civil rights groups, despite their criticism of the EEOC, probably would resist diverting the handling of discrimination cases to another forum. Similarly, the plaintiff bar probably prefer to litigate in courts of general jurisdiction.

Generally, the discrete parts of American labor law have evolved toward greater cohesion. First comes executive, legislative, and judicial action to protect particular groups from harm resulting from particular acts, replaced in time with a more comprehensive statutory arrangement protecting an entire class and affording greater predictability for those who wish to conform their conduct to the legal standards.[61] The same course would be desirable with respect to wrongful dismissal.

§ 9.4 The Politics of Statutory Reform

Legislative action occurs when the balance of political power favors change.[62] The balance of political power generally is determined by the strength and intensity of feeling of groups within the larger society perceiving that they have similar

---

[61] *See* G. Calabresi, A Common Law for the Age of Statutes (1982) (criticism of the "orgy of statute making" characteristic of contemporary American law). The development of the law of collective bargaining and of employment discrimination exemplifies this evolutionary approach. Changes in collective bargaining law began with changes in the common law of conspiracy and justification. *See* Commonwealth v. Hunt, 4 Mass. 111 (1842) (conspiracy); Vegelahn v. Guntner, 167 Mass. 92, 44 N.E.2d 1077 (1896); H. Perritt, Labor Injunctions ch. 1-2 (1986) (history of labor injunction before enactment of Norris LaGuardia Act). Then states and the federal government enacted statutes providing for collective bargaining in certain sectors, notably railroading. Finally, the Congress enacted a comprehensive statute governing virtually all employees affecting interstate commerce. Changes in discrimination law began with federal prohibitions against discrimination in the administration of the Unemployment Relief Act of 1933, 48 Stat. 22 (1933). Then the federal government moved more broadly with the promulgation of Exec. Order No. 8587, 5 Fed. Reg. 445 (1940), prohibiting race and religious discrimination in the federal civil service, and Executive Order No. 8802, 6 Fed. Reg. 3109 (Jun. 25, 1941) prohibiting race discrimination in employment by war contractors. Nondiscrimination in the civil service was ratified by the Congress in the Ramspeck Act, 54 Stat. 1211 (1940). Meanwhile at the state level, New York enacted the first state fair employment practices act in 1945, but had moved earlier to prohibit employment discrimination in certain industries, for example by public utilities. By the time Title VII of the Civil Rights Act of 1964 was enacted, more than half the states had fair employment practices legislation. Overlapping these statutory and executive branch developments were judicial decisions prohibiting race discrimination in collective bargaining, in Steele v. Louisville & N.R.R., 232 U.S. 192 (1944) (Railway Labor Act), and Wallace Corp. v. NLRB, 323 U.S. 248 (1944) (National Labor Relations Act). *See generally* Jones, *The Development of Modern Equal Employment Opportunity and Affirmative Action Law: A Brief Chronological Overview,* 20 How. L. J. 74 (1977); M. Sovern, Legal Restraints on Racial Discrimination in Employment (1966).

[62] *See* V.O. Key, Politics, Parties and Pressure Groups 7-8 (1942); The Federalist No. 10 (J. Madison).

interests on a particular subject.[63] Usually an extended period of active public discussion and debate precedes legislative action, while interest groups develop their positions and move a subject higher on their agendas.[64] Additional legislation protecting against wrongful discharge appears to be in the early stages of political evolution.[65] The concept does not appear to be high on the agenda of any relevant interest group. On the other hand, the political equation may change in reaction to common law developments.

The political alignment of six salient interests groups will determine the fate of any proposed wrongful discharge legislation. They are: employers, the defense bar, trade unions, the plaintiff bar, nonunion employees and academic lawyers.

Employers historically have opposed any legislative or judicial action that would restrict their employment practices or impose increased liability for adverse action against employees.[66] Employers are well organized politically and are influential in legislative assemblies. These factors suggest that employers would exert effective pressure to oppose legislation expanding legal protections against wrongful discharge. But employers also historically have favored legislation as an alternative to common law liability when it seemed that legislation would permit greater predictability of outcome and limit the size of damage awards.[67] The continued rapid growth in common law liability for wrongful discharge could shift the preference of this key group toward legislation of an appropriate form.

The defense bar generally opposes legislative measures that would increase exposure to liability by defendants. This predisposition would militate against support of wrongful discharge legislation by this group. But for the same reasons that employer preferences may shift—the burden of increased common law liability

---

[63] *See generally* Sunstein, *Factions, Self-Interest, and the APA: Four Lessons Since 1946,* 72 Va. L. Rev. 271, 281-87 (1986); Sunstein, *Interest Groups in American Public Law,* 38 Stan. L. Rev. 29 (1985); J. Hurst, *Dealing With Statutes 1*–29 (1982). Professor Hurst discusses the limitations that resources, diffusion of interests, and other factors may present in obtaining legislative response. Fundamentally, he suggests, legislatures are instructions that provide broad arenas for bargaining among diverse interests. *Id.* at 19. Most people interest themselves, however, in the legislative process only when a matter under consideration has material importance for them. *Id.* at 23. J. Grenzke, Influence, Change and the Legislative Process (1982) is an excellent study of how legislators change policy as a result of lobbying and election pressures.

[64] Agenda refers to the relative priority of issues for an interest group, determining how much scarce political capital will be devoted to some issues as opposed to others. *See generally* J. Grenzke, Influence, Change and the Legislative Process (1982).

[65] Wrongful discharge bills introduced in the legislatures of Pennsylvania and Michigan have received little support. See § **9.10**. The author has participated in seminars and bar committees considering wrongful dismissal legislation since December, 1982. The subject usually draws yawns from practicing lawyers. Plaintiff counsel are happy with common law litigation. Defense counsel fear further erosion of the Employment-at-Will Rule.

[66] For example, employers appeared as amici curiae in Toussaint v. Blue Cross & Blue Shield, 408 Mich. 579, 609-10, 292 N.W.2d 880, 890 (1980), Brockmeyer v. Dun & Bradstreet, 113 Wis. 561, 562-63, 335 N.W.2d 834, 835 (1983), and *Brief of Amicus Curiae Merchants & Mfrs. Ass'n,* Foley v. Interactive Data Corp., ___ Cal. 3d ___, 712 P.2d 891, 222 Cal. Rptr. 740 (1986), arguing against relaxation of the Employment-at-Will Rule.

[67] An example is the position of major segments of the business community on products liability legislation.

and the desire for predictability and order through statutory reform--the preferences of this group also may change in favor of comprehensive legislation.

Ironically, the three groups who would benefit most from wrongful dismissal legislation are either too poorly organized to effect a change or are simply ambivalent toward such a change.

Trade unions historically have favored legislation granting new rights to employees.[68] Furthermore, the trade union movement is well organized and influential with legislators.[69] These factors suggest that this group would favor, and that its support could be effective in behalf of, wrongful discharge legislation. Yet, the trade union movement has become increasingly aware in recent years that statutory expansion of employee rights may dilute the incentive for employees to organize.[70] It is well recognized that one of the benefits that union organizers can offer to employees is protection against arbitrary dismissal. Accordingly, trade union groups have been ambivalent toward proposals for wrongful discharge statutes.[71] The ambivalence will be tested by a committee appointed to work with the AFL-CIO's general counsel to develop a position on wrongful dismissal legislation, in response to a resolution introduced at the AFL-CIO convention by the United Auto Workers.

The plaintiff bar apparently is ambivalent also. Plaintiff lawyers make their living by litigating and by receiving portions of judgments or settlements large enough to compensate them for work done on cases in which the plaintiff receives nothing—a form of cross-subsidy. This segment of the bar has favored expansion of common law wrongful dismissal doctrines,[72] but that does not translate into support of legislation. Wrongful dismissal legislation would most likely include a cap on damages,

---

[68] *See* J. Greenstone, Labor in American Politics 342 (1977) (position of AFL-CIO on equal employment legislation).

[69] *See* Kau & Rubin, *The Impact of Labor Unions on the Passage of Economic Legislation,* 2 J. Lab. Res. 133 (1981). The Kau and Rubin study presents empirical evidence that union membership in legislative districts and union campaign contributions affect congressional voting behavior on economic legislation.

[70] Reportedly, the Canada Labour Congress argued against enactment of federal wrongful dismissal legislation in Canada in 1978. Letter from Gilles Trudeau, École de Relations Industrielles, Université de Montréal to author, Sept. 19, 1983. Mr. Trudeau has investigated the effect of the Canadian legislation on union organizing efforts in his S.J.D. thesis, under the supervision of Professor Paul Weiler at Harvard Law School. Mr. Trudeau concludes that such legislation does not have an adverse effect on unionization.

[71] On July 29, 1983, New York Governor Mario Cuomo vetoed Assembly Bill Number 6610-B, entitled, "AN ACT to amend the labor law, in relation to unfair labor practices against an employee who is a licensed professional." The bill would have given a cause of action to a licensed professional employee who was discharged for refusal to engage in conduct that would violate professional ethical standards. One of the reasons cited in the Governor's veto message was the uncertain effect of the bill on collectively negotiated grievance mechanisms. It is reasonable to infer that organized labor played a role in this veto by a Democratic governor.

[72] The Wisconsin Academy of Trial Lawyers appeared as an amicus curiae in Brockmeyer v. Dun & Bradstreet, 113 Wis. 561, 563, 335 N.W.2d 834, 835 (1983), urging that recovery be permitted on one or more wrongful discharge theories. Similarly, in Hansen v. Harrah's, 100 Nev. 60, 675 P.2d 394 (1984) the Nevada Trial Lawyer's Association filed an amicus brief urging

thus limiting the opportunity for cross-subsidy of plaintiff litigation. On the other hand, to the extent that legislation simplifies litigation or provides for attorneys' fee awards, it could reduce the need for large potential damage awards to provide cross-subsidy. Also, if legislation broadens the substantive rights of dismissed employees, it could increase the probability of success for plaintiffs and their lawyers. Plaintiff lawyers may oppose or favor wrongful dismissal legislation, depending on its content.

Undoubtedly, nonunion employees would benefit most from expanded protection against wrongful discharge. Such protection would enhance their economic security without imposing any identifiable costs directly on them. But this interest group is poorly organized and probably largely ignorant of the legal issues involved. Moreover, there is no public interest group that regularly speaks for nonunion employees. Accordingly, the preferences of nonunion employees are unlikely to be influential unless the subject of wrongful discharge gains prominence in election politics, so that the individual votes of employees are influenced by candidates' positions on the wrongful discharge issue. Wrongful discharge has not become such a prominent issue yet.

There really is only one group which seems strongly to support wrongful dismissal legislation of the type most frequently discussed: academic lawyers. Law professors generally have favored legislative initiatives expanding legal protection for individual employees. This predisposition has been manifest with respect to wrongful discharge law. Indeed, the common law wrongful discharge concepts may be attributed in part to the academic legal literature.[73] Academic lawyers are influential because they provide technical assistance to legislators and because they link new proposals to well-accepted legal doctrines, and thus improve the perceived legitimacy of proposals for legislative change.[74] At present, there is no indication that this group will lessen its support of comprehensive wrongful discharge legislation.

The foregoing interest group analysis suggests that the balance of political power would shift in favor of wrongful discharge legislation only if employers and the defense bar react against expanded common law liability for wrongful discharge, and if the plaintiff bar perceives that proposed legislation would enhance—or at least would not diminish—the economic feasibility of representing dismissed employees.[75] If these groups decide that legislation is a desirable alternative to

---

adoption of the public policy tort theory. *Id.* at 62 n.4, 675 P.2d at 395 n.4. *See also Application by California Trial Lawyers Ass'n Amicus Curiae Committee,* Foley v. Interactive Data Corp., ___ Cal. 3d ___, ___ P.2d ___, ___ Cal. Rptr. ___, Case No. LA 32148 (arguing for expansive interpretation of implied covenant).

[73] See § 1.11.

[74] The influence of law writers on the development of laissez faire judicial doctrines is reviewed in C. Jacobs, Law Writers and the Courts (1954).

[75] A group or a political actor may favor a legislative initiative but place much lower priority on action in that area than in others. More intense interest in wrongful discharge legislative action would have the effect of raising its priority, relative to other issues.

§ 9.4 STATUTORY REFORM

continued expansion of common law liability,[76] they may become proponents of legislative action.

Clearly, the groups' needs and desires are at variance and therefore compromises must be made. Wrongful dismissal legislation is unlikely unless it satisfies the essential needs of the major groups.

Employers seek order and predictability. To meet these needs, legislation attractive to employers must include:

1. Clear criteria to distinguish legitimate from prohibited dismissals
2. A means to screen frivolous claims
3. Protection against multiple claims
4. A cap on damages
5. Limited expansion of existing prohibitions (i.e., retention of the employment-at-will doctrine to the extent possible)
6. Deference to voluntarily adopted internal grievance mechanisms.

The preferences of the defense bar parallel those of employers.

Trade unions are likely to want:

1. Increased protection of employees
2. Protection of incentives to unionize
3. Decreased volume of fair representation claims against unions.

Nonunion employees need:

1. Low cost claim assertion
2. Closest thing possible to just cause protection
3. Protection of private off-duty conduct and freedom of speech
4. Maximum potential damages
5. Speedy claim resolution
6. The opportunity to present claims in as many forums as possible and with maximum opportunity for review.

The plaintiff bar would like:

1. The potential for large damage awards
2. The opportunity to present claims in as many forums as possible
3. Statutory award of attorneys' fees.

---

[76] Such benefit could come from simplification of litigation machinery and modification of procedural fairness standards in the direction suggested in §§ 9.25–9.32.

Academic lawyers, for the most part, have supported legislation providing:

1. Just cause protection
2. Arbitration of claims of wrongful dismissal.

§ 9.5 Statutory Models

A number of models exist for wrongful dismissal legislation at both the federal and the state level. In addition, Britain and Canada have taken somewhat different approaches to providing statutory protection against wrongful dismissal. **Sections 9.6 through 9.12** review these models. Broader models for wrongful dismissal legislation proposed by commentators or borrowed from the law of private associations are treated separately in **§§ 9.13 through 9.17**.

The statutory models fall into two general groups. The first group is the only type of statute that has been enacted in the United States: a group of statutes enumerating reasons for which dismissal is not permitted. Some of these statutes establish special administrative or arbitral institutions to adjudicate claims of violation; others leave adjudication to the common law courts. The second group contains statutes prohibiting dismissal except for just cause. This approach has been followed in England[77] and in Canada,[78] and has been reflected in a number of bills considered by state legislatures but not enacted. Virtually all of these proposals establish a special institution, usually an arbitral one, to adjudicate claims of violation.

Enumerated reasons are found in two types of statutes: (1) those enacted with the primary purpose of addressing the employment relationship (labor statutes); and (2) those enacted with the primary purpose of addressing a nonemployment problem (e.g., a statute regulating water pollutants). At the federal level, *enumerated reasons* statutes appear in both contexts, protecting against adverse employer action based on specific employee conduct or characteristics.[79] Similarly, at the state level, *enumerated reasons* statutes can be found in both contexts, but only those with the primary purpose of addressing wrongful dismissal are addressed in this chapter.[80]

§ 9.6 —Federal Wrongful Dismissal Statutes

As the structure of **Chapter 2** suggests, federal statutes limiting employee dismissals fall into two general groups—those prohibiting dismissals based on membership in specified classes, and those prohibiting dismissals for engaging in specified conduct. Both types of statutes are of the enumerated reasons type. In

---

[77] See § **9.11**.
[78] See § **9.12**.
[79] See §§ **2.2–2.24**.
[80] **App. A** lists all state statutes protecting against employment termination.

other words, employees can show a violation only by showing that the employer made the termination decision based on a reason prohibited by the statute.

With a few exceptions, the federal statutes erect an administrative mechanism to handle claims of violation. Under Title VII[81] and the Age Discrimination in Employment Act,[82] claims of violation must be considered initially by a federal or state administrative agency, but the federal agencies only have the power to conciliate. The employee retains the ultimate right to an adjudicatory decision either in federal court or before a state administrative agency with ultimate judicial review. The choice whether to proceed at the state or federal level is the employee's. The statutes protecting employee conduct permit the employee to claim a violation before an administrative agency. The paradigm is the National Labor Relations Act.[83] A number of other statutes require that claims of violation be presented to the Secretary of Labor. Access to the courts is, for the most part, restricted to judicial review of administrative agency decisions.[84] Generally, litigation before administrative agencies is undertaken at public cost on behalf of the employee.

§ 9.7 —State Whistleblower Statutes

Nine states have enacted statutes with the primary purpose of protecting specific employee conduct, termed generally as *whistleblower* acts.[85] These whistleblower statutes allow a civil action to be brought directly in the state courts.[86] Of the nine states that have enacted whistleblower acts, only six protect employees outside the public sector.[87]

---

[81] 42 U.S.C. § 2000e (1982).

[82] 29 U.S.C. § 621 (1982).

[83] See § **2.16**.

[84] See §§ **2.18–2.24**.

[85] Cal. Lab. Code § 1102.5 (West 1971 & Supp. 1986); Iowa Code Ann. § 79.28 (West 1973 & Supp. 1985); Conn. Gen. Stat. Ann. § 31.51m (West Supp. 1986); Me. Rev. Stat. Ann. tit. 26, § 831 (1974 & Supp. 1985); Mich. Comp. Laws Ann. § 15.361 (West 1981 & Supp. 1985); 1986 N.J. Sess. Law Serv. ch. 105 (approved Sept. 5, 1986) (West); (N.Y. Lab. Law § 740 (Consol. 1977 & Supp. 1986); R.I. Gen. Laws § 36-15-1 (1984 & Supp. 1985); Utah Code Ann. § 67-21-1 (1985–1986).

[86] Cal. Lab. Code § 1102.5 (West 1971 & Supp. 1986); Conn. Gen. Stat. Ann. § 31.51m(c) (West Supp. 1986) (after exhausting administrative remedies); Iowa Code Ann. § 79.28 (West 1973 & Supp. 1985); Me. Rev. Stat. Ann. tit. 26, § 834 (1974 & Supp. 1985) (requires use of employer procedures; action must be brought within 90 days after alleged violation or within 60 days if a grievance procedure or similar process used); Mich. Comp. Laws Ann. § 15.363 Sec. 3(1) (West 1981 & Supp. 1985) (within 90 days after alleged violation of act); N.Y. Lab. Law § 740(3) (Consol. 1977 & Supp. 1986) (within one year after alleged "retaliatory personnel action was taken"); R.I. Gen. Laws § 36-15-4(a) (1984 & Supp. 1985); Utah Code Ann. § 67-21-4(1) (1985–1986) (within 90 days after alleged violation of this chapter); S.D. Codified Laws Ann. § 60-1-3 (1969 & Supp. 1985).

[87] Cal. Lab. Code § 1102.5 (West 1971 & Supp. 1986); Conn. Gen. Stat. Ann. § 31.51m (West Supp. 1986); Me. Rev. Stat. Ann. tit. 26, § 831 (1974 & Supp. 1985); Mich. Comp. Laws Ann. § 15.361 (West 1981 & Supp. 1985); 1986 N.J. Sess. Law Serv. ch. 105 (approved Sept. 5, 1986) (West); N.Y. Lab. Law § 740 (Consol. 1977 & Supp. 1986).

The whistleblower statutes generally prohibit dismissing employees because the employees report employer violations of law. Each of these six states has a different standard on the correctness of a charge by an employee that his employer was in violation of law.[88] The California, Connecticut, Michigan, and Maine statutes are similar, except that the Maine statute is slightly broader. The California, Connecticut, and Michigan statutes protect reports of violations of law to public agencies.[89] The Maine statute protects reports of violations of law either to the employer or to a public agency.[90] New York and New Jersey, in addition to protecting reports to the employer or to a public agency, protect employees who refuse to take part in "any activity which the employee reasonably believes is in violation of the law, is criminal, or is incompatible with the clear mandate of public policy concerning health, safety or welfare."[91]

Maine, New Jersey, and New York require that the violation first be brought to the attention of the employer.[92] Iowa, Rhode Island, and Utah's public sector whistleblower statutes offer similar protections.[93]

Whistleblower statutes codify the substantive fairness principles developed in the limited area characterized by the public policy tort. The California statute gives a state administrative agency jurisdiction to investigate complaints,[94] but expressly preserves "other rights and remedies under any other provisions of law."[95] Maine's statute explicitly preserves common law rights. The Michigan statute is silent as to its effect on common law rights, but New York's statute explicitly effects a waiver of common law rights covered by the statute.[96]

---

[88] California requires that the employee have "reasonable cause to believe that the information discloses a violation of state or federal statute, or . . . regulation." Cal. Lab. Code § 1102.5(b) (West Supp. 1986). Similarly, Maine requires that the employee be "acting in good faith" and with "reasonable cause to believe" a violation is being reported. Me. Rev. Stat. Ann. tit. 26, § 833 (1974 & Supp. 1985). Michigan allows recovery unless the "employee knows that the report is false." Mich. Comp. Laws Ann. § 15.362 Sec. 3(1) (West 1981 & Supp. 1985). Connecticut applies the same knowledge of falsity standard as Michigan. Conn. Gen. Stat. Ann. § 31.51m(b) (West Supp. 1986). New York allows the court in its discretion to order reasonable attorneys' fees and court costs and disbursements where it is determined that the action was "without basis in law or in fact." N.Y. Lab. Law § 740(6) (Consol. 1977 & Supp. 1986).

[89] See Conn. Gen. Stat. Ann. § 31.51m (West Supp. 1986) (any public agency); Mich. Comp. Laws Ann. § 15.362 (West 1981); Cal. Lab. Code § 1102.5 (West Supp. 1986) (violation of state or federal statute or violation or noncompliance with state or federal regulation).

[90] Me. Rev. Stat. Ann. tit. 26, § 833 (Supp. 1985).

[91] S.1105, 202nd N.J. Leg. (1986), approved Sept. 5, 1986, Ch. 105, Laws of 1986; N.Y. Lab. Law § 740 (McKinney Supp. 1986) ("objects to, or refuses to participate in any such activity, policy or practice in violation of a law, rule or regulation.").

[92] Me. Rev. Stat. Ann. tit. 26, § 833 (1974 & Supp. 1985); N.Y. Lab. Law § 740(3) (Consol. 1977 & Supp. 1986).

[93] See Iowa Code Ann. § 79.28 (West 1973 & Supp. 1985); R.I. Gen. Laws § 36-15-1 (1984 & Supp. 1985); Utah Code Ann. § 67-21-1 (1985–1986).

[94] Cal. Lab. Code § 98.7 (West Supp. 1986).

[95] Cal. Lab. Code § 98.7(f) (West Supp. 1986).

[96] Me. Rev. Stat. Ann. tit. 26, § 840 (1974 & Supp. 1985). See also Cal. Lab. Code § 1102.5 (West 1971 & Supp. 1986); Mich. Comp. Laws Ann. § 15.361 (West 1981 & Supp. 1985); N.Y. Lab. Law § 740(7) (Consol. 1977 & Supp. 1986).

§ 9.8 — State Employment Term Statutes

A South Dakota statute established a presumption that employment is to continue for a period of time defined by pay interval.[97] Thus, an employee paid once per week was presumed to have a contract of employment for one week. An employee paid once per month was presumed to have a contract of employment for one month, and so on.[98] This statute was recently amended to do away with the presumption that the length of time the parties adopt for the estimation of wages equals the period for which the employee was hired.[99] This length of time is now deemed relevant to the determination of the employment term.[1] In effect, the statute has been weakened by this revision.

§ 9.9 — State Service Letter Statutes

Missouri has a *service letter statute*,[2] which requires employers to give employees a letter accurately specifying the reason for their termination. Employees recover substantial damages for violation of the requirement.[3]

§ 9.10 — State Just Cause Proposals

Many states have considered proposals to afford protection against dismissals without just cause. Only Puerto Rico has such a statute.[4] The Pennsylvania,[5]

---

[97] S.D. Codified Laws Ann. § 60-1-3 (1978). If there is no agreement or custom respecting wages, the hiring is presumed to be for a one-month term. *Id.* § 60-1-4. *See* Bushman v. Pure Plant Food Int'l, Ltd., 330 N.W.2d 762 (S.D. 1983) (statute implied a contract in an action for fringe benefits brought by employees who resigned).

[98] S.D. Codified Laws Ann. § 60-1-3 (1969 & Supp. 1985).

[99] For example, as the statute originally read, "[a] hiring at a yearly rate [was] presumed to be for one year." Now the hiring at a yearly rate would only be "relevant to a determination of the term of employment." *Compare* S.D. Codified Laws Ann. § 60-1-3 (1969) *with* S.D. Codified Laws Ann. § 60-1-3 (Supp. 1985).

[1] S.D. Codified Laws Ann. § 60-1-3 (Supp. 1985).

[2] Mo. Rev. Stat. § 290.140 (1978).

[3] *See* Boyle v. Vista Eyewear, Inc., 700 S.W.2d 859 (Mo. Ct. App. 1985) (affirming $15,000 punitive and $1.00 compensatory damages for service letter containing incorrect reason for termination).

[4] *See* L.P.R.A. § 185a–i (1985); Vargas v. Royal Bank of Can., 604 F. Supp. 1036, 1039 (D.P.R. 1985) (statute provides exclusive remedy).

[5] Pa. House Bill No. 1742, Session of 1981, introduced July 1, 1981, referred to the Committee on Labor Relations. The 1981 bill died in committee, but the bill was reintroduced in 1983 and again in 1985. The current version is House Bill No. 1020, introduced in 1985, and referred on April 23, 1985 to the House Labor Relations Committee.

Michigan,[6] New York,[7] and Connecticut[8] state legislatures have considered, but have not enacted,[9] bills that would afford general protection against wrongful discharge. A bar committee in California has proposed such legislation. This section summarizes the generally similar approach taken by these proposals.

All of the bills prohibit dismissals without just cause, leaving just cause to be defined in individual cases.[10] The Pennsylvania and Michigan bills applied to all employees who were not covered by collective bargaining agreements.[11] The Pennsylvania bill exempted from coverage employees with written employment contracts of two years or more in duration providing for at least six months' notice of termination.[12] The Michigan bill covered all employees who had been employed for at least fifteen hours per week for six months or more,[13] and confidential, managerial and other employees with written contracts of employment for two years or more providing for at least six months' notice of termination.[14] The Michigan bill expressly did not supersede employer arbitration procedures.[15]

Under both bills, employees believing they had been dismissed for reasons other than just cause could file complaints with a state administrative agency.[16] Both bills provided for a two-step procedure for handling complaints. The first step was to be mediation conducted by a mediator appointed from the panel of mediators maintained by the commission.[17] If mediation of the dispute was not successful, arbitration was available on request of the employee.[18] Arbitrators were to be selected from lists maintained by the Michigan agency,[19] but the Pennsylvania bill specified no means for appointment of an arbitrator. Arbitration fees were to be paid by the parties.[20] If the arbitrator determined the discharge to be unjust, the arbitrator was authorized to order reinstatement with no, partial, or full back pay, or to award a severance payment.[21]

---

[6] 1983 House Bill No. 5155, introduced Nov. 1, 1983, referred to House Judiciary Committee.

[7] N.Y. Assembly Bill No. 2126, N.Y. Senate Bill No. 1153, 1983-84 Regular Session. The Governor's veto of a similar bill is discussed in § **9.4**.

[8] Connecticut subsequently enacted a whistleblower law. Conn. Gen. Stat. Ann. § 31.51m (West Supp. 1986). See § **9.7**.

[9] The Michigan, Maine and New York legislatures have enacted more limited whistleblower bills. See § **9.7**.

[10] Mich. House Bill at § 3(a).

[11] Pa. House Bill No. 1020, § 3 (definition of *employee*); Mich. House Bill No. 5755, § 2.

[12] *Id.*

[13] Mich. House Bill § 2(e).

[14] *Id.*

[15] Mich. House Bill No. 5155, § 14.

[16] *Id.* § 3(1); Pa. House Bill No. 1020, § 5.

[17] Mich. House Bill No. 5155, § 4(1); Pa. House Bill No. 1020, § 6.

[18] Mich. House Bill No. 5155, § 5; Pa. House Bill No. 1020, § 7.

[19] Mich. House Bill No. 5155, § 5(3).

[20] Mich. House Bill No. 5155, § 6; Pa. House Bill No. 1020, § 10.

[21] Mich. House Bill No. 5155, § 10; Pa. House Bill No. 1020, § 8.

§ 9.10 STATE JUST CAUSE PROPOSALS

Enforcement under the bills also was similar. Arbitration awards could be enforced in the courts of general jurisdiction.[22] Noncompliance with an award was to be punishable by contempt penalties, not exceeding $250 per day.[23] Judicial review of awards was limited to the grounds that the arbitrator exceeded her jurisdiction, or that the award was procured by fraud or collusion.[24] In addition, the Michigan bill provided that awards could be set aside if the award was not supported by substantial evidence on the whole record.[25]

The Pennsylvania bill expressly stated that the statutory procedures were not to supplant any employer grievance procedure that terminated with final and binding arbitration.[26] Presumably, this savings provision was intended to cover arbitration procedures adopted by nonunion employers, since the basic coverage of the bill was limited to employees not covered by collective agreements.[27]

A special committee of the State Bar of California has endorsed a comprehensive legislative scheme establishing a just cause standard for dismissal, arbitration, and reinstatement, with back pay as the primary remedy.[28] In the committee's opinion, legislating a just cause standard would remedy the existing tension between the California Labor Code (codifying the terminable at-will rule) and the California cases adopting: (1) the public policy tort; (2) the implied covenant of good faith and fair dealing; and (3) the breach of implied contract action.[29]

The committee articulated several reasons in support of arbitration. It avoids long and expensive litigation which necessarily discourages legitimate claimants. Arbitration utilizes the expertise of labor arbitrators which makes the process more predictable. Because juries erratically award punitive and compensatory damages, employers may hold inefficient employees who would otherwise be dismissed. Predictability underlay the committee's proposal to legislate reinstatement with back pay as the appropriate remedy and eliminate punitive and compensatory damages. The committee also believed that the average employee would prefer reinstatement.

---

[22] Pa. House Bill No. 1020, §§ 9, 11, 12.

[23] Mich. House Bill No. 5155, § 13; Pa. House Bill No. 1020, § 12.

[24] Mich. House Bill No. 5155, § 12; Pa. House Bill No. 1020, § 11.

[25] Mich. House Bill No. 5155, § 12.

[26] Pa. House Bill No. 1020, § 13.

[27] A special committee appointed by the Philadephia Bar Association questioned whether deferral to voluntary employer procedures was workable, raised constitutional questions about establishing an exclusive arbitral forum, and noted that an enumerated prohibitions approach should be considered as an alternative to the just cause approach embodied in the bill. The author of this treatise served as a member of the committee.

[28] *See* Adhoc Committee on Termination at Will and Wrongful Discharge Appointed by the Labor and Employment Law Section of The State Bar of California, *To Strike a New Balance* (Feb. 8, 1984).

[29] *See* Tameny v. Atlantic Richfield Co., 27 Cal. 3d 167, 610 P.2d 1330, 164 Cal. Rptr. 839 (1980) (public policy tort); Cleary v. American Airlines, Inc., 111 Cal. App. 3d 443, 168 Cal. Rptr. 722 (1980) (implied covenant); Pugh v. See's Candies, Inc., 116 Cal. App. 3d 311, 171 Cal. Rptr. 917 (1981) (implied-in-fact contract).

A minority of the committee refused to endorse any legislation which would add to existing federal, state and common law remedies protecting against wrongful dismissal. That minority believed that a proper balance already had been struck and that another forum would cause overlapping remedies.

§ 9.11 —The British Model

British labor law provides a comprehensive remedy for employees believing they have been subjected to unfair dismissal. The concept of unfair dismissal dates from the Industrial Relations Act of 1971,[30] which was a comprehensive reform of British labor law. The provision of the Act relating to trade union matters was repealed by the Trade Union and Labor Relations Act of 1974,[31] but the unfair dismissal procedures remained intact with certain minor amendments effected in 1980.[32]

The statute affords protection to employees who have been employed continuously by a large employer (one with more than twenty employees)[33] for six months,[34] and to employees who have been employed continuously by small employers for two years.[35] Employees with employment contracts for a fixed term of one year or more are excluded from the protection.[36] Employees covered by a "dismissal procedures agreement," providing for arbitration as the terminal step, similarly are excluded from the statutory protections, if the private agreement has been approved by the government.[37]

Dismissals are declared to be unfair unless the employer can show that the dismissal was for a reason:

1. Related to the employee's capability or qualifications
2. Related to the conduct of the employee

---

[30] Section 22, Industrial Relations Act, 1971 ch. 72, 41 Halsbury's Statutes 2088 (1971 Cont. Vol.). *See* P. Davies & M. Freedland, Labour Law Text and Materials 348 (1979).

[31] Section 1, Trade Union and Labor Relations Act 1974, 44 Halsbury's Statutes 1768 (1974 Cont. Vol.). Section 1(2)(b) of the 1974 Act reenacted the unfair dismissal provisions of the 1971 Act, which were consolidated and reenacted again by the Employment Protection (Consolidation) Act 1978 ch.44, 48 Halsbury's Statutes 452 (1978 Cont. Vol.).

[32] *See* §§ 6-10, Employment Act 1980, 50(1) Halsbury's Statutes 387 (1980 Cont. Vol.).

[33] Section 64A(1)(b), Employment Protection (Consolidation) Act 1978, as amended by § 8(1), Employment Act 1980, 50(1) Halsbury's Statutes 390 (1980 Cont. Vol.).

[34] Section 64, Employment Protection (Consolidation) Act 1978, 48 Halsbury's Statutes 516 (1978 Cont. Vol.), amended by § 8(1), Employment Act 1980, 50(1) Halsbury's Statutes 390 (1980 Cont. Vol.).

[35] Section 64A, Employment Protection (Consolidation) Act 1978, as amended by § 8(1), Employment Act 1980, 50(1) Halsbury's Statutes 390 (1980 Cont. Vol.).

[36] Section 142(1), Employment Protection (Consolidation) Act 1978, 48 Halsbury's Statutes 603 (1978 Cont. Vol.), as amended by § 8(2), Employment Act 1980, 50(1) Halsbury's Statutes 391 (1980 Cont. Vol.).

[37] Section 65, Employment Protection (Consolidation) Act 1978, 48 Halsbury's Statutes 517 (1978 Cont. Vol.).

3. Related to lack of work for the employee
4. Related to contravention of law
5. Related to "some other substantial reason of a kind such as to justify the dismissal of an employee holding the position which that employee held."[38]

The House of Lords has interpreted the statute to permit a finding of unfair dismissal when the employee is deprived of an internal appeal process in violation of an employer-union agreement.[39]

An employee believing that he has been dismissed unfairly can file a complaint with an industrial tribunal within three months after the dismissal.[40] An industrial tribunal is a three-person arbitration panel[41] which may order reinstatement and award monetary damages sufficient to make the employee whole.[42] Industrial tribunals also have jurisdiction over discharges violating discrimination statutes.[43] Awards of industrial tribunals may be appealed as of right to the Employment Appeal Tribunal (EAT), a special court composed of high court judges sitting in rotation, and a number of lay members equally divided between employee and management interest.[44] The statutory standards of review for industrial tribunal awards accord substantial deference to the tribunal.[45] Decisions of the EAT are appealable to the Court of Appeal as judgments of any court of general jurisdiction.[46]

Unfair dismissal complaints account for about 80 percent of the cases brought before industrial tribunals.[47] Only about 35 percent of the cases proceed to a

---

[38] Section 57(2), Employment Protection (Consolidation) Act 1978, 48 Halsbury's Statutes 506 (1978 Cont. Vol.).

[39] *See* West Midlands Co-Operative Soc'y v.Tipton, [1986] I.C.R. 192, 204 (H.L.).

[40] Section 67, Employment Protection (Consolidation) Act 1978, 48 Halsbury's Statutes 518 (1978 Cont. Vol.).

[41] Industrial tribunals originally were established under the Industrial Training Act 1964, 12 Halsbury's Statutes 230 (1969). The Royal Commission on Trade Unions and Employers' Association (the Donovan Commission) recommended that the tribunals be given jurisdiction over all disputes arising between employers and employees, arising from their contracts of employment or under statutes governing the employment relationship. P. Davies & M. Freedland, Labour Law Text and Materials 727-28 (1979). Section 67, Employment Protection (Consolidation) Act 1978, 48 Halsbury's Statutes 518 (1978 Cont. Vol.) gives the tribunals jurisdiction over unfair dismissal complaints.

[42] Section 69 (reinstatement), §§ 72-74 (compensation), Employment Protection (Consolidation) Act 1978, 48 Halsbury's Statutes 520, 524 (1978 Cont. Vol.).

[43] *See, e.g.,* Owen & Briggs v. James, I.C.R. 618 (C.A. 1982) (affirming decision of industrial tribunal finding discriminatory refusal to hire).

[44] The EAT was established by § 87 of the Employment Protection Act 1975, 45 Halsbury's Statutes 366 (1975 Cont. Vol.). That section was replaced by § 135 of the Employment Protection (Consolidation) Act 1978, 48 Halsbury's Statutes 592 (1978 Cont. Vol.), which restructured the EAT. *See* P. Davies & M. Freedland, Labour Law Text and Materials 742-43 (1979).

[45] § 136, Employment Protection (Consolidation) Act 1978, 48 Halsbury's Statutes 593 (1978 Cont. Vol.) (appeals over questions of law).

[46] *See id.,* § 136(4); P. Davies & M. Freedland, Labour Law Text and Materials 742-43 (1979).

[47] Remarks of Prof. Benjamin Aaron Before Oxford/BNA Symposium on Comparative Industrial Relations, held Aug. 3-17, 1983, *reprinted in* Daily Labor Reporter (BNA) No. 170, at D-1, D-2 (Aug. 31, 1983).

hearing.[48] The remainder are settled or withdrawn before a hearing. The average time from the filing of a claim to the first hearing before a tribunal is about 10 weeks.[49] Hearings usually take no more than one day, and are informal.[50] About 35 percent of employees and 51 percent of employers are represented by counsel.[51] Between April 1978 and March 1980 the industrial tribunals decided about 14,000 cases.[52] Of these, appeals were taken in only 602 cases, and only 10 percent of these appeals were allowed.[53]

In evaluating the results of the British unfair dismissal process, it should be recalled that grievance arbitration under collective bargaining agreements is relatively rare in Britain.[54]

§ 9.12 — The Canadian Model

Federal law in Canada has provided comprehensive remedies for unjust dismissal since 1978,[55] and three provinces provide at least limited protection.[56] The federal statute covers all employees within the constitutional reach of the federal parliament,[57] unless a "procedure for redress has been provided elsewhere in or under this or any other Act of Parliament."[58] Complaints respecting layoffs because of a lack of work or because of the discontinuance of an employer function are excluded specifically.[59]

The statute does not define *unjust dismissal,* but leaves it to the discretion of the persons designated under the statute to determine whether a dismissal was

---

[48] *Id.* at D-3.

[49] *Id.*

[50] *Id.*

[51] *Id.*

[52] *Id.* at D-4.

[53] *Id.*

[54] *Id.* at D-1. The prevalence of arbitration of discharge disputes under collective bargaining agreements in the United States is discussed in § 3.3.

[55] Section 21 of the 1978 Act to Amend the Canada Labour Code, 26–27 Eliz. II c.27, 1977–78 Can. Stat. 614, added a new Division V.7, § 61.5, to the Canada Labour Code, 5 Can. Rev. Stat. ch. L-1. The federal statute is discussed in Simmons, *Unjust Dismissal of the Unorganized Workers in Canada,* 20 Stan. J. Int'l L. 473 (1984). Proposals and provincial experience that shaped the federal legislation in Canada are discussed in England, *Recent Developments in Wrongful Dismissal Laws and Some Pointers for Reform,* 16 Alberta L. Rev. 470, 495 (1978). For an overview of Canadian wrongful dismissal law, see H. Levitt, The Law of Dismissal in Canada (1985).

[56] C. 45, § 124, 1979 Que. Rev. Stat. (protecting employees with five or more years of service against dismissal without "good and sufficient cause"); Blanchard v. Control Data Canada Ltd., 14 D.L.R.4th 289 (1984) (reviewing arbitration award under Quebec statute); c.10, § 68, 1972 N.S. Rev. Stat. (requiring up to eight weeks' notice before dismissal); c.137, §§ 4, 40, Ont. Rev. Stat. (same); Fanaken v. Bell, 9 D.L.R.(4th) 637 (Ont. 1984) (interpreting Ontario statute).

[57] Canada Labour Code, 5 Can. Rev. Stat. L-1, § 61.5 (1977).

[58] *Id.* § 61.5(3)(b).

[59] *Id.* § 61.5(3)(a).

unjust.[60] A person believing dismissal was unjust may file a complaint with the Minister of labor within 30 days after the dismissal.[61] The statute provides for a two-step procedure for handling such complaints. The first step is conciliation, conducted under the auspices of the Minister of Labor.[62] During this step, the employer is required to provide a written statement of the reasons for dismissal.[63] If conciliation is not successful, the Minister *may* appoint "any person he considers appropriate" as an "adjudicator" to decide whether the dismissal was unjust.[64] An adjudicator may order reinstatement and award compensation not exceeding the remuneration that would have been paid by the employer if the dismissal had not occurred.[65] Decisions of adjudicators are insulated from any judicial review,[66] but may be filed in the Federal Court of Canada, in which case they are to be afforded the same effect as a judgment of that court.[67]

Civil remedies that employees may have against their employers expressly are not affected by the unjust dismissal statutes.[68]

§ 9.13 —Commentators' Models

In addition to the concrete proposals enacted in other countries or by state legislatures or proposed to those legislatures, American commentators have proposed model doctrines to limit employment terminations. They include Professor Clyde Summers' proposal to prohibit dismissals except for just cause and to provide state funded arbitration to adjudicate claims of violation, Professor Selznick's proposal to impose due process requirements on private employers, and Professor Bellace's proposal to integrate new statutory just cause protection with the existing state unemployment compensation machinery. Sections **9.14** through **9.16** address these theoretical ideas, comparing them with doctrines used to permit or to limit judicial review of the decisions of other types of private associations.

The Summers and Bellace proposals are more concrete than the Selznick proposal in that they suggest specific mechanisms for deciding wrongful dismissal disputes. The Selznick proposal offers more than the Summers or Bellace proposals in terms of doctrinal justification for some kind of legal intervention in dismissal decisions.

---

[60] *Id.* § 61.5(8).

[61] *Id.* § 61.5.

[62] *Id.* § 61.5(5).

[63] *Id.* § 61.5(4).

[64] *Id.* § 61.5(6).

[65] *Id.* § 61.5(9).

[66] *Id.* § 61.5(10). *But see* Pioneer Grain Co. v. Kraus, [1981] 2 F.C. 815, 824–25 (Ct. App.) (federal court has jurisdiction to review decision of unfair dismissal adjudicator as to jurisdiction and compliance with statutory formula for damages), Attorney General of Canada v. Gautheir, 34 N.R. 549, [1980] 2 F.C. 393, 398 (Ct. App.) (federal court has jurisdiction to reverse and remand adjudicator decision that decided dismissal on legal, as opposed to factual, grounds).

[67] Canada Labour Code, 5 Can. Rev. Stat. L-1, § 61.5(12), (13) (1977).

[68] *Id.* § 61.5(14).

§ 9.14 —The Summers Concept

Most of the state just cause proposals[69] derive from Professor Clyde Summers' 1976 proposal for enactment of legislation at the state level to protect all employees against unjust dismissal.[70] He preferred legislative action at the state, instead of the federal, level to maintain simplicity, to provide more accessible forums, and to permit variety and experimentation.[71]

Professor Summers proposed the statutory granting to employees of a right not to be disciplined or discharged except for just cause and channelling adjudication of cases arising under the statute into the arbitration process.[72] He urged that any such statute not define *just cause,* preferring the existing body of arbitral precedent which gives workable content to the phrase, while "preserving its flexibility to accommodate special circumstances and changed conditions."[73] Professor Summers noted that a number of states already maintain panels of arbitrators for use in union-management disputes, and proposed reliance on these panels for selection of arbitrators under the new statute.[74]

A number of issues necessarily would be resolved in the enactment of a statute such as proposed by Professor Summers. He noted the arguments for and against public funding of the costs of arbitration, and proposed the imposition of a fee, equivalent to one week's takehome pay, on the complaining employee to discourage frivolous claims.[75] He proposed exempting new employees during a probationary period of six months from the just cause requirement and the arbitration procedures.[76] He opposed a small employer exemption.[77] He recognized the inappropriateness of including highly paid executive employees within the statute's protections, and favored he English approach to this problem: exempting employees covered by written employment contracts of two or more years in duration providing for at least six months' notice of termination.[78]

Finally, Professor Summers considered the relationship between the proposed statute and existing, collectively bargained arbitration remedies.[79] He proposed that employees covered by collective agreements containing just cause and

---

[69] See § 9.10.

[70] Summers, *Individual Protection Against Unjust Dismissal: Time for a Statute,* 62 Va. L. Rev. 481 (1976).

[71] *Id.* at 521.

[72] *Id.* at 521–22.

[73] *Id.* at 521.

[74] *Id.* at 522.

[75] *Id.* at 524.

[76] *Id.* at 525. Summers noted that situations requiring a longer probation could be accommodated by a proviso that if the contract were for one year or more, employment would be protected only past the initial time period. He also recommended flexible application of just cause to accommodate the employer's need and ability to judge the suitability of the new worker.

[77] *Id.* at 525: "The personal relationship element could be better accommodated by an arbitrator in applying the just cause standard . . . ."

[78] *Id.* at 526.

[79] *Id.* at 528.

arbitration provisions be required to resort to those procedures in lieu of the statutory procedures.[80] He would, however, expand judicial review of the collectively bargained arbitration awards to ensure they met standards of procedural fairness appropriate to determination of statutory as well as contractual rights.[81] He would allow existing statutory protections and remedies to remain.

Several other commentators have suggested variants of the Summers proposal, but their proposals have not yet received the wide attention given to Professor Summers' 1976 proposal.

Kenneth Mennemeier examined various alternatives for dealing with employee discharge disputes.[82] He concludes that judicial recognition of a cause of action for wrongful discharge has disadvantages that outweigh the advantages. Judicial recognition is available to employees without waiting for the legislatures to act, and the common law is inherently adaptable to the facts of particular cases. On the other hand, litigation is slow and expensive, and adaptability, which is an advantage, means that the outcomes are uncertain and nonuniform. Judges lack specialized expertise regarding workplace disputes. Judicial remedies are limited. The adversarial character of the judicial process reduces the possibility of an amicable resolution of the dispute.[83] Statutory recognition of a wrongful discharge cause of action presents only slight advantages, in Mennemeier's opinion, if claims are heard by courts or administrative agencies.[84]

Mennemeier prefers enactment of statutes that permit discharge disputes to be heard and decided by arbitrators. He evaluates issues related to coverage of employees,[85] selection of arbitrators,[86] coverage of disputes,[87] remedies,[88] judicial review,[89] and allocation of cost burdens.[90] He concludes that the bill introduced in the Michigan legislature[91] strikes the right balance on most of these issues.[92]

---

[80] *Id.*

[81] *Id.* at 529. Protection of a worker's procedural rights would require that the worker had the chance to be present at a hearing, to hear the evidence, to cross-examine witnesses and to present evidence on his own behalf. Summers would also confer a right to be represented by counsel of his own choosing upon the worker.

[82] Mennemeier, *Protection from Unjust Discharges: An Arbitration Scheme,* 19 Harv. J. on Legis. 49 (1982).

[83] *Id.* at 65–67.

[84] *Id.* at 70–74.

[85] *Id.* at 78–82.

[86] *Id.* at 83–84.

[87] *Id.* at 84–85.

[88] *Id.* at 85–86.

[89] *Id.* at 86–87.

[90] *Id.* at 89–90.

[91] The Michigan bill is described in **§ 9.10**.

[92] Mennemeier would prefer two modifications in the Michigan bill. First, he thinks the arbitration system should have jurisdiction over a broader class of employee disputes than discharges. Mennemeier, *Protection from Unjust Discharges: An Arbitration Scheme,* 19 Harv. J. Legis. 49, 84–85 (1982). Second, he would impose a filing fee on the employee bringing a claim rather than requiring that the employee bear half the costs. *Id.* at 89–90.

A 1983 article in the *Journal of Law Reform*[93] contains a draft state statute that would prohibit dismissals except for just cause,[94] and would provide for mediation/arbitration under the supervision of courts of general jurisdiction.[95] A discharged employee could file a complaint with the court, and the court would be required to appoint a mediator/arbitrator to hear the dispute.[96] Both parties would be required to pay $300 before arbitration would proceed. The proposed bill adds little to other proposals that have been advanced. Its provision for judicial review of the mediation/arbitration award on a substantial evidence standard[97] misapprehends the nature of mediation, which is promoted as an advantage of the proposal.[98]

§ 9.15 — The Selznick Concept

Professor Selznick, writing in 1969, proposed that constitutional due process concepts be applied to private employers. He saw private employment relations law as presenting an "historical opportunity" to apply public policy in a way that would promote industrial justice.[99] He perceived governance in the workplace as raising problems fundamentally similar to the problems of administrative law—the law of bureaucracy.[1] "For the basic problem is the same, in both spheres: 'how executive power can be controlled by law and also, so to speak, colonized by legal principles of fair and proper procedure.'"[2] Professor Selznick sought to justify the application to private work organizations of the principles of due process hitherto restricted to public government.[3] He began with the proposition that the cardinal principle of public law in American jurisprudence is due process.[4] Then he proposed that due process norms ought to be applied to private organizations performing the functions of governments.[5] He explained why he considered employers to be performing governmental functions and therefore why he believed they should be held to due process standards.[6] Professor Selznick described due process in terms

---

[93] *Reforming At-Will Employment Law: A Model Statute*, 16 J.L. Ref. 389 (1983).

[94] *Id.* at 417.

[95] *Id.* at 418–19.

[96] *Id.* at 420.

[97] *Id.* at 432.

[98] *Id.* at 406.

[99] P. Selznick, Law, Society and Industrial Justice (1969).

[1] *Id.* at 243.

[2] *Id.*

[3] *Id.* at 244.

[4] *Id.* at 250.

[5] *Id.* at 256–76.

[6] *Id.* at 264–66. Private employers resemble governments because they make and enforce rules having substantial impact on the interests of those governed by the rules—employees. See §§ **8.3–8.4** for other commentators' views on the subject of employer rules.

§ 9.15   SELZNICK CONCEPT

of five special ideals.[7] With slight modification, those ideals can be applied to workplace governance in the following terms:

1. Actions should be restrained by a proper regard for all legal interests affected. This ideal encompasses the interest balancing required in adjudicating wrongful discharge cases under the public policy tort theory. It suggests that legitimate employer interests must be weighed against other employee and societal interests
2. The making and application of rules should promote rationality. This ideal precludes arbitrary and capricious action. It suggests that employer actions be scrutinized to ensure that the employer can articulate a reason for her action, and that the reason bears a legitimate relationship to the interests of the business
3. A reliable assessment of fact should be assured. This ideal suggests that the employer have a procedure for ascertaining whether the facts justify adverse action against the employee under standards meeting ideals numbered 1 and 2
4. Legitimacy of authority should be assured. This ideal, though stated vaguely by Selznick, seems to suggest that the employer's agent responsible for making the decision adverse to an employee be clothed with legitimate authority to do so by the employer
5. A basic minimum of rights of personality should be protected. This ideal encompasses an employee's right to be heard and to be entitled to minimum rights of privacy and to minimum rights to lead her own life in ways bearing no legitimate relationship to the employer's interests.

Ideals 1 and 2 are associated with concepts of substantive fairness, and ideals 3 and 4 are associated with procedural fairness concepts discussed in § 9.2. Ideal 5 is mixed. The first element is procedural, and the remaining elements are substantive.[8]

Professor Selznick stops short of proposing specific legal changes necessary to ensure adherance to these norms by employers. He limits himself to the argument that these due process ideals are intertwined with the common law, and thus need not be limited to public law problems in which the phrase *due process* in the Constitution is applicable.[9] His concept can form a useful foundation for the decisional rules to be applied under a variety of common law or statutory procedures to protect against wrongful dismissal.

Two legal philosophers have espoused theories similar to Selznick's. Professor Lon Fuller argues that as an organization moves through its normal course of development, the principle by which the group conducts itself changes from that

---

[7] P. Selznick, Law, Society and Industrial Justice 252–55 (1969).

[8] Professor Selznick discussed the connection between substantive and procedural fairness only briefly. *See id.* at 256.

[9] *Id.* at 75.

of shared commitment toward a common goal to that of function by legal principle.[10] The second phase of development requires the organization to use formal standards of review for actions taken[11] similar to standards used by courts when reviewing actions taken by the state against individuals. The Fuller conception suggests that due process requirements be imposed on employers.

Professor Willard Hurst suggests that, because of technological advances, private organizations have attained substantial powers of compulsion.[12] A consequence of this newly gained power is that the public has insisted through the legal process that private organizations be required to exercise their powers responsibly.[13]

§ 9.16 — The Bellace Concept

Professor Janice Bellace, writing in a 1983 symposium, proposed state enactment of just cause protection, with powers of enforcement placed in existing unemployment compensation tribunals.[14] She argued that integration of wrongful dismissal protection with the existing unemployment compensation system would result in low cost, avoidance of additional government bureaucracy, and relieving the courts of a flood of new cases.[15] She explained that the unemployment compensation referees are accustomed to deciding most of the same questions confronting labor arbitrators hearing dismissal cases because of the frequency with which employers allege misconduct as grounds for denying unemployment compensation.[16]

Professor Bellace would modify unemployment compensation procedure in one important respect. Under the existing system, a hearing before a referee usually is available only if compensation is denied by the local office.[17] After the right to be dismissed only for just cause is added to the unemployment compensation statute, she would grant a hearing in any case in which the employee claimed unfair dismissal as well as, or in lieu of, seeking benefits.[18]

---

[10] Fuller, *Two Principles of Human Association,* Nomos XI, Voluntary Associations 14 (1969).

[11] Fuller cites the example of the university use of formal disciplinary proceedings. He concludes that, while using formal standards for decisions distracts the university from its educational goals, it is not too high a price to pay for the knowledge that the internal disciplinary proceedings will be upheld upon review by an outside authority. *Id.* at 20.

[12] Hurst, *Constitutional Ideals and Private Associations,* Nomos XI, Voluntary Associations 64 (1969).

[13] Hurst defines constitutionalism as "the ideal that all powers of compulsion created by social organization over men's wills and lives should be responsibly exercised." He mentions the growth of the administrative process as being the most tangible reflection of the trend toward the constitutionalization of private associations. *Id.* at 63, 64.

[14] Bellace, *A Right of Fair Dismissal: Enforcing a Statutory Guarantee,* 16 U. Mich. J.L. Ref. 207 (1983).

[15] *Id.* at 208, 232.

[16] *Id.* at 236–37. The misconduct standard is explained in **§ 2.36**.

[17] Bellace, *A Right of Fair Dismissal: Enforcing a Statutory Guarantee,* 16 U. Mich. J.L. Ref. 207, 235 (1983).

[18] *Id.* at 239.

She disfavored reinstatement as the standard remedy for unfair dismissal, fearing that nonunion employees would be subject to harassment with no union to protect them.[19] Instead, she proposed a remedial scheme composed of a basic award, supplemented by a compensatory award in appropriate cases.[20]

§ 9.17 Judicial Control of Other Types of Associations

Suits for wrongful dismissal require courts to scrutinize decisions of a particular type by private associations. Courts have passed judgment on other actions by private associations for many years,[21] basing their jurisdiction on the protection of property, contract, or personal rights of members.[22] Sometimes the degree of judicial intrusion can be substantial. In *Reid v. Gholson,*[23] the Virginia Supreme Court affirmed the appointment of a commissioner in chancery to preside over a church meeting to ensure fair treatment of dissenters threatened with expulsion by the pastor and his adherents. The court observed that, in the absence of an established body of substantive and procedural church rules, "simple and fundamental principles of democratic government which are universally accepted in our society" could be enforced by a court of equity.[24] Private association decisional law should be reviewed in conjunction with any attempt to formulate a coherent doctrine of wrongful dismissal.

Legal philosophers long have recognized that as institutions mature, they increasingly rely on formal decision making to resolve conflicts between individual rights and institutional authority. This evolutionary tendency is true of governments and of private voluntary associations.[25] As an association's own procedures become more formal, courts are more willing to enforce compliance with the procedures.

Once a court decides it has jurisdiction over an intra-associational dispute, it needs standards by which to review the association's action. Courts examine the

---

[19] *Id.* at 241.

[20] *Id.*

[21] For a detailed, though dated, discussion of judicial intervention in intra-association disputes, *see Developments in the Law—Judicial Control of Actions of Private Associations,* 76 Harv. L. Rev. 983 (1963).

[22] *Id.* at 998–1005. Courts utilize several theories for jurisdiction because each theory has deficiencies. *See* Note, *Common Law Rights for Private University Students: Beyond the State Action Principle,* 84 Yale L.J. 120, 137 (1974).

[23] 229 Va. 179, 192, 327 S.E.2d 107, 115 (1985).

[24] 229 Va. at 188–89, 327 S.E.2d at 113.

[25] Fuller, *Two Principles of Human Association,* XI Nomos, Voluntary Associations 14 (1969) (institutions self-impose a form of due process as they mature); Hurst, *Constitutional Ideals and Private Associations,* XI Nomos, Voluntary Associations 14 (1969) (public has insisted through the legal process that private organizations be required to exercise their powers responsibly).

association's authority to act,[26] examine compliance with the association's own rules, and compare the procedures under which the association acted with common law due process standards.[27] Occasionally courts invalidate associations' acts on the basis of public policy.[28] The judicially imposed constraints on private associations implicate both substantive and procedural fairness, though courts rarely distinguish the two.

When reviewing intra-association disputes, courts act much as they do in administrative law cases by refusing de novo decision on the facts of the disputes, relying instead upon internal factfinding procedures.[29] Courts defer to the rules of the associations,[30] as they do to rules of administrative agencies, and permit promulgators to change rules as long as alleged violators are afforded the procedures in effect at the time of the incident under review.[31]

The basic principles derived from these private association cases generally are consistent with wrongful dismissal concepts. Employment and nonemployment cases adopt a rationality standard for substantive fairness, evaluating the association's basis for taking adverse action by balancing the needs of the association against external public policy criteria.[32] In addition to this externally imposed substantive fairness criterion, the cases also enforce promises made by the association to its members, as a matter of substantive fairness.[33]

The cases adopt a relatively nonintrusive approach to procedural fairness, according substantial deference to facts found by private associations following their own procedures.[34]

Any wrongful dismissal legislation will reflect, however unconsciously, a synthesis of principles that frame other governmental inquiries into private decisions affecting individual rights.[35]

---

[26] *See* Atlanta Nat'l League Baseball Club, Inc. v. Kuhn, 432 F. Supp. 1213, 1226 (N.D. Ga. 1977) (baseball commissioner's deprivation of a draft choice ultra vires and therefore void).

[27] *See* 7 C.J.S. *Associations* § 29 at 74 (1980).

[28] See 7 C.J.S. *Associations* § 25 at 66 (1980).

[29] As long as procedural fairness exists and the findings are supported by substantial evidence, courts do not disturb an administrative decision. *See generally* Mathews v. Eldridge, 424 U.S. 319 (1976) (declining to impose additional procedures in connection with social security disability determinations).

[30] *See* Coveney v. President & Trustees of Holy Cross College, 388 Mass. 16, 19, 445 N.E.2d 136, 138–39 (1983).

[31] *Id.* at 19, 445 N.E.2d at 139; Randolph v. First Baptist Church, 53 Ohio Op. 288, 299–300, 120 N.E.2d 485, 498 (1954).

[32] See § **5.1** (synthesizing a balancing formula from wrongful dismissal tort cases); §§ **7.10–7.16** (demonstrating formula in trial proof terms).

[33] See **ch. 4** (explaining implied contract theories for wrongful dismissal recovery).

[34] See §§ **7.25–7.26** (reviewing court deference to employer decisions).

[35] In 1969, Professor Selznick proposed that constitutional due process concepts be applied to private employers. P. Selznick, Law, Society and Industrial Justice (1969). He perceived governance in the workplace as raising problems fundamentally similar to the problems of administrative law, the law of bureaucracy. *Id.* at 243. The Selznick ideas are probed in greater detail in § **9.15**.

§ 9.18 A Proposed Wrongful Dismissal Statute: Introduction

Two realities make new wrongful dismissal legislation desirable. The first is the uncertainty confronting common law courts in developing appropriate criteria for substantive and procedural fairness.[36] The second is the proliferation of remedies for wrongful dismissal involving diverse statutory and common law rights in multiple arbitral, administrative, and judicial forums. Articulation of a comprehensive doctrine even without legislation can facilitate sounder common law judicial decisions, if the doctrine is perceived as fair and practical. Integrating the various remedies requires legislative action. Sections **9.19** through **9.34** are intended to contribute to the achievement of both types of improvement in the law.

First, it is useful to develop in more detail the basic approaches to substantive and procedural fairness articulated in skeletal form in § **9.2**.[37] Some specific institutional problems are considered, such as election and preclusion,[38] treatment of employer dismissal procedures,[39] integration with collectively bargained arbitration[40] and with the unemployment compensation system,[41] forum selection,[42] burdens of proof,[43] remedies,[44] and costs of litigation.[45] Most of the suggestions offered in these areas could be adopted judicially or legislatively. Draft legislation for consideration at the state and federal levels is presented in **Appendix C**. The last section of this chapter estimates the case volume that might be expected if the legislation is enacted.[46]

§ 9.19 Legislative Drafting Pitfalls

The remainder of this chapter considers several issues that must be confronted in drafting a wrongful dismissal statute. It is a mistake, however, for any legislature or interest group to address discrete provisions of a wrongful dismissal statute without considering the interrelationship among the parts. For example, it is difficult to draft language that imposes the burden of proof on the employee-claimant to

---

[36] The concepts of substantive and procedural fairness are explained in § **9.2**.

[37] A proposed substantive fairness criterion is developed in §§ **9.20–9.24**. A proposed procedural fairness criterion is developed in §§ **9.25–9.33**.

[38] See § **9.26**.

[39] See § **9.27**.

[40] See § **9.28**.

[41] See § **9.30**.

[42] See § **9.29**.

[43] See § **9.31**.

[44] See § **9.32**.

[45] See § **9.33**.

[46] See § **9.34**.

establish wrongful dismissal under a statute that prohibits dismissals except for just cause. The practical effect of just cause protection is to shift the burden of proof to the employer to establish just cause for the dismissal.[47] The order of proof articulated by the Supreme Court in *McDonnell Douglas v. Green*,[48] and similar formulations utilized under other federal labor statutes, depend for their logic upon a prohibition against a specific motive or type of conduct.

The political tradeoff among (1) the scope of the statute, (2) the reasons for which the statute prohibits dismissal, (3) remedies available for violation of the statute, and (4) attorneys' fees for plaintiff's counsel, is important. If a new statute limits the amount recoverable, as it surely must to have any hope of attracting employer support, the statute presents a potentially serious threat to the plaintiff bar. This threat can be mitigated and a statute made attractive to the plaintiff bar if the statute provides for awards of attorneys' fees to plaintiffs' counsel. Similarly, if the statute preempts other kinds of claims for wrongful dismissal either directly or by requiring a binding election of remedies by a claimant who files under the statute, the potential threat to plaintiffs' counsel's contingency fees is greater. Conversely, the attractiveness to employers is greater.

It is important to understand that possible wrongful dismissal statutes lie on a continuum ranging from a simple codification of existing common law theories based on implied contract or public policy tort at the most limited end, to a broad prohibition against dismissals without just cause.

If the statute prohibits dismissal for enumerated reasons, comprehensive preemption is difficult to achieve; otherwise an employee dismissed for a *bad* reason not covered by the statute would be without remedy unless the statute is amended. Moreover, it is not entirely clear how preemption can be framed to exclude employer conduct ancillary to the discharge that falls within recognized tort categories, such as intentional infliction of emotional distress, defamation, fraudulent misrepresentation, and invasion of privacy.[49] The enumeration of prohibited reasons for dismissal inherently makes the statute more complex. An enumerated reasons statute may be difficult to enforce fairly by claimants not represented by counsel. Moreover, it may be difficult to provide an enforcement procedure that is truly speedy. A just cause statute has the virtue of simplicity.

Arbitration forums are attractive for the reasons explained in § **9.29**. Yet drafting a statute that sends wrongful dismissal claims to arbitration presents a number of difficulties. A practical difficulty is deciding where the arbitrators will come from and how they will be certified and assigned. If a new agency must be established to administer an arbitration system, one of the advantages of arbitration as opposed to administrative adjudication may be diluted.

A philosophical difficulty arises from the inapplicability of *stare decisis* in most arbitral systems. One of the ways in which a statute is expected to improve the

---

[47] See §§ **9.21, 9.31**.

[48] 411 U.S. 792 (1973); see §§ **2.3, 2.4 & 7.6**. An employee-plaintiff in a Title VII case has the burden of proof to show that a discriminatory motive existed.

[49] See §§ **5.22–5.26**.

law of dismissal is by making the law more predictable. Yet if arbitrators decide claims and do not report their decisions, or if their rules of decision are not reviewable, this sought-after predictability may not be achieved.

A number of constitutional problems also may arise if the statute forces claims presently litigated by the regular courts into arbitration. All but two states have statutes affording the right to jury trial in civil cases. Presumably, a legislature can abolish a cause of action and, in creating a replacement cause of action, require that this replacement cause of action be litigated in whatever form the legislature deems appropriate. But it is easy to imagine that a wrongful dismissal statute could be drafted initially to abolish tort and contract causes of action for dismissal but might have that abolition stricken from the statute during the legislative process. In such a circumstance, the statute well might be unconstitutional.

§ 9.20 Possible Substantive Fairness Standards

The starting point for writing a wrongful dismissal statute is to select a substantive fairness standard. This section reviews the alternatives introduced in § 9.2, and concludes that an enumerated prohibition approach is preferable to a just cause or good faith approach. An enumerated prohibitions approach follows the pattern set by Congress and state legislatures over many years, rejecting the approach suggested by most commentators. Section 9.2 observed that substantive fairness requires accommodating interests already afforded legal recognition,[50] balancing them against employer and societal interests in effective management of organizations.[51] Employees should be protected, but employers should not be burdened with litigation whenever an employee is terminated. Litigation is expensive and fundamentally at odds with the preference for regulating economic relations by market forces instead of by law.

A workable substantive fairness standard should reflect this tension and should draw upon the experience of the common law courts and the expressions of the legislature in balancing different interests involved in workplace governance. As § 9.2 explained, the balancing required has intellectual roots in substantive due process scrutiny of public employer decisions,[52] and in employer justification of class-based discrimination by bona fide occupational qualification or business necessity grounds.[53] Defining the scope of legitimate rights and needs accomplishes the hardest part of the substantive fairness analysis.[54]

---

[50] These interests are discussed in connection with the public policy tort cases in **ch. 5**. They include interests in the jury system, in the workers' compensation system, in safe products, in free speech, and in privacy.

[51] *See* Note, *Limiting the Right to Terminate At Will Employees—Have the Courts Forgotten the Employer?*, 35 Vand. L. Rev. 201 (1982).

[52] See § **6.13**.

[53] See §§ **2.3 & 2.7**.

[54] The legitimacy of employee and employer interests is explored in § **9.2**.

Section **9.2** reviewed the prima facie tort concept,[55] under which liability is imposed on one who intentionally, without justification, causes legal injury to another.[56] Legal injury to the plaintiff is weighed against the legitimate needs of the defendant attempting to justify his action.[57] In prima facie tort anlysis, as in constitutional due process analysis, legitimacy enters into the equation on both plaintiff's and defendant's sides. If the plaintiff has been injured in some way not recognized as legal injury, prima facie tort will afford him no damages and no injunction.[58] Once the plaintiff proves legal injury (and causation, of course), if the defendant cannot offer legally recognized justification, his conduct will subject him to liability.[59]

Section **9.2** suggested an historical perspective for law in the United States in which legally recognized employee interests have been expanding. The courts and legislatures have expanded recognized employee interests in the following ways:

First, when the reason for the termination is race, gender, age, religion, marital status, or sexual orientation, or when it is based on certain conduct, legislatures say that the termination is at least prima facie illegal, and has afforded remedies to employees terminated for these reasons, unless the employer can offer overriding justification.[60]

Second, when the termination violates constitutional prohibitions[61] against governmental interference with free speech, association, privacy, and religion,

---

[55] Essentially the same analytical structure is involved in constitutional substantive due process analysis. In substantive due process analysis, the needs of the state are weighed against the rights of the individual claiming denial of due process. *See* Beller v. Middendorf, 632 F.2d 788, 807 (9th Cir. 1980); Major v. Hampton, 413 F. Supp. 66, 69 (E.D. La. 1976); J. Nowak, R. Rotunda & J. Young, Constitutional Law 404 (1978). The balancing process is not necessary unless the person claiming denial of due process can implicate rights recognized as appropriate for constitutional protection: liberty. *See* Connick v. Myers, 461 U.S. 138 (1983); Loehr v. Ventura County Community College Dist., 743 F.2d 1310, 1317 (9th Cir. 1984) (failure to demonstrate property interest does not defeat properly asserted liberty interest claim). *See* Cleveland Bd. of Educ. v. Loudermill, 470 U.S. 532 (1985); Perry v. Sindermann, 408 U.S. 593 (1972); Board of Regents v. Roth, 408 U.S. 564 (1972). Once either of these rights is shown to be involved, the decision under scrutiny can be sustained only if a legitimate state interest in making the scrutinized decision can be shown. *Compare* Connick v. Myers, 461 U.S. at 154 (decision justified) *with* Norton v. Macy, 417 F.2d 1161 (D.C. Cir. 1969) (decision not justified). The analogy between the property or liberty interest in constitutional analysis and the individual right in substantive fairness analysis is obvious. Similarly, the legitimate state interest is analogous to the institutional employer need in substantive fairness analysis.

[56] Restatement (Second) of Torts § 870 (1979).

[57] *Id.* comment k.

[58] *Id.* at comment e.

[59] *Id.*

[60] Statutory prohibitions against class-based discharges are considered in §§ **2.2–2.14**. Statutory prohibitions against conduct-based discharges are considered in §§ **2.15–2.24**.

[61] With few exceptions, *see* Novosel v. Nationwide Ins. Co., 721 F.2d 894 (3d Cir. 1983) (recognizing public policy tort for private sector employee, based on First Amendment), the conduct restricted by the Constitution is conduct of the state or its instrumentalities.

§ 9.20 SUBSTANTIVE FAIRNESS STANDARDS

the termination is prima facie illegal.[62] A governmental employer must offer legally adequate justification to escape liability.

Third, when the reason for the termination is conduct that is protected by public policy, the discharge is a tort, unless the employer can offer justification.[63]

Fourth, when the employer has promised that it will terminate only for certain reasons, or only after following certain procedures, the employee's expectations created thereby will be protected by enforcing the employer's promise in a common law breach of contract suit,[64] or, if the employer is the government, in an action under the constitutional guarantee against governmental deprivation of property without due process.[65]

Fifth, when an employer acts unfairly or in bad faith, some states permit a terminated employee to recover for breach of the implied covenant of good faith and fair dealing.[66]

Formulating a standard for substantive fairness in wrongful discharge legislation requires consideration of all of the recognized interests enumerated above.[67] In some cases, societal interests reinforce employee interests.[68]

However, there are interests on the other side also. Employees should not be free to perform badly or to engage in misconduct. Supervisors should not be discouraged from managing effectively by the threat of lawsuits or administrative proceedings.[69] An employer should be allowed to justify removing an employee

---

[62] These liberty interests are considered in § **6.11**. Use of the term *prima facie* indicates that the employer can assert sufficiently compelling state interests to justify the invasion of liberty interests. Assessing the justification is at the heart of substantive due process analysis. See § **6.13**.

[63] The public policy tort concept is considered in **ch. 5**.

[64] Contract theories are considered in **ch. 4**.

[65] Due process protection of property rights rooted in promises of employment tenure is considered in § **6.10**.

[66] See § **4.11**.

[67] A major weakness in most of the proposals found in the law review literature is that they address only one or a few of the types of substantive fairness. *See, e.g.*, Pierce, Mann & Roberts, *Employee Termination at Will: A Principled Approach*, 28 Vill. L. Rev. 1, 46 (1982–1983) (definition of *just cause* primarily by reference to whistleblowing). Some proposals have addressed the relationship between wrongful discharge actions and collectively bargained arbitration. *See, e.g.*, Summers, *Individual Protection Against Unjust Dismissal: Time for a Statute*, 62 Va. L. Rev. 481 (1976). Some have proposed arbitral, rather than judicial, adjudication of wrongful discharge cases. *See, e.g., id.*; see also the Pennsylvania and Michigan bills discussed in § **9.10**. However, none has proposed a mechanism that would encompass all forms of substantive fairness identified in the text, especially those relating to statutory discrimination. In contrast, the British system of industrial tribunals provides just such a mechanism. See § **9.11**. Strictly speaking, the institutional factors mentioned in the text have more to do with procedural fairness than substantive fairness.

[68] These interests are recognized by the public policy tort. See **Ch. 5**. They include interests in the jury system, in the workers' compensation system, and in safe products.

[69] *See* Note, *Limiting the Right to Terminate At Will Employees—Have the Courts Forgotten the Employer?*, 35 Vand. L. Rev. 201 (1982).

when these interests in efficient enterprise management outweigh the adverse effect on legitimate employee interests.

§ 9.21 — Just Cause Standard

A simple substantive fairness standard would prohibit dismissals except for just cause. Such a substantive standard inherently balances employer and employee interests. This is the approach taken or suggested by most of the unfair dismissal schemes reviewed earlier in this chapter.[70] Imposing such a standard, however, would have the effect of making private employment similar to public employment, in that employees would enjoy something resembling civil service tenure. Such a standard would represent a revolutionary change in private sector employment relations. A for cause standard is undesirable for the reasons explained in § **9.23**, and almost certainly is unfeasible politically.

§ 9.22 — Good Faith Standard

Another simple substantive fairness possibility is a requirement that employer dismissal actions be accomplished in good faith.[71] Good faith is a less burdensome standard for employers than a for cause requirement;[72] the employer's action would be allowed to stand based on the subjective nature of the employer's decision, rather than on application of an external standard.

§ 9.23 — Weakness of Simple Standards

A weakness with either a just cause or a good faith standard for substantive fairness is that both are inherently vague, and therefore invest in individual decisionmakers outside the workplace broad discretion to make basic value tradeoffs.[73] The acceptability of the substantive standard may depend on who the external decisionmaker is. If common law judges make the tradeoffs, the appellate process can correct major excursions from rules of decision that reflect competing societal values. But the price is high in time and expense and in the resulting uncertainty

---

[70] See §§ **9.10–9.16**.

[71] *See* Brockmeyer v. Dun & Bradstreet, 113 Wis. 2d 561, 569, 335 N.W.2d 834, 838 (1983) (discussing alternative standards).

[72] In Wadeson v. American Family Mut. Ins. Co., 343 N.W.2d 367 (N.D. 1984), for example, the court approved a jury instruction on good faith, but rejected the unsuccessful plaintiff's argument that the covenant requires the employer to discharge only for good cause. *Id.* at 370. It reviewed earlier covenant of good faith cases as stopping short of requiring good cause for discharge. *Id.*

[73] Professor Unger has noted this problem with broad standards. *See* R. Unger, Law in Modern Society 193–94, 197 (1976).

before basic standards of conduct can stabilize. If arbitrators make the tradeoffs, the resulting transfer of authority over employment decisions is potentially greater. The advantages of arbitration flow in part from its simplicity, and in part from its insulation from subsequent review on the merits of individual cases. This may not be a problem in the collective bargaining context, where union and management negotiators can change or make more definitive the basic document that arbitrators are interpreting. But in the wrongful dismissal setting, the discretion of an arbitrator to give her own interpretation to a statutory term such as just cause or good faith is troublesome, because it is difficult to provide a convenient means of channeling the arbitrator's exercise of discretion in specific cases without vitiating the advantages of arbitration. Adopting a broad general substantive fairness standard almost certainly would result in reduced acceptance of the system and less predictability in employment relations.[74]

§ 9.24 —Enumerated Prohibitions

An enumerated prohibitions approach, being more specific, constrains the role of an external decisionmaker more than a just cause or a good faith standard. Legislatures make threshold interest balancing decisions.[75] This would result in a more complex set of rules, but would be consistent with an attempt to rationalize, rather than to revolutionize, the law of employee dismissal. This approach to substantive fairness would incorporate into one wrongful dismissal doctrine the various standards contained in the Constitution and in state and federal statutes, and articulated in common law cases. In essence the legislature would codify common law wrongful dismissal rules. This is what the legislatures have done in part when they have enacted whistleblower statutes.[76] The order and predictability stemming from this consolidation could reduce employer opposition.

The major weakness of an enumerated prohibitions statute is that it is more difficult to preempt other legal theories for an employment termination.[77]

The first step in developing such a standard is to identify those types of employee interests that are entitled to legal protection under existing law. Each of these interests should be incorporated in the new substantive fairness standard.

The interests of employees to be free from discrimination based on race, religion, gender, age, marital status, or sexual orientation should be recognized. These interests presently are variously protected by statute in all or some jurisdictions, and it is unlikely that any credible opposition to including them in a comprehensive wrongful discharge doctrine could be mounted. Interests of employees to be

---

[74] *See* Brockmeyer v. Dun & Bradstreet, 113 Wis. 2d 561, 596, 335 N.W.2d 834, 838 (1983) (problems with a good faith requirement).

[75] *See* Murphy v. American Home Prods. 58 N.Y.2d 293, 448 N.E.2d 86, 461 N.Y.S.2d 232 (1983) (rejecting public policy tort because legislature should make policy judgments involved).

[76] See § **9.7**.

[77] The desirability of preemption is discussed in § **9.26**.

free from discrimination based on specified conduct also are recognized to some extent by statutory law, and also should be protected in conjunction with protections afforded presently under public policy tort concepts.[78]

The expections of employees, generally protected under common law contract principles,[79] in having employers live up to their promises also should be recognized. Recognition of these contract principles does not greatly involve external reviewers of termination decisions in striking difficult balances among competing interests; the employer itself has struck the balance when it makes the promise of employment tenure. If the employer wishes to change the way the balance is struck, it can forbear to make the promise.[80] This part of an enumerated prohibitions statute should address the form of promises that give rise to rights under the statute and the consideration issue.[81] ERISA may not be a bad model, statutorily providing for enforcement of employer promises of fringe benefits.[82]

Inclusion of these protections in a new substantive fairness standard would not tilt the balance of interests appreciably against employers. On the contrary, codification would reduce uncertainty and permit responsible employers to design better employee policies and thus from a political standpoint would attract employer support.

Incorporation of two other, overlapping, categories of existing common law protection presents more difficult questions of balance. These categories relate to off-duty conduct, and to liberty interests protected by the Constitution against governmental interference.

Including termination for off-duty conduct in an enumerated prohibitions statute has two virtues: it would not jeopardize legitimate employer interests[83] though it undeniably diminishes employer power, and it would protect certain interests recognized by the Constitution without eviscerating the state-action barrier to full constitutional scrutiny of private employer decisions. Off-duty conduct protection, widely afforded by labor arbitrators,[84] shields employee interests in privacy and

---

[78] The statutory conduct-based protection is discussed in §§ **2.15–2.24**. Conceptually, it is hard to distinguish from the conduct-based protection afforded by the public policy tort doctrines discussed in **ch. 5**.

[79] See generally **ch. 4**.

[80] The right of the employer to define the terms of employment is emphasized in the *Pine River State Bank v. Mettille* (333 N.W. 2d (Minn. 1983)) jury instruction quoted in § **7.28**.

[81] See §§ **4.6–4.16**.

[82] Indeed a statute could require that employers give to their employees an "employment document," similar to the "summary plan description" required under Employee Retirement Income Security Act. *See* 29 U.S.C. § 1021(a) (1982). Such a document would set out the legally enforceable terms of employment. I am indebted to John W. Rowe for the idea, which merits further thought. The ERISA concepts could be followed, however, even without requiring such a document.

[83] *See* Slohoda v. United Parcel Serv., Inc., 193 N.J. Super. 586, 594, 475 A.2d 618, 622 (1984) (reversing summary judgment for employer; inquiry by an employer into extramarital sexual activities can give rise to tort liability if employee discharged for that reason); Wagenseller v. Scottsdale Memorial Hosp., 147 Ariz. 370, 710 P.2d 1025 (1985) (reversing dismissal of plaintiff's claim and holding that nurse dismissed for refusing to "moon" on off-duty rafting trip could recover on public policy tort theory).

[84] See § **3.8**.

personal freedom from employer coercion unrelated to employer economic interests. Unless the employer can sustain the burden of demonstrating a nexus with its business needs, it should not escape liability for terminating employees on the basis of political views expressed outside the workplace, marital status, or sexual orientation. Affording protection to off-duty conduct is not the same thing as imposing a just cause requirement. Adding off-duty conduct to the enumerated reasons for which dismissal is not permitted leaves the burden of proof on the employee to demonstrate that he was fired for off-duty conduct. A just cause protection burdens the employer to articulate the reason for the dismissal and to demonstrate that the reason amounted to just cause.[85]

Other constitutionally protected interests also might be included as sources of public policy.[86]

These substantive fairness rules might be expressed in a statute like this:

A discharge of an employee shall be wrongful if one or more of the following was a determining factor in the discharge:
(i) The employee's age, sex, race, religion, national origin, marital status, or sexual orientation;
(ii) The employee's exercise of rights of political expression, religious activities, association or privacy guaranteed under the United States Constitution against governmental interference;
(iii) The employee's performance of an act or refusal to perform an act, the performance or refusal being in furtherance of public policy, as expressed in statute, administrative regulation, or formal statements of professional ethics applicable to the employee;
(iv) Off-duty conduct of the employee bearing no reasonable relationship to the employee's job performance; or
A discharge of an employee shall be wrongful if the discharge occurred in violation of an employer's express or implied promise that the employer would dismiss the employee only for certain reasons or only after following certain procedures.

None of the suggested enumerated rights would be absolute; employers would escape liability for infringing the rights when they can show legitimate business reasons for doing so.[87] This is not a revolutionary proposal; virtually all of these grounds

---

[85] Off-duty private conduct and employee free speech are constitutional liberty interests protected against infringement by public employers. Exercise of constitutional rights by public employees is protected both because adverse employment action by a public employer is state action potentially triggering due process protections, and because many public employees have a statutory right to be dismissed only for cause. See **ch. 6**. These interests historically were not protected against infringement by private sector employers. *But see* Novosel v. Nationwide Ins. Co., 721 F.2d 894 (3d Cir. 1983) (public policy tort claim can be pleaded under Pennsylvania law for discharge interfering with First Amendment political expression rights).

[86] *See* Novosel v. Nationwide Ins. Co., 721 F.2d 894 (3d Cir. 1983) (public policy tort claim pleaded under Pennsylvania law for dismissal for refusing to testify before state legislative committee in support of employer's position; based on policy of First Amendment).

[87] Such justification occurs in applying substantive due process scrutiny to public employer decisions, and when an employer is allowed to justify class-based discrimination on Bona Fide Occupational Qualification (BFOQ) or business-necessity grounds recognized in the discrimination statutes. A BFOQ is a defense to a prima facie case of sex, religious, or age discrimination,

for dismissal would give rise to statutory or common law liability under present law. The political motivation for this approach to substantive fairness is the need to attract support from employers and the defense bar; the needs of the plaintiff bar are addressed primarily through the selections made regarding procedural fairness.

§ 9.25 Procedural Fairness

Once a policy decision is made regarding substantive fairness, drafters of a statute must resolve the threshold procedural fairness question: who decides whether a particular termination violated the substantive fairness standard? Whether a wrongful dismissal statute should send claims to arbitration, to an administrative agency, or directly to the regular courts is a procedural fairness question, as is the standard these forums should use in reviewing employer decisions.

Procedural fairness is a relative, rather than an absolute, concept. At minimum, it requires some external check on the decision procedures utilized by employers, as a counterweight to natural employer interests potentially antagonistic to employee interests. Procedural fairness can be ensured by a review of employer decisions made under procedures used by the employer or it can involve a de novo decision by an external tribunal. Determining the appropriate level of procedural fairness, like determining the appropriate approach to substantive fairness, requires a balancing of values.[88]

Most of the proposals for comprehensive wrongful dismissal legislation contemplate some form of arbitration. As §§ **9.26** through **9.33** show, however, there are potentially insuperable problems in designing a satisfactory statutory arbitration system. The most practical course of action may be to establish administrative procedures or to send claims to the regular common law courts.

§ 9.26 —Preemption, Election, Exhaustion, and Preclusion

Sections **9.2** and **9.3** explained that one major shortcoming of present employment law is that employers are subjected to multiple litigation in various forums

---

recognized by § 703(e) of Title VII, 42 U.S.C. § 2000e-2(e) (1984), and by § 623(f) of the Age Discrimination in the Employment Act, 29 U.S.C. § 623(f) (1984). See §§ **2.3, 2.6**.

[88] Acceptance of this proposition is reflected in the balancing approach to procedural due process adopted by the Supreme Court in Mathews v. Eldridge, 424 U.S. 319 (1976).

§ 9.26 PREEMPTION, ELECTION, EXHAUSTION

over adverse employment actions. A particular employee may be able to arbitrate a grievance over her discharge, file a charge with the NLRB, file a complaint with the EEOC alleging sex, race, or age discrimination, and file a suit alleging wrongful discharge.[89] In *Olguin v. Inspiration Consolidated Copper Co.*,[90] the employee filed a state public policy tort action for wrongful dismissal after having administrative claims dismissed under the Mine Safety and Health Act and the National Labor Relations Act. He also filed a grievance under the collective agreement, which the union refused to take to arbitration.[91]

It is wasteful and confusing for all these separate claims to be tried independently. Enactment of comprehensive protection against wrongful discharge creates an opportunity to simplify dismissal litigation.

Any wrongful discharge statute should force all legal claims related to a discharge into a single proceeding, and should preclude relitigation of the discharge in any other forum.[92] Of course this objective is difficult to meet entirely through state legislation. Federal preemption would guarantee employees access to federal forums despite establishment of new state remedies.[93]

State legislation could be framed, however, to preclude access to the state forum by an employee electing to pursue federal forums. The employee still would have access to multiple forums, but it is unlikely that an employee would choose to litigate several narrow federal causes of action to the exclusion of the broad state causes of action for implied-in-fact contract and public policy tort claims. Thus, protection against multiple claims is established indirectly by abolishing the two causes of action at common law, including them in a comprehensive state statute and disallowing actions under this statute when a federal claim is pursued in a federal forum. The difficulty with this approach is that it penalizes those with federal claims, potentially raising supremacy clause problems.

If the employee presents a claim to the new state tribunal, loses, and then proceeds to a federal forum, the federal forum might apply judgment- or issue-preclusion

---

[89] *See* Alexander v. Gardner-Denver, 415 U.S. 36 (1974) (both collectively bargained arbitration and Title VII available for same claim), NLRB v. Plasterers Local 79, 404 U.S. 116, 136 (1971) (unfair labor practice and arbitration potentially available for same claim); Johnson v. Railway Express Agency, Inc., 421 U.S. 454 (1975) (Title VII and 42 U.S.C. § 1981 available for same discrimination claim); W.R. Grace & Co. v. Rubber Workers Local 759, 461 U.S. 757 (1983) (conflicting arbitration award and Title VII decree allowed to stand); Belknap, Inc. v. Hale, 463 U.S. 491 (1983) (potentially conflicting unfair labor practice proceeding and state lawsuit by discharged striker replacements permitted); Taylor v. NLRB, 786 F.2d 1516 (11th Cir. 1986) (vacating NLRB order deferring to arbitration award denying grievance of truck driver dismissed for refusal to drive unsafe truck); *id.* at 1518–20 (reviewing history of deferral doctrine).

[90] 740 F.2d 1468 (9th Cir. 1984).

[91] *Id.* at 1470–71.

[92] Section 11 of the proposed state and federal statutes accomplish this. See **App. C**.

[93] Federal preemption is discussed in **§§ 2.27–2.34**. *See also* Alexander v. Gardner-Denver, 415 U.S. 36 (1974) (arbitration award not entitled to preclusive effect in Title VII discrimination litigation). *But see* Darden v. Illinois Bell Tel. Co., 797 F.2d 497 (7th Cir. 1986) (affirming dismissal of Title VII suit, based on great weight given to arbitration award).

principles, though preclusion would be uncertain.[94] It is important that a new wrongful dismissal statute unequivocally declare its policy in favor of preclusion, because of the weight the *Restatement (Second) of Judgments* gives to policy in resolving questions of administrative preclusion.[95]

A number of problems arise in connection with defining the appropriate relationship between new wrongful dismissal tribunals and administrative agencies already established to hear issues related to a wrongful dismissal claim. The problem is evident currently when an employee brings a common law public policy tort claim premised on employer violation of health or safety regulations. Health or safety regulations commonly are enforced by administrative agencies. If the agency decides that a health or safety violation did not occur, the question of what effect this should have on the wrongful dismissal case then arises.[96] One can argue that, since the agency did not decide the retaliatory dismissal question, the administrative decision should have no effect. Conversely, one can argue that the public policy basis for the wrongful dismissal claim evaporates when the responsible agency has found that there was nothing wrong with the employer's conduct. The soundest view is that the issue is not whether the employee was *correct* in her complaints; rather the issue should be whether the employee's right to complain *in good faith* without fear of retaliation promotes public policy. Accordingly, a finding of a serious violation by the responsible administrative agency would be persuasive evidence that the employee's concern was in good faith. A finding of no violation might support an argument that the employee's complaint was frivolous.

When the responsible agency has not yet addressed the employer's compliance with law, exhaustion-of-remedies principles should preclude a decision on the

---

[94] *Compare* University of Tenn. v. Elliott, ___ U.S. ___, 106 S. Ct. 3220 (1986) (unreviewed state administrative decision entitled to preclusive effect in § 1983 suit, but not in Title VII suit) *and* Buckhalter v. Pepsi-Cola Gen. Bottlers, 768 F.2d 842 (7th Cir. 1985) (dismissal of state discrimination claim by administrative agency precluded relitigation under 42 U.S.C. § 1981) *and* Gorin v. Osborne, 756 F.2d 834, 836 (11th Cir. 1985) (§ 1983 claim barred by res judicata effect of state court decision affirming state personnel board on "any evidence" to support decision) *with* Bottini v. Sadore Management Corp., 764 F.2d 116, 120 (2d Cir. 1985) (state administrative proceedings do not bar subsequent federal court action under Title VII) *and* Heath v. John Morrell & Co., 768 F.2d 245, 248 (8th Cir. 1985) (reversing district court for giving res judicata effect to unemployment compensation board decision in Title VII and § 1981 case; state board had no jurisdiction over discrimination law issues) *and* Griffen v. Big Spring Indep. School Dist., 706 F.2d 645, 655 (5th Cir. 1983) (denying res judicata or collateral estoppel effect to state administrative appeals board determination because of gross irregularity of procedure, though procedure before hearing officer was adequate).

[95] *See* Restatement (Second) of Judgments § 83(4) (1982).

[96] This problem is addressed more fully in § **7.34**.

wrongful dismissal claim prior to the agency having an opportunity to interpret its own statute or regulation.[97]

§ 9.27 —Deference to Employer Procedures

Voluntarism decentralizes decisionmaking, thereby reducing the load on central political institutions. It permits experimentation, provides opportunities for employers and employees to participate directly in making decisions that affect them, and usually results in procedures and substantive norms that are tailored to the needs and priorities of a particular enterprise and its employees.[98] A wrongful dismissal statute that promotes voluntarism is more likely to be favored by the employers because it allows them to design dispute resolution procedures that accommodate the needs of a particular workplace.

Voluntarism can be promoted by ensuring that substantial deference is paid by legal institutions to procedures adopted by employers for deciding discharge controversies voluntarily. Some state courts have suggested that the external legal machinery should not decide de novo whether an employee was discharged wrongfully; rather the inquiry should be whether the employer fairly followed the procedures that the employer itself voluntarily promised to follow.[99] Major impediments to this type of voluntarism exist under present law.[1]

As explained in § **9.2**, two basic alternatives can be identified. The first is to permit employers to make discharge decisions, immune from external review, so long as they follow formal processes with the rudiments of procedural fairness (e.g., giving of notice, appointment of an unbiased decisionmaker, and affording of an opportunity for the employee to tell his side of the story to that decision-

---

[97] *Compare* Gaibis v. Werner Continental, Inc., 565 F. Supp. 1538 (W.D. Pa. 1983) (refusing to defer to administrative agency decision that no safety violation occurred), *rev'd sub nom.* Vosch v. Werner Continental, Inc., 734 F.2d 149 (3d Cir. 1984), *cert. denied,* 469 U.S. 1108 (1985) *with* Cavoli v. A.R.A. Serv., Inc., Civil No. 83-3764 (D.N.J. Jan. 24, 1984) (staying public policy tort action until administrative agency could address safety question).

[98] *See* Dunlop, *The Limits of Legal Compulsion,* 27 Lab. L. J. 67 (1976).

[99] *See* Rap, Inc. v. District of Columbia Comm'n on Human Rights, 485 A.2d 173, 179 (D.C. 1984) (employer mistake in internal investigation does not necessarily show prohibited intent). *But see* Doe v. St. Joseph's Hosp., 788 F.2d 411 (7th Cir. 1986) (declining to accept argument that Title VII plaintiff must exhaust administrative remedies under defendant hospital's internal procedures and bylaws).

[1] *See* Alexander v. Gardner-Denver, 415 U.S. 36 (1974) (grievance arbitration not entitled to preclusive effect in Title VII case); Barrantine v. Arkansas-Best Freight Sys., 450 U.S. 728 (1981) (discussed in § **3.27**); University of Tenn. v. Elliott, ___ U.S. ___, 106 S. Ct. 3220 (1986) (unreviewed state administrative decision not entitled to preclusive effect in Title VII case). *But see* Darden v. Illinios Bell Tel. Co., 797 F.2d 497 (7th Cir. 1986) (affirming dismissal of Title VII suit, based on great weight given to arbitration award).

maker).[2] The other alternative is a trial de novo of the fairness of the discharge decision by a jury in a regular court of law.[3]

Section **9.2** also suggested an intermediate approach, borrowed from administrative law.[4] Under this approach, employer decisions meeting basic requirements of procedural fairness[5] would be accepted[6] unless they were arbitrary and capricious,[7] or made in bad faith.[8]

---

[2] This is similar to the minimum due process required for student suspensions in Goss v. Lopez, 419 U.S. 565, 581 (1975) (notice of charges, explanation of evidence against student, and an opportunity to present student's side of story). In Judge Friendly's list of ingredients of procedural due process, this would include only the first three rights: (1) an unbiased tribunal, (2) notice, and (3) an opportunity to present reasons for which the proposed actions should not be taken. See Friendly, *"Some Kind of Hearing,"* 123 Pa. L. Rev. 1267, 1279-94 (1975). The Oregon Supreme Court essentially has embraced this approach in Simpson v. Western Graphics Corp., 293 Or. 96, 643 P.2d 1276, 1278 (Or. 1982), though it is not clear that it would impose *any* procedural requirements, as opposed to deferring to the employer regardless of the procedure followed. An alternative, adopted by the Montana Supreme Court in Gates v. Life of Mont. Ins. Co., 196 Mont. 178, 638 P.2d 1063 (1982), would permit the employer to define the procedures for decisionmaking, but let the jury decide whether it followed them. Professor Summers's proposed statute would apply similar procedural scrutiny to collectively bargained procedures. See Summers, *Individual Protection Against Unjust Dismissal: Time for a Statute,* 62 Va. L. Rev. 481, 529 (1976). The Summers proposal is discussed fully in § **9.14**.

[3] This is essentially the approach adopted by the Michigan Supreme Court in Toussaint v. Blue Cross & Blue Shield, 408 Mich. 579, 621-23, 292 N.W.2d 880, 896 (1980) (jury decides facts, and whether facts amount to cause). Obviously even if a jury is to decide the termination question de novo, presumptions and burdens of proof materially can affect the relative weight given to employer and employee interests. See Grey, *Procedural Fairness and Substantive Rights,* Nomos XVIII, Due Process 182, 183 (1977). Presumptions and burdens of proof are discussed in **ch. 7**.

[4] The administrative law analogy is imperfect. Judicial review of administrative agency decisions proceeds from constitutional due process and legislative delegation doctrines, and is intended to enforce compliance with the agency's statutory mandate. External review of private employer decisions would be premised instead on public principles derived through the common law or expressed in statutes.

[5] The Administrative Procedure Act imposes detailed procedural requirements for adjudication. See 5 U.S.C. §§ 554, 556-557 (1982), but the courts allow agencies some discretion respecting compliance with these requirements. See Richardson v. Perales, 402 U.S. 389, 409-10 (1971); American Trucking Ass'n v. United States, 627 F.2d 1313, 1321 (D.C. Cir. 1980) (agencies have broad discretion to fashion own procedures); Verkuil, *The Emerging Concept of Administrative Procedure,* 78 Colum. L. Rev. 258, 313 (1978) (noting flexibility provided by present APA adjudication requirements). Much more flexibility is permitted under procedural due process constitutional requirements. See Schweiker v. McClure, 456 U.S. 188 (1982) (agency adjudicatory functions can be delegated to private hearing officer pursuant to statute without violating due process); Mathews v. Eldridge, 424 U.S. 319 (1976); Richardson v. Perales, 402 U.S. 389 (1971) (informal adjudication by the Social Security Administration).

[6] Whether the employer followed the procedure adopted voluntarily or imposed on it externally is of course a separate question. See Gates v. Life of Mont. Ins. Co., 196 Mont. 178, 638 P.2d 1063 (1982) (jury should decide whether employer followed its own policies).

[7] One of the difficulties with the administrative model is that it tends toward imposition of greater procedural obligations, over time, on the decisionmaker. For example, a requirement that a factual decision be supported by *substantial evidence,* see Universal Camera v. NLRB, 340 U.S. 474 (1951), implies that a record must be generated which, in turn, implies certain procedural

If an employer affords no procedures protective of employee rights, then an external tribunal should decide the merits of a wrongful discharge claim. However, if the employer does have formal procedures within which the grounds for discharge are adjudicated, then the external tribunal should confine itself to an appellate role, ensuring that those procedures are followed. Decisions reached by the employer in compliance with those procedures should be final and binding, unless there is a substantive fairness problem. Substantive issues need not be reached until it is determined that employer procedures were followed.

Such an approach will provide incentives for employers to continue to adopt their own disciplinary procedures and may reduce employer resistance to new wrongful dismissal legislation. Any other approach would create a disincentive for the continuation or adoption of such procedures because the employer always would face the threat of relitigation of questions already decided in its own internal procedures. Precedent for a deferential approach to procedural fairness includes arbitral review of discharges in the railroad industry[9] and court review of public employee discharges under the civil service laws.[10]

Despite the desirability of deferring to certain employer decisions, however, a number of difficulties arise. One obvious difficulty is deciding what standards the employer-established procedure must meet in order to be entitled to deferral. Whether procedural fairness existed in the employer's forum cannot be determined by an external decisionmaker without scrutinizing what the employer did, and what the employee was allowed to say in his defense. It is difficult for an external decisionmaker to ensure procedural fairness without having before it a record of the employer's proceedings or else retrying the case on the merits. But requiring employers to make transcripts or otherwise to create a record formalizes employer procedures, creating economic and other disincentives for adoption of such procedures.

The underlying premise of a deferential approach to procedural fairness is that the employer's substantive decision to terminate employment will be allowed to stand if the employee has been afforded procedural fairness in the employer's forum.

For example, suppose the employer discharged an employee because the employee threatened his supervisor and the employer claims that the decision should not be reviewed on its merits because the employee was afforded procedural fairness in the employer's forum. The employer explains that the employee was given notice

---

requirements. *See* Camp v. Pitts, 411 U.S. 138 (1973). *See generally* Pittston Stevedoring Corp. v. Dellaventura, 544 F.2d 35 (2d Cir. 1976), for Judge Friendly's discussion of the standards for judicial review of administrative agency action.

[8] *See* Gates v. Life of Mont. Ins. Co., 196 Mont. 178, 638 P.2d 1063 (1982) (covenant of good faith violated by failure to follow procedures).

[9] *See* McDonald v. Penn Cent. Transp. Co., 337 F. Supp. 803, 805–06 (D. Mass. 1972). A general review of the functioning of the National Railroad Adjustment Board is found in Garrison, *The National Railroad Adjustment Board: A Unique Administrative Agency,* 46 Yale L.J. 567 (1937). For a general discussion of the arbitrator's role as an appellate reviewer or de novo decisionmaker, *see* O. Fairweather, Practice and Procedure in Arbitration 244 (1983).

[10] See §§ **6.4–6.6**.

that dismissal was contemplated because he threatened his supervisor and was afforded an opportunity to present his version of the facts to the president of the employing enterprise. The president did not believe the employee's presentation and decided that his employment should be terminated.

The employee's version of what happened is somewhat different. The employee alleges that he was given no real opportunity to present his story to the president; that the president gave him only 60 seconds to make his presentation saying, "Make it quick. This is all a farce, anyway." Under these circumstances, it is difficult for the external decisionmaker to make a meaningful decision unless he hears complete testimony about the decisionmaking process engaged in by the employer, or unless he has a verbatim transcript of proceedings before the employer. Transcripts are available to the external reviewer in administrative law cases and in railroad adjustment board cases—the two analogies offered. But requiring employers to make transcripts significantly reduces employer procedural flexibility, the underlying reason for deference to employer procedures.

The procedural fairness standard offered in § 7(b) of the proposed statutes in **Appendix C** attempts to deal with this problem in two ways. First, it confines the arbitrator to the question of whether the employer procedures were fair before he can proceed to address the substantive fairness question. In this first stage, evidence could be offered as to procedures actually followed by the employer. In the hypothetical case in this section, the arbitrator could hear testimony and decide whether the employee was given a meaningful opportunity to present his version of the facts to the president of the employing enterprise. Only if the arbitrator determines that the procedures followed by the employer were unfair can she proceed to hear evidence on the merits. This compromise is far from perfect, but it represents a reasonable attempt to defer to employer procedures without rendering the opportunity for external review entirely illusory.

At the very least, a new statute should ensure the finality of final and binding arbitration agreed to in individual cases or in a class of cases. In those states adopting the Uniform Arbitration Act[11] or similar statutes, little more will be necessary than a savings clause preserving the effect of such statutes. In other states, specific language should be included.[12]

§ 9.28 —Treatment of Collectively Bargained Arbitration

Employees with a right to be discharged only for cause and to litigate the fairness of terminations within collectively bargained procedures should not gain the right to relitigate such claims in a new external forum.[13] Exclusions of statutory coverage

---

[11] See § **3.22** notes.

[12] Section 11(c) of the proposed state statute, and section 11(d) of the proposed federal statute accomplish this. See **App. C** for the proposed statutes.

[13] Courts hearing common law claims for wrongful dismissal can require that the claims be litigated in collectively bargained arbitration, as a matter of common law. *See* Burkhart v. Mobil Oil Corp.,

for employees covered by collective agreements is one way to preclude such relitigation. This approach appears in the British statute and in the Pennsylvania and Michigan bills and was suggested by Professor Summers.[14]

One of the difficulties with this proposal is that union control over the arbitration process reduces individual employee discretion to press a claim as far as possible,[15] since the standard of review of collectively bargained decisions is so deferential that it makes meaningful merits review impracticable.

There are signs, moreover, that some unions are willing to support wrongful dismissal legislation only if the legislation gives a choice: the union may submit a dismissal claim to collectively bargained arbitration or the individual employee may submit it under a new statutory procedure. The rationale for this position is that giving an individual employee access to a forum not controlled by the union probably would lessen the number of subsequent fair representation claims against the union.[16]

§ 9.29 —Selection of Forum

A new statute could direct wrongful discharge disputes to any one of three forums: the regular courts, an existing or new administrative agency, or alternative dispute resolution tribunals, such as arbitration. As noted earlier, most of the wrongful dismissal statutes involve an arbitration forum. Most of the statutes actually enacted involve a judicial forum.

Permitting the regular courts to decide claims would facilitate preclusion of other independent proceedings.[17] This approach also eliminates potential problems with state constitutional rights to jury trial. On the other hand, traditional litigation is expensive and slow. The serious burden on regular courts by the existing volume of civil litigation militates against sending additional wrongful dismissal claims directly to court.[18] A search for civil litigation alternatives enjoys wide support within the legal community and elsewhere.[19] Legislative action perceived as increasing burdens on the courts would contravene the movement to reduce the

---

[13] 143 Vt. 123, 463 A.2d 226 (1983) (reversing judgment for plaintiff who failed to use arbitration to contest dismissal). See also §§ **4.25, 5.20**.

[14] See §§ **9.10, 9.14**.

[15] *See* McDonald v. City of W. Branch, 466 U.S. 284, 291 n.10 (1984) (noting union control over arbitration as one reason why an adverse arbitration award should not preclude access to the courts).

[16] The rationale for bypassing arbitration when an employee can prove breach of the duty of fair representation is that the union controls access to the arbitral forum. See §§ **3.25-3.26**.

[17] *See* University of Tenn. v. Elliot, ___ U.S. ___, 106 S. Ct. 3220 (1986) (state court decision entitled to res judicata effect in Title VII case, but not unreviewed state administrative decision).

[18] *See* Perritt, *And the Whole Earth Was of One Language: A Broad View of Dispute Resolution,* 29 Vill. L. Rev. 1049 (1984).

[19] *See id.*; 2 Politics of Informal Justice 1 (R. Abel ed. 1982); Warren E. Burger, *Isn't There a Better Way,* Annual Report by the Chief Justice of the United States on the State of the Judiciary, American Bar Association Mid Winter Meeting, January 4, 1982; Mennemeier, *Protection from Unjust Discharges: An Arbitration Scheme,* 19 Harv. J. on Legis. 49 (1982).

burden. Additionally, poor plaintiffs depend on the willingness of contingent fee attorneys to take their cases. Thus, access to the judicial forum frequently depends on attorney availability and attorney evaluation of the case. This presents a barrier to forum access, but also helps to screen claims lacking merit.

Administrative forums traditionally are used in twentieth century labor legislation.[20] This approach provides easier access, is usually more expeditious than the judicial process, requires no payment by the claimant, and benefits from a mature scheme of judicial review. On the other hand, administrative regulation has been subjected to increasing criticism since 1970, and regulatory reform has been high on the priorities of the last two Presidents of the United States.[21] Early experience of the EEOC shows that a free administrative forum for employment grievances can become completely overwhelmed by the number of cases.

The arbitration alternative is attractive because it avoids the problems with judicial and administrative alternatives. In addition, arbitration already is in wide use to protect against wrongful discharge in the private union and government sectors of society and has proven to be generally successful in protecting the legitimate rights of both employers and employees. Also, presumably the economic barriers to arbitral resolution are lower for the dismissed employee than the barriers to judicial litigation. A California study has estimated that plaintiff legal fees for wrongful dismissal cases that go to trial average $7500–$8000 per case.[22] A typical labor arbitration case probably costs about $1,000. It is not surprising that many of the concrete proposals for wrongful discharge legislation, and the methods actually adopted in Britain and Canada, utilize some form of arbitration.

Arbitration has a number of disadvantages, however. The civil courts already exist, and referring claims under a new wrongful dismissal statute to the courts has the virtue of avoiding the establishment of a new institution. Moreover, the constitutions of all but one state afford the right to a jury trial for common law claims. Serious constitutional issues may be raised by a statute that apparently leaves intact common law tort and contract claims for wrongful dismissal[23] and purports to require that they be heard in a nonjudicial forum.

Also, statutory arbitration suffers from disadvantages not present with collectively bargained arbitration. Individual claimants, unlike unions, are largely ignorant of the qualifications and biases of potential arbitrators. Selection of neutral arbitrators thus may be a problem. Of course, it is possible that the plaintiff bar could develop knowledge about potential arbitrators commensurate with that exercised by unions on behalf of grievants.

---

[20] Most of the statutes discussed in **ch. 2** provide for disputes to be referred, at least initially, to an administrative agency.

[21] President Carter promulgated Exec. Order No. 12,044 to improve regulation. 43 Fed. Reg. 12661 (Mar. 23, 1978). President Reagon promulgated Exec. Order No. 12,291 for the same purpose. 46 Fed. Reg. 13193 (Feb. 17, 1981). *See* 5 U.S.C. § 553 note, § 601 note (1982).

[22] *See* Ad Hoc Committee on Termination at Will and Wrongful Discharge Appointed by the Labor and Employment Law Section of The State Bar of California, *To Strike a New Balance* 8 (Feb. 8, 1984).

[23] The constitutional problem might be avoided if a new statute expressly extinguishes the common law claims and substitutes a new statutory claim.

Employers lose more control over workplace decisions if arbitration is selected as the forum. If common law judges review dismissals, the appellate process can control review of employer action. If arbitrators decide the cases, their decisions are largely insulated from judicial review. In the collective bargaining context, union and management negotiators can change the basic document that arbitrators are interpreting. But under a statute, the discretion of an arbitrator to give her own interpretation to a statutory term such as *cause* or *good faith* is great. If greater judicial scrutiny of arbitral decisionmaking is provided, the system reduces the advantages of arbitration: simplicity, cheapness, and speed.[24]

Until someone offers a way of solving these problems with arbitration, the best approach is to refer claims of statutory violation to the regular courts, as the legislatures' enactment of whistleblower statutes have done,[25] or utilize existing administrative tribunals, as suggested in the next section.

§ 9.30 — Integration of Wrongful Dismissal and Unemployment Compensation Systems

One possibility for statutory wrongful dismissal protection is to integrate the machinery for adjudicating wrongful dismissal complaints with the existing unemployment compensation system.[26] The British unfair dismissal system is a model for such integration.[27] The industrial tribunals under the British system award *redundancy pay* (unemployment compensation) as well as deciding claims of unfair dismissal. The advantages of such integration are the following:

1. The unemployment compensation system already exists in every state, and has an administrative mechanism for deciding individual cases involving termination of employment[28]
2. Unemployment compensation tribunals already must decide certain factual issues that may be outcome determinative in claims of wrongful dismissal[29]
3. The unemployment compensation system affords limited monetary relief to dismissed employees. It would be necessary in any event to address how this type of relief should be integrated with new remedies under a wrongful dismissal statute.

---

[24] See § **3.17**, explaining that courts do not require opinions or reasoning from arbitrators as prerequisites to enforcement of their decisions.

[25] See § **9.7**.

[26] Such integration was suggested by Professor Bellace. See § **9.16**.

[27] See § **9.11**.

[28] §§ **2.36–2.37** describe the unemployment compensation system.

[29] See § **7.35** (explaining relationship between findings of misconduct in claims for unemployment compensation and factual issues in wrongful dismissal cases.

Integration of a comprehensive wrongful dismissal scheme with unemployment compensation would be relatively simple. The unemployment compensation statute could be amended to provide a schedule of payments, ranging from present compensation for no-fault termination to higher levels of monetary compensation or reinstatement for employees dismissed in violation of the new rights granted by the wrongful dismissal statute.[30] Integration of wrongful dismissal with unemployment compensation would be equally feasible, regardless of whether a legislation elects a just cause approach or an enumerated prohibitions approach.[31]

§ 9.31 —Burdens of Proof

Any balancing approach to substantive fairness is sensitive to the burdens of proof and presumptions imposed on the parties. The prevailing approach under existing enumerated prohibitions statutes and under the common law theories[32] is to saddle the employee with the ultimate burden of persuasion. This burden can be retained under the proposed enumerated prohibitions approach to substantive fairness. It is more difficult to retain under a just cause or good faith standard.[33]

Most experienced practitioners know that a terminated plaintiff's chances of recovery are substantial if he can get the case to a jury. Conversely, employers hope that cases can be decided on the pleadings or at the summary judgment stage rather than by a jury. Burdens of production and persuasion frequently are outcome determinative at the summary judgment stage. If the plaintiff is burdened to produce evidence that the termination was motivated by a prohibited reason, the case can be ended in a summary judgment proceeding if the plaintiff is unable to marshal evidence during discovery from which a prohibited motive may be inferred by a reasonable factfinder.

But if the employee is obligated only to show that he was terminated without just cause, the practical burden of production is shifted to the employer to adduce some evidence of a legitimate reason. Even if a legitimate reason is a permissible inference, it is likely that a factfinder would be allowed to choose between the allowable inferences. It is difficult to structure burdens of proof under a just cause statute to keep many cases from the jury.

§ 9.32 —Remedies

Deciding on the remedies to be afforded under a wrongful dismissal statute presents several difficult questions:

---

[30] § **9.32** considers various approaches to remedies.

[31] See §§ **9.20–9.24** (weighing the advantages of just cause, good faith, and enumerated prohibitions approaches to substantive fairness).

[32] See generally **ch. 7**.

[33] As §§ **3.5 & 3.15** explain, the practical burden is always placed on the employer to show just cause.

§ 9.32 REMEDIES

1. Should reinstatement be allowed?
2. Should front pay[34] be allowed?
3. Should plaintiff or defense attorneys' fees be recoverable?
4. Should compensatory damages be "capped"?
5. Should punitive damages be allowed?

The remedies question is inseparable from politics. Adjusting remedies is an important way to build support for a proposed statute in the employer and plaintiff bar communities. Only the first issue, reinstatement, is relatively noncontroversial. Reinstatement is almost universally available under existing statutory[35] and common law[36] wrongful dismissal doctrines, and therefore is included as an available remedy in the proposed statutes in **Appendix C**.

Employer support for a wrongful dismissal statute can be increased by a cap on damages[37] and the possibility of attorneys' fees awards to employers exposed to frivolous claims. The draft statutes in **Appendix C** meet these two desires.[38]

Plaintiff bar support can be increased primarily by providing for an award of attorneys' fees to successful plaintiffs.[39] This should make legal representation more widely available to dismissed employees despite the prospect of relatively small damage awards.

Front pay and punitive damages provisions afford additional opportunities to structure a political accommodation between employer and employee interests.

---

[34] Front pay is pay for lost earnings in the future, after the date of judgment, as opposed to back pay, which is pay between the date of dismissal and the date of judgment. Front pay as a common law contract remedy is considered in **§ 4.28**.

[35] Statutes prohibiting discharge based on defined characteristic or conduct commonly provide for reinstatement as a remedy. See **ch. 2**. The best known statutes are probably the National Labor Relations Act, 29 U.S.C. § 160(c) (authorizing NLRB to order reinstatement), and Title VII of the Civil Rights Act of 1964; 42 U.S.C. § 2000e-5(g) (authorizing affirmative relief explicitly including reinstatement). The Supreme Court has noted that, since one of the central purposes of Title VII is to make injured persons whole, broad equitable discretion, including the power to order reinstatement, is vested in the judiciary. See Franks v. Bowman Transp. Co., 424 U.S. 747 (1976). Section 1983 of the Reconstruction Civil Rights Acts, 42 U.S.C. § 1983 (1982), also allows reinstatement as a remedy. See Allen v. Autauga County Bd. of Educ., 685 F.2d 1302, 1305–06 (11th Cir. 1982) (reinstatement required in suit be discharged nontenured teacher asserting First Amendment rights); Clary v. Irvin, 501 F. Supp. 706, 713 (E.D. Tex. 1980) (reinstatement of discharged police officers ordered even though bitterness and tension might result). Civil Service statutes (see **§§ 6.3–6.6**) usually provide for reinstatement when the government body fails to follow procedures. See, e.g., Chavers v. State Personnel Bd., 357 So. 2d 662 (Ala. Civ. App.), cert. denied, 357 So. 2d 664 (Ala. 1978); Massman v. H.U.D., 332 F. Supp. 894 (D.D.C. 1963). Reinstatement is also granted when the government body fails to demonstrate a nexus between the act charged and the employee's job performance. See, e.g., Bonet v. United States Postal Serv., 661 F.2d 1021 (5th Cir. 1981).

[36] Reinstatement is available in common law actions as a form of injunctive relief, either mandatory or prohibitory. See **§§ 4.28, 5.33**.

[37] See **§ 9.4**.

[38] See § 9 of the federal statute and § 9 of the state statute, in **App. C**.

[39] See **§ 9.4**.

The draft statutes[40] allow for front pay but do not permit punitive damages or compensatory damages for emotional injury. This represents a compromise between the common law contract rule, which permits expectation damages when a breach of contract has been shown,[41] and the tort[42] and statutory rules, which generally would permit only back pay, but which frequently also permit exemplary damages. The compromise position also is congruent with the majority rule applied under the Age Discrimination in Employment Act.[43] An obvious alternative to the proposal would be to permit only a limited amount of front pay, perhaps up to two years' worth. This also would be congruent with the liquidated damages approach of the ADEA, which permits penalty damages equal to the amount of compensatory damages, but not in excess of them.

The proposed statute provides for the award of attorneys' fees to the prevailing party. This is done to make it easier for discharged employees of modest means to obtain counsel, as noted earlier in this section, and to provide a further disincentive for the filing of frivolous claims.

§ 9.33 —Costs of Litigation

The volume of litigation is controlled in part by economic barriers to litigation.[44] Such controls are present in common law court litigation.[45] They also are present in conventional labor arbitration, in which the union and the employer usually share the costs of arbitration.[46] They are absent in administrative adjudication under the National Labor Relations Act and the discrimination statutes.[47] A system of

---

[40] *See* § 9(d) of the draft state and federal statutes in **App. C**.

[41] See § **4.28** for a discussion of contract damages principles.

[42] Tort damages can include amounts for posttrial pecuniary loss. *See* Restatement (Second) of Torts § 910 (1979). Comment d to § 924, however, could be construed to bar recovery for future earnings, unless the dismissal has impaired the plaintiff's capacity to seek and find work. Tort damage principles are discussed generally in § **5.33**. The cases discussed in that section can be read to permit front pay as an element of damages.

[43] See § **2.6**.

[44] The economic burden of attorneys' fees has been the frequent subject of litigation. *See* Hensley v. Eckerhart, 461 U.S. 424 (1983) (award of attorneys' fees under 42 U.S.C. § 1988 should depend on extent of success); New York Gaslight Club, Inc. v. Carey, 447 U.S. 54, 63 (1980) (allowing attorneys' fees in state administrative litigation under § 706(k) of Civil Rights Act of 1964). The history of the American and English Rules regarding court costs and attorneys' fees is reviewed in Alyeska Pipeline Serv. Co. v. Wilderness Soc'y, 421 U.S. 240 (1975). The economic burden of court costs also has been considered by the Supreme Court. *See* Ortwein v. Schwab, 410 U.S. 656 (1973) (fees for judicial review of administrative denial of welfare benefits); United States v. Kras, 409 U.S. 434 (1973) (fees for bankruptcy filing); Boddie v. Connecticut, 401 U.S. 371 (1971) (fees for divorce). In these cases, the Supreme Court has recognized that many cases would not be litigated by private plaintiffs unless the economic burden of litigation is reduced.

[45] *See generally* 20 Am. Jur. 2d *Costs* §§ 1–25 (1965).

[46] *See* O. Fairweather, Practice and Procedure in Labor Arbitration 522 (1983).

[47] No fee is imposed for filing an unfair labor practice charge with the NLRB or for filing an EEOC complaint.

free arbitration is provided for under the Railway Labor Act.[48] The caseload under a comprehensive wrongful discharge statute could be large, as projected in § **9.34**. Imposing a threshold cost on claimants therefore is desirable to reduce the incidence of frivolous claims.

Special provision for imposing an *entry fee* to the forum is necessary only if attorneys are not needed to commence a wrongful dismissal case. If attorneys are required, an attorney's willingness to take a case depends to some degree on its merit;[49] the attorney will not get paid for his work if the plaintiff does not win.

Professor Summers has a good idea on how to impose reasonable costs to potential claimants without barring access to the procedures by poor but deserving employees. His suggestion for imposing a fee equivalent to a week's pay seems sound,[50] and is reflected in the draft statutes. In addition, the provision in the New York whistleblower statute, permitting employers to recover attorneys' fees and costs when frivolous claims are presented, is worthy of consideration.[51]

As noted in § **9.32**, the proposed statute provides for the award of attorneys' fees to the prevailing party, to make it easier for discharged employees to obtain counsel, and to reduce the incidence of frivolous claims.

§ 9.34 Estimation of Case Volume

The enactment of a statute giving rise to a new or unified wrongful dismissal remedy brings up the question of the number of complaints likely to be filed under the new statute. Labor statistics were analyzed, using a simple model, to determine a potential range of the number of complaints.

The first step in the analysis was to determine what percentage of terminated employees protest their termination. In the discussion that follows, this is called the *propensity to litigate*. The raw data were obtained from three sources[52] and

---

[48] Under § 3 of the Railway Labor Act, 45 U.S.C. § 153 (1982), partisan members of adjustment boards are compensated by the parties they represent, and neutrals are compensated by the government.

[49] This is true if attorneys are compensated primarily on a contingent fee basis, or if statutory award of attorneys' fees depends, as it does under 42 U.S.C. § 1988 (1982), on achieving a successful outcome for the client. The screening phenomenon discussed in the text is ineffective as to cases brought by clients who are wealthy enough to pay counsel on an hourly or retainer basis.

[50] See § **9.14**. *But see* Mennemeier, *Protection from Unjust Discharges: An Arbitration Scheme,* 19 Harv. J. on Legis. 49, 89 (1982). The entire Mennemeier proposal is discussed in § **9.14**. He mentions the possibility of the state bearing the costs while pointing out that such a scheme might encourage frivolous claims. He also notes that employees cannot deduct arbitration costs from their taxes, as can employers.

[51] *See* N.Y. Lab. Law § 740(6) (McKinney Supp. 1986), discussed in § **9.7**.

[52] The annual reports of the Equal Employment Opportunity Commission from 1969 through 1983; the Handbook of Labor Statistics by the Bureau of Labor Statistics (BLS), U.S. Department of Labor (1975 & 1985); telephone conversation with Railroad Retirement Board (railroad employment data); and the National Railroad Adjustment Board annual reports: 1969–1983, encompassed in the 35th through 49th annual reports of the National Mediation Board.

Table 9-1

PROBABILITY OF LITIGATION: CLAIMS FILED, PER 100 DISCHARGED EMPLOYEES

Year	Race[53]	Railroad[54]	Gender[55]
1983	2.1		0.8
1982	1.9		0.7
1981	2.7		0.9
1980	3.1	2.0	0.9
1979	3.3	2.6	1.0
1978	3.2	2.4	0.9
1977	3.2	2.3	0.8
1976	3.4	1.9	0.8
1975	1.6	2.2	0.4
1974	2.5	3.9	0.6
1973	2.4	2.4	0.5
1972	0.6	1.0	0.1
1971	1.1	0.6	0.1
1970	0.6	2.7	0.1
1967	0.4	2.9	0.1
Average 1967–83	2.1	2.2	0.6
Average 1976–83	2.9	2.2	0.9

analyzed as follows: The percentage of discharged employees who file claims with the Equal Employment Opportunity Commission (EEOC) or National Railroad Adjustment Board (NRAB) was calculated. The number of job losers by class (race, sex, or railroad employee)[56] was divided into the number of complaints filed with the EEOC[57] or with the NRAB. The quotient is the estimate of the propensity to litigate for each group (**Table 9-1**). Stock unemployment figures were used to represent job losses because they were readily available. Changes in the employment status of employees would be more accurate as a measure of the group likely to file complaints. Figures on change in status, however, are more difficult to obtain for selected groups; thus, the stock numbers for unemployment were substituted.

---

[53] Claims of race discrimination in private employer discharge decisions filed with the EEOC, divided by total private sector black unemployed due to discharge.

[54] Claims filed with the NRAB, divided by total railroad unemployment. The Railroad Retirement Board was unresponsive to requests for more current railroad unemployment data. A review of NRAB claims filed for 1978–1983, and of unemployment statistics for the entire transportation industry, suggests that the propensity of railroad employees to file NRAB claims has not changed significantly since 1980.

[55] Claims of sex discrimination in private employer discharge decisions filed with the EEOC, divided by total private sector female unemployment due to discharge.

[56] Job losers were taken from Bureau of Labor Statistics unemployment figures for the appropriate period.

[57] Only complaints classified by the EEOC as private employer discharge were used. These cases were further subdivided by the EEOC as religion, race, sex, national origin, color, unspecified, and no basis.

Table 9-2

**PROJECTIONS OF CASE VOLUME
UNDER PROPOSED STATUTE
BASED ON HISTORICAL
DATA**
(000 omitted)

	PROJECTIONS BASED ON PROPENSITY FOR LITIGATION BY:		
Year	Race	Railroad	Gender
1983	133		50
1982	119		44
1981	113		39
1980	117	77	35
1979	84	66	26
1978	82	60	23
1977	100	73	24
1976	123	67	29
1975	70	94	16
1974	56	85	13
1973	40	39	9
1972	13	20	1
1971	25	14	3
1970	11	48	1
1969	5	29	0.5
Based on Average 1969–83	73	56	21
Based on Average 1976–83	109	69	34

The number of job losers as a percentage of total unemployed is approximately 50 percent, generally increasing in years of slow economic growth or recession and decreasing in years of high growth.

The second step in the analysis was to extrapolate the propensity to litigate for the three groups shown in **Table 9-1** to the total workforce. The number of potential complaints under a new statute was estimated by multiplying the propensity to litigate by the total number of job losers. The results appear in **Table 9-2**. The EEOC received a dramatically increased number of cases in 1972 and 1973 and again in 1975 and 1976; both were times of economic downturn. The number of complaints filed annually with the EEOC has increased every year since 1972. Moreover, the percentage increase in complaints filed has been greater than the steady percentage increase in total job losers. The overall trend is mirrored in both race and gender classes. This probably results from increased awareness of EEOC relief.

The propensity to litigate is highest for employees of railroads and employees complaining of race discrimination, far greater than the probability of litigation for employees complaining of gender-based discrimination (**Table 9-1**). This may be due to a lack of alternative jobs open to both minorities and specialized railway workers. The lack of job opportunities would tend to encourage suit over the loss of a job. The propensity for suits based on gender discrimination has increased over the 13-year period just described but remains approximately half of the incidence of suits in race and railroad arenas.

The projections of the number of complaints under proposed statutes (see **Table 9-2**) are estimations of the caseload which might have been experienced in the past had statutes similar to the proposed state and federal statutes been enacted. The projections are not estimations of future complaints because they do not include estimations of future unemployment and causes for unemployment. If job loss becomes more or less prevalent in the future, the projections will be correspondingly under- or overstated.

The projections in **Table 9-2** indicate that a minimum of approximately 60,000 cases could be filed annually under the proposed statutes. A much higher caseload would be projected if only the years since the latest jump in EEOC case volume (1976) are analyzed. Averaging the years 1976 through 1982, the projected volume is 103,000 cases annually.

In sum, the number of cases could range from 30,000 to 103,000, based on five-year averages, which is a substantial number of potential claims by any estimation.[58] The size of the pool of arbitrators would have to be commensurately large in order to accommodate the projected case volume. The costs of administering the arbitration procedures outlined in the suggested statutes would be proportionately large.

The number of claims filed probably would be larger if all 50 states enacted wrongful dismissal statutes than if a single federal statute were enacted. This would be so because the number of claim locations probably would be higher under state statutes than under a federal statute.

The estimates do not take into account the deterrent effect that the proposed prepayment of the arbitration fee will have on the number of claims. The absence of any cost to the charging party probably results in a higher number of charges being filed with the Equal Employment Opportunity Commission and the National Labor Relations Board than under the proposed statutes.

---

[58] Rough projections derived from experiences under the British unfair dismissal system (see § **9.11**) are of the same magnitude. Adjusting British unfair dismissal claims volume upwards for differences in labor force size yields a projected United States claim volume of 65,000 annually. Another commentator has estimated potential complaint volume under a comprehensive wrongful discharge program as ranging from 12,000 to 300,000 cases per year. His estimates were based on the propensity of employees covered by collective bargaining agreements to arbitrate discharge cases, extrapolated based on the proportion of the workforce not covered by collective agreements. *See* Peck, *Unjust Discharges from Employment: A Necessary Change in the Law,* 40 Ohio St. L. J. 1, 10 (1979).

APPENDIXES

A. State Statutes
B. Discovery
C. Draft Statutes
D. In-House Counsel Checklist for Wrongful Dismissal Litigation
E. Criticism of the Laws of Damage in Dismissal Cases
F. Implied-in-Fact Contract Theory and the Employment Relation

APPENDIX A
STATE STATUTES

NOTE: Because these laws are subject to change, the reader is advised to use this table as a means of accessing current material.

APPENDIX A

	Alabama (Ala. Code)	**Alaska** (Alaska Stat.)
Discrimination based on race, sex, religion, national origin		§ 18.80.220 (1981) (color, age, physical handicap, marital status, changes in marital status, pregnancy or parenthood)
Age discrimination		§ 18.80.220 (1981)
Handicap discrimination	§ 21-5-1 (1984) (creation of Governor's committee to promote employment of handicapped)	§ 18.80.220 (1981) (physical)
Collective bargaining retaliation		
Occupational safety and health		§§ 18.60.010–18.62.080 (1981) (§ 18.60.089 (retaliation))
Environmental statutes		
Fair labor standards		
Consumer credit protection		
Employee retirement income security		
Jury duty	§ 12-16-8.1 (Supp. 1985)	
Whistleblower statutes		
Service letter statutes		
Garnishment	§ 6-10-7 (1977 & Supp. 1986)	§ 47.23.070(d) (1984) (prohibiting termination due to wage attachment)
Military service		
Union activity	§ 25-7-35 (1977)	
Political expression	§§ 17-23-10 & 17-23-11 (1977)	§ 14.20.100 (1982) (protects teachers in public schools)
Employment at will		
Miscellaneous	§ 22-33-8 (Supp. 1985) (toxic substances in the workplace) § 13A-11-123 (1982) (blacklisting) §§ 39-3-2; 39-3-3 (1977) (Resident Workmen's Act)	§ 23.10.37 (1984) (polygraph tests) § 47.30.865 (1984) (mental illness) § 23.10.135 (1985) (wage complaint)

APPENDIX A

	Arizona (Ariz. Rev. Stat. Ann.)	Arkansas (Ark. Stat. Ann.)
Discrimination based on race, sex, religion, national origin	§ 41-1463 (1985) (color, handicap, age)	§ 81-333 (Supp. 1985) (only covers sex discrimination with regard to wages)
Age discrimination	§ 41-1463 (1985)	§ 12-3502 (1979) (protects public employees)
Handicap discrimination	§ 41-1463 (1985)	§ 82-2901 (Supp. 1985) (state and state supported)
Collective bargaining retaliation	§ 23-1385 (1983) (protects agricultural workers)	
Occupational safety and health	§§ 23-401–23-491.16 (1983 & Supp. 1985) (§ 23-425 (retaliation))	§ 81-108 & §§ 81-401–81-509 (1976 & Supp.1985)
Environmental statutes		
Fair labor standards		
Consumer credit protection	§ 844-1691(4), 44-1693(A)(3); 44-1693(D) (West. Supp. 1985)	
Employee retirement income security		
Jury duty	§ 21-2361 (Supp. 1985).	§§ 12-2105 & 12-2106 (1979) (protect public employees)
Whistleblower Statutes		
Service Letter Statutes		
Garnishment	§ 25-323 (Supp. 1985–86)	
Military service	§ 26-167 (Supp. 1985–86)	
Union activity	§ 23-1342 (1983)	Const. amend. 34, § 1 (1979) & Stat. Ann. § 81-202 (1976)
Political expression	§ 16-1012 (1984)	
Miscellaneous	§ 36-506 (1986) (mental illness) Const. art. 18, § 9 (1984) & Rev. Stat. § 23-1361 (1983) (blacklists) § 23-203 (1983) (coercion) § 23-202 (1983) (extortion) §§ 23-329, 23-355, 23-356 (1983) (wage complaint)	§ 81-329 (1976) (wage complaint) § 81-211 (1976) (blacklists) § 81-310 (1976) (additional damages for wrongful discharge of employee hired for definite period of time)

APPENDIX A

	California (Cal. ___ Code) (West)	Colorado (Colo. Rev. Stat.)
Discrimination based on race, sex, religion, national origin	Gov't § 12940 (Supp. 1986) (color, ancestry, physical handicap, medical condition, marital status)	§ 24-34-402 (1982) (handicap, color, ancestry)
Age discrimination	Gov't § 12941 (Supp. 1986)	§ 8-2-116 (1974)
Handicap discrimination	Gov't § 12940 (Supp. 1986) (physical)	§ 24-34-402 (1982)
Collective bargaining retaliation		§ 8-3-108 (1) (1974)
Occupational safety and health	Lab. §§ 6300-9061 (1971 & Supp. 1986) (§ 6310 (retaliation))	
Environmental statutes		
Fair labor standards	Lab. § 50.6 (1971)	
Consumer credit protection	Lab. § 2929(e) (Supp. 1986)	
Employee retirement income security		
Jury duty	Lab. § 230 (Supp. 1986)	§ 13-71-118 (1974)
Whistleblower statutes	§ 1102.5 (Supp. 1986)	
Service letter statutes	Lab. § 1053 (1971); Lab. § 1055 (1971) (public utility)	
Garnishment	Lab. § 2929(b) (Supp. 1986)	§ 5-5-106 (1974)
Military service	Mil. & Vet. § 394 (1955)	§ 28-3-506 (1982)
Union activity	Lab. § 922 (1971)	§§ 8-2-102, 8-2-103 (1974)
Political expression	Lab. § 1102 (1971)	§§ 1-7-102 & 1-13-719 (1980); § 8-2-108(1) & (2) (1974)
Employment at will	Lab. § 2922 (1971 & Supp. 1986)	
Miscellaneous	Gov't § 9414 (1980) (witness); Health & Safety § 17031.7 (1984) (employee housing complaints); Lab. Code & § 1196 (Supp. 1971) (wage complaint); Gov't § 12945.5 (1980) (sterilization); Gov't § 12943 (1980) (pregnancy); Lab. § 1051 (1971) (photo, fingerprints); Lab. § 432.7(a) (Supp. 1986) (arrest record); Lab. § 1198.3(b) (Supp. 1986) (hours); Lab. § 1050 (Supp. 1986) (misrepresentation); Lab. § 432.2 (1971) (polygraph tests)	§§ 8-2-110, 8-2-111, 8-2-114 (1974) (blacklists); § 8-6-115 (1974) (wage complaint); § 24-5-101 (Supp. 1985) (public employment of reformed convicts)

APPENDIX A

	Connecticut (Conn. Gen. Stat. Ann.)(West)
Discrimination based on race, sex, religion, national origin	Conn. Gen. Stat. Ann. § 46a-60 (Supp. 1986) (color, age, marital status, ancestry, present or past history of mental disorder, mental retardation or physical disability, including, but not limited to blindness); § 46a-70 (Supp. 1986) (no discrimination by state agencies)
Age discrimination	§ 46a-60 (Supp. 1986)
Handicap discrimination	§ 46a-60 (Supp. 1986)
Collective bargaining retaliation	§ 35-105(1) (1972)
Occupation safety and health	§§ 31-367–31-385 (Supp. 1986) (§ 31-371 (retaliation))
Environmental statutes	
Fair labor standards	
Consumer credit protection	
Employee retirement income security	
Jury duty	§ 51-247a (1985)
Whistleblower statutes	§ 31-51m (Supp. 1986)
Service letter statutes	
Garnishment	§ 52-361a (j) (Supp. 1986) (employer justified in discharge if number of wage executions is over seven in one calendar year)
Military service	§§ 28-17, 27-33 & 27-33a (1975)
Union activity	§§ 31-105(2), (4), (5) & (9) (1972)
Political expression	§ 9-365 (1967)
Employment at will	
Miscellaneous	§ 31-40o (Supp. 1986) (toxic substances in the workplace); § 31-69 (1972) (wage complaint); § 2-3a (Supp. 1986) (protects running for or serving in state legislature); § 53-303e (a) (1985) (protects refusal to work over six days in a row); § 53-303e (b) (1985) (Sabbath); § 31-51g (Supp. 1986) (polygraph tests); § 31-51q (Supp. 1986) (prohibits discharge for exercise of constitutional rights); § 31-290a (Supp. 1986) (discrimination for filing workers' compensation claim); § 31-51 (Supp. 1986) (blacklisting); § 31-48b (Supp. 1986) (electronic surveillance); § 46a-80 (Supp. 1986) (employment discrimination based on prior convictions and arrests)

APPENDIX A

	Delaware (Del. Code Ann.)	District of Columbia (D.C. Code Ann.)
Discrimination based on race, sex, religion, national origin	tit. 19, § 711 (1985) (color, age, marital status)	§ 1-2512 (1981) (color, age, marital status, personal appearance, sexual orientation, family responsibilities, physical handicap, matriculation or political affiliation)
Age discrimination	tit. 19, § 711 (1985)	§ 1-2512 (1981)
Handicap discrimination		§ 1-2512 (1981) (physical)
Collective bargaining retaliation		
Occupational safety and health	tit. 19, § 106 (1985)	§§ 36-201–36-232 (1981); (§ 36-214 (3) (1981) (retaliation))
Environmental statutes		
Fair labor standards		
Consumer credit protection		
Employee retirement income security		
Jury duty	tit. 10, § 4505(c) (Supp. 1984)	
Whistleblower statutes	tit. 19, § 5115(a) to (e) (1983) (public employees only)	
Service letter statutes		
Garnishment	tit. 10, § 3509 (1975)	§ 16-584 (1981)
Military service	tit. 20, § 905 (1985)	
Union activity	tit. 19, § 1303 (1985) (protects public employees)	
Political expression	tit. 15, §§ 5161, 5162, 5163 (1981)	§ 1-2512 (1981)
Employment at will		
Miscellaneous	tit. 19, § 910 (1985) (wage complaint) tit. 19, § 704 (1985) (polygraph tests) tit. 19, § 805 (1985) (employer taking of employee inventions)	§ 36-214 (3) (1981) (wage complaint) § 36-342 (1981) (workers' compensation claims) § 36-802 (1981) (polygraph tests)

APPENDIX A

	Florida (Fla. Stat. Ann.)(West)	Georgia (Ga. Code Ann.)
Discrimination based on race, sex, religion, national origin	§ 760.10 (1986) (color, age, handicap or marital status)	§ 34-5-3 (1982) (only covers sex discrimination with regard to wages)
Age discrimination	§ 760.10 (1986)	§ 34-1-2 (1982)
Handicap discrimination	§ 760.10 (1986)	§ 34-6A-4 (1982)
Collective bargaining retaliation		
Occupational safety and health	§ 440.56 (1981 & Supp. 1986)	§ 34-2-10 (1982)
Environmental statutes		
Fair labor standards		
Consumer credit protection		
Employee retirement income security		
Jury duty	§ 40.271 (Supp. 1986)	
Whistleblower statutes	§ 112.3187(1–8) (Supp. 1986) (effective July, 1986)	
Service letter statutes	§ 351.22 (1968)	
Garnishment	§ 61.12 (1985)	§ 18-4-7 (1982)
Military service	§ 295.14(1) and (2) (Supp. 1986)	§ 38-2-280(e) (1982)
Union activity	Const. art. I, § 6 (1970)	§§ 34-6-6, 34-6-21 & 34-6-22 (1982)
Political expression	§ 104.081 (1982)	
Employment at will		§ 34-7-1 (1982 & Supp. 1986)
Miscellaneous	§ 448.03 (1981) (coercion) § 532.04 (2) (Supp. 1986) (direct deposit) § 448.075 (1981) (sickle-cell anemia)	§§ 43-36-12, 43-36-13, 43-36-14, 43-36-15 (Supp. 1986) (polygraph)

	Hawaii (Haw. Rev. Stat.)	Idaho (Idaho Code)
Discrimination based on race, sex, religion, national origin	§ 378-2 (1985) (age, color, ancestry, physical handicap, marital status, or arrest and court record)	§ 67-5909 (Supp. 1986) (color, age)
Age discrimination	§ 378-2 (1985)	§ 67-5909 (Supp. 1986)
Handicap discrimination	§ 378-2 (1985) (physical)	§ 56-707 (Supp. 1986) (state and state supported)
Collective bargaining retaliation	§ 377-6(1) (1985)	
Occupational safety and health	§§ 396-1 to 396-16 (1985) (§ 396-8 (e) (retaliation))	§ 44-104 (1977)
Environmental statutes		
Fair labor standards		
Consumer credit protection		
Employee retirement income security		
Jury duty	§ 612-25 (1976)	§ 2-218 (1979)
Whistleblower statutes		
Service letter statutes		
Garnishment	§ 378-32 (1) (1985)	§ 28-35-106 (1980)
Military service	§ 121-43 (1985)	§ 46-407(a) to (d) (Supp. 1986)
Union activity	§ 377-6 (3) (1985)	§ 44-2003 (Supp. 1986) § 18-2319 (1979)
Political expression		
Employment at will		
Miscellaneous	§ 378-32 (2) (1985) (workers' compensation claims) § 387-12(a)(3) (1985) (wage complaint) § 378-26 (1985) (polygraph tests) § 377-6(11) (1985) (blacklists)	§ 44-1509 (1977) (wage complaint) § 44-903 (1971) (polygraph tests)

APPENDIX A

	Illinois (Ill. Ann. Stat.) (Smith-Hurd)	Indiana (Ind. Code Ann.)(West)
Discrimination based on race, sex, religion, national origin	Const. art. 1, §§ 17, 18 & 19 (1971) & Ann. Stat. ch. 68, § 2-102 (Supp. 1986) (color, sex, ancestry, age, marital status, physical or mental handicap, unfavorable discharge from military service)	§ 22-9-1-3 (1) (Supp. 1985) (color, handicap, ancestry)
Age discrimination	ch. 68, § 2-102 (Supp. 1986)	§ 22-9-2-2 (1981)
Handicap discrimination	Const. art. 1, § 19 (1971) & Ann. Stat. ch. 68, § 2-102 (Supp. 1986)	§ 22-9-1-3 (Supp. 1985)
Collective bargaining retaliation		
Occupational safety and health	ch. 48, §§ 137.1–137.21 (1969)	§§ 22-8-1.1-1–22-8-1.1-50 (1981 & Supp. 1985) (§ 22-8-1.1-38.1 (retaliation))
Environmental statutes	ch. 111½, §§ 1001–1052 (1977 & Supp. 1986) (ch. 111½, § 1052 (retaliation))	
Fair labor standards		
Consumer credit protection		
Employee retirement income security	ch. 108½, §§ 20-101 to 20-133 (1964 & Supp. 1986)	
Jury duty	ch. 78, § 4.1 (Supp. 1986)	§ 35-44-3-10 (1978)
Whistleblower statutes		
Service letter statutes		§ 22-6-3-1 (1981)
Garnishment	ch. 62, § 88 (1972)	§ 24-4.5-5-106 (1980)
Military service	ch. 126½, § 33 (1967) & ch. 129, §§ 220.100 & 307 (Supp. 1986)	§ 10-2-4-2 (1982)
Union activity	ch. 48, § 2b (1969)	§§ 22-7-1-2 & 22-7-1-3 (1981)
Political expression		§ 3-4-7-3 (1981)
Employment at will		
Miscellaneous	ch. 48, § 1414 (Supp. 1986) (toxic substances in the workplace); ch. 48, § 138.4(h) (Supp. 1986) (workers' compensation claims); ch. 48, § 1011(c) (Supp. 1986) (wage complaint); ch. 38, § 155-3 (Supp. 1986) (witness); ch. 48, § 2001–2012 (1986) (limiting use of personnel records)	§ 22-2-2-11 (Supp. 1985) (wage complaint) §§ 22-5-3-1 & 22-5-3-2 (1981) (blacklists)

APPENDIX A

	Iowa (Iowa Code Ann.) (West)	Kansas (Kan. Stat. Ann.)
Discrimination based on race, sex, religion, national origin	§ 601A.6 (1975 & Supp. 1986) (age, color, disability)	§ 44-1009 (1981) (color, physical handicap, ancestry)
Age discrimination	§ 610A.6 (1975 & Supp. 1986)	§ 44-1113 (Supp. 1985)
Handicap discrimination	§ 610A.6 (1975 & Supp. 1986)	§ 44-1009 (1981) (physical)
Collective bargaining retaliation	§ 20.10 (1978) (protects public employees)	
Occupational safety and health	§§ 88.1–88.21 (1984 & Supp. 1986) (§ 88.9 (3) (retaliation))	§ 44-636 (1981)
Environmental statutes		
Fair labor standards		
Consumer credit protection		
Employee retirement income security		
Jury duty		
Whistleblower statutes	§ 19A-19 (Supp. 1986) (public employees)	
Service letter statutes		
Garnishment	§ 598.23 (Supp. 1986)	§ 60-2311 (1983)
Military service	§ 29A.43 (Supp. 1986)	
Union activity	§ 731.1 (1979)	§§ 44-803 & 44-808 (1981)
Political expression	§ 49.110 (Supp. 1986)	§ 25-418 (1981)
Employment at will		
Miscellaneous	§ 91A.10(5) (Supp. 1986) (wage complaint); § 730.4 (Supp. 1986) (polygraph tests); § 321.283(8) (1985) (drunk driving); § 730.1 & 730.2 (1979) (blacklists); § 455D.9 (Supp. 1986) (hazardous substances in the workplace)	§ 44-1210 (1981) (wage complaint) § 44-112 (1981) (blacklists) § 75-4316 (1984) (bankruptcy for public employees)

APPENDIX A

	Kentucky (Ky. Rev. Stat.) (Michie/Bobbs-Merrill)	Louisiana (La. Rev. Stat. Ann.)(West)
Discrimination based on race, sex, religion, national origin	§ 344.040 (1983) (color, age)	§ 23:1006 (1985) (color)
Age discrimination	§ 344.040 (1983)	§ 23:972 (1985)
Handicap discrimination	§ 207.150 (1982)	§ 46:2254 (1982)
Collective bargaining retaliation	§ 336.130 (1983)	
Occupational safety and health	§§ 338.011–338.991 (1983 & Supp. 1984) (§ 338.12 (retaliation))	§§ 23:481–23:542 (1985)
Enviromental statutes		§§ 30:1051–30-1150.79 (1975 & Supp. 1986) (§ 30:1074.1 (retaliation))
Fair labor standards		
Consumer credit protection		
Employee retirement income security		
Jury duty	§ 29A.160 (1985)	§ 23:965 (1985)
Whistleblower statutes	ch. 301 (1986 Advance Leg. Service) (public employees)	§ 23:964 (1985)
Service letter statutes		
Garnishment	§ 427.140 (1972)	§ 23:731(c) (1985)
Military service	§ 38A.460 (1985)	§ 29:38 (1975)
Union activity	§ 336.130 (1983)	§ 23:983 (1985)
Political expression	§ 121.310 (1982)	§§ 23:961 & 23:962 (1985)
Employment at will		Civ. Code Ann. art. 2747 (1952) (applies to hired servants attached to the employer's person or family)
Miscellaneous	§ 337.992 (1983) (wage complaint) § 337.415 (1983) (witness) § 436.165 (4) (b) (1985) (Sabbath)	§ 23:1361 (1985) (workers' compensation claims) § 23:1002 (1985) (sickle-cell anemia)

APPENDIX A

	Maine (Me. Rev. Stat. Ann.)	Maryland (Md. Ann. Code)
Discrimination based on race, sex, religion, national origin	tit. 5, § 4572 (1979 & Supp. 1985) (color, physical or mental handicap, ancestry, age)	art. 49B, § 16 (1979) (color, age, marital status, physical or mental handicap)
Age discrimination	tit. 5, § 4572 (1979 & Supp. 1985)	art. 49B, § 16 (1979)
Handicap discrimination	tit. 5, § 4572 (1979 & Supp. 1985)	art. 49B, § 16 (1979)
Collective bargaining retaliation		art. 100, § 63 (1985)
Occupational safety and health	tit. 26, §§ 81–581 (1974 & Supp. 1985) (tit. 26, § 570 (retaliation))	art. 89, §§ 28–49D (1985) (art. 89, § 43 (retaliation))
Environmental statutes		
Fair labor standards		
Consumer credit protection		
Employee retirement income security		
Jury duty	tit. 14, § 1218 (Supp. 1985)	Cts. & Jud. Proc. Code Ann. § 8-105 (1984)
Whistleblower statutes	tit. 26, § 833 (Supp. 1985)	art. 64A, § 12(G) (1983) (public employees)
Service letter statutes		
Garnishment	tit. 9-A, § 5-106 (1980)	Com. Law Code Ann. § 15-606 (1983)
Military service	tit. 37-A, §§ 1110 & 1111 (1978)	art. 64A, § 18B (1983) (state employees)
Union activity		art. 100, § 63 (1985)
Political expression		
Employment at will		
Miscellaneous	tit. 5, § 4572-A (Supp. 1985) (pregnancy) tit. 26, § 671 (1974) (wage complaint) tit. 32, § 7166 (Supp. 1985) (polygraph tests) tit. 26, § 594 (Supp. 1985) (extortion) tit. 17, § 401 (1983) (blacklists)	art. 100, § 89 (1985) (wage complaint) art. 101, § 39A (1985) (workers' compensation claims) art. 100, § 95 (1985) (polygraph tests) art. 49B, § 17 (Supp. 1985) (pregnancy)

APPENDIX A

	Massachusetts (Mass. Gen. Laws Ann.) (West)	Michigan (Mich. Comp. Laws)
Discrimination based on race, sex, religion, national origin	ch. 151B, § 4 (Supp. 1986) (color, ancestry, age, handicap)	§ 37.2202 (1985) (color, age, marital status, height, weight)
Age discrimination	ch. 151B, § 4 (Supp. 1986) & ch. 149, § 24A (Supp. 1986)	§ 37.2202 (1985)
Handicap discrimination	ch. 151B, § 4 (Supp. 1986)	§ 37.1202 (1985)
Collective bargaining retaliation		§ 423.16 (1978)
Occupational safety and health		§§ 408.1001–408.1094 (1985 & Supp. 1986) (§ 408.1065 (retaliation))
Environmental statutes		
Fair labor standards		
Consumer credit protection	ch. 93 § 62 (1984) (denial of employment because of adverse credit report)	
Employee retirement income security		
Jury duty	ch. 268, § 14A (1970)	§ 600.1348 (Supp. 1986)
Whistleblower statutes		§ 15.362 (1981)
Service letter statutes		
Garnishment		§§ 600.8307 & 600.4015 (Supp. 1986)
Military service		§ 750.398 (1968)
Union activity	ch. 149, § 20 (West 1982)	§ 423.161 (1978)
Political expression	ch. 56, § 33 (West 1975)	§§ 15.402 & 15.403 (1981 & West Supp. 1986) (public employees)
Employment at will		
Miscellaneous	ch. 151, § 19 (1982) (wage complaint); ch. 149, § 159 (1982) (employers demanding notice of termination from employees must give like notice to employees before termination); ch. 149, § 19B (Supp. 1986) (polygraph tests); ch. 111F, §§ 1–21 (Supp. 1986) (hazardous substances in the workplace) (ch. 111F, § 13 (retaliation)); ch. 111 § 70F (Supp. 1986) (AIDS testing as condition of employment)	§§ 408.395 & 408.396 (1985) (wage complaint) § 418.125 (1985) (workers' compensation claims) § 37.203 (1985) (polygraph tests)

APPENDIX A

	Minnesota (Minn. Stat. Ann.)(West)	Mississippi (Miss. Code Ann.)
Discrimination based on race, sex, religion, national origin	§ 363.03 (Supp. 1986) (color, marital status, status with regard to public assistance, disability or age)	§ 25-9-149 (Supp. 1985) (protects state service employees from discrimination based on Title VII categories and color, age, handicap)
Age discrimination	§ 363.03 (Supp. 1986)	§ 25-9-149 (Supp. 1985) (protects state service employees)
Handicap discrimination	§ 363.03 (Supp. 1986)	§ 25-9-149 (Supp. 1985) (protects state service employees)
Collective bargaining retaliation		
Occupational safety and health	§§ 182.65–182.675 (Supp. 1986) (§ 182.669 (retaliation))	§§ 71-1-1–71-1-53 (1972)
Environmental statutes		
Fair labor standards		
Consumer credit protection		
Employee retirement income security		
Jury duty	§ 593.50 (Supp. 1985)	§ 13-5-23 (Supp. 1985)
Whistleblower statutes		
Service letter statutes		
Garnishment	§ 571.61 (Supp. 1985)	
Military service	§ 192.34 (Supp. 1986)	§ 33-1-15 (Supp. 1985)
Union activity	§§ 179.12, 179.19 & 179.60 (1966 & Supp. 1986)	Const. art. 7, § 198-A (1972) & Code Ann. § 71-1-47 (1972)
Political expression	§ 210A.14 (Supp. 1986)	§ 23-3-29 (1972)
Employment at will		
Miscellaneous	§ 176.82 (Supp. 1986) (workers' compensation claims); § 177.32 (Supp. 1986) (wage complaint); §§ 179.12(6) & 179.60 (1966 & Supp. 1986) (blacklists); § 179.60 (1966) (extortion); § 3.083 (Supp. 1986) (legislators); § 3.088 (Supp. 1986) (public officials)	

APPENDIX A

	Missouri (Mo. Ann. Stat.)(Vernon)	Montana (Mont. Code Ann.)
Discrimination based on race, sex, religion, national origin	§ 296.020 (Supp. 1986) (color, ancestry, handicap)	§ 49-2-303 (1985) (age, physical or mental handicap, marital status, color, sex distinction)
Age discrimination		§ 49-2-303 (1985)
Handicap discrimination	§ 296.020 (Supp. 1986)	§ 49-2-303 (1985)
Collective bargaining retaliation	Const. art. 1, § 29 (1970 & Supp. 1986)	
Occupational safety and health	§§ 292.010–292.570 (1965 & Supp. 1986)	§§ 50-71-101–50-71-334 (1985) (§ 50-71-322 (retaliation))
Environmental statutes		
Fair labor standards		
Consumer credit protection		
Employee retirement income security		
Jury duty		
Whistleblower statutes		§ 49-2-301 (1985)
Service letter statutes	§ 290.140 (Supp. 1986)	§ 39-2-302 (1985)
Garnishment	§ 525.030(5) (Supp. 1986)	§ 39-2-303 (1985)
Military service	§ 41.730 (1969)	§ 10-1-603 & 10-1-604 (1985)
Union activity	Const. art. 1, § 29 (1970 & Supp. 1986)	
Political expression	§ 130.028 (1980)	§ 13-35-226 (1985)
Employment at will		§ 39-2-503 (1985)
Miscellaneous	§ 287.780 (Supp. 1986) (workers' compensation claims) § 290.130 (1965) (contract) § 578.115 (1979) (Sabbath)	§ 39-2-304 (1985) (polygraph tests) § 39-2-301 (1985) (refusal to pay cost of medical exam) § 39-2-803 (1985) (blacklists) § 49-2-310 (1985) (pregnancy)

APPENDIX A

	Nebraska (Neb. Rev. Stat.)	Nevada (Nev. Rev. Stat.)
Discrimination based on race, sex, religion, national origin	§ 48-1104 (1984) (color, marital status, disability)	§ 613.330 (1986) (age, color, physical, aural or visual handicap)
Age discrimination	§ 48-1001 (1984)	§ 613.330 (1986)
Handicap discrimination	§ 48-1104 (1984)	§ 613.330 (1986) (physical, aural or visual handicap)
Collective bargaining retaliation		§ 614.080 (1986)
Occupational safety and health		§§ 618.005–618.720 (1986) (§ 618.445 (retaliation))
Environmental statutes		
Fair labor standards		
Consumer credit protection		
Employee retirement income security		
Jury duty	§ 25-1640 (1985)	§ 6.190 (1986)
Whistleblower statutes		§ 613.340 (1986)
Service letter statutes		
Garnishment	§ 25-1558(6) (1985)	
Military service	§ 55-166 (1984)	§ 412.139 (1986) (National Guard)
Union activity		§§ 613.130 & 614.080 (1986)
Political expression	§§ 32-1050, 32-1050.01 & 32-1223 (1984)	§§ 293.585 & 613.040 (1986)
Employment at will		
Miscellaneous	§ 81-1932 (1984) (polygraph)	§ 50.070 (1986) (witness) § 613.210 (1986) (blacklists) § 613.140 (1986) (coercion) § 608.015 (1986) (wage complaint) § 613.120 (1986) (extortion)

APPENDIX A

	New Hampshire (N.H. Rev. Stat. Ann.)	New Jersey (N. J. Stat. Ann.)(West)
Discrimination based on race, sex, religion, national origin	§ 354-A:8 (1984) (age, physical or mental handicap, marital status)	§ 10:5-12 (Supp. 1986) (age, color, ancestry, marital status, atypical hereditary cellular or blood trait or service in the armed forces)
Age discrimination	§ 354-A:8 (1984)	§ 10:5-12 (Supp. 1986)
Handicap discrimination	§ 354-A:8 (1984)	§ 10:5-12 (Supp. 1986); § 10:5-29.1 (Supp. 1986) (protects the blind and deaf)
Collective bargaining retaliation		
Occupational safety and health	§ 125:15a–125:95 (Supp. 1985)	§§ 34:6A-25–34:6A-49 (Supp. 1986) (protects public employees) (§ 34:6A-45 (retaliation))
Environmental statutes		
Fair labor standards		
Consumer credit protection	§ 359:B:1–B:21 (1984 & Supp. 1985)	
Employee retirement income security		
Jury duty	§ 500-A:14 (1983)	§ 2A:69-5 (1976)
Whistleblower statutes		1986 N.J. Sess. Law Serv. ch. 105 (Conscientious Employee Protection Act)
Service letter statutes		
Garnishment		§ 2A:170-90.4 (1985)
Military service	§ 110-B:65 (Supp. 1985) (National Guard)	§§ 10:5-12 (Supp. 1986) & 38A:14-4 (1968)
Union activity	§ 275:1 (1977)	
Political expression	§ 98-E (Supp. 1985) (public employees)	§ 19:34-27 (1964)
Employment at will		
Miscellaneous	§ 275:40 (1977) (wage complaint)	§ 34:15-39.1 (Supp. 1986) (workers' compensation claims); § 34:11-56a24 (Supp. 1986) (wage complaint); §§ 34:5A-1–34:5A-31 (Supp. 1986) (hazardous substances in the workplace); § 34:5A-17 (retaliation); § 2C:40A-1 (Supp. 1986) (polygraph)

APPENDIX A

	New Mexico (N.M. Stat. Ann.)	**New York** (N.Y. ___ Law)(McKinney)
Discrimination based on race, sex, religion, national origin	§ 28-1-7 (1978) (age, physical or mental handicap, ancestry, color)	Exec. § 296 (1982 & Supp. 1986) (age, disability, marital status)
Age discrimination	§ 28-1-7 (1978)	Exec. § 296 (1982 & Supp. 1986)
Handicap discrimination	§ 28-1-7 (1978)	Exec. § 296 (1982 & Supp. 1986); Civ. Rights § 47-a (Supp. 1986)
Collective bargaining retaliation		
Occupational safety and health	§§ 50-9-1–50-9-25 (1978 & Supp. 1985) (§ 50-9-25 (retaliation))	Lab. §§ 27–41 (1986) (protects public employees), (§ 27-a (10) (retaliation))
Environmental statutes		
Fair labor standards		
Consumer credit protection	§ 56-3-5 (1986)	
Employee retirement income security		
Jury duty	§ 35-5-18 (Supp. 1986)	Jud. § 532 (1975)
Whistleblower statutes		Lab. §§ 740-1–740-7 (1986); 1986 Laws ch. 899 (public employees)
Service letter statutes		
Garnishment		Civ. Prac. L. & R. § 5252 (Supp. 1986)
Military service	§ 28-15-1 & 28-15-2 (1978); § 20-9-6 (1978) (National Guard)	Mil. § 251–252 (Supp. 1986)
Union activity	§ 50-2-4 (1978)	
Political expression	§ 1-20-13 (Supp. 1985)	Elec. Law § 150 (1978)
Employment at will		
Miscellaneous	§ 30-13-3 (1984) (blacklisting) § 30-13-5 (1984) (coercion)	Work. Comp. § 120 (Supp. 1986) (workers' compensation claims) Lab. § 736 (Supp. 1986) (polygraph tests) Lab. § 215 (Supp. 1986) (wage complaint) 1986 Laws ch. 744 (retaliation for reporting violation of labor laws) Lab. § 201-a (1974) (fingerprinting)

APPENDIX A

	North Carolina (N.C. Gen. Stat.)	North Dakota (N.D. Cent. Code)
Discrimination based on race, sex, religion, national origin	§ 143-422.2 (1983) (age, color, handicap)	§ 34-01-19 (1980) (color) & § 14-02.4-03 (Supp. 1985) (color, age, physical or mental handicap, status with respect to marriage or public assistance)
Age discrimination	§ 143-422.2 (1983)	§ 34-01-17 (1980) & § 14-02.4-03 (Supp. 1985)
Handicap discrimination	§§ 143-422.2 (1983) & 168A-5 (Supp. 1985)	§ 14-02.4-03 (Supp. 1985)
Collective bargaining retaliation		
Occupational safety and health	§§ 95-126–95-218 (1985) (§ 95-130 (8) (retaliation))	
Environmental statutes		
Fair labor standards		
Consumer credit protection		
Employee retirement income security		
Jury duty		§ 27-09.1-22 (Supp. 1985)
Whistleblower statutes		
Service letter statutes		
Garnishment		§ 32-09.1-18 (Supp. 1985)
Military service	§ 127B-14 (Supp. 1985); § 127A-202 (1981) (National Guard)	§ 37-01-25 (Supp. 1985)
Union activity	§§ 95-80 & 95-81 (1985)	§ 34-01-14 (1980)
Political expression	§§ 126-14 & 126-14.1 (Supp. 1985) (public employees)	
Employment at will		§ 34-03-01 (1980)
Miscellaneous	§ 97-6.1 (1985) (workers' compensation claims) § 95-28.1 (1985) (sickle cell anemia) § 95-25.20 (1985) (wage complaint) § 14-355 (1986) (blacklisting)	Const. art. XII § 17 (blacklists) § 34-06-18 (1980) (wage complaint)

APPENDIX A

	Ohio (Ohio Rev. Code Ann.) (Anderson)	Oklahoma (Okla. Stat. Ann.)(West)
Discrimination based on race, sex, religion, national origin	§ 4112.02 (Supp. 1985) (age, handicap, ancestry, color)	tit. 25, § 1302 (Supp. 1985) (age, handicap, color)
Age discrimination	§§ 4101.17 (1980) & 4112.02 (Supp. 1985)	tit. 25, § 1302 (Supp. 1985)
Handicap discrimination	§ 4112.02 (Supp. 1985)	tit. 25, § 1302 (Supp. 1985)
Collection bargaining retaliation		
Occupational safety and health	§ 4101.12 (1980)	tit. 40, §§ 401–424 (1986) (§ 412 (retaliation))
Environmental statutes		
Fair labor standards		
Consumer credit protection		
Employee retirement income security		
Jury duty	§ 2313.18 (Supp. 1986)	tit. 38, § 34 (Supp. 1985)
Whistleblower statutes		
Service letter statutes		tit. 40, § 171 (1986)
Garnishment		tit. 56, § 250.2(E)(5) (Supp. 1985); tit. 12, § 1171.1(E)(5) (Supp. 1985); & tit. 14A, § 5-106 (1983)
Military service	§ 5903.08 (Supp. 1986)	tit. 44, § 208 (1979); tit. 44, § 71 (1979) (National Guard)
Union activity		
Political expression	§§ 3599.05 & 3599.06 (1972)	tit. 26, §§ 7-110 & 16-113 (1976)
Employment at will		
Miscellaneous	§ 4111.13 (1980) (wage complaint)	tit. 40, § 172 (1986) (blacklists) tit. 25, § 1452(10) (Supp. 1985) (employee housing complaints) tit. 40, § 199 (1986) (wage complaint)

APPENDIX A

	Oregon (Or Rev. Stat.)	Pennsylvania (Pa. Stat. Ann.)(Purdon)
Discrimination based on race, sex, religion, national origin	§ 659.030 (1985) (age, color, marital status) (§ 659.029 sex includes pregnancy, childbirth, and related medical condition)	tit. 43, § 955 (Supp. 1986) (age, ancestry, nonjob related handicap or disability)
Age discrimination	§ 659.030 (1985)	tit. 43, § 955 (Supp. 1986)
Handicap discrimination	§ 659.425 (1985)	tit. 43, § 955 (Supp. 1986)
Collective bargaining retaliation	§ 663.120 (1985)	tit. 43, § 211.6 (1964)
Occupational safety and health	§§ 654.001–654.991 (1985) (§ 654.062(5)(a) (retaliation))	
Environmental statutes		
Fair labor standards	§ 653.055 (1985) (wage and hour complaints)	
Consumer credit protection		
Employee retirement income security		
Jury duty	§ 10.090 (1985)	tit. 42, § 4563 (Supp. 1986)
Whistleblower statutes	§ 659.035 (1985)	tit. 43, § 1101.1201 (Supp. 1986) (public employees); tit. 43, § 211.6 (1964) (employees generally)
Service letter statutes		
Garnishment	§ 23.185(7) (1985)	
Military service	§ 408.240 (1985) (public employees)	tit. 51, § 7309 (1976)
Union activity	§§ 663.120, 663.125, 663.145 (1985) (honoring pickets of another employer), 243.672 (public employees), & 662.735 (1985) (nurses)	tit. 43, § 206(e) (1964)
Political expression	§ 260.432 (1985) (public employees)	tit. 25, § 3547 (1963)
Employment at will		tit. 43, § 1101.706 (Supp. 1986) (termination always for just cause)
Miscellaneous	§ 659.030 (1985) (juvenile arrest record); § 659.225 (1985) (polygraph tests/breathalyzer); § 659.230 (1985) (blacklists); § 659.270 (1985) (witness); § 659.410 (1985) (workers' compensation claims); §§ 653.355, 652.990(7) & 653.060 (1985) (wage complaint); § 163.500 (compelling buying at a particular place); § 658.452 (farm labor wage claim)	tit. 43, § 955.1 (Supp. 1986) (Sabbath (public employees)); tit. 43, § 955.2 (Supp. 1986) (no physician terminated for refusal to perform abortion); tit. 43, § 1201 (Supp. 1986) (protects volunteer firemen in performance of their duties); tit. 18, § 7321 (1983) (polygraph tests); tit. 43, § 333.112 (Supp. 1986) (wage complaint)

APPENDIX A

	Rhode Island (R.I. Gen. Laws)	South Carolina (S.C. Code Ann.)(Law. Coop.)
Discrimination based on race, sex, religion, national origin	§ 28-5-7 (Supp. 1985) (color, handicap, age); § 28-6-17-18 (equal pay)	§ 1-13-80 (1986) (color, age)
Age discrimination	§ 28-5-7 (Supp. 1985)	§ 1-13-80 (1986)
Handicap discrimination	§ 28-5-7 (Supp. 1985)	§ 43-3.3-60 (1985) (state and state supported)
Collective bargaining retaliation	§ 28-7-13 (1979) (including blacklisting); § 36-11-2 (1984) (public employees)	
Occupational safety and health	§§ 28-20-2–28-20-30 (1979 & Supp. 1985) (§ 28-20-21 (retaliation))	§§ 41-15-10–41-15-640 (1986) (§ 41-15-510 (retaliation))
Environmental statutes		
Fair labor standards		
Consumer credit protection		
Employee retirement income security		
Jury duty	§ 9-9-28 (1985)	
Whistleblower statutes	§§ 36-15-2–36-15-9 (Supp. 1985)	
Service letter statutes		
Garnishment		§§ 37-5-104, 37-5-106 & 37-5-202 (Supp. 1985)
Military service	§§ 30-11-6–30-11-9 (1982)	§ 25-1-2190 & §§ 25-1-2310 to 2340 (Supp. 1985)
Union activity		§§ 41-1-20 & 41-7-70 (1986)
Political expression	§ 17-23-6 (1981)	§ 16-17-560 (1985)
Employment at will		
Miscellaneous	§ 28-12-16 (1979) § 28-6.1-1 (1979) (polygraph tests) §§ 28-21-1–28-21-21 (1979 & Supp. 1985) (hazardous substances in the workplace) (§ 28-21-8 (retaliation))	

APPENDIX A

	South Dakota (S.D. Codified Laws Ann.)	Tennessee (Tenn. Code Ann.)
Discrimination based on race, sex, religion, national origin	§ 20-13-10 (Supp. 1986) (disability, ancestry); §§ 60-12-15 & 60-12-16 (1985) (equal pay)	§ 4-21-401 (1985) (color, age); § 50-2-202 (1986)
Age discrimination		§ 4-21-401 (1985)
Handicap discrimination	§ 20-13-10 (Supp. 1986); § 20-13-10.1 (Supp. 1986) (blind, partially blind)	§ 8-50-103 (1980)
Collective bargaining retaliation	§§ 60-9A-2 & 60-9A-12(3) (1978); § 3-18-3.2 (1985) (public employees)	§ 50-1-201 (1983)
Occupational safety and health		§ 50-3-101–50-3-918 (1983) (§ 50-3-106 (retaliation)); § 50-3-409 (1983) (same)
Environmental statutes		
Fair labor standards		
Consumer credit protection		
Employee retirement income security		
Jury duty	§ 16-13-41.1 (1979)	§ 39-5-523 (1982)
Whistleblower statutes		
Service letter statutes		
Garnishment		
Military service	§ 33-17-15 (1977)	§ 58-1-604 (1980)
Union activity	Const. art. VI, § 2 & Codified Laws Ann. § 60-9A-12 (1978)	
Political expression	§ 12-26-13 (1982)	§ 2-19-134 (1985)
Employment at will	§ 60-4-4 (1978)	
Miscellaneous	§ 60-11-17.1 (1978) (wage complaint)	§ 62-27-128 (1986) (polygraph)

APPENDIX A

	Texas (Tex. Rev. Civ. Stat. Ann.) (Vernon)	**Utah** (Utah Code Ann.)
Discrimination based on race, sex, religion, national origin	art. 5221K(5.01) (Supp. 1986) (age, color, handicap); art. 5197 (1962) (all discrimination in employment)	§ 34-35-6 (Supp. 1983) (age, ancestry, color, handicap)
Age discrimination	art. 5221K(5.01) (Supp. 1986)	§ 34-35-6 (Supp. 1983)
Handicap discrimination	art. 5221K(5.01) (Supp. 1986)	§ 34-35-6 (Supp. 1983)
Collective bargaining retaliation	art. 5207a (1962)	§ 34-20-8(a) (1974)
Occupational safety and health	arts. 5182a–5182b (Supp. 1986) (art. 5182b (15(b)) (retaliation))	§§ 35-9-1–35-9-22 (1974 & Supp. 1983) (§ 35-9-11 (retaliation))
Environmental statutes		
Fair labor standards		
Consumer credit protection		
Employee retirement income security		
Jury duty	Civ. Prac. & Rem. Code Ann. § 122.001 (1986)	§ 78-46-21 (Supp. 1983)
Whistleblower statutes	art. 6252-16a (Supp. 1986)	
Service letter statutes	art. 5196(3) (1962) (letter must be furnished within 10 days upon request)	
Garnishment	Fam. Code Ann. § 14.43 (1986) (court-ordered child support withholding)	§§ 708-5-106, 708-5-202 & 78-45-9.1 (1986)
Military service	art. 5196(7A) (Supp. 1986)	§ 39-1-36 (1981)
Union activity		§§ 34-34-2, 34-34-8 & 34-34-9 (1974)
Political expression		Const. art. XVI, § 3 (Supp. 1983) & Utah Code Ann. § 20-13-18 (1984); § 20-13-7 (1986) (influencing vote of employees)
Employment at will		
Miscellaneous	art. 5196d (Supp. 1986) (blacklists) art. 8307c (Supp. 1986) (workers' compensation claims) art. 5196g (Supp. 1986) (coercion)	Const. art. XVI, § 4 § 34-37-16 (Supp. 1983) (polygraph tests) § 34-24-1 (1974) (blacklists) § 34-22-12 (1974) (wage complaint)

APPENDIX A

	Vermont (Vt. Stat. Ann.)	Virginia (Va. Code Ann.)
Discrimination based on race, sex, religion, national origin	tit. 21, § 495 (Supp. 1985) (color, ancestry, place of birth, age, physical or mental condition)	Const. art. I, § 11 (1979) (government) & Va. Code Ann. § 2.1-375 (1979) (prohibits discrimination by contractors with the government for contracts over $10,000.); § 40.1-28.6 (1986) (equal pay)
Age discrimination	tit. 21, § 495 (Supp. 1985)	
Handicap discrimination	tit. 21, § 495 (Supp. 1985)	§ 51.01-41 (Supp. 1986)
Collective bargaining retaliation	tit. 21, § 1621(4) (1978); tit. 31, § 961(3) and (4) (1985) (public employees)	
Occupation safety and health	tit. 21, §§ 201–264 (1978 & Supp. 1985) (tit. 21, § 231 (retaliation))	§§ 40.1-44.1–40.1-51.19 (1986) (§ 40.1-51.2:1 (retaliation))
Environmental statutes		
Fair labor standards		
Consumer credit protection		
Employee retirement income security		
Jury duty	tit. 21, § 499(a) (1978)	§ 18.2-465.1 (Supp. 1986)
Whistleblower statutes		
Service letter statutes		
Garnishment	tit. 12, § 3172 (Supp. 1985)	§ 34-29(f) (1984); § 63.1-271 (Supp. 1986) (support lien)
Military service	tit. 21, § 491 (1978)	
Union activity		§§ 40.1-60 & 40.1-61 (1986)
Political expression		
Employment at will		
Miscellaneous	tit. 21, § 494a(3)(b) (Supp. 1985) (polygraph tests) tit. 21, § 394(a) (1978) (wage complaint) tit. 21, § 499(b) (1978) (witness)	§ 40.1-28.1 (1986) (each employee entitled to 24-hour rest period within each calendar week); § 40.1-28.2 (1986) (employee entitled to choose Sunday as day off); § 40.1-28.3 (1986) (Sabbath); § 40.1-27 (1986) (blacklists); § 40.1-51.4:3 (1986) (prohibits polygraph test relating to sexual activities)

APPENDIX A

	Washington (Wash. Rev. Code Ann.)	West Virginia (W. Va. Code)
Discrimination based on race, sex, religion, national origin	§ 49.60.180 (Supp. 1986) (age, marital status, color, sensory, mental or physical handicap)	§ 21-5C-7(b) (1985) (color, age); § 21-58-3 (1985) (sex)
Age discrimination	§ 49.60.180 (Supp. 1986)	§ 21-5C-7 (b) (1985)
Handicap discrimination	§ 49.60.180 (Supp. 1986)	§ 5-11-9 (Supp. 1985)
Collective bargaining retaliation		
Occupational health and safety	§§ 49.17.010–49.17.910 (1962 & Supp. 1986) (§ 49.17.160 (retaliation))	
Environmental statutes		
Fair labor standards		
Consumer credit protection		
Employee retirement income security		
Jury duty		§ 52-3-1 (1981)
Whistleblower statutes	§ 42.40.10–42.40.900 (Supp. 1986)	§ 21-5C-7(a) (1985)
Service letter statutes		
Garnishment	§§ 7.33.160, 26.18.110(8) & 74.20A.230 (Supp. 1986)	§ 46A-2-131 (1986); § 48A-5-3 (1986) (support liens)
Military service	§ 38.40.050 (1964)	§§ 15-1F-8, 15-1-1 (1985)
Union activity		
Political expression		§ 3-9-20 (1979)
Employment at will		
Miscellaneous	§ 49.60.030(f) (Supp. 1986) (blacklists) §§ 49.70.010–49.70.905 (1962 & Supp. 1986) (hazardous substances in the workplace) § 49.70.110 (retaliation) § 49.44.120–49.44.130 (Supp. 1986) (polygraph)	§ 23-5A-1 (1985) (workers' compensation claims) § 21-5-5b (1985) (polygraph) § 21-5-5 (1985) (coercion)

APPENDIX A

	Wisconsin (Wis. Stat. Ann.) (West)
Discrimination based on race, sex, religion, national origin	§ 111.321 & 111.322 (Supp. 1985) (age, color, handicap, marital status, ancestry, arrest record or conviction record); § 111.36 (1986) (sex includes sexual orientation); § 103.20 (Supp. 1986) (AIDS tests)
Age discrimination	§§ 111.321, 111.322 & 111.33 (Supp. 1985)
Handicap discrimination	§§ 111.321, 111.322 & 111.34 (Supp. 1985)
Collective bargaining retaliation	§ 111.06(1)(C)(1) (1974); § 111.84(1)(C) (1974) (public employees); § 111.70(3)(a)(3) (1974) (municipal employees)
Occupational safety and health	§ 101.595(2) (Supp. 1986) (retaliation)
Environmental statutes	
Fair labor standards	§ 104.10 (1974) (retaliation)
Consumer credit protection	
Employee retirement income security	
Jury duty	§ 756.25 (1981)
Whistleblower statutes	§§ 230.80–230.83 (Supp. 1986)
Service letter statutes	
Garnishment	§ 425.110 (1974) & § 767.265(3) (Supp. 1985); § 812.235 (1977)
Military service	
Union activity	
Political expression	§ 103.18 (1974)
Employment at will	
Miscellaneous	§ 103.87 (Supp. 1985) (witness); § 103.17 (1974) (employers demanding notice of termination from employees must give like notice to employees before termination); § 134.02 (1974) (blacklists); § 134.02 (1974) (coercion); § 102.35 (Supp. 1985) (workers' compensation claims); § 111.37 (Supp. 1985) (polygraph tests)

	Wyoming (Wyo. Stat.)
Discrimination based on race, sex, religion, national origin	§ 27-9-105 (Supp. 1985) (color, ancestry, handicap, age); § 27-4-301–27-4-304 (1983) (equal pay)
Age discrimination	§ 27-9-105 (Supp. 1985)
Handicap discrimination	§ 27-9-105 (Supp. 1985)
Collective bargaining retaliation	
Occupational safety and health	§§ 27-11-101–27-11-114 (1983) (§ 27-11-109 (retaliation))
Environmental statutes	
Fair labor standards	
Consumer credit protection	
Employee retirement income security	
Jury duty	§ 1-11-401 (Supp. 1985)
Whistleblower statutes	
Service letter statutes	
Garnishment	§ 40-14-506 (1977)
Military service	§ 19-2-505 (1977)
Union activity	§§ 27-7-109 & 27-7-110 (1983)
Political expression	§ 22-26-116 (1977)
Employment at will	
Miscellaneous	

APPENDIX B
DISCOVERY

General Considerations

Modern discovery can be accomplished in one of four ways: through depositions, through interrogatories, through requests for production of documents, and through requests for admissions.[1] Additionally, counsel for plaintiff should not ignore important prelitigation sources of discovery materials.[2] Depositions are relatively more expensive than other methods, and involve other disadvantages as well.[3]

On the other hand, depositions are unique in that they provide an opportunity to interact with key witnesses on a spontaneous basis, and provide counsel with an opportunity to pursue lines of inquiry interactively.[4] These features can make depositions of certain key personnel significantly superior to written discovery methods.[5]

Counsel should formulate a rational discovery plan[6] that includes a sense of where depositions fit in the overall plan.[7] It may be desirable to schedule depositions only after interrogatories have been answered and documents produced.[8] In other

---

[1] *See* Fed. R. Civ. P. 23(a). The list of methods in the text omits permission to inspect, and physical and mental examinations, which are unlikely to be involved in wrongful dismissal litigation. *See also* M. Dichter, A. Gross, D. Morikawa & S. Sauntry, Employee Dismissal Law: Forms and Procedures § 4.7 (complaint strategy), § 4.9 (complaints as a discovery device), §§ 4.10–4.29 (complaint forms) (1986).

[2] For a full discussion of these sources, *see* M. Dichter, A. Gross, D. Morikawa, S. Sauntry, Employee Dismissal Law: Forms and Procedures § 4.5 (1986).

[3] *See* Suplee, *Depositions: Objectives, Strategies, Tactics, Mechanics, and Problems*, 2 Rev. of Litig. 255, 258–59 (1982).

[4] *See* R. Keeton, Trial Tactics and Methods 400 (1973).

[5] J. Underwood, A Guide to Federal Discovery Rules 65–66 (1979) (taking deposition of key personnel gives an excellent opportunity to catch deponent in inaccuracy, exaggeration, or in an outright lie).

[6] The client should be advised of the plan as well, so that she can assist in its ongoing revision as new information and events surface. M. Dichter, A. Gross, D. Morikawa & S. Sauntry, Employee Dismissal Law: Forms and Procedures § 4.3 at 133 (1986).

[7] Depositions may be taken for two basic reasons: recording of testimony and discovery. P. Keeton, Trial Tactics and Methods 390 (1973).

[8] W. Glaser, Pretrial Discovery and the Adversary System 151 (1968)

cases, counsel may prefer to begin discovery with a deposition of a key actor to facilitate development of more focused interrogatories and requests for production of documents.[9] Another set of interrogatories may be served after depositions to elicit answers to questions omitted in depositions, or to expand on lines of inquiry developed in the depositions.

A number of general principles of discovery are applicable in wrongful dismissal cases.[10] They can be summarized as follows:

1. Prepare. Read the pleadings. Investigate. Think out your own theory of the case, with particular emphasis on burdens of proof.[11]

2. Know the purpose of each discovery activity.[12] Some of these will depend upon the manner in which you expect the case to develop.[13] In any deposition there are multiple purposes; e.g., determining the opposing party's evidence and legal theories,[14] assessing the witness's demeanor,[15] assessing the competence of opposing counsel,[16] and revealing to opposing counsel the lack of merit in his case.[17]

3. Make a rational decision regarding whom to take from your side to a deposition.[18] Having a knowledgeable person present may discourage misrepresentation of the facts.[19] Such a knowledgeable person can suggest useful questions to the attorney conducting the deposition. In addition, exposing

---

[9] *See* Suplee, Strategies, Tactics, Objectives, Depositions, Mechanics and Problems, 2 Rev. of Litig. 255, 260 (1982). The Federal Rules of Civil Procedure prescribe few limitations on the order in which discovery tools may be used. *See* Fed. R. Civ. P. 26(d). For a detailed discussion of considerations involved in the use of requests for the production of documents, see M. Dichter, A. Gross, D. Morikawa & S. Sauntry, Employee Dismissal Law: Forms and Procedures § 4.50 (1986). Sample requests may be found in *id.* §§ 4.51–4.56.

[10] *See generally* B. Schlei & P. Grossman, Employment Discrimination Law 1271–85 (1983).

[11] *See* R. Keeton, Trial Tactics and Methods Ch. 7 (1973); *see also* Schlei & Grossman, Employment Discrimination Law 595–603 (1983). Wrongful dismissal burdens of proof are discussed in **ch. 7** of this treatise.

[12] Be certain that the discovery plan will gather facts helpful in overcoming judicial resistance to allowing employee dismissal cases to get to juries. *See* M. Dichter, A. Gross, D. Morikawa & S. Sauntry, Employee Dismissal Law: Forms and Procedures § 4.6 (1986).

[13] Counsel's task is strategically to use all of the discovery tools available under the federal rules to learn the facts involving the opponent's claims, and to limit the client's exposure to irrelevant and unnecessarily burdensome discovery. Mazaroff, *Surviving the Avalanche: Defendant's Discovery in Title VII Litigation,* 4 Litig. Mag. 17 (1977).

[14] *See* R. Keeton, Trial Tactics and Methods 411 (1973).

[15] *See id.* § 11.4 (preparing a deponent).

[16] W. Glaser, Pretrial Discovery and the Adversary System 66–67 (1968).

[17] J. Kestler, Questioning Techniques and Tactics 234 (1982).

[18] *See* M. Dichter, A. Gross, G. Morikawa & S. Sauntry, Employee Dismissal Law: Forms and Procedures § 4.4 (Use of the Plaintiff as a Discovery Resource) (1986).

[19] W. Glaser, Pretrial Discovery and the Adversary System 63 (1968).

the client to the opposing side's testimony can enhance a realistic client view of the case.[20]

4. In interrogatories, ask if the opposing party disagrees with any of your answers to the other side's interrogatories. This will help narrow the factual issues for trial.[21]

5. Use requests for admissions to reduce your trial burdens.[22] Such requests are underutilized.[23] Make sure that the requests are framed so that if the proffered admission is denied, the opposing party is called upon to set forth her version of the facts.[24] Also, in requests for admissions, the opposing party should be asked to admit that she contends that _____ [key facts]. Interrogatories should be appended to the requests for admission asking the opposing party to describe evidentiary support for the factual contentions admitted pursuant to the request for admissions.[25] And if the opposing party does assert such a contention, then she should be asked to set forth the facts supporting the contention. Requests for admissions should include requests that the authenticity of key documents be admitted.

Counsel for both parties should review the questions set out below for both plaintiff and defendant. The discovery questions for the opposing side may suggest new theories for establishing liability or for defenses. For the same reason that opposing counsel may want to consult the questions in this appendix for the other side, counsel for whom the questions are intended probably will want to avoid asking some of them lest she suggest ideas to the opponent.

---

[20] *See* R. Keeton, Trial Tactics and Methods 392 (1973). For specific guidance concerning the preparation and conduct of the deposition, see M. Dichter, A. Gross, D. Morikawa & S. Sauntry, Employee Dismissal Law: Forms and Procedures §§ 4.57–4.59 (1986)

[21] M. Callahan & B. Bramble, Discovery in Construction Litigation 111 (1983).

[22] Request for admissions are better suited than interrogatories for committing an adverse party to his admissions for your use at trial, because the statements can be phrased as you prefer them, thereby making it more difficult for the adverse party to thwart your efforts with an evasive or ambiguous answer. R. Keeton, Trial Tactics and Methods 417 (1973). *But see* M. Dichter, A. Gross, D. Morikawa & S. Sauntry, Employee Dismissal Law: Forms and Procedures 141, 199 (1986) (use of requests for admission usually meet only with objections and when filed close to trial, may detract from trial preparation; if valuable admissions appear in depositions and interrogatories, turning the admissions into requests for admission may provide an opportunity for the opponent to explain away or deny the damaging testimony).

[23] *See* B. Schlei & P. Grossman, Employment Discrimination Law 1272 (1983). Requests for admission under Federal Rule of Civil Procedure 36 commonly are not used until completion of discovery, since the preparation of the requests presupposes that counsel knows the facts desired to be admitted.

[24] Interrogatories are more useful than a request for admissions if your information is incomplete; that is, interrogatories are more suitable for discovery purposes. R. Keeton, Trial Tactics and Methods 412–13 (1973).

[25] M. Dichter, A. Gross, D. Morikawa & S. Sauntry, Employee Dismissal Law: Forms and Procedures 231 (1986).

Plaintiff's Discovery: In General

The following sections are intended to be used as a checklist for discovery by the plaintiff in a wrongful dismissal case. Dichter, Gross, Morikawa and Sauntry suggest the following elements for a plaintiff discovery plan:

1. A well-conceived and thoroughly researched complaint, with or without accompanying discovery requests
2. A first set of interrogatories and requests for production of documents
3. A list of witnesses for deposition, together with the order in which they are to be deposed
4. Follow-up discovery after each deposition.[26]

Plaintiffs frequently serve interrogatories with their complaint.[27] Accordingly, many of the basic questions[28] could be included in such interrogatories and followed up in depositions.[29] Frequently, plaintiffs are forced to hold down the costs of wrongful dismissal litigation more than defendants,[30] and therefore may prefer to use interrogatories to a greater extent than a discovery strategy not constrained by costs would suggest.[31]

The following questions relate to the basic conditions under which the plaintiff was employed, the reasons proffered by the employer for terminating the plaintiff, and the manner in which the termination was effected. They serve the discovery

---

[26] *Id.* at 142.

[27] B. Schlei & P. Grossman, Employment Discrimination Law 1272 (1983). If this is done, defendant has 45 days rather than the normal 30 days within which to answer under Fed. R. Civ. P. 33(a). The same rule applies to requests for production of documents pursuant to Rule 34(b). For a more detailed discussion of the practical aspects of this strategy, *see* M. Dichter, A. Gross, D. Morikawa & S. Sauntry, Employee Dismissal Law: Forms and Procedures § 4.8 (1986).

[28] R. Keeton, Trial Tactics and Methods 39–40, 390–92 (1973). For sample interrogatory questions to be served *after* defendant has answered the complaint, *see* M. Dichter, A. Gross, D. Morikawa & S. Sauntry, Employee Dismissal Law: Forms and Procedures §§ 4.32–4.49 (1986).

[29] W. Glaser, Pretrial Discovery and the Adversary System 67 (1968). *See also* M. Dichter, A. Gross, D. Morikawa & S. Sauntry, Employee Dismissal Law: Forms and Procedures § 4.30 (listing 10 questions to be included in interrogatories rather than depositions), § 4.30 (identifying kinds of questions to be asked in a first, and then a second, set of interrogatories), § 4.31 (sample interrogatories regarding insurance coverage) (1986).

[30] Funds for the prosecution of a wrongful dismissal action usually are limited, thereby making interrogatories the most attractive discovery tool, due to their low cost. A notice to produce is also desirable, since it involves no direct cash outlay unless someone must be hired to copy documents. It is usually the second most inexpensive method of discovery. Depositions are rather expensive. Therefore, they should be saved for situations in which their use is absolutely necessary. *See Employment Discrimination Action Under Federal Civil Rights Acts,* 21 Am. Jur. *Trials* § 122 (1974).

[31] *See* R. Keeton, Trial Tactics and Methods 393 (1973) (probability of victory in trial is factor determining effect of expense on advisability of depositions.)

objective of revealing the employer's position and serve a potential admission objective respecting key factual elements of an implied-in-fact contract or public policy tort case.

Contract Formation and Terms of the Employment Relation

1. Was the plaintiff covered by a collective bargaining agreement?[32] If the answer is yes, please provide a copy of the agreement.
2. Was the plaintiff ever told anything, orally, or in writing, respecting how long her employment would last or the conditions under which the employment would end?[33]
3. Did you ever tell the plaintiff that it would take a certain discrete period of time fully to complete the task or tasks for which she was hired? If so, state the date and circumstances under which the statement was made, and the time period mentioned.
4. Did you ever represent to the employee that her job was for a certain length of time? If so, how long?
5. Did you ever represent to the employee that her job was dependent on the performance of tasks, or on the fulfilling of certain conditions? If so, please specify the date upon which the representations were made, by whom, in what form, and the precise details of the tasks or the conditions.
6. Did you ever represent to the employee that she would never have to worry about being discharged? If so, state the time, place, and form of the representation.
7. Did you ever represent to the employee that all employees of the company would be treated fairly? If so, state the time, date, and place such representations were made, and the party who made the representations.
8. Do you believe that you treat your employees fairly? If so, please state your reasons why. How do you ensure that your first-level supervisors treat your employees fairly?
9. Do you have a written personnel policy or handbook or an employee manual? If so, please state when it was created, describe any revisions made to it since it was created, and describe its contents.[34] Please provide a copy.
10. Please describe the purpose of the employee handbook or manual.

---

[32] If the answer is "yes," the plaintiff probably must pursue his claim under the agreement. See **ch. 3**.
[33] Questions 2 through 18 relate to the employer's promise. See §§ **7.18–7.19**.
[34] See § **4.8** for an analysis of when such policies or handbooks may be enforceable contracts.

11. Do you give the employee manual or policy handbook to employees who are hired? If so, please state when the handbook or policy book is given to employees.
12. Was the employee handbook or manual given to the plaintiff when she first began work? If so, please state the time, date, and place of the distribution.
13. Was the handbook or policy manual accompanied by an explanation as to its meaning by a person authorized to make representations on your behalf? If so, please state the name of the person who made the representation, his address, the position of the person and a description of the explanation given at the time the distribution was made.
14. Do documents exist that were written in connection with the creation of the employee handbook or manual? If so, please describe their content.
15. Who wrote the employee handbook or manual? Please state their names, addresses, and positions.
16. Do you believe the employee handbook or manual to be a part of the plaintiff's employment contract with you? If not, please state your reasons.
17. Did you think that the plaintiff would believe that you would follow the policies articulated or procedures outlined in the handbook or manual? If not, please give your reasons.
18. When you gave the plaintiff the handbook or manual, did you intend to be bound by it? If not, please explain why.
19. Why do you think the plaintiff came to work for you?[35]
20. After you hired the plaintiff, were you ever aware of any offers made to her for new employment? If so, please state the date and substance of the offers, to the best of your knowledge.
21. After you agreed to hire the plaintiff, did she arrive for work at the stated time? Please state the date upon which work began.

Reasons for Termination and Employer Justification[36]

22. Why was the plaintiff terminated?
23. Are there any documents reflecting this reason? Please briefly describe each document. Please provide copies of the documents.
24. What, if anything, was the plaintiff told was the reason for her termination? By whom? When? Please give dates, names of persons participating, and describe what was said on each occasion to plaintiff and by plaintiff.

---

[35] Questions 19 through 21 relate to the reliance necessary to establish consideration. See § **7.20**.

[36] The reasons for the termination are material to proving a public policy tort (see §§ **7.13–7.15**) and breach of contract (see §§ **7.22–7.28**).

25. When did you begin contemplating discharge of the plaintiff? Please state the exact date.

26. Were you aware of any attempt at any time on the part of the plaintiff to encourage the formation of a union or other labor organization during the time she was employed by you or by any other employer? If so, state, to the best of your knowledge, the date and place such attempts were made, and the manner by which you gained your knowledge of the attempts.

27. Were you ever aware of any attempt by the plaintiff to take time off from work for you or any other employer to perform jury duty? If so, state the date at which you became aware of the attempt, the employer under whom the plaintiff made the attempt, and the manner by which you gained your knowledge of the attempt.

28. Were you ever aware of any attempt by the plaintiff to file a request for workers' compensation benefits during the time when she was employed by you, or by anyone else? If so, state the date at which you became aware of the attempts, the date the attempts were made, and the manner by which you gained your knowledge of the attempts.

29. Were you ever aware of any off-duty conduct or status by the plaintiff of which you disapproved? If so, please describe the action exactly, the date on which the action occurred, the time at which the action occurred, and the manner by which you became aware of the action.[37]

30. Please describe the incident or series of incidents that prompted you first to think about terminating the plaintiff. In your answer, please describe exactly what the plaintiff did or did not do.

31. Please describe your response to the conduct of the plaintiff. Include the date, the name of any person designated to act in your behalf, and the action you took.

32. If you told the plaintiff anything about her conduct, please state as well as you can what you said, and state the time, date, and place. If you communicated to the plaintiff in writing, please describe the content of the communication, and state the date the communication was sent or given to the plaintiff.

33. If the plaintiff was terminated for violating a company rule,[38] what is the rule? What is the justification for the rule?

34. Why do you feel that the plaintiff's conduct could not be tolerated, consistent with your firm's business needs?[39]

---

[37] Some examples of active conduct might be getting a divorce, marital status, sexual conduct, drug or alcohol use, attending a meeting, or writing a letter to the local newspaper. An example of inactive conduct might be a refusal to do something requested by a supervisor.

[38] The rule itself might violate public policy. See generally §§ **5.8–5.18**.

[39] This question has a discovery objective of pinning down the employer's *business necessity* defense on a tort claim (see § **7.15**) or position on what constitutes *cause* in a breach of contract claim (see § **7.26**).

Procedures Utilized in Connection with the Termination[40]

35. What procedure was followed in the plaintiff's case? Please list each step, the result, the date upon which the step was taken, and the person in charge of administering the particular steps.
36. Please describe any additional actions that you took, or the actions taken by any person designated by you to act, in response to any conduct of the plaintiff.
37. If you told the plaintiff anything in response to her conduct, please state as well as you can what you said, the date, time, and place.
38. If you communicated anything written to the plaintiff in response to her conduct, please describe the content of the communication and the date on which it was sent or given to the plaintiff.
39. Did you at any time cause anyone to investigate any fact of the plaintiff's life, including conduct on the job or off the job? If so, please state the investigator's name, his address, and the time period during which investigations were conducted.
40. If an investigation was made of the plaintiff, were reports made to you? If so, please state the date on which reports were made, the nature of the reports, and their contents.
41. What means were used to investigate the plaintiff? Please describe the means in detail.
42. If an investigation of the plaintiff was made, were any reports made? If so, please state the dates of the reports, and their nature and content.
43. Did you ever tell the employee that she would be terminated on a date other than the date plaintiff actually was terminated? If so, please state the date and place such statements were made, the person who made the statements, and his address and position.
44. If you never told plaintiff prior to the date she was terminated that she would be terminated, please explain why you did not.
45. Was the decision to terminate the plaintiff reviewed by anyone else before the termination was effected? By whom?
46. Before you terminated the plaintiff's employment, did you think about how the plaintiff would feel when she was terminated? If you did, please describe your thoughts at the time.
47. Do you believe the plaintiff should have expected to be terminated? If so, please state why you believe she should have so expected.
48. Was the plaintiff afforded any kind of internal hearing or review before she was terminated? If she was, please describe, giving dates and persons

---

[40] These questions relate to compliance with the covenant of good faith and fair dealing (see §§ **4.11, 4.23, 7.23**), and to traditional tort claims such as defamation (§ **5.25**), invasion of privacy (§§ **5.26–5.27**), or intentional infliction of emotional distress (§ **5.23**).

participating in each step. Are there any written records or documents summarizing or otherwise memorializing what transpired as these procedures were being followed? Please describe each of these documents.

49. If you personally terminated the employee, please describe the plaintiff's reaction to the termination. If another person terminated the employee, please state the person's name, address, and position.

50. When you were contemplating terminating the plaintiff's employment, did you communicate about the pending decision with anyone? If so, please state the other person's name, address, and position, if your employee, and describe the nature and content of the communication.

51. During the termination, was any other person present? If so, state the other person's name, address, and position, if your employee.

52. Did the plaintiff undertake to arbitrate or mediate her termination? If so, please describe the steps taken, the results, the dates upon which the steps were taken, and the names and addresses of any persons involved.

53. After the employee's termination, did you communicate with any other person about the decision, excluding attorneys? If so, state the other person's name, address, and position, if your employee, and describe the nature and content of the discussion.

Employer's Assessment of Plaintiff's Job Performance

The following questions relate to the plaintiff's job performance. Depending on the answers obtained, they may serve the admission objective of undercutting a proffered explanation that the plaintiff was terminated for misconduct or poor performance.[41]

54. Are there any written evaluations[42] of plaintiff's performance during her tenure with the company? Do you have any other documents showing the employee's job performance during the time she was employed by you? If so, please describe. Please provide copies of the documents.

---

[41] If financial resources permit, the officials proposing and deciding upon the discipline should be deposed and all facets of the adverse action should be explored. Supervisors should be questioned about the alleged misconduct or poor performance, the past record of the client, the use of a table of penalties, the number and context of counseling discussions, the conferences among the managers concerning the adverse action to be taken, and the existence of supervisor's notes, logs, tape recordings, or other records concerning the client that agency representatives may be reluctant to identify in response to interrogatories or document requests. Broida, *What to Do When Representing a Federal Employee in an Adverse Action Appeal,* 28 Prac. Law. 42, 53 (1982).

[42] *See* B. Schlei & P. Grossman, Employment Discrimination Law 604 (1983) (counsel should obtain access to discharged employee's personnel file, paying special attention to evaluations and warnings or the lack thereof; counsel also should obtain access to significant number of personnel files of comparably situated majority group members, potentially revealing pattern of discriminatory evaluations.

55. Do you have documents describing your evaluation of the plaintiff before she first began working for you? Please describe them, and provide copies.
56. Do you have documents describing your disciplinary actions taken against the plaintiff? If so, please describe, and provide copies.
57. Was the plaintiff counseled[43] in any way respecting her performance or conduct? Please give dates and the names of persons participating. What was said on each occasion to plaintiff and by plaintiff?
58. How would you characterize the plaintiff's job performance?
59. Why was the plaintiff continued as an employee for as long as she was?
60. Did the plaintiff ever receive any awards or commendations? Please give dates and describe.

Discovering Similarly Situated Personnel

Another initial discovery objective should be to identify personnel similarly situated with the plaintiff. This information will be essential in proving a statutory discrimination case,[44] and may be helpful in connection with an implied-in-fact contract or public policy tort case.[45]

61. Have any other employees been terminated for the same reason as the plaintiff? Please give names and dates of termination.
62. What other employees performed functions similar to those performed by the plaintiff, and engaged in conduct similar to the plaintiff's? Please give names and a brief summary of (a) performance, (b) conduct, and (c) any personnel action taken.
63. Is anyone now filling the plaintiff's job? Who?
64. Is anyone else now performing the plaintiff's job duties? Who?
65. Ask for an explanation of any apparent disparate treatment (in deposition) shown by answers to questions in this section.

Background Information About the Employer

It also is important early in discovery to ascertain the organizational structure of the defendant,[46] and to identify the relevant management personnel and to find

---

[43] Discovery of any possible management attempts to alert the plaintiff to the poor job performance will greatly affect the possibility of a negligence theory. See § **5.29**.

[44] *See* the discussion of disparate treatment theory in §§ **2.3 & 2.4**.

[45] In organizations without written disciplinary procedures, demonstrating that the plaintiff's discharge was an extreme, unprecedented reaction of management would support an argument of bad faith. See § **7.23**. It also would undercut an employer's *business necessity* defense. See § **7.15**.

[46] To facilitate discovery, especially requests for documents, knowledge of who may have the information or documents is important in order to avoid fruitless effort. 8 C. Wright & A. Miller, Federal Practice and Procedure § 2207 (1970).

out what their functions are. It also is desirable to ascertain whether the discharge may be deemed *state action*.[47]

66. Describe the nature of your business. Include the number of employees, the type of work they do, and the institutions or persons they serve, if applicable.
67. Are you required to be licensed by the state, local or federal governments to perform your business functions? If so, please describe the licenses held and the issuing agency, including its address.
68. Are you subject to any local, state or federal regulations of the conduct of your business? If so, please briefly describe the nature of the regulations, or state specifically in what publication they may be found.
69. Are you subject to any state or federal civil service laws or regulations? If so, please briefly describe their nature, or state in what publication they may be found.
70. When did the plaintiff first begin working for you? State the exact date.
71. Who was the plaintiff's supervisor?
72. Who made the decision to terminate the plaintiff?
73. Has this person terminated any other employees? Please give names and dates.

Witness Identification

Another objective of discovery is to identify potential witnesses, either for trial or for further discovery.

74. What are the names, phone numbers, and addresses of coworkers who can testify as to employer policies or statements or conduct showing employer policy or practice and performance or conduct of the plaintiff?

Other Formal Proceedings Related to the Termination

75. Was any hearing held on an unemployment claim by the plaintiff?[48] Was a transcript made? Were any other documents or records made memorializing the hearing?
76. Did the company contest any claim for unemployment benefits made by the plaintiff? If not, why not? Do you have any internal procedures for grievance processing? If so, please state when they came into effect, the name, address, and position of the person or persons responsible for administering them, and the nature of the procedures.

---

[47] See § **6.2**.

[48] See § **7.35** for the possible preclusive effect of unemployment benefit determinations. *See also* B. Schlei & P. Grossman, Employment Discrimination Law 605 (1983).

77. Did you have in effect any arbitration or mediation procedure, whether formal or informal, at the time of the plaintiff's termination? If so, please describe the steps to be taken under the procedure, and describe the procedure as a whole.

78. Do you know of any company or official investigation or inquiry into the circumstances of the plaintiff's termination?

Defendant Discovery: In General

The following sections are intended to be used as a checklist in discovery by the defendant in a wrongful dismissal case. The choice among discovery methods and the style to be utilized with respect to any of these methods depends on the probable course of the litigation.[49] One possibility is that the case will go to trial. In these circumstances, the defendant will want to find out what the plaintiff will say in his testimony, what kind of witnesses will be called and what kinds of documents will be introduced.[50] In this posture, the risk of educating the plaintiff by complete discovery is relatively low.[51] Another possibility is that the case may settle short of trial. In these circumstances discovery can serve the purpose, among others, of communicating to the plaintiff and his attorney that a trial would be difficult and expensive.[52] A third possibility is that summary judgment in the defendant's favor can be obtained. In these circumstances, the purpose of discovery is to show that there are no material issues of disputed fact for trial.[53]

Counsel should analyze the defendant's case to determine if a pretrial motion for judgment on the pleadings or for summary judgment would be advantageous. Then counsel should make a thorough initial investigation and interview possible witnesses in order to determine the validity of the employer's reasons for terminating the plaintiff. This investigation also will reveal possible affirmative defenses so that they can be preserved in the answer to the complaint and in discovery.

---

[49] Because only 10 percent of all cases actually go to trial, the deposition frequently is the most significant event in a lawsuit. Successfully conducted depositions eliminate the need for trial. The deposition provides an opportunity to discover the facts and nail down the testimony of opposing witnesses. J. Kestler, Questioning Techniques and Tactics § 7.01 at 233 (1982). For a complete discussion of effective deposition strategies and techniques in the wrongful dismissal context, *see* M. Dichter, A. Gross, D. Morikawa & S. Sauntry, Employee Dismissal Law: Forms and Procedures § 5.17 at 218–21 (1986).

[50] *See* B. Schlei & P. Grossman, Employment Discrimination Law at 1276–77 (1983) (information that defendant should get as soon as possible).

[51] R. Keeton, Trial Tactics and Methods 398 (1954).

[52] *See* J. Kestler, Questioning Techniques and Tactics 234 (1982). "It . . . provides a forum for the litigator to display a most effective weapon: himself or herself. In psychological terms, the deposition should be viewed as the functional equivalent of a May Day parade in Moscow's Red Square. In the deposition room, the litigator can display the knowledge, resources, and skills that can be brought to bear against the opponent in an ultimate confrontation. This message is conveyed from the moment the examining counsel is introduced to the opponent and her counsel, and continues to be transmitted throughout the course of the deposition both on and off the record."

[53] *See* Fed. R. Civ. p. 56.

Defense counsel should formulate a theory of the facts, and ensure that discovery develops evidence supporting such a theory.

Order of Discovery

Different lawyers have different views on the order in which different types of discovery should be used.[54] Counsel may also want to consider certain forms of informal discovery.[55] In general, however, it usually is accepted that a deposition elicits the plaintiff's answers while interrogatories elicit those of her attorney.[56] Accordingly, taking the plaintiff's deposition before serving interrogatories can help confine the plaintiff to particular theories and one version of the facts.[57] On the other hand, some questions are better asked and answered in interrogatories:[58] dates, the type of public policy relied upon under a public policy tort theory, the names of witnesses, and the names of similarly situated people. Some information, such as the plaintiff's employment history, is obtained more efficiently through interrogatories because of the likelihood that there will be no controversy over such facts, because of length, detail, and the need for accuracy. Accordingly, the defendant may wish to serve interrogatories before the deposition. Regardless of whether this is done, a set of interrogatories may be served after the deposition to elicit answers to questions omitted in the deposition, to expand on lines of inquiry developed in the deposition.[59]

The defendant may wish to save his own documents for trial if he expects a trial.[60] On the other hand, if he is hopeful of obtaining summary judgment in his

---

[54] *See* W. Glaser, Pretrial Discovery and the Advisory System 58–62 (1968). *See also* M. Dichter, A. Gross, D. Morikawa & S. Sauntry, Employee Dismissal Law: Forms and Procedures § 5.3 at 204–05 (one view of best order of discovery for defendant), § 5.2 (need to anticipate opponent's reaction to discovery, and who will be most educated by discovery; need for strategic plan for nature and timing of likely discovery battles) (1986).

[55] The advantages and disadvantages of this tactic are discussed in M. Dichter, A. Gross, D. Morikawa & S. Sauntry, Employee Dismissal Law: Forms and Procedures § 5.6 at 206–08 (1986).

[56] *Id.* at 66.

[57] J. Kestler, Questioning Techniques and Tactics § 7.01 at 234 (1982). "[A]t the deposition, the witness does not have the opportunity to run through a story prior to your questioning (as she would under direct testimony at trial). In fact, the witness' lawyer may very well have paid little attention to the task of getting her ready to present her version of the facts as counsel would in preparing for direct examination. It is more likely that opposing counsel has told the witness not to volunteer information, and then concentrated on a series of defenses related to your probable lines of questioning during cross. The result is that the witness may not have her story straight at this stage of the litigation. At least, she will be less prepared to tell it."

[58] W. Glaser, Pretrial Discovery and the Advisory System 63 (1968). *See* M. Dichter, A. Gross, D. Morikawa & S. Sauntry, Employee Dismissal Law: Forms and Procedures §§ 5.10–5.16 (sample questions better suited to interrogatories), § 5.18 (deposition checklist) (1986).

[59] Postdeposition strategy is discussed more fully in M. Dichter, A. Gross, D. Morikawa & S. Sauntry, Employee Dismissal Law: Forms and Procedures § 5.4 at 205 (1986).

[60] Retaining documents may surprise the adversary; a diligent opponent, however, normally will obtain the documents in the due course of discovery. Moreover, a purpose behind Federal Rule of Civil Procedure 34 is to eliminate strategic surprise, 8 C. Wright & A. Miller, Federal Practice and Civil Procedure § 2202 (1970).

favor, it is important to get the plaintiff's acknowledgment of the documents' authenticity.[61] If a motion for summary judgment is contemplated, any possible advantage from surprise at trial would be eliminated in any event by the papers filed in the summary judgment proceeding. In a summary judgment proceeding, the results of thorough discovery can educate the judge and influence opposing counsel as to the insubstantiality of his position on factual disputes.

It is useful to get the plaintiff's documents before deposing the plaintiff.[62] Either a formal request for production of documents should be served before the deposition[63] or an informal request should be made of the plaintiff's attorney that the documents be brought to the deposition.[64] If a large number of documents have been requested, it may be desirable to postpone the deposition until the documents can be reviewed. This course of action will avoid wasting time on unnecessary questions in the deposition.

There are arguments in favor of obtaining discovery of the plaintiff before permitting discovery against the defendant.[65] Such an order of discovery permits the plaintiff's theory to be pinned down more narrowly. On the other hand, in an especially strong case for the defendant, letting the plaintiff depose the defense witnesses first may enhance settlement possibilities. Another consideration arises when a terminated employee claims damages for emotional distress allegedly caused by the defendant. In this situation, the defendant must decide whether and when to request a mental or physical examination of the plaintiff pursuant to Federal Rule of Civil Procedure 35.[66]

Depending on whether the defendant wishes to blur his theory of the case, the order of questions in the deposition of the plaintiff should not be followed by a highly structured pattern or logical progression.[67] An overly logical framework of questions can reveal to the plaintiff the kinds of factual answers that will

---

[61] To obtain summary judgment, the moving party must show that there was no genuine issue on any material fact. 10 C. Wright, A. Miller, & M. Kane, Federal Practice and Civil Procedure § 2714 (2d ed. 1983).

[62] Examination of documents prior to deposition will enable the attorney to develop a line of questioning to obtain the most useful information. If, during deposition, other documents are indicated which may have a bearing on the case, these may be requested. 8 C. Wright & A. Miller, Federal Practice and Civil Procedure § 2047 (1970).

[63] Compulsory process includes the following: a subpoena *duces tecum* in connection with a deposition; a bill of discovery under equity principles or a modified form adopted by decision, rule, or statute; and a motion for discovery under Federal Rule of Civil Procedure 34 or under rules or statutes of some of the states. R. Keeton, Trial Tactics and Methods 412-13 (1973). *See* M. Dichter, A. Gross, D. Morikawa, S. Sauntry, Employee Dismissal Law: Forms and Procedures § 5.19 (considerations surrounding requests for the production of documents) and § 5.20 (sample document requests) (1986).

[64] Generally a request for production of documents will be complied with by the opposing attorney. W. Glaser, Pretrial Discovery and the Adversary System 135 (1968).

[65] R. Keeton, Trial Tactics and Methods 382 (1973) (plaintiff has less opportunity to learn of your theories). *But see* Fed. R. Civ. P. 26(d) (discovery permitted in any order).

[66] Various strategies are considered in M. Dichter, A. Gross, D. Morikawa & S. Sauntry, Employee Dismissal Law: Forms and Procedures § 5.5 at 205-06; § 5.23 at 231-32 (1986).

[67] *See* R. Keeton, Trial Tactics and Methods 404 (1973).

jeopardize her case. Accordingly, the questions in the following sections should not be asked in the order given, and defense counsel may wish to intersperse questions of lesser importance so that the purposes of the questions is not obvious.[68] On the other hand, if the primary purpose of discovery is to convince the plaintiff that her chances for success are not good, then a more structured and concise approach to deposing the plaintiff may be called for.[69]

Regardless of whether interrogatories are to be *served* before the plaintiff's deposition, the interrogatories should be *drafted* before the deposition so that rational decisions can be made regarding what information should be sought in the deposition and what should be reserved for the interrogatories.[70]

Counsel should also be alert to the possible usefulness, as well as the pitfalls involved, in the use of requests for admissions.[71]

General Questions

The questions in this section are intended to elicit the plaintiff's basic position and to reveal his attitude toward the employer's personnel policy. Answers to these questions should reveal the legal theory or theories on which the plaintiff relies. More specific questions related to each discrete theory are contained in following sections. The questions relating to the plaintiff's attitude toward personnel policy are useful primarily for impeachment at trial and to refute the reasonableness of reliance by the plaintiff on any implied promises that may be asserted.

1. Do you believe that the employer's criteria for termination are valid in general?[72]
2. While you were employed there, did you ever terminate anyone, or were you involved in any terminations? What criteria were utilized in deciding to terminate such employees? (Emphasize those cases in which the grounds for termination appear to be similar to those related to the plaintiff's discharge.)[73]
3. Please explain the rationale for the actions you took vis-a-vis your subordinates. Please identify as specifically as you can any performance evaluations you did on your subordinates.

---

[68] *See* J. Kestler, Questioning Techniques and Tactics § 7.01 at 249 (1982).

[69] *See* R. Keeton, Trial Tactics and Methods 404 (1973).

[70] The deposition, especially when taken primarily for use at trial, should be as complete as possible. Thorough preparation will insure that nothing is overlooked while allowing the attorney to follow any paths of questioning which arise during deposition. *Id.* at 389–90.

[71] *See* M. Dichter, A. Gross, D. Morikawa & S. Sauntry, Employee Dismissal Law: Forms and Procedures §§ 5.21–5.22 at 228–31 (1986).

[72] Questions 1 through 5 are intended to elicit the plaintiff's attitude toward the employer's personnel policies in general.

[73] See §§ **4.6–4.11,** and §§ **7.18–7.19** relating to proof of implied promises.

4. Were you ever involved in recruiting new employees? What promises or assurances of employment security did you make in such recruiting activities?[74] Did you understand those assurances to be legally binding?[75]
5. How would you have treated a subordinate who went public with a managerial disagreement?[76]
6. What criteria for performance and conduct do you think were applied in your case[77] Were they the same criteria applied in other cases? Do you think those criteria are unfair? (If the plaintiff says that the criteria are unfair, ask if the plaintiff ever raised objections to the criteria.)
7. Why did you fail to meet the criteria?
8. Please describe discrete periods in your employment history.[78] (Attempt to obtain an admission that nothing unfair happened to the plaintiff during each discrete period.)
9. What warnings, poor performance ratings, or disciplinary measures were imposed on you?[79] Did you protest any such corrective actions or warnings?
10. (If the plaintiff says he received commendations, attempt to obtain an admission that commendations routinely were handed out to large numbers of people.)
11. Please explain the factual basis for your legal claim.[80] Is it based on an employer's promise?[81] Is it based on the perceived unfairness of the reason for termination? Is it based on your activities outside the workplace?
12. What policies, documents, or oral representations do you rely upon for any implied contract theory? When did you receive them? In what way did you rely upon them?[82]
13. What public policy do you believe is jeopardized[83] by your discharge?
14. Were you involved in any disagreements over company policy?[84]
15. What else should the company have done in the circumstances leading up to your discharge?

---

[74] *Id.*

[75] *Id.*

[76] See § **5.16**.

[77] Questions 6 and 7 ask the plaintiff to relate her discharge to the employer's general policies.

[78] Questions 8 through 10 ask the plaintiff for general information about her employment history.

[79] *See* B. Schlei & P. Grossman, Employment Discrimination Law 604 (1983).

[80] Questions 11 through 14 ask the plaintiff to identify the bases for her claim in general. These questions should be supplemented with more detailed questions pertinent to specific theories of wrongful dismissal contained in the following sections.

[81] See the section of this appendix entitled *Contract Theories* for other theories.

[82] See *id.* for other questions related to contract theories.

[83] See the section of this appendix entitled *Tort Theories* for other questions related to public policy tort theories.

[84] The purpose of this question is to support an argument that the cause of the discharge was a managerial disagreement rather than *whistleblowing*.

16. Did you utilize any internal grievance procedure?[85] Whether or not you did, do you consider the internal grievance procedure to be unfair, and if so why?
17. Please give me the names of all the people you believe treated you unfairly.
18. (With respect to each discrete time period and at the end of any deposition,) was there *anything* else unfair that happened to you?

Statutory Discrimination

The plaintiff's pleadings usually will reveal whether the plaintiff claims discrimination prohibited by statute, as described in **Chapter 2**. Defendant should concentrate on finding out information tending to show that the plaintiff was not a member of a protected class, or that her conduct was not protected, that she was not discharged because of her class or conduct, or that if she was, the employer was acting pursuant to a bona fide occupational qualification (BFOQ).

19. Why do you believe that the termination was initiated because of the your [conduct or status]? Please relate in detail any discussion, memoranda or other instances on which you base your belief.
20. Have you ever spoken to any person, excluding attorneys, about the termination and your belief that it occurred because of your [conduct or status]? Please state the names, addresses, and, if employed by defendant, the positions of any such persons.
21. Do you know of any other persons employed by defendant in your situation who were dismissed for the same or similar reasons as you contend? If so, please state the names and addresses of such persons, and the date upon which they were dismissed, to the best of your recollection.
22. Do you know of any persons in the defendant's employ who [acted as you did or were of the same status as you] and were treated differently than you were? Please state names and positions of any such person.

Counsel facing a claim of violation of the major federal discrimination statutes are advised to look into specialized discovery techniques outlined in various handbooks.[86]

Collectively Bargained Arbitration

Arbitration, if it occurs, necessarily involves the employer. Thus, the employer should have access to internal information that will minimize surprise. It may,

---

[85] See the section of this appendix entitled *Collectively Bargained Arbitration* for additional questions related to exhaustion of internal procedures. *See* Johnson v. General Motors Corp., 641 F.2d 1075 (2d Cir. 1981) (reversing summary judgment; plaintiff failed to exhaust internal remedies but disputed question of fact existed whether remedies were adequate).

[86] *See generally* B. Schlei & P. Grossman, Employment Discrimination Law 1276 (1983).

however, be worthwhile to find what part of the dispute resolution procedure the plaintiff considers defective.[87]

23. Did your union refuse to file a grievance on your behalf? Did the union refuse to arbitrate your grievance on your behalf?

24. If you undertook to resolve your termination by arbitration, did you consider any part of the procedures utilized to be defective? If so, describe the defective procedure, state the date upon which it occurred, name the person in charge of the proceeding and his position, and state why you believe the procedure was defective.

25. If the procedure was defective, state what procedure should have occurred, and whether the different procedure would have resulted in a different outcome. State why the new procedure would have resulted in a different outcome.

Contract Theories

Because of the employer's recordkeeping capacity, it is likely that it will have records duplicating anything the plaintiff could bring forth. Defendant will be interested mostly in what theories plaintiff intends to use at trial with respect to an implied contract theory. Defendant also will be interested in the extent to which plaintiff mitigated his damages.

26. If you are relying on an employee handbook or manual, state the date upon which you first became aware of any provisions in the employee handbook or manual relating to terminations.[88]

27. State the date upon which you first read the provisions relating to terminations.

28. Did defendant or defendant's agents ever represent to you that you would not be dismissed? If so, please state the name of the person making the representation, his position, the nature of the representation (written or oral), the date upon which the representation was made, and the circumstances under which the representation was made.

29. Did defendant or defendant's agents ever represent to you that you would be dismissed only after certain procedures were followed? If so, state the name of the person making the representation, his position, the date upon which the representation was made, the nature of the representation (written or oral), and the circumstances under which the representation was made.

30. Did defendant or defendant's agents ever represent to you that you would be treated fairly? If so, please state the name of the person who made the

---

[87] See § **3.25** on the duty of fair representation.

[88] Questions 26 through 32 relate to proof of a promise on which the plaintiff might have relied. See §§ **7.18–7.19**.

representation, his position, the date, the nature of the representation, and the circumstances under which the representation was made.

31. When you were working for defendant, did any event occur which led you to believe that your employment was secure? If so, please describe the event in detail, including the names, addresses, and, if employed by defendant, the positions of any persons involved.[89]

32. When you first began working for defendant, how long did you anticipate working there? Explain why you believed as you did.

33. What do you consider to be proper grounds for discharge by the defendant? Explain your reasons for your thinking.[90]

34. When you first decided to go to work for the defendant, did you have any other job offers open to you?[91] If so, please state the name of the person making the offer, his position, the date upon which the offer was made, the rate of compensation offered, whether the offer was written or oral, and the nature of the employment offered.

35. When you were employed with the defendant, did you ever receive an offer of employment with another party? If so, please state the name of the person making the offer, his position, the date upon which the offer was made, the rate of compensation offered, whether the offer was written or oral, and the nature of the employment.

36. Why did you go to work for the defendant? In your answer describe any conversations, memoranda, or other communications which played a part in your decision. State the names of any persons with whom you spoke regarding the offer by the defendant, their addresses, their positions if employed by defendant, and the dates upon which communications occurred. Describe the content of the conversations, memoranda or other communications.

37. Was anyone else employed by the defendant ever terminated for the same reason that you were terminated? If so, please state the person's name and address and the approximate date of termination.

38. Why do you believe your dismissal was inconsistent with any of the statements made to you by the defendant or his agents?

39. If you were dismissed for conduct, do you dispute whether the conduct occurred? If so, state what conduct you think occurred.[92]

40. If you acted as the defendant claims you did, do you believe such conduct was grounds for dismissal? If you base your belief on a list of forbidden

---

[89] Questions 31 and 32 relate to the plaintiff's subjective belief in the employer's promise.

[90] This question seeks to pin down the plaintiff's understanding of the content of the promise on which she relied.

[91] Questions 34 through 36 relate to detrimental reliance by the plaintiff on the employer's promise. See § **7.20** for a discussion of proof of consideration.

[92] Questions 39 through 42 relate to factual assertions by the plaintiff that might show a breach of an implied promise of employment security. Proof of breach is treated in §§ **7.22–7.28**.

conduct or on oral representations by the defendant or defendant's agents, state the origin of the list or the date upon which the representations were made to you, and the name of the person making the representations, and the circumstances of the representations.

41. Do you contend that procedures that should have been followed in your termination were not? If so, please describe the procedures that should have been followed.

42. If the procedures that you believe should have been followed had been followed, what result would have occurred? Explain why the result would have occurred.

Tort Theories

In tort cases, the employer usually possesses most of the documentation necessary, but may wish to find out more about the plaintiff's legal theories. The plaintiff has unique knowledge about his mental state, for instance, and will be able to disclose information about witnesses unknown to defendant.

43. What conduct do you believe led to your dismissal? Give a detailed description of your conduct.

44. Why do you believe that dismissal interferes with the public policy you have said exists? Explain your belief in detail.

45. If the conduct [of plaintiff] which prompted the dismissal involved discussions, memoranda or other communications with you, please state the date upon which each communication occurred, the circumstances, the nature of the communication, the name and position of each person with whom communication was made, and the content of the communication. If written please attach copies.

46. Was your dismissal based on an employer rule or regulation? Did the defendant or any agent of defendant ever explain the reason or justification for this rule or regulation? Please state the date upon which the statement was made, the name and position of the person making the statement, and the circumstances under which the statement was made. If the statement was written, please attach copies.[93]

47. Why do you believe that it is possible for the defendant to conduct his business when employees act as you acted? Give details.

48. If the defendant dismissed you because of your conduct at work, is there a reason why your actions had to take place at work? Explain why your action could not have taken place anywhere else.

---

[93] Questions 46 through 48 relate to the employer's justification for a dismissal that arguably jeopardizes public policy. See § **7.15** for a discussion of proof of such a *business necessity* defense.

49. What was your state of mind upon first being told of the possibility of your dismissal? Please describe fully.[94]
50. Was there any person present at the time you were told of your possible dismissal apart from the person or persons who told you of the possible dismissal? Please state their names and, if employed by the defendant, their positions; if not employed by the defendant, their addresses.
51. Did you talk or write to any other person about your feelings regarding the possible dismissal? If so, please state their names, addresses, the date upon which the communication occurred, the nature of the communication, and, if employed by the defendant, their positions.
52. What was your state of mind upon being told of your dismissal? If there was present at the dismissal any person or persons other than the dismissing person and yourself, please state their names, and, if employed by the defendant, their positions; if not employed by the defendant, their addresses.
53. Did you talk to or write to any person or persons regarding your dismissal? If so, please state their names, addresses, and, if employed by the defendant, their positions; the date upon which the communication occurred, and the content of the communication.
54. How did defendant or defendant's agent act when you were dismissed? Please describe as exactly as you can the dismissing person's demeanor, tone of voice, and the physical circumstance at the time of the dismissal.
55. Do you believe defendant ever did anything that interfered with your chance of getting another job? If so, please state the nature of the action, the date upon which the action occurred, and the name of the person taking the action.[95]
56. Do you believe the defendant ever wrote or said anything about you that was untrue and that hurt your reputation? If so, please state the content of the statements, the dates upon which they were made, the persons to whom they were directed, and the medium by which they were expressed.[96]
57. If you believe your name has been blackened, what procedures could take place to clear your name?
58. State your basis for believing that untrue information has been communicated to others. If events occurred which substantiate your belief, give the date and place at which such events occurred.

---

[94] Questions 49 through 54 relate to the emotional injury and outrageous conduct elements necessary to sustain a claim for intentional infliction of emotional distress. See § **5.23** for a description of this theory.

[95] This question relates to the tort of intentional interference with contractual relations. See § **5.22**.

[96] Questions 56 through 58 relate to a claim for defamation, discussed in § **5.25**, or to a due process liberty impairment claim by a public employee. See § **6.11**.

59. When did you first begin to suspect that the defendant was investigating you? Please state the time, date, place, and circumstances of your discovery.[97]
60. Did you ever tell or write to anyone that you believed defendant was investigating you? If so, please give the date upon which you so stated, the nature of the statements, the content of the statements; the names, and, if employed by the defendant, positions of such persons; and, if not employed by the defendant, their addresses.
61. If you had anticipated that you might be discharged for your private conduct, would this have caused you to refrain from the conduct?[98]
62. If you were periodically evaluated by the defendant with regard to job performance, do you believe that defendant adequately evaluated you? If not, please state your reasons, and give specific instances of inadequate evaluations.[99]
63. Why do you believe that you were entitled to advance notice of your dismissal? Explain as completely as possible.

Public Employment

The factual issues under most of the public employment theories discussed in **Chapter 6** coincide with the factual issues under contract and tort theories. Counsel desiring public employment questions for defendant are advised to use the tort and contract sections of this appendix for questions on expectations and other theories of public employment liability.

Damages

Damages are a question of great importance in wrongful dismissal litigation. The defendant should seek information tending to show the plaintiff's lack of effort to find new employment in order to argue lack of mitigation.

64. Have you sought employment elsewhere since defendant dismissed you? If so, please state the names of places to which you applied, the dates of application, the positions for which you applied, the rate of pay of those positions, and the names of any persons who handled your applications.

---

[97] Questions 59 and 60 relate to well-established doctrines of invasion of privacy on the *intrusion* ground. See § **5.26**.

[98] This question relates to an extension of the invasion of privacy doctrine to cover dismissals for private conduct. See § **5.27** for an explanation of this theory.

[99] Questions 62 and 63 relate to a negligence theory. See § **5.29**.

65. Did you contact any employment services or agencies after being dismissed? If so, please state the names, addresses, and the dates upon which you contacted them.
66. Did you leave the immediate area to seek employment? If so, state the date you left, the places you went, and the names and addresses of any prospective employers to which you submitted applications for employment. Include the nature of the positions for which you submitted applications, and the rate of pay for each.
67. When did you return to the area from seeking employment elsewhere? Please give the exact date.
68. Give the places where you stayed while out of the area, the cost of staying there, and their addresses and phone numbers.
69. Have you received any offers of employment since you were dismissed? Please give the names and addresses of the parties offering employment, the nature of the positions, and the rate of pay.

Final Note

The defendant ordinarily will concentrate on discovery of the plaintiff for information about expectations, reliance, damages, and the like, but may be able to obtain substantial amounts of useful information from his own employees as well.[1] Accordingly, the defendant should interview his own employees and prepare affidavits for them to sign. In addition, the defendant should consider deposing his own employees. This has the benefit of preserving his employees' testimony for trial, since it is possible that an employee could become disenchanted with the defendant and refuse to testify or change his story later.

---

[1] See **App. D**.

APPENDIX C
DRAFT STATUTES

Draft State Bill

Section 1. Short Title

This act shall be known and may be cited as the "Wrongful Dismissal Act."

Section 2. Definitions

The following words and phrases shall have the following meanings when used in this act, unless the context clearly indicates otherwise:

(a) "Board": The Board of Labor Arbitration.[1]
(b) "Costs": Includes the arbitrator's fee as established in § 12(b)(vii).[2]
(c) "Determining factor": A factor, in the absence of which a discharge would not have occurred.
(d) "Discharge": Any termination of employment effected by an employer, including a resignation induced by unreasonable employer conduct.[3]
(e) "Employee": Any natural person in the employment of the same employer for at least 15 hours per week over a six-month period prior to discharge[4] and not covered by a collective bargaining agreement[5] or written contract of

---

[1] The name *Board of Labor Arbitration* is used in this draft bill as a surrogate for the name of an existing agency in the state with responsibility for union-management relations in the private sector. Accordingly, no language respecting the general organization or powers of the agency is included. If no such agency exists in the state, a section should be added to the bill establishing a Board of Labor Arbitration.

[2] This definition is intended to work in conjunction with § 9 of the Act to impose the costs of arbitration, including the arbitrator's fee, on the losing party. It is preferable not to provide for free adjudication of claims to reduce the incidence of frivolous claims.

[3] This definition is intended to permit allegedly improper layoffs to be challenged, and to include *constructive discharge* within the ambit of the Act.

[4] This part of the definition is intended to provide for a probationary period during which employees could be dismissed for any reason. See Mennemeier, *Protection from Unjust Discharges: An Arbitration Scheme,* 19 Harv. J. on Legis. 49, 81–82 (1982). Mr. Mennemeier's views are discussed in **§ 9.11**.

[5] This part of the definition is intended to exclude employees covered by collective agreements, so as to prevent interference with union organization or the functioning of collective bargaining.

employment of two or more years in duration,[6] including a person who has been dismissed in violation of § 5 of this Act.[7]

(f) "Employer": Any person who employs more than 10 employees.

(g) "Employment": The performance of duties defined by an employer, under the supervision of the employer,[8] but which does not include the performance of duties pursuant to a collective bargaining agreement.

(h) "Fair termination procedure": Any procedure actually followed by an employer prior to discharge of an employee that includes notice to the employee, provision of an impartial decisionmaker,[9] and an opportunity for the employee to present argument,[10] but excluding procedures required under a collective bargaining agreement.

(i) "Person": One or more individuals, labor organizations, partnerships, associations, corporations, legal representatives, trustees, trustees in bankruptcy, or receivers.

(j) "Termination procedures": Any actions taken by an employer prior to the discharge of an employee in connection with the discharge.

Section 3. Policy

The Legislature finds that employers are now able to dismiss employees on grounds which conflict with public policies and with laws barring discriminatory practices, and which interfere with commerce and the economic health and welfare of this state. The Legislature finds it necessary to regulate the discharge practices of employers and to create a uniform method of dealing with complaints of wrongful discharge. The Legislature finds it inappropriate to prohibit discharges in the private sector except for *cause*.

Section 4. Jurisdiction and Administrative Provisions

The Board has original and exclusive jurisdiction over any case of wrongful discharge as defined in § 5 of this Act. Tort and contract causes of action arising out of discharges covered by this Act hereby are abolished.[11]

---

[6] This part of the definition is intended to exclude executives and other employees who have sufficient bargaining power to negotiate traditional contracts of employment.

[7] This part of the definition is intended to foreclose any argument that an employee, once dismissed, lacks standing to bring a claim under the statute.

[8] This is intended to exclude termination of independent contractor relations.

[9] *Impartial decisionmaker* is intended to include a senior official of the employer not directly involved in the dismissal decision, to protect the integrity of adequate internal employer procedures.

[10] These are the minimum elements of procedural fairness discussed in **§§ 9.2, 9.25 & 9.27**.

[11] If the state has a constitutional provision protecting the right to a jury trial for causes of action recognized at common law, it is necessary to include language extinguishing the common law cause of action. *See, e.g.,* Singer v. Sheppard, 464 Pa. 387, 400, 346 A.2d 897, 903–04 (1975) (Pennsylvania no-fault act constitutional; tort liability abolished).

Section 5. Standards of Employer Conduct

(a) A discharge of an employee shall be wrongful if one or more of the following was a determining factor in the discharge:
   (i) The employee's age, sex, race, religion, national origin, handicap, marital status, or sexual orientation;[12]
   (ii) The employee's exercise of rights of political expression, religious activities, association, or privacy guaranteed under the United States or this states's Constitution against governmental interference;[13]
   (iii) The employee's performance of an act or refusal to perform an act, the performance or refusal being in furtherance of public policy, as expressed in statutes, administrative regulations, formal statements of professional ethics applicable to the employee, or well-settled common law principles;[14]
   (iv) Off-duty conduct of the employee bearing no reasonable relationship to the employee's job performance; or [15]
(b) A discharge of an employee shall be wrongful if the discharge occurred in violation of an employer's express or implied promise that the employer would continue employment for a particular period of time, would dismiss the employee only for cause or only for certain reasons or only after following certain procedures, including a fair termination procedure or termination procedure.[16] This subsection shall apply regardless of whether the employee gave anything in return for the employer's promise.
(c) A discharge of an employee shall not be wrongful under § 5(a)(i) when the employee was discharged for failure to meet a bona fide occupational qualification reasonably necessary to the proper performance of the duties of the position.[17]

Section 6. Claim Procedures

(a) A claim for wrongful discharge is commenced by filing a notice with the Board and paying an arbitration fee in accordance with § 6(c).[18]
(b) Time Limitations
   (i) No claim for wrongful discharge may be filed under this section by any employee unless the claim is filed within six months of the discharge;[19]

---

[12] This is intended to encompass claims arising under federal, state, or municipal employment discrimination statutes.

[13] This is intended to protect the employee's federal constitutional rights against interference by private employers.

[14] This is intended to encompass the public policy tort discussed in **Ch. 5**.

[15] This is intended to encompass the right of privacy, possibly cognizable under tort concepts discussed in **§ 5.27**.

[16] This is intended to encompass the implied contract cause of action discussed in **Ch. 4**.

[17] This is intended to preserve the employer's bona fide occupational qualification (BFOQ) defense recognized under the federal discrimination statutes.

[18] This is intended to effect Professor Summers's suggestion regarding the economic burden of litigating wrongful discharge disputes.

[19] A relatively short statute of limitations is provided.

(ii) The Board shall send notice to the former employer of the employee within five days of the filing of a claim.
(c) Arbitration Fee
(i) Tender of fee. Upon filing a claim, the employee shall tender an amount equivalent to one week's net pay for the employee to the Board. If the employee prevails on his complaint, the arbitrator shall assess the prepaid fee as part of the award in the employee's favor.
(ii) Waiver of Arbitrator's Fee. Upon application by the employee, the Board may waive the prepayment requirement of § 6(c)(i) for good cause. The Board shall waive the prepayment requirement when prepayment would result in substantial hardship. If the prepayment requirement is waived, the Board shall compensate the arbitrator from public funds in the event that an award is made in the employer's favor.

Section 7. Scope of Review of Employer's Action

(a) Preliminary findings. Upon receipt of a wrongful discharge claim notice, the Board shall make a preliminary review of the complaint.[20]
(i) The Board shall select an arbitrator pursuant to § 12 to hear the claim if it finds that the claim alleges that the discharge was in violation of the standards set forth in § 5 of this Act; or
(ii) The Board shall enter an award finding for the employer if it finds the claim does not allege a violation of § 5 of this Act. The Board shall notify both parties within five working days of its finding;
(iii) In making findings under this subsection, the Board shall not consider evidence other than the claim filed under § 6(a). No hearing shall be held, and the employee shall not have the right to appear or to present evidence or argument beyond the original claim;
(iv) The Board may issue regulations permitting claims to be dismissed without prejudice to their resubmission in appropriate circumstances.
(b) Finding by Arbitrator
(i) The arbitrator shall determine whether the termination procedures were fair termination procedures, as defined in § 2(h) of this Act. If fair termination procedures were followed, the arbitrator shall not hear evidence on the facts decided in the fair termination procedures, but shall confine his findings to whether the discharge was made in good faith, not involving a violation of § 5 of this Act.[21]
(ii) If the arbitrator determines that the employer did not afford the employee fair termination procedures as defined in § 2(h), the arbitrator shall proceed to hear evidence on the actual cause for the discharge and the employer's justification

---

[20] The Board makes a threshold determination to avoid appointment of an arbitrator when there are no legally material facts to try.

[21] This paragraph is intended to protect the integrity of internal employer procedures meeting the requisites of procedural fairness. Unless the employee can establish lack of substantive fairness, de novo trial by the arbitrator is precluded.

for using such cause as grounds for discharge. The burden of persuading the arbitrator shall be on the employee;[22]

(iii) If the arbitrator determines that a wrongful discharge occurred, he shall enter an award in the employee's favor.

Section 8. Procedure Before Arbitrator

(a) Time of Hearing. After being appointed, the arbitrator shall arrange a time and place, reasonably convenient for the parties, to hear the claim. The arbitrator shall notify the parties of the time and place not less than five working days prior to the hearing.

(b) Conduct of Hearing. The proceedings before the arbitrator shall be informal. The arbitrator may conduct the hearing in whatever manner he or she reasonably believes will permit the full and expeditious presentation of the evidence and arguments of the employer and employee. Formal rules of evidence shall not apply.[23]

(c) Production of Evidence. The arbitrator may issue subpoenas to compel production of evidence. Such subpoenas shall have full force of law and failure to comply shall be considered as contempt. The arbitrator may invoke the aid of a court of general jurisdiction to enforce his subpoenas. Such court is authorized to enforce subpoenas issued under this section through any of its inherent powers.[24]

(d) Award. Within 15 working days of the close of the hearing, the arbitrator shall make an award and shall notify the parties of the award. The arbitrator shall support the award with written findings and shall send a copy of the findings to each party with the notice of award.

Section 9. Remedies

(a) If the arbitrator determines that a discharge is wrongful, the arbitrator may order reinstatement and may award the employee lost earnings, as he deems fair.[25] Costs and attorneys' fees shall be awarded to the prevailing party.

(b) If the arbitrator determines that a discharge is not wrongful, the arbitrator may award the employer costs and attorneys' fees.[26]

---

[22] Imposing the burden of proof on the employee differs from the collectively bargained arbitration practice, but it conforms with the majority rule in tort, contract, and statutory discrimination suits. See § **9.31**.

[23] The procedure to be followed by the arbitrator is intended to be flexible. This language is borrowed from the rules of the American Arbitration Association for labor arbitration.

[24] This will extend subpoena power to the arbitrator in the absence of the Uniform Arbitration Act.

[25] These remedies are more extensive than those provided for in the draft Pennsylvania, New York or Michigan statutes, but they give the employee part of what he could obtain in a common law contract or tort action.

[26] This is intended to reduce the incidence of frivolous claims, and to make the bill more acceptable to employers.

(c) Award of punitive damages is specifically prohibited.[27]

(d) *Lost earnings,* for purposes of this section, means all wages lost by reason of the discharge up to the date at which the employee obtains or is likely to obtain employment at the same wage rate lost by the discharge. An award may be reduced if the arbitrator finds the employee has not used reasonable effort to find similar employment at the same or a higher wage rate.[28]

Section 10. Enforcement of Board Awards

(a) Awards of arbitrators under this Act shall be deemed to be awards of the Board and be final and binding except to the extent they are reviewable under this section.

(b) An award of an arbitrator shall be mailed to all parties appearing in the case and filed in the Board's offices within 15 days after the arbitrator's decision.

(c) Any party may file an arbitration award filed under § 10(b) of this Act in the clerk's office of the _____ court with jurisdiction over the employer.

(d) An award filed as provided for in §§ 10(b) and (c) shall be conclusive as to the merits and facts of the controversy submitted to the Board, unless, within 10 days after the filing of the award, a petition to impeach the award, on grounds specified in this section, is filed in the clerk's office of the court in which the award has been filed. Unless a petition to impeach is filed, the court shall enter judgment on the award, which judgment shall be final and conclusive on the parties.[29]

(e) A petition for impeachment of any award shall be entertained by the court only on one or more of the following grounds:[30]

(i) The award does not conform or confine itself to the remedies available under § 9 of this act; or

(ii) The proceedings were not in substantial conformity with this Act; or

(iii) The Board or arbitrator was guilty of fraud, collusion, or corruption; or

(iv) A party to the proceedings under this Act practiced fraud or corruption which affected the result of the proceedings.

(f)(i) If the court determines that part or all of the award is invalid under § 10(e), the award shall be invalid only to that extent, and the remaining valid severable portions of the award shall be final and conclusive on the parties.

(ii) The part of the determination declared invalid under § 10(f)(i) shall be remanded to the Board for new proceedings.

---

[27] This is intended to make the bill more acceptable to employers. Moreover, it comports with the usual rule prohibiting punitive damages in contract actions.

[28] See **§ 4.28**, regarding front pay.

[29] This procedure is intended to provide an enforcement mechanism for a money award, and to satisfy any constitutional requirement for access to the courts.

[30] This is intended to prevent relitigation of controversies on the merits.

APPENDIX C

(g) Any employer or employee willfully disobeying an award properly filed under § 10(d) may be held in contempt. The punishment for each day of contempt shall be 25 percent of the total monetary award, including fees and expenses.[31]

Section 11. Claim and Issue Preclusion

(a) If any claim respecting discharge is brought under this statute, that claim and any other claim respecting that discharge which is brought, or could have been brought pursuant to this statute may not be asserted in any forum except as provided in § 10.[32]

(b) If a claim or claims arising from a single discharge is brought pursuant to any state or federal statute other than this statute, no claim respecting that termination may be asserted under this statute.[33]

(c) If a claim arising from a single termination has been brought or could be brought under an arbitration agreement, no claim respecting that termination may be asserted under this statute.

Section 12. Appointment of Arbitrators

(a) The employer and the discharged employee may select as arbitrator any person who is acceptable to both parties, and notify the Board of the selection. Upon receiving such notification, the Board shall appoint such person.[34]

(b) If the parties are unable to agree on an arbitrator under § 12(a):

(i) The Board shall select five available arbitrators from a list that the Board maintains of available impartial, competent, and reputable arbitrators who are not employees of this state;

(ii) Within five days of receipt of the names of the nominees, the employer and employee peremptorily may strike two of the nominees and rank the remainder of the nominees;

(iii) Within seven days after the five-day period, the Board shall appoint as arbitrator the nominee with the lowest combined rank;

(iv) If the appointed arbitrator is unable to serve, the next lowest combined rank nominee shall be appointed;

(v) If either party fails to return the list properly ranked within five days, the selection shall be based on the ranking of the returned, properly ranked list;

---

[31] This is necessary to permit enforcement of awards for other than monetary sums. Monetary awards would be enforced like any other judgment.

[32] This is consistent with the basic concept of forcing all wrongful discharge litigation into a single forum. It is intended to prevent an employee from "splitting his claim," and subsequently litigating part of a claim covered by this statute in another forum.

[33] This requires an employee to elect his forum. The forum established by this statute is not available unless the employee litigates all of the claims related to a particular dismissal in this forum. This is consistent with the basic concept of forcing all wrongful discharge litigation into a single forum.

[34] This language is borrowed from the draft Michigan statute. It permits the parties to select their own arbitrator. The Michigan bill would permit the board to appoint another arbitrator should the selected arbitrator be unable to serve.

(vi) If neither party returns the list properly ranked within five days of receipt, then the Board shall appoint an arbitrator from the list of nominees;
(vii) The arbitrator's fee shall be set by the Board according to a schedule of general applicability.

Section 13. Posting a Copy of Act

(a) The employer shall post a copy of this Act together with the following notice in a conspicuous place.
(b) The notice is as follows:
"As an employee, you may have certain legal rights should you believe you have been discharged for reasons unrelated to your job performance. Contact the Board of Labor Arbitration for further information."

APPENDIX C

Draft Federal Statute

AN ACT[35] To govern the practices of employers in discharge of employees, to provide for the review of complaints of wrongful discharge, and other purposes.

Be it enacted by the Senate and the House of Representatives of the United States of America in Congress assembled:

Section 1. Short Title

This Act may be cited as "The Wrongful Dismissal Act of 1987."

Section 2. Definitions

The following words and phrases shall have the following meanings when used in this Act, unless the context clearly indicates otherwise.

(a) "Commission": The Equal Employment Opportunity Commission established by 78 Stat. 253 (1964), Pub. L. No. 88-352, 42 U.S.C. § 2000e-4.

(b) "Costs": Includes the arbitrator's fee as established in § 4(c)(ii).[36]

(c) "Determining factor": A factor in the absence of which a discharge would not have occurred.

(d) "Discharge": Any termination of employment effected by an employer, including a resignation induced by unreasonable employer conduct.[37]

(e) "Employee": Any natural person in the employment of the same employer for at least 15 hours per week over a six-month period prior to discharge[38] and not covered by a collective bargaining agreement[39] or written contract of employment of two or more years in duration,[40] including a person who has been dismissed in violation of § 5 of this Act.[41]

(f) "Employer": Any person who employs more than 10 employees.

---

[35] The section numbers of the federal statute are the same as the corresponding section numbers of the state statute.

[36] This definition is intended to work in conjunction with § 9 to impose the costs of arbitration, including the arbitrator's fee, on the losing party. It is preferable not to provide for a free adjudication of claims to reduce the incidence of frivolous claims.

[37] This definition is intended to permit allegedly improper layoffs to be challenged, and to include *constructive discharge* within the ambit of the Act.

[38] This part of the definition is intended to provide for a probationary period during which employees could be dismissed for any reason. See Mennemeier, *Protection from Unjust Discharges: An Arbitration Scheme,* 19 Harv. J. on Legis. 49, 81–82 (1982).

[39] This part of the definition is intended to exclude employees covered by collective agreements, so as to prevent interference with union organization or the functioning of collective bargaining.

[40] This part of the definition is intended to exclude executives and other employees who have sufficient bargaining power to negotiate traditional contracts of employment.

[41] This part of the definition is intended to foreclose any argument that an employee, once dismissed, lacks standing to bring a claim under the statute.

(g) "Employment": The performance of duties defined by an employer, under the supervision of the employer,[42] but which does not include the performance of duties pursuant to a collective bargaining agreement.

(h) "Fair termination procedure": Any procedure actually followed by an employer prior to discharge of an employee that includes notice to the employee, provision of an impartial decisionmaker,[43] and an opportunity for the employee to present argument, but excluding procedures required under a collective bargaining agreement.[44]

(i) "Person": One or more individuals, labor organizations, partnerships, associations, corporations, legal representatives, trustees, trustees in bankruptcy or receivers.

(j) "Service": The Labor Arbitration Service.

(k) "Termination procedures": Any actions taken by an employer prior to the discharge of an employee in connection with the discharge.

Section 3. Policy

The Congress finds that employers are now able to dismiss employees on grounds which conflict with public policies and with laws barring discriminatory practices, and which interfere with interstate commerce. Congress finds it necessary to regulate the discharge practices of employers and to create a uniform method of dealing with complaints of wrongful discharge. Congress finds it inappropriate to prohibit discharges in the private sector except for *cause*.

Section 4. Jurisdiction and Administrative Provisions

(a) Labor Arbitration Service. There is created within the Commission a Labor Arbitration Service.

(b) Jurisdiction. The Service has original and exclusive jurisdiction over any case of wrongful discharge as defined in § 5 of this Act.[45]

(c) Powers and Duties of the Commission. The Commission shall have the power and duty to:

(i) Exercise general supervision of and make regulations for the governance of the Service;

(ii) Prescribe uniform rules pertaining to selection of arbitrators, the fees for arbitrators, the filing of arbitration reports, and the filing of requests for arbitration;

(iii) Supervise the fiscal affairs of the Service;

---

[42] This is intended to exclude termination of independent contractor relations.

[43] *Impartial decisionmaker* is intended to include a senior official of the employer not directly involved in the dismissal decision, to protect the integrity of adequate internal employer procedures.

[44] These are the minimum elements of procedural fairness discussed in §§ **9.2, 9.25,** and **9.27**.

[45] It should be constitutional to require that wrongful discharge claims proceed to arbitration. See Crowell v. Benson, 285 U.S. 22 (1932) (Constitution permits nonjudicial factfinding, subject to judicial review); Atlas Roofing Co. v. O.S.H.R.C., 430 U.S. 442 (1977) (administrative adjudication permitted with respect to rights and duties created by statute).

(iv) Prescribe the qualifications of, appoint, remove, and fix the compensation of Service employees;
(v) Organize and administer the service so as to comply with the requirements of this Act;
(vi) Keep an accurate and complete record of all proceedings under this Act;
(vii) Make recommendations and an annual report to the Congress;
(viii) Exercise any other power necessary to standardize administration, expedite Service business, assure the establishment of fair rules and promote the efficiency of the Service.
(d) The Service shall consist of the Director, arbitrators, and such staff as the Commission deems necessary for the functioning of the Service.

Section 5. Standards of Employer Conduct

(a) A discharge of an employee shall be wrongful if one or more of the following was a determining factor in the discharge:
(i) The employee's age, sex, race, religion, national origin, handicap, marital status, or sexual orientation;[46]
(ii) The employee's exercise of rights of political expression, religious activities, association, or privacy guaranteed under the United States or any State Constitution against governmental interference;[47]
(iii) The employee's performance of an act or refusal to perform an act, the performance or refusal being in furtherance of public policy, as expressed in statutes, administrative regulations, formal statements of professional ethics applicable to the employee, or well-settled common law principles;[48]
(iv) Off-duty conduct of the employee, if the conduct is not reasonably related to the employee's work performance.[49]
(b) A discharge of an employee shall be wrongful if the discharge occurred in violation of an employer's express or implied promise that the employer would continue employment for a particular period of time, would dismiss the employee only for cause or only for certain reasons or only after following certain procedures, including a fair termination procedure or termination procedure.[50] Enforcement of this subsection shall not depend on the employee having given anything in return for the employer's promise.
(c) A discharge of an employee shall not be wrongful under § 5(a)(i) when the employee was dismissed for failure to meed a bona fide occupational

---

[46] This is intended to encompass claims arising under the federal (or comparable state) employment discrimination statutes.

[47] This is intended to protect employees' federal constitutional rights against interference by private employers.

[48] This is intended to encompass the public policy tort discussed in **Ch. 5**.

[49] This is intended to encompass the right of privacy, possibly cognizable under the tort concepts discussed in **§ 5.27**.

[50] This is intended to encompass the implied contract cause of action discussed in **Ch. 4**.

qualification reasonably necessary to the proper performance of the duties of the position.[51]

Section 6. Claim Procedures

(a) A claim for wrongful discharge is commenced by filing a notice with the Service and paying an arbitration fee in accordance with § 6(c).[52]

(b) Time Limitations

(i) No claim for wrongful discharge may be filed under this section by any employee unless the claim is filed within six months of the discharge;[53]

(ii) The Service shall send notice to the former employer of the employee within five days of the filing of a claim.

(c) Arbitration Fee

(i) Tender of fee. Upon filing a claim, the employee shall tender to the Service an amount equivalent to one week's net pay for the employee. If the employee prevails on his claim, the arbitrator shall assess the prepaid fee as part of the award in the employee's favor.

(ii) Waiver of Arbitrator's Fee. Upon application by the employee the Service may waive the prepayment requirement of 6(c)(i) for good cause. The Service shall waive the prepayment requirement when prepayment would result in substantial hardship. If the prepayment requirement is waived, the Service shall compensate the arbitrator from public funds in the event that an award is made in the employer's favor.

Section 7. Scope of Review of Employer's Action

(a) Preliminary Findings. Upon receipt of a wrongful discharge claim, the Service shall make a preliminary review of the claim.[54]

(i) The Service shall select an arbitrator pursuant to § 12 to hear the claim if it finds that the claim alleges that the discharge was in violation of the standards set forth in § 5 of this Act;

(ii) The Service shall enter an award finding for the employer if it finds the claim does not allege a violation of § 5 of this Act. The Service shall notify both parties within five working days of its finding;

(iii) In making findings under this subsection, the Service shall not consider evidence other than the claim filed under § 6(a). No hearing shall be held, and the employee shall not have the right to appear or to present argument or evidence beyond the original claim;

---

[51] This is intended to preserve the employer's BFOQ defense recognized under the federal discrimination statutes.

[52] This is intended to effect Professor Summers's suggestion regarding the economic burden of litigating wrongful discharge disputes.

[53] A relatively short statute of limitations is provided.

[54] The Service makes a threshold determination to avoid appointment of an arbitrator when there are no legally material facts to try.

(iv) The Service may issue regulations permitting claims to be dismissed without prejudice to their resubmission in appropriate circumstances.
(b) Finding by Arbitrator.
(i) The arbitrator shall determine whether the termination procedures were fair termination procedures, as defined in § 2(h) of this Act. If fair termination procedures were followed, the arbitrator shall not hear evidence on the facts decided in the fair termination procedures, but shall confine his findings to whether the discharge was made in good faith, not involving a violation of § 5 of this Act.[55]
(ii) If the arbitrator determines that the employer did not afford the employee fair termination procedures as defined in § 2(h), the arbitrator shall proceed to hear evidence on the actual cause for the discharge and the employer's justification for using such cause as grounds for discharge. The burden of persuading the arbitrator shall be on the employee;[56]
(iii) If the arbitrator determines that a wrongful discharge occurred, he shall enter an award in the employee's favor.

Section 8. Procedure Before Arbitrator

(a) Time of Hearing. After being appointed, the arbitrator shall arrange a time and place, reasonably convenient for the parties, to hear the claim. The arbitrator shall notify the parties of the time and place not less than five working days prior to the hearing.
(b) Conduct of Hearing. The procedures utilized in the hearing shall be informal. The arbitrator may conduct the hearing in whatever manner he or she reasonably believes will permit the fullest and most expeditious presentation of the evidence and arguments. Formal rules of evidence shall not apply.[57]
(c) Production of Evidence. The arbitrator may issue subpoenas to compel the production of evidence. Such subpoenas shall have the full force of law, and failure to comply shall be considered as contempt. The service may invoke the aid of district courts in enforcing subpoenas, and district courts are authorized to enforce subpoenas issued under this section.[58]
(d) Award. Within 15 working days of the close of the hearing, the arbitrator shall make an award and shall notify the parties of the award. The arbitrator shall support the award with written findings and shall send a copy of the findings to each party with the notice of award.

---

[55] This paragraph is intended to protect the integrity of internal employer procedures meeting the requisites of procedural fairness. Unless the employee can establish lack of substantive fairness, de novo trial by the arbitrator is precluded.

[56] Imposing the burden of proof on the employee differs from the collectively bargained arbitration practice, but it conforms with the majority rule in tort, contract, and statutory discrimination suits. See § **9.31**.

[57] The procedure to be followed by the arbitrator is intended to be flexible. This language is borrowed from the rules of the American Arbitration Association for labor arbitration.

[58] This extends subpoena power to the arbitrator.

Section 9. Remedies

(a) If the arbitrator determines that a discharge is wrongful, the arbitrator may order reinstatement and may award the employee lost earnings as he deems fair.[59] Costs and attorneys' fees shall be awarded to the prevailing party.

(b) If the arbitrator determines that a discharge is not wrongful, the arbitrator may award the employer costs and attorneys' fees.[60]

(c) Award of punitive damages is specifically prohibited.[61]

(d) *Lost earnings,* for purposes of this section, means all wages lost by reason of the discharge up to the date at which the employee obtains employment or is likely to obtain employment at the same wage rate lost by the discharge. An award may be reduced if the arbitrator finds the employee has not used reasonable effort to find similar employment at the same or a higher wage rate.

Section 10. Enforcement of Awards

(a) Binding Nature of Award. Awards of arbitrators under this Act[62] shall be deemed to be awards of the Service and shall be final and binding except to the extent they are reviewable under this section.

(b) Mailing of Award. An award of an Arbitrator shall be mailed to all parties appearing in the case and filed in the Service's offices within 15 days after the arbitrator's decision.

(c) Filing of Award. Any party may file an award in the clerk's office of the district court with jurisdiction over the employer. If, after 10 working days, no petition has been filed to impeach the award, the district court shall enter judgment on the award, and it shall be final and conclusive on the parties.

(d) Impeachment Petition. Within 10 working days of the award, any party may file a petition to impeach the award in the clerk's office of the district court with jurisdiction over the employer.

(e) Granting of Impeachment Petition. The district court shall entertain a petition for impeachment only on one or more of the following grounds:[63]

(i) The award does not conform or confine itself to the remedies available under this Act;

(ii) The proceedings were not in substantial conformity with this Act;

(iii) There was fraud or collusion in the determination of the award;

---

[59] These remedies are more extensive than those provided for in the draft Pennsylvania, New York or Michigan statutes, but they give the employee part of what he could obtain in a common law contract or tort action.

[60] This is intended to reduce the incidence of frivolous claims, and to make the bill more acceptable to employers.

[61] This is intended to make the bill more acceptable to employers. The prohibition also comports with the usual rule barring punitive damages in contract actions.

[62] This procedure is intended to provide an enforcement mechanism for a money award, and to satisfy any constitutional requirement for access to the courts.

[63] This is intended to prevent relitigation of controversies.

APPENDIX C

(iv) A party to the determination practiced fraud or collusion which affected the outcome. Should the court find grounds for impeachment, it shall invalidate only the impeachable portion and shall remand only that portion to the Service for further proceedings.

(f) Noncompliance. Any party willfully disobeying an award properly filed in district court may be held in contempt and fined 25 percent of the total monetary award for each day of noncompliance.[64]

Section 11. Preclusion

(a) In keeping with the public policy of reducing repetitious and unnecessary litigation, any claim arising from a single discharge may be brought once only under this Act or under any one of the following acts:[65]
(i) The Civil Rights Act of 1964, 42 U.S.C. § 2000e;
(ii) The Age Discrimination in Employment Act, 29 U.S.C. §§ 621–634;
(iii) The Rehabilitation Act of 1973, Pub. L. No. 93–112, 82 Stat. 355 (codified as amended in scattered sections of 29 U.S.C.);
(iv) The Reconstruction Civil Rights Acts, 42 U.S.C. §§ 1981, 1985(3);
(v) The Federal Employers' Liability Act, 45 U.S.C. §§ 55, 60;
(vi) The Federal Railroad Safety Act, 45 U.S.C. § 441;
(vii) The Clean Air Act, 42 U.S.C. § 7622(a);
(viii) The Fair Labor Standards Act, 29 U.S.C. § 215(a)(3);
(ix) The Consumer Credit Protection Act, 15 U.S.C. § 1674;
(x) The Clean Water Act, 33 U.S.C. § 1367;
(xi) The Resource Conservation and Recovery Act, 42 U.S.C. § 6971;
(xii) The Toxic Substances Control Act, 15 U.S.C. § 2622;
(xiii) The Energy Reorganization Act of 1974, 42 U.S.C. § 5851;
(xiv) The Employee Retirement Income Security Act, 29 U.S.C. § 1140 (1982);
(xv) Any other Act which provides for the protection of employees against discriminatory employment practices.
(b) No court of the United States or of any state shall entertain any action for wrongful discharge unless such suit is brought under this Act or under any of the acts listed in § 11(a)(i)–(xv).
(c) If any claim respecting a single instance of discharge is brought under any of the statutes identified in § 11(a), then neither that claim nor any other claim respecting that discharge may be brought under this Act or any other act.[66]

---

[64] This is necessary to permit enforcement of awards for other than monetary sums. Monetary awards would be enforced like any other judgment.

[65] This is consistent with the basic concept of forcing all wrongful discharge litigation into a single forum. It is intended to prevent an employee from "splitting his claim," and subsequently litigating part of a claim covered by this statute in another forum.

[66] This requires an employee to elect his remedy. The remedies established by this statute are not available unless the employee litigates all of the claims related to a particular dismissal in this forum. This is consistent with the basic concept of forcing all wrongful discharge litigation into a single forum.

(d) If a claim arising from a single termination has been brought or could be brought under an arbitration agreement, no claim respecting that termination may be asserted under this Act.

Section 12. Appointment of Arbitrators

(a) The employer and the discharged employee may select as arbitrator any person who is acceptable to both parties, and notify the Service of the selection. Upon being notified, the Service shall appoint the person so selected.
(b) If the parties are unable to agree on an arbitrator under § 12(a):
(i) Then the Service shall select five available arbitrators from a list that the Service maintains of available impartial, competent, and reputable arbitrators who are not employees of the federal government;
(ii) Within five days of receipt of the names of the nominees, the employer and employee peremptorily may strike two of the nominees and rank the remainder of the nominees;
(iii) Within seven days after the five-day period, the Service shall appoint as arbitrator the nominee with the lowest combined rank;
(iv) If the appointed arbitrator is unable to serve, the next lowest combined rank nominee shall be appointed;
(v) If either party fails to return the list properly ranked within five days, the selection shall be based on the ranking of the returned, properly ranked list;
(vi) If neither party returns the list properly ranked within five days of receipt, then the Service shall appoint an arbitrator from the list of nominees

Section 13. Exceptions, Provisos and Saving Clauses

(a) Administrative Procedure Act. The provisions of the Administrative Procedure Act, 5 U.S.C. § 551 *et seq.*, are not applicable to actions taken by arbitrators appointed by the service.
(b) Severability. Should § 10 of this Act be held invalid by a court of competent jurisdiction, the remaining sections shall not be affected.

APPENDIX D

IN-HOUSE COUNSEL CHECKLIST FOR WRONGFUL DISMISSAL LITIGATION[1]

1. Reviewing Complaint
   a. Is service good or defective?
   b. Determine who the defendants are: parent company, subsidiaries, individuals, etc.
   c. Determine causes of actions, including any novel theories
   d. Forum and preemption issues
      (i) Is removal available?
      — If not now, maybe later
      (ii) If removal is available, is it desirable?
      — Evaluation of courts, judges, appeal potential
   e. Related actions
2. Applying of Employee Defense Policy
   a. Pennsylvania business corporation law requires a determination of whether company will defend individually sued employee/defendants
   b. Evaluate conflicts and stress for employee/defendants
      — Does individual defendant fear the company will make him a *sacrificial lamb*?
      — Is there corporate and departmental political pressure?
      — Evaluate the great need for personal reassurance by the attorney
3. Evaluating the Complaint from a Corporate Policy Standpoint
   a. Identify who is entitled to evaluate policy implications: divisions, subsidiaries, departments, etc.

---

[1] Developed by Dennis Alan Arouca, Partner, Pepper, Hamilton & Sheetz; formerly General Counsel, Labor and Employment, Consolidated Rail Corporation. Reprinted with permission.

b. Identify policy issues
      - Effect on collective bargaining or other labor relations issues
      - Community impact and publicity
      - Systemic personnel policies implications
      - Trade association implications and resources
   c. Evaluate appropriateness of forum: is the case suitable for alternative dispute resolution because of, for example, need for speed or confidentiality?
   d. Manage or develop corporate response to policy issues raised in (b) and (c)
4. Determining Who Should Handle the Case
   a. Law department philosophy influences the viewpoint from which the determinations described below are made
      - Managing outside counsel vs. direct handling by in-house counsel
      - Quality control on management
   b. Review allegations against management/supervisors
      i. Allegations of impropriety/unlawful behavior
         Investigation may reveal matters that
         - Need corporate attention beyond immediate concerns of litigation
         - Need ad hoc determination of whether to attack pattern or systemic action until the lawsuit is over
         - Might hurt chances in litigation
      ii. Actions beyond scope of position/duties
   c. Evaluation of in-house capacity
      - Policy
      - Workload
      - Experience; jury and nonjury
      - Sophistication of issues
      - Efficiency (travel)
      - Relationships with courts, agencies, arbitrators
      - Training
      - Budgets
      - Confidentiality
      - Politics
   d. Evaluation of outside counsel
      - Policy
      - Experience (jury and nonjury) and sophistication of issues

- Track record
- Location
- Relationships with courts, agencies, arbitrators
- Efficiency
- Ability to work with in-house counsel
- Confidentiality
- Politics

5. Assigning the Case to Outside Counsel
    a. Important that initial communications be clear and complete
    b. Establish a team relationship between in-house and outside attorneys, if possible
    c. Explicit decision on who is *first chair*, and who controls communications to the client
        - Short and longterm implications for you, your in-house colleagues, interested departments, company clients
    d. Framework and method for supervising work
6. Assigning the Case to In-house Counsel
    a. Make sure resources are available; clerical support, legal research—investigatory and pretrial—and time
    b. Training considerations
        - Relationship to outside counsel
        - Perception by peers and superiors
    c. Framework and method for supervising work
    d. Corporate communications
7. Investigating the Complaint
    a. Identifying people and records
        - In-house counsel usually are better positioned to do this
    b. Establishing document repository and retrieval
    c. Deploy resources effectively
        - Attorney vs. paralegal vs. other type of company employee
        - Attorney supervision of nonlawyers, to ensure privilege
    d. Interview witnesses
        - Names/positions
        - Decisionmakers
        - Employee's supervisors, both immediate and up the chain of command
        - Coworkers—have they been approached by plaintiff or counsel?
        - Asked for statements

- Advantages/disadvantages of in-house counsel doing the interviewing
- Will you need to work with these people on corporate policy matters, and if so, in what capacity?
- Will interview promote or retard that relationship?

    e. Obtain documents
- Named in complaint
- Labor contract/employee handbooks/guidebooks
- Personnel files/other files on employee (Labor Relations, EEO, and so forth)/employee performance appraisals.

    f. Inside counsel usually knows better what is available, and where
- Very rarely is there only one file. Be conscious of continuing discovery obligation

    g. Need to develop
- Plaintiff's employment history/record
- Employment records of significant actors
- Supervisors and comparably positioned co-workers
- Plaintiff's postdischarge employment record, especially as to earnings

    h. Give the client something to do; create teamwork and commitment

8. Preparing Witnesses

    a. Early identification and contact
- Witnesses can "disappear," especially former employees[2]
- Experts
- Get to key ones before the plaintiff

    b. Coworkers
- Their status can work for and against you
- Coworker-witnesses may perceive threats to their status, tell you a favorable story but break down at trial

    c. Witness meetings
- Separate meetings, with different agenda, for discovery; factfinding; deposition preparation; trial preparation
- Use written, audio, and visual aids, and mock deposition or trials, to educate them on their role
- Be conscious of group dynamics
- A strong personality can help bring reluctant witnesses into line or place others in doubt

---

[2] Consider where former employees come within attorney-client relationship. Also, production of former employees by Company and underwriting costs thereof can be a source of leverage in negotiations.

9. Settlement
   a. Evaluating the case for settlement
      i. Begin evaluating as soon as the complaint is served, if not sooner. Encourage the client to think the same way
      ii. Take care to distinguish case-handling activities on the basis of pretrial or settlement activities
         — Evidentiary impact
      iii. Settlement considerations
         — Merits of action
         — Jury vs. nonjury trial
      iv. Exposure: Settlement should be considered even if you have a strong position on the merits, because you can't ever be sure of what will happen at trial. Decision risk analysis, which can't be done by the lawyer alone, requires close client participation
      v. Policy, personnel and labor relations ramifications
         — Beware of the disruptive effect of personalities on an organization
         — There often can be company and industry ramifications
      vi. Publicity and company image
         — Outside the company
         — Inside the company, especially other employees' perceptions
         — Effect of unhappy employee "badmouthing" the company, or sharing trade secrets
         — Nature of the case
         — Will this be an industry or area test case, or just one of routine, recurring discipline? More precedent associated with the former, but perhaps more signals sent to coworkers on company policy and position with the latter
         — Effect on future litigation
         — Fairness to or equity for the plaintiff employee
         — Balance company errors vs. quality/type of employee
         — Company does have a conscience
         — Other litigation with same employee
      (vii) Consider use of neutral sounding board, within or without the company, to test your perceptions of fairness or equity and chances for success at trial
      (viii) Consider again alternative dispute resolution. Facts of case, or status of litigants may make private proceedings desirable and therefore a source of leverage.

b. Methods to promote settlement
   i. Discussions with opposing counsel
   ii. Letters demanding withdrawal
      – Sanctions can attach to frivolous cases or those brought in bad faith
      – Costs, attorneys' fees
      – Don't overlook establishing deadlines and declining monetary amounts. The latter can be effective if opposing counsel is sophisticated and realistic, and your initial offer is not frivolous
   iii. Rule 68 offers of judgment
   iv. Offers to counsel vs. offers to plaintiff[3]
   v. Court assistance
      – Judge-supervised settlement conferences: local counsel often is invaluable here
      – File dispositive motions: the effect of this tactic depends on who has the better side of the merits, the judge, and skill/realism of opposing counsel
c. Keys to Settlement
   i. Try to centralize communication in one defense counsel. There is a great tendency in labor relations and personnel matters for multiple channels of communication to open up, which can lead to "forum shopping" and affect your leverage
   ii. Forge a consensus among different corporate actors, otherwise implementing the settlement may be frustrated and your reputation damaged, especially with the court
   iii. Settlement documents
      A. Settlement agreement
         – Nonadmission clause
         – Termination of employment rights
         – Confidentiality and *no publicity* clauses
         – Don't forget about plaintiff's attorney
         – Personnel files and job references.

         These are important settlement tools, because they cost the company very little but are very important to the plaintiff.
      B. Release and waiver
         – Knowing and voluntary declaration

---

[3] Be sure you understand applicable prohibitions in the Code of Professional Responsibility against contacting person represented by counsel.

- Duress, coercion could vitiate settlement
C. Court involvement
- Consent decrees
- Stipulated, or ordered dismissals
10. Implementing Settlements and Trial Determinations
  a. Need for clear, express company communication. Assumptions can lead to unintended personnel consequences
  b. Anticipate, and deal with, effect on company departments, supervisors, and co-workers
  c. Implement remedial action, if any
  d. Settlement is still an option after an adverse trial decision
      - Beware of any angry, victorious employee returning to a hostile environment
      - Advantages to both parties for cash settlement and clean personnel records
  e. Professional responsibilities—beware of characterizations that could damage the reputation of the court and the law

APPENDIX E
CRITICISM OF THE LAWS OF DAMAGE IN DISMISSAL CASES[1]

The law of damages is not fair to most victims of wrongful discharge. The occasional, gigantic, highly publicized six to seven figure verdicts are misleading.

In most litigated cases, plaintiffs receive only modest sums by suit or settlement. First of all, many wrongfully dismissed employees cannot afford to hire a lawyer. The potential damages are usually too small to warrant a lawyer taking the case on a contingency fee basis. The employee cannot afford to pay a substantial retainer or an hourly rate. In common law cases, there are no court awarded fees for the winner. Without an incentive to attract a lawyer, the employee has no remedy in court.

Theoretically, the law of damages does remedy any loss of income to date of trial. The right to back pay is undisputed. But other important damages—emotional distress, loss of front pay, and loss of future pension benefits—are difficult and sometimes impossible to collect.

Under Title VII, the NLRA, the ADEA, and most federal anti-discrimination acts, damages for loss of self-esteem, mental anguish, humiliation, harm to reputation, and emotional distress are non-recoverable. Similarly, labor arbitrators do not award damages for pain and suffering. Employees claiming a breach of contract—be it a fixed term, implied-in-fact, verbal or express, or a contract based on an employee handbook, policy manual, custom or practice—cannot generally recover for their emotional distress. Yet the emotional wounds run deep, endure, and cry out for relief.

In other fields of law, the courts have no trouble in awarding damages extending beyond the date of trial, such as lost profits. However, judges have been particularly cautious before permitting employees to receive prospective loss of earnings damages and front pay. In breach of contract and discrimination cases, courts often hold that awards for time periods extending for more than three to four years after trial are too speculative. Loss of pension benefits can be a devastating blow for an employee. The courts will permit damages for ascertainable pension losses

---

[1] Paul H. Tobias, Esq., 911 Mercantile Library Bldg., 414 Walnut Street, Cincinnati, Ohio 45202; (513) 241-8137.

up to the date of trial but, again, may be reluctant to permit juries to speculate upon the present value of pension benefits payable at expected date of retirement.

The duty to mitigate doctrine punishes those who are most diligent and aggressive in their post discharge job search. Those who have intelligence, emotional strength, initiative, a network of friends, and marketable skills usually obtain an equivalent job quickly. They, of course, will then be deemed to have little or no lost earnings. Those who are lazy or have less initiative often will be unable to find a job or obtain work of any kind. They will have the largest back pay claims.

Many defendants seek to minimize damages by making offers of reinstatement to positions which are somewhat comparable, though less attractive, than the prior job. Most employees are too psychologically upset by the dismissal trauma to go back into a work environment they view as hostile. Yet the law of damages requires the plaintiff to accept the job or risk losing all right to any damages from the date of the offer.[2] If the wrongful discharge has caused the employee to be fearful and emotionally upset about returning to a hostile workplace, he should not be required to accept an offer of reinstatement or to request reinstatement as a condition precedent to obtaining front pay.

The result is that an employee in his late thirties with ten to fifteen years service, who has been the victim of a cruel, outrageous discharge, may have no remedy at all. His ego and self-esteem may be shattered. The dismissal is a blow to his reputation, his long range career plans, and the amount of his pension at age 70. If he gets a job equivalent to his former job within a few months, he probably will have such modest damages that no lawyer will take his case, even if liability is clear.

Hopefully, the courts will be more willing to award emotional distress damages in breach of contract cases. The possibility of damages are foreseeable and within the contemplation of the parties and, therefore, should be recoverable under traditional contract law.[3] In addition, an employment contract should be viewed as personal as well as commercial, thus permitting emotional distress damages.[4]

The tort-contract dichotomy which permits the award of punitive damages in tort cases but generally not in contract cases often makes no sense.[5] The better

---

[2] Ford Motor Co. v. EEOC, 458 U.S. 219 (1982) (unconditional offer tolls running of back pay).

[3] For breach of employment contract cases in which emotional damages have been allowed, see Westesen v. Olathe State Bank, 78 Colo. 217, 240 P. 689 (1925); Burrus v. Nevada–Cal.–Ore. R. R. Co., 38 Nev. 156, 145 P. 926 (1915) (delay in running a special train to transport son for medical treatment); Lewis v. Holmes, 109 La. 1030, 34 So. 66 (1903) (bride's wedding clothing). The Restatement permits recovery for emotional disturbance when the breach was of a type particularly likely to produce serious emotional disturbance. Restatement (Second) of Contracts § 353 (1981). Some courts have allowed damages for mental suffering connected with breaches of special types of contractual relationships. *See* J.Murray, Murray on Contracts § 232 at 471–72 (1974).

[4] Lamm v. Shingleton, 231 N.C. 10, 55 S.E.2d 810 (1949) (leaking casket; foreseeable mental distress damages recoverable); *cf.* Valentine v. General American Credit, Inc., 420 Mich. 256, 362 N.W.2d 628 (1984).

[5] Victims of racial discrimination and constitutional torts can recover punitive damages under 42 U.S.C. §§ 1981 and 1983. *See* §§ **2.8, 6.19**.

rule is that an employee who has been discharged out of malice or in deliberate violation of his rights should be awarded punitive damages.[6]

The California rule, which recognizes the duty of good faith and fair dealing and awards punitive damages, is realistic by providing a deterrent against the wrongdoer and restitution for the victim.[7] More jurisdictions should adopt the rule.

There are a few cases holding that the duty of mitigation does not apply where there is a malicious discharge.[8] Hopefully other courts will soon adopt such an approach. The constructive service doctrine utilized in some jurisdictions also eliminates the need of mitigation for the unfinished term of a fixed term contract and could also be the basis for future erosion of the mitigation rule.[9]

Some wrongfully discharged employees would prefer a substantial lump sum-severance pay type award, based in part on income and years of service, obtainable without a lawyer and without regard to mitigation or offset rules. Legislation establishing an administrative small claims court for some employees would be helpful. Obviously such a system would not provide a deterrent or an adequate remedy in egregious cases.

The law of employment damages is a hodgepodge of conflicting rules and statutes. The lack of uniformity of the rules is unfortunate but perhaps an inevitable byproduct of our complicated legal system. It is unlikely Congress will ever devise one system of damages for all victims. However our courts can continue to strive for improvement in rules, designed in the nineteenth century, which often make no sense as we near the twenty-first century.

---

[6] There are a few contract cases which permit punitive damages when the defendant acts maliciously. *See* Mobile & O.R.R. Co. v. Moreland, 104 Miss. 312, 61 So. 424 (1913) (failure of train to stop at station to permit visit to sick daughter); Scheps v. Giles, 222 S.W. 348 (Tex. Civ. App. 1920); Smith v. Fleischman, 214 S.C. 263, 52 S.E.2d 199 (1949) (fraudulent act accompanying breach); Restatement (Second) of Contracts § 355, illustration 2 (1981); J. Murray, Murray on Contracts § 231 at 471 (1974).

[7] Rulon-Miller v. IBM, 162 Cal. App. 3d 241, 208 Cal. Rptr. 524 (1984).

[8] A few courts have awarded victims of a malicious breach of contract punitive damages in exceptional cases. *See* Mason County Bd. of Educ. v. Superintendent of Schools, 295 S.E.2d 719 (W. Va. 1982); Steranko v. Inforex, Inc., 5 Mass. App. Ct. 523, 362 N.E.2d 222 (1977), *appeal after remand,* 8 Mass. App. Ct. 523, 395 N.E.2d 1303 (1979); Turner v. Winn Dixie La., Inc., 474 So. 2d 966 (La. Ct. App. 1985).

[9] Ware v. Woodward Iron Co., 271 Ala. 462, 124 So. 2d 84 (1960); Dixie Glass Co. v. Pollak, 341 S.W.2d 530 (Tex. Civ. App. 1960).

APPENDIX F

IMPLIED-IN-FACT CONTRACT THEORY AND THE EMPLOYMENT RELATION

David F. Girard-diCarlo*
Peter S. Pantaleo*

THE EXPANSION OF EMPLOYER LIABILITY BEYOND THE "JUST CAUSE" STANDARD

I. Introduction

Earlier portions of this treatise explain the three basic exceptions to the Employment-at-Will Rule: the public policy tort,[1] the implied-in-fact contract,[2] and the implied covenant of good faith and fair dealing.[3]

In addition to relying on the implied-in-fact contract theory to challenge terminations, employees have asserted contractual rights concerning benefits, promotions, and working conditions. This appendix discusses the various contexts in which employees have attempted to equate employer statements, promises, and actions regarding benefits, promotions, and working conditions with contractual obligations. In analyzing relevant case law, the discussion offers employers guidance in preventing or successfully defending this additional category of implied-in-fact contract lawsuits.

II. Development of the Implied-in-Fact Contract Theory in the Employment Arena

Most employee lawsuits claiming implied-in-fact contracts involve terminated employees asserting promises of continued employment.[4] Successful claims have

---

* Partner, Blank, Rome, Comisky & McCauley, Philadelphia, Pennsylvania. The authors gratefully acknowledge the assistance of Paul A. Tufano and Caren Litvin Sacks, associates, Blank, Rome, Comisky & McCauley.

[1] See §§ 5.8–5.20.
[2] See ch. 4.
[3] See §§ 4.11, 4.23.
[4] See ch. 4.

been established where a defendant-employer promises, either orally or through statements in an employee handbook, that employees will be terminated only for just cause or after utlization of specific procedures.[5]

III. Employee Claims of Contractual Rights to Benefits, Promotions, and Working Conditions

A. Pre-Employment Promises

The cases in which plaintiff-employees have challenged employers' breaches of pre-employment promises have centered on promises of new or improved positions.[6] The implied-in-fact contract theory may provide a successful strategy for employees seeking large damage awards from employers. In July of 1986, a federal jury awarded a former executive of Exxon $10 million in damages for Exxon's failure to compensate and promote as promised.[7] The plaintiff, Ian J. Dowie, left his position as a marketing executive with IBM to accept a position as vice president of Exxon's Office Products Division.[8] Dowie was promised the opportunity to run the Division in return for over $1 million in salary, bonuses, and stock options.[9] Exxon subsequently passed over Dowie for the top position of the division, as well as for other executive promotions.[10] In addition, Dowie never received the salary Exxon had promised and lost the $1 million stock option he had initially received, when the division was reorganized.[11]

---

[5] See §§ 4.6–4.11.

[6] This section discusses the potentially actionable promises or representations of employers prior to the formation of the employment relation. For a discussion of the implied-in-fact contract theory as a basis for employee actions regarding the post-hiring relationship, see part III.B (1)–(3) of this appendix and notes therein.

[7] Gombossy, *Jury Tells Exxon to Pay $10 Million to Fired Executive*, National Law Journal, Aug. 4, 1986, pg. 8. The jury awarded Dowie $9 million in punitive damages, $1 million plus interest for breach of contract, $1,000 for fraud and $25,000 for pain and suffering. *Id.*

[8] *Id.* Dowie was National Marketing Director for IBM's Canadian subsidiary at the time he decided to join Exxon. Phillips, *$10 Million Broken Promise*, Philadelphia Inquirer, September 25, 1986, pg. 10-D [hereinafter cited as Phillips]. He had been with IBM for seventeen years. *Id.*

[9] Gombossy, *supra* note 35, at 8. Exxon offered Dowie an annual salary of $82,000 if he would leave his $75,000 per year position at IBM. *Id.* He was promised approximately $1 million in stock options in order to compensate him for forfeiting the stock option and pension he had with IBM. Phillips, *supra* note 36, pg. 10-D.

[10] Andresky, *Fire-Proof Executives?*, Forbes, October 6, 1986, pg. 104 [hereinafter cited as Andresky]. When Dowie started at Exxon he held the position of Vice President for Marketing of QYX, Inc., a division of Exxon Enterprises. Phillips, *supra* note 36, pg. 10-D. In his lawsuit, Dowie asserted that Exxon promised that he would run Exxon Office Systems, a company created to market products from Exxon Enterprises' units. *Id.* Exxon filled the position with a different person. *Id.*

[11] Phillips, *supra* note 36, pg. 10-D. Exxon recalled the stock option when the Office Products Division was reorganized. *Id.* Dowie complained to his supervisors regarding this as well as being denied the promotion. *Id.* He stated that the Exxon officials responded by labeling him a "trouble-maker"

In his suit against Exxon, Dowie alleged breach of contract and fraud.[12] He maintained that some of Exxon's promises were in writing, while others were oral.[13] Exxon officials have responded to the jury's award by referring to it as "totally unjustified."[14] Exxon plans to appeal the verdict.[15]

In *Sea-Land Service, Inc. v. O'Neill*,[16] the plaintiff sued her former employer for breach of contract and fraud after the employer induced her to resign from one position by promising employment in another position.[17] The plaintiff, a sales representative, requested a transfer to her former job as a teletype operator-messenger[18] in order to pursue a college education at night.[19] Several supervisors approved the transfer and informed O'Neill that she would have to resign from her position as sales representative in order to effect the transfer.[20] O'Neill's supervisor announced the transfer on the same day that she tendered her letter of resignation.[21] When O'Neill reported to her new job, a supervisor who had originally approved the transfer said she was over-qualified for the position[22] and could not have the job.[23] The company did not permit O'Neill to rescind her letter of resignation.[24]

In upholding the jury award in favor of O'Neill,[25] the Supreme Court of Virginia rejected Sea-Land's contention that since the employment was terminable at-will,

---

and accusing him of wasting his time rather than selling Exxon's products. *Id.* Dowie was subsequently offered the position of Director of Worldwide Distribution Strategy, a position outside of the reorganized division. *Id.*

[12] *Id.* Dowie contended that Exxon defrauded him by "misrepresenting what I was going to do." *Id.* "If I had known, I wouldn't have left IBM. They defrauded me out of what I had there." *Id.*

[13] *Id.*

[14] *Id.*

[15] *Id.*

[16] 224 Va. 343, 297 S.E.2d 647 (1982), discussed in §§ **4.14–4.15**.

[17] 224 Va. at 346, 297 S.E.2d at 648. O'Neill started with Sea-Land in 1970 as a teletype operator-messenger and worked her way up to a position in management as a sales representative. *Id.*

[18] *Id.* at 346, 297 S.E.2d at 649. O'Neill believed that the lack of travel involved with the teletype operator position, unlike her sales representative position, would enable her to attend school at night. *Id.* at 346, 297 S.E.2d at 648.

[19] *Id.* at 346, 297 S.E.2d at 648. O'Neill's appraisal form included a suggestion that she attend junior college. This suggestion was listed in a space entitled "performance improvement plan" which is agreed upon by the evaluator and the employee. *Id.*

[20] *Id.* at 347, 297 S.E.2d at 649.

[21] *Id.* In her letter of resignation, O'Neill also accepted the position of teletype operator. *Id.*

[22] *Id.* The terminal manager told O'Neill that all he needed was "somebody with two legs and a driver's license." *Id.*

[23] *Id.*

[24] *Id.* The Sea-Land official whom O'Neill contacted told her that " 'it was too late' to retract the letter and that she should wait for other opportunities at Sea-Land that might open up." *Id.* O'Neill never obtained a position with Sea-Land after this incident. *Id.*

[25] *Id.* at 344–45, 297 S.E.2d at 653. The jury awarded O'Neill $125,000 in compensatory damages. *Id.* at 346, 297 S.E.2d at 648.

"there was no contract whatsoever."[26] Reasoning that the disputed agreement for the transfer was a separate undertaking from the existing employment relationship, the court concluded that when O'Neill performed her part of the bargain by resigning, Sea-Land was obligated to place her in the new job.[27] The court held further that O'Neill's reliance on Sea-Land's promise, demonstrated through her resignation, furnished adequate consideration to support the agreement.[28]

The United States Supreme Court has also encountered the implied-in-fact contract theory with respect to pre-employment promises. In *Hishon v. King & Spalding*,[29] the Court held that a female attorney's action for discrimination based on her failure to attain partnership status stated a claim under Title VII of the Civil Rights Act of 1964.[30] The attorney had asserted that the prospect of partnership in five to six years was an inducement the law firm utilized in recruiting her to become an associate.[31] She was not asked to join the partnership after the sixth or seventh year of her association with the firm.[32]

In concluding that the attorney's complaint stated a Title VII claim, the Court determined that the employment relationship was contractual in nature.[33] The Court stated that if the attorney was able to prove at trial that the promise of partnership was used to attract young lawyers to the firm, it would demonstrate that partnership was a term or condition of employment.[34]

---

[26] *Id.* at 348, 297 S.E.2d at 650. Sea-Land cited a decision in which the court held that where a specific term for duration of employment is not fixed, the relationship is presumed to be at-will, leaving the dismissed employee without a basis for recovery. *Id.* at 349, 297 S.E.2d at 650. (citing Hoffman Specialty Co. v. Pelouze, 158 Va. 586, 164 S.E. 397 (1932)).

[27] 224 Va. at 349, 297 S.E.2d at 650.

[28] *Id.* at 350, 297 S.E.2d at 651. The court noted a rule it had approved in a prior case:
[w]here one makes a promise conditioned upon the doing of an act by another, and the latter does the act, the contract is not void for want of mutuality, and the promisor is liable . . . . Upon the performance of the condition by the promisee, the contract becomes clothed with a valid consideration which renders the promise obligatory.

Id. (citing Twohy v. Harris, 194 Va. 69, 72 S.E.2d 329 (1952)).

[29] 467 U.S. 69 (1984).

[30] *Id.* at 73.

[31] *Id.* at 71-72. The attorney contended that the law firm indicated that "advancement to partnership after five or six years was a 'matter of course' for associates 'who receive[d] satisfactory evaluations' and that associates were promoted to partnership 'on a fair and equal basis'." *Id.* She asserted that she relied on this promise in accepting employment with the firm. *Id.* at 72.

[32] *Id.* at 72. The firm's policy provided that associates who were passed over for partnership were to be notified to look for new employment. The attorney's employment terminated after she was denied partnership status a second time. *Id.*

[33] *Id.* at 74. The Court noted that the existence of a contractual relationship was essential to the applicability of Title VII's provision regarding "terms, conditions or privileges of employment." *Id.*

[34] *Id.* at 76.

B. Post-Employment Promises

Employer policies, actions, or statements communicated to current employees have given rise to numerous implied-in-fact contract actions challenging compensation, benefits, and working conditions. A review of the pertinent case law demonstrates the vulnerability of employers who promise without delivering.

1. Compensation Upon Termination of Employment

Employers who promise their employees compensation upon termination of employment, in the form of severance pay, accrued vacation pay or pensions, may create implied-in-fact contracts for those benefits. Courts have frequently held that at-will employees are contractually entitled to severance pay.[35] In *Gaydos v. White Motor Corp.*,[36] the Michigan Court of Appeals rejected the notion that severance pay was merely a unilaterally-promulgated policy or gratuity and held that the defendant-employer's adoption of such a policy constituted a contractual offer.[37] Other courts concur with this view and hold that consideration for the employer's offer of a unilateral contract is supplied by the employee's continued work.[38] As

---

[35] *See, e.g.,* Dahl v. Brunswick Corp., 277 Md. 471, 356 A.2d 221 (1976); Kulins v. Malco, 121 Ill. App. 3d 520, 459 N.E.2d 1038 (1984); Langdon v. Saga Corp., 569 P.2d 524 (Okla. Ct. App. 1977); O'Shea v. RCA Global Communications, 117 L.R.R.M. 2880 (D.N.J. 1984). The decisions enforcing an employee's contractual right to severance pay have usually been based on employer's policies in handbooks or company statements. *See, e.g.,* Bolling v. Clevepak Corp., 20 Ohio App. 3d 113, 484 N.E.2d 1367 (1984) (severance pay policy in manual entitled "Benefit Plan and Personnel Policies for Salaried Employees" distributed to all employees); Adcock v. Firestone Tire & Rubber Co., 616 F. Supp. 409 (M.D. Tenn. 1985) (severance pay plan described in "Salaried Employees Handbook" distributed to all employees); Kulins v. Malco, 121 Ill. App. 3d 520, 459 N.E.2d 1038 (1984) (written policy statement made available to employees). Several courts, however, have not accorded the same treatment to severance pay provisions modifying employee rights contained in confidential personnel manuals. In Adcock v. Firestone & Rubber Co., 616 F. Supp. 409 (M.D. Tenn. 1985), the court held that it would not consider Firestone's confidential Salaried Personnel Manual which contained approximately 30 pages of information regarding the administration of the severance pay plan. *Id.* at 419. It noted that Firestone's efforts in keeping the manual confidential demonstrated that the severance pay procedures were not communicated to the employees and thus, were not included in the severance pay offer. The court stated that it would be "highly inequitable to give effect to those provisions contained in the confidential manual that would operate to limit the scope or amount of the plaintiff employees' severance pay benefits." *Id. See also* Dependahl v. Falstaff Brewing Corp., 491 F. Supp. 1188 (E.D. Mo. 1980) (modification of severance pay benefits contained in confidential manual ineffective).

[36] 54 Mich. App. 143, 220 N.W.2d 697 (1974).

[37] 54 Mich. App. at 148, 220 N.W.2d at 700. The employer pled an affirmative defense that its severance pay policy was "merely an expression of desire or good intention, without any binding commitment for the benefit of the employees concerned." *Id.*

[38] *Id.* at 148–49, 220 N.W.2d at 700. See § **4.16**.

one court noted, "severance pay is not analogous to unemployment compensation but rather is 'a kind of accumulated compensation for past services and a material recognition of their past value.' "[39]

A similar analysis has been applied to the payment of retirement and disability benefits. In *Nicely v. Bank of Virginia Trust Co.*,[40] the Supreme Court of Virginia considered a non-contributory pension and profit-sharing plan an offer of a unilateral contract.[41] The offer, according to the court, takes the form of the employer's "promise to pay benefits upon the fulfillment of certain conditions by [the employees] or upon the happening of certain events, such as retirement after a specified term of service or sustaining a permanent disability."[42] An employee accepts the offer by fulfilling any applicable conditions.[43]

In *Dahl v. Brunswick Corp.*,[44] the Court of Appeals of Maryland held that the fact that a corporate practice of paying two weeks' compensation in lieu of two weeks' notice of termination was not in writing and did not prevent it from being enforced as a contract.[45] As with severance pay policies, the court regarded this practice as a unilateral contract offer which the employees accepted by continuing to work in reliance thereon.[46]

---

[39] 54 Mich. App. at 148–49, 220 N.W.2d at 700 (citing Willets v. Emhart Mfg. Co., 52 Conn. 487, 490–491, 208 A.2d 546, 548 (1965)).

[40] 221 Va. 1084, 277 S.E.2d 209 (1981).

[41] *Id.* at 1089, 277 S.E.2d at 211–12. The plaintiff asserted that upon his dismissal from employment due to disability, he was entitled to all amounts credited to his account under a profit-sharing and trust plan. *Id.* at 1086, 277 S.E.2d at 210. The plan provided that such amounts would be paid in cases involving the permanent disability of an employee-participant. *Id.* at 1087, 277 S.E.2d at 210. Although the court affirmed the denial of the employee's claim for reasons related to the profit-sharing plan's claim rules, the court's opinion noted that the "better reasoned decisions" in cases involving retirement and profit-sharing plans characterize the plan as a unilateral contract. *Id.* at 1089, 277 S.E.2d at 211–12 (citing Amicone v. Kennecott Copper Corp., 19 Utah 2d 297, 300, 431 P.2d 130, 132 (1967)).

[42] *Id.* at 1089, 277 S.E.2d at 212.

[43] *Id.* (citing Matthew v. Swift & Co., 465 F.2d 814, 818 (5th Cir. 1972); Rochester Corp. v. Rochester, 450 F.2d 118, 120–21 (4th Cir. 1971); Twohy v. Harris, 194 Va. 69, 81, 72 S.E.2d 329, 336 (1952)).

[44] 277 Md. 471, 356 A.2d 221 (1976).

[45] *Id.* at 487, 356 A.2d at 231. In addition to their claim for two weeks' compensation in lieu of the traditional notice, the plaintiffs-employees sued Brunswick for severance pay and accrued vacation due to their involuntary termination resulting from the sale of their division. *Id.* at 474, 356 A.2d at 223. The court characterized the issue as follows:

> [W]hether, when employees have neither a written employment contract nor a collective bargaining agreement, an unwritten general practice of an employer constitutes, like a written company policy, an offer of a unilateral contract.

Id. at 488, 356 A.2d at 231.

[46] *Id.* at 488, 356 A.2d at 231. The court cited the decision in Morschauser v. American News Co., 6 A.D.2d 1028, 178 N.Y.S.2d 279 (1958) (per curiam):

> "If the defendant engaged in a practice of making severance payments to non-union employees on the termination of employment, and if such employees relied on this practice

2. Reinstatement After Leave of Absence

Employees on a leave of absence who have asserted a contractual right to reinstatement have had less consistent results than those involving severance pay or retirement benefits.[47] In *White v. I.T.T.*,[48] the Eleventh Circuit held that an employee did not have a contractual right to reinstatement following her maternity leave, despite the employer's written policy providing reinstatement following a leave of absence.[49] The court reasoned that the employer did not have a contractual obligation to reinstate the employee since the employment was terminable at will,[50] and thus any executory promises were unenforceable.[51]

Similarly, in *Gillespie v. Equitable Life Assurance Society*,[52] the court denied the plaintiff's claim that he was contractually entitled to re-employment after a leave of absence.[53] The employee contended that the employer's refusal to reinstate him violated a "mutual agreement" he had with a company official, which granted

---

in accepting or continuing their employment, plaintiffs have a cause of action against the defendant, 178 N.Y.S.2d at 280."

Id. at 489, 356 A.2d at 231.

[47] Cases regarding employee contract actions for severance pay and retirement benefits are discussed in part III.B.1 of this appendix.

[48] 718 F.2d 994 (11th Cir. 1983), *cert. denied,* 466 U.S. 938 (1984).

[49] *Id.* at 996. Aetna's maternity leave policy appeared in the "Management Manual" which White was given upon her hiring. *Id.* at 995. The policy provided in pertinent part:

A six month Leave of Absence for Maternity purposes will be granted only to those pregnant employees fully intending to work after the birth of their child. A . . . Leave of Absence form must be submitted indicating the maternity leave . . . A pregnant employee may continue working for as long as she desires before delivery and then be granted a leave of absence at the end of which she may return to her old position or another of similar content and pay.

Id. Another section of the manual outlined the procedure for obtaining a maternity leave of absence, requiring employees to complete a "Request for Leave of Absence Form." *Id.* A sample of this form appeared in the manual:

When I return to work at the expiration of my leave of absence, I may return to the position I held prior to this leave of absence or to another position comparable in function and compensation; *if an opening then exists*. If there are no positions available at the time I am scheduled to return to work, I understand that I will be re-employed in the first position which becomes available for which I am qualified.

Id. (emphasis in original).

[50] *Id.* at 997. The court cited the Georgia law of employment-at-will and noted that White admitted that her employment would continue "[f]or as long as I done my duties like I was supposed to . . . ." *Id.*

[51] *Id.*

[52] 590 F. Supp. 1111 (D. Del. 1984).

[53] (referring to the decision in White v. I.T.T., 718 F.2d 994 (11th Cir. 1983), *cert. denied,* 466 U.S. 938 (1984)). The court, applying Pennsylvania law in a diversity action, also relied on the decision in Brown v. Carnegie-Illinois Steel Corp., 168 Pa. Super. 380, 77 A.2d 655, *aff'd,* 368 Pa. 166, 81 A.2d 562 (1951), in which the court held that an employer was free to dismiss an at-will employee who was on leave of absence. *Id.*

him a leave of absence without pay, in response to his arrest on charges of sodomy and solicitation.[54] The employer subsequently rescinded this action by discharging the employee and refusing his request for re-employment 16 years later, after he was pardoned.[55] The court held that since the plaintiff was an at-will employee, the granting of the leave of absence did not limit the company's right to terminate his employment.[56]

In sharp contrast to these decisions, in *Sepanske v. Bendix*,[57] the Michigan Court of Appeals held that an employer's establishment of a reinstatement policy for employees on an employer-sponsored social leave of absence was a contractual obligation.[58] Citing the Michigan Supreme Court's decision in *Toussaint v. Blue Cross & Blue Shield*,[59] the court stated that although the employer was not obligated to initiate such a policy, once it was in place, the employees could expect compliance

---

[54] *Id.* at 1113. Upon learning of the charges against Gillespie from the police department directly, Gillespie's immediate supervisor initially told him that he would have to end his employment with Equitable and sent a letter the next day, September 29, 1965, informing him that his services were "terminated". *Id.* However, the supervisor sent another letter on September 30, 1965, informing Gillespie that he was being place on "leave of absence without pay,', effective September 29, 1965. *Id.*

[55] *Id.* Equitable rescinded the leave of absence in a letter dated October 21, 1965, informing Gillespie that his termination was effective September 28, 1965 (one day prior to the grant of the leave of absence). The court noted that this action was apparently influenced by a telephone call from Gillespie to his supervisor (while Gillespie was under the influence of alcohol) in which he threatened to "appeal" his situation to the Chairman of the Board. *Id.*

[56] *Id.* at 1116.

[57] 147 Mich. App. 819, 384 N.W.2d 54 (1985).

[58] *Id.* at 826, 384 N.W.2d at 58. The plaintiff participated in Bendix's social service leave program, which enabled employees to work for a charitable organization and still receive their salary from Bendix. Bendix's policy manual provided:

G. REINSTATEMENT FROM A SOCIAL LEAVE OF ABSENCE.

1. Upon completion of the assignment, the employee will be reinstated to his former position or to a position of equivalent or greater responsibility at the same location from which leave was granted.

Id. at 822, 384 N.W.2d at 56. At the time of his leave of absence, plaintiff was a member of the pension and payroll department at Bendix. When he returned to Bendix after his leave expired (one year later), he was told that his former position was no longer available and was assigned to a similar position in the tax department. *Id.* at 823–24, 384 N.W.2d at 57. His action for breach of contract was based, in part, on a letter he received from the personnel manager:

We are pleased to advise you that your request for social leave of absence has been approved for the period August 1, 1974 through July 31, 1975. Please report to the Personnel Department at 2:00 p.m. on July 31, for your leave processing. Upon completion of your assignment you are scheduled to return to your former position with the Corporate Pension and Payroll Department. Also, you are requested to provide written and/or verbal reports concerning your social service leave assignment to Mr. K. Pearce and me.

Id. at 823, 384 N.W.2d at 57.

[59] For a discussion of the court's decision in *Toussaint v. Blue Cross & Blue Shield*, 408 Mich. 579, 292 N.W.2d 880 (1980), see §§ **4.7–4.17**.

by the employer.[60] The court found that "[s]uch statements of company policy and procedure create enforceable contract rights."[61]

3. Compensation

The treatment accorded employee claims for compensation based on an implied-in-fact contract theory has varied. In *Muller v. Stromberg Carlson Corp.*,[62] the employee asserted that an employer's extensive policy governing the advancement of employees within the company constituted an enforceable contract upon which he based a claim for a salary increase.[63] The employer's "Merit Pay Plan" required annual evaluations of an employee's progress in achieving the objectives he had established with his supervisor.[64] The salary recommendations were made by the employee's supervisor and reviewed by upper management and the parent company.[65] In addition, the policy provided that pay raises were not to be given to all employees.[66]

The court rejected the employee's contention that the merit review policy established a contractual right to salary increases for his three years of satisfactory performance.[67] The court noted that enforcement of the policy as a contract would necessitate judicial involvement wherever employees who have performed well were dissatisfied with the employer-determined compensation.[68] In addition, the court pointed to the Florida law of employment-at-will and resisted joining the

---

[60] 384 N.W.2d at 58. Although the court recognized the implications of the employment-at-will doctrine, it stated that "the employment relationship is enhanced where, as here, the employer establishes specific personnel policies and practices." *Id.*

[61] *Id.* The court ultimately decided that the evidence did not support the jury's determination that Bendix promised Sepanske his same position in the pension and payroll department upon his return. It believed that the letter from the personnel manager, note 80, *supra,* did not prevent Bendix from returning plaintiff to another position of equal or greater responsibility, as provided in the policy manual. *Id.* at 827, 384 N.W.2d at 58.

[62] 427 So. 2d 266 (Fla. Dist. Ct. App. 1983).

[63] 427 So. 2d at 268. Muller contended that he was given no salary increases in three fiscal years in spite of his receiving satisfactory evaluations, fulfilling his annual objectives, and receiving comments from supervisors that his performance warranted increases. *Id.*

[64] *Id.*

[65] *Id.*

[66] *Id.* This policy was included in a memorandum issued to supervisors. *Id.*

[67] *Id.* Muller argued that Stromberg Carlson's policy of conducting annual reviews created "a series of annual employment contracts" and that the Merit Review Plan contractually bound Stromberg Carlson to give him salary increases. *Id.*

[68] *Id.* at 269. The court expressed concern with the resolution of cases

> in the more common circumstances of simply having an employee for a probationary period after which he would be considered as a permanent employee and could expect salary increases if he did good work. If those circumstances entitled dissatisfied employees to relief,

movement to give employer policies the contractual status accorded by such courts as the Supreme Court of Michigan in *Toussaint*.[69]

The analysis used in many severance pay actions[70] has been used to impose a contractual obligation on an employer to pay accrued sick leave benefits.[71] In *Gilman v. County of Chesire*,[72] the Supreme Court of New Hampshire upheld a decision awarding an employee's accrued sick leave benefits to his estate.[73] The Court, noting a difference of opinion in other jurisdictions,[74] held that payment for sick leave was "not a mere gratuity, but constituted compensation for services rendered."[75] The employer in *Gilman* had an established policy concerning sick

---

the courts would be potentially flooded with claims asking that judicial discretion be substituted for employer discretion.

Id. An incentive plan's level of sophistication, the court concluded, should not be used as a standard in deciding its contractual status. *Id.*

The court also agreed with Muller's argument that the "balance of power" often shifts in favor of the employer. *Id.* at 270. However, the court stated that "mere unequal bargaining power of the parties in business relationships has never been a basis on which to either create or terminate contracts. *Id.*

[69] *Id.* at 270 (citing, as an example, Toussaint v. Blue Cross & Blue Shield, 408 Mich. 579, 292 N.W.2d 880 (1980)). Although the court viewed the *Toussaint* opinion as providing "food for profound thought," it concluded that adoption of a similar position would be inappropriate, in light of the fact that Florida law did not reflect the same views as expressed in *Toussaint*. Those views, the court noted, were based on "a perception of social or economic policy thought to be beneficial." The function of law, according to the court, is to "foster certainty in business relationships, not to create uncertainty by establishing ambivalent criteria for the construction of those relationships." *Id.*

[70] See Part III.B.1. of this appendix and notes therein.

[71] For a discussion of the analysis used in employee actions for severance pay, see Part III.B.2 of this appendix and notes therein.

[72] 126 N.H. 445, 493 A.2d 485 (1985).

[73] *Id.* at 450, 493 A.2d at 489. The administrator of the estate asserted that the deceased employee was entitled to accrued sick leave compensation pursuant to a sick leave policy adopted by the county (the deceased employees' employer):

Accrued Sick Pay Payment: After five (5) years of continuous employment, if an employee terminates voluntarily for other than cause, all accrued sick pay will be paid at the regular rate (in existence at the time of retirement or termination) in weekly payments until all accrued sick benefits are used up. Except that if any employee retires, he will be paid in a lump sum at the time of his or her retirement.

Id. at 446, 493 A.2d at 486.

[74] *Id.* at 448, 493 A.2d at 488. The court prefaced its discussion with a reference to decisions holding that sick leave benefits are "mere contingencies or gratuities, creating only an expectancy in a future benefit which can be abolished at the will of the public employer." *Id.* (citing, as examples, City of North Little Rock v. Vogelgesang, 273 Ark. 390, 619 S.W.2d 652 (1981); Marsille v. City of Santa Ana, 64 Cal. App. 3d 764, 134 Cal. Rptr. 743 (Ct. App. 1977); McCarty v. City of Rockford, 96 Ill. App. 3d 531, 421 N.E.2d 576 (1981)).

[75] *Id.* at 449, 493 A.2d at 488. The court stated that the right to receive the benefit rested upon the employee's rendering his services. It noted that its holding was in accordance with several other jurisdictions. *Id.* (citing, as examples Logue v. City of Carthage, 612 S.W.2d 148 (Mo. App. 1981); Vangilder v. City of Jackson, 492 S.W.2d 15 (Mo. App. 1973); Christian v. County

leave under which the deceased employee had earned deferred benefits through the rendering of his services.[76] According to the court, consideration for the promise contained in the employer's policy was furnished by the employee's continued employment with the knowledge that he would receive accrued sick leave benefits upon his leaving the employer.[77] In addition, the court noted that the enforcement of such a promise prevented the primary purpose of providing benefits—inducing people to enter and remain in employment—from being undermined.[78]

In *Hance v. United Family Life Insurance Co.*,[79] an opposite approach was taken by the Tennessee Court of Appeals in resolving an employee's contract claim for an employer-provided incentive trip. The employee, an insurance agent, was awarded a trip to a company sales conference in recognition of his meeting a certain sales quota.[80] However, in the period between the presentation of the award and the date of the trip, the employee's sales declined substantially and he was dismissed.[81] He brought suit against the employer for the cost of the trip, contending that his qualifications for receiving the trips supported his claim for recovery.[82]

On appeal, the court agreed with the employer that the employee did not have a contractual right to the trip, which was only a gratuity.[83] The court cited decisions of other jurisdictions which held that an employer's promise to pay a bonus is not a contractual obligation if the employee is not required to do something for which he was not already obligated.[84] The court noted further that the employee

---

of Ontario, 92 Misc. 2d 51, 399 N.Y.S.2d 379 (Sup. Ct. 1977); South Euclid Fraternal Order of Police v. D'Amico, 13 Ohio App. 3d 46, 468 N.E.2d 735 (1983); City of Orange v. Chance, 325 S.W.2d 838 (Tex. Civ. App. 1959)).

[76] *Id.* The employer changed its sick leave policy prior to the employee's death. The estate of the employee sought the benefits which vested under the former policy. The court held that, although the employee's sick leave benefits were deferred compensation, "the employer could not impair its obligation to pay those benefits by changing its sick leave policy after the compensation was earned so as to divest the rights of those already benefitting from it." *Id.*

[77] *Id.* at 450, 493 A.2d at 489.

[78] *Id.* at 449, 493 A.2d at 488. The court added:

Benefits would serve as little inducement if they could be whisked away at the whim of the public employer. In many instances, the employee would have no assurance of receiving promised benefits unless he terminated employment while favorable policies were still in effect. Moreover, in the end, benefits would become merely a snare and a delusion to the unwary.

Id.

[79] C/A No. 1073, slip op. at 3 (Tenn. Ct. App. Oct. 9, 1986).

[80] *Id.* The plaintiff received a letter from the vice president of the company, inviting him to attend the 1983 presidential sales conference aboard a cruise ship. In order to win the trip, the plaintiff was required to maintain a specific sales quota for one year. *Id.*

[81] *Id.*

[82] *Id.*

[83] *Id.* at 7. The court held that the trial court was in error in awarding the plaintiff the cost of the trip. *Id.* at 4.

[84] *Id.* at 7 (citing Annotation, 81 A.L.R.2d 1066, Section 4 at 1075).

was an employee-at-will and that the employer's rules required the award recipient to be an employee at the time of the trip.[85]

4. Disability Benefits

Two recent cases involving employee claims for disability benefits demonstrate the nexus between a jurisdiction's support for the employment-at-will doctrine and the effectiveness of the implied-in-fact contract theory. In *LaRocca v. Xerox Corp.*,[86] a terminated employee sought recovery of disability benefits he contended were promised in a company manual.[87] The court, in granting the employer's motion for summary judgment, noted the reluctance of Florida courts to grant contractual status to employer policies in the absence of express references in the policy to the term of employment and associated benefits.[88] The court found that the lack of any statement in the manual providing that it constituted an independent contract[89] required the court to dismiss the employee's complaint.[90]

Similarly, in *Stewart v. Ethicon, Inc.*,[91] the court held that the at-will nature of the employment relationship prevented the employee from recovering disability benefits under the employer's "Long-Term Disability Plan."[92] The court relied on the fact that, under Georgia law, an employer may discharge an at-will employee with impunity.[93]

---

[85] *Id.* at 8. Although the plaintiff had a written contract with the company, the court still concluded that he was an at-will employee. The court noted that the contract provided for its termination by either party "by notice in writing mailed to the last known address of either party." *Id.* at 6.

[86] 587 F. Supp. 1002 (S.D. Fla. 1984).

[87] *Id.* at 1003. The plaintiff ceased working for Xerox temporarily after suffering a disability. Xerox attempted to find work for him when he informed them that he could perform light work. During this period, Xerox provided him with disability benefits. Xerox terminated plaintiff's employment status and disability benefits when it was unable to find work that the plaintiff was willing to perform. *Id.*

[88] *Id.*. (citing Muller v. Stromberg Carlson Corp., 427 So. 2d 266, 268–70 (Fla. Dist. Ct. App. 1983)). The court stated that it was unable to determine whether the employer made any reference to the policy manual when the plaintiff was hired. Noting that the employment contract was oral, the court stated that such representations would require it to find that the personnel manual was an independent contract. *Id.*

[89] The court noted that the plaintiff was "caught on the horns of a dilemma" since the old policy manual produced by the plaintiff, which lacked any reference to its potential status as a contract, was too general and the newer manual produced by the employer specifically disclaimed any independent contractual status. *Id.* at 1004.

[90] The court also rejected the plaintiff's contention that the policy manual was a separate contract obligating the employer to "agressively pursue" other employment for the employee during his period of disability, referring to its analysis regarding the employee's other contract claims. *Id.*

[91] 642 F. Supp. 7 (N.D. Ga. 1983).

[92] *Id.* at 8. The employee admitted that a written employment contract did not exist. The employer's "Long Term Disability Plan" expressly provided for the automatic termination of coverage upon the date of the termination of the employee's employment. *Id.*

[93] *Id.*

5. Miscellaneous Aspects of the Employment Relationship

Lieber v. Union Carbide Corp., Nuclear Division,[94] provides one of the clearest examples of the attractiveness of the implied-in-fact contract theory to employees seeking contractual protection for various aspects of the employment relationship. The plaintiff, a retired employee, sued Union Carbide for breach of an implied contractual right to receive an annual performance appraisal.[95] As a result of the company's failure to provide such evaluations, the retired employee contended that he was unable to ameliorate his job performance, which would have resulted in salary increases and, ultimately, enhanced pension benefits.[96] In support of this contractual claim, the plaintiff pointed to Union Carbide's practice of providing employees with annual reviews and the company's written endorsement of such reviews in both a confidential supervisory manual and a policy statement issued by Union Carbide's president to all employees.[97]

Union Carbide argued that the confidential manual was a "managerial tool to be used in the discretion of the supervisor."[98] It explained that Lieber was given annual reviews although not conducted in conformance with the established review procedures, in which he was told that his work was unsatisfactory.[99] The lack of compliance with the procedures, Union Carbide contended, was not the proximate cause of denying Lieber salary increases.[1]

Noting the dearth of Tennessee decisions considering the contractual status of employer policy statements in non-handbook cases,[2] the court focused on whether a "meeting of the minds existed," and looked to the conduct and circumstances of the parties and the language contained in the Union Carbide Policy Statement.[3]

---

[94] 577 F. Supp. 562 (E.D. Tenn. 1983).

[95] *Id.* at 563.

[96] *Id.* The plaintiff's suit sought the additional salary and pension benefits he claimed he would have received. *Id.*

[97] *Id.* Union Carbide adopted a policy of reviewing salaried employee performance annually and printed the review procedures in a manual distributed only to supervisory personnel. *Id.* at 564. The policy statement issued by the president constituted page 1 of the manual and was posted on the bulletin board at the facility plaintiff worked and provided:

> The policy of the Union Carbide Corporation, Nuclear Division, is to have a performance review annually with each salaried employee in order to relate organizational and individual goals, to review actual performance in the light of established goals, to lay a firm basis for further individual development, and to serve as an input for career planning and salaried action.

Id.

[98] *Id.* at 563.

[99] *Id.*

[1] *Id.*

[2] *Id.* at 564. The court noted that in one case a Tennessee court found that a statement in an employer's handbook guaranteeing that the company would comply with certain policies, practices and procedures, created contractual rights. *Id.* (citing Hamby v. Genesco, 627 S.W.2d 373 (Tenn. Ct. App. 1981)). However, general statements in employee handbooks were held to not create any contractual rights. *Id.* (citing Whitaker v. Care-More, Inc., 621 S.W.2d 395 (Tenn. Ct. App. 1981)).

[3] *Id.* (citing Judd v. Heitmann, 402 F. Supp. 929, 933 (M.D. Tenn. 1975)).

The court concluded that the annual performance review policy was an internal guide for managing the facility and that neither the policy, nor the practice of conducting annual reviews, created any contractual rights.[4]

Employee claims for promotional opportunities or "bumping" rights have also relied on the implied-in-fact contract theory. In *Lakeside v. Freightliner Corp.*,[5] the court considered whether a personnel policy in which the company offered lower positions to employees scheduled to be laid-off was contractually binding on the employer.[6] The plaintiff claimed that Freightliner breached its contractual obligation by not considering her for certain promotions for which she was qualified, failing to accord her preferential treatment over outside employee candidates, and dismissing her as a result of a layoff without considering her for alternative positions.[7]

In its defense, Freightliner cited the fact that the policy was contained in an external policy guide for management which was never distributed to employees.[8] The company added that Lakeside was never informed that the manual was a part of the terms and conditions of her employment.[9] The employee argued that Freightliner's actions supported the inference that the manual did create a contract of employment, pointing to a letter from the president encouraging employee compliance with company procedures and the vice president's statement that the manual represented the company's position with which all departments were required to comply.[10]

Noting the limited access employees had to the manual,[11] the court held that the manual was not part of the terms and conditions of employment. In addition, the court noted that Freightliner never informed the employees that the manual constituted a contract and made an effort to restrict employee access to the manual.[12] The court concluded that neither the documentation of policies for management's use nor the accessibility of a manual by employees could establish a contractual obligation.[13]

In *Knox v. American Sterilizer Co.*,[14] a discharged employee asserted a contractual right to promotion, in addition to other employment benefits. The plaintiff

---

[4] *Id.*

[5] 612 F. Supp. 10 (D. Or. 1984).

[6] *Id.*

[7] *Id.*

[8] *Id.* at 4. Freightliner asserted that Lakeside failed to offer evidence that Freightliner informed her of the sections from the manual which were the basis of the contract action. *Id.*

[9] *Id.*

[10] *Id.* at 4–5. The president's letter emphasized to the employees that "teamwork results from 'well-designed and documented procedures which are followed by the people responsible'." *Id.* at 5.

[11] *Id.* at 6. Employees were only able to read the manual at different managers' desks or work areas. *Id.*

[12] *Id.* Consequently, the court found that the company intended the manual to instruct managers in the methods of responding to personnel policy issues. *Id.*

[13] *Id.*

[14] 117 L.R.R.M. 2341 (M.D. Ala. 1984).

asserted that pursuant to the company handbook he was "contractually entitled to, among other things, safe working conditions, excellent wages, excellent employee benefits, and opportunity for advancement."[15] The court, in dismissing the action, held that the manual did not manifest the parties' intention to enter into such a mutual contract.[16]

One court has recognized implied-in-fact contracts to protect the privacy of employees. A California appellate court, in *Rulon-Miller v. I.B.M.*,[17] upheld a jury verdict awarding $300,000 to an employee who was constructively dismissed in contravention of a company policy regarding privacy.[18] The employee, a marketing manager with IBM, was initially told by her supervisor that her romantic relationship with an official from QYX, an IBM competitor, did not present any problems.[19] However, the same supervisor subsequently told the employee that her relationship "constituted a 'conflict of interest' and told her to stop dating Blum or lose her job."[20] Although he told her he would give her approximately a week to consider her choices, he informed her the next day that he "had made up her mind for her," resulting in the employee's protest and her dismissal.[21]

On appeal of the jury's award, the court concluded that IBM's policy statements regarding privacy of employees and conflicts of interest ensured employees "both the right of privacy and the right to hold a job even though 'off-the-job behavior' might not be approved of by the employee's manager."[22] While the court's analysis

---

[15] *Id.* at 2342. In addition, the employee claimed that he was permanently employed and could only be terminated for cause. *Id.*

[16] *Id.* The court also concluded that, even if a contract did exist, the employee offered only general allegations of breach and failed to produce substantive evidence to support a breach. *Id.*

[17] 162 Cal. App. 3d 241, 208 Cal. Rptr. 524 (1984).

[18] *Id.* at 243, 208 Cal. Rptr. at 527. The plaintiff won a jury verdict awarding her $100,000 in compensatory damages and $200,000 in punitive damages on claims of wrongful dismissal and intentional infliction of emotional distress. *Id.* at 406.

[19] *Id.* at 245, 208 Cal. Rptr. at 528. The supervisor's statement was made in conjunction with his pledging his support for the plaintiff with respect to a pending promotion. *Id.*

[20] *Id.* at 246, 208 Cal. Rptr. at 528.

[21] *Id.* The supervisor fired the employee in response to her protesting his decision regarding her relationship. IBM and the supervisor claimed that the employee was merely "transferred" to another division. *Id.* at 246, 208 Cal. Rptr. at 28-29.

[22] *Id.* at 249, 208 Cal. Rptr. at 530. A policy regarding employee privacy was issued by the chairman of IBM prior to the incident involving the plaintiff. It provided, in pertinent part:

TO ALL IBM MANAGERS:

The line that separates an individual's on-the-job business life from his other life as a private citizen is at times well-defined and at other times indistinct. But the line does exist, and you and I as managers in IBM, must be able to recognize that line.

I have seen instances where managers took disciplinary measures against employees for actions or conduct that are not rightfully the company's concern. These managers usually justified their decisions by citing their personal code of ethics and morals or by quoting some fragment of company policy that seem to support their position. Both arguments proved unjust on close examination. What we need, in every case, is balanced judgment which weighs the needs of the business and the rights of the individual.

* * *

of the wrongful dismissal claim focused primarily on the implied covenant of good faith and fair dealing, it is interesting to note that the court stated that in the initial confrontation between the employee and her supervisor, "the assertion of the right to be free of inquiries concerning her personal life was based on substantive direct contract rights she had flowing from IBM policies."[23] The willingness of courts to fashion contractual remedies on a similar basis would significantly expand an employer's vulnerability to employee lawsuits.

IV. Analysis

Despite the lack of consistency among various jurisdictions, the cases discussed above demonstrate that employers today are becoming increasingly more vulnerable to challenges from at-will employees seeking contractual rights beyond continued employment. The successful assertion of the implied-in-fact contract theory in cases involving pre-employment promises and employee privacy warrants some degree of alarm by employers.[24] The extent to which an at-will employee will be able to impose an implied-in-fact contract on his or her employer well may depend on a particular jurisdiction's tolerance for the employment-at-will doctrine.[25] Nonetheless, employers should adopt measures which will reduce their exposure to

---

> We have concern with an employee's off-the-job behavior only when it reduces his ability to perform regular job assignments, interferes with the job performance of other employees, or if his outside behavior affects the reputation of the company in a major way. When on-the-job performance is acceptable, I can think of a few situations in which outside activities could result in disciplinary action or dismissal.
>
> * * *
>
> IBM's first basic belief is respect for the individual, and the essence of the belief is a strict regard for his right to personal privacy. This idea should never be compromised easily or quickly.
>
> *Id.* at 248–49, 208 Cal. Rptr. at 530. IBM's policies concerning employee conduct were maintained in a "Performance and Recognition Manual". In regards to conflicts of interest, it provided, in pertinent part:
>
> > A conflict of interest can arise when an employee is involved in activity for personal gain, which for any reason is in conflict with IBM's business interests. Generally speaking, 'moonlighting' is defined as working at some activity for personal gain outside of your IBM job. If you do perform outside work, you have a special responsibility to avoid any conflict with IBM's business interests.
> >
> > * * *
> >
> > Employees must be free of any significant investment or association of their own or of their immediate family's [sic], in competitors or suppliers, which might interfere or be thought to interfere with the independent exercise of their judgment in the best interest of IBM.
>
> *Id.* at 249–50, 208 Cal. Rptr. at 530–31.
>
> [23] *Id.* at 251, 208 Cal. Rptr. at 532.
>
> [24] For a discussion of cases involving pre-employment promises, see part III.A of this appendix, and notes therein. For a discussion of *Rulon-Miller v. I.B.M.*, involving employee contractual rights to privacy, see part III.B.5 of this appendix and notes therein.
>
> [25] For a discussion of cases in which the court's position in favor of the employment-at-will doctrine was the basis for denying an employee's contractual claim, see part III.B. 2–4 and notes therein.

contractual liability. Employers' efforts in preventing implied-in-fact contractual liability must focus on the entire employment relationship—from pre-employment promise to termination-related policies.

The recruiting process is the first area in which preventive measures should be enacted. Employers must sensitize employees involved in "selling" job opportunities to the potential liability of implied-in-fact contracts. These employers must refrain from "puffing"—from making offers or promises to job candidates which the employer may not be willing or even able to keep. In addition, any literature utilized in conjunction with interviews should be drafted in accordance with this perspective.

Another preventive measure which employers should consider is the use of disclaimers, in both job applications and employee handbooks.[26] In *Toussaint v. Blue Cross & Blue Shield*,[27] the court noted that the employer could have required employee-candidates to acknowledge that they would be serving at the pleasure of the employer.[28] The insertion of a disclaimer in an employment application, signed by the employee, provides significant evidence in proving that the employment relationship was at will—a status which was dispositive in many of the cases discussed.[29] Employment application disclaimers have been proven to be successful in achieving this objective.[30]

The insertion of disclaimers in employee handbooks offers a means of defending and perhaps preventing employee litigation over the terms and conditions of employment.[31] In *LaRocca v. Xerox Corp.*,[32] the court stated that such a statement would defeat an employee's attempt to obtain contractual relief.[33]

Employers should consider, however, the potential negative aspects of handbook disclaimers. A disclaimer which is not clearly written may alienate employees by appearing to obscure the employer's policies.[34] Handbook disclaimers might

---

[26] *See* §§ **4.10, 8.7–8.9**.

[27] 408 Mich. 579, 292 N.W.2d 880 (1980).

[28] *Id.* at 612, 292 N.W.2d at 891.

[29] See § **4.10**.

[30] *See, e.g.,* Novosel v. Sears, Roebuck & Co., 495 F.Supp. 344 (E.D. Mich. 1980) (employer did not have duty to dismiss for just cause only where employment application contained disclaimer of definite period of employment).

[31] Decker, *Handbooks and Employment Policies as Express or Implied Guarantees of Employment—Employer Beware!,* 5 Journal of Law and Commerce 207, 223 (1985).

[32] 587 F. Supp. 1002 (S.D. Fla. 1984).

[33] 587 F. Supp. at 1004. *See also* Woolley v. Hoffman-LaRoche, *supra* note 19.

[34] Decker, *supra* note 157, at 223. Decker offers several examples of disclaimers to be placed at the beginning of employee handbooks:

> None of the benefits or policies in this handbook is intended by reason of their publication to confer any rights or privileges upon you, or to entitle you to be or remain employed by the Company. The contents of this handbook are presented as a matter of information only. While the Company believes wholeheartedly in the plans, policies, and the procedures described herein, they are not conditions of employment.
>
> or
>
> This is not a contract of employment. Any individual may voluntarily leave employment upon proper notice, and may be terminated by the employer at any time and for any reason.

be used by union organizers in an attempt to persuade employees into believing that they do not have job security.

Supervisory personnel manuals and memoranda have also been relied upon, somewhat successfully, by employees in establishing contractual rights.[35] Employers should take steps to maintain the confidentiality of such managerial literature. In *Lakeside v. Freightliner*,[36] the employer's efforts in restricting employee access to such a manual was a significant factor in preventing the formation of a contractual relationship.[37] Indeed, employee access to such information is arguably not essential to promoting better employee relations.

Employers' promulgation of policy statements or memoranda may also present employers with a dilemma. Recent employee lawsuits based, in part, on such statements, suggest the curtailment or severe limitation on this practice.[38] However, open lines of communication between management and employees are essential to the operator of a business, as well as to employee morale. In drafting policy statements or internal memoranda for employee-wide distribution regarding benefits, promotional opportunities, and working conditions, employers should structure them carefully, avoiding any commitments which they cannot honor.

Management or supervisory employees who are responsible for interacting with employees should be cautioned, through training, that their oral statements may constitute enforceable contracts of employment. They should be instructed not to make promises or representations implying that employment is other than at-will. In addition, employers should implement some form of objective employee performance evaluation system. An integral part of any such program should be a written evaluation of the employee's performance, which is placed into his or her personnel file. It is critical that evaluations be candid and accurately reflect the employee's actual job performance. If an evaluation overrates an average or below-average performer, it may prove to be very useful to an employee seeking benefits or compensation on the basis of an alleged "untarnished" job performance record.

> Any oral or written statements or promises to the contrary are hereby expressly disavowed and should not be relied upon by any prospective or existing employee. The contents of this handbook are subject to change at any time at the discretion of the employer.
>
> or
>
> The foregoing personnel policies are not a binding contract, but a set of guidelines for the implementation of personnel policies. The Company explicitly reserves the right to modify any of the provisions of these policies at any time and without notice. Notwithstanding any of the provisions of these policies, employment may be terminated at any time, either by the employee or by the Company, with or without cause.

Id.

[35] For a discussion of cases involving employee claims based on supervisory personnel manuals and memoranda, see part ____ of this appendix.

[36] See part III.B.5 of this appendix and notes therein.

[37] *Lakeside, supra* note 5.

[38] For a discussion of cases in which employees relied on employer policy statements or memoranda, see part III.B.5 of this appendix and notes therein.

V. Conclusion

The expansion of employer liability on an implied-in-fact contract basis is another sign of the gradual erosion of the employment-at-will doctrine. Employees have made significant inroads toward achieving contractual protection from many aspects of the employment relationship. By enacting several simple measures, employers may effectively limit employee claims for contractual relief for benefits, promotions, and working conditions.

Although companies should attempt to prevent written policies from attaining contractual status, it is oversimplistic to suggest that employers can disavow on page 25 what they have promised on pages 1 through 24. Moreover, employers cannot completely avoid breach of contract claims even if they completely avoid documentation, since oral assurances may trigger lawsuits as well.

Recent cases expanding protections for at-will employees suggest that individuals are no longer the "property" of their masters, but rather enjoy certain property rights in their employment. Employers may no longer assume that they can unilaterally dictate policy changes or aberrations. The imposition of implied contractual liability on employers will undeniably reduce arbitrary and capricious employer conduct. Unfortunately, it will frustrate employers' communications to employees about future hopes and expectations as well.

CONVERSION TABLE
First Edition to Second Edition
Section Numbers

First Edition & Cumulative Supplement	Second Edition	First Edition & Cumulative Supplement	Second Edition
§ 1.1	§ 1.1	§ 2.21	§ 2.24
§ 1.2	§ 1.3	§ 2.22	§ 2.25
§ 1.3	§ 1.4	§ 2.23	§ 2.26
§ 1.4	§ 1.5	§ 2.24	§ 2.26
§ 1.5	§ 1.6	§ 2.25	§ 2.27
§ 1.6	§ 1.7	§ 2.26	§ 2.28
§ 1.7	§ 1.8	§ 2.26A	§§ 2.29, 2.30
§ 1.8	§ 1.9	§ 2.27	§ 2.31
§ 1.9	§ 1.10	§ 2.28	§ 2.32
§ 1.10	§ 1.11	§ 2.28A	§ 2.33
§ 1.11	§ 1.12	§ 2.28B	§ 2.34
§ 1.11A	§ 1.14	§ 2.29	§ 2.35
§ 1.12	§ 1.2	§ 2.30	§ 2.36
§ 1.13	§ 1.15	§ 2.31	§ 2.37
§ 1.14	§ 1.16	§ 2.32	§ 7.29
§ 1.15	§ 1.17	§ 2.33	§ 7.35
§ 2.1	§ 2.1	§ 3.1	§ 3.1
§ 2.2	§ 2.2	§ 3.2	§ 3.2
§ 2.3	§ 2.3	§ 3.3	§ 3.3
§ 2.4	§ 2.4	§ 3.4	§ 3.4
§ 2.4A	§ 2.5	§ 3.5	§ 3.5
§ 2.5	§ 2.6	§ 3.6	§ 3.6
§ 2.6	§ 2.7	§ 3.7	§ 3.7
§ 2.7	§ 2.8	§ 3.8	§ 3.8
§ 2.8	§ 2.9	§ 3.9	§ 3.9
§ 2.9	§ 2.10	§ 3.10	§ 3.10
§ 2.10	§ 2.13	§ 3.11	§ 3.12
§ 2.11	§ 2.14	§ 3.12	§ 3.13
§ 2.11A	§ 2.11	§ 3.13	§ 3.14
§ 2.12	§ 2.15	§ 3.14	§ 3.15
§ 2.13	§ 2.16	§ 3.15	§ 3.16
§ 2.14	§ 2.17	§ 3.16	§ 3.18
§ 2.15	§ 2.18	§ 3.17	§ 3.19
§ 2.16	§ 2.19	§ 3.18	§ 3.20
§ 2.17	§ 2.20	§ 3.19	§ 3.21
§ 2.18	§ 2.21	§ 3.20	§ 3.22
§ 2.19	§ 2.22	§ 3.21	§ 3.23
§ 2.20	§ 2.23	§ 3.22	§ 3.25

CONVERSION TABLE

First Edition & Cumulative Supplement	Second Edition	First Edition & Cumulative Supplement	Second Edition
§ 3.23	§ 3.26	§ 5.21	§ 5.24
§ 3.24	§ 3.24	§ 5.22	§ 5.25
§ 3.25	§ 3.27	§ 5.23	§§ 5.26, 5.27
§ 3.26	§ 3.28	§ 5.24	§ 5.29
§ 3.27	§ 3.29	§ 5.24A	§ 5.30
		§ 5.25	§ 5.31
§ 4.1	§ 4.1	§ 5.26	§ 5.32
§ 4.2	§ 4.2	§ 5.27	§ 5.33
§ 4.3	§ 4.3		
§ 4.4	§ 4.4	§ 6.1	§ 6.1
§ 4.5	§ 4.5	§ 6.2	§ 6.2
§ 4.6	§ 4.6	§ 6.3	§ 6.3
§ 4.7	§ 4.8	§ 6.4	§ 6.4
§ 4.8	§ 4.9	§ 6.5	§ 6.5
§ 4.9	§ 4.11	§ 6.6	§ 6.6
§ 4.10	§ 4.12	§ 6.7	§ 6.7
§ 4.11	§ 4.12	§ 6.7A	§ 6.8
§ 4.12	§§ 4.12, 4.14	§ 6.8	§ 6.9
§ 4.13	§§ 4.15, 4.16	§ 6.9	§ 6.10
§ 4.14	§ 4.17	§ 6.10	§ 6.11
§ 4.15	§ 4.13	§ 6.11	§ 6.12
§ 4.16	§ 4.20	§ 6.12	§ 6.13
§ 4.17	§§ 4.21, 4.23	§ 6.13	§ 6.14
§ 4.18	§§ 4.22, 4.24	§ 6.14	§ 6.15
§ 4.19	§ 4.1	§ 6.15	§ 6.16
§ 4.20	§ 4.25	§ 6.16	§ 6.17
§ 4.21	§ 4.26	§ 6.17	§ 6.18
§ 4.22	§ 4.27	§ 6.18	§ 6.19
§ 4.23	§ 4.28	§ 6.19	§ 6.20
§ 5.1	§ 5.1	§ 7.1	§ 7.1
§ 5.2	§ 5.3	§ 7.2	§ 7.2
§ 5.3	§ 5.4	§ 7.3	§§ 7.3, 7.4
§ 5.4	§ 5.5	§ 7.4	§ 7.5
§ 5.5	§ 5.6	§ 7.5	§ 7.6
§ 5.6	§ 5.7	§ 7.6	§ 7.7
§ 5.7	§ 5.8	§ 7.7	§ 7.8
§ 5.8	§ 5.9	§ 7.7A	§ 7.9
§ 5.9	§§ 5.10, 5.11	§ 7.8	§ 7.10
§ 5.10	§ 5.12	§ 7.9	§ 7.11
§ 5.10A	§ 5.13	§ 7.10	§ 7.12
§ 5.11	§ 5.14	§ 7.11	§§ 7.13, 7.14
§ 5.12	§§ 5.15–5.18	§ 7.12	§ 7.15
§ 5.13	§§ 5.15–5.18	§ 7.13	§§ 7.13–7.15
§ 5.14	§ 5.19	§ 7.14	§ 7.16
§ 5.15	§§ 5.1, 5.2	§ 7.15	§ 7.17
§ 5.16	§§ 5.9–5.14	§ 7.16	§§ 7.18, 7.19
§ 5.17	§§ 5.14–5.18	§ 7.16A	§ 7.21
§ 5.18	§ 5.21	§ 7.17	§ 7.20
§ 5.19	§ 5.22	§ 7.18	§§ 7.22, 7.23
§ 5.20	§ 5.23	§ 7.19	§§ 7.22, 7.24

CONVERSION TABLE

First Edition & Cumulative Supplement	Second Edition	First Edition & Cumulative Supplement	Second Edition
§ 7.20	§§ 7.25, 7.26	§ 9.2	§ 9.2
§ 7.21	§ 7.27	§ 9.3	§ 9.3
§ 7.22	§ 7.28	§ 9.4	§ 9.4
§ 7.23	§ 7.29	§ 9.5	§ 9.5
§ 7.24	§ 7.30	§ 9.6	§ 9.11
§ 7.25	§ 7.31	§ 9.7	§ 9.12
§ 7.26	§§ 7.32–7.35	§ 9.8	§ 9.15
		§ 9.9	§ 9.14
§ 8.1	§ 8.1	§ 9.10	§§ 9.7–9.10
§ 8.2	§ 8.2	§ 9.11	§ 9.14
§ 8.3	§ 8.3	§ 9.12	§ 9.17
§ 8.4	§ 8.4	§ 9.13	§ 9.18
§ 8.5	§ 8.5	§ 9.13A	§ 9.19
§ 8.6	§ 8.6	§ 9.14	§§ 9.20–9.24
§ 8.7	§ 8.7	§ 9.15	§ 9.25
§ 8.8	§ 8.8	§ 9.16	§ 9.29
§ 8.9	§ 8.9	§ 9.17	§ 9.27
§ 8.10	§ 8.11	§ 9.18	§ 9.28
§ 8.11	§ 8.12	§ 9.19	§ 9.27
§ 8.12	§ 8.13	§ 9.20	§ 9.26
§ 8.13	§ 8.14	§ 9.21	§ 9.31
§ 8.14	§ 8.15	§ 9.22	§ 9.32
		§ 9.23	§ 9.33
§ 9.1	§ 9.1	§ 9.24	§ 9.34

TABLE OF CASES

Case	Book §
Abood v. Board of Educ., 431 U.S. 209 (1979)	§ 6.11
Abrams v. Department of Navy, 714 F.2d 1219 (3d Cir. 1983)	§§ 6.4, 6.18
Abrisz v. Pulley Freight Lines, Inc., 270 N.W.2d 454 (Iowa 1978)	§ 1.12
Ackman v. Ohio Knife Co., 589 F. Supp. 768 (S.D. Ohio 1984)	§ 4.17
Adair v. United States, 208 U.S. 161 (1908)	§§ 1.4, 1.7
Adams v. Budd Co., 583 F. Supp. 711 (E.D. Pa. 1984)	§§ 4.9, 5.11
Adams v. Frontier Airlines Fed. Credit Union, 691 P.2d 352 (Colo. Ct. App. 1984)	§§ 4.28, 7.25
Ad-Art, Inc. v. NLRB, 645 F.2d 669 (9th Cir. 1980)	§ 3.27
Adcock v. Firestone Tire & Rubber Co., 616 F. Supp. 409 (M.D. Tenn. 1985)	app. F
Adler v. American Standard Corp., 538 F. Supp. 572 (D. Md. 1982)	§§ 2.35, 5.25, 7.11
Adler v. American Standard Corp., 291 Md. 31, 432 A.2d 464 (1981)	§§ 1.10–1.12, 5.7, 5.17, 5.31, 7.11
Adolph v. Cookware Co. of Am., 283 Mich. 561, 278 N.W. 687 (1938)	§ 1.4
A.F.S.C.M.E. Council 96 v. Arrowhead Regional Corrections Bd., 356 N.W.2d 295 (Minn. 1984)	§ 6.15
Agarwal v. Regents of Univ. of Minn., 788 F.2d 504 (8th Cir. 1986)	§§ 6.12, 6.13
Agis v. Howard Johnson Co., 371 Mass. 140, 355 N.E.2d 315 (1976)	§ 5.23
Aikens v. Wisconsin, 195 U.S. 194 (1904)	§ 5.4
Air Force Logistics Command, 75 Lab. Arb. (BNA) 597 (1980) (Johannes, Arb.)	§ 3.15
Ajax Paving Indus., Inc. v. NLRB, 713 F.2d 1214 (6th Cir. 1983)	§ 2.16
Akron Beacon Journal Publishing Co., 85 Lab. Arb. (BNA) 314 (1985) (Oberdank, Arb.)	§ 3.5
Alaniz v. San Isidro Indep. School Dist., 589 F. Supp. 17 (S.D. Tex. 1983), aff'd, 742 F.2d 207 (5th Cir. 1984)	§ 5.33
Albemarle Paper Co. v. Moody, 422 U.S. 405 (1975)	§ 7.6
Albert v. Davenport Osteopathic Hosp., 385 N.W.2d 237 (Iowa 1986)	§§ 1.12, 4.12
Albright v. Upjohn Co., 788 F.2d 1217 (6th Cir. 1986)	§ 4.28
Alexander v. Gardner-Denver Co., 415 U.S. 36 (1974)	§§ 2.3, 2.8, 2.32, 3.27, 7.31, 8.9, 9.3, 9.26, 9.27
Alexander v. Kay Finlay Jewelers, Inc., 208 N.J. Super. 503, 506 A.2d 379 (1986)	§ 7.15
Alexander v. Phillips Oil Co., 707 P.2d 1385 (Wyo. 1985)	§ 1.12
Alford v. Harold's Club, 99 Nev. 670, 669 P.2d 721 (1983)	§§ 7.12, 7.34

CASES

Case	Book §
Alizadeh v. Safeway Stores, Inc., 802 F.2d 111 (5th Cir. 1986)	§ 2.8
Al-Khazraji v. St. Francis College, 784 F.2d 505 (3d Cir. 1986)	§ 2.8
Allegheny, County of v. Allegheny City Prison Employees Indep. Unions, 476 Pa. 27, 381 A.2d 849 (1978)	§ 6.16
Allegri v. Providence-St. Margaret Health Center, 9 Kan App. 2d 659, 684 P.2d 1031 (1984)	§§ 4.9, 7.19
Alleluia Cushion Co., 221 NLRB 999 (1975)	§ 2.16
Alleman v. T.R.W., Inc., 419 F. Supp. 625 (M.D. Pa. 1976)	§ 2.12
Allen v. Amalgamated Transit Union, Local 788, 554 F.2d 876 (8th Cir.), *cert. denied,* 434 U.S. 891 (1977)	§ 2.8
Allen v. Autauga County Bd. of Educ., 685 F.2d 1302 (11th Cir. 1982)	§ 9.32
Allen v. Greenville County, 712 F.2d 934 (4th Cir. 1983)	§ 2.32
Allied Chem. Workers Local 1 v. Pittsburgh Plate Glass Co., 404 U.S. 157 (1971)	§ 4.19
Allis-Chalmers v. Lueck, 471 U.S. 202, 105 S. Ct. 1904 (1985)	§§ 2.27, 5.30
A.L.P.A. v. Northwest Airlines, 627 F.2d 272 (D.C. Cir. 1980)	§ 3.19
Alvey, Inc., 74 Lab. Arb. (BNA) 835 (1980) (Roberts, Arb.)	§ 3.7
Alyeska Pipeline Serv. Co. v. Wilderness Soc'y, 421 U.S. 240 (1975)	§§ 2.25, 4.28, 5.33, 9.33
Amalgamated Meat Cutters v. Great W. Food Co., 712 F.2d 122 (5th Cir. 1983)	§ 3.24
Amaro v. Continental Can Co., 724 F.2d 747 (9th Cir. 1984)	§§ 2.23, 7.31
Amato v. Western Union Int'l, Inc., 733 F.2d 1402 (2d Cir. 1985)	§ 4.19
American Freightways Co., 124 N.L.R.B. 146 (1959)	§ 7.7
American Motors Corp. v. Labor & Indus. Review Comm'n, 119 Wis. 2d 706, 350 N.W.2d 120 (1984)	§ 2.12
American Road Serv. Co. v. Inmon, 394 So. 2d 361 (Ala. 1980)	§ 5.23
American Ship Bldg. Co. v. NLRB, 380 U.S. 300 (1965)	§ 2.16
American Tel. & Tel. Co., 6 Lab. Arb. (BNA) 31 (1947) (Wallen, Arb.)	§ 3.16
American Trucking Ass'n v. United States, 627 F. 2d 1313 (D.C. Cir. 1980)	§§ 9.2, 9.27
Amicone v. Kennecott Copper Corp., 19 Utah 2d 297, 431 P.2d 130 (1967)	app. F
Anaconda Copper Co., N.M. Div., 78 Lab. Arb. (BNA) 690 (1982) (Cohen, Arb.)	§ 3.7
Anco Constr. Co. v. Freeman, 236 Kan. 626, 693 P.2d 1183 (1985)	§§ 1.12, 2.28
Anderberg v. Georgia Elec. Membership Corp., 175 Ga. App. 14, 332 S.E.2d 326 (1985)	§ 1.12
Anderson v. Alpha Portland Indus., Inc., 727 F.2d 177 (8th Cir. 1984), *reh'g en banc,* 752 F.2d 1293 (1985)	§ 4.19
Anderson v. Ford Motor Co., 803 F.2d 953 (8th Cir. 1986)	§ 5.30
Anderson v. Labor & Indus. Review Comm'n, 111 Wis. 2d 245, 330 N.W.2d 594 (1983)	§ 2.12
Anderson v. Liberty Lobby, Inc., ___ U.S. ___, 106 S. Ct. 2505 (1986)	§ 5.25
Anderson v. Low Rent Hous. Comm'n, 304 N.W.2d 239 (Iowa 1981)	§ 5.26

Case *Book §*

Case	Book §
Anderson v. National R.R. Passenger Corp., 754 F.2d 202 (7th Cir. 1985)	§§ 3.24, 6.2
Andolsun v. Berlitz School of Languages, Inc., 196 A.2d 926 (D.C. 1964)	§ 5.33
Andress v. Augusta Nursing Facilities, 156 Ga. App. 775, 275 S.E.2d 368 (1980)	§ 1.12
Andrews v. Drew Mun. Separate School Dist., 507 F.2d 611 (5th Cir. 1975)	§ 6.11
Andrews v. Louisville & N.R.R., 406 U.S. 320 (1972)	§§ 1.10, 2.31, 4.25
Andrew Williams Meat Co., 8 Lab. Arb. (BNA) 518 (1947) (Chency, Arb.)	§ 3.12
Anselmo v. Ailes, 344 F.2d 607 (2d Cir. 1965)	§ 6.3
Anselmo v. Manufacturers Life Ins. Co., 771 F.2d 417 (8th Cir. 1985)	§ 8.10
Anselmo v. Manufacturers Life Ins. Co., 595 F. Supp. 541 (W.D. Mo. 1984)	§§ 4.20, 5.21, 5.31
Antinore v. New York, 49 A.D. 2d 6, 371 N.Y.S.2d 213, *aff'd*, 358 N.E.2d 268 (1975)	§§ 6.15, 6.16
Aranson, *In re*, 6 Lab. Arb. (BNA) 1033 (1946) (Botein, Arb.)	§ 3.12
Arie v. Intertherm, 648 S.W.2d 142 (Mo. Ct. App. 1983)	§ 1.12
Armstrong v. Freeman United Coal Mining Co., 112 Ill. App. 3d 1020, 446 N.E.2d 296 (1983)	§ 2.12
Armstrong v. Richland Clinic, Inc., 42 Wash. App. 181, 709 P.2d 1237 (1985), *review denied,* 105 Wash. 2d 1009 (1986)	§ 7.18
Arnett v. Kennedy, 416 U.S. 134 (1974)	§ 6.10
Arvie v. Century Tel. Enters., Inc., 452 So. 2d 392 (La. Ct. App. 1984)	§ 1.12
Athan v. P.A.T.C.O., 672 F.2d 706 (8th Cir. 1982)	§ 7.32
Atkins v. Bridgeport Hydraulic Co., 5 Conn. App. 643, 501 A.2d 1223 (1985)	§§ 5.9, 7.12
Atlanta Nat'l League Baseball Club, Inc. v. Kuhn, 432 F. Supp. 1213 (N.D. Ga. 1977)	§ 9.17
Atlas Roofing Co. v. O.S.H.R.C., 430 U.S. 442 (1977)	app. C
Attorney Gen. of Can. v. Gauthier, 34 N.R. 549, [1980] 2 F.C. 393 (Ct. App.)	§ 9.12
AT&T Technologies, Inc. v. Communications Workers, ___ U.S. ___, 106 S. Ct. 1415 (1986)	§§ 3.1, 3.19, 3.21, 3.23
Authier v. Ginsberg, 757 F.2d 796 (6th Cir. 1985)	§§ 2.34, 7.11
Avco Corp. v. Aerolodge No. 735, 390 U.S. 557 (1968)	§ 2.29
Averyt v. Doyle, 456 So. 2d 1096 (Ala. Civ. App. 1984)	§ 6.6
Awbrey v. Great Atl. & Pac. Tea Co., 505 F. Supp. 604 (N.D. Ga. 1980)	§ 5.26
Azzi v. Western Elec. Co., 19 Mass. App. Ct. 406, 474 N.E.2d 1166 (1985)	§§ 4.11, 4.25
Bachand v. Connecticut Gen. Life Ins. Co., 101 Wis. 2d 617, 305 N.W.2d 149 (Ct. App. 1981)	§ 2.12
Bader v. Alpine Ski Shop, 505 A.2d 1162 (R.I. 1986)	§ 7.18

CASES

Case	Book §
Baker v. Kaiser Aluminum & Chem. Corp., 608 F. Supp. 1315 (N.D. Cal. 1984)	§ 2.34
Baker v. Penn Mut. Life, 788 F.2d 650 (10th Cir. 1986)	§ 1.12
Baker v. Pennsylvania Human Relations Comm'n, 75 Pa. Commw. 366, 462 A.2d 301 (1983), aff'd as modified, 507 Pa. 325, 489 A.2d 1354 (1984)	§ 2.12
Baker Bus Serv., Inc. v. Keith, 416 A.2d 727 (Me. 1980)	§ 6.2
Bakery Salesmen v. ITT Continental Baking Co., 692 F.2d 29 (6th Cir. 1982)	§ 3.1
Bakker v. Metropolitan Pediatric, 355 N.W.2d 330 (Minn. Ct. App. 1984)	§ 7.18
Bale v. General Tel. Co., 795 F.2d 775 (9th Cir. 1986)	§ 2.29
Balicao v. University of Minn., 737 F.2d 747 (8th Cir. 1984)	§ 7.5
Baltimore & A.R.R. v. National Mediation Bd., 321 F. Supp. 51 (D. Md. 1970)	§ 3.19
Banas v. Matthews Int'l Corp., 348 Pa. Super. 464, 502 A.2d 637 (1985)	§§ 4.6, 4.16, 5.25, 7.18
Barnes v. Costle, 561 F.2d 983 (D.C. Cir. 1977)	§ 2.5
Barr v. Kelso-Burnett Co., 106 Ill. 2d 520, 478 N.E.2d 1354 (1985)	§§ 5.12, 5.15, 7.11
Barrentine v. Arkansas-Best Freight Sys., 450 U.S. 728 (1981)	§§ 3.27, 7.31, 8.9, 9.27
Bartley v. University Asphalt Co., Inc., 111 Ill. 2d 318, 489 N.E.2d 1367 (1986)	§§ 2.30, 5.30
Bazor Express, Inc., 46 Lab. Arb. (BNA) 307 (1966) (Duff, Arb.)	§ 3.8
Beard v. General Servs. Admin., 801 F.2d 1318 (Fed. Cir. 1986)	§ 6.4
Beardon & Co., 272 NLRB 135 (1984)	§ 2.16
Beasley v. Affiliated Hosp. Prods., 713 S.W.2d 557 (Mo. Ct. App. 1986)	§§ 1.12, 5.18, 5.19
Beauvoir v. Rush-Presbyterian-St. Luke's Medical Center, 137 Ill. App. 3d 294, 484 N.E.2d 841 (1985)	§ 8.10
Beckman v. Harris, 756 F.2d 1032 (4th Cir. 1985)	§§ 6.10, 6.11
Becton v. Detroit Terminal of Consol. Freightways, 687 F.2d 140 (6th Cir. 1982)	§ 3.27
Beers v. Southern Pac. Transp. Co., 703 F.2d 425 (9th Cir. 1983)	§ 2.31
Belcher v. Little, 315 N.W.2d 734 (Iowa 1982)	§ 5.25
Belknap, Inc. v. Hale, 463 U.S. 491 (1983)	§§ 2.27, 2.28, 9.3, 9.26
Beller v. Middendorf, 632 F.2d 788 (9th Cir. 1980)	§§ 6.13, 9.2, 9.20
Bell Tel. & Tel. Co. v. Mobile Am. Corp., 291 So. 2d 199 (Fla. 1974)	§ 2.27
Benoir v. Ethan Allen, Inc., ___ Vt. ___, 514 A.2d 716 (1986)	§§ 1.12, 4.8, 7.21
Benson v. Little Rock Hilton Inn, 742 F.2d 414 (8th Cir. 1984)	§ 2.17
Berdin v. Duggan, 701 F.2d 909 (11th Cir.), cert. denied, 464 U.S. 893 (1983)	§§ 6.11, 6.19
Berg v. LaCrosse Coller Co., 612 F.2d 1041 (7th Cir. 1980)	§ 2.17
Bernardine v. City of N.Y., 294 N.Y. 361, 62 N.E.2d 604 (1945)	§ 6.20
Bernstein v. Birch Wathen School, 71 A.D.2d 129 (1979), aff'd, 51 N.Y.2d 932, 415 N.E.2d 982, 434 N.Y.S.2d 994 (1980)	§ 7.35
Bertrand v. Quincy Mkt. Cold Storage & Warehouse Co., 728 F.2d 568 (1st Cir. 1984)	§§ 4.11, 4.25, 5.23

Case *Book §*

Bethel School Dist. No. 403 v. Fraser, ___ U.S. ___, 106 S. Ct. 3159 (1986) — § 9.2

Bethlehem Mines Corp. v. United Mine Workers, 344 F. Supp. 1161 (W.D. Pa. 1972), *aff'd,* 494 F.2d 726 (3d Cir. 1974) — §§ 3.22, 3.23

Beye v. Bureau of Nat'l Affairs, 59 Md. App. 642, 477 A.2d 1197 (1984), *cert. denied,* 301 Md. 369, 484 A.2d 274 (1984) — § 5.6

Bibbs v. Block, 778 F.2d 1318 (8th Cir. 1985) — § 7.6

Bichan v. Chemetron Corp., 681 F.2d 514 (7th Cir. 1982) — § 5.19

Biggins v. Hanson, 252 Cal. App. 2d 16, 59 Cal. Rptr. 897 (1967) — § 5.25

Bihlmainer v. Carson, 603 P.2d 790 (Utah 1979) — § 1.12

Bishop v. Wood, 426 U.S. 341 (1976) — §§ 6.10, 6.11

Bishopp v. District of Columbia, 788 F.2d 781 (D.C. Cir. 1986) — § 2.5

Bittner v. Sadoff & Rudoy Indus., 728 F.2d 820 (7th Cir. 1984) — § 2.23

Bivens v. Six Unknown Agents, 403 U.S. 388 (1971) — § 6.9

Black-Clawson Co. v. Machinists, Lodge 355, 313 F.2d 179 (2d Cir. 1962) — § 3.9

Blackwell v. Sun Elec. Corp., 696 F.2d 1176 (6th Cir. 1983) — § 7.8

Blake v. State Personnel Bd., 25 Cal. App. 3d 541, 102 Cal. Rptr. 50 (1972) — § 6.5

Blanchard v. Control Data Can. Ltd., 14 D.L.R.4th 289 (1984) — § 9.12

Blanton v. Griel Memorial Psychiatric Hosp., 758 F.2d 1540 (11th Cir. 1985) — § 6.10

Blizard v. Frechette, 601 F.2d 1217 (1st Cir. 1979) — § 2.3

Block v. R.H. Macy & Co., 712 F.2d 1241 (8th Cir. 1983) — § 2.8

Blum v. Gulf Oil Co., 597 F.2d 936 (5th Cir. 1979) — § 2.3

Board of Educ. v. Associated Teachers of Huntington, Inc., 30 N.Y.2d 122, 282 N.E.2d 109, 331 N.Y.S.2d 17 (1972) — § 6.15

Board of Educ. v. Philadelphia Fed'n of Teachers, 464 Pa. 92, 346 A.2d 35 (1975) — § 6.16

Board of Educ. v. Yonkers Fed'n of Teachers, 46 N.Y.2d 727, 385 N.E.2d 1297, 413 N.Y.S.2d 370 (1978) — § 6.16

Board of Regents v. Roth, 408 U.S. 564 (1972) — §§ 4.9, 6.10, 6.19, 9.2, 9.20

Bobo v. ITT, Continental Baking Co., 662 F.2d 340 (5th Cir. 1981) — § 2.8

Boddie v. Connecticutt, 401 U.S. 371 (1971) — §§ 1.10. 9.33

Bolling v. Clevepak Corp., 20 Ohio App. 3d 113, 484 N.E.2d 1367 (1984) — app. F

Bondi v. Jewels by Edwar, Ltd., 267 Cal. App. 2d 672, 73 Cal. Rptr. 494 (1968) — § 5.24

Bonet v. United States Postal Serv., 661 F.2d 1071 (5th Cir. 1981) — § 6.4

Boniuk v. New York Medical College, 535 F. Supp. 1353 (S.D.N.Y. 1982) — § 5.12

Borg-Warner Corp., 3 Lab. Arb. (BNA) 423 (1944) (Gilden, Arb.) — § 3.13

Borrell v. United States Int'l Communications Agency, 682 F.2d 981 (D.C. Cir. 1982) — § 6.6

Borumka v. Rocky Mountain Hosp. & Medical Serv., 599 F. Supp. 857 (D. Colo. 1984) — § 2.35

Bottini v. Sadore Management Corp., 764 F.2d 116 (2d Cir. 1985) — §§ 3.27, 7.31, 9.26

Bouchet v. National Urban League, Inc., 730 F.2d 799 (D.C. Cir. 1984) — § 2.35

Bowen v. United States Postal Serv., 459 U.S. 212 (1983) — §§ 3.9, 3.26

CASES

Case	Book §
Bower v. Bunker Hill Co., 725 F.2d 1221 (9th Cir. 1984)	§ 4.19
Bowman v. State Bank of Keysville, 229 Va. 534, 331 S.E.2d 797 (1985)	§§ 1.12, 5.17, 7.11, 7.12
Boyd v. United States Postal Serv., 752 F.2d 410 (9th Cir. 1985)	§ 6.6
Boyle v. Vista Eyewear, Inc., 700 S.W.2d 859 (Mo. Ct. App. 1985)	§§ 1.12, 5.8, 9.9
Boyle v. Carnegie Mellon Univ., 648 F. Supp. 1318 (W.D. Pa.), *mandamus denied*, No. 85-3619 (3d Cir. 1986)	§ 2.38
Boynton Cab Co. v. Department of Indus., 96 Wis. 2d 396, 291 N.W.2d 850 (1980)	§ 2.12
Bradkin v. Leverton, 26 N.Y.2d 192, 257 N.E.2d 643, 309 N.Y.S.2d 192 (1970)	§ 4.11
Brantley v. Surles, 765 F.2d 478 (5th Cir. 1985)	§ 6.11
Bratt v. International Business Machs. Corp., 785 F.2d 352 (1st Cir. 1986)	§ 5.26
Brennan v. Braswell Motor Freight Lines, Inc., 396 F. Supp. 704 (N.D. Tex. 1975)	§ 2.21
Brewster v. Martin Marietta Aluminum Sales, Inc., 145 Mich. App. 641, 378 N.W.2d 558 (1985)	§§ 4.28, 5.29, 7.19
Brezinski v. F.W. Woolworth Co., 626 F. Supp. 240 (D. Colo. 1986)	§§ 1.12, 2.26, 4.26, 5.31
Brieck v. Harbison-Walker Refractories, 624 F. Supp. 363 (W.D. Pa. 1985)	§§ 7.8, 7.18
Briggs v. Mid-State Oil Co., ___ N.C. App. ___, 280 S.E.2d 501 (1981)	§ 5.24
Briggs v. North Muskegon Police Dep't, 563 F. Supp. 585 (W.D. Mich. 1983)	§ 5.27
Bringle v. Methodist Hosp., 701 S.W.2d 622 (Tenn. Ct. App. 1985)	§ 1.12
Brink's Inc. v. City of N.Y., 533 F. Supp. 1123 (S.D.N.Y. 1982)	§§ 5.12, 5.23
Briscoe v. LaHue, 460 U.S. 325 (1983)	§ 6.19
B&R Motor Express v. NLRB, 413 F.2d 1021 (1969)	§ 2.16
Brockell v. Norton, 732 F.2d 664 (8th Cir. 1984)	§ 6.11
Brockert v. Skornicka, 711 F.2d 1376 (7th Cir. 1983)	§ 6.10
Brockmeyer v. Dun & Bradstreet, Inc., 113 Wis. 2d 561, 335 N.W.2d 834 (1983)	§§ 1.2, 4.6, 4.11, 4.23, 4.28, 9.4, 9.22, 9.23
Broniman v. Great Atl. & Pac. Tea Co., 353 F.2d 559 (6th Cir. 1965)	§ 3.9
Bronx County Pharmaceutical Ass'n, 16 Lab. Arb. (BNA) 835 (1951)	§ 3.10
Brooks v. Trans World Airlines, 574 F. Supp. 805, 114 L.R.R.M. 3136 (D. Colo. 1983)	§§ 1.12, 5.24, 5.29
Brookshaw v. South St. Paul Feed, Inc., 381 N.W.2d 33 (Minn. Ct. App. 1986)	§§ 1.12, 4.16, 7.18, 7.20
Broussard v. C.A.C.I., Inc., 780 F.2d 162 (1st Cir. 1986)	§§ 4.6, 5.24
Browder v. Tipton, 630 F.2d 1149 (6th Cir. 1980)	§ 2.9
Brower v. Holmes Transp., Inc., 140 Vt. 114, 435 A.2d 952 (1981)	§ 7.20
Brown v. Alabama State Tenure Comm'n, 349 So. 2d 56 (Ala. Civ.	

Case Book §

App. 1977) § 6.5
Brown v. Board of Educ., 347 U.S. 483 (1954) § 1.10
Brown v. Carnegie-Illinois Steel Corp., 168 Pa. Super. 380, 77 A.2d 655, *aff'd,* 368 Pa. 166, 81 A.2d 562 (1951) app. F
Brown v. G.S.A., 425 U.S. 820 (1976) § 6.8
Brown v. Physicians Mut. Ins. Co., 679 S.W.2d 836 (Ky. Ct. App. 1984) § 1.12
Brown & Root, Inc. v. Donovan, 747 F.2d 1029 (5th Cir. 1984) §§ 2.24, 5.12, 5.14, 7.15
Bruffet v. Warner Communications, Inc., 692 F.2d 910 (3d Cir. 1982) §§ 2.12, 2.26, 5.19, 7.11
Bryant v. St. Helena Parish School Bd., 561 F. Supp. 239 (M.D. La. 1983) § 6.11
Buchanan v. Boh Bros. Constr. Co., 741 F.2d 750 (5th Cir. 1984) §§ 2.24, 5.11
Buchanan v. Martin Marietta Corp., 494 A.2d 677 (Me. 1985) § 7.18
Buchholz v. Symons Mfg. Co., 445 F. Supp. 706 (E.D. Wis. 1978) § 2.6
Buckhalter v. Pepsi-Cola Gen. Bottlers, 768 F.2d 842 (7th Cir. 1985) §§ 7.33, 9.26
Buckley v. Hospital Corp. of Am., 758 F.2d 1525 (11th Cir. 1985) §§ 2.6, 2.7
Bucyrus-Erie Co. v. State, Dep't of Indus., Labor & Human Relations, Equal Rights Div., 90 Wis. 2d 408, 280 N.W.2d 142 (1979) § 2.12
Buell v. Atchison, T.&S.F. Ry., 771 F.2d 1320 (9th Cir. 1985) § 2.31
Bueno v. City of Donna, 714 F.2d 484 (5th Cir. 1983) §§ 6.10, 6.11
Buethe v. Britt Airlines, Inc., 749 F.2d 1235 (7th Cir. 1984), *later appeal,* 787 F.2d 1194 (7th Cir. 1986) §§ 1.2, 1.12, 1.15, 2.35, 5.19, 7.11
Buice v. Gulf Oil Corp., 172 Ga. App. 93, 322 S.E.2d 103 (1984) § 1.12
Bullard v. OMI Ga., 640 F.2d 632 (5th Cir. 1981) § 2.8
Bullock v. Automobile Club of Mich., 146 Mich. App. 711, 381 N.W.2d 793 (1985) § 4.19
Bundy v. Jackson, 641 F.2d 934 (D.C. Cir. 1981) §§ 2.3, 2.5
Burke v. Compania Mexicana de Aviacion, S.A., 433 F.2d 1031 (9th Cir. 1970) § 2.26
Burkett v. United States, 402 F.2d 1002 (Ct. Cl. 1968) § 6.4
Burkhart v. Mobil Oil Corp., 143 Vt. 123, 463 A.2d 226 (1983) §§ 3.21, 4.25, 9.28
Burkhart v. Randles, 764 F.2d 1196 (6th Cir. 1985) § 6.11
Burnette v. Walsh, 284 Or. 705, 588 P.2d 1105 (1978) § 5.19
Burney v. Polk Community College, 728 F.2d 1374 (11th Cir. 1984) § 7.30
Burnham City Hosp. v. Human Relations Comm'n, 126 Ill. App. 3d 999, 467 N.E.2d 635 (1984) § 2.12
Burns v. Preston Trucking Co., Inc., 621 F. Supp. 366 (D. Conn. 1986) § 1.14
Burroughs v. Great Atl. & Pac. Tea Co., 462 So. 2d 353 (Ala. 1984) § 2.6
Burrus v. Nevada-Cal.-Or. R.R., 38 Nev. 156, 145 P.2d 926 (1915) app. E
Burton v. Wilmington Parking Auth., 365 U.S. 715 (1961) § 6.2
Buscemi v. McDonnell Douglas Corp., 736 F.2d 1348 (9th Cir. 1984) § 2.29
Buschi v. Kirven, 775 F.2d 1240 (4th Cir. 1985) §§ 2.9, 6.11, 6.12, 6.19

CASES

Case	Book §
Bush v. Lucas, 462 U.S. 367 (1983)	§§ 1.6, 1.10, 6.4, 6.6, 6.9, 6.18, 8.11
Bushko v. Miller Brewing Co., 396 N.W.2d 167, 170 (Wis. 1986)	§ 5.17
Bushman v. Pure Plant Food Int'l, Ltd., 330 N.W.2d 762 (S.D. 1983)	§ 9.8
Butz v. Economou, 438 U.S. 478 (1978)	§ 6.18
Cagle v. Burns & Roe, Inc., 106 Wash. 2d 911, 726 P.2d 434 (1986)	§ 5.33
Cahill v. Board of Educ., 187 Conn. 94, 444 A.2d 907 (1982)	§ 6.20
Calhoun v. Falstaff Brewing Corp., 478 F. Supp. 357 (E.D. Mo. 1979)	§ 2.23
California Fed. Sav. & Loan Ass'n v. Guerra, 758 F.2d 390 (9th Cir. 1985) aff'd, ___ U.S. ___, 55 U.S.L.H. 4077 (Jan. 13, 1987)	§ 2.32
Callahan v. Scott Paper Co., 541 F. Supp. 550 (E.D. Pa. 1982)	§ 5.19
Camacho v. Ritz-Carlton Water Tower, 786 F.2d 242 (7th Cir.), cert. denied, ___ U.S. ___, 106 S. Ct. 3282 (1986)	§ 3.25
Cameron Iron Works Inc., 25 Lab. Arb. (BNA) 295 (1955) (Boles, Arb.)	§ 3.5
Camp v. Pitts, 411 U.S. 138 (1973)	§§ 9.2, 9.27
Campbell v. Eli Lilly & Co., 413 N.E.2d 1054 (Ind. Ct. App. 1980), aff'd, 421 N.E.2d 1099 (1981)	§ 5.17
Campbell v. Ford Indus., 274 Or. 243, 546 P.2d 141 (1976)	§ 5.15
Campbell v. State, 259 Ind. 55, 284 N.E.2d 733 (1972)	§ 6.20
Campbell Soup Co., 2 Lab. Arb. (BNA) 27 (1946) (Lohman, Arb.)	§ 3.13
Cancellier v. Federated Dep't Stores, Inc., 672 F.2d 1312 (9th Cir.), cert. denied, 459 U.S. 859 (1982)	§§ 2.32, 4.23, 7.11
Cannon v. Geneva Wheel & Stamping Corp., 172 Ga. App. 20, 322 S.E.2d 69 (1984)	§ 5.24
Cannon v. University of Chicago, 441 U.S. 677 (1979)	§ 2.14
Capital Area Transp. Auth., 79 Lab. Arb. (BNA) 665 (1982) (Fieger, Arb.)	§ 3.6
Capone v. Chesebrough Pond's, Inc., 112 A.D.2d 779, 492 N.Y.S.2d 277 (1985), appeal dismissed, 67 N.Y.2d 904, 492 N.E.2d 1230, 501 N.Y.S.2d 814 (1986)	§ 7.27
Cappiello v. Ragen Precision Indus., Inc., 192 N.J. Super. 523, 471 A.2d 432 (1984)	§ 4.28
Caproom v. G.D. Searle Co., ___ F. Supp. ___, No. 84-0640-Civ-Marcus (S.D. Fla., filed Nov. 21, 1986)	§ 5.23
Carbonell v. Louisiana Dep't of Health & Human Servs., 772 F.2d 185 (5th Cir. 1985)	§ 6.6
Carlson v. Green, 446 U.S. 14 (1980)	§ 6.9
Carmichael v. Birmingham Saw Works, 738 F.2d 1126 (11th Cir. 1984)	§ 2.3
Carpenters v. Scott, 463 U.S. 825 (1983)	§§ 2.9, 5.12
Carrillo v. Illinois Bell Tel. Co., 538 F. Supp. 793 (N.D. Ill. 1982)	§§ 2.26, 5.23
Carter v. Board of Trustees of Univ. of Ala., 431 So. 2d 529 (Ala. 1983)	§ 6.20
Carter v. United States, 407 F.2d 1238 (D.C. Cir. 1968)	§ 2.24
Carver v. Sheller-Globe Corp., 636 F. Supp. 368 (W.D. Mich. 1986)	§ 1.14
Casey v. City of Fairbanks, 670 P.2d 1133 (Alaska 1983)	§ 6.15

Case	Book §
Castelli v. Douglas Aircraft Co., 752 F.2d 1480 (9th Cir. 1985)	§§ 3.9, 3.25
Caster v. Hennessey, 727 F.2d 1075 (11th Cir. 1984)	§ 1.12
Castiglione v. Johns Hopkins Hosp., ___ Md. App. ___, ___, 517 A.2d 786, 793 (1986)	§ 4.10
Cauley v. Jacksonville, 403 So. 2d 329 (Fla. 1981)	§ 6.20
Cavoli v. A.R.A. Servs., Inc., Civ. No. 83-3764 (D.N.J. letter op., filed Jan 24, 1984)	§§ 7.34, 9.26
Cecil v. Department of Transp., 767 F.2d 892 (Fed. Cir. 1985)	§ 6.4
Cederstrand v. Lutheran Bhd., 263 Minn. 520, 117 N.W.2d 213 (1962)	§ 7.20
Central Soya Co., 74 Lab. Arb. (BNA) 1084 (1980) (Cantor, Arb.)	§ 3.8
Chai v. Michigan Technical Univ., 493 F. Supp. 1137 (W.D. Mich. 1980)	§ 2.9
Chamberlain v. Bissell, Inc., 547 F. Supp. 1067 (W.D. Mich. 1982)	§ 5.29
Chandler v. City of Lanett, 424 So. 2d 1307 (Ala. 1982)	§ 6.5
Charles Dowd Box Co. v. Courtney, 368 U.S. 502 (1962)	§ 2.29
Charles Todd Uniform Rental Serv. Co., 77 Lab. Arb. (BNA) 144 (1981) (Hutcheson, Arb.)	§ 3.6
Chastain v. Kelly-Springfield Tire Co., 733 F.2d 1479 (11th Cir. 1984)	§§ 4.8, 4.17, 4.28
Chas. Wolff Packing Co. v. Court of Industrial Relations, 262 U.S. 522 (1923), 267 U.S. 552 (1925)	§ 3.3
Chatelain v. Mount Sinai Hosp., 580 F. Supp. 1414 (S.D.N.Y. 1984)	§ 7.35
Cha-Tsu Siu v. Johnson, 748 F.2d 238 (4th Cir. 1984)	§ 6.12
Chavers v. State Personnel Bd., 357 So. 2d 662 (Ala. Civ. App.), cert. denied, 357 So. 2d 664 (Ala. 1978)	§§ 6.5, 9.32
Chin v. American Tel. & Tel. Co., 96 Misc. 2d 1070, 410 N.Y.S.2d 737 (1978)	§ 5.12, 5.21
Choudhury v. Polytechnic Inst., 735 F.2d 38 (2d Cir. 1984)	§§ 2.17, 7.9
Christian v. County of Ontario, 92 Misc. 2d 51, 399 N.Y.S.2d 379 (Sup. Ct. 1977)	app. F
Cilley v. New Hampshire Ball Bearings, Inc., ___ N.H. ___, 514 A.2d 818 (1986)	§§ 1.12, 7.13, 7.16
Cinefot Int'l Corp. v. Hudson Photographic Indus., 13 N.Y.2d 249, 196 N.E.2d 54, 246 N.Y.S.2d 345 (1963)	§§ 4.19, 7.19
Cipov v. International Harvester Co., 134 Ill. App. 3d 522, 481 N.E.2d 22 (1985)	§ 7.11
Cisco v. United Parcel Serv., Inc., 328 Pa. Super. 300, 476 A.2d 1340 (1984)	§ 7.15
Clafin v. Houseman, 93 U.S. 130 (1876)	§ 2.27
Clanton v. Cain Sloan Co., 677 S.W.2d 441 (Tenn. 1984)	§§ 1.12, 5.11, 5.33
Clark v. Times Square Stores Corp., 469 F. Supp. 654 (S.D.N.Y. 1979)	§ 2.8
Clary v. Irvin, 501 F. Supp. 706 (E.D. Tex. 1980)	§ 9.32
Clayton v. Automobile Workers, 451 U.S. 679 (1981)	§ 4.25
Cleary v. American Airlines, Inc., 111 Cal. App. 3d 443, 168 Cal. Rptr. 722 (1980)	§§ 4.8, 4.9, 4.11, 4.12, 4.23, 5.9, 7.10, 9.10
Cleasby v. Leo A. Daly Co., 221 Neb. 254, 376 N.W.2d 312 (1985)	§ 7.18

CASES

Case	*Book §*
Cleveland Bd. of Educ. v. Loudermill, 470 U.S. 532 (1985)	§§ 6.10, 6.12, 9.2, 9.20
Clifford v. Cactus Drilling Corp., 419 Mich. 356, 353 N.W.2d 469 (1984)	§ 5.11
Cline v. Roadway Express, Inc., 689 F.2d 481 (4th Cir. 1982)	§§ 2.3, 2.6, 7.7, 7.8
Cloutier v. Great Atl. & Pac. Tea Co., 121 N.H. 915, 436 A.2d 1140 (1981)	§§ 1.2, 1.9, 1.12, 2.18, 5.9, 5.18, 5.31, 7.11, 7.13, 7.16, 7.28
Cloverleaf Butter v. Patterson, 315 U.S. 148 (1942)	§ 2.27
Coburn v. Pan Am. World Airways, 711 F.2d 339 (D.C. Cir. 1983)	§§ 2.6, 2.7
Codd v. Velger, 429 U.S. 624 (1977)	§§ 6.10, 6.11
Cohen v. City of Philadelphia, 736 F.2d 81 (3d Cir.), *cert. denied,* 469 U.S. 1019 (1984)	§ 6.6
Collins v. MBPXL Corp., 9 Kan. App. 2d 363, 679 P.2d 746 (1984)	§§ 2.28, 5.24
Colorado Springs Coach Co. v. Colorado Civil Rights Comm'n, 35 Colo. App. 378, 536 P.2d 837 (1975)	§ 7.35
Comerio v. Beatrice Foods Co., 600 F. Supp. 765 (E.D. Mo. 1985)	§ 4.9
Commonwealth v. Hunt, 4 Mass. 111 (1842)	§ 9.3
Commonwealth v. Social Servs. Union, 82 Pa. Commw. 200, 475 A.2d 133 (1984)	§ 6.15
Community College, 85 Lab. Arb. (BNA) 687 (1985) (Goldberg, Arb.)	§ 3.8
Compo Machining Co. v. Machinists Local 1926, 536 F.2d 330 (10th Cir. 1976)	§ 3.18
Concrete Pipe Prods., Daily Lab. Rep. 2 (Sept. 18, 1986) (Caraway, Arb.)	§ 3.7
Conley v. Gibson, 355 U.S. 41 (1957)	§§ 4.26, 5.31
Connelly v. United States, 554 F. Supp. 1250 (Cl. Ct. 1982), *cert. denied,* 465 U.S. 1065 (1984)	§§ 6.4, 6.18
Conner v. Fort Gordon Bus Co., 761 F.2d 1495 (11th Cir. 1985)	§ 7.6
Conner v. United States Civil Serv. Comm'n, 721 F.2d 1054 (6th Cir. 1983)	§ 6.4
Connick v. Myers, 461 U.S. 138 (1983)	§§ 6.11, 6.13, 7.5, 9.2, 9.20
Connor v. B.R.A.C., 496 F. Supp. 154 (M.D. Pa. 1980)	§ 3.19
Connors v. Connolly, 86 Conn. 641, 86 A. 600 (1913)	§ 3.21
Consolidated Edison Co. v. Donovan, 673 F.2d 61 (2d Cir. 1982)	§ 2.24
Consolidated Rail Corp. v. Darrone, 465 U.S. 624 (1984)	§ 2.10
Consolidated Coal Co. v. Federal Mine Safety & Health Review Comm'n, 795 F.2d 364 (4th Cir. 1986)	§ 2.18
Continental Air Lines, Inc. v. Keenan, ___ Colo. ___, ___ P.2d ___, No. 84SC460 (filed Jan. 20, 1987)	§§ 1.12, 4.17
Contreras v. Crown Corp., 88 Wash. 2d 735, 565 P.2d 1173 (1977)	§ 5.23
Cook v. Alexander & Alexander of Conn., Inc., 40 Conn. Supp. 246, 488 A.2d 1295 (1985)	§ 4.11, 7.11
Cook v. Heck's Inc., 342 S.E.2d 453 (W. Va. 1986)	§§ 1.12, 4.13, 4.16, 7.18
Cook Paint & Varnish Co. v. NLRB, 648 F.2d 712 (D.C. Cir.	

Case	Book §
1981)	§ 3.28
Cooper v. United States, 639 F.2d 727 (Ct. Cl. 1980)	§ 6.4
Cooper Thermometer, 154 NLRB 502 (1965)	§ 2.16
Coppage v. Kansas, 236 U.S. 1 (1915)	§§ 1.4, 1.7
Corbin v. Sinclair Mktg., Inc., 684 P.2d 265 (Colo. Ct. App. 1984)	§ 5.9
Corder v. Champion Road Mach. Int'l, 283 S.C. 520, 324 S.E.2d 79 (1984)	§§ 5.23, 5.27
Cordle v. General Hugh Mercer Corp., 325 S.E.2d 111 (W. Va. 1984)	§ 7.11
Corporon v. Safeway Stores, Inc., 708 P.2d 1385 (Colo. Ct. App. 1985)	§ 1.12
Cort v. Ash, 422 U.S. 66 (1975)	§§ 2.22, 2.26, 5.19
Cort v. Bristol-Myers Co., 385 Mass. 300, 431 N.E.2d 908 (1982)	§ 5.26
Cory v. White, 457 U.S. 85 (1982)	§ 6.19
Costa v. Stephens-Adamson, Inc., 142 Ill. App. 3d 798, 491 N.E.2d 490 (1986)	§ 8.10
Costello v. Shelter Mut. Ins. Co., 697 S.W.2d 236 (Mo. Ct. App. 1985)	§ 5.21
County College of Morris Staff Ass'n v. County College of Morris, 100 N.J. 383, 495 A.2d 865 (1985)	§ 6.16
Covell v. Spengler, 141 Mich. App. 76, 366 N.W.2d 76 (1985)	§§ 1.12, 2.26, 5.9
Coveney v. President & Trustees of Holy Cross College, 388 Mass. 16, 445 N.E.2d 136 (1983)	§ 9.17
Cox v. Dardanelle Pub. School Dist., 790 F.2d 668 (8th Cir. 1986)	§§ 6.11, 7.5
Cox v. Resilient Flooring Div., 638 F. Supp. 726 (C.D. Cal. 1986)	§§ 1.15, 1.16, 5.7
C.&P. Tel. Co. v. NLRB, 687 F.2d 633 (2d Cir. 1982)	§ 3.28
Craig v. Alabama State Univ., 804 F.2d 682, 686 (11th Cir. 1986)	§ 2.3
Crenshaw v. Bozeman Deaconess Hosp., ___ Mont. ___, 693 P.2d 487 (1984)	§§ 4.11, 4.23, 4.28, 5.29, 7.23
Crews v. Memorex Corp., 588 F. Supp. 27 (D. Mass. 1984)	§§ 2.26, 2.27, 5.9, 5.11
Criswell v. Western Airlines, Inc., 514 F. Supp. 384 (C.D. Cal. 1981)	§ 2.6
Croker v. Boeing Co., 662 F.2d 975 (3d Cir. 1981)	§ 2.8
Cronan v. New Eng. Tel. & Tel. Co., 41 F.E.P. Cas. (BNA) 1273 (Mass. Super. Ct. 1986)	§ 2.12
Crossman v. Trans World Airlines, 777 F.2d 1271 (7th Cir. 1985)	§§ 1.14, 5.24
Crowell v. Benson, 285 U.S. 22 (1932)	app. C
Cuddy v. Carmen, 694 F.2d 853 (D.C. Cir. 1982)	§§ 2.6, 7.8
Cummings v. National R.R. Passenger Corp., 343 Pa. Super. 137, 494 A.2d 393 (1985)	§ 2.31
Cutter v. Lincoln Nat'l Life Ins. Co., 794 F.2d 352 (8th Cir. 1986)	§§ 1.12, 4.10, 7.18
Cybyske v. Independent School Dist. No. 196, 347 N.W.2d 256 (Minn.), *cert. denied,* 469 U.S. 933 (1984)	§ 5.27
Czosek v. O'Mara, 397 U.S. 25 (1970)	§ 3.26
Dahl v. Brunswick Corp., 277 Md. 471, 356 A.2d 221 (1976)	app. F
Daigle v. Gulf State Utils. Co., 794 F.2d 974 (5th Cir. 1986)	§ 2.9
Dair v. NLRB, 801 F.2d 1404 (D.C. Cir. 1986)	§ 3.27
Dake v. Tuell, 687 S.W.2d 191 (Mo. 1985)	§§ 1.12, 5.21
Dale v. Chicago Tribune Co., 797 F.2d 458 (7th Cir. 1986)	§ 7.8

CASES

Case	*Book §*
D'Amato v. Wisconsin Gas Co., 760 F.2d 1474 (7th Cir. 1985)	§ 2.10
Damrow v. Thumb Coop. Terminal Inc., 126 Mich. App. 354, 337 N.W.2d 338, *appeal denied,* 418 Mich. App. 899 (1983)	§§ 4.22, 7.24
Dangott v. ASG Indus., Inc., 558 P.2d 379 (Okla. 1976)	§§ 4.8, 4.18
Danzer v. Professional Insurors, Inc., 101 N.M. 178, 679 P.2d 1276 (1984)	§ 7.25
Darden v. Illinois Bell Tel. Co., 797 F.2d 497 (7th Cir. 1986)	§§ 7.31, 8.9, 9.26, 9.27
Dare v. Montana Petroleum Mktg. Co., ___ Mont. ___, 687 P.2d 1015 (1984)	§§ 1.12, 4.11
Darlington v. General Elec. Co., 350 Pa. Super, 183, 504 A.2d 306 (1986)	§ 1.12, 4.12, 4.21, 7.17, 7.18, 7.20
Darnell v. Impact Indus., 105 Ill. 2d 158, 473 N.E.2d 935 (1984)	§ 5.11
Daubert v. United States Postal Serv., 733 F.2d 1367 (10th Cir. 1984)	§ 2.10
Davis v. Combustion Eng'g, Inc., 742 F.2d 916 (6th Cir. 1984)	§ 2.6
Davis v. Scherer, 468 U.S. 183 (1984)	§ 6.19
Davis v. State Univ., 802 F.2d 638 (2d Cir. 1986)	§ 7.6
Davis v. Western-Southern Ins. Co., 34 F.E.P. Cases (BNA) 97 (N.D. Ohio 1984)	§ 2.5
Day v. South Park Indep. School Dist., 768 F.2d 696 (5th Cir. 1985)	§ 6.11
Day v. Wayne County Bd. of Auditors, 749 F.2d 1199 (6th Cir. 1984)	§ 6.8
Dayton Power & Light Co., 80 Lab. Arb. (BNA) 19 (1982) (Heinsz, Arb.)	§ 3.7
Dean v. American Sec. Ins. Co., 559 F.2d 1036 (5th Cir. 1977), *cert. denied,* 434 U.S. 1066 (1978)	§ 2.6
Deaton Truck Line v. Teamsters Local 612, 314 F.2d 418 (5th Cir. 1962)	§ 3.23
DeBriar v. Minturn, 1 Cal. 450 (1851)	§ 1.4
DeCinto v. Westchester County Medical Center, 807 F.2d 304 (2d Cir. 1986)	§ 2.3
DeHorney v. Bank of Am., 777 F.2d 440 (9th Cir. 1985), *withdrawn & reh'g stayed,* 784 F.2d 339 (9th Cir. 1986)	§§ 2.8, 2.35, 4.11, 5.22, 7.23
Delaney v. Taco Time Int'l, Inc., 297 Or. 10, 681 P.2d 114 (1984)	§§ 2.26, 5.8, 5.9, 5.18, 5.19, 7.11
DelCasal v. Eastern Airlines, Inc., 634 F.2d 295 (5th Cir.), *cert. denied,* 454 U.S. 892 (1981)	§ 3.25
DelCostello v. Teamsters, 462 U.S. 151 (1983)	§§ 2.38, 3.24, 4.25
DeLury v. Kretchover, 66 Misc. 2d 897, 322 N.Y.S.2d 517 (Sup. Ct. 1971)	§ 5.26
Delzell v. Pope, 200 Tenn. 641, 294 S.W.2d 690 (1956)	§§ 4.9, 7.18
DeMarco v. Thatcher Furnace Co., 102 N.J. Super. 258, 245 A.2d 773 (1968)	§ 7.35
Denver Public Warehouse Co. v. Holloway, 34 Colo. 432, 83 P. 131 (1905)	§ 5.25
Department of Corrections v. Gandy, 374 So. 2d 1081 (Fla. Dist. Ct. App. 1979)	§ 6.5
Department of Defense v. Federal Labor Relations Auth., 659 F.2d	

Case	Book §
1140 (D.C. Cir. 1981)	§ 6.16
Department of Transp. v. Pennsylvania Human Relations Comm'n, 84 Pa. Commw. 98, 480 A.2d 342 (1984)	§ 2.12
Dependahl v. Falstaff Brewing Corp., 491 F. Supp. 1188 (E.D. Mo. 1980), *modified,* 653 F.2d 1208 (8th Cir. 1981)	§§ 4.19, app. F
Deretich v. Office of Admin. Hearings, 798 F.2d 1147 (8th Cir. 1986)	§§ 6.12, 6.13, 7.30
DeRose v. Putnam Management Co., 398 Mass. 205, 496 N.E.2d 428 (1986)	§§ 1.12, 4.11, 4.23, 7.23
Derr v. Gulf Oil Corp., 796 F.2d 340 (10th Cir. 1986)	§ 2.5
DeSantis v. Pacific Tel. & Tel. Co., 608 F.2d 327 (9th Cir. 1979)	§§ 2.3, 2.9
Deschler v. Brown & Williamson Tobacco Co., 797 F.2d 695 (8th Cir. 1986)	§ 7.18
Detroit & Toledo Shore Line R.R. v. U.T.U., 413 F. Supp. 681 (E.D. Mich. 1976)	§ 3.19
Devine v. White, 697 F.2d 421 (D.C. Cir. 1983)	§§ 3.27, 6.16
Devore v. Edgefield County School Dist., 68 F.R.D. 423 (D.S.C. 1975)	§ 2.9
Diaz v. Pan Am. World Airways, Inc., 442 F.2d 385 (5th Cir.), *cert. denied,* 404 U.S. 950 (1971)	§ 2.3
Diaz v. Schwerman Trucking Co., 709 F.2d 1371 (11th Cir. 1983)	§ 3.24
Dinger v. Anchor Motor Freight, Inc., 501 F. Supp. 64 (S.D.N.Y. 1980)	§§ 2.29, 4.25, 5.9
Dioguardi v. Durning, 139 F.2d 774 (2d Cir. 1944)	§§ 4.26, 5.31
Dixie Glass Co. v. Pollak, 341 S.W.2d 530 (Tex. Civ. App. 1960)	app. E
Doe v. St. Joseph's Hosp., 788 F.2d 411 (7th Cir. 1986)	§§ 2.3, 2.8, 2.11, 2.20, 9.27
Doe v. United States Dep't of Justice, 753 F.2d 1092 (D.C. Cir. 1985)	§§ 6.3, 6.11, 6.12
Dombrowski v. Dowling, 459 F.2d 190 (7th Cir. 1972)	§ 2.9
Donnellon v. Fruehauf Corp., 794 F.2d 598 (11th Cir. 1986)	§§ 2.17, 7.6
Donnely v. United Fruit Co., 40 N.J. 61, 190 A.2d 825 (1963)	§ 3.9
Donovan v. George Lai Contracting, Ltd., 629 F. Supp. 121 (W.D. Mo. 1985)	§ 2.18
Donovan v. Hahner, Foreman & Harness, Inc., 736 F.2d 1421 (10th Cir. 1984)	§§ 2.18, 7.34
Donovan v. Peter Zimmer Am., Inc., 557 F. Supp. 642 (D.S.C. 1982)	§§ 2.18, 7.35
Donovan v. Stafford Constr. Co., 732 F.2d 954 (D.C. Cir. 1984)	§ 2.18
Dorak v. Shapp, 403 F. Supp. 863 (M.D. Pa. 1975)	§ 6.9
Dorr v. County of Butte, 795 F.2d 875 (9th Cir. 1986)	§ 6.10
Dorr v. First Ky. Nat'l Corp., 796 F.2d 179 (6th Cir. 1986)	§ 5.28
Dorsey v. Chesapeake & O. R.R., 476 F.2d 243 (4th Cir. 1973)	§ 3.19
Dothard v. Rawlinson, 433 U.S. 321 (1977)	§§ 2.3, 6.7
Douglas v. Anderson, 656 F.2d 528 (9th Cir. 1981)	§§ 2.7, 8.15
Dowd Box Co. v. Courtney, 368 U.S. 502 (1962)	§ 4.25
Doyle v. Veterans Admin., 667 F.2d 70 (Ct. Cl. 1981)	§ 6.4
Dresser Indus., Inc., 83 Lab. Arb. (BNA) 577 (1984) (Harrison, Arb.)	§ 3.6
Drutrisac v. Caterpillar Tractor Co., 749 F.2d 1270 (9th Cir. 1983)	§ 3.25

CASES

Case	*Book §*
Dryden v. Tri-Valley Growers, 65 Cal. App. 3d 990, 135 Cal. Rptr. 720 (1977)	§ 5.22
Ducote v. J.A. Jones Constr. Co., 471 So. 2d 704 (La. 1985)	§ 5.11
Duffy v. Wheeling Pittsburgh Steel Corp., 738 F.2d 1393 (3d Cir.), *cert. denied,* 469 U.S. 1087 (1984)	§§ 2.6, 2.7, 7.8
Duhon v. Slickline, Inc., 449 So. 2d 1147 (La. Ct. App. 1984)	§ 4.28
D'Ulisse-Cupo v. Board of Directors of Notre Dame High School, 6 Conn. App. 153, 503 A.2d 1192, *cert. granted,* 199 Conn. 806, 508 A.2d 32 (1986)	§ 4.17
Dumas v. Kessler & Maguire Funeral Home, Inc., 380 N.W.2d 544 (Minn. Ct. App. 1986)	§§ 1.12, 7.18
Dunham v. Brock, 794 F.2d 1037 (5th Cir. 1986)	§ 2.24
Durabond Prods., Inc. v. Steelworkers, 421 F. Supp. 76 (N.D. Ill. 1976)	§ 3.18
Dvorak v. Pluswood Wis., Inc., 121 Wis. 2d 218, 358 N.W.2d 544 (1984)	§ 4.28
Eales v. Tanana Valley Medical-Surgical Group, Inc., 663 P.2d 958 (Alaska 1983)	§ 1.12
Early v. Eastern Transfer, 669 F.2d 552 (1st Cir. 1983)	§ 3.25
Eastex, Inc. v. NLRB, 437 U.S. 556 (1978)	§ 2.16
Eatmon v. Bristol Steel & Iron Works, Inc., 769 F.2d 1503 (11th Cir. 1985)	§ 2.13
Ebling v. Masco Corp., 408 Mich. 579, 292 N.W.2d 880 (1980)	§ 4.7
Edelman v. Jordan, 415 U.S. 651 (1974)	§ 6.19
Edwards v. Citibank, 74 A.D. 2d 553, 425 N.Y.S.2d 327, *appeal dismissed,* 51 N.Y.2d 875, 414 N.E.2d 400, 433 N.Y.S.2d 1020 (1980)	§ 4.26
Edwards v. Lutheran Senior Servs. of Dover, Inc., 603 F. Supp. 315 (D. Del. 1985)	§ 6.2
EEOC v. CBS, Inc., 743 F.2d 969 (2d Cir. 1984)	§ 2.6
EEOC v. Contour Chair Lounge Co., 596 F.2d 809 (8th Cir. 1979)	§ 2.3
EEOC v. Henry Beck Co., 729 F.2d 301 (4th Cir. 1984)	§ 2.3
EEOC v. Liberty Trucking Co., 695 F.2d 1038 (4th Cir. 1982)	§ 2.3
EEOC v. Pierce Packing Co., 669 F.2d 605 (10th Cir. 1982)	§ 2.3
EEOC v. Prudential Fed. Sav. & Loan Ass'n., 741 F.2d 1225 (10th Cir. 1984), *on remand,* 763 F.2d 1166 (10th Cir. 1985)	§ 2.6
EEOC v. Safeway Stores, Inc., 714 F.2d 567 (5th Cir. 1983)	§ 2.3
EEOC v. Wyoming, 460 U.S. 226 (1983)	§§ 2.6, 6.7
EEOC v. Zippo Mfg. Corp., 713 F.2d 32 (3d Cir. 1983)	§ 2.6
Eichelberger v. NLRB, 765 F.2d 851 (9th Cir. 1985)	§ 3.9
Eichman v. Linden & Sons, Inc., 752 F.2d 1246 (7th Cir. 1985)	§ 2.25
Eiland v. City of Montgomery, 797 F.2d 953 (11th Cir. 1986)	§ 6.11
Eklund v. Vincent Brass & Aluminum Co., 351 N.W.2d 371 (Minn. Ct. App. 1984)	§§ 4.17, 5.23
Elbe v. Wausau Hosp. Center, 606 F. Supp. 1491 (W.D. Wis. 1985)	§§ 2.12, 5.22
Electrical Workers Local 369 v. Olin Corp., 471 F.2d 468 (6th Cir. 1972)	§ 3.18
Elgin, Joliet & E. Ry. v. Burley, 325 U.S. 711 (1945)	§ 3.19
Elia v. Industrial Personnel Corp., 125 Ill. App. 3d 1026, 466 N.E.2d 1054 (1984)	§§ 5.20, 7.12

Case — Book §

Eller v. Houston's Restaurants, 117 L.R.R.M. 2651 (D.D.C. 1984) — § 8.8
Elliott v. Kupferman, 58 Md. App. 510, 473 A.2d 960 (1984) — §§ 6.5, 6.20
Ellis v. El Paso Natural Gas Co., 754 F.2d 884 (10th Cir. 1985) — §§ 4.8, 5.2, 7.18
Ellis v. Glover & Gardner Constr. Co., 562 F. Supp. 1054 (M.D. Tenn. 1983) — § 2.22
Elrod v. Burns, 427 U.S. 347 (1980) — § 6.11
Embry v. Pacific Stationery & Printing Co., 62 Or. App. 113, 659 P.2d 436 (1983) — § 2.29
Emporium Capwell Co. v. Western Addition Community Org., 420 U.S. 50 (1975) — §§ 2.16, 7.15
Enis v. Continental Ill. Nat'l Bank, 582 F. Supp. 876 (N.D. Ill. 1984) — § 1.12
Enterprise Wire Co., 46 Lab. Arb. (BNA) 359 (1966) (Daugherty, Arb.) — § 3.5
Enyeart v. Shelter Mut. Ins. Co., 693 S.W.2d 120 (Mo. Ct. App. 1985) — §§ 1.12, 4.18
Erickson v. Goodell Oil Co., 384 Mich. 207, 180 N.W.2d 798 (1970) — § 4.1
Erie R.R. v. Thompkins, 304 U.S. 64 (1938) — § 1.14
Espaillat v. Berlitz School of Languages, Inc., 383 F.2d 220 (D.C. Cir. 1967) — § 5.33
Evans v. Fluor Distrib. Co., 799 F.2d 364 (7th Cir. 1986) — § 4.20
Ewing v. Board of Trustees of Pulaski Memorial Hosp., 486 N.E.2d 1094 (Ind. Ct. App. 1985) — §§ 1.12, 7.18
Ewing v. NLRB, 768 F.2d 51 (2d Cir. 1985) — § 2.16

Fairchild Indus., 75 Lab. Arb. (BNA) 288 (1980) (Groshong, Arb.) — § 3.7
Falcone v. Columbia Pictures Indus., Inc., 805 F.2d 115, 119 (2d Cir. 1986) — § 4.18
Fanaken v. Bell, 9 D.L.R.4th 637 (Ont. 1984) — § 9.12
Farkus v. Texas Instruments, Inc., 375 F.2d 629 (5th Cir. 1967) — § 2.13
Farmer v. Carpenters Local 25, 430 U.S. 290 (1977) — §§ 2.28, 2.29, 5.9
Farrell v. Automobile Club, ___ Mich. App. ___, ___ N.W.2d ___, No. 82916 (Oct. 6, 1986) — §§ 4.19, 7.19
Fausto v. United States, 783 F.2d 1020 (Fed. Cir.), *on reh'g,* 791 F.2d 1554 (Fed. Cir. 1986) — § 6.18
Fentron Indus., Inc. v. National Shopmen Pension Fund, 674 F.2d 1300 (9th Cir. 1982) — § 4.19
Ferguson v. Freedom Forge Corp., 604 F. Supp. 1157 (W.D. Pa. 1985) — §§ 5.12, 7.20
Ferraro v. Koelsch, 119 Wis. 2d 407, 350 N.W.2d 735 (Ct. App. 1984), *aff'd by different rationale,* 124 Wis. 2d 154, 368 N.W.2d 666 (1985) — §§ 1.12, 4.13, 7.20, 7.26, 8.7
Fine v. Semet, 699 F.2d 1091 (11th Cir. 1983) — § 4.19
Finley v. Aetna Life & Casualty Co., 5 Conn. App. 394, 499 A.2d 64, *cert. granted,* 198 Conn. 802, 501 A.2d 1213 (1985) — §§ 1.12, 4.17, 7.20, 7.21
Firestone Textile Co. v. Meadows, 666 S.W.2d 730 (Ky. 1983) — §§ 1.12, 7.14
Fischer v. Sears, Roebuck & Co., 107 Idaho 197, 687 P.2d 587 (Ct. App. 1984) — § 5.9

CASES

Case	Book §
Fisher v. Illinois Office Supply Co., 130 Ill. App. 3d 996, 474 N.E.2d 1263 (1984)	§§ 2.29, 5.25
Fisher v. Snyder, 476 F.2d 375 (8th Cir. 1973)	§ 6.11
Fisher Foods, Inc., 80 Lab. Arb. (BNA) 133 (1983) (Abrams, Arb.)	§ 3.7
Fitzgerald v. Norwest Corp., ___ Minn. App. ___, 382 N.W.2d 290 (1986), *review denied* (Apr. 24, 1986)	§ 4.8
Fitzpatrick v. Bitzer, 427 U.S. 445 (1975)	§ 6.19
Flagg Bros., Inc. v. Brooks, 436 U.S. 149 (1978)	§ 6.2
Flanigan v. Prudential Fed. Sav. & Loan Ass'n, ___ Mont. ___, 720 P.2d 257 (1986)	§§ 1.12, 4.23, 4.28, 5.29, 7.18, 7.23
Fleming v. Kids & Kin Head Start, 71 Or. App. 718, 692 P.2d 1363 (1985)	§ 7.26
Fletcher v. Wesley Medical Center, 585 F. Supp. 1260 (D. Kan. 1984)	§§ 1.12, 5.22, 5.23
Flight Attendants v. American Airlines, Inc., 767 F.2d 1331 (9th Cir. 1985)	§ 3.27
Flight Attendants v. Pan Am. World Airways, Inc., 789 F.2d 139 (2d Cir. 1986)	§ 2.31
Florida Lime & Avocado Growers v. Paul, 373 U.S. 132 (1963)	§ 2.27
Foley v. Interactive Data Corp., 174 Cal. App. 3d 282, 219 Cal. Rptr, 866 (1985), *review granted,* ___ Cal. 3d ___, 712 P.2d 891, 222 Cal. Rptr. 740 (1986)	§§ 2.8, 2.35, 4.11, 4.23, 5.22, 7.23, 9.4
Foley v. Philadelphia Civil Serv. Comm'n, 55 Pa. Commw. 594, 423 A.2d 1351 (1980)	§ 6.5
Ford Motor Co. v. EEOC, 458 U.S. 219 (1982)	app. E
Ford Motor Co. v. Huffman, 345 U.S. 330 (1953)	§ 3.25
Forman v. B.R.I. Corp., 532 F. Supp. 49 (E.D. Pa. 1982)	§§ 1.12, 7.18
Forrisi v. Bowen, 794 F.2d 931 (4th Cir. 1986)	§ 2.10
Fortune v. National Cash Register Co., 373 Mass. 96, 364 N.E.2d 1251 (1977)	§§ 1.9, 1.11, 1.12, 4.11, 4.22, 4.23, 7.11, 7.23
Fountain v. Safeway Stores, 555 F.2d 753 (9th Cir. 1977)	§ 3.25
Frampton v. Central Ind. Gas Co., 260 Ind. 249, 297 N.E.2d 425 (1973)	§§ 1.12, 5.10, 5.11, 7.14
Franceski v. Plaquemines Parish School Bd., 772 F.2d 197 (5th Cir. 1985)	§ 6.12
Franklin Mining Co. v. Harris, 24 Mich. 115 (1871)	§ 1.4
Franks v. Bowman Transp. Co., 424 U.S. 747 (1976)	§ 9.32
Frankson v. Design Space Int'l, 394 N.W.2d 140 (Minn. 1986)	§ 5.25
Frazier v. Colonial Williamsburg Found., 574 F. Supp. 318 (E.D. Va. 1983)	§§ 1.12, 2.32
Frazier v. Ford Motor Co., 364 Mich. 648, 112 N.W.2d 80 (1961)	§ 2.29
French v. Dillard Dep't Stores, Inc., 285 Ark. 332, 686 S.W.2d 435 (1985)	§ 1.12
Freuhauf Trailer Co., 16 Lab. Arb. (BNA) 666 (1951)	§ 3.5

Case *Book §*

Froelich v. Werbin, 219 Kan. 461, 548 P.2d 482 (1976)	§ 5.26
Frontiero v. Richardson, 411 U.S. 677 (1973)	§ 1.10
Fulford v. Burndy Corp., 623 F. Supp. 78 (D.N.H. 1985)	§ 7.11
Furr's, Inc., 83 Lab. Arb. (BNA) 279 (1984) (Daughton, Arb.)	§ 3.6
Fye v. Central Transp., Inc., 487 Pa. Super. 137, 409 A.2d 2 (1979)	§ 2.12
Gahr v. Trammel, 796 F.2d 1063 (8th Cir. 1986)	§ 7.30
Gaibis v. Werner Continental, Inc., 565 F. Supp. 1538 (W.D. Pa. 1983), *rev'd sub nom.* Vosch v. Werner Continental, Inc., 734 F.2d 149 (3d Cir. 1984), *cert. denied,* 469 U.S. 1108 (1985)	§§ 7.34, 9.26
Galante v. Sandoz, 196 N.J. Super. 568, 483 A.2d 829 (1984)	§ 7.15
Garcia v. Aetna Fin. Co., 752 F.2d 488 (10th Cir. 1984)	§§ 1.12
Garcia v. NLRB, 785 F.2d 807 (9th Cir. 1986)	§ 2.16
Garibaldi v. Lucky Food Stores, Inc., 726 F.2d 1367 (9th Cir. 1984), *cert. denied,* 471 U.S. 1099 (1985)	§§ 2.29, 3.27, 5.20, 5.30, 7.31
Garment Workers v. Quality Mfg. Co., 420 U.S. 276 (1975)	§ 3.9
Garry v. TRW, Inc., 603 F. Supp. 157 (N.D. Ohio 1985)	§ 2.23
Gas Serv. Co., 39 Lab. Arb. (BNA) 1025 (1962) (Granoff, Arb.)	§ 3.8
Gates v. Life of Mont. Ins. Co., 196 Mont. 178, 638 P.2d (1982), *later appeal,* 668 P.2d 213 (1983)	§§ 1.12, 4.11, 4.22, 4.23, 5.23, 5.24, 7.23, 9.2, 9.27
Gattis v. Gravett, 806 F.2d 778, 781 (8th Cir. 1986)	§ 6.12
Gaulden v. Emerson Elec. Co., 284 Ark. 149, 680 S.W.2d 92 (1984)	§ 4.26
Gaydos v. White Motor Corp., 54 Mich. App. 143, 220 N.W.2d 697 (1974)	app. F
Gay Law Students Ass'n v. Pacific Tel. & Tel. Co., 24 Cal. 3d 458, 595 P.2d 592, 156 Cal. Rptr. 14 (1979)	§ 5.12
Geary v. United States Steel Corp., 456 Pa. 171, 319 A.2d 174 (1974)	§§ 1.11, 1.12, 5.1, 5.6, 5.7, 5.13, 5.14, 5.17, 5.18, 5.21, 5.22, 7.14, 7.15
Gee v. Alabama State Tenure Comm'n, 419 So. 2d 227 (Ala. Civ. App.), *cert. denied,* 410 So. 2d 227 (Ala. 1982)	§ 6.5
Geller v. Markham, 635 F.2d 1027 (2d Cir. 1980), *cert. denied,* 451 U.S. 945 (1981)	§§ 2.6, 7.8
General Bldg. Contractors Ass'n v. Pennsylvania, 458 U.S. 375 (1982)	§ 2.8
General Elec. Co., 74 Lab. Arb. (BNA) 290 (1979) (MacDonald, Arb.)	§ 3.6
General Elec. Co., 71 Lab. Arb. (BNA) 884 (1978) (Abrams, Arb.)	§ 3.7
General Elec. Co. v. Electrical Workers Local 205, 353 U.S. 547 (1957)	§ 3.22
General Mills, Inc. v. Hathaway, 694 S.W.2d 96 (Tex. Ct. App. 1985)	§ 4.19

CASES

Case	*Book §*
General Tel. Co. of Cal., 73 Lab. Arb. (BNA) 531 (1979) (Richman, Arb.)	§ 3.15
Genuine Parts Co., 79 Lab. Arb. (BNA) 220 (1982) (Reed, Arb.)	§ 3.5
George v. Aztec Rental Center, Inc., 763 F.2d 184 (5th Cir. 1985)	§ 2.18
Georgia Power Co. v. Busbin, 242 Ga. 612, 250 S.E.2d 442 (1978)	§ 1.12
Gianaculas v. T.W.A., Inc., 761 F.2d 1391 (9th Cir. 1985)	§§ 1.14, 4.18, 7.23
Gibbs v. United Mine Workers, 383 U.S. 715 (1966)	§ 2.35
Gibson v. Hummel, 688 S.W.2d 4 (Mo. Ct. App. 1985)	§ 5.23
Gil v. Metal Serv. Corp., 412 So. 2d 706 (La. Ct. App.), *cert. denied*, 414 So. 2d 379 (La. 1982)	§§ 1.12, 5.12, 5.17
Gilchrist v. Metal Polishers, 113 A. 320 (N.J. Ch. 1919)	§ 4.5
Gillespie v. Equitable Life Assurance Soc'y, 590 F. Supp. 1111 (D. Del. 1984)	§§ 1.14, 7.11, app. F
Gillespie v. St. Joseph's Univ., ___ Pa. Super. ___, 513 P.2d 471 (1986)	§ 7.11
Gilman v. County of Cheshire, 126 N.H. 445, 493 A.2d 485 (1985)	app. F
Giudice v. Drew Chem. Corp., 210 N.J. Super. 32, 509 A.2d 200 (1986)	§ 5.17
Glasgow v. Georgia-Pacific Corp., 103 Wash. 2d 401, 693 P.2d 708 (1985)	§ 2.5
Glenn v. Clearman's Golden Cock Inn, 192 Cal. App. 2d 793, 13 Cal. Rptr. 769 (1961)	§ 5.9
Goclowski v. Penn Cent. Transp. Co., 571 F.2d 747 (3d Cir. 1978)	§ 3.19
Goldberg v. Kelly, 397 U.S. 254 (1970)	§ 1.10
Golden v. Board of Educ., 285 S.E.2d 665 (W. Va. 1981)	§ 5.27
Golden v. Shapell Indus., 24 F.E.P. Cas. (BNA) 1283 (N.D. Cal. 1980)	§ 2.9
Golden Eagle Distrib. Co. v. Burroughs Corp., 801 F.2d 1531 (9th Cir. 1986)	§ 4.28
Goldman v. Cohen, 222 A.D. 631, 227 N.Y.S. 311 (1928)	§§ 3.21, 4.5
Gomez v. Texas Dep't of Mental Health, 794 F.2d 1018 (5th Cir. 1986)	§ 6.11
Gomez v. Toledo, 446 U.S. 635 (1980)	§§ 6.17, 6.19
Gonzales v. Southern Pac. Transp. Co., 773 F.2d 637 (5th Cir. 1985)	§§ 2.19, 3.27, 8.9
Gonzalez v. Stanford Applied Eng'g, 597 F.2d 1298 (9th Cir. 1979)	§ 2.8
Goodman v. Heublein, Inc., 645 F.2d 127 (2d Cir. 1981)	§ 7.16
Gordon v. Lancaster Osteopathic Hosp. Assoc., 340 Pa. Super. 253, 489 A.2d 1364 (1985)	§§ 5.22, 5.25, 5.31
Gorham v. City of Kansas City, 225 Kan, 369, 590 P.2d 1051 (1979)	§ 6.15
Gorin v. Osborne, 756 F.2d 834 (11th Cir. 1985)	§§ 7.32, 9.26
Gorrill v. Icelander/Flugleidir, 761 F.2d 847 (2d Cir. 1985)	§ 4.16
Goss v. Exxon Office Sys. Co., 747 F.2d 885 (3d Cir. 1984)	§ 2.3
Goss v. Lopez, 419 U.S. 565 (1975)	§§ 9.2, 9.27
Goss v. Revlon, Inc., 548 F.2d 405 (2d Cir. 1976), *cert. denied*, 434 U.S. 968 (1977)	§ 2.8
Gould v. Campbell's Ambulance Serv., 111 Ill. 2d 54, 488 N.E.2d 993 (1986)	§ 7.11
Graf v. Elgin, J.&E. Ry., 790 F.2d 1341 (7th Cir. 1986)	§ 2.31

Case   *Book §*

Graf v. Elgin, J.&E. Ry., 697 F.2d 771 (7th Cir. 1983)	§ 3.25
Graham v. F.B. Leopold Co., 602 F. Supp. 1423 (W.D. Pa. 1985)	§ 7.8
Grahams Serv. Co. v. Teamsters Local 975, 700 F.2d 420 (8th Cir. 1982)	§ 3.22
Gram v. Liberty Mut. Ins. Co., 391 Mass. 333, 461 N.E.2d 796 (1984)	§ 4.28
Graves v. Duganne, 581 F.2d 222 (10th Cir.), *on reh'g*, 620 F.2d 749 (10th Cir. 1978)	§ 5.27
Gray v. Superior Court (Cipher Data), 181 Cal. App. 3d 813, 226 Cal. Rptr. 570 (1986)	§§ 4.11, 4.23, 7.12, 7.23
Grayson v. American Airlines, Inc., 803 F.2d 1097 (10th Cir. 1986)	§ 4.23
Great Am. Fed. Sav. & Loan Ass'n v. Novotny, 442 U.S. 366 (1979)	§ 2.9
Green v. American Cast Iron Pipe Co., 446 So. 2d 16 (Ala. 1984)	§ 8.14
Green v. Illinois Dep't of Transp., 609 F. Supp. 1021 (N.D. Ill. 1985)	§ 6.8
Green v. Finley, 749 F.2d 467 (7th Cir. 1984)	§ 6.12
Greene v. McElroy, 360 U.S. 474 (1959)	§ 1.10
Greenwood v. Atchison, T.&S.F. Ry., 129 F. Supp. 105 (S.D. Cal. 1955)	§ 2.19
Greyhound Lines, Inc., 79 Lab. Arb. (BNA) 422 (1982) (Larkin, Arb.)	§ 3.6
Griffen v. Big Spring Indep. School Dist., 706 F.2d 645 (5th Cir. 1983)	§ 9.26
Griffin v. Breckenridge, 403 U.S. 88 (1971)	§ 2.9
Griffin v. U.A.W., 469 F.2d 181 (4th Cir. 1972)	§ 3.25
Griffin v. Sollay Found. Drilling, Inc., 373 So. 2d 979 (La. Ct. App. 1979)	§ 4.7
Griggs v. Duke Power, 401 U.S. 424 (1971)	§ 2.3
Griswold v. Connecticut, 381 U.S. 479 (1965)	§ 1.10, 5.27
Grossart v. Dinaso, 758 F.2d 1221 (7th Cir. 1985)	§ 6.11
Grouse v. Group Health Plan, Inc., 306 N.W.2d 114 (Minn. 1981)	§§ 4.17, 4.28
Grove City College v. Bell, 465 U.S. 555 (1984)	§§ 2.10, 2.14
Grubb v. W.A. Foote Memorial Hosp., Inc., 741 F.2d 1486 (6th Cir. 1984)	§§ 2.3, 2.6, 4.21, 7.6, 7.24
Grywczynski v. Shasta Beverages, Inc., 606 F. Supp. 61 (N.D. Cal. 1984)	§ 2.23
Grzyb v. Evans, 700 S.W.2d 399 (Ky. 1985)	§§ 1.12, 1.15, 5.9
Guard v. Kilburn, 5 Ohio St. 3d 21, 448 N.E.2d 1153, *cert. denied*, 464 U.S. 893 (1983)	§ 6.11
Guevara v. K-Mart Corp., 629 F. Supp. 1189 (S.D. W. Va. 1986)	§ 5.9
Gulf Consol. Int'l, Inc. v. Murphy, 658 S.W.2d 565 (Tex. 1983)	§ 4.28
Gulf Offshore Co. v. Mobil Oil Co., 453 U.S. 473 (1981)	§ 2.27
Gulf States Tel. Co. v. Electrical Workers Local 1692, 416 F.2d 198 (5th Cir. 1969)	§ 3.18
Gulla v. Barton, 164 A.D. 293, 149 N.Y.S. 952 (1924)	§ 3.21
Gully v. First Nat'l Bank, 299 U.S. 109 (1936)	§ 2.35
Gunderman v. Pennsylvania Unemployment Compensation Bd. of Review, ___ Pa. Commw. ___, 505 A.2d 1112 (1986)	§ 2.36
Guthrie v. J.C. Penney Co., 803 F.2d 202 (5th Cir. 1986)	§ 7.8

CASES

Case	Book §
Gutierrez v. City of Chicago, 605 F. Supp. 973 (N.D. Ill. 1985)	§§ 2.26, 2.27, 5.9, 6.1
Haines v. Kerner, 404 U.S. 519 (1972)	§ 7.1
Haith v. Model Cities Health Corp., 704 S.W.2d 684 (Mo. Ct. App. 1986)	§§ 1.12, 5.26
Haldeman v. Total Petroleum, Inc., 376 N.W.2d 98 (Iowa 1985)	§§ 1.12, 5.23, 5.25
Hall v. Board of Comm'rs, 509 F. Supp. 841 (E.D. Md. 1981)	§ 2.35
Hall v. Farmers Ins. Exch., 713 P.2d 1027 (Okla. 1986)	§§ 1.12, 7.23
Hall v. Hotel l'Europe, Inc., 69 N.C. App. 664, 318 S.E.2d 99 (1984)	§§ 4.28, 7.18
Hall v. Integon Life Ins. Co., 454 So. 2d 1338 (Ala. 1984)	§§ 1.12, 5.22, 5.24
Hamby v. Genesco, 627 S.W.2d 373 (Tenn. Ct. App. 1981)	app. F
Hamer v. Sidway, 124 N.Y. 538, 27 N.E. 256 (1891)	§ 4.14
Hammermill Paper Co. v. NLRB, 658 F.2d 155 (3d Cir. 1981), *cert. denied*, 460 U.S. 1080 (1983)	§ 3.27
Hance v. United Family Life Ins. Co., Civ. No. 1073, slip. op. (Tenn. Ct. App. Oct. 9, 1986)	app. F
Hanley v. Lamb, 312 A.2d 330 (Del. Super. Ct. 1973)	§ 1.12
Hanlon v. MacFadden Publications, Inc., 302 N.Y. 502, 99 N.E.2d 546 (1951)	§ 5.33
Hansen's v. Harrah's, 100 Nev. 60, 675 P.2d 394 (1984)	§§ 1.12, 9.4
Hansome v. Northwestern Coop. Co., 679 S.W.2d 273 (Mo. 1984)	§ 5.11
Hardwick v. Bowers, 106 S. Ct. 2841 (1986)	§§ 5.28, 6.11
Hargrove v. Town of Cocoa Beach, 96 So. 2d 130 (Fla. 1957)	§ 6.20
Haring v. C.P.C. Int'l, Inc., 664 F.2d 1234 (5th Cir. 1981)	§ 7.16
Harless v. First Nat'l Bank, 289 S.E.2d 692 (W. Va. 1982)	§§ 5.17, 5.23, 5.33, 7.14, 7.16
Harless v. First Nat'l Bank, 246 S.E.2d 270 (W. Va. 1978)	§§ 1.11, 1.12, 5.17, 7.14
Harman v. LaCrosse Tribune, 117 Wis. 2d 448, 344 N.W.2d 536 (1984)	§§ 5.12, 5.22, 7.15
Harper v. Cedar Rapids Tel. Co., 244 N.W.2d 782 (Iowa 1976)	§§ 4.9, 7.19
Harper v. I.B.E.W. Local 520, 48 S.W.2d 1033 (Tex. Civ. App. 1932)	§ 4.5
Harris v. Arkansas Book Co., 287 Ark. 353, 700 S.W.2d 41 (1985)	§§ 4.20, 5.23
Harris v. Hubbert, 588 F.2d 167 (5th Cir. 1979)	§ 6.2
Harris v. Parmley, 480 So. 2d 500 (La. Ct. App. 1985)	§ 1.12
Harris v. Richards Mfg. Co., 511 F. Supp. 1193 (W.D. Tenn. 1981), *modified*, 675 F.2d 811 (6th Cir. 1982)	§ 2.8
Harrison v. U.T.U., 530 F.2d 558 (4th Cir. 1975)	§ 3.19
Hartman v. C.W. Travel, Inc., 792 F.2d 1179 (D.C. Cir. 1986)	§ 7.18
Harvey Aluminum, Inc. v. Steelworkers, 263 F. Supp. 488 (C.D. Cal. 1967)	§ 3.12
Hayes v. McIntosh, 604 F. Supp. 10 (N.D. Ind. 1984)	§ 2.21
Hays v. Potlatch Forests, Inc., 465 F.2d 1081 (8th Cir. 1972)	§ 2.32
Healy v. James, 408 U.S. 169 (1972)	§ 6.11
Heat & Frost Insulators v. General Pipe Covering, 613 F. Supp. 858 (D. Minn. 1985)	§ 3.11
Heath v. John Morrell & Co., 768 F.2d 245 (8th Cir. 1985)	§§ 7.35, 9.26
Heaven Hill Distilleries, Inc., 74 Lab. Arb. (BNA) 42 (1980) (Beckman, Arb.)	§ 3.8

Case *Book §*

Heideck v. Kent Gen. Hosp., Inc., 446 A.2d 1095 (Del. 1982) — § 1.12
Helle v. Landmark, Inc., 15 Ohio App. 3d 1, 472 N.E.2d 765 (1984) — § 4.19
Heller v. Dover Warehouse Mkt., Inc., 515 A.2d 178 (Del. Super. Ct. 1986) — §§ 1.12, 2.26
Hendley v. Central of Ga. R.R., 609 F.2d 1146 (5th Cir. 1980), *cert. denied,* 449 U.S. 1093 (1981) — § 12.19
Hennebury v. T.W.U., 485 F. Supp. 1319 (D. Mass. 1980) — § 3.19
Hennis Freight Liners, 44 Lab. Arb. (BNA) 711 (1964) (McGury, Arb.) — § 3.13
Henry v. Anderson County, 522 F. Supp. 1112 (E.D. Tenn. 1981) — § 2.24
Henry v. Delta Air Lines, 759 F.2d 870 (11th Cir. 1985) — § 3.24
Henry v. Radio Station KSAN, 374 F. Supp. 260 (N.D. Cal. 1974) — § 2.8
Hensley v. Eckerhart, 461 U.S. 424 (1983) — §§ 2.25, 9.33
Hepp v. Lockheed-California Co., 86 Cal. App. 3d 714, 150 Cal. Rptr. 408 (1978) — §§ 4.12, 4.16
Herring v. Prince Foods-Canning Div., 799 F.2d 120 (3d Cir. 1986) — § 7.12
Herring v. Prince Foods-Canning Div., 611 F. Supp. 177 (D.N.J. 1985) — §§ 5.20, 5.30
Herrmann v. Moore, 576 F.2d 453 (2d Cir. 1977), *cert. denied,* 439 U.S. 1003 (1978) — § 2.9
Hewitt v. Grabicki, 794 F.2d 1373 (9th Cir. 1986) — §§ 6.9, 6.18
Hicks v. Tulsa Dynaspan, Inc., 695 P.2d 17 (Okla. Ct. App. 1985) — § 7.13
High v. Sperry Corp., 581 F. Supp. 1246 (S.D. Iowa 1984) — § 4.11
Hill v. Coca Cola Bottling Co., 786 F.2d 550 (2d Cir. 1986) — § 7.35
Hillsman v. Sutter Community Hosps., 153 Cal. App. 3d 743, 200 Cal. Rptr. 605 (1984) — § 7.19
Hilo Coast Processing Co., 74 Lab. Arb. (BNA) 236 (1980) (Tanake, Arb.) — § 3.7
Hines v. Anchor Motor Freight, Inc., 424 U.S. 554 (1976) — §§ 3.23, 3.25, 3.26, 4.25
Hishon v. King & Spalding, 467 U.S. 69 (1984) — app. F
Hochstadt v. Worcester Found. for Experimental Biology, Inc., 545 F.2d 222 (1st Cir. 1976) — §§ 2.17, 7.16
Hodge v. Evans Fin. Corp., 707 F.2d 1566 (D.C. Cir. 1983), *later appeal,* 778 F.2d 794 (D.C. Cir. 1985) — §§ 1.12, 4.20
Hodges v. Atchison, T. & S.F. Ry., 728 F.2d 414 (10th Cir.), *cert. denied,* 469 U.S. 822 (1984) — §§ 2.10, 2.31
Hoffman Specialty Co. v. Pelouze, 158 Va. 586, 164 S.E. 397 (1932) — § 1.9, app. F
Hogan v. Forsyth Country Club Co., 79 N.C. App. 483, 340 S.E.2d 116, *review denied,* 317 N.C. 334, 346 S.E.2d 140 (1986) — §§ 5.22, 5.23, 5.31, 7.11
Hogue v. Clinton, 791 F.2d 1318 (8th Cir. 1986) — §§ 6.10, 6.11
Holden v. Owens-Illinois, Inc., 793 F.2d 745 (6th Cir. 1986) — §§ 2.17, 5.31
Holien v. Sears, Roebuck & Co., 298 Or. 76, 689 P.2d 1292 (1984) — § 2.5
Holland v. Beto, 309 F. Supp. 785 (S.D. Tex. 1970) — § 2.32
Hollenback v. Carnegie Free Library, 439 U.S. 1052 (1978) — § 6.11
Holliday v. Civil Serv. Comm'n, 121 Ill. App. 3d 763, 460 N.E.2d 358 (1984) — § 6.5
Holloway v. K-Mart Corp., 113 Wis. 2d 143, 334 N.W.2d 570 (1983) — § 8.7

CASES

Case	Book §
Holmes v. Jones, 738 F.2d 711 (5th Cir. 1984)	§ 6.15
Holt v. Gamewell Corp., 797 F.2d 36 (1st Cir. 1986)	§§ 2.6, 7.8
Hoover v. Livingston Bank, 451 So. 2d 3 (La. Ct. App. 1984)	§ 1.12
Hopes v. Black Hills Power & Light Co., 386 N.W.2d 490 (S.D. 1986)	§§ 1.12, 7.18
Horacek v. Smith, 33 Cal. 2d 186, 199 P.2d 929 (1948)	§§ 4.9, 7.19
Horn v. Duke Homes, 755 F.2d 599 (7th Cir. 1985)	§ 2.5
Hoska v. United States Dep't of the Army, 677 F.2d 131 (D.C. Cir. 1982)	§ 6.4
Hospital Employees v. NLRB, 613 F.2d 1102 (D.C. Cir. 1979)	§ 3.27
Hostettler v. Pioneer Hi-Bred Int'l, Inc., 624 F. Supp. 169 (S.D. Ind. 1985)	§ 1.12
Hoteles Conado Beach v. Union de Tronquistas Local 901, 763 F.2d 34 (1st Cir. 1985)	§ 3.10
Howard v. Dorr Woolen Co., 120 N.H. 295, 414 A.2d 1273 (1980)	§§ 4.11, 4.23
Howard Univ. v. Best, 484 A.2d 958 (D.C. 1984)	§ 5.25
Howard Univ. v. Best, 117 L.R.R.M. 3241 (D.C. 1984)	§ 5.23
Hrab v. Hayes-Albion Corp., 103 Mich. App. 90, 302 N.W.2d 606 (1981)	§ 5.10
Hubbard v. United States E.P.A., ___ F.2d ___ (D.C. Cir. 1986)	§ 6.6
Hudgens v. NLRB, 424 U.S. 507 (1976)	§ 6.2
Hudson v. Cincinnati Ry., 152 Ky. 711, 154 S.W. 47 (1913)	§ 3.21
Huffman v. Westinghouse Elec. Corp., 752 F.2d 1221 (7th Cir. 1985)	§ 4.25
Hughes Air Corp., 73 Lab. Arb. (BNA) 148 (1979) (Barsamian, Arb.)	§ 3.8
Hughes Aircraft Corp., 49 Lab. Arb. (BNA) 535 (1967) (Doyle, Arb.)	§ 3.14
Humphrey v. Moore, 375 U.S. 335 (1964)	§§ 3.25, 4.25
Hunt v. Department of Health & Human Servs., 758 F.2d 608 (Fed. Cir. 1985)	§§ 6.4, 6.16
Hunt v. I.B.M. Mid Am. Employees Fed. Credit Union, 384 N.W.2d 853 (Minn. 1986)	§§ 4.9, 4.16, 7.18
Hunt v. Northwest Airlines, 600 F.2d 176 (8th Cir.), *cert. denied,* 444 U.S. 946 (1979)	§ 3.19
Hunter v. Port Auth. of Allegheny County, 277 Pa. Super. 4, 419 A.2d 631 (1980)	§ 5.12
Hurn v. Oursler, 289 U.S. 238 (1933)	§ 2.35
Hurst v. Farmer, 40 Wash. App. 116, 697 P.2d 280 (1985)	§ 5.23
Hutchinson v. Board of Trustees of Univ. of Ala., 288 Ala. 20, 256 So. 2d 281 (1971)	§ 6.20
Hyland v. New Haven Radiology Assocs., Inc., 794 F.2d 793 (2d Cir. 1986)	§ 2.6
I.A.M. v. Central Airlines, 372 U.S. 682 (1963)	§ 3.19
Imbler v. Pachtman, 424 U.S. 409 (1976)	§ 6.19
Inda v. United Air Lines, Inc., 565 F.2d 554 (9th Cir. 1977), *cert. denied,* 435 U.S. 1007 (1978)	§ 2.3
Indian Head, Inc., 71 Lab. Arb. (BNA) 82 (1978) (Rimer, Arb.)	§ 3.8
Industrial Gas Antitrust Litig., *In re,* 681 F.2d 514 (7th Cir. 1982)	§ 2.26
Industrial Workers v. Exxon, 712 F.2d 161 (5th Cir. 1983)	§ 3.23

Case	Book §
Instrument Workers v. Minneapolis-Honeywell Co., 54 L.R.R.M. (BNA) 2660 (E.D. Pa. 1963)	§ 3.12
Interboro Contractors, Inc., 157 NLRB 1295 (1966), *enforced*, 388 F.2d 495 (2d Cir. 1967)	§ 2.16
Interior Alterations, Inc. v. NLRB, 738 F.2d 373 (10th Cir. 1984)	§§ 2.16, 7.34
Ising v. Barnes Hosp., 674 S.W.2d 623 (Mo. Ct. App. 1984)	§§ 5.9, 7.11
Iticho v. First Nat'l Bank, No. AP 85-533 (W.D. Cal., filed Oct. 9, 1986)	§ 2.24
Ivy v. Army Times, 428 A.2d 831 (D.C. 1981)	§ 1.11
Jack v. Texaco Research Center, 743 F.2d 1129 (5th Cir. 1984)	§§ 2.17, 7.6
Jackson v. City of Killeen, 654 F.2d 1181 (5th Cir. 1981)	§ 2.8
Jackson v. Consolidated Rail Corp., 717 F.2d 1045 (7th Cir. 1983)	§§ 2.19, 2.31
Jackson v. Cox, 540 F.2d 209 (5th Cir. 1976)	§ 2.32
Jackson v. Kinark Corp., 282 Ark. 548, 669 S.W.2d 898 (1984)	§ 1.12
Jackson v. Metropolitan Edison Co., 419 U.S. 345 (1974)	§ 6.2
Jackson v. Minidoka Irrigation, 98 Idaho 330, 563 P.2d 54 (1977)	§ 5.10
Jacobs v. Georgia-Pacific Corp., 172 Ga. App. 319, 323 S.E.2d 238 (1984)	§ 5.24
Jadison v. Missouri Pac. R.R., 803 F.2d 401 (8th Cir. 1986)	§ 7.6
James v. F.E.R.C., 747 F.2d 1581 (Fed. Cir. 1984)	§ 6.4
Janda v. Iowa Indus. Hydraulics, Inc., 326 N.W.2d 339 (Iowa 1982)	§ 1.12
Janmort Leasing Inc. v. Econo-Car Int'l, 475 F. Supp. 1282 (E.D.N.Y. 1979)	§ 5.22
Janusaitis v. Middlebury Volunteer Fire Dep't, 607 F.2d 17 (2d Cir. 1979)	§ 6.2
Jennings v. Tinley Park Community Consol. School Dist. 146, 796 F.2d 962 (7th Cir. 1986)	§ 7.6
Jerviss v. School Dist. No. 294, 273 N.W.2d 638 (Minn. 1978)	§ 6.15
J.I. Case Co. v. NLRB, 321 U.S. 332 (1944)	§§ 2.30, 3.9, 4.25
J.&J. Enters. v. Martignetti, 369 Mass. 535, 341 N.E.2d 645 (1976)	§ 2.27
Joachim v. AT&T Information Sys., 793 F.2d 113 (5th Cir. 1986)	§ 1.12
Johns-Manville Sales Corp. v. Machinists Local 1609, 621 F.2d 756 (5th Cir. 1980)	§ 3.27
Johnson v. Al-Tech Specialties Steel Corp., 731 F.2d 143 (2d Cir. 1984)	§ 2.6
Johnson v. Ford Motor Co., 690 S.W.2d 90 (Tex. Ct. App. 1985)	§ 1.12
Johnson v. General Motors Corp., 641 F.2d 1075 (2d Cir. 1981)	app. B
Johnson v. Hussman Corp., ___ F.2d ___, 123 L.R.R.M. (BNA) 3074 (8th Cir. 1986)	§ 2.29
Johnson v. Jefferson County Bd. of Health, 662 P.2d 463 (Colo. 1983), *later appeal*, 674 P.2d 952 (1984)	§ 6.13
Johnson v. Railway Express Agency, 421 U.S. 454 (1975)	§§ 2.8, 2.32, 9.3, 9.26
Johnson v. World Color Press, Inc., 147 Ill. App. 3d 746, 498 N.W.2d 575 (1986)	§§ 7.11, 7.34
John Wiley & Sons v. Livingston, 376 U.S. 543 (1964)	§ 3.21
Joint School Dist. v. Jefferson Educ. Ass'n, 78 Wis. 2d 94, 253 N.W.2d 536 (1977)	§ 6.16
Jones v. Alfred H. Mayer Co., 392 U.S. 409 (1973)	§ 2.8
Jones v. Continental Corp., 789 F.2d 1225 (6th Cir. 1986)	§ 4.28
Jones v. East Center for Community Mental Health, Inc., 19 Ohio App. 3d 19, 482 N.E.2d 969 (1984)	§ 4.17

Case	*Book §*
Jones v. Farm Credit Admin., 702 F.2d 160 (8th Cir. 1983)	§ 6.6
Jones v. Flagship Int'l, 793 F.2d 714 (5th Cir. 1986)	§§ 2.5, 2.17
Jones v. Keogh, 137 Vt. 562, 409 A.2d 581 (1979)	§ 1.11
Jones v. Memorial Hosp. Sys., 677 S.W.2d 221 (Tex. Ct. App. 1984)	§§ 5.12, 7.11
Jones v. Seaboard Sys. R.R., 783 F.2d 639 (6th Cir. 1986)	§ 3.24
Jones v. State Bd. of Regents, 385 N.W.2d 240 (Iowa 1986)	§ 6.20
Jones & Laughlin Corp., 29 Lab. Arb. (BNA) 778 (1957) (Cahn, Arb.)	§ 3.13
Jong-Yul Lim v. International Inst. of Metropolitan Detroit, 510 F. Supp. 722 (E.D. Mich. 1981)	§ 2.35
Jorden v. National Guard Bureau, 799 F.2d 99 (3d Cir. 1986)	§ 6.19
Joy Mfg. Co., 68 Lab. Arb. (BNA) 697 (1977) (Freeman, Arb)	§ 3.8
Joyner v. AAA Cooper Transp., 597 F. Supp. 537 (M.D. Ala.), aff'd without opinion, 749 F.2d 732 (5th Cir. 1983)	§§ 2.5, 5.28
J.R. Simplot Co. v. State, 110 Idaho 762, 718 P.2d 1200 (1986)	§ 1.12
Judd v. Heitmann, 402 F. Supp. 929 (M.D. Tenn. 1975)	app. F
Juvenile Diabetes Research Found. v. Rievman, 370 So. 2d 33 (Fla. Dist. Ct. App. 1979)	§ 4.28

Case	*Book §*
Kalman v. Grand Union Co., 183 N.J. Super. 153, 443 A.2d 728 (1982)	§ 5.18
Kamens v. Summit Stainless, Inc., 586 F. Supp. 324 (E.D. Pa. 1984)	§§ 2.26, 4.11, 5.9
Kaminski v. United Parcel Srv., 120 A.D.2d 409, 501 N.Y.S.2d 871 (1986)	§ 5.22
Kane Gas Light & Heating Co. v. Firemen & Oilers, 687 F.2d 673 (3d Cir. 1982)	§ 3.18
Kansas Gas & Elec. Co. v. Brock, 780 F.2d 1505 (10th Cir. 1985), cert. denied, ___ U.S. ___, 106 S. Ct. 3311 (1986)	§ 2.24
Karren v. Far West Fed. Sav., 79 Or. App. 131, 717 P.2d 1271 (1986)	§§ 5.13, 5.27, 7.11
Kaschak v. Consolidated Rail Corp., 707 F.2d 902 (6th Cir. 1983)	§ 3.19
Katz v. Dole, 709 F.2d 251 (4th Cir. 1983)	§ 2.5
Kavanagh v. KLM Royal Dutch Airlines, 566 F. Supp. 242 (N.D. Ill. 1983)	§§ 5.10, 5.11
Kay v. United Technologies Corp., 757 F.2d 100 (6th Cir. 1985)	§ 7.18
Keddie v. Pennsylvania State Univ., 412 F. Supp. 1264 (M.D. Pa. 1976)	§ 5.25
Kellums v. Freight Sales Centers, Inc., 467 So. 2d 816 (Fla. Dist. Ct. App. 1985)	§ 8.10
Kelly v. American Standard, Inc., 640 F.2d 974 (9th Cir. 1981)	§ 2.6
Kelly v. Mississippi Valley Gas Co., 397 So. 2d 874 (Miss. 1981)	§ 1.12
Kelly v. Smith, 764 F.2d 1412 (11th Cir. 1985)	§ 6.12
Kelly v. Wauconda Park Dist., 801 F.2d 269 (7th Cir. 1986)	§ 2.6
Kelsay v. Motorola, Inc., 74 Ill. 2d 172, 384 N.E.2d 353 (1978)	§§ 1.12, 5.10, 5.11, 5.16, 5.33
Kemper v. Worcester, 106 Ill. App. 3d 121, 435 N.E.2d 827 (1982)	§ 5.22
Kenneally v. Orgain, 186 Mont. 1, 606 P.2d 127 (1980)	§ 5.17
Kent Jenkins Sales, Inc. v. Angelo Bros. Co., 804 F.2d 482, 485 (8th Cir. 1986)	§ 4.9

Case   *Book §*

Kern v. South Baltimore Gen. Hosp., 66 Md. App. 441, 504 A.2d
    1154 (1986) — §§ 1.12, 7.11
Keyishian v. Board of Regents, 385 U.S. 589 (1967) — §§ 1.10, 6.11
Khalifa v. Henry Ford Hosp., ___ Mich. App. ___, ___ N.W.2d
    ___, No. 84582 (Dec. 2, 1986) — §§ 8.9, 8.14
Khanna v. Microdata Corp., 170 Cal. App. 3d 250, 215 Cal. Rptr.
    860 (1985) — §§ 4.23, 7.23
Kilpatrick v. Delaware County Soc'y for Prevention of Cruelty to
    Animals, 632 F. Supp. 542 (E.D. Pa. 1986) — §§ 2.33, 7.11, 7.12
Kimble v. D.J. McDuffy, Inc., 648 F.2d 340 (5th Cir. 1981) — § 2.9
Kinoshita v. Canadian Pac. Airlines, Ltd., 724 P.2d 110 (Haw.),
    after certification, 803 F.2d 471 (9th Cir. 1986) — §§ 1.12, 4.16, 4.18, 7.15
Klaxon Co. v. Stenton Elec. Mfg. Co., 313 U.S. 487 (1941) — § 1.14
Knight v. American Guard & Alert, Inc., 714 P.2d 788 (Alaska
    1986) — §§ 1.12, 7.11
Knowles v. Unity College, 429 A.2d 220 (Me. 1981) — § 4.8
Knox v. American Sterilizer Co., 117 L.R.R.M. 2341 (M.D. Ala.
    1984) — app. F
Kofoid v. Woodard Hotels, Inc., 78 Or. App. 283, 716 P.2d 771
    (1986) — §§ 2.27, 5.9, 7.12
Kotarski v. Cooper, ___ F.2d ___ (9th Cir. Sept. 16, 1986) — § 6.6
Kovalesky v. A.M.C. Associated Merchandising Corp., 551 F. Supp.
    544 (S.D.N.Y. 1982) — § 5.12
Kravetz v. Merchants Distribs., Inc., 387 Mass. 457, 440 N.E.2d
    1278 (1978) — §§ 7.23, 7.27
Kremer v. Chemical Constr. Co., 456 U.S. 461 (1982) — §§ 2.3, 2.8, 2.32, 2.35, 7.29, 7.30, 7.32, 7.33
Krodel v. Young, 748 F.2d 701 (D.C. Cir. 1984), *cert. denied,* ___
    U.S. ___, 106 S. Ct. 62 (1985) — § 7.8
Kroger Co., 25 Lab. Arb. (BNA) 906 (1955) (Smith, Arb.) — § 3.15
Kroger Co. v. Teamsters Local 661, 380 F.2d 728 (6th Cir. 1967) — § 3.18
Kropiwka v. Department of Indus., Labor & Human Relations, 87
    Wis. 2d 709, 275 N.W.2d 881, *cert. denied,* 444 U.S. 852
    (1979) — § 2.12
Kross v. Western Elec. Co., Inc., 534 F. Supp. 251 (N.D. Ill.
    1982), *aff'd in part, rev'd in part,* 701 F.2d 1238 (7th Cir.
    1983) — § 2.23
Krystad v. Lau, 65 Wash. 2d 827, 400 P.2d 72 (1965) — § 5.9
Kulins v. Malco, 121 Ill. App. 3d 520, 459 N.E.2d 1038 (1984) — §§ 4.17, app. F
Kump v. Department of Transp., 767 F.2d 889 (Fed. Cir. 1985) — § 6.4
Kumpf v. Steinhaus, 779 F.2d 1323 (7th Cir. 1985) — §§ 5.21, 5.22
Kurtz v. City of Waukesha, 91 Wis. 2d 103, 280 N.W.2d 757
    (1979) — § 2.12
Kush v. Rutledge, 460 U.S. 719 (1983) — § 2.9

LaBeach v. Beatrice Foods Co., 461 F. Supp. 152 (S.D.N.Y. 1978) — § 8.10
LaChapelle v. Owens-Illinois, Inc., 513 F.2d 286 (5th Cir. 1975) — § 2.6
Ladesic v. Servomation Corp., 140 Ill. App. 3d 489, 488 N.E.2d
    1355 (1986) — § 1.12

CASES

Case	*Book §*
LaGrant v. Gulf & W. Mfg. Co., 748 F.2d 1087 (6th Cir. 1984)	§ 7.8
Lakeside v. Freightliner Corp., 612 F. Supp. 10 (D. Or. 1984)	§ 4.18, app. F
Lally v. Copygraphics, 85 N.J. 668, 428 A.2d 1317 (1981)	§ 5.10
Lamb v. Briggs Mfg., 700 F.2d 1092 (7th Cir. 1983)	§ 5.20
Lambert v. Equinox House, Inc., 126 Vt. 229, 227 A.2d 403 (1967)	§ 7.27
Lamm v. Shingleton, 231 N.C. 10, 55 S.E.2d 810 (1949)	app. E
Lampe v. Presbyterian Medical Center, 41 Colo. App. 465, 590 P.2d 513 (1978)	§ 1.12
Lancaster v. Buerkle Burch Honda Co., 39 F.E.P. Cas. (BNA) 721 (D. Minn. 1985)	§ 2.6
Lancaster v. Norfolk & W. Ry., 773 F.2d 807 (7th Cir. 1985)	§ 2.19
Landfried v. Terminal R.R. Ass'n, 721 F.2d 254 (8th Cir. 1983), *cert. denied,* 466 U.S. 928 (1984)	§ 2.19
Langdon v. Saga Corp., 569 P.2d 524 (Okla. Ct. App. 1977)	§§ 1.12, 4.8, 4.14, app. F
LaRocca v. Xerox Corp., 587 F. Supp. 1002 (S.D. Fla. 1984)	app. F
LaRocca v. Bakwin, 108 Ill. App. 3d 723, 439 N.E.2d 537 (1982)	§ 5.22
Larose v. Agway, Inc., ___ Vt. ___, 508 A.2d 1364 (1986)	§§ 1.12, 4.14, 4.17, 7.20
Larrabee v. Penobscot Frozen Foods, Inc., 486 A.2d 97 (Me. 1984)	§§ 1.12, 2.26
Larson v. Domestic & Foreign Commerce Corp., 337 U.S. 682 (1949)	§ 6.18
Laugesen v. Anaconda Co., 510 F.2d 307 (6th Cir. 1975)	§§ 2.6, 2.7, 7.8
Laureano-Agosto v. Garcia-Caraballo, 731 F.2d 101 (1st Cir. 1984)	§ 6.11
Lawson v. Sheriff of Tippecanoe County, 725 F.2d 1136 (7th Cir. 1984)	§ 6.11
Leahy v. Federal Express Corp., 609 F. Supp. 668 (S.D.N.Y. 1985)	§§ 1.12, 8.7
Ledl v. Quik Pik Food Stores, Inc., 133 Mich. App. 529, 349 N.W.2d 529 (1984)	§ 4.10
Lee v. Western Reserve Psychiatric Habilitation Center, 747 F.2d 1062 (6th Cir. 1984)	§§ 6.12, 6.19
Leftwich v. Harris-Stowe State College, 702 F.2d 686 (8th Cir. 1983)	§§ 2.6, 7.8
Legal Aid Soc'y v. Brennan, 608 F.2d 1319 (9th Cir. 1979), *cert. denied sub nom* Chamber of Commerce v. Legal Aid Soc'y, 447 U.S. 921 (1980)	§ 2.13
Leikvold v. Valley View Hosp., 141 Ariz. 544, 688 P.2d 170 (1984)	§ 1.12
Lentsch v. Marshall, 741 F.2d 301 (10th Cir. 1984)	§§ 6.10, 6.11
LeSassier v. Chevron USA, Inc., 776 F.2d 506 (5th Cir. 1985)	§ 2.34
LeVick v. Skaggs Co., 701 F.2d 777 (9th Cir. 1983)	§§ 2.22, 2.26
Lew v. Kona Hosp., 754 F.2d 1420 (9th Cir. 1985)	§ 6.12
Lewis v. Equitable Life Assurance Soc'y, 389 N.W.2d 876 (Minn. 1986)	§ 5.25
Lewis v. Equitable Life Assurance Soc'y, 361 N.W.2d 875 (Minn. Ct. App. 1985)	§ 7.18
Lewis v. Hillsborough Transit Auth., 726 F.2d 668 (11th Cir.), *cert. denied,* 469 U.S. 822 (1984)	§§ 6.6, 6.12
Lewis v. Holmes, 109 La. 1030, 34 So. 66 (1903)	app. E
Lewis v. I.B.M., 393 F. Supp. 305 (D. Or. 1974)	§ 7.35
Lewis v. Smith, 731 F.2d 1535 (11th Cir. 1984)	§ 2.3
Lewy v. Southern Pac. Transp. Co., 799 F.2d 1281 (9th Cir. 1986)	§ 2.31

Case | *Book §*

Case	Book §
Lieber v. Union Carbide Corp., 577 F. Supp. 562 (E.D. Tenn. 1983)	§§ 5.29, 8.15, app. F
Life Ins. Co. of N. Am. v. Reichardt, 591 F.2d 499 (9th Cir. 1979)	§ 2.9
Litman v. Massachusetts Mut. Life Ins. Co., 739 F.2d 1549 (11th Cir. 1984)	§§ 4.17, 5.25, 7.20
Littlejohn v. Rose, 768 F.2d 765 (6th Cir. 1985), *cert. denied,* ___ U.S. ___, 106 S. Ct. 1260 (1986)	§ 6.11
Livingston v. Roadway Express, Inc., 802 F.2d 1251 (10th Cir. 1986)	§ 2.3
Livingston Export Packing, Inc., 83 Lab. Arb. (BNA) 270 (1984) (Ives, Arb.)	§ 3.8
Lockheed Aircraft Corp., 27 Lab. Arb. (BNA) 709 (1956) (Maggs, Arb.)	§ 3.13
Locomotive Eng'rs v. Missouri-Kansas-Texas R.R., 363 U.S. 528 (1960)	§ 3.23
Locomotive Eng'rs v. St. Louis S.W. Ry., 757 F.2d 656 (5th Cir. 1985)	§ 3.24
Loehr v. Ventura County Community College Dist., 743 F.2d 1310 (9th Cir. 1984)	§§ 6.11, 9.2, 9.20 app. F
Logue v. City of Carthage, 612 S.W.2d 148 (Mo. Ct. App. 1981)	
Longley v. Blue Cross & Blue Shield, 136 Mich. App. 336, 356 N.W.2d 20 (1985)	§§ 4.10, 8.7
Longshoremen v. Pacific Maritime Ass'n, 773 F.2d 1012 (9th Cir. 1985)	§ 3.24
Love v. Pullman Co., 404 U.S. 522 (1972)	§ 2.3
Love v. RE/MAX of Am., Inc., 738 F.2d 383 (10th Cir. 1984)	§§ 2.21, 7.9, 7.34
Lubin v. Crittenden Hosp. Ass'n, 713 F.2d 416 (8th Cir. 1983)	§ 6.2
Lucas v. Brown & Root, Inc., 736 F.2d 1202 (8th Cir. 1984)	§§ 1.2, 1.12, 5.13, 7.11
Ludwick v. This Minute of Carolina, Inc., 287 S.C. 219, 337 S.E.2d 213 (1985)	§§ 1.12, 5.10
Lukus v. Westinghouse Elec. Corp., 276 Pa. Super. 232, 419 A.2d 431 (1980)	§ 2.12
Lumber Prod. Workers Local 2812 v. Missoula White Pine Sash Co., 734 F.2d 1384 (9th Cir. 1984)	§ 4.25
Lumbley v. Gye, 118 Eng. Rep. 749 (Q.B. 1853)	§ 1.3
MacDonald v. Eastern Fine Paper, Inc., 485 A.2d 228 (Me. 1984)	§ 5.11
MacDonald v. Santa Fe Trail Transp. Co., 427 U.S. 273 (1976)	§ 2.8
Mack v. Cape Elizabeth School Bd., 553 F.2d 720 (1st Cir. 1977)	§ 7.6
Mack v. South Bay Beer Distribs., 798 F.2d 1279 (9th Cir. 1986)	§ 7.35
Mackowiak v. University Nuclear Sys., Inc., 735 F.2d 1159 (9th Cir. 1984)	§ 2.24
MacNeil v. Minidoka Memorial Hosp., 108 Idaho 588, 701 P.2d 208 (1985)	§ 1.12
Maddaloni v. Western Mass. Bus Lines, 12 Mass. App. Ct. 236, 422 N.E.2d 1379 (1981), *modified,* 386 Mass. 877, 438 N.E.2d 351 (1982)	§§ 1.12, 4.23
Magnan v. Anaconda Indus., Inc., 193 Conn. 558, 479 A.2d 781 (1984)	§§ 4.11, 4.23, 7.23, 7.28

CASES

Case	*Book §*
Maguire v. American Family Life Assurance Co., 442 So. 2d 321 (Fla. Dist. Ct. App. 1983), *review denied,* 451 So. 2d 849 (Fla. 1984)	§ 1.12
Mahan v. Reynolds Metals, 569 F. Supp. 488 (E.D. Ark. 1983)	§ 3.27
Mahdavi v. Fair Employment Practice Comm'n, 67 Cal. App. 3d 326, 136 Cal. Rptr. 421 (1977)	§ 2.12
Mailhandlers v. United States Parcel Serv., 751 F.2d 834 (6th Cir. 1985)	§§ 3.10, 3.24
Maine v. Thiboutot, 448 U.S. 1 (1980)	§§ 2.9, 6.9
Maine School Dist. No. 33 v. Teacher Ass'n, 395 A.2d 461 (Me. 1978)	§ 6.16
Major v. Hampton, 413 F. Supp. 66 (E.D. La. 1976)	§§ 6.13, 9.2, 9.20
Majors v. United States Air, 544 F. Supp. 752 (D. Md. 1982)	§ 2.31
Maley v. John Hancock Mut. Life Ins. Co., 609 F. Supp. 621 (E.D. Pa. 1985)	§ 5.24
Malia v. RCA Corp., 794 F.2d 909 (3d Cir. 1986)	§ 2.30
Malik v. Apex Int'l Alloys, Inc., 762 F.2d 77 (10th Cir. 1985)	§ 5.33
Mallard v. Boring, 182 Cal. App. 2d 390, 6 Cal. Rptr. 171 (1960)	§ 5.10
Malley v. Briggs, ___ U.S. ___, 106 S. Ct. 1092 (1986)	§ 6.19
Manzaneres v. Safeway Stores, Inc., 593 F.2d 968 (10th Cir. 1979)	§ 2.8
Mares v. Marsh, 777 F.2d 1066 (5th Cir. 1985)	§ 2.3
Marlowe v. Fisher Body, 489 F.2d 1057 (6th Cir. 1973)	§ 2.9
Marriott In-Flite Servs. v. Air Transp. Div. Local 504, 557 F.2d 295 (2d Cir. 1977)	§ 3.19
Marsh v. Alabama, 326 U.S. 501 (1946)	§ 6.2
Marshall v. Georgia Southwestern College, 489 F. Supp. 1322 (M.D. Ga. 1980)	§ 2.21
Marshall v. Sun Oil Co. (Del.), 605 F.2d 1331 (5th Cir. 1979), *cert. denied,* 444 U.S. 826 (1979)	§ 2.6
Marsille v. City of Santa Ana, 64 Cal. App. 3d 764, 134 Cal. Rptr. 743 (Ct. App. 1977)	app. F
Martin v. Capital Cities Media, Inc., 354 Pa. Super. 199, 511 A.2d 830 (1986)	§§ 1.12, 2.28, 4.14, 5.7, 5.12, 7.18
Martin v. Federal Life Ins. Co., 109 Ill. App. 3d 596, 440 N.E.2d 998 (1982)	§§ 1.4, 4.15, 4.20
Martin v. New York Life Ins. Co., 148 N.Y. 117, 42 N.E. 416 (1895)	§ 1.4
Martin v. Platt, 179 Ind. App. 688, 386 N.E.2d 1026 (1979)	§ 5.17
Martin v. Southern R.R., 240 S.C. 460, 326 S.E.2d 365 (1962)	§ 7.25
Martin v. Unified School Dist. No. 434, 728 F.2d 453 (10th Cir. 1984)	§§ 6.10, 6.11
Martino v. Transport Workers, 505 Pa. 391, 480 A.2d 242 (1984)	§§ 3.19, 6.15
Mason County Bd. of Educ. v. Superintendent of Schools, 295 S.E.2d 719 (W. Va. 1982)	app. E
Massman v. H.U.D., 332 F. Supp. 894 (D.D.C. 1963)	§ 9.32
Mastriano v. F.A.A., 714 F.2d 1152 (Fed. Cir. 1983)	§ 6.4
Mathews v. Eldridge, 424 U.S. 319 (1976)	§§ 6.5, 6.12, 9.2, 9.17, 9.25, 9.27
Matthew v. Swift & Co., 465 F.2d 814 (5th Cir. 1972)	app. F
Maus v. National Living Centers, Inc., 633 S.W.2d 674 (Tex. Ct.	

Case | *Book §*

App. 1982)	§ 5.17
Maxfield v. Sinclair Int'l, 766 F.2d 788 (3d Cir. 1985), *cert. denied*, ___ U.S. ___, 106 S. Ct. 796 (1986)	§ 7.8
M.B.M. Co. v. Counce, 268 Ark. 269, 596 S.W.2d 681 (1980)	§ 5.23
McCabe v. City of Eureka, 664 F.2d 680 (8th Cir. 1981)	§ 2.22
McCarthy v. Bark Peking, 676 F.2d 42 (2d Cir. 1982)	§ 2.18
McCartin v. Norton, 674 F.2d 1317 (9th Cir. 1982)	§ 6.18
McCarthy v. City of Rockford, 96 Ill. App. 3d 531, 421 N.E.2d 576 (1981)	app. F
McCauley v. Thygerson, 732 F.2d 978 (D.C. Cir. 1984)	§§ 4.17, 6.3, 6.10
McClary v. United States, 775 F.2d 280 (Fed. Cir. 1985)	§ 6.18
McClendon v. Continental Group, Inc., 602 F. Supp. 1492 (D.N.J. 1985)	§ 8.9
McCluskey v. Unicare Health Facility, Inc., 484 So. 2d 398 (Ala. 1986)	§ 1.12
McCone v. New Eng. Tel. & Tel. Co., 393 Mass. 231, 471 N.E.2d 47 (1984)	§§ 4.11, 4.23, 5.25, 8.15
McConnell v. Anderson, 451 F.2d 193 (8th Cir. 1971), *cert. denied*, 405 U.S. 1046 (1972)	§ 6.13
McCormack v. Jermyn, 351 Pa. 161, 40 A.2d 477 (1945)	§ 4.15
McCorstin v. United States Steel Corp., 621 F.2d 749 (1980)	§ 7.8
McDonald v. City of W. Branch, 466 U.S. 284 (1984)	§§ 2.8, 3.27, 6.15, 7.31, 9.28
McDonald v. Penn. Cent. Transp. Co., 337 F. Supp. 803 (D. Mass. 1972)	§ 9.27
McDonald v. Santa Fe Trail Transp. Co., 427 U.S. 273 (1976)	§§ 2.3, 7.6
McDonnell Douglas Corp. v. Green, 411 U.S. 792 (1973)	§§ 2.3, 2.4, 7.6–7.8, 7.13, 7.27, 7.32, 7.33, 9.19
McGeehan v. Bank of N.H., 123 N.H. 83, 455 A.2d 1054 (1983)	§ 4.27
McGinley v. Burroughs Corp., 407 F. Supp. 903 (E.D. Pa. 1975)	§ 2.6
McGinnis v. Joyce, 507 F. Supp. 654 (N.D. Ill. 1981)	§ 2.23
McKay v. Capital Cities Communications, Inc., 605 F. Supp. 1489 (S.D.N.Y. 1985)	§ 2.23
McKinney v. County of Santa Clara, 110 Cal. App. 3d 787, 168 Cal. Rptr. 89 (1980)	§ 5.25
McKinney v. Kimberly-Clark Corp., 449 So. 2d 790 (Ala. Civ. App. 1982), *aff'd*, 449 So. 2d 794 (1983)	§ 5.6
McKinney v. Missouri-Kansas-Texas R.R., 357 U.S. 265 (1958)	§ 3.27
McKinney v. National Dairy Council, 491 F. Supp. 1108 (D. Mass. 1980)	§ 4.23
McLeod v. Department of Army, 714 F.2d 918 (9th Cir. 1983)	§ 6.4
McMullen v. Carson, 754 F.2d 936 (11th Cir. 1985)	§ 6.13
McMurphy v. City of Flushing, 802 F.2d 191 (6th Cir. 1986)	§ 6.13
McNeese v. Board of Educ., 373 U.S. 608 (1963)	§ 2.32
McNeil v. Economics Laboratory, Inc., 800 F.2d 111 (7th Cir. 1986)	§ 7.8
McNulty v. Borden,Inc., 474 F. Supp. 1111 (E.D. Pa. 1979)	§ 5.21
McPherson v. Rankin, 786 F.2d 1233 (5th Cir. 1986)	§ 6.11

CASES

Case	Book §
McQuary v. Bel Air Convalescent Home, Inc., 69 Or. App. 107, 684 P.2d 21 (1985)	§§ 5.16, 7.12, 7.34
McQuitty v. General Dynamics Corp., 204 N.J. Super. 514, 499 A.2d 526 (1985)	§ 4.25
Medina v. Spotnail, Inc., 591 F. Supp. 190 (N.D. Ill. 1984)	§§ 2.26, 2.27, 2.35, 5.9
Meeks v. Opps Cotton Mills, Inc., 459 So. 2d 814 (Ala. 1984)	§ 1.12
Mein v. Masonite Corp., 124 Ill. App. 3d 617, 464 N.E.2d 1137 (1984), *aff'd,* 109 Ill. 2d 1, 485 N.E.2d 312 (1985)	§ 5.9
Melchi v. Burns Int'l Sec. Serv., Inc., 597 F. Supp. 575 (E.D. Mich. 1984)	§ 7.13
Melley v. Gillette Corp., 19 Mass. App. Ct. 511, 475 N.E.2d 1227 (1985)	§§ 2.26, 5.9
Mendelson v. Macy, 356 F.2d 796 (D.C. Cir. 1966)	§ 6.4
Meredith v. C.E. Walther, Inc., 422 So. 2d 761 (Ala. 1982)	§ 1.12
Meritor Sav. Bank v. Vinson, ___ U.S. ___, 106 S. Ct. 2399 (1986)	§ 2.5
Merkel v. Scovill, Inc., 787 F.2d 174 (6th Cir. 1986)	§ 7.8
Mers v. Dispatch Printing Co., 19 Ohio St. 3d 100, 483 N.E.2d 150 (1985)	§§ 1.12, 4.17
Meyers Indus., 268 NLRB 493 (1984)	§ 2.16
Midgett v. Sackett-Chicago, Inc., 105 Ill. 2d 143, 473 N.E.2d 1280 (1984)	§§ 5.20, 5.30, 7.12
Midland Heights Homes, Inc. v. Pennsylvania Human Relations Comm'n, 478 Pa. 625, 387 A.2d 664 (1978)	§ 2.12
Migra v. Warren City School Dist. Bd. of Educ., 465 U.S. 75 (1984)	§§ 2.8, 3.27, 6.15
Miles v. M.N.C. Corp., 750 F.2d 867 (11th Cir. 1985)	§ 7.6
Miller v. International Tel. & Tel. Corp., 755 F.2d 20 (2d Cir. 1985)	§ 2.6
Miller Brewing Co. v. Brewery Workers Local 9, 739 F.2d 1159 (7th Cir. 1984)	§§ 3.18, 3.22, 3.24
Milton v. Illinois Bell Tel. Co., 101 Ill. App. 3d 75, 427 N.E.2d 829 (1981)	§ 5.31
Milwaukee Newspaper & Graphic Communications Union Local 23 v. Newspapers, Inc., 586 F.2d 19 (7th Cir. 1978)	§ 3.3
Mine Safety Appliances Co. v. Forrestal, 326 U.S. 371 (1945)	§ 6.18
Minehart v. Louisville & N.R.R., 731 F.2d 342 (6th Cir. 1984)	§ 2.19
Minihan v. American Pharmaceutical Ass'n, 624 F. Supp. 345 (D.D.C. 1985)	§§ 1.12, 4.17
Misco, Inc. v. Paperworkers, 768 F.2d 739 (5th Cir. 1985)	§ 3.24
Misericordia Hosp. Medical Center v. NLRB, 623 F.2d 808 (2d Cir. 1980)	§ 2.16
Mistretta v. Sandia Corp., 649 F.2d 1383 (10th Cir. 1981)	§ 7.8
Mitchell v. Baldridge, 759 F.2d 80 (D.C. Cir. 1985)	§ 7.6
Mitchell v. Keith, 752 F.2d 385 (9th Cir. 1985)	§§ 2.8, 7.9, 8.9
Mitchell v. National Broadcasting Co., 553 F.2d 265 (2d Cir. 1977)	§ 2.8
Mitchell v. Pepsi-Cola Bottlers, Inc., 772 F.2d 342 (7th Cir. 1985), *cert. denied,* ___ U.S. ___, 106 S. Ct. 1266 (1986)	§ 5.30
Mitchell v. Robert DeMario Jewelry, Inc., 361 U.S. 288 (1960)	§ 2.21
Mizell v. North Broward Hosp. Dist., 427 F.2d 468 (5th Cir. 1970)	§ 2.9

Case | *Book §*

Case	Book §
Mobil Coal Producing, Inc. v. Parks, 704 P.2d 702 (Wyo. 1985)	§ 1.12
Mobil & O. R.R. v. Moreland, 104 Miss. 312, 61 So. 424 (1913)	app. E
Moffett v. Gene B. Glick Co., 604 F. Supp. 229 (N.D. Ind. 1984)	§§ 5.23, 5.24, 5.27
Mohasco v. Silver, 447 U.S. 807 (1979)	§ 2.3
Molder v. Southwestern Bell Tel. Co., 665 S.W.2d 175 (Tex. Ct. App. 1983)	§ 4.20
Monell v. Department of Social Servs., 436 U.S. 658 (1978)	§§ 6.17, 6.19
Monge v. Beebe Rubber Co., 114 N.H. 130, 316 A.2d 549 (1974)	§§ 1.2, 1.9, 1.11, 1.12, 4.11, 4.28, 7.11, 7.23
Moniodis v. Cook, 64 Md. App. 1, 494 A.2d 212 (1985)	§§ 2.26, 5.23, 5.33, 7.11, 7.12
Monroe v. Pape, 365 U.S. 167 (1961)	§ 6.19
Montalvo v. Zamora, 7 Cal. App. 3d 69, 86 Cal. Rptr. 401 (1970)	§ 5.9
Monteiro v. Poole Silver Co., 615 F.2d 4 (1st Cir. 1980)	§ 2.17
Montgomery v. Big B, Inc., 460 So. 2d 1286 (Ala. 1984)	§ 5.25
Moore v. General Motors Corp., 739 F.2d 311 (8th Cir. 1984)	§§ 2.29, 5.24
Moore v. Illinois Cent. R.R., 312 U.S. 630 (1941)	§§ 1.10, 2.31
Moore v. McDermott, Inc., 481 So. 2d 602 (La. 1986)	§§ 7.10, 7.13
Moore v. Sun Oil Co., 636 F.2d 154 (6th Cir. 1980)	§ 2.8
Moran v. Lasete, 221 A.D. 118, 223 N.Y.S. 283 (1927)	§ 3.21
Morgan Drive Away, Inc. v. Brant, 479 N.E.2d 1336 (Ind. Ct. App. 1985), *rev'd,* 489 N.E.2d 933 (Ind. 1986)	§§ 1.12, 5.11
Morris v. Hartford Courant Co., 200 Conn. 676, 513 A.2d 66 (1986)	§§ 5.23, 7.11
Morris v. Lutheran Medical Center, 215 Neb. 677, 340 N.W.2d 388 (1983)	§§ 1.4, 1.12
Morris v. Owens-Illinois, 544 F. Supp. 752 (S.D. W. Va. 1982)	§ 2.29
Morschauser v. American News Co., 6 A.D.2d 1028, 178 N.Y.S.2d 279 (1958)	app. F
Motor Vehicle Mfrs. Ass'n v. State Farm Mut., 463 U.S. 29 (1982)	§ 4.19
Mouser v. Granite City Steel Div., 121 Ill. App. 3d 834, 460 N.E.2d 115 (1984)	§§ 5.20, 7.12
Mt. Healthy City School Dist. v. Doyle, 429 U.S. 274 (1977)	§§ 6.13, 7.5–7.7
Mueller v. Chicago & N.W. Ry., 194 Minn. 83, 259 N.W. 798 (1935)	§ 3.21
Mueller v. Union Pac. R.R., 220 Neb. 742, 371 N.W.2d 732 (1985)	§§ 1.12, 5.24, 7.18
Muller v. Stromberg Carlson Corp., 427 So. 2d 266 (Fla. Dist. Ct. App. 1983)	§ 1.12, app. F
Muller Optical Co. v. EEOC, 743 F.2d 380 (6th Cir. 1984)	§ 2.6
Munsell v. Ideal Food Stores, 208 Kan. 909, 494 P.2d 1063 (1972)	§ 5.25
Munson v. Friske, 754 F.2d 683 (7th Cir. 1985)	§§ 2.9, 2.25, 6.10, 6.11
Murphree v. Alabama Farm Bureau Ins. Co., 449 So. 2d 1218 (Ala. 1984)	§§ 1.4, 1.12, 4.15
Murphy v. American Home Prods. Corp., 58 N.Y.2d 293, 448 N.E.2d 86, 461 N.Y.S.2d 232 (1983)	§§ 1.2, 1.4, 1.9, 1.12, 4.11, 4.20, 5.6, 5.9, 5.12, 5.15, 5.17, 5.21, 5.23, 7.11, 9.24

CASES 675

Case	*Book §*
Murphy v. City of Topeka-Shawnee County Dep't of Labor Servs., 6 Kan. App. 2d 488, 630 P.2d 186 (1981)	§ 5.10
Murphy v. Publicker Indus., Inc., ___ Pa. Super. ___, 516 A.2d 47 (1986)	§ 7.21
Murphy v. Villanova Univ., 520 F. Supp. 560 (E.D. Pa. 1981)	§ 2.9
Murray v. Bridgeport Hosp., 40 Conn. Supp. 56, 480 A.2d 610 (1984)	§§ 5.22, 5.23
Murray v. Commercial Union Ins. Co., 782 F.2d 432 (3d Cir. 1986)	§§ 5.9, 7.12, 7.18
Murray v. Consolidated Rail Corp., 736 F.2d 372 (6th Cir. 1984)	§ 3.19
Murray v. Kaiser Aluminum & Chem. Corp., 591 F. Supp. 1550 (S.D. W. Va. 1984)	§ 4.10
Muskego-Norway Consol. Schools v. Wisconsin Employee Relations Bd., 35 Wis. 2d 540, 151 N.W.2d 617 (1967)	§ 7.7
Muskopf v. Corning Hosp. Dist., 55 Cal. 2d 211, 359 P.2d 457, 11 Cal. Rptr. 89 (1961)	§ 6.20
Musso v. Suriano, 586 F.2d 59 (7th Cir. 1978)	§ 6.2
Myers v. Bethlehem Shipbuilding Corp., 303 U.S. 41 (1938)	§ 2.16
Myron v. Consolidated Rail Corp., 752 F.2d 50 (2d Cir. 1985)	§§ 3.24, 6.2
Myrtle Springs Reverted Indep. School Dist. v. Hogan, 705 S.W.2d 707 (Tex. Ct. App. 1985)	§§ 4.6, 4.28, 6.20
Nader v. Allegheny Airlines, 426 U.S 290 (1976)	§ 2.27
Nader v. Bork, 366 F. Supp. 104 (D.D.C. 1973)	§ 4.19
Napier v. Atlantic Coast Line, 272 U.S. 605 (1926)	§ 2.27
Nasem v. Brown, 595 F.2d 801 (D.C. Cir. 1979)	§ 7.32
Naval Air Rework, 72 Lab. Arb. (BNA) 1266 (1979) (Mire, Arb.)	§ 3.6
Nederlandsch ASM v. Stevedores, 265 F.397 (E.D. La. 1920)	§ 4.5
Nees v. Hocks, 272 Or. 210, 536 P.2d 512 (1975)	§§ 1.9, 1.11, 1.12, 5.10, 5.12, 5.21, 5.33, 7.10, 7.15
Neighbors v. Kirksville College of Osteopathic Medicine, 694 S.W.2d 822 (Mo. Ct. App. 1985)	§ 5.25
Nelson v. City of Moss Point, 701 F.2d 556 (5th Cir. 1983)	§ 2.8
Nelson v. Piedmont Aviation, 750 F.2d 1234 (4th Cir. 1984)	§ 2.26
Neulist v. County of Nassau, 50 A.D.2d 803, 375 N.Y.S.2d 402 (1975)	§ 2.32
Newman v. Legal Servs. Corp., 628 F. Supp. 535 (D.D.C. 1986)	§ 1.12
Newport, City of v. Fact Concerts, 453 U.S. 247 (1981)	§ 6.19
Newton v. Brown & Root, 280 Ark. 337, 658 S.W.2d 370 (1983)	§ 1.12
New York City Transit Auth. v. Beazer, 440 U.S. 568 (1979)	§ 6.7
New York Gaslight Club, Inc. v. Carey, 447 U.S. 54 (1980)	§ 9.33
New York Pub. Library v. New York P.E.R.B., *In re,* 37 N.Y.2d 752, 377 N.E.2d 136, 374 N.Y.S.2d 625 (1975)	§ 6.2
New York Times Co. v. Sullivan, 376 U.S. 254 (1964)	§ 5.25
Nicely v. Bank of Va. Trust Co., 221 Va. 1084, 277 S.E.2d 209 (1981)	app. F
Nix v. WLCY Radio, 738 F.2d 1181 (11th Cir. 1984)	§§ 2.3, 2.4, 7.6
NLRB v. Acme Indus. Co., 385 U.S. 432 (1967)	§ 3.28
NLRB v. Associated Milk Producers, Inc., 711 F.2d 627 (5th Cir. 1983)	§ 2.16
NLRB v. Babcock & Wilcox Co., 351 U.S. 105 (1956)	§ 2.16

Case	Book §
NLRB v. Bliss & Laughlin Steel Co., Inc., 754 F.2d 229 (7th Cir. 1985)	§ 2.16
NLRB v. Burnup & Sims, 379 U.S. 21 (1964)	§ 2.16
NLRB v. City Disposal Sys., Inc., 465 U.S. 822 (1984)	§ 2.16
NLRB v. Columbus Printing Pressmen, 543 F.2d 1161 (5th Cir. 1976)	§ 3.3
NLRB v. Container Corp. of Am., 649 F.2d 1213 (6th Cir. 1981)	§ 3.27
NLRB v. Erie Resistor Corp., 373 U.S. 221 (1963)	§ 2.16
NLRB v. Esco Elevators, Inc., 736 F.2d 295 (5th Cir. 1984)	§ 2.16
NLRB v. Fleetwood Trailer Co., 389 U.S. 375 (1967)	§ 2.16
NLRB v. Great E. Color Lithographic Corp., 309 F.2d 352 (2d Cir. 1962)	§ 7.7
NLRB v. Pace Motor Lines, 703 F.2d 28 (2d Cir. 1983)	§ 2.16
NLRB v. Plasterers Local 79, 404 U.S. 116 (1971)	§§ 3.27, 9.3, 9.26
NLRB v. Transportation Management Corp., 462 U.S. 393 (1983)	§§ 7.3, 7.6, 7.7
NLRB v. Weingarten, Inc., 420 U.S. 251 (1975)	§ 3.9
Nolde Bros., Inc. v. Bakery Workers, 430 U.S. 243 (1977)	§ 3.19
Nolting v. Yellow Freight Sys., 799 F.2d 1192 (8th Cir. 1986)	§ 2.6
Norfolk S. Ry. Co. v. Harris, 190 Va. 966, 59 S.E.2d 110 (1950)	§§ 1.9, 1.10
Norfolk & W. Ry. Co. v. B.R.A.C., 657 F.2d 596 (4th Cir. 1981)	§ 3.18
North Haven Bd. of Educ. v. Bell, 456 U.S. 512 (1982)	§ 2.14
North Little Rock, City of v. Vogelgesang, 273 Ark. 390, 619 S.W.2d 652 (1981)	app. F
Norton v. Macy, 417 F.2d 1161 (D.C. Cir. 1969)	§§ 6.11, 6.13, 9.2, 9.20
Novosel v. Nationwide Ins. Co., 721 F.2d 894 (3d Cir. 1983), *on remand*, 118 L.R.R.M. 2779 (W.D. Pa. 1985)	§§ 1.2, 1.9, 1.12, 5.12, 5.28, 7.11, 7.15, 9.20, 9.24
Novosel v. Sears, Roebuck & Co., 495 F. Supp. 344 (E.D. Mich. 1980)	§§ 4.10, 8.7, 8.8, app. F
Novotny v. Great Am. Fed. Sav. & Loan Ass'n, 584 F.2d 1235 (3d Cir. 1978)	§ 2.9
Nugent Sand Co., 71 Lab. Arb. (BNA) 585 (1978) (Kanner, Arb.)	§ 3.8
Nye v. Department of Livestock, 196 Mont. 222, 639 P.2d 498 (1982)	§§ 1.12, 5.15, 6.5
Oakley v. St. Joseph's Hosp., 116 A.D.2d 911, 498 N.Y.S.2d 218 (1986)	§ 7.18
O'Brien v. Papa Gino's, 780 F.2d 1067 (1st Cir. 1986)	§§ 5.26, 5.27, 5.33, 7.16
O'Connor v. Donaldson, 422 U.S. 563 (1975)	§ 6.19
O'Connor v. Eastman Kodak Co., 65 N.Y.2d 724, 481 N.E.2d 549, 492 N.Y.S.2d 9 (1985)	§ 7.18
Ogletree v. Chester, 682 F.2d 1366 (11th Cir. 1982)	§ 6.10
Ohanian v. Avis Rent a Car Sys., Inc., 779 F.2d 101 (2d Cir. 1985)	§§ 4.2, 4.7, 4.10, 4.20, 4.28, 7.18
Oklahoma City, City of v. Tuttle, 471 U.S. 808 (1985)	§ 6.19
Olguin v. Inspiration Consol. Copper Co., 740 F.2d 1468 (9th Cir. 1984)	§§ 2.29, 7.29, 7.31, 9.26

CASES

Case	Book §
Olin v. Prudential Ins. Corp., 781 F.2d 1 (1st Cir. 1986)	§ 7.21
Olin Corp., 268 N.L.R.B. 268 (1984)	§ 3.27
O'Neill v. ARA Servs., Inc., 457 F. Supp. 182 (E.D. Pa. 1978)	§ 4.15
Ontario Knife Co. v. NLRB, 637 F.2d 840 (2d Cir. 1980)	§ 2.16
Operating Eng'rs v. Shank-Artukovich, 751 F.2d 364 (10th Cir. 1985)	§ 3.18
Operating Eng'rs Local 926 v. Jones, 460 U.S. 669 (1983)	§ 2.28
Orange, City of v. Chance, 325 S.W.2d 838 (Tex. Civ. App. 1959)	app. F
Orloski v. Pennsylvania Unemployment Compensation Bd. of Review, 52 Pa. Commw. 254, 415 A.2d 720 (1980)	§ 7.35
Ortwein v. Schwab, 410 U.S. 656 (1973)	§ 9.33
Oscar Mayer & Co. v. Evans, 441 U.S. 750 (1979)	§§ 2.6, 2.32
O'Shea v. RCA Global Communications, 117 L.R.R.M. 2880 (D.N.J. 1984)	app. F
Osman v. Hialeah Hous. Auth., 785 F.2d 1550 (11th Cir. 1986)	§ 6.10
Osterkamp v. Alkota Mfg., Inc., 332 N.W.2d 275 (S.D. 1983)	§§ 1.12, 4.22, 4.28, 7.28
Ostrofe v. Crocker Co., 670 F.2d 1378 (9th Cir. 1982), *vacated & remanded,* 460 U.S. 1007 (1983), *on remand,* 740 F.2d 739 (9th Cir. 1984), *cert. dismissed,* 469 U.S. 1200 (1985)	§§ 2.26, 5.19
Overman v. Flour Constructors, Inc., 797 F.2d 217 (5th Cir. 1986)	§ 7.19
Owen v. City of Independence, 445 U.S. 622 (1980)	§§ 6.17, 6.19
Owenboro Shovel & Tool Co. v. Moore, 154 Ky. 431, 157 S.W. 1121 (1913)	§ 4.20
Owen & Briggs v. James, [1982] I.C.R. 618 (C.A.)	§ 9.11
Pacheco v. Advertisers Lithographing, Inc., 657 F.2d 191 (8th Cir. 1981)	§ 2.8
Padway v. Palches, 665 F.2d 965 (9th Cir. 1982)	§ 2.9
Palmateer v. International Harvester Co., 85 Ill. 2d 124, 421 N.E.2d 876 (1981)	§§ 1.12, 5.16
Palmer v. United States, 794 F.2d 534 (9th Cir. 1986)	§ 7.8
Paolino v. Channel Home Centers, 668 F.2d 721 (3d Cir. 1981)	§ 7.1
Papapetropoulous v. Milwaukee Transp. Servs., Inc., 795 F.2d 591 (7th Cir. 1986)	§ 6.12
Parnar v. Americana Hotels, Inc., 65 Haw. 370, 652 P.2d 625 (1982)	§§ 1.10–1.12, 7.13, 7.14
Parsons v. Yellow Freight Sys., Inc., 741 F.2d 871 (6th Cir. 1984)	§ 2.3
Patsy v. Florida Bd. of Regents, 457 U.S. 496 (1982)	§§ 6.6, 6.19
Patterson v. American Tobacco Co., 586 F.2d 300 (4th Cir. 1978)	§ 2.3
Patterson v. McLean Credit Union, 805 F.2d ___ (4th Cir. 1986)	§ 2.8
Patton v. J.C. Penney Co., 301 Or. 117, 719 P.2d 854 (1986)	§§ 5.12, 5.13, 5.23, 5.27, 7.11
Pavlo v. Stiefel Laboratories, Inc., 22 F.E.P. Cas. (BNA) 489 (S.D.N.Y. 1979)	§ 2.9
Pavolini v. Bard-Air Corp., 645 F.2d 144 (2d Cir. 1981)	§ 2.18
Payne v. McLemore's Wholesale & Retail Stores, 654 F.2d 1130 (5th Cir. Sept. 1981), *cert. denied,* 455 U.S. 1000 (1982)	§§ 2.17, 7.15, 7.34
Pedersen v. South Williamsport Area School Dist., 677 F.2d 312 (3d Cir.), *cert. denied,* 459 U.S. 972 (1982)	§ 6.15

Case   *Book §*

Pennsylvania Labor Relations Bd. v. Neshaminy School Dist., 43 Pa.
    Commw. 377, 403 A.2d 1003 (1979)   § 6.15
Pennsylvania Labor Relations Bd. v. West Middlesex Area School
    Dist., 55 Pa. Commw. 404, 423 A.2d 781 (1980)   § 6.15
Pennsylvania State Police v. Pennsylvania Human Relations Comm'n,
    72 Pa. Commw. 520, 457 A.2d 584 (1983)   § 2.12
Perks v. Firestone Tire & Rubber Co., 611 F.2d 1363 (3d Cir.
    1979)   § 5.9
Perry v. Hartz Mountain Corp., 537 F. Supp. 1387 (S.D. Ind. 1982)   §§ 5.19, 5.23,
                                                                                                                5.25, 7.11
Perry v. Sindermann, 408 U.S. 593 (1972)   §§ 1.10, 4.9, 6.10,
                                                                                                                6.19, 7.19, 9.2,
                                                                                                                9.20
Petermann v. Teamsters, 174 Cal. App. 2d 184, 344 P.2d 25 (1959)   §§ 1.2, 1.9, 1.11,
                                                                                                                4.11, 4.23, 5.10,
                                                                                                                5.18
Peterson v. Air Line Pilots' Ass'n, 759 F.2d 1161 (4th Cir. 1985)   § 2.31
Petrik v. Monarch Printing Corp., 143 Ill. App. 3d 1, 493 N.E.2d
    616 (1986)   § 5.17
Petrovich v. New Canaan Bd. of Educ., 189 Conn. 585, 457 A.2d
    315 (1983)   § 6.5
Peytan v. Ellis, 200 Conn. 243, 510 A.2d 1337 (1986)   § 5.25
Philadelphia Hous. Auth. v. Security Officers, 500 Pa. 213, 455
    A.2d 625 (1983)   § 6.16
Philadelphia Newspapers, Inc. v. Hepps, ___ U.S. ___, 106 S. Ct.
    1558 (1986)   § 5.25
Phillips v. Babcock & Wilcox, 349 Pa. Super. 351, 503 A.2d 36
    (1986)   §§ 5.20, 5.30, 7.12
Phillips v. Smalley Maintenance Serv., Inc., 711 F.2d 1524 (11th
    Cir. 1983)   §§ 2.35, 5.26
Phung v. Waste Management, Inc., 23 Ohio St. 3d 100, 491 N.E.2d
    1114 (1986)   §§ 1.2, 1.12
Piacitelli v. Southern Utah State College, 636 P.2d 1063 (Utah 1981)   § 8.5
Pickering v. Board of Educ., 391 U.S. 563 (1968)   §§ 1.10, 6.11, 6.13
Pierce v. Ortho Pharmaceutical Corp., 84 N.J. 58, 417 A.2d 505
    (1980)   §§ 1.11, 1.12, 5.7,
                                                                                                                5.18, 5.31, 5.33,
                                                                                                                7.11
Pierce v. Stinson, 493 F. Supp. 609 (E.D. Tenn. 1980)   § 2.9
Pine River State Bank v. Mettille, 333 N.W.2d 622 (Minn. 1983)   §§ 1.9–1.12, 4.8,
                                                                                                                4.12, 4.13, 4.15,
                                                                                                                4.16, 4.19, 4.21,
                                                                                                                4.22, 4.28, 7.18,
                                                                                                                7.20, 7.24, 7.27,
                                                                                                                7.28, 8.13, 8.14,
                                                                                                                9.24
Pinsof v. Pinsof, 107 Ill. App. 3d 1031, 438 N.E.2d 525 (1982)   §§ 4.7, 5.22
Pioneer Grain Co. v. Kraus, [1981] 2 F.C. 815 (Ct. App.)   § 9.12
Pirne v. Loyola Univ., 803 F.2d 351 (7th Cir. 1986)   § 2.3
Pittsburgh Joint Collective Bargaining Comm. v. City of Pittsburgh,
    481 Pa. 66, 391 A.2d 1318 (1978), *rev'g* 351 A.2d 304 (1976)   § 6.15

Case	Book §
Pittston Stevedoring Corp. v. Dellaventura, 544 F.2d 35 (2d Cir. 1976)	§§ 9.2, 9.27
Placos v. Cosmair, Inc., 517 F. Supp. 1287 (S.D.N.Y. 1981)	§§ 2.6, 5.9
Plumbers v. Kahme, 6 N.Y.S.2d 589 (N.Y. Sup. Ct. 1937)	§ 4.5
Poledna v. Bendix Corp., 360 Mich. 129, 103 N.W.2d 789 (1960)	§ 5.25
Polk v. Yellow Freight Sys., Inc., 801 F.2d 190 (6th Cir. 1986)	§§ 5.23, 7.13, 7.35
Polsky v. Radio Shack, 666 F.2d 824 (3d Cir. 1981)	§ 5.9
Portillo v. G.T. Price Prods., Inc., 131 Cal. App. 3d 285, 182 Cal. Rptr. 291 (1982)	§ 5.11
Postal Workers v. United States Postal Serv., 789 F.2d 1 (D.C. Cir. 1986)	§§ 3.13, 3.24, 3.27
Poughkeepsie School Dist., City of v. Poughkeepsie Pub. Teachers Ass'n, 35 N.Y.2d 599, 324 N.E.2d 144, 364 N.Y.S.2d 492 (1974)	§ 6.15
Powell v. Rockwell Int'l Corp., 788 F.2d 279 (5th Cir. 1986)	§ 7.8
Powermatic Houdaille, Inc., 71 Lab. Arb. (BNA) 54 (1978) (Cocalis, Arb.)	§ 3.7
Powers v. Delnor Hosp., 135 Ill. App. 3d 317, 481 N.E.2d 968 (1985)	§ 7.11
Price v. Carmack Datsun, Inc., 124 Ill. App. 3d 979, 464 N.E.2d 1245 (1984), aff'd, 109 Ill 2d 65, 485 N.E.2d 359 (1985)	§§ 5.9, 7.11
Price v. Mercury Supply Co., 682 S.W.2d 924 (Tenn. Ct. App. 1984)	§§ 4.18, 4.20, 5.24
Price v. United Parcel Serv., Inc., 601 F. Supp. 20 (D. Mass. 1984)	§ 4.11
Priest, In re, 47 Pa. Commw. 320, 408 A.2d 547 (1979), aff'd, 497 Pa. 202, 439 A.2d 671 (1982)	§ 6.5
Prill v. NLRB, 755 F.2d 941 (D.C. Cir. 1985)	§ 2.16
Prochaska v. Fediaczko, 458 F. Supp. 778 (W.D. Pa. 1978)	§ 2.9
Procunier v. Navarette, 434 U.S. 555 (1978)	§ 6.19
Protos v. Volkwagen of Am., Inc., 797 F.2d 129 (3d Cir. 1986)	§ 2.3
Pugh v. See's Candies, Inc., 116 Cal. App. 3d 311, 171 Cal. Rptr. 917 (1981)	§§ 1.12, 4.8, 4.9, 4.12, 4.15, 4.16, 4.23, 7.18, 7.27, 9.10
Pullman Standard v. Swint, 624 F.2d 525 (5th Cir. 1980) rev'd. 456 U.S. 273 (1982), on remand, 692 F.2d 1031 (5th Cir. 1982)	§ 2.3
Pullman Standard Car Mfg. Co. v. Local 2928, 152 F.2d 493 (7th Cir. 1945)	§ 3.21
Quern v. Jordan, 440 U.S. 332 (1979)	§ 6.19
Raab v. Keystone Ins. Co., 271 Pa. Super. 185, 412 A.2d 638 (1979)	§ 5.22
Rabidue v. Osceola Refining Co., ___ F.2d ___, 42 Fair Empl. Prac. 631 (6th Cir. 1986)	§ 2.5
Rachford v. Evergreen Int'l Airlines, 596 F. Supp. 384 (N.D. Ill. 1984)	§§ 2.26, 5.17, 7.11
Radio Officers Union v. NLRB, 347 U.S. 17 (1954)	§ 2.16
Railroad Trainmen v. Central of Ga. Ry., 305 F.2d 605 (5th Cir. 1962)	§ 3.23

Case	Book §
Railroad Trainmen v. Jacksonville Terminal Co., 394 U.S. 369 (1969)	§§ 3.19, 3.22
Ralph's Grocery Co., 77 Lab. Arb. (BNA) 867 (1981) (Kaufman, Arb.)	§ 3.8
Ramos v. Henry C. Beck Co., 711 S.W.2d 331 (Tex. Ct. App. 1986)	§ 5.25
Randolph v. First Baptist Church, 53 Ohio Op. 288, 120 N.E.2d 485 (1954)	§ 9.17
Rap, Inc. v. District of Columbia Comm'n on Human Rights, 485 A.2d 173 (D.C. 1984)	§§ 2.3, 7.6, 9.27
Rasch v. City of E. Jordan, 141 Mich. App. 336, 367 N.W.2d 856 (1985)	§ 7.25
Ratliff v. City of Milwaukee, 795 F.2d 612 (7th Cir. 1986)	§§ 6.8, 6.10, 6.11
Raus v. B.R.C., 663 F.2d 791 (8th Cir. 1981)	§ 3.19
Ray-O-Vac, Div. of E.S.B., Inc. v. Wisconsin Dep't of Indus., Labor & Human Relations, 70 Wis. 2d 919, 236 N.W. 2d 209 (1975)	§ 2.12
Reed v. Famous Barr Div., 518 F. Supp. 538 (E.D. Mo. 1981)	§ 2.4
Reed v. Sale Memorial Hosp. & Clinic, 698 S.W.2d 931 (Mo. Ct. App. 1985)	§§ 5.33, 7.16
Reich v. Holiday Inn, 454 So. 2d 982 (Ala. 1984)	§ 1.12
Reid v. Gholson, 229 Va. 179, 327 S.E.2d 107 (1985)	§ 9.17
Reid v. Sears, Roebuck & Co., 790 F.2d 453 (6th Cir. 1986)	§ 4.10
Reid v. Sears, Roebuck & Co., 588 F. Supp. 558 (E.D. Mich. 1984)	§ 8.8
Rendell-Baker v. Kohn, 457 U.S. 830 (1982)	§ 6.2
Renny v. Port Huron Hosp., ___ Mich. ___, ___ N.W.2d ___, No. 74884 (Dec. 1986)	§ 4.28
Republic Aviation Corp. v. NLRB, 324 U.S. 793 (1945)	§ 2.16
Republic Steel Corp. v. Maddox, 379 U.S. 650 (1965)	§§ 3.9, 4.25, 5.9
Reuther v. Fowler & Williams, Inc., 255 Pa. Super. 28, 386 A.2d 119 (1978)	§§ 5.10, 7.14
Reynolds v. Humko Prods., 756 F.2d 469 (6th Cir. 1985)	§ 2.4
Rice v. Grant County Bd. of Comm'rs, 472 N.E.2d 213 (Ind. Ct. App. 1984)	§§ 4.26, 5.31
Rice v. Santa Fe, 331 U.S. 218 (1947)	§ 2.27
Rice v. United Ins. Co., 465 So. 2d 1100 (Ala. 1984)	§ 2.32
Richardson v. Alaska Airlines, Inc., 750 F.2d 763 (9th Cir. 1984)	§ 2.25
Richardson v. Charles Cole Memorial Hosp., 320 Pa. Super. 106, 466 A.2d 1084 (1983)	§ 4.8
Richardson v. Perales, 402 U.S. 389 (1971)	§§ 9.2, 9.27
Richins v. Southern Pac. Co., 620 F.2d 761 (10th Cir. 1980), *cert. denied*, 449 U.S. 1110 (1981)	§ 3.19
Ridenour v. Lawson Co., 791 F.2d 52 (6th Cir. 1986)	§ 7.8
Ridley School Dist. v. Ridley Educ. Ass'n, 84 Pa. Commw. 117, 479 A.2d 641 (1984)	§ 6.15
Riggins v. Board of Regents of Univ. of Neb., 790 F.2d 707 (8th Cir. 1986)	§ 6.12
Riggs v. Commonwealth of Ky., 734 F.2d 262 (6th Cir.), *cert. denied*, 469 U.S. 857 (1984)	§§ 6.10, 6.19
Ring v. River Walk Manor, Inc., 596 F. Supp. 393 (D. Md. 1984)	§§ 5.12, 7.11
Ringwelkski v. Sears, Roebuck & Co., 636 F. supp. 519 (E.D. Mich. 1985)	§§ 4.10, 8.7

Case	Book §
Risner v. Federal Aviation Admin., 677 F.2d 36 (8th Cir. 1982)	§ 6.4
Riverside, City of v. Rivera, ___ U.S. ___, 106 S. Ct. 2686 (1986)	§ 2.25
Roach v. Consolidated Forwarding Co., 665 S.W.2d 675 (Mo. Ct. App. 1984)	§ 7.28
Roadway Express, Inc. v. Donovan, 603 F. Supp. 249 (N.D. Ga. 1985)	§ 2.24
Roadway Express, Inc. v. NLRB, 647 F.2d 415 (4th Cir. 1981)	§ 3.27
Roberts v. Atlantic Richfield Co., 88 Wash. 2d 887. 568 P.2d 764 (1977)	§ 4.15
Roberts v. Citicorp Diners Club, Inc., 597 F. Supp. 311 (D. Md. 1984)	§ 2.35
Roberts v. Van Buren Pub. Schools, 773 F.2d 949 (8th Cir. 1985)	§§ 6.11, 7.5
Roberts v. Wake Forest Univ., 55 N.C. App. 430, 286 S.E.2d 120, *review denied,* 305 N.C. 586, 292 S.E.2d 571 (1982)	§§ 4.9, 7.35
Rochester Corp. v. Rochester, 450 F.2d 118 (4th Cir. 1971)	app. F
Rodgers v. Norfolk School Bd., 755 F.2d 59 (4th Cir. 1985)	§ 6.12
Rodriguez v. MSPB, 804 F.2d 673, 675 (Fed. Cir. 1986) (federal employee must elect either arbitration or MSPB review; cannot have both);	§ 6.15
Roe v. Wade, 410 U.S. 113 (1973)	§ 1.10
Rogers v. Exxon Research & Eng'g Co., 550 F.2d 834 (3d Cir. 1977), *cert. denied,* 434 U.S. 1022 (1978)	§ 2.6
Rompf v. John. Q. Hammons Hotels, Inc., 685 P.2d 25 (Wyo. 1984)	§§ 4.1, 4.21, 4.23, 7.20, 7.24
Rose v. Allied Dev. Co., 719 F.2d 83 (Utah 1986)	§§ 1.12, 4.17
Rose v. Secretary of Labor, 800 F.2d 563 (6th Cir. 1986)	§ 2.38
Roseborough v. N.L. Indus., 10 Ohio St. 3d 142, 462 N.E.2d 384 (1984)	§ 7.13
Ross v. Communications Satellite Corp., 759 F.2d 355 (4th Cir. 1985)	§§ 7.6, 7.35
Ross v. Life Ins. Co., 273 S.C. 764, 259 S.E.2d 814 (1979)	§ 5.22
Ross v. Montana R.R., ___ Pa. Super. ___, 516 A.2d 29 (1986)	§§ 4.12, 4.26
Rosser v. Laboreres, 616 F.2d 221 (5th Cir.), *cert. denied,* 449 U.S. 886 (1980)	§§ 2.17, 7.15
Rossi v. Pennsylvania State Univ., 340 Pa. Super. 39, 489 A.2d 828 (1985)	§§ 5.21, 5.31, 7.11
Ross-Meehan Foundries, 55 Lab. Arb. (BNA) 1078 (1970) (King, Arb.)	§ 3.13
Rotert v. Jefferson Fed. Sav. & Loan Ass'n, 623 F. Supp. 1114 (D. Conn. 1985)	§ 7.35
Rotondo v. Seaboard Foundry, Inc., 440 A.2d 751 (R.I. 1981)	§ 1.12
Rouse v. Peoples Natural Gas Co., 605 F. Supp. 230 (D. Kan. 1985)	§ 1.12
Rowe v. Noren Pattern & Foundry Co., 91 Mich. App. 254, 283 N.W.2d 713 (1979)	§ 4.15
Rubin v. Rudolf Wolff Commodity Brokers, Inc., 636 F. Supp. 258 (N.D. Ill. 1986)	§§ 1.14, 4.20, 7.18
Ruch v. Strawbridge & Clother, Inc., 115 L.R.R.M. 2044 (E.D. Pa. 1983)	§ 7.18
Ruiz v. Miller Curtain Co., 686 S.W.2d 671 (Tex. Ct. App. 1985)	§ 2.28

Case	Book §
Rulon-Miller v. I.B.M. 162 Cal. App. 3d 241, 208 Cal. Rptr. 524 (1984)	§§ 4.11, 5.27, 7.23, 7.28, app. E
Runyan v. National Cash Register Corp., 787 F.2d 1039 (6th Cir. 1986)	§§ 2.6, 2.21
Runyon v. McCrary, 427 U.S. 160 (1976)	§ 2.8
Rupinsky v. Miller Brewing Co., 627 F. Supp. 1181 (W.D. Pa. 1986)	§ 1.14
Russell v. Geis, 251 Cal. App. 2d 560, 59 Cal. Rptr. 569 (1967)	§ 5.25
Ruzicka v. General Motors Corp., 523 F.2d 306 (6th Cir. 1975)	§ 3.25
Ryan v. New York Tel. Co., 62 N.Y.2d 494, 467 N.E.2d 487, 478 N.Y.S.2d 823 (1984)	§ 7.35
Saal v. Middendorf, 427 F. Supp. 192 (N.D. Cal. 1977)	§ 6.11
Sabetay v. Sterling Drug, Inc., 114 A.D.2d 6, 497 N.Y.S.2d 655, *appeal granted,* 68 N.Y.2d 605, 497 N.E.2d 708, ___ N.Y.S.2d ___ (1986)	§§ 4.16, 7.18, 7.20
Sabine Pilot Serv., Inc. v. Hauck, 687 S.W.2d 733 (Tex. 1985)	§§ 1.12, 7.14
Safeway Stores, Inc., 74 Lab. Arb. (BNA) 1293 (1980) (Doyle, Arb.)	§ 3.8
Salanger v. United States Air, 611 F. Supp. 427 (N.D.N.Y. 1985)	§§ 7.20, 7.24
Salary Policy Employee Panel v. T.V.A., 731 F.2d 325 (6th Cir. 1984)	§ 6.15
Salazar v. Furr's, Inc., 629 F. Supp. 1403 (D.N.M. 1986)	§§ 5.9, 7.11
Samini Line Ltd. v. Altamar Navegacion S.A., 605 F. Supp. 72 (S.D.N.Y. 1985)	§ 3.18
Sanders v. Broadwater, 402 So. 2d 1035 (Ala. Civ. App. 1981)	§ 6.5
San Diego Bldg. Trades Council v. Garmon, 359 U.S. 236 (1959)	§§ 2.16, 2.28
San Diego County Dist. Council v. Cory, 685 F.2d 1137 (9th Cir. 1982)	§ 3.22
Satterfield v. Western Elec. Co., 758 F.2d 1252 (8th Cir. 1985)	§ 2.28
Saucedo v. Brothers Well Serv., Inc., 464 F. Supp. 919 (S.D. Tex. 1979)	§ 2.4
Savage v. Holiday Inn Corp., 603 F. Supp. 311 (D. Nev. 1985)	§§ 1.12, 2.26, 5.9
Savodnik v. Korvettes, Inc., 488 F. Supp. 822 (E.D.N.Y. 1980)	§§ 4.20, 5.9
Saye v. St. Vrain Valley School Dist., 785 F.2d 862 (10th Cir. 1986)	§ 6.11
Scheller v. Health Care Serv. Corp., 138 Ill. App. 3d 219, 485 N.E.2d 26 (1985)	§ 5.6
Scheps v. Giles, 222 S.W. 348 (Tex. Civ. App. 1920)	app. E
Scherk v. Alberto-Culver Co., 417 U.S. 506 (1974)	§ 3.22
Scheuer v. Rhodes, 416 U.S. 232 (1974)	§ 6.19
Schipani v. Ford Motor Co., 102 Mich. App. 606, 302 N.W.2d 307 (1981)	§§ 4.10, 8.8
Schlesinger v. Quinto, 201 A.D. 487, 194 N.Y.S. 401 (1922)	§§ 3.21, 4.5
Schmidly v. Perry Motor Freight, Inc., 735 F.2d 1086 (8th Cir. 1984)	§ 7.27
Schmidt v. Yardney Elec. Corp., 4 Conn. App. 69, 492 A.2d 512 (1985)	§ 7.11
Schneider v. Jax Shack, Inc., 794 F.2d 383 (8th Cir. 1986)	§ 2.5
Scholtes v. Signal Delivery Serv. Inc., 548 F. Supp. 487 (W.D. Ark. 1982)	§§ 1.12, 4.13, 4.17

CASES

Case	Book §
School Comm. of Danvers v. Tyman, 372 Mass. 106, 360 N.E.2d 877 (1977)	§ 6.16
School Dist. v. Marshall, 657 F.2d 16 (3d Cir. 1981)	§ 2.20
Schrachta v. Curtis, 752 F.2d 1257 (7th Cir. 1985)	§ 2.26
Schroeder v. Dayton-Hudson Corp., 448 F. Supp. 910 (E.D. Mich. 1977)	§ 5.9
Schubbe v. Diesel Serv. Unit Co., 71 Or. App. 232, 692 P.2d 132 (1984)	§§ 5.33, 7.14
Schuhl v. United States, 3 Cl. Ct. 207 (1983)	§ 6.18
Schwartz v. Cigar Makers, 219 Mich. 589, 189 N.W. 55 (1922)	§ 3.21
Schwartz v. Driscoll, 217 Mich. 384, 186 N.W. 522 (1922)	§ 3.21
Schweiker v. McClure, 456 U.S. 188 (1982)	§ 9.2, 9.27
Scott v. Lane, 409 So. 2d 791 (Ala. 1982)	§ 1.12
Scott v. Moore, 680 F.2d 979 (5th Cir. 1982), *rev'd on other grounds,* 463 U.S. 825 (1983)	§ 2.9
Scott v. Sears, Roebuck & Co., 798 F.2d 210 (7th Cir. 1986)	§§ 2.5, 4.10
Scott v. Sears, Roebuck & Co., 605 F. Supp. 1047 (N.D. Ill. 1985)	§ 1.12
Scott v. Union Tank Car, 402 N.E.2d 922 (Ind. Ct. App. 1980)	§ 5.11
Scroggins v. Kansas Dep't of Human Resources, 802 F.2d 1289 (10th Cir. 1986)	§ 7.30
Scroghan v. Kraftco Corp., 551 S.W.2d 811 (Ky. Ct. App. 1977)	§ 1.12
Sea-Land Serv., Inc. v. O'Neal, 224 Va. 343, 297 S.E.2d 647 (1982)	§§ 1.12, 4.14, app. F
Sears, Roebuck & Co. v. San Diego County Dist. Council of Carpenters, 436 U.S. 180 (1978), *on remand,* 25 Cal. 3d 317, 599 P.2d 676, 158 Cal. Rptr. 370 (1979), *cert. denied,* 447 U.S. 935 (1980)	§ 2.28
Sedlacek v. Hach, 752 F.2d 333 (8th Cir. 1984)	§ 2.3, 2.6
Sengupta v. Morrison-Knudson Co., 804 F.2d 1072, F.2d 1072, 1076 (9th Cir. 1986)	§ 2.3
Sepanske v. Bendix Corp., 147 Mich. App. 819, 384 N.W.2d 54 (1985)	§§ 4.6, 4.28, app. F
Service Employees v. Office Center Servs., Inc., 670 F.2d 404 (3d Cir. 1982]	§ 3.22
Setser v. Novack Inv. Co., 638 F.2d 1137 (8th Cir.), *another part modified (en banc),* 657 F.2d 962 (8th Cir.), *cert. denied,* 454 U.S. 1064 (1981)	§§ 2.8, 2.17
Seymor v. Olin Corp., 666 F.2d 202 (5th Cir. 1985)	§ 3.9
Shah v. American Synthetic Rubber Corp., 655 S.W.2d 489 (Ky. 1983)	§ 1.12
Shaitelman v. Phoenix Mut. Life Ins. Co., 517 F. Supp. 21 (S.D.N.Y. 1980)	§ 5.12
Shanahan v. WITI-TV, Inc., 565 F. Supp. 219 (E.D. Wis. 1982)	§ 2.12
Shapiro v. Wells Fargo Realty Advisors, 152 Cal. App. 3d 467, 199 Cal. Rptr. 613 (1984)	§ 4.11
Sharon Steel Corp. v. V.J.R. Co., 604 F. Supp. 420 (W.D. Pa. 1985)	§§ 5.22, 5.31
Shaw v. Burchfield, 481 So. 2d 247 (Miss. 1985)	§§ 1.12, 7.18
Shaw v. Russell Trucking Line, Inc., 542 F. Supp. 776 (W.D. Pa. 1982)	§§ 5.19, 5.22
Shawgo v. Spradlen, 701 F.2d 470 (5th Cir. 1983)	§ 5.27

Case   *Book §*

Case	Book §
Sheets v. Teddy's Frosted Foods, Inc., 179 Conn. 471, 427 A.2d 385 (1980)	§§ 1.9, 1.11, 1.12, 2.26, 2.35, 5.1, 5.17, 7.14
Sheffens v. Railway Clerks, 797 F.2d 442 (7th Cir. 1986)	§ 3.24
Shelby v. Zayre Corp., 474 So. 2d 1069 (Ala. 1985)	§§ 5.24, 8.8
Sherman v. Alexander, 684 F.2d 464 (7th Cir. 1982)	§ 6.4
Sherman v. Rutland Hosp., Inc., 146 Vt. 204, 500 A.2d 230 (1985)	§§ 1.12, 7.21
Sherman v. St. Barnabas Hosp., 535 F. Supp. 564 (S.D.N.Y. 1982)	§ 5.9
Shipper v. Avon Prods., Inc., 605 F. Supp. 701 (S.D.N.Y. 1985)	§ 5.24
Shore v. Federal Express Corp., 777 F.2d 1155 (6th Cir. 1985)	§ 2.3
Shoultz v. Monfort of Colo., Inc., 754 F.2d 318 (10th Cir. 1985)	§§ 2.9, 2.26, 6.6, 6.8
Shuman v. City of Philadelphia, 470 F. Supp. 449 (E.D. Pa. 1979)	§ 5.27
Shuttleworth v. Broward County, 639 F. Supp. 654 (S.D. Fla. 1986)	§ 2.10
Sias v. City Demonstration Agency, 588 F.2d 692 (9th Cir. 1978)	§ 2.17
Sibley Memorial Hosp. v. Wilson, 488 F.2d 1338 (D.C. Cir. 1973)	§ 2.3
Sides v. Duke Hosp., 74 N.C. App. 331, 328 S.E.2d 818, *review denied,* 314 N.C. 331, 333 S.E.2d 490 (1985)	§§ 1.12, 5.10
Siles v. Travenol Laboratories, 13 Mass. App. 354, 433 N.E.2d 103, *writ denied,* 386 Mass. 1103, 440 N.E.2d 1176 (1982)	§ 4.23
Silkwood v. Kerr-McGee Corp., 464 U.S. 238 (1984)	§ 2.33
Silver v. K.C.A., Inc., 586 F.2d 138 (9th Cir. 1978)	§ 2.17
Simmons v. Southwestern Bell Tel. Co., 452 F. Supp. 392 (W.D. Okla. 1978)	§ 5.26
Simpson v. Van Ryzin, 289 Ala. 22, 265 So. 2d 569 (1972)	§ 6.5
Simpson v. Western Graphics Corp., 53 Or. App. 205, 631 P.2d 805 (1981), *aff'd,* 293 Or. 96, 643 P.2d 1276 (1982)	§§ 1.11, 4.8, 4.24, 7.25, 8.9, 9.2, 9.27
Singer v. Sheppard, 464 Pa. 387, 346 A.2d 897 (1975)	app. C
Sisco v. J.S. Alberici Constr. Co., Inc., 655 F.2d 146 (8th Cir. 1981), *cert. denied,* 455 U.S. 976 (1982)	§ 2.17
Sitek v. Forest City Enters., Inc., 587 F. Supp. 1381 (E.D. Mich. 1984)	§ 2.28
Sivell v. Conwed Corp., 605 F. Supp. 1265 (D. Conn. 1985)	§ 1.14
Slatin v. Stanford Research Inst., 590 F.2d 1292 (4th Cir. 1979)	§ 2.6
Slochower v. Board of Higher Educ., 350 U.S 551 (1956)	§ 1.10
Slohoda v. United Parcel Serv., Inc., 193 N.J. Super. 586, 475 A.2d 618 (App. Div. 1984), *appeal after remand,* 207 N.J. Super. 145, 504 A.2d 53 (1986)	§§ 5.13, 5.27, 9.24
Slover v. Brown, 140 Ill. App. 3d 618, 488 N.E.2d 1103 (1986)	§ 7.15
Smalley v. City of Eatonville, 640 F.2d 765 (5th Cir. 1981)	§ 2.17
Smith v. Atlas Off-Shore Boat Serv., Inc., 653 F.2d 1057 (5th Cir. Aug. 1981)	§§ 5.11, 5.33
Smith v. CMTA-IAM Pension Trust, 746 F.2d 587 (9th Cir. 1984)	§ 2.23
Smith v. Consolidated Mut. Water Co., 787 F.2d 1441 (10th Cir. 1986)	§§ 2.6, 7.8
Smith v. Cotton Bros. Backing Co., Inc., 609 F.2d 738 (5th Cir.), *cert. denied,* 449 U.S. 821 (1980)	§ 2.22
Smith v. Evening New Ass'n, 371 U.S. 195 (1962)	§§ 3.9, 3.23, 4.25
Smith v. Fleischman, 214 S.C. 263, 52 S.E.2d 199 (1949)	app. E
Smith v. Greyhound Lines, Inc., 614 F. Supp. 558 (W.D. Pa. 1984)	§§ 5.20, 5.30, 7.12

CASES

Case	Book §
Smith v. Hussman Refrigerator Co., 619 F.2d 1229 (8th Cir. 1980)	§ 3.25
Smith v. Kansas City Title & Trust Co., 255 U.S. 180 (1921)	§ 2.35
Smith v. Kerrville Bus Co., Inc., 709 F.2d 914 (5th Cir. 1983), *later appeals,* 748 F.2d 1049 (5th Cir. 1984), 799 F.2d 1079 (5th Cir. 1986)	§§ 2.28, 3.5, 4.25, 7.25, 7.26
Smith v. Monsanto Chem. Co., 770 F.2d 719 (8th Cir. 1985), *cert. denied,* ___ U.S. ___, 106 S. Ct. 1273 (1986)	§ 2.3
Smith v. Piezo Technology & Professional Admin., 427 So. 2d 182 (Fla. 1983)	§ 1.12
Smith v. United States, 654 F.2d 50 (Ct. Cl. 1981)	§ 6.18
Smith v. University of N.C., 632 F.2d 316 (4th Cir. 1980)	§ 7.16
Smith v. Updegraff, 744 F.2d 1354 (8th Cir. 1984)	§ 7.30
Smithberg v. Merico, Inc., 575 F. Supp. 80 (C.D. Cal. 1983)	§ 2.12
Snuffer v. Motorists Mut. Ins. Co., 636 F. Supp. 430 (S.D.W. Va. 1986)	§ 5.31
Social Sec. Admin., 80 Lab. Arb. (BNA) 725 (1983) (Lubic, Arb.)	§ 3.8
Soderbeck v. Burnett County, 752 F.2d 285 (7th Cir. 1985)	§ 6.11
Southern Bell Tel. & Tel. Co., 75 Lab. Arb. (BNA) 409 (1980) (Seibel, Arb.)	§ 3.8
Southern Bell Tel. & Tel. Co., 25 Lab. Arb. (BNA) 85 (1955) (Alexander, Arb.)	§ 3.15
South Euclid Fraternal Order of Police v. D'Amico, 13 Ohio App. 3d 46, 468 N.E.2d 735 (1983)	app. F
Southland Corp. v. Keating, 465 U.S. 1 (1984)	§ 8.9
South Penn Oil Co., 29 Lab. Arb. (BNA) 718 (1957) (Duff, Arb.)	§ 3.12
Southwest Elec. Co., 54 Lab. Arb. (BNA) 195 (1969) (Bothwell, Arb.)	§ 3.6
Southwest Gas Corp. v. Ahmad, 99 Nev. 594, 668 P.2d 261 (1983)	§§ 1.12, 4.16
Spagnola v. Mathis, ___ F.2d ___ (D.C. Cir. 1986)	§ 6.6
Spagnuolo v. Whirlpool Corp., 641 F.2d 1109 (4th Cir. 1981)	§ 7.16
Spaur v. City of Greeley, 150 Colo. 346, 372 P.2d 730 (1962)	§ 6.20
Spielmann v. Anchor Motor Freight, Inc., 551 F. Supp. 817 (S.D.N.Y. 1982)	§ 2.29
Sprott v. Avon Prods., Inc., 596 F. Supp. 178 (S.D.N.Y. 1984)	§ 4.9
Squier Distrib. Co. v. Teamsters Local 7, 801 F.2d 238 (6th Cir. 1986)	§ 2.16
Stacey v. Allied Stores Corp., 768 F.2d 402 (D.C. Cir. 1985)	§ 7.8
Staggs v. Blue Cross, 61 Md. App. 381, 486 A.2d 798 (1985)	§§ 4.8, 5.6, 5.31
Stancil v. Mergenthaler Linotype Co., 589 F. Supp. 78 (D. Haw. 1984)	§§ 1.12, 5.24, 7.20
Stanton v. State Personnel Bd., 105 Cal. App. 3d 729, 164 Cal. Rptr. 557 (1980)	§ 6.5
Stark v. Burlington, 538 F. Supp. 1061 (D. Colo. 1982)	§ 2.19
State Tenure Comm'n v. Madison County Bd. of Educ., 282 Ala. 658, 213 So. 2d 823 (1968)	§ 6.5
Staton v. Amax Coal Co., 122 Ill. App. 3d 631, 461 N.E.2d 612 (1984)	§§ 4.24, 4.28, 7.26
Stearns v. Consolidated Mgmt., Inc., 747 F.2d 1105 (7th Cir. 1984)	§ 2.6
Stearns v. Ohio Sav. Ass'n, 15 Ohio App. 3d 18, 472 N.E.2d 372 (1984)	§§ 5.25, 7.19
Steele v. Louisville & N. R.R., 323 U.S. 192 (1944)	§ 1.8

Case	*Book §*

Case	Book §
Steelworkers v. American Mfg. Co., 363 U.S. 564 (1960)	§§ 2.29, 3.21
Steelworkers v. Enterprise Wheel & Car Corp., 363 U.S. 593 (1960)	§§ 2.29, 3.21, 3.24, 4.25
Steelworkers v. Warrior & Gulf Navigation Co., 363 U.S. 574 (1960)	§§ 2.29, 3.9, 3.21, 3.23, 4.25
Steinberg v. St. Regis/Sheraton Hotel, 583 F. Supp. 421 (S.D.N.Y. 1984)	§ 2.25
Stepanischen v. Merchants Despatch Transp. Corp., 722 F.2d 922 (1st Cir. 1983)	§§ 2.26, 5.25
Stephens v. Norfolk & W. Ry., 792 F.2d 576 (6th Cir. 1986)	§ 2.31
Steranko v. Inforex, Inc., 5 Mass. App. Ct. 253, 362 N.E.2d 222 (1977), *appeal after remand,* 8 Mass, App. Ct. 523, 395 N.E.2d 1303 (1979)	app. E
Sterner v. Department of Army, 711 F.2d 1563 (Fed. Cir. 1983)	§ 6.4
Stewart v. Ethicon, Inc., 642 F. Supp. 7 (N.D. Ga. 1983)	app. F
St. Louis Theatrical Co. v. St. Louis Theatrical Bhd. Local 6, 715 F.2d 405 (8th Cir. 1983)	§ 3.18
Stockholm Pipe Fittings Co., 4 Lab. Arb. (BNA) 744 (1946) (McCoy, Arb.)	§ 3.12
Stoecklein v. Illinois Tool Works, Inc., 589 F. Supp. 139 (E.D. Ill. 1984)	§ 2.12
Stoetzel v. Continental Textile Corp., 768 F.2d 217 (8th Cir. 1985)	§ 7.18
Stone v. White, 301 U.S. 532 (1937)	§ 4.3
Straube v. Larson, 287 Or. 357, 600 P.2d 371 (1979)	§ 5.22
St. Regis Paper Co., Consumer Prods. Div., 74 Lab. Arb. (BNA) 1281 (1980) (Kaufman, Arb.)	§ 3.7
Strong v. Demopolis City Bd. of Educ., 515 F Supp. 730 (S.D. Ala. 1981)	§ 2.14
Stylemaster, Inc., 79 Lab. Arb. (BNA) 76 (1982) (Winton, Arb.)	§ 3.5
Suchodolski v. Michigan Consol. Gas. Co., 412 Mich. 692, 316 N.W.2d 710 (1982)	§ 5.17
Sugar Creek Packing, Inc. v. Food & Allied Workers, 526 F. Supp. 809 (S.D. Ohio 1981)	§ 3.18
Sullivan v. Boorstin, 484 F. Supp. 836 (D.D.C. 1980)	§ 2.4
Sutton v. Weirton Steel Div., 724 F.2d 406 (4th Cir. 1983)	§ 4.19
Sventko v. Kroger Co., 69 Mich. App. 644, 245 N.W.2d 151 (1976)	§§ 5.10, 5.11, 7.14
Swift v. United States, ___ F. Supp. ___, 42 Fair Empl. Prac. Cas. (BNA) 787 (D.D.C. 1986)	§ 6.11
Sykes v. McDowell, 786 F.2d 1098 (11th Cir. 1986)	§§ 6.11, 7.5
Takahashi v. Board of Trustees, 783 F.2d 848 (9th Cir.), *cert. denied,* ___ U.S. ___, 106 S. Ct. 2916 (1986)	§§ 2.8, 7.30
Tameny v. Atlantic Richfield Co., 27 Cal. 3d 167, 610 P.2d 1330, 164 Cal. Rptr. 839 (1980)	§§ 1.11, 1.12, 4.6, 5.10, 5.18, 7.14, 9.10
Tatterson v. Suffolk Mfg. Co., 106 Mass. 56 (1870)	§ 1.4
Taylor v. Atchison, T.&S.F. Ry., 92 F. Supp. 968 (W.D. Mo. 1950)	§ 5.33
Taylor v. Brighton Corp., 616 F.2d 256 (6th Cir. 1980)	§ 2.18

CASES

Case	Book §
Taylor v. Crane, 24 Cal. 3d 442, 595 P.2d 129, 155 Cal. Rptr. 695 (1979)	§ 6.16
Taylor v. General Motors Corp., 588 F. Supp. 562 (E.D. Mich. 1984)	§ 4.21
Taylor v. Gordon Flesch Co., 793 F.2d 858 (7th Cir. 1986)	§ 2.3
Taylor v. Missouri Pac. R.R., 794 F.2d 1082 (5th Cir. 1986)	§ 3.9
Taylor v. NLRB, 786 F.2d 1516 (11th Cir. 1986)	§§ 3.27, 9.26
Teamsters v. United States, 431 U.S. 324 (1977)	§ 2.3
Teamsters Local 174 v. Lucas Flour Co., 369 U.S. 95 (1962)	§§ 2.29, 3.21
Teamsters Local 542, 223 N.L.R.B. 533 (1976)	§ 3.25
Teays v. Supreme Concrete Block, Inc., 51 Md. App. 166, 441 A.2d 1109 (1982)	§ 5.17
Tenedios v. Wm. Filene's Sons Co., 20 Mass. App. Ct. 252, 479 N.E.2d 723 (1985)	§ 7.23
Terrell v. University of Tex. Sys. Police, 792 F.2d 1360 (5th Cir. 1986)	§ 6.11
Terrio v. Millinocket Community Hosp., 379 A.2d 135 (Me. 1977)	§§ 4.7, 7.18
Texas Dep't of Community Affairs v. Burdine, 450 U.S. 248 (1981)	§§ 2.3, 2.4, 2.12, 7.3, 7.6, 7.7
Texas & Pac. Ry. v. Abilene Cotton, 204 U.S. 426 (1907)	§ 2.27
Texas State Fed'n of Labor v. Brown & Root, 246 S.W.2d 938 (Tex. Civ. App. 1952)	§ 2.27
Textile Workers v. American Thread Co., 113 F. Supp. 137 (D. Mass. 1953)	§§ 3.22, 3.23
Textile Workers v. Darlington Mfg. Co., 380 U.S. 263 (1965)	§ 2.16
Textile Workers Union v. Lincoln Mills, 353 U.S. 448 (1957)	§§ 2.29, 3.3, 3.21–3.23, 4.5, 4.25
Thebner v. Xerox Corp., 480 So. 2d 454 (La. Ct. App.), *cert. denied*, 484 So. 2d 139 (1986)	§§ 1.12, 4.17, 4.26
Thibodeau v. Foremost Ins. Co., 605 F. Supp. 653 (N.D. Ind. 1985)	§§ 2.35, 7.29
Thomas v. Atascadero Unified School Dist., ___ F. Supp. ___, Civ. 86-6609 (C.D. Cal. 1986)	§ 5.28
Thomas v. General Elec. Co., 207 F. Supp. 792 (W.D. Ky. 1962)	§ 5.26
Thomas v. Kroger Co., 583 F. Supp. 1031 (S.D. W. Va. 1984)	§ 2.35
Thomas v. Review Bd. of Ind. Employment Sec. Div., 450 U.S. 707 (1981)	§ 5.27
Thomas v. Washington Gas Light Co., 448 U.S. 261 (1980)	§ 7.32
Thomas v. Zamberletti, 134 Ill. App. 3d 387, 480 N.E.2d 869 (1985)	§§ 5.31. 7.11
Thompkins v. Stuttgart School Dist. No. 22, 787 F.2d 439 (8th Cir. 1986)	§ 2.35
Thompson v. American Motor Inns, 623 F. Supp. 409 (W.D. Va. 1985)	§§ 1.12, 4.16, 7.20
Thompson v. St. Regis Paper Co., 102 Wash. 2d 219, 685 P.2d 1081 (1984)	§§ 1.12, 4.8, 4.10, 4.11, 4.16, 5.17, 7.10, 7.11, 7.14
Titsch v. Reliance Group, Inc., 548 F. Supp. 983 (S.D.N.Y. 1982)	§§ 5.9, 5.17
Todd v. South Carolina Farm Bureau Mut. Ins. Co., 283 S.C. 155, 321 S.E.2d 602 (1984), *cert. granted*, 285 S.C. 84, 328 S.E.2d	

Case   *Book §*

479, *verdict for plaintiff reinstated,* 287 S.C. 190, 336 S.E.2d 472 (1985) .... §§ 5.22, 5.23, 7.11
Tombollo v. Dunn, 342 N.W.2d 23 (S.D. 1984) .... § 5.9
Torres v. Wisconsin Dep't of Health & Social Servs., 592 F. Supp. 922 (E.D. Wis. 1984) .... § 6.8
Tourville v. Inter-Ocean Ins. Co., ___ Pa. Super. ___, 508 A.2d 1263 (1986) .... § 5.21
Toussaint v. Blue Cross & Blue Shield, 408 Mich. 579, 292 N.W.2d 880 (1980) .... §§ 1.4, 1.9–1.12, 4.1, 4.7, 4.8, 4.10, 4.13, 4.14, 4.16, 4.19, 4.24, 4.28, 5.24, 7.18, 7.20, 7.24–7.27, 8.9, 8.13, 9.2, 9.4, 9.27, app. F
Town House Apartments, 83 Lab. Arb. (BNA) 538 (1984) (Roumell, Arb.) .... § 3.6
Townsend v. L.W.M. Management, Inc., 64 Md. App. 55, 494 A.2d 239 (1985) .... § 7.12
Trailways Southeastern Lines, Inc. & Amalgamated Transit Union, 83-2 Arb. (CCH) ¶ 8519 (1983) (Gibson, Arb.) .... § 3.27
Tramble v. Coverters Ink Co., 343 F. Supp. 1350 (N.D. Ill. 1972) ... § 2.17
Transamerica Mortgage Advisors, Inc. v. Lewis, 444 U.S. 11 (1979) ... § 2.26
Treasury Employees v. Federal Labor Relations Auth., 800 F.2d 1165 (D.C. Cir. 1986) .... § 6.15
Tribble v. Westinghouse Elec. Corp., 669 F.2d 1193 (8th Cir. 1982), *cert. denied,* 460 U.S. 1080 (1983) .... §§ 2.7, 7.16
Trigg v. Fort Wayne Community Schools, 766 F.2d 299 (7th Cir. 1985) .... § 6.8
Trought v. Richardson, 78 N.C. App. 758, 338 S.E.2d 617 (1986), *review denied,* 316 N.C. 557, 344 S.E.2d 18 (1986) ... § 1.12
Troutman v. Facetglas, Inc., 281 S.C. 598, 316 S.E.2d 424 (1984) .... § 5.21
Troy v. Interfinancial, Inc., 171 Ga. App. 763, 320 S.E.2d 872 (1984) .... §§ 1.12, 5.22
Truex v. Garrett Freightlines, Inc., 784 F.2d 1347 (9th Cir. 1985) ... § 2.29
Truxes v. Kenco Enter., 80 S.D. 104, 119 N.W.2d 914 (1963) .... § 5.26
Tuohy v. Ford Motor Co., 675 F.2d 842 (6th Cir. 1982) .... § 7.3
Turner v. Letterkenny Fed. Credit Union, 351 Pa. Super. 51, 505 A.2d 259 (1985) .... § 7.11
Turner v. Winn Dixie La., Inc., 474 So. 2d 966 (La. Ct. App. 1985) .... app. E
Twohy v. Harris, 194 Va. 69, 72 S.E.2d 329 (1952) .... app. F

U.A.W. v. Yard-Man, Inc., 716 F.2d 1476 (6th Cir. 1983), *cert. denied,* 465 U.S. 1007 (1984) .... § 4.19
Union Camp Corp., 71 Lab. Arb. (BNA) 883 (1978) (Hardy, Arb.) ... § 3.7
Union Pac. R.R. v. Sheehan, 439 U.S. 89 (1978) .... § 4.25
United States v. Dusquesne Light Co., 423 F. Supp. 507 (W.D. Pa. 1976) .... § 2.13
United States v. Hayes Int'l Corp., 6 F.E.P. Cas. (BNA) 1328 (N.D. Ala. 1973), *aff'd,* 507 F.2d 1279 (5th Cir. 1975) ... § 7.6

CASES

Case	Book §
United States v. Hopkins, 427 U.S. 123 (1967)	§ 6.18
United States v. Kras, 409 U.S. 434 (1973)	§ 9.33
United States v. Lee, 106 U.S. 196 (1882)	§ 6.18
United States v. Mendoza, 464 U.S. 154 (1984)	§ 7.29
United States v. O'Brien, 391 U.S. 367 (1968)	§ 4.19
United States v. Stauffer Chem. Co., 464 U.S. 165 (1984)	§ 7.29
United States v. Testan, 424 U.S. 392 (1976)	§ 6.17
United States v. Utah Constr. & Mining Co., 384 U.S. 394 (1966)	§§ 7.32, 7.33
United States v. Western Pac. R.R., 352 U.S. 59 (1956)	§ 2.27
United States v. Bulk Carriers, Inc. v. Arguelles, 400 U.S. 351 (1971)	§ 3.27
United States v. Dep't of Transp. v. Paralyzed Veterans, ___ U.S. ___, 106 S. Ct. 2705 (1986)	§ 2.10
United States Postal Serv. v. Postal Workers, 736 F.2d 822 (1st Cir. 1984)	§ 6.16
United States Steel & Carnegie Pension Fund v. McSkining, 759 F.2d 269 (3d Cir. 1985)	§ 3.27
United Technologies Corp., 268 N.L.R.B. 557 (1984)	§ 3.27
Universal Camera v. NLRB, 340 U.S. 474 (1951)	§ 9.2, 9.27
University of Tenn. v. Elliott, ___ U.S. ___, 106 S. Ct. 3220 (1986)	§§ 2.8, 7.33, 9.3, 9.26, 9.27, 9.29
Upshur v. Love, 474 F. Supp. 332 (N.D. Cal. 1979)	§ 2.12
Usery v. Sun Oil Co. (Del.), 423 F. Supp. 125 (N.D. Tex. 1976), aff'd in part, rev'd in part, 605 F.2d 1331 (5th Cir. 1979)	§ 2.6
U.T.U. v. Long Island R.R., 455 U.S. 678 (1982)	§ 6.2
Vaca v. Sipes, 386 U.S. 171 (1967)	§§ 3.9, 3.19, 3.25, 3.26, 4.25, 6.15
Vail v. Board of Educ., 706 F.2d 1435 (7th Cir. 1983), aff'd by an equally divided Court, 466 U.S. 377 (1984)	§§ 6.10, 6.20
Vail v. Pennsylvania R.R., 103 N.J.L. 213, 136 A. 425 (1927)	§ 5.25
Valdes v. Lumberman's Mut. Cas. Co., 507 F. Supp. 10 (S.D. Fla. 1980)	§ 2.3
Valentine v. General Am. Credit, Inc., 420 Mich. 256, 362 N.W.2d 628 (1984)	§ 4.28, app. E
Valenzuela v. Kraft, Inc., 739 F.2d 434 (9th Cir. 1984)	§§ 2.3, 2.32
Vallone v. Agip Petroleum Co., 705 S.W.2d 757 (Tex. Ct. App. 1986)	§§ 4.11, 4.26
Vane v. Nocella, 303 Md. 362, 494 A.2d 181 (1985)	§ 2.28
Vangilder v. City of Jackson, 492 S.W.2d 15 (Mo. Ct. App. 1973)	app. F
Vantine v. Elkhart Brass Mfg. Co., 762 F.2d 511 (7th Cir. 1985)	§ 5.30
VanTran Elec. Corp. v. Thomas, 708 S.W.2d 527 (Tex. Ct. App. 1986)	§ 5.11
Vargas v. Royal Bank of Can., 604 F. Supp. 1036 (D.P.R. 1985)	§ 9.10
Varnum v. Nu-Car Carriers, ___ F.2d ___, 123 L.R.R.M. (BNA) 3068 (11th Cir. 1986)	§ 2.29
Vasquez v. Eastern Airlines, Inc., 579 F.2d 107 (1st Cir. 1978)	§ 2.6
Vaughn v. Pacific Northwest Bell Tel. Co., 289 Or. 73, 611 P.2d 281 (1980)	§ 5.9
Vegelahn v. Guntner, 167 Mass. 92, 44 N.E. 1077 (1896)	§ 9.3
Veno v. Meredith, ___ Pa. Super. ___, 515 A.2d 571 (1986)	§§ 1.15, 5.1, 7.11

Case	Book §
Verway v. Blincoe Packing Co., 108 Idaho 315, 698 P.2d 377 (1985)	§ 1.12
Veterans Admin. Medical Center v. Federal Labor Relations Auth., 675 F.2d 260 (11th Cir. 1982)	§ 6.16
Video Elecs., Inc. v. Tedder, 470 So. 2d 4 (Fla. Dist. Ct. App. 1985)	§ 7.26
Vietnam Fisherman's Ass'n v. Knights of Ku Klux Klan, 518 F. Supp. 933 (S.D. Tex. 1981)	§ 2.8
Viggiano v. Shenango Chica Div., 750 F.2d 276 (3d Cir. 1984)	§ 4.19
Vigil v. Arzola, 101 N.M. 687, 687 P.2d 1038 (1984)	§ 1.12
Vinson v. Taylor, 753 F.2d 141 (D.C. Cir. 1985), aff'd & remanded sub nom Meritor Sav. Bank v. Vinson, ___ U.S. ___, 106 S. Ct. 2399 (1986)	§ 2.5
Vinyard v. King, 728 F.2d 428 (10th Cir. 1984)	§§ 1.12, 6.10, 6.20, 7.5
Vokas Provision Co. v. NLRB, 796 F.2d 864 (6th Cir. 1986)	§ 7.7
Vosch v. Werner Continental, Inc., 734 F.2d 149 (3d Cir. 1984)	§§ 3.24, 5.18, 5.19
Waddell v. Small Tube Prods., Inc., 799 F.2d 69 (3d Cir. 1986)	§ 7.6
Wadeson v. American Family Mut. Ins. Co., 343 N.W.2d 367 (N.D. 1984)	§§ 1.12, 4.11, 4.23, 7.23, 7.28, 9.22
Wagenseller v. Scottsdale Memorial Hosp., 147 Ariz. 370, 710 P.2d 1025 (1985)	§§ 1.2, 1.4, 1.11, 1.12, 4.6, 4.8, 4.11, 4.18, 4.23, 5.13, 5.22, 7.11
Wager v. Hasenkrug, 486 F. Supp. 47 (D.C. Mont. 1980)	§ 2.9
Wakefield v. Northern Telecom, Inc., 769 F.2d 109 (2d Cir. 1985)	§ 4.11
Walden v. Teamsters Local 71, 468 F.2d 196 (4th Cir. 1972)	§ 3.25
Walker v. Modern Realty, 675 F.2d 1002 (8th Cir. 1982)	§§ 4.12, 4.15, 4.17
Walker v. Pettit Constr. Co., 605 F.2d 128 (4th Cir.), modified sub nom Frith v. Eastern Airlines, 611 F.2d 950 (4th Cir. 1979)	§ 2.6
Walker v. Westinghouse Elec. Corp., 79 N.C. App. 253, 335 S.E. 2d 79 (1985)	§§ 1.12, 7.34
Wallace v. Civil Aeronautics Bd., 755 F.2d 861 (11th Cir. 1985)	§ 3.17
Wallace Corp. v. NLRB, 323 U.S. 248 (1944)	§ 9.3
Walsh v. Consolidated Freightways, Inc., 278 Or. 347, 563 P.2d 1205 (1977)	§§ 2.18, 2.26, 5.9, 5.18
Walters v. City of Atlanta, 803 F.2d 1135 (11th Cir. 1986)	§ 7.6
Wampler v. Palmerton, 250 Or. 65, 439 P.2d 601 (1968)	§ 5.22
Wandry v. Bull's Eye Credit Union, 129 Wis. 2d 37, 384 N.W.2d 325 (1986)	§§ 1.1, 1.12, 5.19, 7.11
Ward v. Consolidated Food Corp., 480 S.W.2d 483 (Tex. Ct. App. 1972)	§ 7.25
Ware v. Woodward Iron Co., 271 Ala. 462, 124 So. 2d 84 (1960)	app. E
Warren v. A.F.G.E. Local 1759, 764 F.2d 1395 (11th Cir. 1985)	§ 6.15
Washington Welfare Ass'n, v. Poindexter, 116 L.R.R.M. 3438 (D.C. App. 1984)	§ 4.27

CASES

Case	Book §
Washington Welfare Ass'n, Inc. v. Wheeler, 496 A.2d 613 (D.C. 1985)	§§ 1.12, 4.28, 7.27
Watassek v. Michigan Dep't of Mental Health, 143 Mich. App. 556, 372 N.W.2d 617 (1985)	§§ 1.12, 6.20
Waterbury Teachers Ass'n v. City of Waterbury, 164 Conn. 426, 324 A.2d 267 (1973)	§ 6.15
Waters v. Steelworkers, 427 F.2d 476 (7th Cir.), *cert. denied,* 400 U.S. 911 (1970)	§ 2.8
Watson v. Idaho Falls Consol. Hosp., Inc., 111 Idaho 44, 720 P.2d 632 (1986)	§§ 1.12, 4.8, 4.13, 4.16, 4.18, 5.9
Wayne v. Rollins Int'l, Inc., 169 Cal, App. 3d 1, 215 Cal. Rptr. 59 (1985)	§ 7.19
Weaver v. Gross, 605 F. Supp. 210 (D.D.C. 1985)	§§ 1.12, 5.22
Webb v. Board of Educ., 471 U.S. 234 (1985)	§ 2.25
Webb v. Dayton Tire & Rubber Co., 697 P.2d 519 (Okla. 1985)	§ 5.11
Weber v. Logan Country Home for the Aged, 623 F. Supp. 711 (D.N.D. 1985)	§ 2.24
Weeks v. Southern Bell Tel. & Tel. Co., 408 F.2d 228 (5th Cir. 1969)	§ 2.3
Weiner v. McGraw-Hill, Inc., 57 N.Y.2d 458, 443 N.E.2d 441, 457 N.Y.S.2d 193 (1982)	§§ 1.4, 1.9–1.12, 4.7, 4.8, 4.12,–4.15, 4.17, 4.20, 7.18, 7.20, 7.27, 8.5, 8.12
Weiss v. Syracuse Univ., 522 F.2d 397 (2d Cir. 1975)	§ 2.13
Welch v. Brown's Nursing Home, 20 Ohio App. 3d 15, 484 N.E.2d 178 (1985)	§ 7.12
Welch v. Kennedy Piggly Wiggly Stores, Inc., 63 Bankr. 888 (W.D. Va. 1986)	§ 5.22
Wells v. Doland, 711 F.2d 670 (5th Cir. 1983)	§§ 6.11, 6.12
Wells v. Thomas, 569 F. Supp. 426 (E.D. Pa. 1983)	§ 5.22
West v. Butler, 621 F.2d 240 (6th Cir. 1980)	§ 2.23
Westbrook School Comm'n v. Westbrook Teachers Ass'n, 404 A.2d 204 (Me. 1979)	§ 6.16
Western Air Lines v. Criswell, 472 U.S. 400 (1985)	§ 2.7
Westesen v. Olathe State Bank, 78 Colo. 217, 240 P.2d 689 (1925)	app. E
West Midlands Co-Operative Soc'y v. Tipton, [1986] I.C.R. 192 (H.L.)	§ 9.11
West Va. Dep't of Corrections v. Lemasters, 313 S.E.2d 436 (W. Va. 1984)	§ 6.5
West Va. Glass Specialty Co. v. Guice & Walshe, Inc., 170 Ga. App. 556, 317 S.E.2d 592 (1984)	§ 5.22
Weyerhauser Co., 83 Lab. Arb. (BNA) 365 (1984) (Shearer, Arb.)	§ 3.6
Whalen v. Roe, 429 U.S. 589 (1977)	§§ 5.27, 6.11
Wheeler v. Caterpillar Tractor Co., 108 Ill. 2d 502, 485 N.E.2d 372 (1985), *cert. denied,* ___ U.S. ___, 106 S. Ct. 1641 (1986)	§§ 2.33, 5.9, 7.11, 7.12
Wheeling-Pittsburgh Steel Corp., 83 Lab. Arb. (BNA) 318 (1984) (Leahy, Arb.)	§ 3.6
Whirlpool Corp. v. Marshall, 445 U.S. 1 (1980)	§§ 2.18, 7.34

Case *Book §*

Whitaker v. Care-More, Inc., 621 S.W.2d 395 (Tenn. Ct. App. 1981) — app. F

White v. I.T.T., 718 F.2d 994 (11th Cir. 1983), *cert. denied*, 466 U.S. 938 (1984) — §§ 1.12, 5.24, app. F

White v. Thomas, 660 F.2d 680 (5th Cir.), *cert. denied*, 455 U.S. 1027 (1982) — § 6.9

Whitehead v. Telesphere Int'l, Inc., 611 F. Supp. 961 (N.D. Ill. 1985) — § 7.18

Whitfield v. City of Knoxville, 756 F.2d 455 (6th Cir. 1985) — §§ 2.6, 7.30

Whitfield v. Finn, 731 F.2d 1506 (11th Cir. 1984) — § 6.10

Whiting v. Jackson State Univ., 616 F.2d 116 (5th Cir. 1980) — § 7.6

Whitlock v. Haney Seed Co., 110 Idaho 347, 715 P.2d 1017 (Ct. App. 1986) — §§ 1.12, 4.12

Whittlesay v. Union Carbide Co., 742 F.2d 724 (2d Cir. 1984) — § 2.6

Wieman v. Updegraff, 344 U.S. 183 (1952) — § 1.10

Wilder v. United States, 5 Ct. Cl. 462 (1869) — § 1.4

Willets v. Emhart Mfg. Co., 52 Conn. 487, 208 A.2d 546 (1965) — app. F

Williams v. Caterpillar Tractor Co., 786 F.2d 928 (9th Cir.), *cert. granted*, ___ U.S. ___, No. 86-526 (Nov. 17, 1986) — §§ 2.29, 2.30

Williams v. Delta Haven, Inc., 416 So. 2d 637 (La. Ct. App. 1982) — § 5.25

Williams v. Treen, 671 F.2d 892 (5th Cir. 1982) — § 6.9

Wilmington v. J.I. Case Co., 793 F.2d 909 (8th Cir. 1986) — §§ 2.8, 2.25, 7.6, 7.31

Wilson v. Airline Coal Co., 215 Iowa 855, 246 N.W. 753 (1933) — § 3.21

Wilson v. City of Littleton, 732 F.2d 765 (10th Cir. 1984) — § 6.11

Wilson v. Riverside Hosp., 18 Ohio St. 3d 8, 479 N.E.2d 275 (1985) — § 5.11

Wilson v. Taylor, 733 F.2d 1539 (11th Cir. 1984) — §§ 5.27, 6.11

Wimberly v. Mission Broadcasting Co., 523 F.2d 1260 (10th Cir. 1975) — § 2.24

Windsor v. Tennessean, 726 F.2d 277 (6th Cir. 1984) — § 6.3

Wing v. JMB Management Corp., 714 P.2d 916 (Colo. App. 1985) — § 1.12

Winn v. Trans World Airlines, Inc., 75 Pa. Commw. 366, 462 A.2d 301 (1983), *aff'd*. 506 Pa. 484 A.2d 392 (1984) — § 2.12

Winston v. Lear Siegler, Inc., 558 F.2d 1266 (6th Cir. 1977) — § 2.17

Winston-Salem Printing Press v. Piedmont Publishing Co, 393 F.2d 221 (4th Cir. 1968) — § 3.3

Wirtz v. C.H. Valentine Lumber Co., 236 F. Supp. 616 (E.D.S.C. 1964) — § 2.21

Wirtz v. Ross Packaging Co., 367 F.2d 549 (5th Cir. 1966) — § 2.21

Wisconsin Dep't of Indus. v. Gould, Inc., ___ U.S. ___, 106 S. Ct. 1057 (1986) — § 2.28

Wisconsin Employee Relations Comm'n v. Teamsters Local 567, 75 Wis. 2d 602, 250 N.W.2d 696 (1977) — § 6.16

Wisconsin Tissue Mills, 63 Lab. Arb. (BNA) 917 (1974) (Hilpert, Arb.) — § 3.8

Wise v. Pressed Steel Car Co., 19 Dist. 112 (1909) — § 3.3

Wiskotoni v. Michigan Nat'l Bank W., 716 F.2d 378 (6th Cir. 1983) — §§ 5.10, 7.10–7.12, 7.14, 7.16, 7.18, 8.12

CASES

Case	Book §
Witter v. Pennsylvania Nat'l Guard, 462 F. Supp. 299 (E.D. Pa. 1978)	§ 2.24
Wolber v. Service Corp., 612 F. Supp. 235 (D. Nev. 1985)	§§ 2.32, 5.9
Wolfe v. Graether, 389 N.W.2d 643 (Iowa 1986)	§ 7.21
Wolk v. Saks Fifth Ave., Inc., 728 F.2d 221 (3d Cir. 1984)	§§ 1.14, 2.26, 2.27, 5.9
Womack v. Munson, 619 F.2d 1292 (8th Cir. 1980), *cert. denied,* 450 U.S. 979 (1981)	§ 2.17
Wood v. Strickland, 420 U.S. 308 (1975)	§ 6.19
Woolley v. Hoffman-LaRoche, Inc., 99 N.J. 284, 491 A.2d 1257, *modified,* 101 N.J. 10, 499 A.2d 515 (1985)	§§ 1.12, 1.15, 1.17, 4.1, 4.8, 4.16, 4.18, 7.20
Woolridge v. National R.R. Passenger Corp., 800 F.2d 647 (7th Cir. 1986)	§ 2.31
World Airways v. Teamsters, 578 F.2d 800 (9th Cir. 1978)	§ 3.27
Worthington Pump & Mach. Corp. v. Local 259, 63 F. Supp. 411 (D. Mass. 1945)	§ 3.21
W.R. Grace & Co. v. Rubber Workers Local 759, 461 U.S. 757 (1983)	§§ 2.3, 3.21, 3.27, 9.3, 9.26
Wright v. Methodist Youth Servs. Inc., 511 F. Supp. 307 (N.D. Ill. 1981)	§§ 2.3, 2.5, 5.28
Wrighten v. Metropolitan Hosps., Inc., 726 F.2d 1346 (9th Cir. 1984)	§ 2.17
Wright Line & Bernard R. Lamoureux, 251 N.L.R.B. 1083 (1980), *enforced,* 662 F.2d 899 (1st Cir. 1981), *cert. denied,* 455 U.S. 989 (1982)	§§ 7.3, 7.7, 7.14
Wyant v. S.C.M. Corp., 692 S.W.2d 814 (Ky. Ct. App. 1985)	§ 7.11
Wyatt v. Bronner, 500 F. Supp. 817 (M.D. Ala. 1980)	§ 6.3
Wyman v. Osteopathic Hosp. of Me., Inc., 493 A.2d 330 (Me. 1985)	§ 7.27
Wyman Gordon Co. v. Steelworkers, 613 F. Supp. 626 (N.D. Ill. 1985)	§ 3.17
Wynn v. Boeing Military Airplane Co., 595 F. Supp. 727 (D. Kan. 1984)	§§ 2.26, 5.9
Yancy v. McDevitt, 802 F.2d 1025 (8th Cir. 1986)	§ 7.30
Yandl v. Ingersoll Rand Co., 281 Pa. Super. 560, 422 A.2d 611 (1981)	§ 5.21
Yanta v. Montgomery Ward & Co., 66 Wis. 2d 53, 224 N.W.2d 389 (1974)	§ 2.12
Yellow Cab Co. v. City of Chicago, 186 F.2d 946 (7th Cir. 1951)	§ 6.20
Yoho v. Triangle P.W.C., Inc., 336 S.E.2d 204 (W. Va. 1985)	§§ 1.12, 7.12
Yonkers, City of v. Cassidy, 44 N.Y.2d 784, 377 N.E.2d 475, 406 N.Y.S.2d 32 (1978)	§ 6.15
Young v. ITT Nesbitt Div., 438 F.2d 757 (3d Cir. 1971)	§ 2.8
Young, *Ex parte,* 209 U.S. 123 (1908)	§ 6.19
Young Radiator Co. v. U.A.W., 734 F.2d 321 (7th Cir. 1984)	§ 3.24
Youngstown Osteopathic Hosp., 224 N.L.R.B. 574 (1976), *enforcement denied,* 574 F.2d 891 (6th Cir. 1978)	§ 7.7

Case	*Book §*
Yount v. Hesston Corp., 124 Ill. App. 3d 943, 464 N.E.2d 1214 (1984)	§ 2.12
Zick v. Verson Allsteel Press Co., 623 F. Supp. 927 (N.D. Ill. 1985)	§§ 4.23, 4.28, 5.33
Zipes v. T.W.A., 455 U.S. 385 (1982)	§ 2.3

TABLE OF STATUTES

Federal Named Statutes	Book §
Administrative Procedure Act	§§ 9.2, 9.27, app. C
Administrative Procedure Act § 702	§ 6.18
Age Discrimination in Employment Act of 1967 (ADEA)	§§ 1.8, 1.10, 2.2, 2.3, 2.6, 2.7, 2.9, 2.12, 2.17, 2.21, 2.25, 2.26, 2.32, 2.35, 2.38, 4.11, 5.9, 6.7, 7.8, 7.16, 7.30, 7.35, 9.6, 9.32, app. C, app. E
ADEA § 4	§ 7.8
ADEA § 7	§ 2.7
ADEA § 11(f)	§ 6.7
ADEA § 15	§ 6.7
ADEA § 623	§ 2.6
ADEA § 623(a)	§ 2.32
ADEA § 623(f)	§ 9.24
Age Discrimination in Employment Act Amendments of 1978, Pub. L. No. 95-256, 92 Stat. 189 (1978)	§ 6.7
Arbitration Act, 25 Stat. 501 (1888)	§ 3.3
Asbestos School Hazard Detection & Control Act of 1980	§ 2.24
Bankruptcy Act	§ 2.24
Civil Rights Act of Apr. 9, 1866, ch. 31, 14 Stat. 27	§ 2.8
Civil Rights Act of 1964 (CRA 1964)	§§ 1.8, 1.10, 2.17, app. C

Federal Named Statutes	Book §
CRA 1964, Title VI	§§ 2.10, 2.11
CRA 1964, Title VII	§§ 2.2–2.9, 2.12, 21.4, 21.7, 2.25, 2.26, 2.32, 2.35, 2.38, 3.27, 5.9, 5.28, 6.7, 6.8, 6.19, 7.4, 7.6–7.9, 7.13, 7.15, 7.27, 7.29–7.31, 7.33–7.35, 8.9, 9.3, 9.6, 9.19, 9.26, 9.27, 9.29, 9.32, app. E, app. F
Civil Rights Act Title IX	§ 2.10
CRA 1964, § 504	§ 7.34
CRA 1964, § 701(a)	§ 6.7
CRA 1964, § 703	§ 7.6
CRA 1964, § 703(e)	§ 9.24
CRA 1964, § 704	§§ 2.17, 7.6
CRA 1964, § 704(a)	§ 2.17
CRA 1964, § 706(g)	§ 7.6
CRA 1964, § 706(k)	§§ 2.25, 9.33
CRA 1964, § 717	§§ 2.10, 6.7
Civil Rights Attorney's Fees Awards Act of 1976	§ 2.25
Civil Service Reform Act of 1978	§§ 2.26, 6.3, 6.4, 6.6, 6.18
Clean Air Act	§ 2.20, app. C
Clean Water Act	§§ 2.20, app. C
Consumer Credit Protection Act	§§ 2.26, app. C
Consumer Credit Protection Act, § 304	§ 2.22
Davis-Bacon Act	§ 2.28

Federal Named Statutes	Book §	Federal Named Statutes	Book §
Education Amendments of 1972, Title IX, Pub. L. No. 92-318, 86 Stat. 373	§ 2.14	Human Relations Act	§ 2.12
		Jones Act	§§ 2.24, 5.11
Employee Retirement Income Security Act (ERISA)	§§ 2.34, 3.27, 4.19, 5.9, 7.11, 7.31, 8.9, 9.24, app. C	Ku Klux Klan Act of 1871, Act of Feb. 1871, ch. 99, 16 Stat. 433	§ 2.9
		Labor Management Relations Act of 1947, Pub. L. No. 80-101, 61 Stat. 136 (1947) (LMRA)	§§ 3.19, 3.21, 3.23, 4.5, 4.25, 7.3, 7.6
ERISA § 502	§ 4.19		
ERISA § 510	§ 2.23		
Energy Reorganization Act of 1974	§§ 2.24, 2.33, 2.38, app. C	LMRA § 203(d)	§ 3.3
		LMRA § 301	§§ 2.28–2.30, 3.1, 3.3, 3.9, 3.21–3.24, 4.5, 4.19, 4.25, 5.9, 5.30
Equal Employment Opportunity Act of 1972, Pub. L. No. 92-261, 86 Stat. 111 (1972)	§ 6.7	LMRA § 301(a)	§ 4.25
Equal Pay Act	§ 7.9	Labor Management Reporting and Disclosure Act, Pub. L. No. 86-257, 73 Stat. 519 (1959)	§ 1.10
Erdman Act, 30 Stat. 424 (1898)	§ 3.3		
Fair Employment Act	§ 2.12		
Fair Labor Standards Act (FLSA)	§§ 2.6, 2.21, 2.26, 3.27, 4.11, 5.9, 5.11, 7.31, 7.34, 8.9, app. C	Landrum-Griffin Amendments, Pub. L. No. 84-257, 73 Stat. 525 (1959)	§ 2.16
		Lloyd-LaFollette Act, 37 Stat. 539 (1912)	§ 1.6
Federal Aviation Act	§§ 2.18, 3.27	Longshoremen's & Harbor Workers' Compensation Act	§§ 2.24, 2.34
Federal Employers' Liability Act (FELA)	§§ 2.19, 2.31, app. C	Mine Safety & Health Act	§§ 2.18, 9.26
FELA § 5	§ 2.19	National Labor Relations Act, ch. 372, 49 Stat. 449 (9135) (NLRA)	§§ 1.4, 1.7, 1.10, 2.16, 2.25, 2.28, 2.31, 2.34, 3.3, 3.9, 3.19, 3.21, 3.25, 3.27, 4.5, 5.9, 5.30, 6.2, 7.3, 7.6, 7.7, 7.15, 7.34, 8.14, 9.3, 9.6, 9.26, 9.32, 9.33, app. E
FELA § 10	§ 2.19		
Federal Meat Inspection Act	§ 2.26		
Federal Motor Carrier Safety Act	§ 7.34		
Federal Railroad Safety Act	app. C		
Federal Railroad Safety Act § 212	§ 2.19		
Federal Tort Claims Act	§ 6.18		
Federal Unemployment Tax Act	§ 2.36		
Foreign Corrupt Practices Act of 1977, Pub. L. No. 95-213, 91 Stat. 1494 (1977)	§§ 5.17, 7.11	NLRA § 2(11)	§ 7.7

STATUTES

Federal Named Statutes	Book §	Federal Named Statutes	Book §
NLRA § 7	§§ 2.16, 2.28, 2.29, 7.7	1211 (1940) Reconstruction Era Civil Rights Acts	§§ 1.8, 9.3 §§ 2.2, 2.8, 2.9, 6.8, app. C
NLRA § 8(a)	§§ 2.16, 7.6, 7.7	Reconstruction Civil Rights Act § 1983	§ 9.32
NLRA § 8(a)(1)	§§ 2.16, 2.28, 7.7	Rehabilitation Act of 1973, Pub. L. No. 93-112, 87 Stat. 355	§§ 1.8, 2.2, 2.10, 2.11, app. C
NLRA § 8(a)(3)	§§ 2.16, 2.28, 7.6, 7.7		
NLRA § 8(a)(4)	§§ 2.16, 2.28, 7.7		
NLRA § 8(a)(5)	§§ 3.28, 4.19	Rehabilitation Act § 503	§§ 2.10, 5.28
NLRA § 8(b)(4)	§ 7.34	Rehabilitation Act § 504	§ 2.10
NLRA § 9(a)	§ 3.9	Rehabilitation Act § 505	§ 2.10
NLRA § 10	§ 2.16	Resource Conservation & Recovery Act	§ 2.20, app. C
NLRA § 10(e)	§ 7.7		
NLRA § 203(d)	§ 3.3		
Newlands Act, 38 Stat. 103 (1913)	§ 3.3	Seaman's Wage Act	§ 3.27
Norris-LaGuardia Act, 47 Stat. 70 (1932)	§§ 1.7, 9.3	Sherman Antitrust Act	§ 5.19
Occupational Safety & Health Act of 1979 (OSHA)	§§ 2.16, 2.18, 2.33, 2.35, 3.27, 5.9, 5.18, 7.11, 7.34, 7.35	Social Security Act §§ 301–303	§ 2.36
		Social Security Act §§ 901–908	§ 2.36
		Surface Transportation Assistance Act	§ 2.24
		Taft-Hartley Act	§§ 3.21, 3.22
OSHA § 11(c)	§ 2.18	Taft-Hartley Amendments, ch. 120, 61 Stat. 136 (1947)	§ 2.16
Omnibus Crime Control Act, Title III, Pub. L. No. 90-351, 82 Stat. 197 (1968)	§ 5.26	Toxic Substances Control Act	§ 2.20, app. C
Pendleton Act, 22 Stat. 403 (1883)	§ 1.6	Transportation Act, ch. 91, 41 Stat. 456 (1920)	§ 3.3
Portal-to-Portal Act of 1947	§ 2.6	Tucker Act, 24 Stat. 505 (1877), 96 Stat. 669 (1982)	§ 6.18
Railway Labor Act (RLA)	§§ 1.8, 2.16, 2.19, 2.26, 2.31, 2.34, 3.3, 3.19, 3.20, 3.22–3.25, 3.27, 4.25, 5.19, 8.9, 9.3, 9.33	Unemployment Relief Act of 1933, 48 Stat. 22 (1933)	§§ 1.8, 9.3
		United States Arbitration Act, 43 Stat. 883	§§ 3.22, 3.23, 8.9
		United States Arbitration Act § 1	§ 3.22
RLA § 2	§ 2.26	Universal Military Training & Service Act	§ 3.27
RL § 3	§§ 3.19, 3.24, 9.33	Veterans Reemployment Act	§ 2.24
RLA § 3, first (q)	§ 3.24		
RLA § 204	§ 3.19	Wagner Act, ch. 372, 49 Stat. 449 (1935)	§ 2.16
Ramspeck Act, 54 Stat.			

Federal Named Statutes	Book §
Act of July 31, 1861, ch. 33, 12 Stat. 284	§ 2.9
Act of Apr. 20, 1871, ch. 22, § 2, 17 Stat. 13	§ 2.9
Act of 1898, 30 Stat. 424	§ 1.7
Act of Mar. 31, 1933, 48 Stat. 22	§ 1.8
Pub. L. No. 88-352, 78 Stat. 253 (1964)	app. C
Pub. L. No. 91-596, § 11, Dec. 29, 1970, 84 Stat. 1602	§ 2.18
Pub. L. No. 97-463, 96 Stat. 2531 (1983)	§ 2.24
Pub. L. No. 98-532, 98 Stat. 2705 (1984)	§ 2.6

United States Code	Book §
5 U.S.C. § 551 *et seq.*	app. C
5 U.S.C. § 553 note (1982)	§ 9.29
5 U.S.C. § 554 (1982)	§§ 9.2, 9.27
5 U.S.C. § 556 (1982)	§§ 9.2, 9.27
5 U.S.C. § 557 (1982)	§§ 9.2, 9.27
5 U.S.C. § 601 note (1982)	§ 9.29
5 U.S.C. § 702 (1982)	§ 6.18
5 U.S.C. § 2102(1) (1982)	§ 6.3
5 U.S.C. § 2301(b)(9)	§ 6.4
5 U.S.C. § 7501 (1982)	§ 6.4
5 U.S.C. § 7503 (1982)	§ 6.4
5 U.S.C. § 7513 (1982)	§ 6.4
5 U.S.C. § 7513(a) (1982)	§ 6.4
5 U.S.C. § 7701(g)(1) (1982)	§ 6.4
5 U.S.C. § 7702	§ 6.7
5 U.S.C. § 7703 (1982)	§ 6.18
9 U.S.C. §§ 1–14 (1982)	§ 3.22
9 U.S.C. §§ 1–4 (1982)	§ 8.9
9 U.S.C. § 1	§ 3.22
11 U.S.C. § 525 (1982)	§ 2.24
12 U.S.C. § 24 Fifth (1976)	§ 4.27
15 U.S.C. § 78m (1982)	§ 7.11
15 U.S.C. § 78dd-1	§ 7.11

United States Code	Book §
15 U.S.C. § 78dd-2 (1982)	§ 7.11
15 U.S.C. § 78ff (1982)	§ 7.11
15 U.S.C. § 1674	§ 2.22, app. C
15 U.S.C. § 1674(a) (1982)	§ 2.26
15 U.S.C. § 2622 (1982)	§ 2.20, app. C
18 U.S.C. § 2511 (1982)	§ 5.26
18 U.S.C. § 2520 (1982)	§ 5.26
19 U.S.C. § 401 (1982)	§ 1.10
20 U.S.C. § 1681 (1982)	§ 2.14
20 U.S.C. § 3608 (1982)	§ 2.24
21 U.S.C. § 601 (1982)	§ 2.26
26 U.S.C. § 3304(a)(10) (1982)	§ 2.36
28 U.S.C. § 1331 (1982)	§ 6.9
28 U.S.C. § 1346 (1982)	§ 6.18
28 U.S.C. § 1346(b) (1982)	§ 6.18
28 U.S.C. § 1445(c)	§ 2.35
28 U.S.C. § 1491 (1982 & Supp. 1984)	§ 6.18
28 U.S.C. § 1738 (1982)	§ 7.30
28 U.S.C. § 1875 (1982)	§ 2.24
29 U.S.C. §§ 101–115 (1982)	§ 1.7
29 U.S.C. §§ 141–197 (1982)	§ 3.21
29 U.S.C. §§ 141–187 (1982)	§ 4.5
29 U.S.C. §§ 151–169 (1982)	§§ 4.5, 7.3, 7.6
29 U.S.C. §§ 151–168 (1982)	§§ 2.16, 2.31
29 U.S.C. § 152(2) (1982)	§ 2.16
29 U.S.C. § 152(3) (1982)	§ 2.16
29 U.S.C. § 152(6) (1982)	§ 2.16
29 U.S.C. § 152(7) (1982)	§ 2.16
29 U.S.C. § 153 (1982)	§ 2.16
29 U.S.C. § 157 (1982)	§§ 1.7, 7.7
29 U.S.C. § 158 (1982)	§ 5.9
29 U.S.C. § 158(a)(1) (1982)	§§ 2.16, 7.7

STATUTES

United States Code	Book §
29 U.S.C. § 158(a)(3) (1982)	§§ 1.7, 2.16, 7.7
29 U.S.C. § 158(a)(4) (1982)	§§ 2.16, 7.7
29 U.S.C. § 159(a)	§ 3.9
29 U.S.C. § 160 (1982)	§ 2.16
29 U.S.C. § 160(b) (1982)	§ 2.38
29 U.S.C. § 160(c)	§ 9.32
29 U.S.C. § 160(e) (1982)	§ 7.7
29 U.S.C. § 173(d)	§ 3.3
29 U.S.C. § 185 (1982)	§§ 2.29, 2.30, 3.21, 3.24, 4.5, 5.30
29 U.S.C. §§ 201–217 (1982)	§ 2.6
29 U.S.C. § 215(a)(3) (1982)	§§ 2.21, 7.9, 7.34, app. C
29 U.S.C. § 216(b) (1982)	§§ 2.6, 2.21
29 U.S.C. § 255(a) (1982)	§ 2.6
29 U.S.C. §§ 621–634 (1982)	§§ 1.8, 1.10, 2.2, 2.6, app. C
29 U.S.C. §§ 621–633a (1982)	§ 6.7
29 U.S.C. § 621 (1982)	§ 9.6
29 U.S.C. § 623 (1982)	§ 2.32
29 U.S.C. § 623(a) (1982)	§§ 2.32, 7.8
29 U.S.C. § 623(d) (1982)	§ 2.17
29 U.S.C. § 623(f) (1982)	§ 2.6
29 U.S.C. § 623(f) (1984)	§ 9.24
29 U.S.C. § 623(f)(1) (1982)	§ 2.6
29 U.S.C. § 623(f)(2) (1982)	§ 2.6
29 U.S.C. § 623(f)(3) (1982)	§ 7.8
29 U.S.C. § 625	§ 2.6
29 U.S.C. § 626(b) (1982)	§ 2.6
29 U.S.C. § 626(c) (1982)	§ 2.6
29 U.S.C. § 626(c)(2) (1982)	§ 2.6
29 U.S.C. § 626(d) (1982)	§§ 2.6, 2.38
29 U.S.C. § 626(d)(1) (1982)	§ 2.6
29 U.S.C. § 626(d)(2) (1982)	§ 2.6
29 U.S.C. § 626(e) (1982)	§ 2.6
29 U.S.C. § 630(b) (1982)	§ 2.6
29 U.S.C. § 631 (1982)	§ 2.6
29 U.S.C. § 633a (1982)	§ 6.7
29 U.S.C. § 633a(a) (1982 Supp.)	§ 6.7
29 U.S.C. § 657(b)	§ 2.18
29 U.S.C. § 657(f)	§ 2.18
29 U.S.C. § 660(c)(1) (1982)	§ 2.18
29 U.S.C. § 660(c)(2)	§ 2.18
29 U.S.C. § 662(d)	§ 2.18
29 U.S.C. §§ 701–709 (1982)	§§ 2.2, 2.10
29 U.S.C. § 707(a) (1982)	§ 2.10
29 U.S.C. §§ 720–724 (1982)	§§ 2.2, 2.10
29 U.S.C. §§ 730–732 (1982)	§§ 2.2, 2.10
29 U.S.C. § 740 (1982)	§§ 2.2, 2.10
29 U.S.C. § 741 (1982)	§§ 2.2, 2.10
29 U.S.C. § 750 (1982)	§§ 2.2, 2.10
29 U.S.C. §§ 760–764 (1982)	§§ 2.2, 2.10
29 U.S.C. §§ 770–776 (1982)	§§ 2.2, 2.10
29 U.S.C. §§ 780–787 (1982)	§§ 2.2, 2.10
29 U.S.C. §§ 790–794 (1982)	§§ 2.2, 2.10
29 U.S.C. § 794 (1982)	§ 2.10
29 U.S.C. § 794a	§ 2.10
29 U.S.C. §§ 1001–1461 (1982)	§ 4.19
29 U.S.C. § 1003 (1982)	§ 4.19
29 U.S.C. § 1201 (1982)	§ 4.19
29 U.S.C. § 1021(a) (1982)	§ 9.24
29 U.S.C. § 1051 (1982)	§ 4.19
29 U.S.C. § 1081 (1982)	§ 4.19
29 U.S.C. § 1101 (1982)	§ 4.19
29 U.S.C. § 1131 (1982)	§ 4.19

United States Code	Book §	United States Code	Book §
29 U.S.C. § 1132(g) (1982)	§ 2.23	42 U.S.C. § 1985(1) (1982)	§§ 2.9, 6.8
29 U.S.C. § 1140 (1982)	§§ 2.23, 2.34, 5.9, app. C	42 U.S.C. § 1985(2) (1982)	§ 2.9
29 U.S.C. § 1144(a) (1982)	§ 5.9	42 U.S.C. § 1985(3) (1982)	§§ 2.2, 2.9, 5.12
30 U.S.C. § 815(c) (1982)	§ 2.18	42 U.S.C. § 1985(c)	§ 2.9
		42 U.S.C. § 1988 (1982)	§§ 2.25, 9.33
30 U.S.C. § 820(b)(1) (1982)	§ 2.18	42 U.S.C. § 2000c app. (1981)	§ 2.13
33 U.S.C. § 902(3) (1982)	§ 2.24	42 U.S.C. § 2000d (1982)	§ 2.10
33 U.S.C. § 902(4) (1982)	§ 2.24	42 U.S.C. §§ 2000d-1 to 2000d-6 (1982)	§ 2.11
33 U.S.C. § 948a (1982)	§ 2.24	42 U.S.C. §§ 2000e to 2000e-17 (1982)	§§ 2.2, 5.28, 6.7
33 U.S.C. § 1367 (1982)	§ 2.20, app. C		
38 U.S.C. § 2021(b)(1)	§ 2.24	42 U.S.C. §§ 2000e-1 to 2000e-17 (1982)	§ 7.6
38 U.S.C. § 2022 (1982)	§ 2.24	42 U.S.C. § 2000e (1982)	§§ 1.8, 1.10, 9.6, app. C
38 U.S.C. § 2023 (1982)	§ 2.24		
38 U.S.C. § 2024 (1982)	§ 2.24	42 U.S.C. § 2000e(b) (1982)	§ 2.3
42 U.S.C. §§ 501–504	§ 2.36		
42 U.S.C. § 503(a)(3) (1982)	§ 2.37	42 U.S.C. § 2000e(c) (1982)	§ 2.3
42 U.S.C. §§ 1101–1108 (1982)	§ 2.36	42 U.S.C. § 2000e(e) (1982)	§ 2.3
42 U.S.C. § 1331	§ 2.13	42 U.S.C. § 2000e-2(a) (1982)	§ 2.3
42 U.S.C. § 1981 (1982)	§§ 2.2, 2.8, 2.17, 2.26, 2.32, 2.35, 3.27, 5.9, 6.8, 7.9, 7.30, 7.31, 7.33, 7.35, 9.3, 9.26, app. C, app. E	42 U.S.C. § 2000e-2(a)(1) (1982)	§§ 2.3, 7.6
		42 U.S.C. § 2000e-2(a)(2) (1982)	§ 7.6
		42 U.S.C. § 2000e-2(b) (1982)	§ 2.3
		42 U.S.C. § 2000e-2(c) (1982)	§ 2.3
		42 U.S.C. § 2000e-2(e) (1984)	§ 9.24
42 U.S.C. § 1982	§ 2.8		
42 U.S.C. § 1983 (1982)	§§ 2.2, 2.8, 2.25, 2.32, 3.27, 6.2, 6.6, 6.8–6.10, 6.13, 6.15, 6.19, 6.20, 7.30, 7.32, 7.33, 7.35, 9.26, 9.32, app. E	42 U.S.C. § 2000e-2(e)(2) (1982)	§ 2.3
		42 U.S.C. § 2000e-2(h) (1982)	§ 2.3
		42 U.S.C. § 2000e-3 (1982)	§ 7.6
		42 U.S.C. § 2000e-3(a) (1982)	§ 2.17
		42 U.S.C. § 2000e-4	app. C
		42 U.S.C. § 2000e-5	§ 2.9
42 U.S.C. § 1985 (1982)	§§ 2.9, 2.25, 2.32, 6.6, 6.8, 7.30	42 U.S.C. § 2000e-5(b) (1982)	§§ 2.3, 2.6
		42 U.S.C. § 2000e-5(c)	

United States Code	Book §	United States Code	Book §
(1982)	§ 2.3	42 U.S.C. § 7622(a) (1982)	§ 2.20, app. C
42 U.S.C. § 2000e-5(e) (1982)	§§ 2.3, 2.38		
42 U.S.C. § 2000e-5(f) (1982)	§§ 2.6, 2.38	42 U.S.C. § 7622(b)(1) (1982)	§ 2.20
42 U.S.C. § 2000e-5(f)(1) (1982)	§ 2.3	42 U.S.C. § 7622(e) (1982)	§ 2.20
42 U.S.C. § 2000e-5(f)(3) (1982)	§ 2.35	45 U.S.C. § 55 (1982)	§ 2.19, app. C
42 U.S.C. § 2000e-5(f)(4) (1982)	§§ 2.3, 2.35	45 U.S.C. § 60 (1982)	§ 2.19, app. C
42 U.S.C. § 2000e-5(g) (1982)	§§ 2.3, 7.6, 9.32	45 U.S.C. § 151 *et seq.* (1982)	§ 3.19
42 U.S.C. § 2000e-5(k) (1982)	§ 2.25	45 U.S.C. §§ 151–164 (1982)	§ 2.31
42 U.S.C. § 2000e-6 (1982)	§ 2.3	45 U.S.C. § 152 (1982)	§ 2.26
42 U.S.C. § 2000e-6(b)	§ 2.3	45 U.S.C. § 153 (1982)	§§ 2.19, 2.31, 3.19, 3.24, 9.33
42 U.S.C. § 2000e-7 (1982)	§ 2.32	45 U.S.C. § 153(q) (1982)	§ 3.24
42 U.S.C. § 2000e-16 (1982)	§ 2.10	45 U.S.C. §§ 181–188 (1982)	§ 2.31
42 U.S.C. § 5851 (1983)	§ 2.24, app. C	45 U.S.C. § 184 (1982)	§ 3.19
42 U.S.C. § 5851(b) (1982)	§ 2.24	45 U.S.C. § 441	app. C
42 U.S.C. § 5851(d) (1982)	§ 2.24	45 U.S.C. § 441(a) (1982)	§ 2.19
42 U.S.C. § 5851(e) (1982)	§ 2.24	45 U.S.C. § 441(b) (1982)	§ 2.19
42 U.S.C. § 6971 (1982)	§ 2.20, app. C	45 U.S.C. § 441(c) (1982)	§ 2.19
42 U.S.C. § 7604 (1982)	§ 2.20	45 U.S.C. § 441(d) (1982)	§ 2.19
42 U.S.C. § 7622 (1982)	§ 2.20	49 U.S.C. § 2305 (1982)	§ 2.24

State Statutes Book §

Note: To ensure complete research, the reader is advised to consult **Appendix A** for a listing of state statutes relating to employment.

Ala. Code § 11-43-182 (Supp. 1986)	§ 6.5
Ala. Code §§ 16-24-2 to 16-24-10 (1977)	§ 6.5
Ala. Code § 21-5-1 (1984)	§ 2.12
Ala. Code § 36-26-10 (1977)	§ 6.3
Ala. Code § 36-26-27 (1975)	§ 6.5
Ala. Code § 36-26-27(a) (1977)	§ 6.5
Alaska Stat. §§ 09.43.010 to 09.43.180 (1985)	§ 3.22
Ariz. Rev. Stat. Ann. §§ 12-1501 to 12-1518 (1982)	§ 3.22

State Statutes *Book §*

Ark. Stat. Ann. §§ 34-511 to 34-532 (Supp. 1985)   § 3.22

Cal. Civ. Proc. Code § 337 (West 1982)   § 2.38
Cal. Civ. Proc. Code § 338 (West 1982)   § 2.38
Cal. Civ. Proc. Code § 339 (West 1982)   § 2.38
Cal. Civ. Proc. Code § 340 (West 1982)   § 2.38
Cal. Civ. Proc. Code §§ 1281–1288 (West 1982)   § 3.22
Cal. Educ. Code § 44882 (West 1980)   § 6.5
Cal. Educ. Code § 44932 (West 1980)   § 6.5
California Fair Employment Practices Act   § 2.12
Cal. Gov't Code § 12903 (West Supp. 1986)   § 2.12
Cal. Gov't Code § 12904 (West Supp. 1986)   § 2.12
Cal. Gov't Code § 12905 (West Supp. 1986)   § 2.12
Cal. Gov't Code § 12920 (West 1980)   § 2.12
Cal. Gov't Code § 12926(c) (West Supp. 1986)   § 2.12
Cal. Gov't Code § 12926(h) (West Supp. 1986)   § 2.12
Cal. Gov't Code § 12930(c) (West Supp. 1986)   § 2.12
Cal. Gov't Code § 12940 (West Supp. 1986)   § 2.12
Cal. Gov't Code § 12940(a) (West Supp. 1986)   § 2.12
Cal. Gov't Code § 12940(a)(1) (West Supp. 1986)   § 2.12
Cal. Gov't Code § 12940(b) (West Supp. 1986)   § 2.12
Cal. Gov't Code § 12940(c) (West Supp. 1986)   § 2.12
Cal. Gov't Code § 12940(d) (West Supp. 1986)   § 2.12
Cal. Gov't Code § 12940(e) (West Supp. 1986)   § 2.12
Cal. Gov't Code § 12940(f) (West Supp. 1986)   § 2.12
Cal. Gov't Code § 12940(i) (West Supp. 1986)   § 2.12
Cal. Gov't Code § 12940(j) (West Supp. 1986)   § 2.12
Cal. Gov't Code § 12960 (West 1980)   § 2.12
Cal. Gov't Code § 12960 (West Supp. 1986)   § 2.12
Cal. Gov't Code § 12963 (West Supp. 1986)   § 2.12
Cal. Gov't Code § 12963.1 (West 1980 & West Supp. 1986)   § 2.12
Cal. Gov't Code § 12963.2 (West 1980 & West Supp. 1986)   § 2.12
Cal. Gov't Code § 12963.3 (West 1980 & West Supp. 1986)   § 2.12
Cal. Gov't Code § 12963.4 (West 1980 & West Supp. 1986)   § 2.12
Cal. Gov't Code § 12963.7(a) (West 1980)   § 2.12
Cal. Gov't Code § 12965 (West Supp. 1986)   § 2.12
Cal. Gov't Code § 12965(b) (West Supp. 1986)   § 2.12
Cal. Gov't Code § 12967 (West 1980)   § 2.12
Cal. Gov't Code § 12970 (West Supp. 1986)   § 2.12
Cal. Gov't Code § 12970(a) (West Supp. 1986)   § 2.12
Cal. Gov't Code § 12970(e) (West Supp. 1986)   § 2.12
Cal. Gov't Code § 12994 (West Supp. 1986)   § 2.12
Cal. Gov't Code § 18528 (West 1980)   § 6.5
Cal. Gov't Code § 19500 (West 1980)   § 6.5
Cal. Gov't Code § 19572 (West 1980)   § 6.5
Cal. Gov't Code § 19574 (West 1980)   § 6.5
Cal. Gov't Code § 19575 (West 1980)   § 6.5
Cal. Gov't Code § 19578 (West 1980)   § 6.5
Cal. Gov't Code §§ 31103–31116   § 6.5
Cal. Gov't Code § 31108 (West 1980)   § 6.5
Cal. Gov't Code §§ 45001–45010 (West 1980)   § 6.5

STATUTES

State Statutes	*Book §*
Cal. Lab. Code § 98.7 (West Supp. 1986)	§ 9.7
Cal. Lab. Code § 98.7(f) (West Supp. 1986)	§ 9.7
Cal. Lab. Code § 1102 (West 1971 & Supp 1986)	§ 2.1
Cal. Lab. Code § 1102.5 (West 1971 & Supp. 1986)	§ 9.7
Cal. Lab. Code § 1102.5(b) (West Supp. 1986)	§ 9.7
Cal. Unemp. Ins. Code §§ 1326–1332 (West 1972 & Supp. 1983)	§ 2.37
Cal. Unemp. Ins. Code § 1326 (West 1972)	§ 2.37
Cal. Unemp. Ins. Code § 1328 (West 1972)	§ 2.37
Cal. Unemp. Ins. Code § 1334 (West 1982)	§ 2.37
Cal. Unemp. Ins. Code § 1334 (West 1972)	§ 7.35
Cal. Unemp. Ins. Code § 1336 (West 1972)	§ 7.35
Cal. Unemp. Ins. Code § 1952 (West 1972)	§ 7.35
Cal. Unemp. Ins. Code § 1953 (West 1972)	§ 2.37
Cal. A.B. 3950 (Jan. 1, 1987)	§ 7.35
Colo. Rev. Stat. §§ 13-22-201 to 13-22-223 (Supp. 1985)	§ 3.22
1915 Colo. Sess. Laws ch. 180	§ 3.3
Conn. Uniform Food Drug & Cosmetic Act, Conn. Gen. Stat. § 19-222	§§ 5.1, 5.17, 7.14
Conn. Gen. Stat. § 21a-93 (1985)	§ 5.17
Conn. Gen. Stat. § 21a-102 (1985)	§ 5.1
Conn. Gen. Stat. Ann. § 31.51m (West Supp. 1986)	§§ 9.7, 9.10
Conn. Gen. Stat. Ann. § 31.51m(b) West Supp. 1986)	§ 9.7
Conn. Gen. Stat. Ann. § 31.51m(c) West Supp. 1986)	§ 9.7
Del. Code Ann. titl. 10, §§ 5701–5725 (1975)	§ 3.22
D.C. Code Ann. § 1-2512 (1981)	§ 5.28
D.C. Code Ann. §§ 16-4301 to 16-4319 (1981)	§ 3.22
D.C. Code Ann. § 22-3502 (1981)	§ 5.28
Fla. Stat. Ann. § 110.061(2)(b) (West 1977)	§ 6.5
Fla. Stat. Ann. § 110.227(4) (West 1982)	§ 6.5
Idaho Code §§ 7-901 to 7-922 (1979)	§ 3.22
Ill. Ann. Stat. ch. 10, §§ 101–123 (Smith-Hurd 1975)	§ 3.22
Ill. Rev. Stat. 1979, ch. 38, para 1-1 *et seq.*	§ 5.16
Ill. Ann. Stat. ch. 48, paras. 450–520 (Smith-Hurd Supp. 1983)	§ 2.37
Ill. Ann. Stat. ch. 48, para. 450 (Smith-Hurd 1966)	§ 2.37
Ill. Ann. Stat. ch. 48, paras. 451–452 (Smith-Hurd Supp. 1983)	§ 2.37
Ill. Ann. Stat. ch. 48, paras. 451–452 (Smith-Hurd 1966)	§ 2.37
Ill. Ann. Stat. ch. 48, para. 453 (Smith-Hurd Supp. 1983)	§ 7.35
Ill. Ann. Stat. ch. 48, para. 471 (Smith-Hurd Supp. 1983)	§ 2.37
Ill. Ann. Stat. ch. 48, para. 474 (Smith-Hurd 1966)	§ 7.35
Ill. Ann. Stat. ch. 48, para. 500 (Smith-Hurd 1966)	§ 2.37
Ill. Ann. Stat. ch. 48, para. 503 (Smith-Hurd 1966)	§ 2.37
Ill. Ann. Stat. ch. 48, para. 520 (Smith-Hurd Supp. 1983)	§ 7.35
Ill. Ann. Stat. ch. 48, para. 2009 (Smith-Hurd Supp. 1986)	§ 5.13
Ill. Ann. Stat. ch. 68, para. 1-103(I)(1) (Smith-Hurd Supp. 1985)	§ 2.12

State Statutes | *Book §*

Statute	Book §
Ill. Ann. Stat. ch. 68, para. 2-101(B)(2) (Smith-Hurd Supp. 1985)	§ 2.12
Ill. Ann. Stat. ch. 68, para. 2-101(B)(b) (Smith-Hurd Supp. 1985)	§ 2.12
Ill. Ann. Stat. ch. 68, para. 2-101(B)(c) (Smith-Hurd Supp. 1985)	§ 2.12
Ill. Ann. Stat. ch. 68, para. 2-101(C) (Smith-Hurd Supp. 1985)	§ 2.12
Ill. Ann. Stat. ch. 68, para. 2-101(D) (Smith-Hurd Supp. 1985)	§ 2.12
Ill. Ann. Stat. ch. 68, para. 2-102(A) (Smith-Hurd Supp. 1985)	§ 2.12
Ill. Ann. Stat. ch. 68, para. 2-102(B) (Smith-Hurd Supp. 1985)	§ 2.12
Ill. Ann. Stat. ch. 68, para. 2-102(C) (Smith-Hurd Supp. 1985)	§ 2.12
Ill. Ann. Stat. ch. 68, para. 2-104(A) (Smith-Hurd Supp. 1985)	§ 2.12
Ill. Ann. Stat. ch. 68, para. 6-101(A) (Smith-Hurd Supp. 1985)	§ 2.12
Ill. Ann. Stat. ch. 68, para. 7-101(A) (Smith-Hurd Supp. 1985)	§ 2.12
Ill. Ann. Stat. ch. 68, para. 7-102(A)(1) (Smith-Hurd Supp. 1985)	§ 2.12
Ill. Ann. Stat. ch. 68, para. 7-102(C)(2) (Smith-Hurd Supp. 1985)	§ 2.12
Ill. Ann. Stat. ch. 68, para. 7-102(C)(3) (Smith-Hurd Supp. 1985)	§ 2.12
Ill. Ann. Stat. ch. 68, para. 7-102(D)(2)(a) (Smith-Hurd Supp. 1985)	§ 2.12
Ill. Ann. Stat. ch. 68, para. 7-102(D)(2)(b) (Smith-Hurd Supp. 1985)	§ 2.12
Ill. Ann. Stat. ch. 68, para. 7-102(F) (Smith-Hurd Supp. 1985)	§ 2.12
Ill. Ann. Stat. ch. 68, para. 8-101(A) (Smith-Hurd Supp. 1985)	§ 2.12
Ill. Ann. Stat. ch. 68, para. 8-101(C)(3) (Smith-Hurd Supp. 1985)	§ 2.12
Ill. Ann. Stat. ch. 68, para. 8-101(D) (Smith-Hurd Supp. 1985)	§ 2.12
Ill. Ann. Stat. ch. 68, para. 8-103 (Smith-Hurd Supp. 1985)	§ 2.12
Ill. Ann. Stat. ch. 68, para. 8-106 (Smith-Hurd Supp. 1985)	§ 2.12
Ill. Ann. Stat. ch. 68, para. 8-106(A) (Smith-Hurd Supp. 1985)	§ 2.12
Ill. Ann. Stat. ch. 68, para. 8-107 (Smith-Hurd 1985)	§ 2.12
Ill. Ann. Stat. ch. 68, para. 8-108(B) (Smith-Hurd Supp. 1985)	§ 2.12
Ill. Ann. Stat. ch. 68, para. 8-108(C) (Smith-Hurd Supp. 1985)	§ 2.12
Ill. Ann. Stat. ch. 68, para. 8-108(D) (Smith-Hurd Supp. 1985)	§ 2.12
Ill. Ann. Stat. ch. 68, para. 8-108(G) (Smith-Hurd Supp. 1985)	§ 2.12
Ill. Ann. Stat. ch. 68, para. 8-111(A)(1) (Smith-Hurd Supp. 1985)	§ 2.12
Ill. Ann. Stat. ch. 68, para. 8-111(A)(2) (Smith-Hurd Supp. 1985)	§ 2.12
Illinois Human Rights Act	§§ 2.12, 2.26, 2.27, 5.9
Illinois Workmen's Occupational Diseases Act	§ 8.10
Ind. Code Ann. §§ 34-4-2-1 to 34-4-2-22 (West 1983)	§ 3.22
Iowa Code Ann. § 79.28 (West 1973 & Supp. 1985)	§ 9.7
Kan. Stat. Ann. §§ 5-401 to 5-422 (1982)	§ 3.22
1920 Kan. Sess. Laws ch. 29	§ 3.3
Me. Rev. Stat. Ann. tit. 14, §§ 5972–5949 (1980)	§ 3.22
Me. Rev. Stat. Ann. tit. 26, § 831 (1974 & Supp. 1985)	§ 9.7
Me. Rev. Stat. Ann. tit. 26, § 833 (1974 & Supp. 1985)	§ 9.7
Me. Rev. Stat. Ann. tit. 26, § 834 (1974 & Supp. 1985)	§ 9.7
Me. Rev. Stat. Ann. tit. 26, § 840 (1974 & Supp. 1985)	§ 9.7
Md. Cts. & Jud. Proc. Code Ann. §§ 3-201 to 3-234 (1984)	§ 3.22
Mass. Gen. L. ch. 93B, § 4(3)(c) (1984)	§ 4.11
Mass. Gen. L. ch. 149, § 24A (1982)	§ 4.23
Mass. Gen. Laws Ann. ch. 251, §§ 1–22 (West 1959)	§ 3.22

STATUTES

State Statutes	*Book §*
Mich. Comp. Laws Ann. § 15.352, sec. 3(1) (West 1981 & Supp. 1985)	§ 9.7
Mich. Comp. Laws Ann. § 15.361 (West 1981 & Supp. 1985)	§ 9.7
Mich. Comp. Laws Ann. § 15.362 (West 1981)	§ 9.7
Mich. Comp. Laws Ann. § 15.363, sec. 3(1) (West 1981 & Supp. 1985)	§ 9.7
Mich. Comp. Laws Ann. §§ 600.5001 to 600.5035 (West 1968)	§ 3.22
Mich. H.B. No. 5155 (1983)	§ 9.10
Mich. H.B. No. 5155, § 2 (1983)	§ 9.10
Mich. H.B. No. 5155, § 2(e) (1983)	§ 9.10
Mich. H.B. No. 5155, § 3(a) (1983)	§ 9.10
Mich. H.B. No. 5155, § 3(1) (1983)	§ 9.10
Mich. H.B. No. 5155, § 4(1) (1983)	§ 9.10
Mich. H.B. No. 5155, § 5 (1983)	§ 9.10
Mich. H.B. No. 5155, § 5(3) (1983)	§ 9.10
Mich. H.B. No. 5155, § 6 (1983)	§ 9.10
Mich. H.B. No. 5155, § 10 (1983)	§ 9.10
Mich. H.B. No. 5155, § 12 (1983)	§ 9.10
Mich. H.B. No. 5155, § 13 (1983)	§ 9.10
Mich. H.B. No. 5155, § 14 (1983)	§ 9.10
Minn. Stat. Ann. §§ 572.08–572.30 (West Supp. 1985)	§ 3.22
Miss. Code Ann. § 71-5-19 (1972)	§ 2.37
Miss. Code Ann. § 71-5-515 (1972)	§ 2.37
Miss. Code Ann. §§ 71-5-517 to 71-5-533 (1972)	§ 2.37
Miss. Code Ann. § 71-5-517 (Supp. 1983)	§ 2.37
Miss. Code Ann. § 71-5-517 (1972)	§§ 2.37, 7.35
Miss. Code Ann. § 71-5-519 (1972)	§ 2.37
Miss. Code Ann. § 71-5-521 (1972)	§ 2.37
Miss. Code Ann. § 71-5-523 (1973)	§ 7.35
Miss. Code Ann. § 71-5-525 (1972)	§ 7.35
Miss. Code Ann. § 71-5-527 (1972)	§ 2.37
Mo. Rev. Stat. § 290.140 (1978)	§ 9.9
Mo. Ann. Stat. §§ 435.350–435.470 (Vernon Supp. 1986)	§ 3.22
Nev. Rev. Stat. §§ 38.015–38.205 (1986)	§ 3.22
N.J. Stat. Ann. § 43:21-6 (West Supp. 1983)	§§ 2.37, 7.35
N.J. Stat. Ann. § 43:21-6(a) (West Supp. 1983)	§ 2.37
N.J. Stat. Ann. § 43:21-6(b)(1) (West Supp. 1983)	§§ 2.37, 7.35
N.J. Stat. Ann. § 43:21-6(c) (West Supp. 1983)	§ 2.37
N.J. Stat. Ann. § 43:21-6(f) (West 1982)	§ 2.37
N.J. Stat. Ann. § 43:21-6(f) (West Supp. 1983)	§ 7.35
1986 N.J. Laws ch. 105 (S. 1105, 202d N.J. Leg.) (Sept. 5, 1986)	§ 9.7
N.M. Stat. Ann. §§ 44-7-1 to 44-7-22 (1978)	§ 3.22
N.Y. Civ. Prac. L.&R. § 213 (McKinney Supp. 1986)	§ 2.38
N.Y. Civ. Prac. L.&R. § 214 (McKinney Supp. 1986)	§ 2.38
N.Y. Civ. Prac. L.&R. § 215 (McKinney Supp. 1986)	§ 2.38

State Statutes | *Book §*

N.Y. Civ. Prac. L.&R. §§ 7501–7514 (McKinney 1980)	§ 3.22
N.Y. Lab. Law § 740 (Consol. 1977 & Supp. 1986)	§ 9.7
N.Y. Lab. Law § 740(3) (Consol. 1977 & Supp. 1986)	§ 9.7
N.Y. Lab. Law § 740(6) (Consol. 1977 & Supp. 1986)	§ 9.7
N.Y. Lab. Law § 740(7) (Consol. 1977 & Supp. 1986)	§ 9.7
N.Y. A.B. No. 6610-B (1983)	§ 9.4
N.C. Gen. Stat. §§ 1-567.1 to 1-567.20 (1983)	§ 3.22
Okla. Stat. Ann. tit. 15, §§ 801–818 (West Supp. 1985)	§ 3.22
42 Pa. Cons. Stat. Ann. § 5522 (Purdon Supp. 1986)	§ 2.38
42 Pa. Cons. Stat. Ann. § 5523 (Purdon Supp. 1986)	§ 2.38
42 Pa. Cons. Stat. Ann. § 5524 (Purdon Supp. 1986)	§ 2.38
42 Pa. Cons. Stat. Ann. § 5525 (Purdon Supp. 1986)	§ 2.38
42 Pa. Cons. Stat. Ann. § 5526 (Purdon Supp. 1986)	§ 2.38
42 Pa. Cons. Stat. Ann. § 5527 (Purdon Supp. 1986)	§ 2.38
42 Pa. Cons. Stat. Ann. §§ 7301–7320 (Purdon 1982)	§ 3.22
Pa. Stat. Ann. tit. 43, § 952 (Purdon Supp. 1985)	§ 2.12
Pa. Stat. Ann. tit. 43, § 954(b) (Purdon Supp. 1985)	§ 2.12
Pa. Stat. tit. 43, § 954(d) (Purdon 1964)	§ 2.12
Pa. Stat. tit. 43, § 954(e) (Purdon 1964)	§ 2.12
Pa. Stat. Ann. tit. 43, § 954(p) (Purdon Supp. 1985)	§ 2.12
Pa. Stat. Ann. tit. 43, § 955 (Purdon Supp. 1985)	§ 2.12
Pa. Stat. Ann. tit. 43, § 955(a) (Purdon Supp. 1985)	§ 2.12
Pa. Stat. Ann. tit. 43, § 955(b) (Purdon Supp. 1985)	§ 2.12
Pa. Stat. Ann. tit. 43, § 955(d) (Purdon Supp. 1985)	§ 2.12
Pa. Stat. Ann. tit. 43, § 955(j) (Purdon Supp. 1985)	§ 2.12
Pa. Stat. Ann. tit. 43, § 956 (Purdon 1964)	§ 2.12
Pa. Stat. Ann. tit. 43, § 957(d) (Purdon 1964)	§ 2.12
Pa. Stat. Ann. tit. 43, § 957(g) (Purdon 1964 & Purdon Supp. 1985)	§ 2.12
Pa. Stat. Ann. tit. 43, § 957(h) (Purdon 1964 & Purdon Supp. 1985)	§ 2.12
Pa. Stat. Ann. tit. 43, § 959 (Purdon Supp. 1985)	§ 2.12
Pa. Stat. Ann. tit. 43, § 959(a) (Purdon Supp. 1985)	§ 2.12
Pa. Stat. Ann. tit. 43, § 959(b) (Purdon Supp. 1985)	§ 2.12
Pa. Stat. Ann. tit. 43, § 959(c) (Purdon Supp. 1985)	§ 2.12
Pa. Stat. Ann. tit. 43, § 959(d) (Purdon Supp. 1985)	§ 2.12
Pa. Stat. Ann. tit. 43, § 959(f) (Purdon Supp. 1985)	§ 2.12
Pa. Stat. Ann. tit. 43, § 959(g) (Purdon Supp. 1985)	§ 2.12
Pa. Stat. Ann. tit. 43, § 960 (Purdon Supp. 1985)	§ 2.12
Pa. Stat. Ann. tit. 43, § 962(c) (Purdon Supp. 1985)	§ 2.12
Pa. Stat. Ann. tit. 53, §§ 12621–12638 (Purdon 1957 & 1983–1984 Supp.)	§ 6.5
Pa. Stat. Ann. tit. 53, §§ 23431–23453 (Purdon 1957 & 1983–1984 Supp.)	§ 6.5
Pa. Stat. Ann. tit. 53, §§ 39401–39408 (Purdon 1957 & 1983–1984 Supp.)	§ 6.5
Pa. Stat. Ann. tit. 53, §§ 55644–55645 (Purdon 1957 & 1983–1984 Supp.)	§ 6.5
Pennsylvania Human Relations Act	§§ 2.12, 2.26, 2.27, 5.9

STATUTES

State Statutes	*Book §*
Pa. H.B. No. 1020 (1985)	§ 9.10
Pa. H.B. No. 1020, § 3 (1985)	§ 9.10
Pa. H.B. No. 1020, § 5 (1985)	§ 9.10
Pa. H.B. No. 1020, § 6 (1985)	§ 9.10
Pa. H.B. No. 1020, § 7 (1985)	§ 9.10
Pa. H.B. No. 1020, § 8 (1985)	§ 9.10
Pa. H.B. No. 1020, § 9 (1985)	§ 9.10
Pa. H.B. No. 1020, § 10 (1985)	§ 9.10
Pa. H.B. No. 1020, § 11 (1985)	§ 9.10
Pa. H.B. No. 1020, § 12 (1985)	§ 9.10
Pa. H.B. No. 1020, § 13 (1985)	§ 9.10
Pa. H.B. No. 1742 (1981)	§ 9.10
P.R. Laws Ann. tit. 29, § 185a-1 (1985)	§ 9.10
R.I. Gen. Laws § 36-15-1 (1984 & Supp. 1985)	§ 9.7
R.I. Gen. Laws § 36-15-4(a) (1984 & Supp. 1985)	§ 9.7
S.C. Code Ann. §§ 15-48-10 to 15-48-240 (Law. Co-op. Supp. 1985)	§ 3.22
S.D. Codified Laws Ann. §§ 21-25A-1 to 21-25A-38 (1978)	§ 3.22
S.D. Codified Laws Ann. § 60-1-3 (1969 & Supp. 1985)	§§ 9.7, 9.8
S.D. Codified Laws Ann. § 60-1-3 (Supp. 1985)	§ 9.8
S.D. Codified Laws Ann. § 60-1-3 (1978)	§ 9.8
S.D. Codified Laws Ann. § 60-1-3 (1969)	§ 9.8
S.D. Codified Laws Ann. § 60-1-4 (1978)	§ 9.8
Tenn. Code Ann. §§ 29-5-301 to 29-5-320 (Supp. 1985)	§ 3.22
Tex. Rev. Civ. Stat. arts. 224 to 238-6 (Vernon 1973)	§ 3.22
Utah Code Ann. § 67-21-1 (1985–86)	§ 9.7
Utah Code Ann. § 67-21-4(1) (1985–86)	§ 9.7
Va. Code Ann. § 13.1-32 (1985)	§ 5.17
Va. Code Ann. § 15.1–17.1 (1981)	§ 6.5
West Va. Consumer Credit & Protection Act, W. Va. Code § 46A-1-101 (1986)	§§ 5.17, 7.16
Wis. Stat. Ann. § 111.31 (West Supp. 1985)	§ 2.12
Wis. Stat. Ann. § 111.31(1) (West Supp. 1985)	§ 2.12
Wis. Stat. Ann. § 111.31(3) (West Supp. 1985)	§ 2.12
Wis. Stat. Ann. § 111.32(6)(a) (West Supp. 1985)	§ 2.12
Wis. Stat. Ann. § 111.32(6)(b) (West Supp. 1985)	§ 2.12
Wis. Stat. Ann. § 111.32(7) (West Supp. 1985)	§ 2.12
Wis. Stat. Ann. § 111.32(8)(a) (West Supp. 1985)	§ 2.12
Wis. Stat. Ann. § 111.32(8)(b) (West Supp. 1985)	§ 2.12
Wis. Stat. Ann. § 111.32(8)(c) (West Supp. 1985)	§ 2.12
Wis. Stat. Ann. § 111.32(9) (West Supp. 1985)	§ 2.12

State Statutes   *Book §*

Wis. Stat. Ann. § 111.34(1)(b) (West Supp. 1985)	§ 2.12
Wis. Stat. Ann. § 111.34(2)(b) (West Supp. 1985)	§ 2.12
Wis. Stat. Ann. § 111.34(2)(c) (West Supp. 1985)	§ 2.12
Wis. Stat. Ann. § 111.36 (West Supp. 1985)	§ 5.28
Wis. Stat. Ann. § 111.39(1) (West Supp. 1985)	§ 2.12
Wis. Stat. Ann. § 111.39(2) (West Supp. 1985)	§ 2.12
Wis. Stat. Ann. § 111.39(3) (West Supp. 1985)	§ 2.12
Wis. Stat. Ann. § 111.39(4)(b) (West Supp. 1985)	§ 2.12
Wis. Stat. Ann. § 111.39(5)(a) (West Supp. 1985)	§ 2.12
Wis. Stat. Ann. § 111.39(5)(b) (West Supp. 1985)	§ 2.12
Wis. Stat. Ann. § 111.39(c) (West Supp. 1985)	§ 2.12
Wis. Stat. Ann. § 111.321 (West Supp. 1985)	§ 5.28
Wis. Stat. Ann. § 111.322 (West Supp. 1985)	§§ 2.12, 5.28
Wis. Stat. Ann. § 111.375 (West Supp. 1985)	§ 2.12
Wis. Stat. Ann. § 111.375(1)	§ 2.12
Wis. Stat. Ann. § 111.395 (West Supp. 1985)	§ 2.12
Wisconsin Fair Employment Act	§ 2.12
Wyo. Stat. §§ 1-36-101 to 1-36-119 (1977)	§ 3.22

INDEX

ABUSIVE DISCHARGE
  Wrongful dismissal, common law recovery § 1.2
ACQUIRED IMMUNE DEFICIENCY SYNDROME
  Discrimination protection under Rehabilitation Act, applicability § 2.10
  Tort theories, dismissal related to AIDS § 5.29
ADMINISTRATIVE DECISIONS
  Comprehensive wrongful discharge legislation § 9.26
  Proof. See PROOF
  Proving jeopardy to public policy § 7.12
ADMINISTRATIVE MODEL
  Employer personnel policy § 8.4
ADMINISTRATIVE REMEDIES
  Employment-at-will, case evaluation checklist § 1.17
  Public employment, exhaustion of administrative remedies § 6.6
  Public policy tort, effect of availability of administrative remedies §§ 5.9, 7.12
  Wrongful dismissal recovery at common law, public policy tort claims § 1.2
AFFIRMATIVE ACTION
  Contract theory, promises derived from statements made to workforce § 4.8
  Executive Order 11,246 § 2.13
AGE DISCRIMINATION IN EMPLOYMENT ACT
  Comprehensive wrongful discharge legislation § 9.6
  Proof of violation §§ 7.8, 7.15, 7.30
  Protection § 2.32
  Public employment discrimination § 6.7
  Statutory protection §§ 2.6, 2.7
AIDS
  See ACQUIRED IMMUNE DEFICIENCY SYNDROME
ALCOHOLISM
  Arbitration, just cause standard, defense § 3.5

ALIENS
  Section 1981 discrimination protection § 2.8
AMERICAN RULE
  Contract theories, § 4.28
  Employment-at-will rule development § 1.4
  Public policy tort actions § 5.33
APPEALS
  Arbitration § 3.19
  Employer personnel policies § 8.14
  Handicap discrimination protection § 2.12
  Proving public policy, judicial or jury decisions § 7.11
  Unemployment compensation benefit eligibility determination § 2.37
APPRAISALS
  Employer personnel policies, appraisal of employees § 8.15
ARBITRATION
  Generally § 3.1
  Awards
  –Compelling compliance by court § 3.23
  –Fair representation duty breach, vacating award § 3.25
  –Form and content of § 3.17
  –Remedies in § 3.18
  Comprehensive wrongful discharge legislation §§ 9.10, 9.19, 9.28, 9.29
  Contract theories, suits by employees covered by collective bargaining agreements § 4.25
  Courts and arbitration
  –Generally § 3.20
  –Compelling arbitration § 3.23
  –Fair representation, duty of §§ 3.25, 3.25
  –Federal common law of arbitration § 3.21
  –Judicial review and enforcement of awards § 3.24
  –Statutes of arbitration § 3.22
  Development in US § 3.3

709

ARBITRATION (*Continued*)
  Employer personnel policies § 8.14
  England, development in § 3.2
  Evidence
  –Generally § 3.12
  –Compulsory process § 3.16
  –Exclusionary and self-incrimination rules § 3.13
  –Fair representation duty of union, breach § 3.25
  –Medical § 3.14
  –Standard of proof § 3.15
  Fair representation
  –Duty of §§ 3.25, 3.26
  –Railway Labor Act § 3.19
  Grievances
  –Defending against § 3.29
  –Handling § 3.28
  –Typical procedure § 3.9
  Hearing
  –Generally § 3.10
  –Evidence, see Evidence, this heading
  –Ex parte hearings § 3.11
  History §§ 3.2, 3.3
  Just cause standards
  –Generally § 3.5
  –Misconduct off job § 3.8
  –Misconduct on job § 3.7
  –Poor performance § 3.6
  Procedural fairness § 9.28
  Procedure, grievance and arbitration § 3.9
  Proof, preclusive effect of decisions § 7.31
  Public employment. See PUBLIC EMPLOYMENT
  Public policy torts § 5.20
  Purpose of § 3.4
  Railway Labor Act § 3.19
  Representation
  –Choice of representative § 3.9
  –Fair representation, duty of §§ 3.19, 3.25, 3.26
  Statutory claims, effect of arbitration awards § 3.27
ASBESTOS SCHOOL HAZARD DETECTION AND CONTROL ACT
  Protection against discrimination § 2.24
ATTORNEY'S FEES
  Arbitration award § 3.18
  Comprehensive wrongful discharge legislation § 9.32
  Contract theories § 4.28

ATTORNEY'S FEES (*Continued*)
  Public employment, civil service protection § 6.4
  Public policy tort actions § 5.33
  Statutory claims § 2.25
AWARDS
  Arbitration. See ARBITRATION
  Public employment, enforceability of grievance arbitration awards § 6.16

BACK PAY
  Comprehensive wrongful discharge legislation § 9.32
  Title VII remedies § 2.3
BAD FAITH
  Proving a breach § 7.23
BLADES, L. E.
  Employment-at-will doctrine § 1.11
BREACH OF CONTRACT
  Contract theories. See CONTRACT THEORIES
  Employment-at-will, choice of law § 1.14
BURDEN OF PROOF
  Comprehensive wrongful discharge legislation §§ 9.19, 9.31
  Contract theories § 4.28
  Just cause standard, arbitration § 3.5
  Procedural fairness § 9.31
  Public policy tort cases § 5.2
BUREAUCRATIC MODEL
  Employer personnel policy § 8.4
BUSINESS NECESSITY
  Proof, public policy torts § 7.15
  Proving justification for dismissal §§ 7.13, 7.15

CANADA
  Comprehensive wrongful discharge legislation § 9.12
CHANDLER, A.
  Personnel policy development § 8.2
CHOICE OF LAW
  Employment-at-will § 1.14
CIRCUMSTANTIAL EVIDENCE
  Generally § 7.2
  Arbitration hearings § 3.12
CIVIL RIGHTS ACTS
  Public employment protection §§ 6.7, 6.8
  Reconstruction acts §§ 2.8, 2.9, 6.8
  Title VI § 2.11
  Title VII. See TITLE VII

INDEX

CIVIL SERVICE
   Employment-at-will rule erosion § 1.6
   Public employment. See PUBLIC EMPLOYMENT
CLASS-BASED DISCRIMINATION
   Employment-at-will rule erosion § 1.8
   Title VII §§ 2.2–2.5
CROSS-EXAMINATION
   Arbitration hearings § 3.10
CULPABILITY
   Public policy tort cases §§ 5.6, 5.7
COLLATERAL ESTOPPEL
   Arbitration hearings, evidence § 3.15
   Proof, preclusive effect of earlier decisions §§ 7.29, 7.30, 7.32
COLLECTIVE BARGAINING
   Comprehensive wrongful discharge legislation §§ 9.2, 9.28
   Procedural fairness § 9.28
COLLECTIVE BARGAINING AGREEMENTS
   Arbitration. See ARBITRATION
   Contract theories. See CONTRACT THEORIES
   Tort theories, employees covered by agreements § 5.20
COMPENSATORY DAMAGES
   Comprehensive wrongful discharge legislation § 9.32
   Contract theories, breach of contract § 4.28
COMPLAINTS
   Contract theories §§ 4.26, 4.27
   Public policy tort cases §§ 5.31, 5.32
COMMON LAW
   Comprehensive wrongful discharge legislation §§ 9.2, 9.4
   Contract theories, history § 4.3
   Contracts. See PROOF
   Discrimination, common law relief § 2.38
   Employment-at-will rule erosion § 1.9
   Preemption. See PREEMPTION
   Tort theories. See TORT THEORIES
   Wrongful dismissal theory § 1.2
COMPREHENSIVE WRONGFUL DISCHARGE LEGISLATION
   Generally § 9.1, app. C
   Commentators' models
   –Generally § 9.13
   –Bellace § 9.16
   –Selznick § 9.15
   –Summers § 9.14

COMPREHENSIVE WRONGFUL DISCHARGE LEGISLATION
(*Continued*)
   Fairness, substantive and procedural § 9.2
   Judicial control of other associations § 9.17
   Legislative drafting § 9.19
   Need for legislation § 9.3
   Procedural fairness
   –Generally § 9.25
   –Burdens of proof § 9.31
   –Case volume estimate § 9.34
   –Collectively bargained arbitration § 9.28
   –Employer procedures, deference to § 9.27
   –Forum selection § 9.29
   –Litigation costs § 9.33
   –Preemption, election, exhaustion, and preclusion § 9.26
   –Remedies § 9.32
   –Wrongful dismissal and unemployment compensation integration § 9.30
   Proposed wrongful dismissal statute § 9.18
   Reform of statutes § 9.4
   Statutory models
   –Generally § 9.5
   –British model § 9.11
   –Canadian model § 9.12
   –Federal wrongful dismissal statutes § 9.6
   –State employment term statute § 9.8
   –State just cause proposal § 9.10
   –State service letter statute § 9.9
   –State whistleblower statute § 9.7
   Substantive fairness standards
   –Generally §§ 9.2, 9.20
   –Enumerated prohibitions § 9.24
   –Good faith § 9.22
   –Just cause § 9.21
   –Simple standards, problems § 9.22
COMPULSORY PRODUCTION
   Arbitration hearings, production of evidence § 3.16
CONDUCT
   Contract theories, promises implied from conduct § 4.9
   Misconduct. See MISCONDUCT
   Proof of promise from conduct § 7.19
CONFIDENTIALITY
   Tort theories, defamation § 5.25

CONFLICTING INTERESTS
Public policy torts § 5.15

CONSIDERATION
Contract theories. See CONTRACT THEORIES
Employment-at-will, case evaluation checklist § 1.17
Proof of consideration, common law contracts § 7.20

CONSPIRACY
Section 1985 protection against discrimination § 2.9

CONSTITUTIONAL LAW
Comprehensive wrongful discharge legislation § 9.20
Proof, preclusive effect of earlier judicial decisions § 7.30

CONSTITUTIONAL RIGHTS
Proof. See PROOF
Public policy torts, termination jeopardizing constitutional rights § 5.12

CONSUMER CREDIT PROTECTION ACT
Statutory protection against discrimination § 2.22

CONTINUING EMPLOYMENT
Contract theories, bargained-for detrimental reliance § 4.16

CONTRACTORS
Affirmative action requirements for federal contractors § 2.13

CONTRACTS
Common law contracts, proof. See PROOF
Proof, jury instructions on common law contract formation § 7.21
Tort theories, intentional interference with contractual relation § 5.22

CONTRACT THEORIES
Generally § 4.1
Breach
–Generally § 4.21
–Employer promise § 4.22
–Good cause, deciding existence of § 4.24
–Good faith covenant § 4.23
–Pleading plaintiff's case § 4.26
Collective bargaining agreements
–Consideration treatment in § 4.5
–Suits by employees covered by § 4.25
Consideration
–Generally §§ 4.1, 4.12

CONTRACT THEORIES (*Continued*)
–Bargained-for detrimental reliance §§ 4.14–4.16
–Collective bargaining agreement § 4.5
–Common law action § 4.3
–Employer modification of promise after consideration given § 4.19
–Pleading defendant's case § 4.27
–Pleading plaintiff's case § 4.26
–Promissory estoppel § 4.17
–Proof of actual reliance § 4.18
–Requirement, history of § 4.4
–Unilateral contracts §§ 4.1, 4.13
Damages § 4.28
Employment security promise
–Generally § 4.6
–Disclaimers § 4.10
–Express commitments made to specific employees § 4.7
–Good faith and fair dealing covenant § 4.11
–Length of service and conduct, promises implied from § 4.9
–Representations made to workforce, promises derived from § 4.8
Frauds, statute of § 4.20
History
–Generally § 4.2
–Common law action § 4.3
–Consideration in collective bargaining agreements § 4.5
–Consideration requirement § 4.4
Pleading
–Defendant's case § 4.27
–Plaintiff's case § 4.26

COSTS
Procedural fairness, cost of litigation § 9.33

COVENANT
Common law action, contract theory § 4.3

DAMAGES
Contract theories. See CONTRACT THEORIES
Criticism of laws app E
Employment-at-will, common law wrongful dismissal § 1.1
Tort theories § 5.33

DEFAMATION
Public employment, liberty interest deprivation § 6.11
Tort theories § 5.25

INDEX

DETRIMENTAL RELIANCE
  Contract theories, bargained-for reliance §§ 4.14–4.16
  Proving contract formation § 7.21
DISCLAIMERS
  Contract theories, employment security promise § 4.10
  Employer personnel policies on terminations §§ 8.7, 8.8
DISCOVERY
  Employment-at-will, case evaluation checklist § 1.17
  Methods app B
DISCRIMINATION
  Arbitration, inconsistent enforcement of company rules § 3.5
  Class-based discrimination. See CLASS-BASED DISCRIMINATION
  Employment-at-will §§ 1.1, 1.8, 1.17
  Handicap. See HANDICAP DISCRIMINATION
  Proof, preclusive effect of administrative decisions § 7.33
  Public employment, federal statute § 6.7
  Statutory protection. See STATUTORY PROTECTION
  Title VII. See TITLE VII
DISPARATE TREATMENT
  Title VII violations § 2.3
DRUG ABUSE
  Arbitration, just cause standard, defense § 3.5
DUE PROCESS
  Public employment. See PUBLIC EMPLOYMENT

EDUCATION ACT
  Statutory protection against discrimination § 2.14
ELECTION
  Procedural fairness § 9.26
EMOTIONAL DISTRESS
  Tort theories, intentional infliction of distress § 5.23
EMPLOYEE HANDBOOKS
  See PERSONNEL MANUALS
EMPLOYEE RETIREMENT INCOME SECURITY ACT
  Contract theories, employer modification of promise after consideration is given § 4.19

EMPLOYEE RETIREMENT INCOME SECURITY ACT (*Continued*)
  Proof, preclusive effect of earlier decisions § 7.31
  Statutory protection against discrimination § 2.23
EMPLOYER PERSONNEL POLICIES
  Generally § 8.1
  Appraisal programs, employee § 8.15
  Contemporary practices § 8.5
  Employer policies on termination
  –Generally § 8.6
  –Internal remedies, limiting relief to § 8.9
  –Limiting authority to make promises § 8.8
  –Releases § 8.10
  –Reserving right to dismiss at will § 8.7
  Function of internal rules § 8.3
  History § 8.2
  Organization theory § 8.4
  Termination in complaint policies
  –Generally § 8.11
  –Personnel manuals. See PERSONNEL MANUALS
  –Procedural fairness policies §§ 8.13, 8.14
  –Substantive fairness policies § 8.12
EMPLOYMENT AT WILL
  Generally § 1.1
  Case evaluation checklist § 1.17
  Choice of law § 1.14
  Commentators § 1.11
  Common law wrongful dismissal theory § 1.2
  Employment tenure rule, before industrial revolution § 1.3
  Erosion of rule
  –Generally § 1.5
  –Civil service protection § 1.6
  –Class-based discrimination, protection against § 1.8
  –Private sector workers, common law protection for § 1.9
  –Reasons for erosion § 1.10
  –Unions, employees represented by § 1.7
  Future of rule § 1.16
  History and development of employment-at-will rule § 1.4
  Role of employment-at-will rule § 1.13
  Status of employment-at-will rule in

INDEX

EMPLOYMENT AT WILL (*Continued*)
   states § 1.12
   Unresolved issues § 1.15
ENERGY REORGANIZATION ACT OF 1974
   Protection against discrimination §§ 2.24, 2.33
ENTRAPMENT
   Arbitration hearings, admissibility of evidence § 3.13
ENUMERATED REASONS STATUTES
   Comprehensive wrongful discharge legislation § 9.5
EQUAL EMPLOYMENT OPPORTUNITY COMMISSION
   Age Discrimination in Employment Act § 2.6
   Discrimination protection § 2.38
   Title VII procedures § 2.3
EQUAL PAY ACT
   Proof of violation § 7.9
ESTOPPEL
   Collateral estoppel. See COLLATERAL ESTOPPEL
   Promissory estoppel. See PROMISSORY ESTOPPEL
EVIDENCE
   Age Discrimination in Employment Act § 2.6
   Arbitration. See ARBITRATION
   Title VII proof of intent § 2.3
EXCLUSIONARY RULES
   Arbitration hearings § 3.13
EXHAUSTION OF ADMINISTRATIVE REMEDIES
   Comprehensive wrongful discharge legislation § 9.6
EX PARTE HEARINGS
   Arbitration hearings § 3.10
EXPECTATION DAMAGES
   Contract theories, breach of contract § 4.28
EXTERNAL POLICY TORTS
   See TORT THEORIES

FAIR DEALING
   Wrongful dismissal, common law recovery for § 1.2
FAIR LABOR STANDARDS ACT
   Statutory protection against discrimination § 2.21
FAIRNESS
   Employer personnel policies, substantive and procedure §§ 8.12–8.14

FAIR REPRESENTATION
   Arbitration, duty of fair representation §§ 3.25, 3.26
FEDERAL CONTRACTORS
   Discrimination by contractors, Executive Order 11,246 § 2.13
FORUM SELECTION
   Comprehensive wrongful discharge legislation §§ 9.26, 9.28
   Procedural fairness § 9.29
FRAUD
   Arbitration award enforcement § 3.24
FRONT PAY
   Comprehensive wrongful discharge legislation § 9.32
FRAUDULENT MISREPRESENTATION
   Tort theories § 5.24
FREEDOM OF CONTRACT
   Employment-at-will rule development § 1.4
FULLER, L.
   Comprehensive wrongful discharge legislation § 9.15

GARNISHMENT
   Consumer Credit Protection Act § 2.22
GOOD CAUSE
   Contract theories, breach, determining existence of good cause § 4.24
   Proving a breach, deciding good cause §§ 7.26, 7.27
GOOD FAITH AND FAIR DEALING COVENANT
   Comprehensive wrongful discharge legislation § 9.20
   Contract theory §§ 4.6, 4.11, 4.23
   Employment-at-will rule § 1.13
   Proving breach of contract §§ 7.23, 7.28
   Substantive fairness standards § 9.22
   Wrongful dismissal, common law recovery for § 1.2
GREAT BRITAIN
   Comprehensive wrongful discharge legislation § 9.11

HANDICAP DISCRIMINATION
   Statutory protection against §§ 2.10–2.12
HARASSMENT
   Title VII protections against sexual harassment § 2.5
HEARINGS
   Arbitration. See ARBITRATION

INDEX

HOLMES, O. W.
    Contract theory § 4.4
    Employment-at-will doctrine § 1.11
    Tort theory § 5.4

HOMOSEXUALITY
    Public policy torts § 5.12
    Title VII protection applicability §§ 2.3, 2.5
    Tort theories, dismissals relating to sexual orientation § 5.28

HUMAN RELATIONS MODEL
    Employer personnel policy § 8.4

HURST, W.
    Comprehensive wrongful discharge legislation § 9.15

ILLEGALITY
    Public policy torts, refusal to follow orders to commit illegal acts § 5.18

IMPLIED-IN-FACT CONTRACTS
    Generally ch. 4
    Contract theories. See CONTRACT THEORIES
    Employment-at-will §§ 1.13, 1.15, 1.16
    Employment incidents other than employment security app F
    Releases, employee § 8.10
    Wrongful dismissal, common law recovery § 1.2

IMPLIED-IN-FACT PROMISE
    Proof of promise, common law contracts § 7.18

INDEBITATUS ASSUMPSIT
    Common law action, contract theory § 4.3

INFERENCES
    Proof inferred from evidence § 7.2

IN-HOUSE COUNSEL
    Checklist for litigation app D

INTENTIONAL INFLICTION OF EMOTIONAL DISTRESS
    Tort theories § 5.23

INTENTIONAL INTERFERENCE WITH CONTRACTUAL RELATIONS
    Tort theories § 5.22

INTERNAL POLICY TORT
    See TORT THEORIES

INVASION OF PRIVACY
    Tort theories. See TORT THEORIES

JEOPARDY
    Proving jeopardy to public policy § 7.12

JOINT AND SEVERAL LIABILITY
    Public policy tort actions, damages § 5.33

JUDICIAL REVIEW
    Arbitration awards review § 3.24

JURISDICTION
    Statutory protection against discrimination, pendent state claims § 2.35

JURORS
    Statutory protection against discrimination, federal jurors § 2.25

JURY DUTY
    Proving jeopardy to public policy § 7.12
    Public policy torts § 5.10

JURY INSTRUCTIONS
    Proof. See PROOF

JUST CAUSE
    Arbitration. See ARBITRATION
    Contract theories §§ 4.21, 4.24
    Demonstrating just cause for termination § 1.1
    Prima facie torts § 5.1
    State proposals § 9.10

JUSTIFICATION
    Proof. See PROOF
    Public policy tort cases § 5.7

LABOR MANAGEMENT RELATIONS ACT
    Arbitration, § 301 preemption § 3.1
    Contract theories, employer modification of promise after consideration is given § 4.19
    Preemption §§ 2.29, 2.30

LABOR STATUTES
    Public policy tort theory § 5.9

LABOR UNIONS
    Arbitration. See ARBITRATION
    Comprehensive wrongful discharge legislation § 9.3
    Employment-at-will rule erosion §§ 1.7, 1.17
    National Labor Relations Act. See NATIONAL LABOR RELATIONS ACT

LANGDELL, C.
    Contract theory § 4.4

LENGTH OF SERVICE
    Contract theories, promises implied from length of service § 4.9

LIBERTY INTERESTS
  Public employment protection, due
    process § 6.11
LIQUIDATED DAMAGES
  Comprehensive wrongful discharge
    legislation § 9.32
LONGSHOREMEN AND HARBOR
  WORKERS COMPENSATION ACT
  Protection against discrimination § 2.24

MALICE
  Proving breach of contract § 7.28
MANDAMUS
  Discrimination by federal contractors
    § 2.13
MASTER-SERVANT RELATIONSHIP
  Employment tenure rule before
    industrial revolution § 1.3
MEDIATION
  Arbitration and mediation §§ 3.1, 3.3
MEDICAL EVIDENCE
  Arbitration hearings § 3.14
MINE HEALTH AND SAFETY ACT
  Statutory protection of employee
    conduct § 2.18
MINNEMEIER, K.
  Comprehensive wrongful discharge
    legislation § 9.14
MINUTE CONTRACTS
  Employment-at-will rule development
    § 1.4
MISCONDUCT
  Arbitration, just cause standards §§ 3.7,
    3.8
  Proof, preclusive effect of earlier
    unemployment compensation
    decisions § 7.35
  Whistleblowing. See
    WHISTLEBLOWING
MISREPRESENTATION
  Tort theories, fraud § 5.24
MODIFICATIONS
  Contract theories, employer modification
    of promise after consideration given
    § 4.19
MOTIVE
  Proof problems §§ 7.3, 7.4

NATIONAL LABOR RELATIONS ACT
  Comprehensive wrongful discharge
    legislation §§ 9.6, 9.33
  Proof of violation §§ 7.3, 7.7
  Statutory protection against
    discrimination §§ 2.16, 2.28

NEGLIGENCE
  Tort theories § 5.29
NOTICE PLEADING
  Contract theories § 4.26
  Public policy tort cases § 5.31

OCCUPATIONAL HEALTH AND
  SAFETY ACT
  Statutory protection against
    discrimination § 2.18
OFF-DUTY MISCONDUCT
  Arbitration, just cause standards § 3.8
  Comprehensive wrongful discharge
    legislation § 9.24
  Proving breach of contract § 7.28
  Public employment, civil service
    protection § 6.4
  Public policy torts § 5.13
ORAL STATEMENTS
  Contract theory, express commitments
    made to employees § 4.7
  Statutes of frauds, oral contracts § 4.20

PENDENT STATE CLAIMS
  Statutory protection. See STATUTORY
    PROTECTION
PENSION BENEFITS
  Employment Retirement Income
    Security Act protection § 2.23
PERSONAL INJURY
  Public policy torts, workers'
    compensation cases § 5.11
PERJURY
  Public policy tort cases § 5.10
PERSONNEL MANUALS
  Contract theories, employment security
    promise made to workforce in general
    §§ 4.1, 4.8, 4.14
  Employer personnel policies. See
    EMPLOYER PERSONNEL
    POLICIES
  Proving an express or implied promise
    of employment security § 7.18
PERSUASION
  Burden of proof. See PROOF
PLEADINGS
  Contract theories. See CONTRACT
    THEORIES
  Tort theories. See TORT THEORIES
POLYGRAPHS
  Tort theories, invasion of privacy
    § 5.26

INDEX

PRECLUSION
  Procedural fairness § 9.26
  Proof. See PROOF
PREEMPTION
  Comprehensive wrongful discharge legislation §§ 9.19, 9.26
  Contract theories, preemption barring recovery § 4.1
  Procedural fairness § 9.26
  Public policy torts and labor statutes §§ 5.9, 5.20
  Statutory protection. See STATUTORY PROTECTION
  Tort theories, LMRA § 301 § 5.30
PRIMA FACIE TORT
  Comprehensive wrongful discharge legislation §§ 9.2, 9.20
  Proof § 7.2
  Tort theories §§ 5.1, 5.7, 5.21
PRIMARY JURISDICTION
  Preemption. See PREEMPTION
PRIVILEGE
  Tort theories, defamation § 5.25
PROCEDURAL FAIRNESS
  Comprehensive wrongful discharge legislation. See COMPREHENSIVE WRONGFUL DISCHARGE LEGISLATION
PRODUCTION
  Burden of proof. See PROOF
PROMISSORY ESTOPPEL
  Contract theory §§ 4.4, 4.12, 4.14, 4.23, 4.27
  Proving consideration §§ 7.20, 7.21
PROOF
  Generally § 7.1
  Age Discrimination in Employment Act violations § 7.8
  Arbitration hearings, standard of proof § 3.15
  Basic concept § 7.2
  Breach, prevent
  –Generally § 7.22
  –Bad faith or unfairness § 7.23
  –Burdens of proof on cause § 7.27
  –Cause for termination § 7.24
  –Employee's conduct § 7.25
  –Good cause, who decides what is § 7.26
  –Jury instructions § 7.28
  Common law contracts
  –Generally § 7.17
  –Conduct, proving promise from § 7.19
  –Consideration, proving § 7.20

PROOF (*Continued*)
  –Express or implied-in-fact promise of employment security, proving § 7.18
  –Jury instructions on contract formation § 7.21
  –Motive of employer § 7.3
  Constitutional and statutory claims
  –Generally § 7.4
  –National Labor Relations Act § 7.7
  –Other statutes § 7.9
  –Public employee constitutional rights § 7.5
  –Title VII violations § 7.6
  Contract theories, proof of actual bargained-for reliance § 4.18
  Employer motive question § 7.3
  Jury instructions
  –Breach § 7.28
  –Contract formation § 7.21
  –Public policy torts § 7.16
  Justification
  –Affirmative defense, justifiable act as § 7.2
  –Public policy torts, see Public policy torts, this heading
  Preclusion by earlier decisions
  –Generally § 7.29
  –Administrative decisions, generally § 7.32
  –Arbitral decisions § 7.31
  –Discrimination findings § 7.33
  –Employer regulatory compliance § 7.34
  –Judicial decisions § 7.30
  –Unemployment compensation § 7.35
  Public policy tort
  –Generally § 7.10
  –Burden of proof, dismissal reason and mixed motive § 7.14
  –Business necessity § 7.15
  –Jeopardy to policy, proving § 7.12
  –Jury instructions § 7.16
  –Motive of employer § 7.3
  –Policy, proof of § 7.11
  –Reason for dismissal, proving lack of justification § 7.13
  –Unemployment compensation, preclusive effect of earlier decisions § 7.35
PROPERTY INTEREST
  Proof, establishing property right §§ 7.1, 7.5
  Public employment protection, due process § 6.10

PROPERTY RIGHTS
  Employment-at-will rule erosion, protected rights based on continued employment expectations § 1.10

PUBLIC EMPLOYMENT
  Generally § 6.1
  Civil service protections
  –Generally § 6.3
  –Exhaustion of administrative remedies § 6.6
  –Federal § 6.4
  –State and local § 6.5
  Discrimination statutes, federal § 6.7
  Due process
  –Generally § 6.9
  –Liberty interests deprivation § 6.11
  –Procedural entitlement § 6.12
  –Property interests deprivation § 6.10
  –Substantive entitlement § 6.13
  Grievance arbitration and civil service laws, interaction
  –Generally § 6.14
  –Enforceability of awards § 6.16
  –Exclusivity, exhaustion and preclusion § 6.15
  Public employer § 6.2
  Reconstruction civil rights acts § 6.8
  Sovereign immunity
  –Generally § 6.17
  –Suits against state and local governments under common law § 6.20
  –Suits against state and local governments under § 1983 § 6.19
  –Suits against U.S. § 6.18

PUBLIC POLICY TORTS
  Generally ch. 5
  Arbitration § 3.27
  Common law recovery § 1.2
  Comprehensive wrongful discharge legislation §§ 9.2, 9.7, 9.20, 9.26
  Employer personnel policy § 8.5
  Employment-at-will rule §§ 1.9, 1.13, 1.15, 1.16
  Injury requirement § 5.16
  Preemption § 2.29
  Private right of action, implying from statute § 2.26
  Proof. See PROOF
  Tort theories. See TORT THEORIES
  Whistleblower protection § 2.33

PUNITIVE DAMAGES
  Arbitration award § 3.18

PUNITIVE DAMAGES (*Continued*)
  Comprehensive wrongful discharge legislation § 9.32
  Contract theories, breach of contract § 4.28
  Tort theories. See TORT THEORIES

QUALITY CIRCLES
  Employer personnel policy § 8.4

RAILROAD SAFETY AND LIABILITY ACTS
  Statutory protection against discrimination §§ 2.19, 2.31

RAILWAY LABOR ACT
  Arbitration under § 3.19
  Comprehensive wrongful discharge legislation § 9.33

REFORM
  Comprehensive wrongful discharge legislation. See COMPREHENSIVE WRONGFUL DISCHARGE LEGISLATION

REGULATORY COMPLIANCE
  Proof, preclusive effect of administrative decisions § 7.34

REHABILITATION ACT OF 1973
  Statutory protection against discrimination §§ 2.10, 2.11

REINSTATEMENT
  Comprehensive wrongful discharge legislation § 9.32
  Public policy tort actions, damages § 5.33

RELEASES
  Employer personnel policies § 8.10

REMEDIES
  Age Discrimination in Employment Act violations § 2.6
  Arbitration §§ 3.18, 3.26
  Environmental statutes, protection against employer retaliation § 2.20
  Fair Labor Standards Act § 2.21
  Handicap discrimination § 2.12
  Procedural fairness § 9.32
  § 1981 actions against discrimination § 2.8
  § 1985 protection against discrimination § 2.9
  Title VII violations § 2.3

REPRESENTATION
  Arbitration. See ARBITRATION
  Contract theories, suits by employees

INDEX

REPRESENTATION (*Continued*)
   covered by collective bargaining agreements § 4.25
   Public employment, duty of fair representation in arbitration process § 6.15

RES JUDICATA
   Preclusive effect of earlier decisions. See PROOF
   Statutory protection against discrimination, preemption §§ 2.27, 2.32

RETALIATION
   Employee conduct. See STATUTORY PROTECTION
   Proof, preclusive effect of earlier administrative decisions § 7.34
   Public policy tort recovery § 5.9

REVIEWS
   Employer personnel policies, appraisal of employees § 8.15

§ 1981
   Proof of violation § 7.9
   Protection § 2.32
   Public employment protection § 6.8
   Statutory protection against discrimination § 2.8

§ 1983
   Proof, preclusive effects of earlier decisions § 7.33
   Public employment protection § 6.8

§ 1985 ACTIONS
   Statutory protection against discrimination §§ 2.9, 2.32

SELF-INCRIMINATION RULES
   Arbitration hearings § 3.13

SELZNICK, PHILIP
   Comprehensive wrongful discharge legislation § 9.15
   Employment-at-will doctrine § 1.11

SERVICE LETTER STATUTES
   State comprehensive wrongful discharge legislation § 9.9

SERVICE TRANSPORTATION ASSISTANCE ACT
   Protection against discrimination § 2.24

SEXUAL HARASSMENT
   Title VII applicability § 2.5

SEXUAL ORIENTATION
   Homosexuality. See HOMOSEXUALITY
   Public policy torts § 5.12

SEXUAL ORIENTATION (*Continued*)
   Title VII protection applicability § 2.3

SOVEREIGN IMMUNITY
   Public employment. See PUBLIC EMPLOYMENT

SPECIAL ASSUMPSIT
   Common law action, contract theory § 4.3

STANDARD OF PROOF
   Arbitration hearings, evidence admissibility § 3.15

STARE DECISIS
   Comprehensive wrongful discharge legislation § 9.19
   Employer personnel policies, termination, substantive fairness § 8.12

STATE STATUTES
   Generally app A

STATUTE OF FRAUDS
   Contract theories §§ 4.1, 4.20

STATUTES
   Draft app C
   State app A

STATUTES OF LIMITATIONS
   Discrimination, statutory protection § 2.38

STATUTORY PROTECTION
   Generally § 2.1
   Age discrimination in employment § 2.32
   Attorneys' fees §§ 2.21, 2.25
   Class-based discrimination
   –Generally § 2.2
   –Age Discrimination in Employment Act §§ 2.6, 2.7
   –Civil Rights Act of 1964, Title VI § 2.11
   –Education Act amendment § 2.14
   –Federal contractors, Executive Order 11,246 § 2.13
   –Handicap Discrimination and Rehabilitation Act § 2.10
   –Handicap discrimination, state law § 2.12
   –Reconstruction civil rights acts §§ 2.8, 2.9
   –Title VII §§ 2.3–2.5
   Employee conduct, statutory protection
   –Generally § 2.15
   –Consumer Credit Protection Act § 2.22
   –Employee Retirement Income Security

STATUTORY PROTECTION
(*Continued*)
  Act § 2.23
  –Fair Labor Standards Act § 2.21
  –National Labor Relations Act § 2.16
  –Occupational Safety and Health Act § 2.18
  –Other federal statutes § 2.24
  –Railroad safety and liability acts § 2.19
  –Retaliation for discrimination opposition § 2.17
  Environmental statutes § 2.20
  Pendent state claims § 2.35
  Preemption
  –Generally § 2.27
  –Discrimination statute § 2.32
  –Labor Management Relations Act §§ 2.29, 2.30
  –National Labor Relations Act § 2.28
  –Other federal statutes § 2.34
  –Railway Labor Act § 2.31
  –Whistleblower statute § 2.33
  Private right of action, implying from statute § 2.26
  Proof. See PROOF
  Reconstruction civil rights acts § 2.32
  Statutory and common law relief, considerations in pursuing § 2.38
  Title VII § 2.32
  Title IX protection § 2.14
  Unemployment compensation
  –Generally § 2.36
  –Eligibility determination procedures § 2.37
STRICT LIABILITY
  Sexual harassment by employees § 2.5
  Title VII applicability to sexual harassment § 2.5
STRIKES
  Employment-at-will rule development § 1.4
SUBPOENAS
  Arbitration, evidence § 3.16
SUBSTANTIVE FAIRNESS
  Comprehensive wrongful discharge legislation. See COMPREHENSIVE WRONGFUL DISCHARGE LEGISLATION
SUMMERS, C. W.
  Comprehensive wrongful discharge legislation §§ 9.14, 9.28, 9.33
  Employment-at-will doctrine § 1.11

SURVEILLANCE
  Arbitration hearings, admissibility of evidence § 3.13

TAFT-HARTLEY ACT
  Arbitration authority § 3.22
TESTIMONY
  Arbitration hearings § 3.10
THEORY Y
  Employer personnel policy § 8.4
THEORY Z
  Employer personnel policy § 8.4
TITLE VII
  Comprehensive wrongful discharge legislation § 9.6
  Proof of violation §§ 7.6, 7.31, 7.33
  Protection under § 2.32
  Public employment protection § 6.7
TITLE IX
  Discrimination, protection against § 2.14
TORT THEORIES
  Generally § 5.1
  AIDS, dismissals related to § 5.28
  Basic tort concepts
  –Generally § 5.3
  –Development of tort action § 5.4
  –§ 870 framework for public policy torts § 5.5
  –§ 870 injury requirement § 5.6
  –§ 870 justification § 5.7
  Categories of torts
  –Generally § 5.9
  –External public policy, see External public policy, this heading
  –Internal public policy torts, see Internal public policy torts, this heading
  –Labor statutes as basis for § 5.9
  Civil remedies for statutory violations, public policy torts as more than § 5.19
  Collective bargaining agreements, employees covered by § 5.20
  Contractual relations, intentional interference with § 5.23
  Damages § 5.33
  Defamation § 5.25
  Emotional distress, intentional infliction of § 5.23
  External public policy
  –Constitutionally recognized rights, termination jeopardizing § 5.12

INDEX

TORT THEORIES (*Continued*)
 –Internal v. external public policy torts § 5.14
 –Jury duty § 5.10
 –Off-duty conduct § 5.13
 –Workers compensation claims § 5.11
 Fraudulent misrepresentation § 5.24
 Good cause, not requiring for dismissal § 5.2
 Internal public policy torts
 –Conflicting interests § 5.15
 –Orders, refusal to follow § 5.18
 –Protest or report to employer § 5.17
 –Whistleblowing § 5.16
 Invasion of privacy
 –Improper acquisition or dissemination of information § 5.26
 –Private conduct, interference with § 5.27
 Labor Management Relations Act § 301, preemption of state claims § 5.30
 Most requiring good cause for dismissal § 5.2
 Negligence § 5.29
 Pleading
 –Defendant's case § 5.32
 –Plaintiff's case § 5.31
 Preemption, LMRA § 301 § 530
 Prima facie torts §§ 5.1, 5.7, 5.21
 Sexual orientation, dismissals related to § 5.28

UNEMPLOYMENT COMPENSATION
 Employment-at-will, case evaluation checklist § 1.17
 Procedural fairness, integration of wrongful dismissal and unemployment compensation § 9.30
 Proof, preclusive effect of administrative decisions § 7.35

UNFAIR LABOR PRACTICES
 National Labor Relations Act protection § 2.16

UNFAIRNESS
 Proving a breach § 7.23

UNIFORM ARBITRATION ACT
 Generally § 3.22

UNILATERAL CONTRACTS
 Contract theories, mutuality of obligation § 4.13

UNIONS
 See LABOR UNIONS

VETERANS REEMPLOYMENT ACT
 Protection against discrimination § 2.24

VOLUNTARISM
 Comprehensive wrongful discharge legislation § 9.27

WAIVER
 Public employment, waiver of due process rights § 6.15

WHISTLEBLOWERS
 Preemption under § 2.33
 Proving public policy in tort actions § 7.11
 Public policy torts § 5.16
 State statutes § 9.7

WILLISTON, S.
 Contract theory § 4.4
 Proving promise from conduct of employer § 7.19

WIRETAPPING
 Tort theories, invasion of privacy § 5.26

WOOD, H. G.
 Employment-at-will doctrine §§ 1.4, 1.11

WORKERS COMPENSATION
 Proving jeopardy to public policy § 7.12
 Public policy torts § 5.11

WRONGFUL DISCHARGE. See PUBLIC POLICY TORT, TORT THEORIES